SOLIDWORKS 2026
Learn by doing

Tutorial Books

SOLIDWORKS 2026 Learn by doing

Download resource files

online.books999@gmail.com

z

Table of Contents

Chapter 1: Getting Started ... 1
Sketch-Based Features ... 2
Placed Features ... 3
Starting SOLIDWORKS ... 4
User Interface ... 5
Quick Access Toolbar ... 5
Menu ... 5
CommandManager ... 6
Features tab ... 6
Evaluate tab ... 6
Sketch tab ... 6
Assemble tab ... 6
Drawing Environment tabs ... 6
Sheet Metal tab ... 7
Collapsing the CommandManager ... 7
FeatureManager Design Tree ... 7
Status bar ... 8
View (Heads Up) Toolbar ... 8
Shortcut Menus ... 8
PropertyManager ... 9
Breadcrumbs ... 9
Mouse Functions ... 10
Customizing the CommandManager, Shortcut Bars, and Menus ... 11
Customizing the Mouse Gestures ... 12
Changing the Background Color ... 14
Chapter 2: Modeling Basics ... 17
TUTORIAL 1 ... 17
Opening a New Part File ... 17
Starting a Sketch ... 17
Adding Dimensions ... 18
Constructing the Base Feature ... 19
Adding an Extruded Feature ... 20
Adding another Extruded Feature ... 22
Saving the Part ... 25
TUTORIAL 2 ... 25
Opening a New Part File ... 26
Sketching a Revolve Profile ... 26
Constructing the Revolved Boss ... 28
Constructing the Cut feature ... 29
Constructing another Cut feature ... 30
Adding a Fillet ... 32
Viewing Parent and Child relationships between features ... 33
Saving the Part ... 34
TUTORIAL 3 ... 34
Opening a New Part File ... 34
Constructing the Cylindrical Feature ... 34
Constructing Cut feature ... 35
Saving and Closing the Part ... 36
TUTORIAL 4 ... 37
Applying Draft ... 37
Saving and Closing the Part ... 38
Chapter 3: Assembly Basics ... 39
TUTORIAL 1 ... 39
Opening a New Assembly File ... 39
Inserting the Base Component ... 39

Adding the second component......40
Applying Mates......40
Adding the Third Component......44
Checking the Interference......46
Saving the Assembly......47
Starting the Main assembly......47
Adding Disc to the Assembly......47
Placing the Sub-assembly......47
Adding Constraints......47
Placing the second instance of the Sub-assembly......48
Saving the Assembly......50
TUTORIAL 2......50
Creating the Exploded View......50
Creating Explode lines......51
Chapter 4: Creating Drawings......57
TUTORIAL 1......57
Opening a New Drawing File......58
Generating the Base View......58
Creating the Section View......59
Creating the Detailed View......60
Creating the Centerline......62
Specifying Dimension Settings......62
Retrieving Dimensions......63
Adding additional dimensions......64
Saving the Drawing......65
TUTORIAL 2......65
Creating a Custom Sheet Format......65
Starting a New drawing......67
Generating the Drawing Views......67
TUTORIAL 3......69
Creating the Isometric View......69
Generating the Exploded View......69
Creating the Bill of Materials......70
Creating Balloons......71
Adding Comments to the Drawing......71
Chapter 5: Sketching......74
Creating Rectangles......74
Creating Polygons......76
Relations......77
Merge......77
Horizontal......77
Vertical......77
Tangent......78
Parallel......78
Perpendicular......78
Midpoint......78
Automatic Relations......78
Deleting Relations......80
Hiding Relations......80
Sketch Numeric Input......80
Replace Entity......81
Path Length Dimension......84
Convert Entities......85
Midpoint line, Perimeter Circle, and SketchXpert......86
Ellipses......88
Partial Ellipse......90

Conic 90
TUTORIAL 1 91
Sketch Fillet 91
Sketch Chamfer 91
Mirror Entities 92
Stretch Entities 93
Move and Rotate Entities 93
Rotate Entities 94
Copy Entities 94
Scale Entities 95
Trim Entities 96
Extend Entities 98
Offset Entities 99
Make Path 100
Circular Sketch Pattern 101
Linear Sketch Pattern 102
Text 103
3D Sketch 104
Mirroring Entities in a 3D Sketch 106
The Slicing command 106
Generic Splines 107
Creating a 3D Curve using the Project Curve command 108
Creating a 3D Curve from two sketches 110
Repairing Dangling Relations 110
TUTORIAL 2 112
TUTORIAL 3 113
TUTORIAL 4 115
Chapter 6: Additional Modeling Tools 120
TUTORIAL 1 120
Creating the Extruded Base Feature 120
Creating the Extruded Cut Features 121
Creating the Extruded Cut feature on the left side 125
Creating the Chamfer 126
Creating the Extruded Cut feature on the left 126
Creating the Extruded Cut feature on the right 127
Adding the Extruded Boss Features 129
TUTORIAL 2 132
Constructing the Helix 132
Adding the Reference Plane 133
Constructing the Swept feature 133
TUTORIAL 3 135
Constructing a Revolved Cut 136
Constructing a Mirror Feature 137
TUTORIAL 4 138
Creating Sections and Guide curves 138
Creating another section 139
Constructing the Lofted feature 140
Constructing the Extruded feature 141
Adding Fillets 141
Shelling the Model 142
Adding the Indent feature 142
Adding Threads 144
TUTORIAL 5 149
Constructing a cylindrical shell 150
Adding a Slot 150
Constructing the Axis 151

Constructing the Linear pattern 151
Constructing the Circular pattern 152
TUTORIAL 6 153
Constructing the first feature 153
Constructing the Second Feature 153
Constructing the third feature 153
Inserting Holes 155
Adding Chamfers 156
Creating Bounding Box 157
TUTORIAL 7 157
Constructing the first feature 157
Constructing the Extruded cut 158
Making the Curve Driven Pattern 159
TUTORIAL 8 160
Start a new part file 160
Creating the second feature 160
Adding Cosmetic Threads 160
Creating Configurations Table 161
TUTORIAL 9 164
Creating the First Feature 164
Creating the Extruded surface 165
Replacing the top face of the model with the surface 165
Creating a Face fillet 166
Creating a Variable Radius fillet 166
Shelling the Model 167
Creating the Mounting Bosses 167
Creating the Vent Feature 169
Creating the Wrap Feature 170
TUTORIAL 10 171
TUTORIAL 11 174
TUTORIAL 12 (CSWA Step 1) 174
Tutorial 13 (CSWA Step 2) 180
Modifying the Global Variable Values 180
Tutorial 14 (CSWA Step 3 and 4) 181
Creating the Extruded Cuts 181
Tutorial 15 186
Chapter 7: Sheet metal Modeling 193
TUTORIAL 1 193
Constructing the Base Flange 193
Adding an Edge flange 194
Constructing the Miter Flange 195
Closing the Corners 197
Adding Corner Reliefs 197
Adding a Tab feature 198
Adding a Jog 199
Unfolding the bends 200
Creating Cuts across bends 200
Folding the Unfolded bends 200
Performing the Forming Operations 200
Making the Linear Pattern 202
Adding a Hem 202
Adding a vent 202
Adding Sheet Metal Gussets 203
Making a Fill Pattern 204
View the Flat Pattern 205
TUTORIAL 2 206

TUTORIAL 3 206
TUTORIAL 4 208
TUTORIAL 5 211
TUTORIAL 6 213
TUTORIAL 7 214
TUTORIAL 8 215
TUTORIAL 9 (MODIFYING FORMING TOOLS) 219
TUTORIAL 10 (THE RIP AND INSERT BENDS COMMANDS) 223
Inserting Bends 225
TUTORIAL 11 (Create Flanges on the Bend Edges) 226
TUTORIAL 12 (Create Sensors) 228
TUTORIAL 13 (USING THE RIP COMMAND FOR THIN CYLINDRICAL OR CONICAL BODIES) 229
TUTORIAL 14 (USING THE STAMP COMMAND) 230
TUTORIAL 15 (CSWPA SAMPLE QUESTION) 231
TUTORIAL 16 (CSWPA SAMPLE QUESTION 2) 236
TUTORIAL 17 (CSWPA SAMPLE QUESTION 3) 237
TUTORIAL 18 (CSWPA SAMPLE QUESTION 3) 238
TUTORIAL 19 240
Chapter 8: Top-Down Assembly 242
TUTORIAL 1 242
Creating a New Assembly File 242
Creating a component in the Assembly 242
Creating the Second Component of the Assembly 244
Creating the third Component of the Assembly 245
Adding Bolt Connections to the assembly 246
Patterning components in an assembly 249
Sectioning an Assembly with Transparency 249
TUTORIAL 2 250
Creating Smart Mates 251
Creating the Limit Mate 252
Creating the Slot Mate 252
TUTORIAL 3 (CSWA Assembly Modeling Sample Question) 254
Chapter 9: Dimensions and Annotations 261
TUTORIAL 1 261
Creating a Model View with Center Marks 262
Creating Centerlines and Center Marks 263
Editing the Hatch Pattern 264
Emphasizing the Outline of the Section View 264
Applying Dimensions 265
Placing the Datum Feature 268
Placing the Feature Control Frame 269
Placing the Surface Texture Symbols 270
Chapter 10: Surface Design 272
TUTORIAL 1 (Extruded Surfaces) 272
TUTORIAL 2 (Revolved Surfaces) 272
TUTORIAL 3 (Swept Surfaces) 273
TUTORIAL 4 (Lofted Surfaces) 274
TUTORIAL 5 (Planar Surfaces) 275
TUTORIAL 6 (Creating a Ruled Surface using the Tangent to Surface option) 276
TUTORIAL 7 (Creating a Ruled Surface using the Normal to Surface option) 277
TUTORIAL 8 (Creating a Ruled Surface using the Tapered to Vector option) 277
TUTORIAL 9 (Creating a Ruled Surface using the Perpendicular to Vector option) 278
TUTORIAL 10 (Creating a Ruled Surface using the Sweep option) 278
TUTORIAL 11 (Offset Surface) 279
TUTORIAL 12 (Knitting Surfaces) 279
Creating a Solid by Knitting Surfaces 280

TUTORIAL 13 (Trimming Surfaces) 280
Trimming a Surface using the Standard option 281
Trimming Surfaces using the Mutual option 282
TUTORIAL 14 (Extending Surfaces) 283
TUTORIAL 15 (Offset on Surface) 284
TUTORIAL 16 (Untrimming a Surface) 285
TUTORIAL 17 (Deleting Holes) 287
TUTORIAL 18 (Filled Surface) 288
TUTORIAL 19 289
TUTORIAL 20 (Converting a Surface to Solid) 290
TUTORIAL 21 (Thickening the Surface) 290
TUTORIAL 22 (Deleting Faces) 291
TUTORIAL 23 (Replacing Faces) 292
TUTORIAL 24 (Cutting with Surfaces) 293
TUTORIAL 25 (Thickened Cut) 293
TUTORIAL 26 (Freeform Surfaces) 294
TUTORIAL 27 (Boundary Surfaces) 298
TUTORIAL 28 (Flatten Surface) 300
Chapter 11: Mold Tools 302
TUTORIAL 1 302
Performing Draft Analysis 302
Applying the Shrinkage allowance 303
Inserting Mold Folders 303
Creating a Parting Line 303
Creating Shut-off Surfaces 304
Creating Parting Surfaces 305
Creating the Tooling Split 306
Performing the Undercut analysis 307
Creating side cores 307
Creating your own surfaces 309
Chapter 12: Weldments 312
TUTORIAL 1 312
TUTORIAL 2 316
Adding Structural members 318
Trimming the Structural Members 320
Creating Gussets 322
Creating Base Plates 323
Mirroring Gussets and Baseplates 324
Creating Fillet Beads 325
Creating Weld Beads 326
TUTORIAL 3 (Creating End Caps) 329
TUTORIAL 4 (Working with Cut lists) 331
Adding a Cut list to the Weldment Drawing 332
Adding Columns to the Cut list table 334
Creating a Bounding box 335
Adding a Weld table to the Weldment Drawing 335
Adding Weld Symbols 335
Creating Sub Weldments 336
TUTORIAL 5 (Creating Custom Profiles for structural members) 337
Chapter 13: MBD Dimensions 339
Geometric Dimensioning and Tolerancing 339
TUTORIAL 1 (Auto Dimension Scheme) 340
TUTORIAL 2 (Adding the GD&T Information Manually) 342
Adding Size Dimensions 343
Adding Location Dimensions 344
Adding Geometric Tolerances 344

Adding other dimensions to Fully-define the part ... 346
TUTORIAL 3 (Using the MBD Dimensions Annotations in drawings) ... 348
TUTORIAL 4 (Pattern Feature) ... 348
TUTORIAL 5 (DimXpert Options) ... 349
TUTORIAL 6 (Insert Dimensions) ... 351
TUTORIAL 7 ... 352
TUTORIAL 8 ... 352
Chapter 14: Appearances and Rendering ... 354
TUTORIAL 1 (Adding Appearances to the Complete Part) ... 354
TUTORIAL 2 (Adding Appearances to Faces, Surfaces, and Features) ... 355
TUTORIAL 3 (Adding Textures) ... 357
TUTORIAL 4 (Texture Mapping options) ... 358
TUTORIAL 5 (Surface Finish) ... 361
TUTORIAL 6 (Illumination) ... 362
Tutorial 7 (Scenes) ... 362
TUTORIAL 8 (Rendering) ... 364
Adding Cameras ... 366
Rendering ... 367
TUTORIAL 9 (Lights) ... 367
Editing the Ambient Light ... 367
TUTORIAL 10 (Working with Directional Lights) ... 368
TUTORIAL 11 (Working with Point Lights) ... 370
TUTORIAL 12 (Working with Spot Lights) ... 370
TUTORIAL 13 (Working with Sun Lights) ... 371
TUTORIAL 14 (Walk-through) ... 372
TUTORIAL 15 (Decals) ... 374
Adding the default Decals to the Model ... 374
Creating your own Decals ... 374
Chapter 15: SimulationXpress ... 377
TUTORIAL 1 ... 377
Creating Fixtures ... 378
Adding Loads ... 379
Adding the Material ... 380
Meshing the model ... 380
Simulating the Model ... 381
Generating Reports ... 382
Optimizing the Model ... 384
Index ... 387

INTRODUCTION

SOLIDWORKS is a package adding a great value to enterprises. It offers a set of tools, which are easy-to-use to design, document and simulate 3D models. Using this software, you can speed up the design process and reduce the product development costs.

This book provides a systematic approach for users to learn SOLIDWORKS. It is aimed at new SOLIDWORKS users. However, users of previous versions of SOLIDWORKS may also find this book useful for them to learn the new enhancements. This book guides the user from starting a SOLIDWORKS Design 2026 session to constructing parts, assemblies, and drawings. Each chapter has components explained with the help of real-world models.

Scope of this book

If you are a student or engineer who is interested to learn SOLIDWORKS Design 2026 for mechanical design, then this book helps you to do it easily and quickly. You will also enjoy the learning process by creating real world models. In addition, if you are a graphical learner, then you will find this book very interesting.

The topics in this book include Getting Started with SOLIDWORKS Design 2026, Basic Part Modeling, Creating Assemblies, Creating Drawings, Additional Modeling Tools, and Sheet Metal Modeling.

Chapter 1 introduces SOLIDWORKS. The user interface and terminology are discussed in this chapter.

Chapter 2 takes you through the creation of your first SOLIDWORKS model. You create simple parts.

Chapter 3 teaches you to create assemblies. It explains the Top-down and Bottom-up approaches for designing an assembly. You create an assembly using the Bottom-up approach.

Chapter 4 teaches you to create drawings of the models created in the earlier chapters. You will also learn to place exploded views, and part list of an assembly.

Chapter 5: In this chapter, you will learn sketch tools.

Chapter 6: In this chapter, you will learn additional modeling tools to create complex models.

Chapter 7: introduces you to Sheet Metal modeling. You will create a sheet metal part using the tools available in the Sheet Metal environment.

Chapter 8: In this chapter, you will learn to create assemblies using Top-down approach and apply some advanced mates.

Chapter 9: In this chapter, you will learn to add annotations to drawings.

Chapter 10: In this chapter, you will learn Surface Modeling tools.

Chapter 11: This chapter introduces you to Mold design.

Chapter 12: In this chapter, you will learn to create Weldments.

Chapter 13: In this chapter, you will learn Model-based dimension tools.

Chapter 14: This chapter introduces you to Appearances and Rendering.

Chapter 15: This chapter introduces you to SimulationXpress.

Chapter 1: Getting Started

In this chapter, you will learn some of the most commonly used features of SOLIDWORKS. Also, you will learn about the user interface.

SOLIDWORKS is a parametric and feature-based system that allows you to create 3D parts, assemblies, and 2D drawings. The following figure shows the design process in SOLIDWORKS.

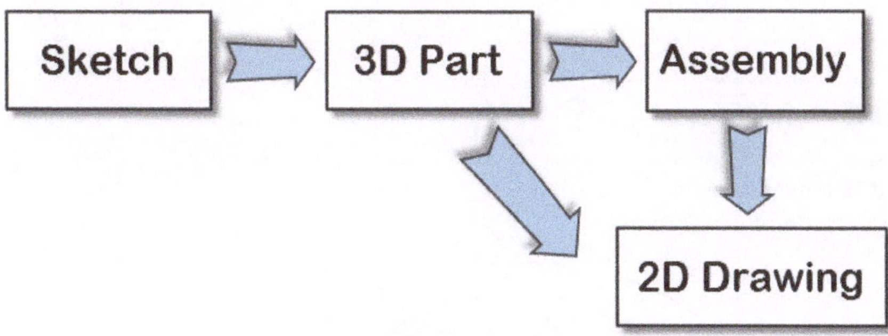

In SOLIDWORKS, you create parts by combining features.

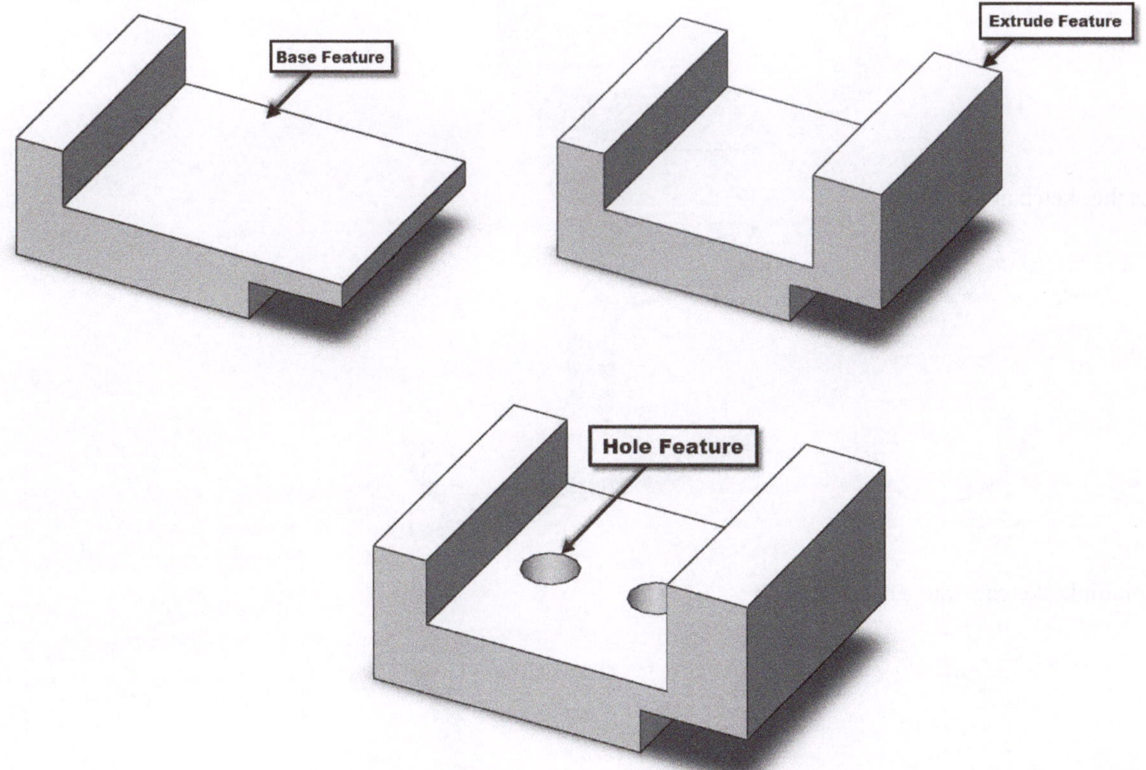

In CAD (Computer-Aided Design), features are categorized into **sketch-based** and **placed** (or "applied") features. Understanding both types is essential for efficient 3D modelling.

Sketch-Based Features

These require a **2D sketch** as their foundation. You draw the sketch first, then use it to generate 3D geometry through operations like:

Extrude: Pulls the sketch into 3D

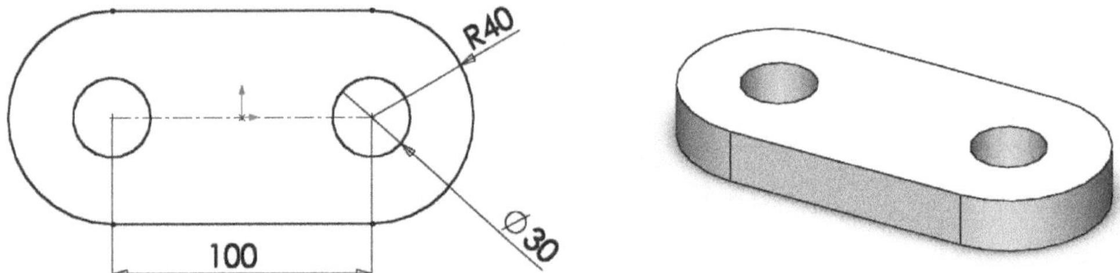

Revolve: Rotates the sketch around an axis

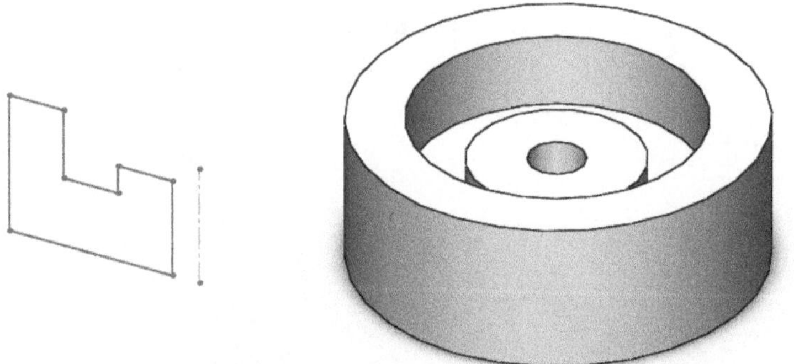

Sweep: Moves the sketch along a path

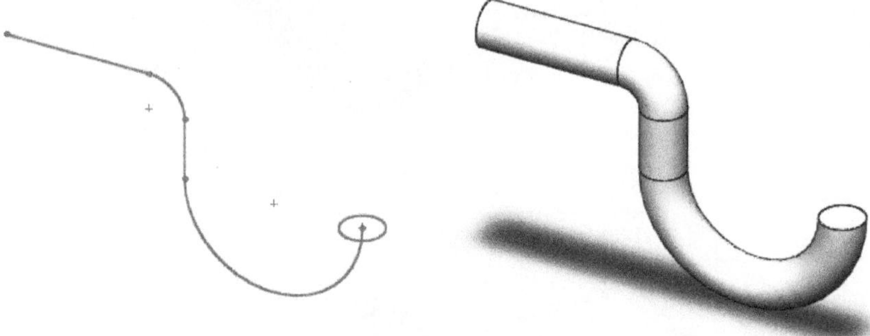

Loft: Blends multiple sketches into a smooth shape

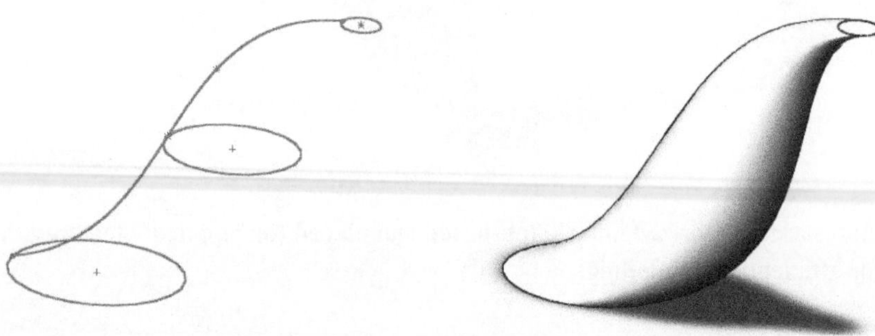

Placed Features

Placed features are applied directly to existing model geometry and do not require a precursor sketch. Common examples include:

- **Holes**: Defined by standard parameters, such as diameter and depth, rather than sketched profiles.
- **Fillets and Chamfers**: Generate rounded or beveled transitions along selected edges based on specified radii or angles.
- **Shell**: Removes internal material from a solid body to create a hollow, thin-walled structure.
- **Draft**: Applies a taper angle to specific faces, typically to facilitate mold release in manufacturing.

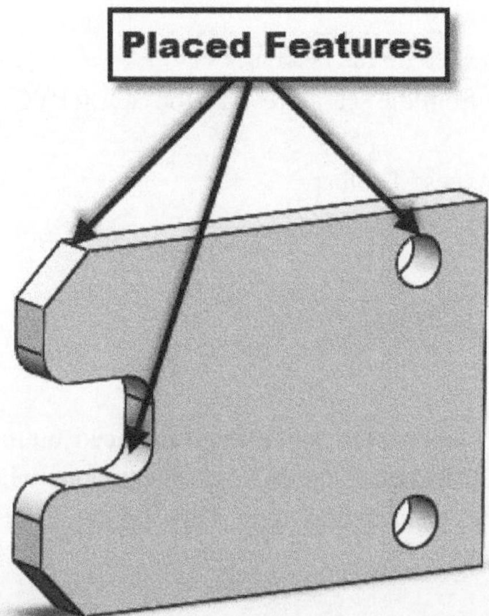

These features are employed to refine or detail existing part geometry, such as incorporating threaded features or modifying edge conditions.

Key Differences between the Sketch-Based and Placed Features

Aspect	Sketch-Based Features	Placed Features
Requires Sketch	Yes	No
Flexibility	High (custom shapes)	Limited (dependent on geometry)
Workflow	Sketch → Operation	Select geometry → Apply feature

In SOLIDWORKS, parameters, dimensions, or relations control everything. For example, if you want to change the hole's position shown in the figure, you need to change the dimension or relation that controls its position.

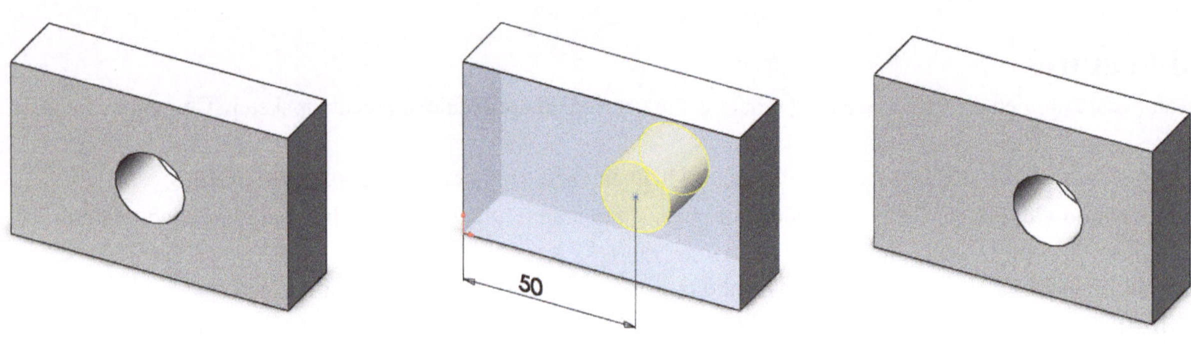

Starting SOLIDWORKS

- Type Solidworks in the search bar located on the taskbar.
- Select SOLIDWORKS Design 2026 from the search results; the SOLIDWORKS Design 2026 application window appears.
- Click the **New** button on the Quick Access Toolbar.

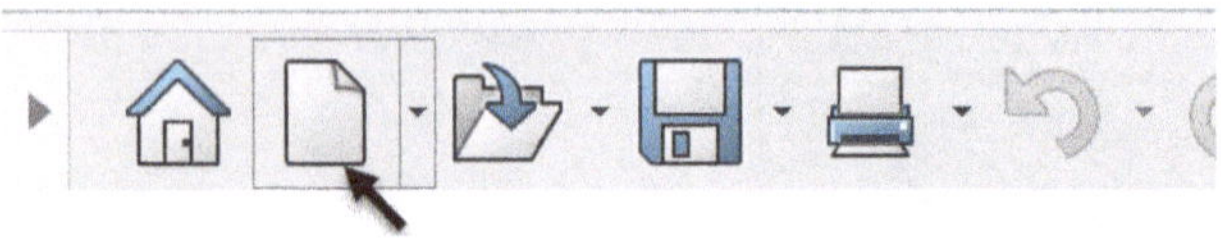

- On the New SOLIDWORKS Document dialog, click the Advanced button located at the bottom left corner. In the Templates tab, you can now choose between Y up or Z up orientations when creating a new document. Unlike earlier versions which defaulted only to Y up, you can now set a Z up orientation as the default for new files.

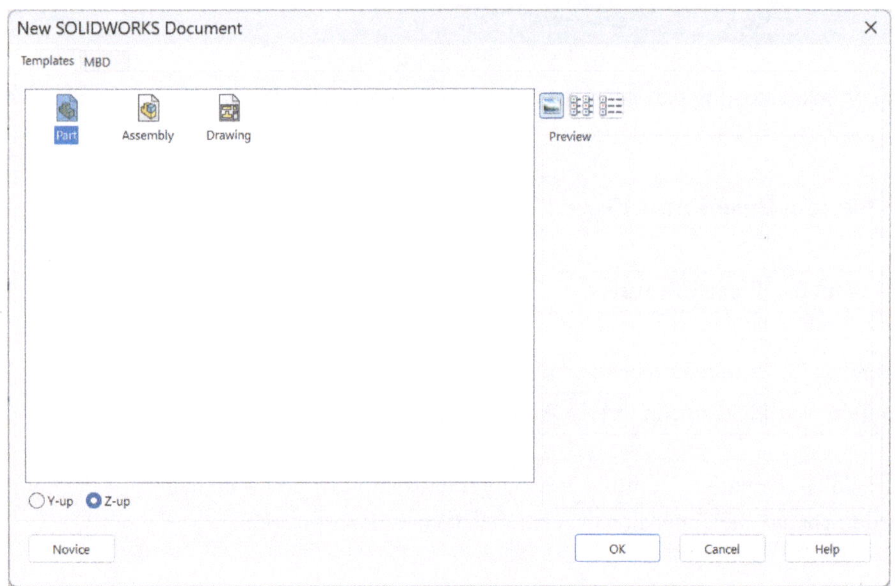

- Click **Part** and then click **OK**.

Notice these important features of the SOLIDWORKS window.

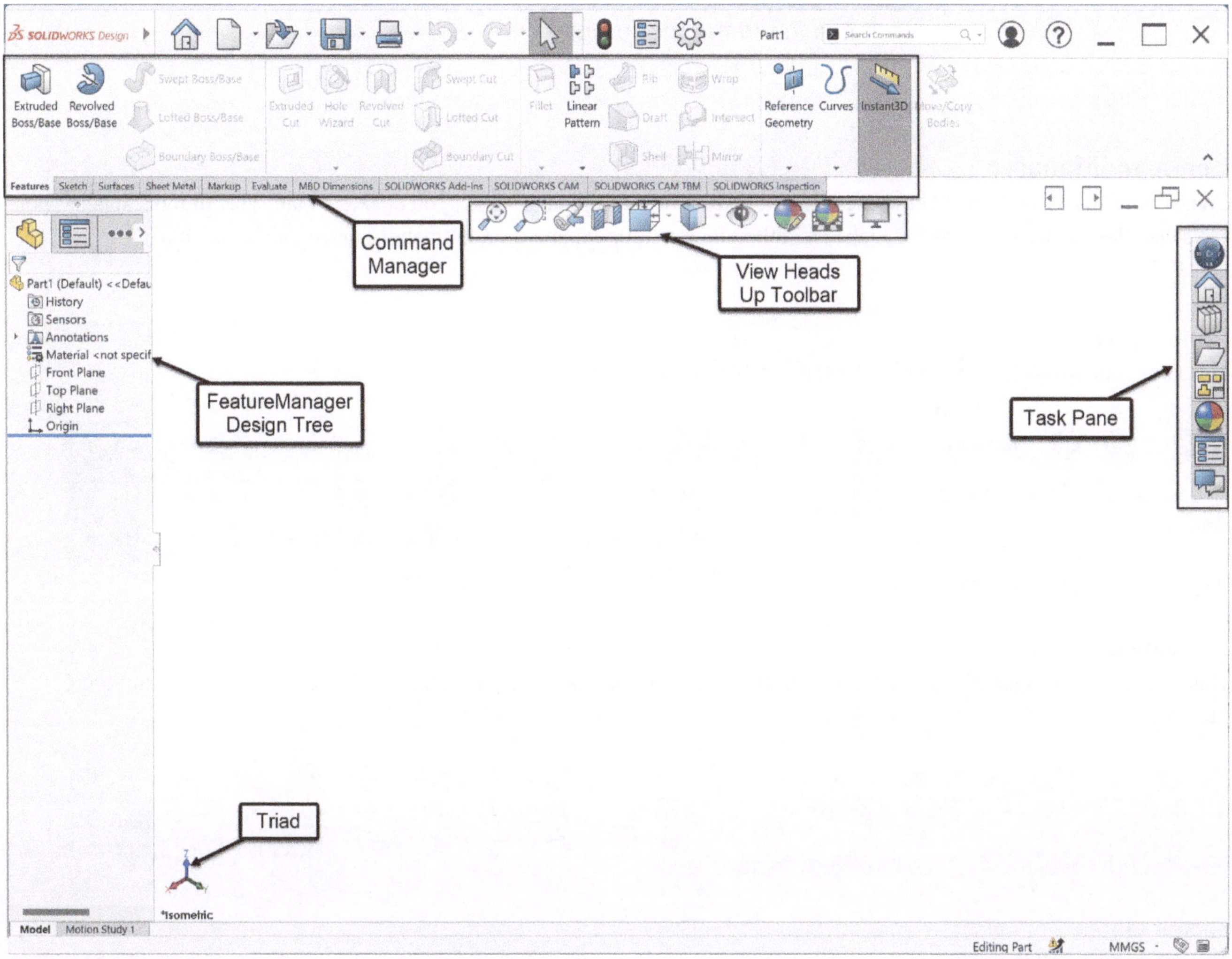

User Interface

The following sections explain various components of the user interface.

Quick Access Toolbar

The Quick Access Toolbar is available at the top of the window. It contains tools such as **New**, **Save**, and **Open**.

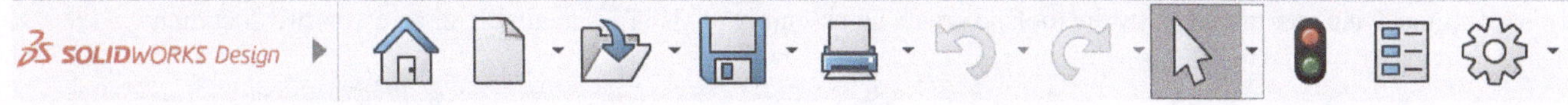

Menu

The menu is located at the top of the window. You can display it by placing the pointer on the arrow located at the top left corner. It has various options (menu titles). When you click on a menu title, a drop-down appears. Select any option from this drop-down.

CommandManager

CommandManager is located below the menu. It consists of various tabs. When you click on a tab, a set of tools appear. You can select the required tool from the tab. The following sections explain the CommandManager tabs available in SOLIDWORKS.

Features tab

This CommandManager tab contains the tools to create 3D features.

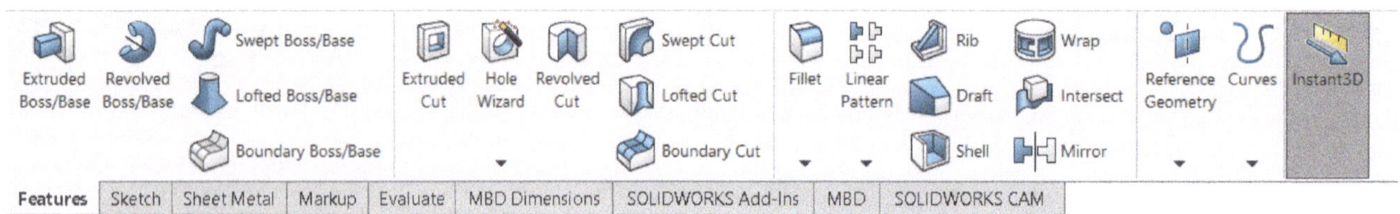

Evaluate tab

This CommandManager tab has the tools to measure the objects. It also has analysis tools to analyze the draft, curvature, surface and so on.

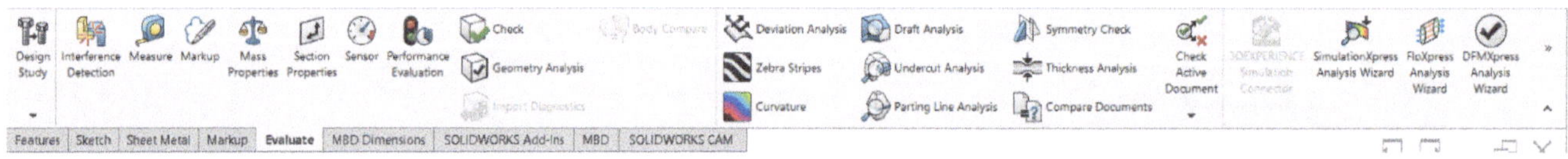

Sketch tab

This tab contains all the sketch tools.

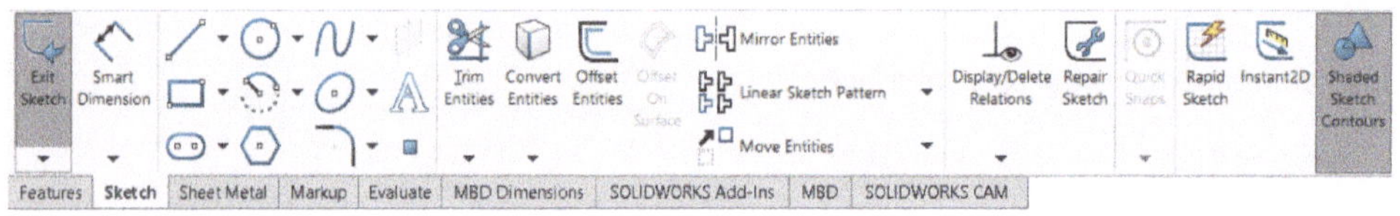

Assemble tab

This CommandManager tab contains the tools to create an assembly. This tab is available in an assembly document.

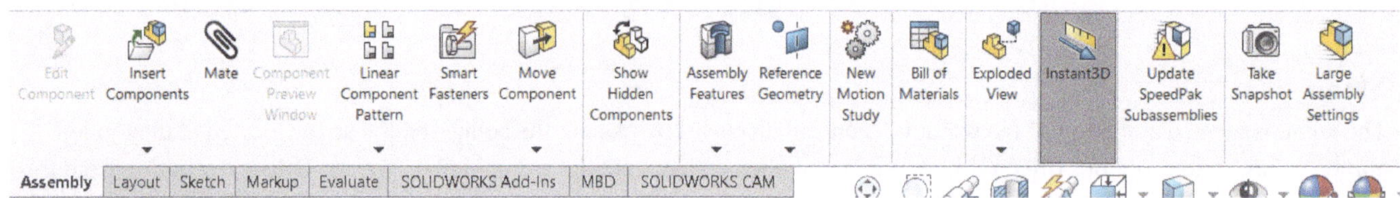

Drawing Environment tabs

In the Drawing Environment, you can create orthographic views of the 3D model. The CommandManager tabs in this environment contain tools to create 2D drawings.

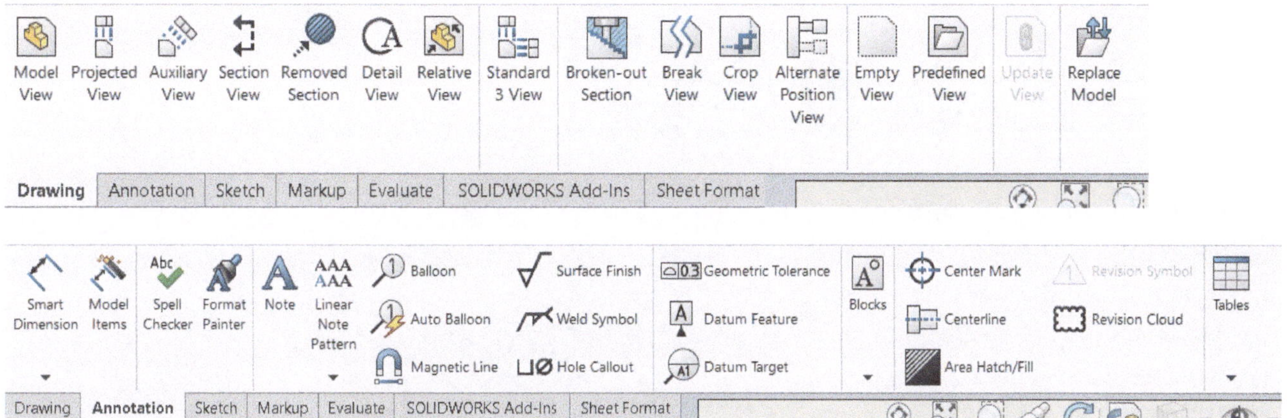

Sheet Metal tab

Use the tools in this tab to create sheet metal components. Note that this tab is not displayed by default. You can display it by right-clicking on anyone of the CommandManager tabs and selecting Sheet Metal from the menu.

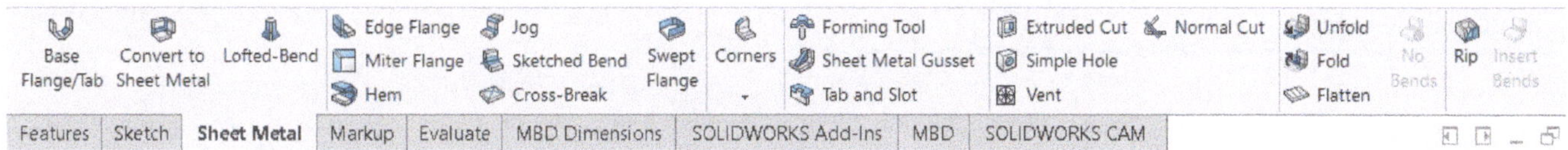

Collapsing the CommandManager

You can also collapse the CommandManager by clicking the **Collapse CommandManager** button located at the bottom right corner of the CommandManager.

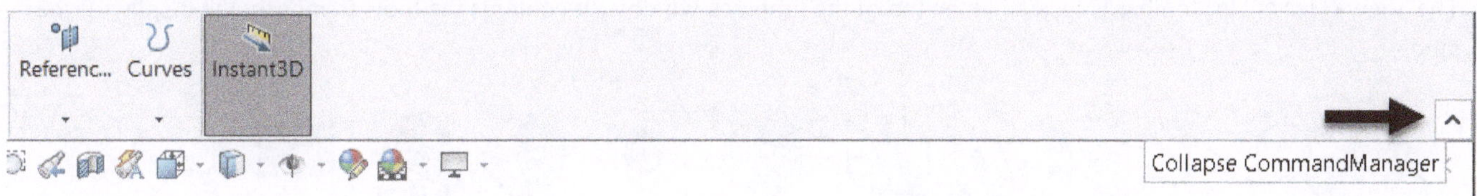

To pin the collapsed CommandManager, click on anyone of the tabs of the CommandManager. Next, click the **Pin CommandManager** button located at the bottom right corner of the CommandManager.

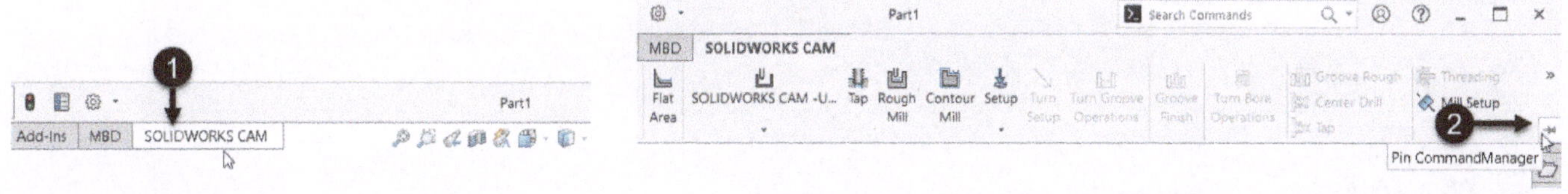

FeatureManager Design Tree

The FeatureManager Design Tree is located on the left pane of the application window. It contains the list of operations carried in a SOLIDWORKS document.

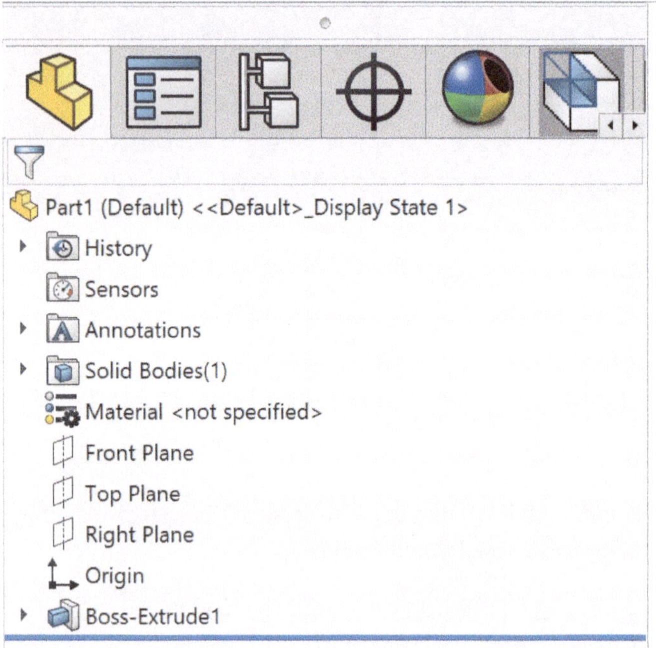

Status bar

The Status bar is available below the graphics window. It displays the status of the SOLIDWORKS document. For example, if you are drawing a sketch, it displays **Editing sketch**.

View (Heads Up) Toolbar

The View (Heads Up) toolbar is located at the top of the graphics window. It contains the tools to modify the display of the model.

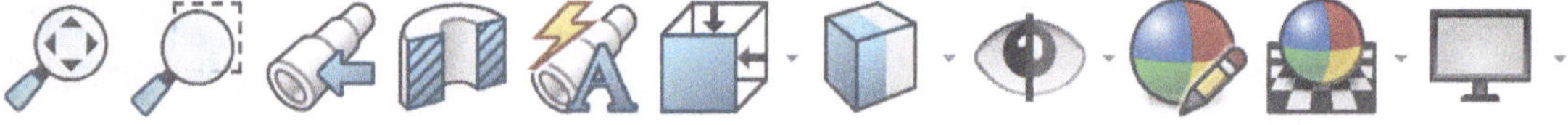

Shortcut Menus

When you click the right mouse button, a shortcut menu appears. A shortcut menu contains a list of some important options that can be accessed very quickly.

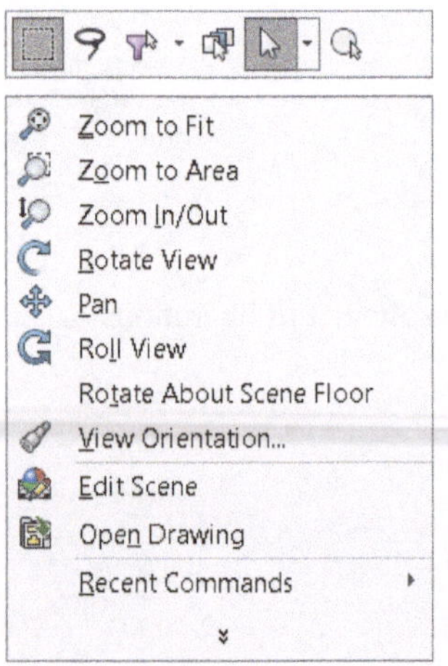

PropertyManager

When you activate any tool in SOLIDWORKS, the PropertyManager related to it appears. It consists of various options that are part of the selected tool. The following figure shows the components of the PropertyManager.

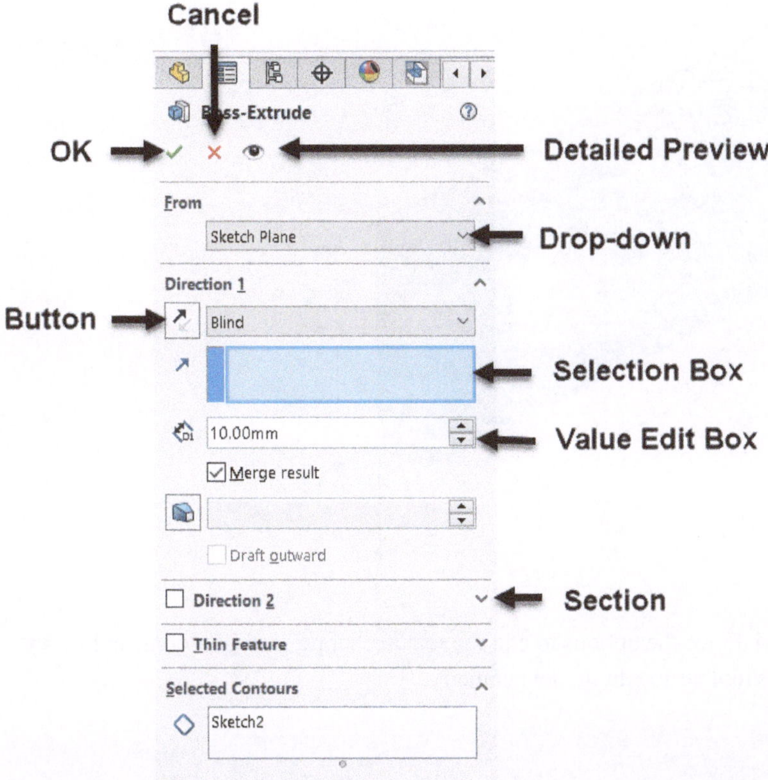

Breadcrumbs

Breadcrumbs is a useful functionality added SOLIDWORKS in recent years. Whenever you click on an item or a feature of the model geometry, the **Breadcrumbs** toolbar appears at the top left corner of the graphics window. For example, click on a face of the part geometry, as shown; the Selection Breadcrumbs toolbar appears, as shown. On the toolbar, you can select the entire part, solid body, feature or sketch related to the feature, or a face.

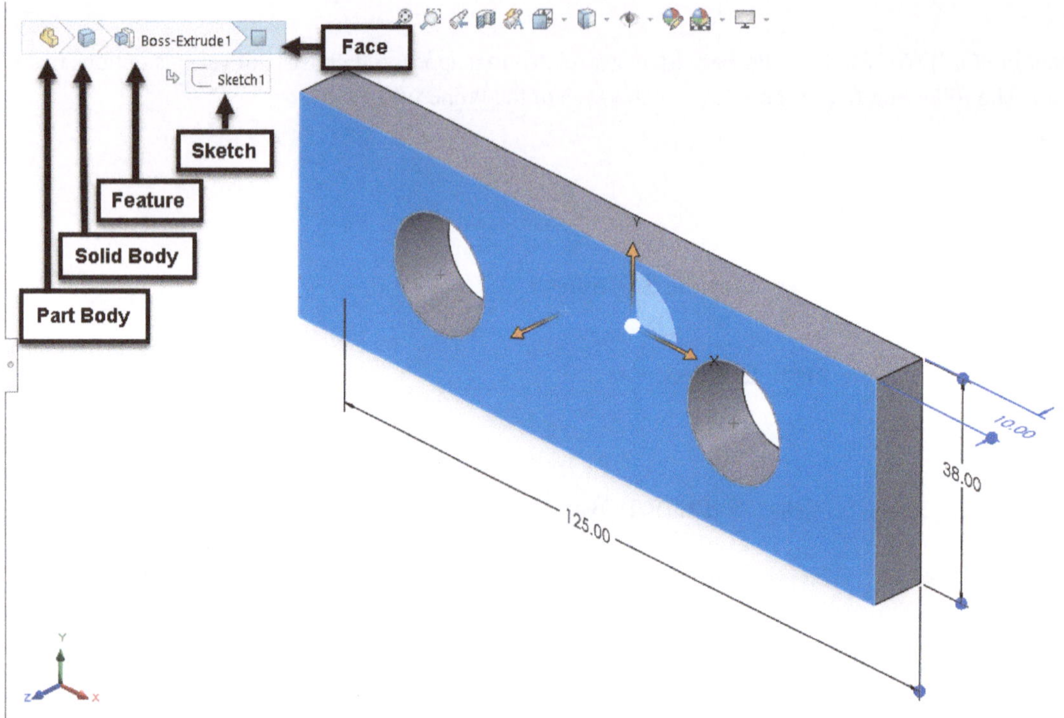

Select the feature from the Breadcrumbs toolbar and notice the options to edit the feature, suppress, hide, zoom, and so on. You can hide the left pane and use the Breadcrumbs toolbar to edit model geometry.

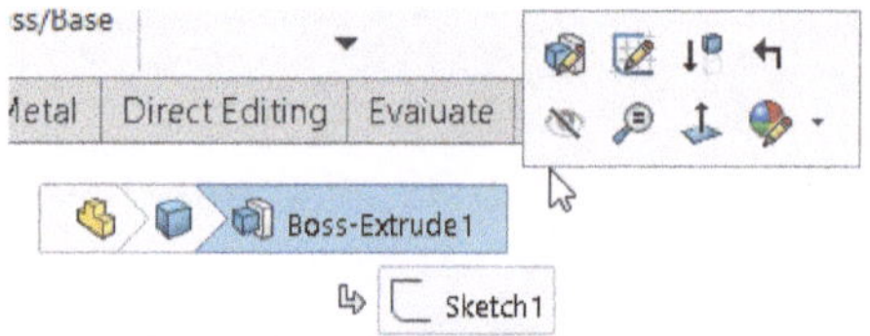

Mouse Functions

Various functions of the mouse buttons are:

Left Mouse button (MB1)

You can select an object, tool, or option using clicking the left mouse button. When you double-click the left mouse button (MB1) on an object, the dimensions related to the object appear. You can then edit the dimensions of the objects.

Middle Mouse button (MB2)

Click and drag this button to rotate the model view.

Right Mouse button (MB3)

Click this button to open a shortcut menu. Click and drag the right mouse button to display the mouse gestures.

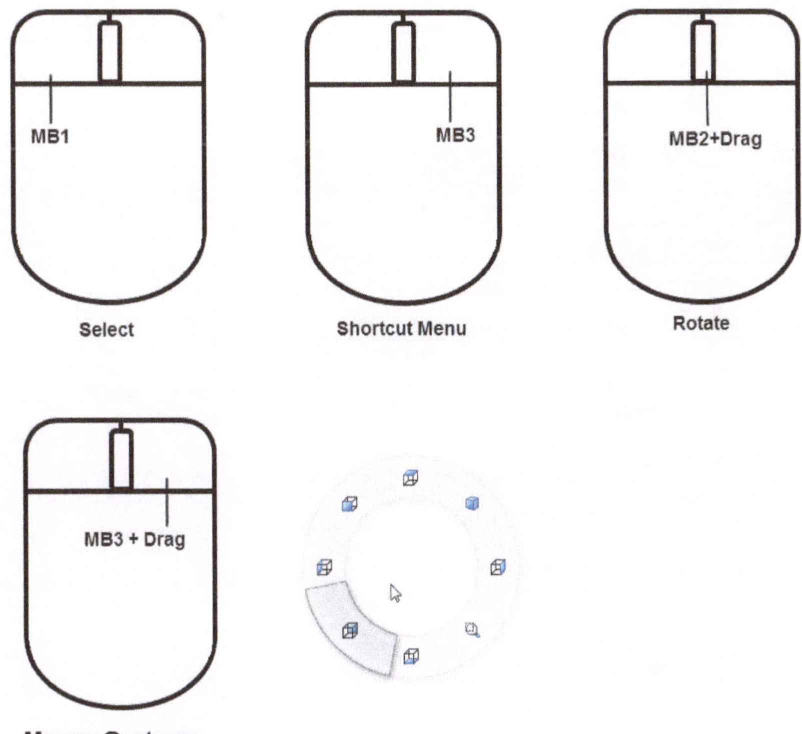

Customizing the CommandManager, Shortcut Bars, and Menus

To customize the CommandManager, shortcut keys, or menus, click **Options > Customize** on the **Quick Access Toolbar**. On the **Customize** dialog, use the tabs to customize the CommandManager or menu or shortcut bars.

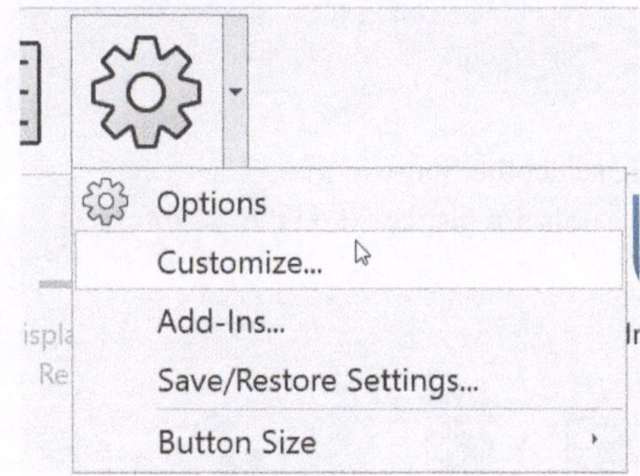

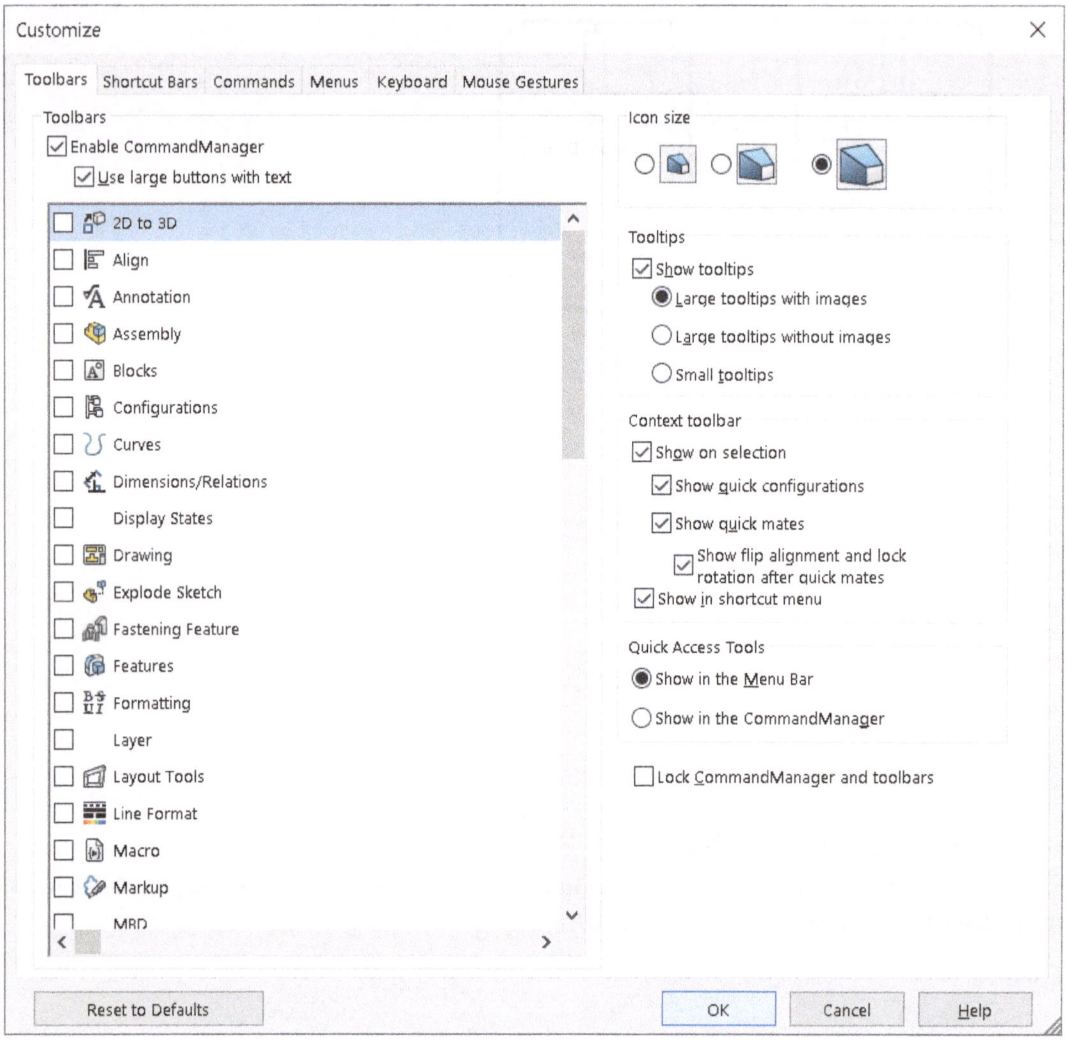

You can also show the Quick Access Toolbar on the CommandManager. To do this, select the Show in the CommandManager option from the **Quick Access Tools** section; the Quick Access Tools are displayed on the CommandManager.

Customizing the Mouse Gestures

To customize the Mouse Gestures, click the right mouse button on the CommandManager and select **Customize** from the menu. Next, click the **Mouse Gestures** tab on the **Customize** dialog and ensure that the **Enable mouse gestures** option is selected. Select the number of commands to be displayed on the gestures from the drop-down available below the **Enable mouse gestures** option. Next, click and drag the required commands from the commands list. Move the pointer and release onto anyone of the mouse gestures (Part, Sketch, Assembly, or Drawing mouse gestures) available on the **Mouse Gestures**

Guide dialog. Click **OK** to close the **Customize** dialog. There are four mouse gestures available on the **Mouse Gestures Guide** dialog: Part, Sketch, Assembly, and Drawing. You can copy a command located on anyone of the mouse gestures onto another mouse gestures. To do this, press the Ctrl key and drag the command onto another mouse gesture.

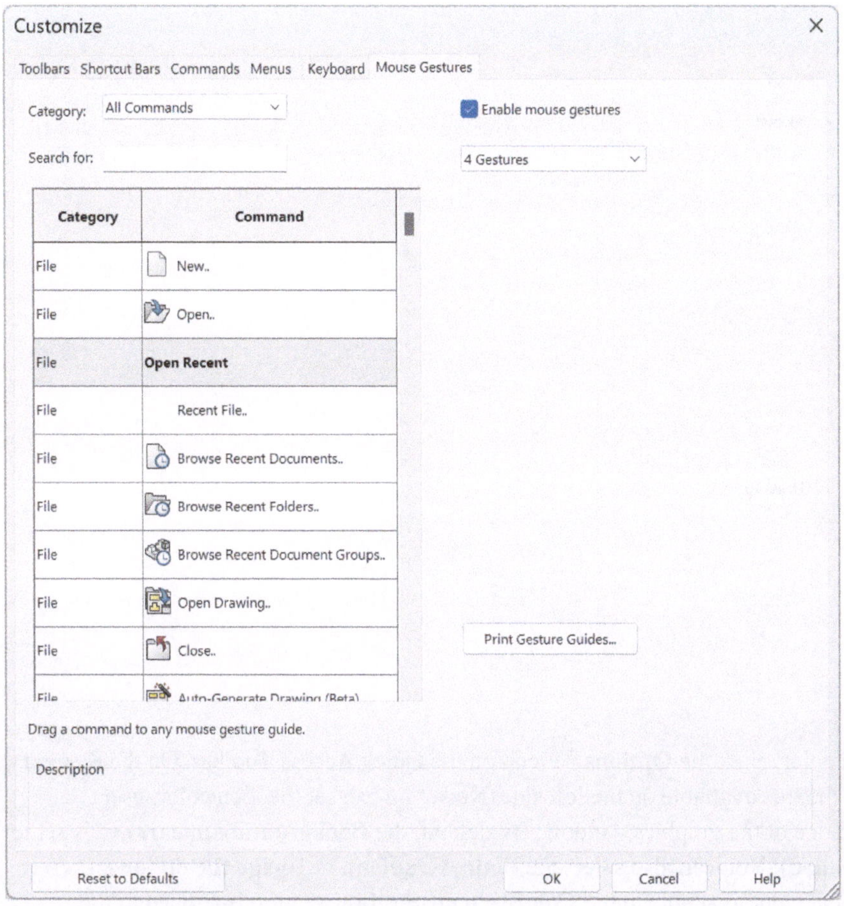

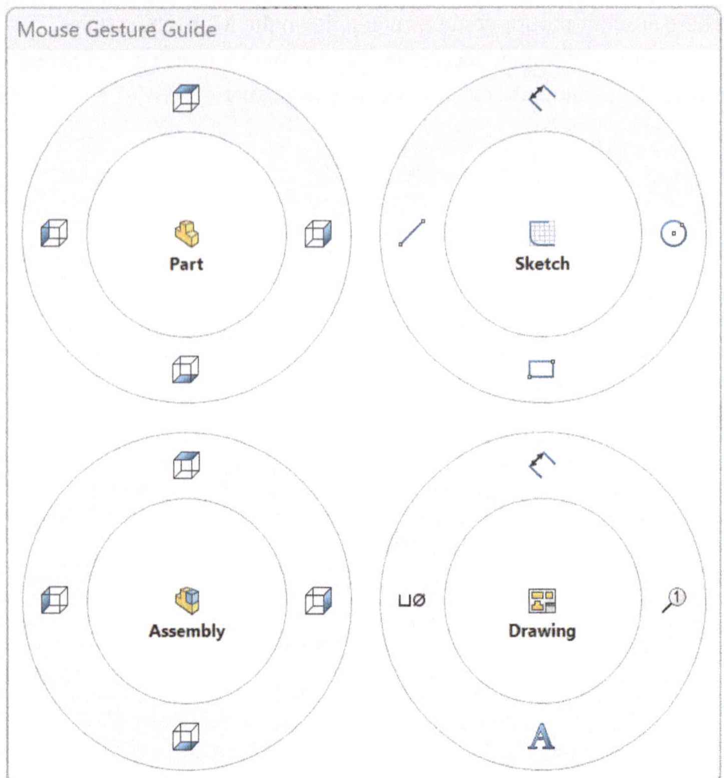

Changing the Background Color

To change the graphics window's background color, click the **Options** icon on the Quick Access Toolbar. On the **System Options** dialog, click the **Colors** option from the tree available on the left side. Now, you can set the icon color, user interface background, and background appearance of the graphics window. By default, the **Background appearance** is set to **Use document scene background(recommended)**. You can also select the **Plain**, **Gradient**, or **Image file options**. If you select the **Plain** option, the viewport background color available in the **Color scheme Settings** section is applied to the background. You can change the viewport background color by clicking the **Edit** button in the **Color scheme Settings** section. Next, select a color from the **Color** dialog, and click **OK**. If you select the **Image file** option from the **Background appearance** section, click the **Browse** button and select an image file from a location on your computer. Next, click **OK** on the **System Options** dialog.

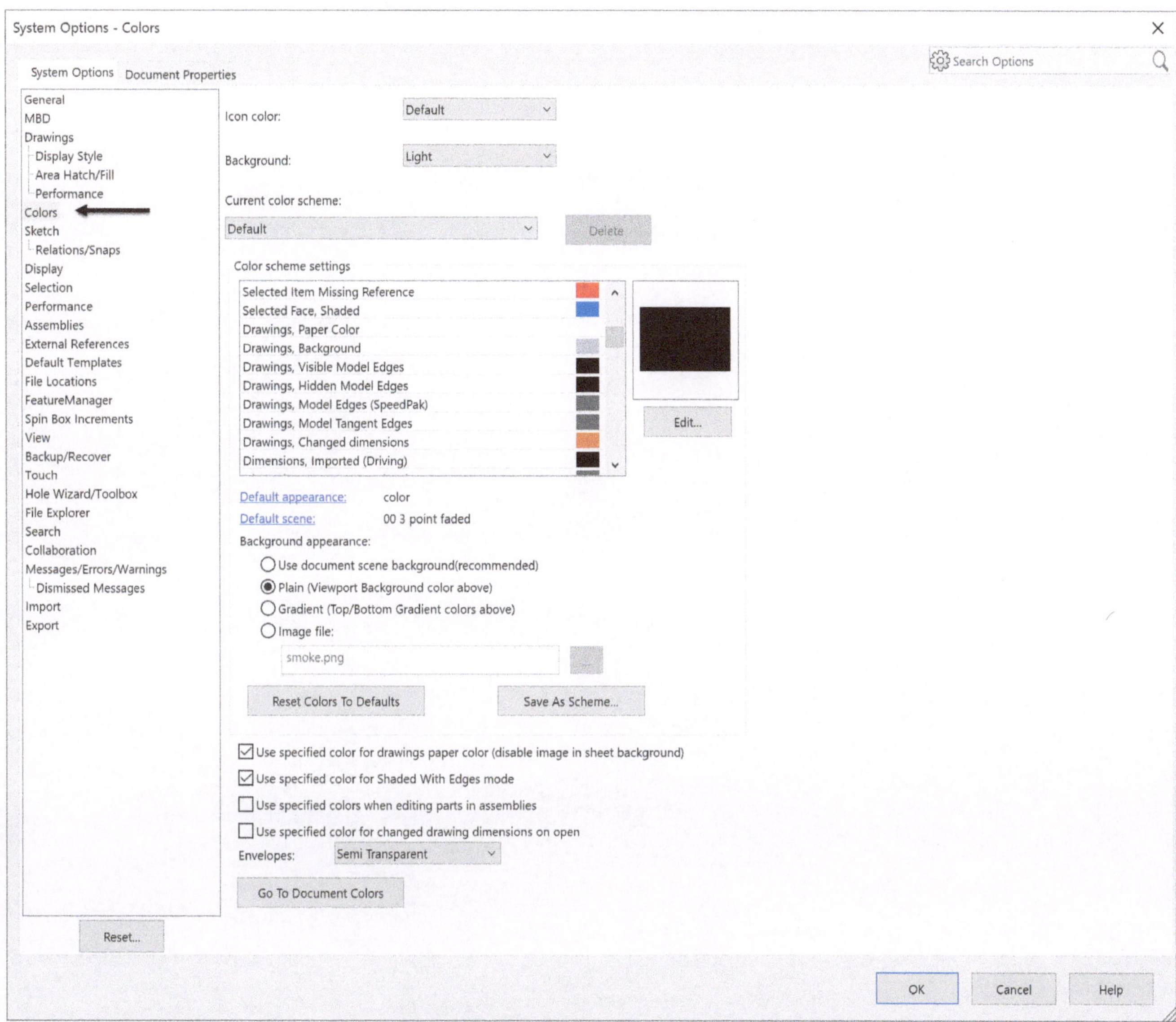
System Options - Colors
System Options
Document Properties
Search Options
General
MBD
Drawings
Display Style
Area Hatch/Fill
Performance
Colors
Sketch
Relations/Snaps
Display
Selection
Performance
Assemblies
External References
Default Templates
File Locations
FeatureManager
Spin Box Increments
View
Backup/Recover
Touch
Hole Wizard/Toolbox
File Explorer
Search
Collaboration
Messages/Errors/Warnings
Dismissed Messages
Import
Export
Icon color:
Default
Background:
Light
Current color scheme:
Default
Delete
Color scheme settings
Selected Item Missing Reference
Selected Face, Shaded
Drawings, Paper Color
Drawings, Background
Drawings, Visible Model Edges
Drawings, Hidden Model Edges
Drawings, Model Edges (SpeedPak)
Drawings, Model Tangent Edges
Drawings, Changed dimensions
Dimensions, Imported (Driving)
Edit...
Default appearance:
color
Default scene:
00 3 point faded
Background appearance:
Use document scene background(recommended)
Plain (Viewport Background color above)
Gradient (Top/Bottom Gradient colors above)
Image file:
smoke.png
Reset Colors To Defaults
Save As Scheme...
Use specified color for drawings paper color (disable image in sheet background)
Use specified color for Shaded With Edges mode
Use specified colors when editing parts in assemblies
Use specified color for changed drawing dimensions on open
Envelopes:
Semi Transparent
Go To Document Colors
Reset...
OK
Cancel
Help

Chapter 2: Modeling Basics

This chapter teaches you to construct your first SOLIDWORKS model. You will construct parts of an Oldham Coupling:

In this chapter, you will:

- Construct Sketches
- Construct a base feature
- Add another feature to it
- Construct revolved features
- Construct cylindrical features and
- Apply draft

TUTORIAL 1

This tutorial takes you through the creation of your first SOLIDWORKS model. You construct the Disc of the Old ham coupling assembly:

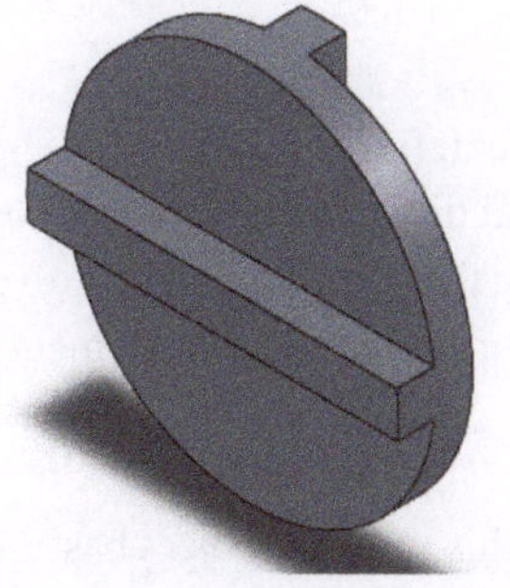

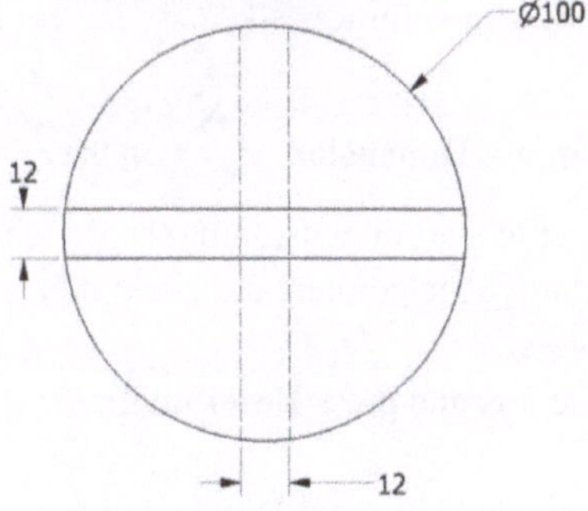

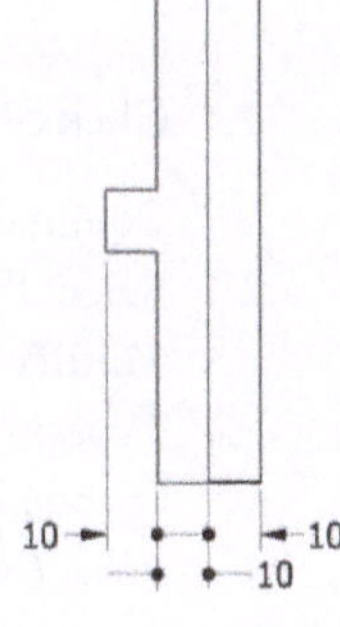

Opening a New Part File

1. Start SOLIDWORKS Design 2026 by clicking the **SOLIDWORKS Design 2026** icon on the desktop; the Welcome window appears.
2. On the Welcome window, click the **Home** tab, and then click the **Part** icon; a new part file is opened.

Starting a Sketch

1. In the SOLIDWORKS Design 2026 window, click the **Unit System** drop-down at the lower right corner.
2. Select **MMGS (millimeter, gram, second)** from the drop-down.

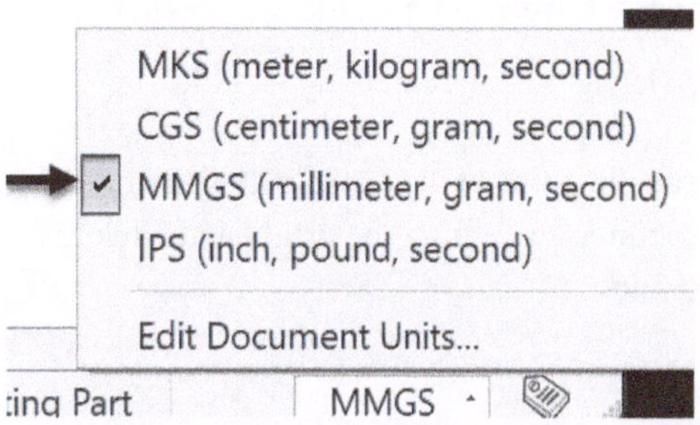

3. To start a new sketch, click **Sketch > Sketch** on the CommandManager.

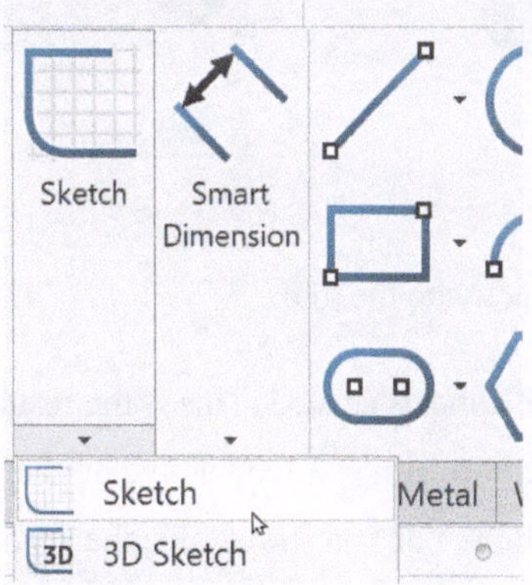

4. Select the front plane.

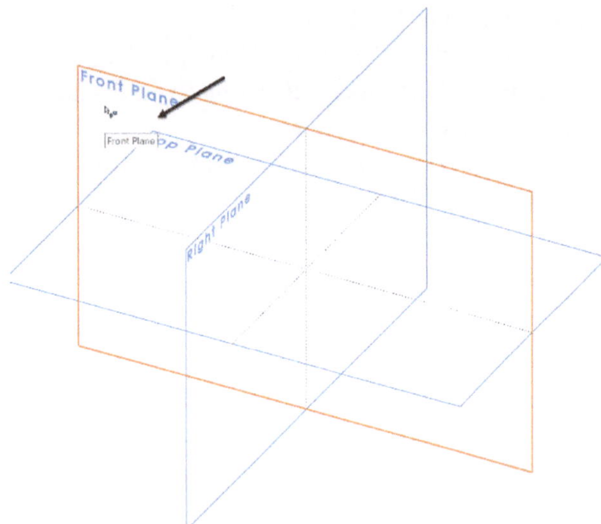

5. Click **Sketch > Circle** on the CommandManager to start creating a circle.

6. Select the origin point of the coordinate system.
7. Move the pointer away from the origin and click to draw the circle.

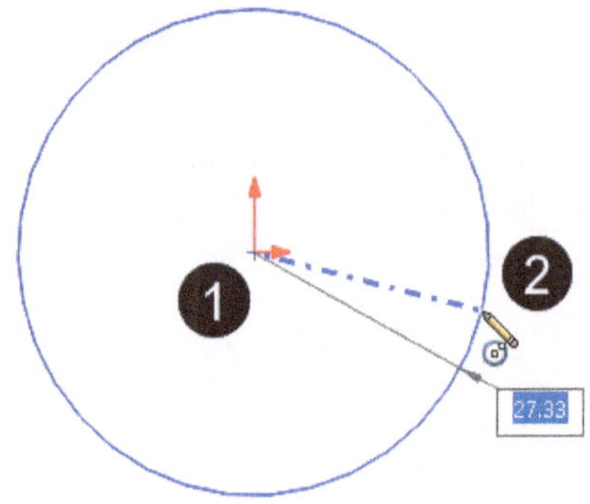

8. Press **ESC** to deactivate the tool.

Notice that the sketch appears shaded. This is the result of the **Shaded Sketch Contours** icon active on the **Sketch** tab of the ribbon. You can show/ hide the shade inside the sketch by turning ON/OFF the **Shaded Sketch Contours** icon.

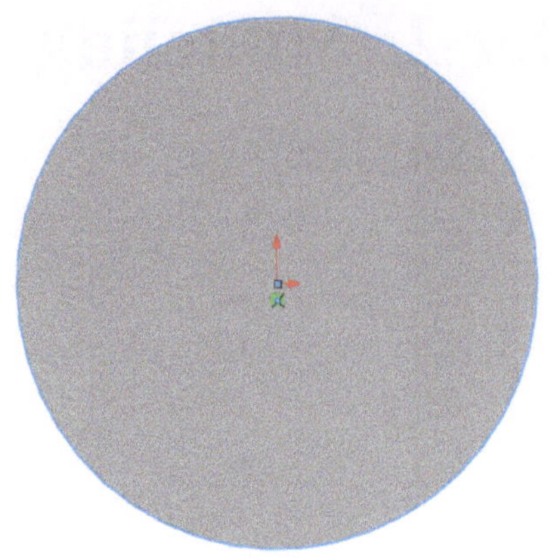

Adding Dimensions

In this section, you will specify the size of the sketched circle by adding dimensions.

As you add dimensions, the sketch can attain any one of the following three states:

Fully Constrained sketch: In a fully constrained sketch, the positions of all the entities are fully described by dimensions, relations, or both. In a fully constrained sketch, all the entities are black.

Under Constrained sketch: To define the geometry completely, you need additional dimensions, relations, or both. In this state, you can drag the sketch elements to modify the sketch. An under constrained sketch element is in blue.

Over Constrained sketch: In this state, an object has conflicting dimensions, relations, or both. An over constraining dimension is in yellow.

1. Click **Sketch > Smart Dimension** on the CommandManager to start dimensioning the sketch.
2. Select the circle, move the pointer, and click; the **Modify** box appears.
3. Type-in **100** in the box and press **Enter** on the keyboard.
4. Press **Esc** to deactivate the **Smart Dimension** tool.

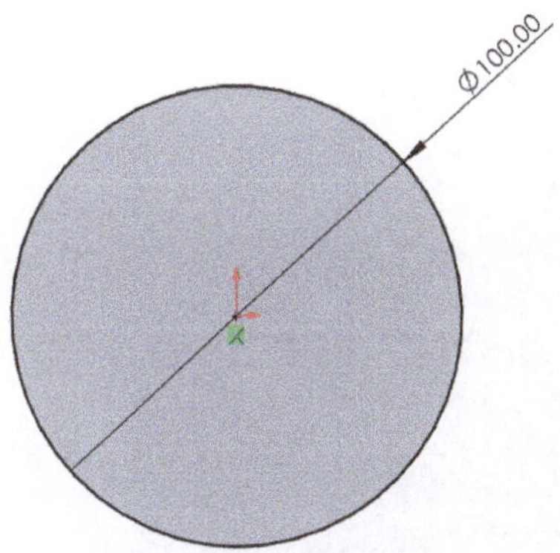

5. To display the entire circle at full size and to center it in the graphics area, use one of the following methods:

• On the **View (Heads Up)** toolbar, click **Zoom to Fit**.

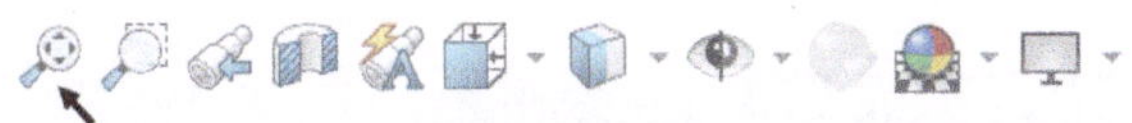

• On the Menu bar, click **View > Modify > Zoom to Fit**.

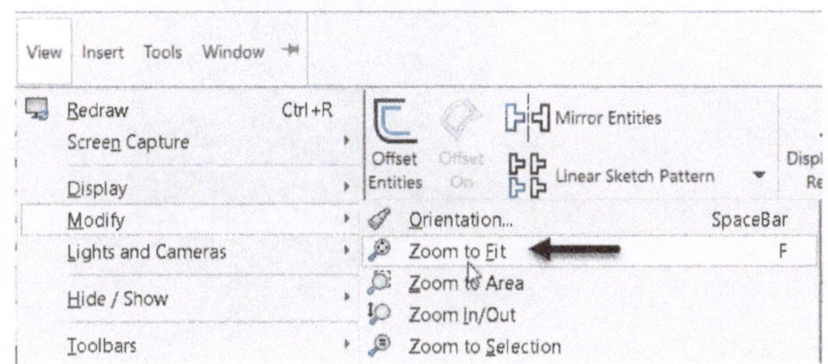

6. On the CommandManager, click **Sketch > Exit Sketch**.

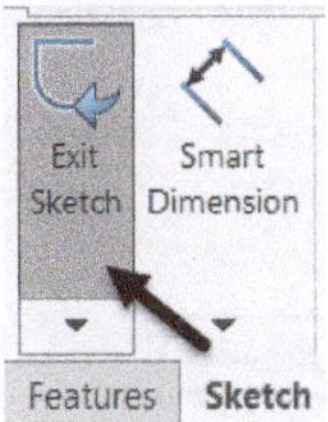

7. On the **View (Heads Up)** toolbar, click **View Orientation > Isometric**.

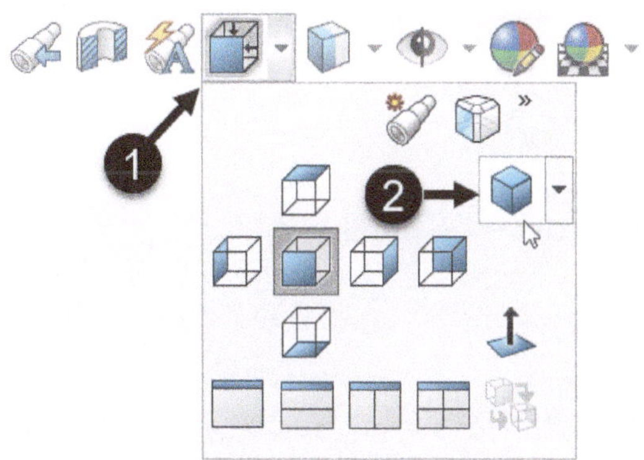

Constructing the Base Feature

You can call the first feature of any part as a base feature. You now construct this feature by extruding the sketched circle.

1. On the CommandManager, click **Features > Extruded Boss/Base** .
2. Click on the sketched circle if it is not already selected.

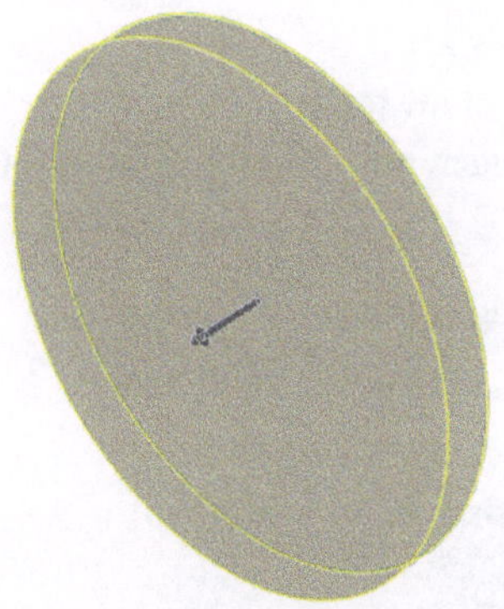

3. On the **Boss-Extrude** PropertyManager, type-in **10** in the **Depth** box, and then click **OK** .

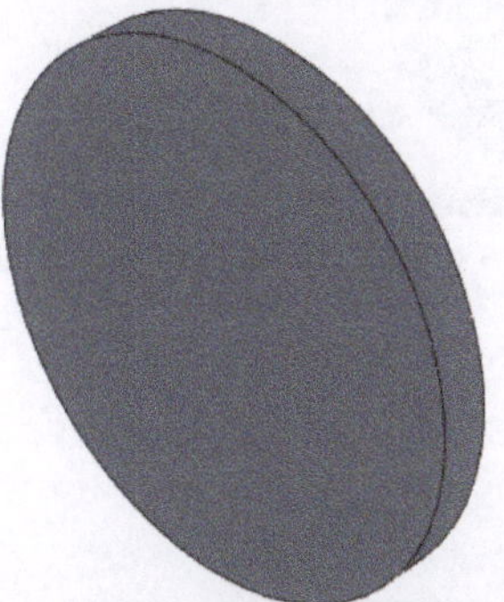

Notice the new feature, **Boss-Extrude1**, in the **FeatureManager Design Tree**.

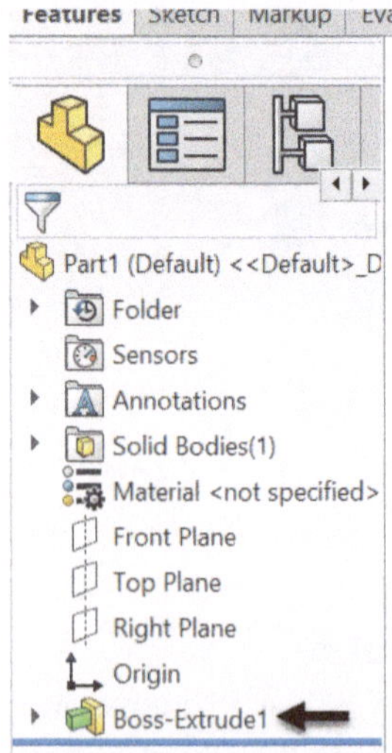

Adding an Extruded Feature

To construct additional features, you must draw sketches on the model faces or planes and then convert them into features.

1. On the CommandManager, click **Features > Extruded Boss/Base** .
2. Click on the front face of the model.
3. On the CommandManager, click **Sketch > Convert Entities** .
4. Click on the circular edge of the model geometry.

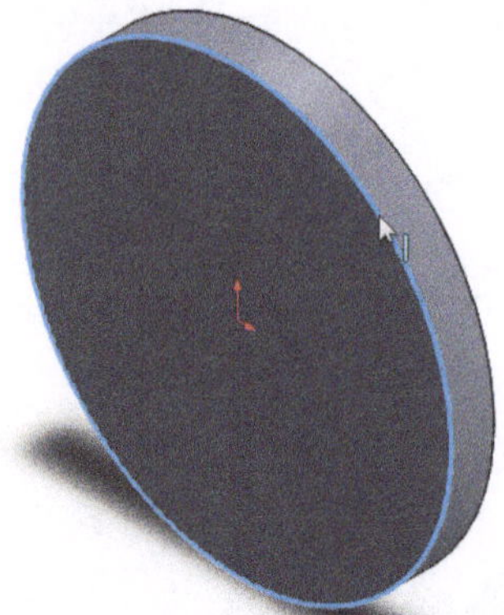

5. On the **Convert Entities** PropertyManager, click **OK** ✓.

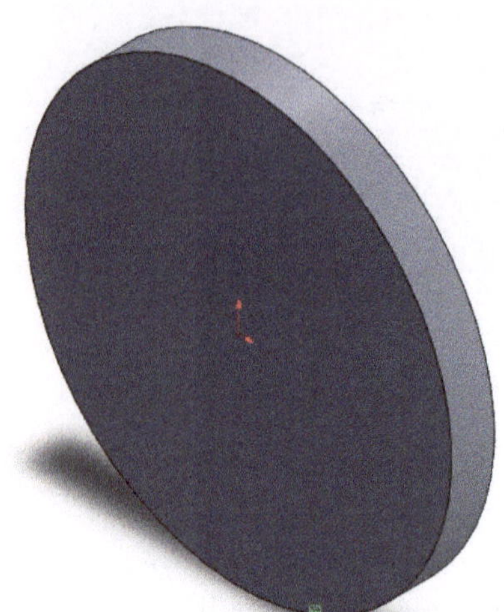

6. On the CommandManager, click **Sketch > Line** .
7. Click on the circular edge to specify the first point of the line, as shown.

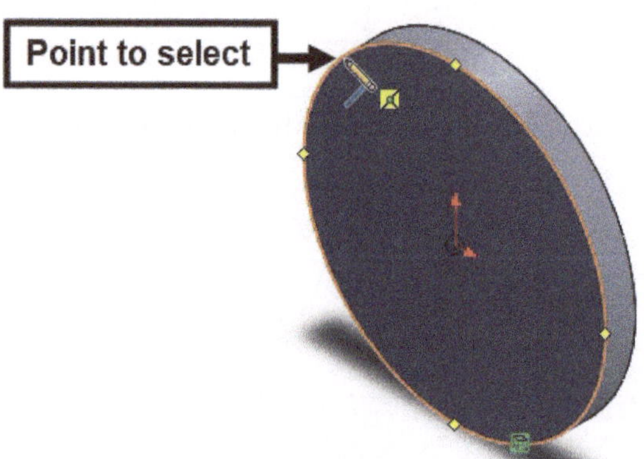

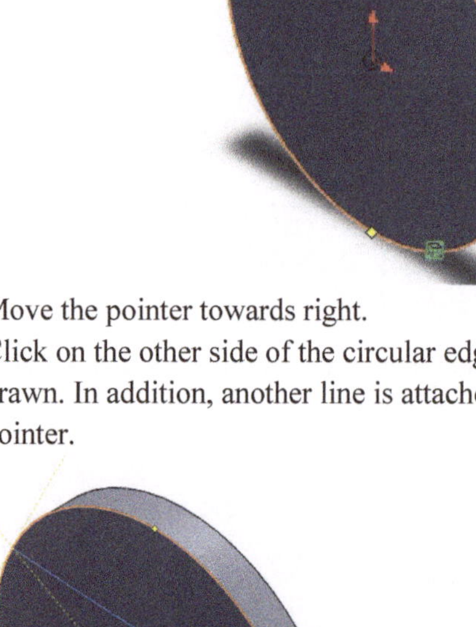

8. Move the pointer towards right.
9. Click on the other side of the circular edge; a line is drawn. In addition, another line is attached to the pointer.

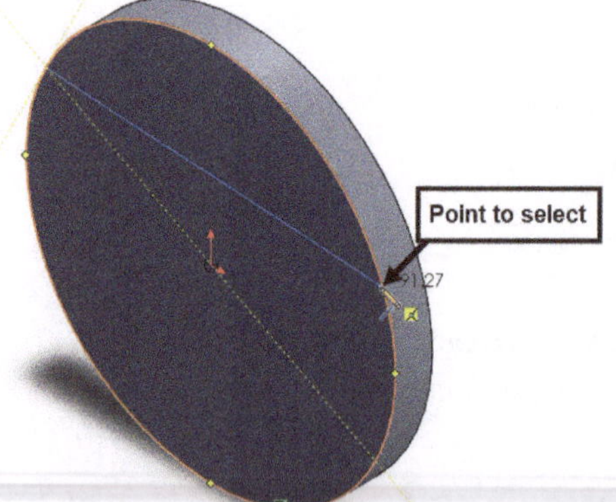

10. Right-click and select **End chain (double-click)** to end the line.

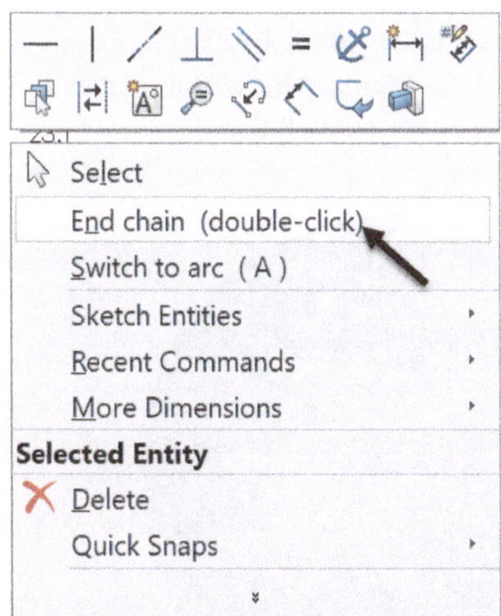

11. Draw another line below the previous line.

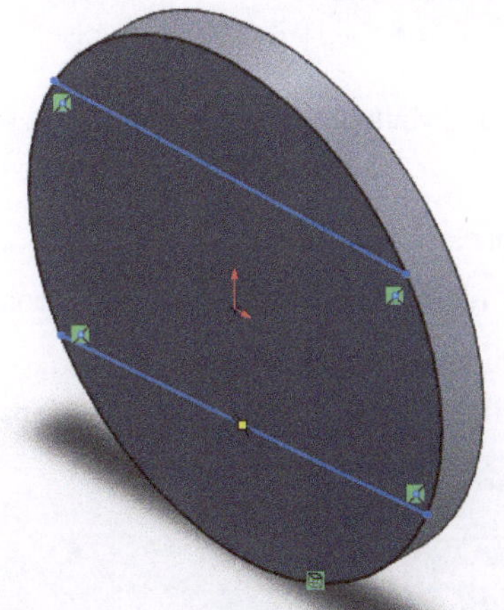

12. Press **Esc** to deactivate the **Line** tool.
13. On the CommandManager, click **Sketch > Display/Delete Relations > Add Relation**.

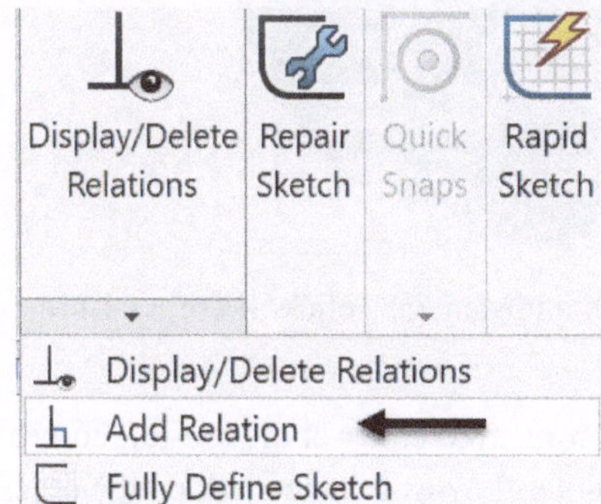

14. Select the two lines.
15. On the **Add Relations** PropertyManager, under the **Add Relations** section, click **Horizontal** to make the two lines horizontal.
16. Under the **Add Relations** section, click **Equal** to make the lines equal in length.

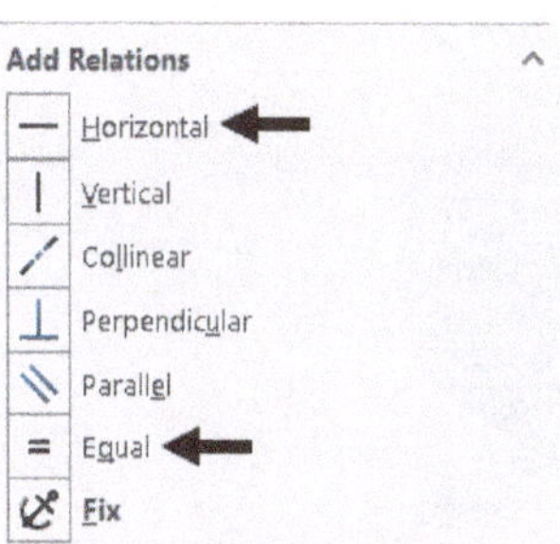

17. Click **OK** on the PropertyManager.
18. On the CommandManager, click **Sketch > Smart Dimension** .
19. Select the two horizontal lines.
20. Move the pointer toward right and click to locate the dimension.
21. Type-in **12** in the Modify box and click **OK**.

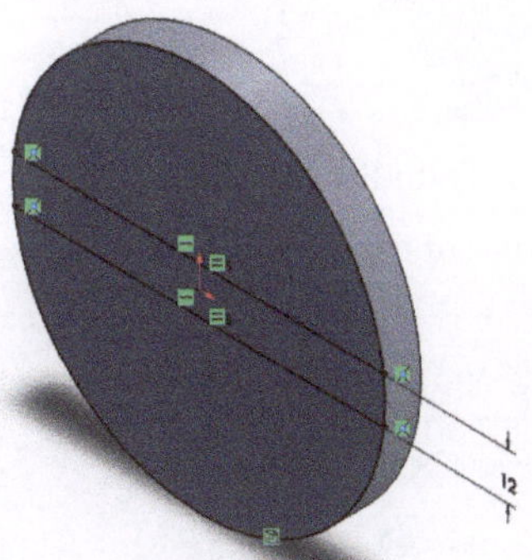

22. On the CommandManager, click **Sketch > Trim Entities** .
23. Click the **Trim to Closest** icon on the PropertyManager.

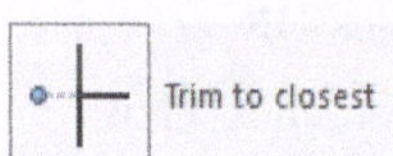

24. Click on the arc portions of the projected entity.

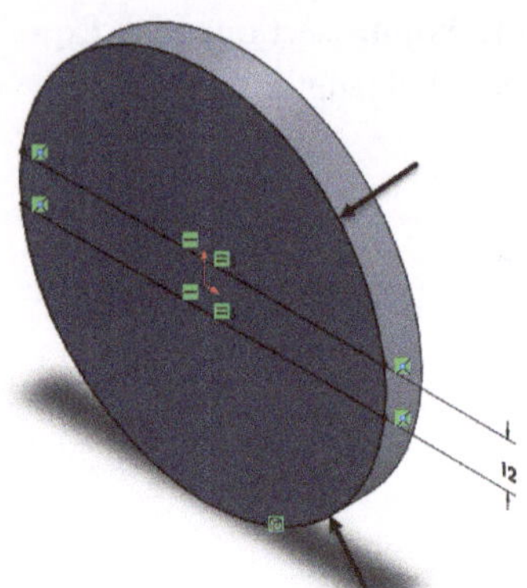

The projected entities are trimmed.

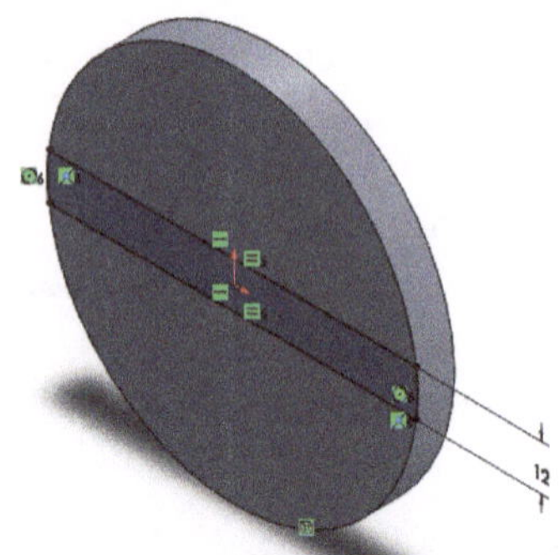

25. Click **OK** ✔ on the **Trim** PropertyManager.
26. On the top right corner of the graphics window, select **Exit Sketch**.

27. On the **Boss-Extrude** PropertyManager, type-in **10** in the **Depth** box, and then click **OK** ✔ .
28. On the **View (Heads Up)** toolbar, click **View Orientation > Isometric**.

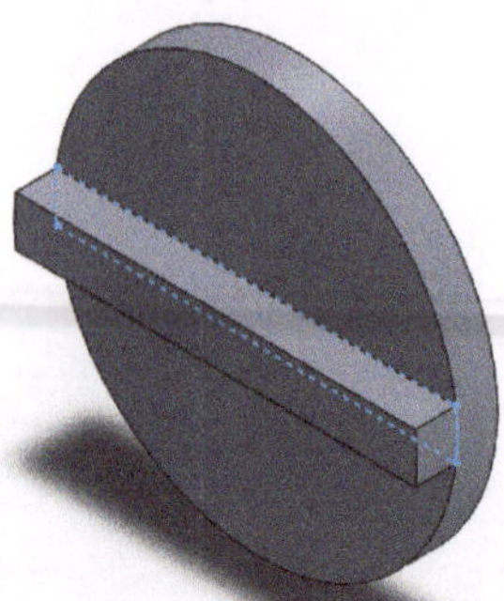

Adding another Extruded Feature

1. Press and hold the Middle Mouse Button and drag the pointer to rotate the part such that the back face of the part is displayed.

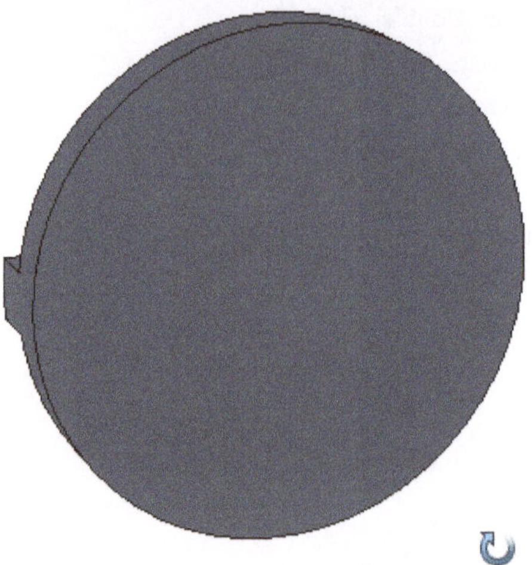

2. On the CommandManager, click **Sketch > Sketch** .
3. Click on the back face of the part.
4. Activate the **Convert Entities** tool and convert the circular edge into a sketch entity.
5. Click **OK** on the Convert Entities PropertyManager.

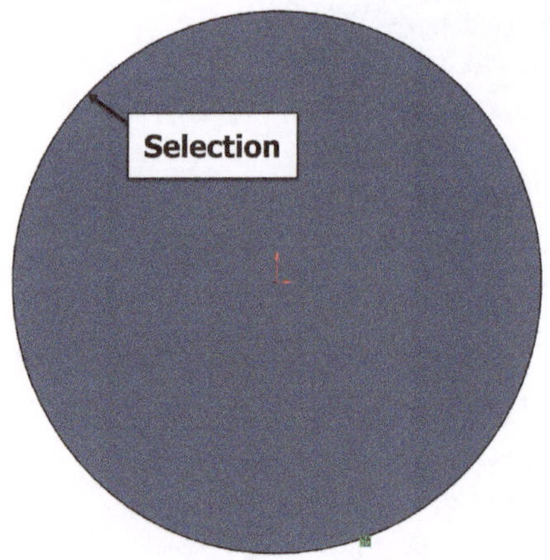

6. On the CommandManager, click **Sketch > Line** .
7. Click on the converted entity at the top-left corner.
8. Move the pointer downward and click on the other side of the converted entity.
9. Right-click and select End Chain.

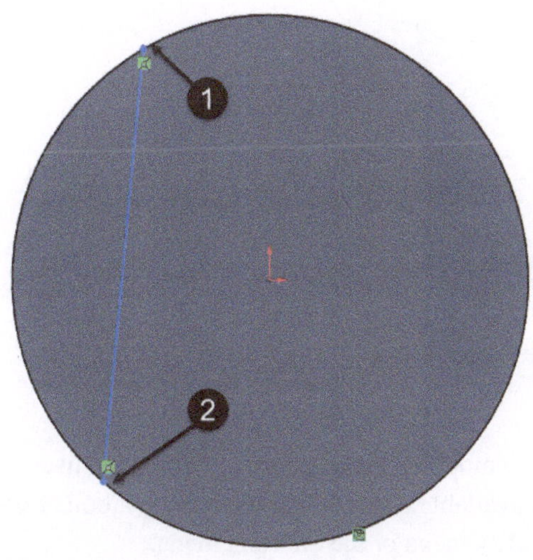

10. Create another line on the right side, as shown.

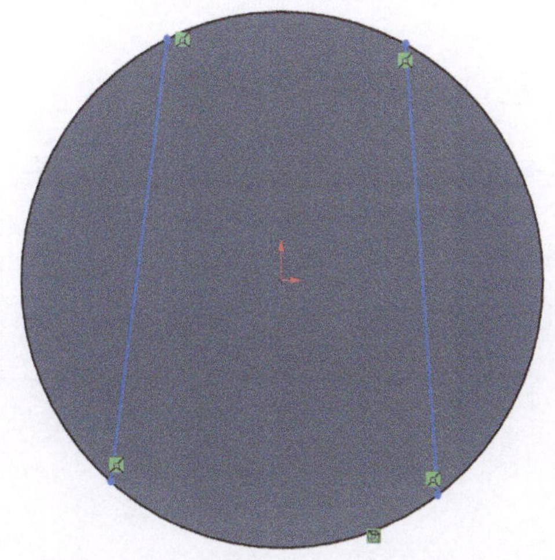

11. Press **Esc** to deactivate the **Line** tool.
12. Press the **Ctrl** key and click on the lines.
13. On the PropertyManager, under the **Add Relations** section, click **Vertical**.
14. Click **Equal**, and then click **OK** on the PropertyManager.

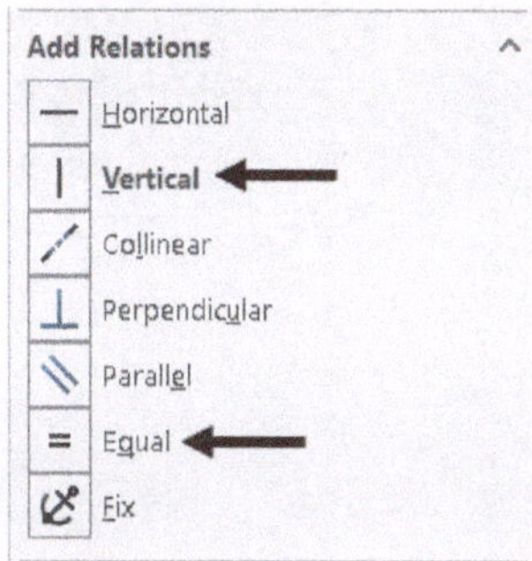

15. Activate the **Smart Dimension** 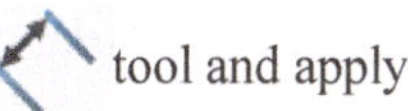 tool and apply a **12** mm distance dimension between the vertical lines (follow the steps to create dimensions, as discussed earlier).

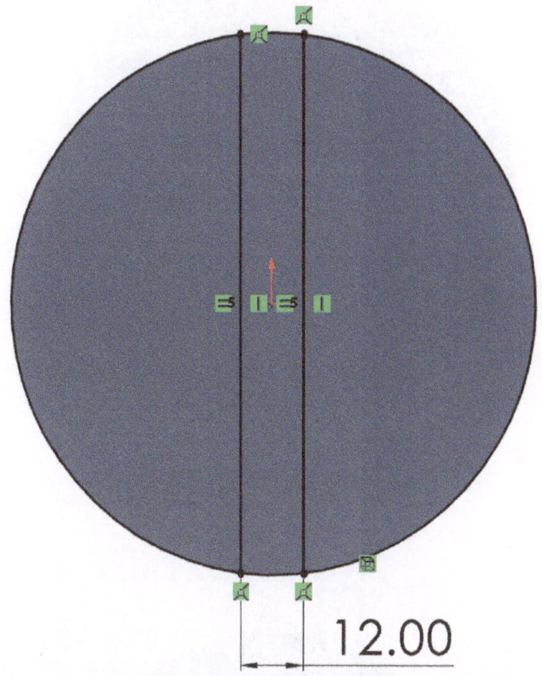

16. Activate the **Trim Entities** tool.
17. Click the **Power Trim** icon on the PropertyManager.

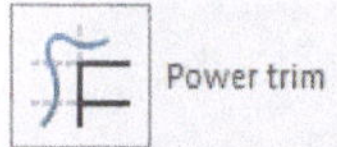

18. Press and hold the left mouse button, and then drag the pointer across the right-side arc; the arc is trimmed.

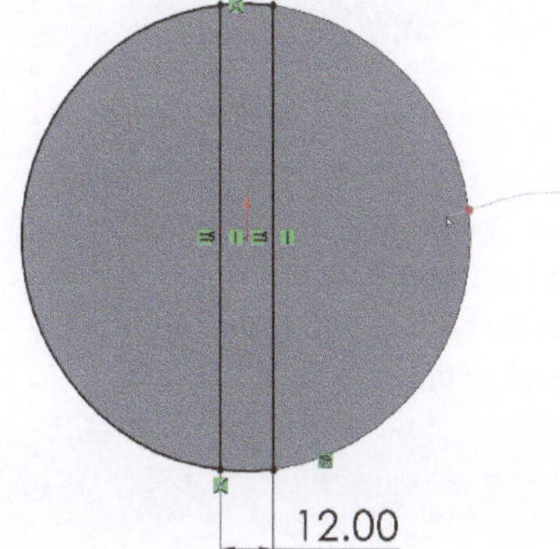

19. Release the left mouse button.

20. Likewise, trim the left side arc by dragging the mouse across it.

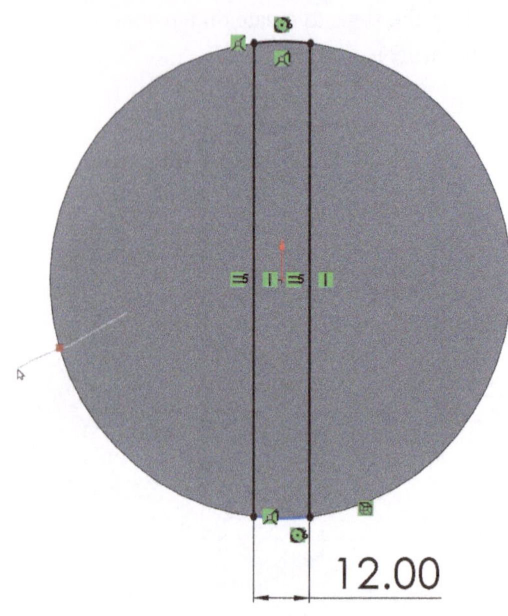

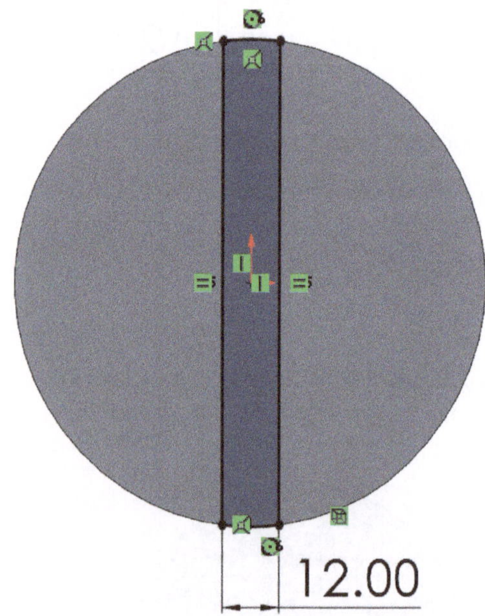

21. Click **Exit Sketch**.
22. Extrude the sketch up to 10 mm depth.
23. Click **OK** on the PropertyManager.

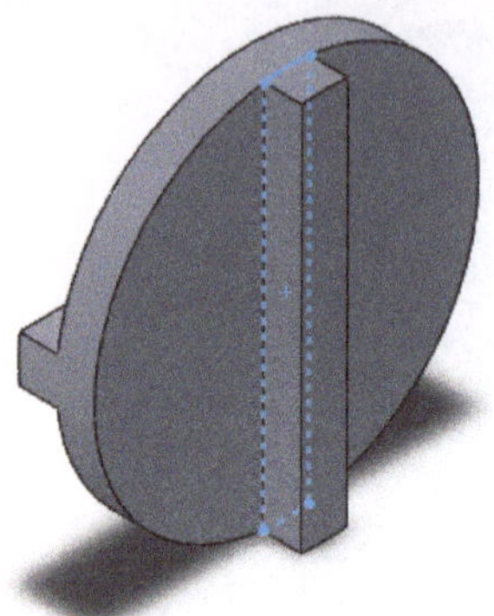

To magnify a model in the graphics area, you can use the zoom tools available on the **View (Heads Up)** toolbar or **View > Modify** menu or the Shortcut menu.

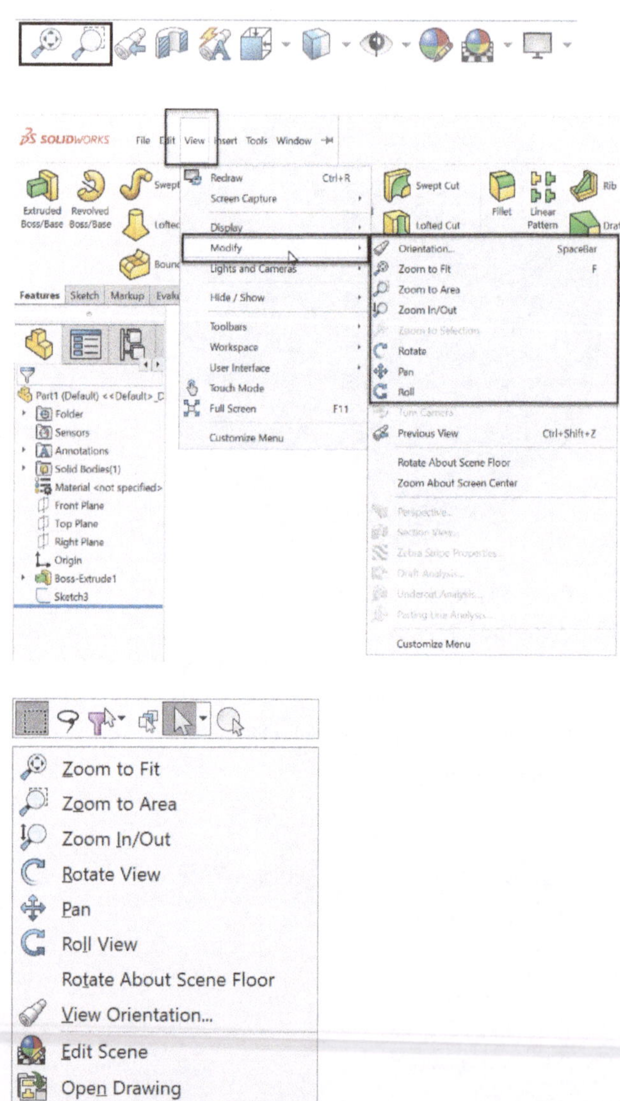

Click **Zoom to Fit** to display the part full size in the current window.

Click **Zoom to Area** , and then drag the pointer to construct a rectangle; the area in the rectangle zooms to fill the window.

Click **Zoom In/Out** , and then drag the pointer. Dragging up zooms in; dragging down zooms out.

Click on a face, edge, vertex or any object, and then click **Zoom to Selection** on the Context Toolbar. You will zoom in to the selection.

To move the part view, click the right mouse button and select **Pan** .

Drag the part to move it around in the graphics area.

Select the **Rotate About Scene Floor** option from the right-click shortcut menu. It helps you to rotate the view about an axis perpendicular to the scene floor. After enabling this option, you can use the **Roll View** option to rotate the view.

Saving the Part

1. Click the **Save** button on the **Quick Access Toolbar**.
2. Enter **Disc** in the **File name** field.
3. Browse to **C:\Users\Username\Documents** folder, and then create a new folder with the name Oldham Coupling.
4. Click **Save** to save the file.
5. Click **File > Close**.

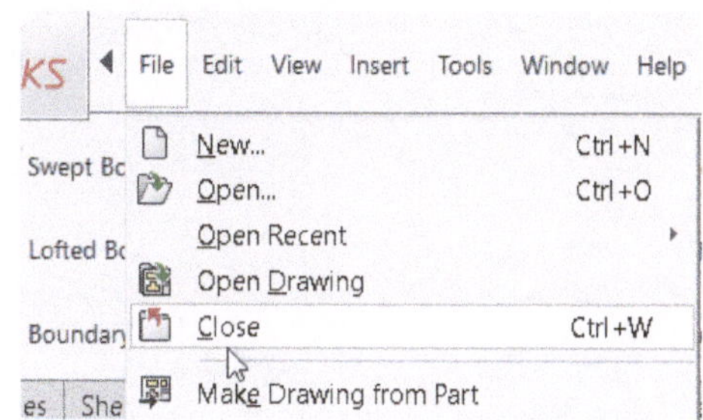

Note:
*.prt or *.sldprt are the file extensions for the files created in the Part environment of SOLIDWORKS.

TUTORIAL 2

In this tutorial, you will construct a flange by performing the following operations:

- Constructing a revolved feature
- Constructing cut features
- Adding Rounds

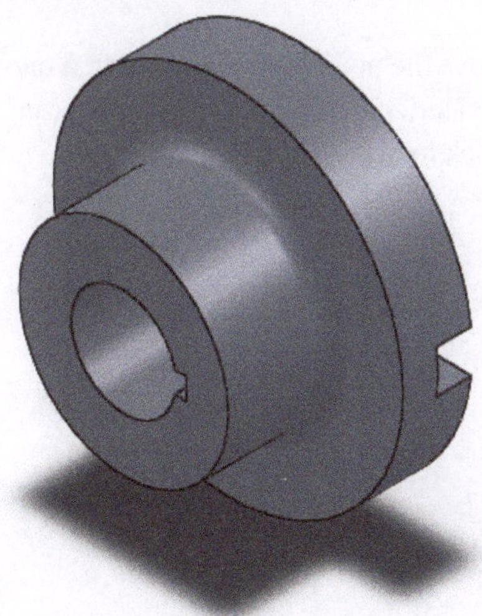

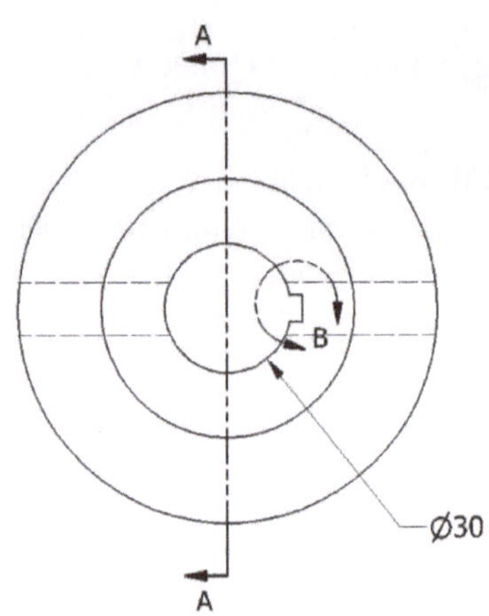

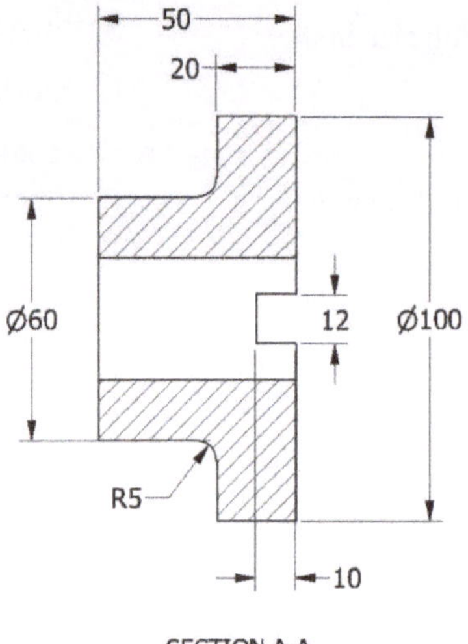

SECTION A-A
SCALE 1 : 1

3
6

DETAIL B
SCALE 2 : 1

Opening a New Part File

1. To open a new part, click the **New** button on the **Quick Access Toolbar**.
2. On the **New SOLIDWORKS Document** dialog, click **Part** and then click **OK**.

Sketching a Revolve Profile

Now, you will construct a sketch for the revolved feature.

1. On the CommandManager, click **Sketch > Sketch** 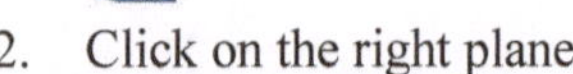.
2. Click on the right plane.
3. Activate the **Line** tool and place the pointer on the sketch origin.
4. Move the pointer upward and notice a dotted line.
5. Click along the dotted line to specify the start point of the line.

6. Move the pointer upwards. You will notice that the Vertical relation symbol appears.
7. Click to draw a vertical line.

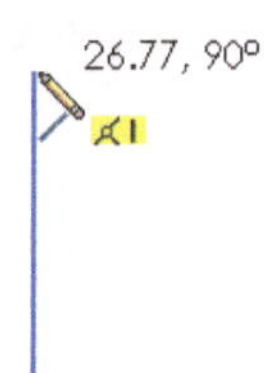

8. Move the pointer toward the left. You will notice that the Horizontal relation symbol appears.
9. Click to draw a horizontal line.

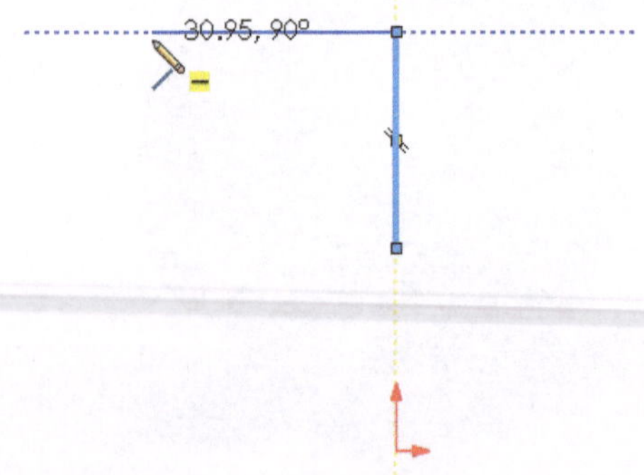

10. Move the pointer vertically downward up to a small distance. Next, click when the Vertical relation symbol appears.

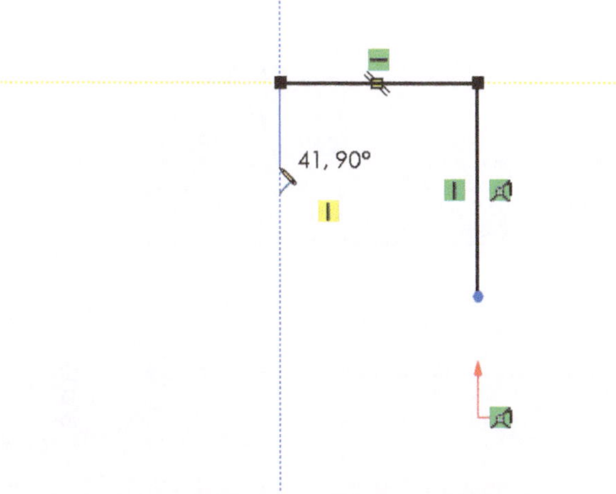

11. Move the pointer toward left horizontally. Next, click when the Horizontal relation symbol appears.

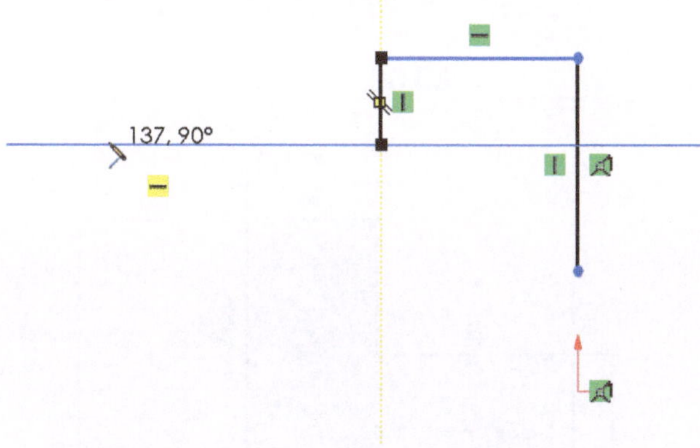

12. Move the pointer vertically downward up to the start point of the first line; a dotted line is displayed between the start point of the first line and the cursor.
13. Click to create the vertical line.

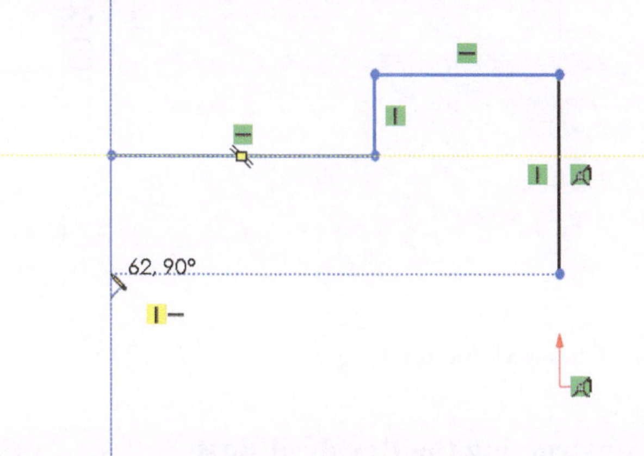

14. Move the pointer horizontally toward right and select the start point of the first line.

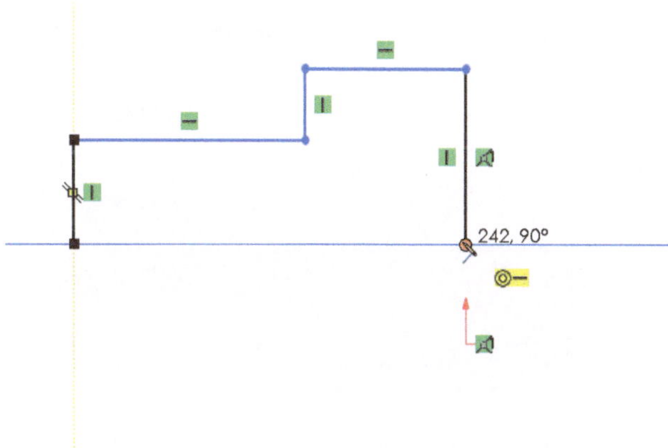

15. On the CommandManager, click **Sketch > Line > Centerline**.

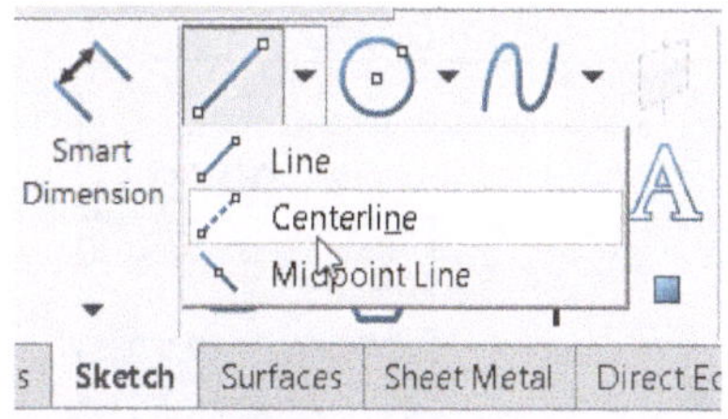

16. Select the sketch origin and move the pointer horizontally toward left and click to create a horizontal centerline.

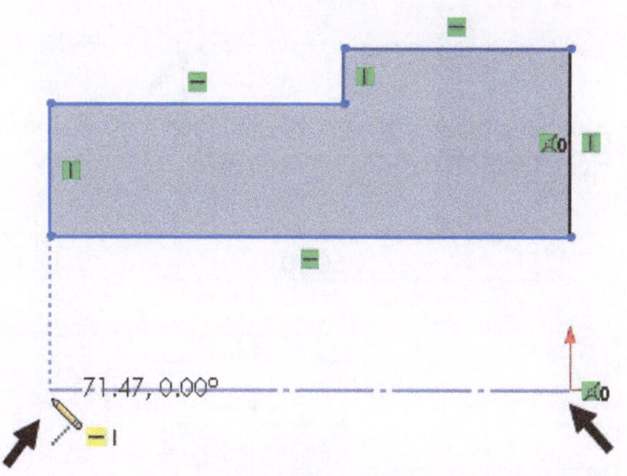

6. Activate the **Smart Dimension** tool and apply two horizontal dimensions (refer to the **Adding Dimensions** section of Tutorial 1).

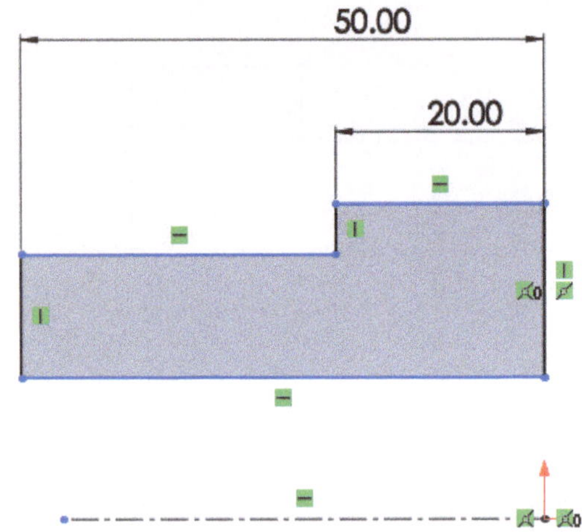

7. Click on the centerline and bottom horizontal line.

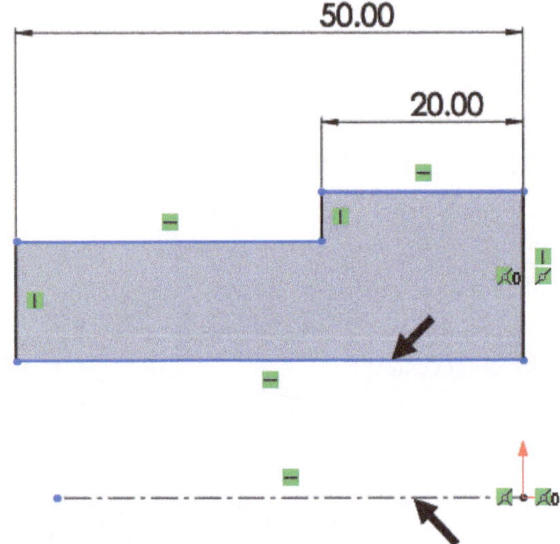

9. Move the pointer downwards and then towards the right. Click to position the dimension.

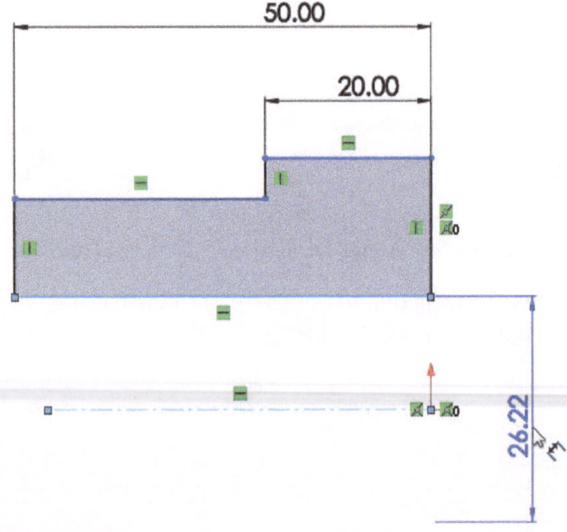

10. Type-in 30 in the **Modify** box and click **OK**.

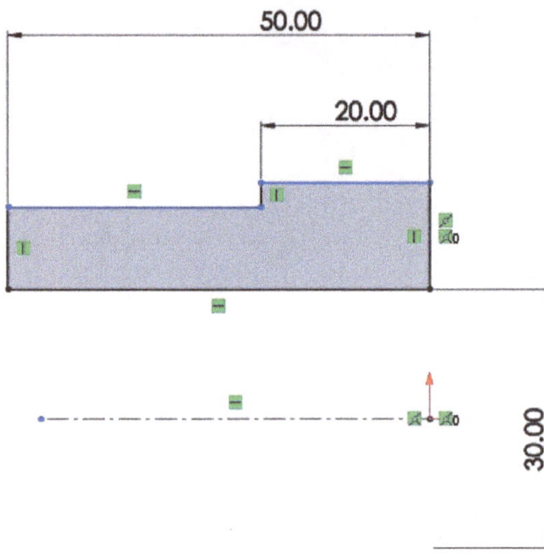

11. Create other symmetric dimensions, as shown.

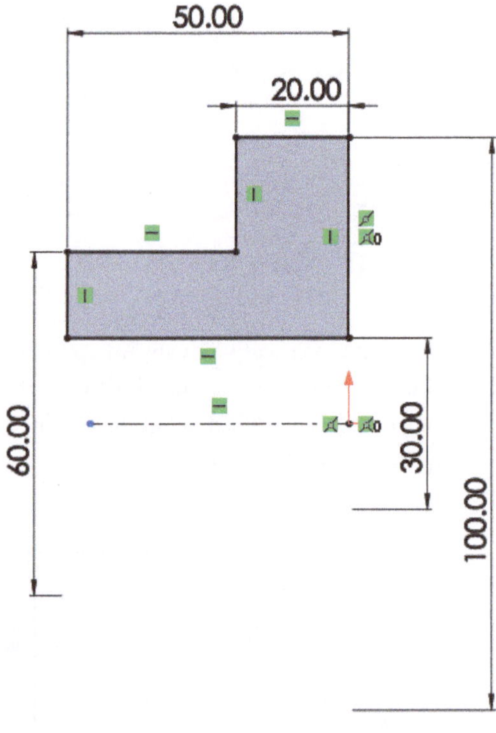

12. Click **Exit Sketch**.

Constructing the Revolved Boss

1. On the CommandManager, click **Features > Revolved Boss/Base**.

2. Select the sketch, if not already selected.

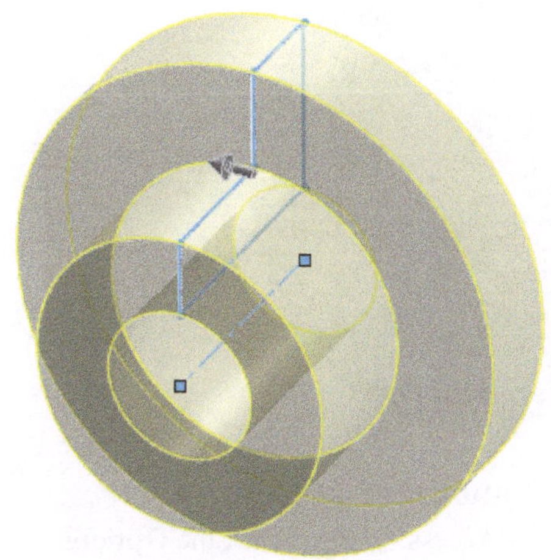

3. On the **Revolve** PropertyManager, set the **Direction1 Angle** value to **360**.

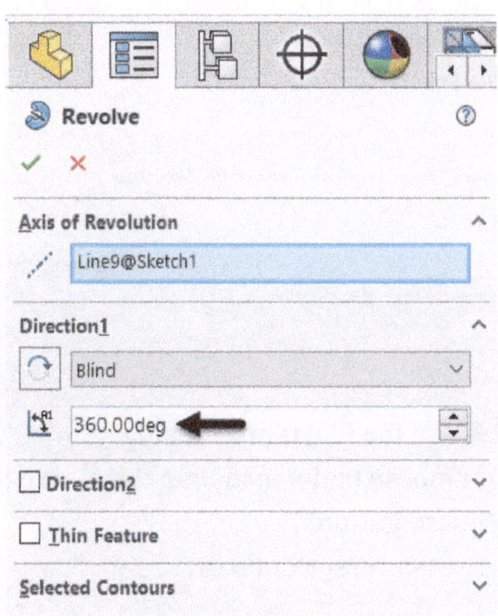

4. Click **OK** ✓.

Constructing the Cut feature

1. Press the CTRL+ 2 keys on your keyboard; the orientation of the model is changed to back.

2. Click on the back face and click **Sketch**.

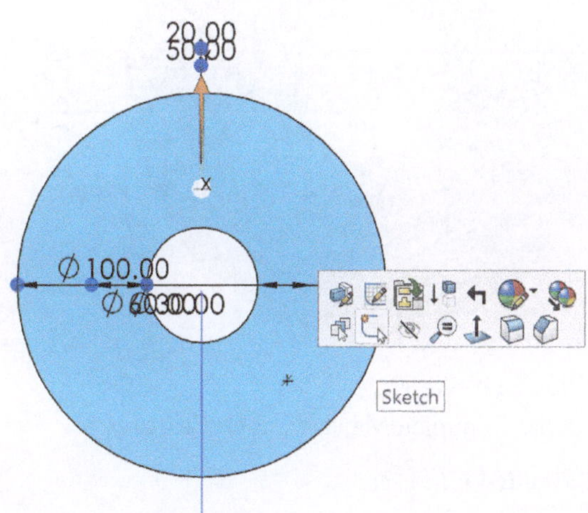

3. On the CommandManager, click **Sketch > Rectangle** drop-down > **Center Rectangle**.

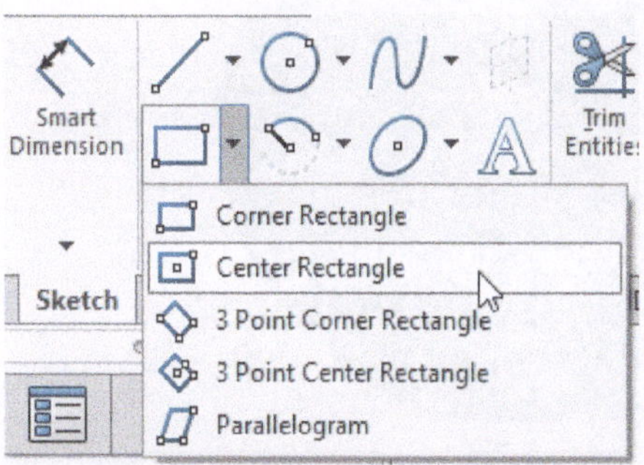

4. Select the origin to define the center point.

5. Move the pointer diagonally toward the right and click to create the rectangle.

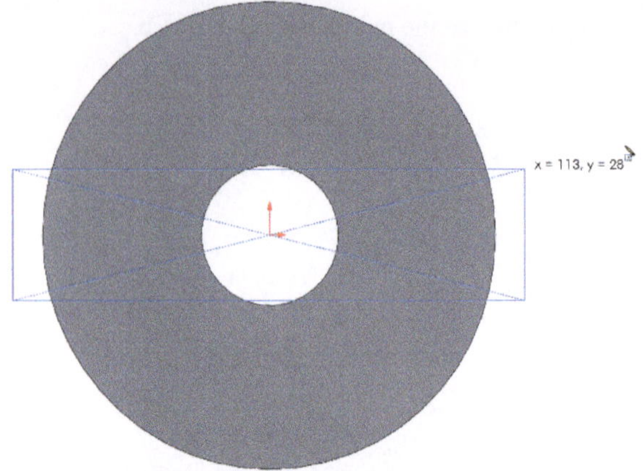

6. Add dimensions to the sketch.

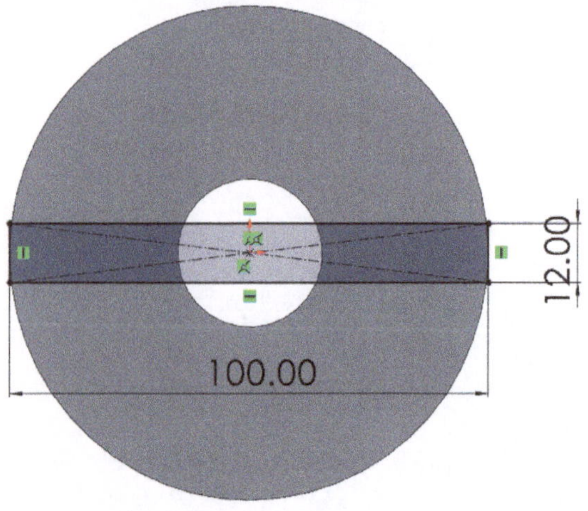

7. Click **Exit Sketch**.
8. On the CommandManager, click **Features > Extruded Cut** .

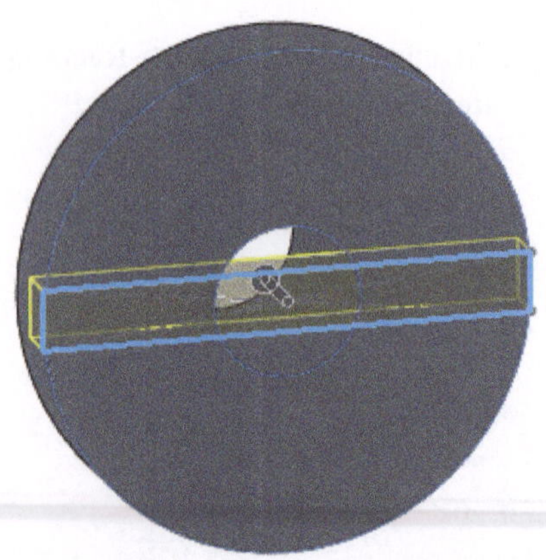

9. On the **Cut-Extrude** PropertyManager, set the **Depth** value to 10 and click **OK** ✔ .

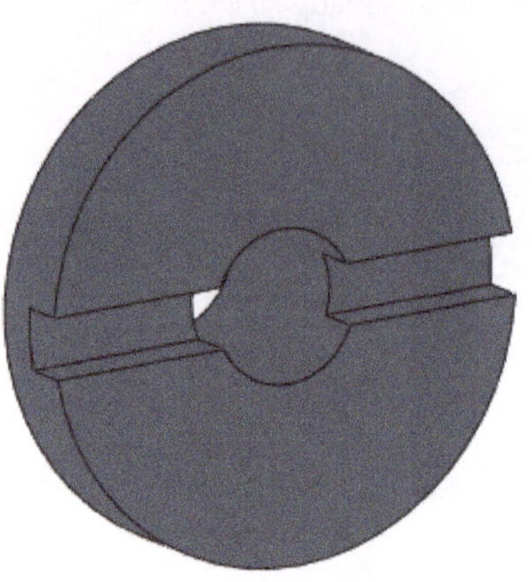

Constructing another Cut feature

1. On the Quick Access Toolbar, click the **Options** drop-down > **Customize**.
2. On the **Customize** dialog, click the **Mouse Gestures** tab.
3. Select **8 Gestures** from the drop-down located on the left side.

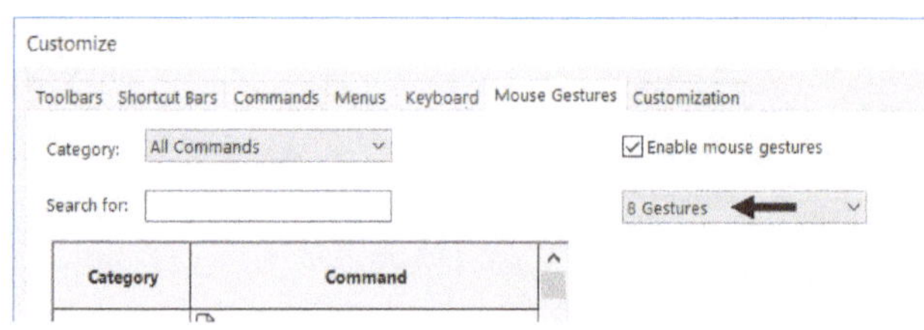

4. Click **OK** to close the **Customize** dialog.
5. Press the right mouse button and drag the mouse to display the Mouse gesture.
6. On the Mouse gesture, select Front.

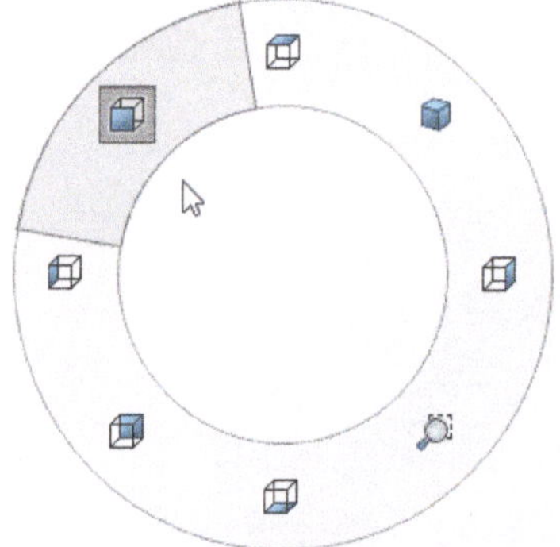

7. On the CommandManager, click **Sketch > Sketch** and click on the front face.
8. Press **S** on the keyboard.
9. On the Flyout Toolbar, click **Rectangle**.

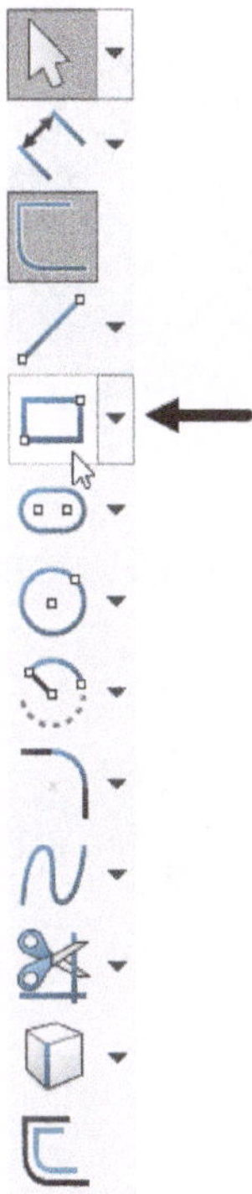

10. On the PropertyManager, select **Corner Rectangle** 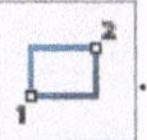.
11. Specify the corners of the rectangle.

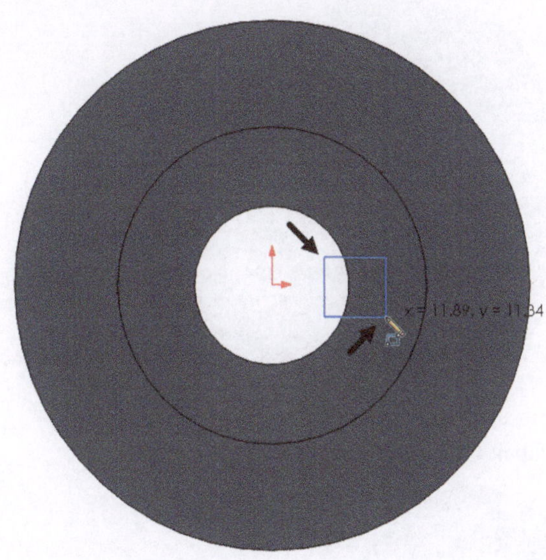

12. On the CommandManager, click **Sketch > Line > Centerline** .
13. Draw a horizontal centerline passing through the origin.

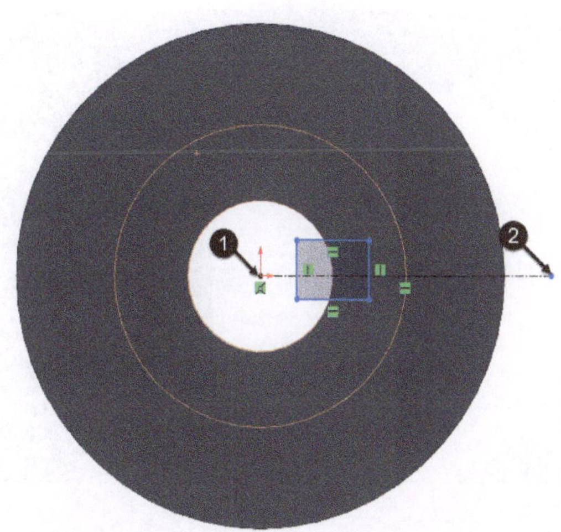

14. Press the Ctrl key and click on the horizontal lines of the sketch.

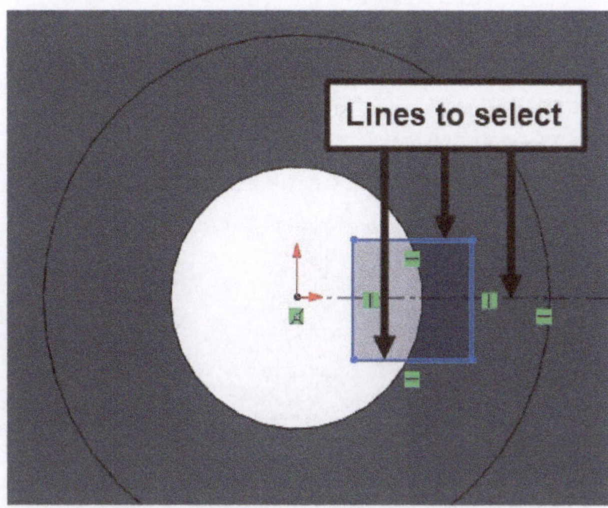

15. On the PropertyManager, under the **Add Relations** section, click **Symmetric**.

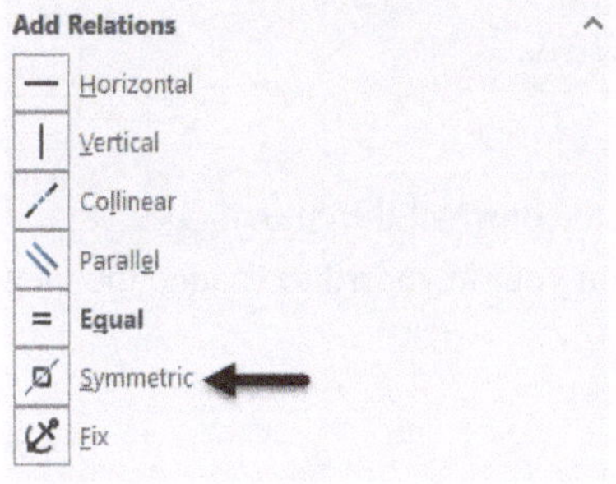

16. Click **OK** .
17. Add dimensions to the sketch.

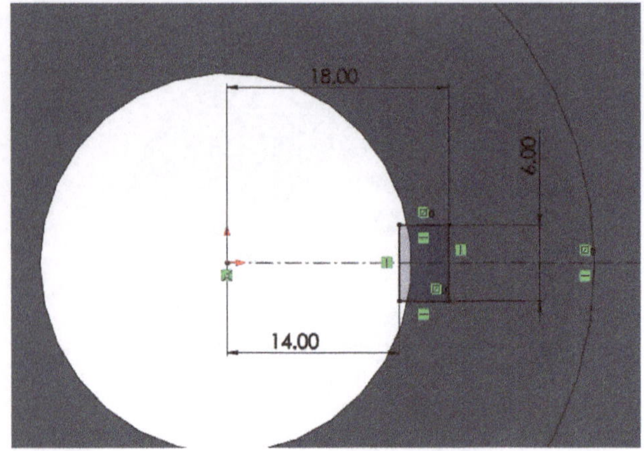

18. Click **Exit Sketch**.
19. On the CommandManager, click **Features > Extruded Cut** .
20. Click on the sketch.
21. On the **Cut-Extrude** PropertyManager, under the **Direction 1** section, select **End Condition > Through All**.

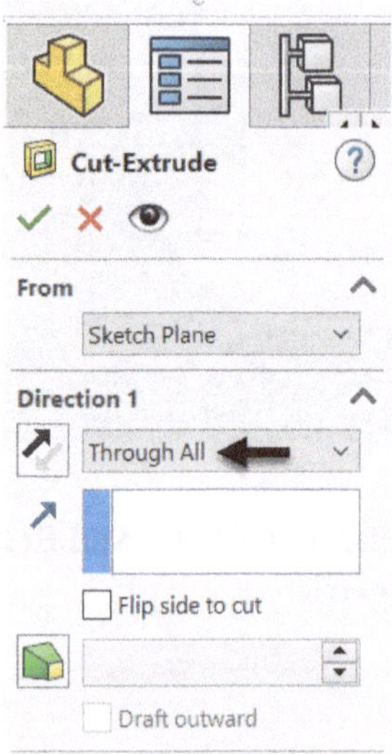

22. Click **OK** to construct the cutout.
23. Press Ctrl+7 on your keyboard to change the view to isometric.

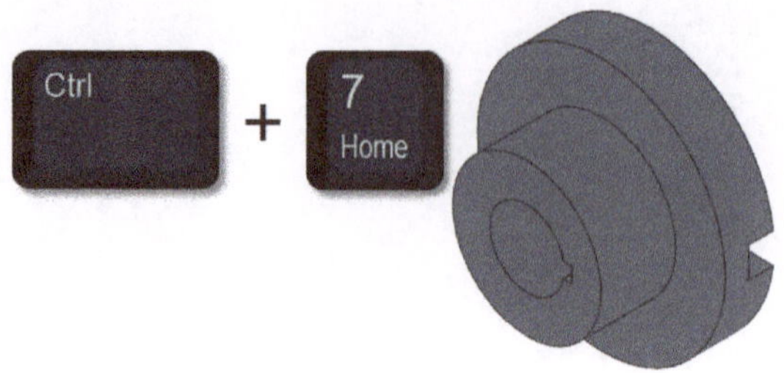

Adding a Fillet

1. Click on the circular edge of the model geometry and select **Fillet**.

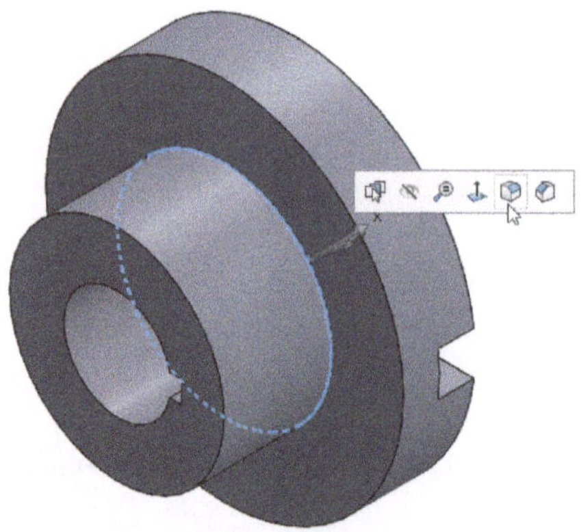

2. Enter **5** in the callout attached to the selected edge.

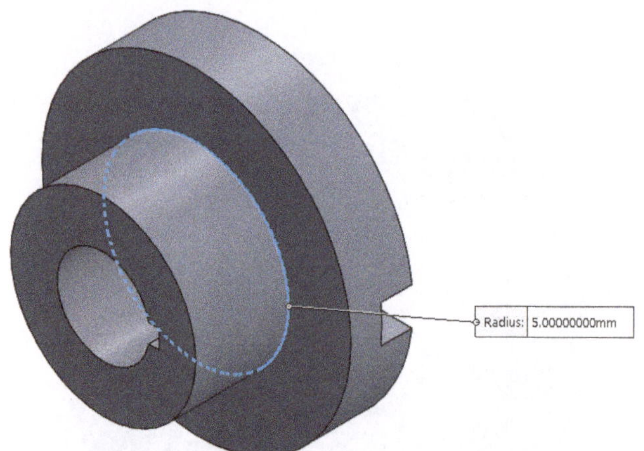

3. Click **OK** to add the fillet.

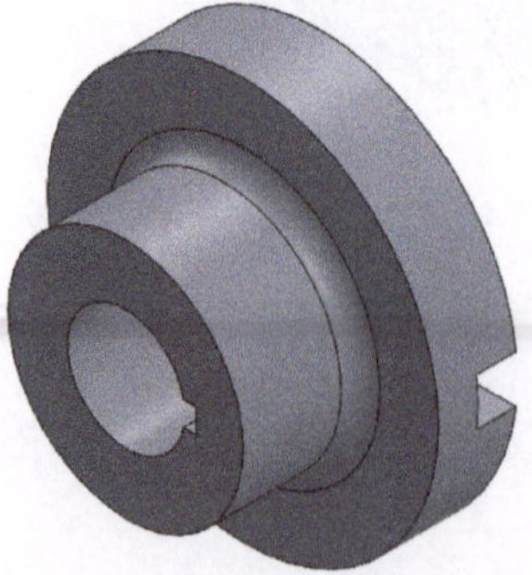

To display the part in different modes, use the **Display Style** menu options on the **View (Heads Up)** toolbar.

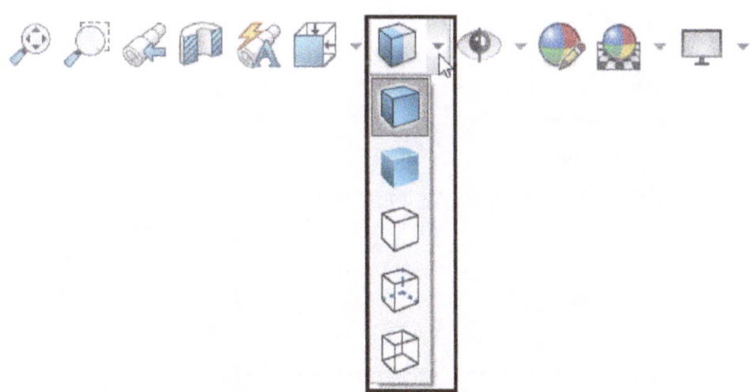

Shaded With Edges

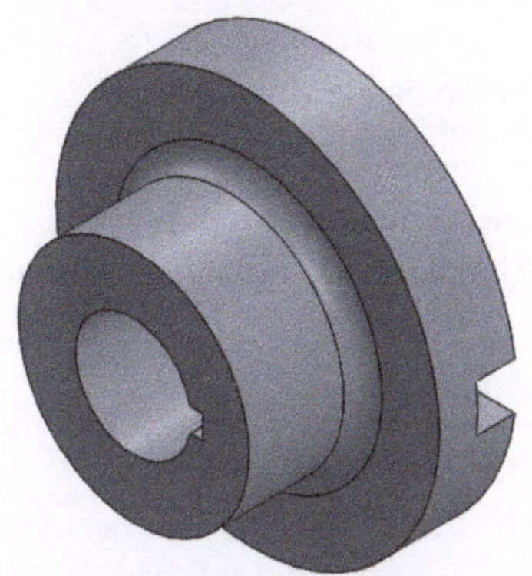

Shaded

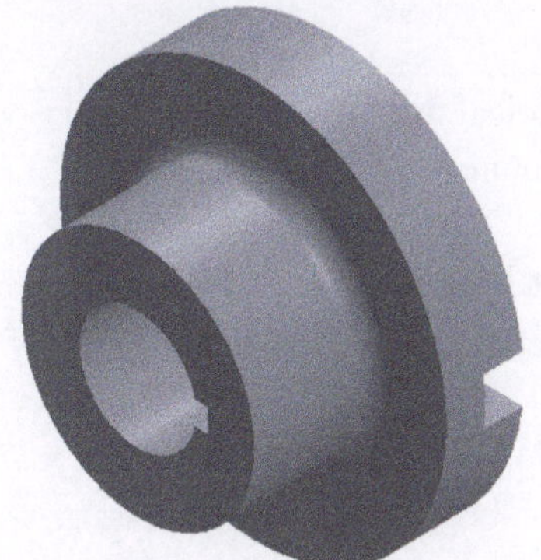

Hidden Lines Removed

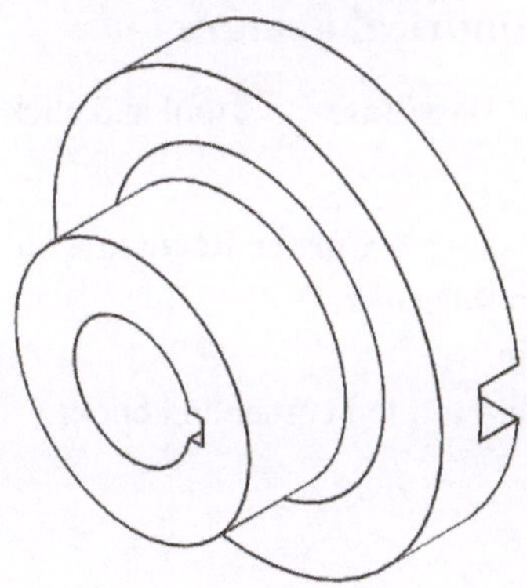

Hidden Lines Visible

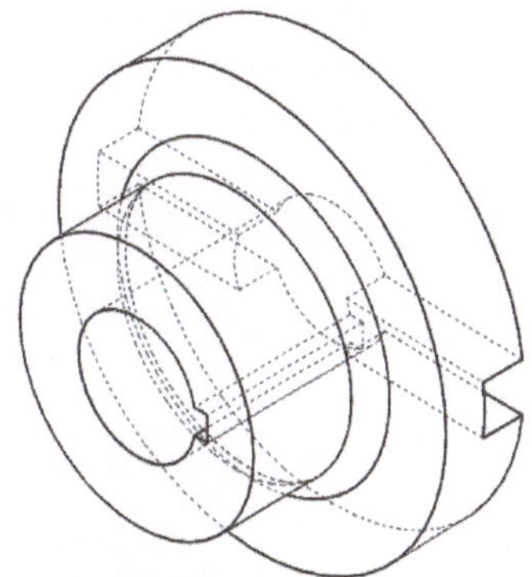

Wireframe

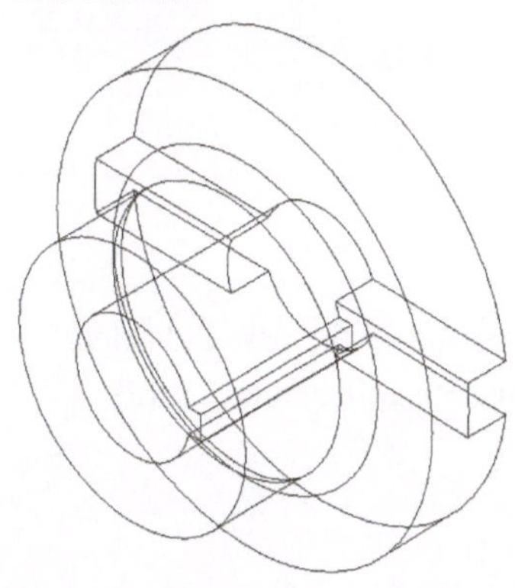

The default display mode for parts and assemblies is **Shaded With Edges**. You may change the display mode whenever you want.

Viewing Parent and Child relationships between features

In SOLIDWORKS, you can view the parent and child relationships between part features using the **Dynamic Reference Visualization** options.

1. On the FeatureManager Design tree, click the right mouse button on the part name, and then select **Dynamic Reference Visualization (Parent).**

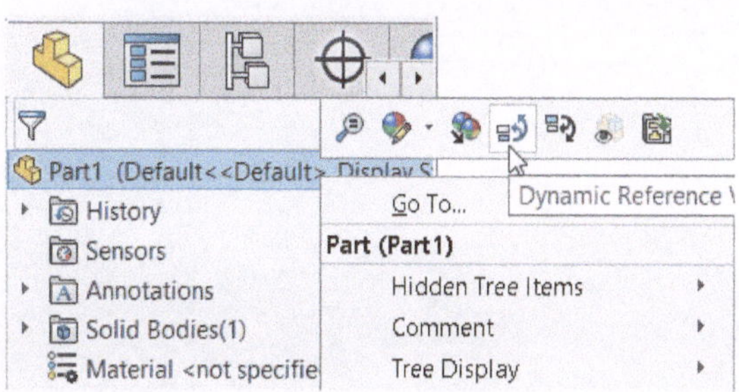

2. On the FeatureManager Design Tree, click the **Fillet** feature and notice an arrow pointing towards the **Revolve** feature. This indicates that the **Revolve** feature is the parent of the **Fillet** feature.

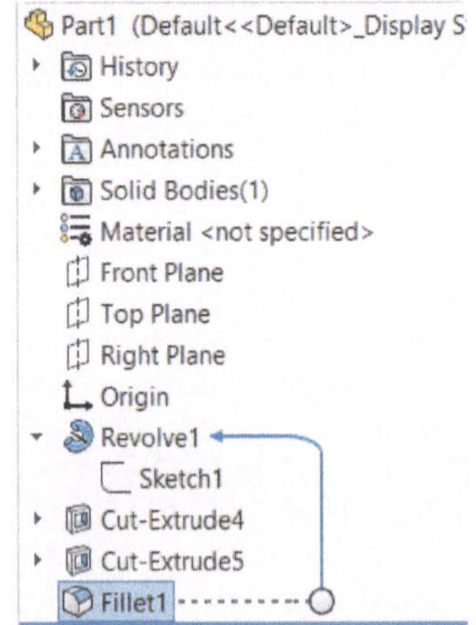

3. Click the right mouse button on the part and select the **Dynamic Reference Visualization (Child)** option.

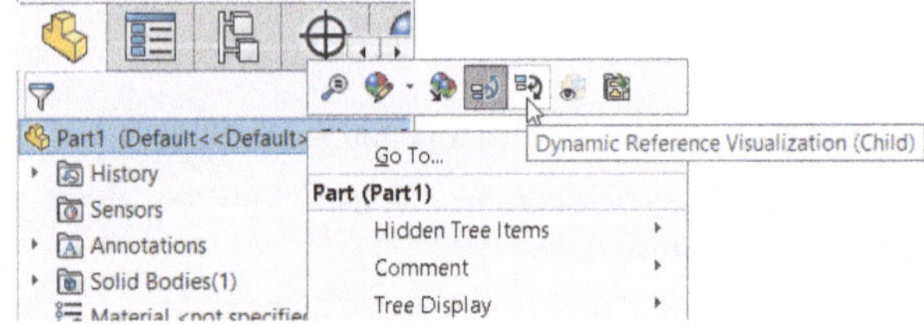

4. Click the **Revolve** feature in the FeatureManager Design Tree. Notice the arrows originating from the Revolve feature and pointing to the Right Plane and Origin. This indicates that they are the parents of the Revolve feature. Also, notice the arrows pointing downwards to the Cut-Extrude and Fillet features. They are the child features of the Revolve feature.

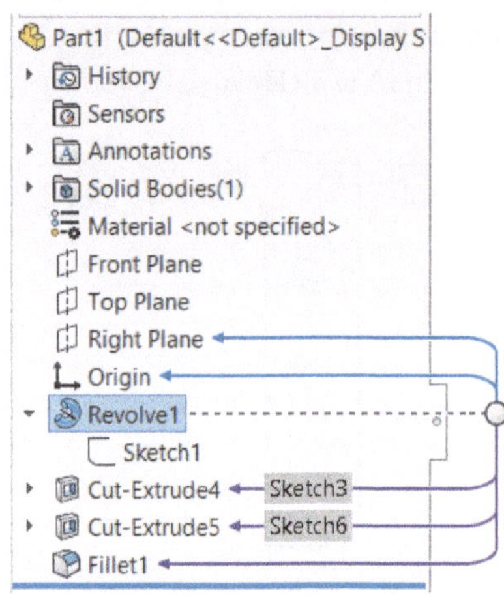

Saving the Part

1. Click the **Save** button on the **Quick Access Toolbar**.
2. Enter **Flange** in the **File name** field.
3. Browse to **C:\Users\Username\Documents\Oldham Coupling** folder.
4. Click **Save** to save the file.
5. Click **File > Close**.

TUTORIAL 3

In this tutorial, you will construct a Shaft by performing the following operations:

- Constructing a cylindrical feature
- Constructing a cut feature

Opening a New Part File

1. To open a new part, click **File > New** on the menu bar.
2. On the **New SOLIDWORKS Document** dialog, click the **Part** button.
3. Click **OK**.

Constructing the Cylindrical Feature

1. Activate the **Revolved Boss/Base** tool and click the right plane.
2. Click **Rectangle** drop-down > **Corner Rectangle** on the **Sketch** CommmandManager.
3. Select the sketch origin.
4. Move the pointer toward top-left corner and click.

5. Add dimensions to the rectangle, as shown.

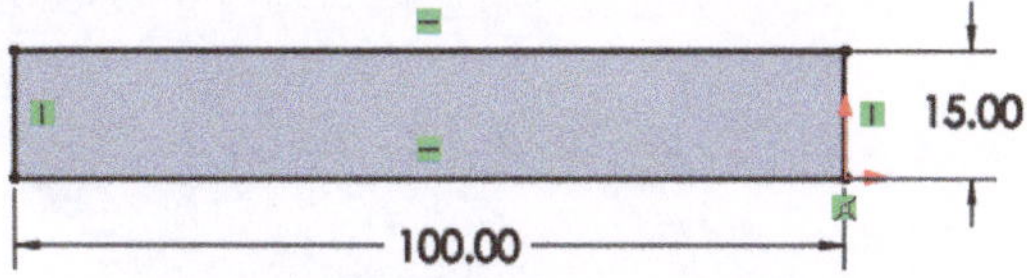

6. Click **Exit Sketch** .
7. Click on the bottom horizontal line of the sketch to define the axis of rotation.

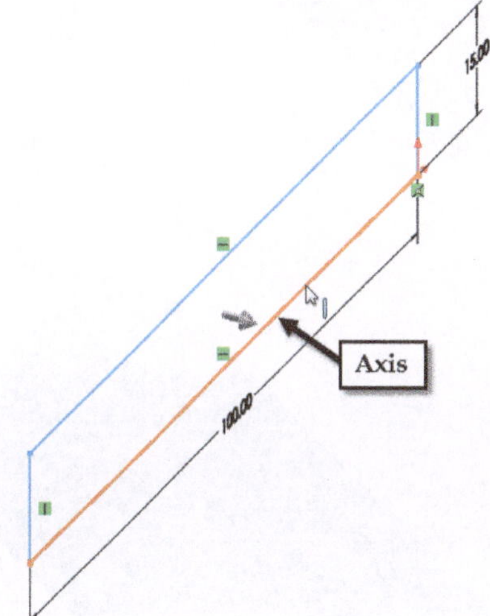

8. Click **OK** .

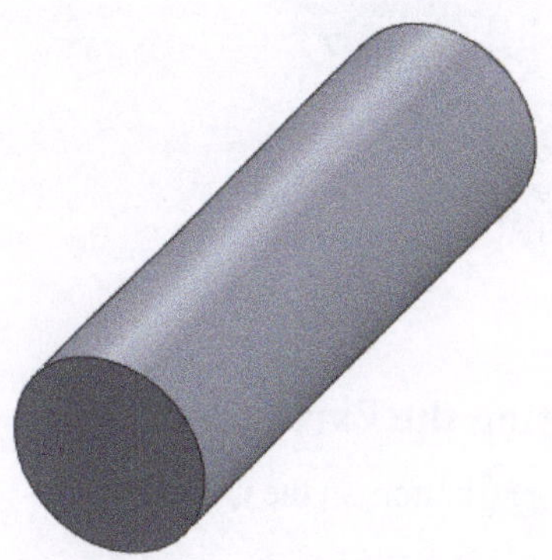

Constructing Cut feature

1. Activate the **Extruded Cut** tool and click on the front face of the model geometry.
2. On the CommandManager, click **Sketch > Center Rectangle** .
3. Click on the top quadrant point of the circular edge.

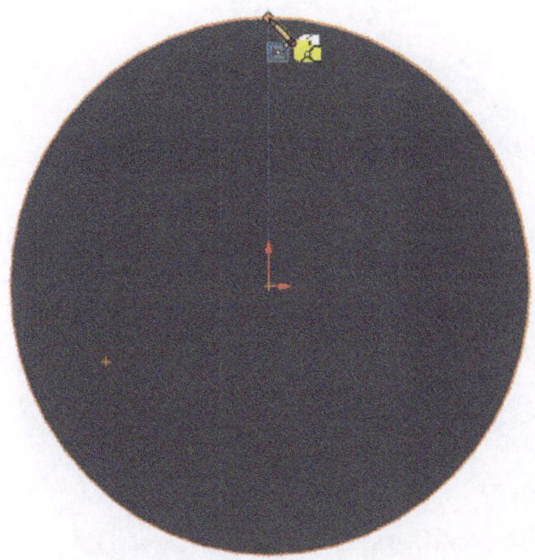

4. Move the pointer away and click to construct the rectangle.

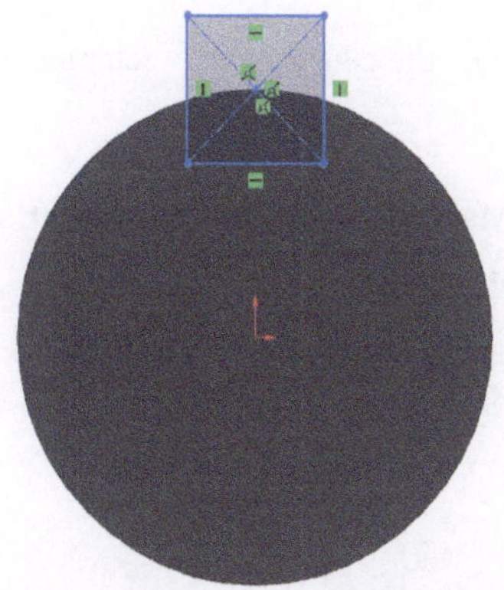

5. On the CommandManager, click **Sketch > Line > Centerline** .
6. Draw a vertical centerline passing through the origin.
7. Press the Ctrl key, and then select the centerline and center point of the rectangle.

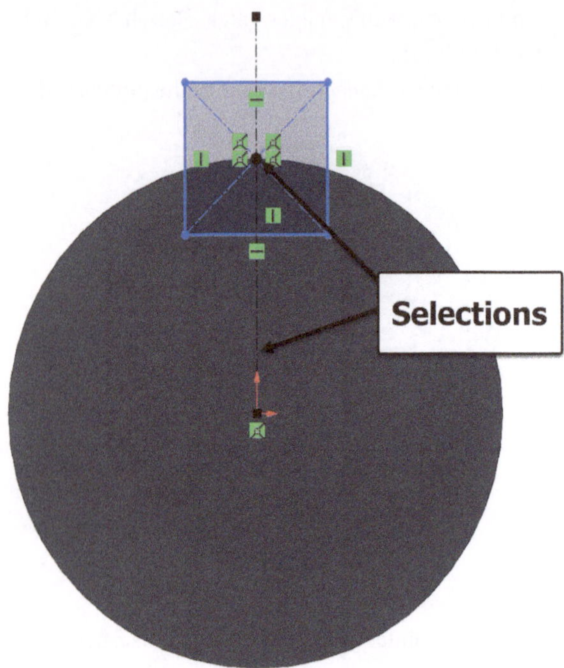

8. Click **Sketch > Display/Delete Relations > Add Relation** on the ribbon.
9. Press Ctrl and select the center of the rectangle and the circular edge.

24. On the PropertyManager, under the **Add Relations** section, click **Coincident** .
10. Add dimensions and relations to constrain the sketch fully.

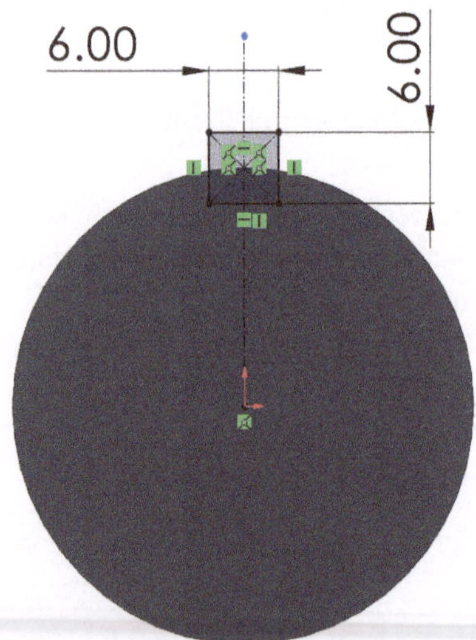

11. Click **Exit Sketch**.
12. On the **View (Heads Up)** toolbar, click **View Orientation > Isometric**.

13. Click on the extrude handle and drag. A scale appears on the model.
14. Release the pointer when the depth is set to 55.

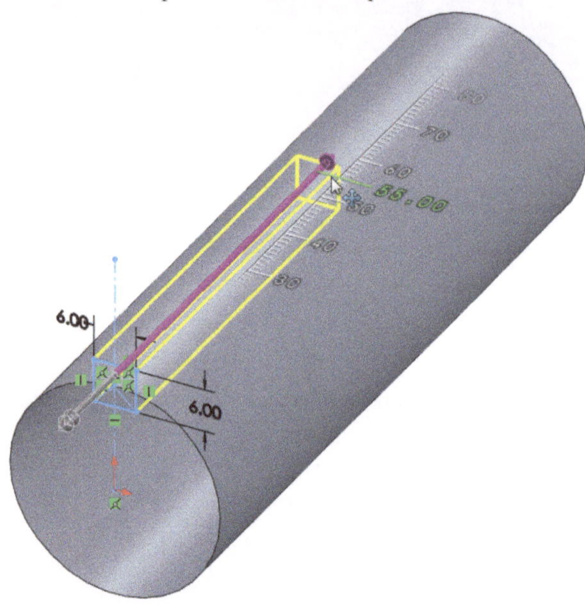

15. Click **OK** .

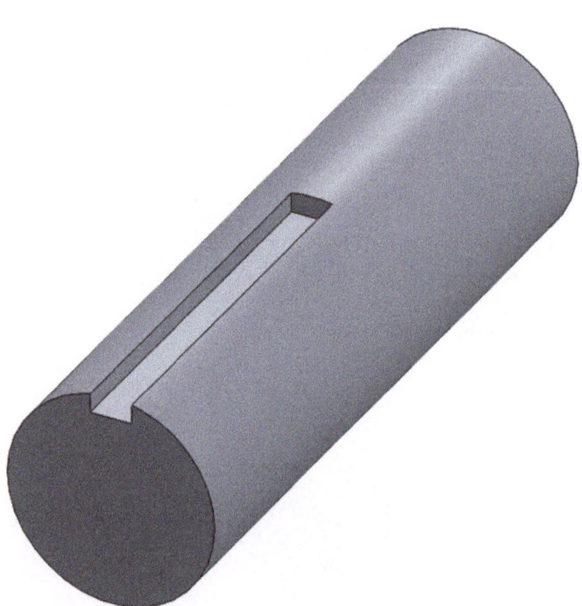

Saving and Closing the Part

1. Click the **Save** button on the **Quick Access Toolbar**.
2. Enter **Shaft** in the **File name** field.
3. Browse to **C:\Users\Username\Documents\Oldham Coupling** folder.
4. Click **Save** to save the file.
5. Click **File > Close**.

TUTORIAL 4

In this tutorial, you construct a Key by performing the following operations:

- Constructing an Extruded Boss
- Applying draft

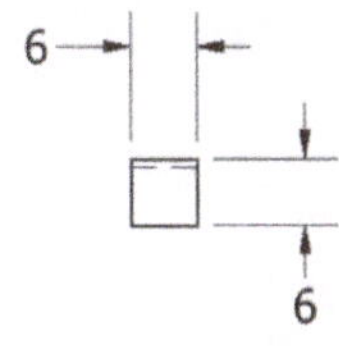

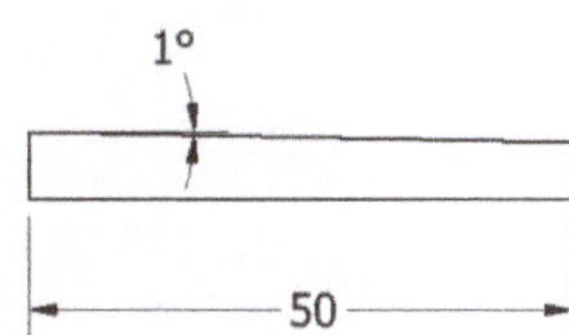

Constructing Extruded Boss

1. To open a new part, click **File > New** on the menu bar.
2. On the **New SOLIDWORKS Document** dialog, click the **Part** button.
3. Click **OK**.
4. On the CommandManager, click **Features > Extruded Boss/Base** .

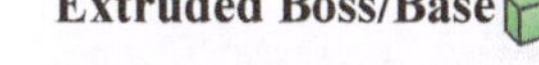

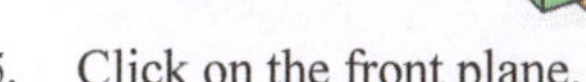

5. Click on the front plane.
6. On the CommandManager, click **Sketch > Center Rectangle** .
7. Select the sketch origin.
8. Move the pointer outward and click.
9. Press and hold the CTRL key and select the horizontal and vertical lines of the rectangle.
10. Click the **Equal** button on the PropertyManager.
11. Click **OK**.
12. Activate the **Smart Dimension** command and select the bottom horizontal line of the rectangle.
13. Type 6 and press ENTER.

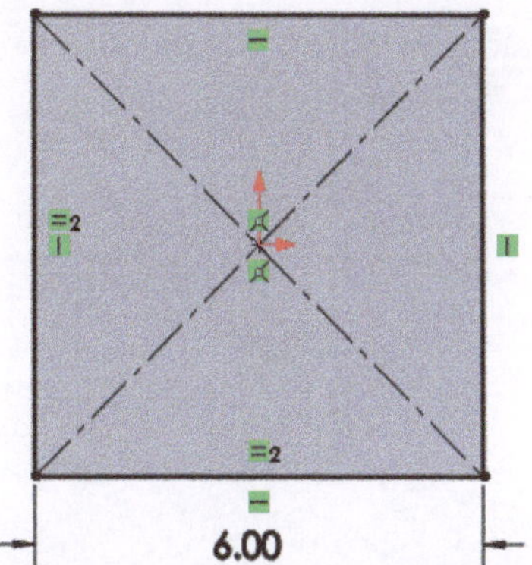

14. Click **Exit Sketch**.
15. On the **Boss-Extrude** PropertyManager, under the **Direction 1** section, set **End Condition** to **Mid Plane**.
16. Set the **Depth** value to 50.
17. Click **OK** to construct the extruded boss.

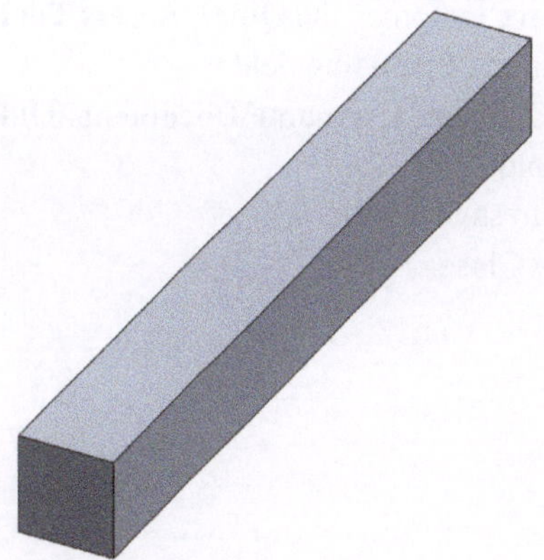

Applying Draft

1. On the CommandManager, click **Features > Draft** .
2. Click on the front face of the model geometry to define the neutral plane
3. Click on the top face to define the draft face.

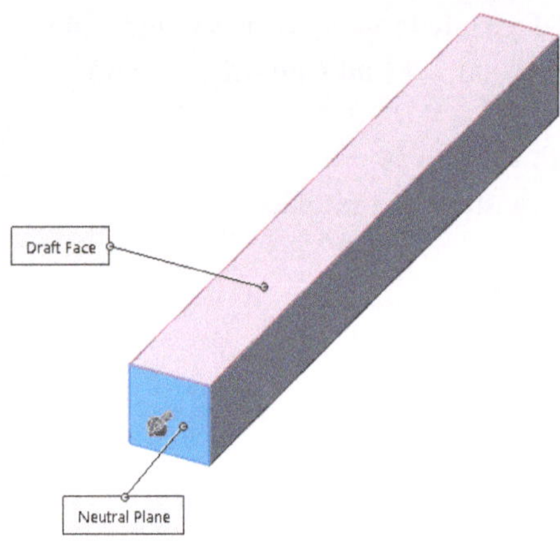

4. Type-in 1 in the **Draft Angle** box and click the **Reverse Direction** button.
5. Click **OK**.

Saving and Closing the Part

1. Click the **Save** button on the **Quick Access Toolbar**.
2. Enter **Key** in the **File name** field.
3. Browse to **C:\Users\Username\Documents\Oldham Coupling** folder.
4. Click **Save** to save the file.
5. Click **File > Close**.

Chapter 3: Assembly Basics

In this chapter, you will:

- Add Components to the assembly
- Apply constraints between components
- Create the exploded view of the assembly

TUTORIAL 1

This tutorial takes you through the creation of your first assembly. You create the Oldham coupling assembly:

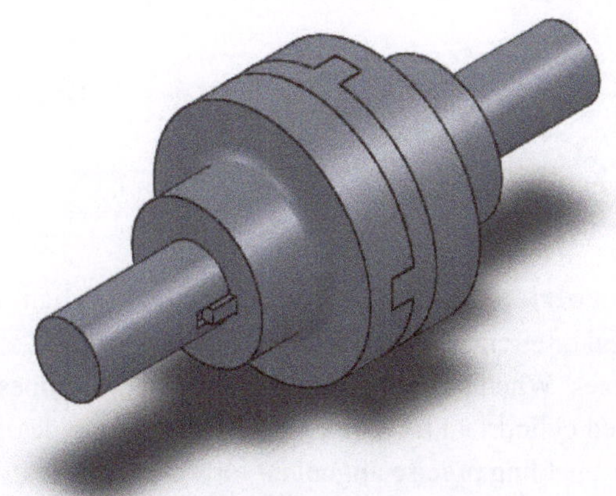

PARTS LIST		
ITEM	PART NUMBER	QTY
1	Disc	1
2	Flange	2
3	Shaft	2
4	Key	2

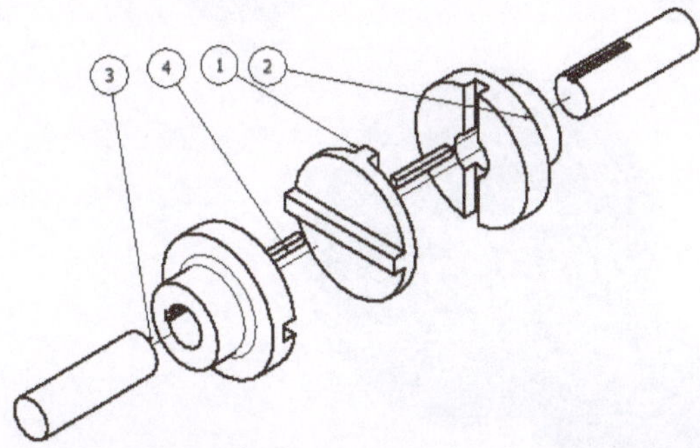

There are two ways to create an assembly model.

- Top-Down Approach
- Bottom-Up Approach

Top-Down Approach

In the Top-Down approach, you will start the assembly document and then construct components in it.

Bottom-Up Approach

In this approach, you will create the components and then add them to the assembly document. In this tutorial, you will create an assembly using this approach.

Opening a New Assembly File

1. To open a new assembly, click New on the **Quick Access Toolbar.**
2. On the **New SOLIDWORKS Document** dialog, click Assembly, and then click **OK**.

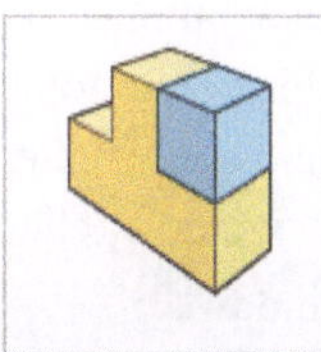

The Assembly window appears along with the **Begin Assembly** PropertyManager located on the left side.

Inserting the Base Component

1. On the Begin Assembly PropertyManager, under the Part/Assembly to Insert section, click the Browse button.
2. Browse to the location: **C:\Users\Username\Documents\Oldham Coupling**
3. Double-click on Flange. This attaches the component to the pointer.
4. Click inside the graphics window to position the component.

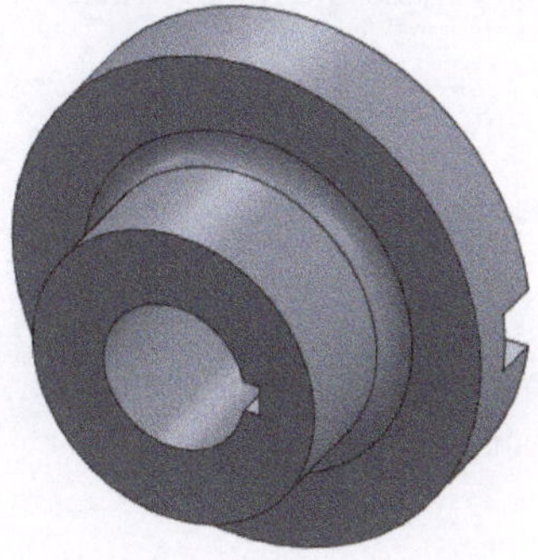

Adding the second component

1. To insert the second component, click **Assembly > Insert Component** on the CommandManager.
2. On the **Insert Component** PropertyManager, click the **Browse** button.
3. Browse to the location **C:\Users\Username\Documents\Oldham Coupling**, and then double-click on **Shaft**.
4. Click inside the graphics window to position the shaft.

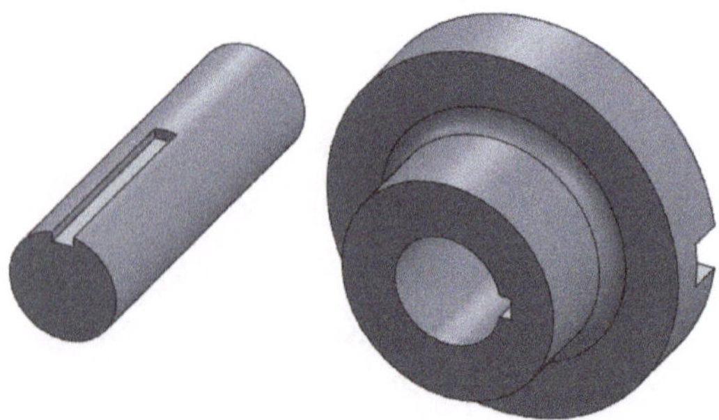

In SOLIDWORKS, you can view a component in a separate preview window. This helps you to rotate or move components independently and apply mates. To view the component in the preview window, click on it and select Component Preview Window.

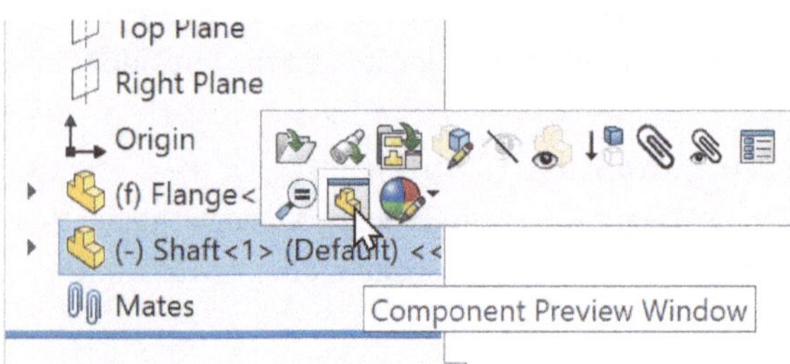

Applying Mates

After adding the components to the assembly window, you have to apply mates between them. By applying mates, you establish real contact and motion between components.

You can apply mates between parts using the **Mate** tool.

The following sections explain some of the assembly mates that you can apply using the **Mate** tool.

Coincident: Using this mate, you can align two faces such that they will point in the same direction.

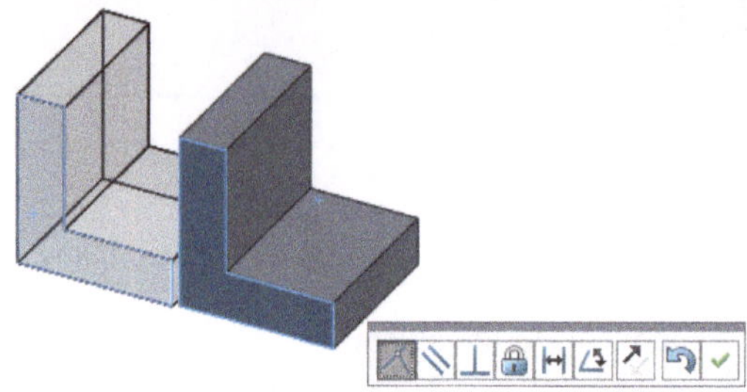

When parts align incorrectly, such as a face flipping inwards instead of outwards, you need to reverse the alignment. Simply click **Flip Mate Alignment** on the context toolbar that pops up in the graphics area..

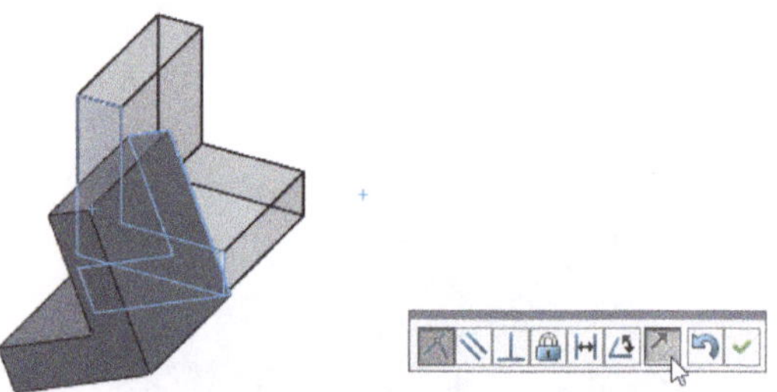

Concentric: The **Concentric** mate is used to align cylindrical or circular components by matching their central axes. When applied, it ensures that the centerlines of selected cylindrical faces (e.g., holes, shafts, or pipes) coincide, enabling precise alignment for assemblies like gears, fasteners, or rotating parts.

Click **Flip Mate Alignment** to flip the alignment direction. Check the **Lock Rotation** option to lock the rotation between components.

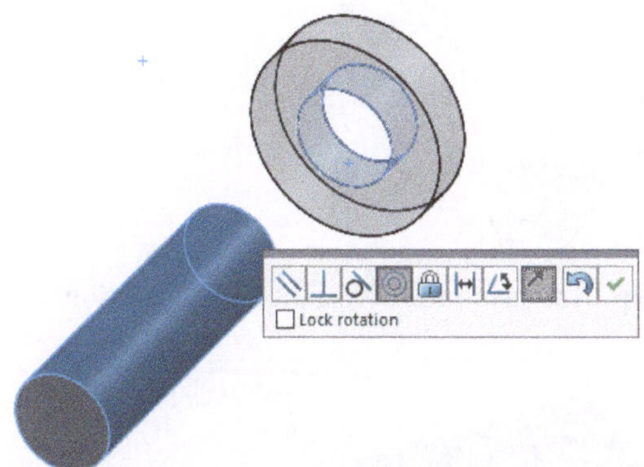

Parallel: The Parallel mate aligns selected axes, faces, or edges of two components to remain parallel without requiring physical contact. Unlike Coincident or Concentric mates, it focuses solely on angular alignment, allowing parts to move freely (e.g., slide or rotate) while maintaining orientation.

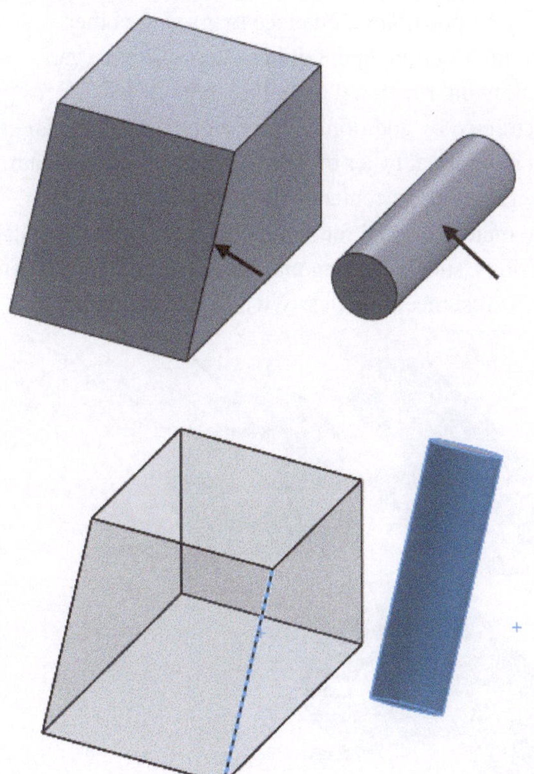

Perpendicular: Using this mate, you can establish a 90-degree orientation between specific features of two parts, such as an axis, face, or edge.

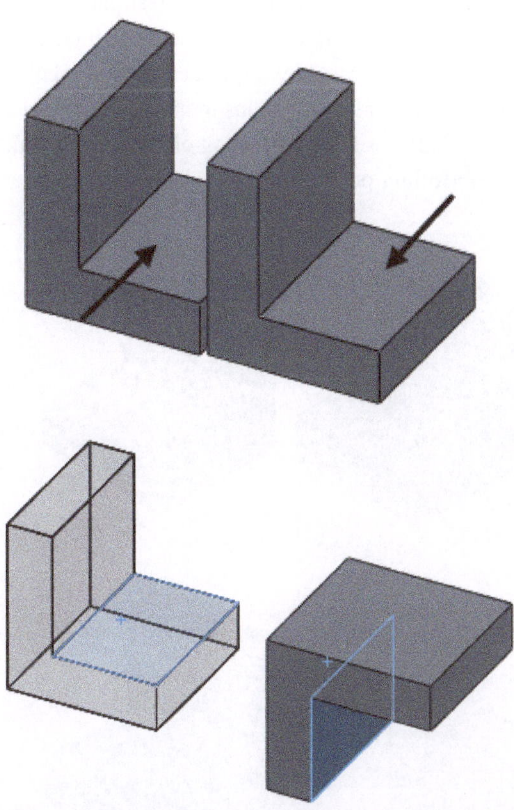

Lock: The **Lock** mate binds parts together as a single rigid unit. When locked, moving one part moves all connected parts simultaneously, keeping their positions fixed relative to each other.

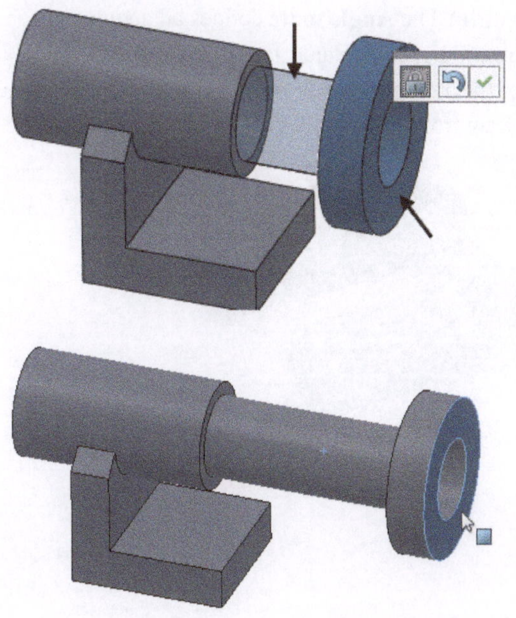

Distance: This mate sets a fixed linear gap between two parts (like faces or edges) in an assembly. It ensures components stay separated by a specific measurement (e.g., 10 mm) while allowing adjustments to the distance value later. This is useful for creating clearances, spacing parts, or controlling positioning in designs.

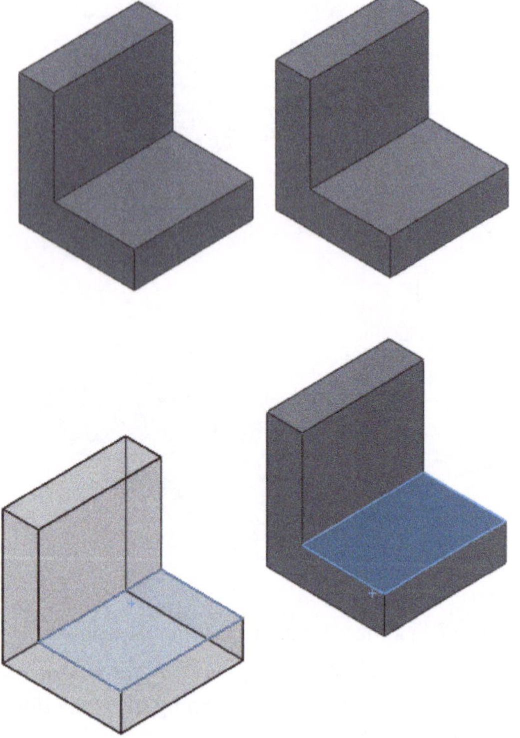

Angle: The **Angle mate** defines an angular relationship between planar faces, edges, or reference axes of two components. You assign a fixed angle (e.g., 30°) to control rotational degrees of freedom.

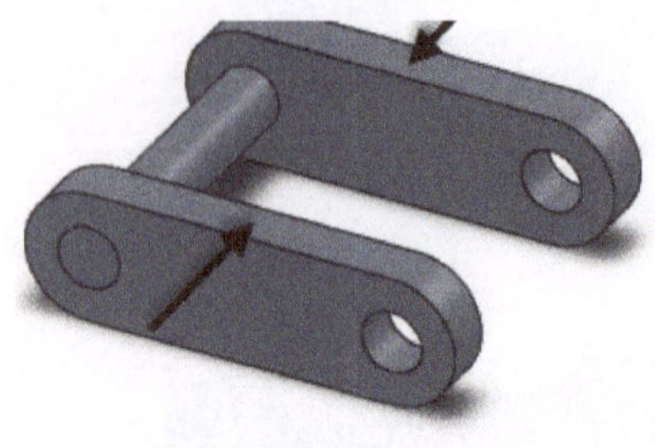

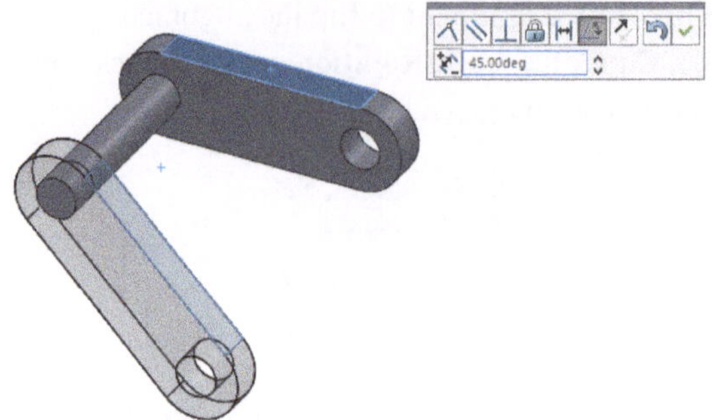

Click **Flip Dimension** to reverse the angle direction.

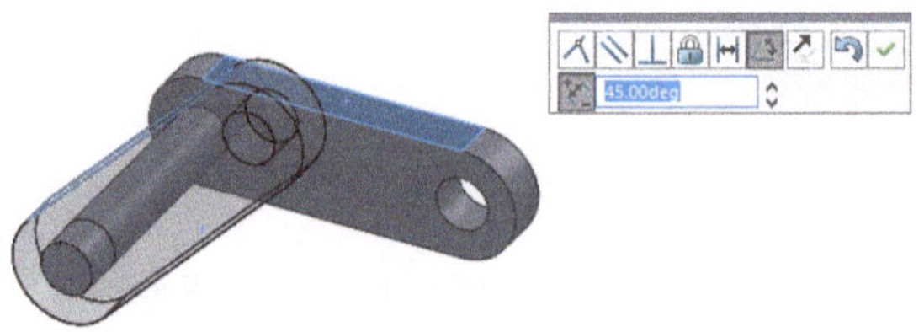

Tangent: The **Tangent** mate aligns two faces (planar, cylindrical, conical, or spherical) such that they touch at a single point or along a continuous line, ensuring smooth transition between surfaces. This mate enforces tangency by positioning one face to graze the other without intersection, maintaining a zero-distance gap while allowing rotational or sliding motion if unconstrained by additional mates. For example, it can align a cylindrical roller to a flat surface or ensure a cam follower remains in contact with a curved profile. The tangent mate is critical for simulating realistic mechanical interactions, such as rolling motion or fluid contact, where surfaces must meet seamlessly without overlapping.

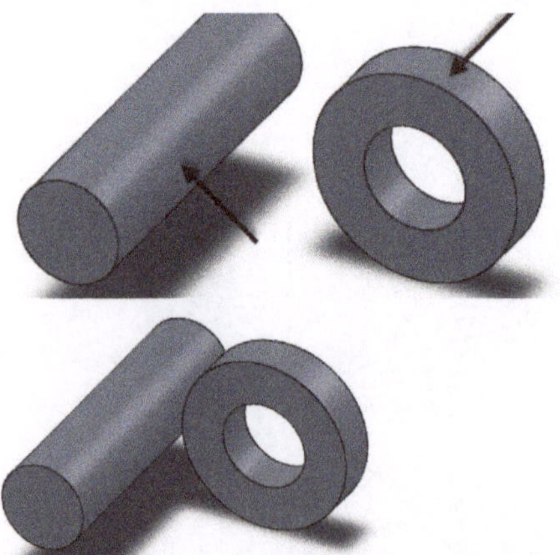

1. On the CommandManager, click **Assembly > Mate** .

2. On the **Mate** PropertyManager, click **Concentric** under the **Mate type** section on the **Standard** tab.
3. Click on the cylindrical face of the Shaft.
4. Click on the inner cylindrical face of the Flange

In SOLIDWORKS, the first selection is made transparent while applying mates. You can turn OFF the transparency by unchecking the **Make first selection transparent** option in the **Options** section of the **Mate** PropertyManager.

5. Click **Add/Finish Mate.**

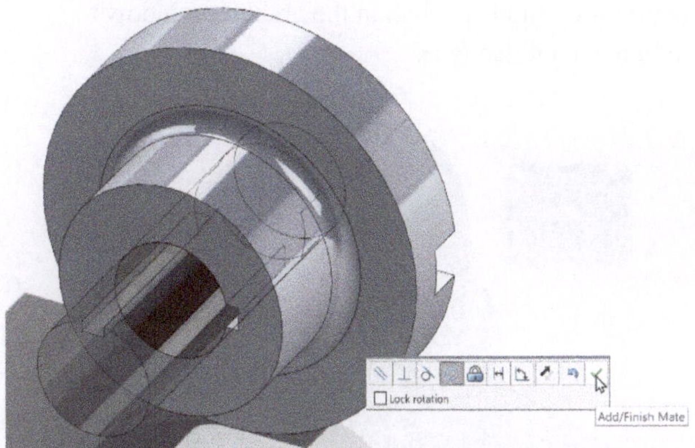

This aligns the Shaft and the Flange axially.

6. On the Mate PropertyManager, click Coincident .
7. Click on the front face of the shaft.

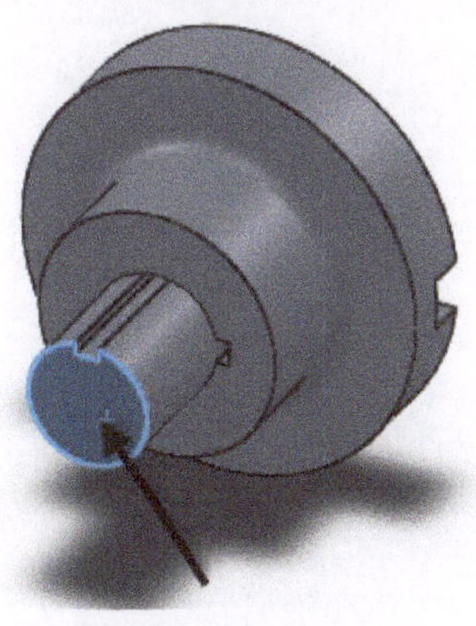

8. Rotate the model.
9. Click on the slot face of the flange, as shown in the figure.

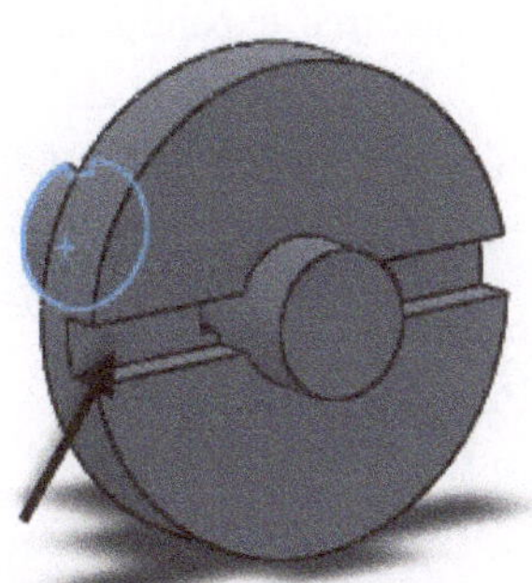

10. On the **Mate** PropertyManager, under the **Mate alignment** section, click the **Aligned** button.

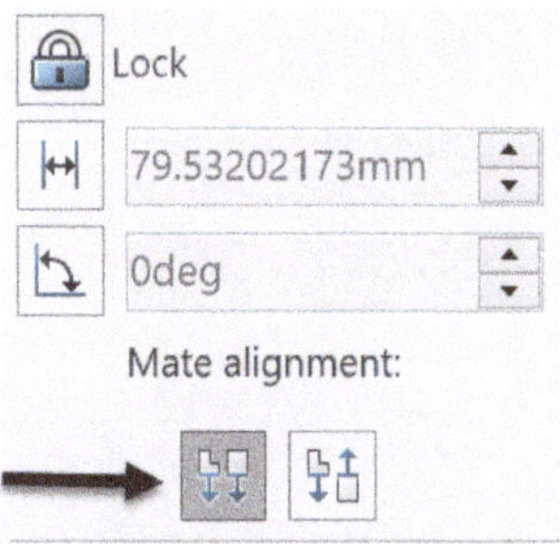

11. Click **OK** on the **SOLIDWORKS** message.

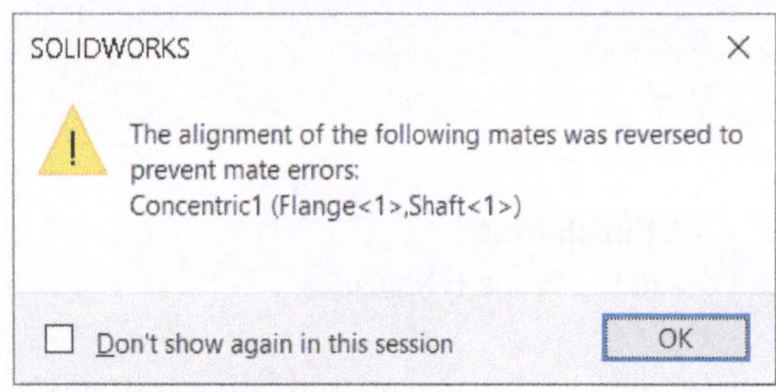

12. Click **Add/Finish Mate.**

This aligns the front face of the Shaft and the slot face of the Flange.

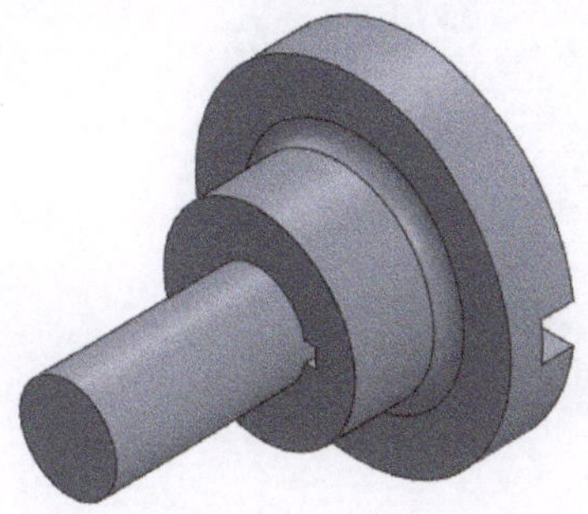

13. On the **Mate** PropertyManager, click **Coincident** .
14. In the FeatureManager tree, expand Flange and select Top Plane.
15. Expand Shaft and select Right Plane.

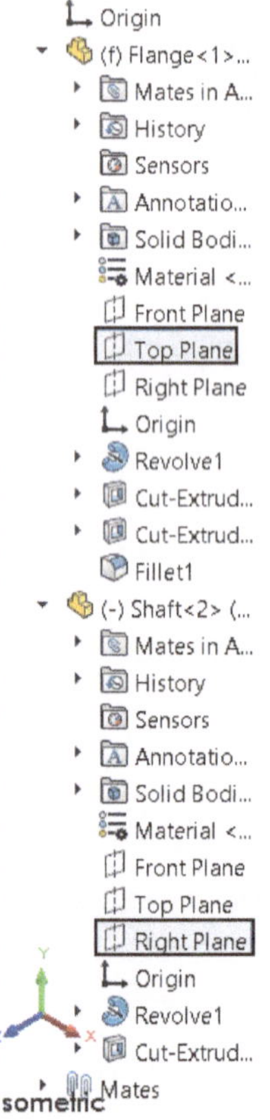

16. Click **Add/Finish Mate**.
17. Click **OK** on the PropertyManager.

This assembles the two components and fully constrains the Shaft.

Adding the Third Component

In order to assemble the third component, you need to hide the Flange.

1. In the FeatureManager Design Tree, click the right mouse button on the Flange and select Hide Components to hide the Flange. Now, it is easy to assemble the third component.

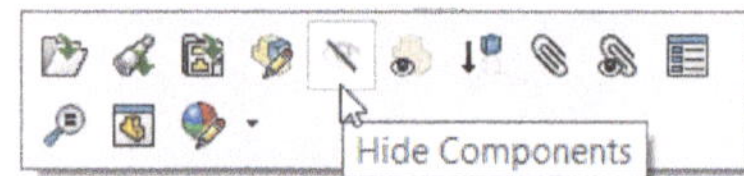

SOLIDWORKS allows you to hide a body, placing the cursor on it and pressing the Tab key. You can unhide the body by placing the cursor at its position and pressing Shift+Tab.

Tip: You can also hide a part face so that the obscured face is visible. To do this, activate the Mate tool, place the pointer on a face, and then press the Alt key; the face is temporarily hidden. Click in the graphics window to unhide the hidden face.

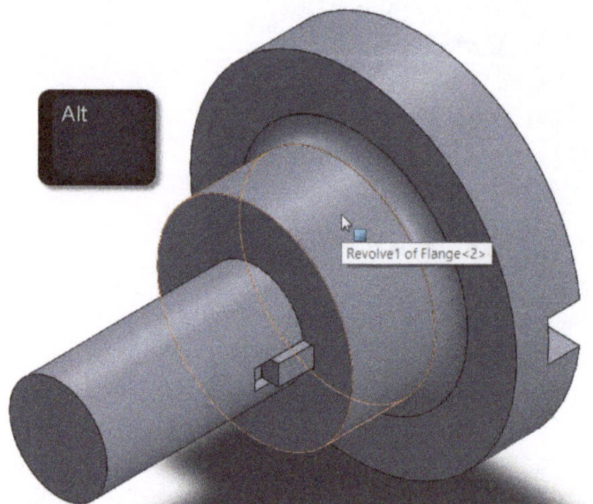

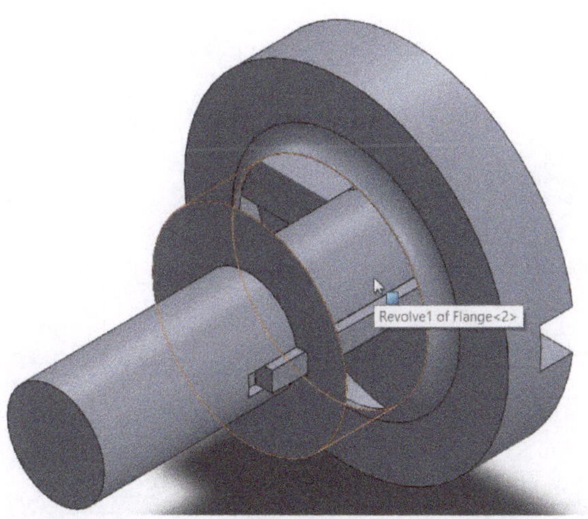

2. To insert the third component, click **Assembly > Insert Component** .
3. On the PropertyManager, click the **Browse** button.
4. Browse to the folder: **C:\Users\Username\Documents\Oldham Coupling, and then double-click on the Key.**
5. Click inside the graphics window to position the key.

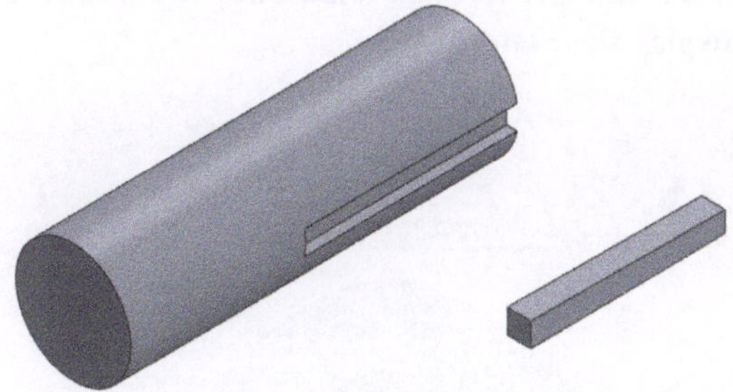

6. Activate the **Mate** tool.
7. On the **Mate** PropertyManager, click **Coincident** .
8. Right-click on the side face of the key and select **Select Other**.

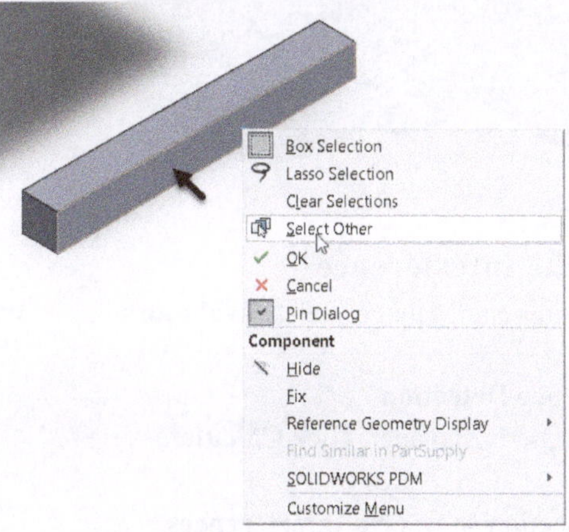

9. From the **Select Other** box, select the bottom face of the Key.

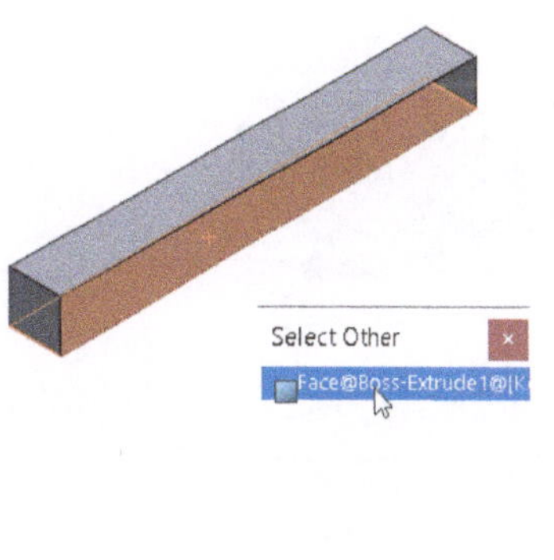

10. Select the bottom face of the slot.

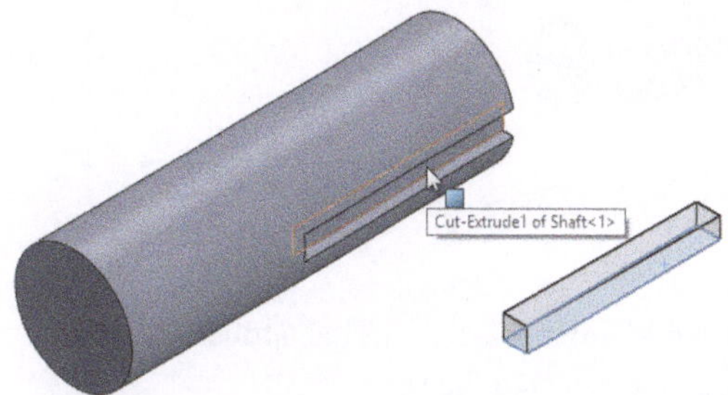

11. Click **Add/Finish Mate** . This aligns the bottom face of the key with the bottom face of the slot.

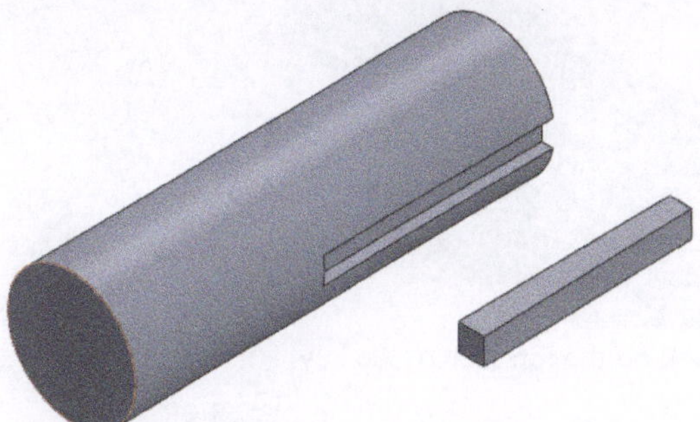

12. Select the front face of the Key and the back face of the Shaft.

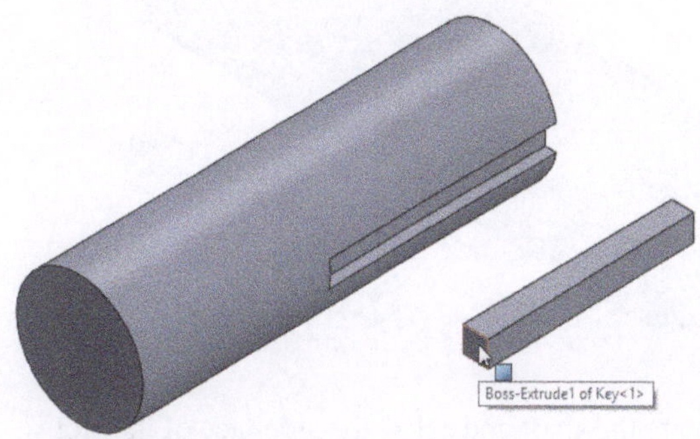

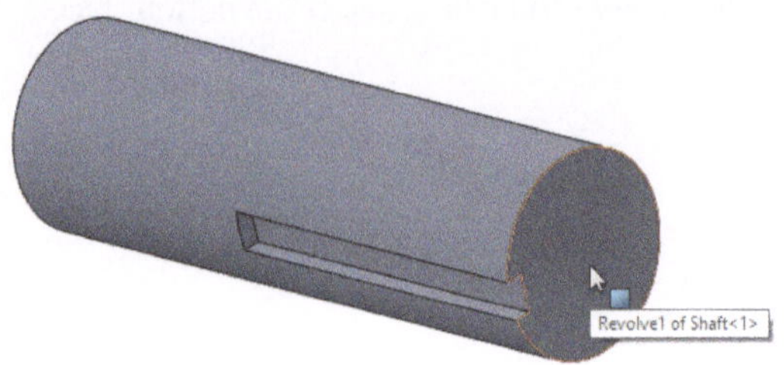

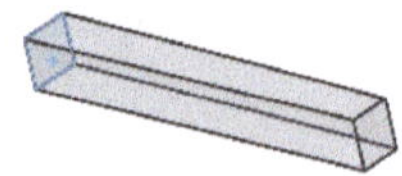

13. Click **Flip Alignment**.

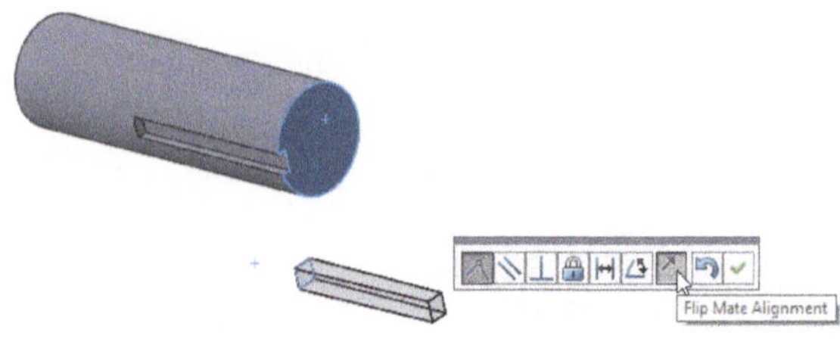

14. Click **Add/Finish Mate** ✓. This applies the mate between the selected faces.

15. Click on the top face of the key.

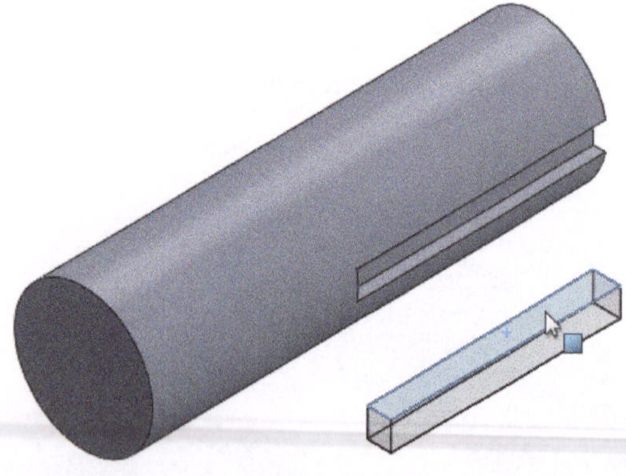

16. Rotate the shaft and select the side face of the slot.

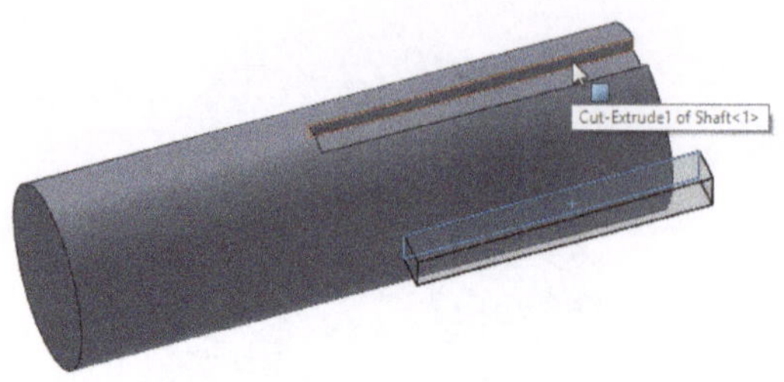

17. Click **Add/Finish Mate**.

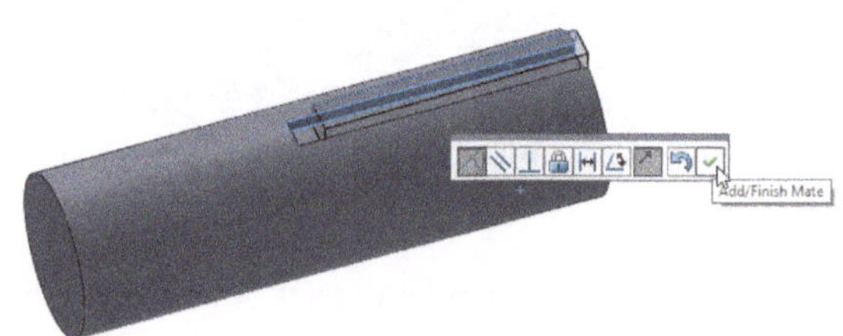

18. Click **OK** ✓ on the PropertyManager.

Now, you have to turn on the display of the Flange.

19. Click the right mouse button on the **Flange** in the **FeatureManager** tree and select **Show Components to display the Flange.**

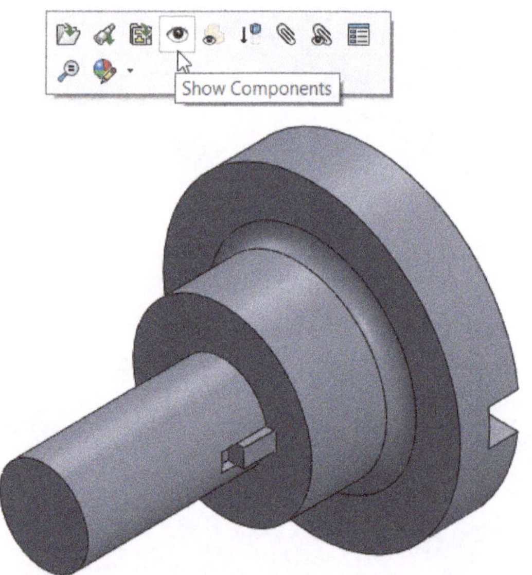

Checking the Interference

1. On the CommandManager, click **Evaluate > Interference Detection** 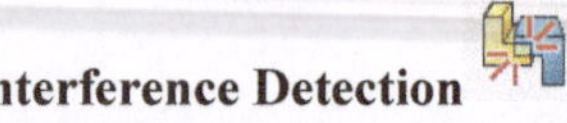.
2. On the PropertyManager, click **Calculate**.

The **Results** section shows **No Interferences.**

3. Click **OK** .

Saving the Assembly

1. Click **Save** on the **Quick Access Toolbar**.
2. Enter **Flange_subassembly** in the **File name field.**
3. Browse to **C:\Users\Username\Documents\Oldham Coupling** folder.
4. Click **Save** to save the file.
5. Click **File > Close**.

Starting the Main assembly

1. Click the **New** button on the Quick Access Toolbar.
2. On the **New SOLIDWORKS Document** dialog, click Assembly, and then click OK.

Adding Disc to the Assembly

1. On the Begin Assembly PropertyManager, click Browse.
2. Browse to the location **C:\Users\Username\Documents\Oldham Coupling** and double-click on **Disc.sldprt**.
3. Click inside the graphics window to place the component at the origin.

Placing the Sub-assembly

1. To insert the sub-assembly, click Assembly > **Insert Components** on the CommandManager.
2. Click **Browse** on the PropertyManager.
3. Browse to the location **C:\Users\Username\Documents\Oldham Coupling** and double-click on **Flange_subassembly.asm**.
4. Click in the window to place the flange sub assembly.

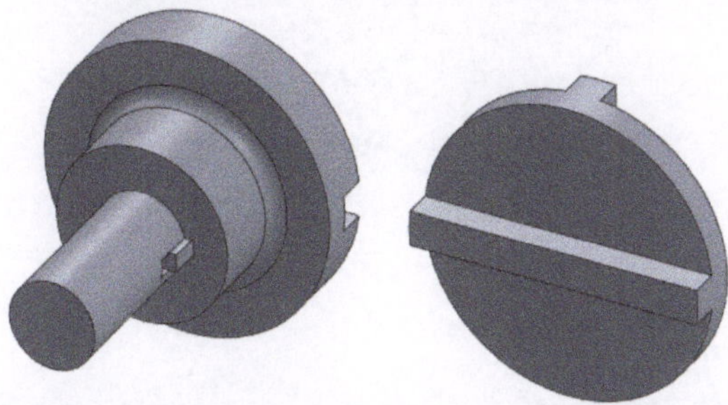

Adding Constraints

1. Activate the **Mate** tool.
2. Click on the front face of the disc and the back face of the flange.

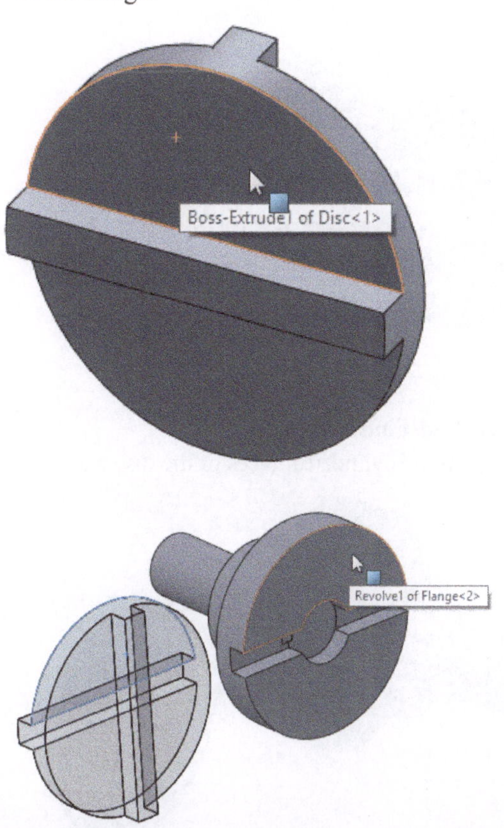

3. Click **Add/Finish Mate**.
4. Click on the flat top face of the disc.

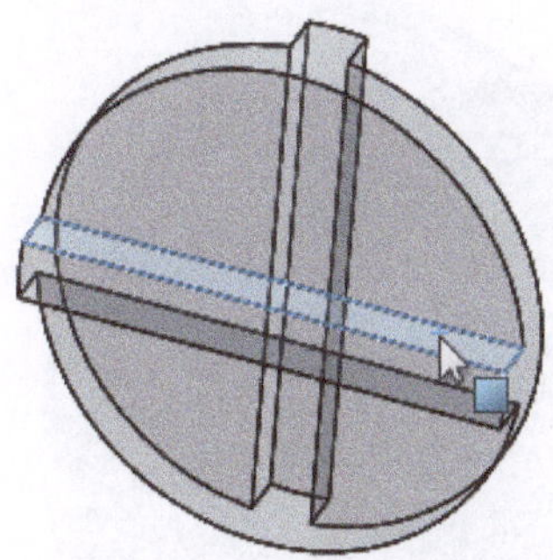

5. Rotate the model geometry and click on the flange's slot face, as shown in the figure.

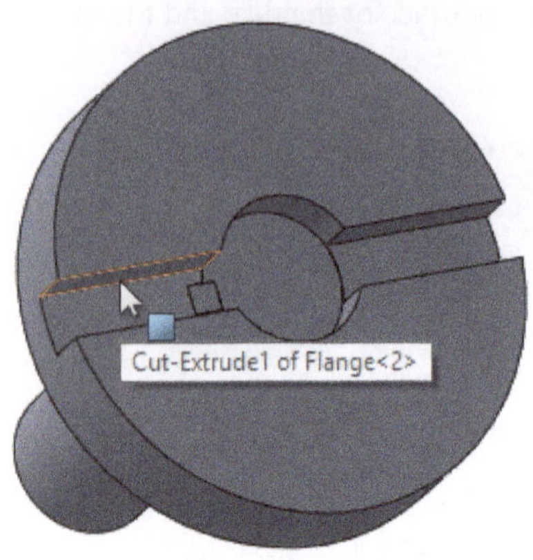

6. Click **Add/Finish Mate**.
7. Click on the cylindrical faces of the disc and flange.

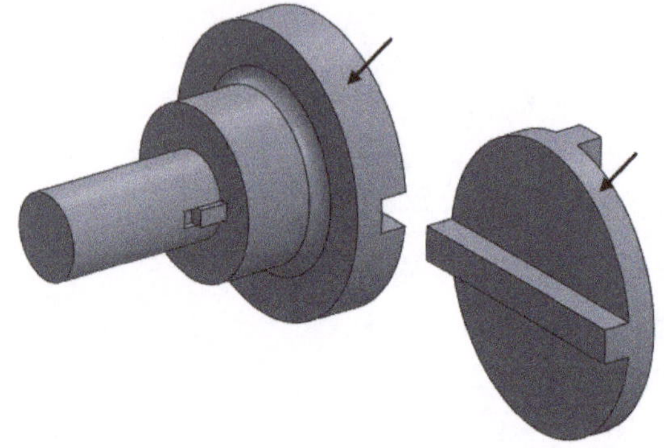

8. Click **Add/Finish Mate**.
9. Click **OK on the Mate** PropertyManager.

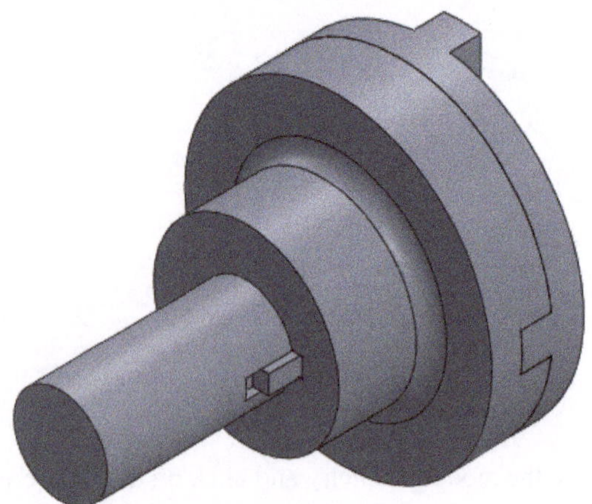

Placing the second instance of the Sub-assembly

1. In the FeatureManager Design Tree, click on the **Flange_subassembly**.
2. Press Ctrl+C on your keyboard to copy the assembly.
3. Press Ctrl+V on your keyboard to paste the assembly. Expand the copied flange assembly in the FeatureManager Design Tree and notice that it is copied along with mates between parts of the sub-assembly.
4. On the **View HeadsUp toolbar**, click **View Orientation > Isometric**. Next, click **View Orientation > View Selector**.

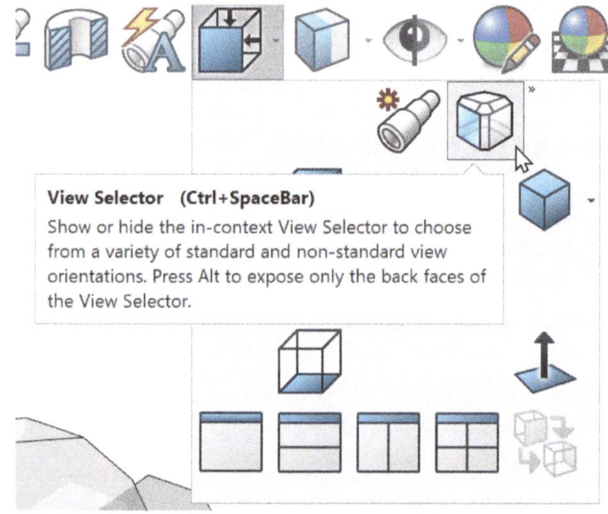

5. Click on the top-right corner of the right face of the View Selector, as shown.

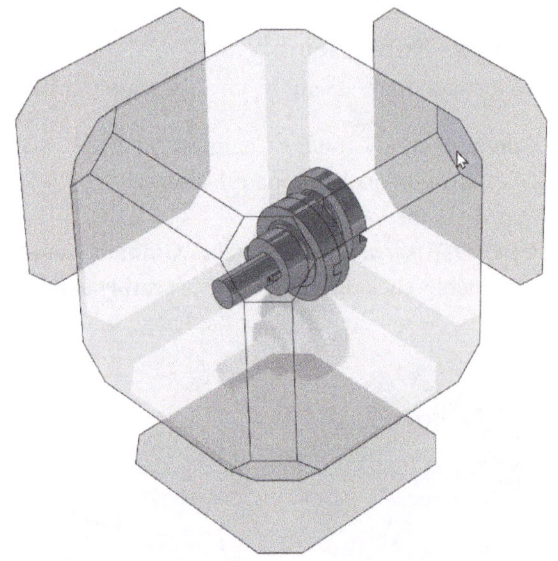

6. On the CommandManager, click **Assembly** tab > **Mate**.
7. Select the two faces of the assembly, as shown.

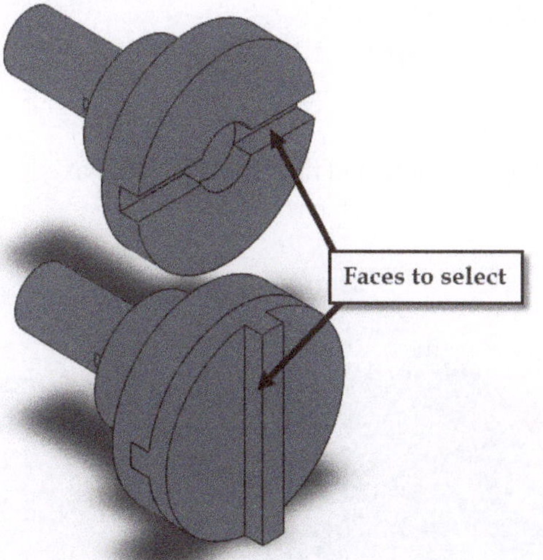

8. Click **OK** on the PropertyManager.
9. Click on the cylindrical faces of the assembly, as shown.

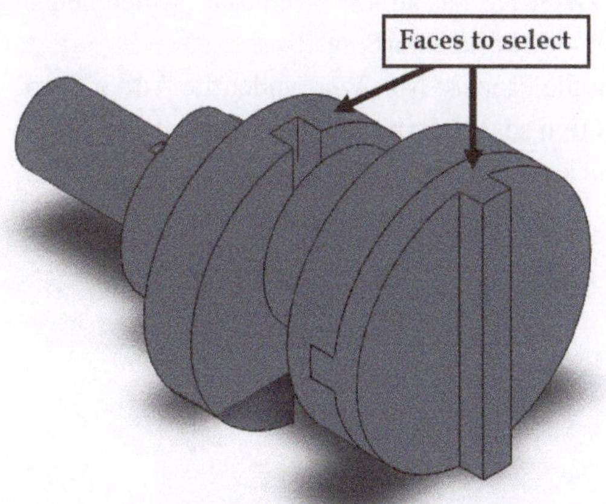

10. Click **OK** on the PropertyManager.

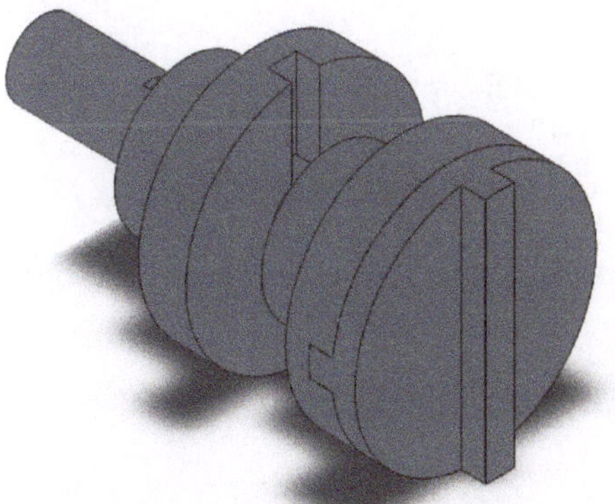

11. Select the flat faces of the assembly, as shown.

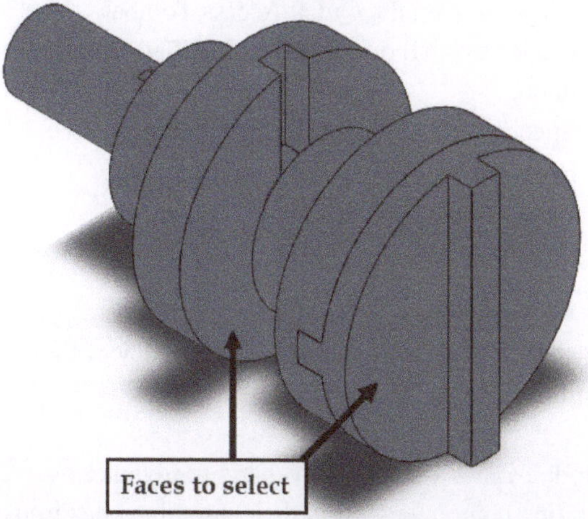

12. Click the **Anti Aligned** icon under the Mate Alignment section of the PropertyManager; the **SOLIDWORKS** dialog shows that the Concentric mate was reversed to prevent any errors.

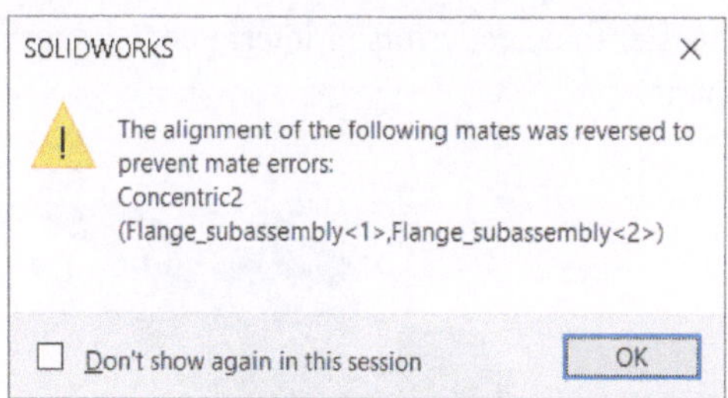

13. Click **OK** on the **SOLIDWORKS** dialog to close it.
14. Click **OK** on the PropertyManager to create the mate.
15. Change the assembly orientation to Isometric.

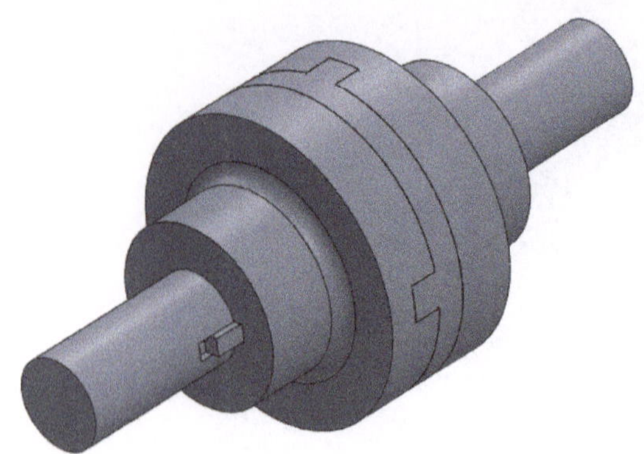

Saving the Assembly

1. Click Save on the Quick Access Toolbar.
2. Click **Save All** on the **Save Modified Documents** dialog.
3. Specify Oldham_coupling as the File name.
4. Browse to the Oldham_coupling folder,.
5. Click Save to save the file.

TUTORIAL 2

In this tutorial, you create the exploded view of the assembly:

Exploded views visualize how parts fit together by separating components from their assembled positions. This displacement reveals internal items, such as fasteners, which are otherwise hidden. These views are essential for creating manufacturing instructions, repair manuals, and technical illustrations. Furthermore, the expanded layout helps you to verify the assembly by making it easier to detect errors or interference issues between parts.

Creating the Exploded View

1. To create the exploded view, click **Assembly > Exploded View** on the CommandManager.
2. On the Explode PropertyManager, under the **Add a Step** section, click Regular Step.
3. On the Explode PropertyManager, under the Options section, check **Select the subassembly parts.**

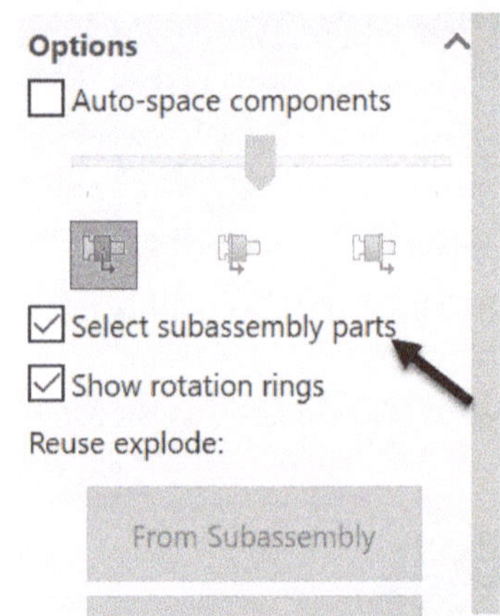

4. Click on the shaft, and then click on the Z-axis.

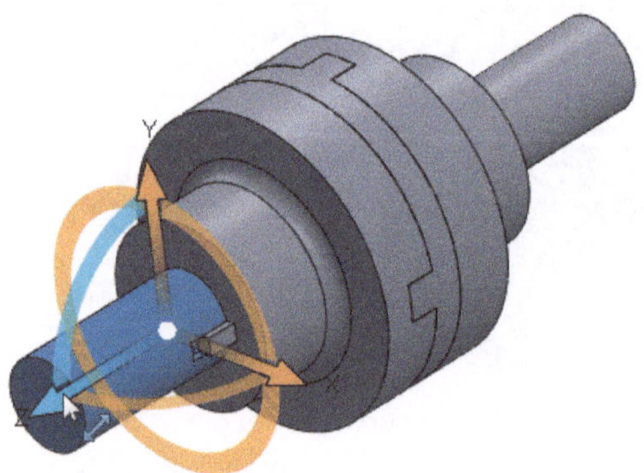

SOLIDWORKS has an improved triad, which helps you to rotate or translate parts easily.

5. On the PropertyManager, under the **Add a Step** section set the **Explode Distance** value to 180.
6. Click **Add Step.**

7. Click on the flange and set the **Explosion Distance** to 100.
8. Click **Add Step**.

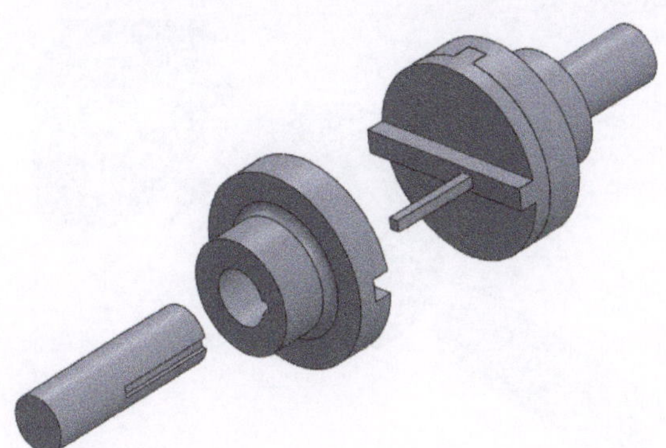

9. Click on the other shaft and set the Explosion Distance to -180.

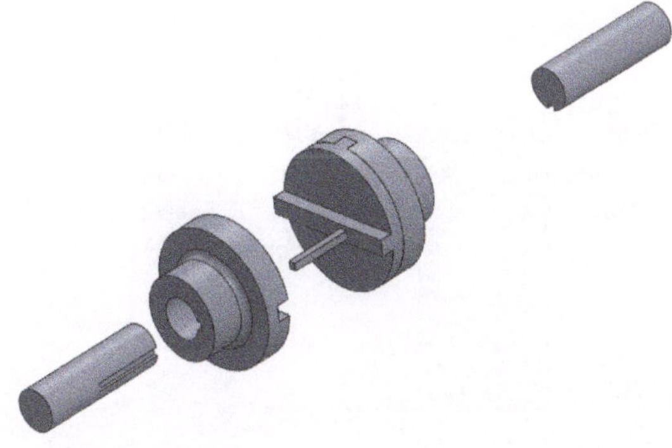

10. Click **Add Step**.
11. Likewise, explode the other flange to -100 mm distance.

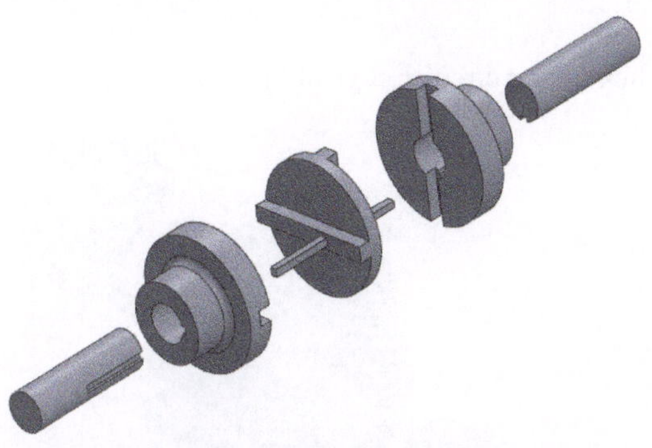

12. Click OK on the PropertyManager.

Creating Explode lines

Exploded lines, also called trajectory lines, indicate how components move in an exploded view. They connect each part to its installed location, so relationships (such as screws to holes) are clear and the assembly or disassembly order is easier to follow. By showing intended movement paths, these lines reduce ambiguity, help reveal potential interferences, and improve the readability of manuals and technical diagrams.

1. To create explode lines, click **Assembly > Exploded View > Explode Line Sketch**.

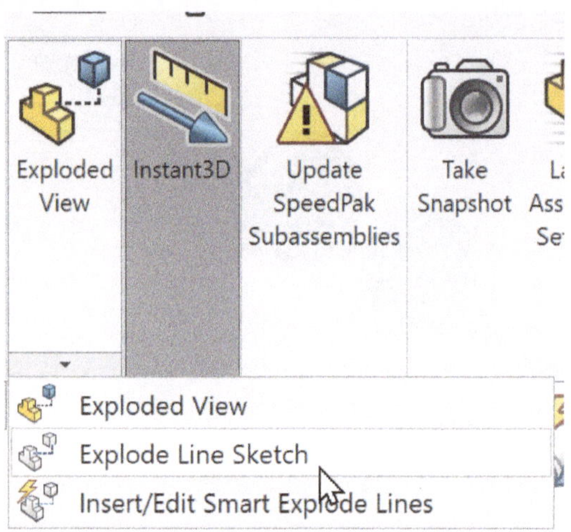

2. Click on the circular edge of the flange.

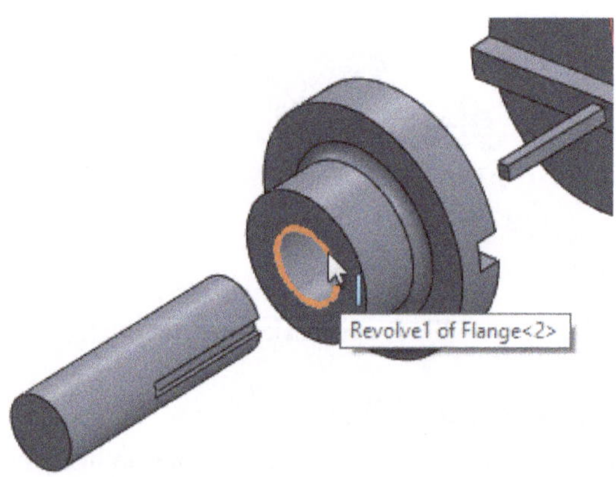

3. On the PropertyManager, under the **Options** section, check the **Reverse** option.

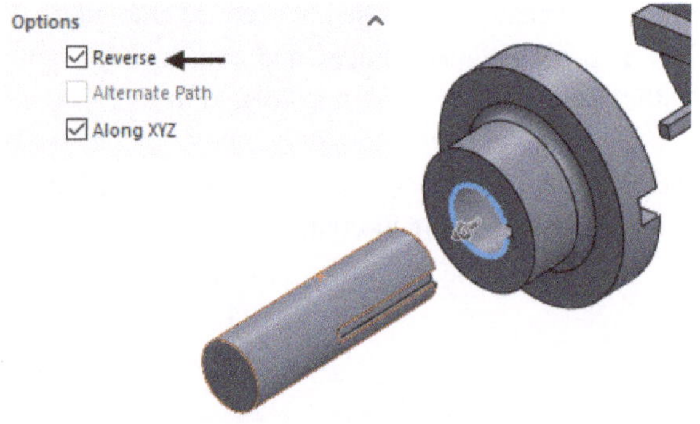

4. Click on the circular edge of the shaft.

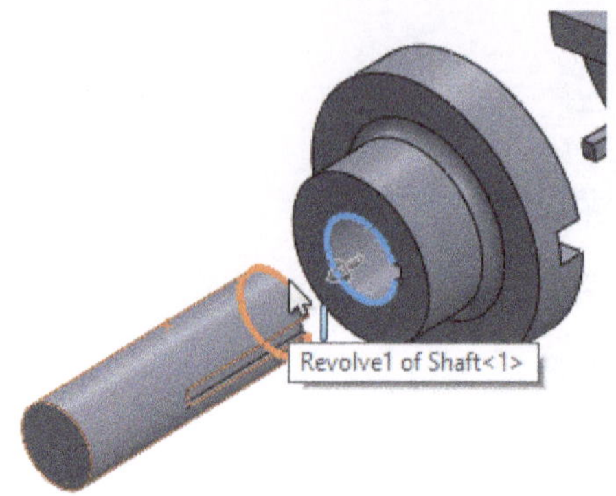

5. Click **OK**.

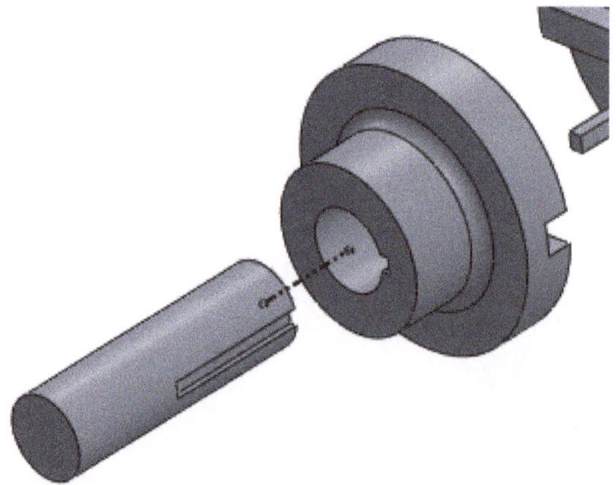

6. Click on the vertices of the flange and key, as shown in figure.
7. Click OK.

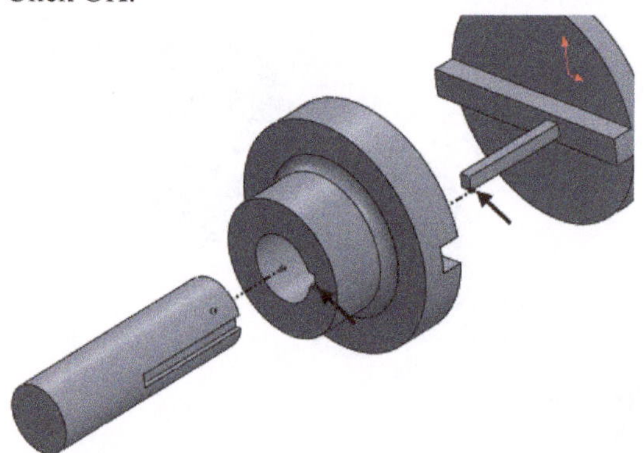

8. Click on the vertices of the flange and disc, as shown in the figure.

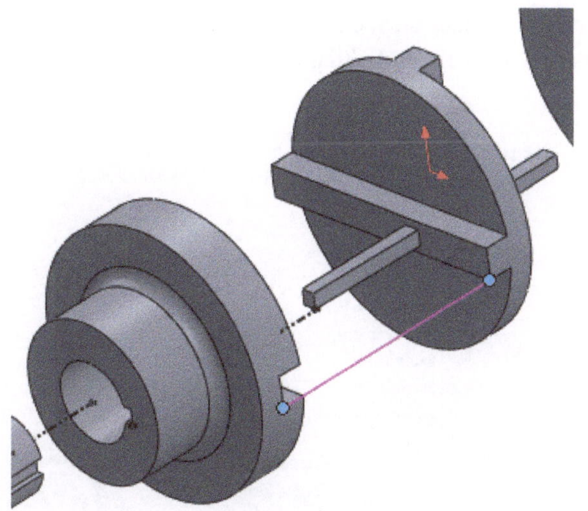

9. Click **OK**.
10. Click the **Jog Line** button located next to the PropertyManager.

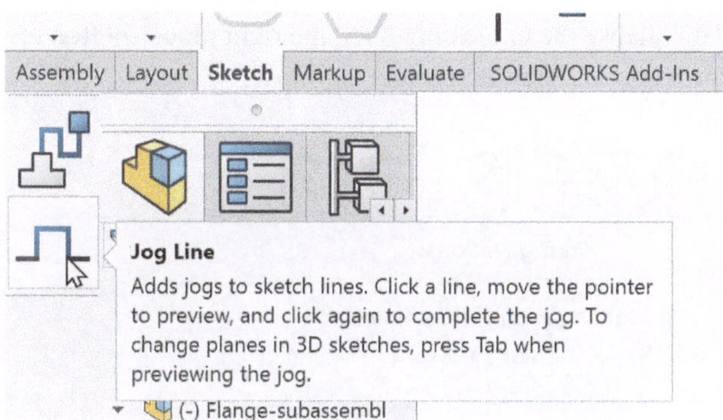

11. Click on the explode line, as shown in the figure.

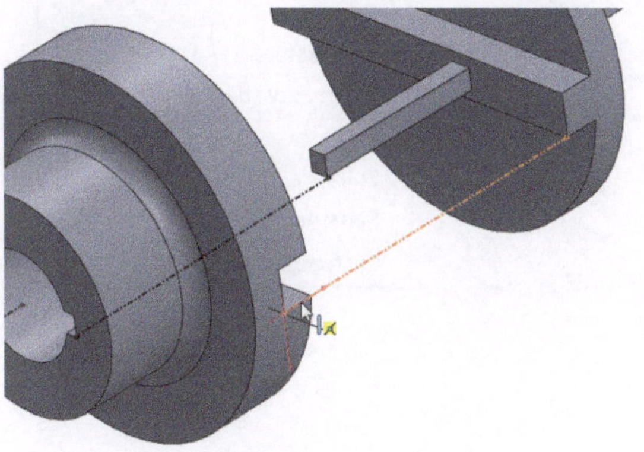

12. Drag the pointer to draw a rectangle.

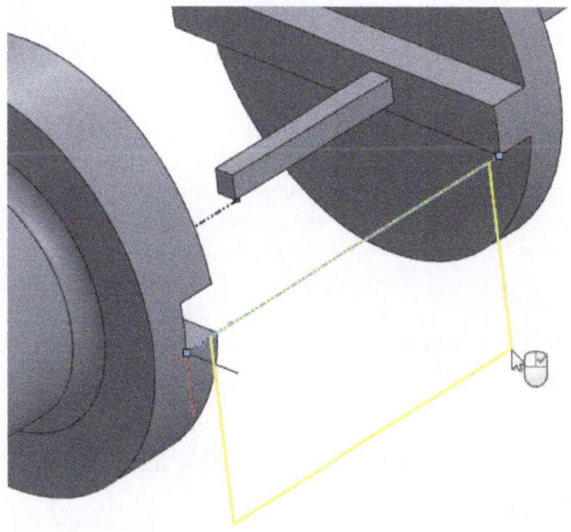

13. Press the Tab key to change the orientation of the sketch line.
14. Click to draw the jogged line.

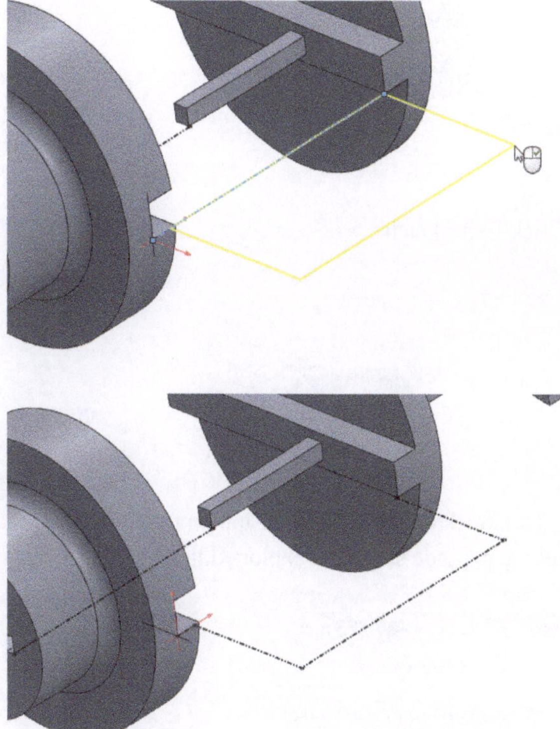

15. Click the **Route Line** icon located next to the PropertyManager.

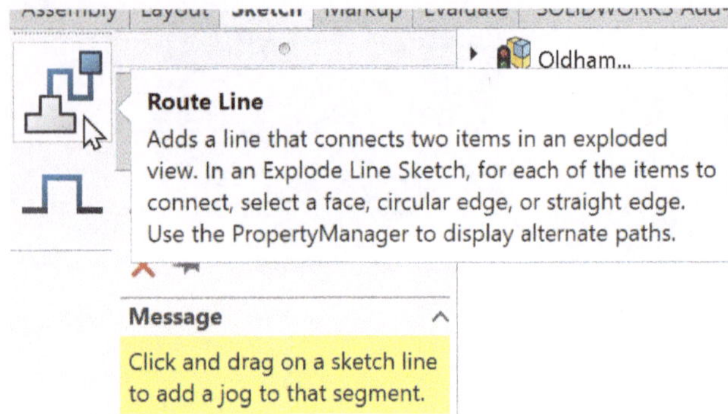

16. Draw the other explode lines. Click **OK** on the PropertyManager.

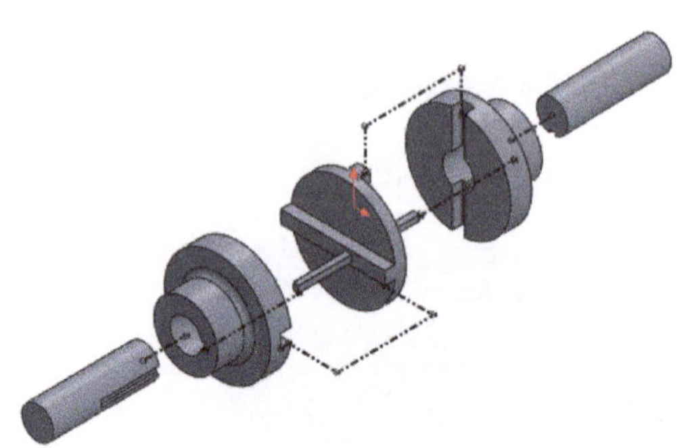

17. Click Exit Sketch.

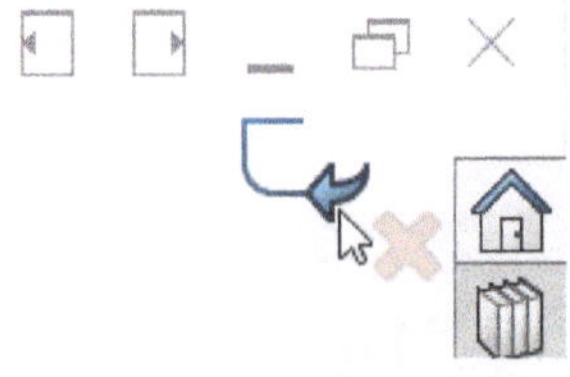

Click the **ConfigurationManager** tab on the left pane; it lists all the explode steps and exploded lines.

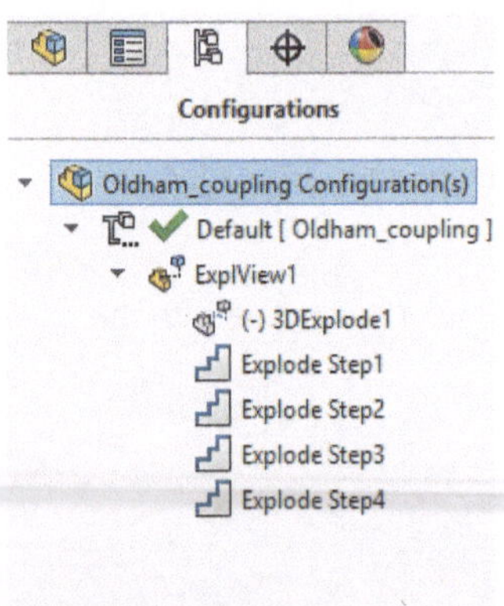

To edit an explode step, click the right mouse button on it and select **Edit Explode Step**.

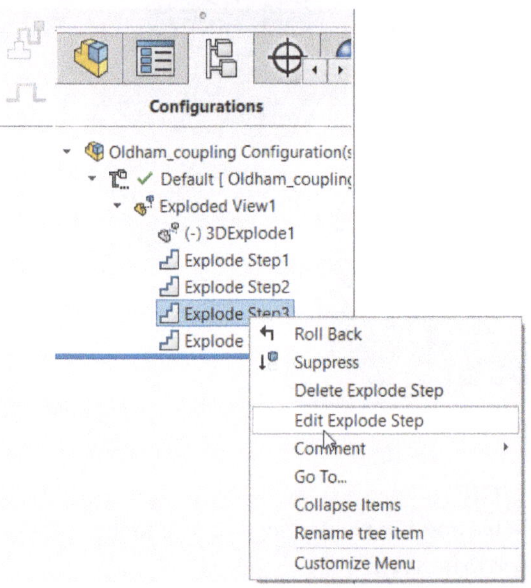

To collapse the explosion, click the right mouse button on the exploded view and select **Collapse**.

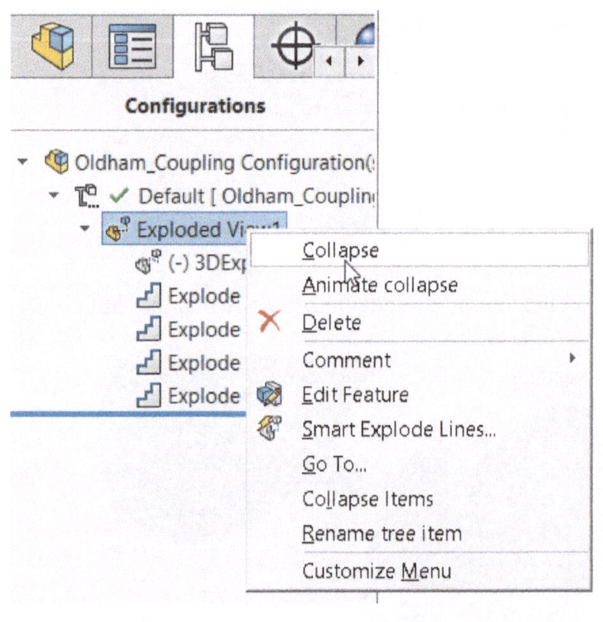

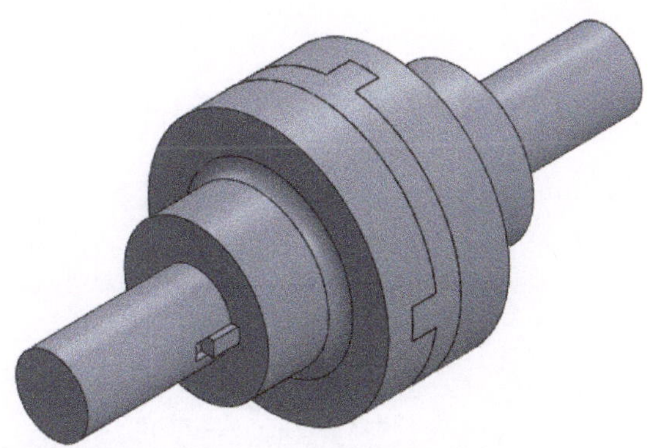

To animate the explosion, select it from the Configurations manager, click the right mouse button, and select **Animate Explode**.

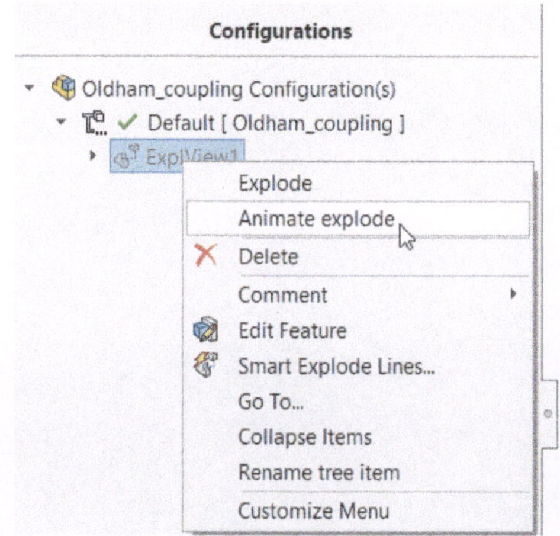

Use the options on the Animation Controller dialog to play, stop, or save the animation.

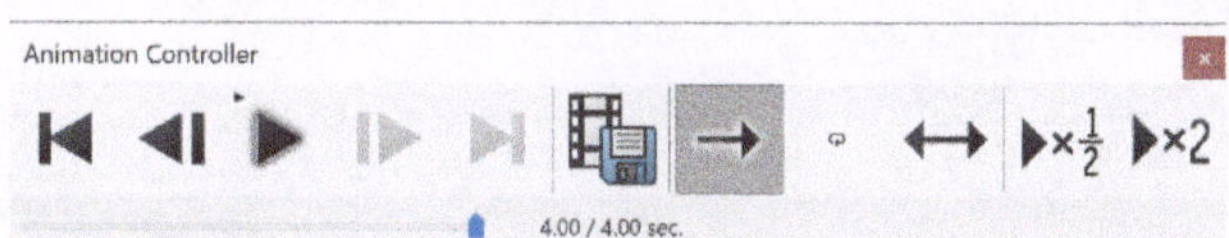

18. Save and close the assembly file.

Chapter 4: Creating Drawings

In this chapter, you create drawings of the parts and assembly from the previous chapters.

In this chapter, you will:

- Create model views
- Create section views
- Create detail views
- Add dimensions and annotations
- Create Custom templates
- Insert exploded view of the assembly
- Insert a bill of materials of the assembly
- Apply balloons to the assembly drawing

TUTORIAL 1

In this tutorial, you will create the drawing of the Flange.sldprt file created in the second chapter.

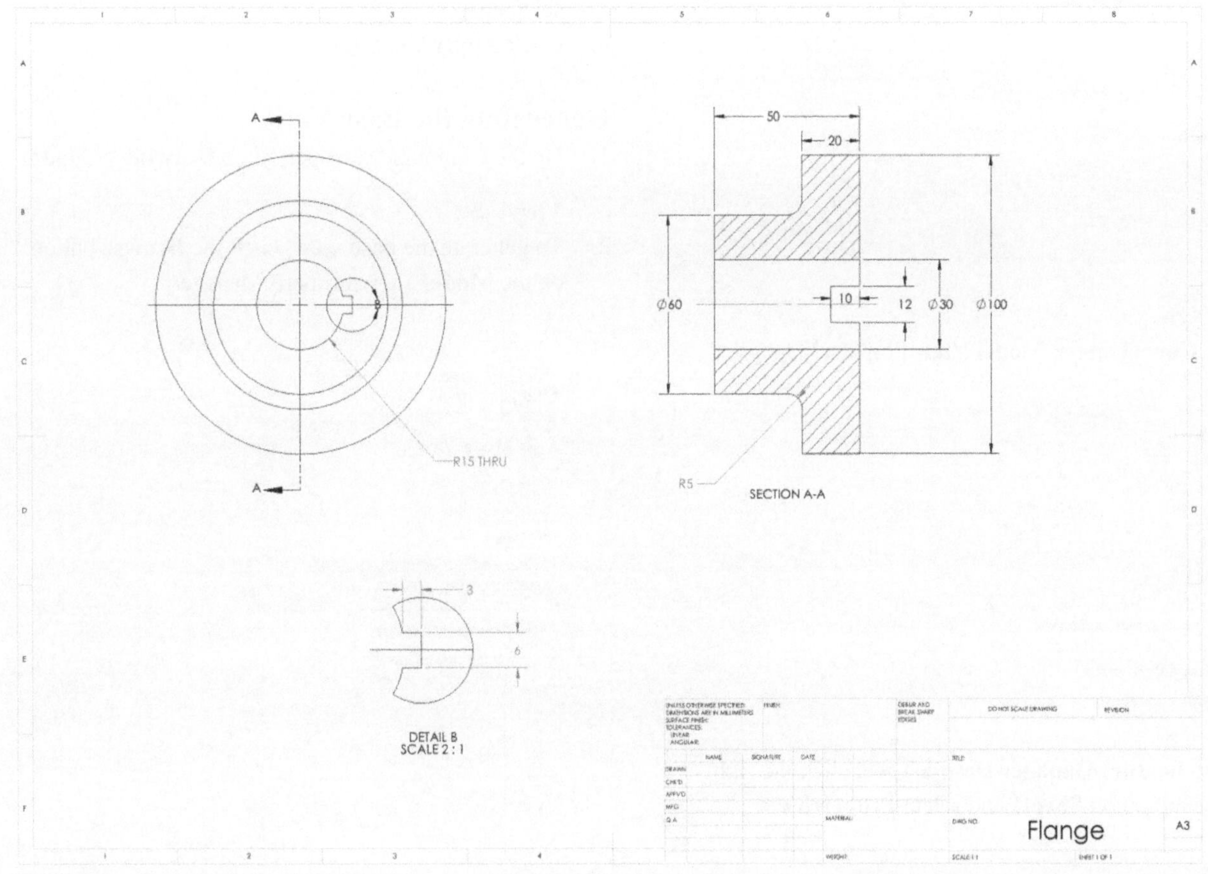

Opening a New Drawing File

1. To open a new drawing, click the **New** button on the **Quick Access Toolbar**.
2. On the **New SOLIDWORKS Document** dialog, select **Drawing** and click **OK**.

3. Select **A3 (ANSI) Landscape** from the list box in the **Sheet Format/Size** dialog.

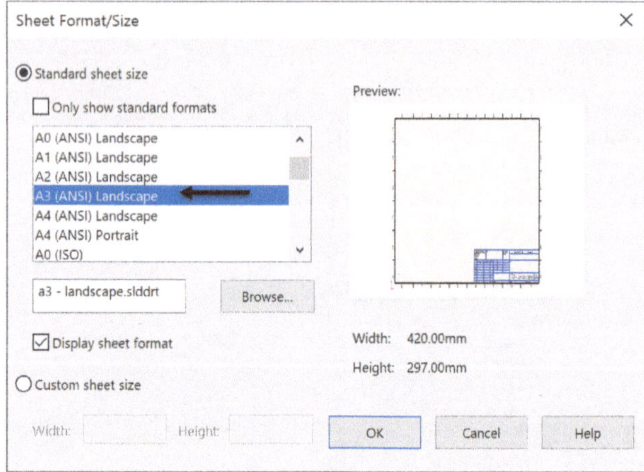

4. Click **OK**.
5. Click **Cancel** on the **Model View** PropertyManager.

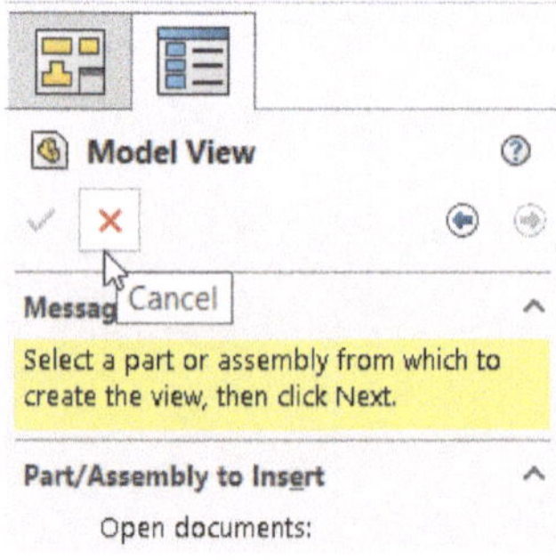

6. On the **FeatureManager Design Tree**, click the right mouse button on **Sheet1** and select **Properties**.

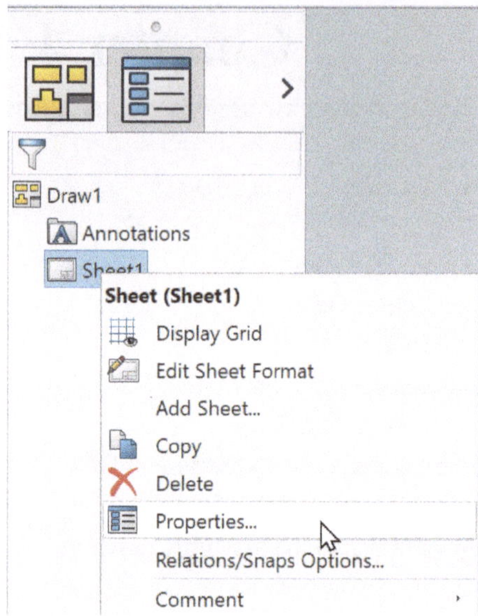

7. On the **Sheet Properties** dialog, set the **Type of projection** to **Third angle** (close the dialog if already selected).
8. Click **Apply Changes**.

Generating the Base View

1. On the CommandManager, click **Drawing > Model View**.
2. To generate the base view, click the **Browse** button on the **Model View** PropertyManager.

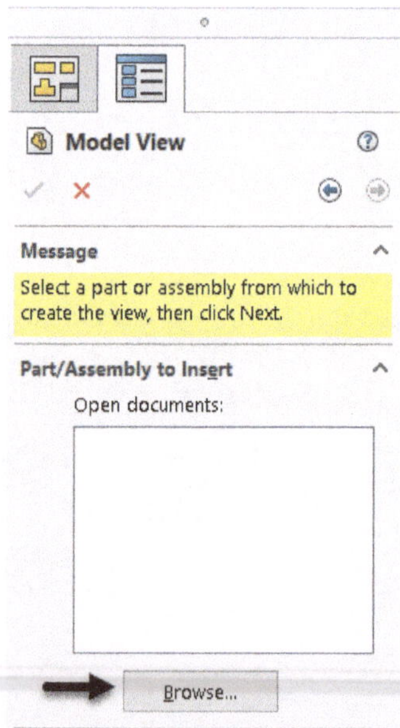

3. Browse to the location **C: /User/Document/Oldham_Coupling** and double-click on **Flange.sldprt**.

4. On the **Model View** PropertyManager, under the **Orientation** section, click **Front**.

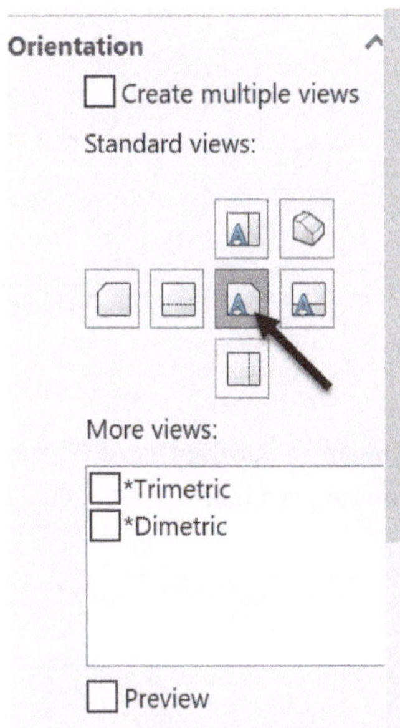

5. Click on the sheet to position the view. The **Projected View** tool gets active.

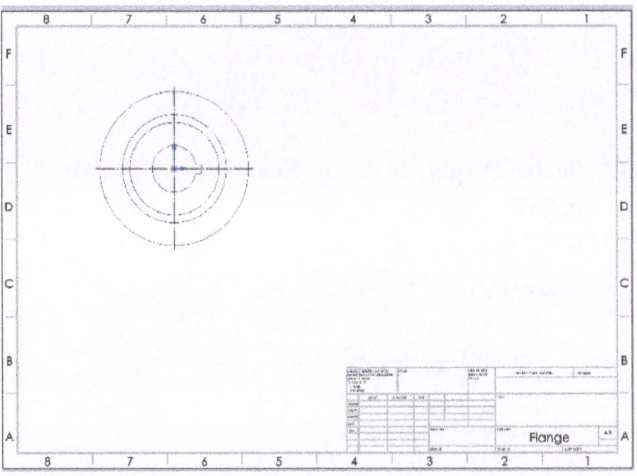

6. Click **OK** on the **PropertyManager**.
7. On the **View Heads-up** toolbar, click the **Hide** flyout and make sure that the **View Origin** icon is deactivated.

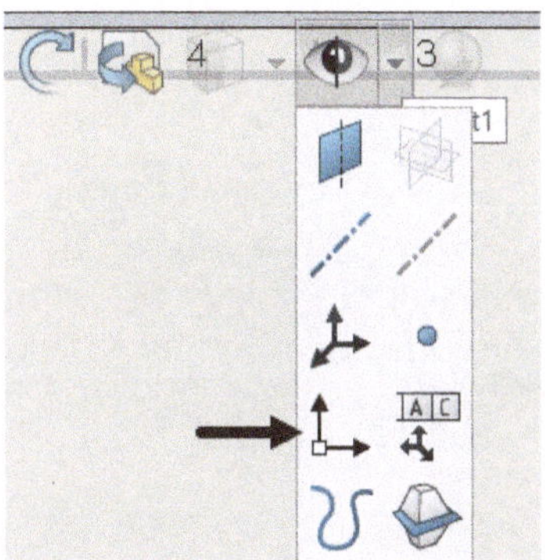

Creating the Section View

Section views are created to reveal internal details of a part or assembly that are hidden in standard views. By cutting through the object along a defined plane, section views provide a clear cross-section of features like holes, cavities, or internal components. This is essential for **design clarity**, **manufacturing guidance**, and **technical documentation**, as it helps visualize hidden geometries, aids fabrication, and ensures accurate assembly.

1. To create the section view, click **Drawing > Section View** on the CommandManager.
2. Snap to the center point of the base view and click to position the section line.

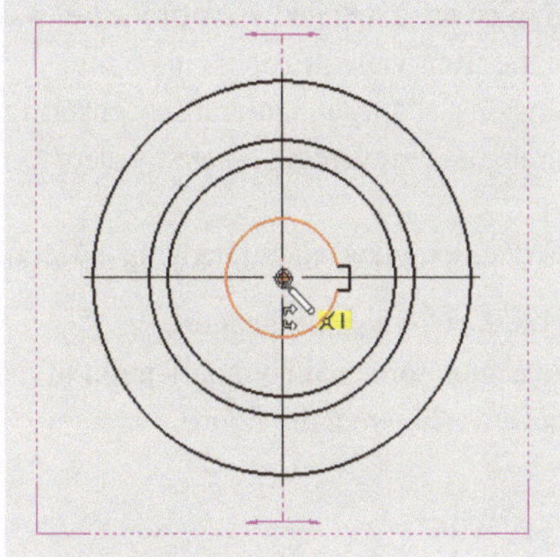

3. Click **OK**.

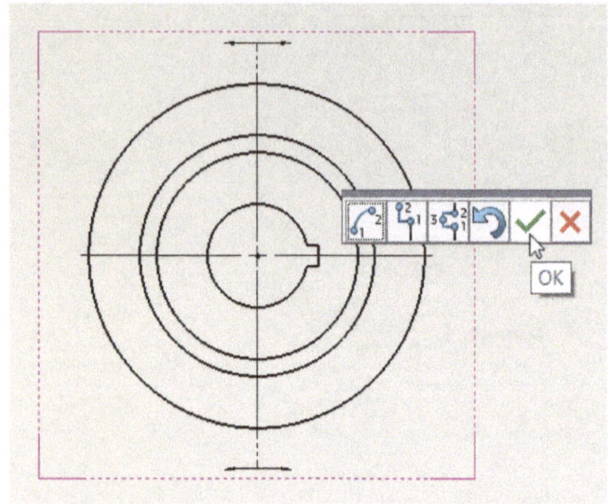

4. Move the pointer toward the right and click to place the section view.
5. Click the green check on the PropertyManager.

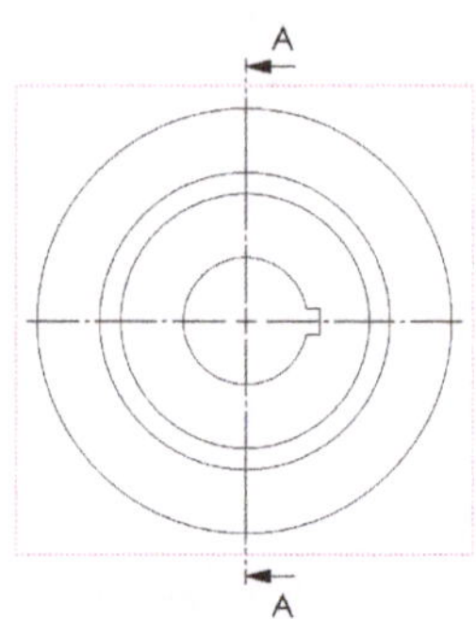

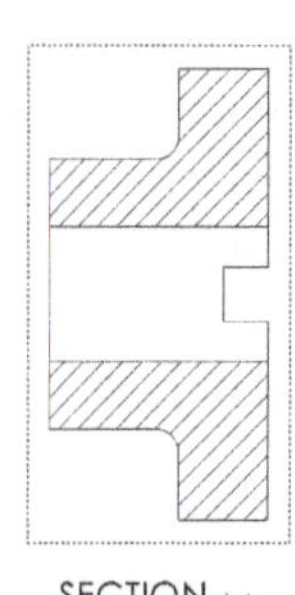

SECTION A-A

Creating the Detailed View

Now, you need to create a detailed view of the keyway that appears on the front view. It zooms in on the keyway's dimensions, shape, and tolerances, ensuring accurate machining and preventing assembly errors.

1. To create a detailed view, click **Drawing > Detail View** on the CommandManager.
2. Specify the center point and boundary point of the detailed view, as shown in the figure.

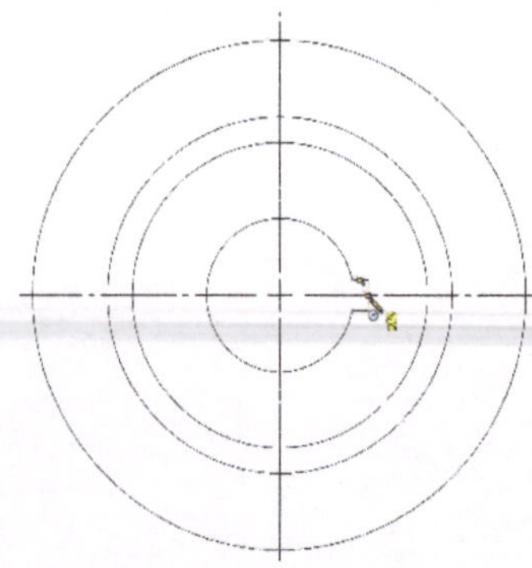

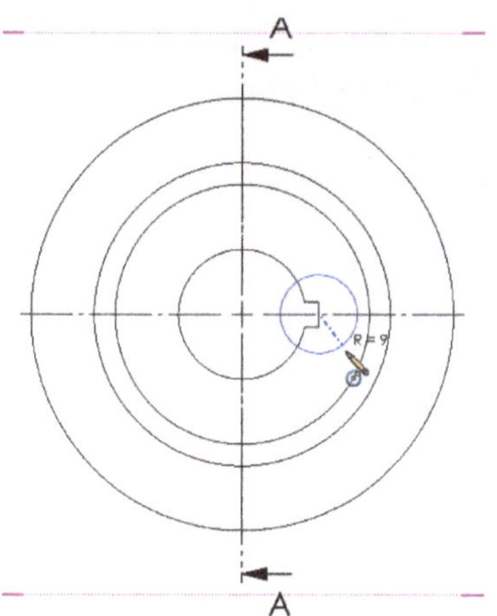

3. On the PropertyManager, under the **Detail Circle** section, set the options shown below.

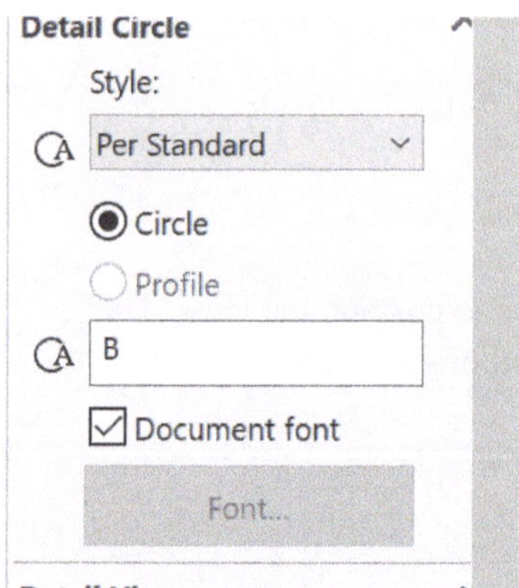

4. Set the **Display Style** and **Scale** options, as shown below.

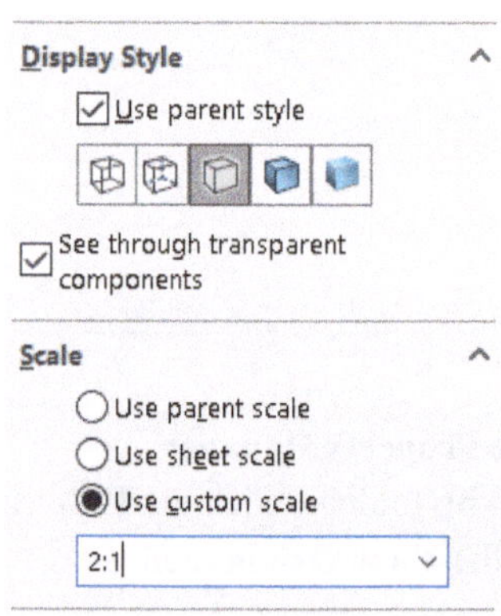

5. Place the detail view below the base view. Click **OK** on the PropertyManager.

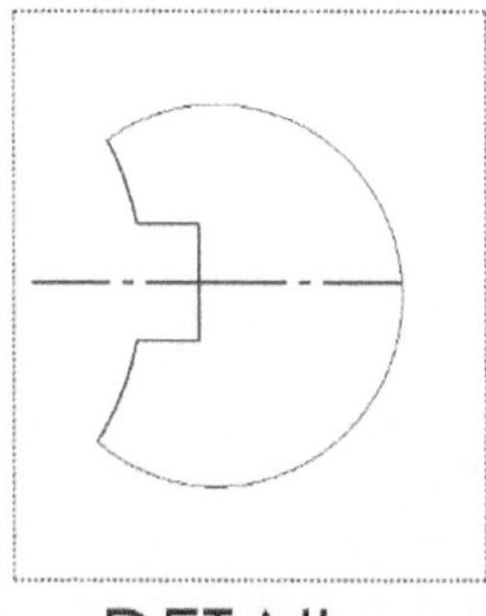

DETAIL B
SCALE 2 : 1

In SOLIDWORKS, you can change the drawing views' scale by using the drop-down available at the bottom right. Note that the scale of the detail view remains unchanged.

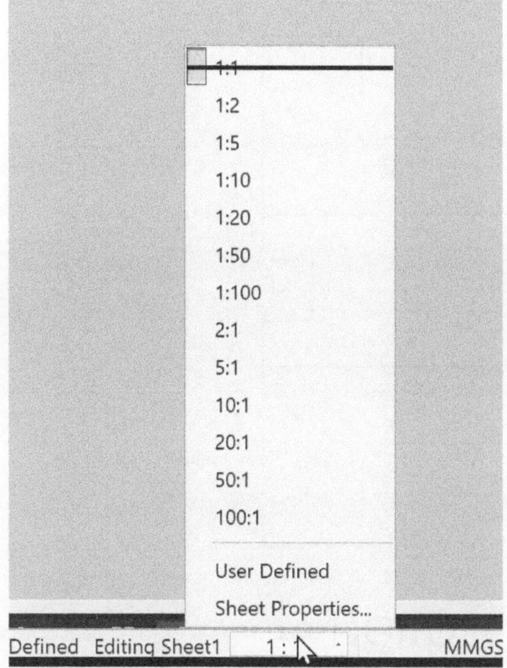

You can change the detailed view outline by using the options in the **Detail View** section of the PropertyManager.

Detail View
- ☐ No outline
- ☐ Full outline
- ☐ Jagged outline
- ☑ Pin position
- ☐ Scale hatch pattern

No outline

The detail view is displayed without any border or outline around it. This creates a clean, minimalistic look but may make it harder to distinguish the detail view from the rest of the drawing.

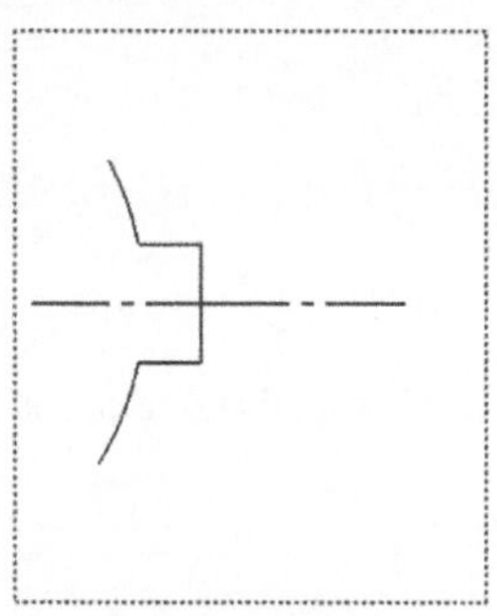

DETAIL B
SCALE 2 : 1

Full outline

The detail view is enclosed with a complete, solid border. This clearly separates the detail view from the main drawing, making it easy to identify.

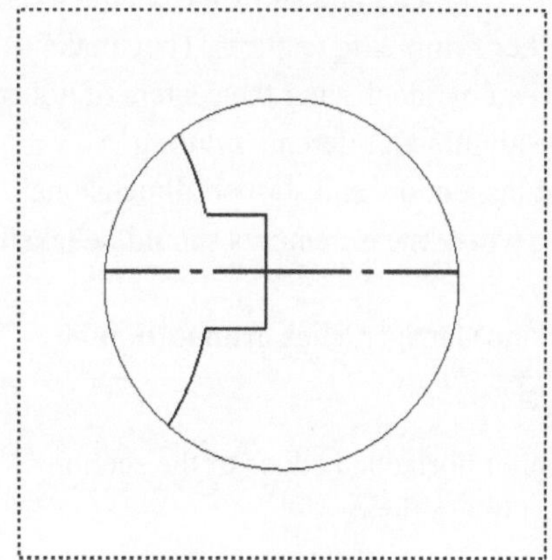

DETAIL B
SCALE 2 : 1

Jagged outline

The detail view is enclosed with a jagged or irregular border, often resembling a hand-drawn break line. This style is commonly used to indicate that the detail view is a "cut-out" or zoomed-in section of the main drawing.

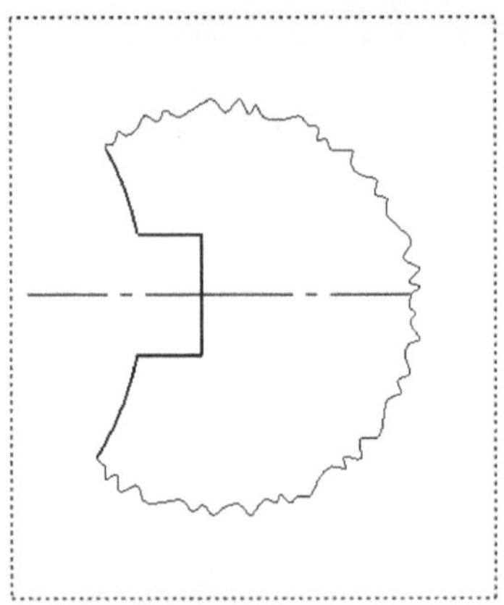

DETAIL B
SCALE 2 : 1

Use the **Shape Intensity** slider to change the size of the jagged shape.

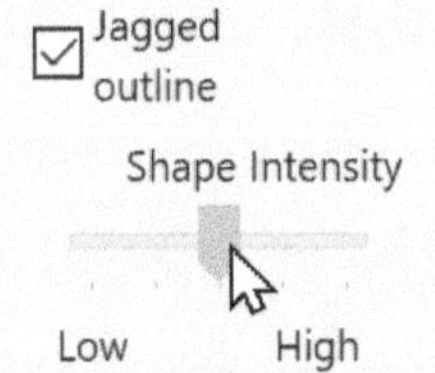

Creating the Centerline

Centerlines indicate symmetry and show the central axis of cylindrical or other symmetric features. They make a drawing easier to read by identifying the centers of holes and shafts, provide alignment references during manufacturing and inspection, and support dimensional checks by showing where measurements should be taken.

1. On the CommandManager, click **Annotation > Centerline** .
2. Click on the inner horizontal edges of the section view, as shown in the figure.

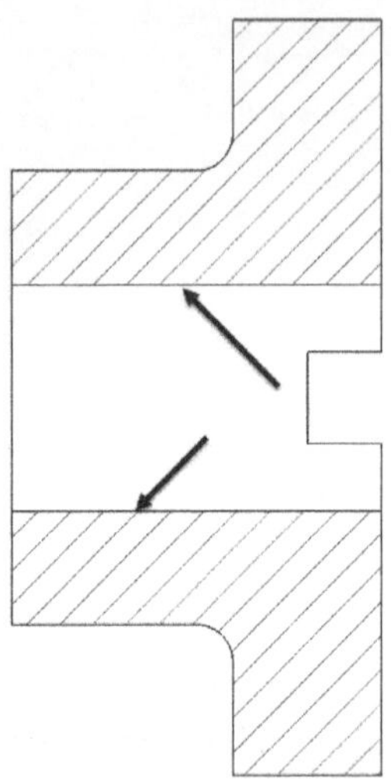

3. Click **OK** on the PropertyManager.

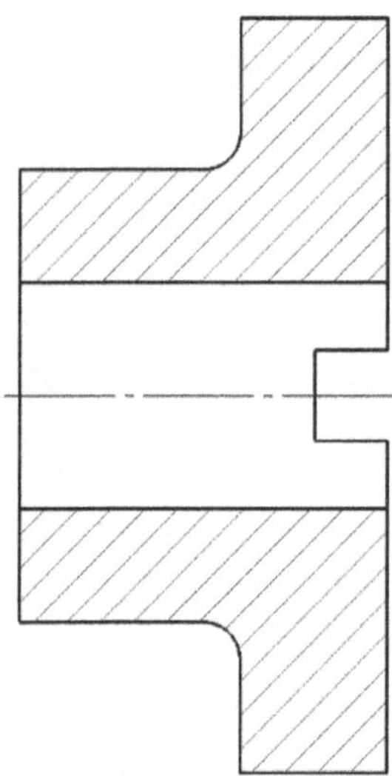

SECTION A-A

Specifying Dimension Settings

1. To specify the dimension settings, click **Options** on the **Quick Access Toolbar**.

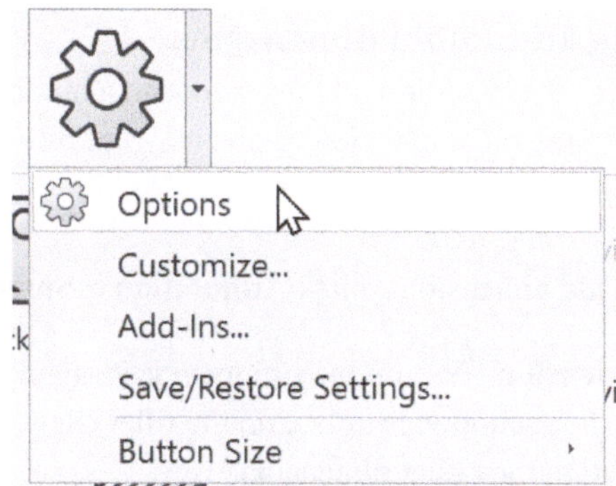

2. On the dialog, under the **Document Properties** tab, click **Drafting Standard**.
3. Select **Overall drafting standard > ANSI**.

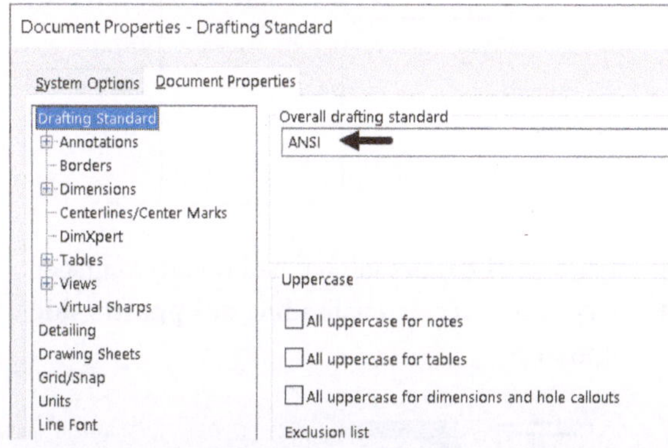

4. Under **Drafting Standard**, click **Dimensions**.

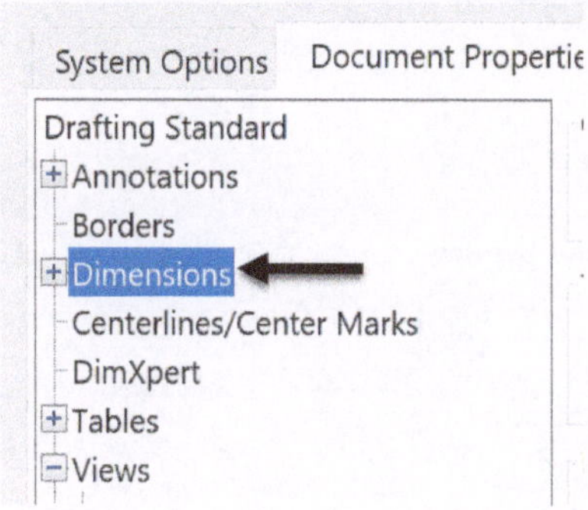

5. Under **Primary Precision**, select **Unit Precision > None**.

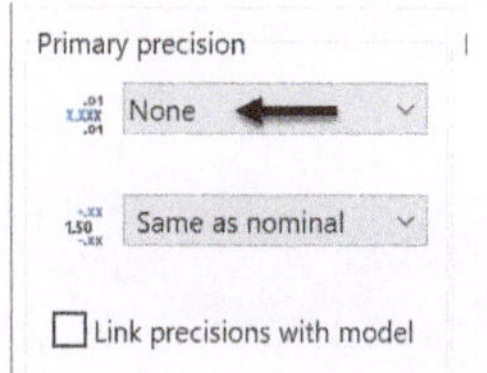

6. At the bottom of the dialog, check the **Center between extension lines**.

☐ Show units of dimensions
☐ Add parentheses by default
☑ Center between extension lines
☐ Include prefix inside basic tolerance box
☐ Display dual basic dimension in one box
☑ Show dimensions as broken in break views

7. Click **OK**.
8. At the bottom of the window, set the **Unit System** to **MMGS**.

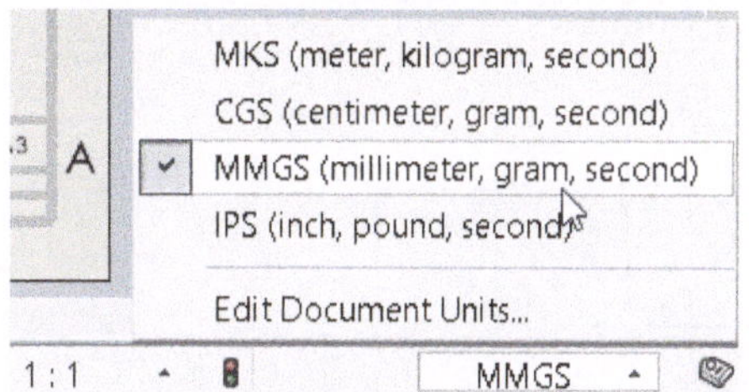

Retrieving Dimensions

Now, you will retrieve the dimensions that were applied to the model while creating it. You retrieve dimensions to access and reuse measurements from a model, ensuring accuracy and consistency in design.

1. To retrieve dimensions, click **Annotation > Model Items** on the CommandManager.
2. On the PropertyManager, select **Source > Entire model**.
3. Uncheck the **Import Items into all views** option.
4. Under the **Dimensions** section, select **Marked for drawing**.

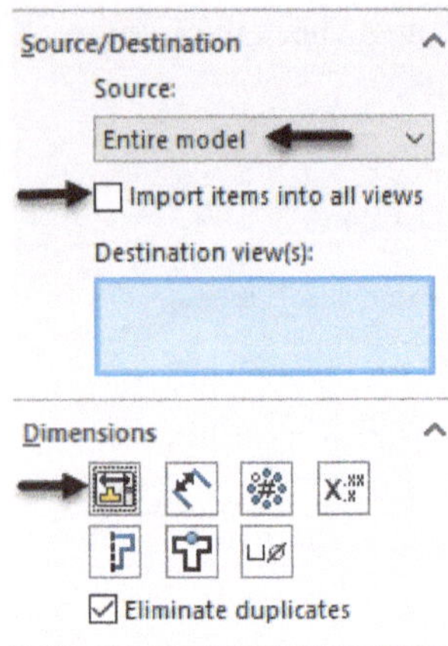

5. Click on the view boundary of the section view and click **OK** on the PropertyManager.

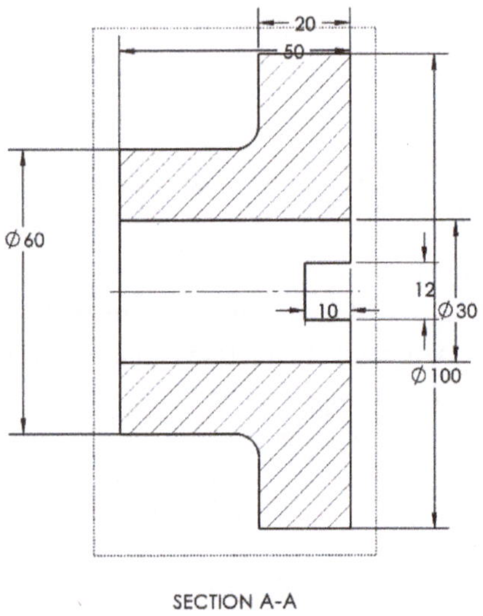

SECTION A-A

6. Drag and arrange the dimensions.

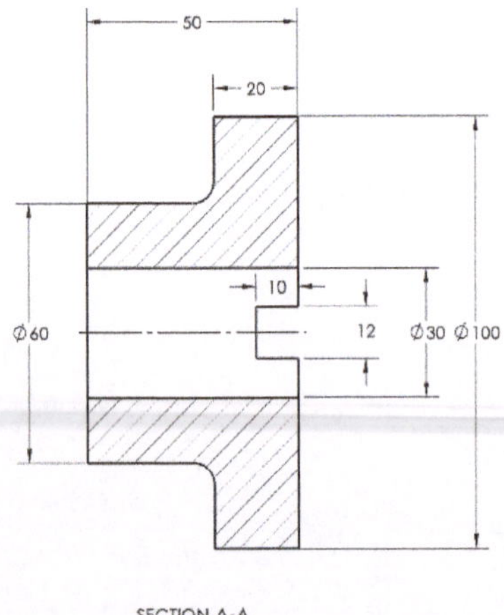

SECTION A-A

Adding additional dimensions

You need to add additional dimensions to a model because retrieved dimensions alone may not fully define the design.

1. To add dimensions, click **Annotation > Smart Dimension** on the CommandManager.
2. On the section view, click on the fillet edge and position the radial dimension.

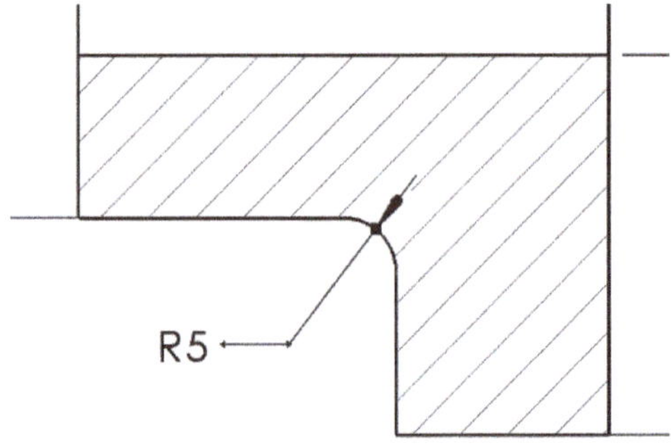

3. Click the **Leaders** tab on the PropertyManager.
4. Check the **Arc extension line or opposite side** option.

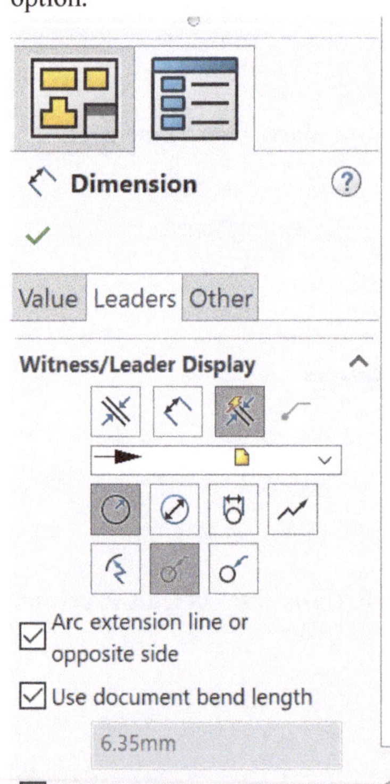

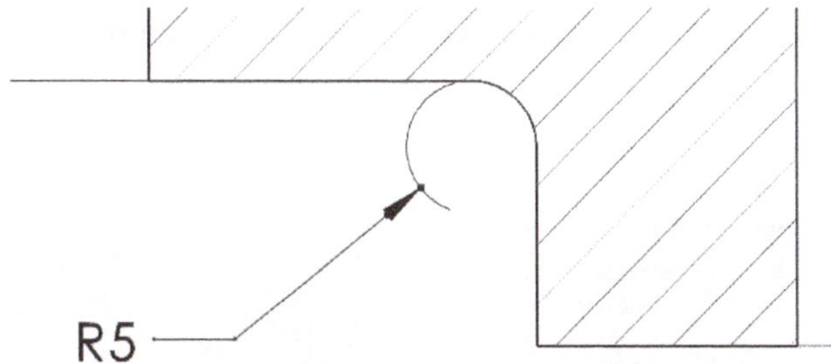

5. On the detail view, click on the vertical edge of the slot and position the dimension.

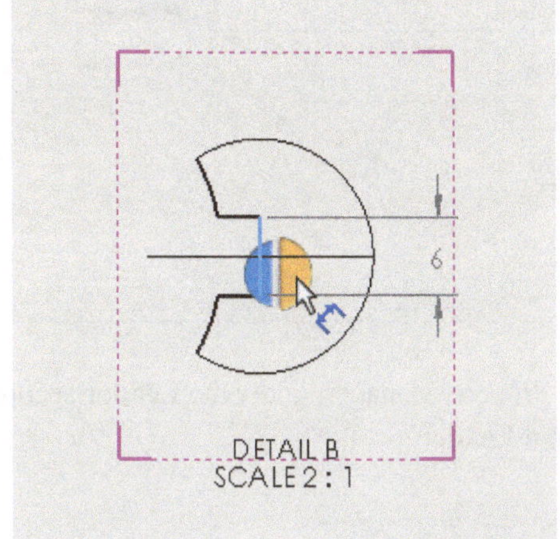

6. Likewise, add dimension to the horizontal edge of the slot.

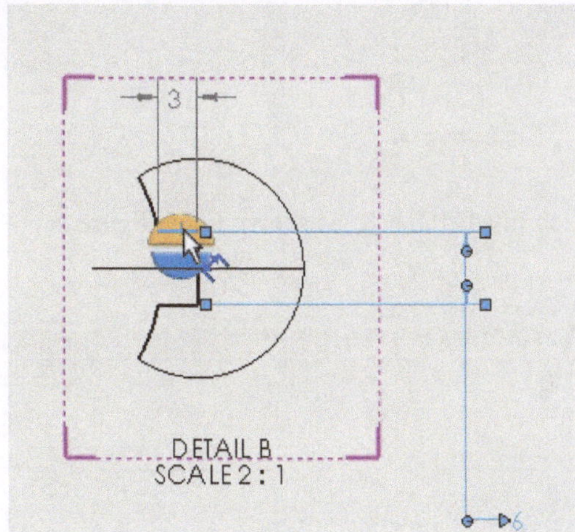

7. Click **OK** on the PropertyManager.
8. On the CommandManager, click **Annotation > Hole Callout**.
9. Click on the innermost circular edge of the front view and position the hole callout.
10. Click **Close Dialog** on the PropertyManager

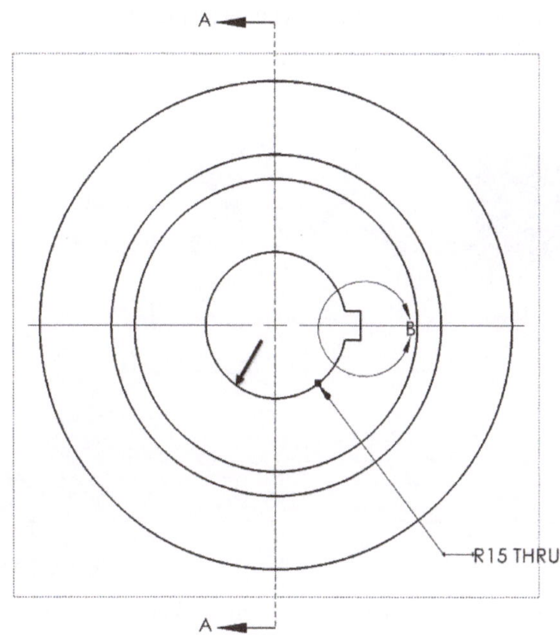

Saving the Drawing

1. Click **Save** on the **Quick Access Toolbar**.
2. Specify **Flange** as **Name**.
3. Browse to **C:\Users\Username\Documents\Oldham Coupling** folder.
4. Click **Save** to save the file.
5. Click **File > Close**.

TUTORIAL 2

In this tutorial, you will create the drawing of the Disc.sldprt file created in the second chapter.

Creating a Custom Sheet Format

1. On Quick Access Toolbar, click the **New** button.
2. On the **New SOLIDWORKS Document** dialog, select **Drawing** and click **OK**.
6. Select **A3 (ANSI) Landscape** from the list box in the **Sheet Format/Size** dialog.
7. Click **OK**.
8. Click **Cancel** on the **Model View** PropertyManager.
9. On the **FeatureManager Design Tree**, click the right mouse button on **Sheet1** and select **Properties**.
10. On the **Sheet Properties** dialog, set the **Type of projection** to **Third angle**. Click **Apply Changes**.
11. On the CommandManager, click **Sheet Format > Edit Sheet Format**.

12. Zoom to the title block, and then select the lines and notes shown in the figure. Press **Delete** on your keyboard.

3. On the CommandManager, click **Sketch > Line** and draw a line on the title block.

4. On the CommandManager, click **Annotation > Note** A.

5. On the PropertyManager, under the **Text Format** section, select **Link to Property**.

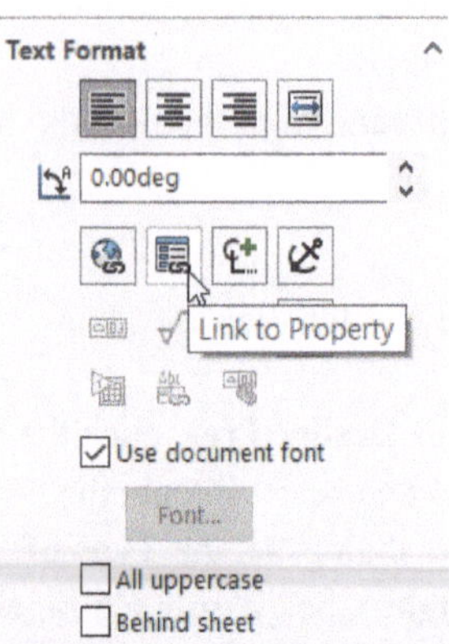

6. On the **Link to Property** dialog, select **Current document**.

7. Select **SW-Author (Author)** from the **Property name** drop-down, and then click **OK**.

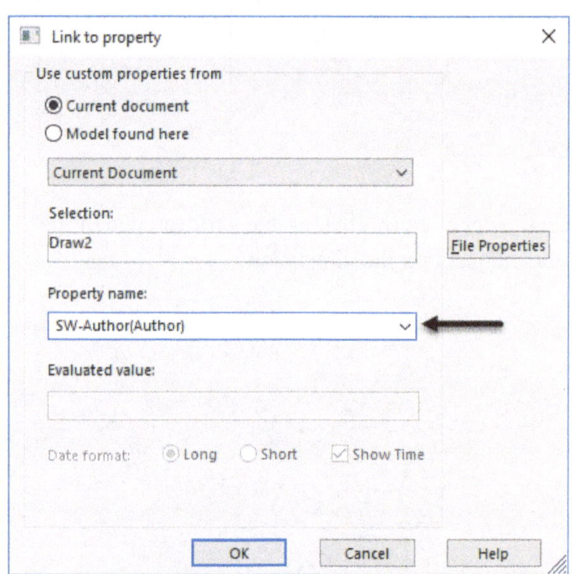

8. On the PropertyManager, under the **Leader** section, select **No Leader**.

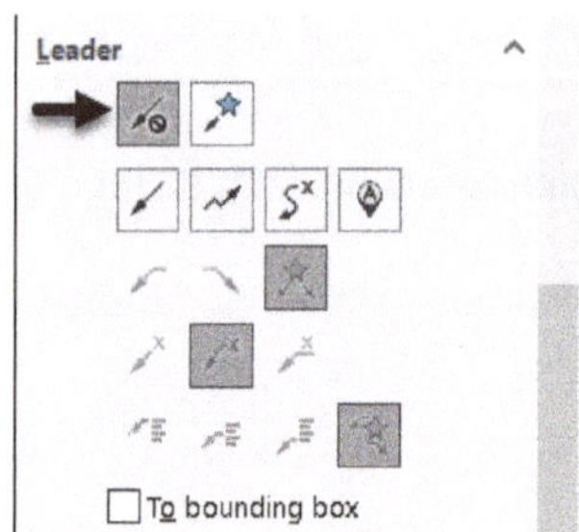

9. Click inside the box, as shown in the figure.

10. On the **Formatting** toolbar, set the font size to 8 and type **Author**.

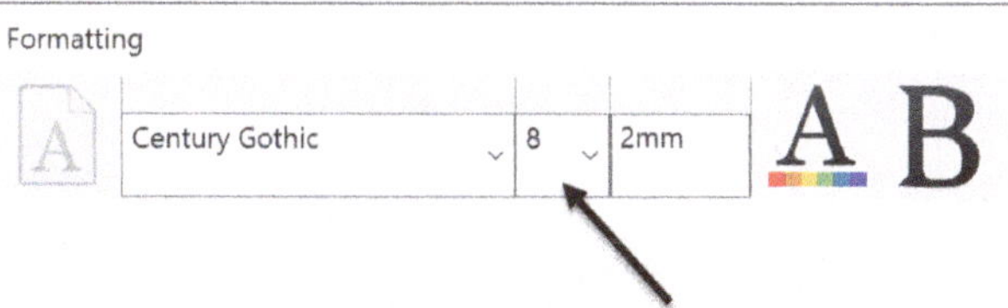

11. Click **OK** on the PropertyManager.

12. On the Menu bar, click **Insert > Picture**.
13. Select your company logo and click **Open**.
14. Resize (click and drag the top right corner of the image) and position the image on the title block.

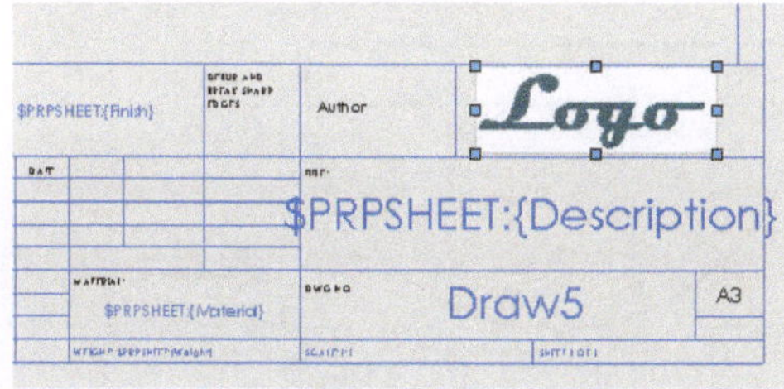

15. Click **OK** on the PropertyManager.
16. Click **Exit Sheet Format**.

17. On the **Quick Access Toolbar**, click **Options**.
18. On the dialog, under the **Document Properties** tab, click **Drafting Standard**.
19. Select **Overall drafting standard** >**ANSI**.
20. Click **Units** and set the **Unit System** to **MMGS**.
21. Click **OK**.
22. Click **File > Save**.
23. On the **Save As** dialog, select **Save as type > Drawing Templates**.
24. Browse to **C:\Users\Username\Documents\Oldham Coupling** folder.
25. Type-in **Sample** in the **File name** box and click **Save**.
26. On the Menu bar, click **File > Close**.

Starting a New drawing

1. On the Quick Access Toolbar, click the **Options** button.
2. On the **System Options** dialog, click **File Locations**.
3. Select **Show folders for > Document Templates** and click the **Add** button.

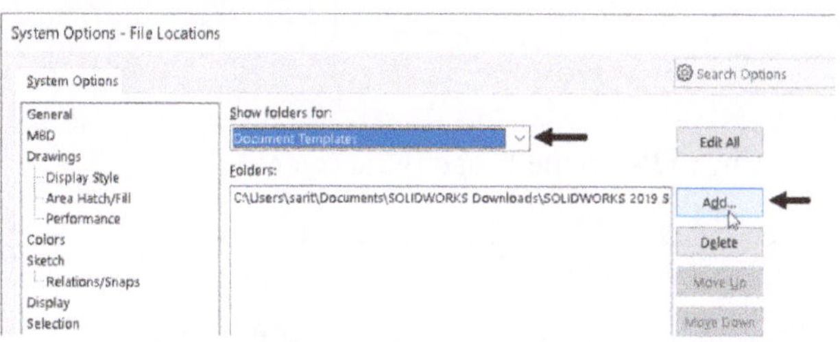

4. Browse to **C:\Users\Username\Documents\Oldham Coupling** folder. Click **Select Folder**.
5. Click **OK** on the **System Options** dialog, and then click **Yes**.
6. On the Quick Access Toolbar, click the **New** button.
7. On the **New SOLIDWORKS Document** dialog, click the **Advanced** button.
8. Under the **Oldham Coupling** tab, select **Sample** and click **OK**.

Generating the Drawing Views

1. On the **Model View** PropertyManager, click the **Browse** button and browse to the location: **C: /User/Document/Oldham_Coupling**
2. Double-click on **Disc.sldprt**.

3. On the PropertyManager, under the **Orientation** section, check the **Create multiple views** option.
4. Select the **Front** and **Bottom** views.

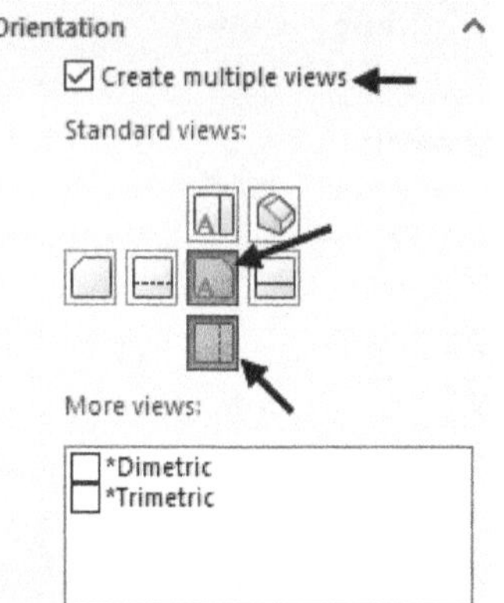

5. Click **OK** on the PropertyManager.

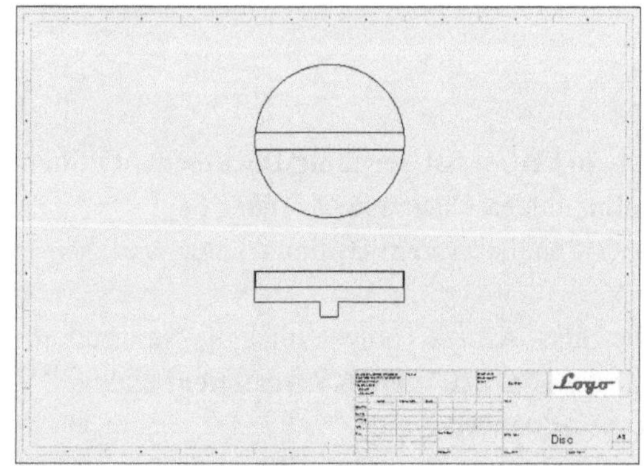

6. On the CommandManager, click **Annotation > Model Items** .
7. On the PropertyManager, select **Source > Entire model**.
8. Click on the two views and click **OK** .

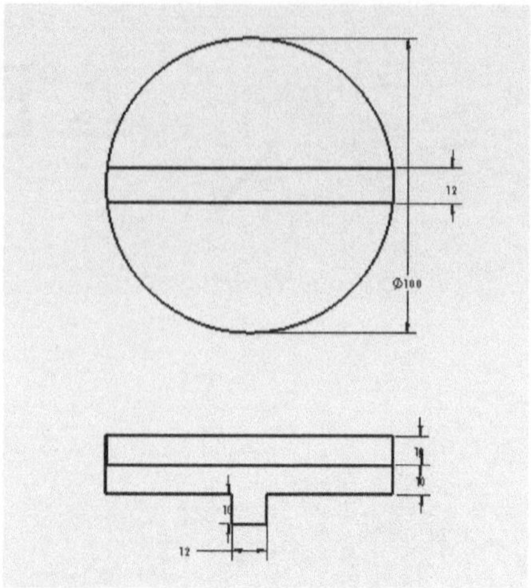

9. Click the right mouse button on the 100-diameter dimension on the front view and select **Display Options > Display as Diameter**.

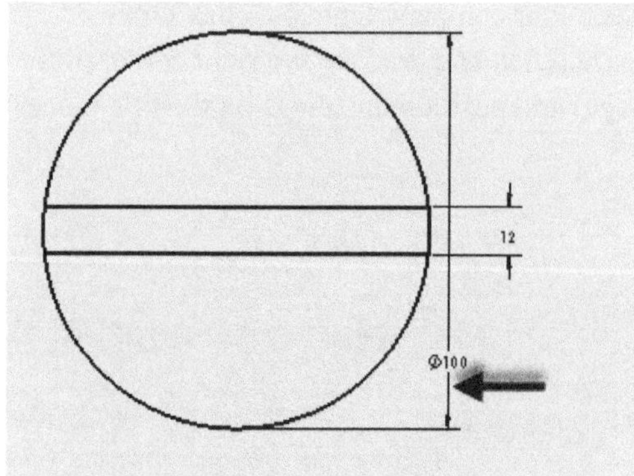

10. Arrange the dimensions by dragging them.

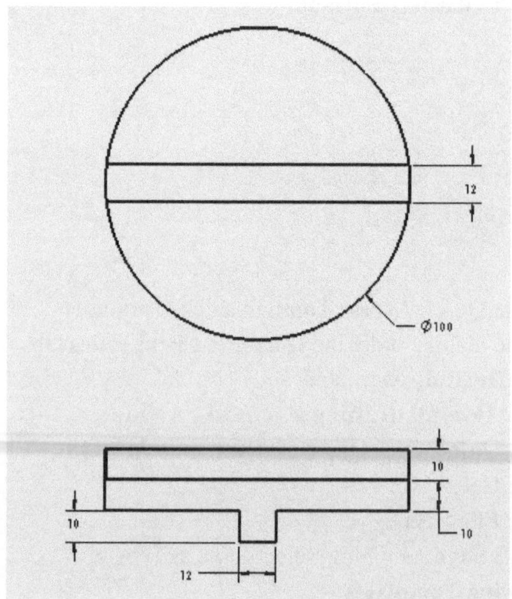

11. Save and close the drawing file.

TUTORIAL 3

In this tutorial, you will create the drawing of the Oldham coupling assembly created in the previous chapter.

Creating the Isometric View

1. Start a new drawing file using the **Sample** template.
2. On the **Model View** PropertyManager, click the **Browse** button.
3. Browse to the location **C: /User/Document/Oldham_Coupling** folder and double-click on **Oldham_Coupling.sldasm**.
4. On the **Model View** PropertyManager, under the **Reference Configuration** section, uncheck the **Show in exploded or model break state** option.
5. Under the **Orientation** section, select **Isometric**.

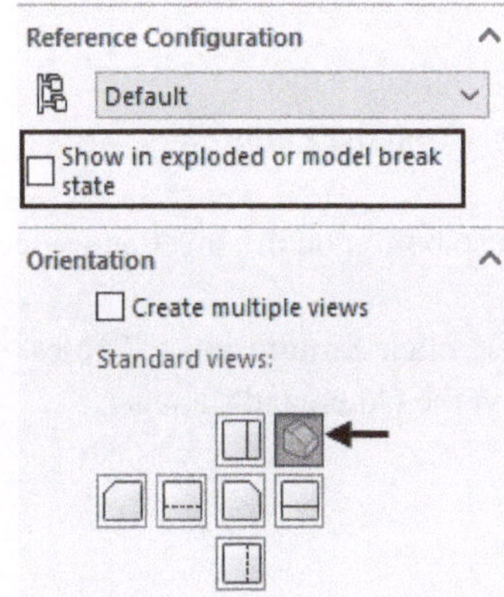

6. Under the **Scale** section, select **Use custom scale** and set the scale factor to **1:2**.

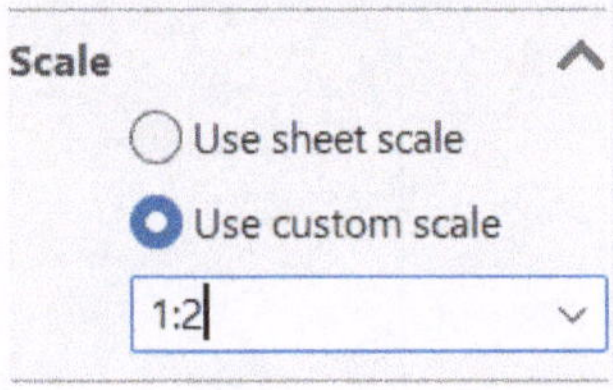

7. Click on the sheet to position the view.

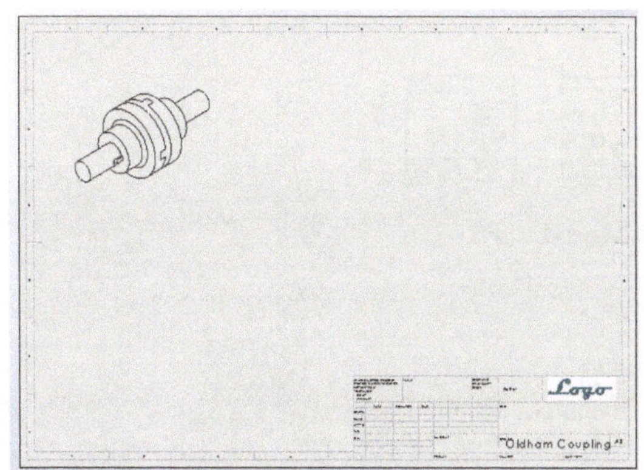

8. Click the green check on the PropertyManager.

Generating the Exploded View

1. On the CommandManager, click **Drawing > Model View**.
2. On the PropertyManager, under the **Part/Assembly to Insert** section, double-click on **Oldham Coupling**.

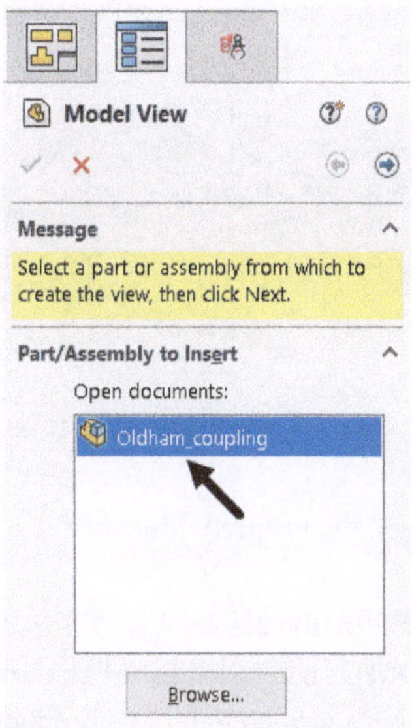

3. Click the **Next** icon on the **Model View** PropertyManager.

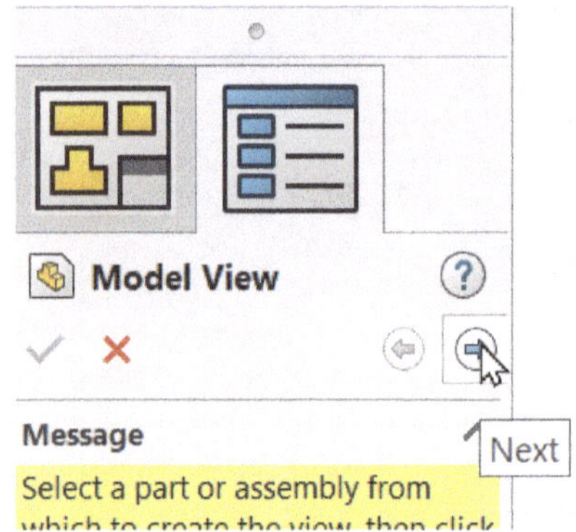

4. Under the **Reference Configuration** section, enable **Shown in exploded or model break state**.
5. Under the **Orientation** section, select **Isometric**.
6. Under the **Scale** section, select **Use custom scale** and set the scale factor to **1:2**.
7. Click on the sheet to position the exploded view.

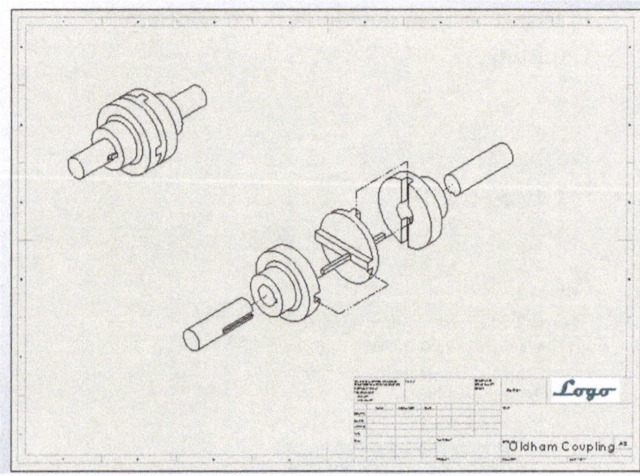

8. Click **Close Dialog** on the Property Manager.

Creating the Bill of Materials

A **Bill of Materials (BOM)** is a detailed list of all parts, materials, and subassemblies needed to build a product. It ensures **clarity in design**, prevents missing components, and guides the assembly process.

1. Click the right mouse button on the sheet and select **Edit Sheet Format**.
2. Click on the top right corner of the sheet border.

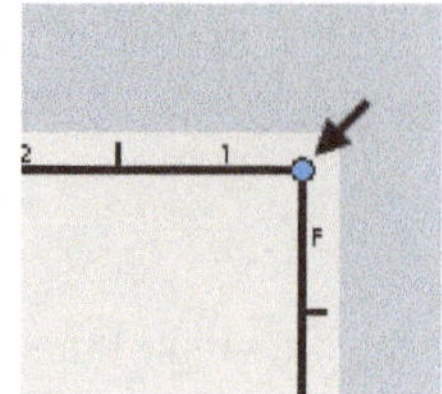

3. Click the right mouse button and select **Set Anchor as > Bill of Materials**.

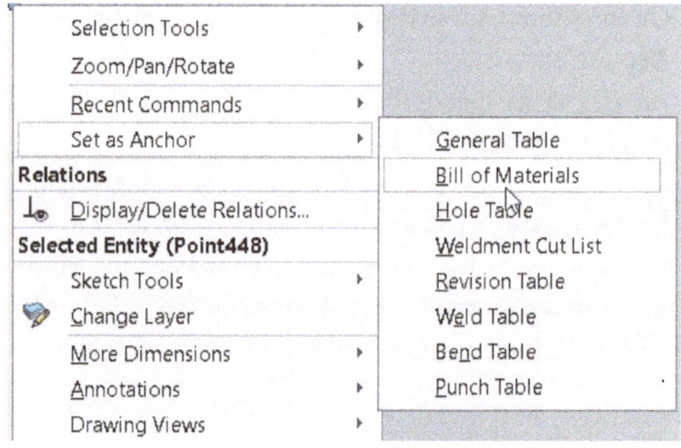

4. Click **Close Dialog** on the **Point** PropertyManager.
5. Click the right mouse button on the sheet and select **Edit Sheet**.
6. To create a parts list, click **Annotation > Tables > Bill of Materials** on the CommandManager.

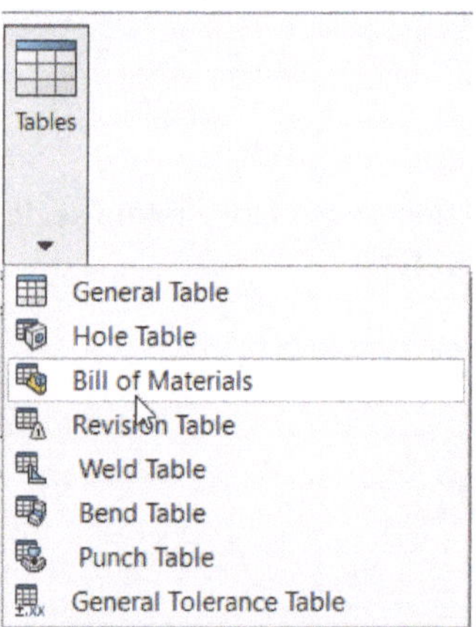

7. Click on the exploded view.
8. On the PropertyManager, under the **Table Position** section, check the **Attach to anchor point** option.
9. Set the **BOM Type** to **Parts only**.

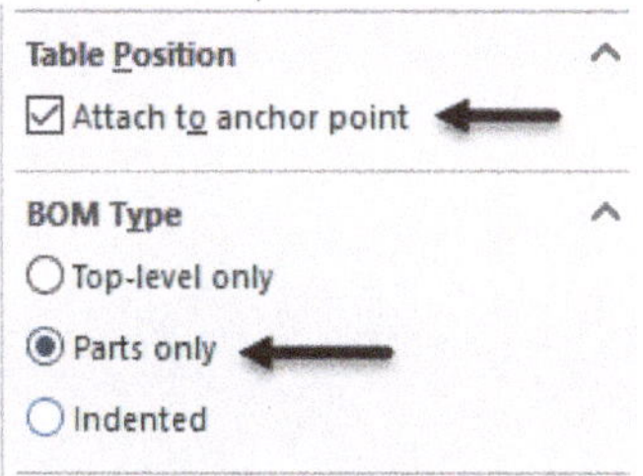

10. Click **OK**. You will notice that the BOM appears outside the sheet.

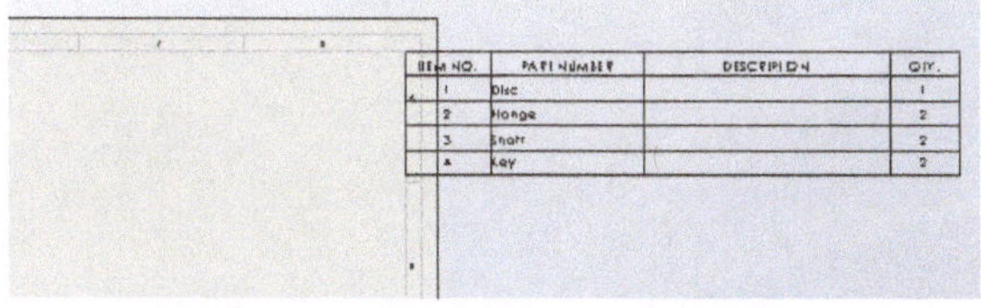

11. Click on the anchor point of the BOM.

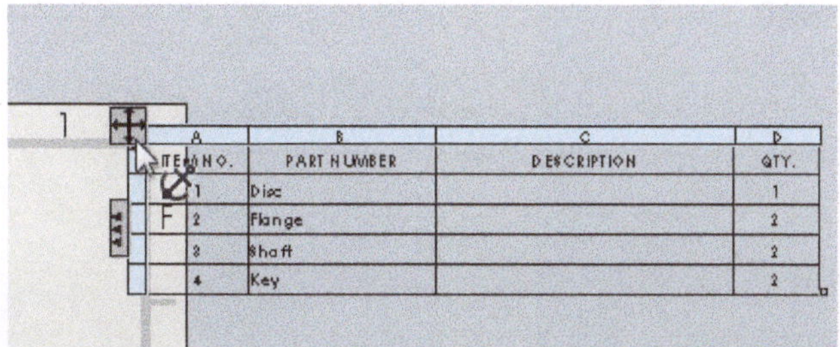

12. On the PropertyManager, under the **Table Position** section, select **Top Right**.

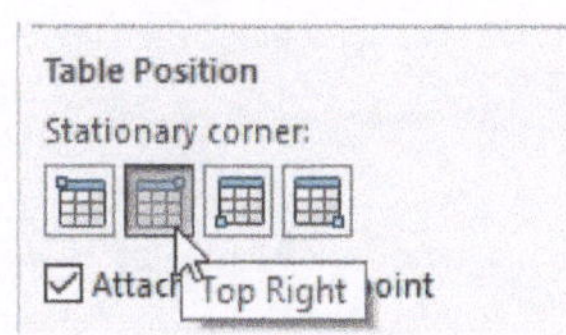

ITEM NO.	PART NUMBER	DESCRIPTION	QTY.
1	Disc		1
2	Flange		2
3	Shaft		2
4	Key		2

13. Click the green check ✓ on the PropertyManager.

Creating Balloons

Balloons are numbered labels with leader lines that point to specific parts, making it easy to identify and reference components. They link the drawing to the **Bill of Materials (BOM)**, ensuring all parts are accounted for.

1. To create balloons, click **Annotation > Auto Balloon** on the CommandManager.
2. On the PropertyManager, under **Balloon Layout** section, select **Layout Balloons to Right**.
3. Click on the exploded view and click **OK** ✓.

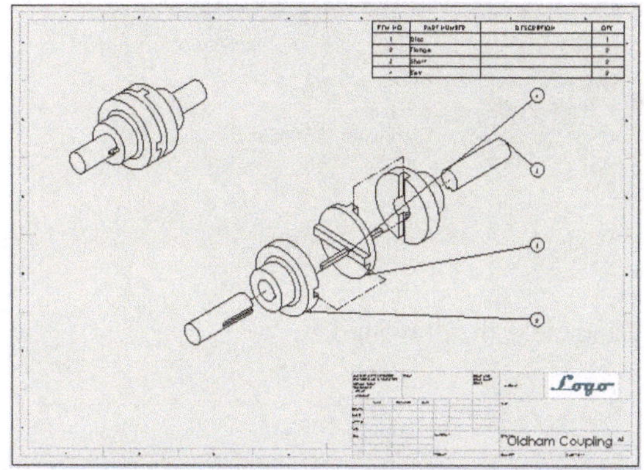

Adding Comments to the Drawing

SOLIDWORKS allows you to add comments to the drawing. This helps you in the inspection process.

1. Place the pointer on the exploded view.
2. Right click when the boundary of the view appears.
3. Select **Comment** > **Add Comment** from the shortcut menu.
4. Type a comment in the comment box.

Also, you can add a timeline, image, or snapshot in the comment.

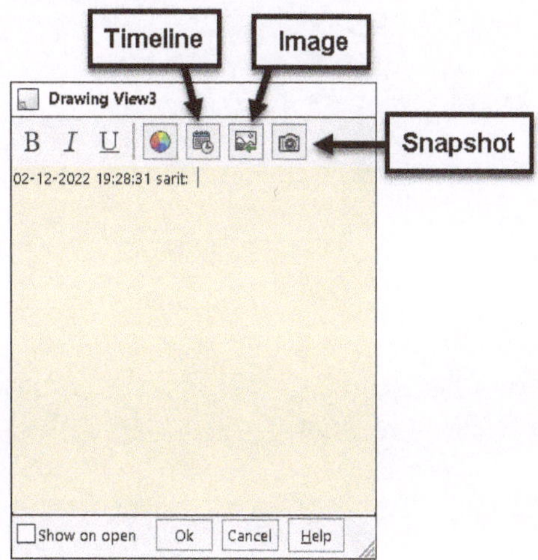

5. Click **Save and Close** on the comment box.
6. On the FeatureManager Design Tree, place the pointer in the Drawing View2 and notice the comment.

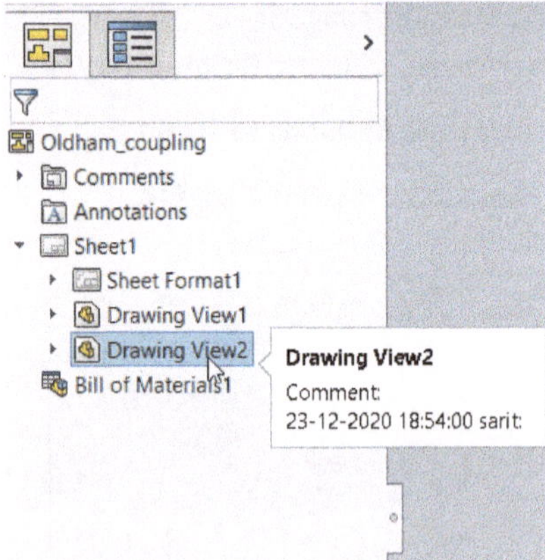

7. Save and close the drawing file.

Chapter 5: Sketching

In this chapter, you will learn the sketching tools. You will learn to do the following:

- Create Rectangles
- Create Polygons
- Resolve Sketch
- Create Relations
- Create Splines
- Create Ellipses
- Move, rotate, scale, copy, and stretch entities
- Create Circles
- Create Arcs
- Create a Circular pattern
- Trim Entities
- Create Fillets and Chamfers

Creating Rectangles

A rectangle is a four-sided object. You can create a rectangle by just specifying its two diagonal corners. However, there are various tools to create a rectangle. You can access these tools from the **Rectangle** drop-down available on the **Sketch** CommandManager. These tools are explained next.

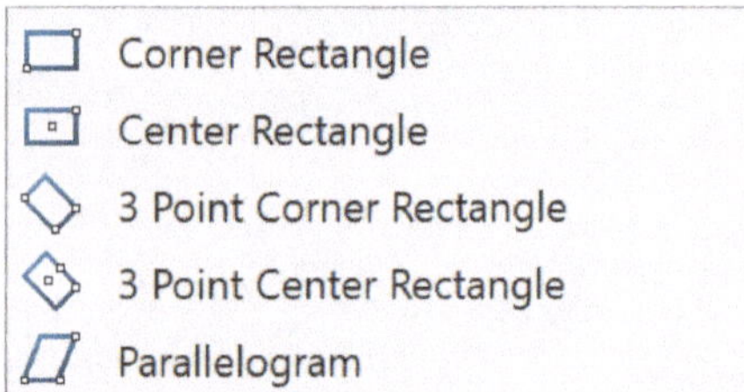

1. On the CommandManager, click **Sketch > Sketch** and select the Front plane.
2. On the CommandManager, click **Sketch > Rectangle Drop-down > Corner Rectangle**.
3. Select the origin point to define the first corner.
4. Move the pointer diagonally and click to define the second corner.

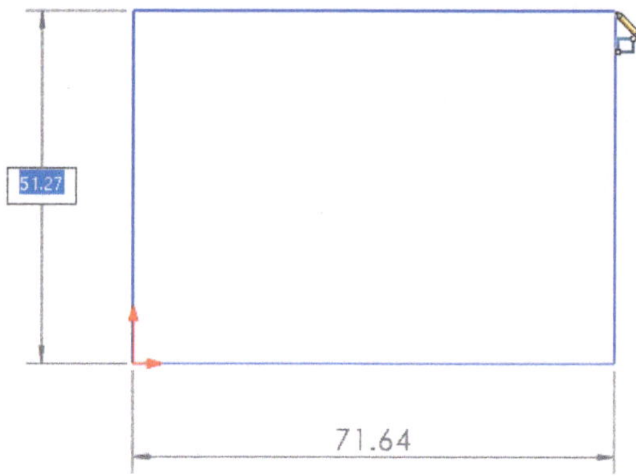

5. On the PropertyManager, click the **Center Rectangle** icon under the **Rectangle Type** section.
6. Click in the graphics window to define the center point.
7. Move the pointer and click to define the corner.

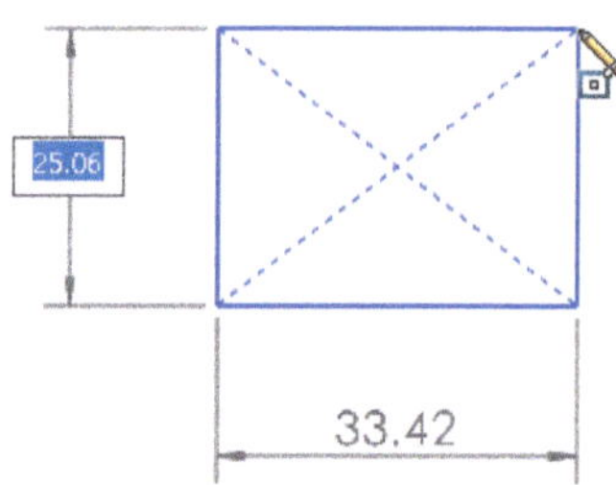

8. On the PropertyManager, select **From Midpoints** under the **Rectangle Type** section.
9. Select the center point and corner point of the rectangle. Two construction lines are created from the midpoints of the rectangle.

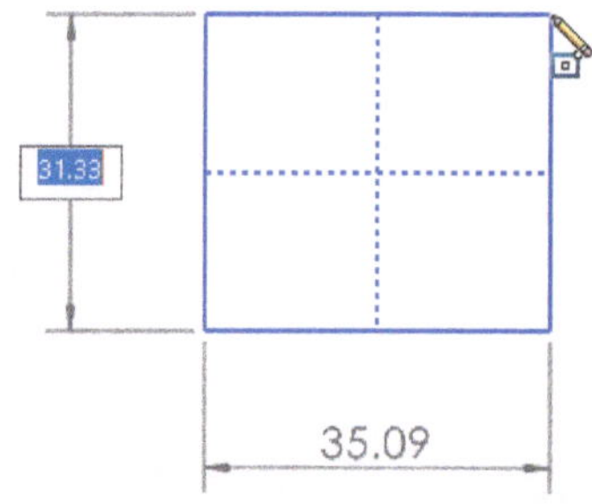

10. On the PropertyManager, click the **3 Point Corner Rectangle** icon under the **Rectangle type** section. This option creates a slanted rectangle. You can also check the **Add construction lines** option to

add construction lines between the corners or midpoints.

11. Select two points to define the width and inclination angle of the rectangle.

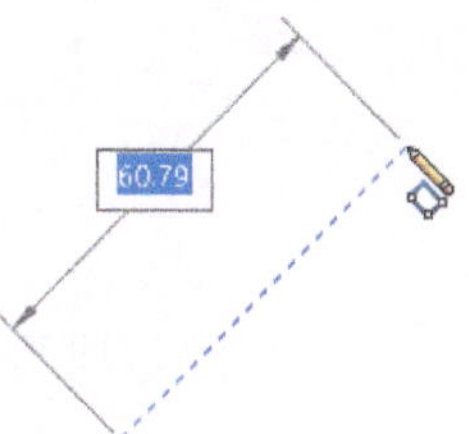

12. Select the third point to define its height.

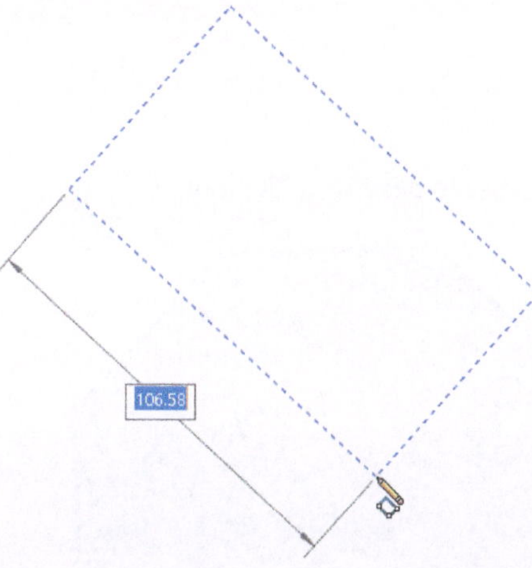

13. On the PropertyManager, click the **3 Point Center Rectangle** icon under the **Rectangle Type** section.
14. Click to define the center point of the rectangle.
15. Move the pointer and click to define the midpoint of one side.

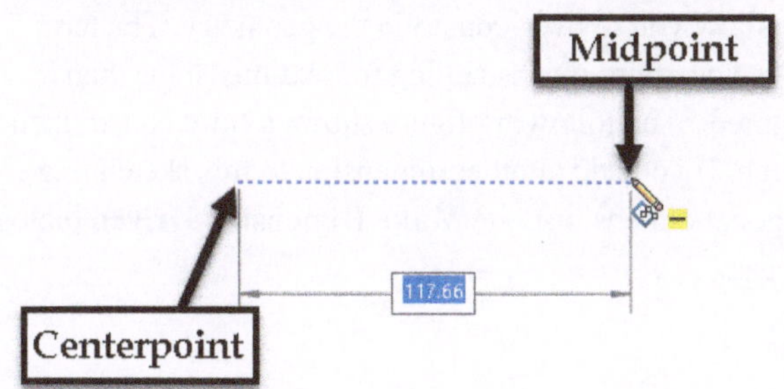

16. Move the pointer and click to define the corner point.

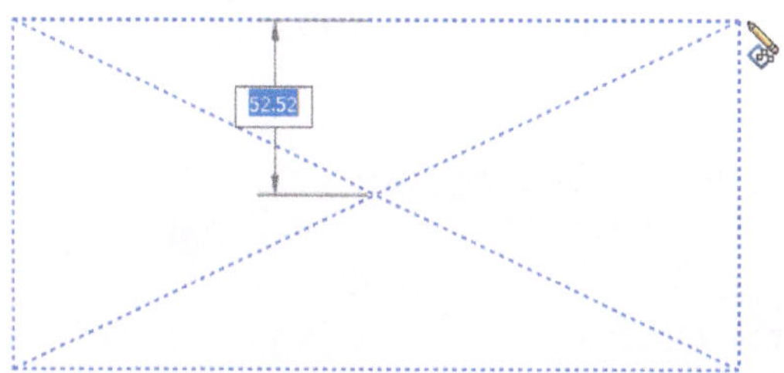

17. On the PropertyManager, click the **Parallelogram** icon under the **Rectangle Type** section. This option creates a parallelogram by using three points that you specify.
18. Select two points to define the width of the parallelogram.

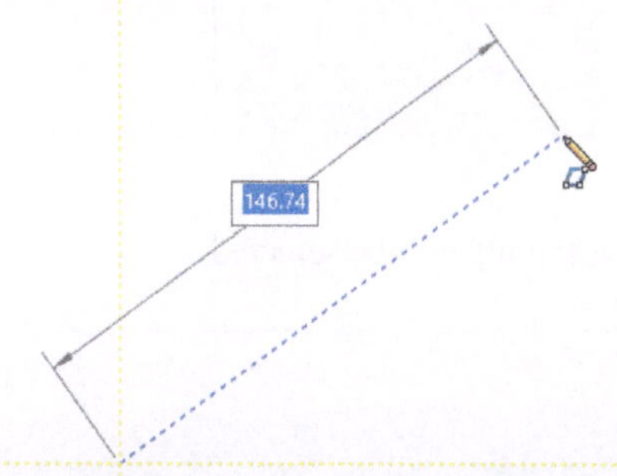

19. Drag the pointer and click to define the height of the parallelogram.

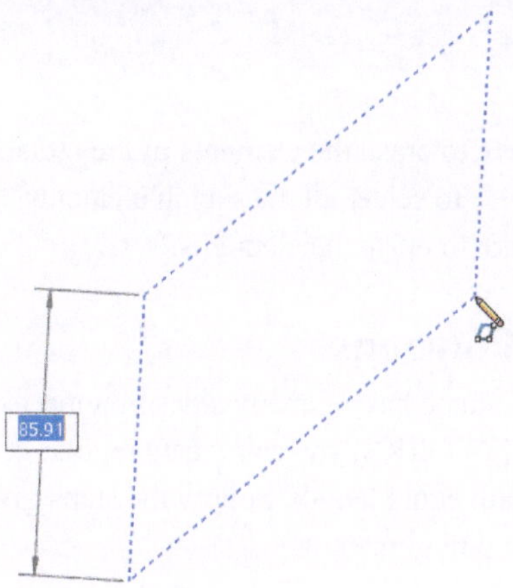

20. Click **Close Dialog** on the PropertyManager.

Lasso Selection

The **Lasso Selection** tool helps you to select multiple elements by dragging the pointer over them.

1. Click the right mouse button in the graphics window and select **Selection Tools > Lasso Selection**.

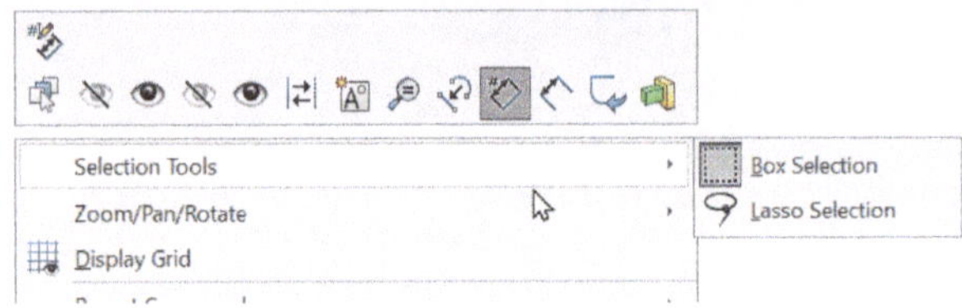

2. Click the left mouse button and drag the pointer from right to left, covering the rectangle's three elements, as shown.

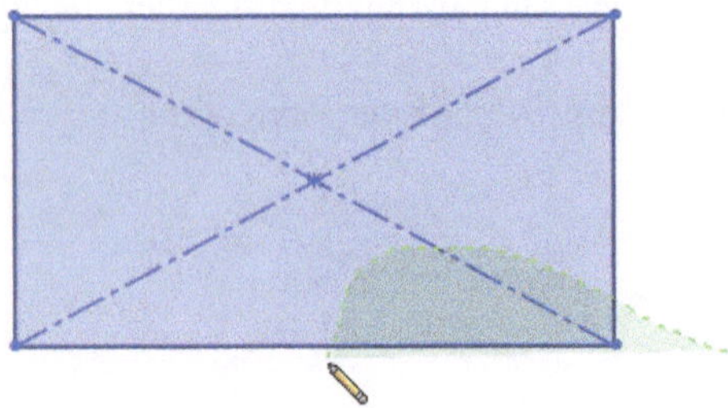

The three elements will be selected.

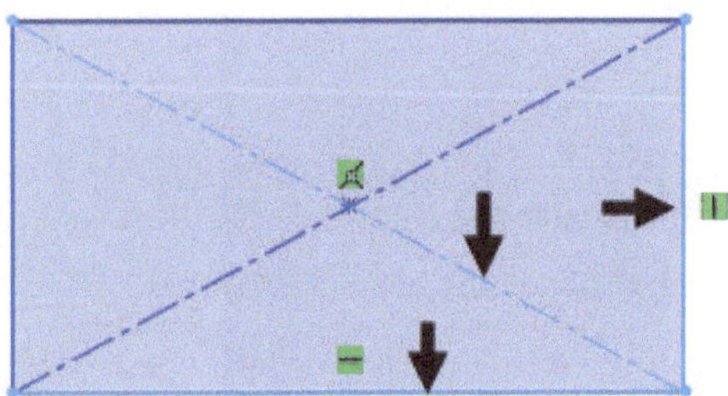

3. Press **Delete** to erase the elements of the rectangle.
4. Press Ctrl+A to select all the sketch elements.
5. Press **Delete** to erase the elements.

Creating Polygons

A Polygon is a shape having many sides ranging from 3 to 1024. In SOLIDWORKS, you can create regular polygons having sides with equal length. Follow the steps given next to create a polygon.

1. Activate the **Sketch** mode.
2. On the CommandManager, click **Sketch > Polygon** .
3. On the PropertyManager, type **8** in the **Number of Sides** box under the **Parameters** section.
4. Select **Inscribed circle**. This option creates a polygon with its sides touching a dotted circle. You can also select the **Circumscribed circle** option to create a polygon with its vertices touching a dotted circle.
5. Click to define the center of the polygon.
6. Move the pointer and click to define the size and angle of the polygon.

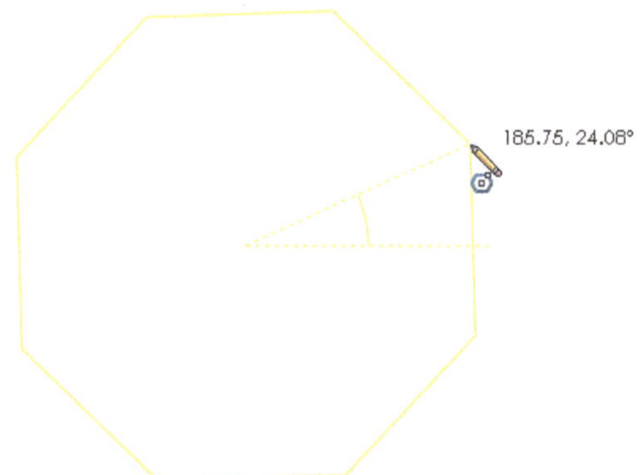

7. Press **Esc** to deactivate the tool.

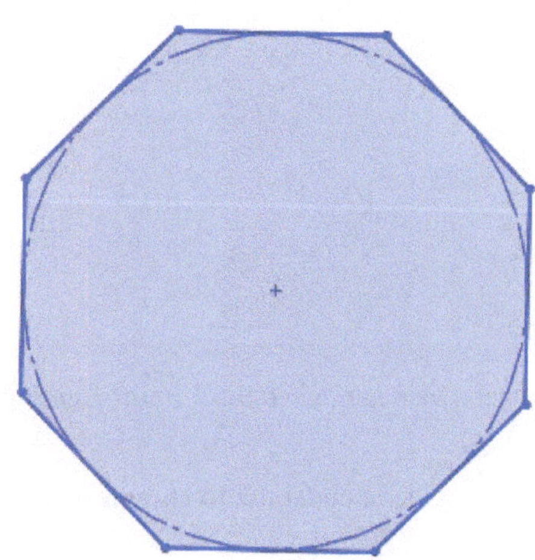

Resolve Sketch

When creating sketches for a part, SOLIDWORKS will not allow you to over-constrain the geometry. The term 'over-constrain' means adding more dimensions than required. The following figure shows a fully constrained sketch. If you add another dimension to this sketch (e.g., diagonal dimension), the **Make Dimension Driven** dialog appears.

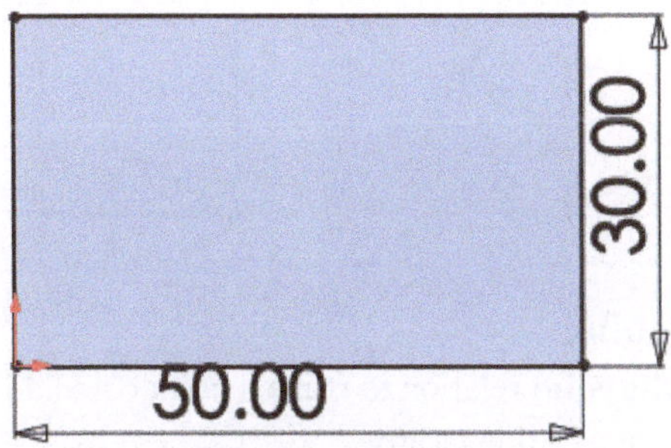

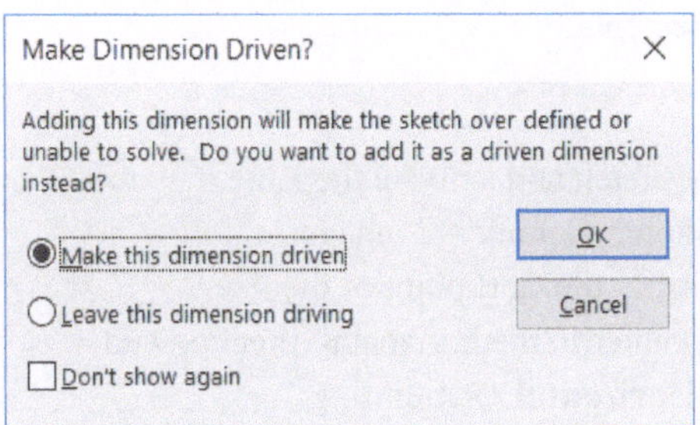
Make Dimension Driven?

Adding this dimension will make the sketch over defined or unable to solve. Do you want to add it as a driven dimension instead?

Make this dimension driven

Leave this dimension driving

Don't show again

OK

Cancel

Now, you have to convert the new dimension into driven. Select **Make this dimension driven** and click **OK**.

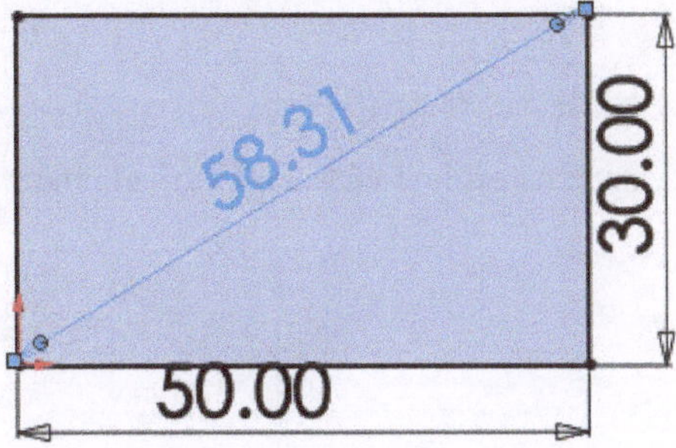

If you change the width's value, the reference dimension along the diagonal updates automatically.

Relations

Relations are used to control the shape of a sketch by establishing relationships between the sketch elements.

You can add relations using the **Add Relation** tool or pop-up toolbar or by selecting sketch elements.

Merge

This relation connects a point to another point.

1. On the **Sketch** tab of the CommandManager, click **Delete/Display Relations > Add Relation** .
2. Select two points.
3. Click **Merge** on the PropertyManager. The selected points will be merged.

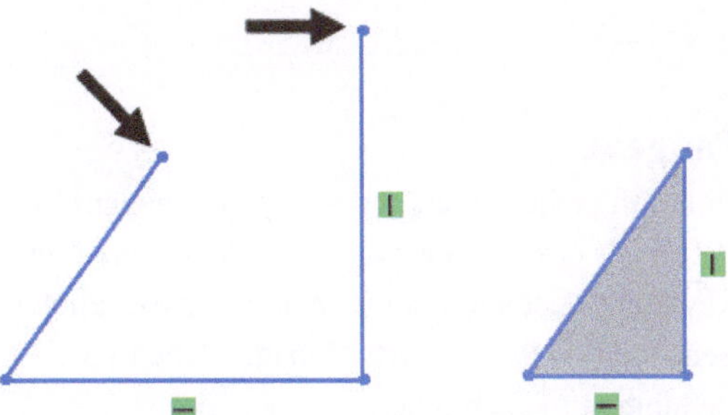

Horizontal

To apply the **Horizontal** relation, click on a line and click the **Horizontal** icon on the context toolbar.

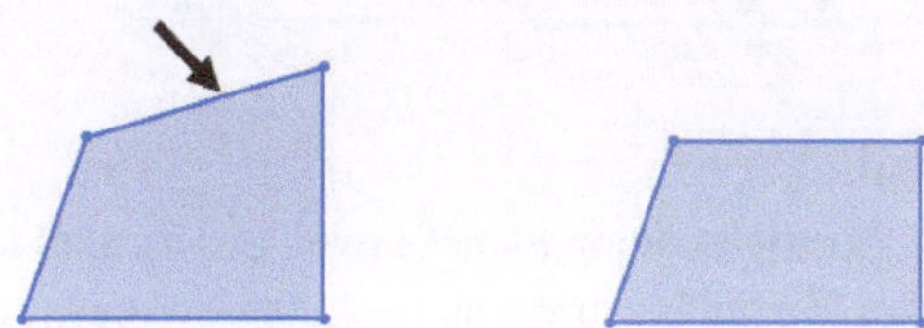

You can also align two points or vertices horizontally. Press the Ctrl key and select the two points. Click the **Horizontal** icon on the PropertyManager.

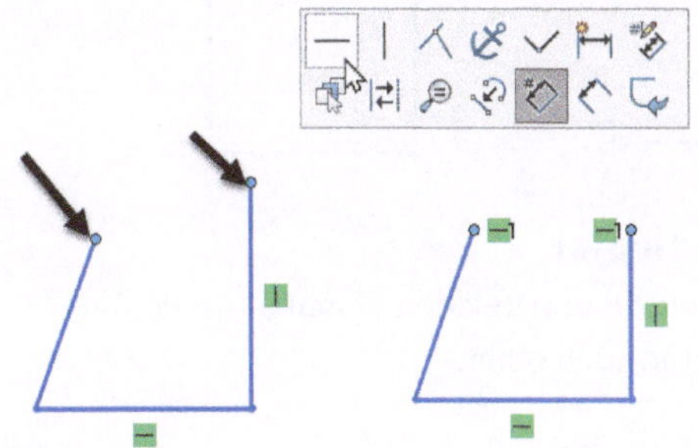

Vertical

Use the **Vertical** relation to make a line vertical. You can also use this relation to align two points or vertices vertically.

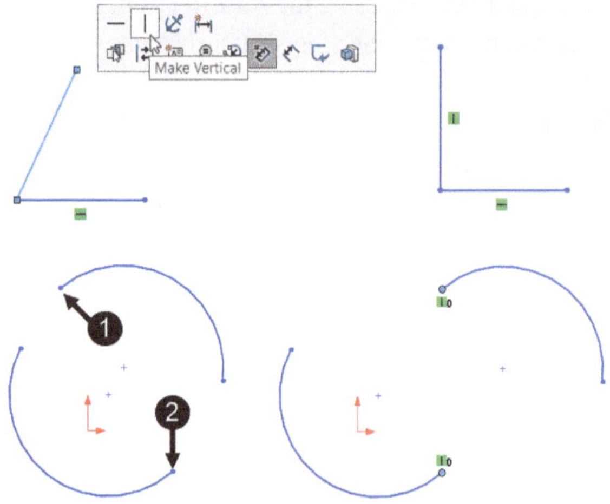

Tangent

This relation makes an arc, circle, or line tangent to another arc or circle. Select a circle, arc, or line. Press the Ctrl key and select another circle or arc. Next, click the **Tangent** icon on the PropertyManager. The two elements will be tangent to each other.

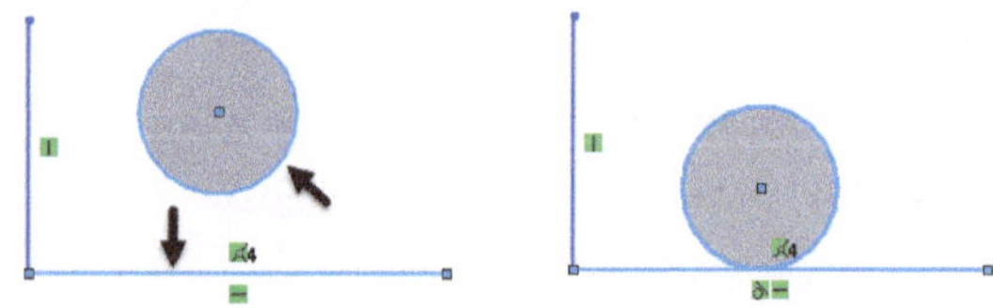

Parallel

Use the **Parallel** relation to make two lines parallel to each other. To do this, press and hold the Ctrl key and select the two lines to be parallel. Next, click the **Parallel** icon on the PropertyManager.

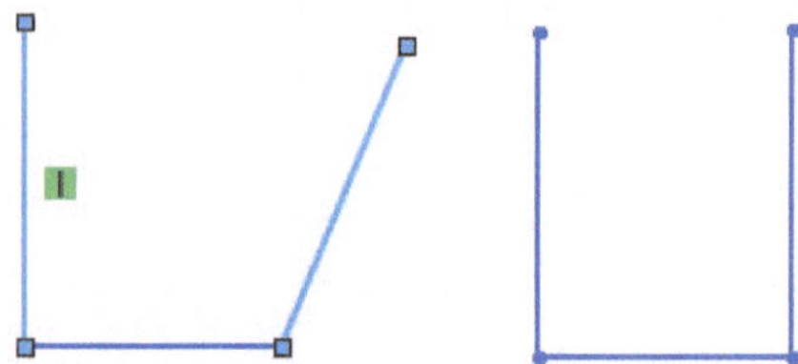

Perpendicular

Use the **Perpendicular** relation to make two entities perpendicular to each other.

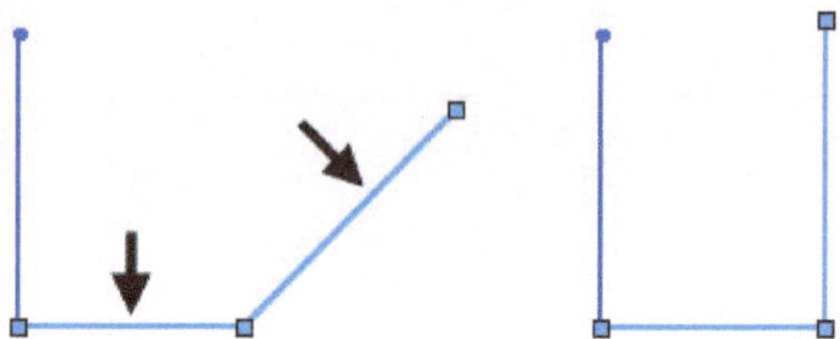

Midpoint

Use the **Midpoint** relation to make a point coincide with the midpoint of a line or arc.

1. Press the Ctrl key and select a line/arc and a point.
2. Click the **Midpoint** icon on the PropertyManager.

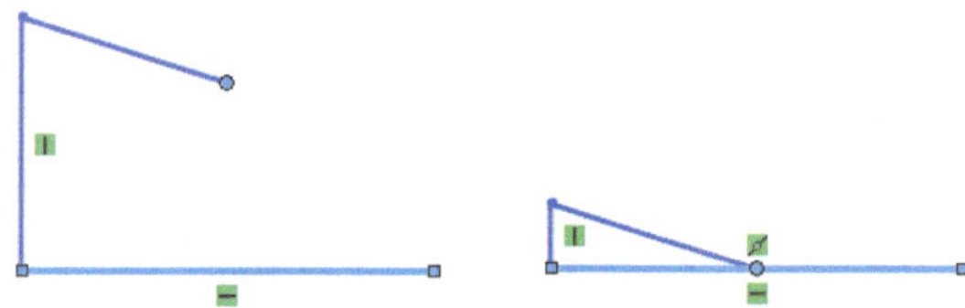

Automatic Relations

SOLIDWORKS automatically adds relations when you create sketch elements.

1. Start a new sketch and activate the **Line** tool from the **Sketch** CommandManager.
2. Click to specify the start point of the line.
3. Move the pointer in the horizontal direction and notice the **Horizontal** relation flag.
4. Click to create a line with the **Horizontal** relation.

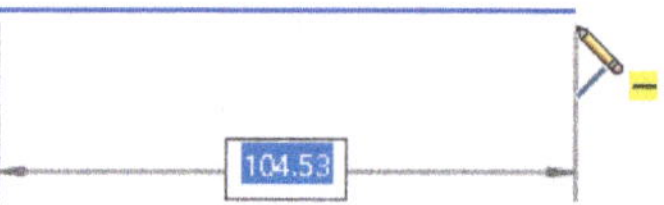

5. Likewise, create a line with the **Vertical** relation.

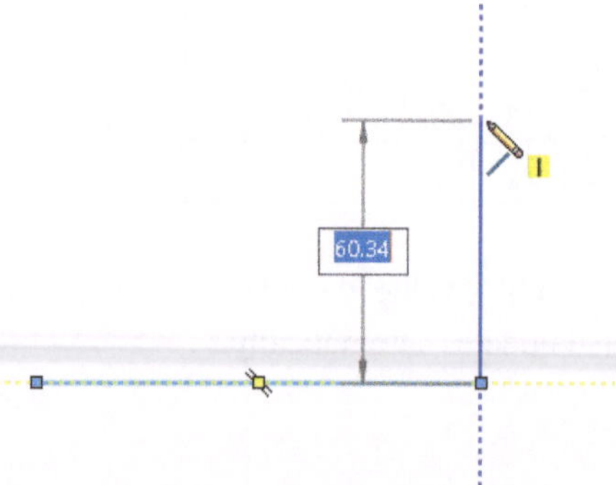

6. Create an inclined line, as shown.

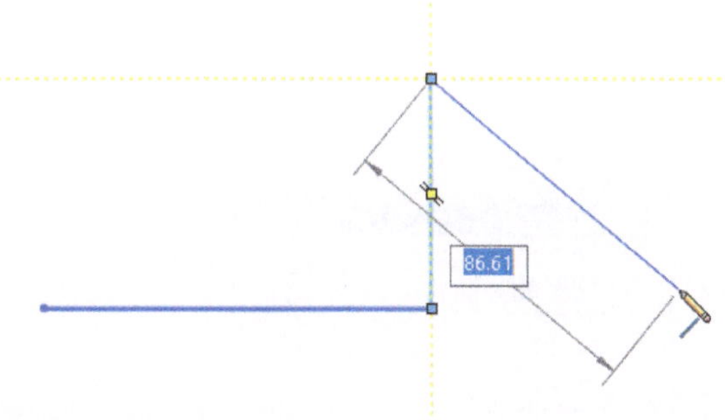

7. Move the pointer along the inclined line and notice the **Collinear** relation flag.

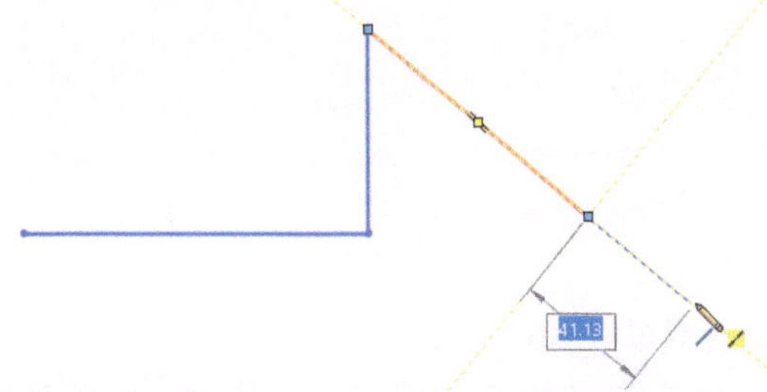

8. Move the pointer in the direction perpendicular to the inclined line and notice the Perpendicular relation flag.
9. Click to create the line with the Perpendicular relation.

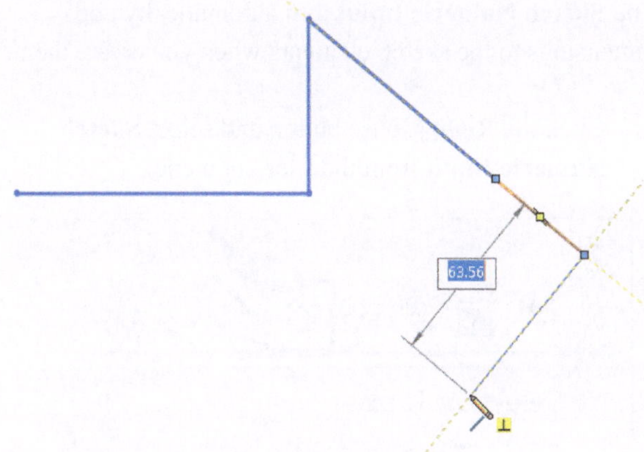

10. Press Esc to deactivate the **Line** tool.
11. Select the perpendicular line.

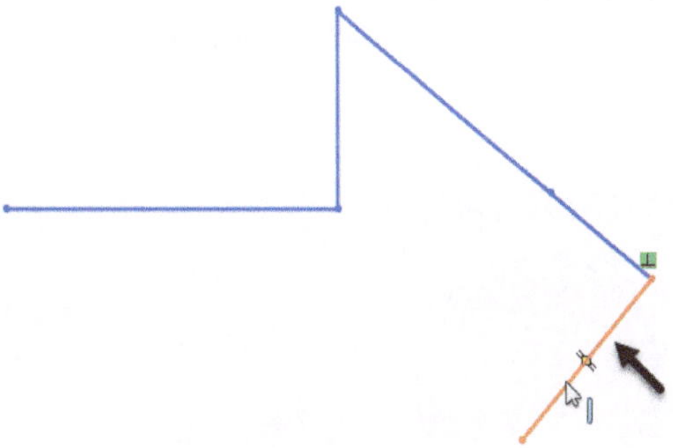

12. Right click and select **Sketch Entities > Line**.
13. Click in the graphics window to specify the start point of the line. Notice the yellow inferred lines with reference to the selected line.
14. Move along the yellow inferred line, notice the **Parallel** relation flag.

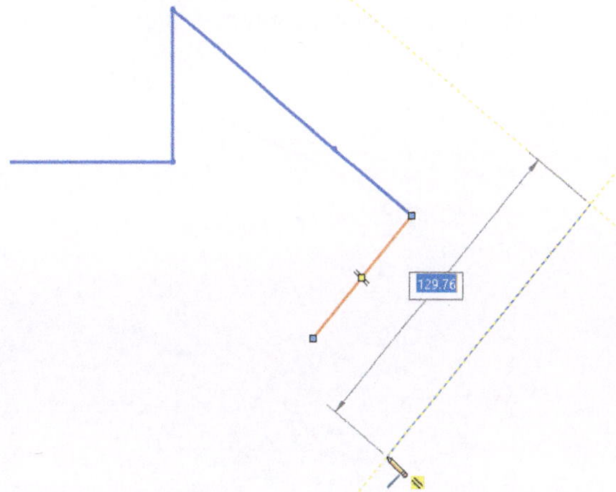

15. Click to create a line parallel to the selected line.
16. Press **Esc** to deactivate the **Line** tool.
17. On the CommandManager, click **Sketch > Circle** , and then create a circle.
18. Activate the **Line** tool and click on the circle.
19. Move the pointer around the circle and notice that the line maintains the **Tangent** relation with the circle.

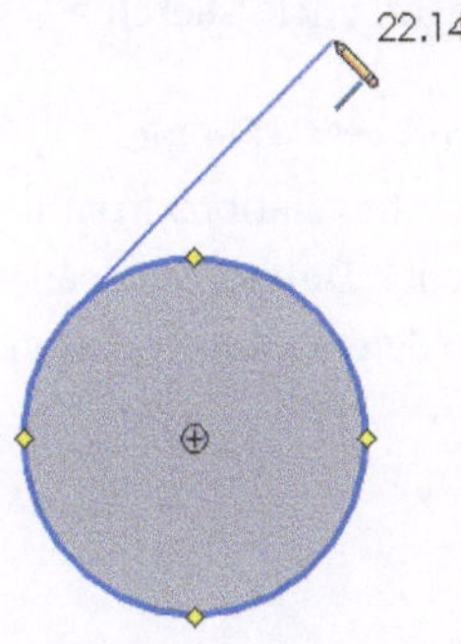

20. Click to create a line that is tangent and coincident to the circle. Right click and select **End chain**.

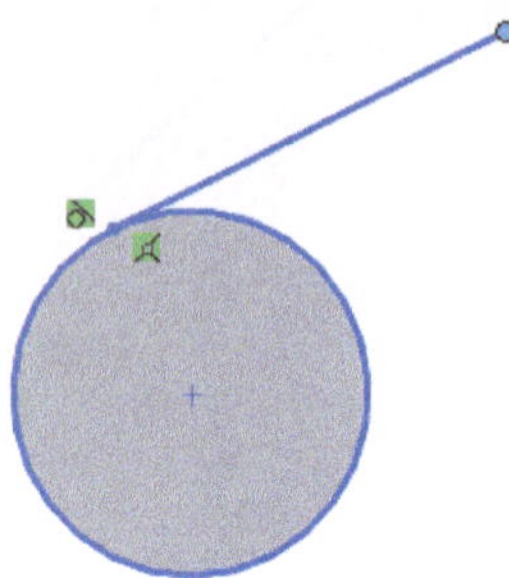

21. Activate the **Line** command.
22. Select a point on the circle and move the pointer.
23. Move the pointer back to the start point of the line.

Notice the **Coincident** relation flag and the yellow inferred lines. You can create a line that is tangent or normal to the circle using the inferred lines.

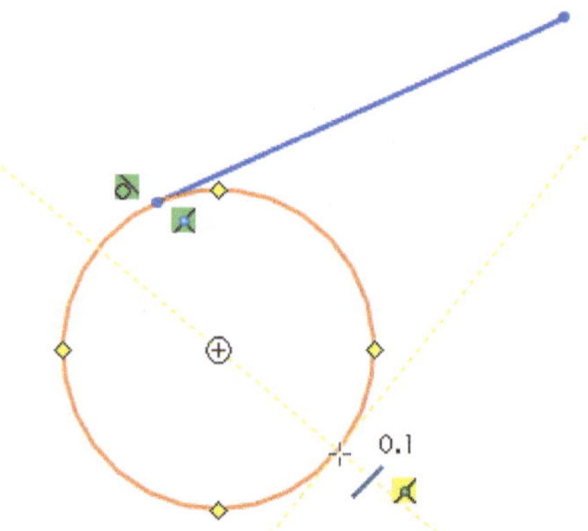

Deleting Relations

You can delete relations by using the following methods.

1. Select the relation and press **Delete**.
2. Select the sketch entity to view all its relations in the PropertyManager. Select the relations from the **Existing Relations** section of the PropertyManager and press **Delete**.
3. On the CommandManager, click **Sketch > Display/Delete Relations**. On the PropertyManager, select the relations from the **Relations** section and click **Delete**. You can also use the **Delete All** button to delete all the relations.

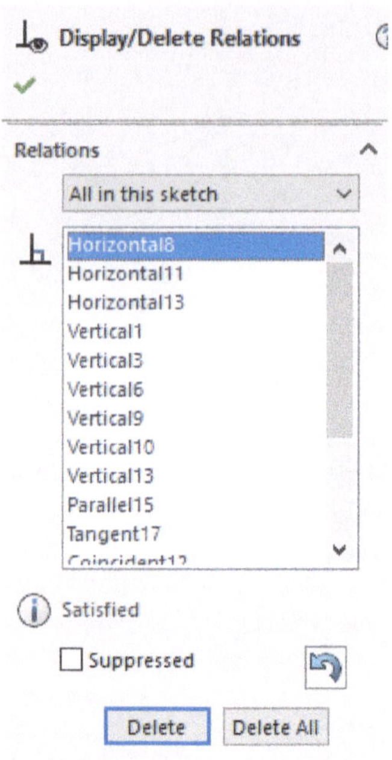

Hiding Relations

Hide sketch relations by clicking the **Hide/Show Items** drop-down on the **View Heads-Up** Toolbar and then deactivating the **View Sketch Relations** icon.

Sketch Numeric Input

The **Sketch Numeric Input** tool automatically adds dimensions to the sketch elements when you create them.

1. Click the Right Mouse button and select **Sketch Numeric Input** from the shortcut menu.

2. Activate a sketching tool and check the **Add Dimensions** option on the PropertyManager. In the case of a circle, you can select the **Diameter dimensions** option to add the diameter dimension to the circle.
3. Start creating the sketch elements. Notice that you can enter the dimension values of the sketch elements. Use the **Tab** key to walk through the dimension values.

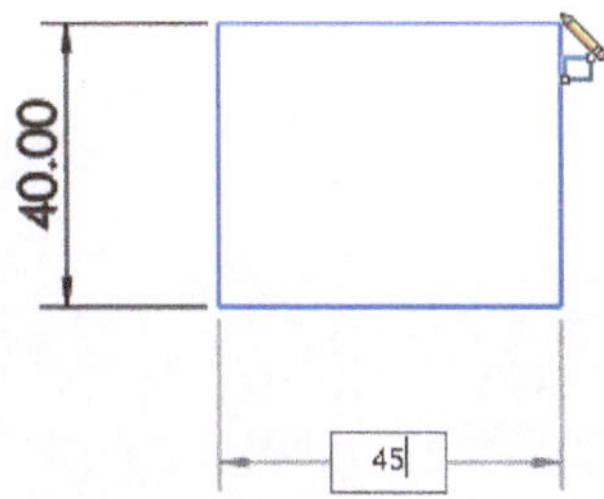

You can change the dimension units from the flyout located at the bottom right corner of the window. The dimension units are reflected in the sketch.

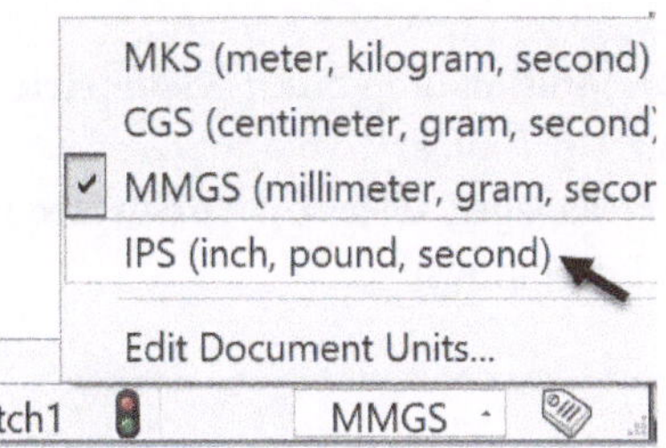

Replace Entity

The **Replace Entity** tool replaces a sketch entity with another one. You can use this tool instead of deleting a sketch entity and creating another one. This tool transfers all the associated features of the replaced entity to the replacement entity. This will avoid any parent-child errors when you modify the sketch. The following example shows the significance of this tool.

1. Start a new sketch on the Front plane and create the sketch, as shown.

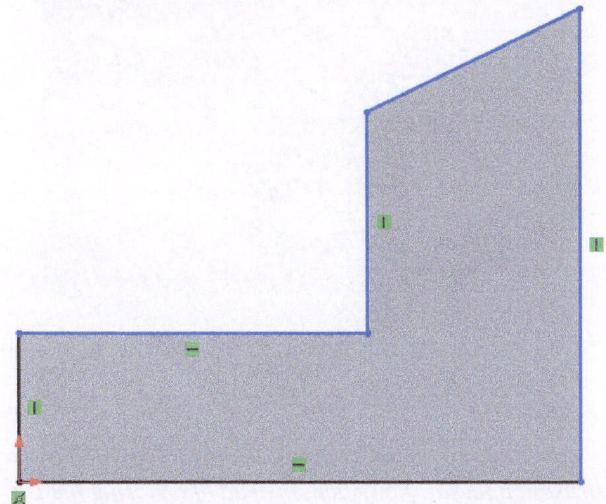

2. On the **Sketch** CommandManager, click the **Smart Dimension** tool.

3. Select the inclined line and the vertical line connected to it.

4. Place the dimension, type 115 in the **Modify** box, and then click **OK**.
5. Select the inclined line and move the pointer. Notice that the orientation of the dimension changes as per the movement of the pointer.
6. Move the pointer vertically upward and right click to lock the orientation of the dimension. Now, the orientation of the dimension does not change with the cursor movement.
7. Place the dimension, and then specify its value as 35.
8. Likewise, add other dimensions to the sketch.

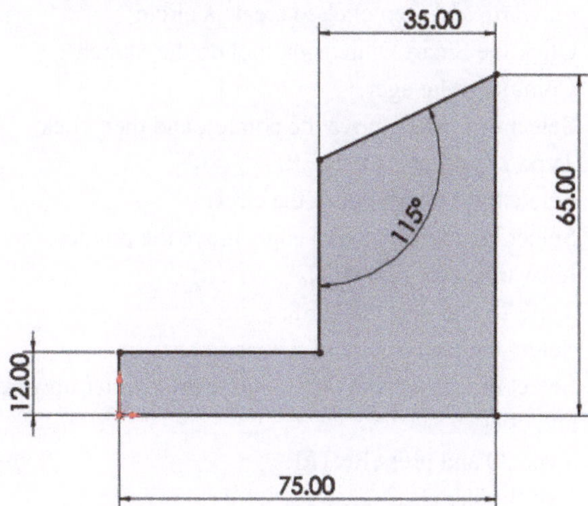

9. Exit the sketch, and then extrude it up to 50 mm distance.

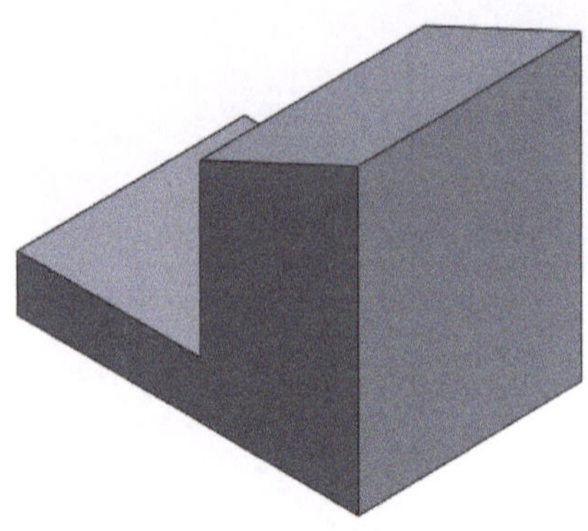

10. Activate the **Extrude Boss/Base** tool and click on the horizontal face of the model.

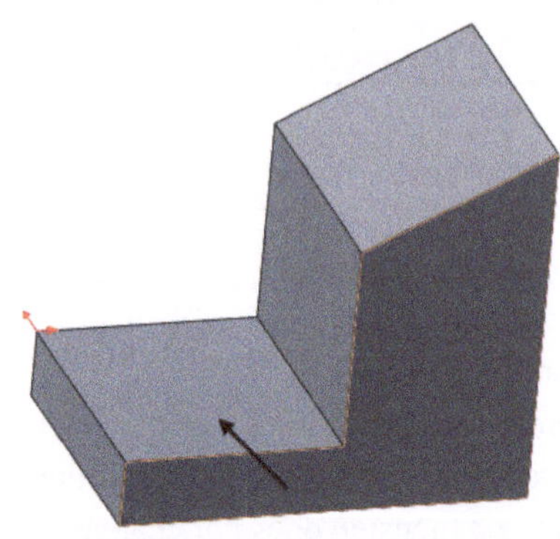

11. Click the **Circle** tool on the **Sketch** CommandManager.
12. Click the pointer on the flat face, move the pointer outward, and then click to create a circle.
13. Click the Smart Dimension tool on the Sketch CommandManager.
14. Select the circle, move the pointer, and then click.
15. Type 22 and press ENTER.
16. Select the centerpoint of the circle.
17. Select the top horizontal edge, move the pointer leftwards, and then click.
18. Type 25 and press ENTER.
19. Select the centerpoint of the circle.
20. Select the left vertical edge, move the pointer upward and click.
21. Type 20 and press ENTER.
22. Exit the sketch.

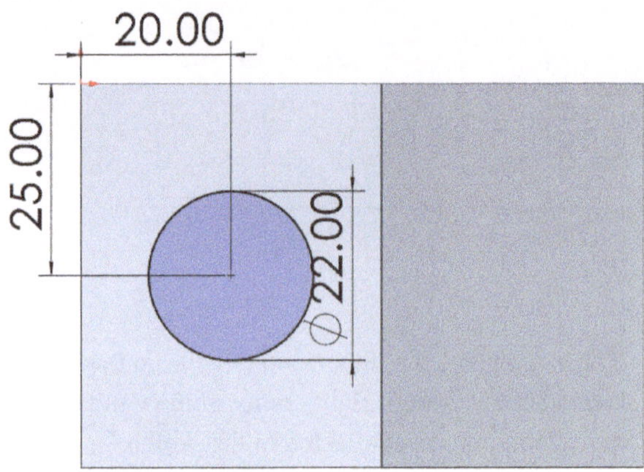

23. Click **View Orientation** drop-down > **Isometric** on the **View HeadsUp** Toolbar.
24. On the PropertyManager, select **Up To Surface** from the **Direction 1** drop-down.

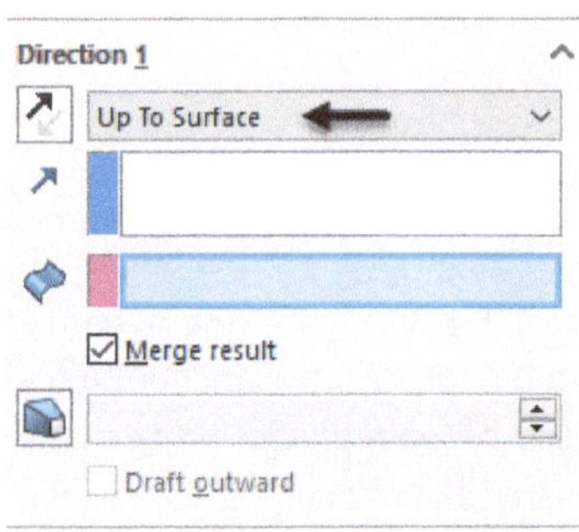

25. Select the inclined face of the model, and then click **OK**.

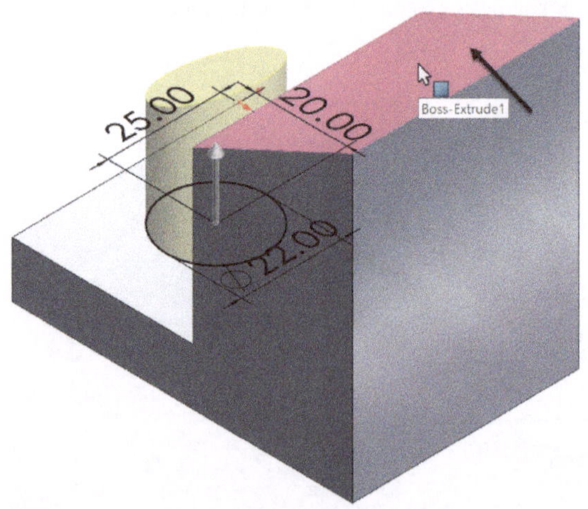

*Double click the inclined face of the model to use it as the extrusion limit for the sketch, instead of choosing the **Up To Surface** option and then selecting the inclined face.*

26. In the FeatureManager Design Tree, expand the Boss-Extrude1, click on the Sketch1, and then select the **Edit Sketch**.

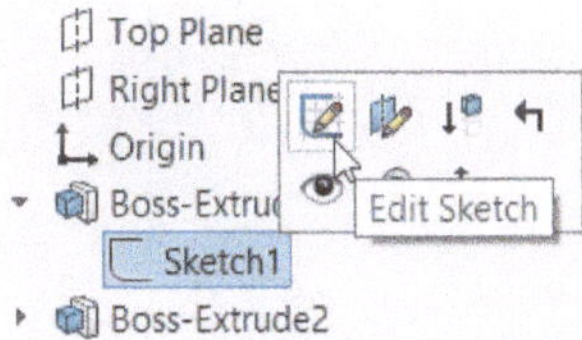

27. Select the inclined line and press **Delete** on your keyboard.

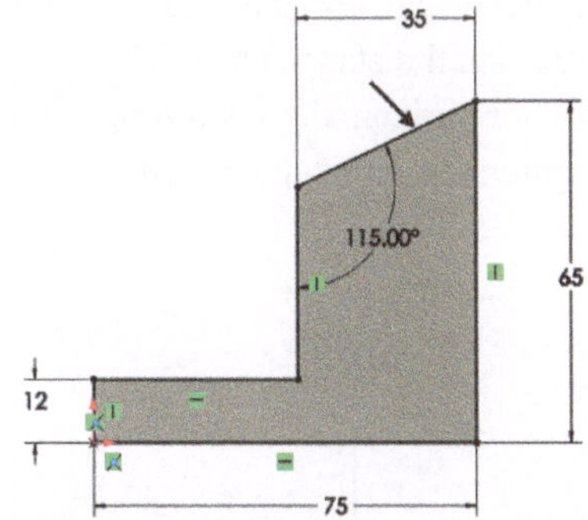

28. Click **Yes**.
29. Click **Arc** drop-down > **3 Point Arc** on the **Sketch** CommandManager.
30. Select the top endpoint of the left vertical line.
31. Select the top endpoint of the right vertical line.
32. Move the pointer upward up to a small distance and click.

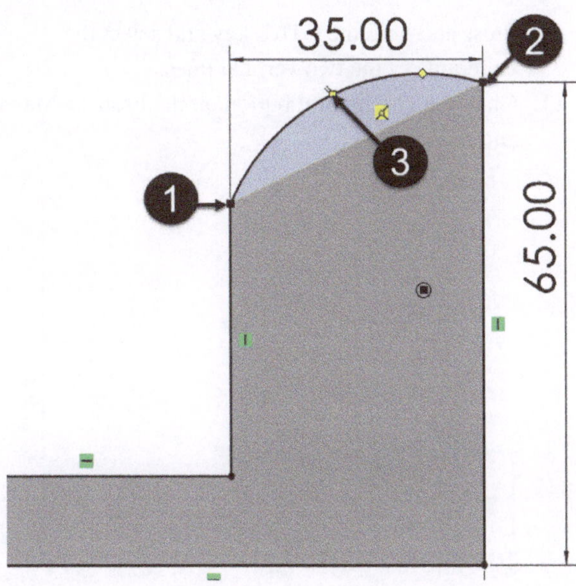

33. Click **Exit Sketch**. The FeatureManager Design Tree shows that the second Boss-Extrude feature fails as it is depended on the first feature.
34. Press Ctrl+Z thrice to undo the changes.
35. Create an arc, as shown. Press Esc to deactivate the **3 Point Arc** command.

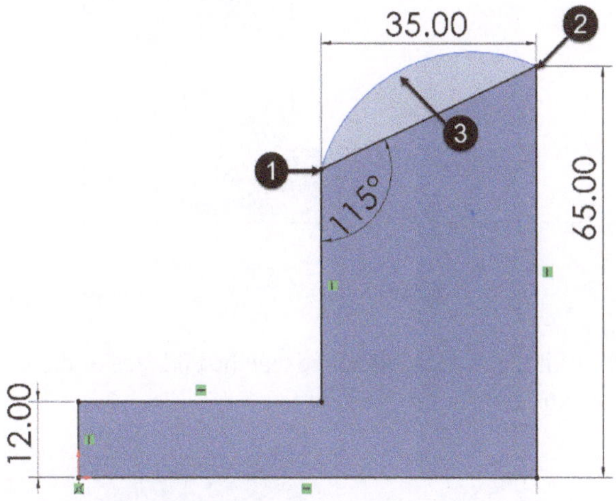

36. Right click in the graphics window and select **Replace Entity** from the shortcut menu.

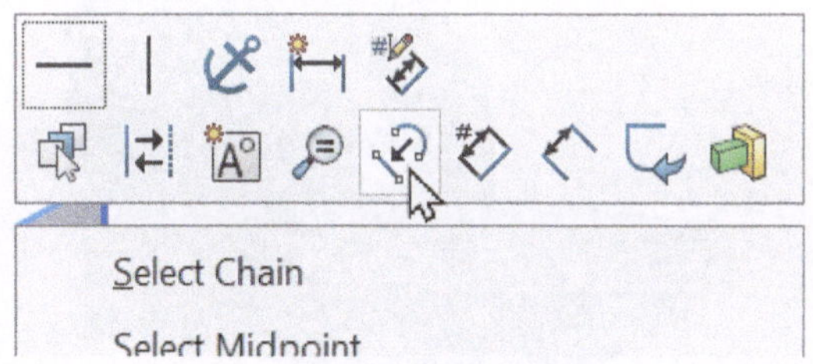

37. Select the inclined line as the entity to be replaced.
38. Select the arc as the replacing entity.
39. Select the **Make construction** option on the PropertyManager, and click **OK** on the **PropertyManager**.
40. Click the **Smart Dimension** tool on the CommandManager and select the arc.
41. Move the pointer and click.
42. Type 50 and press ENTER.

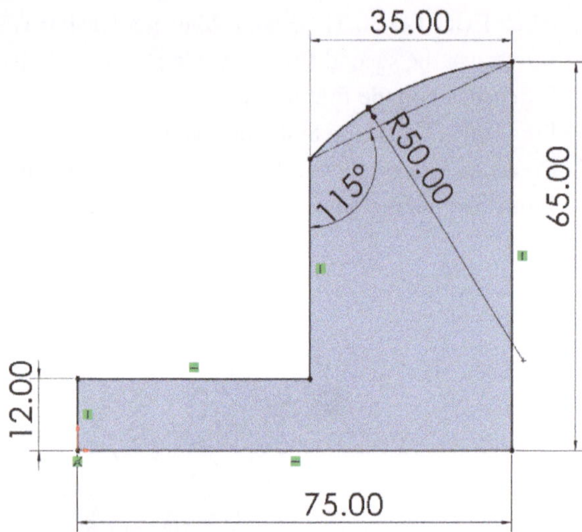

43. Exit the sketch and notice that the end face of the extruded feature is replaced.

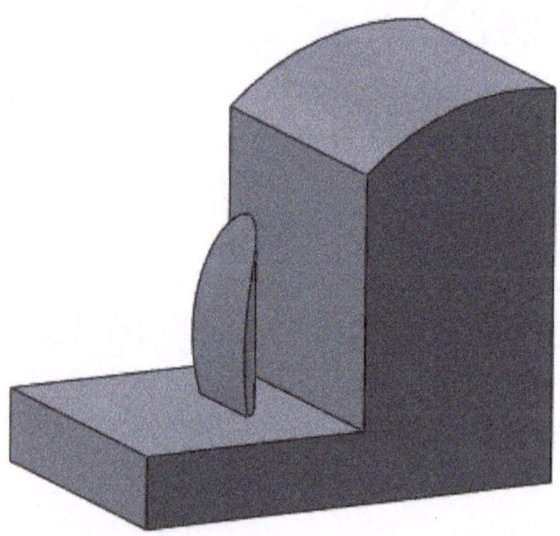

Path Length Dimension

The **Path Length Dimension** tool defines a fixed length for all the sketch entities combined.

1. Start a new sketch on anyone of the planes.
2. Click the **Line** tool on the **Sketch** CommandManager.
3. Select the sketch origin, move the pointer horizontally toward right and click.
4. Move the pointer vertically upward and click.
5. Right-click and select End chain.

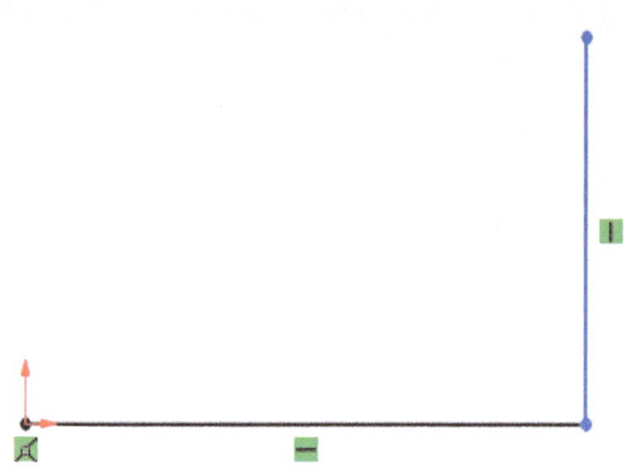

6. Select the sketch origin, move the pointer vertically upward up to a small distance and click.
7. Move the pointer horizontally toward right and click.
8. Move the pointer vertically upward and click.
9. Press **Esc**.

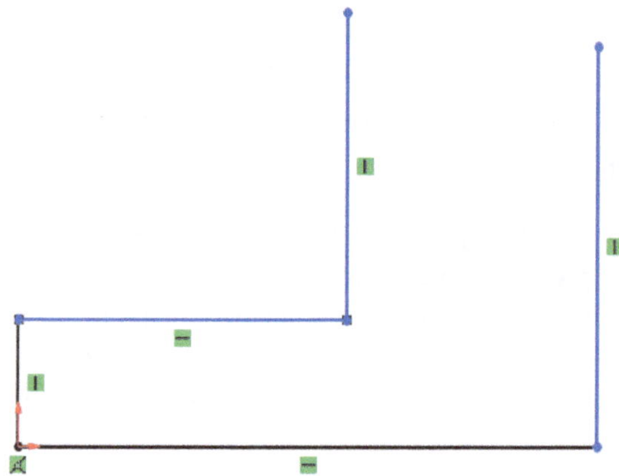

10. Press and hold the CTRL key and select the endpoints of the two vertical lines.
11. Click the **Horizontal** button on the PropertyManager and click **OK**.

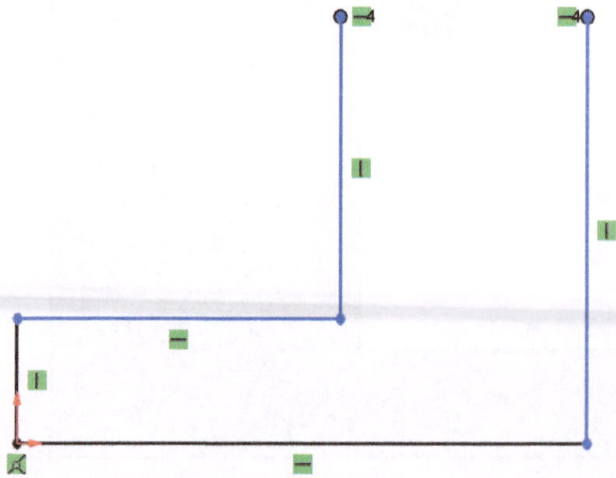

12. Click the **Arc** drop-down > **Tangent Arc** on the Sketch CommandManager.

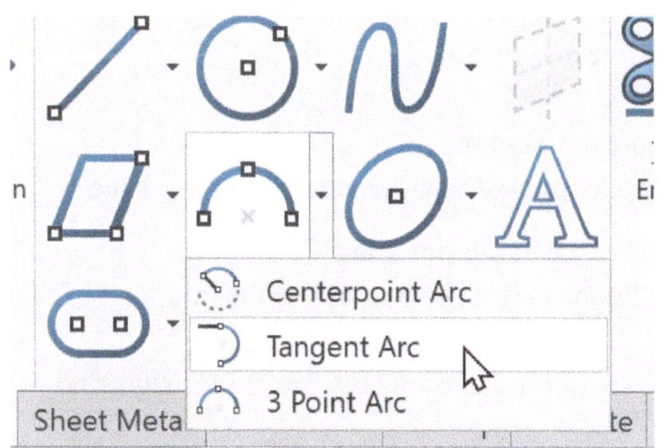

13. Select the endpoint of the right vertical line.
14. Move the pointer upward, and then toward left.
15. Select the endpoint of the left vertical line.

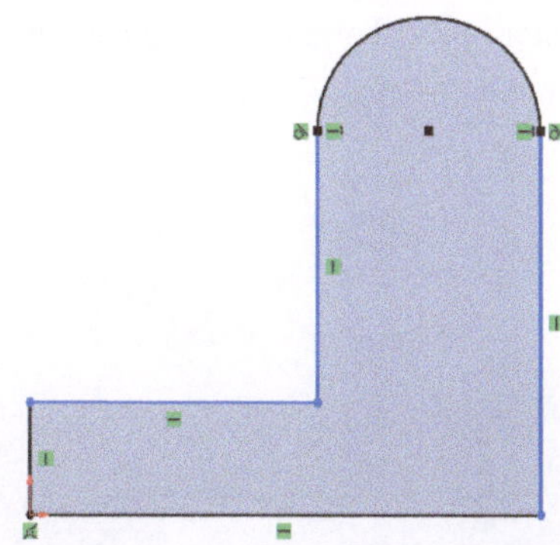

16. On the **Sketch** CommandManager, click **Smart Dimension > Path Length Dimension**.
17. Drag a selection box across all the sketch entities to select them.
18. Click **OK** on the PropertyManager.
19. Double click on the Path Length dimension, type 200, and press Enter.
20. Click and drag the centerpoint of the arc. Notice that the path length is fixed and the sketch shape changes.

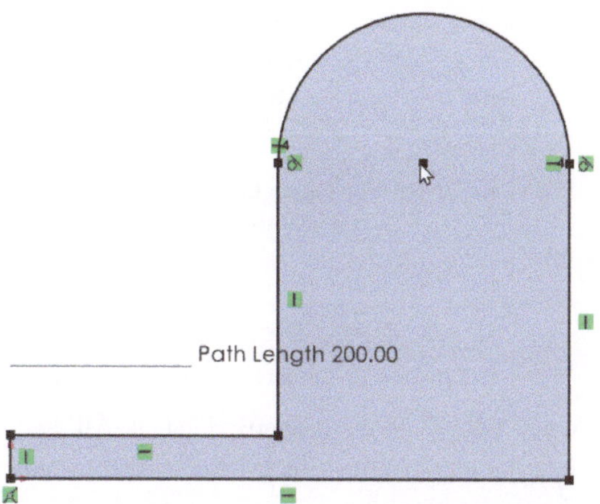

Convert Entities

The **Convert Entities** tool helps you to use the edges of the part geometry to create sketch elements.

1. Download Chapter 5: Sketching folder from the Companion website.
2. Open the Convert_entities part file from the folder.
3. Start a sketch on the plane offset to the model face, as shown.
4. On the **Sketch** CommandManager, click the **Convert Entities** button.
5. Select the face of the model, as shown.

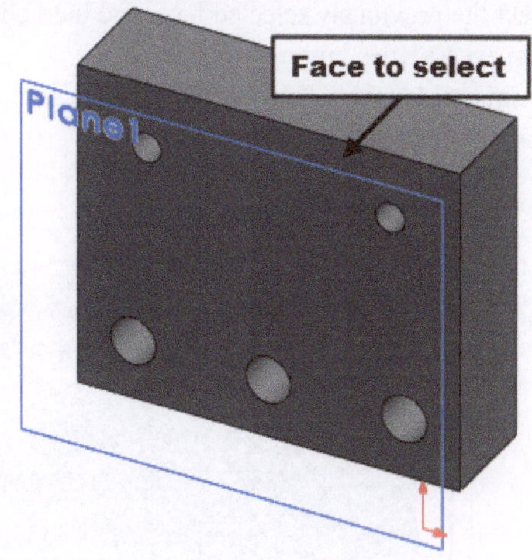

6. On the PropertyManager, click the **Select all inner loops** button to select the face's inner loops.
7. Click on **Face<1>** in the **Entities to convert** selection box, and then select **Delete**.

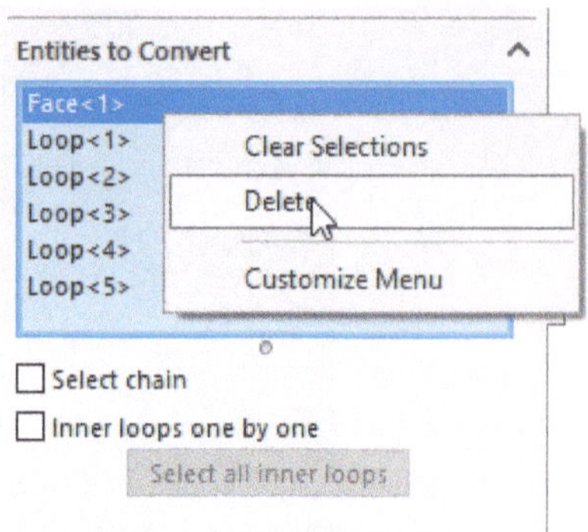

8. Click **OK** on the PropertyManager. All the internal loops of the selected face are projected onto the sketch plane.

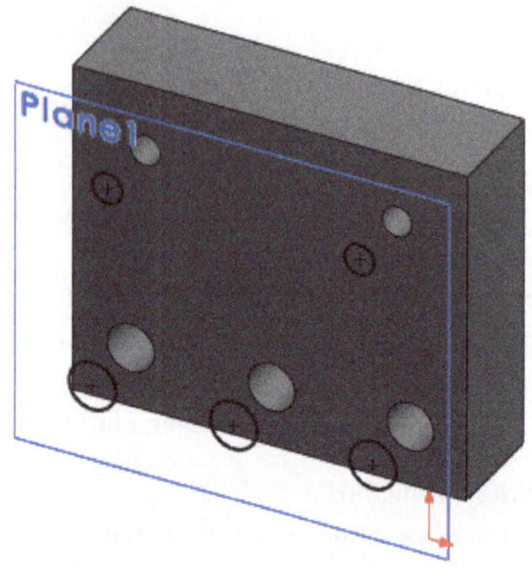

9. Select the previously selected face, and then click the **Convert Entities** button on the **Sketch** CommandManager. The outer loop of the face is converted into sketch elements.

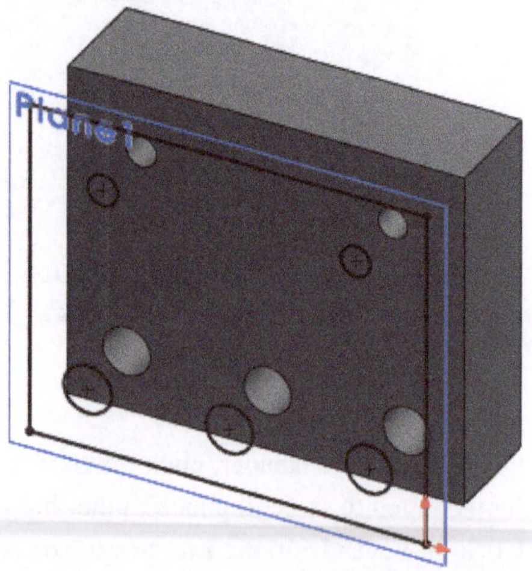

Midpoint line, Perimeter Circle, and SketchXpert

In this tutorial, you will create a sketch using the **Midpoint line** and **Perimeter Circle** tools.

1. Activate the **Sketch** mode.
2. On the CommandManager, click **Sketch > Line** drop-down > **Midpoint Line** .
3. Click on the origin point to define the midpoint of the line.
4. Move the pointer horizontally toward the right and click.

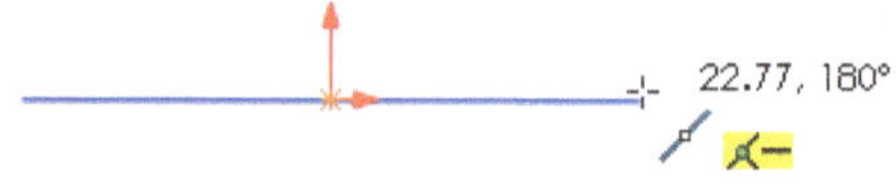

5. Move the pointer upward and click when a dotted line appears.

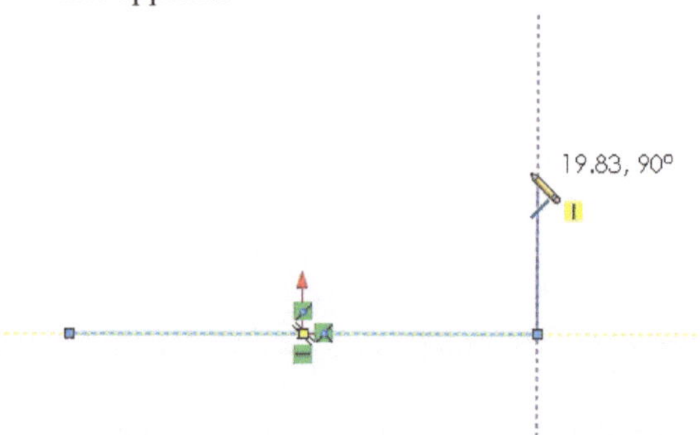

6. Move the pointer away from the endpoint of the vertical line.
7. Move the pointer and place it on the endpoint of the vertical line.
8. Move the pointer horizontally toward the left.
9. Move the pointer diagonally toward the top left corner and click. Next, right click and select **Select**.

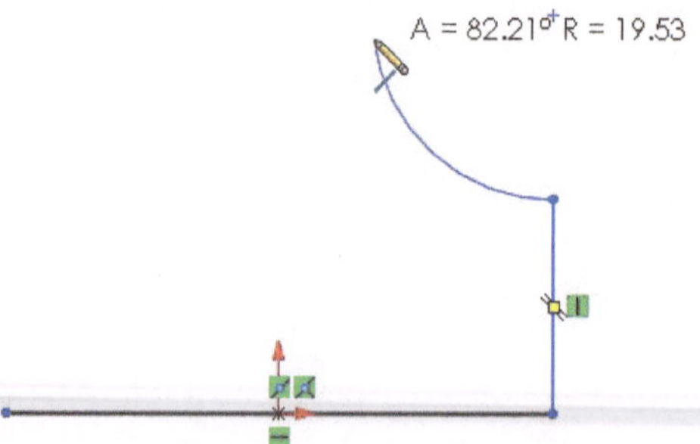

10. On the CommandManager, click **Sketch > Line** drop-down > **Centerline** .

11. Select the origin point of the sketch, move the pointer vertically upwards, and click. Press **Esc**.

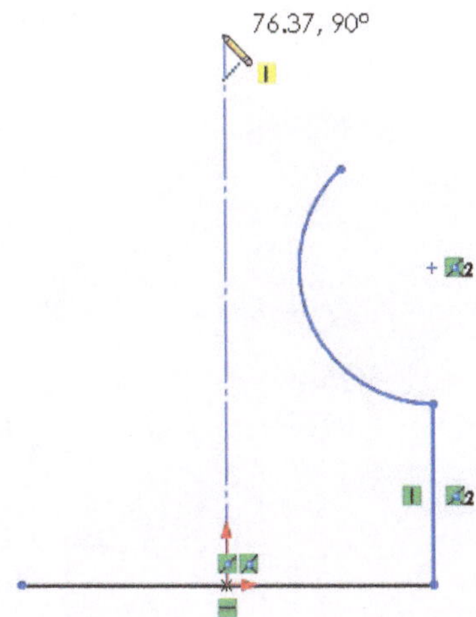

12. On the CommandManager, click **Sketch > Mirror Entities**.
13. Select the arc and right vertical line.
14. On the PropertyManager, click in the **Mirror about** selection box and select the vertical centreline. Click **OK**.

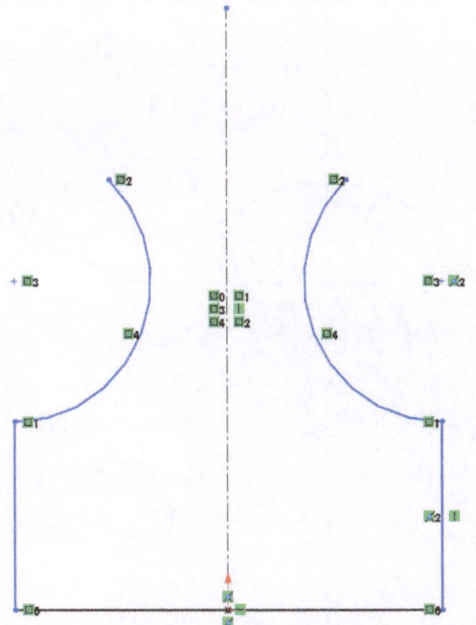

15. Right click and select **Sketch Entities > 3 Point Arc**.

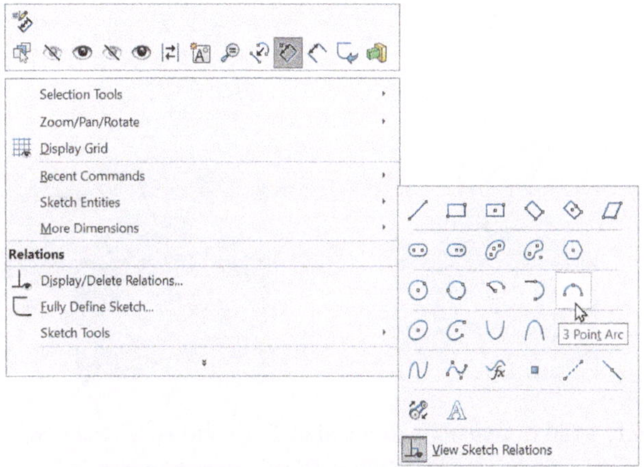

16. Select the endpoint of the left and right arc, and then move the pointer upward.
17. Click to create a three-point arc.

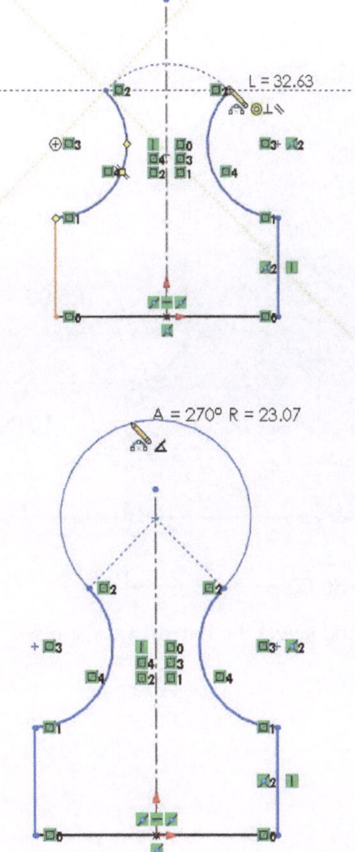

18. On the CommandManager, click **Sketch > Circle**.
19. Place the pointer on the three-point arc to display its centerpoint.
20. Select the centerpoint of the three-point arc, move the pointer outward, and click to create the circle.

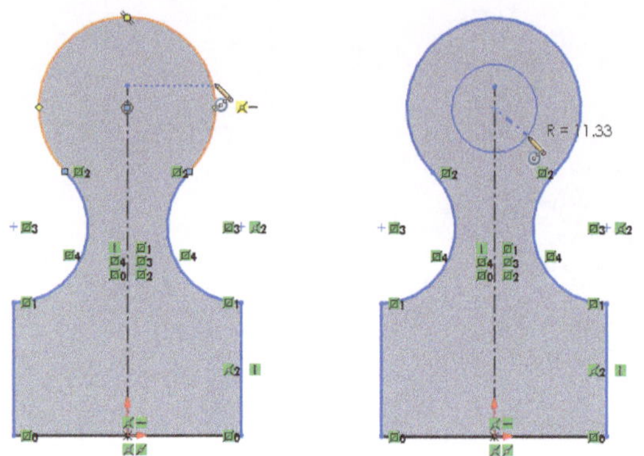

21. Add dimensions to the sketch, as shown. Press ESC to deactivate the **Smart Dimension** command.

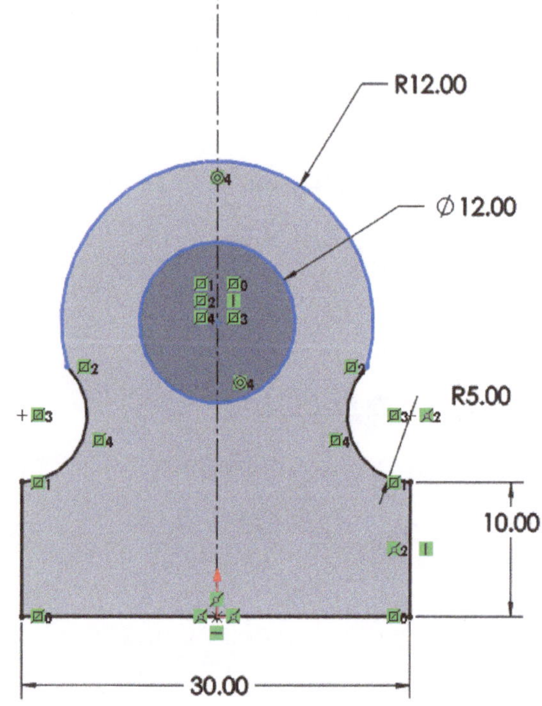

22. Press the Ctrl key and select the two arcs, as shown.

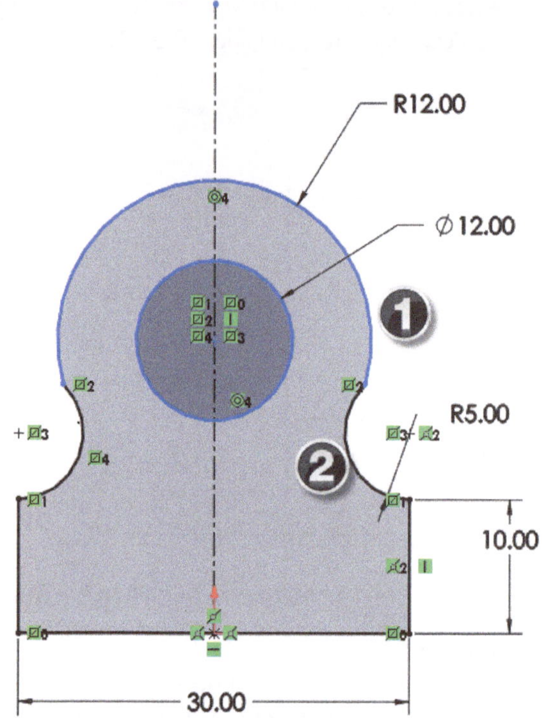

23. Select the **Tangent** icon on the PropertyManager, and click **OK**; the tangent relation is applied between the selected arcs. Also, the sketch is fully constrained.

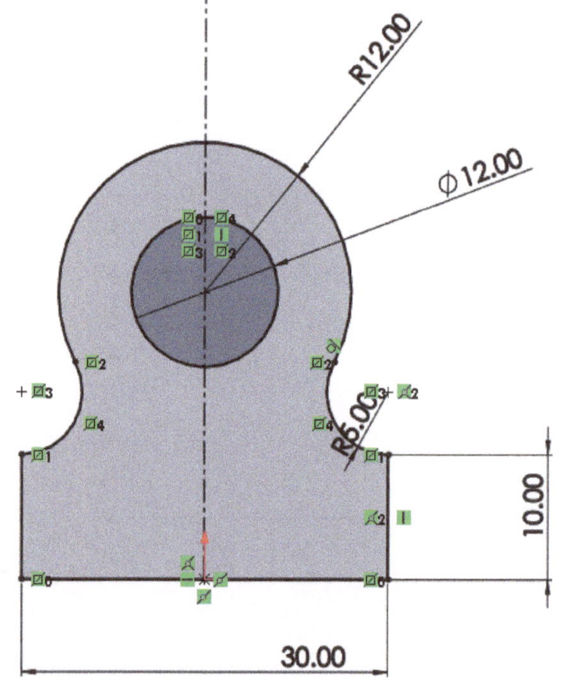

24. Exit the sketch.

Ellipses

Ellipses are **uniform curves** with a regular, closed shape, defined by two axes: the **major axis** (longest diameter) and the **minor axis** (shortest diameter). Ellipses are used in designs requiring symmetrical curves, such as cam profiles, optical lenses, or aerodynamic shapes.

1. Activate the **Sketch** mode.
2. On the CommandManager, click **Sketch > Ellipse** drop-down > **Ellipse**.
3. On the PropertyManager, check the **Add Construction Lines** option under the Options section.

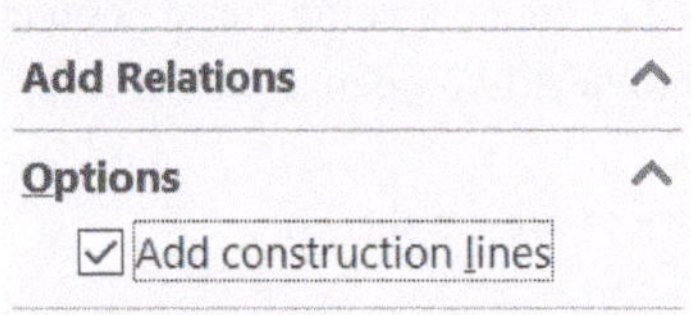

4. Pick a point in the graphics window to define the center of the ellipse.
5. Move the pointer and click to define the radius and orientation of the first axis.

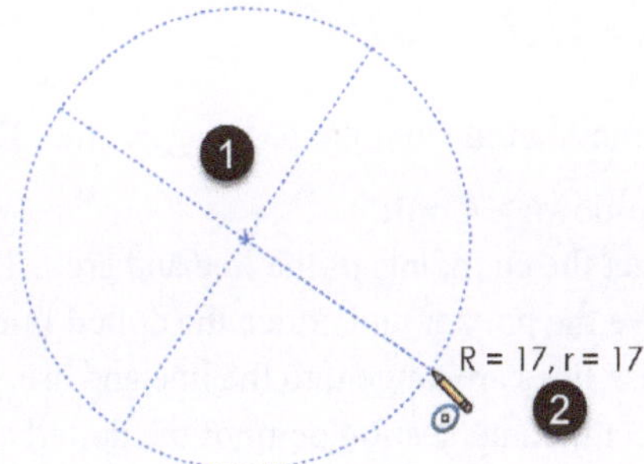

6. Move the pointer and click to define the radius of the second axis.

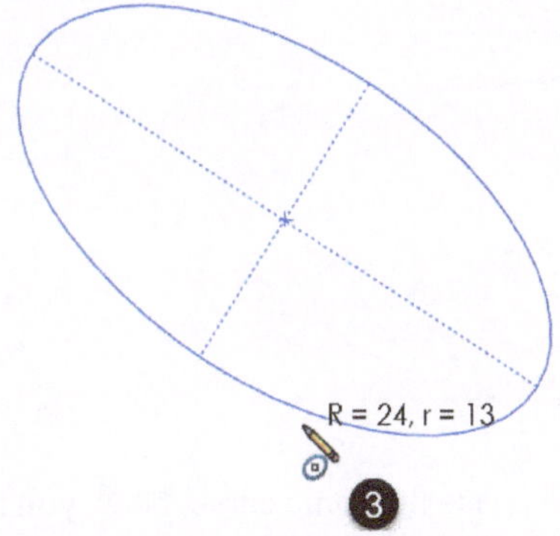

Click and drag the ellipse, notice that it is under-defined. You need to add dimensions and relations to fully define the ellipse.

7. On the **Sketch** CommandManager, click **Line** drop-down > **Centerline**.

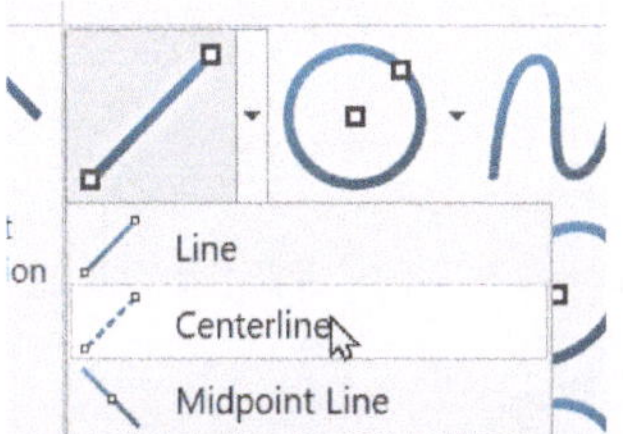

8. Select the center point of the ellipse, move the pointer horizontally toward right and click.

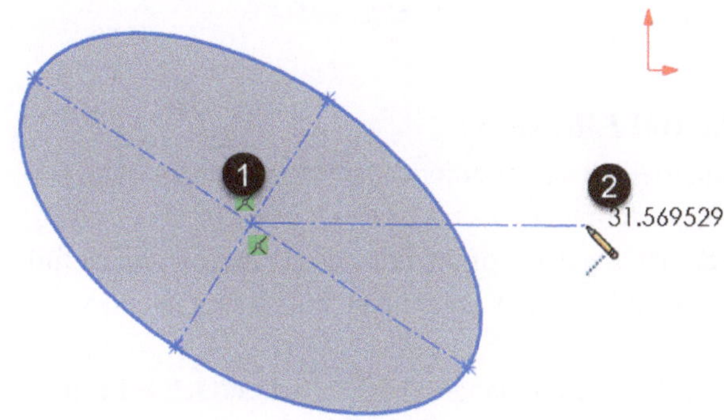

9. Right-click and select **Select**.
10. On the **Sketch** CommandManager, click the **Smart Dimension** tool.
11. Select the major axis line of the ellipse.
12. Select the horizontal construction line. The angled dimension is attached to the pointer.
13. Move the pointer and place the angled dimension.

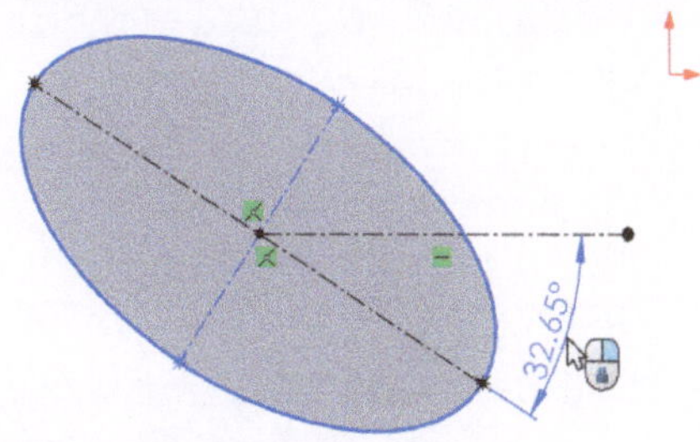

14. Type 15 and click **OK**.
15. Add the major and minor axes dimensions to the sketch.

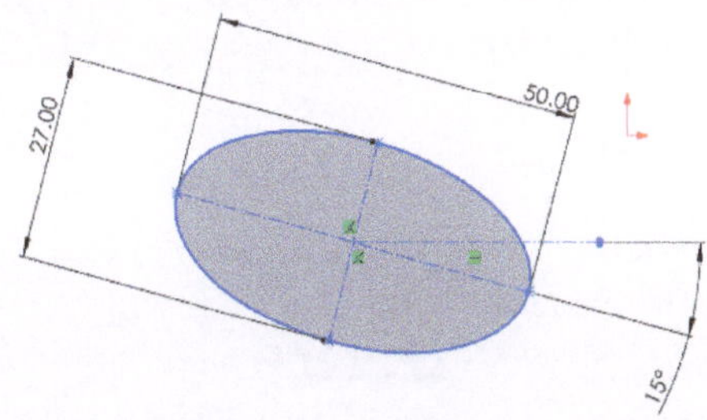

16. Add horizontal and vertical dimensions between the

center point of the ellipse and the sketch origin. This fully-defines the sketch.

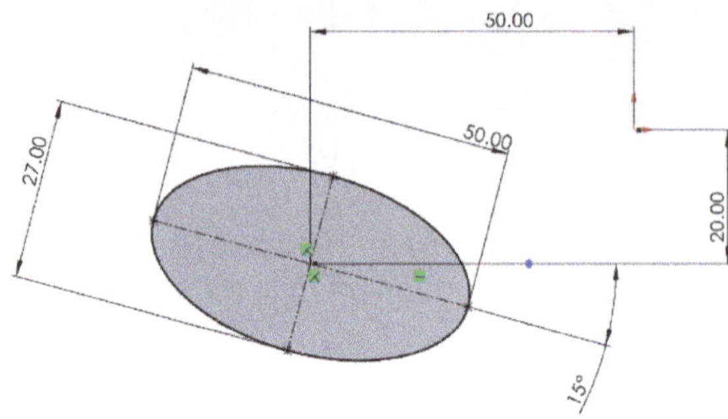

Partial Ellipse

A partial ellipse (or elliptical arc) is a segment of an ellipse, defined by its major and minor axes, but only spanning a portion of the full closed curve. Unlike a full ellipse, it is an open arc with defined start and end angles.

1. On the CommandManager, click **Sketch > Ellipse** drop-down > **Partial Ellipse** .
2. Click to define the center of the partial ellipse.
3. Move the pointer and click to define the radius and orientation of the first axis.

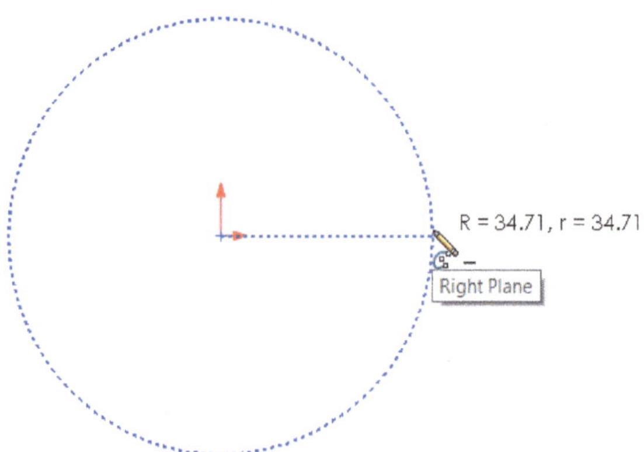

4. Move the pointer and click to define the radius of the second axis and start point.

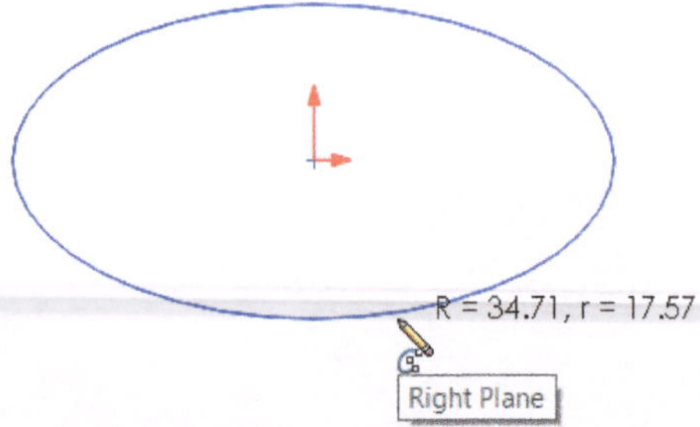

5. Rotate the pointer and click to define the end point.

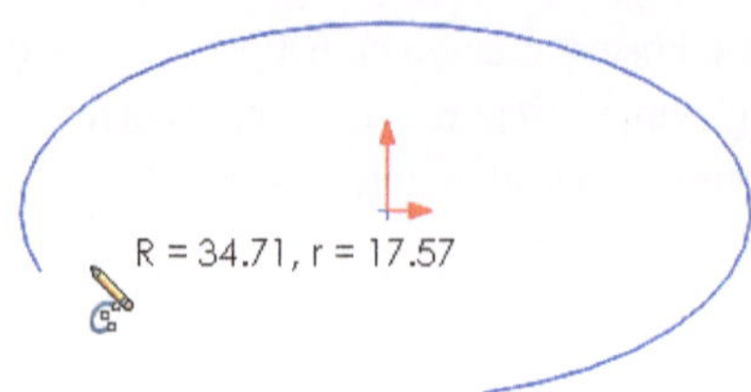

6. Click **Close Dialog** on the PropertyManager.

Conic

The **Conic** tool is used to create a conic curve. You can use a conic curve to connect two open sketch entities.

1. Create a line and arc, as shown.

2. On the **Sketch** CommandManager, click **Ellipse** drop-down > **Conic** .
3. Select the endpoints of the line and arc.
4. Move the pointer and notice the dotted lines. These lines are tangent to the line and arc.
5. Select the intersection point of the dotted tangent lines. Move the pointer and notice the rho value displayed. The rho value defines the type of conic created.

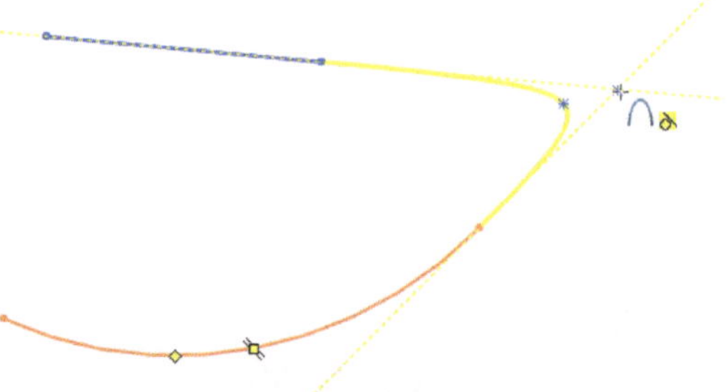

6. Click to create the conic curve. Now, you have to specify the Rho value of the conic curve.
7. Expand the Parameters section of the PropertyManager, and then type 0.5 in the ρ box.
8. Click **Close Dialog** on the PropertyManager.

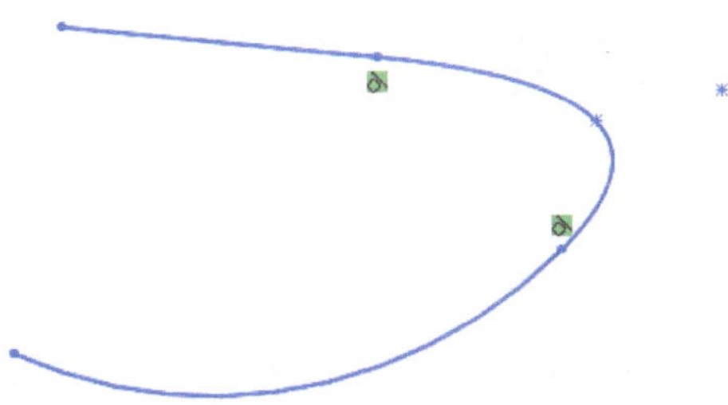

TUTORIAL 1

This tutorial teaches you to use **Sketch Fillet**, **Sketch Chamfer**, **Mirror Entities**, and **Tangent Arc** tools.

Sketch Fillet

The **Sketch Fillet** tool converts the sharp corners into round corners.

1. Draw the lines, as shown below.

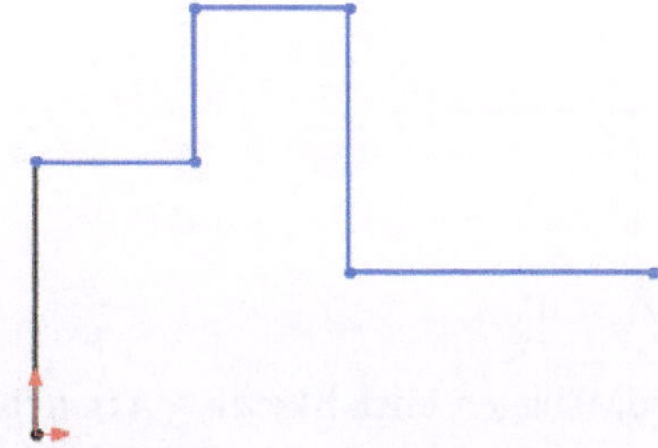

2. Click **Sketch > Sketch Fillet** on the CommandManager.
3. On the PropertyManager, type-in a value in the **Radius** box.
4. Click on the corner, as shown.

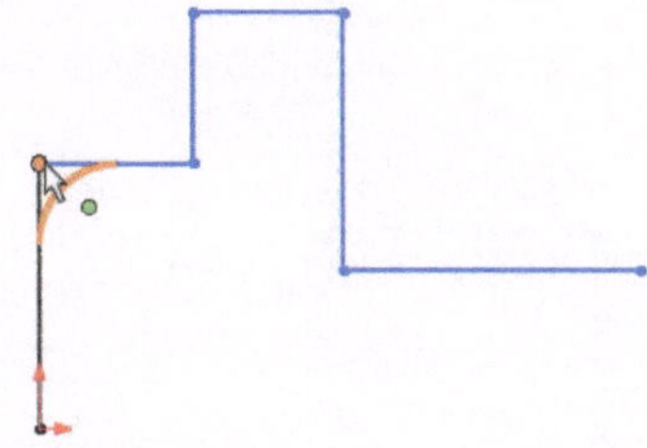

5. Select the vertical and horizontal lines, as shown.

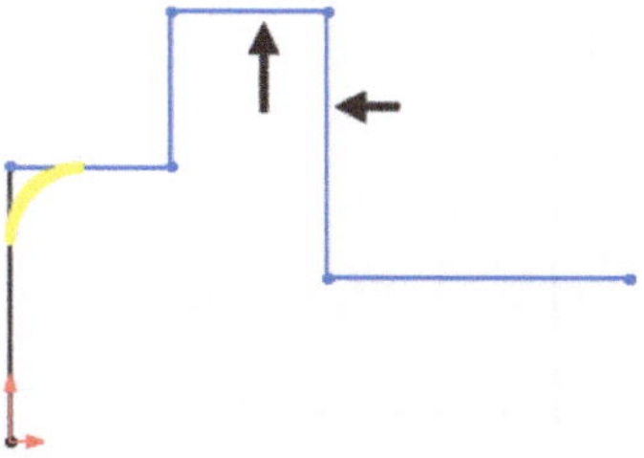

The **Keep constrained corners** option retains all the existing constraints.

The **Dimension each fillet** option dimensions all the fillets created in a single instance. If you uncheck this option, only a single fillet is dimensioned, and the **Equal** relation is applied between all other fillets.

6. Click **OK** on the PropertyManager. The fillets are created. The **Keep visible** icon on the PropertyManager will keep it open. You can select other corners or click the **Close** icon.

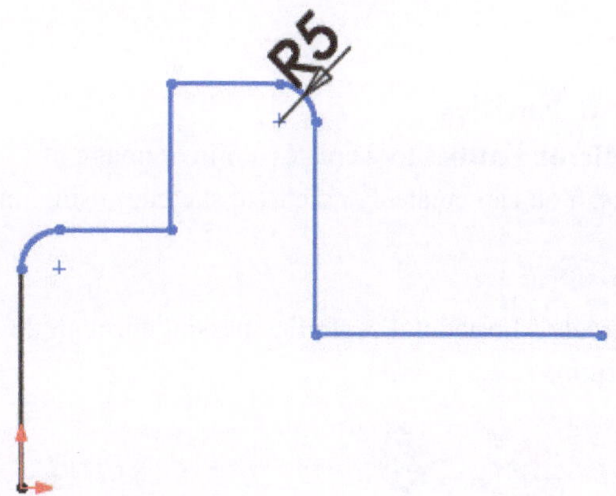

Sketch Chamfer

The **Sketch Chamfer** tool replaces the sharp corners with an angled line. This tool is similar to the **Sketch Fillet** tool, except that an angled line is placed at the corners instead of rounds.

1. Click **Sketch > Sketch Fillet > Sketch Chamfer** on the CommandManager.
2. On the PropertyManager, select the **Distance-distance** option and check the **Equal distance** option.
3. Type-in a value in the **Distance** box.
4. Click on the corner, as shown.

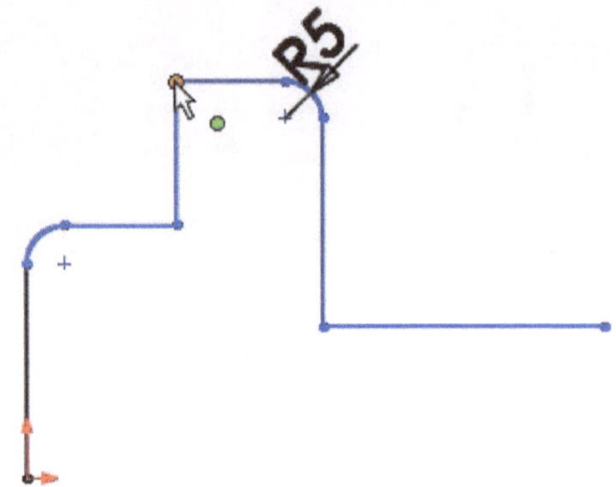

5. Click **OK** on the PropertyManager.

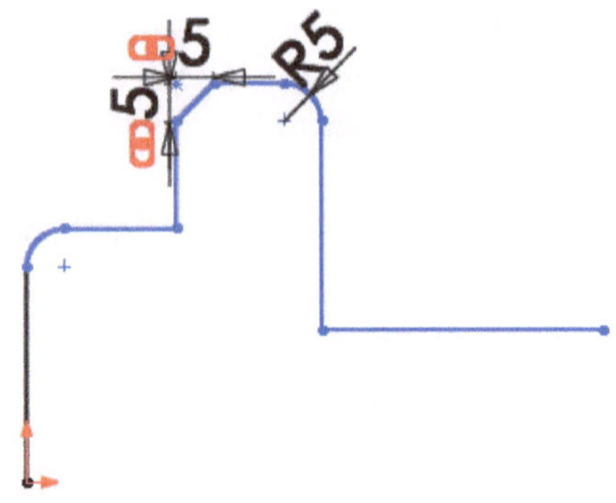

Mirror Entities

The **Mirror Entities** tool creates a mirror image of objects. You can create symmetrical sketches using this tool.

1. Create a horizontal centerline passing through the origin.

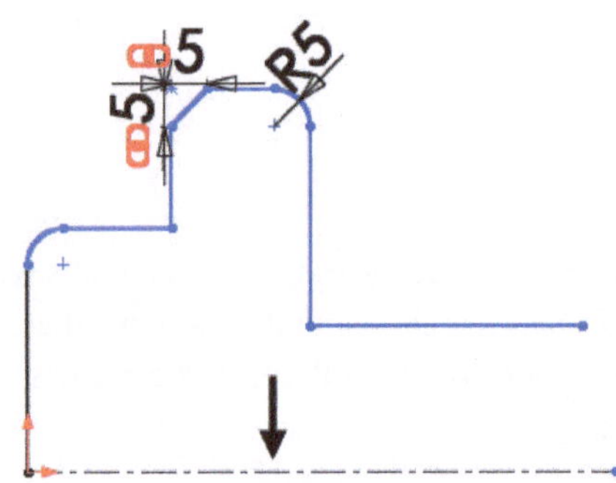

2. On the Command Manager, click **Sketch > Mirror Entities** .
3. Drag a selection box covering all the sketch entities.

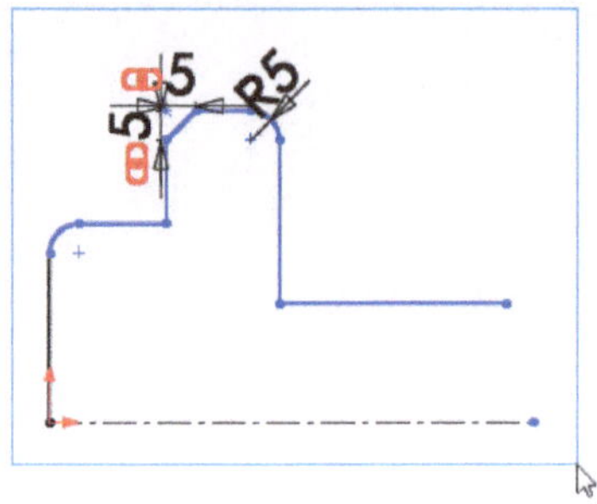

4. On the PropertyManager, click in the **Mirror about** box and select the centerline passing through the origin.
5. Click **OK** to mirror the selected entities.

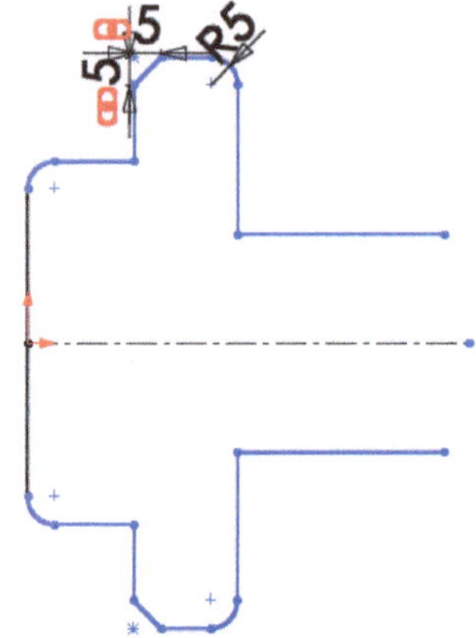

6. On the CommandManager, click **Sketch > Arc drop-down > Tangent Arc** .
7. Select the start point of the arc, as shown below.

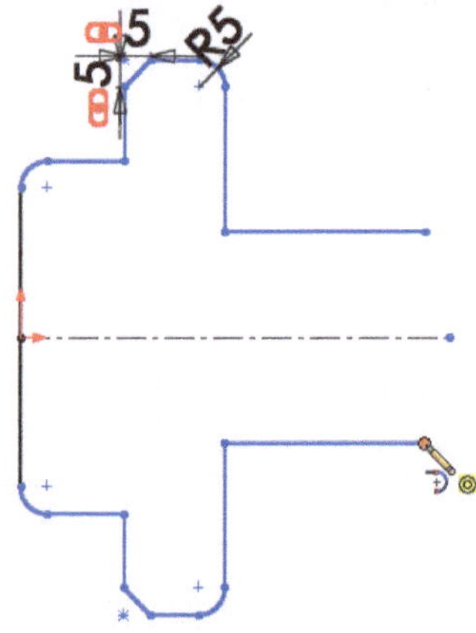

8. Move the pointer and select the endpoint of the arc, as shown below.

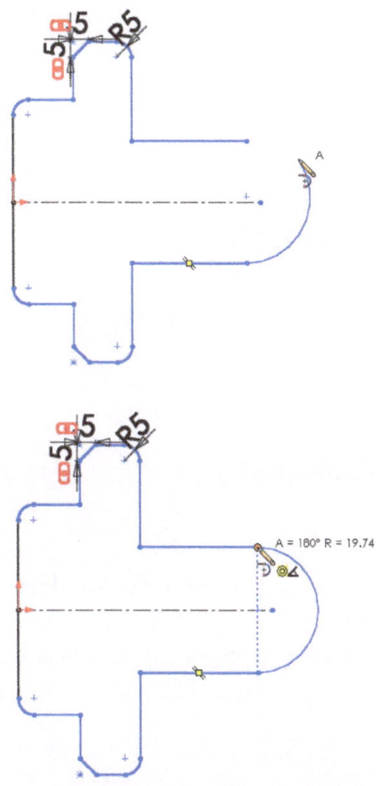

9. Click **OK** on the PropertyManager.

Stretch Entities

The **Stretch Entities** tool lengthens or shortens drawings or parts of sketches. Note that you cannot stretch circles using this tool. Also, you must select the portion of the drawing to be stretched by dragging a selection box.

1. On the CommandManager, click **Sketch > Move Entities > Stretch Entities**.
2. Drag a crossing window to select the objects of the sketch, as shown. Click the right mouse button.

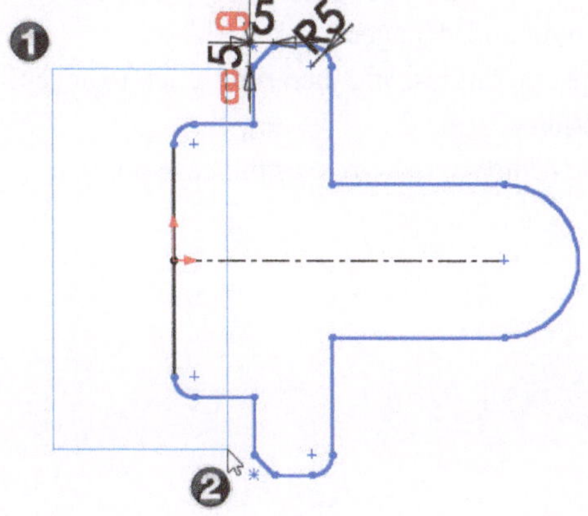

- Select the base point, as shown below.

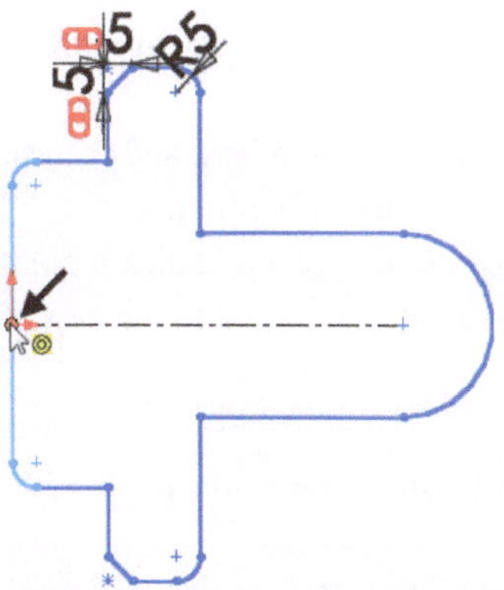

- Move the pointer toward the left and click to stretch the sketch.

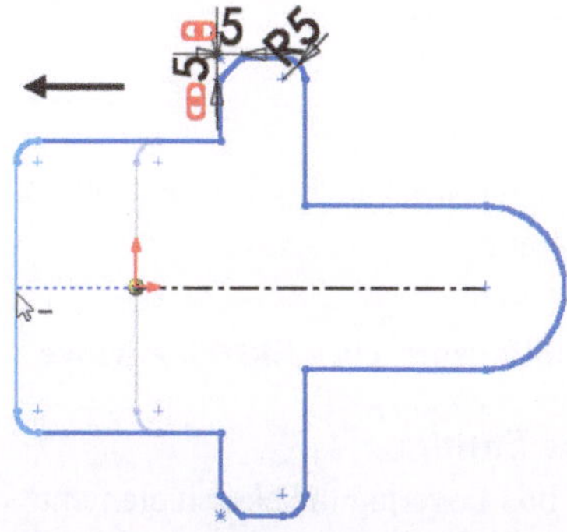

Move and Rotate Entities

The **Move Entities** tool moves a selected object(s) from one location to a new location without changing its orientation. To move objects, you must activate this tool and select the objects from the graphics window. After selecting objects, you must define the 'base point' and 'destination point.'

1. Create the sketch, as shown below.
2. Turn ON the **Shaded Sketch Contours** icon on the **Sketch** tab of the CommandManager.

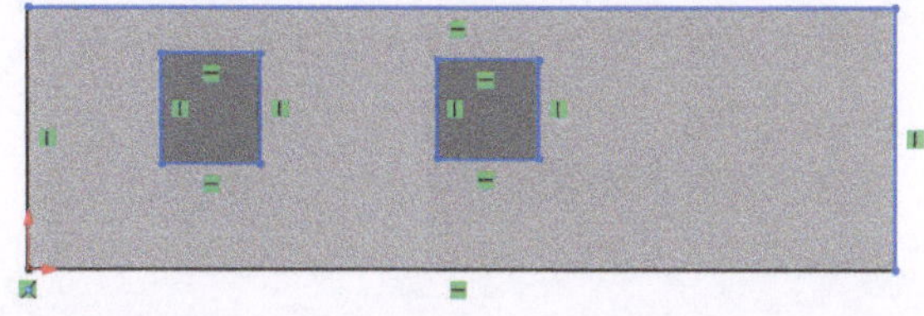

3. Click **Sketch > Move Entities** on the CommandManager.

4. Select the square located at the right-side by clicking inside it.
5. On the PropertyManager, under the **Parameter** section, select **From/To**.
6. Click in the **Start point** selection box, and then select the lower corner point as the base point.
7. Move the pointer toward the right and pick a point, as shown below. This moves the square to the new location.

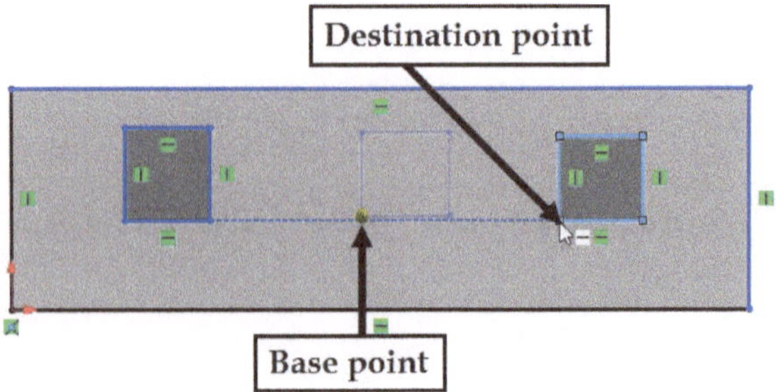

Rotate Entities

The **Rotate Entities** tool rotates an object or a group of objects about a base point.

1. On the CommandManager, click **Sketch > Move Entities > Rotate Entities** .
2. Drag a selection box covering the sketch elements and click the right mouse button.
3. Click to define the base point of the rotation.
4. Click again to specify the second point.

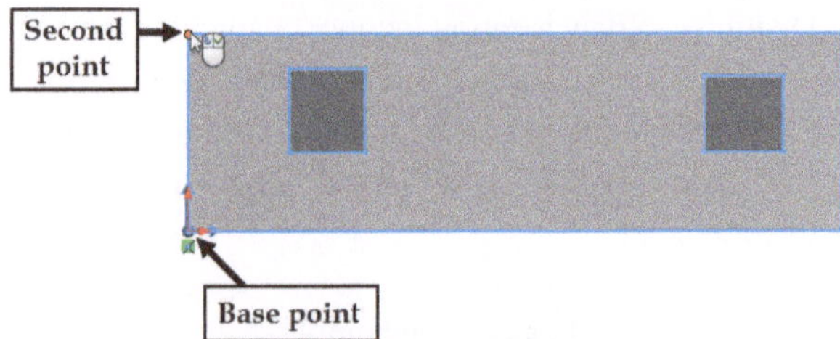

5. Press and hold the left mouse button and drag the cursor; the select sketch elements to rotate. You can also type-in the rotation angle on the PropertyManager.

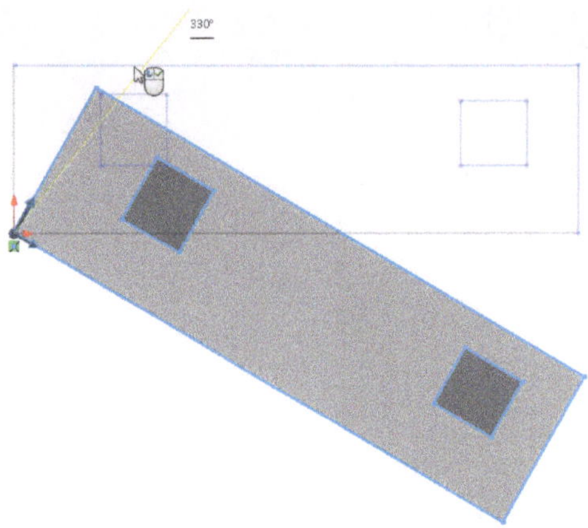

6. Click **OK** on the PropertyManager.

Copy Entities

The **Copy Entities** tool is used to copy objects and place them at a required location. This tool is similar to the **Move Entities** tool, except that object will remain at its original position, and a copy of it will be placed at the new location.

1. Start a new sketch on any one of the planes.
2. Turn OFF the **Shaded Sketch Contours** icon on the **Sketch** tab of the CommandManager.
3. Draw two circles of 80 mm and 140 mm diameter, respectively.

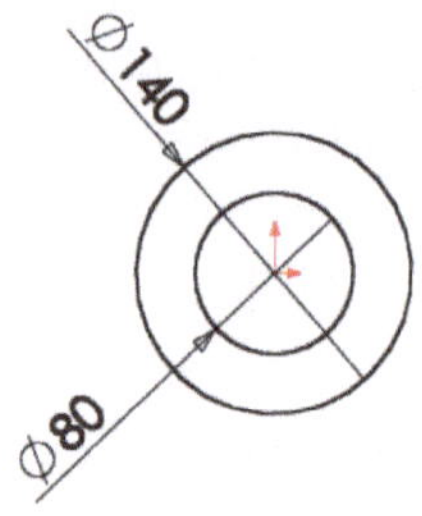

4. Click **Sketch > Move Entities > Copy Entities** on the CommandManager.
5. Select the two circles, and then right-click to accept the selection.
6. Select the center of the circle as the base point.

7. Move the pointer toward the right and click.

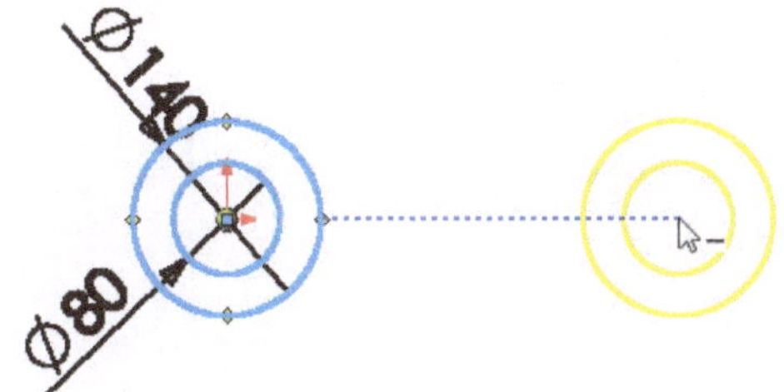

This creates a copy of the circles at the new location.

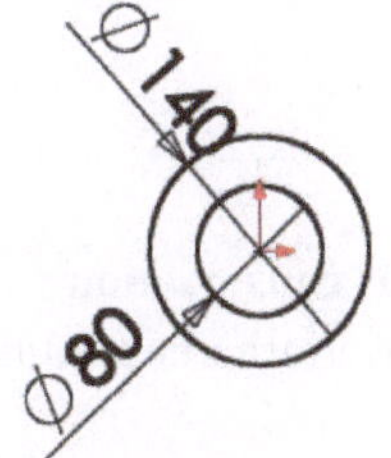

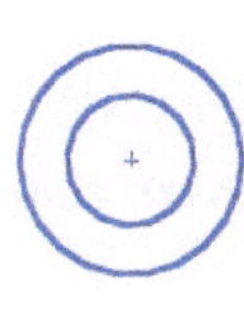

Scale Entities

The **Scale Entities** tool changes the size of objects. It reduces or enlarges the size without changing the shape of an object.

1. Click **Sketch > Move Entities > Scale Entities** on the CommandManager.
2. Select the circles shown below and right-click to accept the selection.

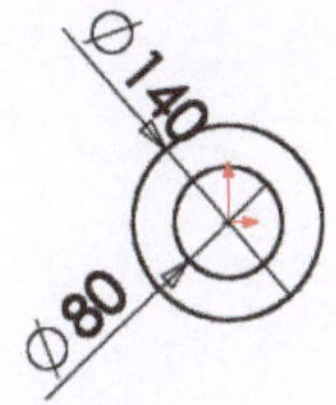

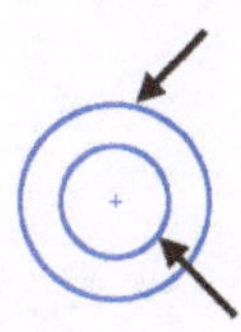

3. Select the center point of the selected circles as the base point.
4. Type 0.6 in the **Scale Factor** box under the **Parameters** section of the PropertyManager.
5. Uncheck the **Copy** option on the PropertyManager and click **OK**.

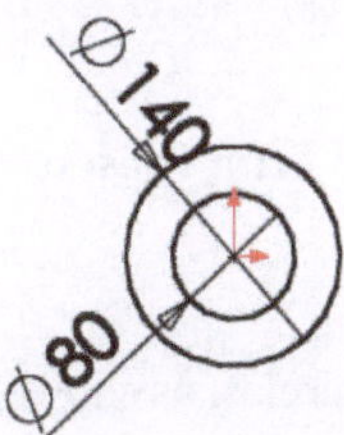

6. Click **Sketch > Circle** drop-down **> Perimeter Circle** on the CommandManager.
7. Select the two circles shown below to define the tangent points.

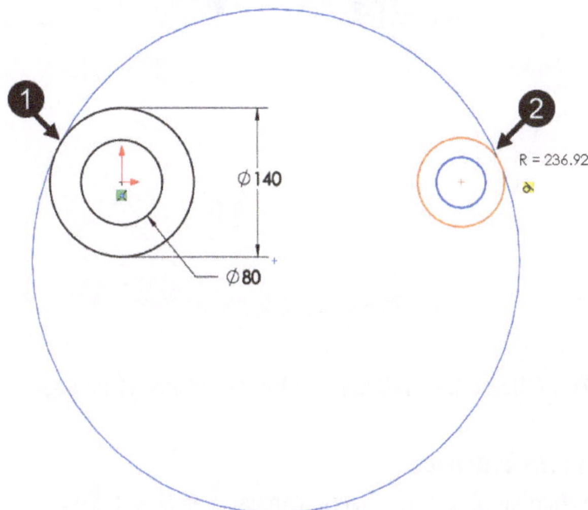

8. Move the pointer down and click to create the circle.

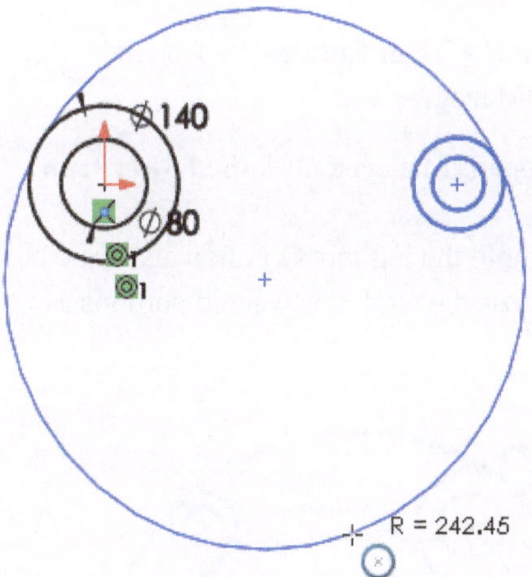

9. Likewise, create another circle by selecting the points as shown.

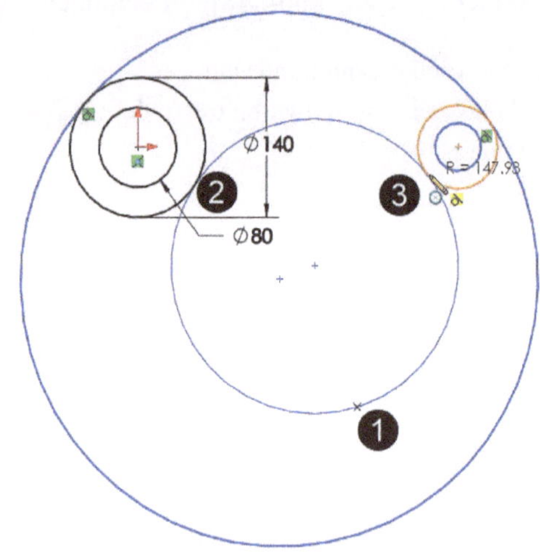

10. Click **Close Dialog** on the PropertyManager.

Trim Entities

When an object intersects with another object, you can remove its unwanted portion using the **Trim Entities** tool.

1. Click **Sketch > Trim Entities** on the CommandManager.
2. On the PropertyManager, click the **Power trim** icon.
3. Press and hold the left mouse button and drag the pointer across the circles' unwanted portions as shown.

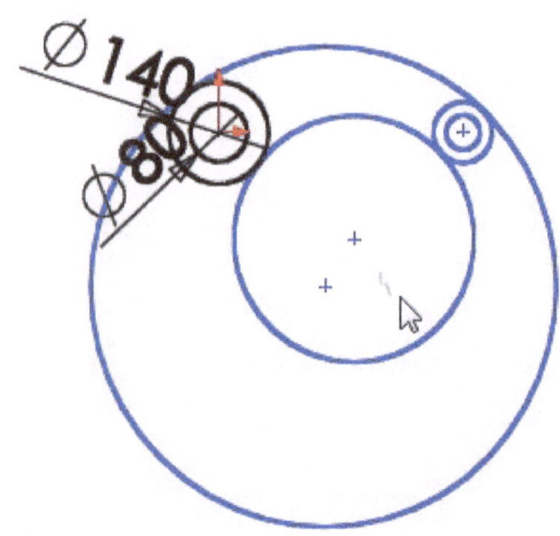

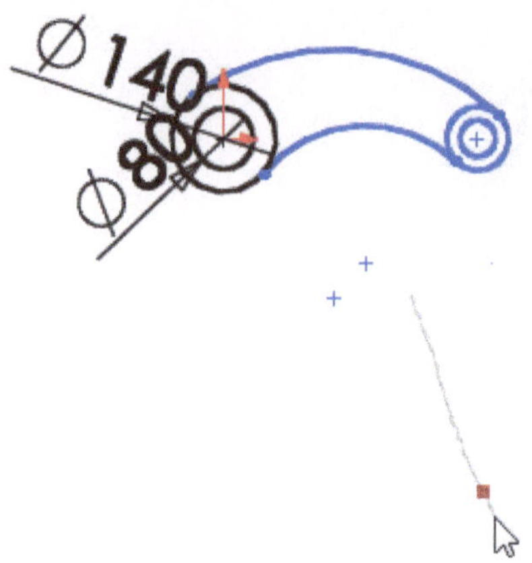

Check the **Keep trimmed entities as construction geometry** option if you want to convert trimmed entities as construction geometry.

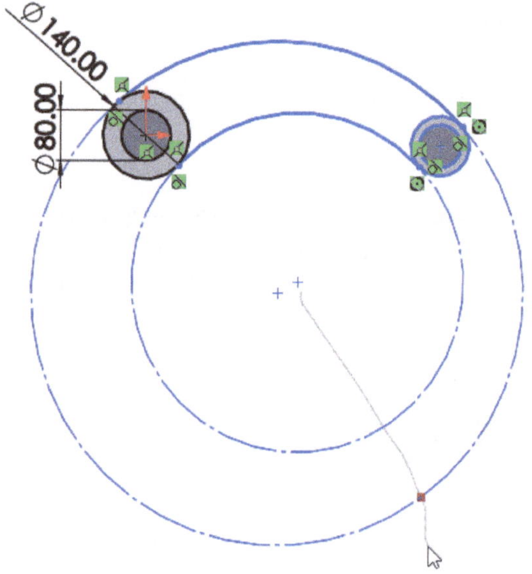

Check the **Ignore trimming of construction geometry** option if you want to leave the construction geometry untrimmed.

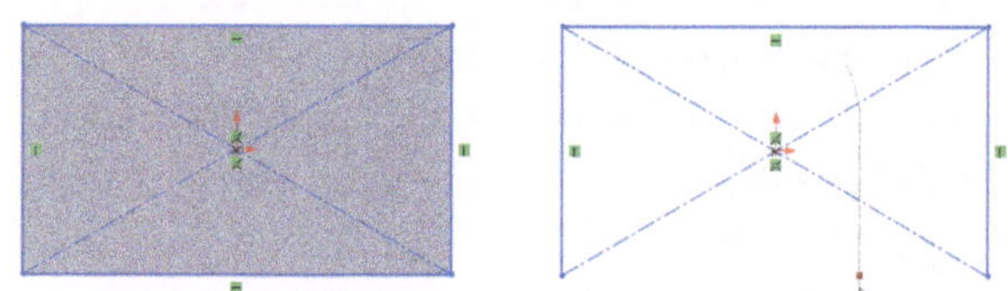

4. On the PropertyManager, click the **Trim Closest** icon.
5. Click on the inner portions of the circles, as shown.

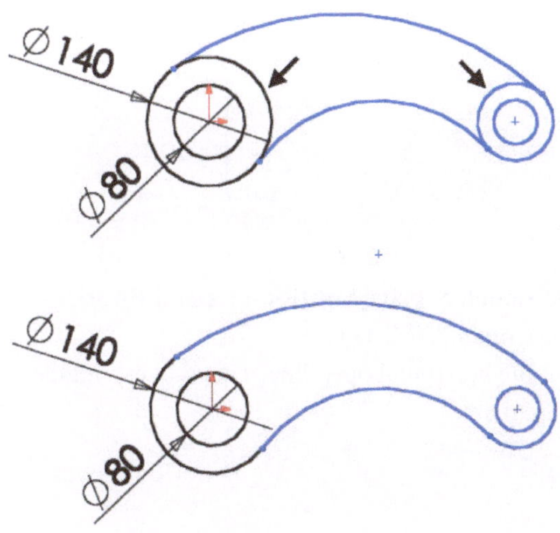

6. Click **Close Dialog** on the PropertyManager.

Another example of the Trim Entities tool

7. On the CommandManager, click **Sketch > Arc drop-down > 3 Point Arc**.
8. Select three points in the graphics window, as shown.

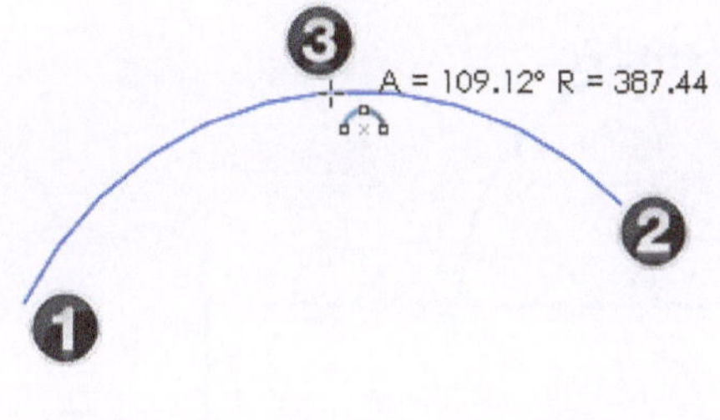

9. Create other arcs using the **3 Point Arc** tool, as shown.

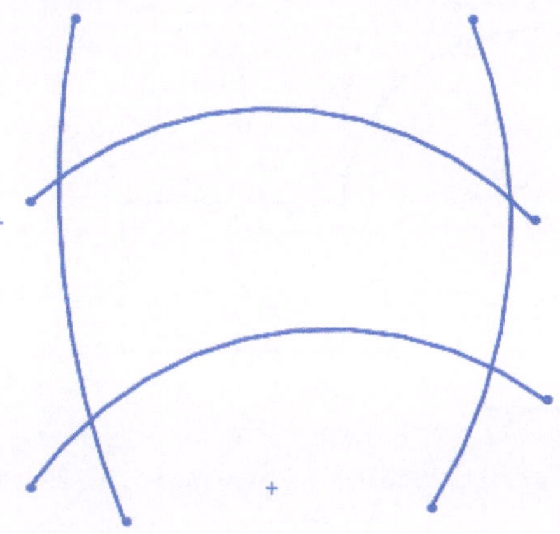

10. On the CommandManager, click **Sketch > Trim Entities**.
11. On the PropertyManager, click the **Trim away inside** icon.
12. Click on the boundary entities, as shown.
13. Click on the entities to trim, as shown.

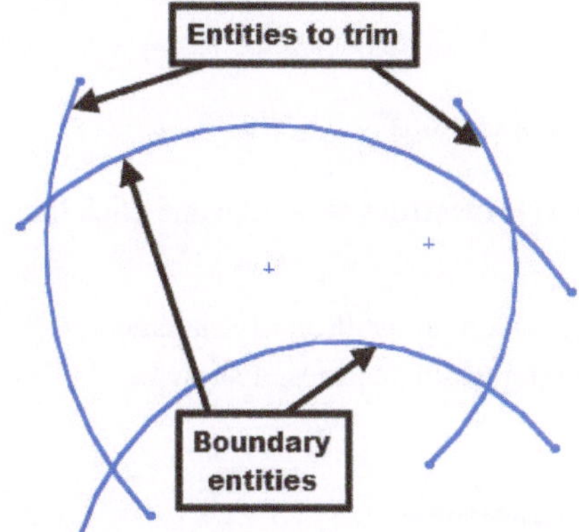

The inner portions of the entities are trimmed.

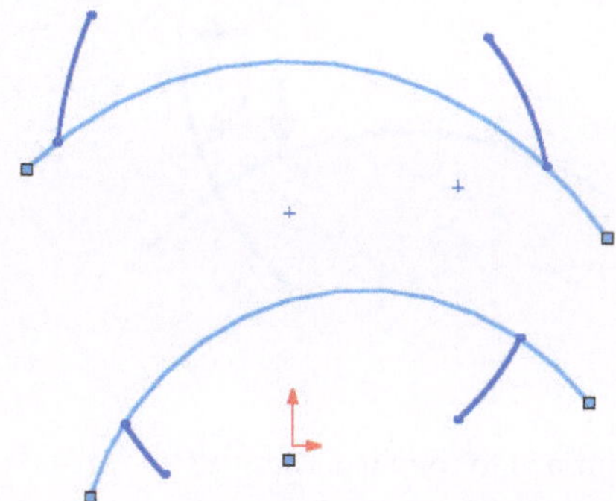

14. Press Ctrl+Z twice to undo the trim operations (or) click **Undo** twice on the Quick Access Toolbar.
15. Activate the **Trim Entities** tool and click the **Trim away outside** icon on the PropertyManager.
16. Click on the boundary and trim entities. The outer portions are trimmed, as shown.

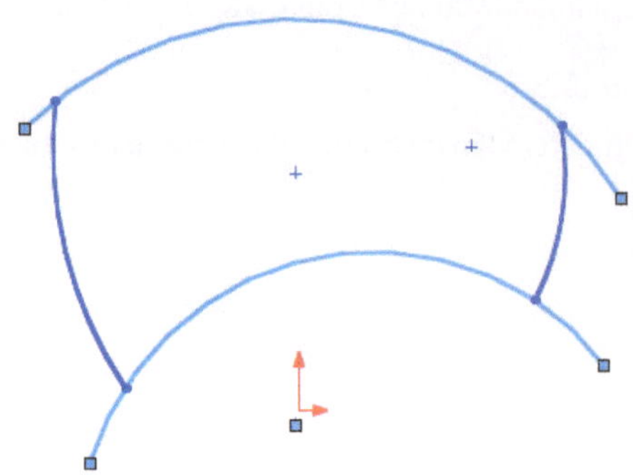

17. Undo the trim operations.
18. Activate the **Trim Entities** tool and click the **Corner** icon on the PropertyManager.
19. Click on the intersecting entities, a shown.

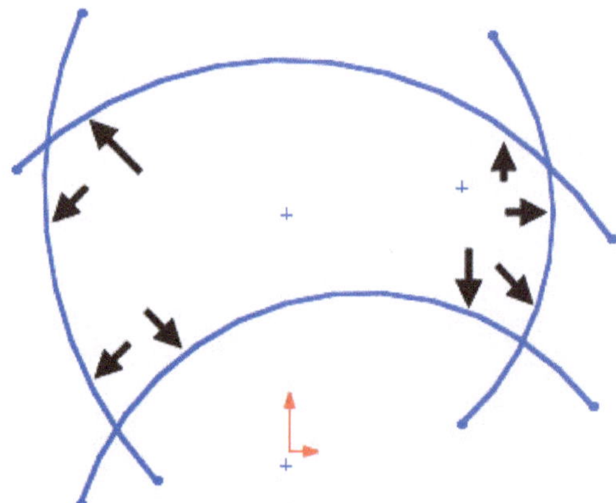

The entities are trimmed to form a corner.

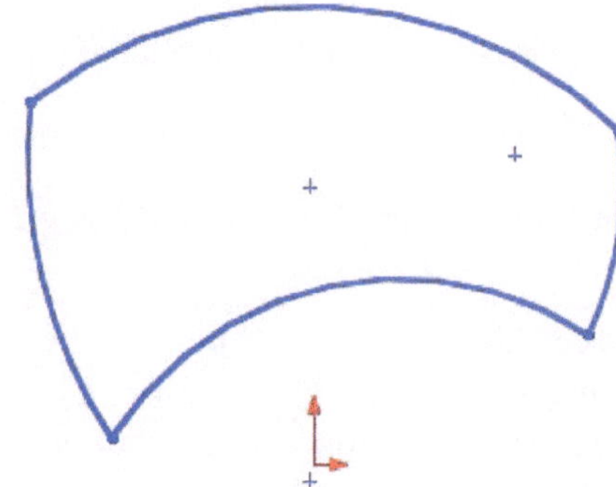

Extend Entities

The **Extend Entities** tool is similar to the **Trim Entities** tool, but its use is the opposite. This tool is used to extend lines, arcs, and other open entities to connect to other objects.

1. Create a sketch, as shown below.

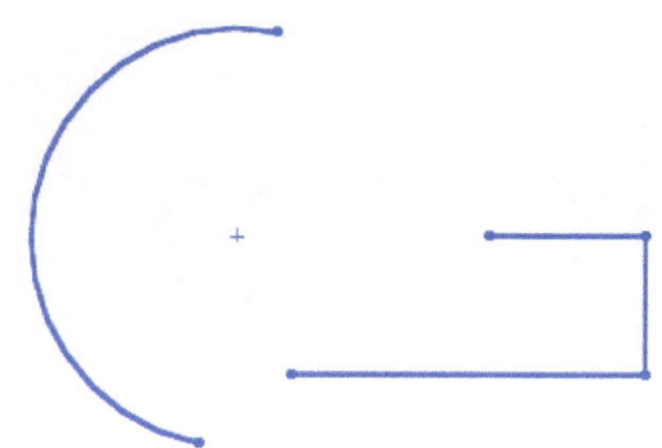

2. Click **Sketch > Trim Entities > Extend Entities** on the CommandManager.
3. Select the horizontal open line. This will extend the line up to arc.

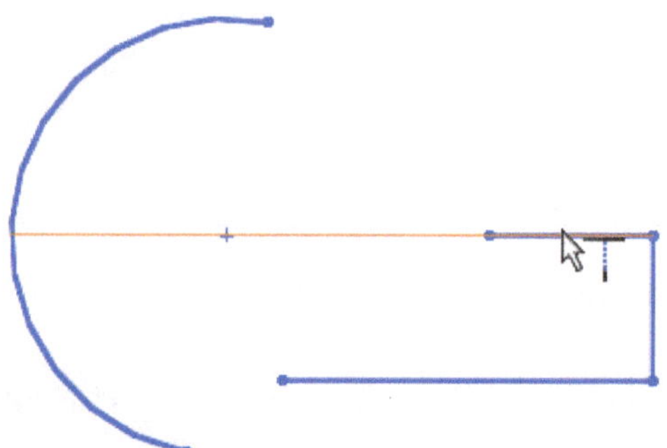

Likewise, extend the other elements, as shown.

4. Trim the unwanted portions.

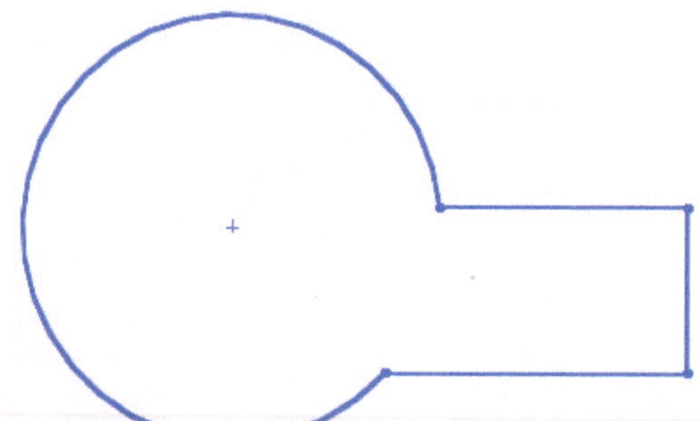

Offset Entities

The **Offset Entities** tool creates parallel copies of lines, circles, and arcs.

1. On the CommandManager, click **Sketch** tab > **Offset Entities** .
2. Check the **Select Chain** option on the PropertyManager to select connected elements.
3. Select an entity and notice that all the connected entities are selected.
4. Type-in the offset distance on the PropertyManager.
5. Click inside or outside the sketch to define the offset side.

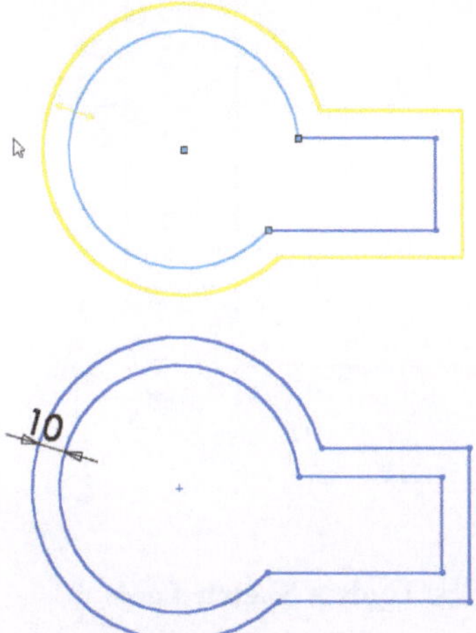

You can also reverse the offset direction by double-clicking on the offset dimension and selecting the **Reverse the sense of direction** button.

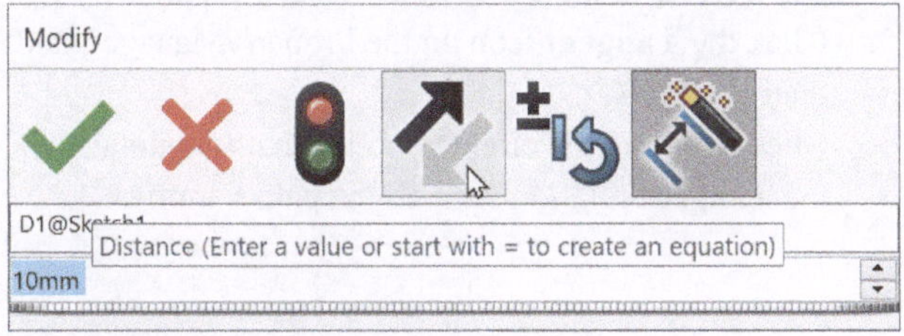

Creating a Bidirectional Offset

1. Click the **Sketch** tool on the **Sketch CommandManager**.
2. Select anyone of the planes.
3. Click the **Line** tool on the **Sketch CommandManager**.
4. Select the sketch origin point, move the pointer horizontally toward right and click; a horizontal line is created.
5. Move the pointer vertically upward and click to create a vertical line.

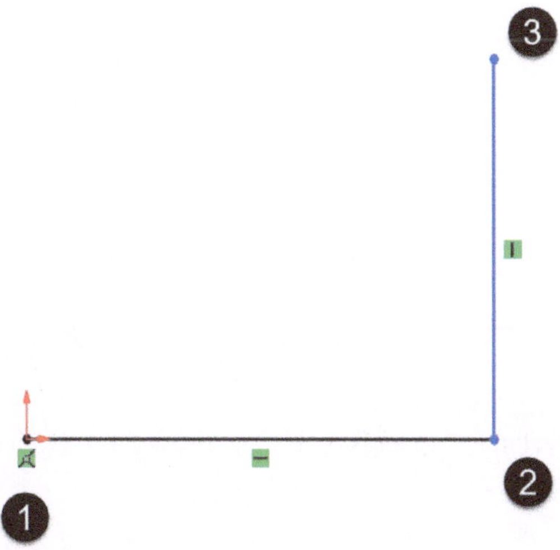

6. Click the **Sketch Fillet** tool on Sketch CommandManager.
7. Select the intersection of the vertical and horizontal lines.
8. Type **20** in the **Fillet Radius** box on the PropertyManager and click **OK**.
9. Add dimensions to the lines, as shown.

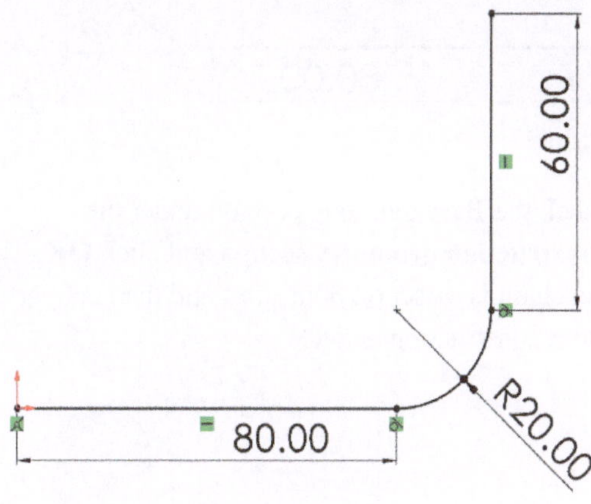

10. Activate the **Offset Entities** tool.
11. Select a line segment and notice that the entire chain is selected.
12. Check the **Bi-directional** option. Notice that the offset preview appears on both sides.

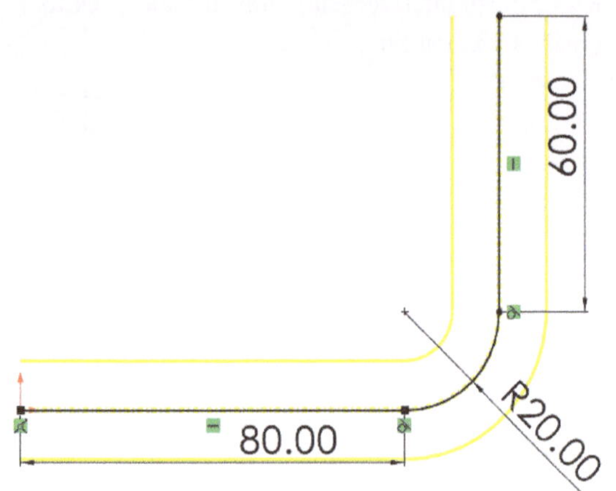

13. Check the **Cap ends** option and select **Arcs**. Notice that the ends are capped with arcs.

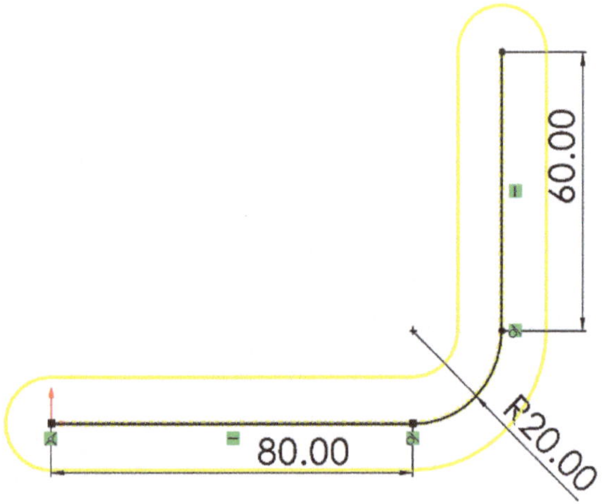

14. Check the **Base geometry** option under the **Construction geometry** section and click **OK**. The line chain is offset on both sides and then converted into a construction entity.

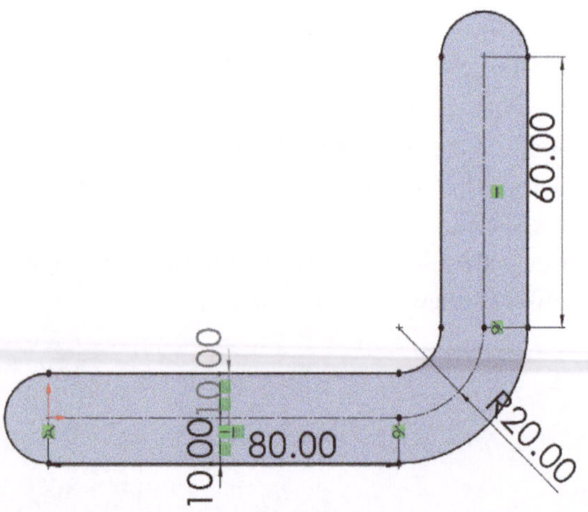

Make Path

The **Make Path** tool creates a path combining all the sketch entities. After creating a path by combining all the sketch entities, you can apply a relation to anyone of its entities; the applied relation will be persistent to all other entities of the path. For example, when you apply the Tangent relation between anyone of the entity of the path and other individual entity, the relation will be persistent through all the path's entities.

1. Create a circle and add dimension to it, as shown.

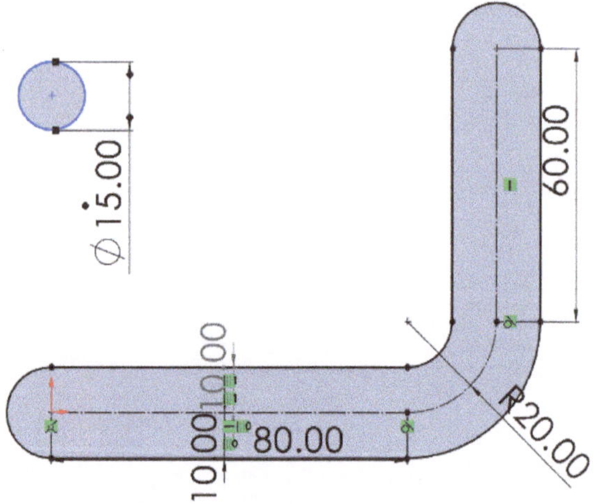

2. On the Menu bar, click **Tools > Sketch Tools > Make Path** .
3. Select all the entities of the closed-loop, and then click **OK** on the PropertyManager.
4. Press and hold the CTRL key and select the circle and anyone of the entity of the closed-loop.
5. Click the **Tangent** icon on the PropertyManager, and then click **OK**.
6. Click and drag the circle to notice that it maintains the **Tangent** relation with all the path's entities.

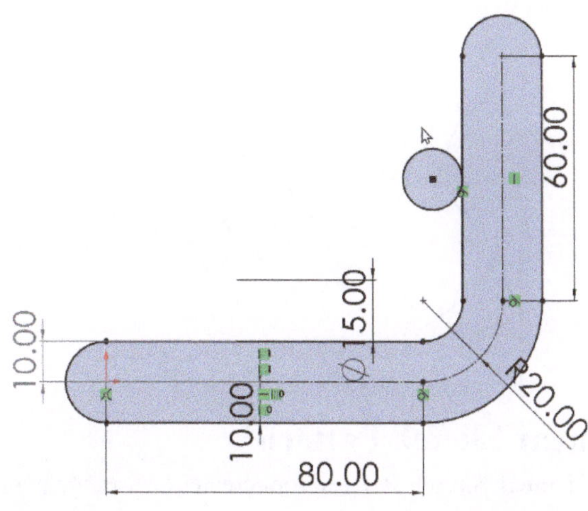

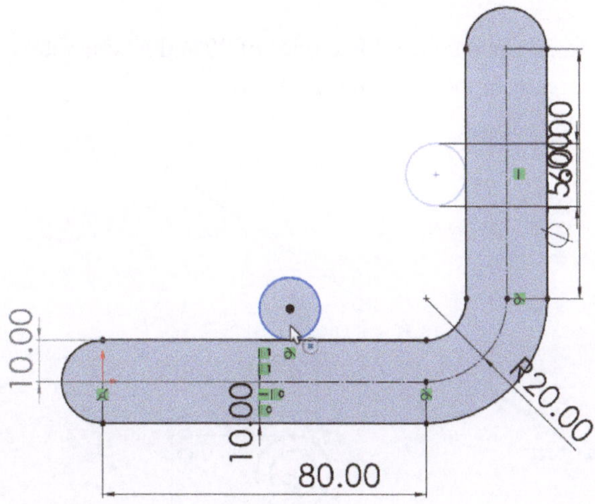

Circular Sketch Pattern

The **Circular Sketch Pattern** tool creates an arrangement of objects around a point in circular form.

1. Create two concentric circles of 140 and 50 diameters.

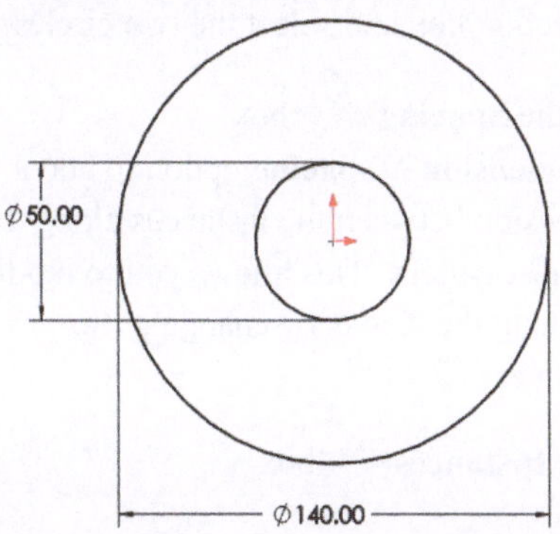

2. On the CommandManager, click **Sketch > Arc drop-down > Centerpoint Arc** .
3. Select the quadrant point of the circle, as shown below.

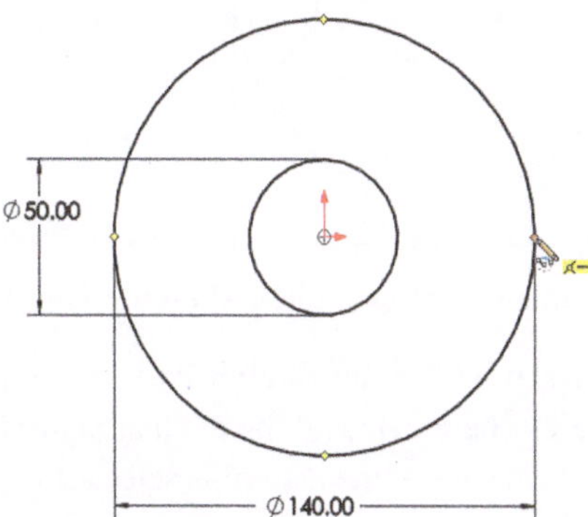

4. Move the pointer down and click on the circle when the **Coincident** symbol appears.

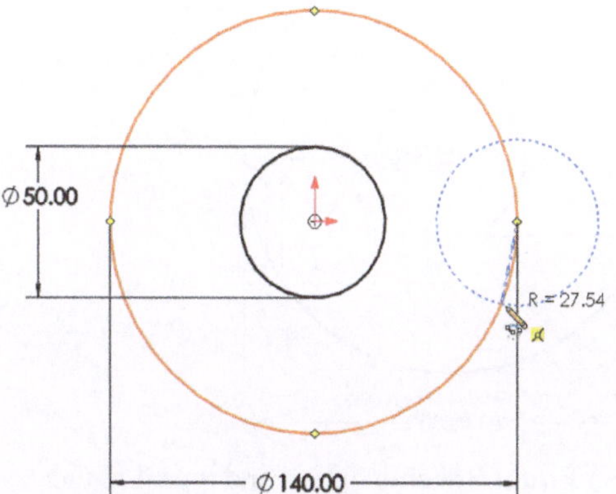

5. Move the pointer leftwards and up.
6. Click on the circle when the Coincident symbol appears.

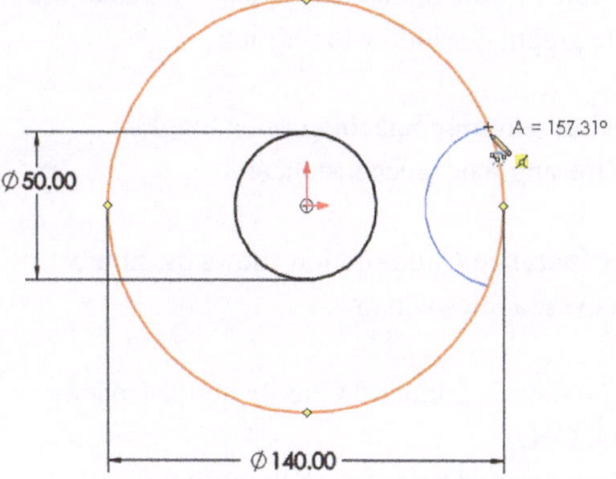

7. Click **Close Dialog** on the PropertyManager.
8. Dimension the arc with radius 30.

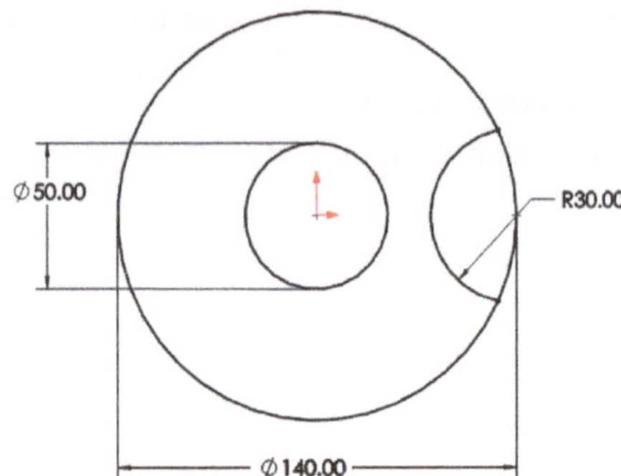

9. On the CommandManager, click **Sketch > Linear Sketch Pattern > Circular Sketch Pattern**.
10. Select the arc. The preview of the circular pattern appears as the center of the pattern is selected automatically.

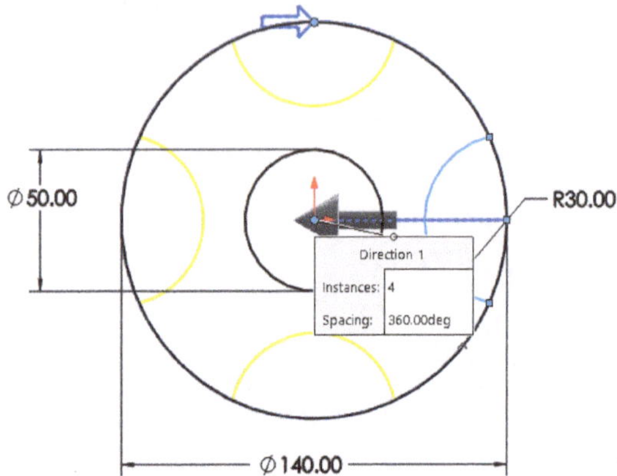

11. Check the **Equal Spacing** option and type **4** in the **Instance Count** box. This enables **uniform angular spacing** between instances

The **Dimension Radius** option displays the radius of the pattern in the graphics window for editing.

The **Dimension Angular Spacing** option toggles visibility of the angle between instances.

The **Display Instance Count** option shows the number of instances in the graphics window.

12. Leave the default options on the PropertyManager and click **OK**.
13. Trim the unwanted portions, as shown below.

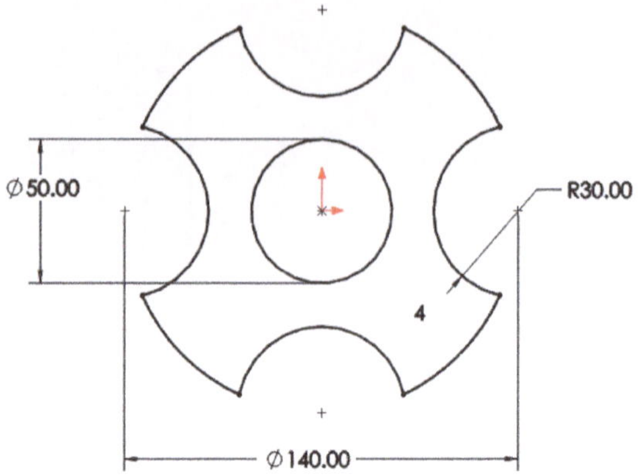

Linear Sketch Pattern

The **Linear Sketch Pattern** tool creates an arrangement of objects along a line.

1. Create two concentric circles of 80 and 50 diameters.
2. Create an inclined line, as shown.

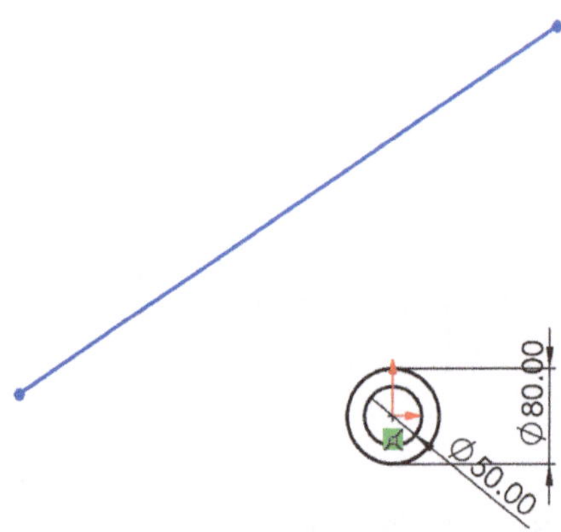

14. On the CommandManager, click **Sketch > Linear Sketch Pattern**.
15. Select the line.
16. On the PropertyManager, click in the **Entities to Patterns** selection box and select the two circles.
17. Type **100** in the **Spacing** box.
18. Check the **Dimension X spacing** option to add a spacing dimension between the instances along the X axis of the linear pattern. This allows you to modify the spacing along the X axis by changing the dimension value.
19. Type **5** in the **Instances** box.

20. Check the **Display instance count** option to display the instance count in the linear pattern. This allows you to change the instance count whenever needed by double-clicking on it.
21. Type 3 in the **Instance Count** box in the **Direction 2** section.
22. Type **100** in the **Distance** box in the **Direction 2**.
23. Check the **Dimension Y spacing** option.

By default, the Y-axis is assigned as **Direction 2**. To change this, you can select any edge, line, or reference geometry to redefine Direction 2. If needed, adjust the angle between Direction 1 and Direction 2 by entering a value in the **Angle** field. Check the **Display angle between axes** option to show this angle visually in the workspace, ensuring precise alignment during design.

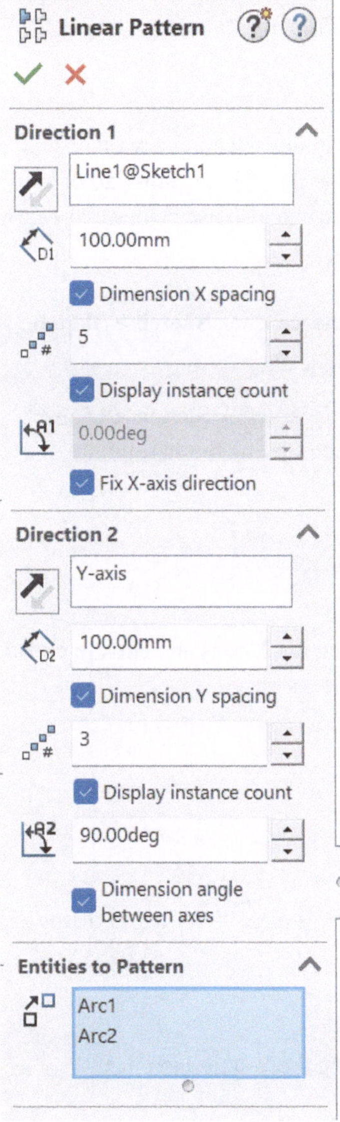

24. Click **OK** to create the linear pattern.

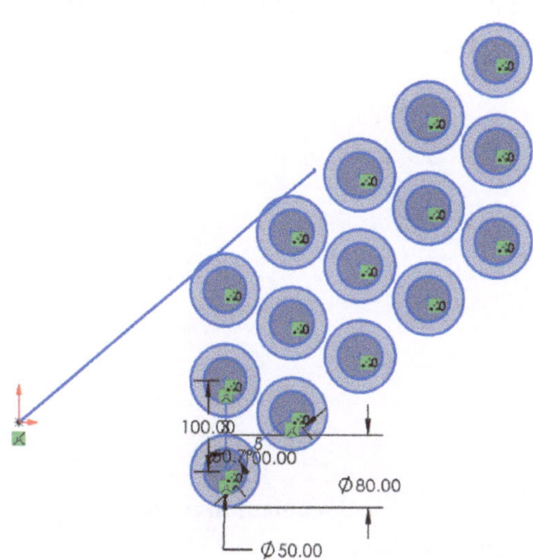

Text

Texts are used to provide information on the models, such as company name and model specifications.

1. Start a new sketch.
2. Create the circle and two lines perpendicular to each other, as shown. Note that you need to check the **For Construction** option in the **Options** section of the PropertyManager while creating sketch elements.

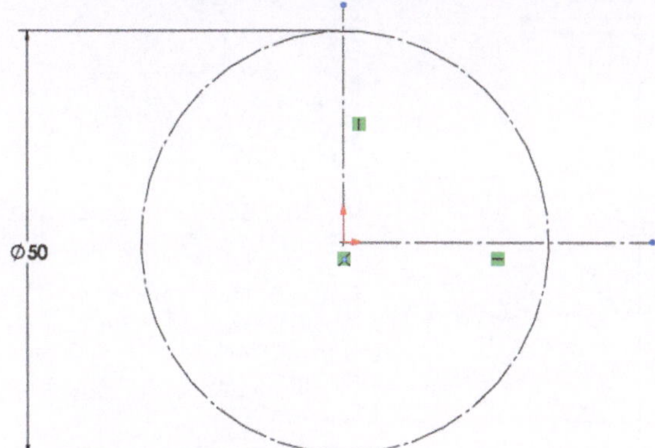

3. On the **Sketch** CommandManager, click the **Text** tool.
4. Select the horizontal line as the supporting curve.
5. Click in the **Text** box in the PropertyManager and type SOLIDWORKS. On the PropertyManager, use the **Alignment** options (**Left Align**, **Center Align**, **Right Align**, and **Full Justify**) to change the text's alignment. Use the **Flip** options (**Flip**

Vertical and **Flip Horizontal**) to flip the text.

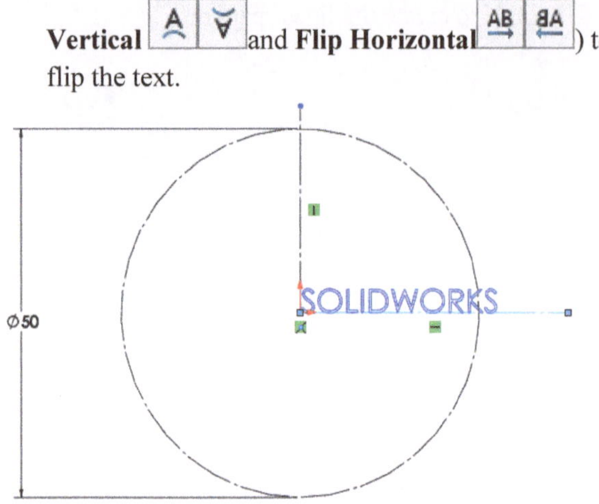

6. Uncheck the **Use document font** option; the font option is available.
7. Click the **Font** button to open the **Choose Font** dialog.
8. On the **Choose Font** dialog, change the font type, font style, height, and spacing between the text. Also, you can apply effects such as strikeout and underline.
9. Click **OK** on the **Choose Font** dialog.
10. Click the right mouse button in the **Curve** box and select the **Clear Selections** option. Next, click on the vertical construction line.

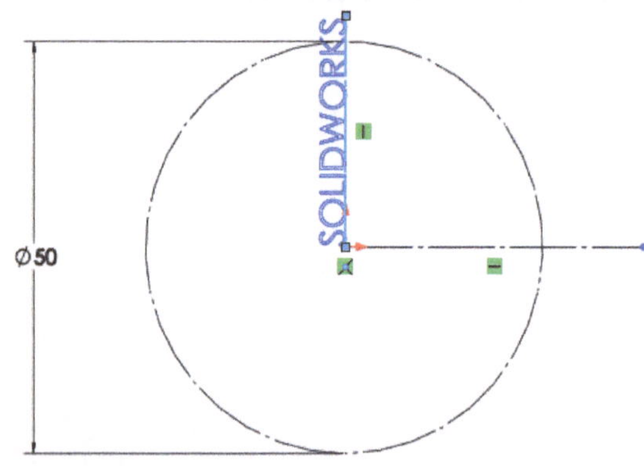

11. Select the text from the **Text** box and click **Rotate**.
12. Change the rotation angle value in the **Text** box, as shown.

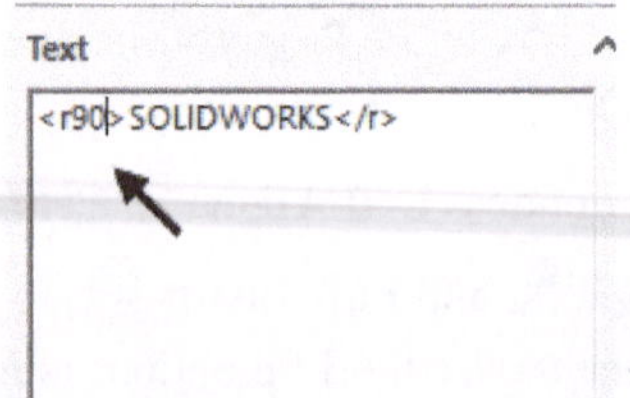

13. Right click in the **Curve** box and select **Clear Selections**.
14. Select the circle as the alignment curve.
15. Select the rotation angle value of the text 0.

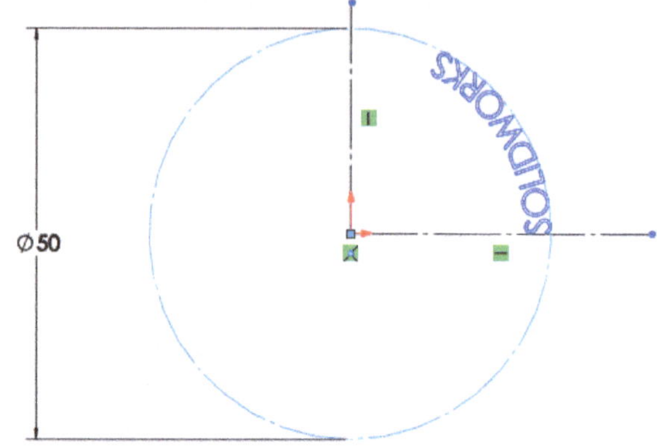

16. Click the **OK** on the PropertyManager.

3D Sketch

3D sketches are created without selecting any plane and sketch elements spread over the 3D space instead of a single plane. However, you can also use planes to create a 3D sketch.

1. On the CommandManager, click **Sketch > Sketch** drop-down **> 3D Sketch** .
2. On the CommandManager, click **Sketch > Line** .
3. Select the origin point to define the start point.

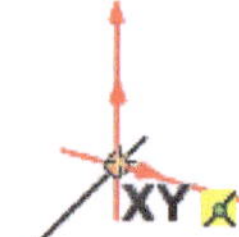

4. Move the pointer along the X-axis and click to create a line.

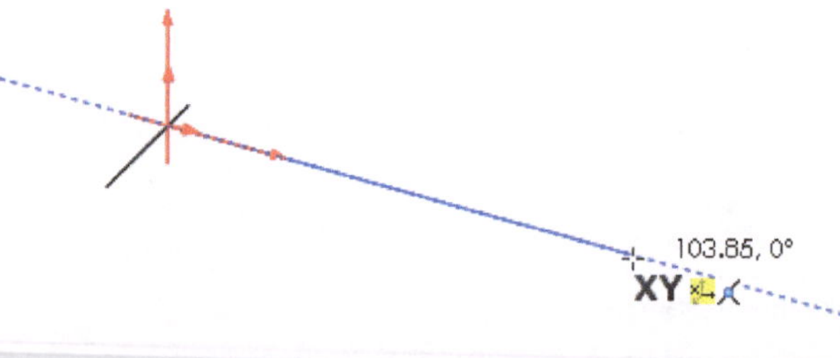

5. Move the pointer along the Y-axis and click.

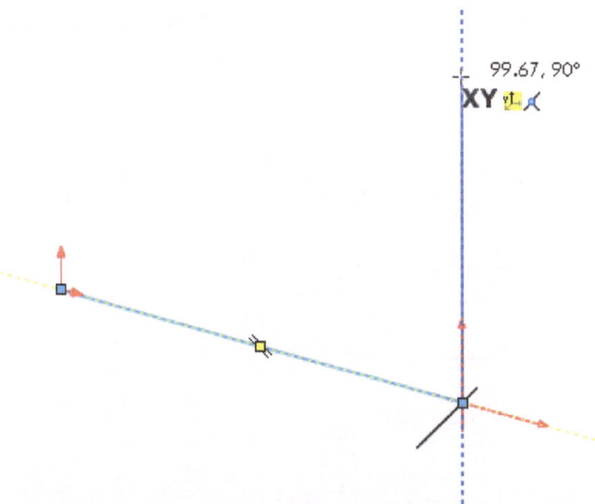

6. Press the Tab key to change the plane.
7. Move the pointer in the Z-direction and click.

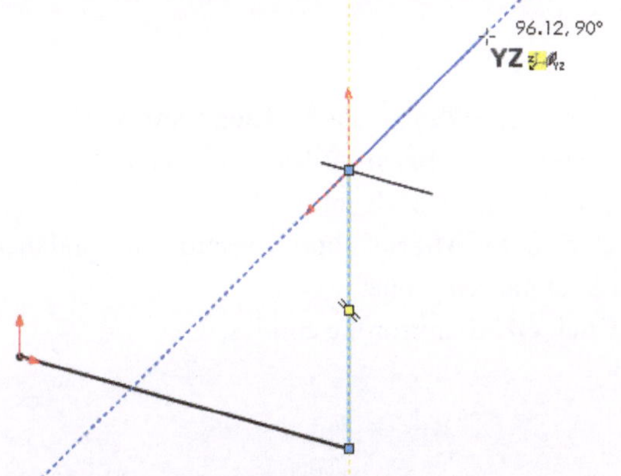

8. Press the Tab key to change the plane.
9. Move the pointer in the X-direction and click.

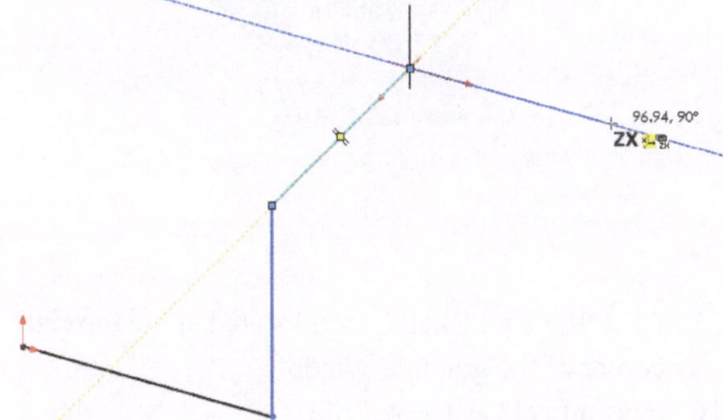

10. Click the right mouse button and select **Select**.
11. On the CommandManager, click **Sketch > Plane** .
12. Press the Ctrl key and select the endpoints as shown.
13. Click **OK** on the PropertyManager.

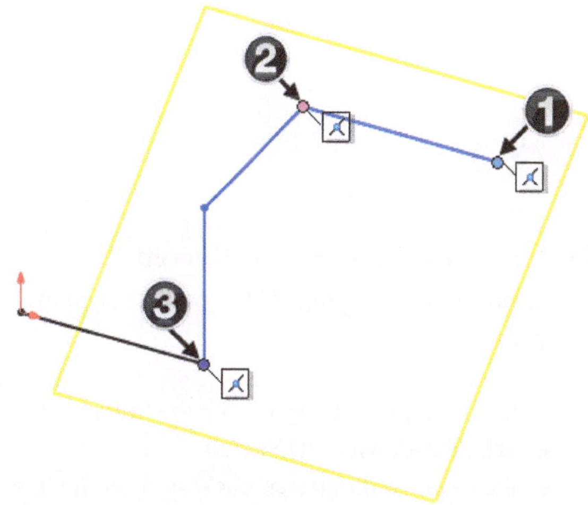

14. Activate the **Line** tool and click the end of the previous line.
15. Move the pointer and click when the **Vertical** symbol appears next to the pointer.

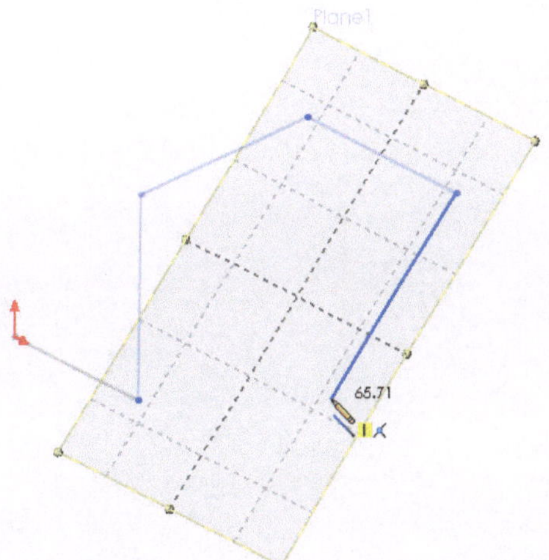

16. Move the pointer and click when the **Horizontal** symbol appears.

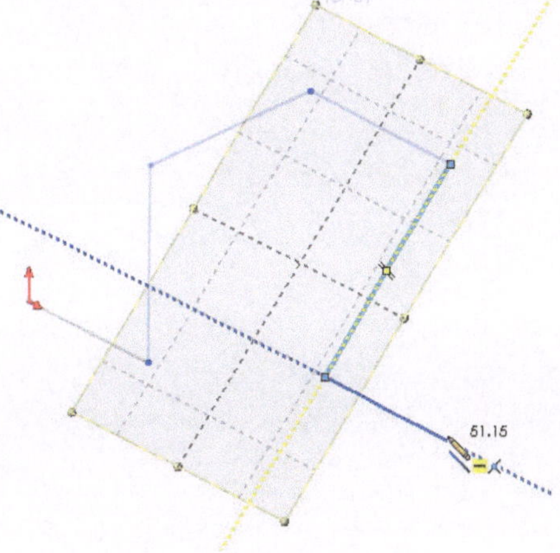

17. Click the right mouse button and select **Select**.
18. Add dimensions and relations, and then click **Exit Sketch**.

Mirroring Entities in a 3D Sketch

In a 3D sketch, you can mirror entities located on the same plane.

1. On the CommandManager, click the **Sketch** tab > **Sketch** drop-down > **3D Sketch**.
2. On the CommandManager, click the **Sketch** tab > **Plane** .
3. Select the Front Plane from the FeatureManager Design Tree.
4. Click the **Coincident** icon on the PropertyManager.
5. Click **OK**.

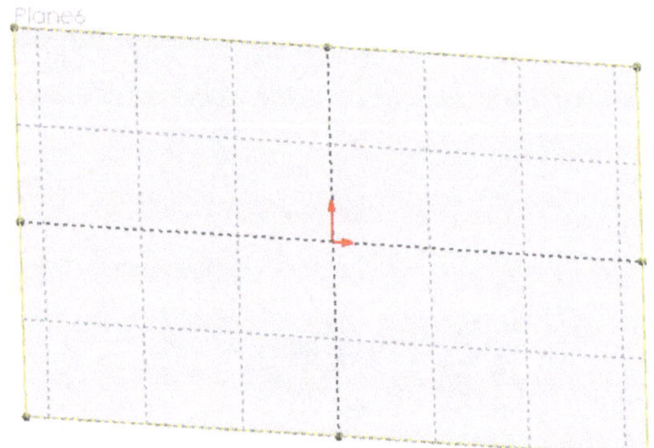

6. On the CommandManager, click the **Sketch** tab > **Line** drop-down > **Centerline**.
7. Select the sketch origin, move the pointer upward, and then click.

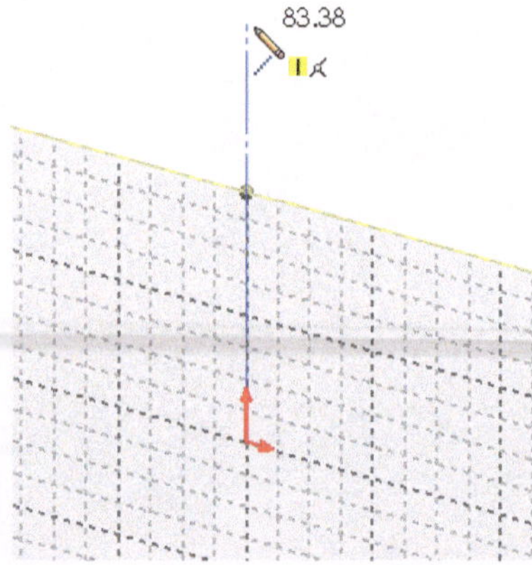

8. Right click and select **Select** from the shortcut menu.
9. Activate the **Line** command, and then create the sketch entities, as shown.

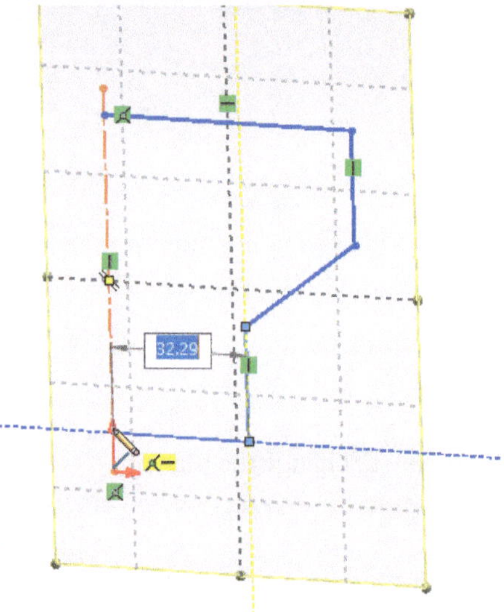

10. Press **Esc** to deactivate the **Line** command.
11. Activate the **Mirror entities** command.
12. Select all the sketch entities.
13. Click in the **Mirror about** selection box, and then select the centreline.
14. Click **OK** to mirror the entities.

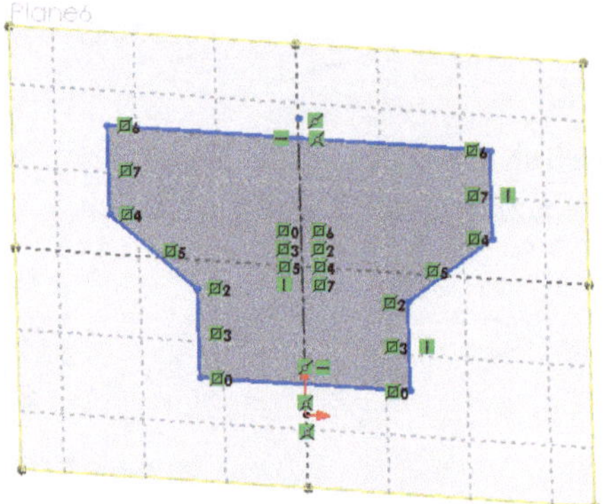

15. Click the **Exit Sketch** icon located at the top right corner of the graphics window.
16. Save and close the part file.

The Slicing command

The **Slicing** command is used to create a sketch using the cross-section at the intersection of a plane and model geometry. This tool is critical for inspecting internal features (e.g., cavities or wall thickness) or reverse engineering complex shapes

1. Download Chapter 5: Sketching files from the companion website.
2. Open the Slicing.sldprt file.
3. On the Menu bar, click **Insert > Slicing** .
4. Select the plane intersecting with the model, as shown.
5. Type 4 in the **Number planes to create** box.
6. Type 20 in the **Offset** box.
7. In the **Options** section, check the **Preview slices (slower)** option to preview the slices.

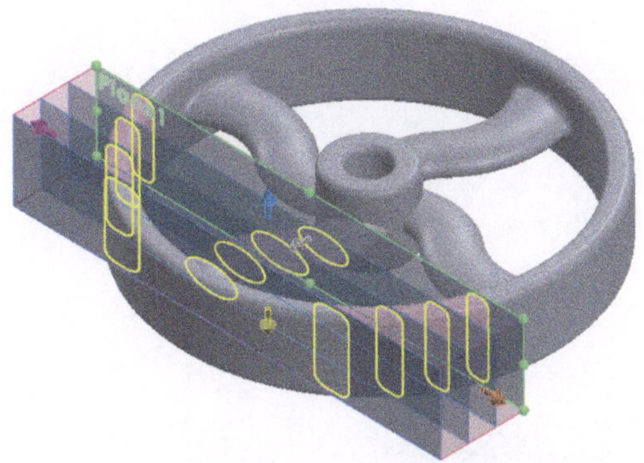

8. Click on the right arrow of the bounding box, and then drag it inside the model.

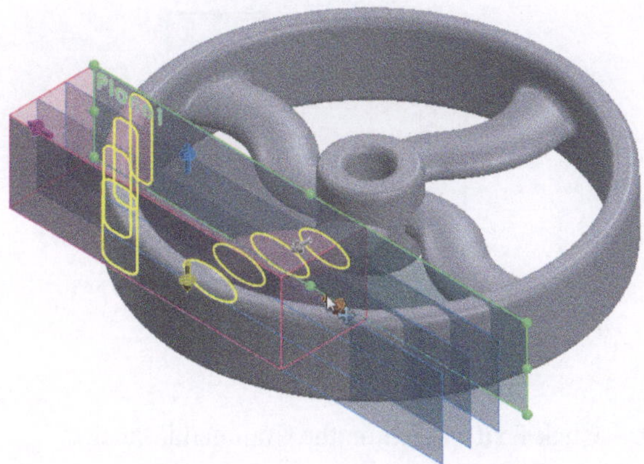

9. Likewise, click and drag the left arrow of the bounding box.

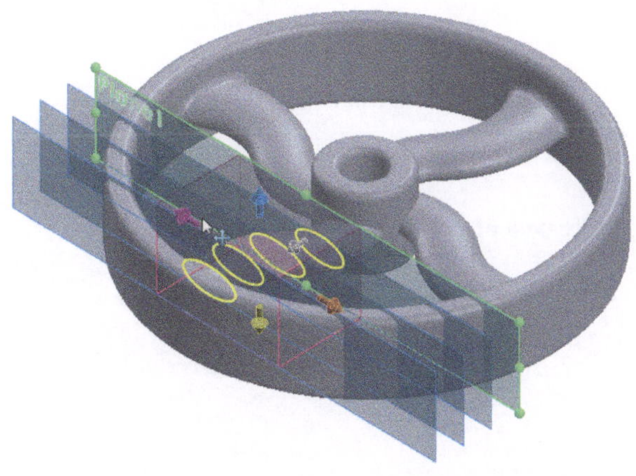

10. Click **OK**.

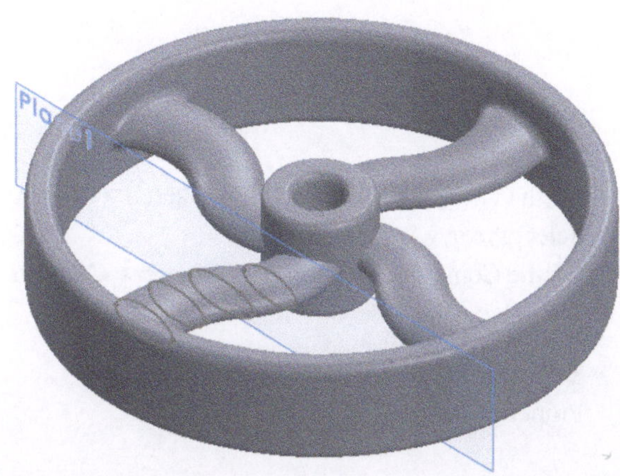

11. Expand the **Slice** folder in the FeatureManager Design Tree, and then notice the sketches and planes created.

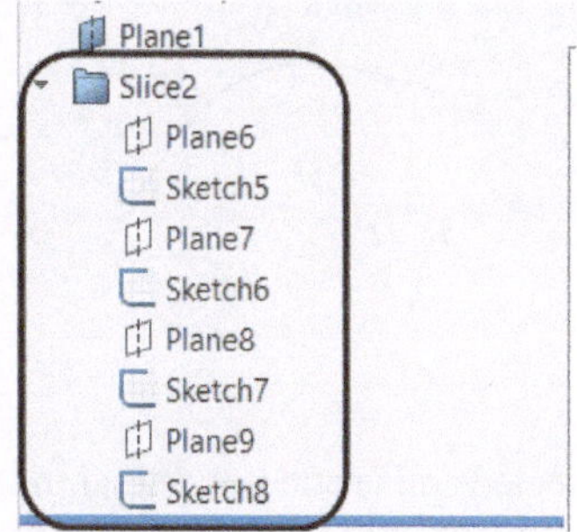

Generic Splines

The generic splines are created when you try to offset or project a spline or create an intersection curve. This makes it easy to edit an entity created by projected or offsetting a spline.

1. Create a spline on the Front plane, as shown.

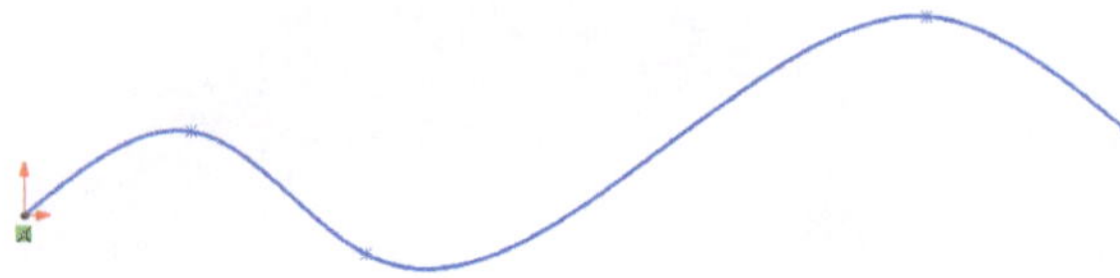

2. Create a plane offset to the Front plane.

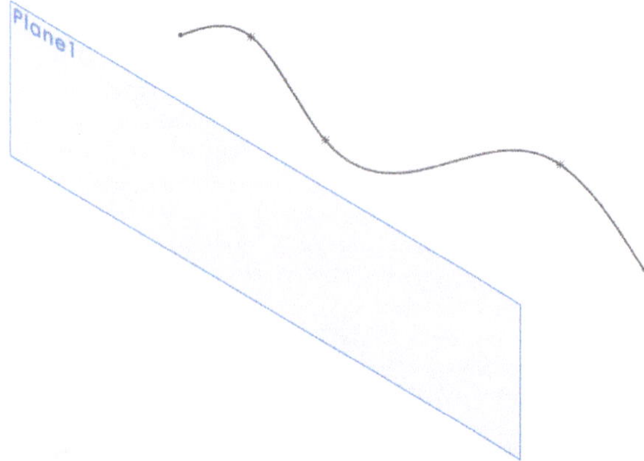

3. On the CommandManager, click **Sketch > Sketch**.
4. Select the newly created plane.
5. On the CommandManger, click **Sketch > Convert Entities**.
6. Select the spline and click **OK** on the PropertyManager.

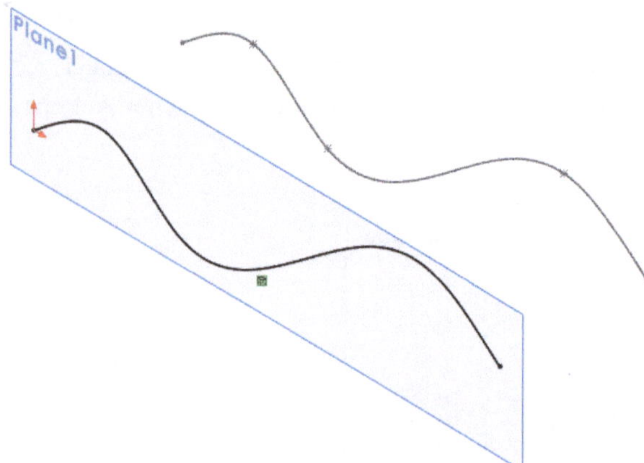

7. Select the projected spline and notice that the **Generic Spline** PropertyManager appears.

On the **Generic Spline** PropertyManager, notice the **On Edge** relation in the **Existing Relations** box.

8. Select the **On Edge** relation in the **Existing Relation** box, and then press **Delete**; the relation is removed, and the generic spline can be edited using the spline editing tools.

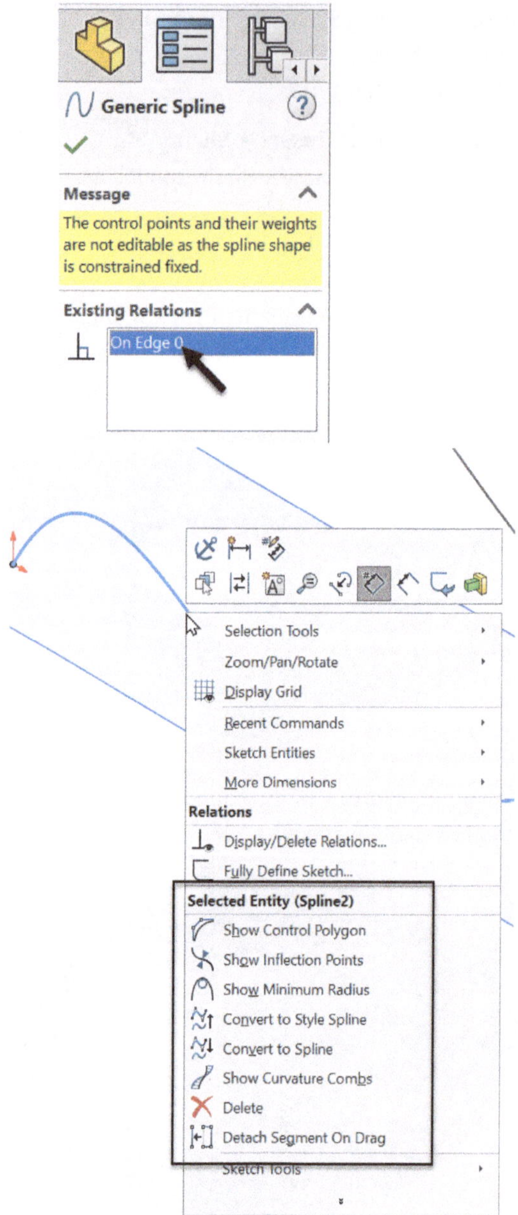

9. Click **Exit Sketch** on the CommandManager.

Creating a 3D Curve using the Project Curve command

The **Project Curve** command allows you to create a 3D curve by projecting a sketch on to a model face. Also, it allows you to create a 3D curve that corresponds to the intersection of two extruded surfaces resulting from sketches on intersecting planes.

1. Create a sphere, as shown.

2. Create a plane offset to the Top plane.

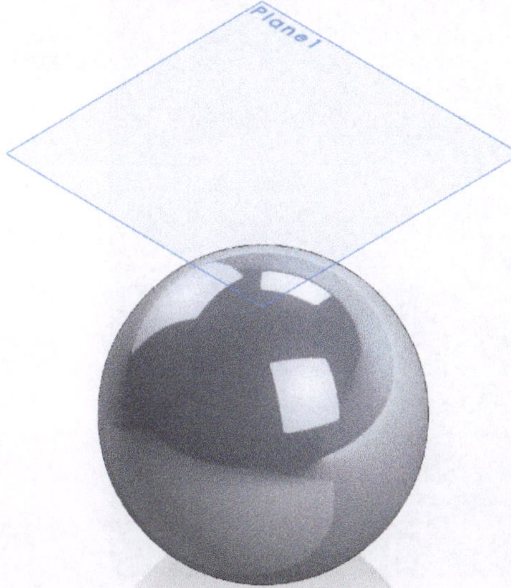

3. On the CommandManager, click **Sketch > Sketch**.
4. Select the newly created plane.
5. Create an ellipse and click **Exit Sketch** on the CommandManager.

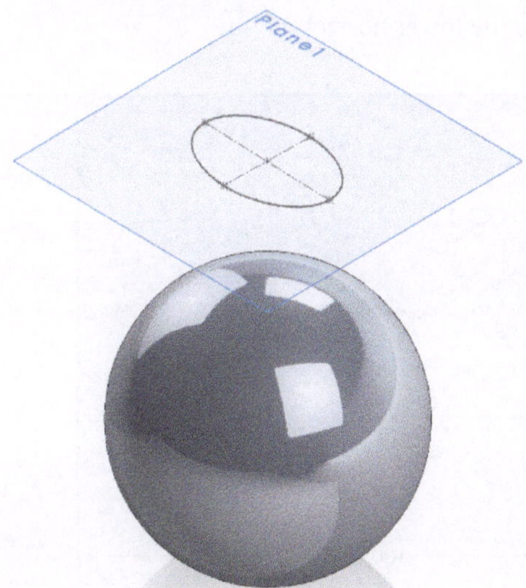

6. On the CommandManager, click **Features** tab > **Insert Curve** drop-down > **Project Curve**.

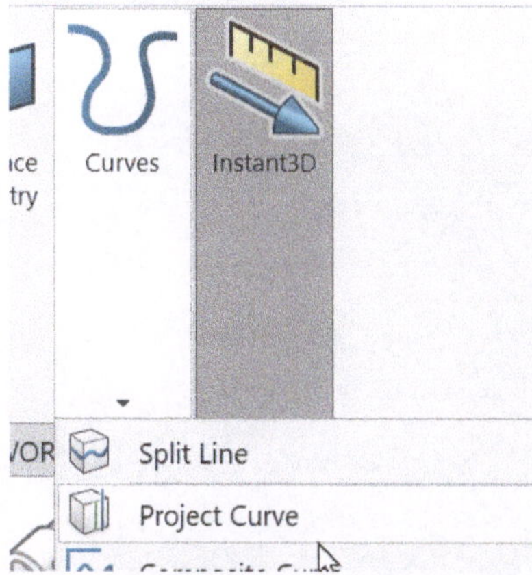

7. On the PropertyManager, select the **Sketch on Faces** option.
8. Select the ellipse from the graphics window.
9. Select the sphere from the graphics window; the ellipse is projected on to the sphere.

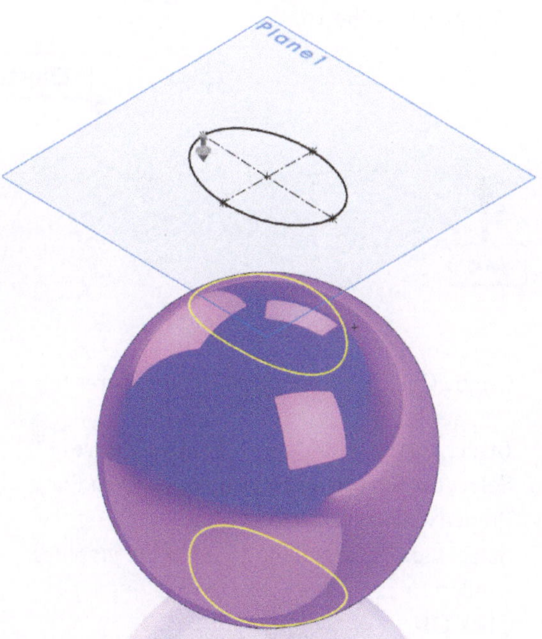

10. Click **OK** to create the projected curve.

Creating a 3D Curve from two sketches

1. Create an ellipse on the Front plane and an arc on the Top plane, as shown.

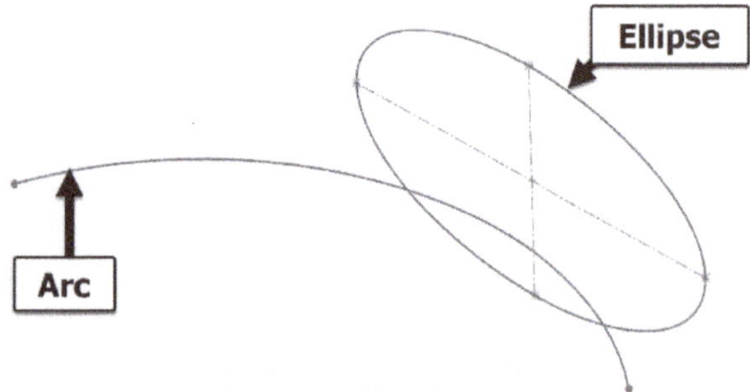

2. On the CommandManager, click **Features** tab >

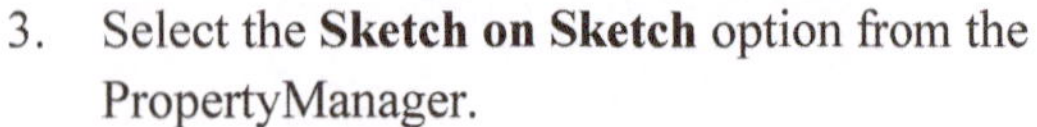

Insert Curve drop-down > **Project Curve** .
3. Select the **Sketch on Sketch** option from the PropertyManager.
4. Select the ellipse and the arc from the graphics window.
5. Click **OK**.

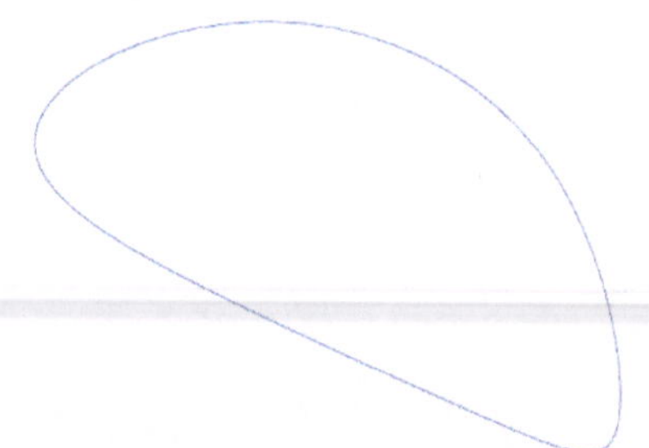

Repairing Dangling Relations

Solidworks provides two options to repair dangling relations: **Find Replacement** and **Repair All Dangling**. These options are available in the **Display/Delete Relations** PropertyManager.

1. Create a rectangular sketch on the top face of the blocks, as shown.

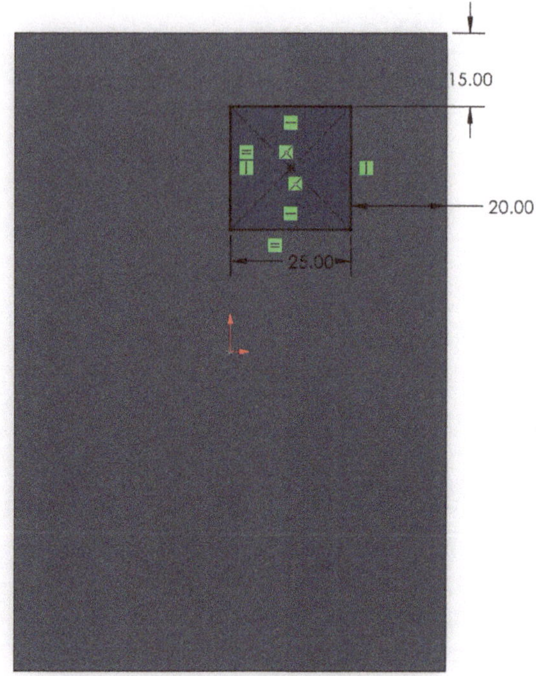

2. Click **Exit Sketch** on the **Sketch** tab of the CommandManager.
3. Click the right-mouse button on the first Boss-Extrude feature and select **Edit Sketch**.
4. Delete the lower horizontal line.

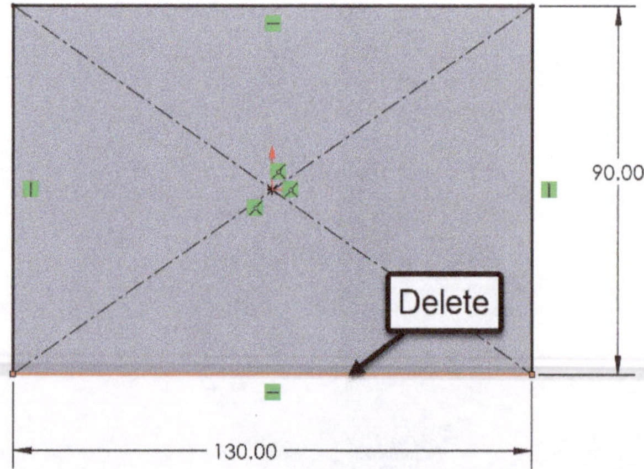

5. Add line segments to the sketch and dimension them.

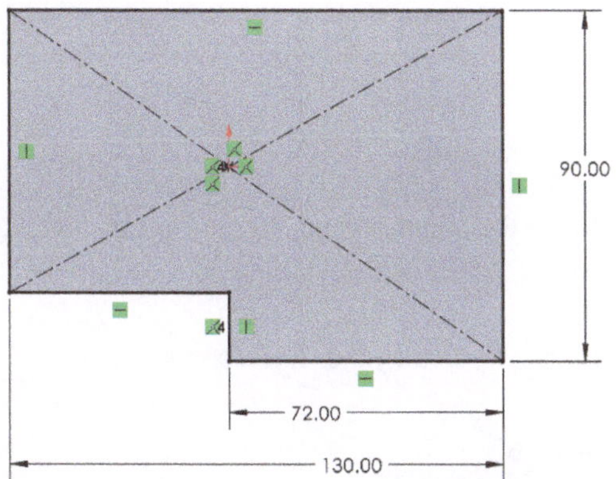

6. Click **Exit Sketch**; the **What's Wrong** message box appears.

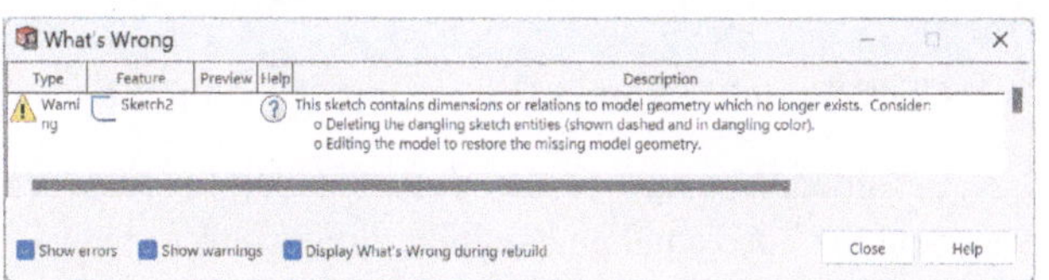

7. Click **Close** button.
8. Right-click on the sketch with the error, and then select **Edit sketch**.

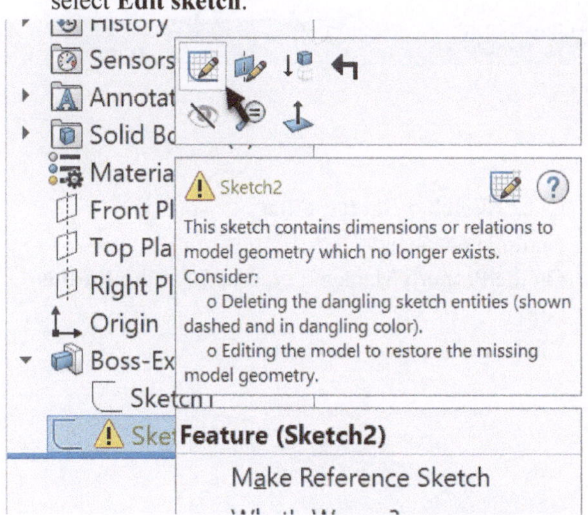

9. Right-click on the dangling dimension and click the **Auto Repair Sketch Relation or Dimension** icon.

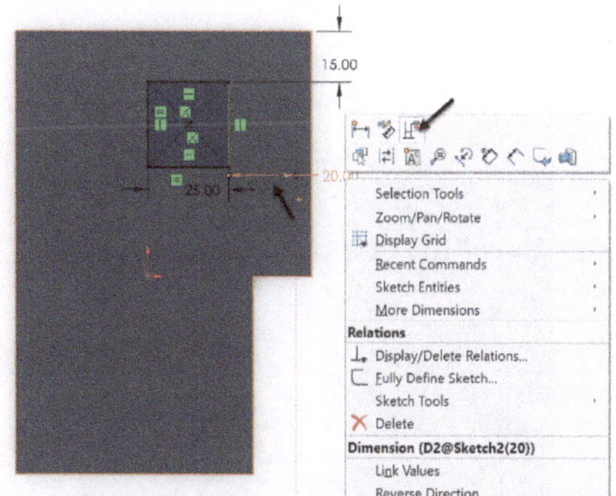

Thee SOLIDWORKS message box appears showing that **No references found for repair**.

10. Click **OK**.
11. Click and drag the dangling dimension downward.
12. To attach the dangling dimension, click and drag its dimension handle and drop it onto the vertical edge. This will anchor the dimension to the edge and resolve the dangling state.

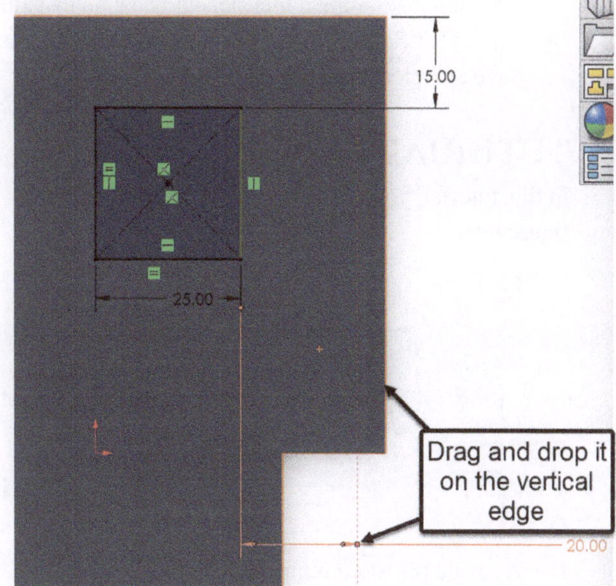

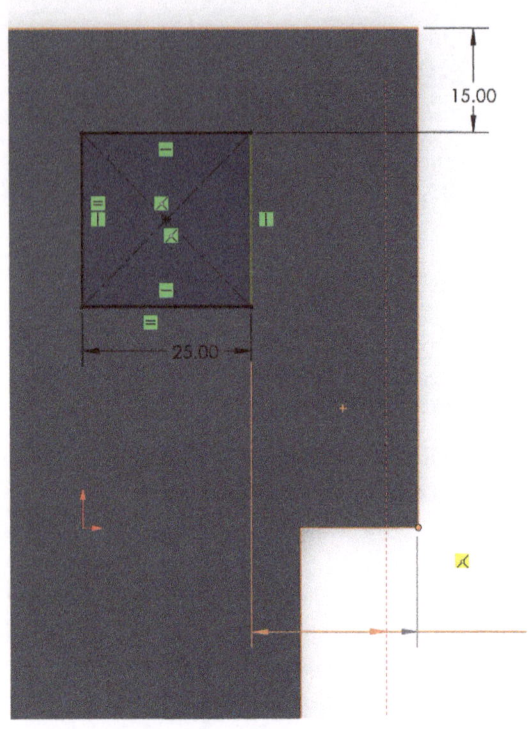

13. Double-click on the dimension and change its value,
14. Click **Exit Sketch** on the CommandManager.
15. Save and close the file.

TUTORIAL 2

In this tutorial, you create the sketch, as shown in the figure next.

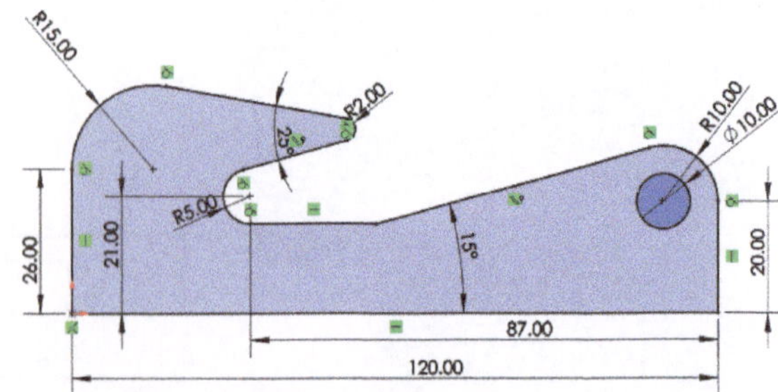

1. Activate the **Sketch** mode.
2. On the CommandManager, click **Sketch > Line**.
3. Click on the origin point to define the start point of the line.
4. Move the pointer horizontally toward the right and click.

5. Move the pointer upward and click when a dotted line appears.

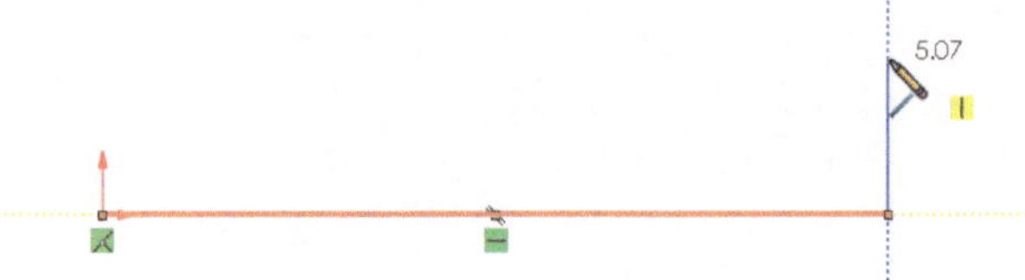

6. Move the pointer diagonally toward bottom right corner, as shown. Next, click to create an inclined line.
7. Likewise, create other lines, as shown.

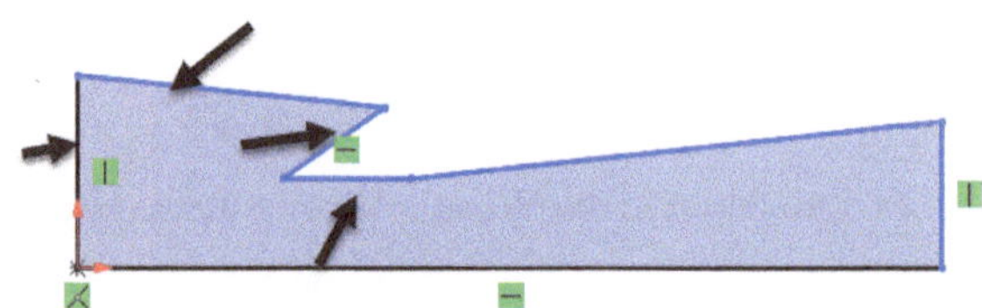

8. Click **Sketch > Smart Dimension**  on the CommandManager to start dimensioning the sketch.
9. Add the horizontal and angular dimensions to the sketch as illustrated. Refer to the previous sections for instructions on applying dimensions.

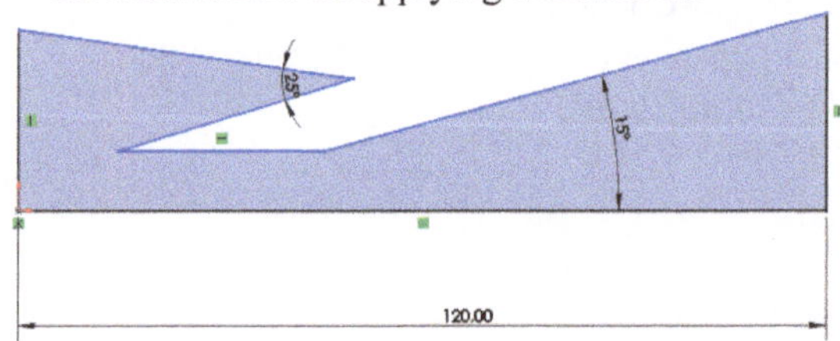

10. Click **Sketch > Sketch Fillet** on the CommandManager.
11. On the PropertyManager, type-in 10 in the **Radius** box.
12. Click on the corner, as shown.

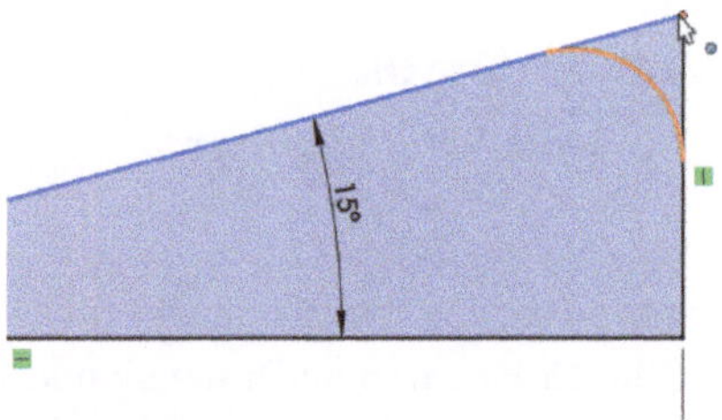

13. Click **OK** on the PropertyManager.
14. On the PropertyManager, type-in **15** in the **Radius** box.
15. Click top-left corner, as shown.

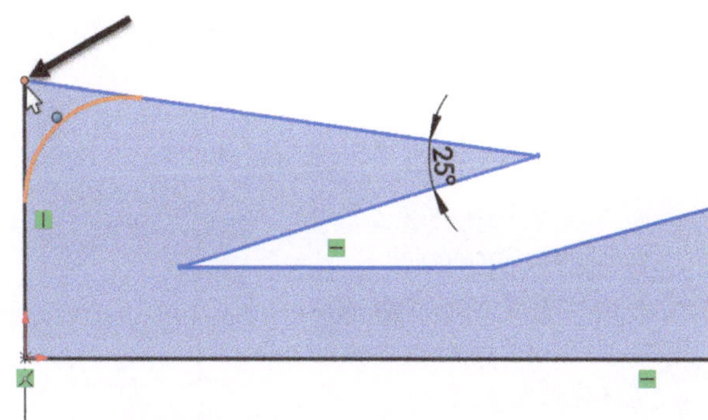

16. Likewise, create two more fillets, as shown. Next, click **Close** on the PropertyManager.

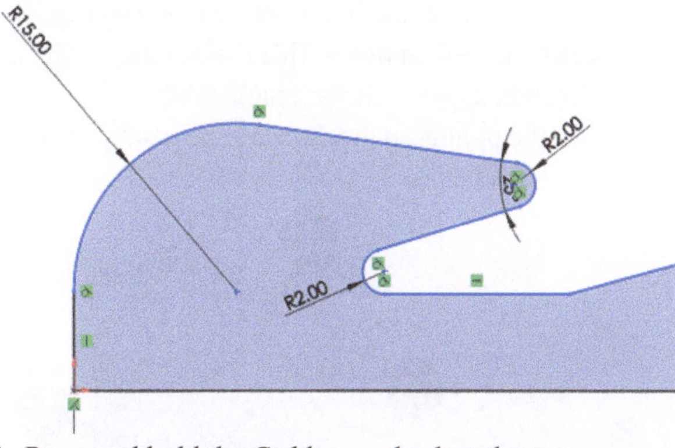

17. Press and hold the Ctrl key and select the two inclined lines, as shown. Next, click the **Parallel** icon on the PropertyManager.

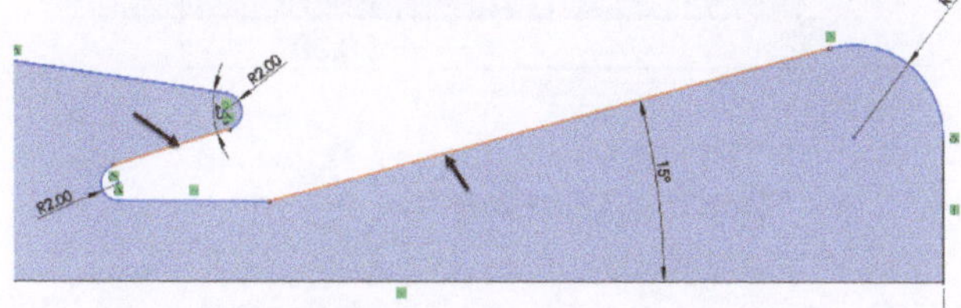

18. On the CommandManager, click **Sketch > Circle**, and then select the center point of the fillet, as show. Move the pointer outward and click to create the circle.

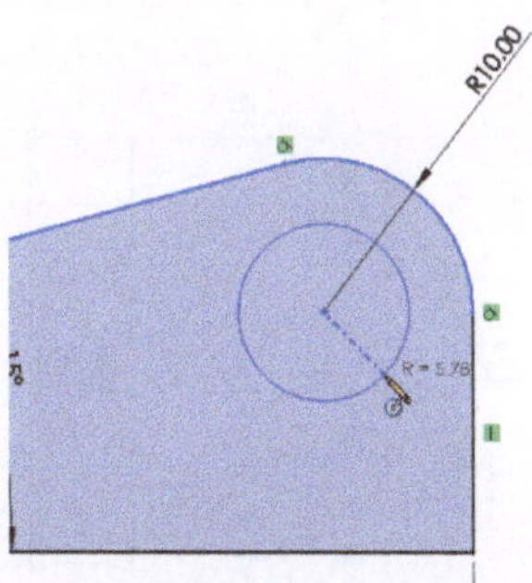

19. Click **Sketch > Smart Dimension** on the CommandManager and add dimensions to the sketch, as shown.

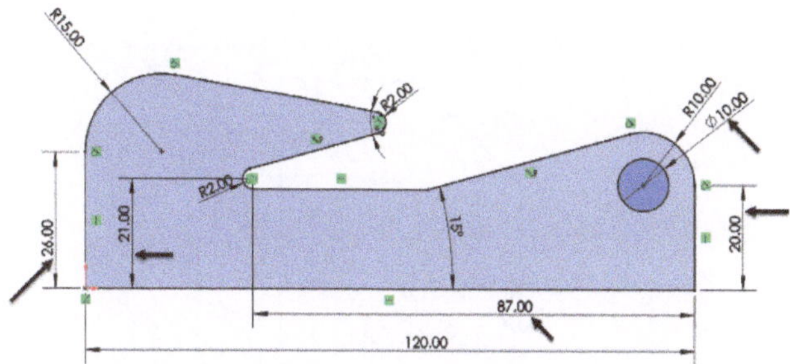

20. Double-click on the radius dimension of the arc, as shown. Next, type **5** in the **Modify** box and click the green check.

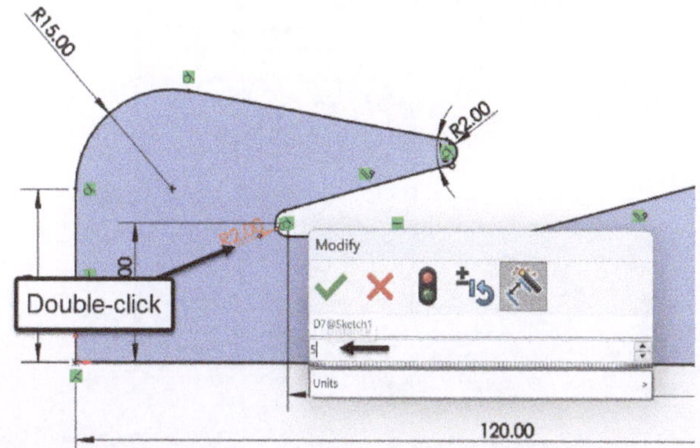

21. Exit the sketch.

TUTORIAL 3

In this tutorial, you create the sketch shown in the figure next.

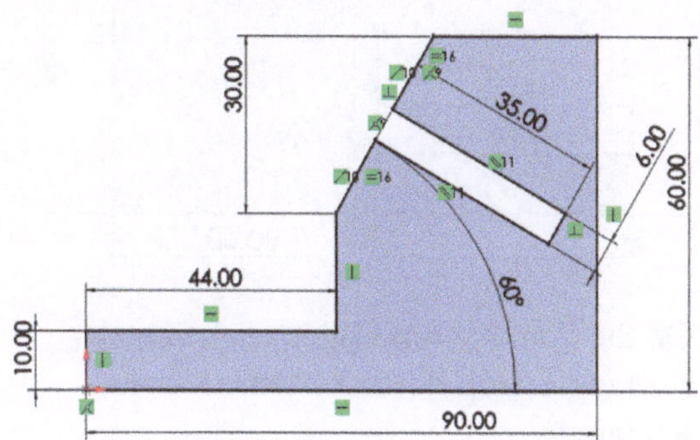

1. On the CommandManager, click **Sketch > Sketch.**
2. Select the Right plane from the graphics window. On the CommandManager, click **Sketch > Line.**
3. Select the sketch origin and move the pointer horizontal toward right.
4. Move the pointer vertically upward and click.

5. Move the pointer horizontally toward left and click.
6. Move the pointer diagonally toward bottom left corner and click.
7. Move the pointer downward and click.

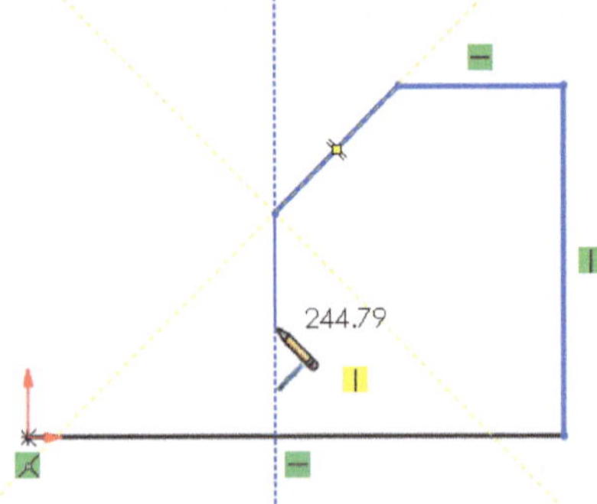

8. Likewise, create the remaining lines, as shown.

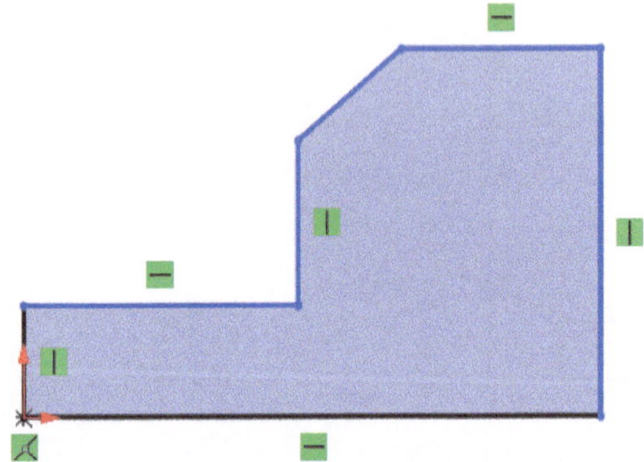

9. Add dimensions to the sketch, as shown.

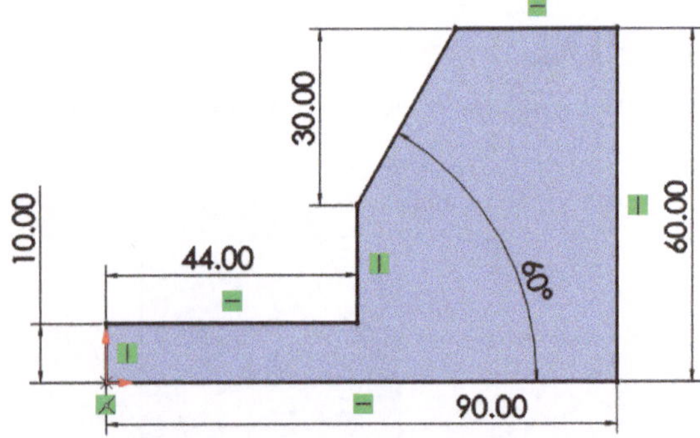

10. On the CommandManager, click **Sketch > Rectangle** drop-down **> 3 Point Corner Rectangle**.

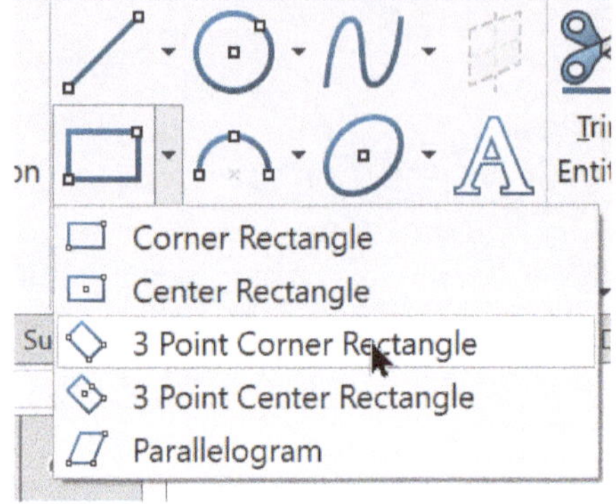

11. Click on the inclined line.
12. Move the pointer along the inclined line and click to specify the second point. This defines the width and inclination angle of the rectangle.
13. Move the pointer in the direction perpendicular to the inclined and click.

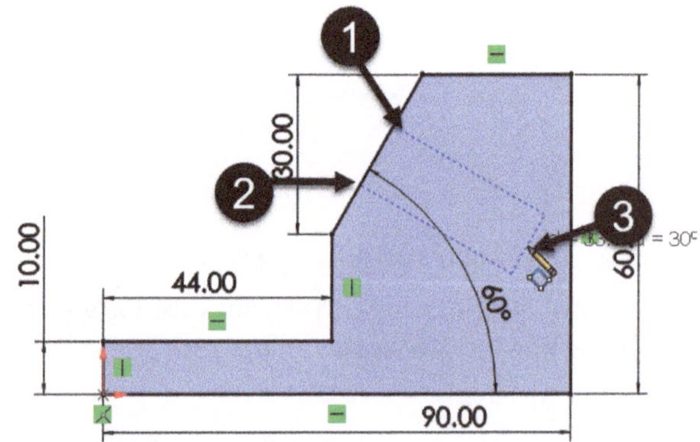

14. Click **Sketch > Trim Entities** on the CommandManager.
15. On the PropertyManager, click the **Power trim** icon.
16. Press and hold the left mouse button and drag the pointer across the width of the rectangle, as shown.

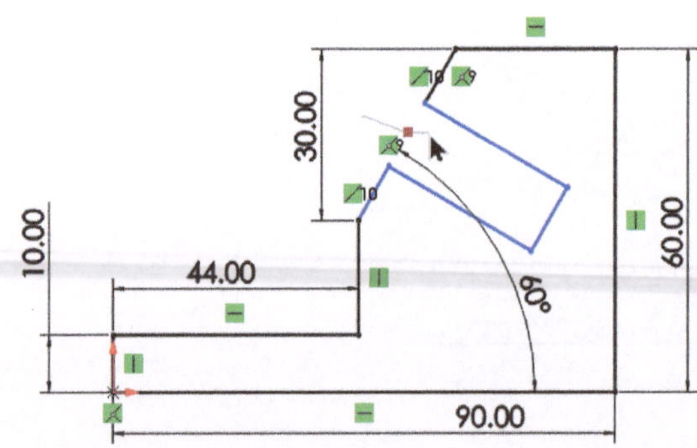

17. Add dimensions to the inclined lines, as shown.

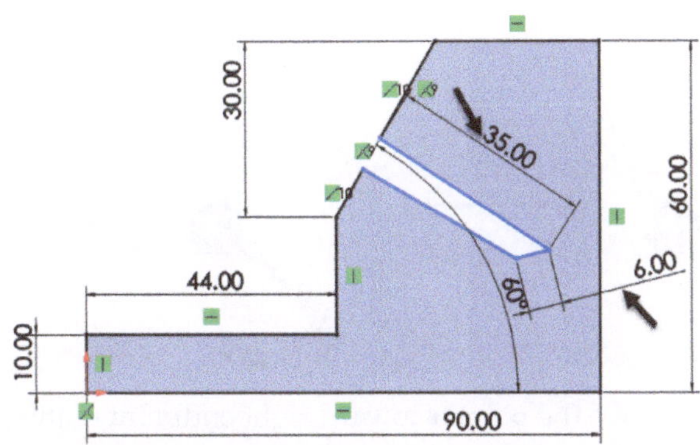

18. Press and hold the Ctrl key and select the two lines, as shown. Next, click the **Parallel** icon on the PropertyManager.

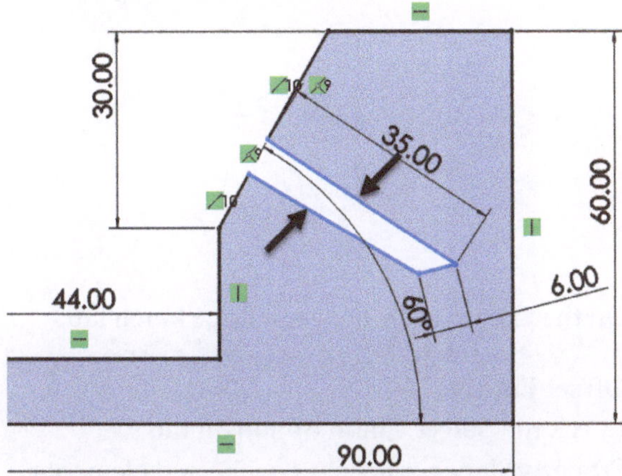

19. Press and hold the Ctrl key and select the two lines, as shown. Next, click the **Pependicular** icon on the PropertyManager.

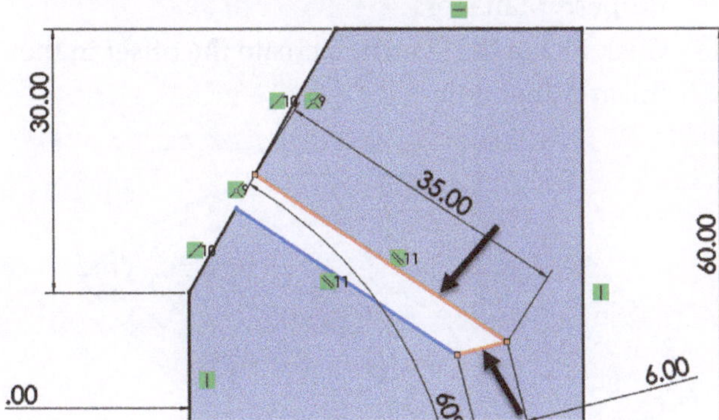

20. Press and hold the Ctrl key and select the two lines, as shown. Next, click the **Pependicular** icon on the PropertyManager.

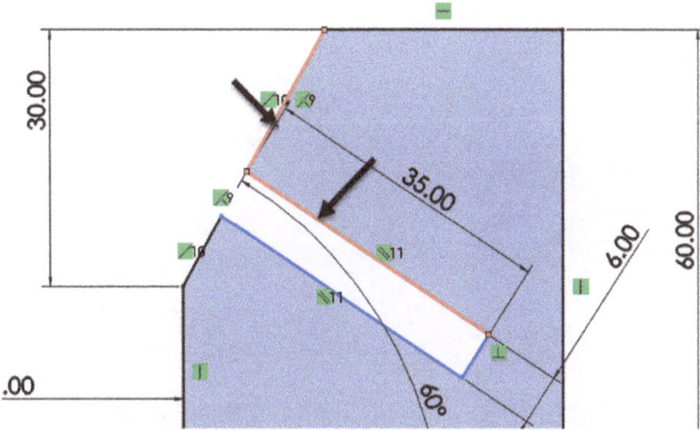

21. Press and hold the Ctrl key and select the two lines, as shown. Next, click the **Equal** icon on the PropertyManager.

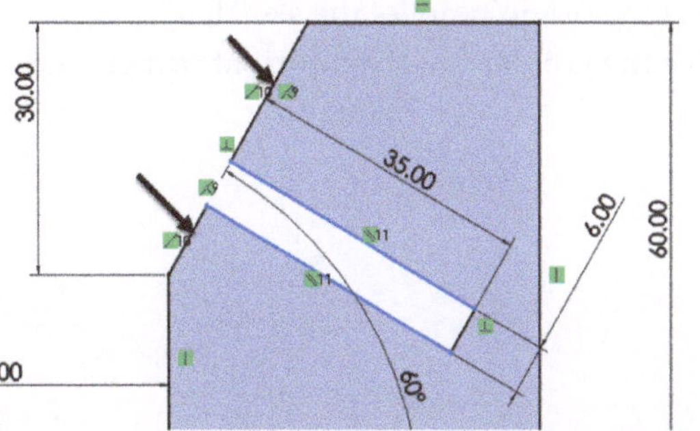

22. Click the **Exit Sketch** on the CommandManager.

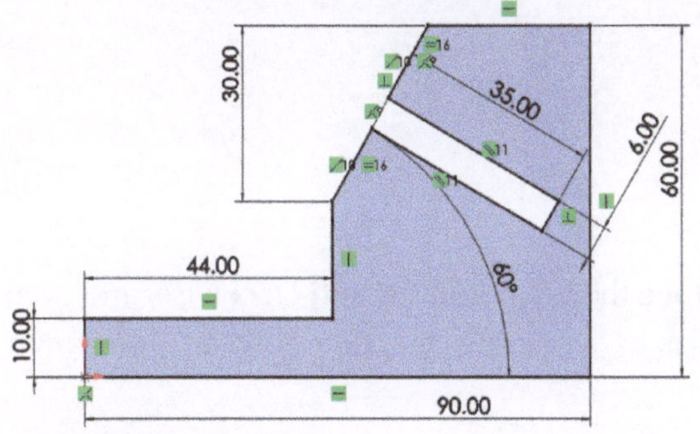

TUTORIAL 4

In this tutorial, you create the sketch, as shown in the figure next.

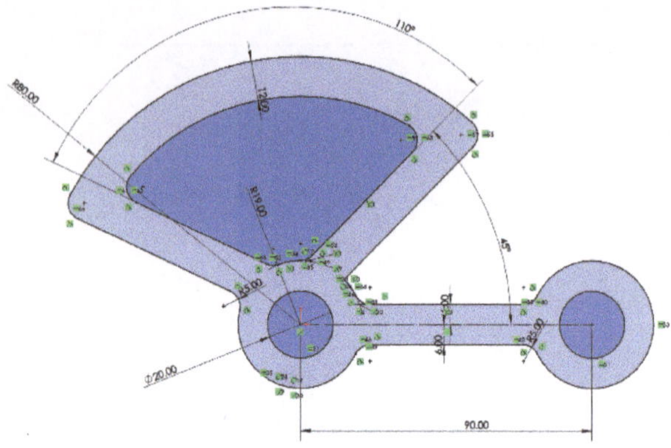

1. Activate the **Sketch** mode.
2. On the CommandManager, click **Sketch** tab > **Arc** drop-down > **Centerpoint Arc**.
3. Select the origin point of the sketch.
4. Move the pointer toward top-right corner, and then specify the start point of the arc, as shown.

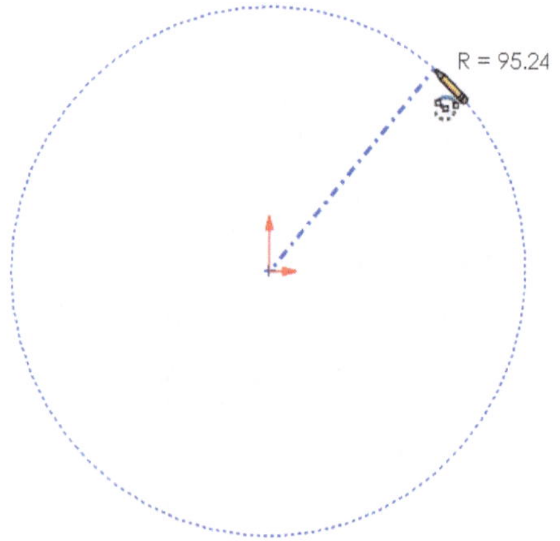

5. Move the pointer in the anti-clockwise, and then click to define the end point of the arc, as shown.

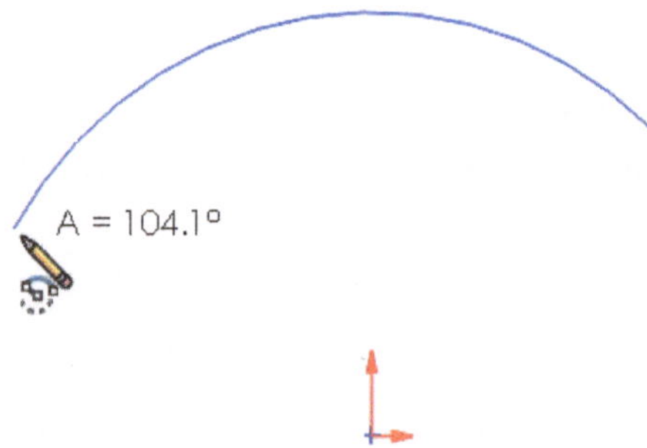

6. On the CommandManager, click **Sketch > Line** .
7. Select the endpoint of the arc, as shown.
8. Move the pointer toward right and select the sketch origin.

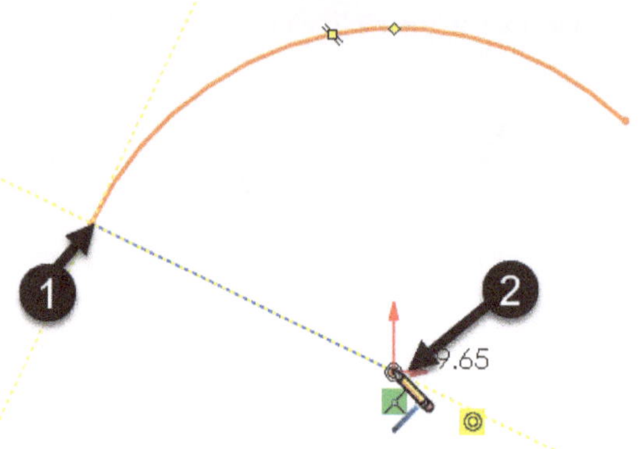

9. Move the pointer toward right endpoint of the arc.

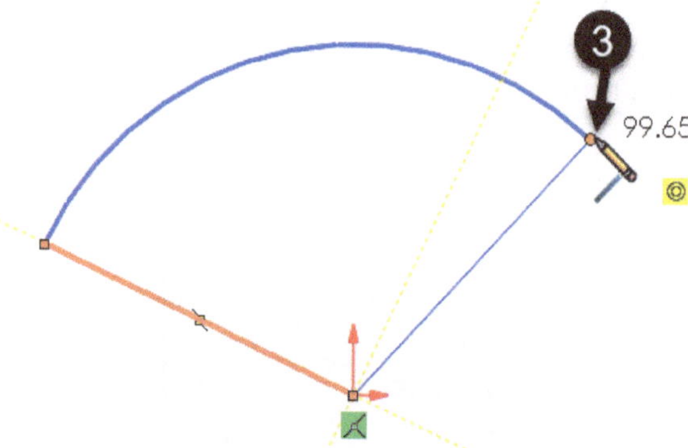

10. On the CommandManager, click **Sketch** tab > **Offset Entities** .
11. Check the **Select Chain** option on the PropertyManager to select connected elements.
12. Select an entity and notice that all the connected entities are selected.
13. Type-in **12** in the **Offset Distance** on the PropertyManager.
14. Click inside the sketch to create the offset in the inward direction.

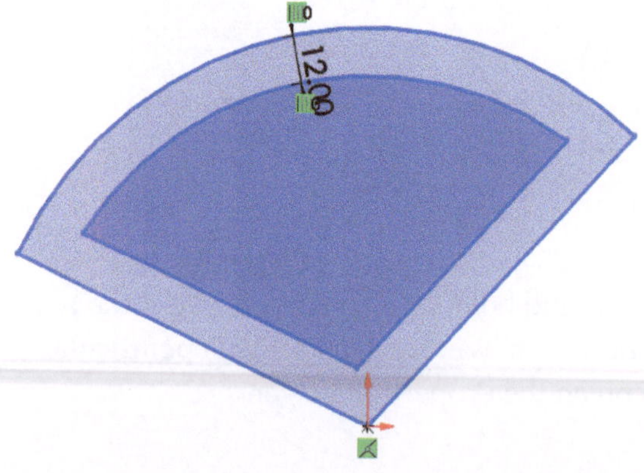

15. On the CommandManager, click **Sketch > Circle**.
16. Select the sketch origin, move the pointer outward and click.
17. Likewise, create another circle concentric to the first one.

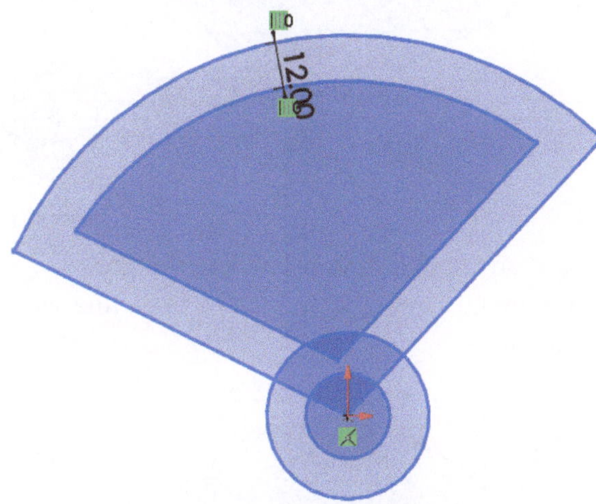

18. On the CommandManager, click **Sketch > Line** .
19. Move the pointer horizontally toward right and click.
20. On the CommandManager, click **Sketch > Circle**.
21. Select the endpoint of the line, move the pointer outward and click.
22. Likewise, create another circle concentric to the first one.

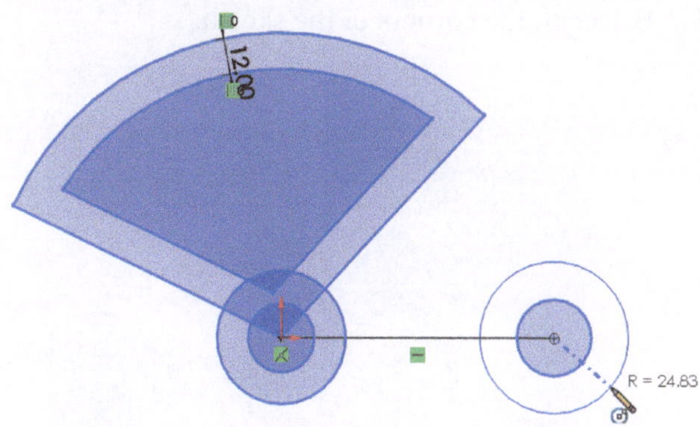

23. On the CommandManager, click **Sketch** tab > **Offset Entities** .
24. Select the newly created horizontal line.
25. Type-in **6** in the **Offset Distance** on the PropertyManager.
26. Check the **Bi-directional** option.
27. Check the **Base geometry** option under the **Construction geometry** section.

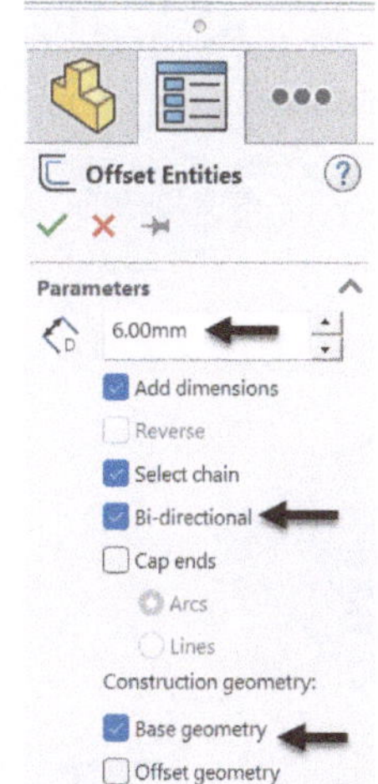

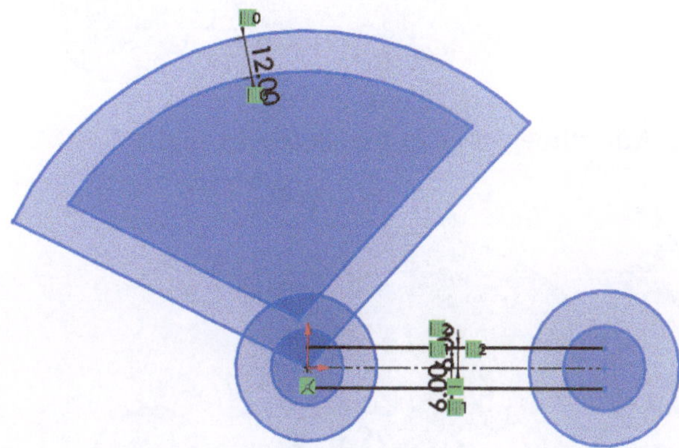

29. On the CommandManager, click **Sketch > Trim Entities** .
30. Click the **Trim to Closest** icon on the PropertyManager.
28. Click on the entities to trim, as shown.

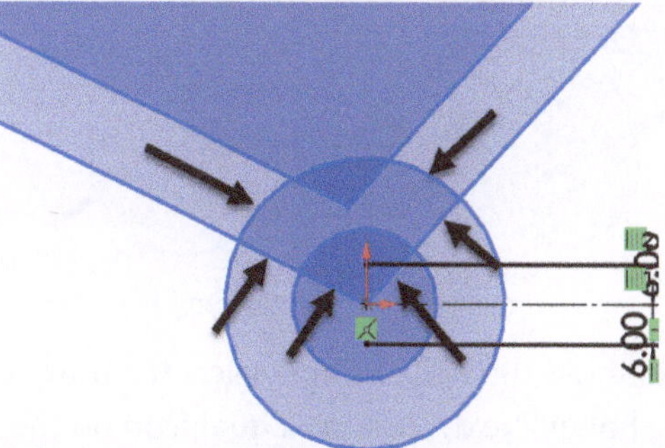

29. Click on the entities to trim, as shown.

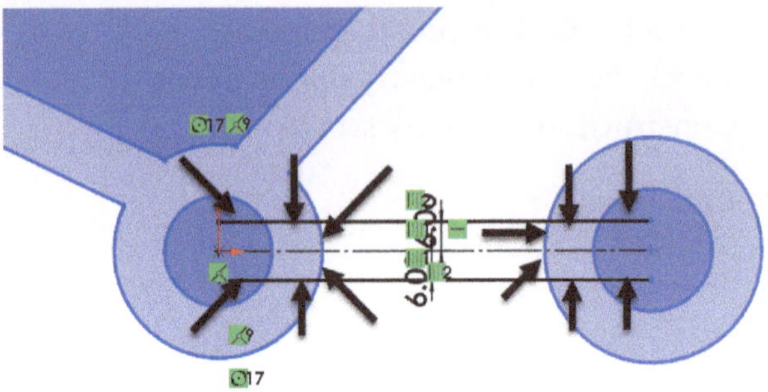

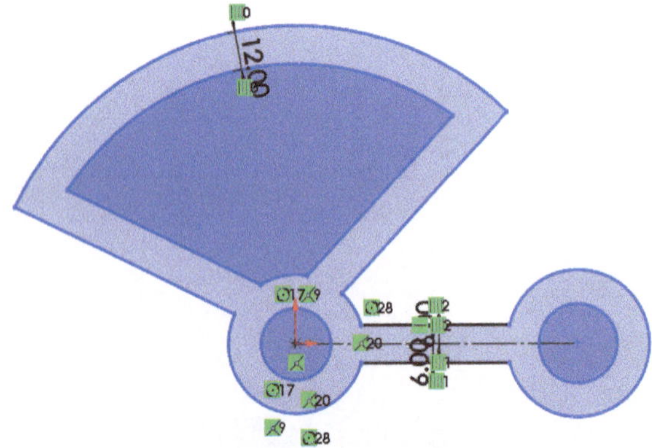

30. Add dimensions to the sketch, as shown.

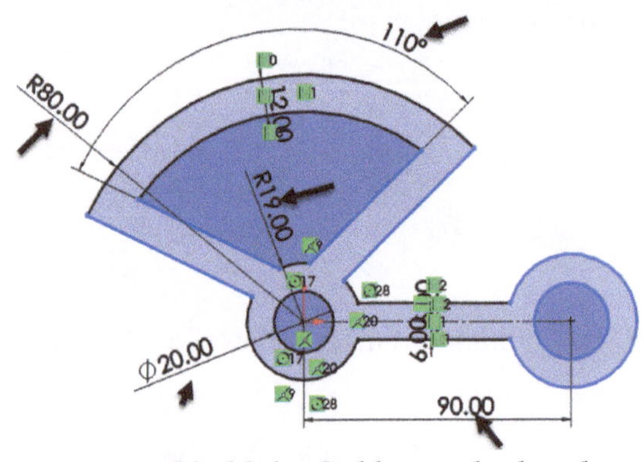

31. Press and hold the Ctrl key and select the two circles, as shown. Next, click the **Equal** icon on the PropertyManager.

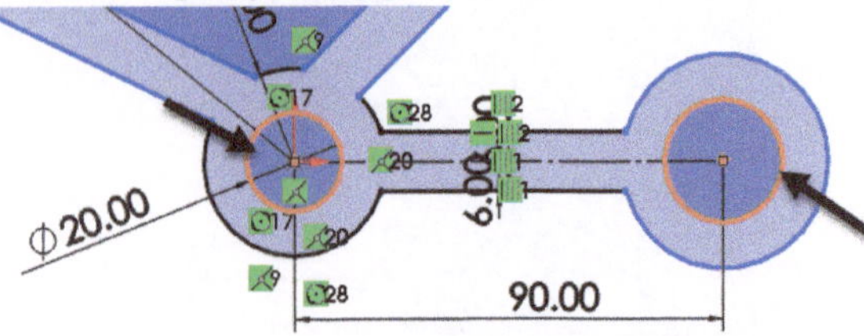

32. Press and hold the Ctrl key and select the four arcs, as shown. Next, click the **Equal** icon on the PropertyManager.

33. 

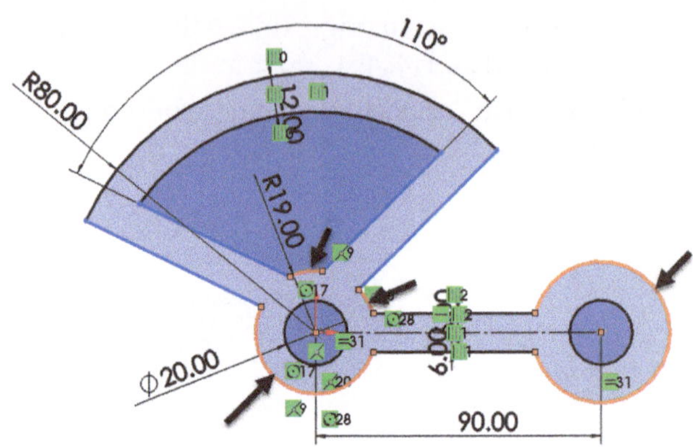

34. Add an angular dimension between the horizontal centerline and the inclined line, as shown.

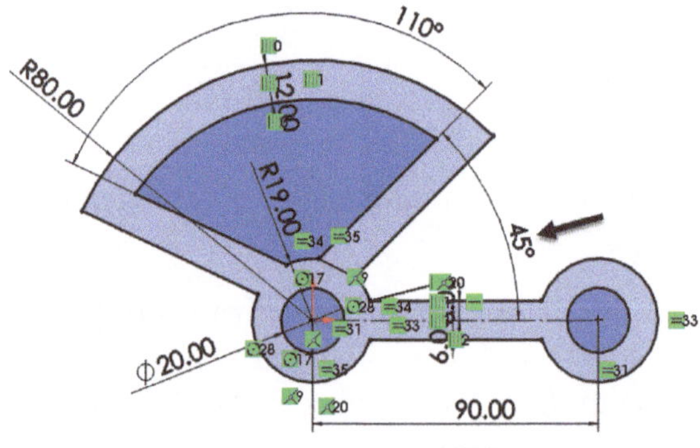

35. Click **Sketch > Sketch Fillet** on the CommandManager.
36. On the PropertyManager, type-in **5** in the **Radius** box.
37. Select all the corners of the sketch.

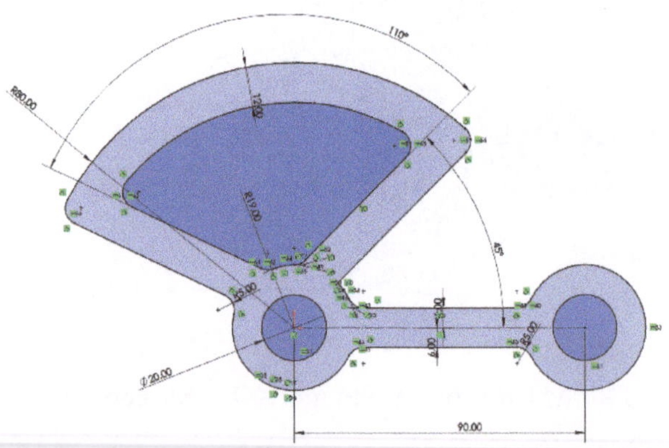

38. Click **Exit Sketch**.

Chapter 6: Additional Modeling Tools

In this chapter, you construct models using additional modeling tools. You will learn to:

- Construct Helixes
- Add Reference Planes
- Construct Swept features
- Construct Revolved Cuts
- Mirror Features
- Construct Loft features
- Create multibody parts
- Add Indent Features
- Shell Models
- Create Helical threads
- Construct rib features
- Insert Holes
- Create Patterns

TUTORIAL 1

In this tutorial, you construct the model shown in the figure.

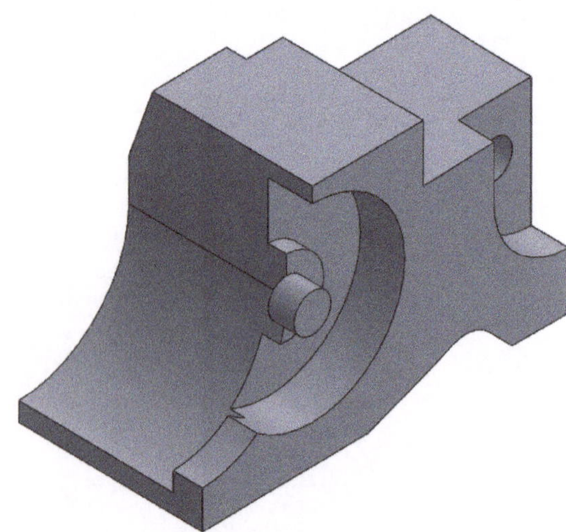

Creating the Extruded Base Feature

1. Open a new SOLIDWORKS part file.
2. Click **Sketch > Sketch** on the CommandManager.
3. Select the Right Plane.
4. Click the **Rectangle** drop-down > **Corner Rectangle** on the **Sketch** tab of the CommandManager.
5. Specify the first and second corners of the rectangle, as shown.

6. Create another rectangle by specifying its first and second corners, as shown.

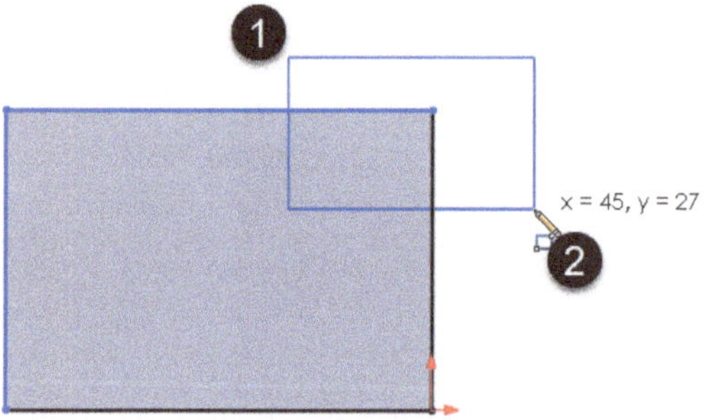

7. Click **Trim Entities** on the **Sketch** tab of the CommandManager.
8. Click the **Trim to closest** icon on the PropertyManager.
9. Select the elements of the rectangles to be trimmed, as shown.

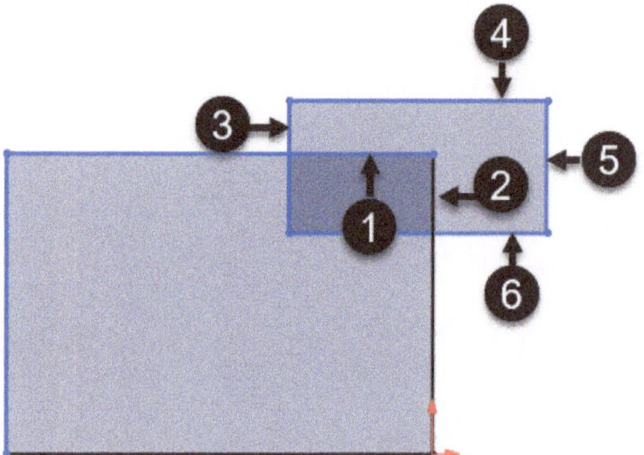

10. Add vertical and horizontal dimensions to the sketch, as shown.

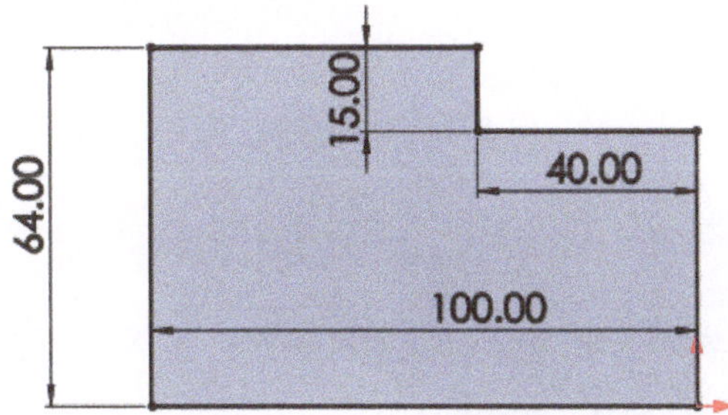

11. Click **Exit Sketch** on the **Sketch** tab of the Command Manager.
12. Click the **Extruded Boss/Base** icon on the **Features** tab of the Command Manager; the sketch is selected automatically.
13. Type 50 in the **Depth** box.
14. Select the **Mid Plane** option from the **End Condition** drop-down.
15. Click **OK**.

Creating the Extruded Cut Features

1. Click **Sketch > Sketch** on the CommandManager.
2. Select the Right Plane.

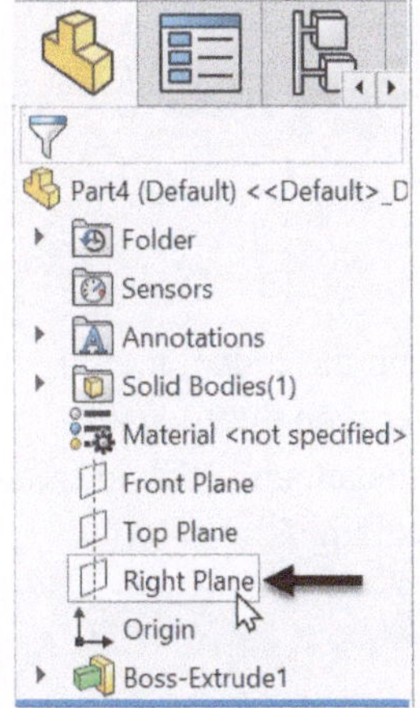

3. Click the **Line** icon on the **Sketch** tab of the CommandManager.
4. Specify the endpoints of the line, as shown.

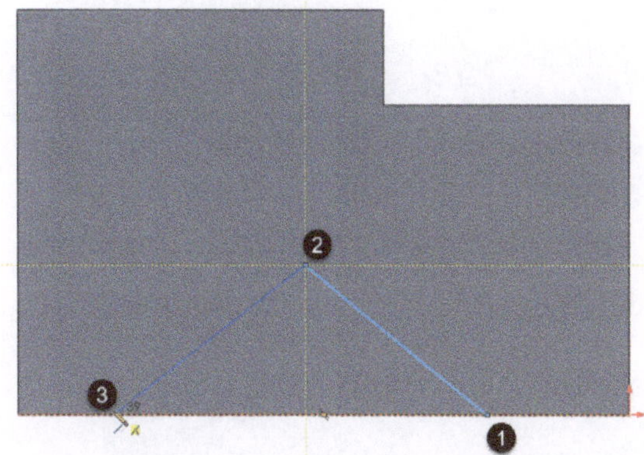

5. Press **Esc**.
6. Click the **Sketch Fillet** icon on the **Sketch** tab of the CommandManager.
7. Select the corner point of the sketch, as shown.
8. Type **10** in the **Fillet Radius** box, and then click **OK**.

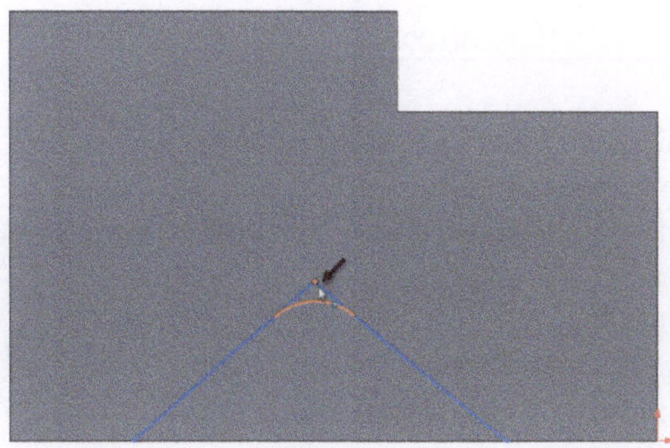

9. Click the **Smart Dimension** icon on the **Sketch** tab of the CommandManager.
10. Select the inclined line and the horizontal edge.
11. Move the pointer between the selected entities, and then click.

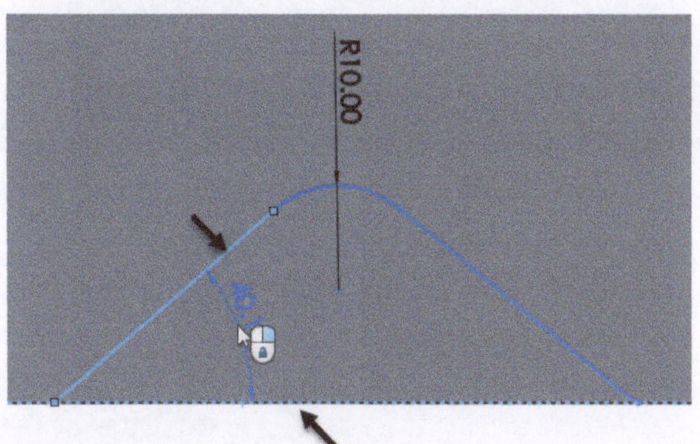

12. Type **20** and click **OK**.
13. Select the other inclined line and the horizontal edge.

14. Type **45** and click **OK**.

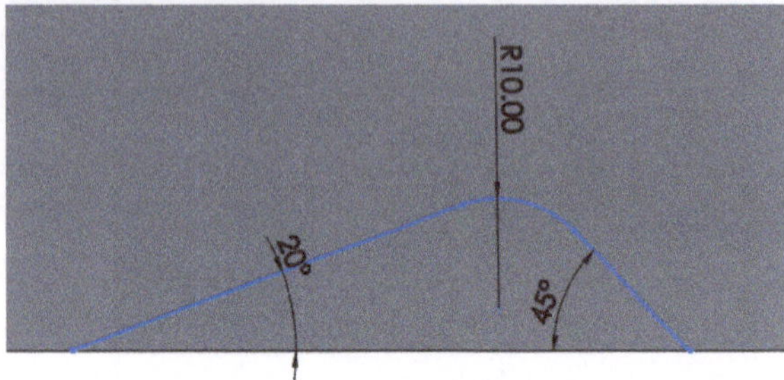

15. Add horizontal dimensions to the sketch, as shown.

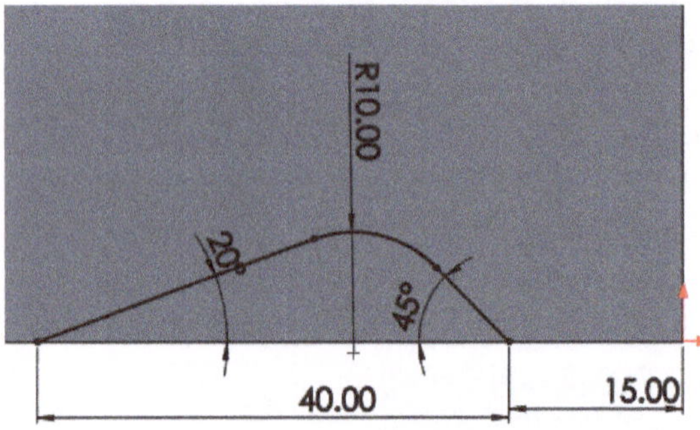

16. Click **Exit Sketch** on the **Sketch** tab of the Command Manager.
17. Click the **Extruded Cut** icon on the **Features** tab of the Command Manager; the sketch is selected automatically.
18. On the **Cut – Extrude** PropertyManager, select **End Condition > Through all - Both**.
19. Make sure that the arrow on the sketch is pointing inside. The arrow appears when the selected sketch is open. It defines the side on which the material will be removed.

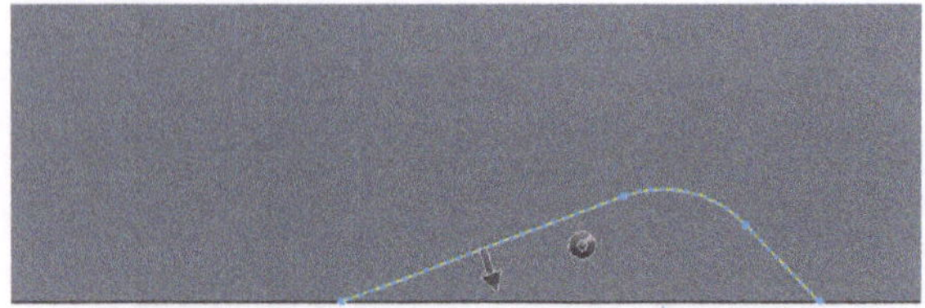

20. Click **OK** to create the extruded cut feature.
21. Press CTRL+7 on your keyboard to change the view orientation to Isometric.

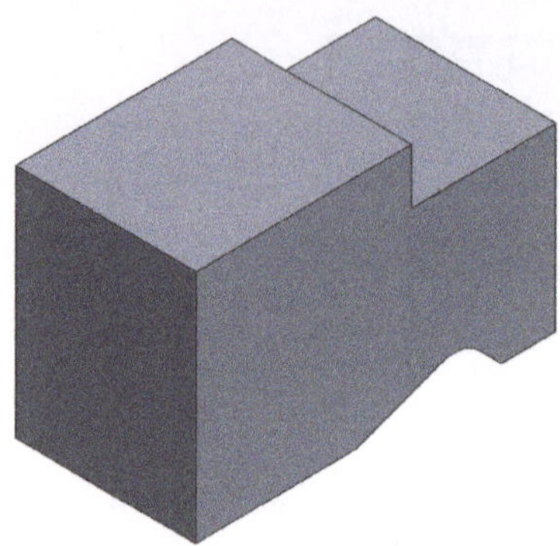

22. Click on the right-side face of the model.
23. Click **Sketch > Sketch** on the CommandManager.
24. Click the **Line** icon on the **Sketch** tab of the CommandManager.
25. Select the corner point of the model, as shown.

26. Move the pointer vertically downward, and then click to create the vertical line.

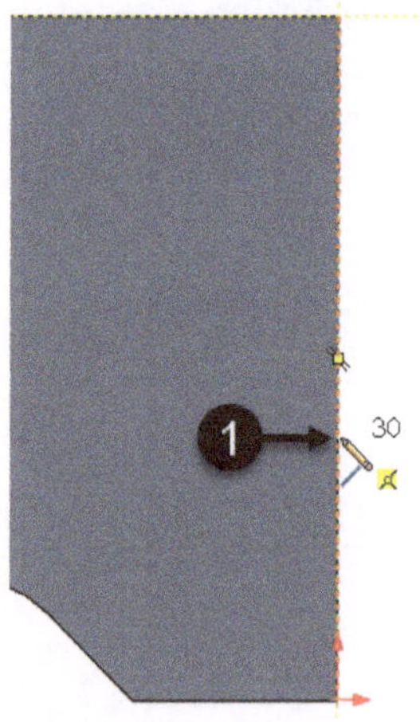

27. Move the pointer away from the endpoint.
28. Move the pointer and hover it on the endpoint.
29. Move the pointer toward the left and click to create an arc normal to the vertical line.

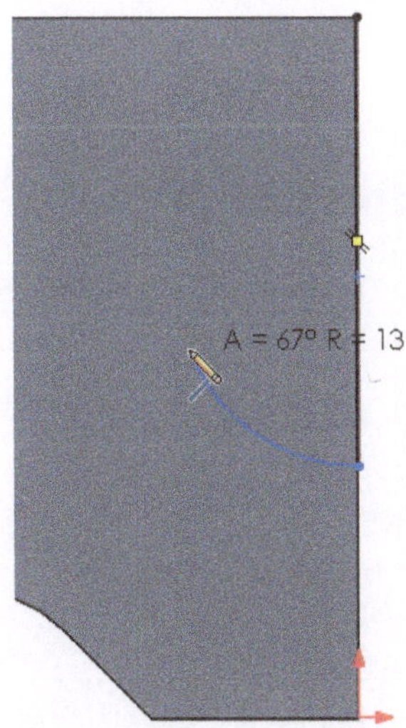

30. Move the pointer vertically upward and click on the horizontal edge.

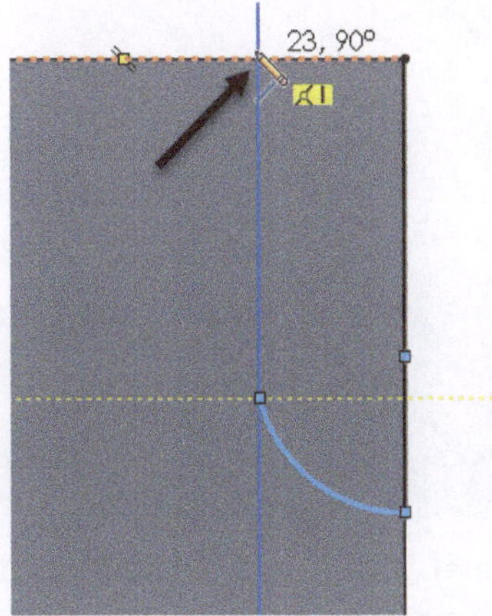

31. Move the pointer toward the right and select the start point of the sketch.

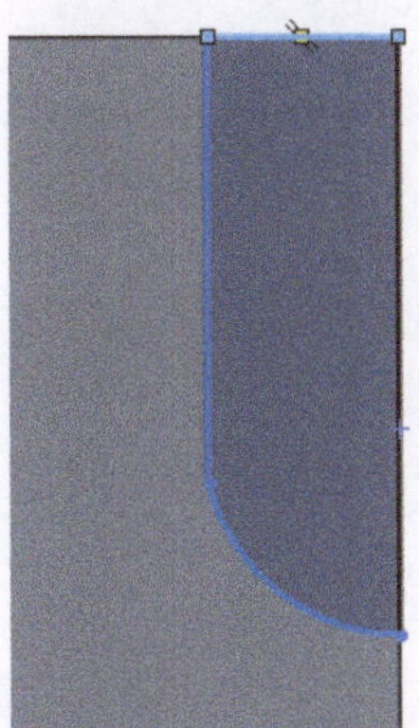

32. Press **Esc**.
33. Press and hold the Ctrl key, and then select the left vertical line and the arc.

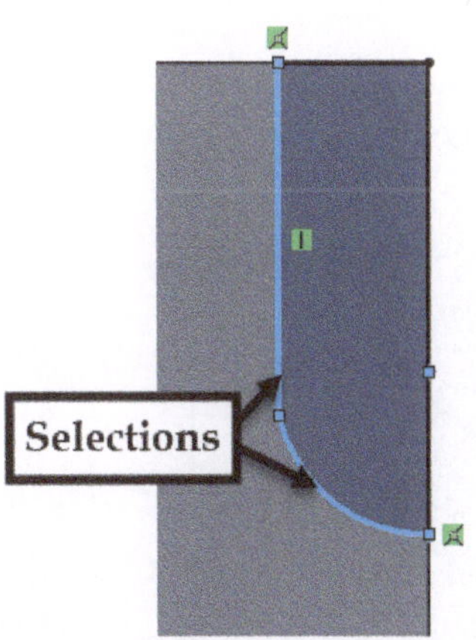

34. Click the **Tangent** icon on the **Add Relations** section of the **Properties** manager.
35. Click the **Smart Dimension** icon on the **Sketch** tab of the CommandManager.
36. Select the arc.
37. Place the dimension.
38. Type **20** and click **OK**.
39. Select the centerpoint of the arc and the sketch origin.

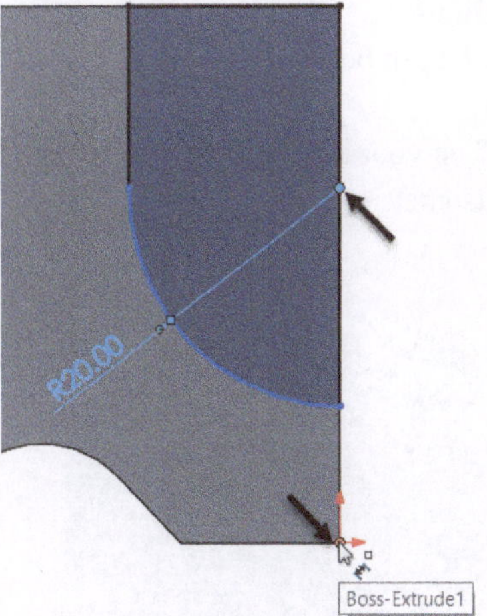

40. Place the dimension.
41. Type **35** and click **OK**.

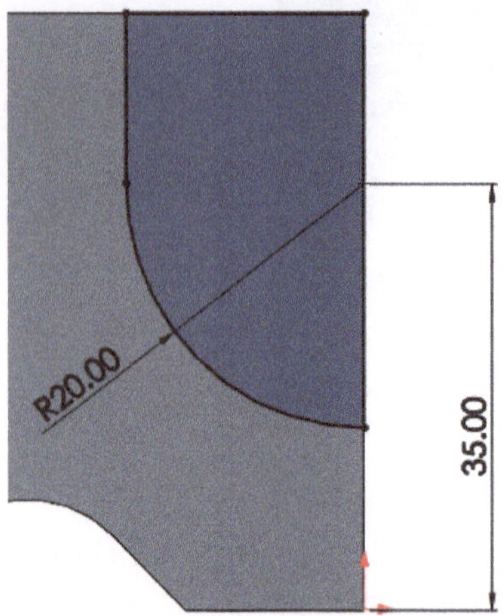

42. Click **Exit Sketch** on the **Sketch** tab of the Command Manager.
43. Click the **Extruded Cut** icon on the **Features** tab of the Command Manager; the sketch is selected automatically.
44. On the **Cut – Extrude** PropertyManager, select **End Condition > Blind**.
45. Type **10** in the **Depth** box.
46. Click **OK**.
47. Press CTRL+7 on your keyboard to change the view orientation to Isometric.

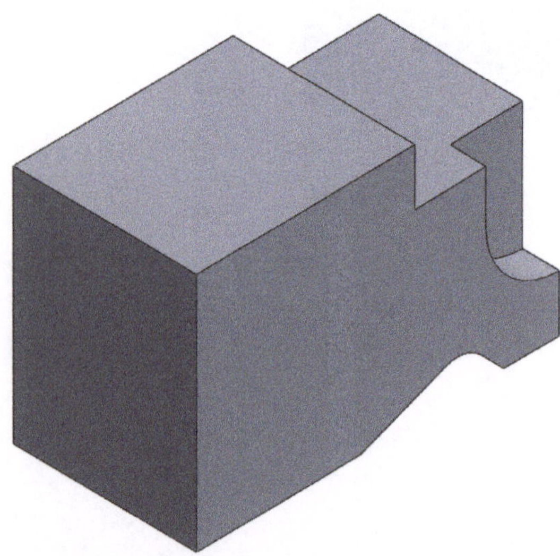

48. Select the flat face of the **Extruded cut** feature.
49. Click the **Sketch** icon on the **Sketch** tab of the CommandManager.
50. Create a circle.
51. Press **Esc**.

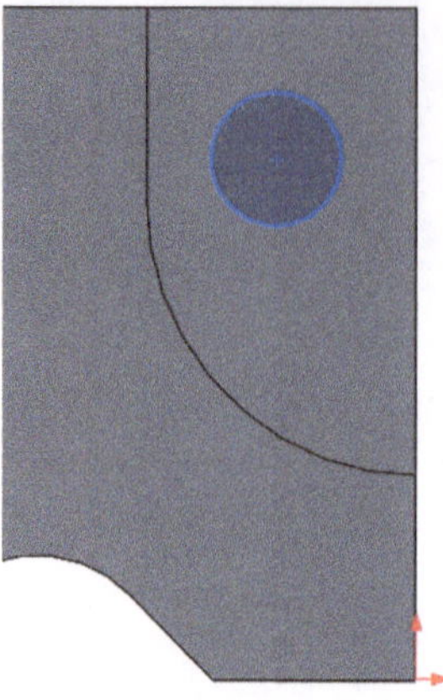

52. Press and hold the Ctrl key.
53. Select the center point of the circle.
54. Select the endpoint of the curved edge.

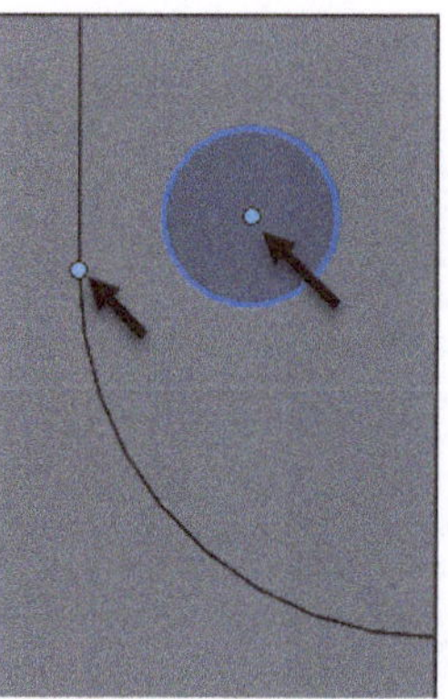

55. Click the **Horizontal** icon on the **Add Relations** section of the **Properties** manager.
56. Press and hold the Ctrl key.
57. Select the midpoint of the horizontal edge.
58. Select the centerpoint of the circle.

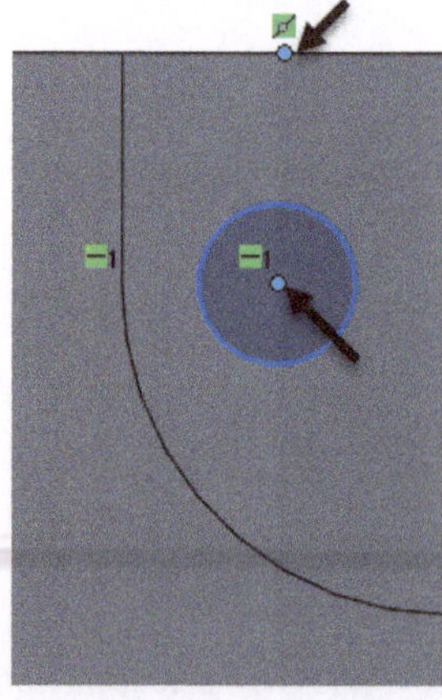

59. Click the **Vertical** icon on the **Add Relations**

section of the **Properties** manager.

60. Add the diameter dimension to the circle.

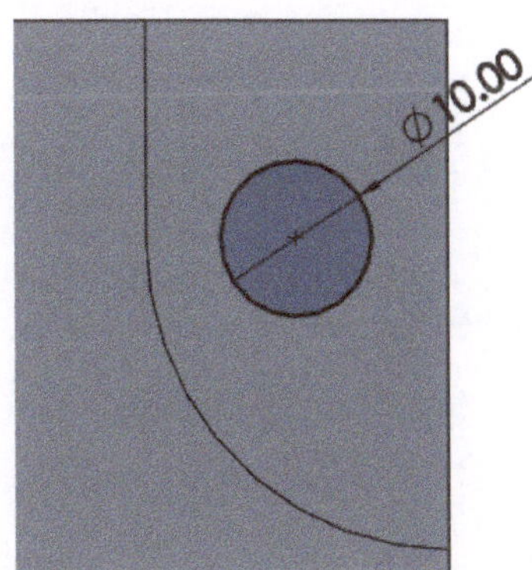

61. Click **Exit Sketch** on the **Sketch** tab of the Command Manager.
62. Click the **Extruded Cut** icon on the **Features** tab of the Command Manager; the sketch is selected automatically.
63. On the **Cut – Extrude** PropertyManager, select **End Condition > Through All**.
64. Click **OK**.

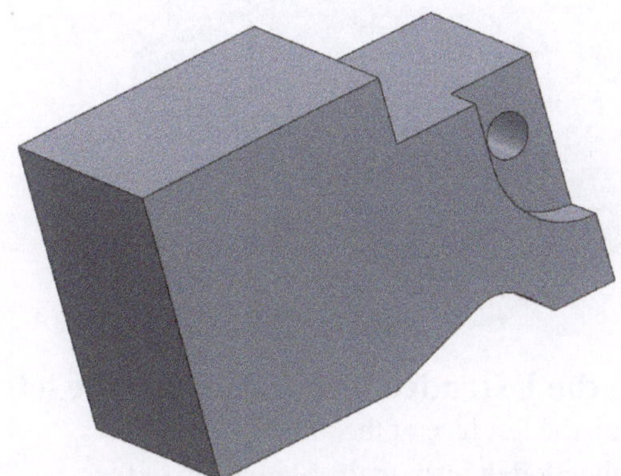

Creating the Extruded Cut feature on the left side

1. Click on the top face of the model.

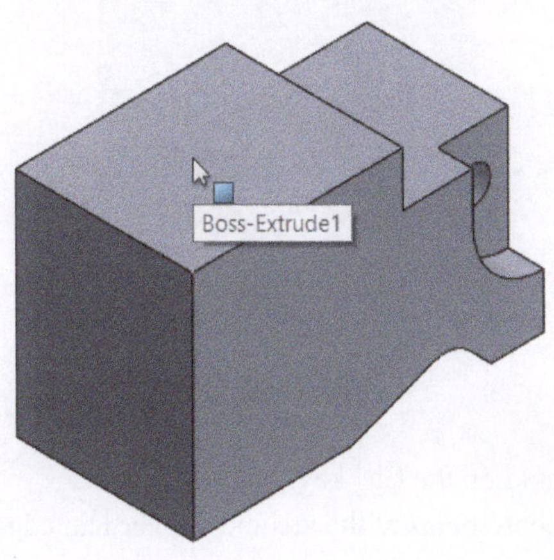

2. Click the **Sketch** icon on the **Sketch** tab of the CommandManager.
3. Create a rectangle by specifying its corners, as shown.

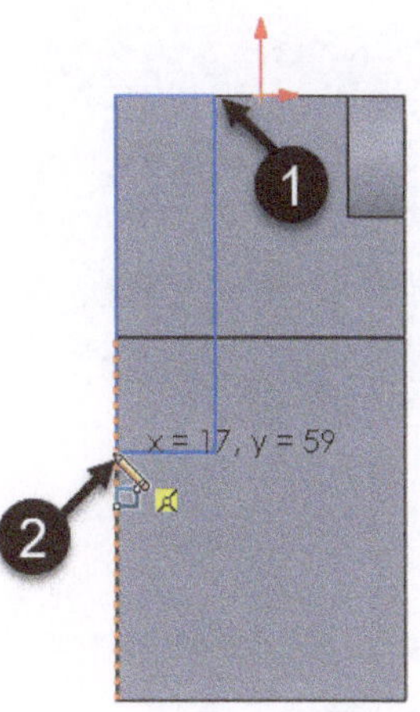

4. Create horizontal and vertical dimensions, as shown.

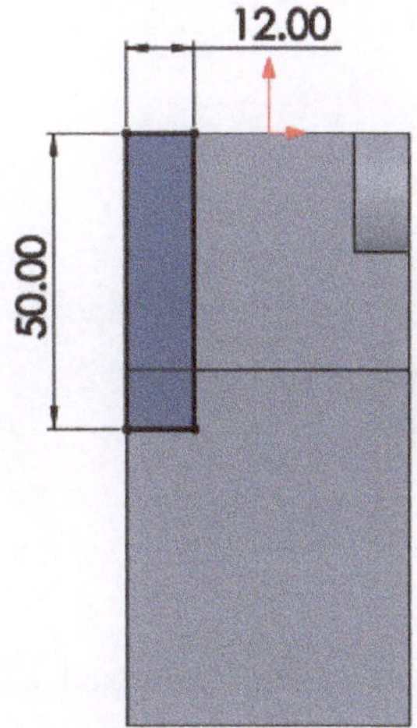

65. Click **Exit Sketch** on the **Sketch** tab of the Command Manager.
66. Click the **Extruded Cut** icon on the **Features** tab of the Command Manager; the sketch is selected automatically.
67. On the **Cut – Extrude** PropertyManager, select **End Condition > Through All**.
68. Click **OK**.

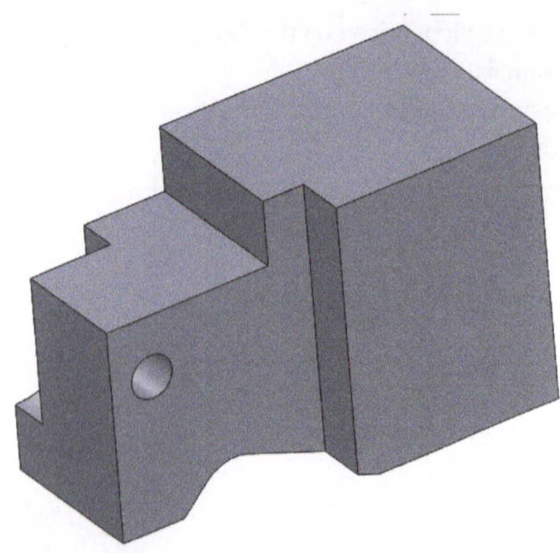

Creating the Chamfer

A chamfer is a **beveled edge** cut at a 45° angle (or specified angle) on a part's corner.

1. On the CommandManager, click **Features > Fillet drop-down > Chamfer**.

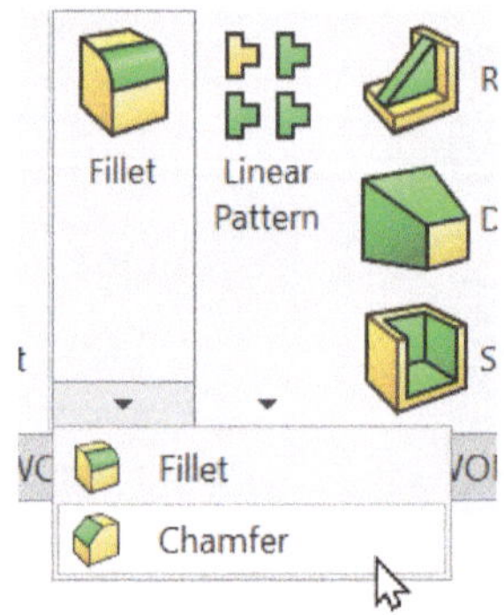

2. Click on the left horizontal edge of the model, as shown.

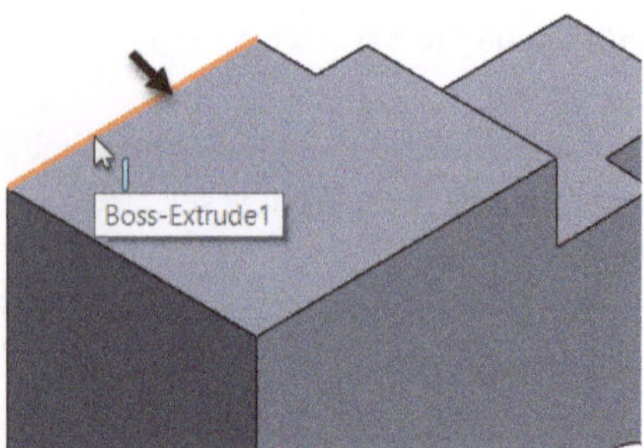

3. Click the **Angle Distance** icon in the **Chamfer Type** section of the **Chamfer** PropertyManager.

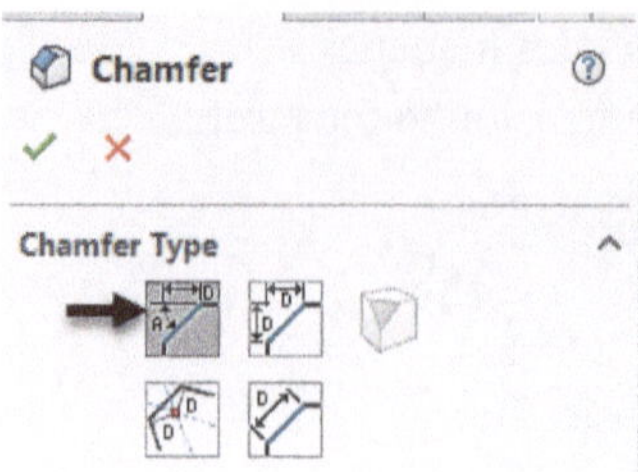

4. Enter 18 and 20 in the **Distance** and **Angle** boxes, respectively.

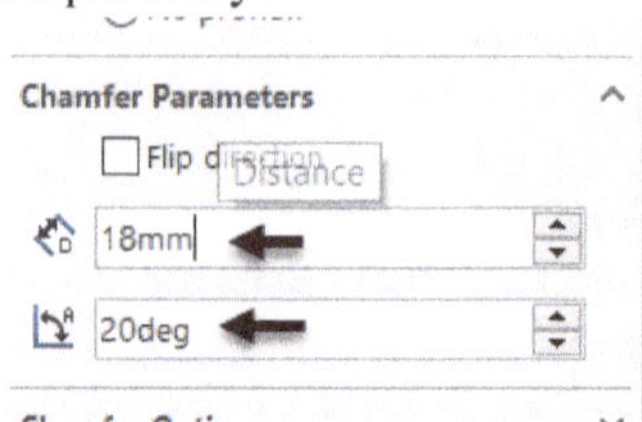

5. Click **OK**.

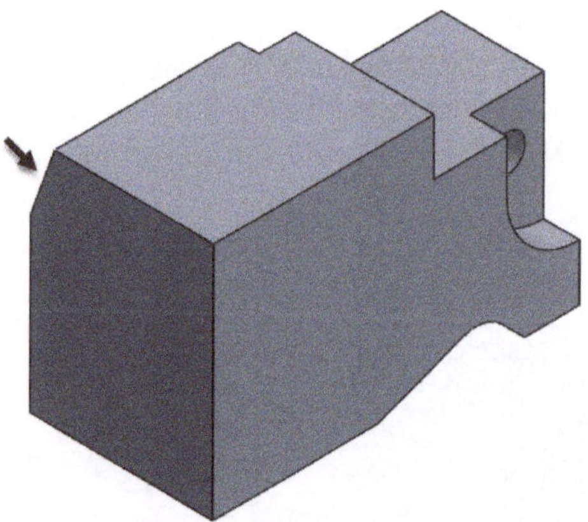

Creating the Extruded Cut feature on the left

1. Click on the left face of the model.
2. Click the **Sketch** icon on the **Sketch** tab of the CommandManager.
3. Create a line and arc, as shown.

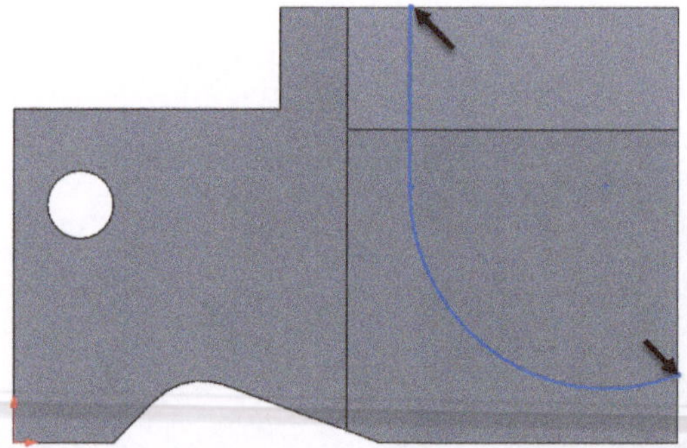

4. Press and hold on the Ctrl key.
5. Select the centerpoint of the arc and the vertical edge,

as shown.

6. Click the **Coincident** icon on the **Add relations** section of the Properties manager.
7. Create the radius and vertical dimensions, as shown.

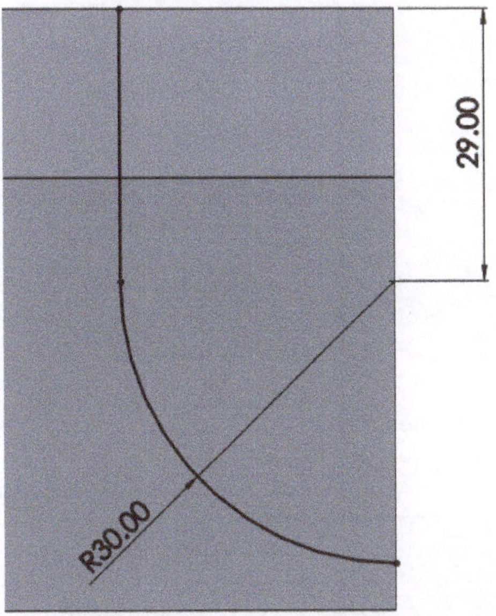

6. Click the **Line** icon on the **Sketch** tab of the CommandManager.
7. Specify the endpoints of the line, as shown.

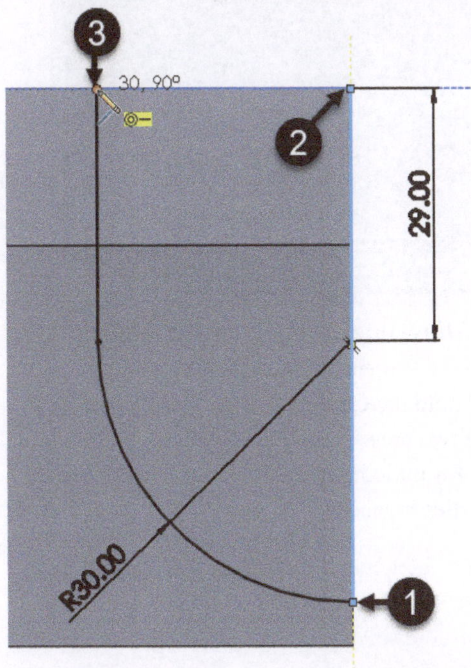

8. Click **Exit Sketch** on the **Sketch** tab of the Command Manager.
9. Click the **Extruded Cut** icon on the **Features** tab of the Command Manager; the sketch is selected automatically.
10. On the **Cut – Extrude** PropertyManager, select **End Condition > Blind.**
11. Type **42** in the **Depth** box.
12. Click **OK.**

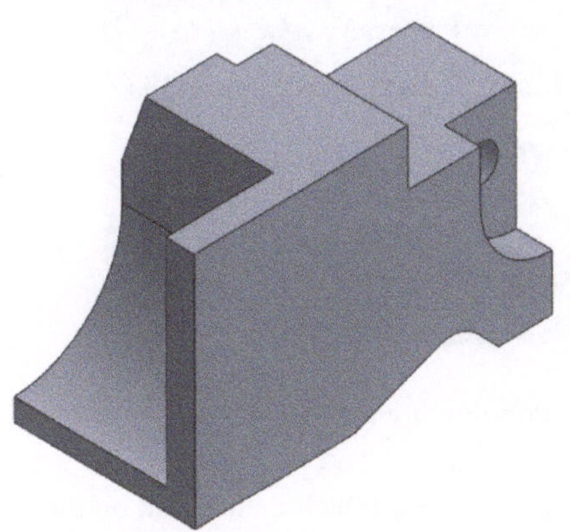

13. Click **OK.**

Creating the Extruded Cut feature on the right

1. Click on the right face of the model.
2. Click the **Sketch** icon on the **Sketch** tab on the CommandManager.
3. Click **Arc** drop-down > **Centerpoint Arc.**

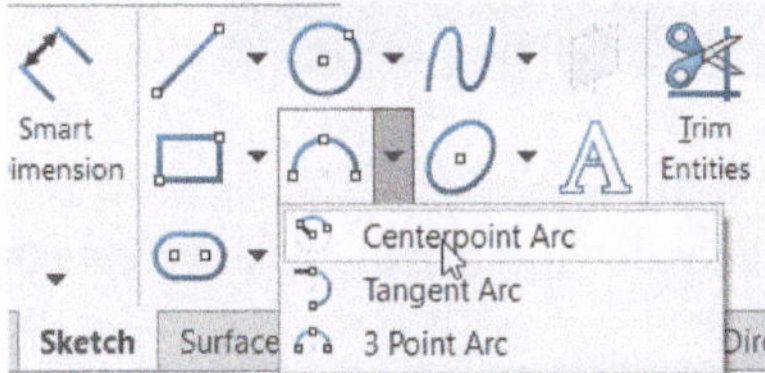

4. Specify the center point of the arc.
5. Move the pointer outward and specify the start and end points of the arc.

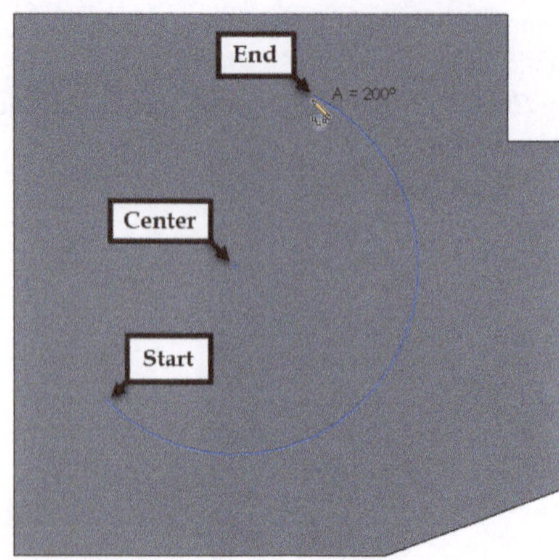

6. Click **Arc** drop-down > **3 Point Arc**.
7. Select the endpoint of the arc.
8. Move the pointer toward the left and click on the vertical edge.

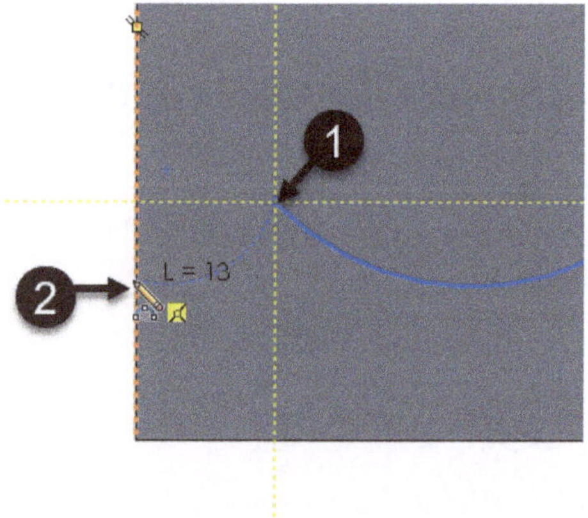

9. Move the pointer downward and click to create the arc.

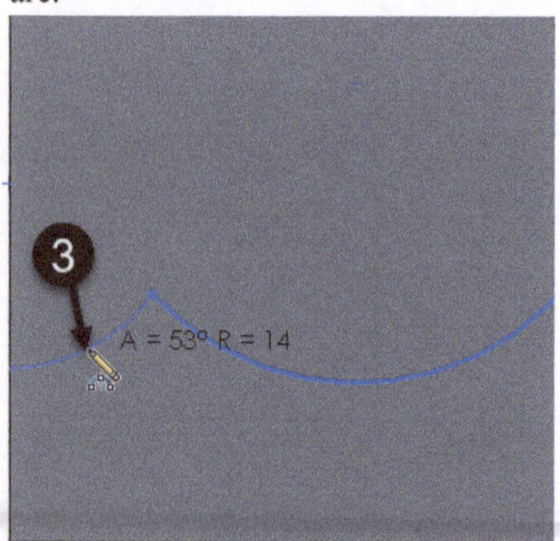

10. Create a vertical line, as shown.

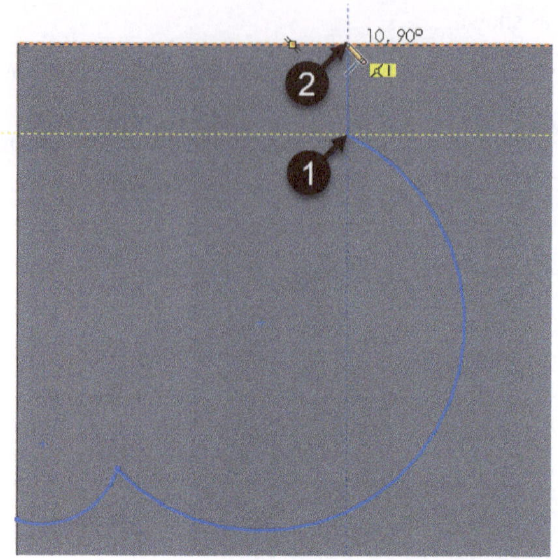

8. Press and hold the Ctrl key.
9. Select the centerpoints of the two arcs.

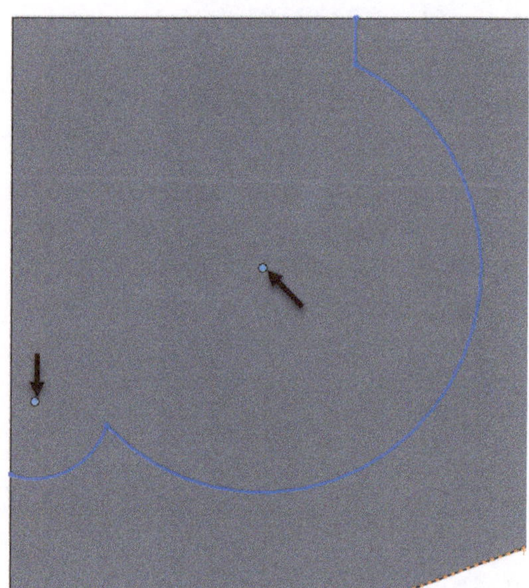

10. Click the **Horizontal** icon on the **Add relations** section of the Properties manager.
11. Press and hold the Ctrl key.
12. Select the two arcs.
13. Click the **Equal** icon on the Add relation section of the Properties manager.

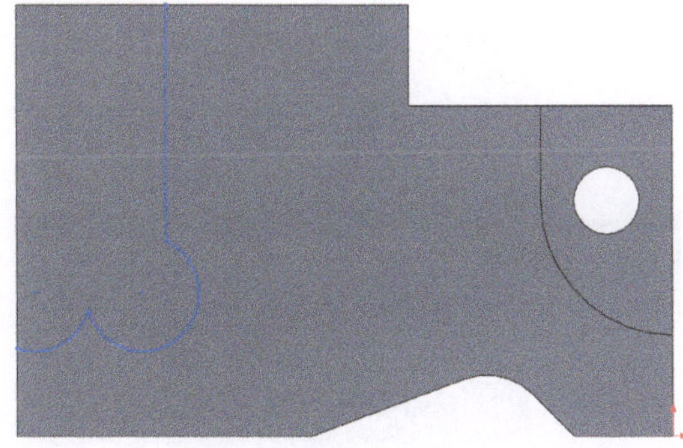

14. Create the radius, vertical and horizontal dimensions, as shown.

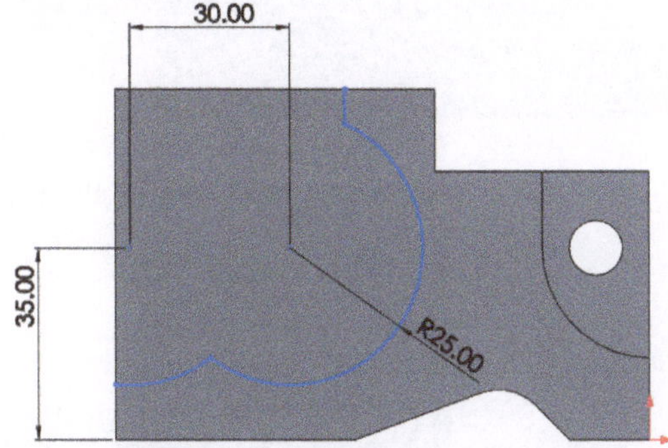

15. Press and hold the Ctrl key.
16. Select the center point and endpoint of the arc, as shown.

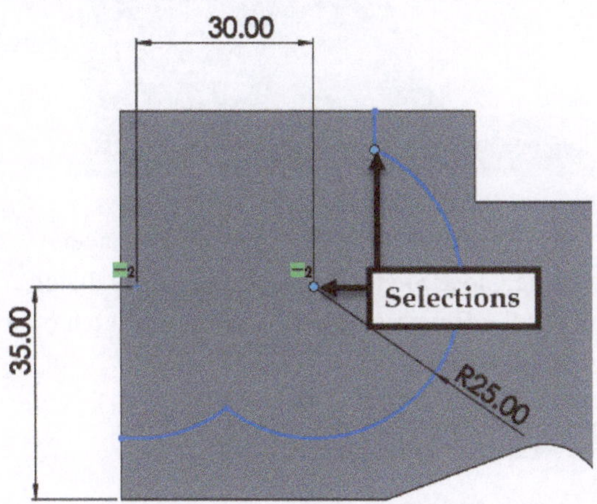

17. Click the **Vertical** icon on the **Add relations** section of the **Properties** manager.
18. Press and hold the Ctrl key.
19. Select the center point of another arc.
20. Select the left vertical edge.
21. Click the **Coincident** icon on the **Add relations** section of the **Properties** manager.

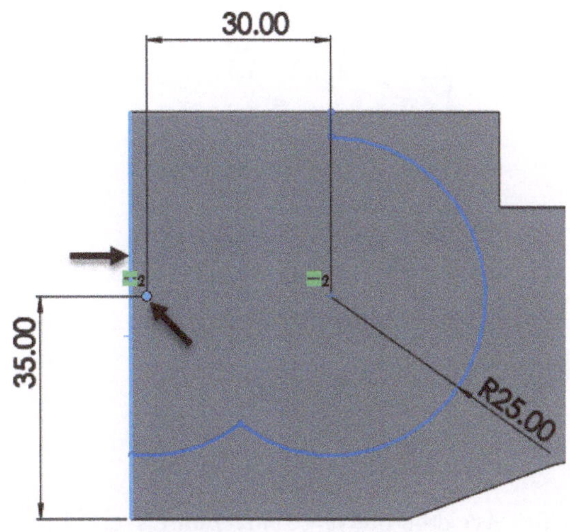

22. Click **Exit Sketch** on the **Sketch** tab of the Command Manager.
23. Click the **Extruded Cut** icon on the **Features** tab of the Command Manager; the sketch is selected automatically.
24. On the **Cut – Extrude** PropertyManager, select **End Condition > Blind**.
25. Type **12** in the **Depth** box.
26. Click **OK**.
27. Press CTRL+7 on your keyboard to change the view orientation to Isometric.

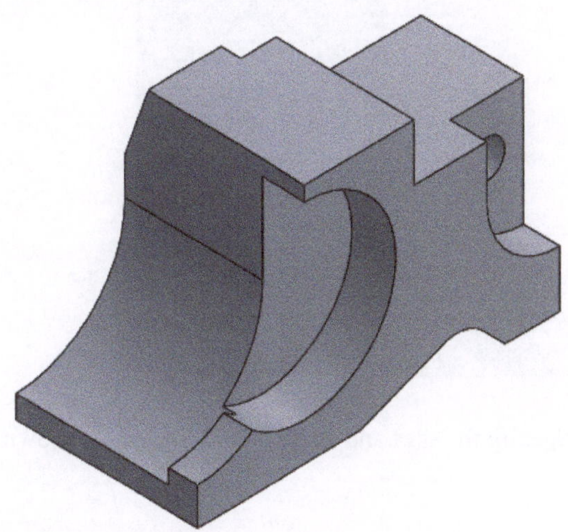

Adding the Extruded Boss Features

1. Click the **Extruded Boss/Base** icon on the **Features** tab of the CommandManager.
2. Click on the flat face of the extruded cut feature.

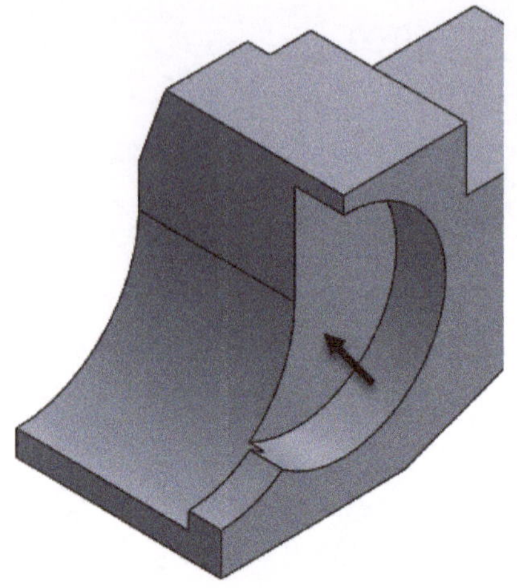

3. Click **Arc** drop-down > **Centerpoint Arc**.

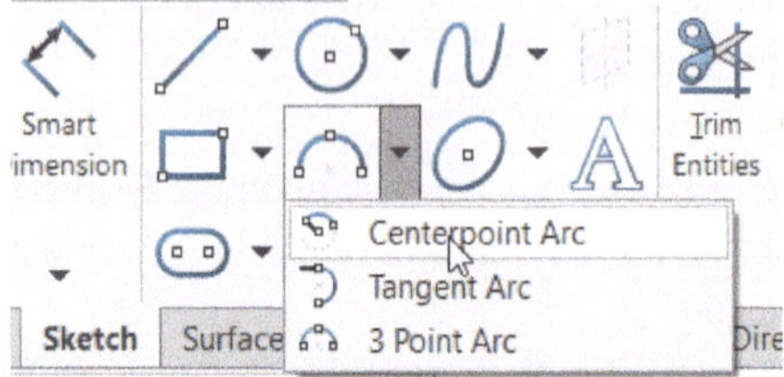

4. Specify the center point of the arc.

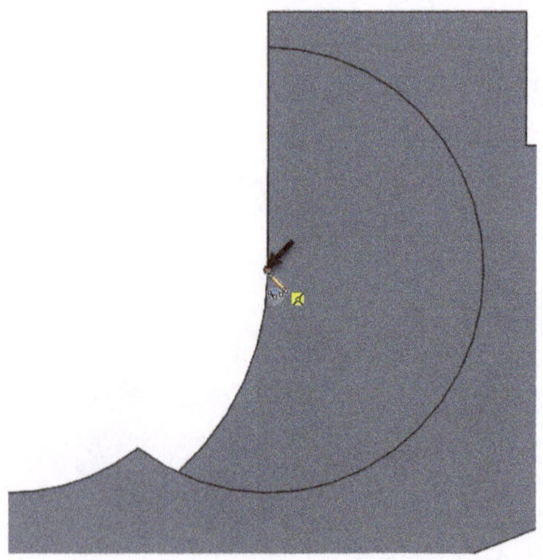

5. Specify the start and endpoints of the arc, as shown.

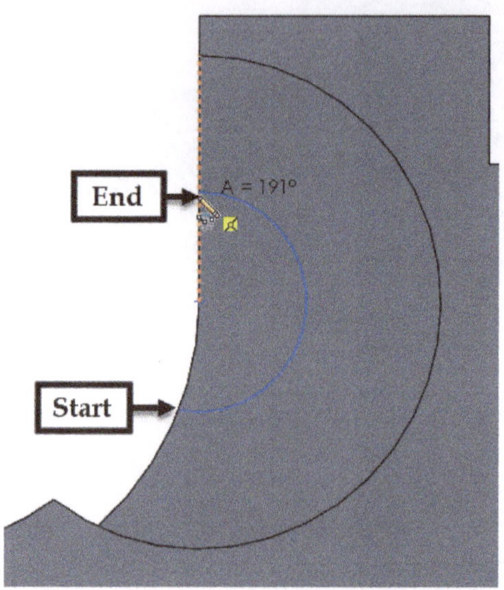

6. Add the radius dimension to the sketch, as shown.

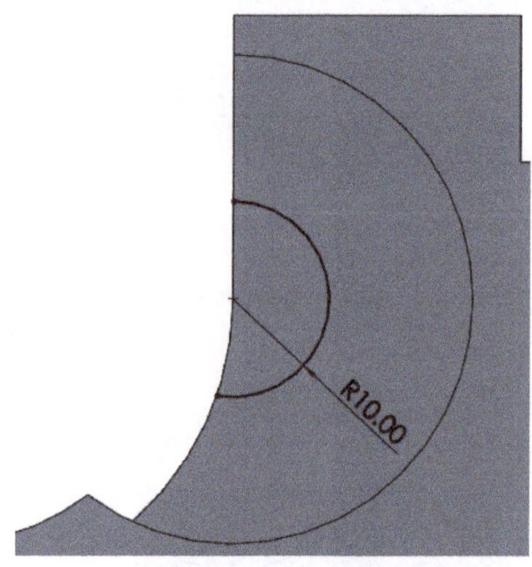

7. Click **Exit Sketch** on the CommandManager.
8. On the **Close Sketch with Model Edges** dialog, check the **Reverse direction to close sketch** option.
9. Click **Yes**.

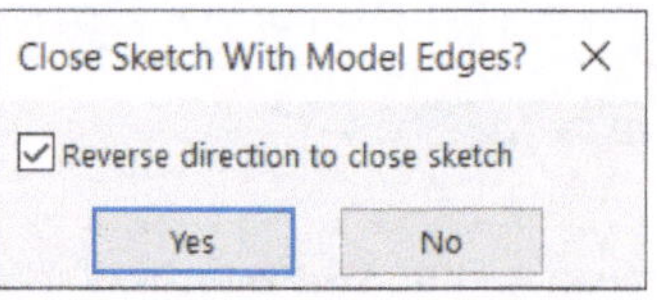

10. Type **5** in the **Depth** box.
11. Click **OK**.

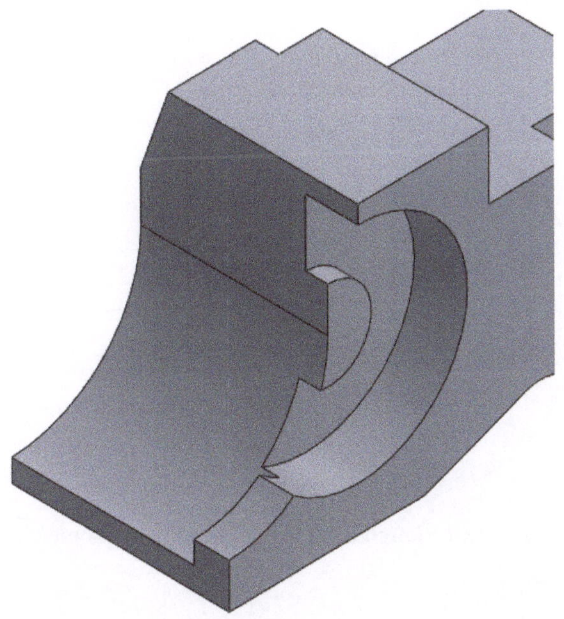

12. Click the **Extruded Boss/Base** icon on the **Features** tab of the CommandManager.
13. Click on the face of the extruded boss feature, as shown.

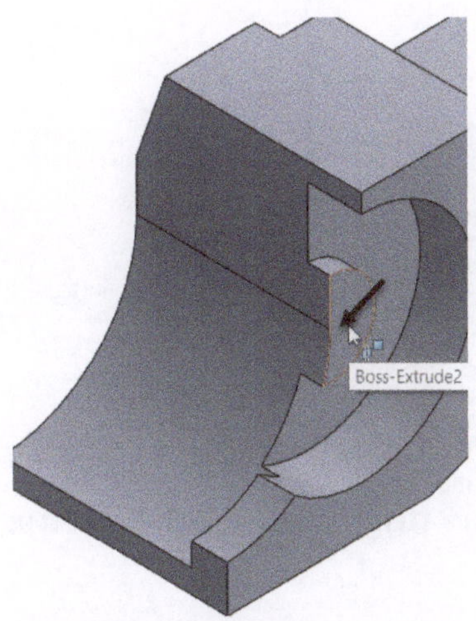

14. Click **Circle** drop-down > **Circle**.
15. Select the centerpoint of the curved edge.

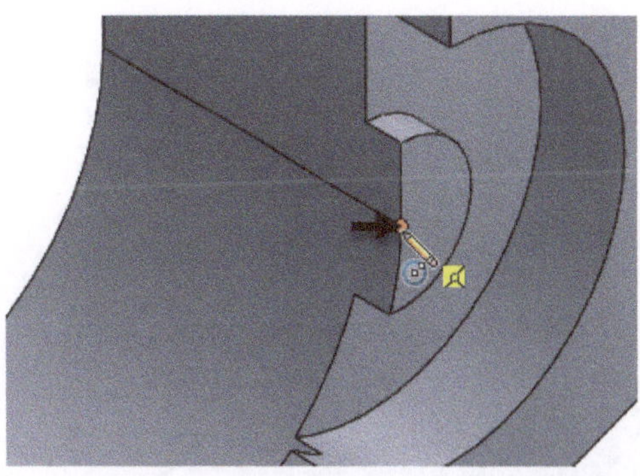

16. Move the pointer outward and click to create a circle.

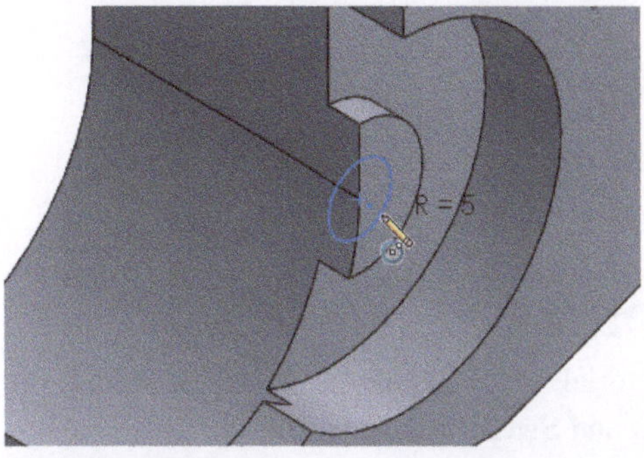

17. Add a diameter dimension to the circle, as shown.

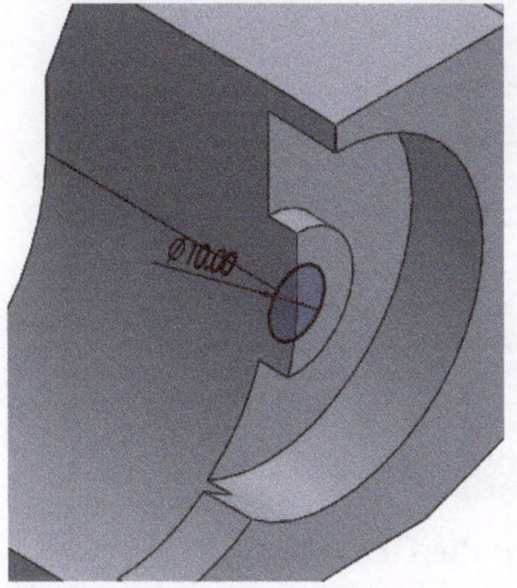

18. Click **Exit Sketch** on the CommandManager.
19. On the **Boss-Extrude** PropertyManager, select **End Condition > Up To Surface**.
20. Select the right face of the model, as shown.

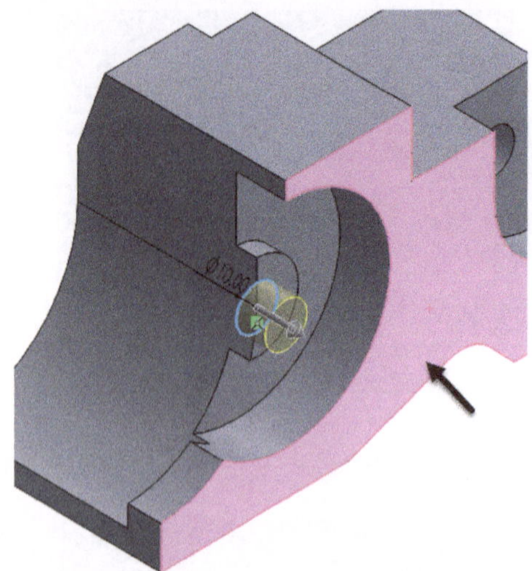

21. Click **OK**.
22. Save and close the model.

TUTORIAL 2

In this tutorial, you will construct a helical spring using the **Helix** and **Swept Boss/Base** tools.

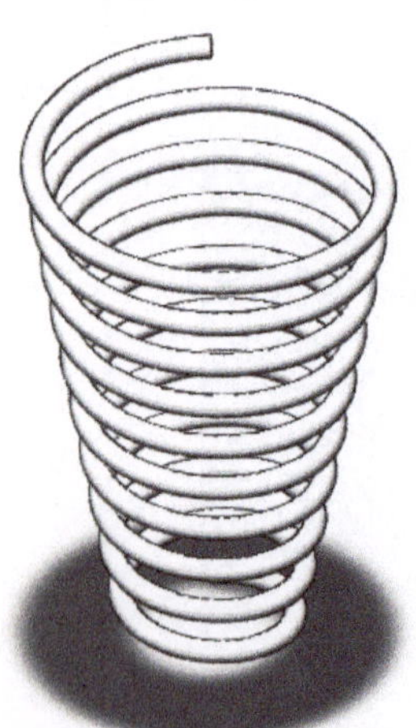

Constructing the Helix

1. Open a new SOLIDWORKS file using the **Part** template.
2. To construct a helix, click **Features > Curves > Helix and Spiral** on the CommandManager.

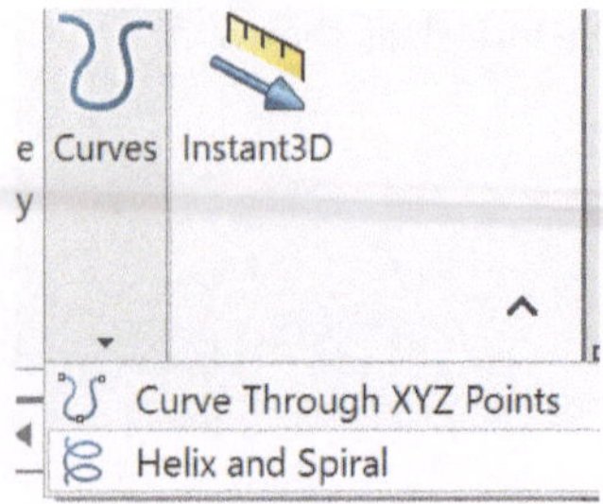

3. Click on the top plane.
4. Draw a circle of diameter 30.

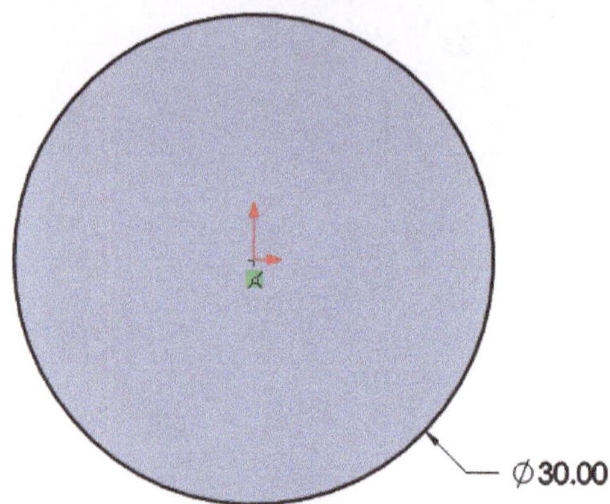

5. Click **Exit Sketch** and change the view to Isometric.

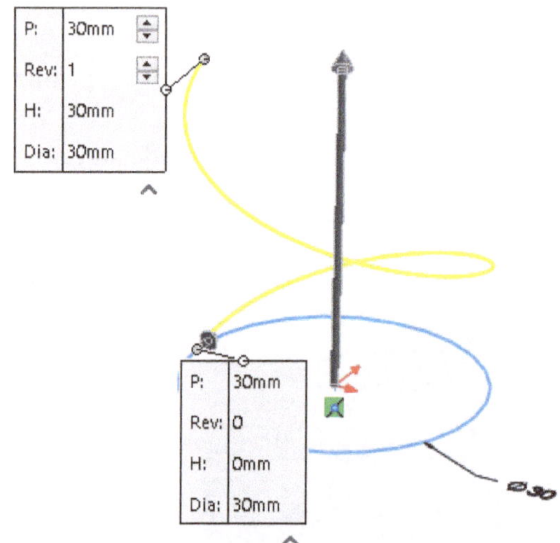

6. On the PropertyManager, set **Pitch** to 10 mm.
7. Set **Revolutions** to 10.
8. Select **Clockwise**.
9. Check the **Taper Helix** option and set **Taper Angle** to 10.
10. Click **OK**.

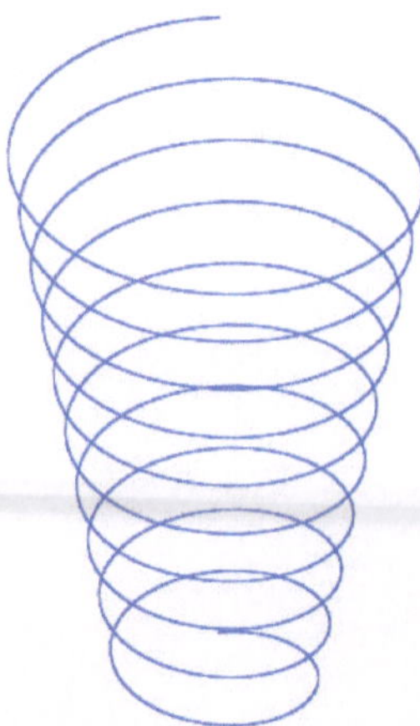

Adding the Reference Plane

1. To add a reference plane, click **Features > Reference Geometry > Plane** on the CommandManager.

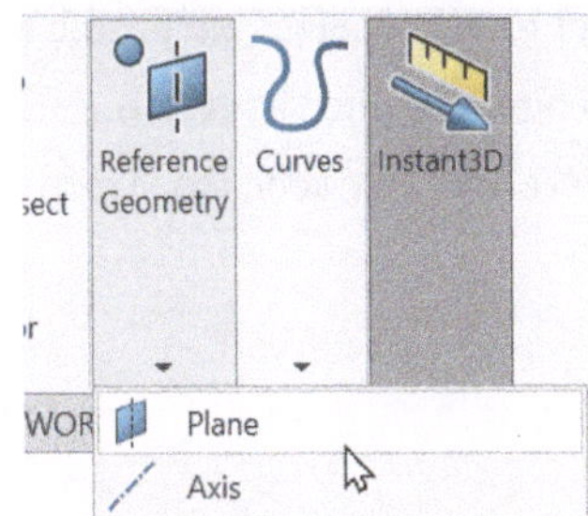

2. Select the helix from the graphics window.
3. Select the end of the helix.

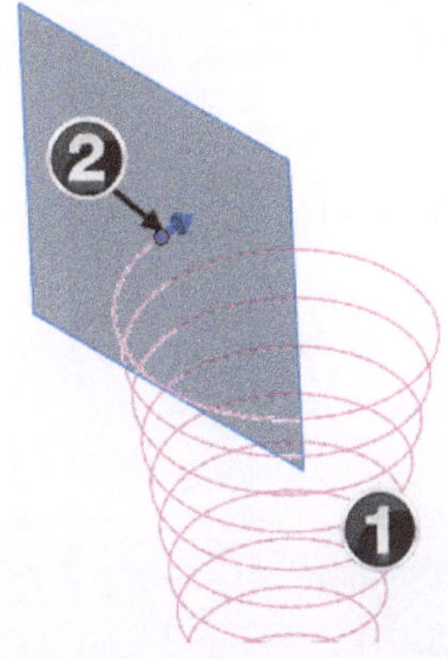

4. Leave the default values and click **OK**.

Constructing the Swept feature

The **Swept** tool is used to create complex 3D geometry by moving a **profile** (cross-section) along a **path** (trajectory). It's used to design complex parts such as **tubes, springs, or wires** that follow precise trajectories. The tool allows control over the profile's orientation (twist, alignment) to avoid distortion, mimics real-world manufacturing (e.g., bending pipes), and ensures parametric updates when edits are made.

1. On the CommandManager, click **Sketch > Sketch**.
2. Select the plane created normal to the helix.
3. Draw a circle of 4 mm in diameter.

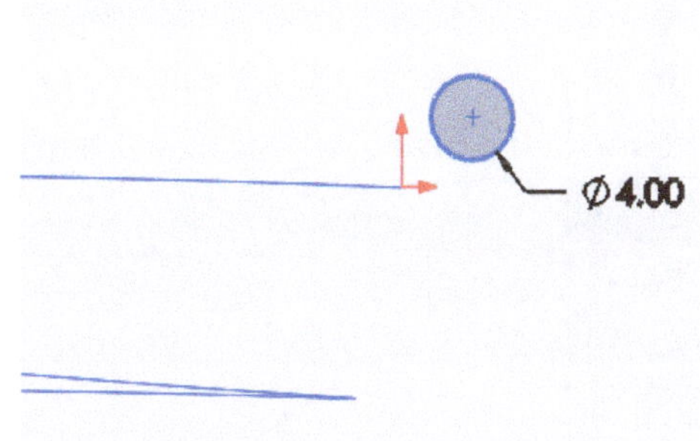

4. On the CommandManager, click **Sketch > Display/Delete Relations > Add Relations**.
5. Click on the center point of the circle.
6. Click on the helix near the sketch origin.
7. On the PropertyManager, under the **Add Relations** section, select **Pierce**.

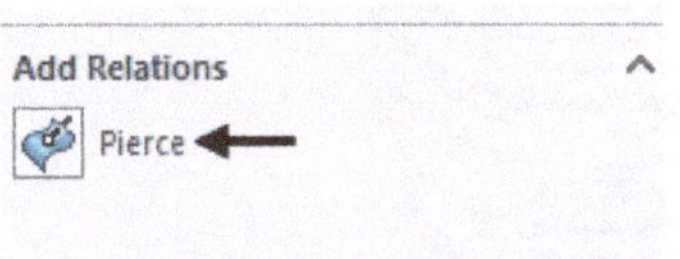

8. Click **OK**.

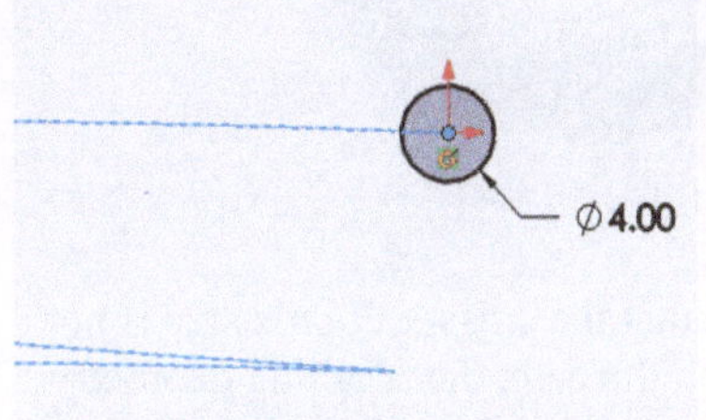

9. Click **Exit Sketch** and change the view orientation to Isometric.
10. To construct a Swept feature, click **Features > Swept Boss/Base**  on the CommandManager.
11. Select the circle to define the profile.
12. On the PropertyManager, click in the **Path** selection box and select the helix to define the path.
13. Leave the default settings and click **OK** to construct the Swept feature.
14. On the **View Heads-Up** toolbar, click the **Visibility** drop-down and turn off the **Plane** and **Curves** icons.

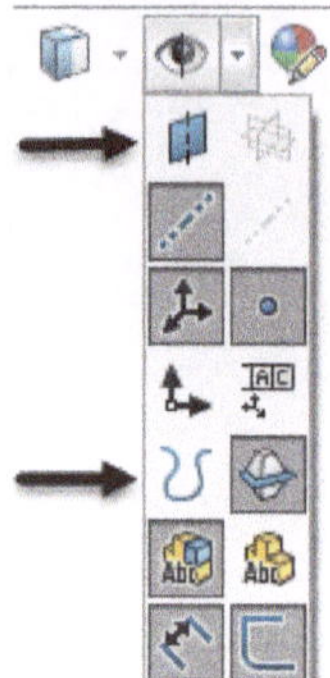

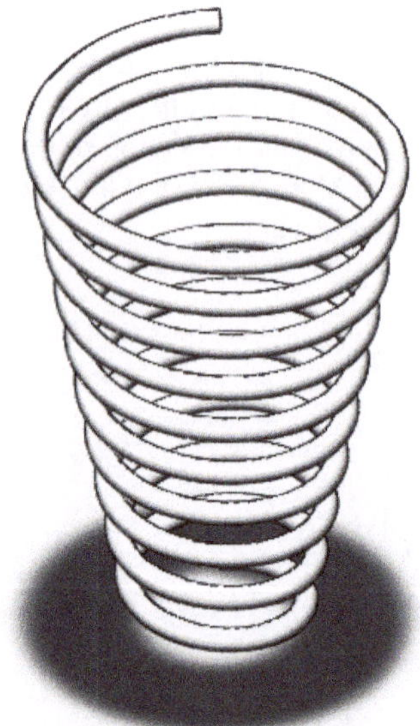

15. Save and close the file.

You need to make sure that the cross-section's size is not larger than the curves on the path, the resulting geometry will intersect, and the Swept will fail.

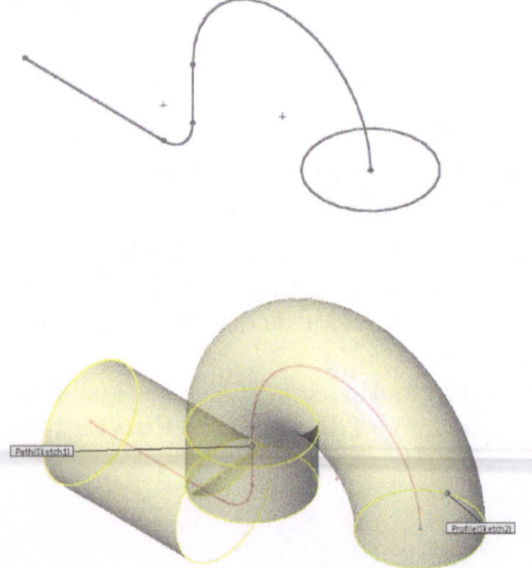

Note: In the above figure, the cross-section plane is normal to the path.

You can create a profile anywhere along the path. For example, create a profile at the middle of the path, as shown. Activate the Swept tool and select the profile and path. On the PropertyManager, use the **Direction 1**, **Bidirectional**, and **Direction 2** icons to sweep the profile.

Direction 1

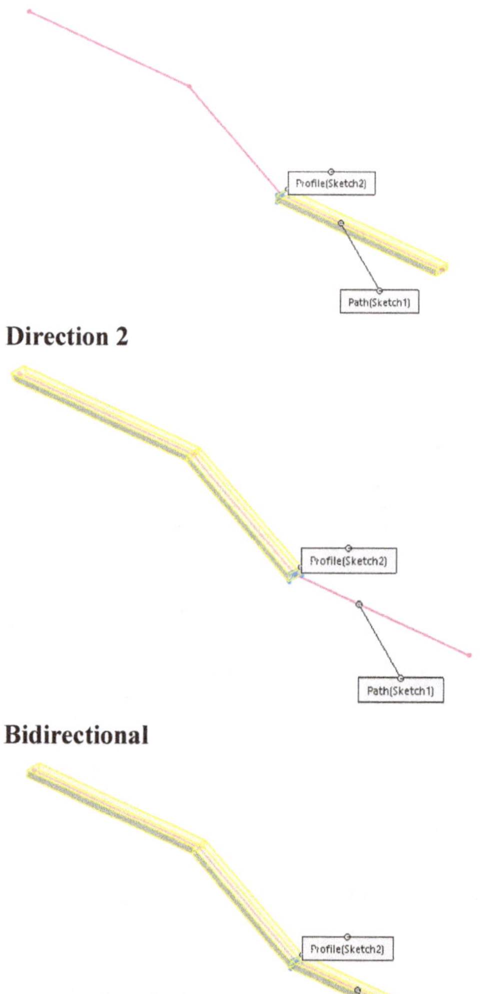

Direction 2

Bidirectional

In SOLIDWORKS, you can select the face of a model to define the swept profile.

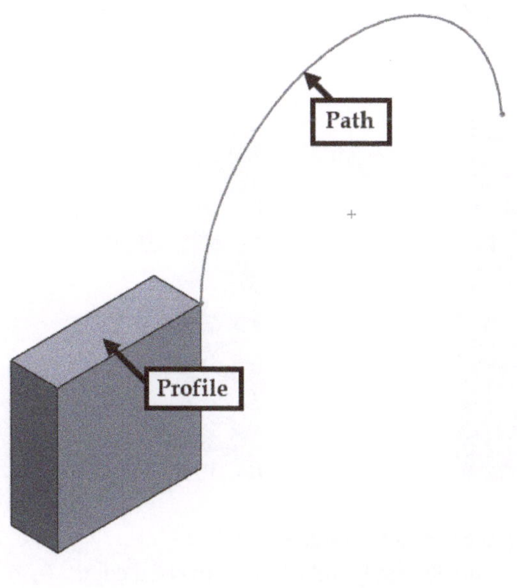

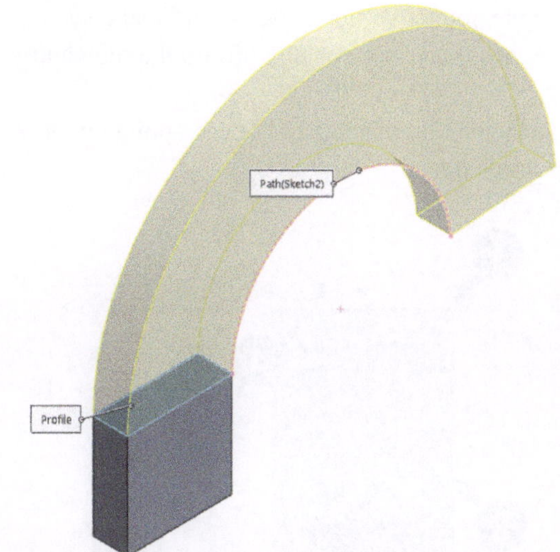

TUTORIAL 3

In this tutorial, you construct a pulley wheel using the **Revolve Boss/Base** and **Revolved Cut** tools.

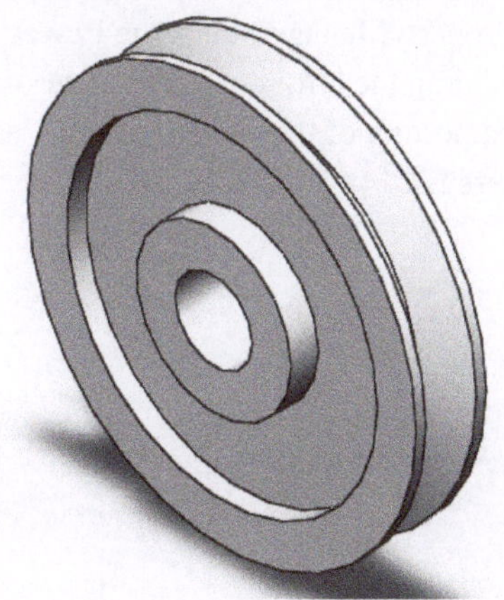

1. Open a new file in the **Part** Environment.
2. On the CommandManager, click **Sketch > Sketch**.
3. Click on the right plane.
4. On the CommandManager, click **Sketch > Line > Centerline**.
5. Check the **Midpoint line** option on the PropertyManager.
6. Select the sketch origin, move the pointer horizontally toward right and click.

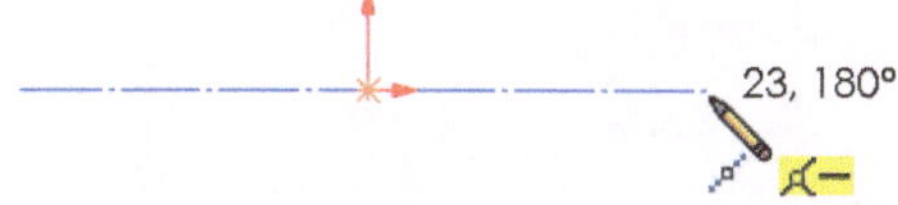

7. Construct the sketch, as shown in the figure.

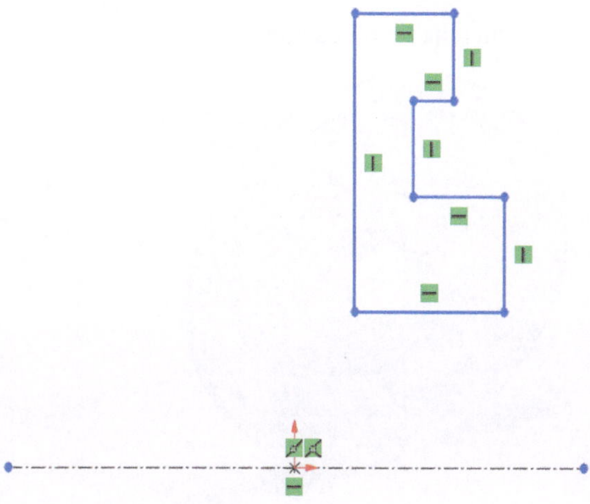

8. Add the **Coincident** relation between the origin and the left vertical line.
9. Add dimensions to the sketch.
10. Next, exit the sketch.

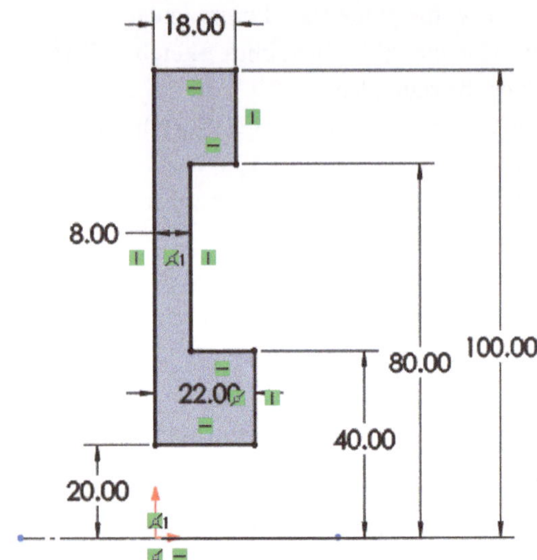

11. Construct the revolved boss.

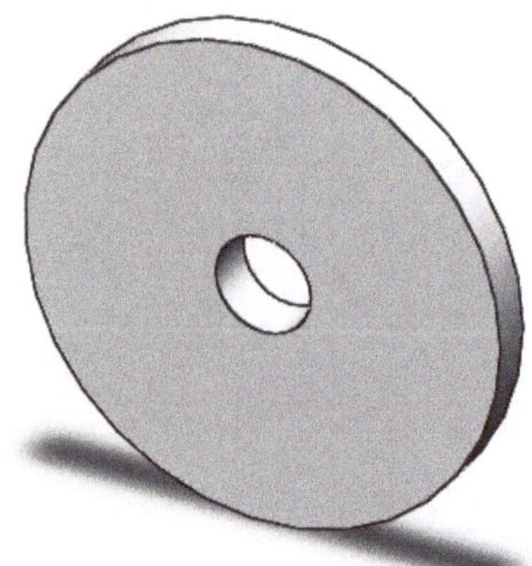

Constructing a Revolved Cut

A **Revolved Cut** removes material by rotating a 2D sketch profile around a central axis, creating symmetrical features like grooves, threads, or radial holes.

1. To construct a revolved cut, click **Features > Revolved cut** on the CommandManager.
2. Expand the **FeatureManager Design Tree** and select the right plane.
3. On the CommandManager, click **Sketch > Convert Entities**.
4. Click on the horizontal edge of the model. Click **OK**.

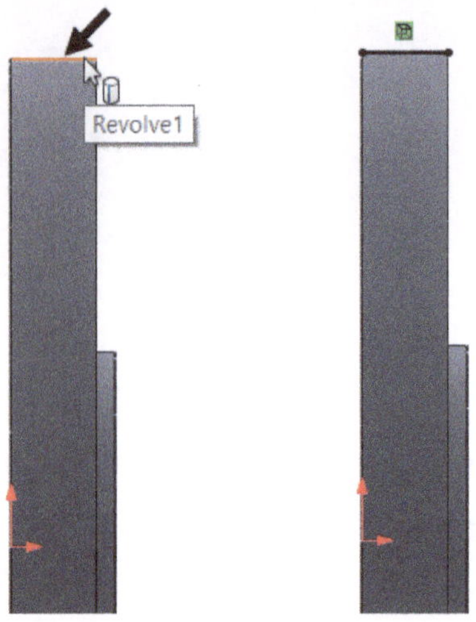

5. Activate the **Line** command.
6. Select the left endpoint of the converted edge.
7. Move the pointer vertically downward and click.
8. Move the pointer horizontally toward the right and click.
9. Move the pointer upward and select a point on the converted edge.

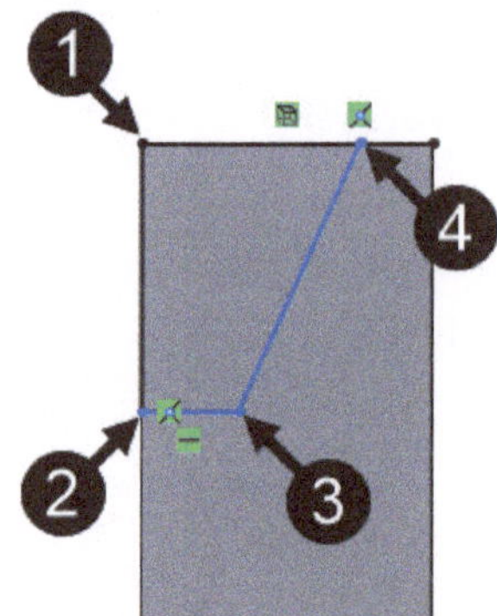

10. On the CommandManager, click **Sketch > Trim Entities**.
11. On the PropertyManager, click the **Power Trim** icon.
12. Click and drag the left mouse button across the unwanted portion of the converted edge, as shown. Next, press Esc.

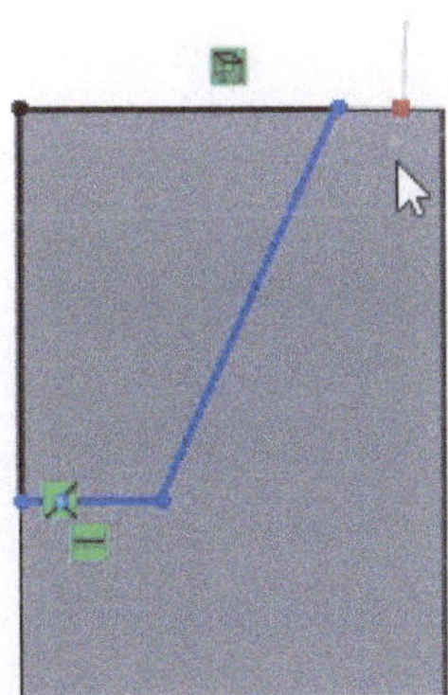

13. Activate the **Smart Dimension** command.
14. Select the inclined and horizontal lines, move the pointer toward the left and click to place the dimension.

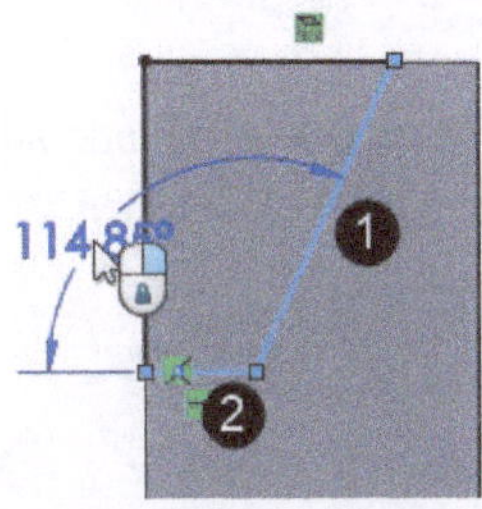

15. Type 110 and press Enter.
16. Select the upper horizontal line, move the pointer upward and click to place the dimension. Type 13 and press Enter.
17. Select the lower horizontal line, move the pointer downward and click to place the dimension. Type 5 and press Enter.
18. Create a horizontal centreline passing through the origin.

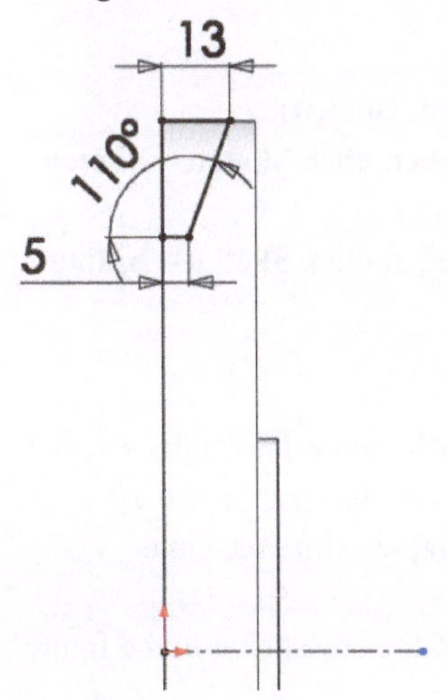

19. Click **Exit Sketch** and click **OK**.

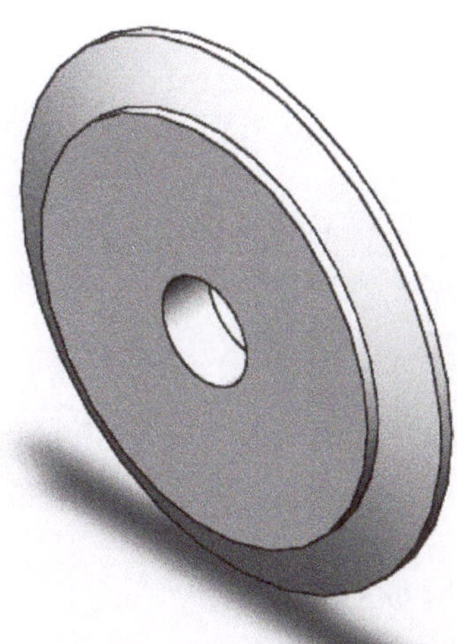

Constructing a Mirror Feature

The Mirror Feature is used to **replicate geometry symmetrically** across a plane, axis, or face.

1. To construct the mirror feature, click **Features > Mirror** on the CommandManager.
2. Click on the flat front face to define the mirror face.

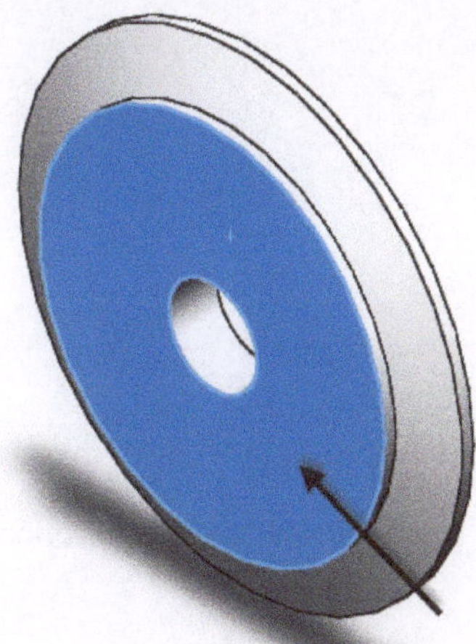

3. On the PropertyManager, expand the **Bodies to Mirror** section and click on the model geometry.
4. Click **OK**.

5. Save and close the model.

TUTORIAL 4

In this tutorial, you construct a shampoo bottle using the **Loft**, **Extrude**, **Shell**, **Indent**, and **Swept** tools.

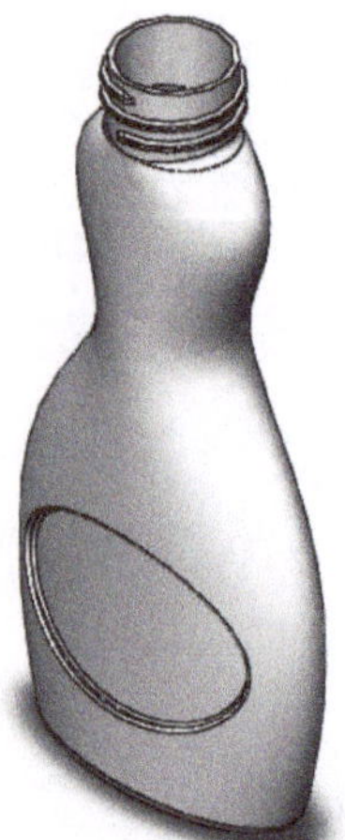

Creating Sections and Guide curves

To construct a lofted boss, you need to create sections and guide curves.

1. Open a new file in the **Part** Environment.
2. On the CommandManager, click **Sketch > Sketch**.
3. Select the top plane.
4. On the CommandManager, click **Sketch > Ellipse** .
5. Select the origin point of the sketch.
6. Move the pointer horizontally and left-click.
7. Move the pointer vertically and left-click.

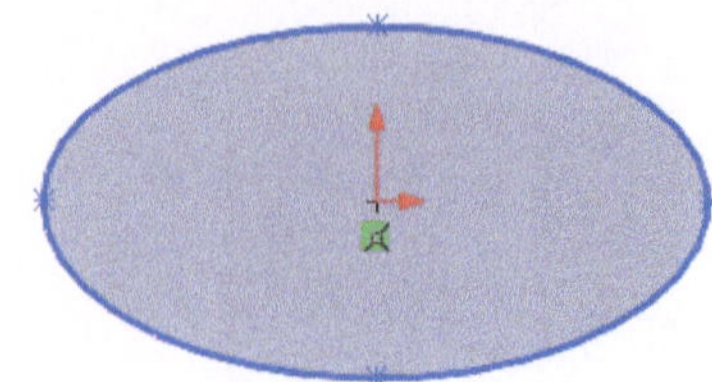

8. Create two centerlines passing to the origin and perpendicular to each other, as shown.

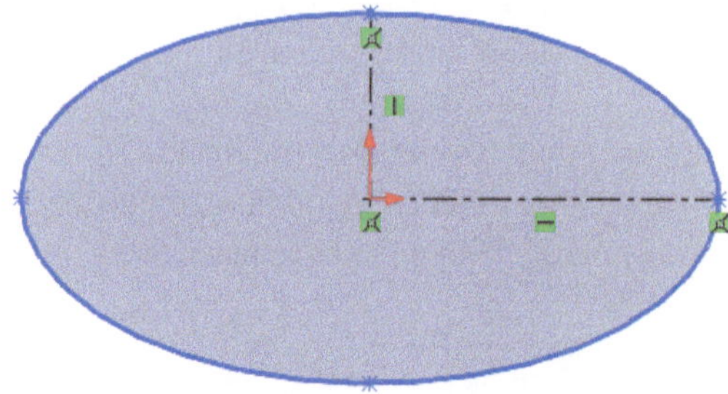

9. Activate the **Smart Dimension** tool and add dimensions to the centerlines, as shown.

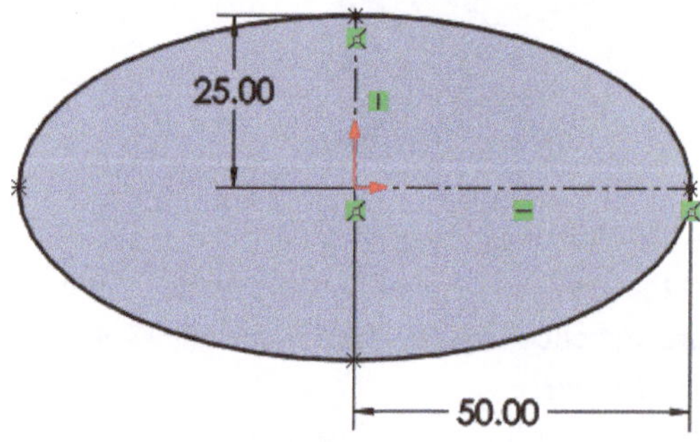

10. Click **Exit Sketch**.

After creating the section, you need to create guide curves.

11. Change the orientation to Isometric.
12. On the CommandManager, click **Sketch > Sketch**.
13. Select the front plane.
14. On the CommandManager, click **Sketch > Spline** .

A **spline** is a **flexible, smooth curve** defined by a series of control points. Unlike arcs or lines, splines can model **complex, organic shapes** with precision.

15. Draw a spline similar to the one shown in the figure.

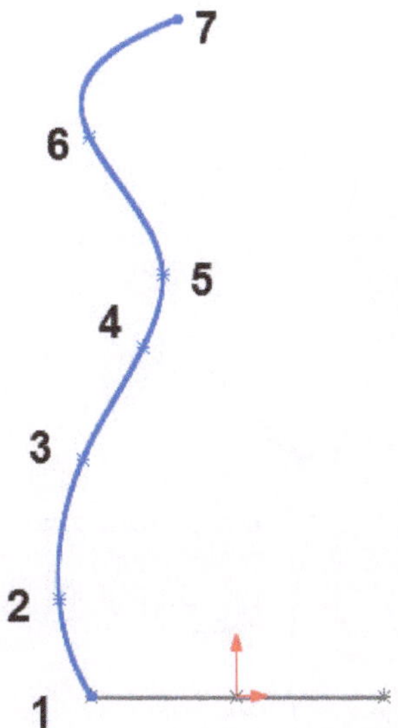

16. Press the Ctrl key and click on the first point of the spline and the previous sketch.
17. On the PropertyManager, under the **Add Relations** section, click **Pierce**.
18. Draw a vertical centreline starting from the origin point.
19. Apply dimensions to the spline, as shown in the figure. First, create the horizontal dimensions, and then create the vertical dimensions in the descending order.

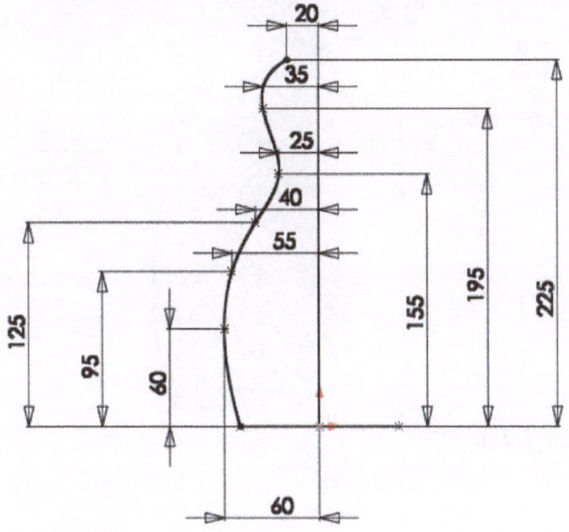

20. On the CommandManager, click **Sketch > Mirror Entities** .
21. Select the spline.
22. On the PropertyManager, click **Mirror about**, and then select the vertical centerline.
23. Click **OK**.

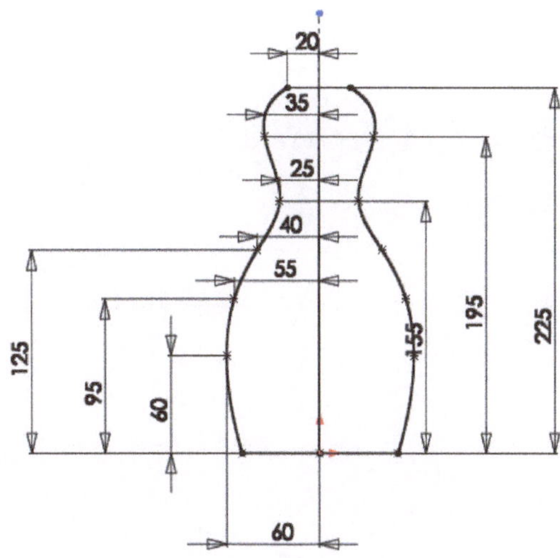

24. Click **Exit Sketch**.
25. Change the view orientation to Isometric.

Creating another section

1. On the CommandManager, click **Features > Reference Geometry > Plane** .
2. Select the top plane from FeatureManager Design Tree.
3. On the PropertyManager, type-in **225** in the **Offset Distance** box.

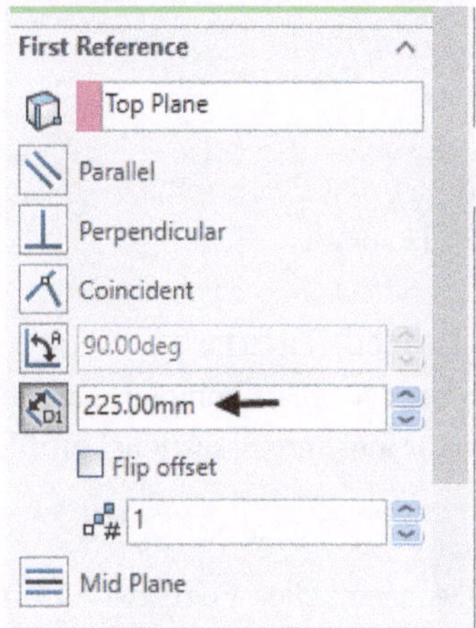

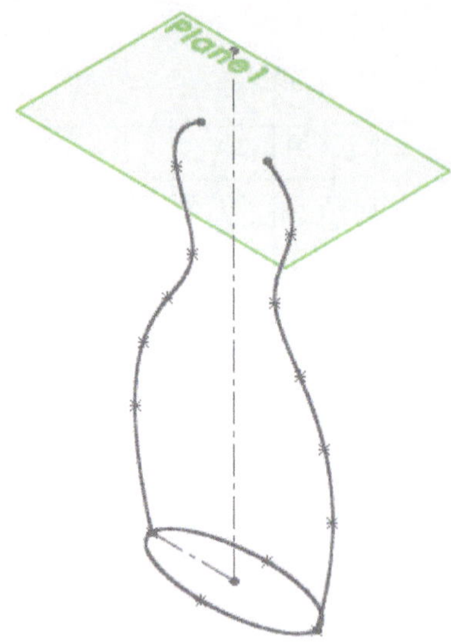

4. Click **OK**.
5. Start a sketch on the new reference plane.
6. Draw a circle of 40 mm in diameter.

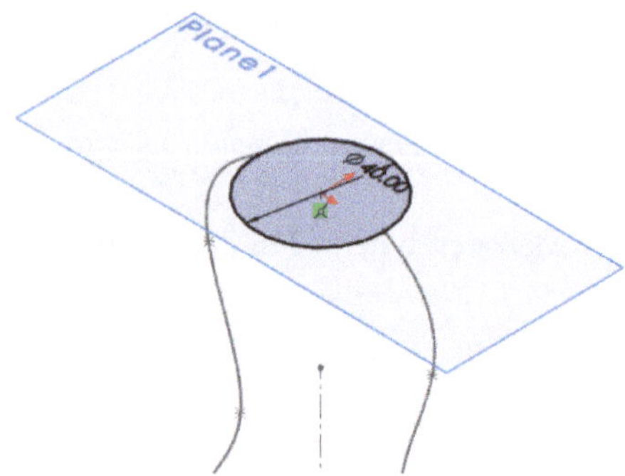

7. Click **Exit Sketch**.
8. Change the view to Isometric.

Constructing the Lofted feature

The **Lofted Feature** is used to create complex, smooth transitions between two or more cross-sectional profiles (sketches or faces).

1. On the CommandManager, click **Features > Lofted Boss/Base**.
2. Select the circle and ellipse.
3. On the PropertyManager, click in the **Guide Curves** selection box, select the first guide curve, as shown. Next, click **OK** on the box.

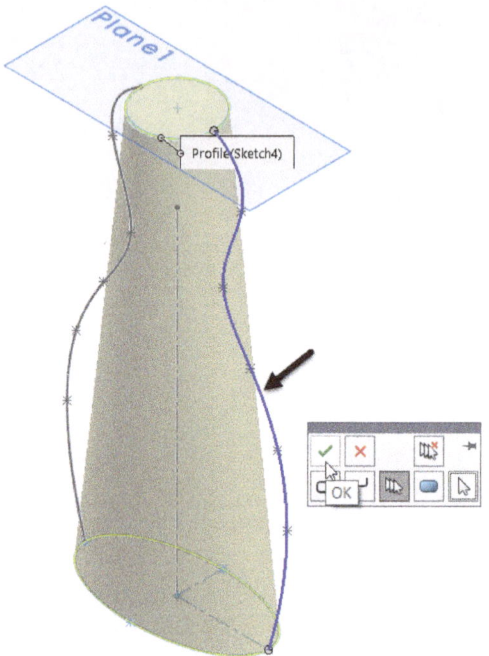

4. Select the second guide curve and click **OK** on the box.

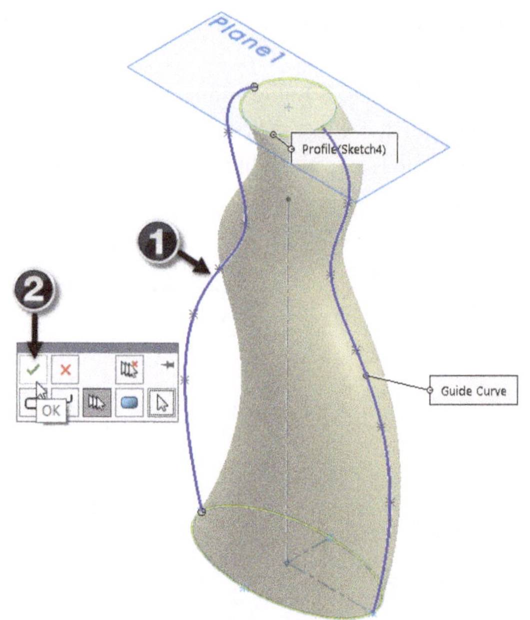

5. Click **OK**.

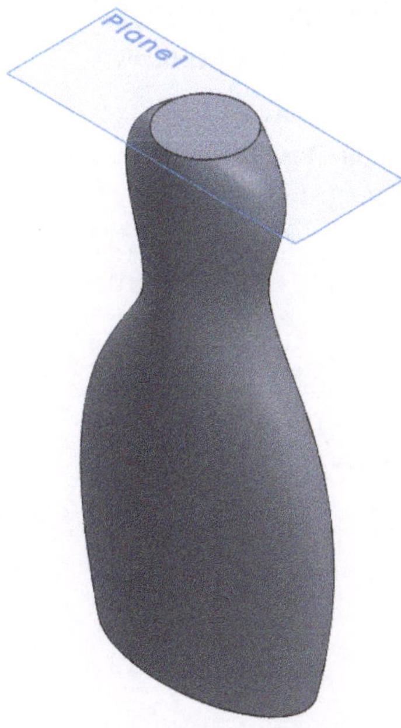

Constructing the Extruded feature

1. In the **FeatureManager Design Tree**, expand the Loft feature and select Sketch 3.

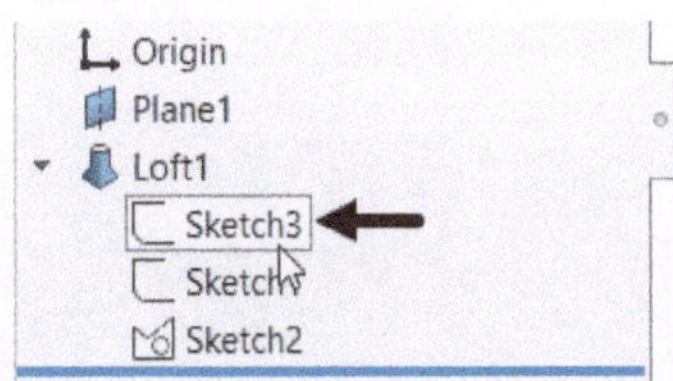

2. Press the Ctrl key and select the reference plane located at the top of the lofted feature.
3. On the Menu bar, click **Insert > Derived Sketch**.

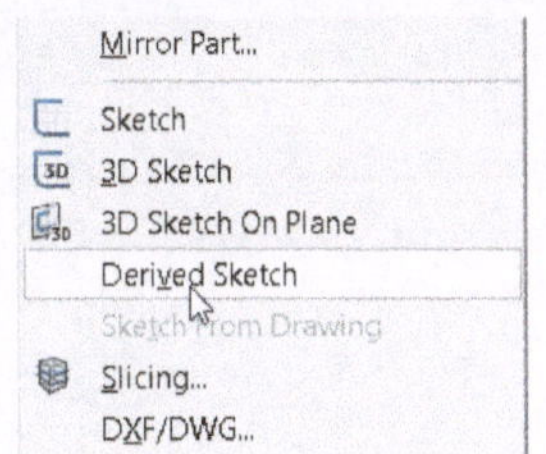

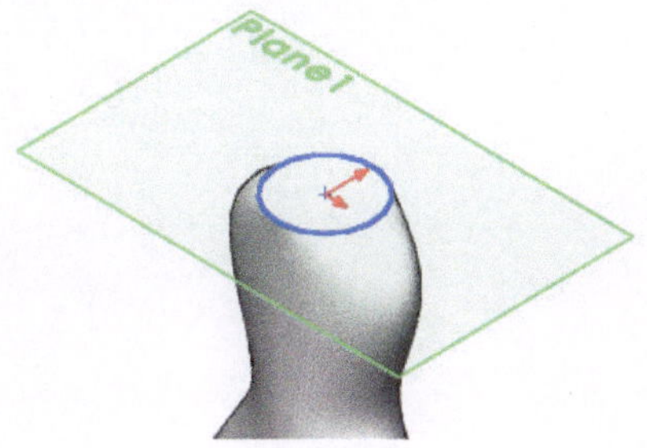

4. Click **Exit Sketch**.
5. Activate the **Extrude Boss/Base** tool and extrude the sketch up to 25 mm depth.

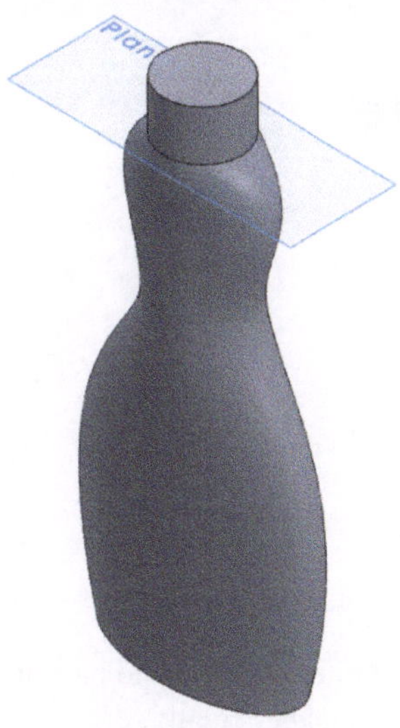

Adding Fillets

1. On the CommandManager, click **Features > Fillet** .
2. On the PropertyManager, click the **FilletXpert** tab.
3. Click on the bottom and top edges of the loft feature.

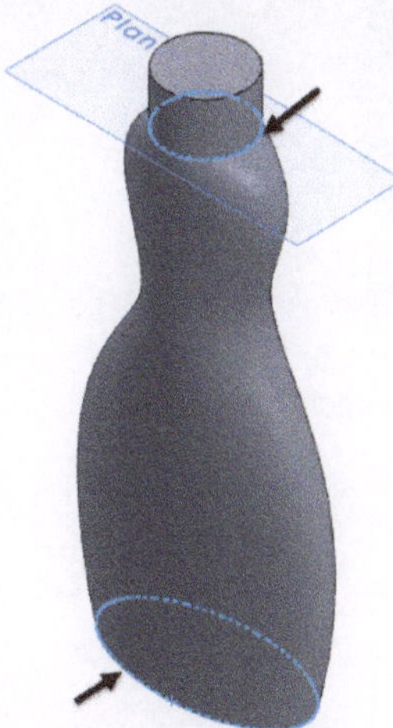

4. Set **Radius** to 5 mm.

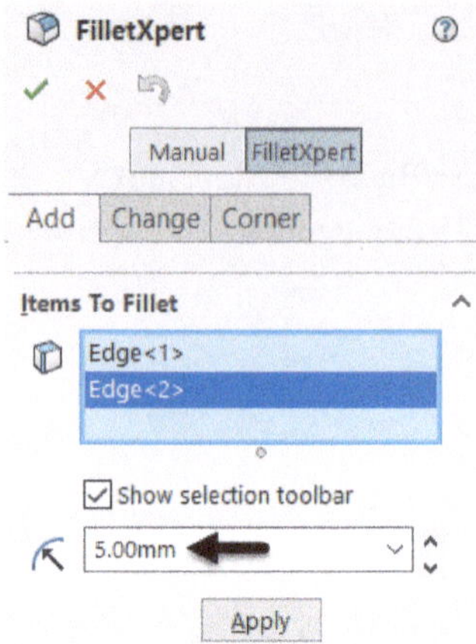

5. Click **OK** to add the fillet.

Shelling the Model

1. On the CommandManager, click **Features > Shell** . The **Shell** tool hollows out a solid part, leaving a uniform or variable-thickness wall.
2. On the PropertyManager, set **Thickness** to 2 mm.
3. Select the top face of the cylindrical feature.

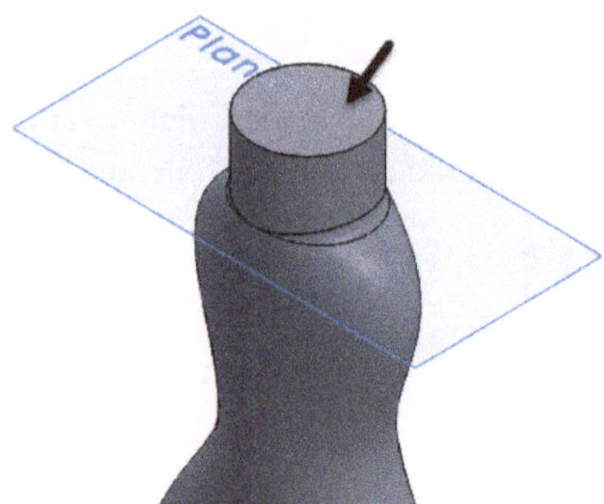

4. Click **OK** to shell the geometry.

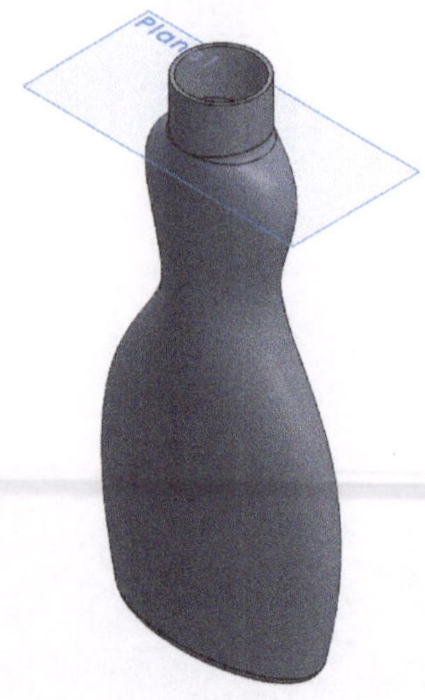

Adding the Indent feature

1. On the CommandManager, click **Features > Reference Geometry > Plane** .
2. In the **FeatureManager Design Tree**, select the Front plane.

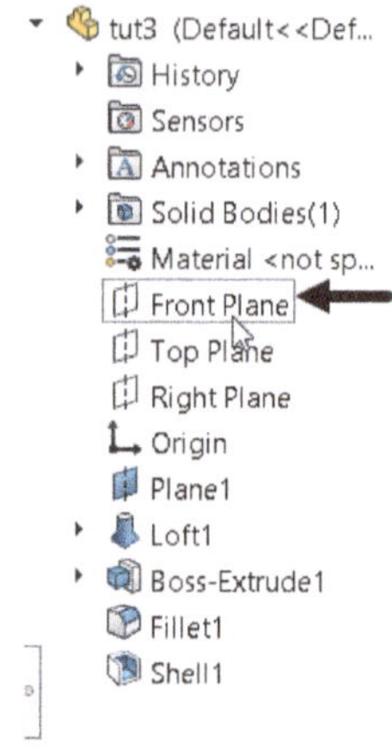

3. On the PropertyManager, type-in **50** in the **Offset distance** box.

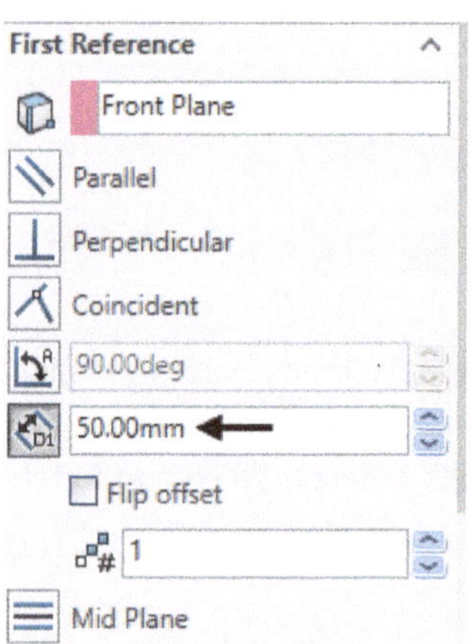

4. Click **OK**.

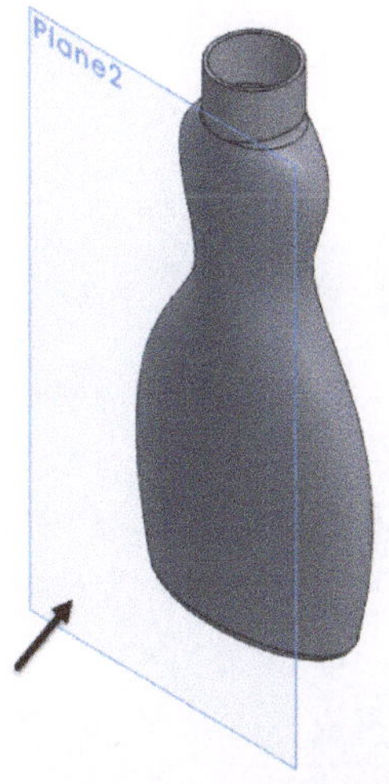

5. Create a sketch on the plane, as shown in the figure.

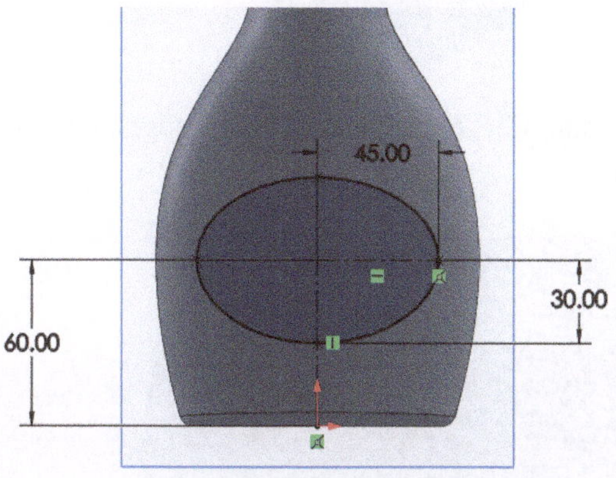

6. Click **Exit Sketch**.
7. On the CommandManager, click **Features > Extruded Boss/Base** .
8. Select the sketch.
9. On the PropertyManager, under the **Direction1** section, select **End Condition > Up To Surface**.
10. On the **PropertyManager**, under **Direction 1**, uncheck **Merge result**.

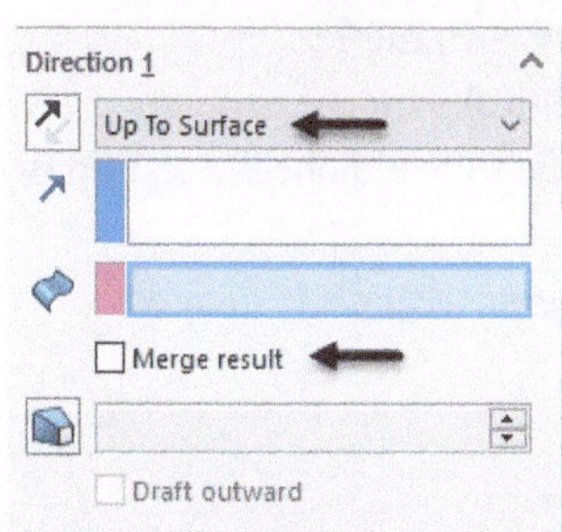

11. Rotate the model and select the inner face of the model geometry.

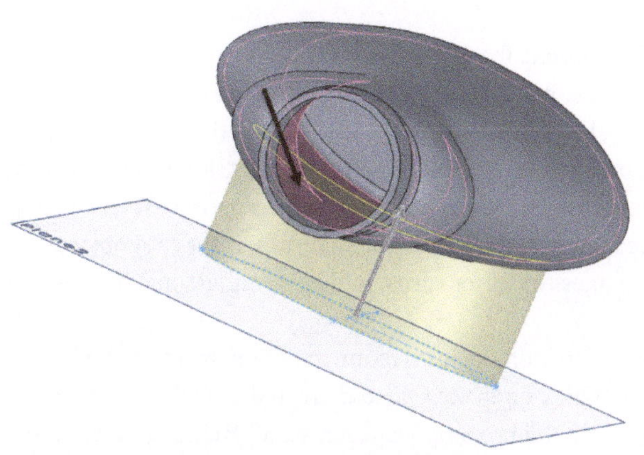

12. Click **OK** to create the separate extruded body.

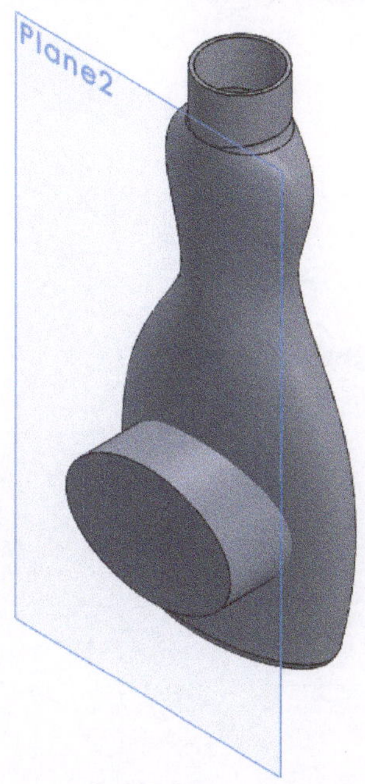

13. On the Menu bar, click **Insert > Features > Indent**.

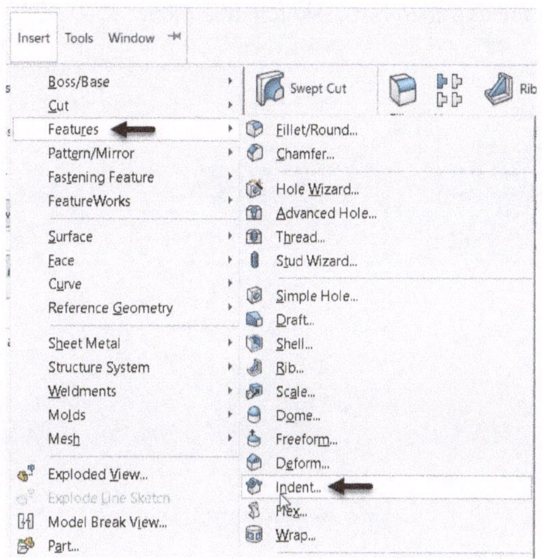

The **Indent** feature creates precise depressions or protrusions on a target body using a tool body. It simplifies designing parts that **fit together** (e.g., battery slots, snap-fit joints) or adding details (logos, textures). It saves time by avoiding manual measurements, ensures accuracy, and updates automatically if the tool object changes. Ideal for cases, molds, or ergonomic designs.

14. Click on the loft feature to define the target body.
15. Click on the extruded body to define the tool body.
16. On the PropertyManager, select **Remove Selections**.
17. Under the **Parameters** section, set the **Thickness** value to 2 and **Clearance** value to 1.

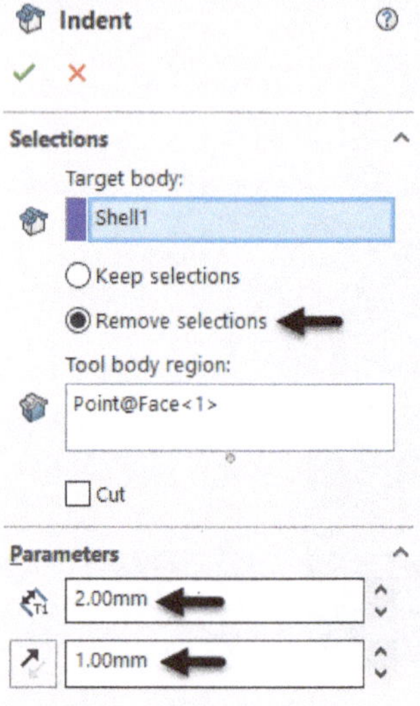

18. Click **OK** to indent the extruded body onto the lofted body.
19. Hide the extruded body, sketch, and plane.

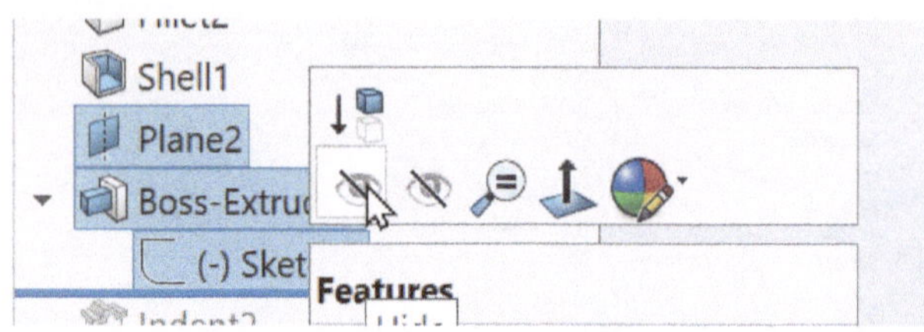

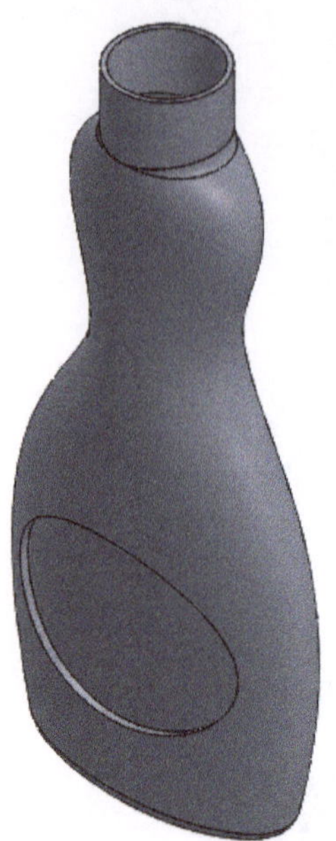

20. Add 1 mm fillet to the inner and outer edges of the indent.

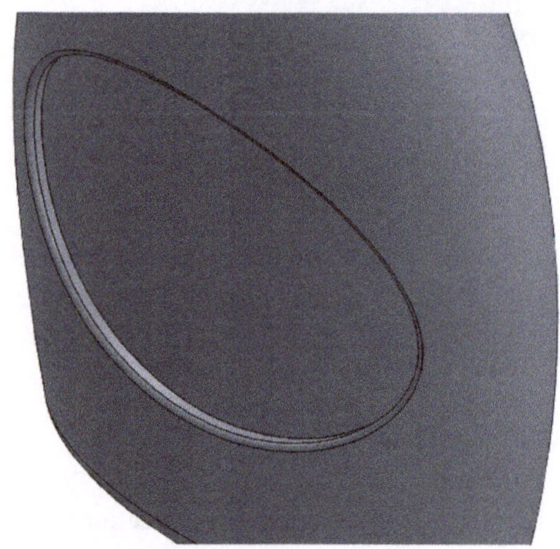

Adding Threads

1. On the CommandManager, click **Features > Reference Geometry > Plane** .
2. Click on the top face of the model geometry.
3. Set the **Distance** value to 5 and check the **Flip offset** option.
4. Click **OK**; a new reference plane is created.

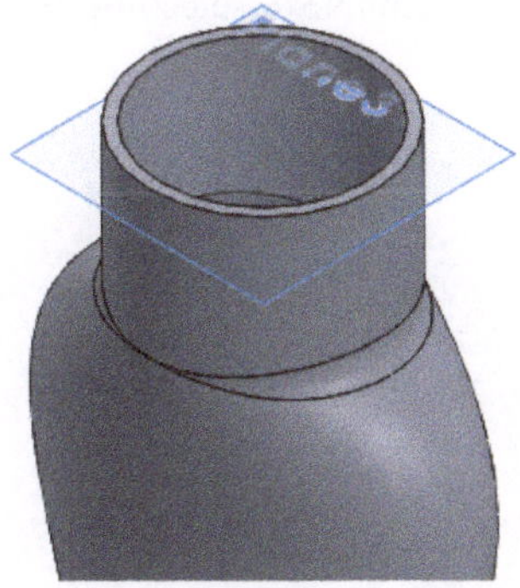

5. Start a sketch on the new reference plane.
6. On the CommandManager, click **Sketch > Convert Entities** .
7. Click on the outer edge of the cylindrical feature and click **OK**.

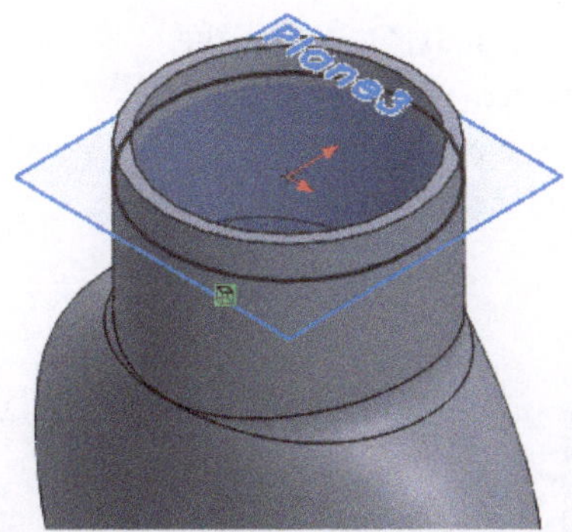

8. Click **Exit Sketch**.
9. On the CommandManager, click **Features > Curves > Helix and Spiral** .
10. Select the circular sketch.
11. On the PropertyManager, select **Constant pitch**.
12. Type-in 7 in the **Pitch** box and check the **Reverse Direction** option.
13. Type-in 2 in the **Revolutions** box.
14. Set the **Start Angle** value to **0**.
15. Uncheck the **Taper Helix** option.
16. Click **OK**.

17. On the CommandManager, click **Features > Reference Geometry > Plane**.
18. Click on the helix and its start point.

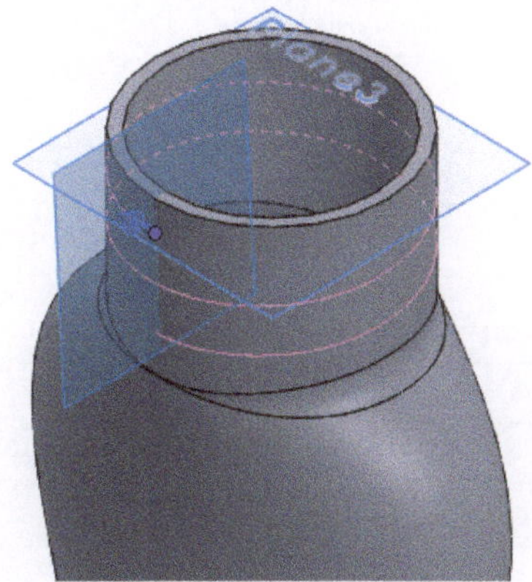

19. Click **OK**.
20. Start a sketch on the new reference plane.
21. On the **View Heads-Up** toolbar, click **View Orientation** drop-down > **Normal To** .
22. Activate the **Line** command and specify the points of the line-chain, as shown.

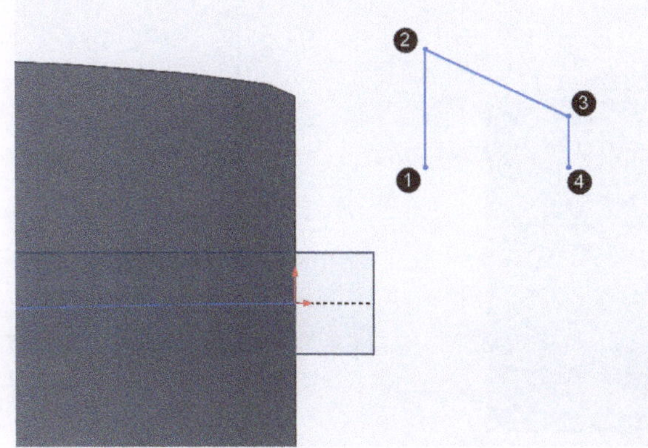

23. Activate the **Centerline** command and create a horizontal line.

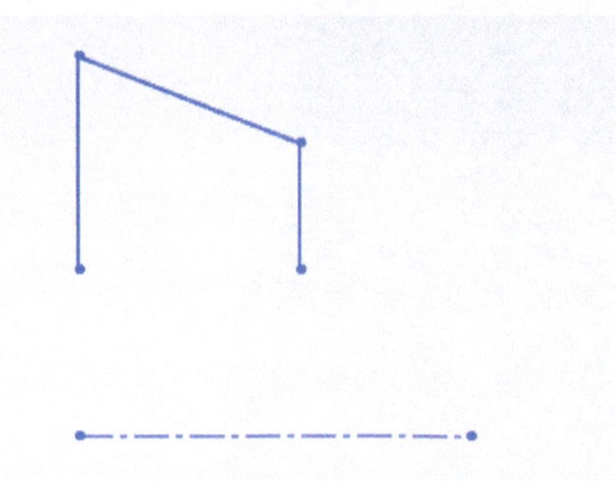

24. Press the Ctrl key and select the left endpoint of the centerline. Next, select the helix.

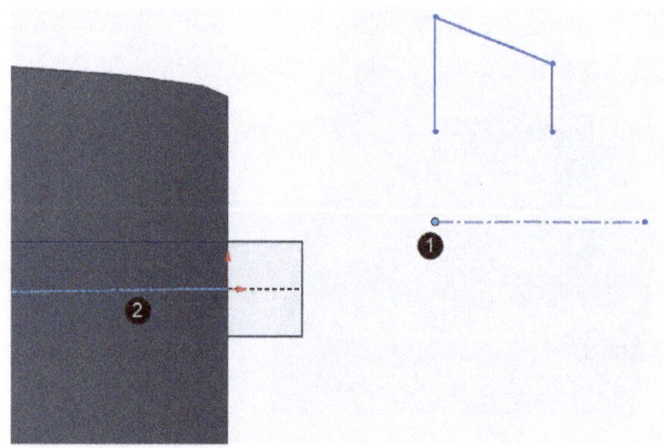

25. On the PropertyManager, click the **Pierce** icon; the endpoint of the centreline is pierced with the endpoint of the helix.

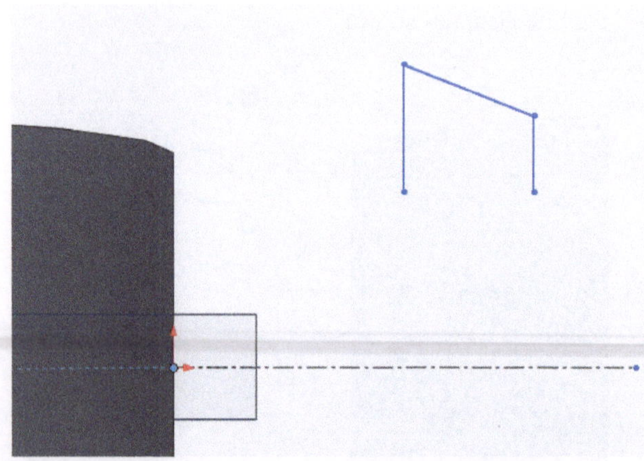

26. Press the Ctrl key and select the lower endpoint of the vertical line of the sketch. Next, select the centreline.

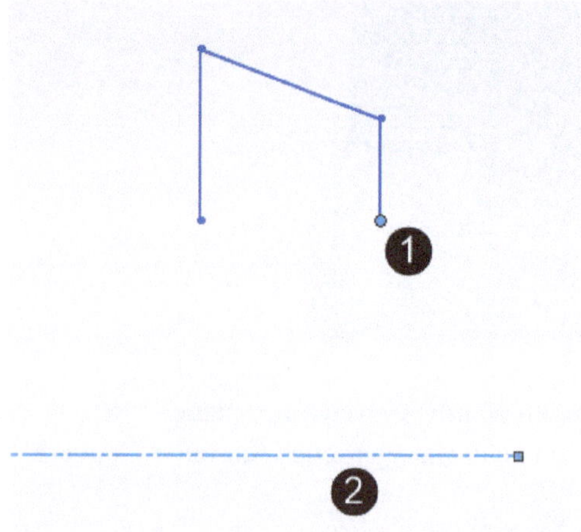

27. Click the **Coincident** icon on the PropertyManager.
28. Click and drag the left vertical line of the sketch such that it is inside the model geometry.

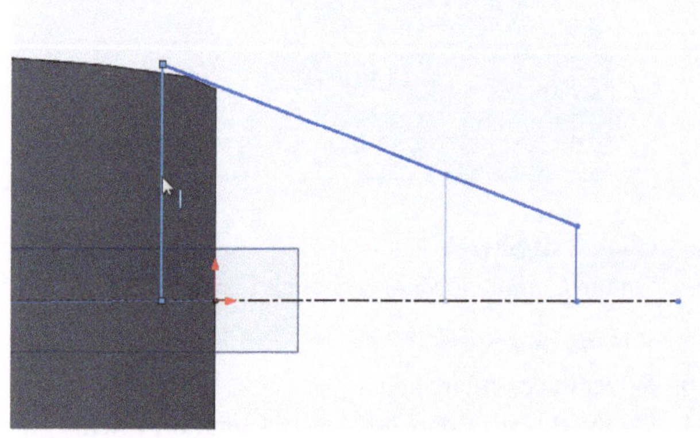

29. Activate the **Sketch Fillet** command and type **0.5** in the **Fillet Radius** box on the PropertyManager.
30. Select the corner point of the right vertical and inclined line, as shown.

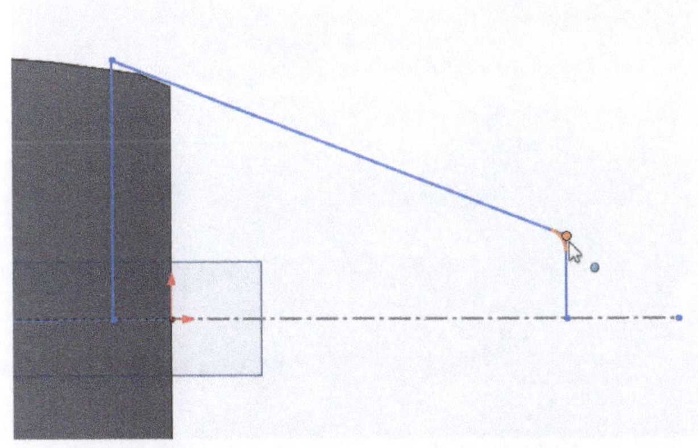

31. Click **OK** on the PropertyManager.
32. On the CommandManager, click the **Mirror Entities** button, and then select all the sketch elements except the centreline.
33. On the PropertyManager, click in the **Mirror about** selection box, and then select the centreline.
34. Click **OK** to mirror the selected elements about the centreline.

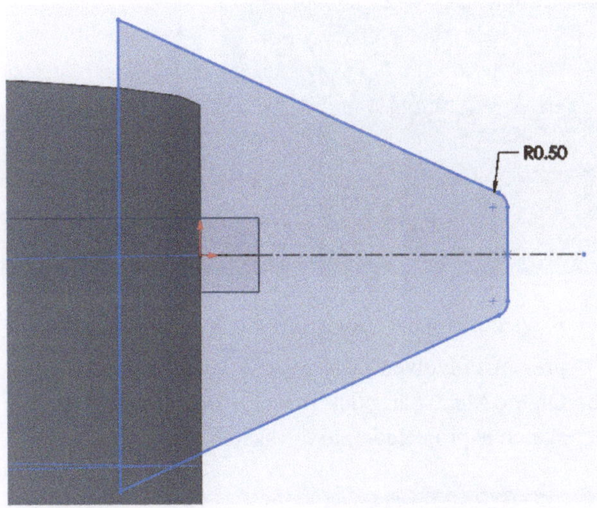

35. Add dimensions to sketch using the **Smart Dimension** command.

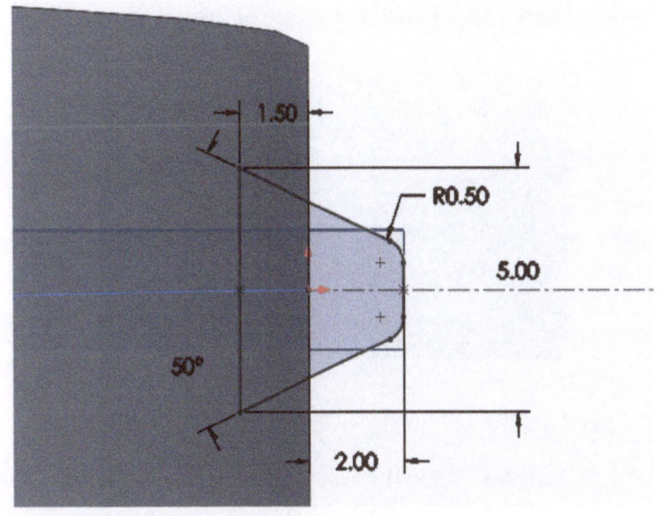

36. Click **Exit Sketch**.
37. On the CommandManager, click **Features > Swept Boss/Base**  .
38. Click on the thread profile and the helix.

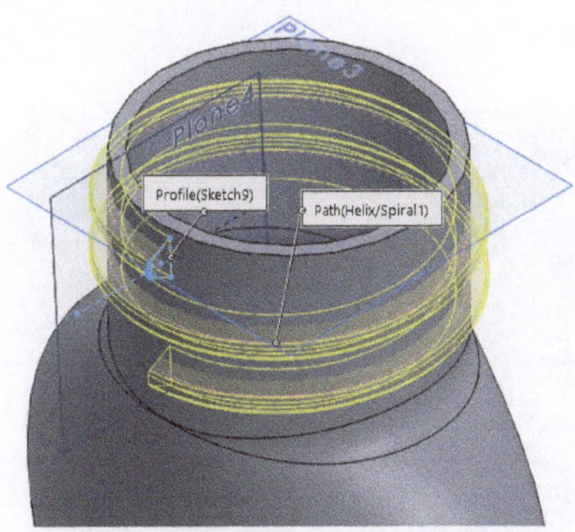

39. On the PropertyManager, expand the **Options** section and check **Merge result**.
40. Click **OK**.

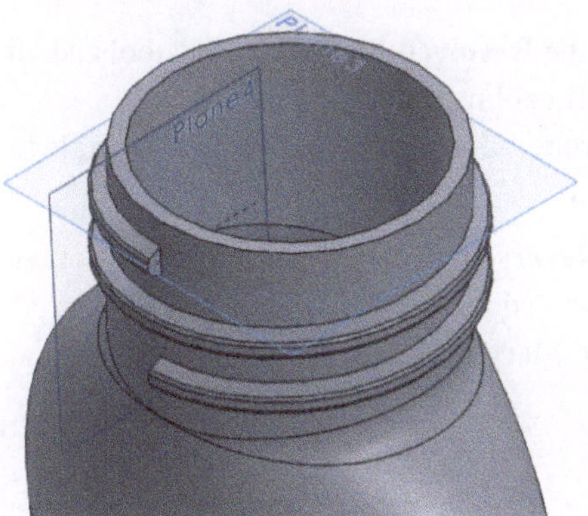

41. Start a sketch on the end face of the thread.

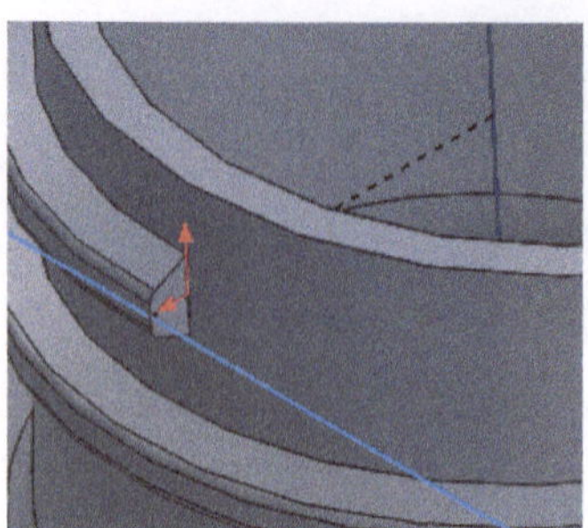

42. On the CommandManager, click **Sketch > Convert Entities** and select the Swept feature's thread profile from the FeatureManager Design Tree.

43. Click **OK**.

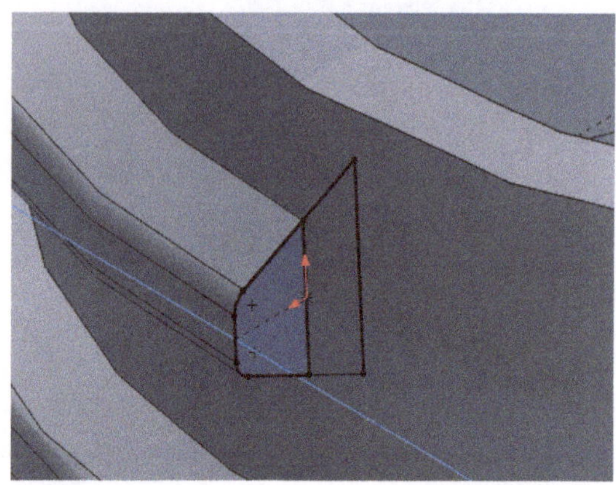

44. Click **Exit Sketch**.
45. Activate the **Revolved Boss/Base** tool and click on the vertical line of the sketch.
46. On the PropertyManager, set **Direction 1 Angle** to **100**.
47. Use the **Reverse Direction** button, if the preview of the revolved feature is displayed inside the model.
48. Check the **Merge result** option.

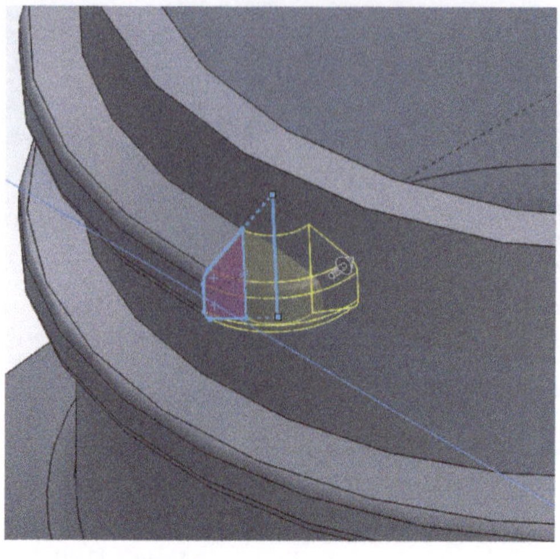

49. Click **OK**.
50. Rotate the model and click on the other end of the thread.

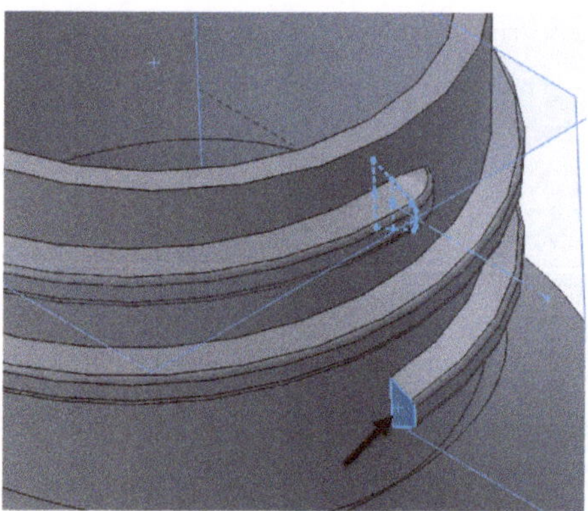

51. Press the Ctrl key and select the sketch used for the previous revolved feature.
52. On the Menu bar, click **Insert > Derived Sketch**; the sketch is projected onto the sketch plane.

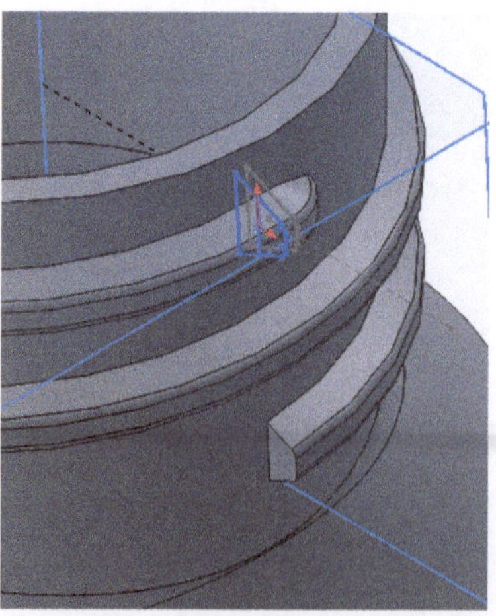

53. Press Esc to deselect the sketch.
54. On the CommandManager, click **Display/Delete Relations > Add Relations**.
55. Click on the inclined line of the sketch and the inclined edge of the end face.

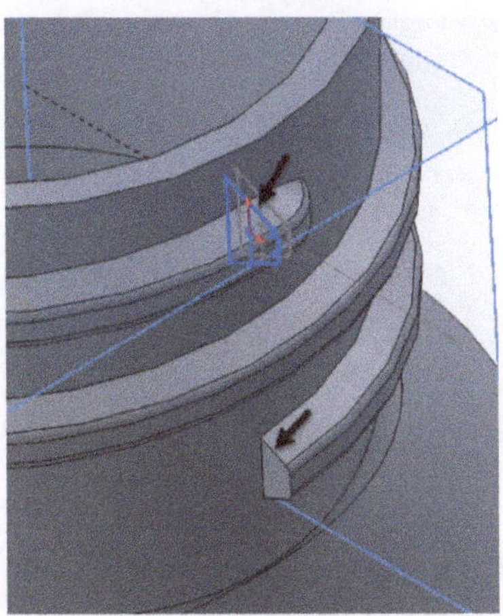

56. On the PropertyManager, click **Collinear**.
57. Press the Ctrl key and click on the end-points, as shown in the figure.

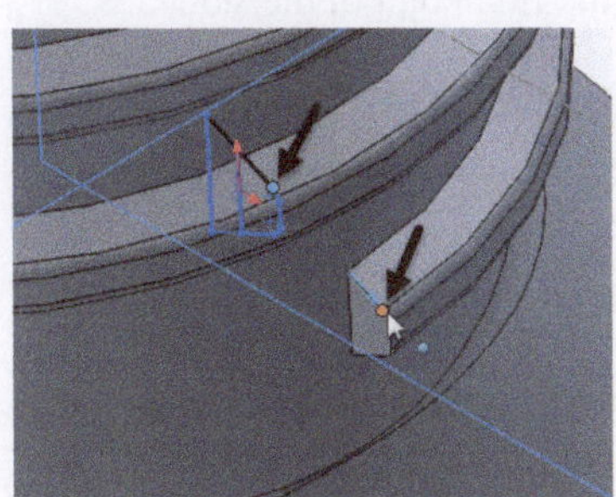

58. On the PropertyManager, click **Coincident**.

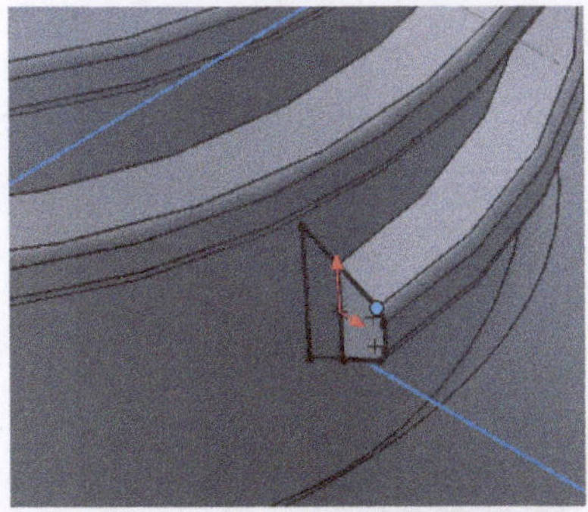

59. Click **OK** on the PropertyManager.
60. Click **Exit Sketch** on the Command Manager.
61. Create a revolved boss using the sketch.

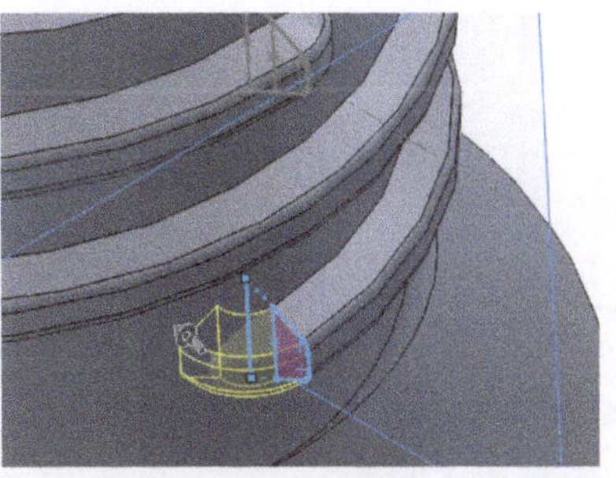

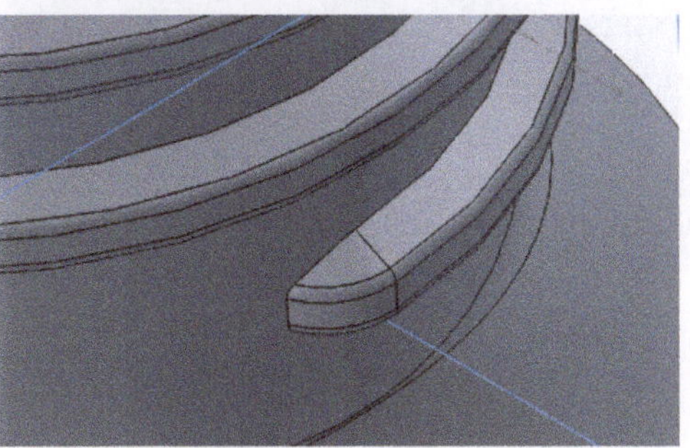

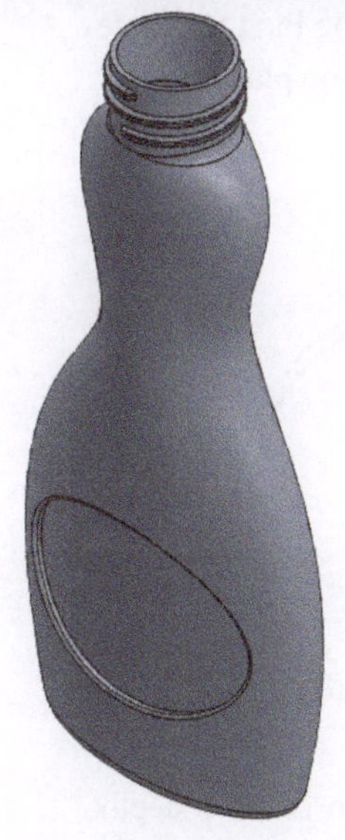

62. Save the model and close it.

TUTORIAL 5

In this tutorial, you construct a patterned cylindrical shell.

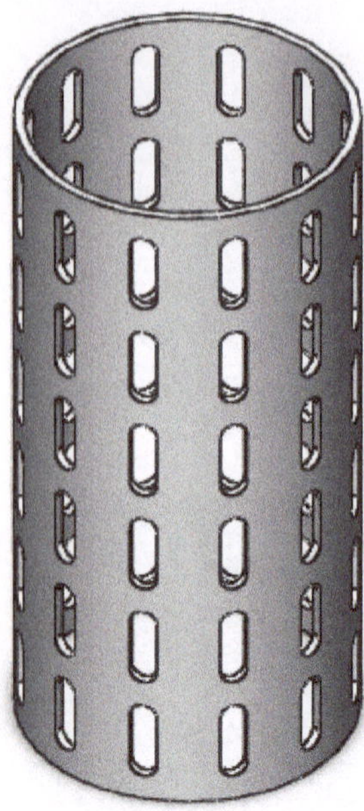

Constructing a cylindrical shell

1. Start a new file using the **Part** template.
2. Create a sketch on the top plane.

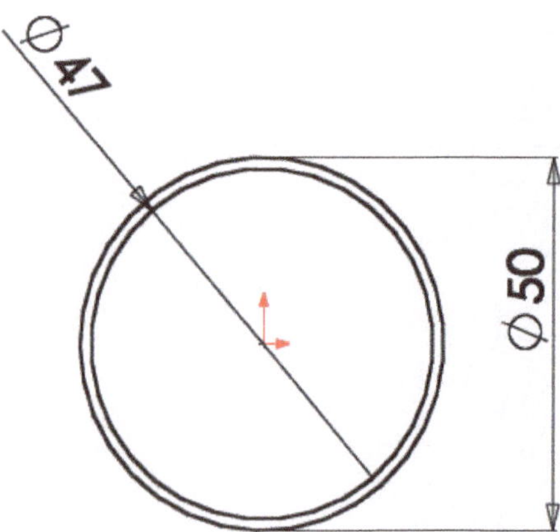

3. Extrude the sketch up to 100 mm depth.

Adding a Slot

1. Activate the **Extruded Cut** tool.
2. Click on the front plane.
3. On the CommandManager, click **Sketch > Straight Slot** .
4. Click to define the first point of the slot.

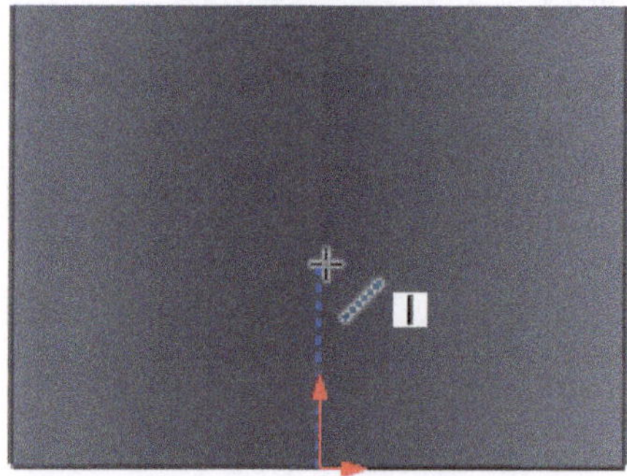

5. Move the pointer up and click to define the second point.

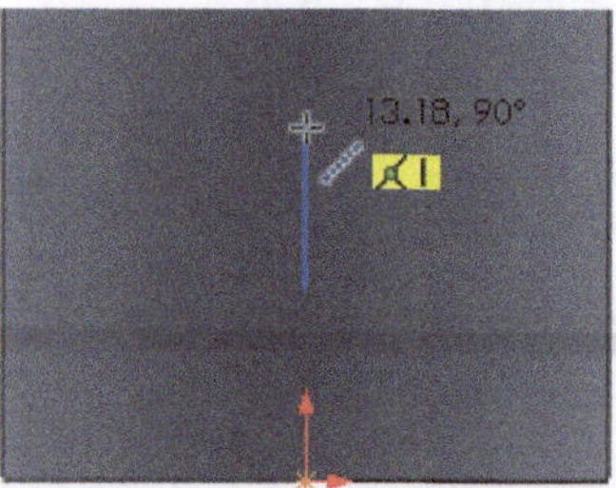

6. Move the pointer and click to create a slot.

7. Add dimensions to the slot.

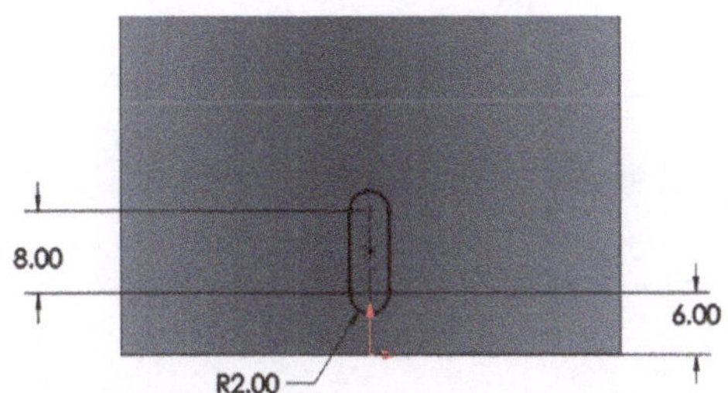

8. Click **Exit Sketch**.
9. On the PropertyManager, select **End Condition > Through All**.
10. Click the **Reverse Direction** button next to the **End Condition** drop-down.

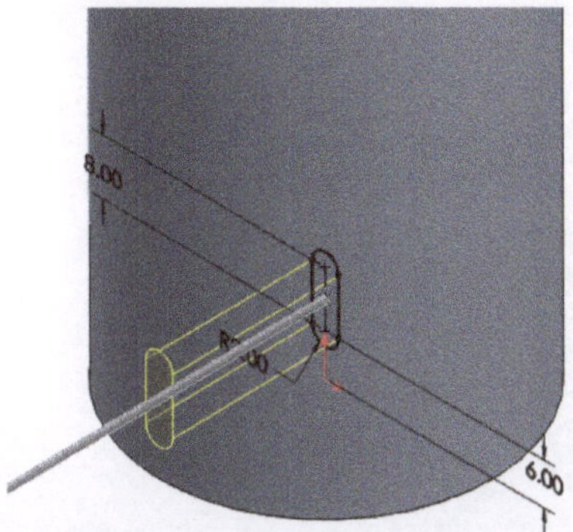

11. Click **OK**.

Constructing the Axis

Axes define the central rotational axis for creating **circular patterns** (e.g., evenly spaced bolts on a flange) or **revolved features** (e.g., cylindrical components like pulleys).

1. On the CommandManager, click **Features > Reference Geometry > Axis** .
2. Click on the inner cylindrical face of the model geometry.

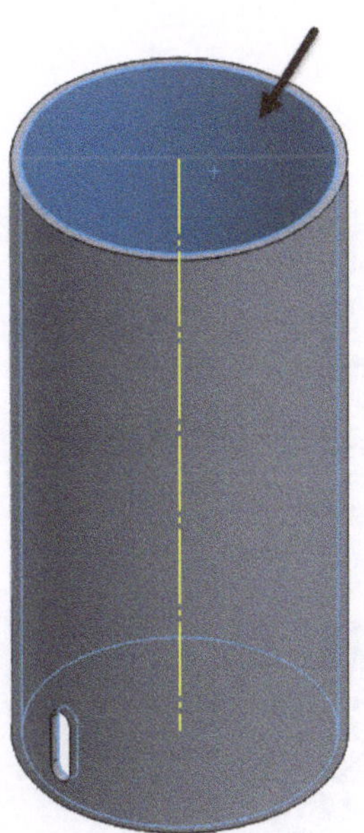

3. Click **OK** to construct the axis.

Constructing the Linear pattern

A linear pattern is used to create multiple, evenly spaced copies of a feature, body, or component along one or two linear directions. It reduces manual modeling time and ensures uniform spacing and alignment of features.

1. On the CommandManager, click **Features > Linear Pattern** .
2. On the PropertyManager, under the **Features and Faces** section, click in the **Features to Pattern** box, and then select the slot.
3. In the FeatureManager Design Tree, select the newly created axis. You can also select the Top Plane from the FeatureManager Design Tree.

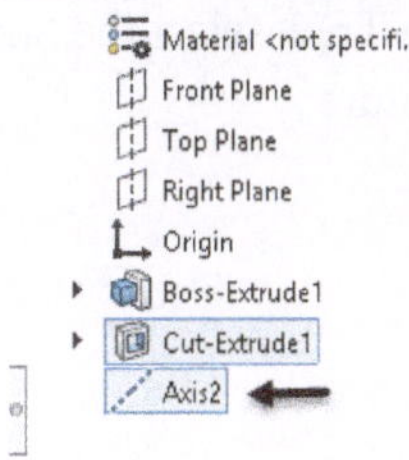

4. On the PropertyManager, under the **Direction1** section, set the **Spacing** value to 16.
5. Set **Number of Instances** to 6.

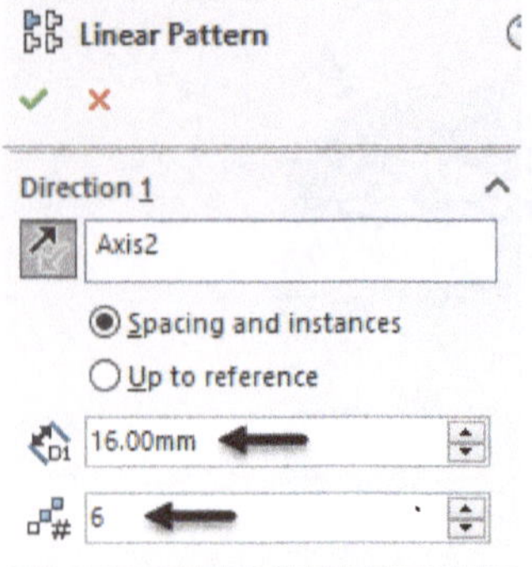

6. Click **OK**.

Constructing the Circular pattern

A **circular pattern** is used to replicate a selected feature, body, or component symmetrically around a defined axis or circular path.

1. On the CommandManager, click **Features > Linear Pattern > Circular Pattern**.
2. In the FeatureManager Design Tree, select the linear pattern and the cut-extrude feature.

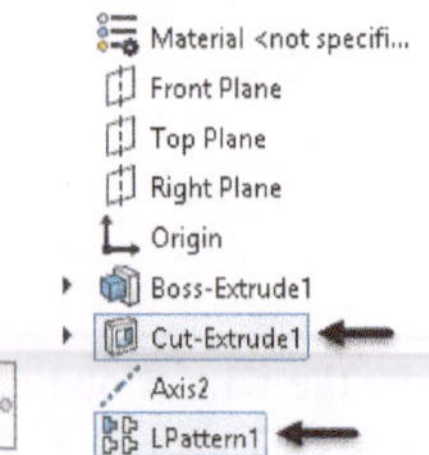

3. On the PropertyManager, click in the **Pattern Axis** selection box and select the model's cylindrical face.

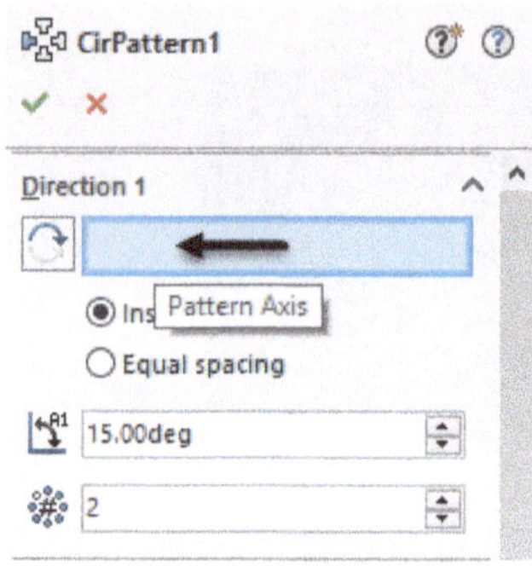

4. Type-in **12** in the **Number of Instances** box.
5. Check the **Equal Spacing** option.
6. Click **OK** to make the circular pattern.

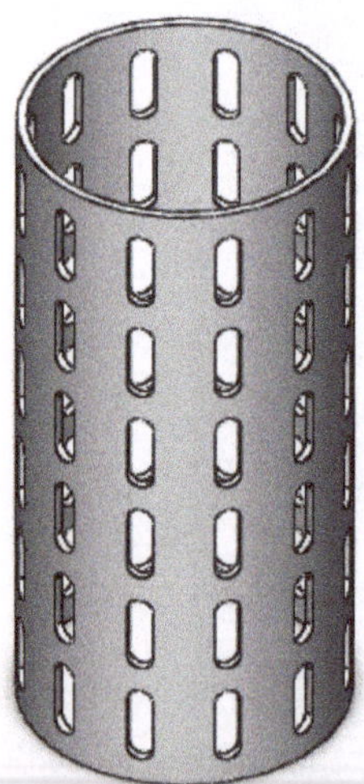

11. Save and close the model.

TUTORIAL 6

In this tutorial, you construct the model shown in the figure.

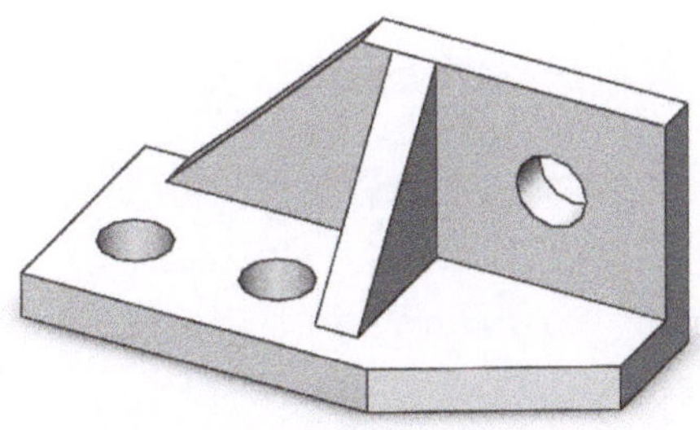

Constructing the first feature

1. Open a new part file.
2. Construct the first feature on the top plane (extrude the sketch up to a distance of 10 mm).

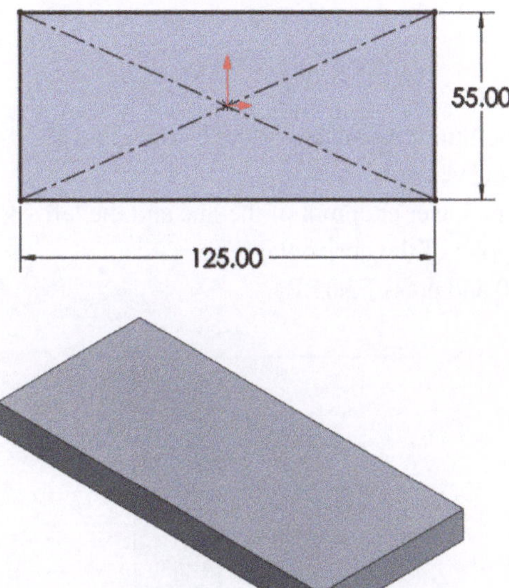

Constructing the Second Feature

1. Draw the sketch on the top face of the first feature.

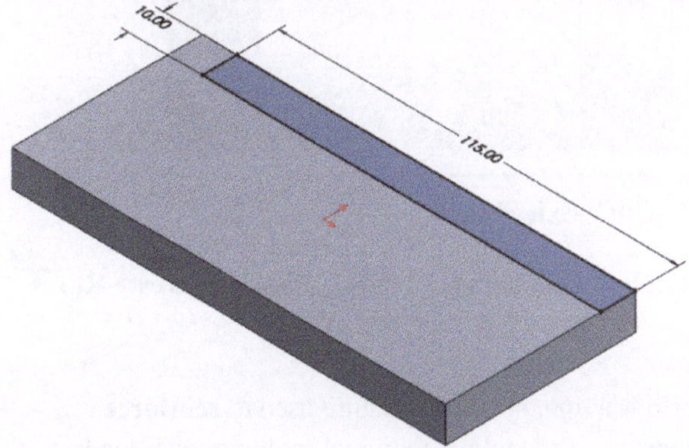

2. Click **Exit Sketch**.
3. On the CommandManager, click **Features > Extruded Boss/Base**.
4. Type-in **45** in the **Depth** box.

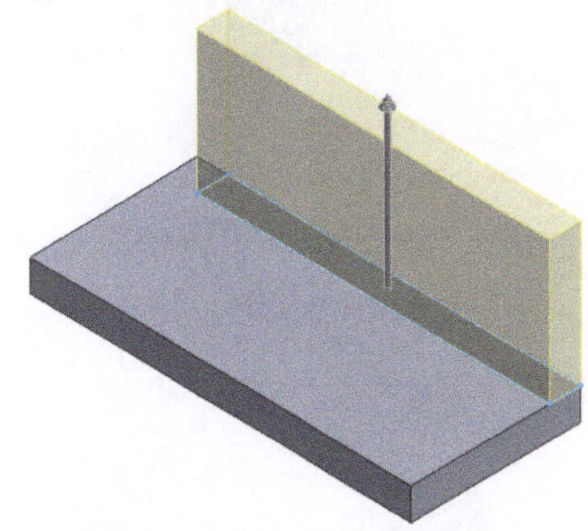

5. Click **OK**.

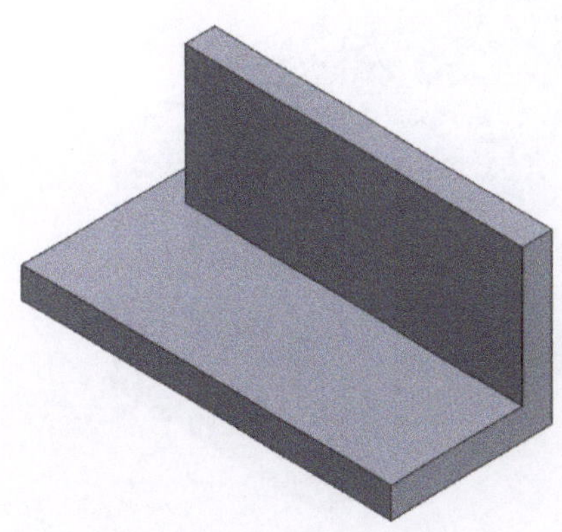

Constructing the third feature

1. On the CommandManager, click **Features > Reference Geometry > Plane**.
2. Click on the right-side face of the model geometry.

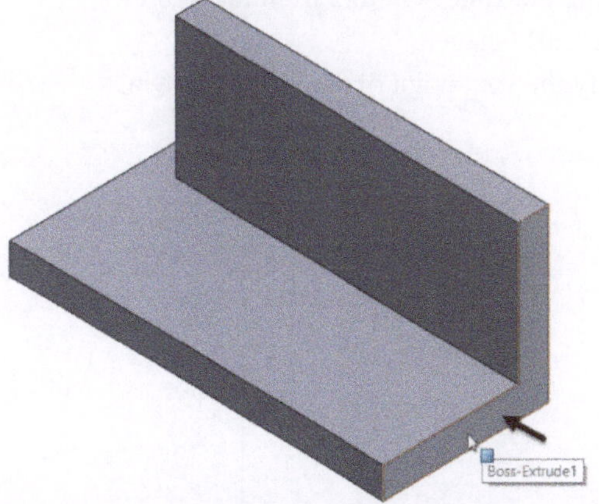

3. Click on the left-side face of the second feature.

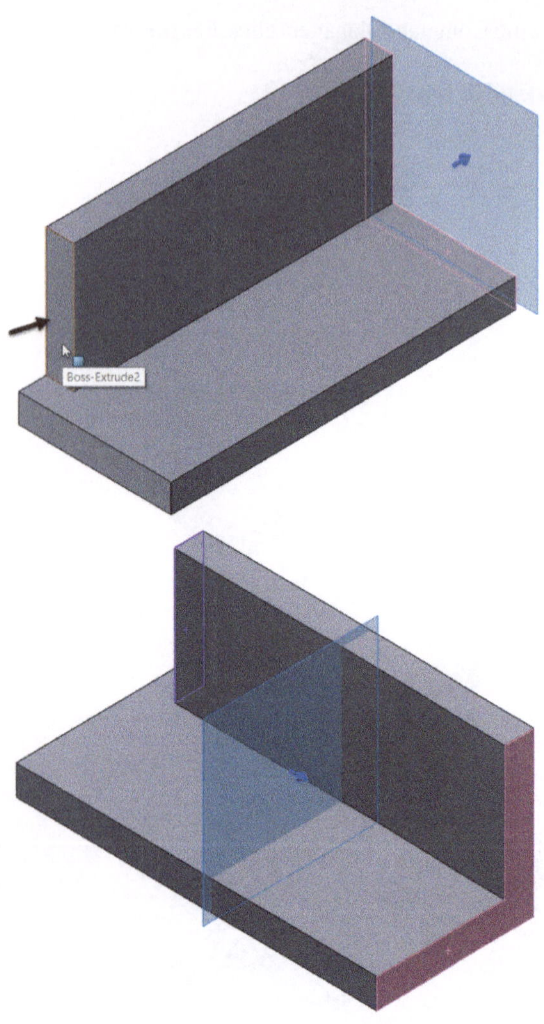

4. Click **OK**.
5. Start a new sketch on the newly created reference plane.
6. Activate the **Line** tool from the **Sketch** CommandManager.
7. Specify the start point of the line, as shown.

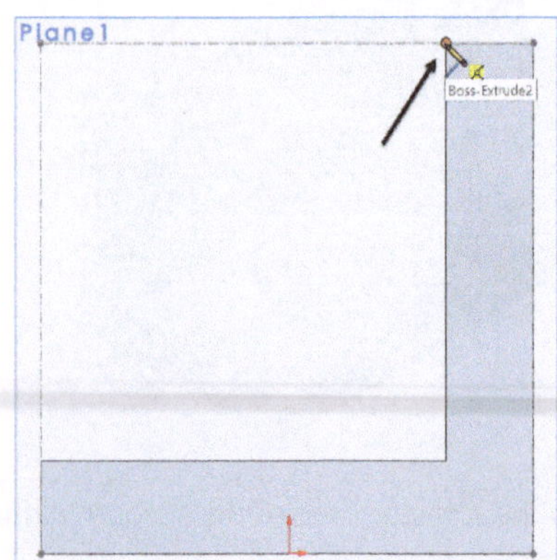

8. Click on the horizontal edge of the model, as shown.

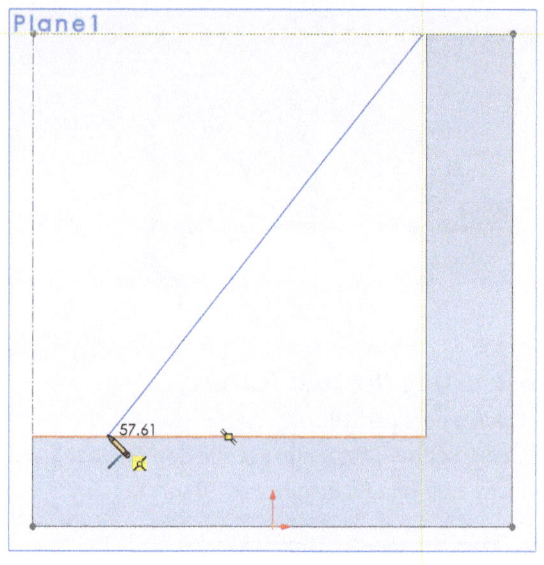

9. Press **ESC**.
10. Click the **Smart Dimension** tool on the Sketch CommandManager.
11. Select the lower endpoint of the line and the left vertex point of the horizontal edge.
12. Type 10 and press ENTER.

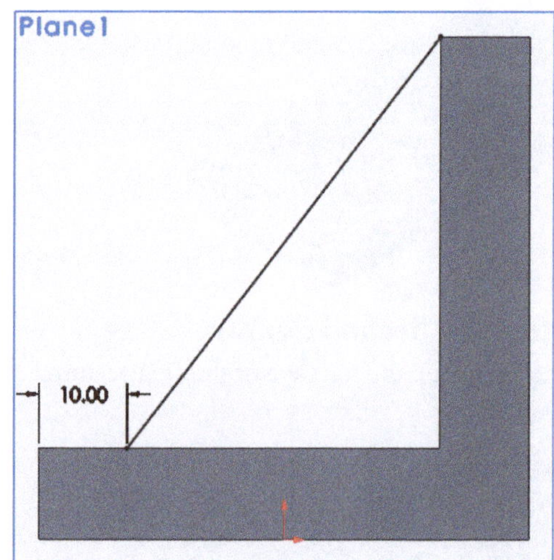

13. Click **Exit Sketch**.
14. On the CommandManager, click **Features > Rib** .

A rib is a thin, structural feature used to **reinforce parts** against bending, torsional, or vibrational loads while minimizing weight and material usage. Ribs are created by extruding a sketched profile perpendicular to a reference plane or face, generating a thin wall that connects to adjacent geometry.

15. On the PropertyManager, click **Thickness > Both Sides**.
16. Set **Rib Thickness** to 10.
17. Select **Extrusion direction > Parallel to Sketch**.
18. Check the **Flip material side** option.
19. Click **OK**.

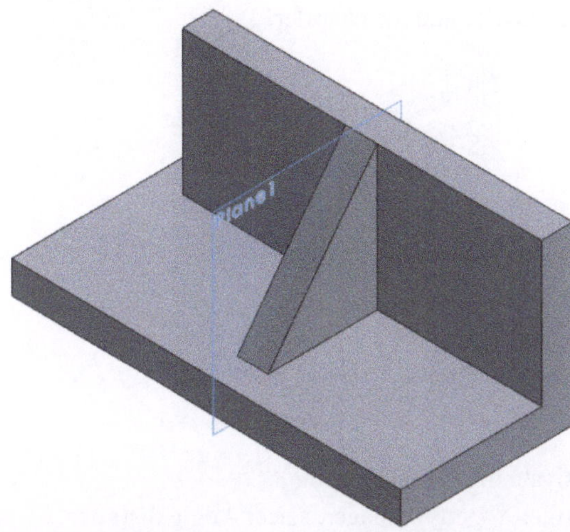

Inserting Holes

1. To insert holes, click **Features > Hole Wizard** on the CommandManager.
2. On the **Hole Specification** PropertyManager, select the **Hole** icon.
3. Select **Standard > ANSI Metric**.
4. Select **Type > Drill Sizes**.
5. Under the **Hole Specifications** section, select **Size > 16**.
6. Select **End Condition > Through All**.
7. Expand the **Tolerance/Precision** section.
8. Select the **Tolerance Type** > **Bilateral**.
9. Type **0.05** in the **Maximum Variation** box.
10. Type **-0.02** in the **Minimum Variation** box.
11. Click the **Positions** tab and click on the top face of the base feature.
12. Place two holes on the top face.

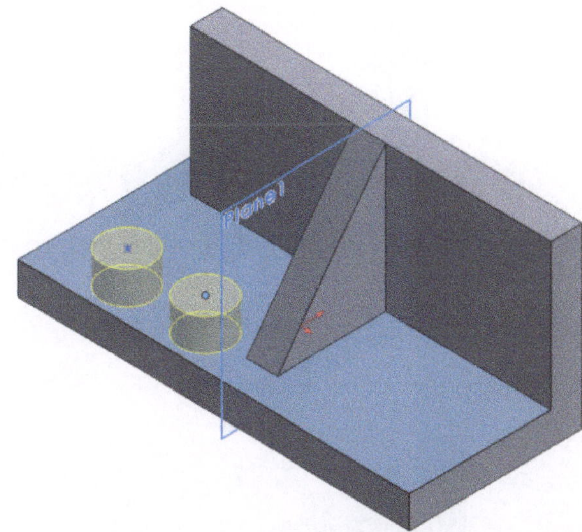

13. Add dimensions to define the hole location.

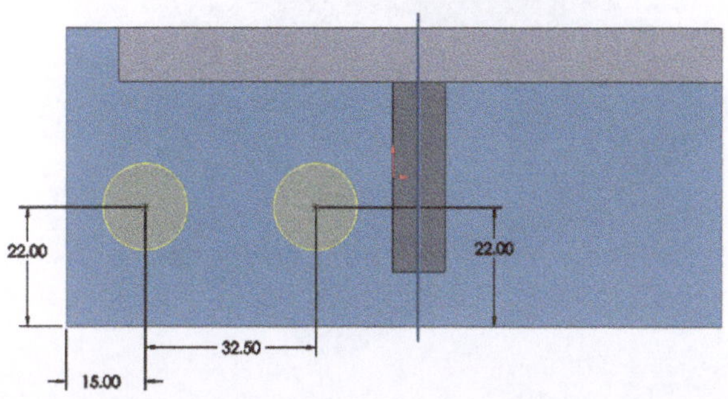

14. Click **OK**.

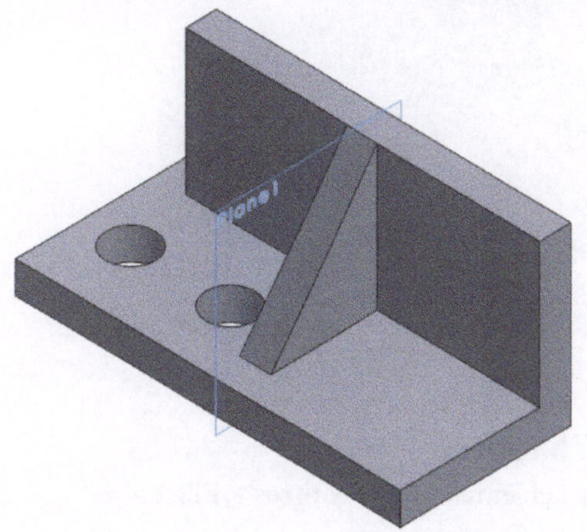

15. Insert another hole on the front face of the second feature.

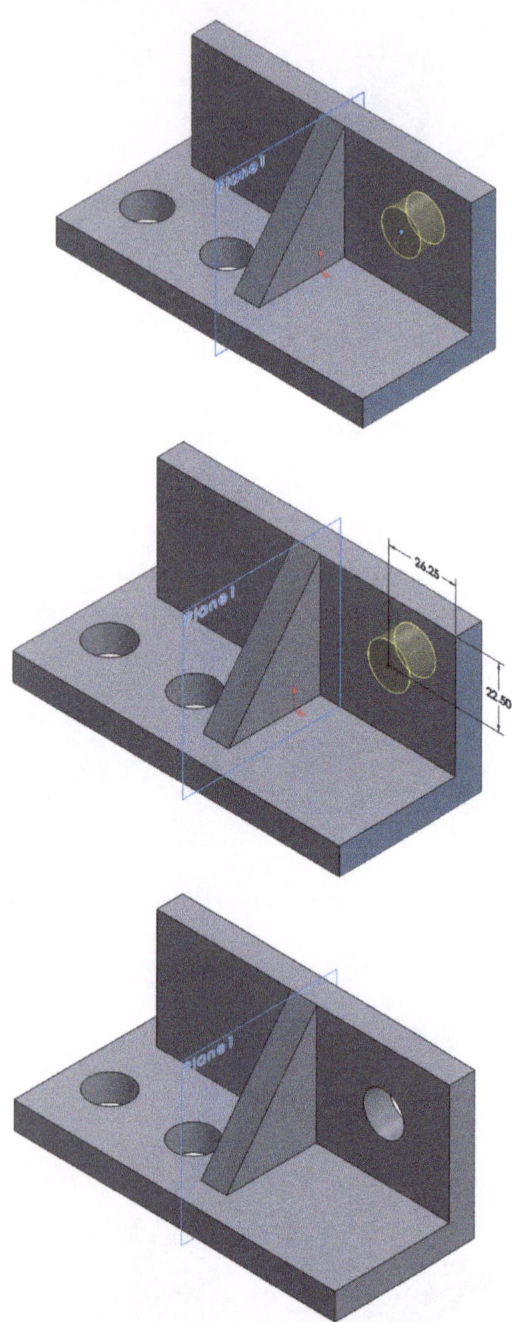

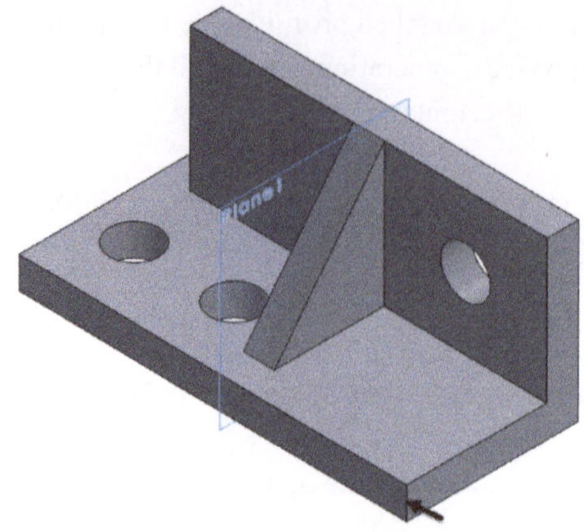

6. Click **OK** to add the chamfer.

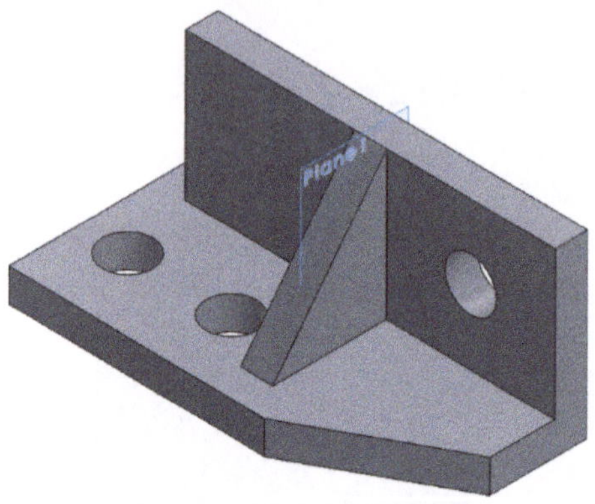

7. Activate the **Chamfer** tool.
8. On the PropertyManager, select **Angle distance**.
9. Type-in **45** in the **Distance** and **Angle** boxes.
10. Click on the corner edge of the second feature.

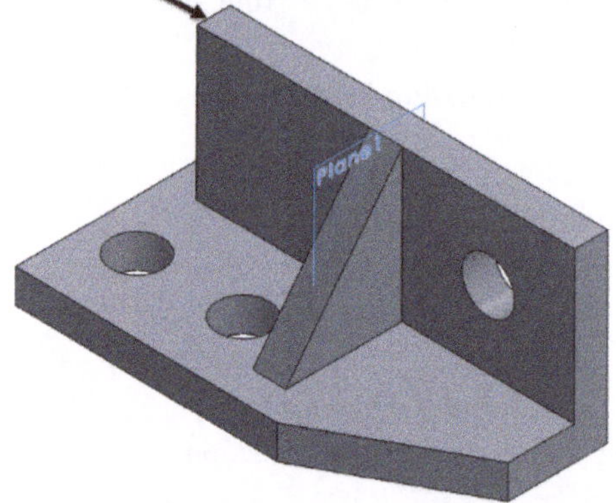

11. Click **OK**.

Adding Chamfers

1. To add a chamfer, click **Features > Fillet > Chamfer** on the CommandManager.
2. On the PropertyManager, select **Distance Distance**.
3. Select **Asymmetric** from the **Chamfer Method** drop-down available in the **Chamfer Parameters** section.
4. Type-in **45** and **25** in the **Distance 1** and **Distance 2** boxes.
5. Click on the corner edge of the first feature.

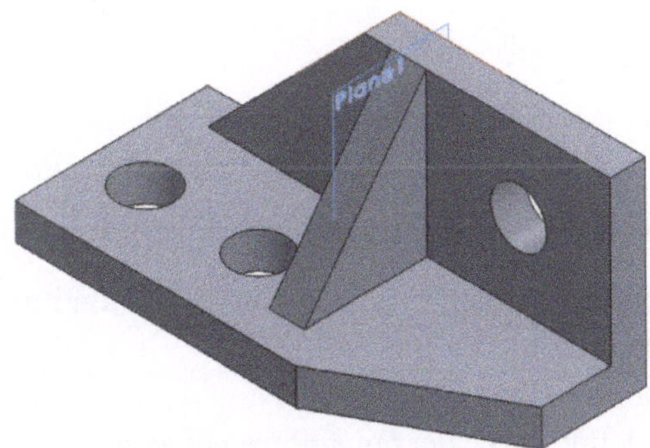

Creating Bounding Box

A bounding box is a rectangular volume that encloses the maximum extents of a part or assembly, automatically calculating its total length, width, and height. You use this feature to determine the minimum raw stock size required for manufacturing, ensuring the chosen material fully covers the part geometry. Bounding boxes also verify if a component fits within defined machine workspaces or packaging constraints. In assemblies, they reduce computational load by simplifying collision detection, checking for overlaps between simple rectangular shapes rather than complex geometry.

You can adjust the bounding box orientation to optimize volume calculations. While default settings align the box with global axes, you can rotate it to align with specific geometry if a part is angled. The bounding box maintains a parametric link to the model, meaning it updates automatically when you change part dimensions. This prevents errors in technical drawings and eliminates the need for manual recalculation.

1. To create a bounding, click **Features > Reference Geometry > Bounding Box** on the CommandManager.
2. On the PropertyManager, select **Best Fit** under the **Reference Face/Plane** section.
3. Click **OK** to create the bounding box.

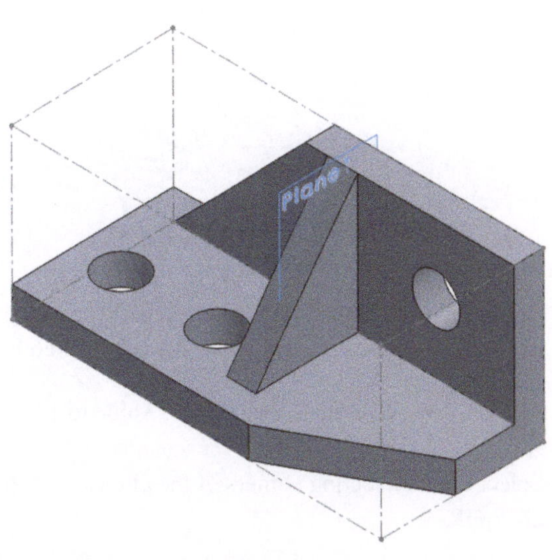

TUTORIAL 7

In this tutorial, you create the model shown in the figure.

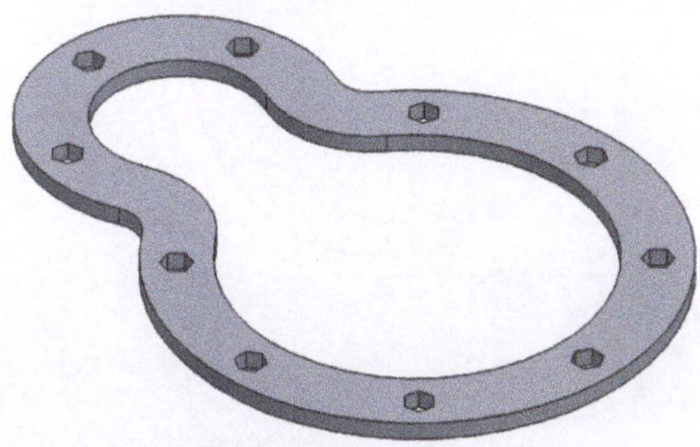

Constructing the first feature

1. Open a new part file.
2. On the CommandManager, click **Features > Extruded Boss/Base**  .
3. Click on the top plane.
4. Construct two circles and add dimensions to them.

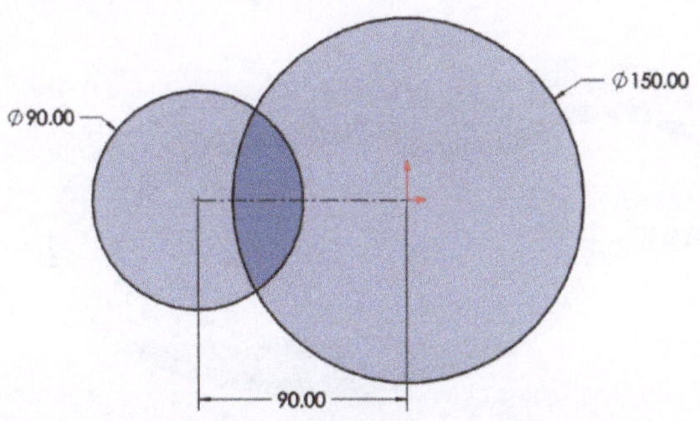

5. On the CommandManager, click **Sketch > Trim Entities**  and trim the intersecting entities.

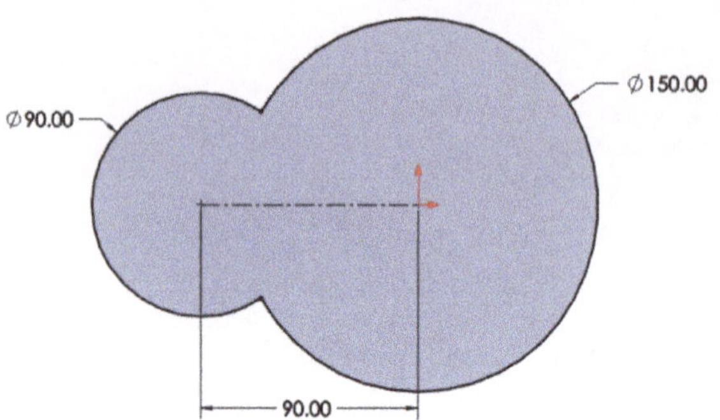

6. On the CommandManager, click **Sketch > Sketch Fillet** and set the **Fillet Radius** value to 10.
7. Select the intersecting corners of the circles, and then click **OK**.

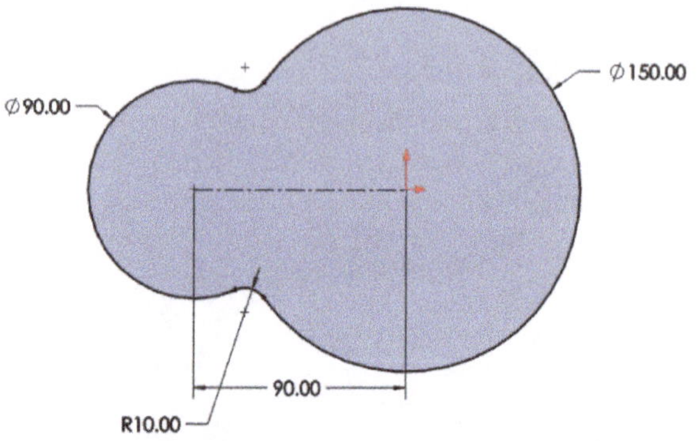

8. Click **Exit Sketch**.
9. On the PropertyManager, type 5 in the **Depth** box.
10. Check the **Thin Feature** option and select **Type > One Direction**.
11. Type 20 in the Thickness box.
12. Use the **Reverse Direction** button next to the **Type** drop-down to ensure that the extruded feature is thickened from inside.
13. Click **OK**.

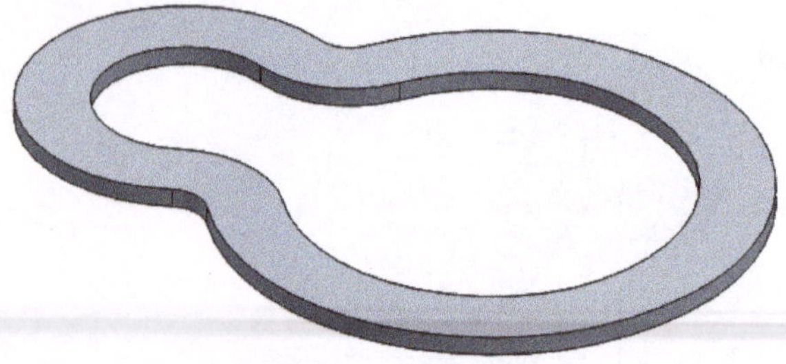

Constructing the Extruded cut

1. On the CommandManager, click **Features > Extruded Cut**.
2. Click on the top face of the model geometry.
3. On the CommandManager, click **Sketch > Polygon**.
4. On the PropertyManager, type-in 6 in the **Number of Sides** box.
5. Select the **Inscribed circle** option.
6. Click to define the center point of the polygon.

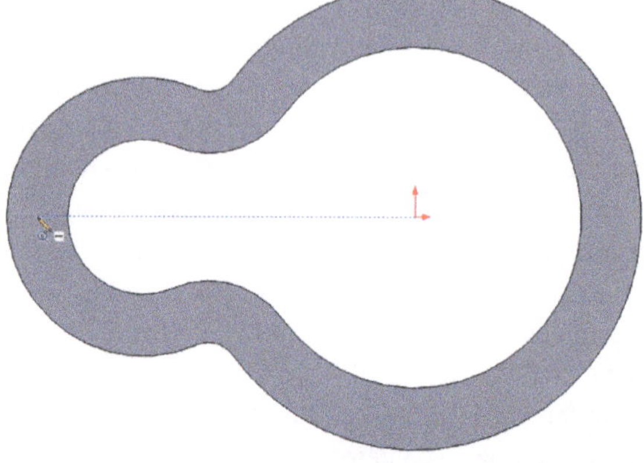

7. Move the pointer and click to construct the polygon.
8. Draw a horizontal centerline connecting the center point of the polygon and sketch origin.

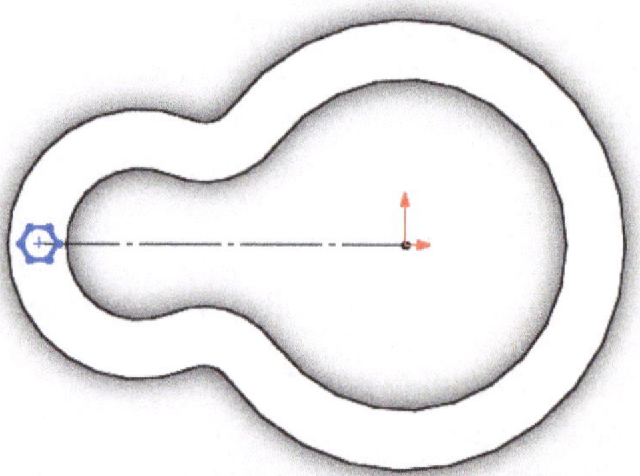

9. On the CommandManager, click **Sketch > Display/Delete Relations > Add Relation**.
10. Click on the horizontal line of the polygon.

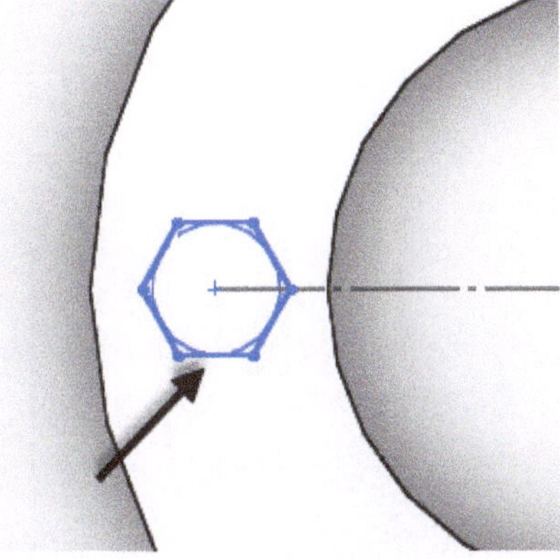

11. On the PropertyManager, click **Horizontal**, and then click **OK**.
12. Activate the **Smart Dimensions** command, zoom into the polygon, and select the construction circle.
13. Place the dimension, type 8, and press Enter.
14. Select the horizontal construction line, place the dimension, and type 125. Next, press Enter.

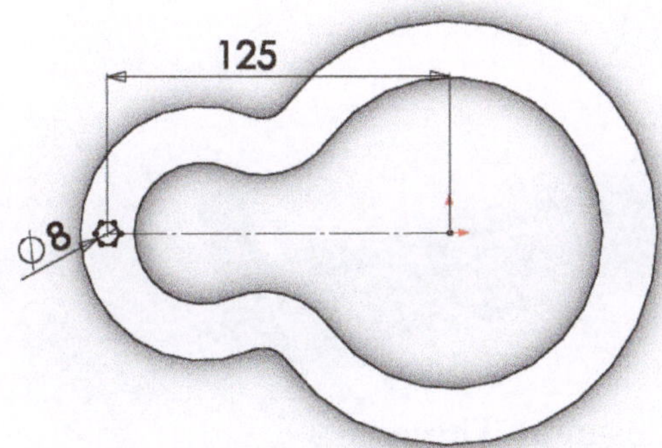

15. Click **Exit Sketch**.
16. Create the cut throughout the body.

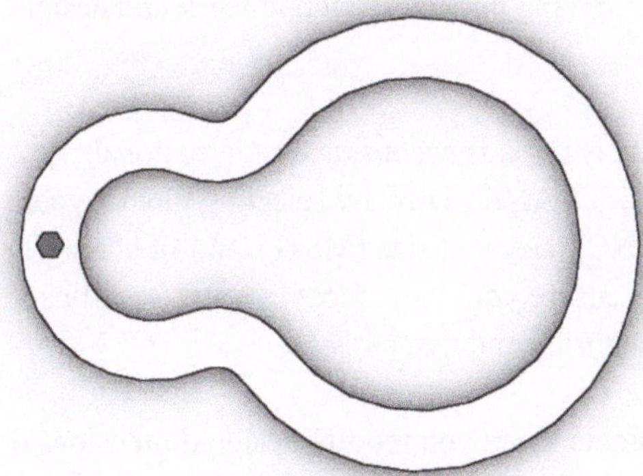

Making the Curve Driven Pattern

The Curve Driven Pattern replicates features, bodies, or components along a user-defined curve. You use this tool to create non-linear distributions, such as vents on curved surfaces or bolts on flanges. To define the pattern, you select a curve (sketch, edge, or composite curve) and set parameters for instance spacing, alignment, and tangent direction. This automates the placement of repetitive elements while maintaining specific geometric constraints.

1. On the CommandManager, click **Features > Linear Pattern > Curve Driven Pattern** .
2. In the FeatureManager Design Tree, select the sketch used to create **Extrude-Thin1**.

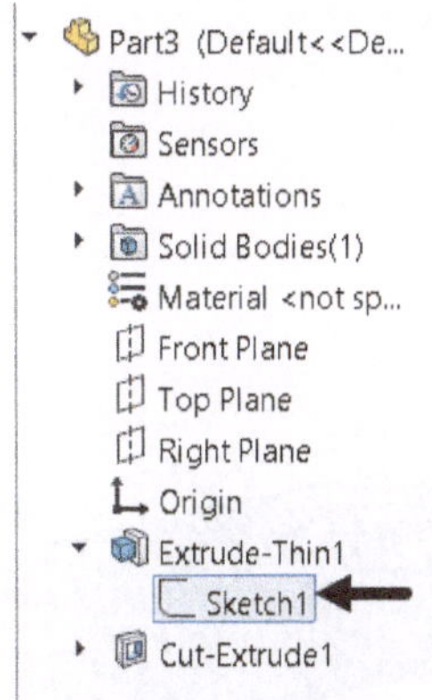

3. Select the polygonal cut to define the feature to pattern.
4. Type-in **10** in the **Number of Instances** box.
5. Check the **Equal Spacing** option.

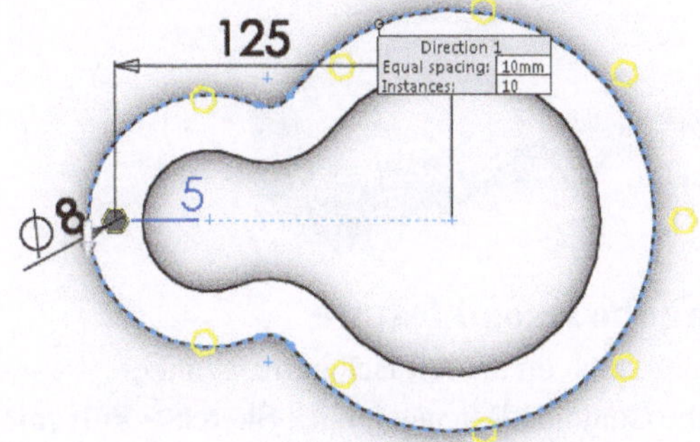

6. Set **Curve method** to **Offset Curve**.
7. Set **Alignment method** to **Tangent to curve**.
8. Click **OK**.

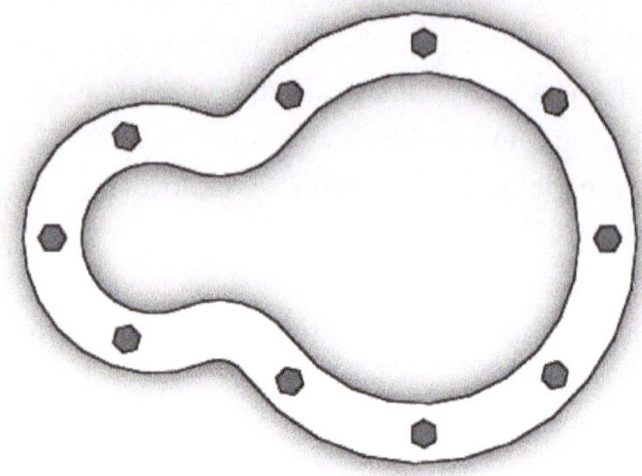

9. Save and close the file.

TUTORIAL 8

In this tutorial, you create a bolt.

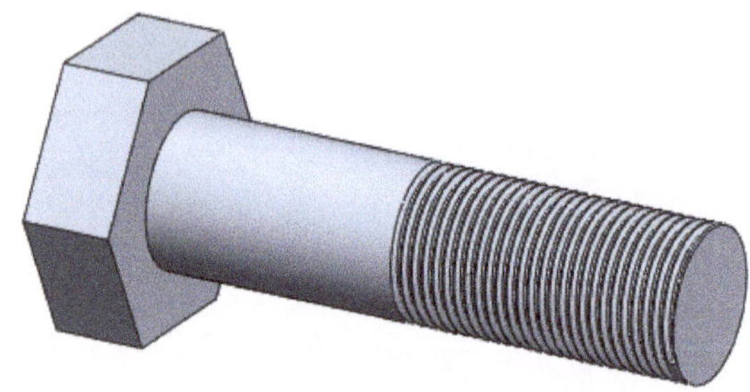

Start a new part file

1. Start a new part file using the **Part** template.
2. Construct a cylindrical feature of 20 mm diameter and 75 mm length.

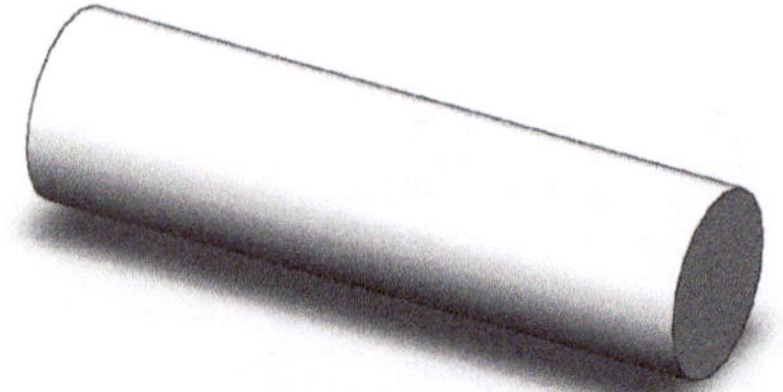

Creating the second feature

1. Start a sketch on the left face of the cylinder.
2. On the CommandManager, click **Sketch > Polygon**.
3. Create a hexagon and dimension it as shown.

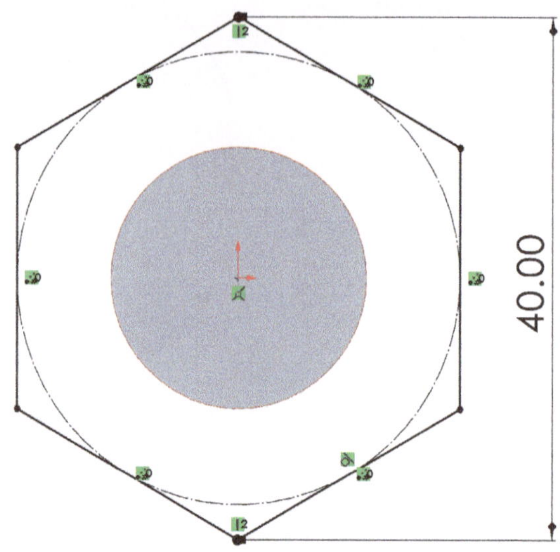

4. Exit the sketch.
5. Extrude the sketch up to 12 mm depth.

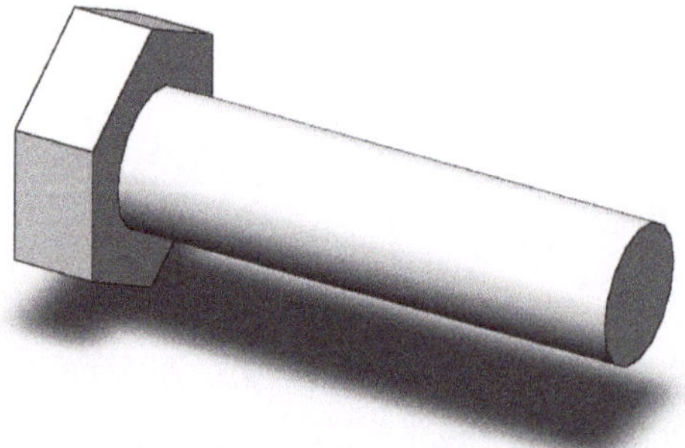

Adding Cosmetic Threads

The Thread tool creates standard internal or external threads in solid models. It generates thread geometry to ensure compatibility with screws, bolts, and other fasteners, reducing manual modeling work and design errors.

You can apply threads according to international standards (ISO, ANSI, DIN) by selecting thread type (Metric, UNC), nominal size (M6x1), and fit class. These parameters ensure your parts meet industry specifications for manufacturing and assembly.

Threads update when you modify design dimensions or change standards. This parametric behavior maintains consistency across assemblies and drawings without requiring manual updates.

You can easily annotate threads in drawings with callouts

that include thread depth, tolerance, and standard references.

1. On the CommandManager, click **Features > Hole Wizard > Thread** .
2. Click on the right circular edge of the model geometry.
3. Select **End Condition > Blind** and type-in 40 in the **Depth** box.
4. On the PropertyManager, select **Type > Metric Die**.
5. Select **Size > M20x1.5**.
6. Click the **Override Diameter** icon below the **Size** drop-down. This will enable you to override the thread diameter.
7. Click **OK** to add the thread.

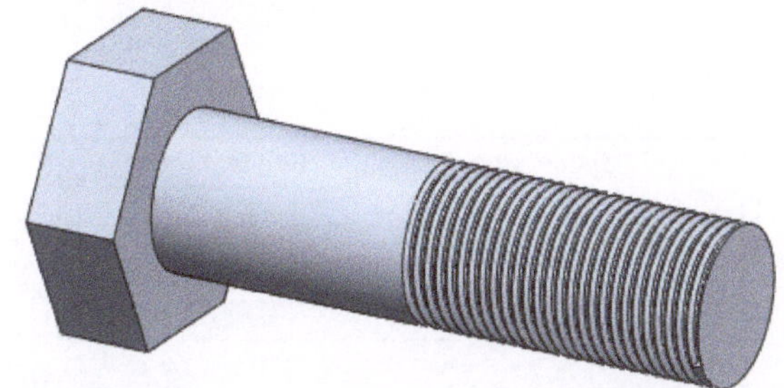

Notice that the starting of the thread is created inside the model.

SOLIDWORKS has options to avoid this undesirable result.

8. On the FeatureManager Design Tree, click on the **Thread** feature and select **Edit Feature**.

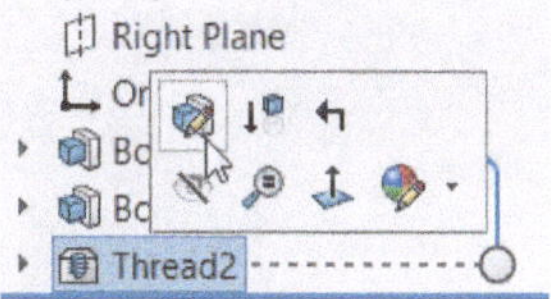

9. On the PropertyManager, under the **Thread Location** section, check the **Offset** option, and then type 1.5 the **Offset Distance** box.
10. Click the **Reverse Direction** button next to the **Offset Distance** box; the thread is offset outside the model.
11. Go to the **Thread Options** section, and then check the **Trim with start face** option; the thread feature is aligned with the model's start face.
12. Click **OK** on the PropertyManager.

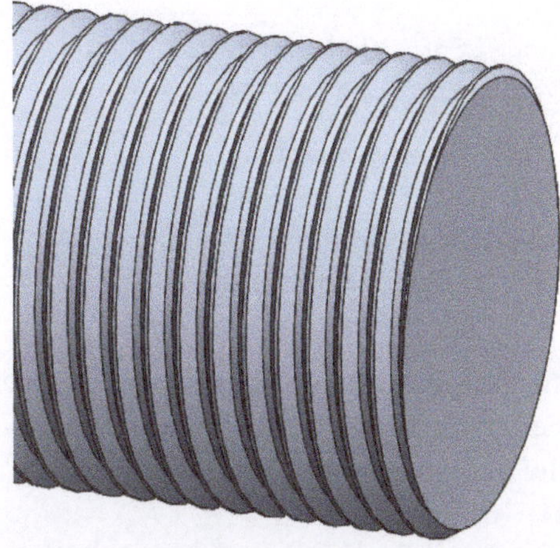

13. Save the file as Tutorial8.sldprt.

Creating Configurations Table

A configurations table manages multiple design variations (configurations) of a part or assembly in a single file. You can use configurations to control dimensions, features, materials, or component states (suppressed/resolved) without creating duplicate files.

You store multiple variants (such as sizes, materials, or optional features) in one file and switch between them as needed. For example, you can create bracket configurations with different hole patterns or thicknesses. You can use an Excel-based table or a SOLIDWORKS Design Table to create configurations automatically. When you link dimensions or features to spreadsheet cells, you keep values consistent across variants and reduce manual entry errors. You can apply equations or table-driven values to adjust parameters. This supports design intent by updating related values across configurations when you define logical links. You can generate configuration-specific bills of materials (BOMs), drawings, or manufacturing specifications. This helps you provide the correct documentation for production or assembly. You can evaluate different design cases (such as stress testing at different thicknesses) without creating separate models.

Now, you will create different variations of the bolt created in the previous section.

1. Click the **Configurations** tab on the left side of the window. Notice that there is only one configuration available in the tree.

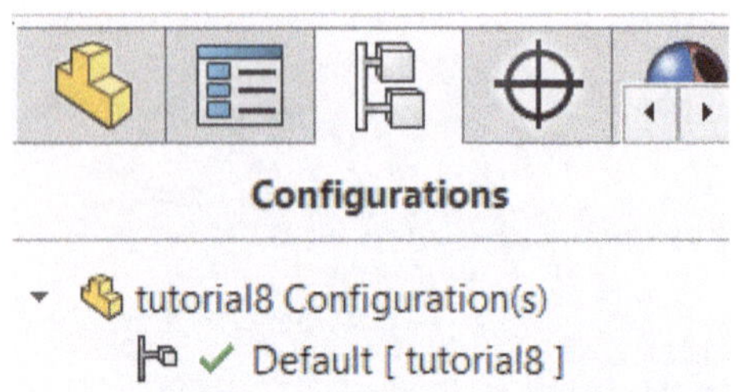

2. Click the **FeatureManager Design Tree** tab.
3. In the FeatureManager Design Tree, expand **Boss-Extrude1** and click the right mouse button on **Sketch1**.
4. Select **Configure Feature** from the shortcut menu.

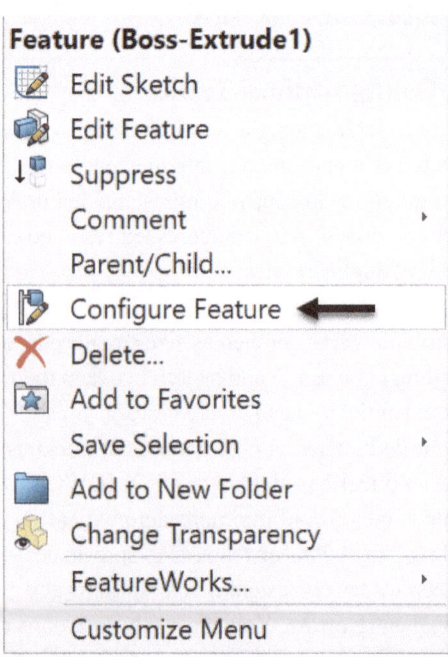

5. On the **Modify Configurations** dialog, click the down-arrow next to **Sketch1** and check **D1**. Click on the dialog to display the Diameter dimension.

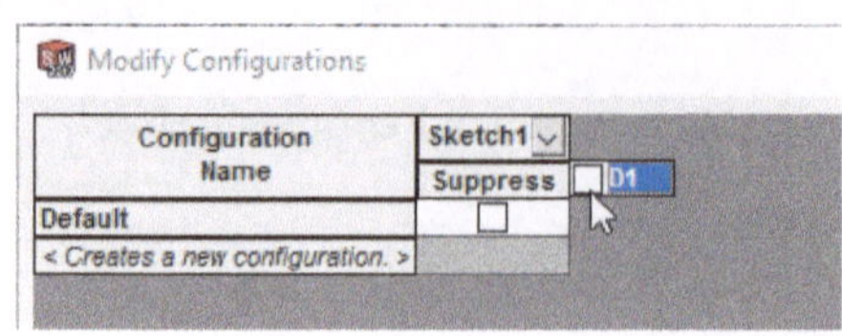

6. On the **Modify Configurations** dialog, click the right mouse button on **Sketch1** and select **Rename**.
7. Type-in **Bolt Diameter** and right-click on the **Modify Configurations** dialog.
8. On the **Modify Configurations** dialog, click in the < *Creates a new configuration.* > cell and type-in Small Diameter. Click on the table to create a new configuration.

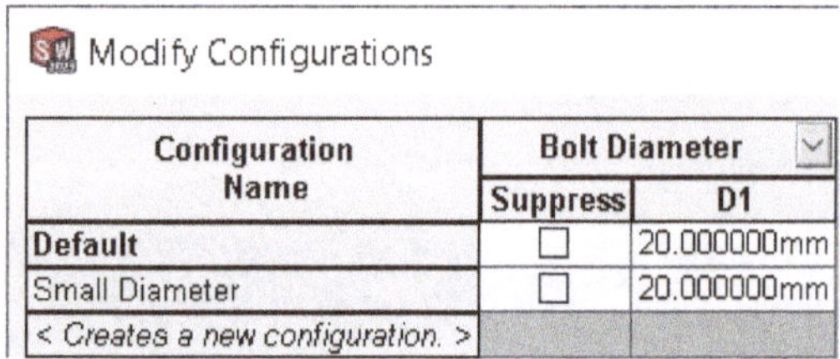

9. Type **12** in the **D1** cell of Small Diameter configuration.

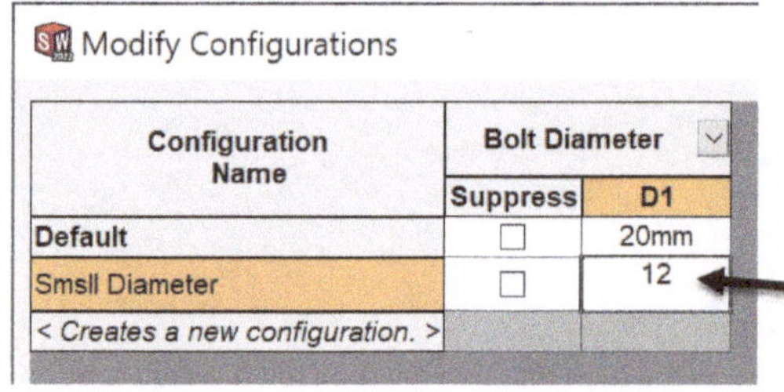

10. In the FeatureManager Design Tree, double-click on **Thread1**, **Boss-Extrude2**, and **Sketch2** to add them to the table.
11. On the **Modify Configurations** dialog, click the right mouse button on the **Boss-Extrude2** column and select **Delete**. The column is removed from the table.
12. Click the drop-down next to the **Thread1** feature.
13. Use the Up and Down arrows and select all the six checkboxes one-by-one.

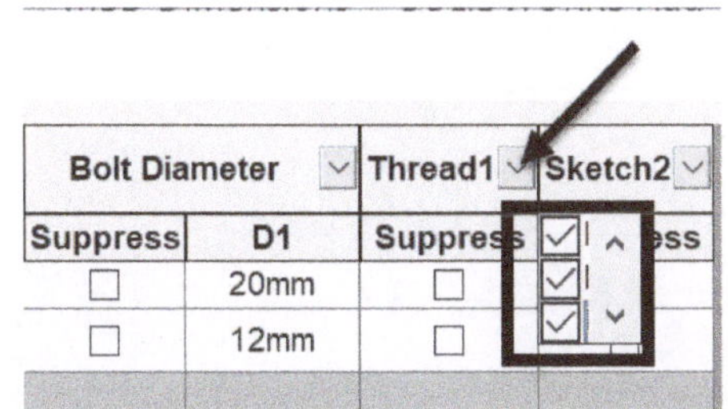

14. Click the down-arrow next to **Sketch2** and check the D1 checkbox.

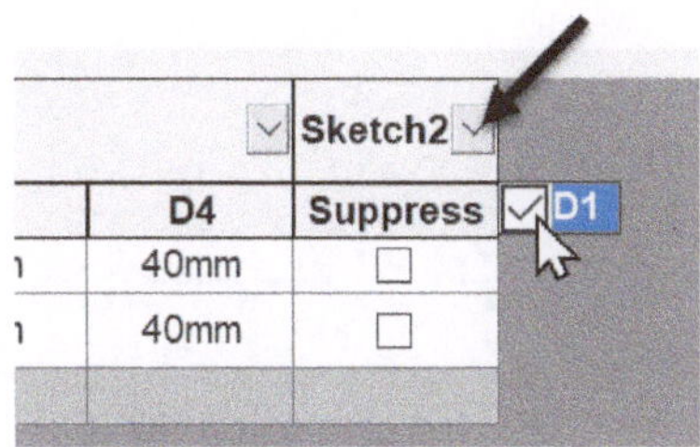

15. Modify the **D6** value of **Thread1** for Small Diameter configuration to 12.

Thread1					
Suppress	D1	D2	D4	D6	D7
☐	0deg	2mm	40mm	20mm	1.500000000
☐	0deg	2mm	40mm	12	1.500000000

16. Modify the **D1** value of the **Sketch2** for Small Diameter configuration to 20.

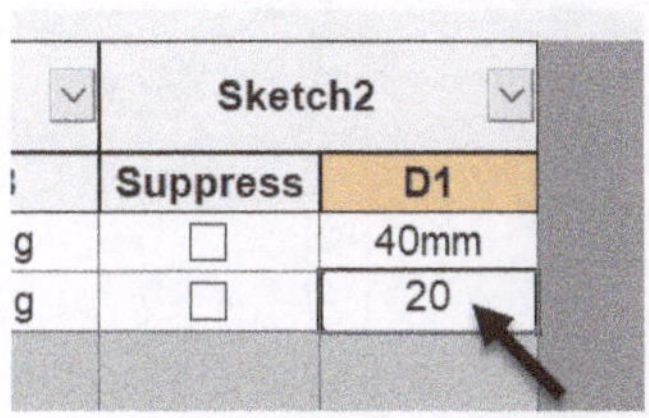

17. On the **Modify Configurations** dialog, type-in **Custom Table** in the box located at the bottom, and then click the **Save table view** button next to it.

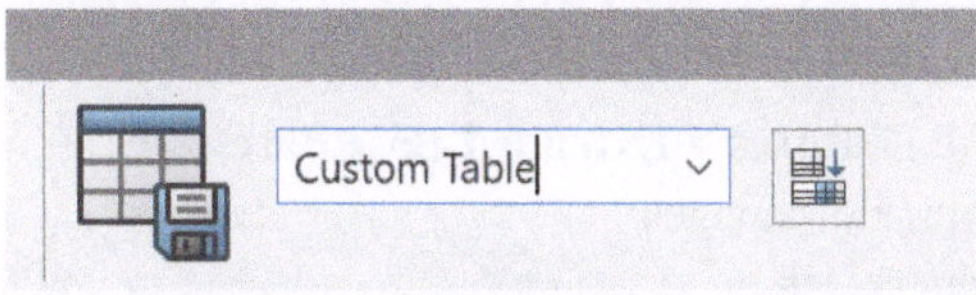

18. Click **OK** to close the dialog.
19. Click the **Configurations** tab on the left-side pane and notice two configurations along with a configurations table.

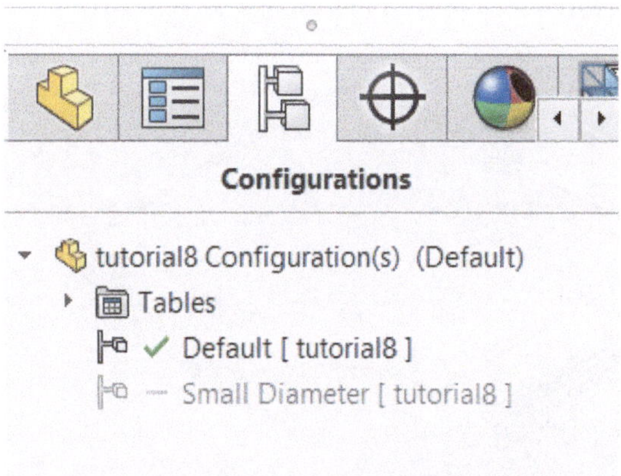

20. Click the right mouse button on the **Small Diameter** configuration and select **Show Configuration**.

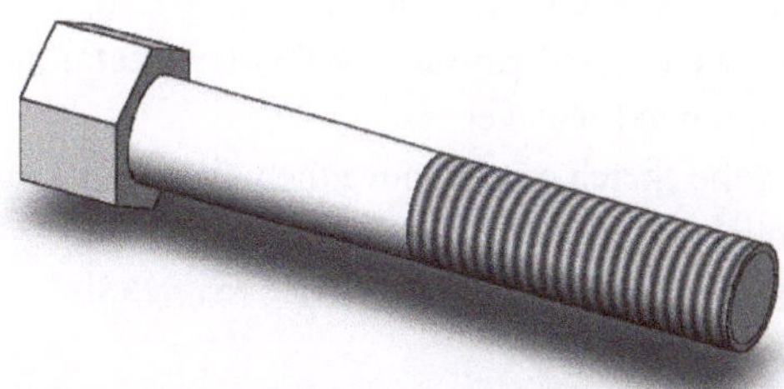

21. To edit the configuration table, click the right mouse button on the **Custom Table** and select **Show Table**. The **Modify Configurations** dialog appears. Change the values or create new configurations, and then click the **Save the table view** 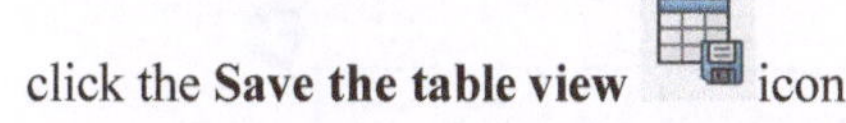 icon.

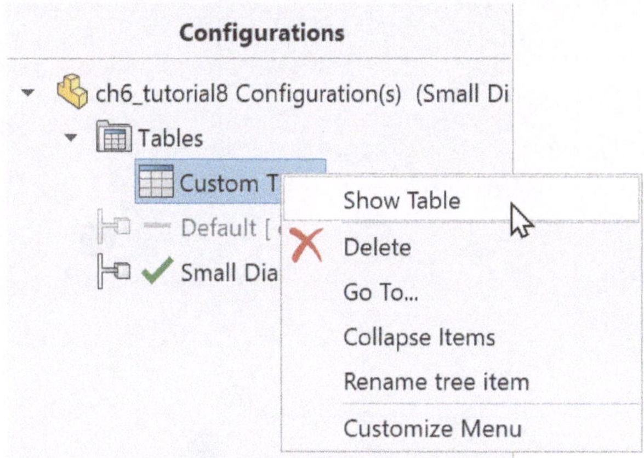

22. Save as **Configurations Table.sldprt** and close the file.

TUTORIAL 9

In this tutorial, you create a plastic casing.

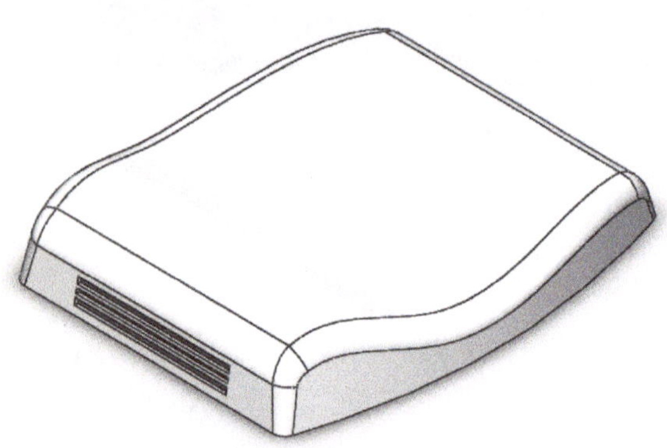

Creating the First Feature

1. Open a new **Part** file.
2. Activate the **Sketch** tool and click on the Top Plane.
3. Click **Rectangle drop-down > Center Rectangle** on the CommandManager.
4. Select the sketch origin, move the pointer outward and click.
5. Click **Arc drop-down > 3 Point Arc** on the CommandManager.
6. Select the top-right corner of the rectangle.
7. Move the pointer downward and select the bottom-right corner of the rectangle.
8. Move the pointer toward right and click to create an arc.

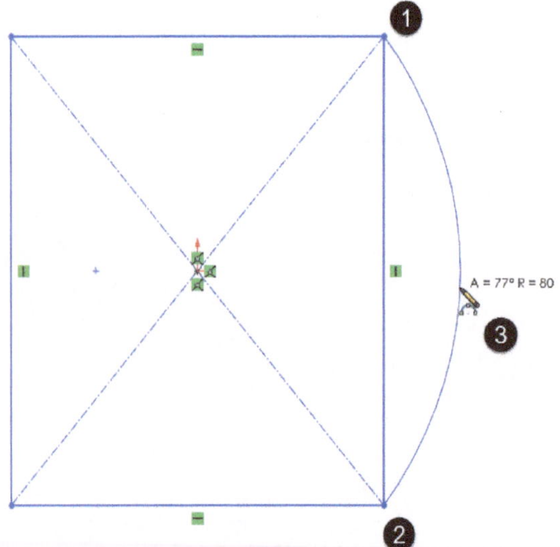

9. Likewise, create another arc on the left side.

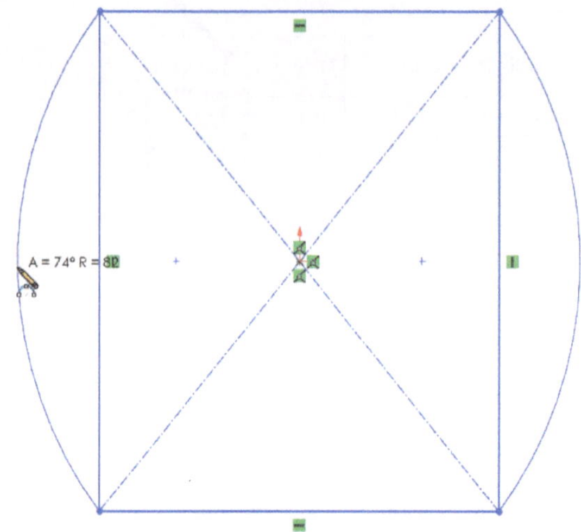

10. Press and hold the CTRL key and select the two vertical lines of the rectangle.
11. Check the **For Construction** option on the PropertyManager; the vertical lines are converted to construction lines.
12. Press and hold the CTRL key and select the two arcs.
13. Click the **Equal** button on the PropertyManager.
14. Add dimensions to the sketch, as shown.

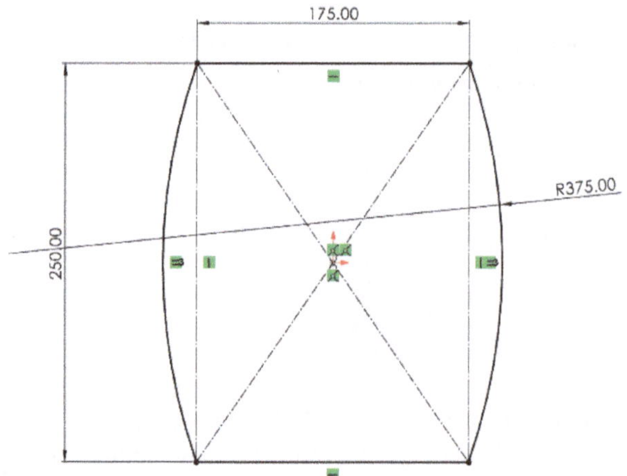

15. Click **Exit Sketch.**
16. Click the **Features > Extruded Boss/Base**  on the CommandManager.
17. Select the sketch.
18. Set the **Distance** to 40.
19. Click the **Draft on/off** icon and set the **Draft Angle** to 10.

20. Click **OK**.

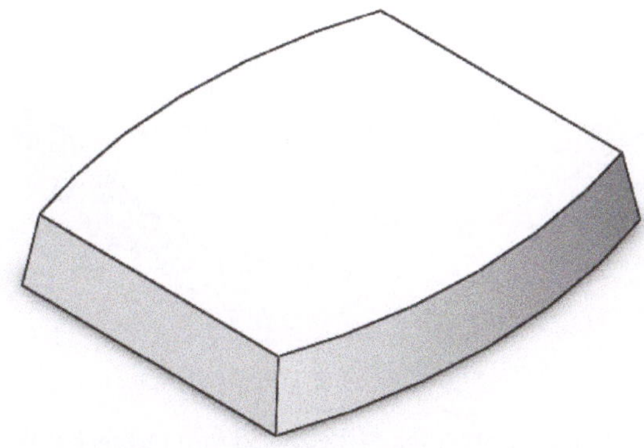

Creating the Extruded surface

1. Click the right mouse button on the CommandManager and select **Tabs** > **Surfaces**.
2. Click **Surfaces > Extruded Surface** on the CommandManager and select the Right Plane.
3. On the View Heads up toolbar, click **View Orientation > Normal To**.
4. Click **Sketch > Spline** on the CommandManager.
5. Create a spline by specifying the spline points from left to right, as shown in the figure.

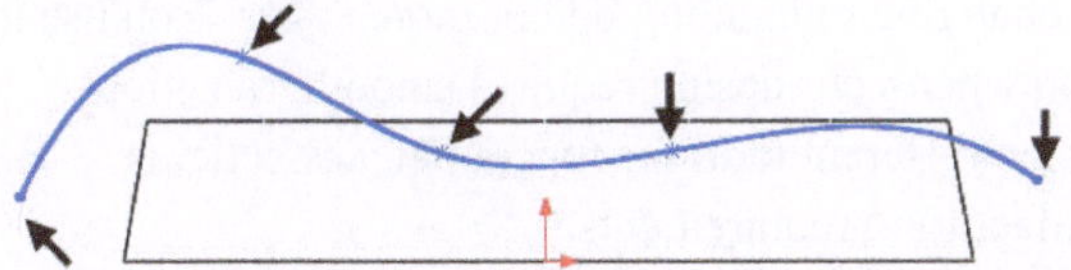

6. Create dimensions between the spline points and the sketch origin, as shown below.

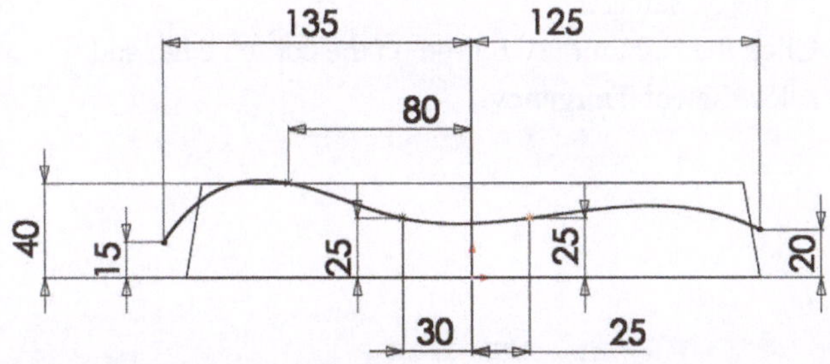

7. Click **Exit Sketch**.
8. Set the **End Condition** type to **Mid Plane**.
9. Type 215 in the **Depth** box and click **OK**.

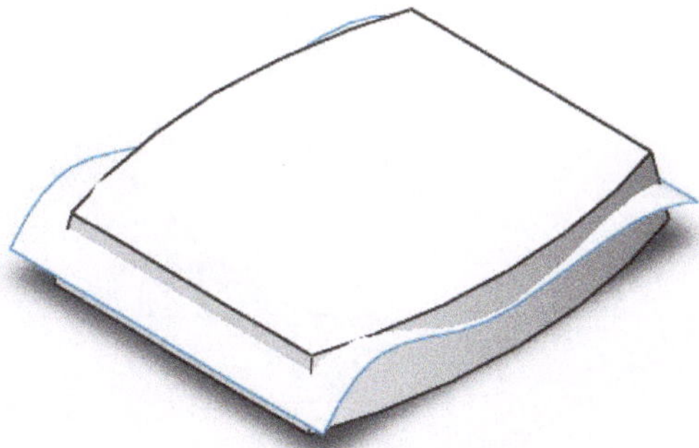

Replacing the top face of the model with the surface

1. On the CommandManager, click **Surfaces > Replace Face**.

Now, you need to select the face to be replaced.

2. Select the top face of the model.

Next, you need to select the replacement face or surface.

3. Click in the **Replacement Face(s)** box on the PropertyManager and select the extruded surface.
4. Click **OK** to replace the top face with a surface.

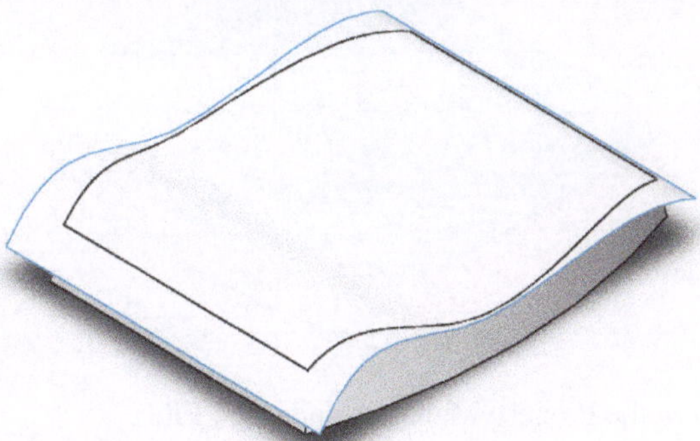

5. Hide the extruded surface by clicking on it and selecting **Hide**.

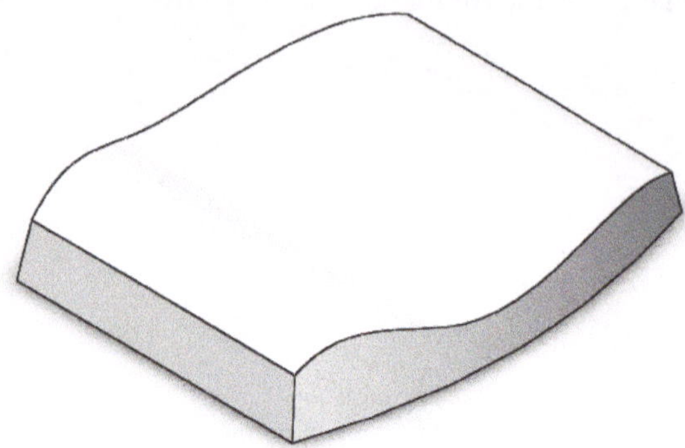

Creating a Face fillet

You use a face fillet to create a rounded transition between two non-adjacent faces or faces with a gap between them. This removes sharp edges and strengthens the part's structure.

1. On the CommandManager, click the **Fillet** icon on the **Features** tab.
2. On the PropertyManager, click the **Manual** tab.
3. Click the **Face Fillet** button on the **Fillet** PropertyManager.
4. Select the top surface as the first face.
5. On the PropertyManager, click in the **Face Set 2** box and select the inclined front face as the second face.

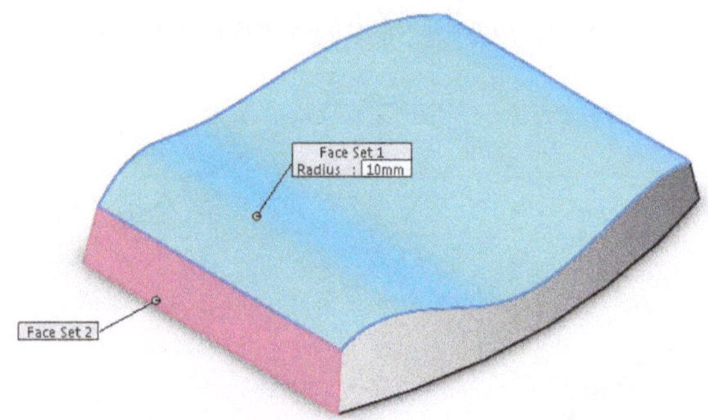

6. On the PropertyManager, under the **Fillet Parameters** section, select **Symmetric** from the drop-down and type 20 in the **Radius** box. Click **OK** to create the face fillet.

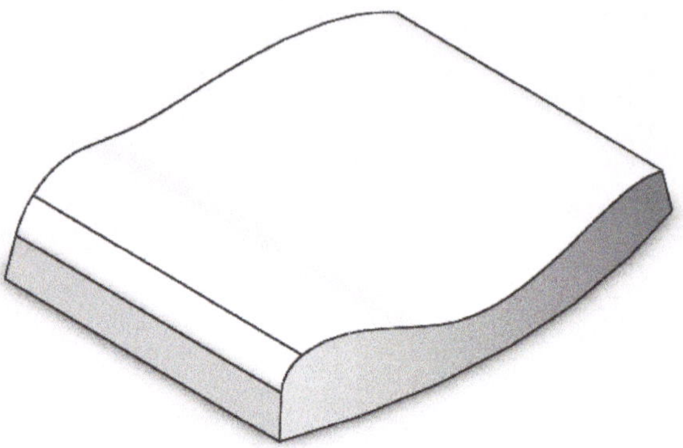

7. Likewise, apply a face fillet of 20 mm radius between the top surface and the inclined back face of the model.

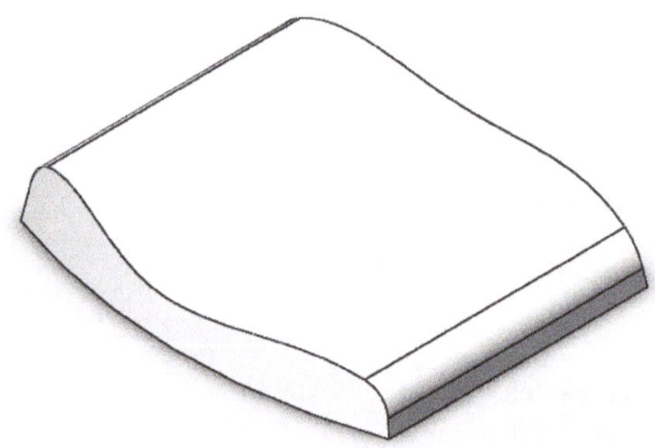

Creating a Variable Radius fillet

The **Variable Size Fillet** option applies a rounded edge with changing radii along one or more edges. You use this option when your design requires smooth transitions between different radii for functional, aesthetic, or manufacturing requirements.

1. Click the **Fillet** icon on the **Features** tab.
2. Click the **Variable Size Fillet** icon on the **Fillet** PropertyManager.
3. Click the right mouse button on the curved edge and select **Select Tangency**.

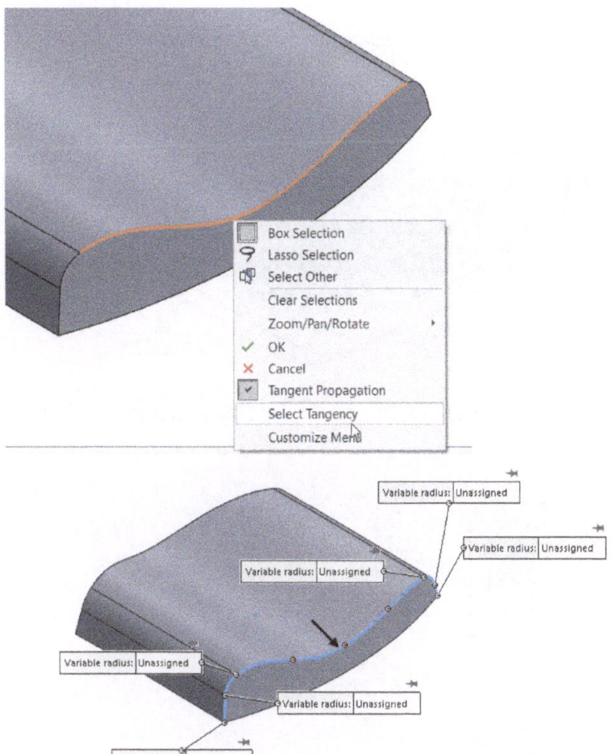

4. Modify the radii values in callouts as shown.

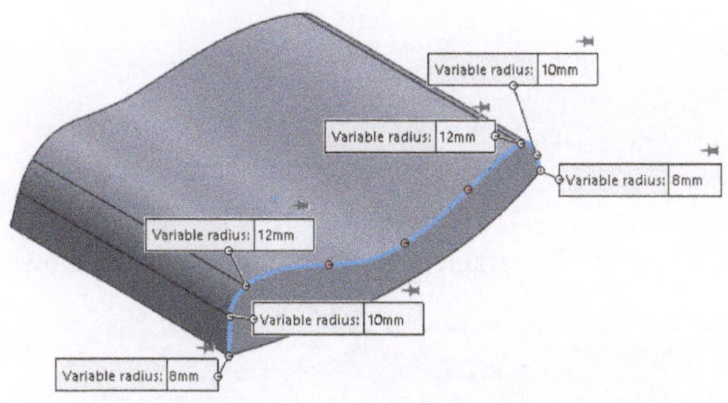

6. Make sure the **Smooth transition** option is checked under the **Profile** drop-down.
7. Expand the **Fillet Options** section and check the **Continuous edge blend** option. This option enables the creation of smoothly blended fillets with variable sizes, ensuring seamless transitions between edges.
8. Click **OK** to create the variable fillet.

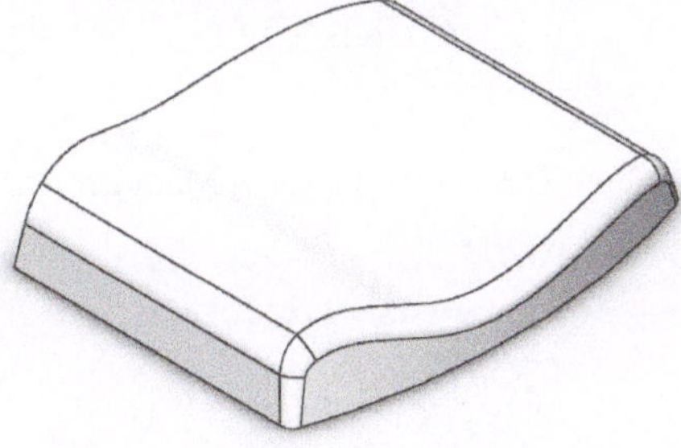

9. Create a variable fillet on another curved edge, as shown.

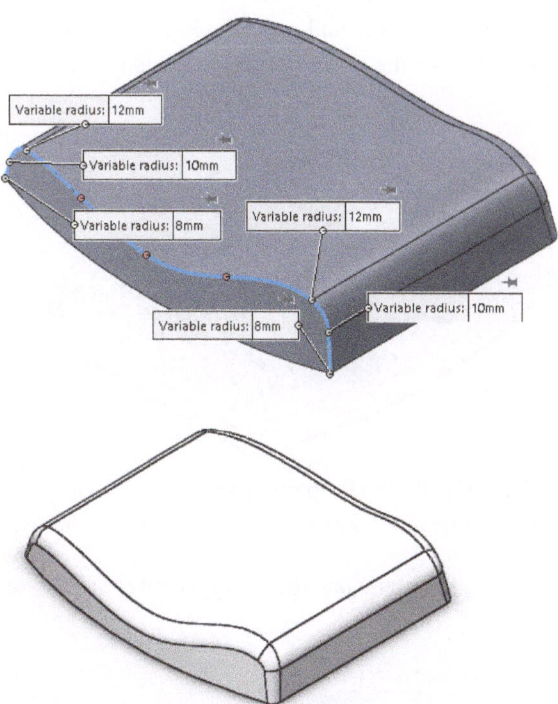

Shelling the Model

1. Click the **Shell** icon on the **Features** tab.
2. On the PropertyManager, type 2.5 mm in the **Thickness** box.
3. Change the orientation of the model and select the bottom face.

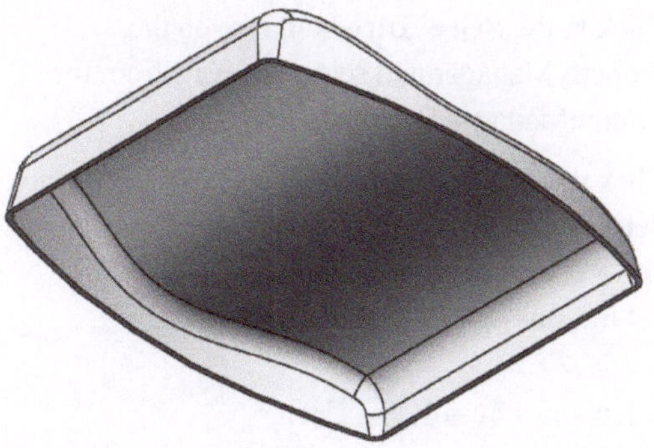

4. Click **OK**.

Creating the Mounting Bosses

A mounting boss is a cylindrical protrusion designed to secure components (e.g., screws, fasteners, or sensors) to a part.

1. On the CommandManager, click **Features > Reference Geometry > Axis** .
2. Press the Ctrl key and select the Right and Front planes from the FeatureManager Design Tree.

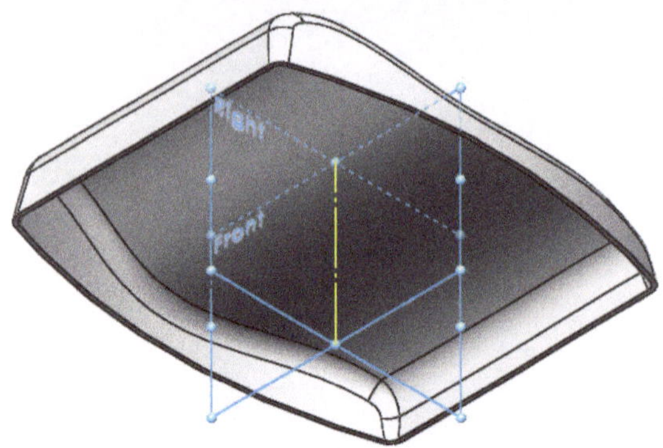

3. Click **OK** on the PropertyManager.
4. Click **Insert > Fastening Feature > Mounting Boss** on the Menu bar and select the inner side of top surface.

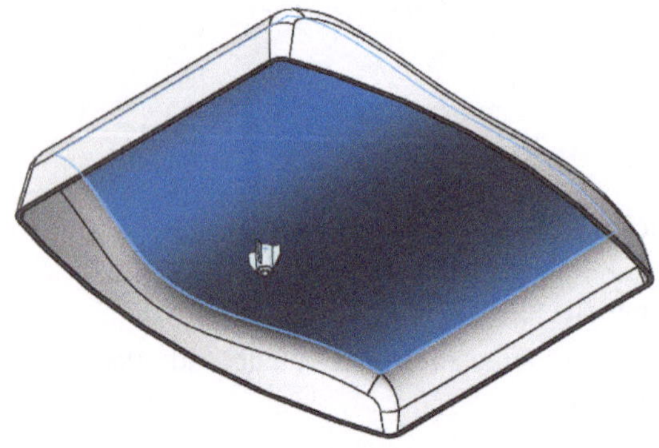

5. Click in the **Select Direction** box on the PropertyManager and select the **Axis** from the FeatureManager Design Tree.
6. Click the **Reverse Direction** icon next to the **Select Direction** box if the mounted boss appears upwards.
7. Set the **Boss Type** to **Hardware Boss**.
8. Select the **Thread** icon.
9. In the **Boss** section, select **Select mating face**.
10. Select the bottom face of the model geometry.

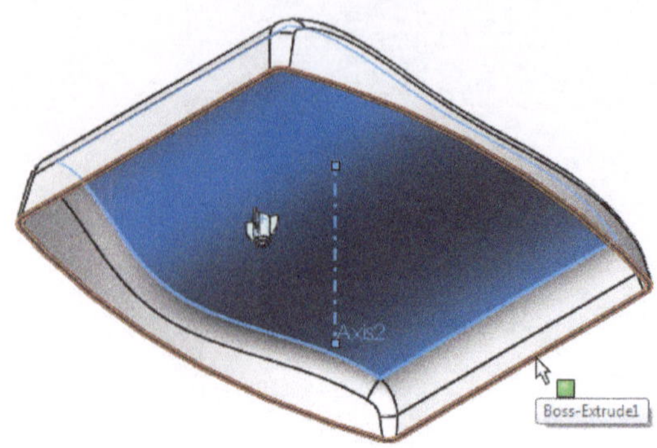

11. Specify the parameters in the **Boss** section, as shown.

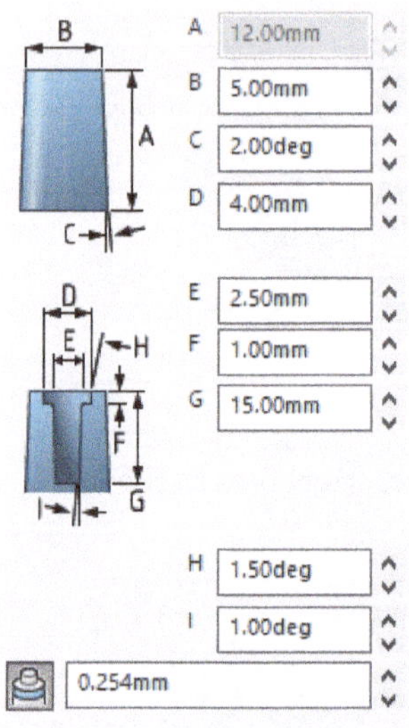

12. Specify the parameters in the **Fins** section, as shown.

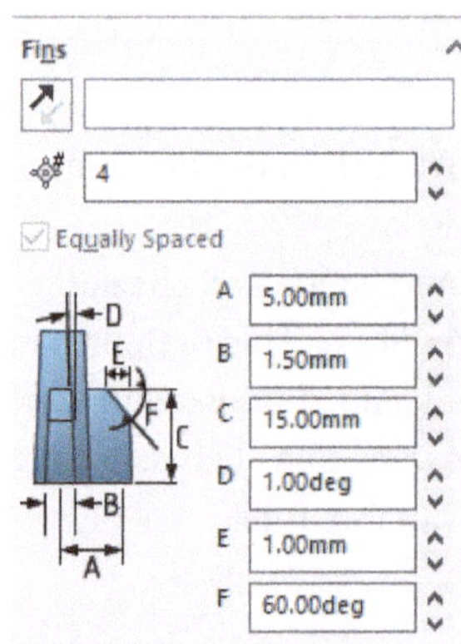

13. Click **OK** on the PropertyManager to create the boss.

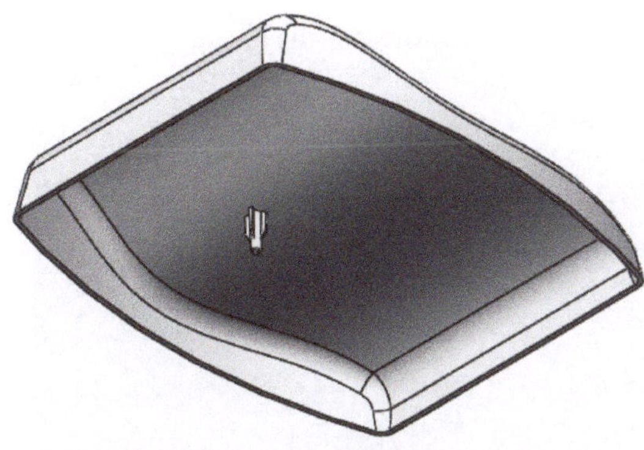

14. In the FeatureManager Design Tree, expand **Mounting Boss1** and notice that a 3D sketch is created.
15. Select **3DSketch1** and click **Edit Sketch**.

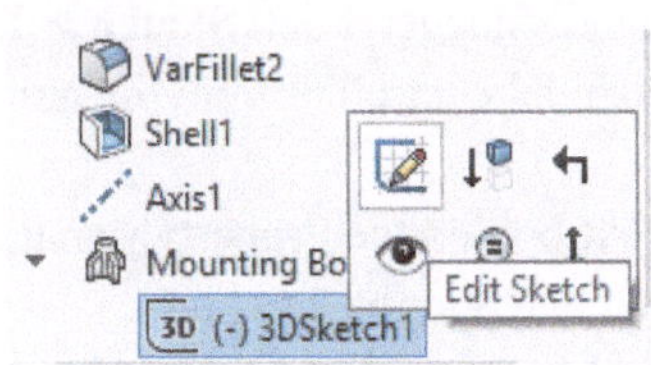

16. Press the Ctrl key and select the points as shown.

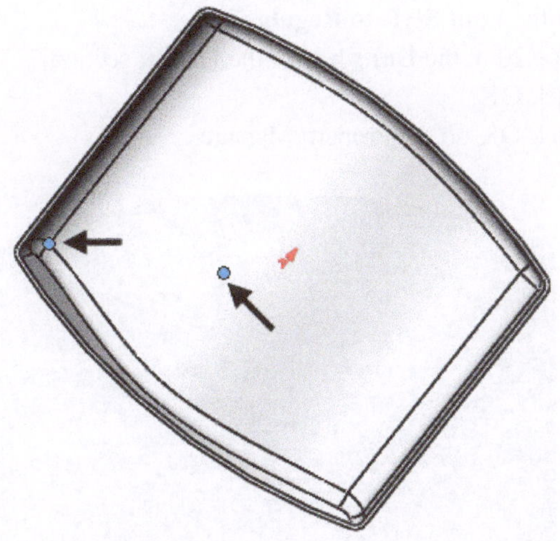

17. Click the **Coincident** icon on the PropertyManager and click **OK**.
18. Click **Exit Sketch**. The position of the mounting boss is changed.

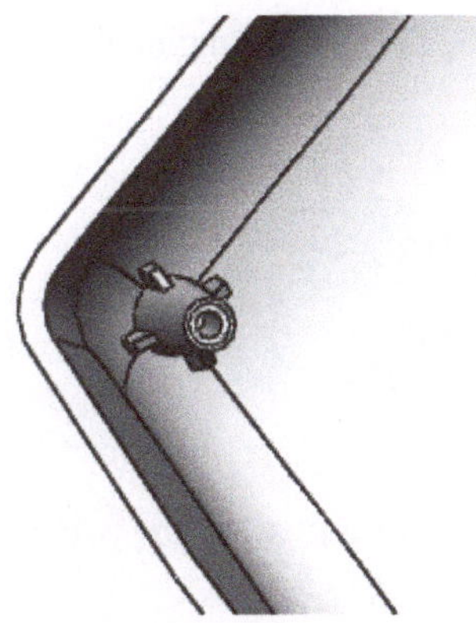

19. Likewise, create other mounting bosses as shown.

Creating the Vent Feature

Vents are designed to enable airflow, reduce pressure buildup, or manage thermal conditions in enclosures, machinery, or consumer products.

1. Create a sketch on the inclined front face.

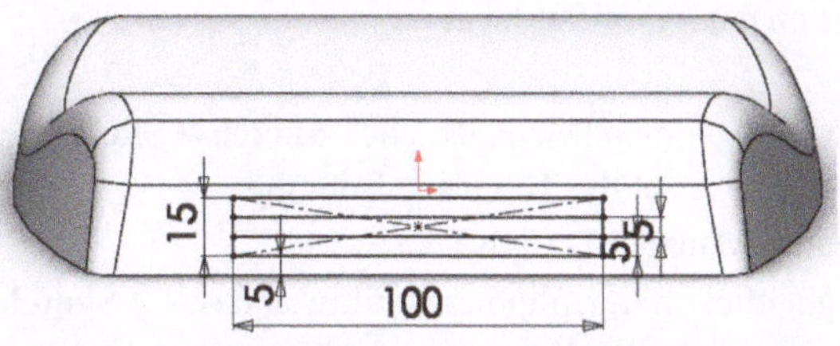

2. Click **Exit Sketch**.
3. On the Menu bar, click **Insert > Fastening Feature > Vent**.

4. Select the four lines of the rectangle to define the boundary.

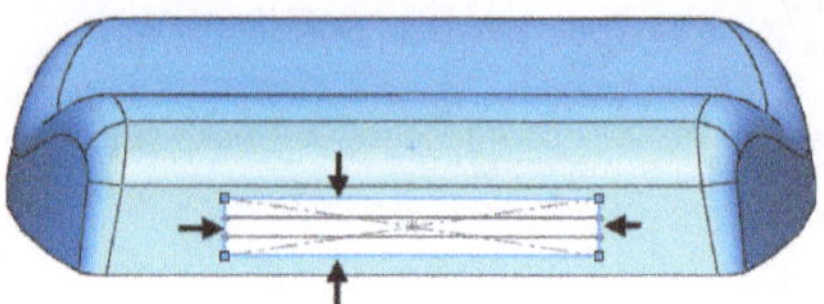

5. Click in the **Ribs** selection box and select the two horizontal lines.
6. Set the rib parameters, as shown below.

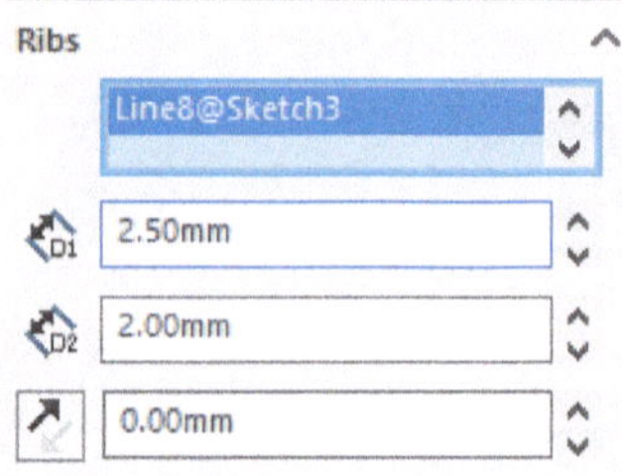

7. Click **OK** to create the vent.

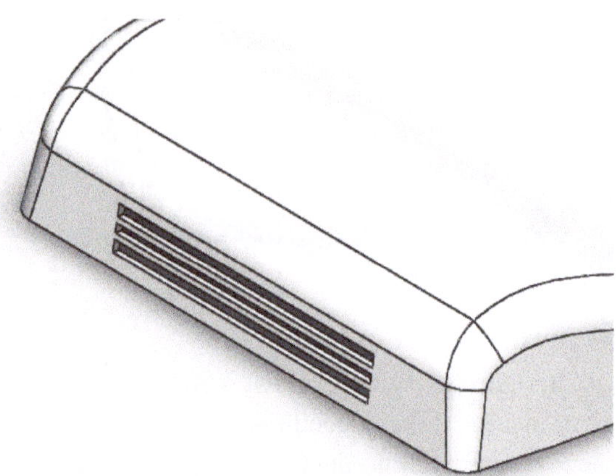

Creating the Wrap Feature

You can use the **Wrap** tool to project a 2D sketch onto a 3D surface. This creates embossed, debossed, or scribed features on curved or flat faces.

1. On the CommandManager, click **Sketch > Sketch**, and then select the Top plane from the FeatureManager Design Tree.
2. Right click in the graphics window and select **Sketch Entities > Centerline**.
3. Create a horizontal centreline passing through the origin.

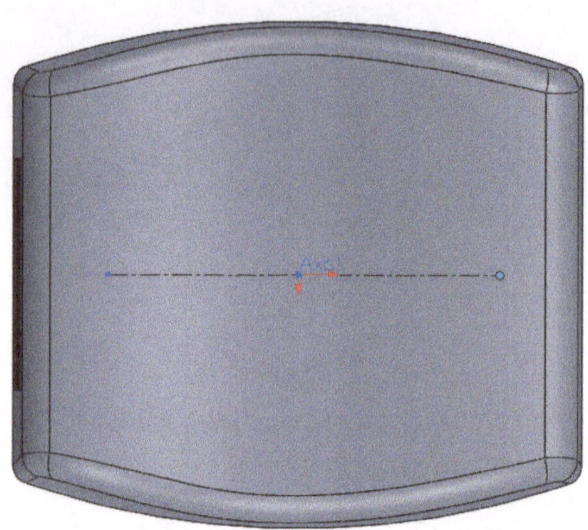

4. On the CommandManager, click **Sketch > Text**.
5. Select the horizontal centreline from the graphics window.
6. Click in the **Text** box on the PropertyManager.
7. Type SOLIDWORKS in the **Text** box.
8. On the PropertyManager, uncheck the **Use document font** option, and then click the **Font** button.
9. Select **SOLIDWORKS GDT** from the **Font** list.
10. Set the **Font Style** to **Regular**.
11. Type 20 in the **Units** box of the **Height** section.
12. Click **OK**.
13. Click **OK** on the PropertyManager.

14. On the CommandManager, click **Sketch > Exit Sketch**.
15. On the CommandManager, click **Features > Wrap**.
16. Click on the centreline of the sketch.

17. On the PropertyManager, click the **Spline Surface** icon under the **Wrap Method** section.
18. Select the **Emboss** icon from the **Wrap Type** section.
19. Click on the top surface of the model.
20. Type 1 in the Thickness box.
21. Click in the **Pull Direction** selection box, and then select the Top plane; the direction perpendicular to the selected plane is defined as the pull direction.
22. Leave the other default options, and then click **OK**.

23. Save the model as a Plastic cover.sldprt and close it.

TUTORIAL 10

In this tutorial, you create Advanced Holes.

The **Advanced Hole** tool creates precise, multi-step holes in a single operation. You can design counterbores, countersinks, tapered holes, and threaded holes without switching between multiple tools.

This feature combines drilling, threading, and chamfering into one parametric operation. You select predefined standards (ANSI, ISO) to match manufacturing specifications for screws, bolts, and pins.

1. Open a new Part file.
2. Create a 50 X 50 X 35 box, as shown.

3. On the FeatureManager Design Tree, click the right mouse button on the **Boss-Extrude1** feature, and then select **Change Transparency**.

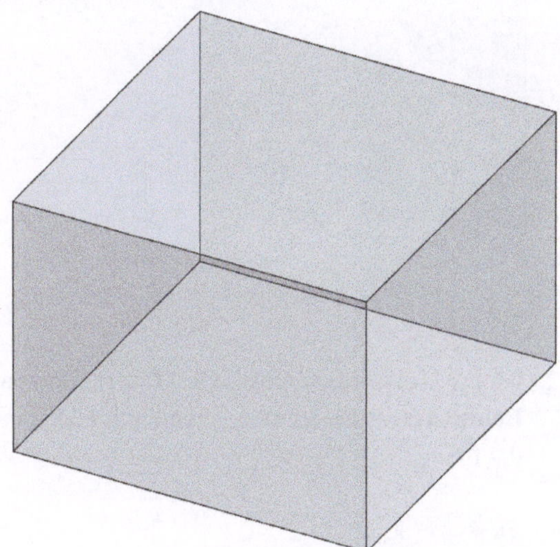

4. On the CommandManager, click **Features > Hole Wizard > Advanced Hole**.
5. Click on the top face of the model.
6. On the **Near Side** toolbar, click the down-arrow next to the **Counterbored hole** button and select **Near Side Counterbore**.

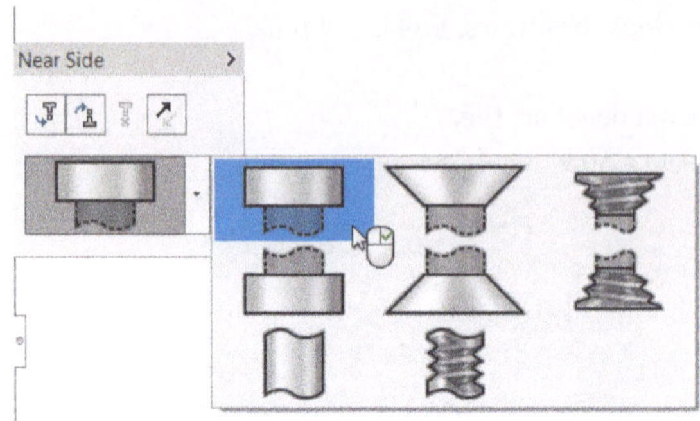

7. On the PropertyManager, select **ISO** from the **Standard** drop-down.
8. Select **Type > Hex Bolt Grade C ISO 4016**.
9. Select **M5** from the **Size** drop-down.
10. Click the **End Condition Override** icon.
11. Type **5** in the **Depth** box.

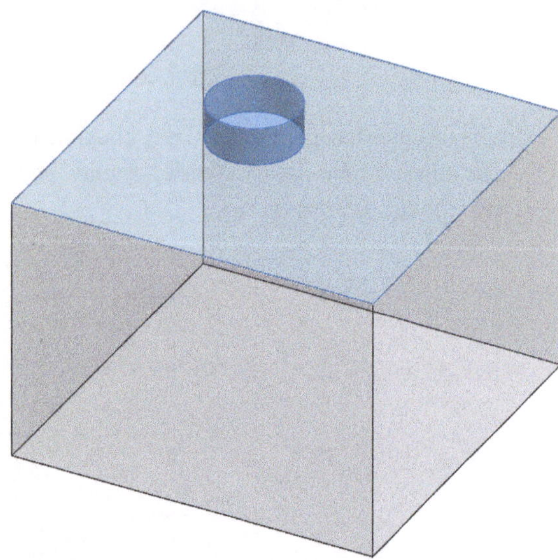

12. On the **Near Side** toolbar, click **Insert Element Below Active Element**; an element is added below the first one.

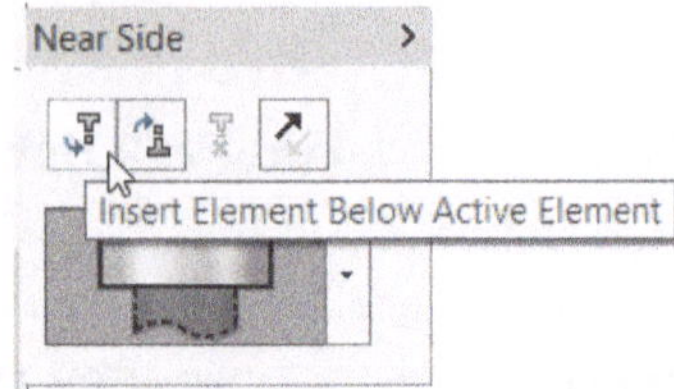

13. Click on the down-arrow next to the second element, and then select **Near Side Countersink**.

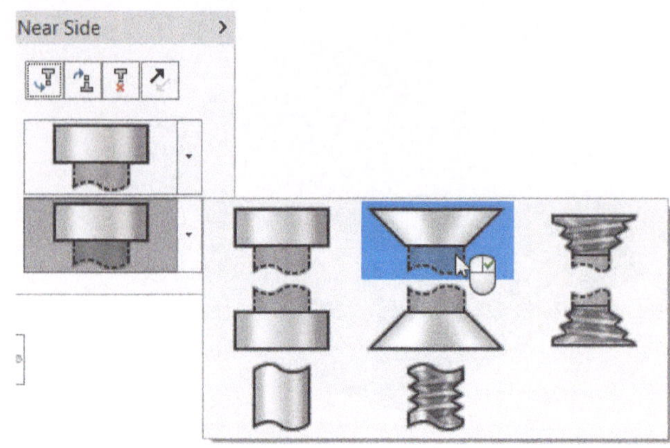

14. Again, click **Insert Element Below Active Element** .
15. Click on the down-arrow next to the third element, and then select **Hole**.

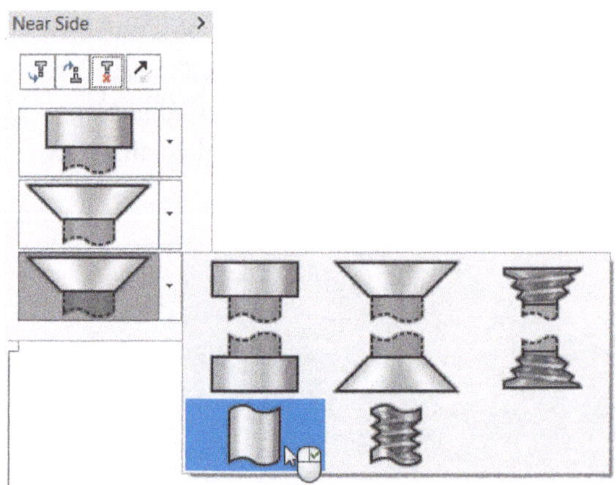

16. Select **Type > Screw Clearances**.
17. Select **M5** from the **Size** drop-down.
18. Select **Up To Next** from the **End Condition** drop-down.
19. Set the **End Shape** to **Flat bottom**.

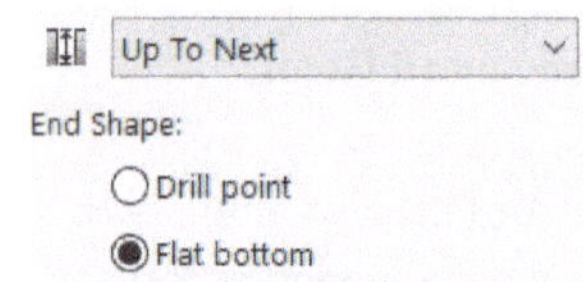

20. Check the **Far Side** option from the **Near And Far Side Faces** section.
21. Rotate the model and select the bottom face of the model geometry.

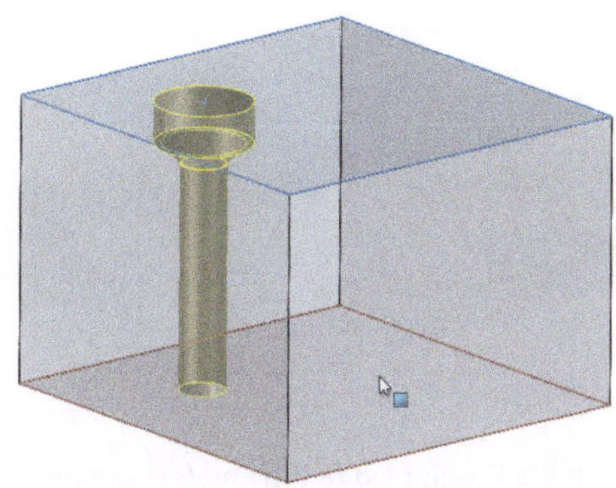

22. Click the down arrow next to the first element of the far side, and then select **Far Side Counterbore**.

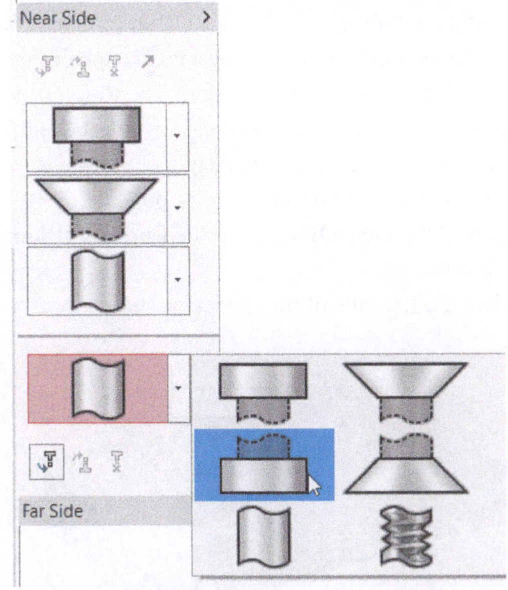

Notice that the model is highlighted in red, which means that there is an error. The third element (hole) extends up to the bottom face of the model. This intersects the far side element. To solve this problem, you need to change the **End Condition** of the third element.

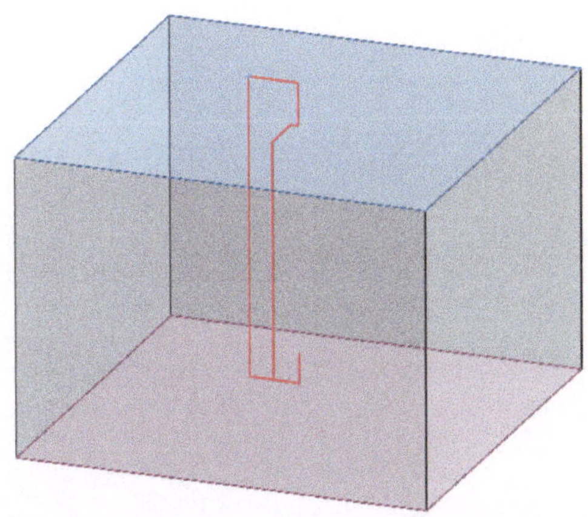

23. Select the third element (Hole) from the **Near Side** toolbar.
24. On the PropertyManager, select **Up To Next Element** from the **End Condition** drop-down.

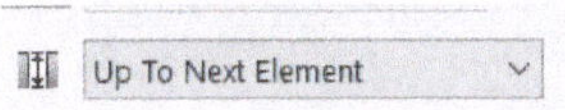

25. Select the far side element.
26. Specify the option in the **Element Specification** section of the PropertyManager.

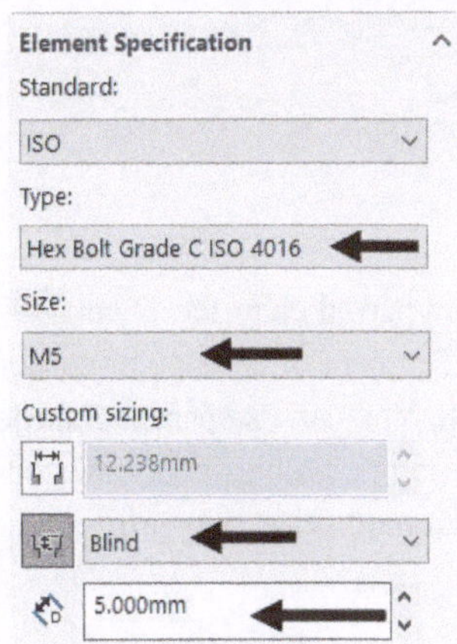

27. Click the **Positions** tab on the PropertyManager.
28. Select the origin point to specify the location of the hole.

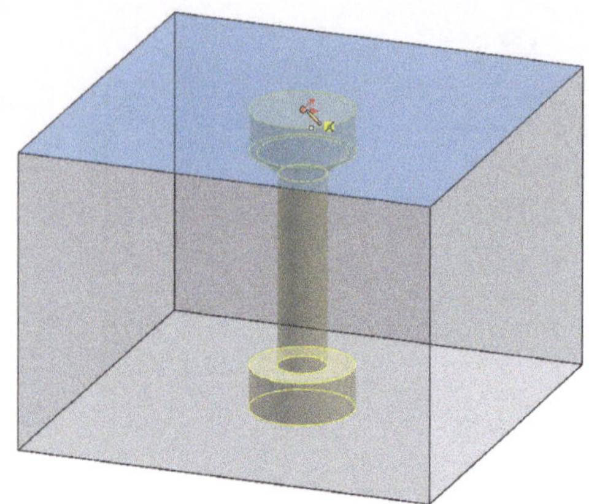

29. Click **OK** on the PropertyManager.

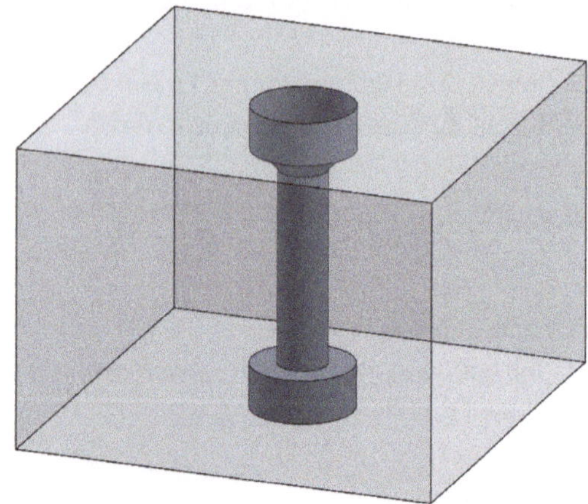

30. Save and close the part file.

TUTORIAL 11

In this tutorial, you create a partial chamfer. A partial chamfer bevels a specific segment of an edge or corner instead of the entire length. You can use partial chamfers to reduce stress at critical points, such as near holes or load bearing edges, without modifying the entire geometry.

1. Download Chapter 6: Additional Modeling Tools files from the companion website.
2. Open the Partial chamfer.sldprt file.
3. On the CommandManager, click **Features** tab > **Fillet** drop-down > **Chamfer**.
4. Click the **Offset Face** icon in the **Chamfer Type** section on the PropertyManager.
5. Select the front edge of the model, as shown.

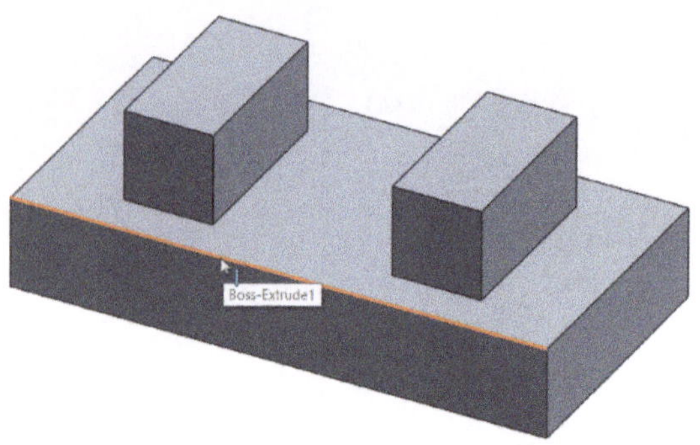

6. Check the **Partial Edge Parameters** option in the PropertyManager.
7. Select the **Distance Offset** option from the **Start condition** drop-down. You can also select the Percentage Offset or Reference Offset options. The Percentage Offset option allows you to specify the offset distance from the start port. The Reference Offset option allows you to create a partial chamfer up to the selected reference face.
8. Type-in 10 in the **Offset distance** box.
9. Select **Reference Offset** from the **End condition** drop-down.
10. Select the flat face of the model, as shown.

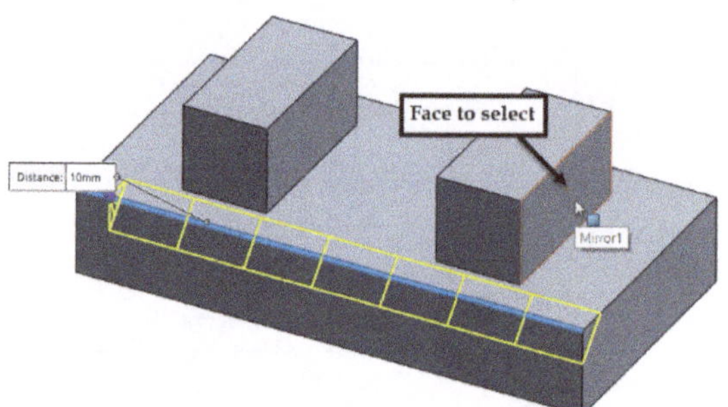

11. Click **OK** on the PropertyManager.

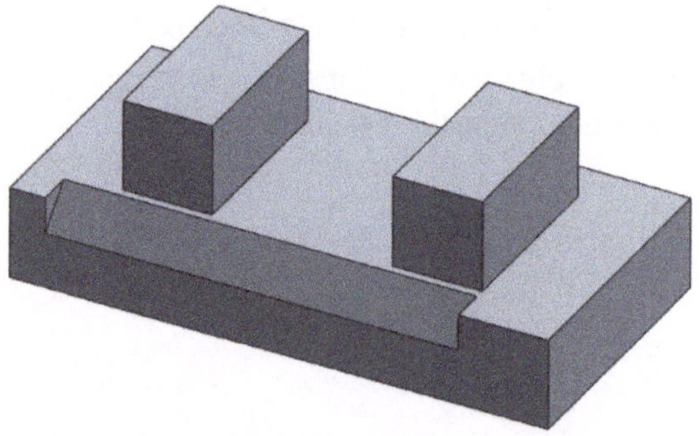

12. Close the file without saving.

TUTORIAL 12 (CSWA Step 1)

In this tutorial, you will create the model given in the CSWA (Certified SolidWorks Associate) sample question. You can get more information about this exam by following the link given below:

https://www.solidworks.com/certifications/mechanical-design-cswa-mechanical-design

1. On the Quick Access Toolbar, click the **New** button.
2. On the **New SOLIDWORKS Document** dialog.
3. Click the **Part** button and click **OK**.
4. Select **MMGS** from the **Unit System** drop-down located at the bottom-right corner.
5. On the menu bar, click **Tools > Equations**.
6. On the **Equations, Global Variables, and Dimensions** dialog, click in the field under the **Global Variables** node, and then type **A**.

In SOLIDWORKS, you can define global variables, which are user-created names assigned numeric values. These variables can be applied in equations or directly in dimensions, making it easier for you to understand and modify equations. You create global variables in either the Equations dialog box or the Modify dialog box for dimensions.

7. Type **81** in the **Value/Equation** field next to the **A** field.
8. Likewise, create other global variables with the values, as shown.

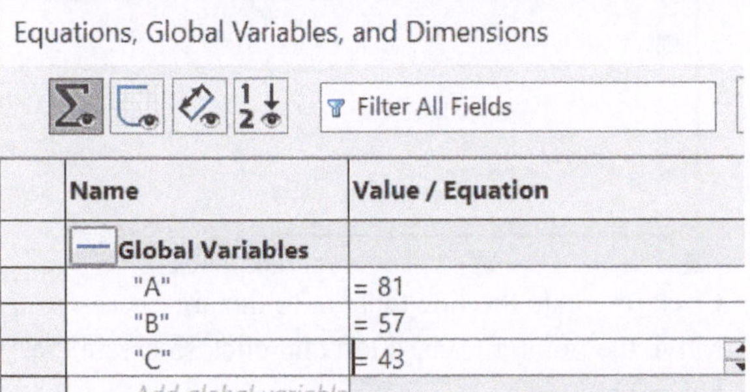

9. On the CommandManager, click **Sketch > Sketch**.
10. Select the Front plane from the graphics window.
11. On the CommandManager, click **Sketch > Line**.
12. Place the pointer on the sketch origin and move the pointer upward; a dotted line is displayed.
13. Click to specify the first point of the line.
14. Move the pointer downward and select the sketch origin.
15. Move the pointer horizontally toward right and click.
16. Move the pointer and place it on endpoint of the horizontal line.
17. Move the pointer away from the endpoint toward right and down.
18. Click to create the arc perpendicular to the horizontal line.

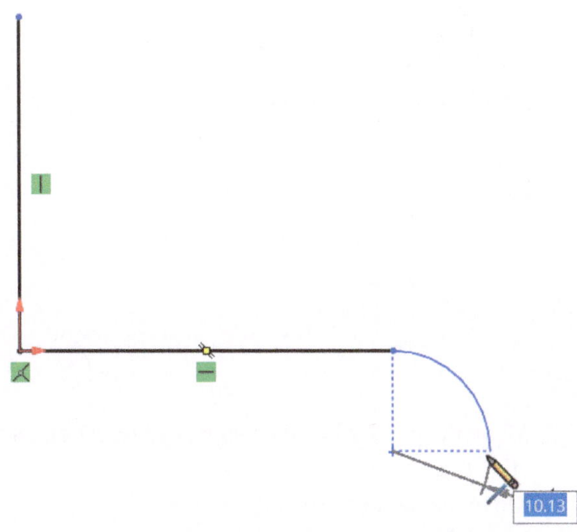

19. Place the pointer on the endpoint of the arc.
20. Move the pointer downward and right, and then click to create an arc, as shown.

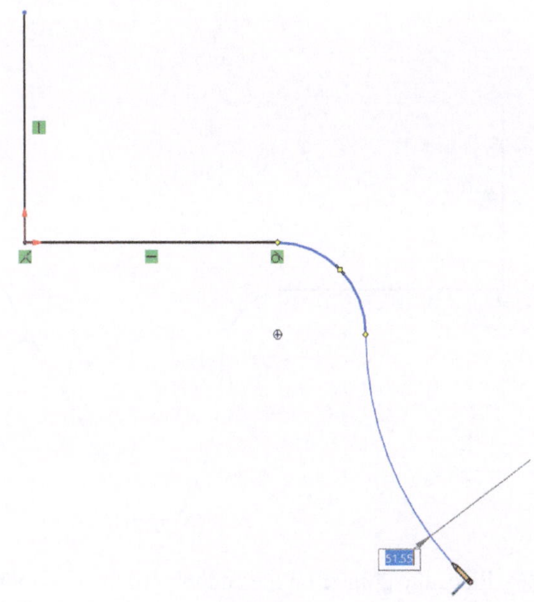

21. Move the pointer horizontally toward right and click.

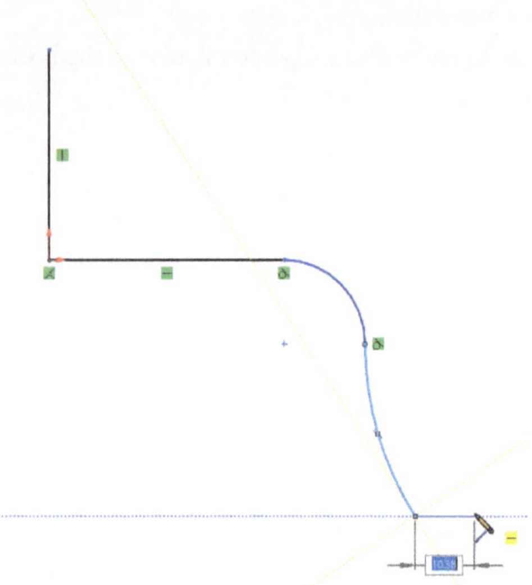

22. Move the pointer in the upward right direction and click to create an inclined line.
23. Move the pointer vertically up and click.
24. Move the pointer toward left-corner up to a small distance and click.
25. Move the pointer horizontally toward left and click.

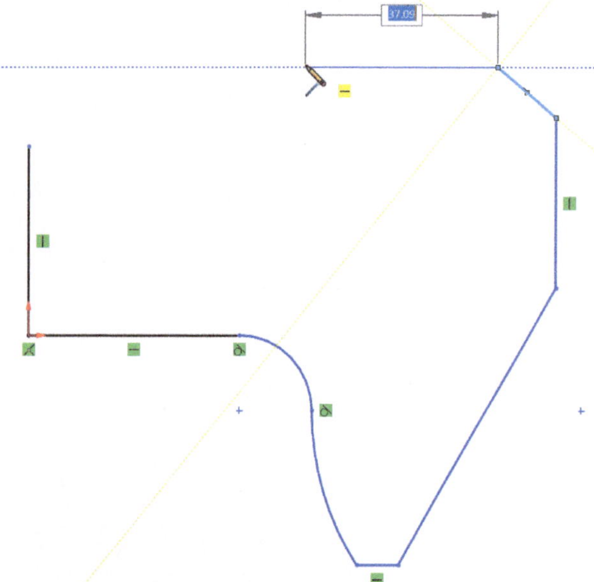

26. Place the pointer on the endpoint of the horizontal line to switch to the **Arc** mode.
27. Move the pointer downward and left, and then click.

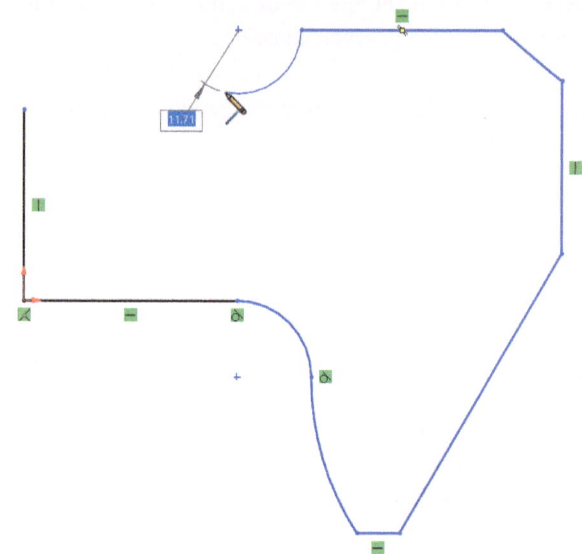

28. Move the pointer along the direction of the arc and notice that the **Tangent** relation is displayed between the line and the arc.

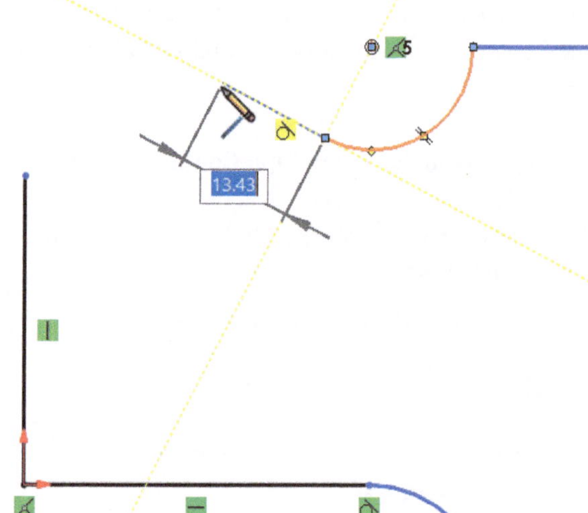

29. Click to create the line tangent to the arc.
30. Move the pointer toward left and click to create the horizontal line.
31. Select the start point of the sketch to create the closed profile.

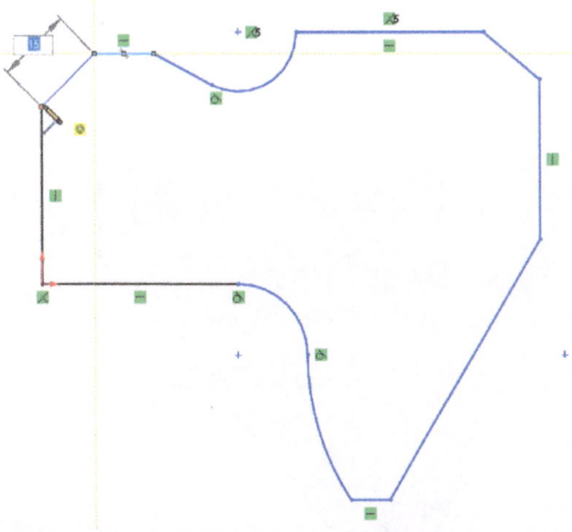

32. On the CommandManager, click **Sketch > Smart Dimension**.
33. Select the small inclined line on the right-side.
34. Position the dimension, type 7 in the Modify box, and then click the green check.

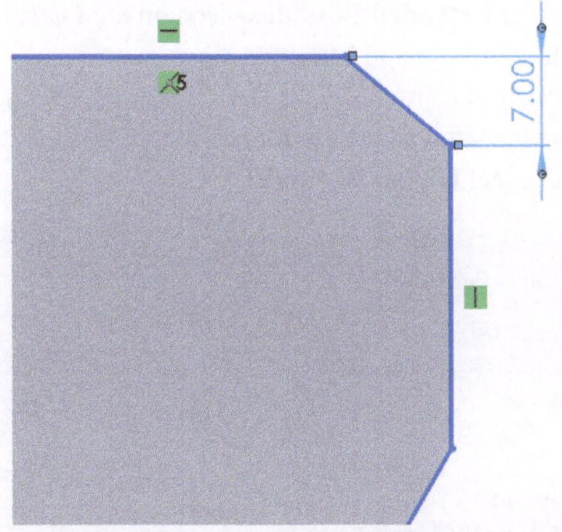

35. Select the top and bottom horizontal lines. Next, position the dimension.
36. On the **Modify** box, select the dimension value and type =.
37. Select **Global Variables > B**. Next, click the green check.

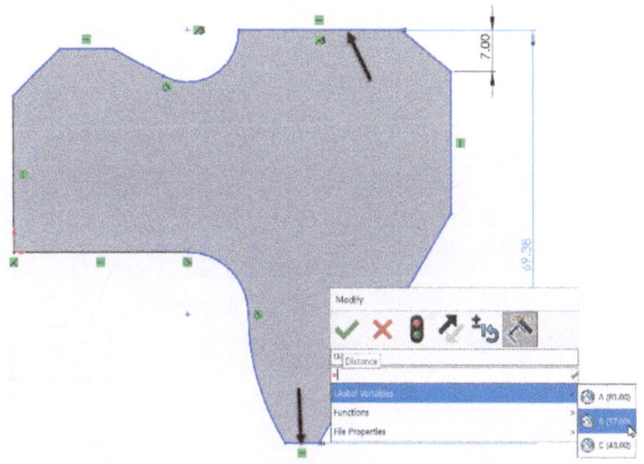

38. Create the other linear dimensions in the sequence given below.

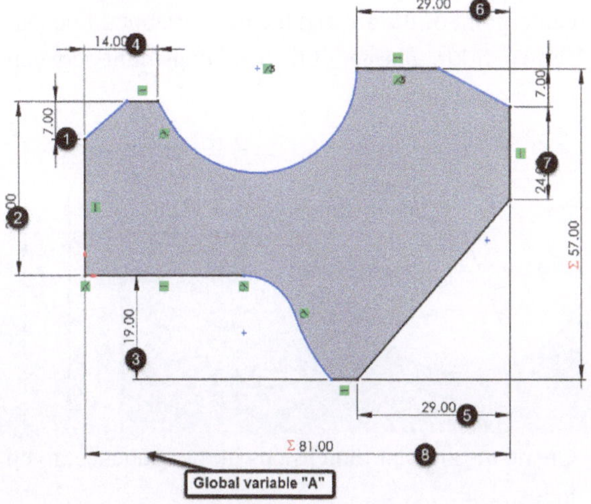

39. Create the radial dimensions in the sequence, as shown.

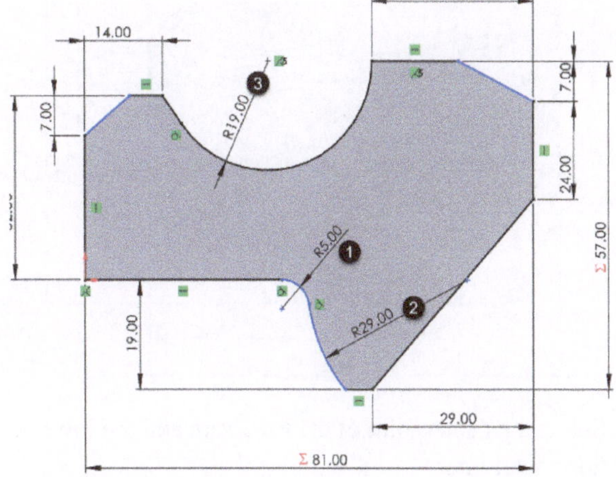

40. Create the Coincident constraint between the centerpoint of the arc and the inclined line, as shown.

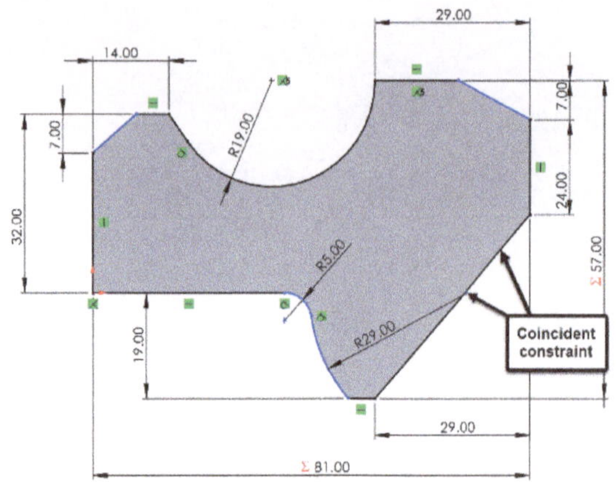

41. Delete the Collinear constraint between the centerpoint of the arc and the top horizontal line, as shown. (Skip this step if there no constraint between the two entities)

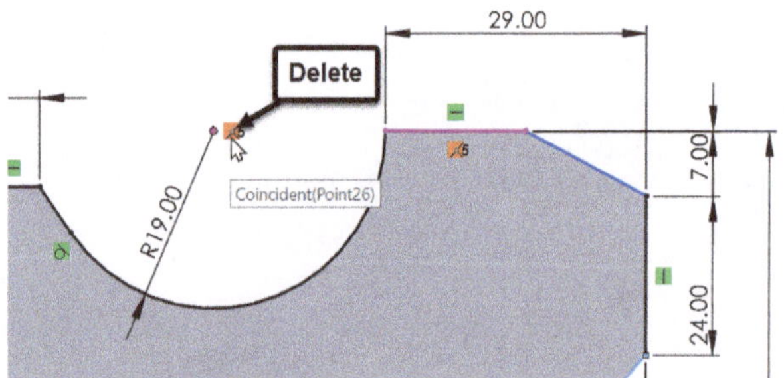

42. Create the angular dimensions in the sequence given below.

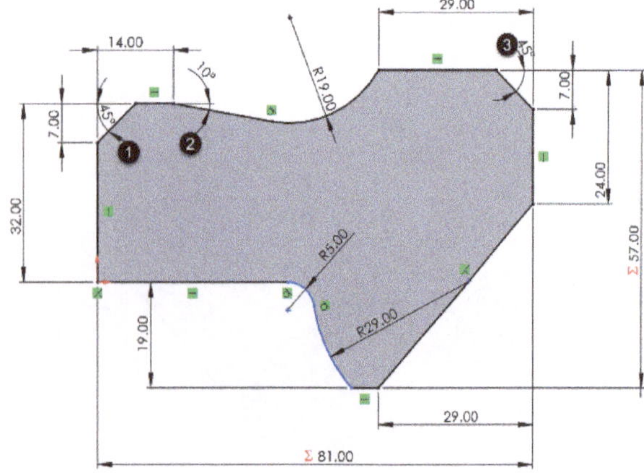

43. Select the centerpoint of the lower arc and the lower horizontal line.
44. Position the dimension, type **19** in the **Modify** box, and click the green check.

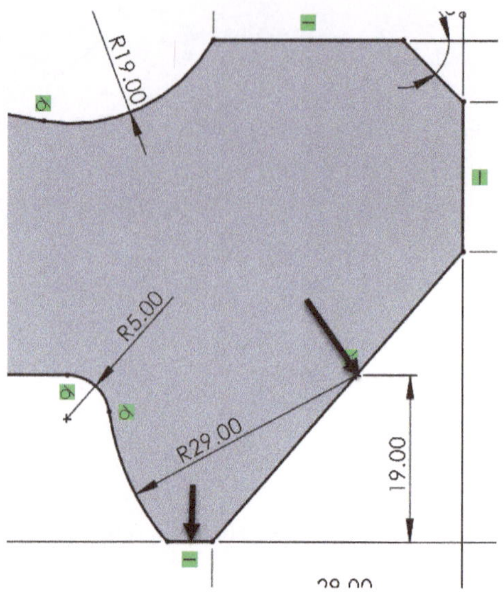

45. Click **Exit Sketch** on the CommandManager.

Extruding the Sketch

1. Click the **Extruded Boss/Base** icon on the **Features** tab of the Command Manager.
2. Select the sketch.
3. Select the value in the **Depth** box and type =.
4. Next, select **Global Variables > C**.

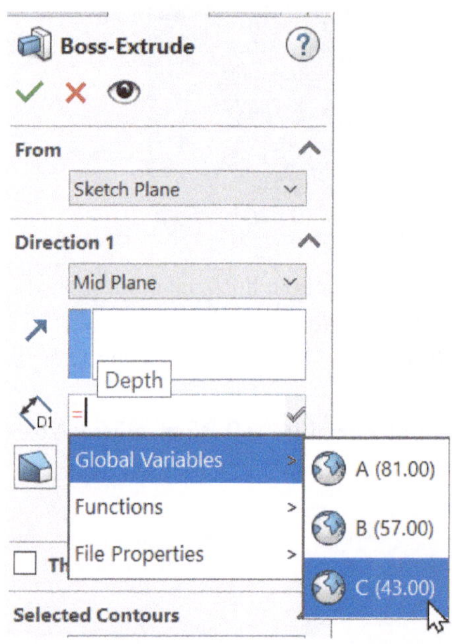

5. Select the **Mid Plane** option from the **End Condition** drop-down.
6. Click **OK**.

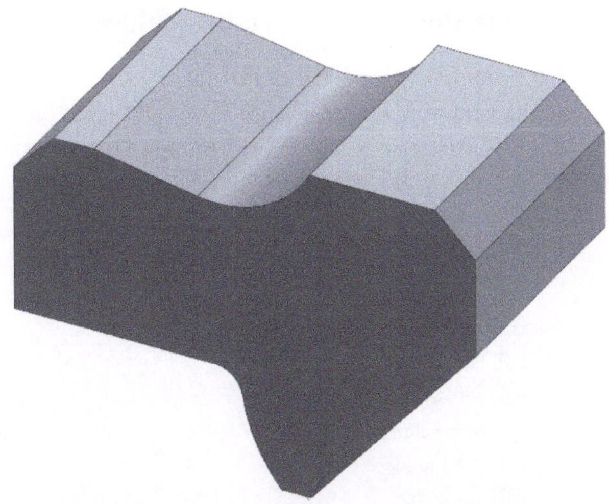

7. On the CommandManager, click **Features** tab > **Extruded Cut**.
8. Click on the front face of the model.
9. Create a circle and add dimensions to it, as shown.

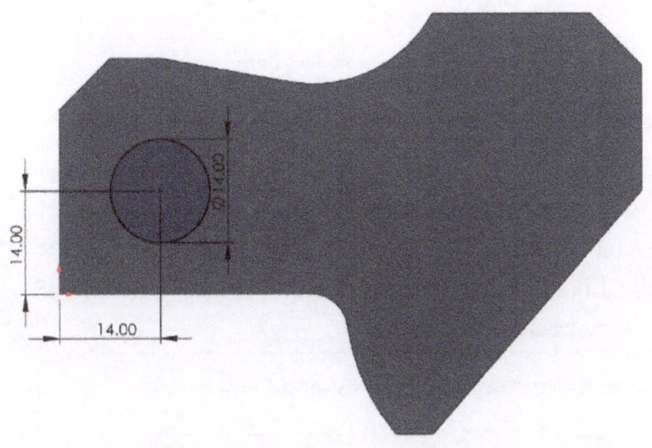

10. Select the **Through all** option from the **End Condition** drop-down.
11. Click **OK** on the PropertyManager.

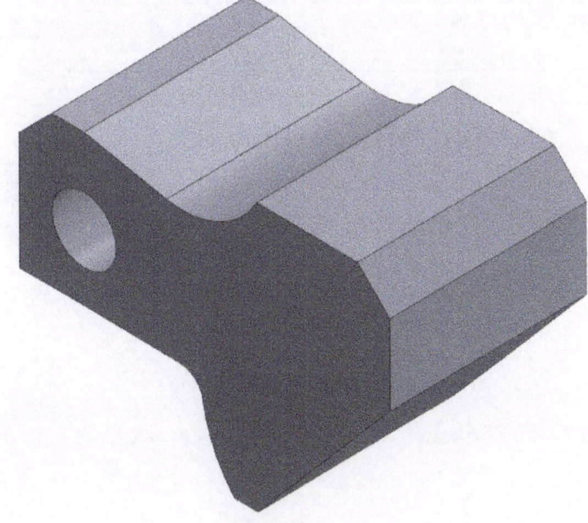

12. On the CommandManager, click **Features** tab > **Fillet** drop-down > **Chamfer**.
13. Click the **Angle Distance** icon in the **Chamfer Type** section on the PropertyManager.
14. Select the lower right edge of the model, as shown.

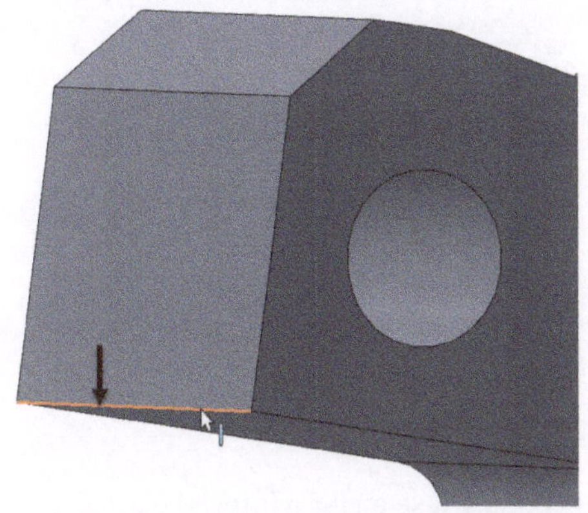

15. Type **7** and **45** in the **Distance** and **Angle** boxes, respectively.
16. Click **OK** on the PropertyManager.

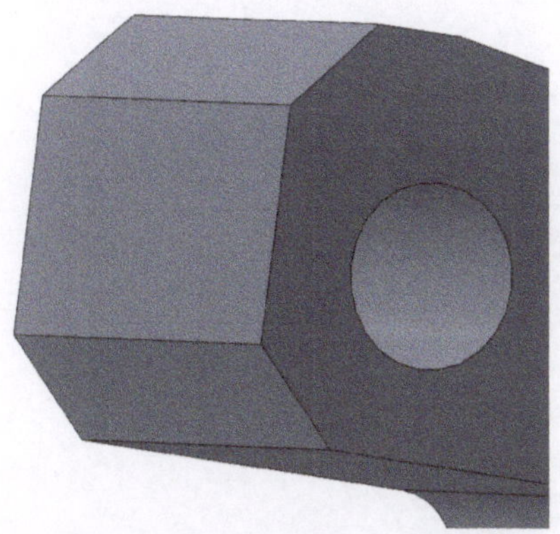

17. In the FeatureManager Design Tree, right-click on the **Material** node and select **Edit Material**.

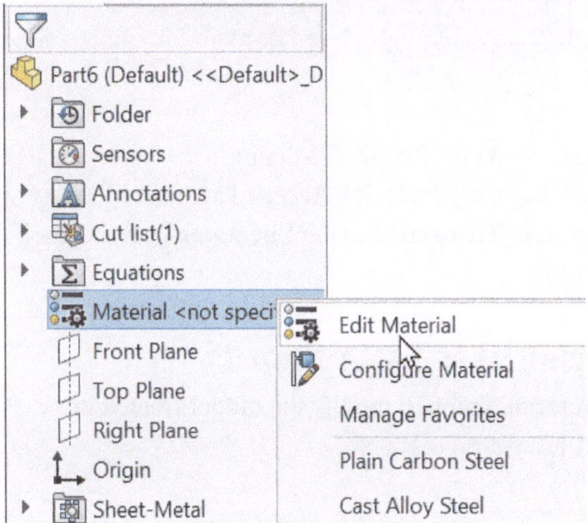

18. On the **Material** dialog, expand the **Aluminium Alloys** folder and select the **1020 Alloy** material.

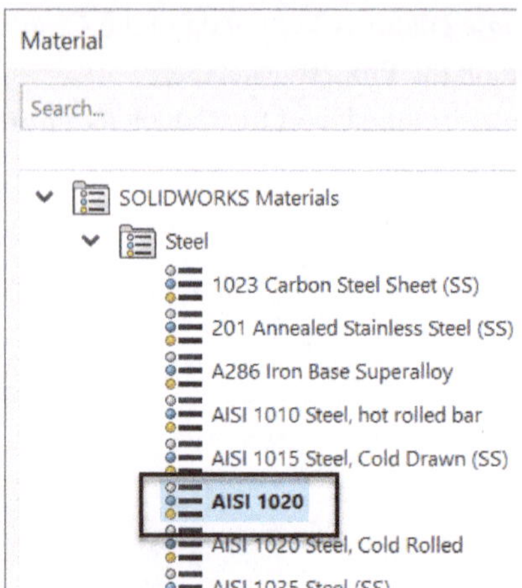

19. Click **Apply** and **Close** on the **Material** dialog.
20. On the CommandManager, click **Evaluate > Mass Properties** ; on the **Mass Properties** dialog, the **Mass** is displayed as 125.6.

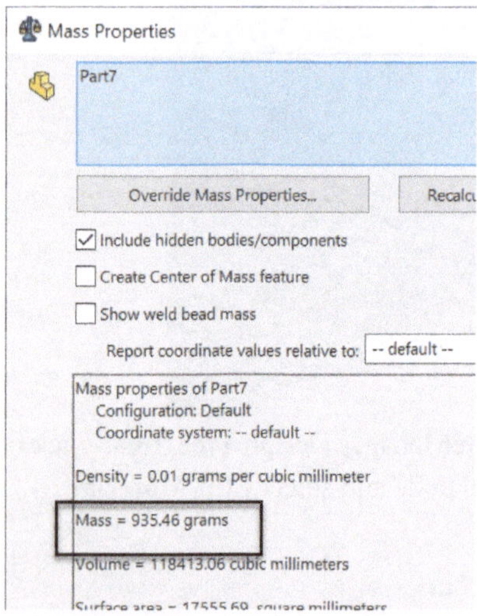

21. Close the **Mass Properties** dialog.
22. Click **Save** on the Quick Access Toolbar.
23. Type **C6_Tutorial12** in the **File name** box and click **Save**.

Tutorial 13 (CSWA Step 2)

In this tutorial, you will modify the model created in Tutorial 12.

Modifying the Global Variable Values

1. Open the file created in Tutorial 12.
2. In the FeatureManager Design Tree, right-click on the **Equations** node and select **Manage Equations**.

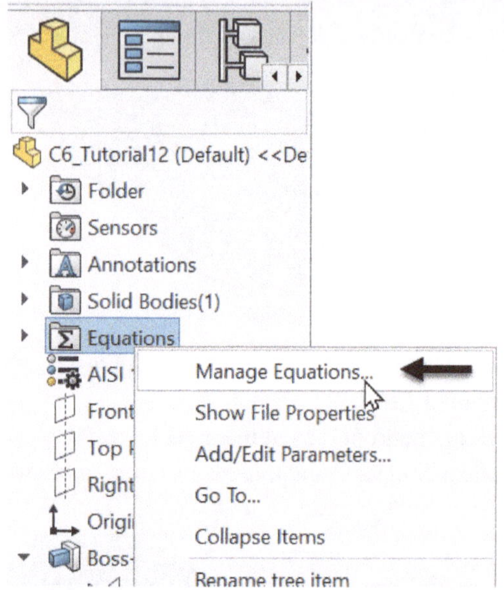

3. On the **Equations, Global Variables, and Dimensions** dialog, select the value in the **Value/ Evaluation** box next to the **A** global variable.
4. Type **84**.
5. Likewise, change the **B** and **C** values to **59** and **45** respectively.

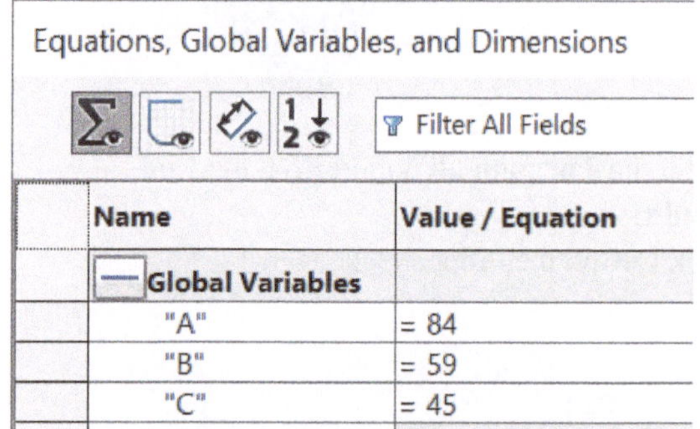

6. Click **OK**; the model is updated.

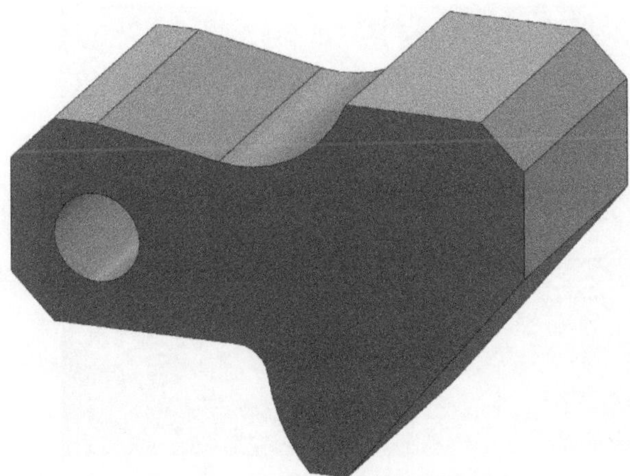

7. Click **Evaluate > Mass Properties** on the CommandManager. The **Mass** value is updated to 1028.05 gms.
8. Close the **Mass Properties** dialog.
9. Save the file as C6_tutorial13 and close it.

Tutorial 14 (CSWA Step 3 and 4)

In this tutorial, you will modify the model created in Tutorial 12.

1. Open the file created in Tutorial 12.
2. In the FeatureManager Design Tree, right-click on the **Equations** node and select **Manage Equations**.
3. On the **Equations, Global Variables, and Dimensions** dialog, select the value in the **Value/ Evaluation** box next to the **A** global variable.
4. Type **86**.
5. Likewise, change the **B** and **C** values to **58** and **44** respectively.
6. Click **OK**; the model is updated.

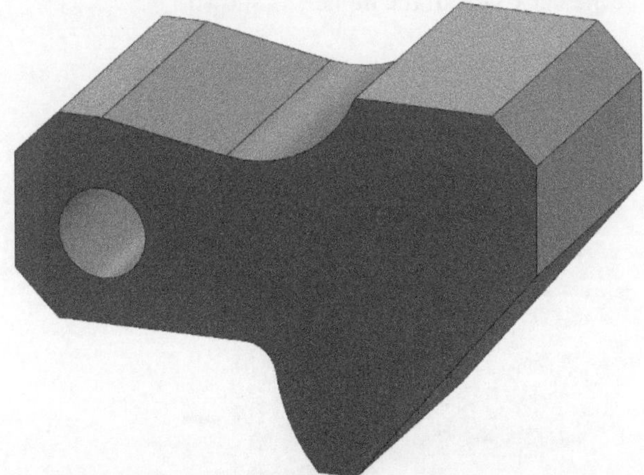

7. Click **Evaluate > Mass Properties** on the CommandManager. The **Mass** value is updated to 1012.88 gms.
8. Close the **Mass Properties** dialog.

Creating the Extruded Cuts

1. On the CommandManager, click **Features > Extruded Cut**.
2. Select the bottom face of the model, as shown.

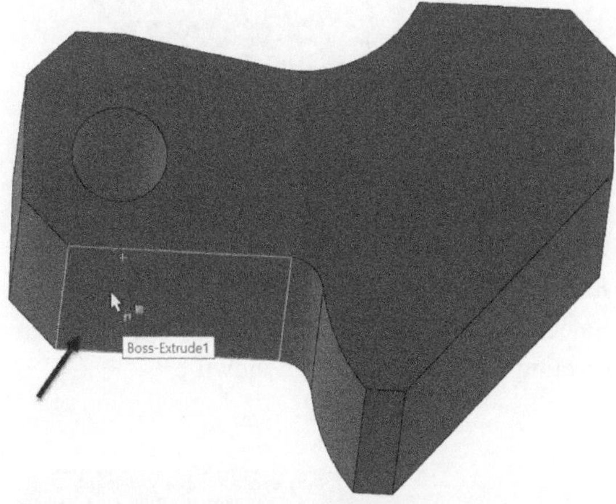

3. On the CommandManager, click **Sketch > Rectangle drop-down > Corner Rectangle**.
4. Select the top right corner vertex of the model.
5. Move the pointer toward right and click.
6. Add dimensions to the rectangle using the **Smart Dimension** command, as shown.

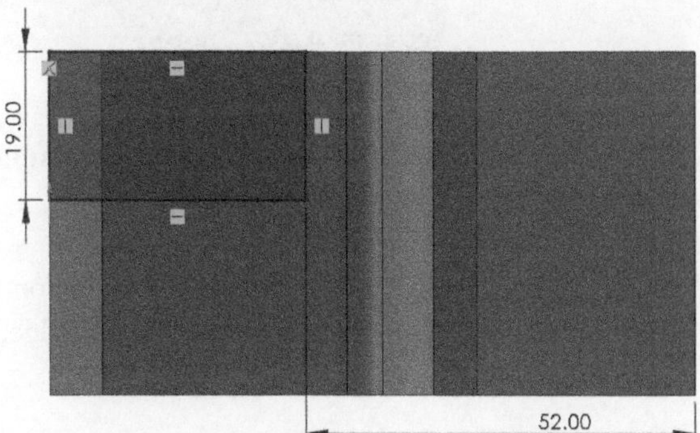

7. Click **Exit Sketch** on the CommandManager.
8. Select **End Condition > Through all** from the PropertyManager. Next, click **OK**.

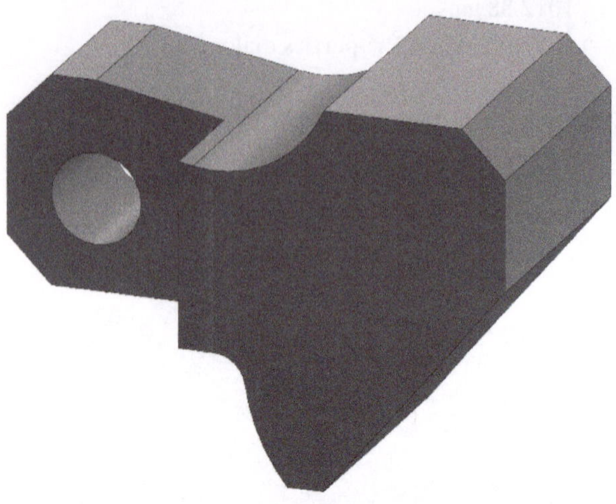

9. On the CommandManager, click **Features > Extruded Cut**.
10. Select the vertical face of the model revealed after creating the extruded cut, as shown.

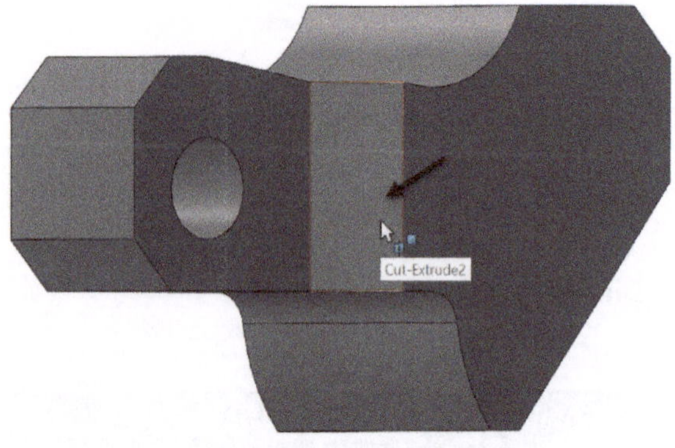

11. On the CommandManager, click **Sketch > Rectangle drop-down > 3-Point Corner Rectangle**.
12. Select the three vertices, as shown.
13. Press and hold the CTRL key, and select the bottom horizontal line of the rectangle and the bottom edge, as shown.
14. Click the **Collinear** icon on the PropertyManager.
15. Click **OK**.

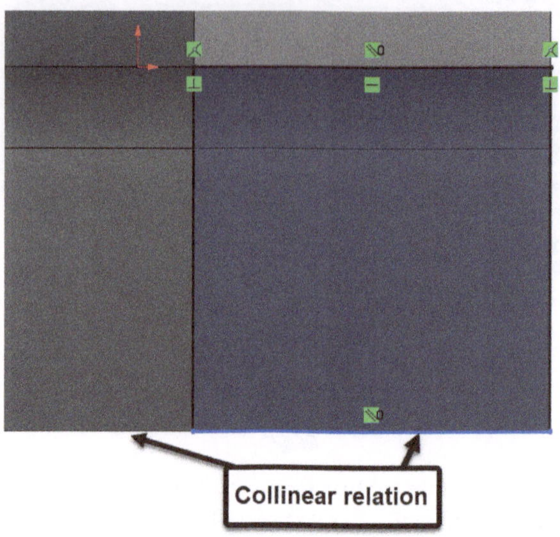

16. Click **Exit Sketch** on the CommandManager.
17. Select **End Condition > Through all** from the PropertyManager. Next, click **OK**.

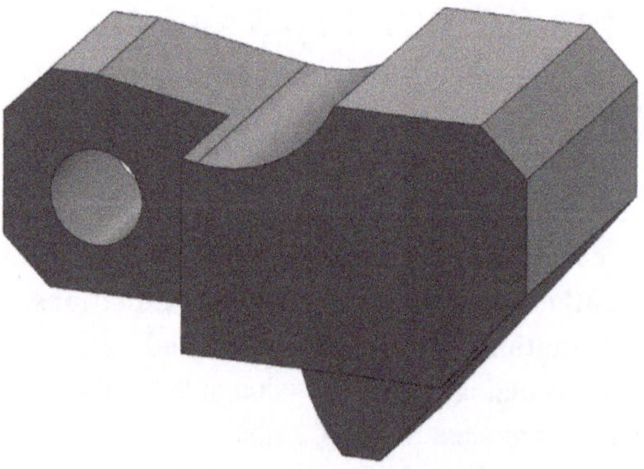

18. On the CommandManager, click **Features > Extruded Cut**.
19. In the graphics window, rotate the model and select the back face of the model, as shown.

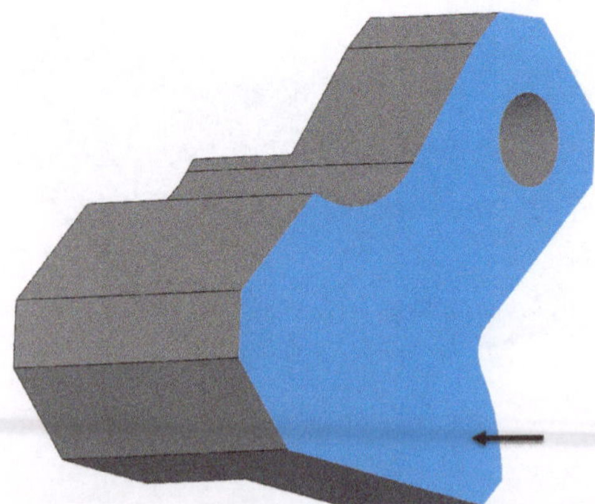

20. On the CommandManager, click **Arc** drop-down > **Centerpoint arc**.

21. Click on the region outside the model, close to the upper-right corner.
22. Move the pointer toward left and click on the curved edge in the top portion of the model.

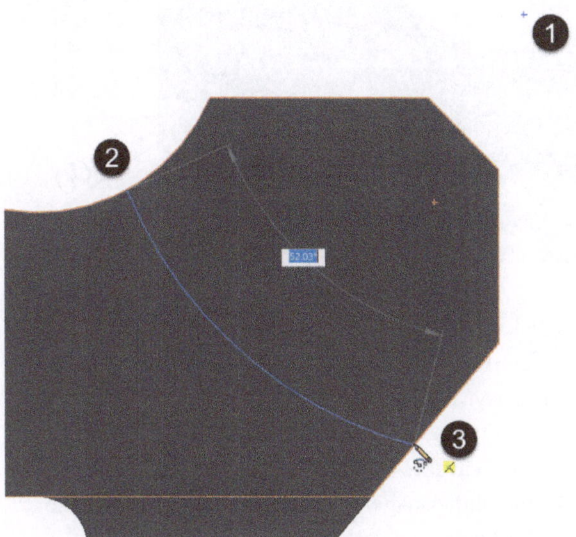

23. Activate the **Line** tool and select the endpoint of the arc, as shown.
24. Move the pointer vertically upward and click.
25. Move the pointer horizontally toward right and click
26. Move the pointer vertically downward and click.
27. Move the pointer toward left and select the lower endpoint of the arc.

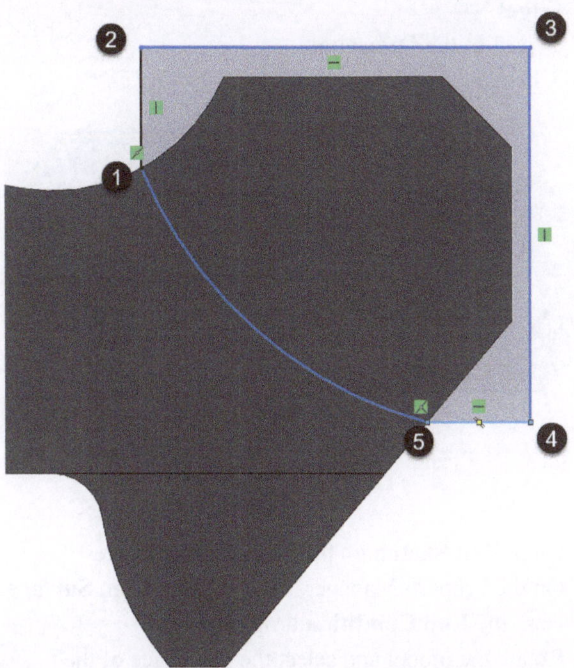

28. Press and hold the CTRL key and select the horizontal line and the top horizontal edge, as shown.
29. Press and hold the CTRL key and select the right vertical line and the vertical edge.

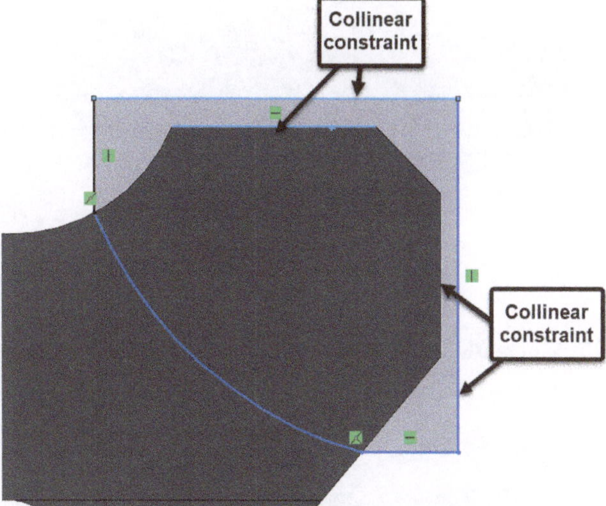

30. Add dimensions to sketch, as shown.

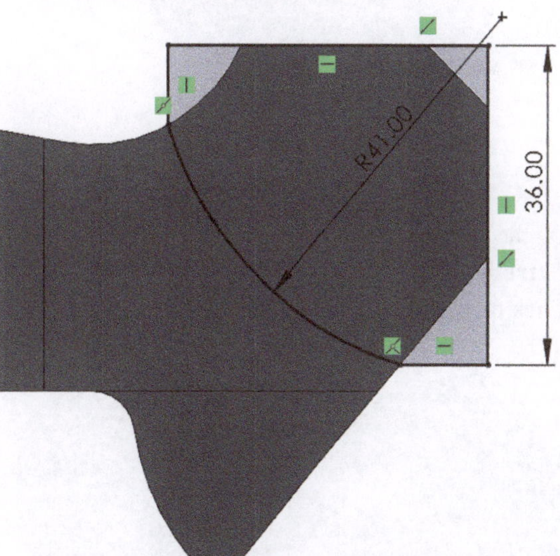

31. Click **Exit Sketch** on the CommandManager.
32. On the PropertyManager, select **Offset** from the **From** drop-down.
33. Type **12** in the **Offset** box.
34. Select **Blind** from the **End Condition** drop-down.
35. Type **24** in the **Depth** box and click the **Reverse Direction** button next to the **End Condition** drop-down.

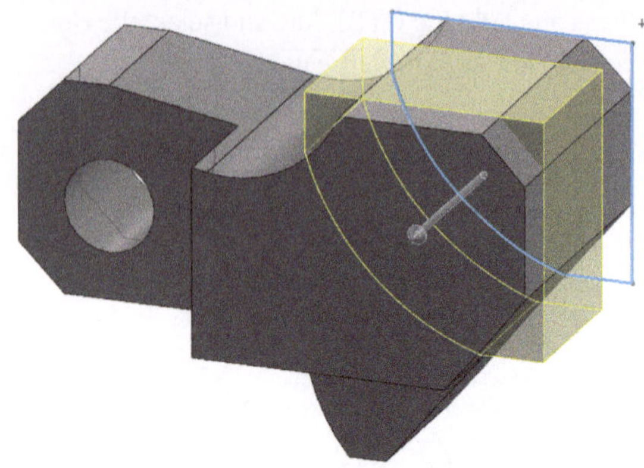

36. Click **OK**.

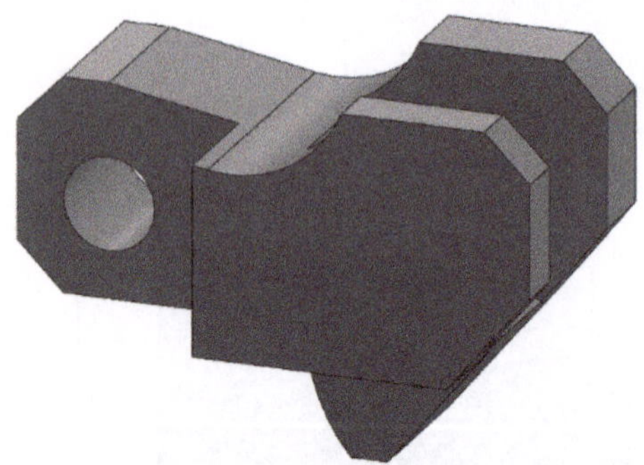

37. On the CommandManager, click **Features > Extruded Cut**.
38. Click on the front face of the model.

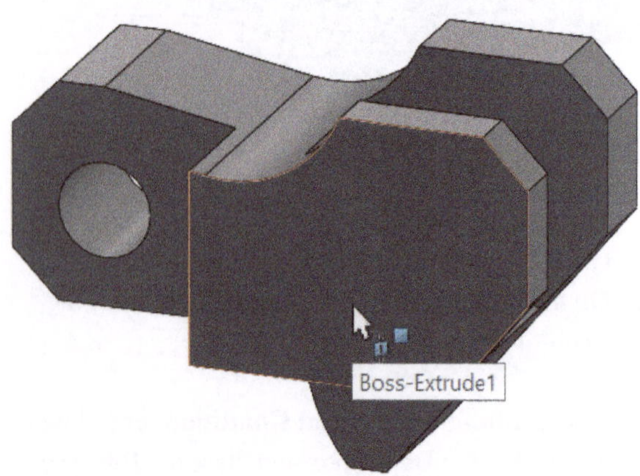

39. Create a circle and add dimensions to it, as shown.

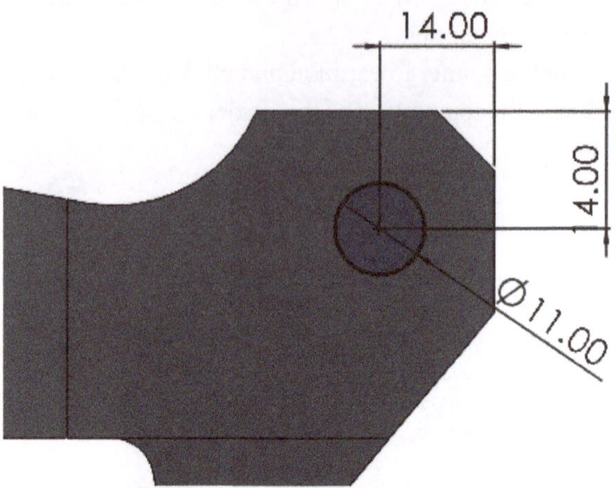

40. Click **Exit Sketch** on the CommandManager.
41. Select **End Condition > Through all** from the PropertyManager.
42. Click **OK** to create the extruded cut.
43. Click **Evaluate > Mass Properties** on the CommandManager. The **Mass** value is updated to 632.32 gms.
44. Close the **Mass Properties** dialog.
45. On the CommandManager, click **Features > Extruded Cut**.
46. Click on the front face of the model.
47. Select the face selected to start the sketch.
48. On the CommandManager, click **Sketch > Offset Edges** .
49. Type **1** in the **Offset** box.
50. Check the **Reverse** option and click **OK**.

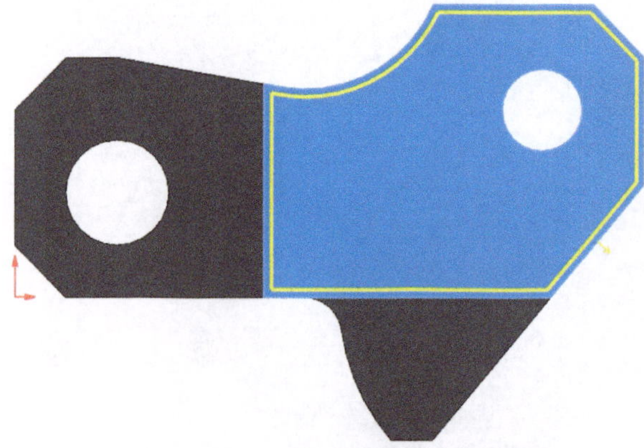

51. Click **Exit Sketch** on the CommandManager.
52. On the PropertyManager, select **Offset from Surface** from the **End Condition** drop-down.
53. Rotate the model and select the inner face of the extruded cut feature, as shown.

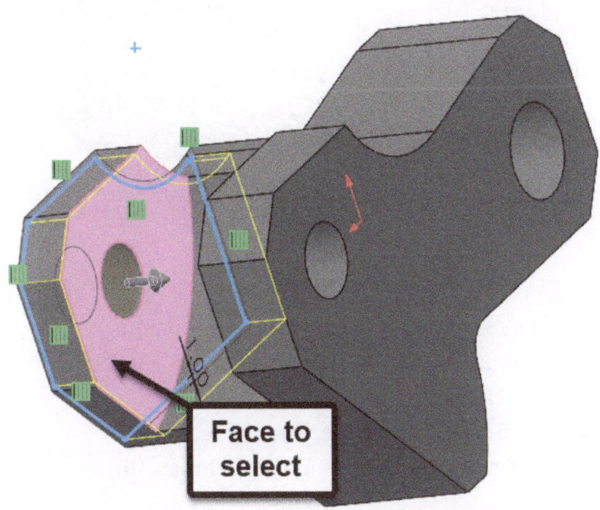

54. Type **1** in **Offset Distance** box.
55. Click **OK**.

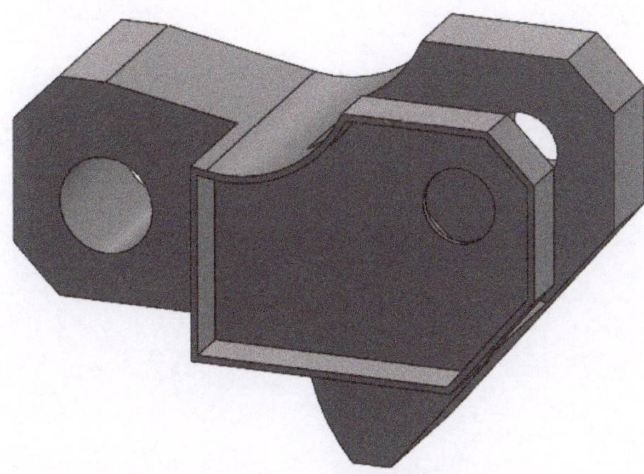

56. On the CommandManager, click **Features > Extruded Cut**.
57. Click on the face revealed after creating the previous extruded cut feature.

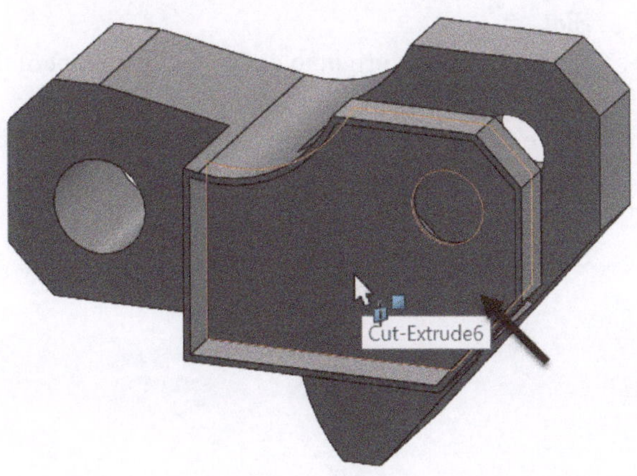

58. On the **View HeadsUp** toolbar, select **Display Style > Wireframe**.
59. On the CommandManager, click **Sketch > Convert Entities**.
60. Select the edges of the model, as shown.

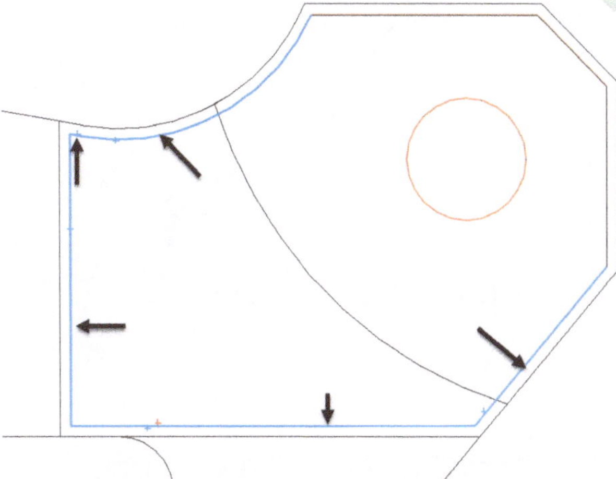

61. Click **OK** on the PropertyManager.
62. On the CommandManager, click **Sketch > Offset Entities**.
63. Type **1** in the **Offset Distance** box and click **OK**.

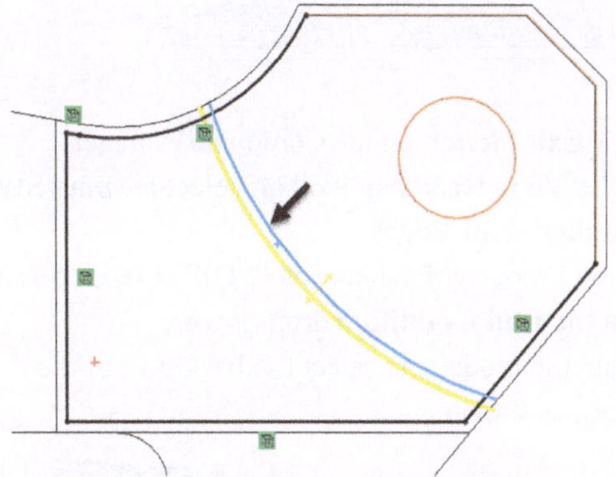

64. On the CommandManager, click **Sketch > Trim Entities**.
65. Select the portions to trim, as shown.

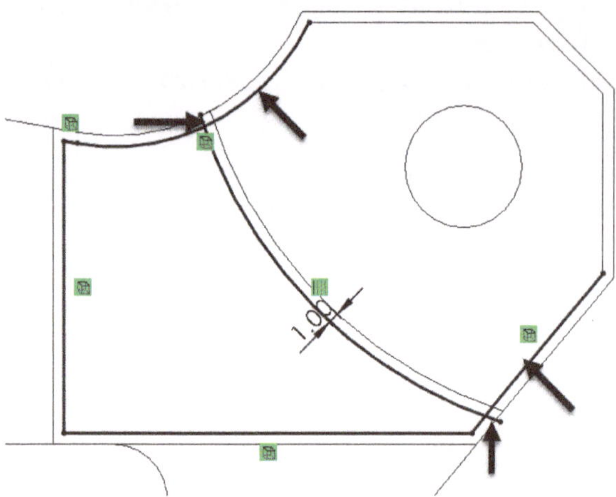

66. Click **OK** on the PropertyManager.

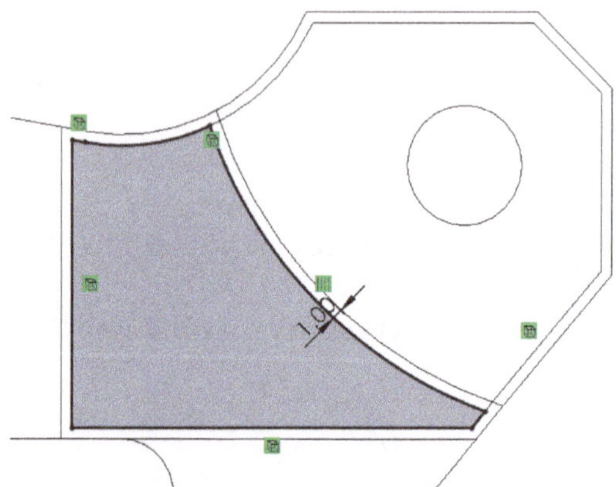

67. Click **Exit Sketch** on the CommandManager.
68. On the **View HeadsUp** toolbar, select **Display Style > Shaded with Edges**.
69. On the PropertyManager, select **Offset from Surface** from the **End Condition** drop-down.
70. Rotate the model and select the back face of the model, as shown.

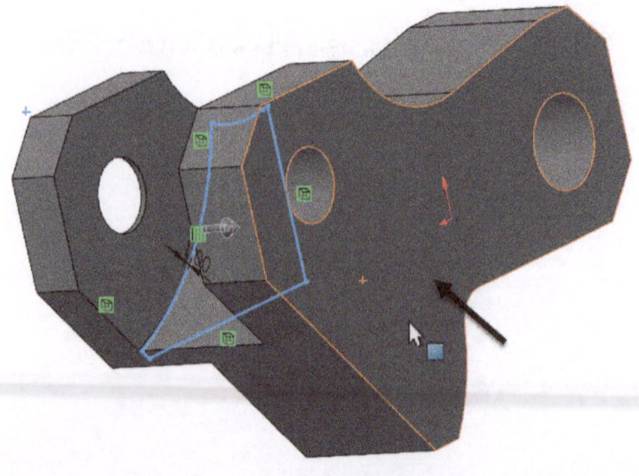

71. Type **12** in **Offset Distance** box.
72. Click **OK**.

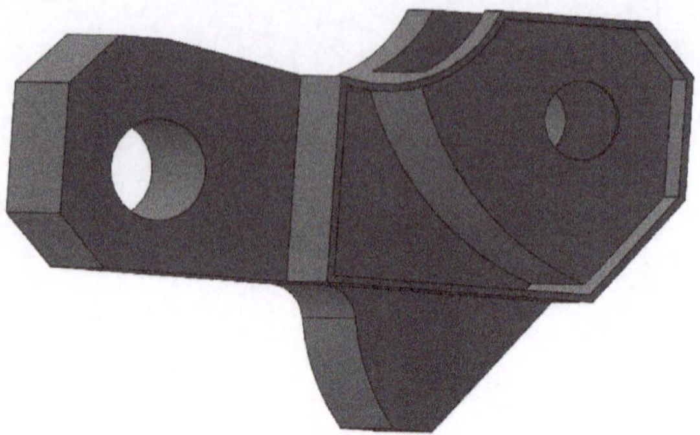

73. Click **Evaluate > Mass Properties** on the CommandManager. The **Mass** value is updated to 431.21 gms.
74. Close the **Mass Properties** dialog.
75. Save and close the file as C6_Tutorial_14.

Tutorial 15

In this tutorial, you will create the part shown in figure below.

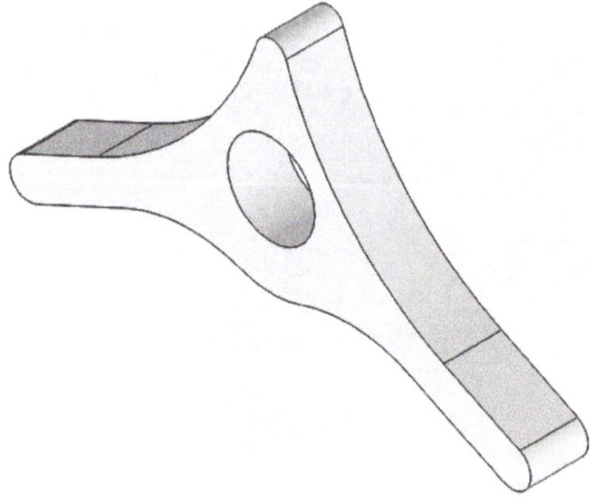

1. Open a new file in the **Part** Environment.
2. On the CommandManager, click **Sketch > Sketch.**
3. Select the front plane.
4. On the CommandManager, click **Sketch > Straight Slot** .
5. Select the sketch origin to define the first point of the slot.
6. Move the pointer diagonally toward bottom-right corner and click.
7. Move the pointer outer up to a small distance and click to specify the slot with.

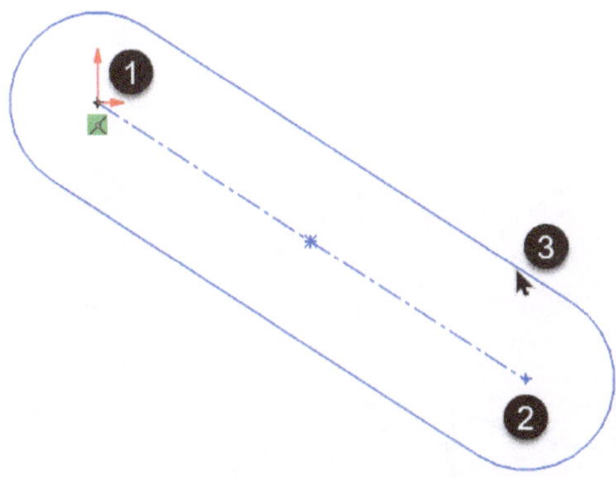

8. On the CommandManager, click **Sketch** tab > **Arc** drop-down > **Centerpoint Arc**
9. Select the origin point of the sketch.
10. Move the pointer vertically downwards, and then specify the start point of the arc, as shown.

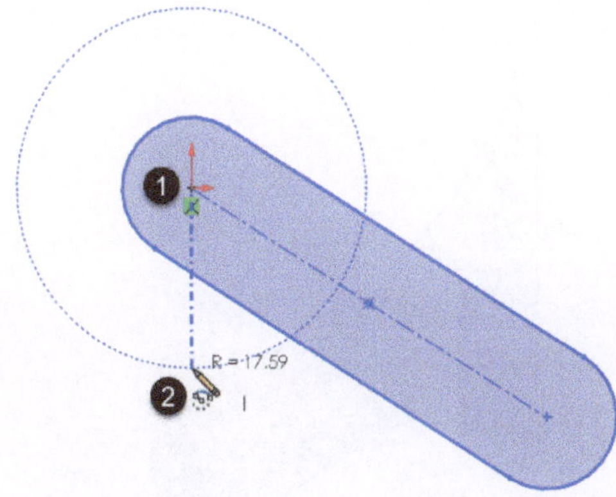

11. Move the pointer in the anti-clockwise, and then click on the slot to define the end point of the arc, as shown.

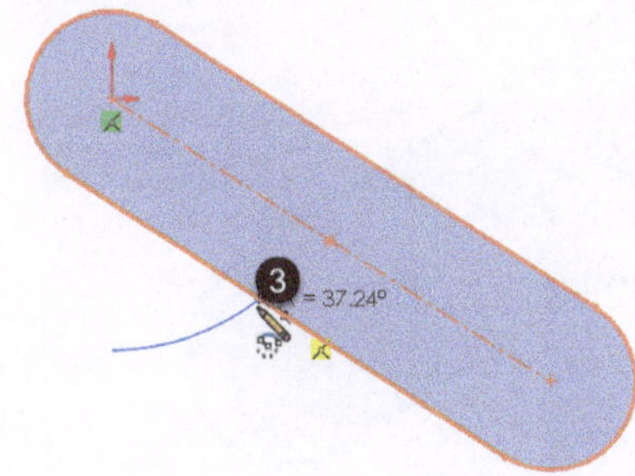

12. On the CommandManager, click **Sketch > Line**.
13. Select the start point of the arc.
14. Move the pointer vertically upward and click.

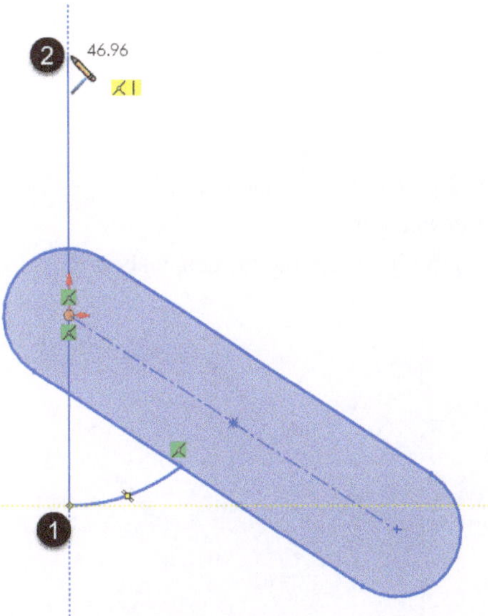

15. On the CommandManager, click **Sketch > Arc drop-down > 3 Point Arc**.
16. Select the top-endpoint of the vertical line.
17. Click on the slot to define the endpoint of the arc.
18. Move the pointer toward left and click to create the arc, as shown.

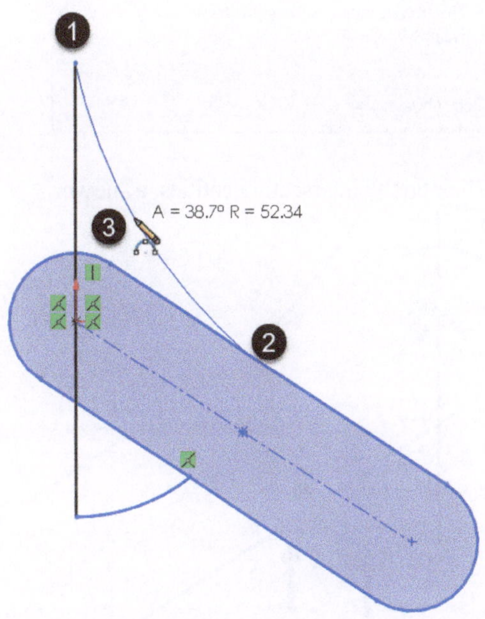

19. Create a three-point arc between the arc and slot, as shown.

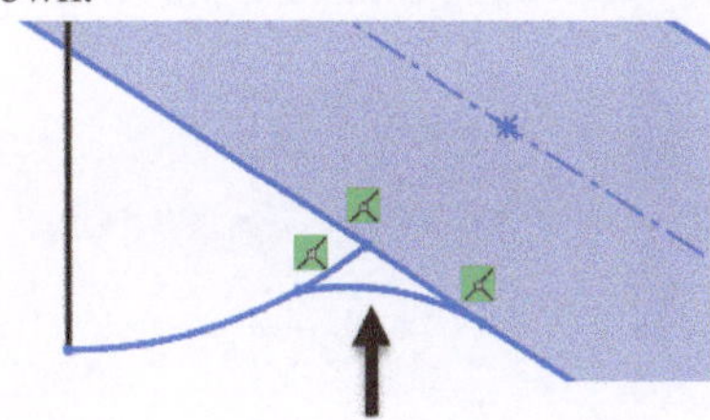

20. Click **Sketch > Trim Entities** on the CommandManager.
21. Click the **Corner** icon on the PropertyManager.
22. Click on the intersecting entities, a shown.

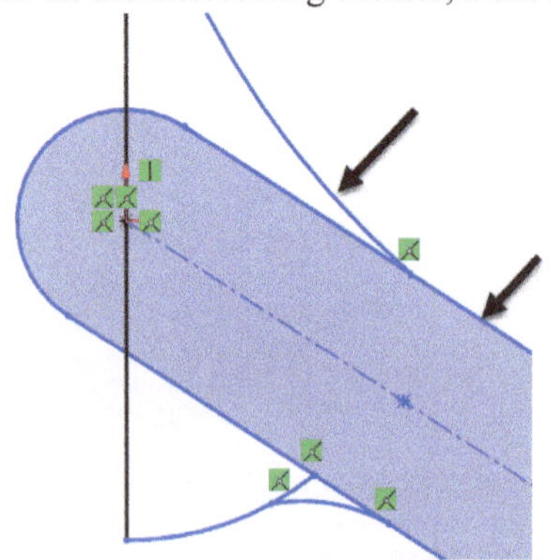

23. Click **OK** on the **SOLIDWORKS Design** message box.

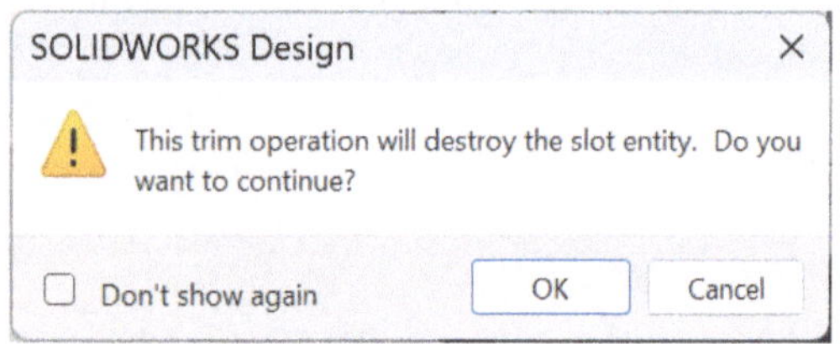

24. Click on the intersecting entities, a shown.

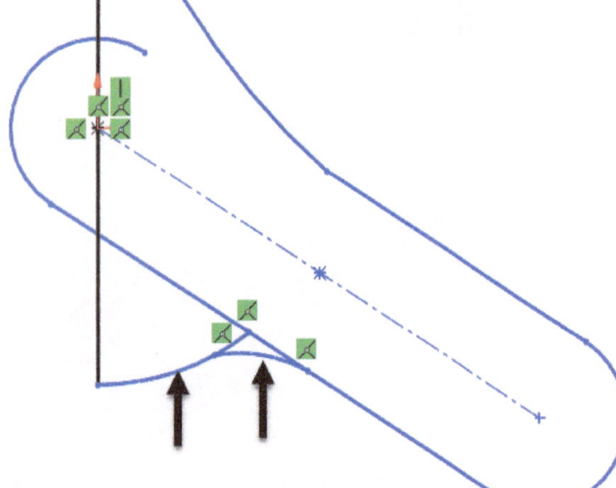

25. Click on the intersecting entities, a shown.

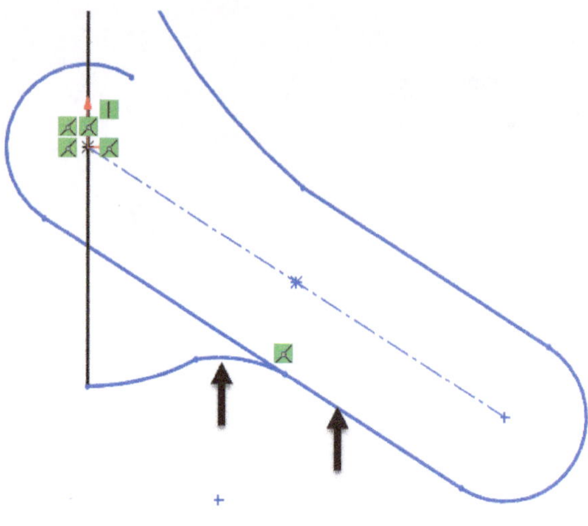

26. Click the **Trim to Closest** icon on the PropertyManager.
27. Click on the arc portions, as shown.

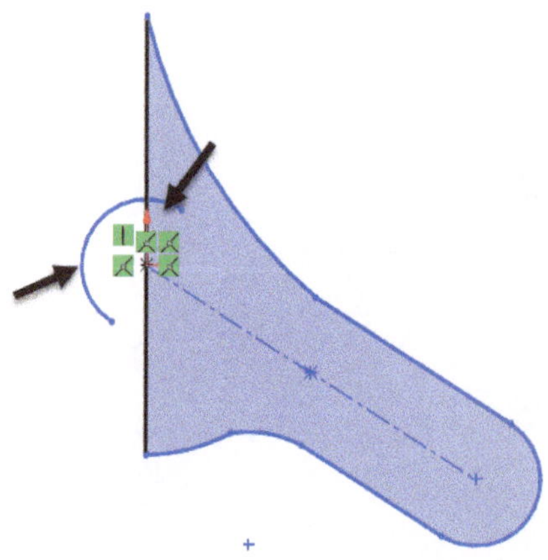

28. Click **OK** on the **Trim** PropertyManager.
29. Press the Ctrl key and select the two arcs, as shown.

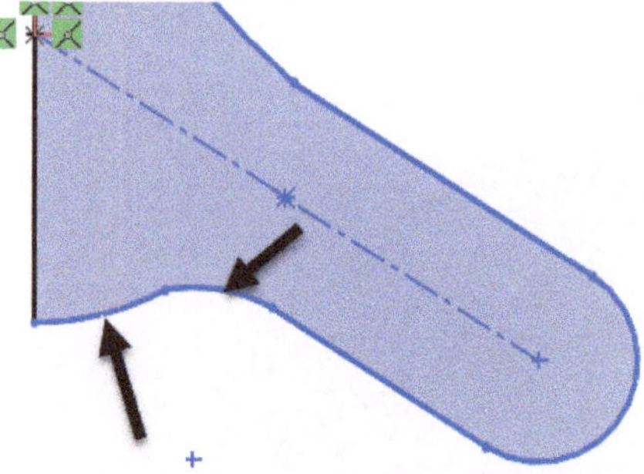

30. Select the **Tangent** icon on the PropertyManager, and click **OK**; the tangent relation is applied between the selected arcs.
31. Likewise, create tangent relations between other entities, as shown.

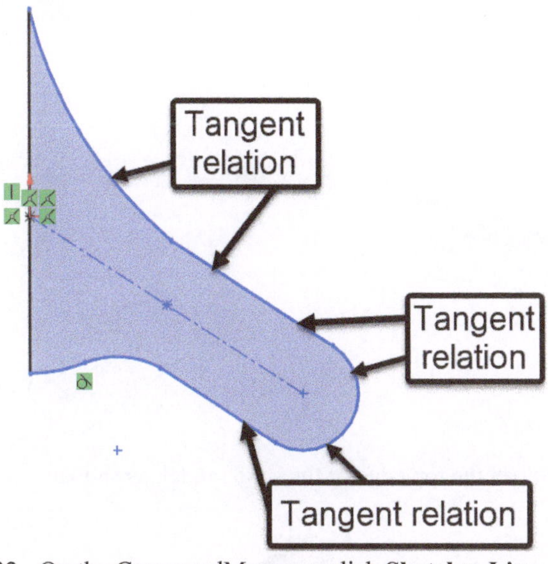

32. On the CommandManager, click **Sketch > Line drop-down > Centerline**.
33. Select the origin point of the sketch, move the pointer horizontally toward right, and click. Press Esc.

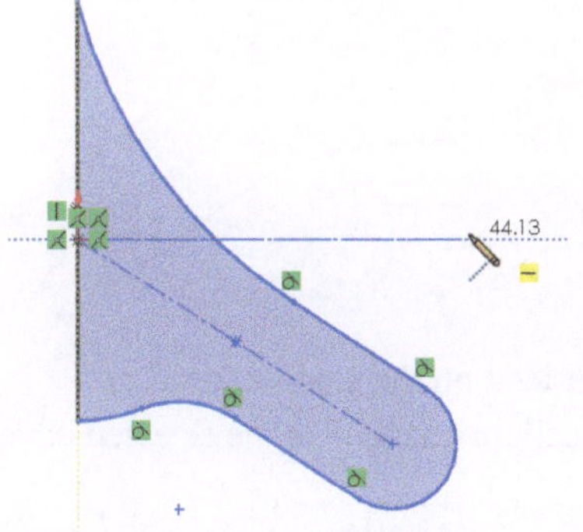

34. Add dimensions to the entities, as shown.

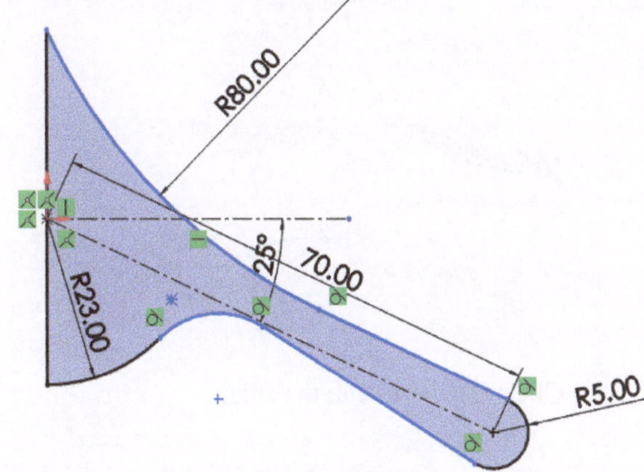

35. Press and hold the Ctrl key and select the two lines and the centerline, as shown. Next, click the **Parallel** icon on the PropertyManager.

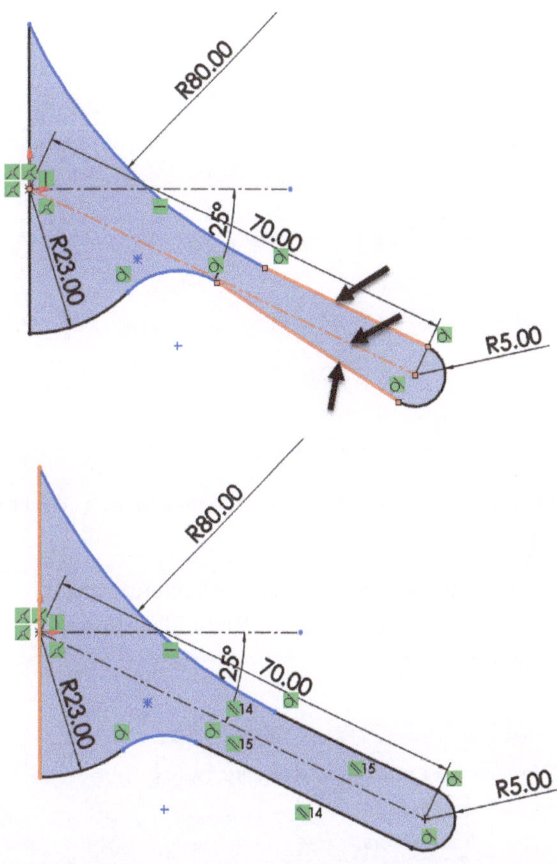

36. Add remaining dimensions, as shown.

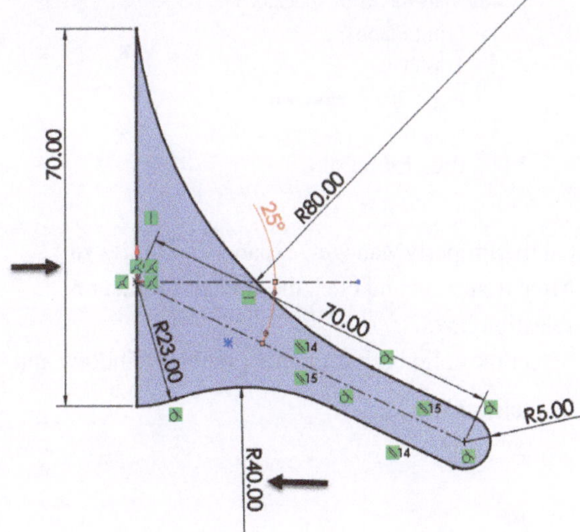

37. Click **Exit Sketch**.
38. Activate the **Extrude Boss/Base** tool and extrude the sketch up to 15 mm depth.

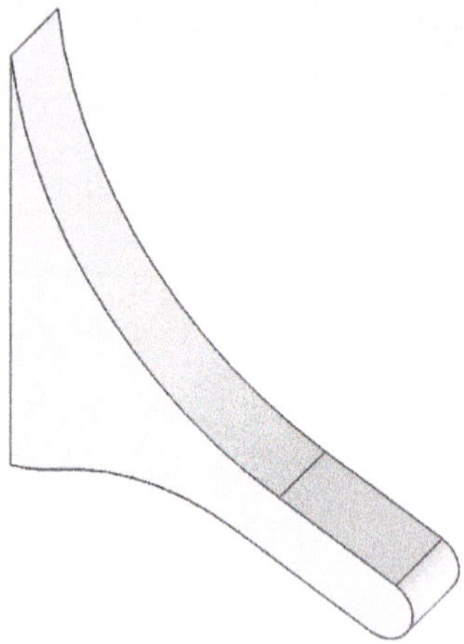

39. On the CommandManager, click **Features > Mirror** .
40. In the graphics area, expand the FeatureManager Design Tree and choose the Right Plane to set it as the mirror plane.

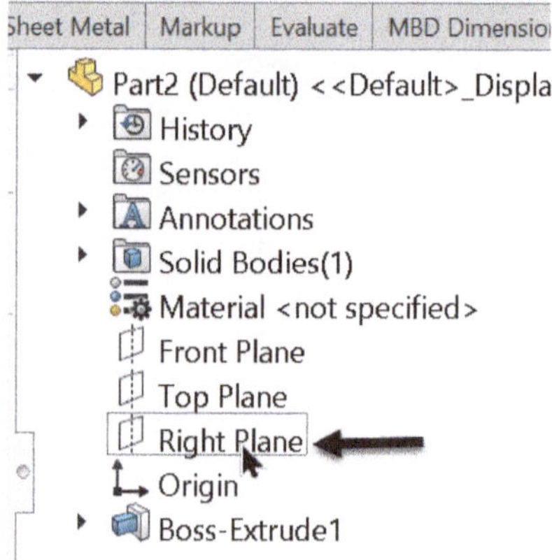

41. On the PropertyManager, expand the **Bodies to Mirror** section and click the **Bodies to mirror** selection box.
42. Select the solid body from the graphics window, and then click **OK**.

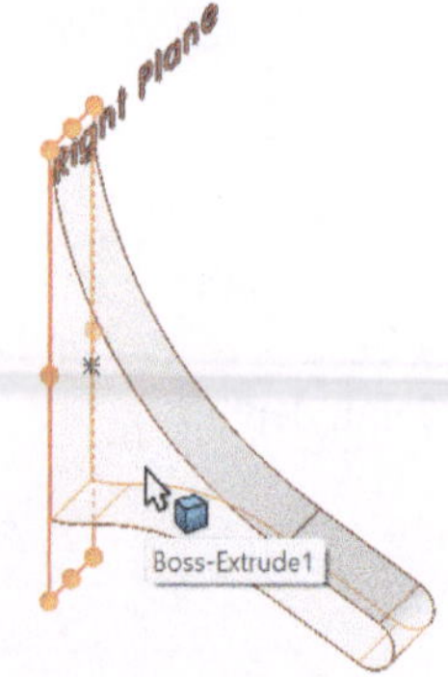

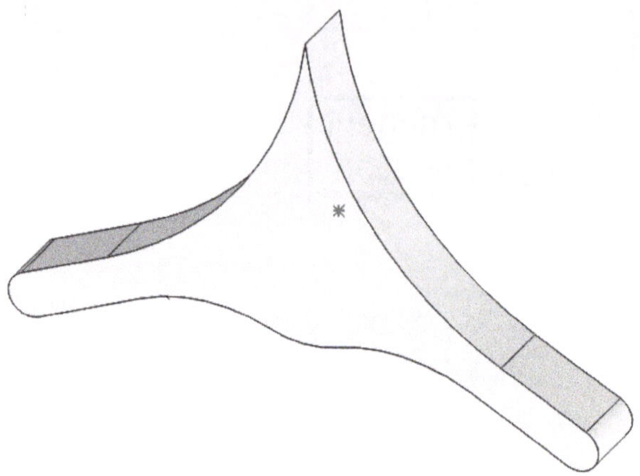

43. Select the top edge of the solid model, as shown.

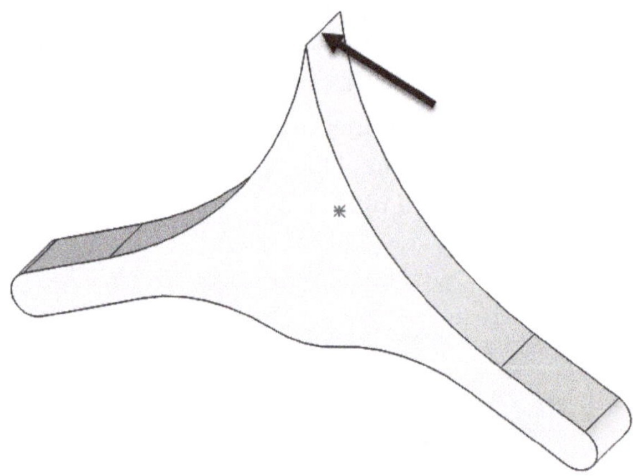

44. Click the **Fillet** icon on the context toolbar.
45. Enter **4** in the callout attached to the selected edge.

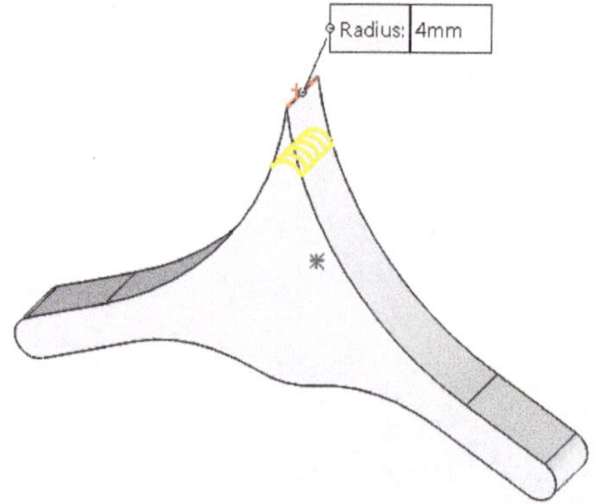

46. Click **OK** to add the fillet.

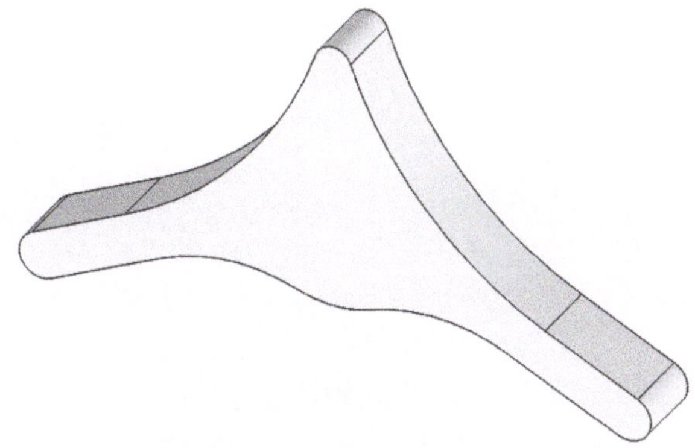

47. Activate the **Extruded Cut** tool and click on the front face of the model geometry.
48. On the CommandManager, click **Sketch > Circle**.
49. Select the sketch origin.
50. Move the pointer away and click to construct the circle.
51. Add diameter dimension to the circle and click **Exit Sketch** on the CommandManager.

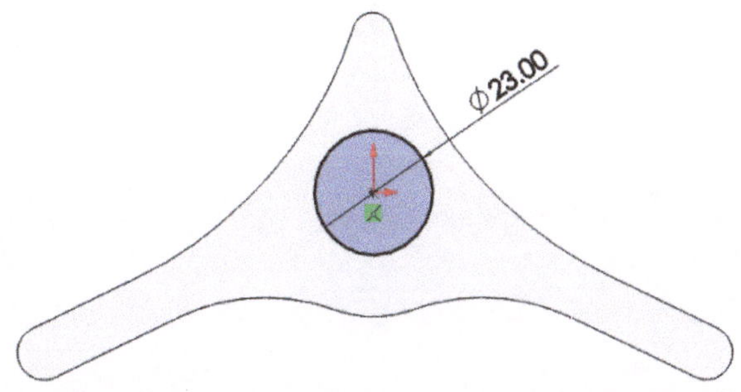

52. On the PropertyManager, select **End Condition > Through All**.
53. Click **OK**.

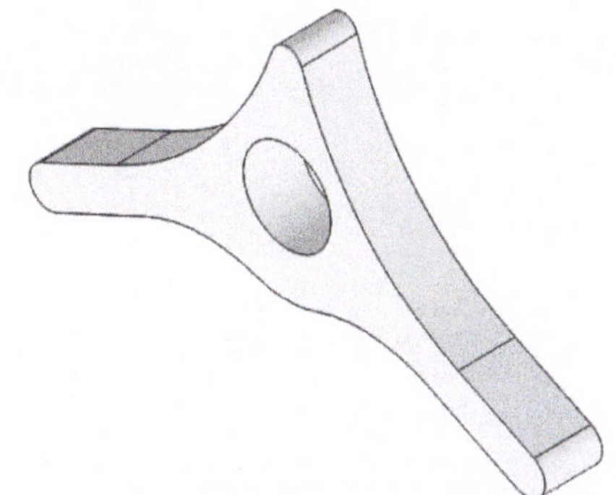

Chapter 7: Sheet metal Modeling

This chapter will show you:

- Construct Base Flange
- Construct Edge Flange
- Construct Miter Flange
- Close Corners
- Apply Corner Treatments
- Add Tab features
- Add Jogs
- Unfold and refold the bends
- Cut across bends
- Perform Forming Operations
- Add Hems
- Add Vents
- Add Gussets
- Make Fill Patterns
- View Flat Pattern

TUTORIAL 1

In this tutorial, you construct the sheet metal model shown in the figure.

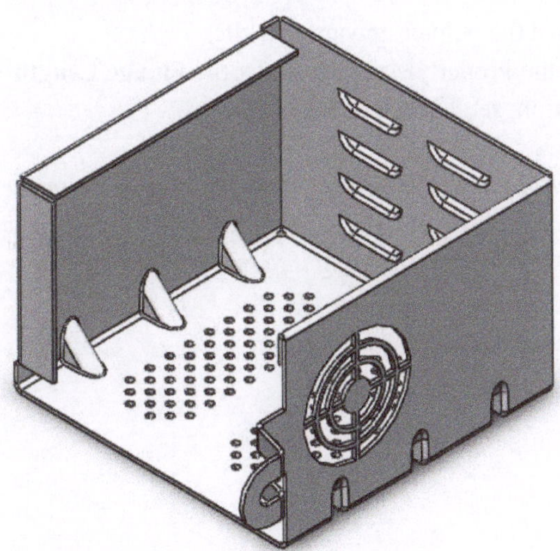

Opening a New File

1. Open a new part file.
2. On the CommandManager, click the right mouse button and select **Tabs > Sheet Metal** if the **Sheet Metal** tab is not displayed.

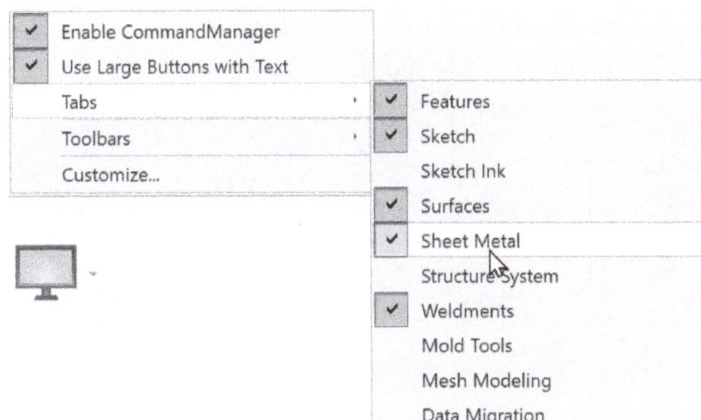

The **Sheet Metal** tab appears.

Constructing the Base Flange

You begin sheet metal design with the base flange or tab. This feature establishes the starting geometry for your 3D model and sets the manufacturing parameters.

The base flange defines three critical specifications:

- Material thickness
- Bend radius
- K factor for bend allowance calculations

These parameters ensure you can flatten the design accurately for fabrication.

1. To construct a base flange, click **Sheet Metal > Base Flange/Tab** on the CommandManager.
2. Select the front plane.
3. Click the **Line** tool on the CommandManager and create three lines, as shown.

4. Press and hold the CTRL key and select the horizontal line and the sketch origin.
5. Click the **Midpoint** icon on the PropertyManager.
6. Click **OK** on the PropertyManager.
7. Press and hold the CTRL key and select the two

vertical lines.

8. Click the **Equal** icon on the PropertyManager.
9. Click **OK** on the PropertyManager.
10. Add dimensions to the sketch, as shown.

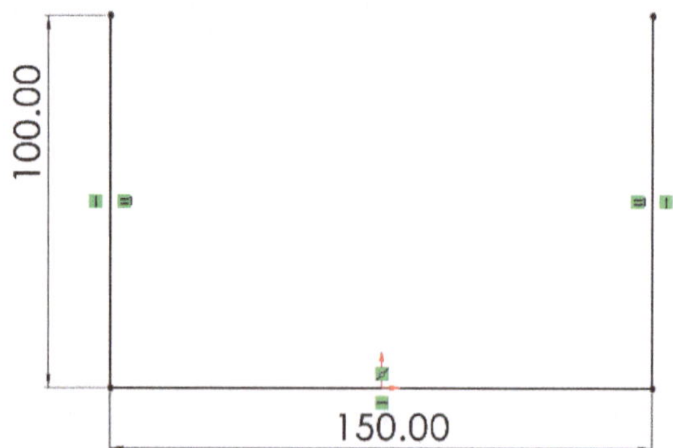

11. Click **Exit Sketch**.
12. On the PropertyManager, under **Direction 1** section, type-in 150 in the **Depth** box.
13. Check the **Use gauge table** option.
14. Select **SAMPLE TABLE –ALUMINIUM-METRIC UNITS.**
15. On the PropertyManager, under the **Sheet Metal Parameters** section, select **Gauge 14.**
16. Set the **Bend Radius** value to **2**.
17. Leave the **Auto Relief** section to default settings.
18. Click **OK** to construct the base flange.

Note: You can check the **Symmetric** option to specify symmetrical thickness that applies the same quantity of material to both sides of the sketch.

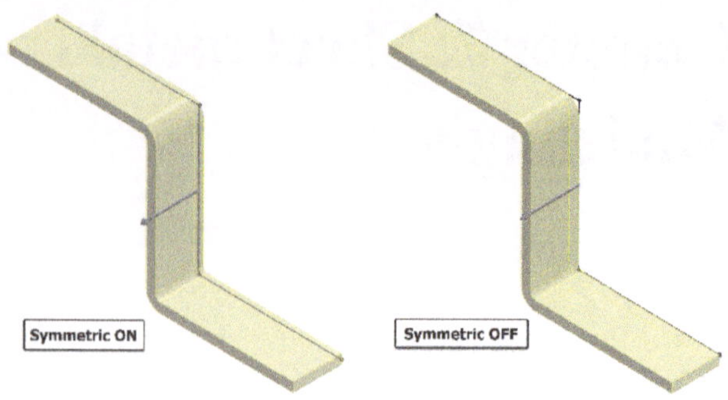

Adding an Edge flange

An edge flange is a sheet metal feature used to extend a flat, bent wall from a selected edge of a base flange or existing face.

1. To add the flange, click **Sheet Metal > Edge Flange**  on the CommandManager.
2. Select the edge on the top face.

3. Move the pointer upward and click.
4. On the PropertyManager, under the **Flange Length** section, set **Length** to 100.

*The **Multi Length Flange** option in the **Flange Length** section allows you to create flanges of different lengths in a single instance by selecting different edges.*

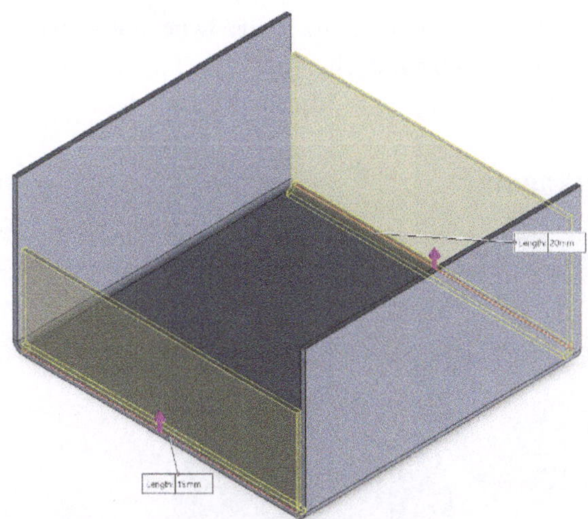

5. Click on the **Inner Virtual Sharp** icon in the **Flange Length** section. This measures the flange length from the outer face.
6. Under the **Flange Position** section, click the **Bend Outside** icon.

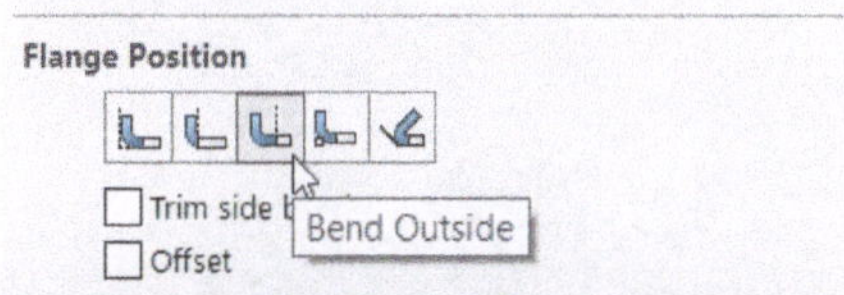

7. Click **OK** to add the flange.

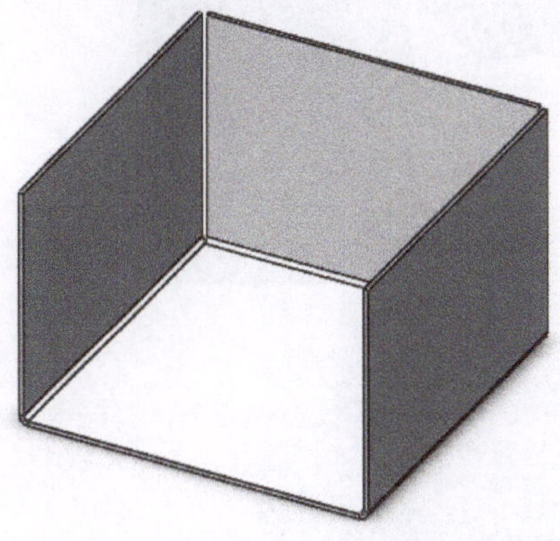

You can use the **Edit Flange Profile** button available on the PropertyManager to change the flange's shape. The sketch mode is activated when you click this button. Use the sketch tools to change the flange shape.

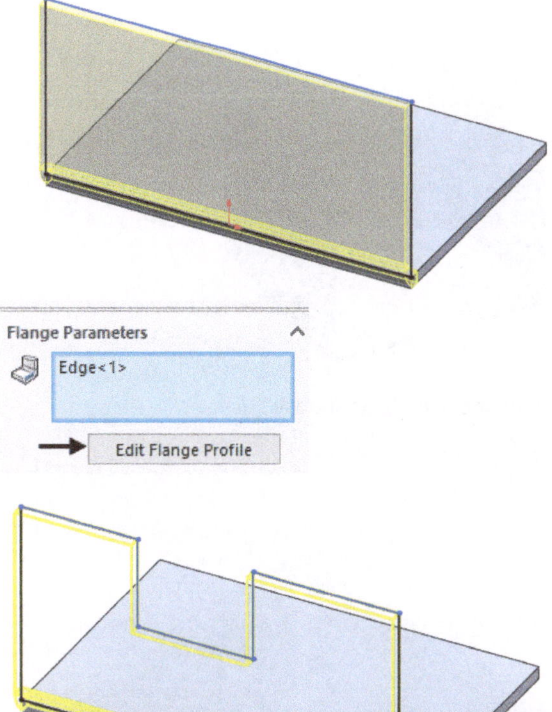

Make sure that the profile is completely closed. Next, click the **Finish** button on the **Profile Sketch** message box.

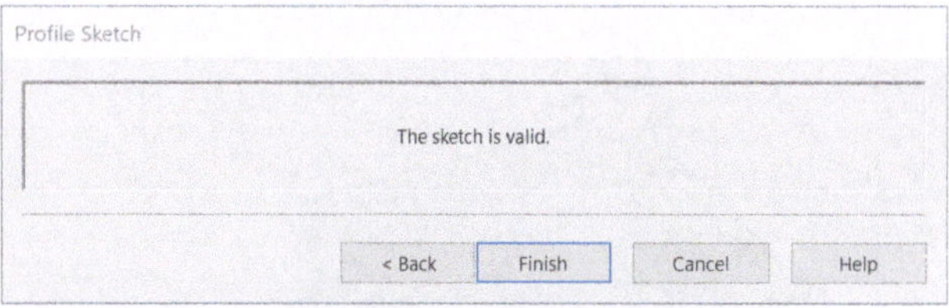

Constructing the Miter Flange

1. To construct the miter flange, click **Sheet Metal > Miter Flange** on the CommandManager.
2. Click the top edge of the left flange.

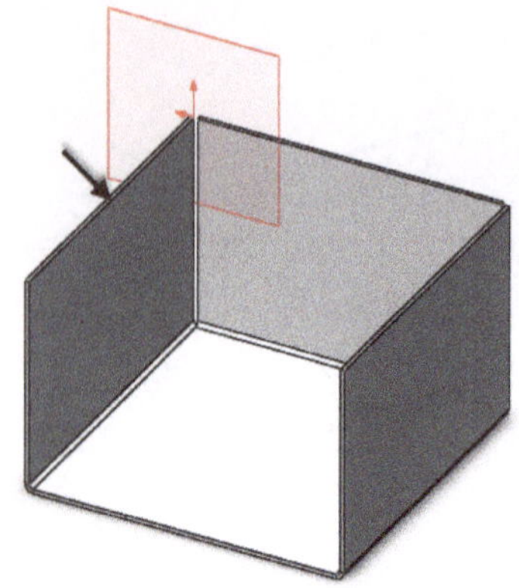

3. Draw the sketch, as shown.

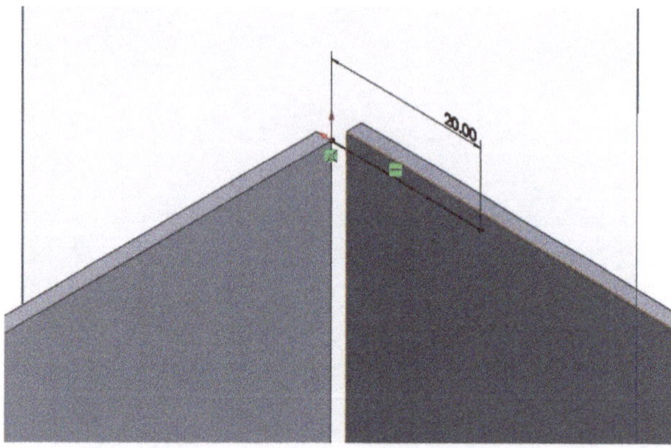

4. Click **Exit Sketch**.
5. Click on the vertical edge of the left flange.

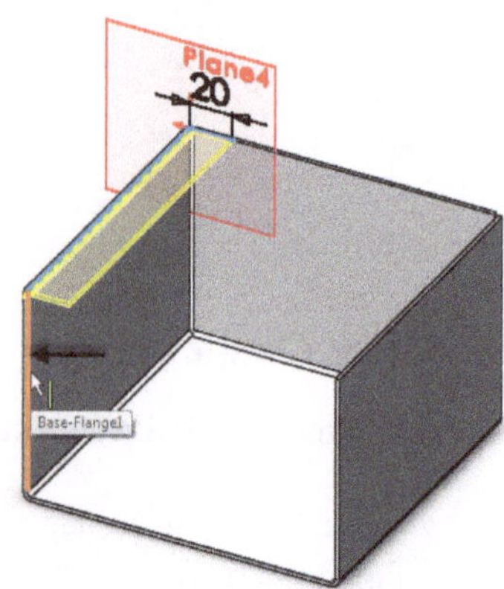

6. On the **Miter Flange** PropertyManager, set the **Flange Position** to **Material Inside** and **Gap distance** to 1.25.
7. Under the **Start/End Offset** section, set the **Start Offset Distance** and **End Offset Distance** to **10**.
8. On the PropertyManager, check the **Custom Relief Type** option.

Notice the three options in the **Relief Type** drop-down: **Rectangular**, **Obround**, and **Tear**. The **Tear** option has two more options under it: **Rip** and **Extended**.

Rectangular

Obround

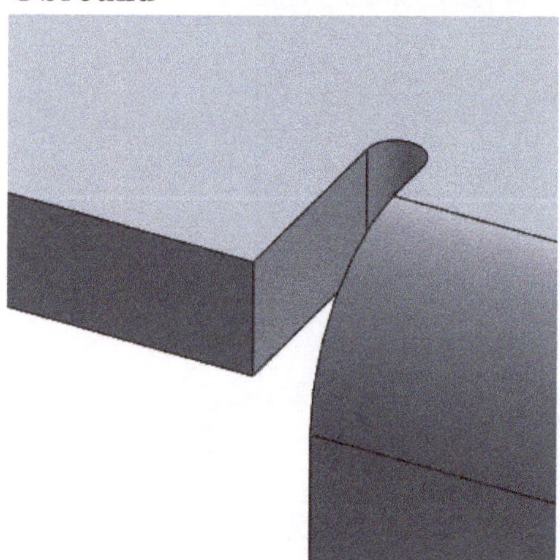

Tear

9. Select the **Rectangular** option from the **Relief Type** drop-down.
10. Check the **Use relief ratio** option.
11. Leave the **Ratio** value to 0.5.

12. Click **OK** to construct the miter flange.

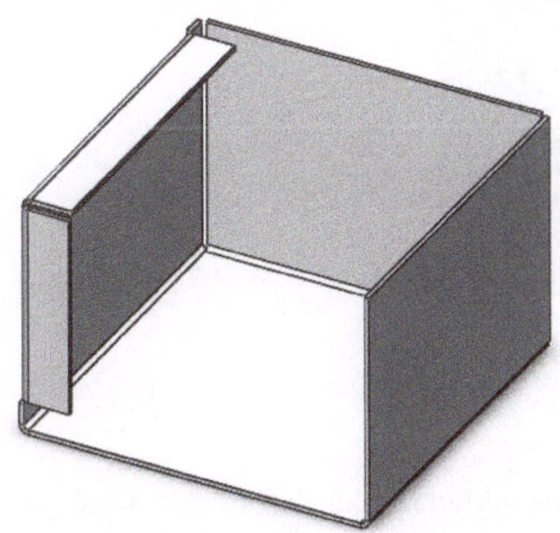

Closing the Corners

1. To close the corners, click **Sheet Metal > Corners > Closed Corner**.
2. Select the corner face of the miter flange.

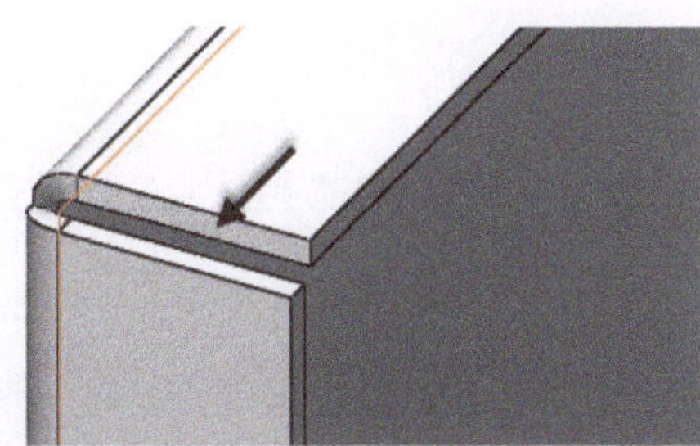

3. On the PropertyManager, set the **Corner type** to **Butt**.
4. Rotate the model and select the other corner faces.

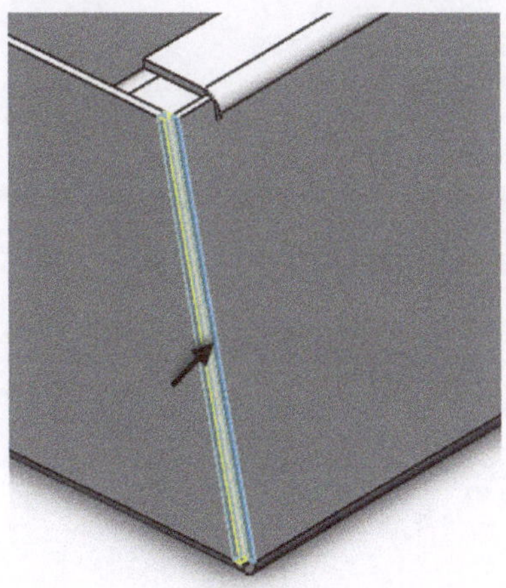

5. Click **OK** to close the corners.

Adding Corner Reliefs

1. To add corner reliefs, click **Sheet Metal > Corners > Corner Relief**. This selects the entire part.
2. Select **2 Bend Corner** from the PropertyManager.
3. On the PropertyManager, under the **Corners** section, click **Collect all corners**.
4. Under the **Relief Options** section, set the **Relief** type **Circular**.
5. Type **2** in the **Slot Width** box.
6. Click **OK** to add the corner relief.

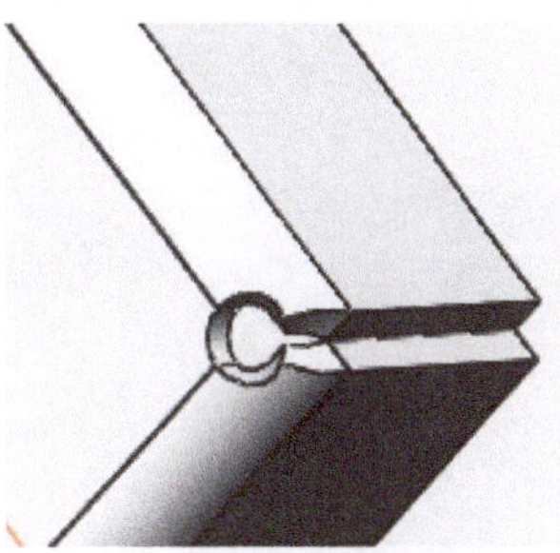

The different types of reliefs are:

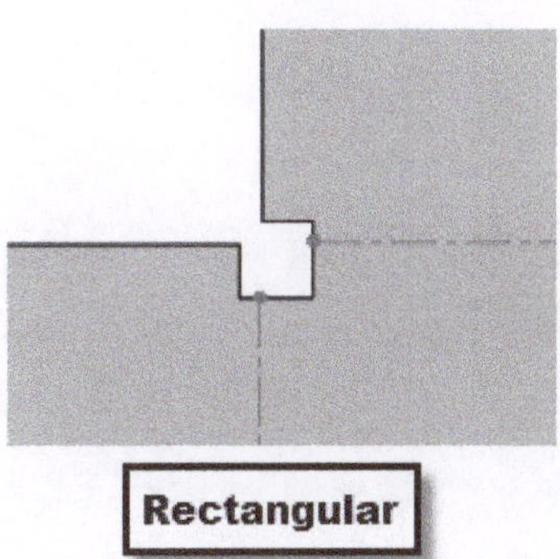

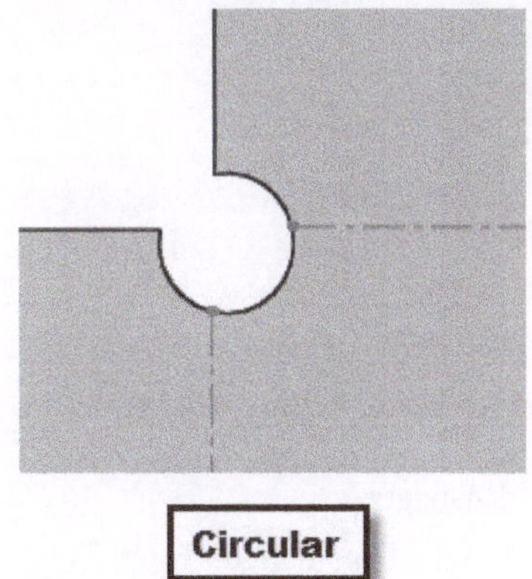

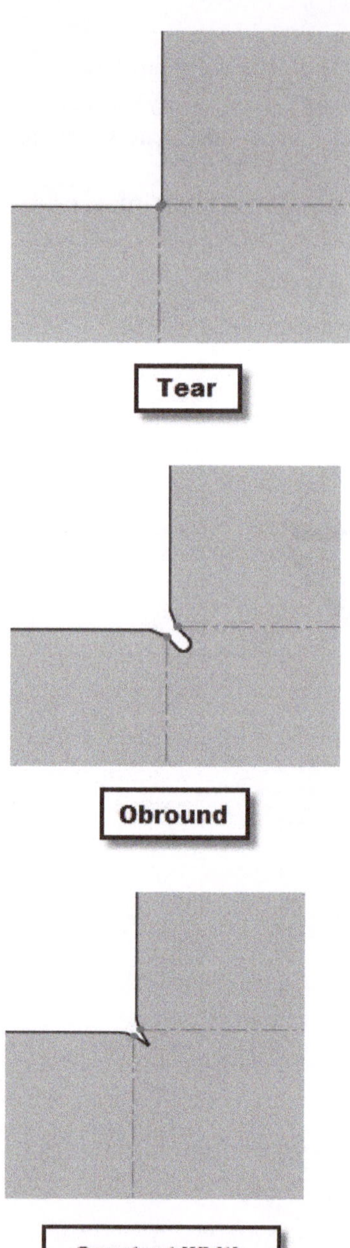

Adding a Tab feature

23. To add a tab, click **Sheet Metal > Base Flange/Tab**

on the CommandManager.

24. Click on the right side of the base flange.

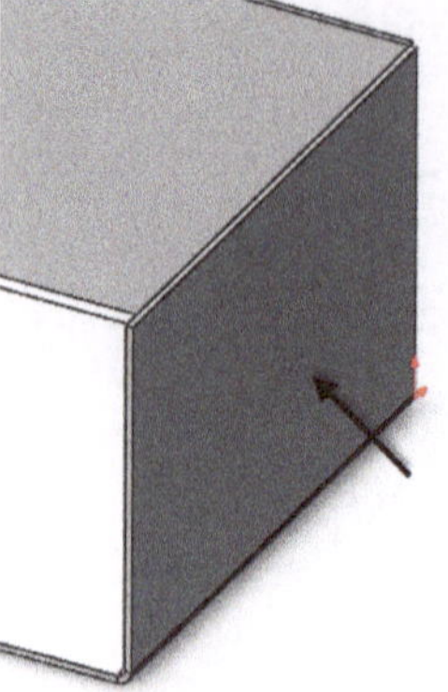

25. On the CommandManager, click **Sketch > Line**.
26. Click on the vertical edge of the face and move the pointer toward left.
27. Again, click to draw a horizontal line.

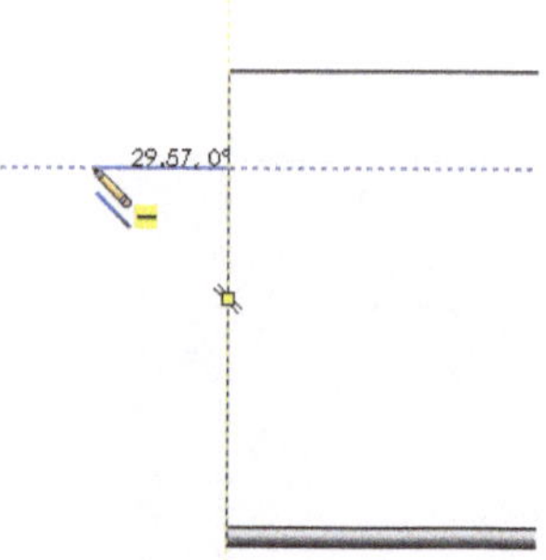

28. Move the pointer toward the endpoint of the line. The arc mode gets active.

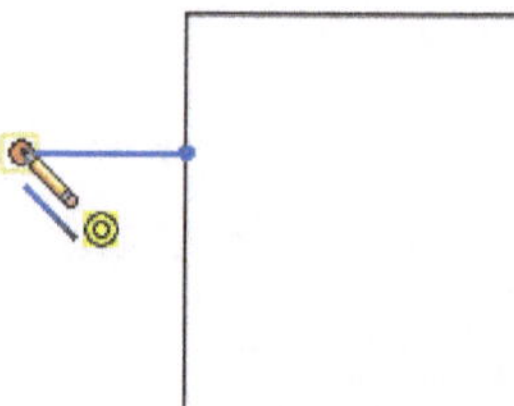

29. Move the pointer toward the left, and then downwards.
30. Click to create an arc.

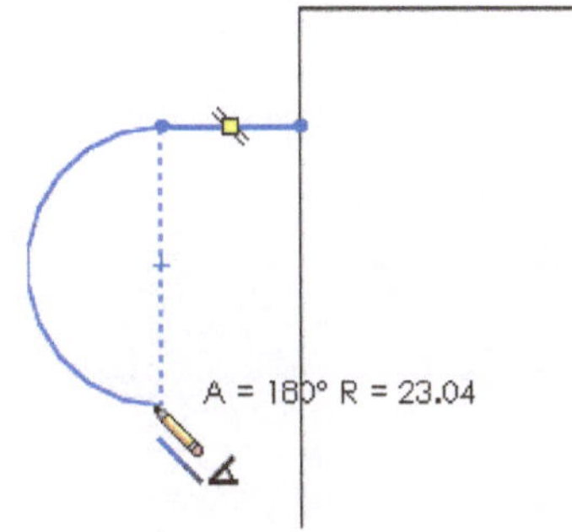

31. Close the sketch and add dimensions.

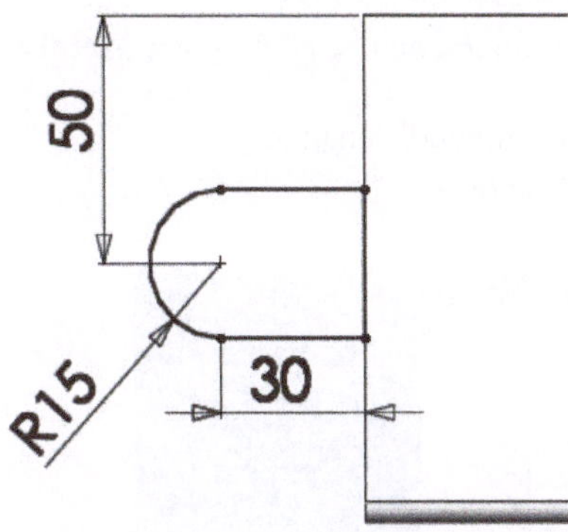

32. Exit the sketch.
33. Select the **Merge result** option and click **OK** on the PropertyManager.

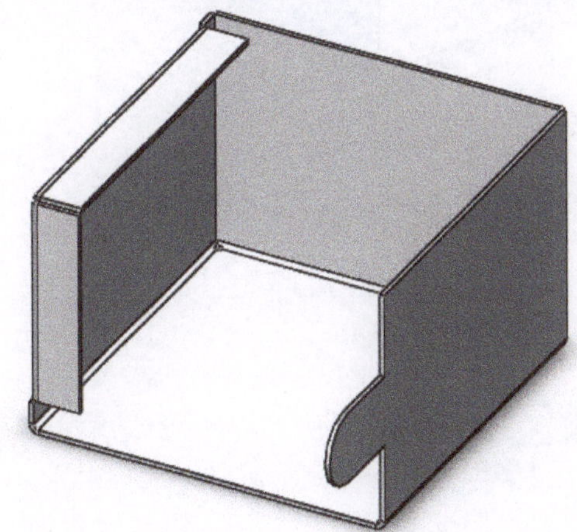

Adding a Jog

1. To add a jog, click **Sheet Metal > Jog** on the CommandManager.
2. Click on the tab face and draw a line.

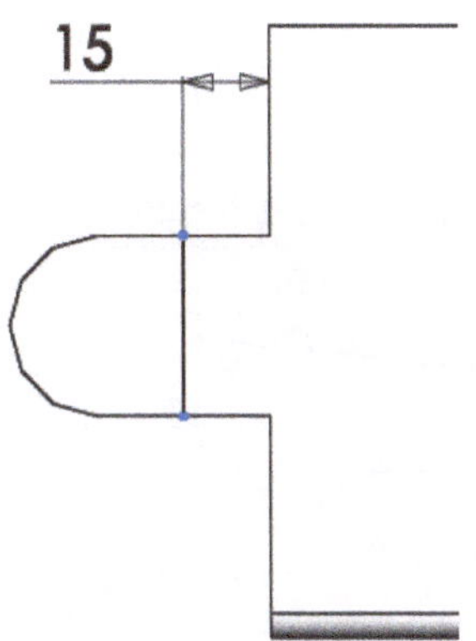

3. Click **Exit Sketch**.
4. Click on the base flange to define the fixed face.

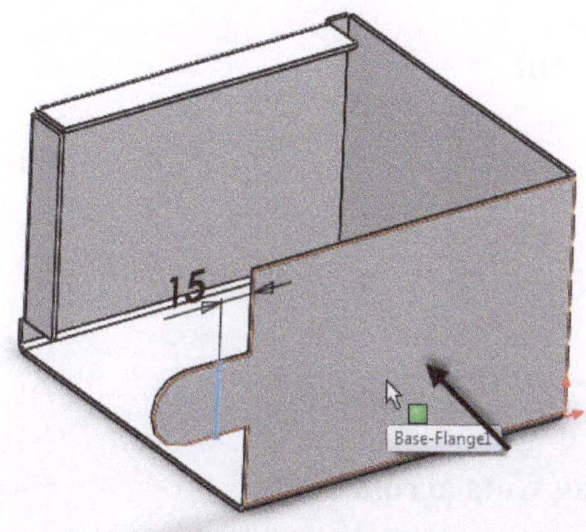

5. On the PropertyManager, under the **Jog Offset** section, set the **Offset Distance** to 20.
6. Set the **Dimension position** to **Outside Offset**.
7. Set the **Jog Position** to **Bend Centerline**.
8. Set the **Jog Angle** to **75**.
9. Click **OK**.

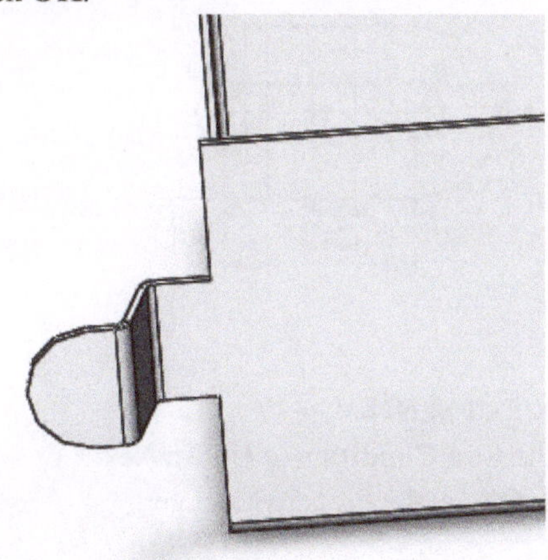

Unfolding the bends

1. To unfold a bend, click **Sheet Metal > Unfold**.
2. Click on the tab face to define the fixed face.
3. Click on the bends of the jog feature.

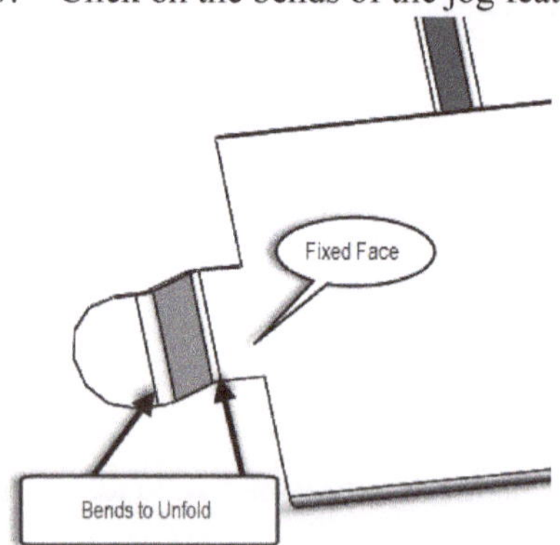

4. Click **OK**.

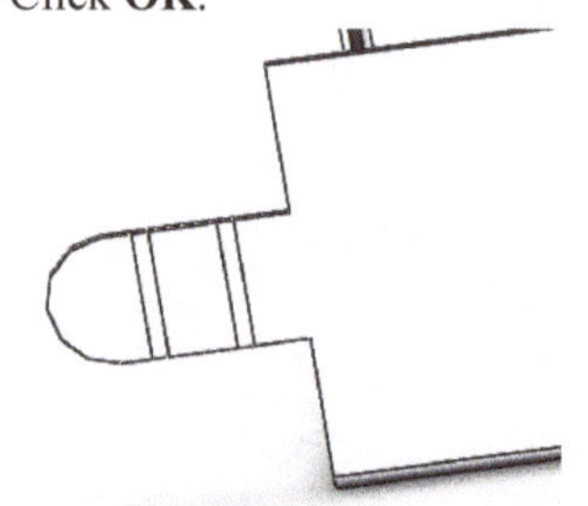

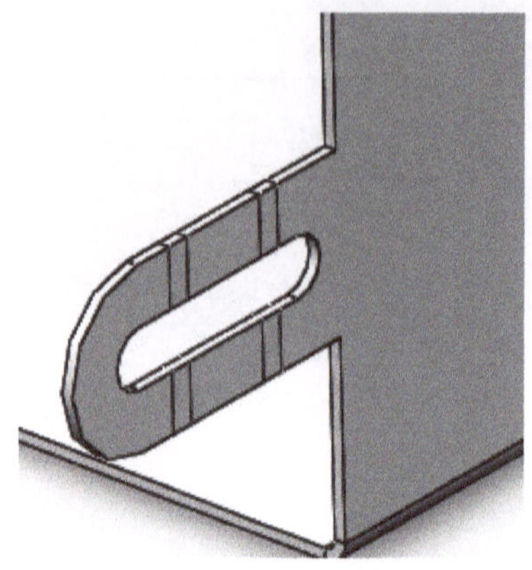

Creating Cuts across bends

1. To create cuts across bends, click **Sheet Metal > Extruded Cut** on the CommandManager.
2. Click on the tab and draw the sketch, as shown. Make sure that the arc is concentric to the circular edge.

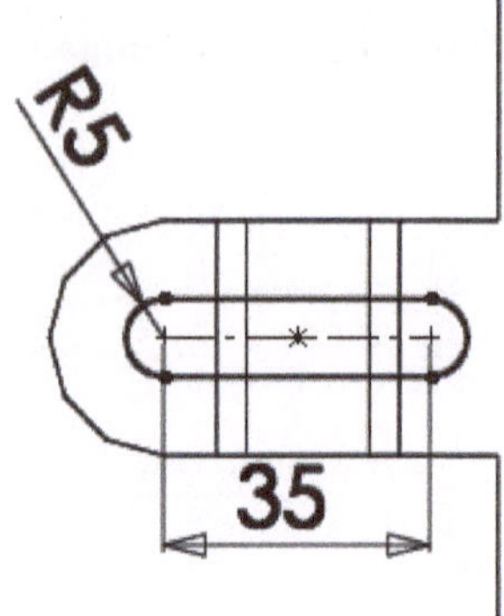

3. Click **Exit Sketch**.
4. Set the **End Condition** to **Up To Next**.
5. Click **OK** on the PropertyManager.

Folding the Unfolded bends

1. To fold the unfolded bends, click **Sheet Metal > Fold** on the CommandManager.
2. Click on the jog bends.

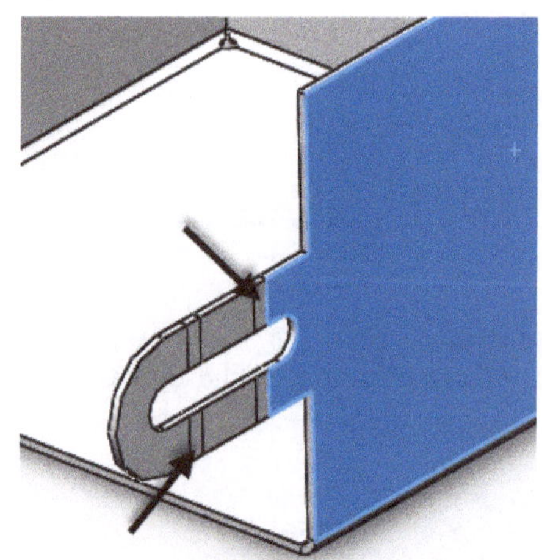

3. Click **OK**.

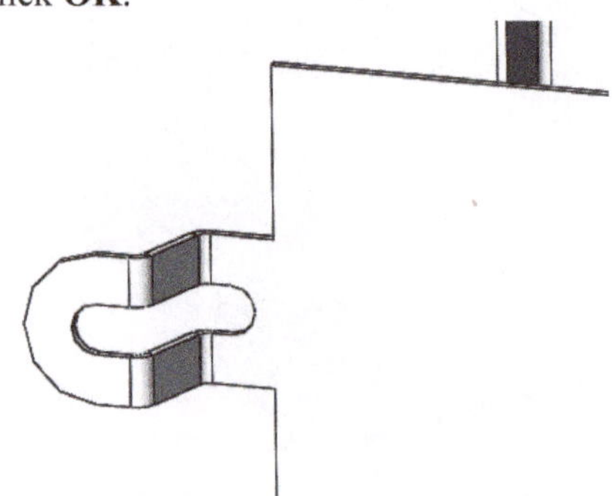

Performing the Forming Operations

1. To perform forming operations, click the **Design Library** on the Task pane.

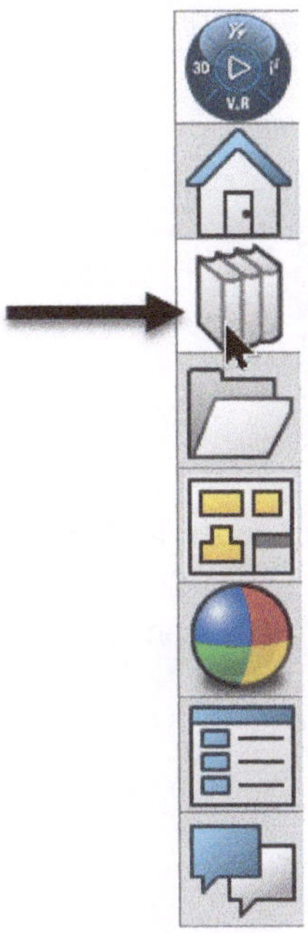

2. If the Design Library is not displayed, click **Add File Location** .
3. Browse to the location: **C:\ProgramData\SOLIDWORKS\SOLIDWORKS 2026\design library**
4. Click **OK**.
5. In the **Design Library**, click the right mouse button on the **forming tools** folder and select **Forming Tools Folder**.
6. Click **Yes** on the **SOLIDWORKS Design** message box.

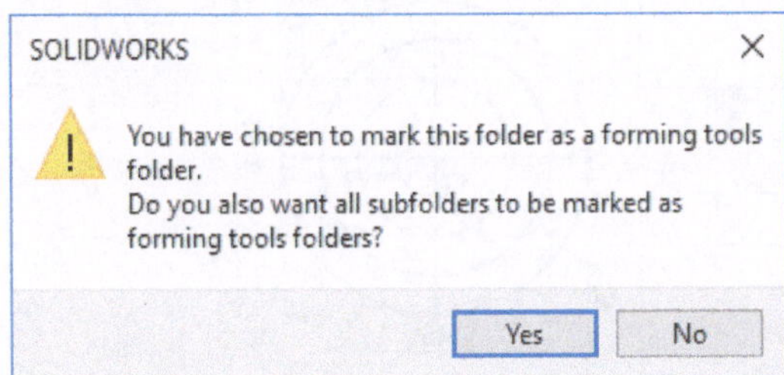

7. Expand the **forming tools** folder and select the **louvers** folder.

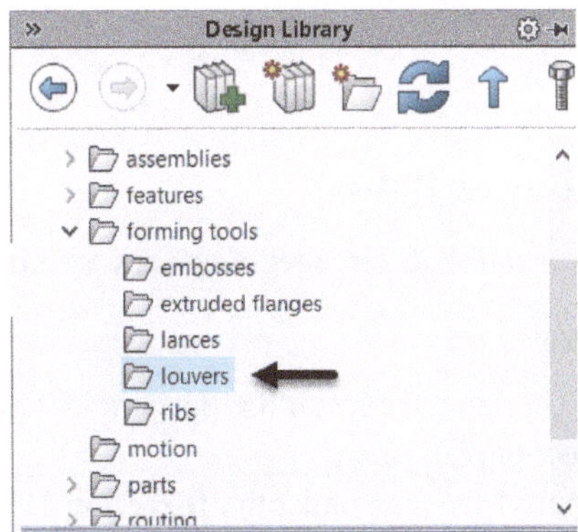

8. Click and drag the Louver onto the flange face.

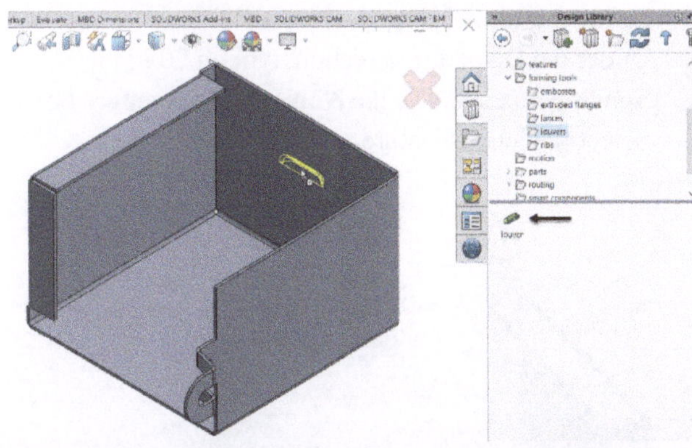

9. On the PropertyManager, type-in 90 in the **Rotation Angle** box.
10. Under the **Link** section, uncheck the **Link to form tool** option.
11. Under the **Flat Pattern Visibility** section, check the **Override document settings** option.
12. On the PropertyManager, click the **Position** tab and add dimensions to position the louver.

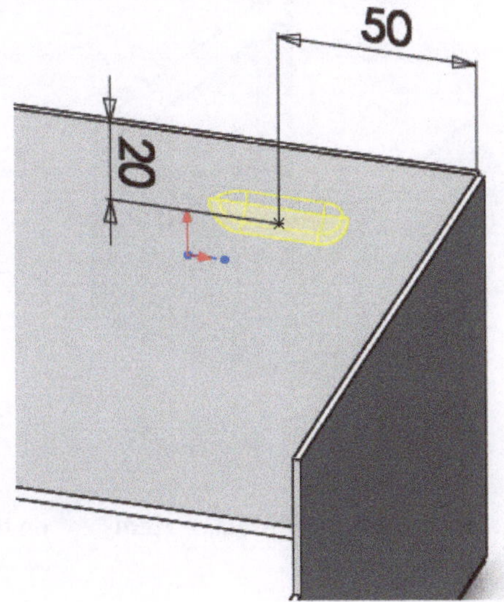

13. Click **OK**.

Making the Linear Pattern

1. On the CommandManager, click **Features > Linear Pattern**.
2. Click on the horizontal edge of the flange to define the first direction.
3. On the PropertyManager, under the **Direction 1** section, type-in 50 in the **Spacing** box and 2 in the **Number of Instances** box.
4. Click on the vertical edge of the flange feature to define the second direction.
5. Under the **Direction 2** section, type-in 20 in the **Spacing** box and 4 in the **Number of Instances** box.
6. Select the louver feature.

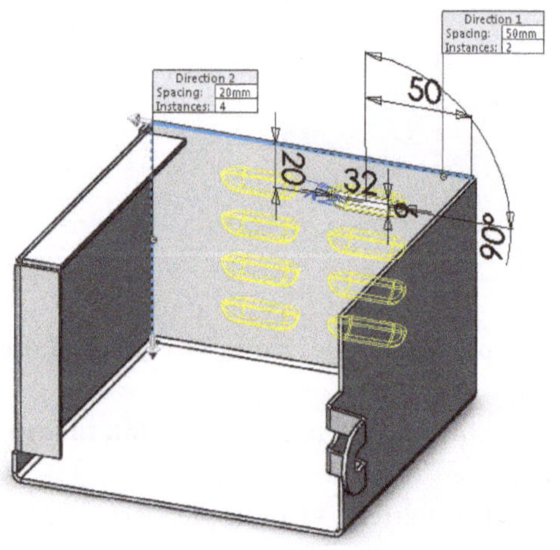

7. Click **OK** to construct the pattern.

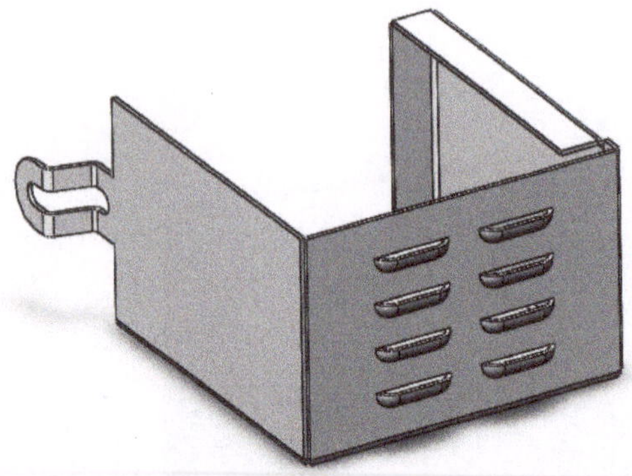

Adding a Hem

1. To add a hem, click **Sheet Metal > Hem**  on the CommandManager.
2. Click on the inner edge of the right-side flange.

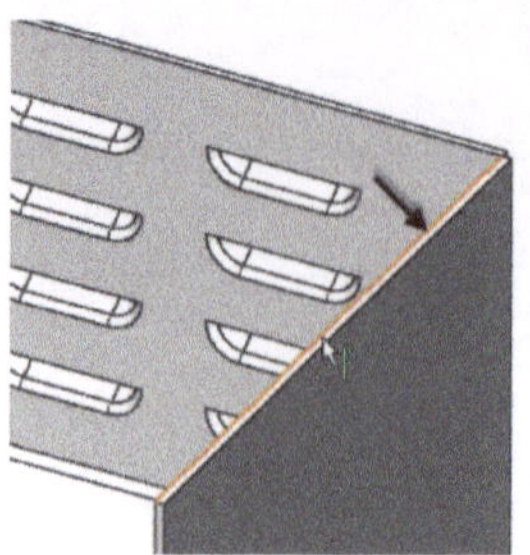

3. On the PropertyManager, under the **Type and Size** section, click the **Closed** icon.
4. Type-in **15** in the **Length** box.
5. Click **OK** to add the hem.

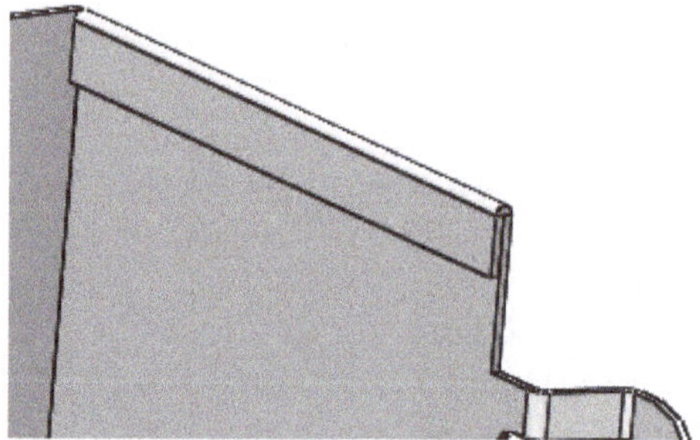

Adding a vent

1. Construct a sketch on the right-side face of the base flange.

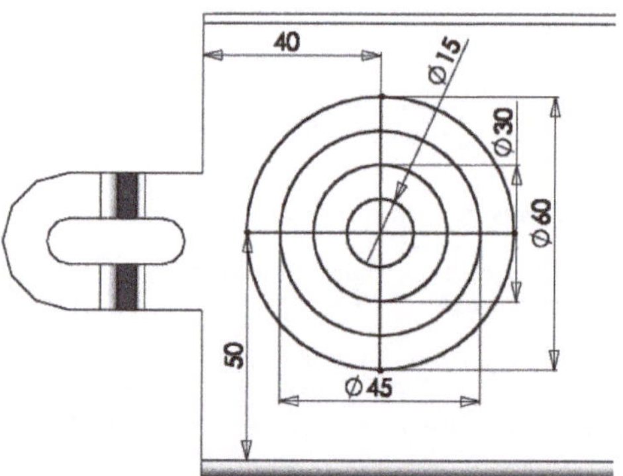

2. Click **Exit Sketch**.
3. On the CommandManager, click **Sheet Metal > Vent**.
4. Click on the outermost circle of the sketch to define the boundary of the vent.

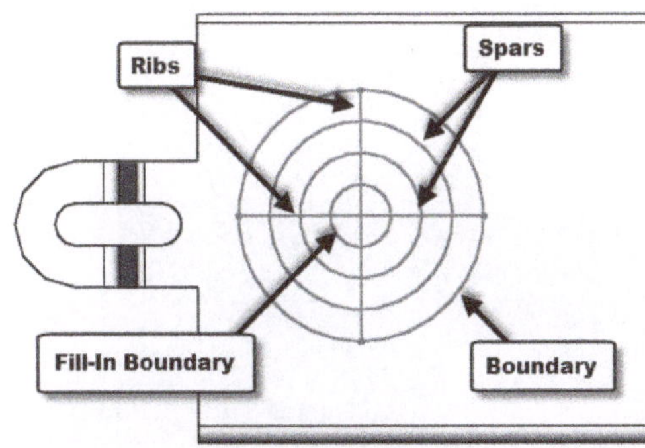

5. On the PropertyManager, click on the **Ribs** selection box and select the line segments from the sketch.
6. Type-in 2 in the **Width** box.
7. Click in the **Spars** selection box and select the two middle circles.
8. Type-in 2 in the **Width** box.
9. Click in the **Fill-In Boundary** selection box and select the innermost circle.
10. Click **OK**.

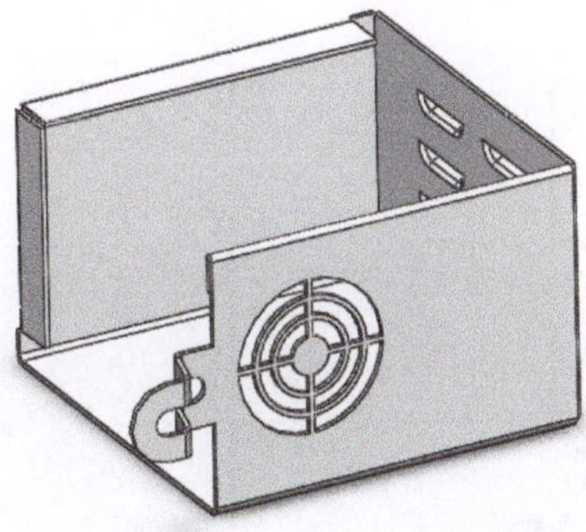

Adding Sheet Metal Gussets

1. To add gussets, click **Sheet Metal > Sheet Metal Gusset** on the CommandManager.
2. Click on the left side bend face of the base flange.

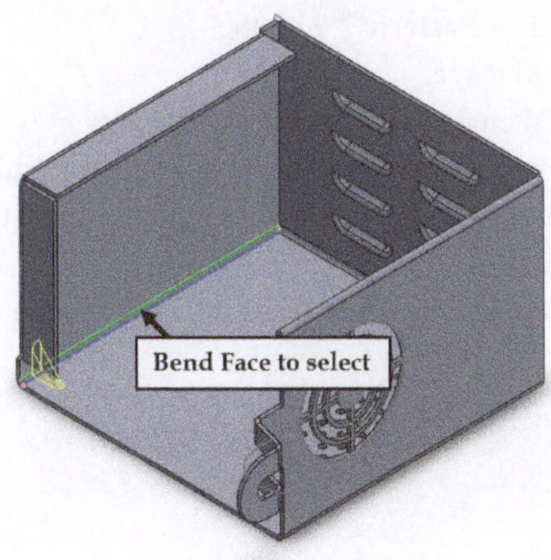

3. On the PropertyManager, under the **Position** section, set the **Offset** value to 30.
4. Under the **Profile** section, set the **Indent depth** to 12.
5. Click the **Rounded gusset** icon.
6. Under the **Dimensions** section, set the **Indent Width** value to 10.
7. Set **Indent Thickness** to **2**.
8. Turn ON the **Side face** icon.
9. Set **Side face draft** to 2.
10. Set **Inner corner fillet** and **Outer corner fillet** to 1 and 2, respectively.

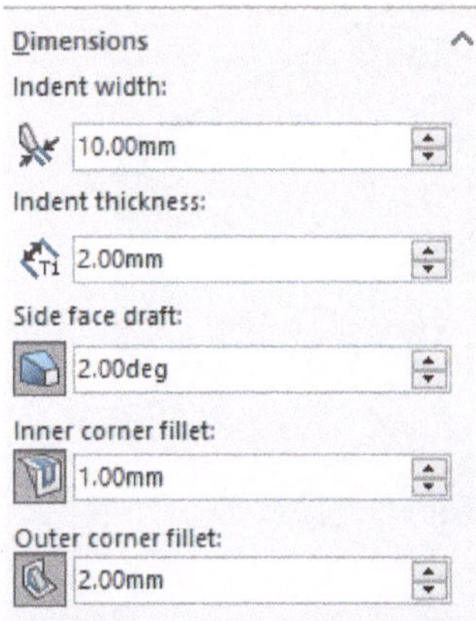

11. Click **OK**.

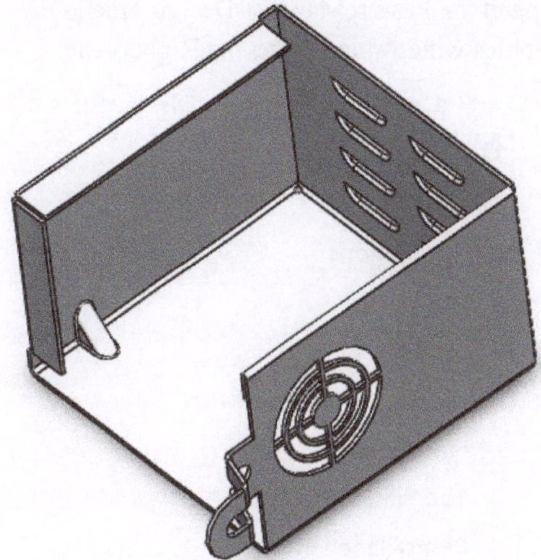

12. On the CommandManager, click **Features > Pattern** drop-down > **Linear Pattern**.
13. Select the edge of the bend on which the gusset is created.
14. Click in the **Features to Pattern** selection box under the **Features and Faces** section.
15. Select the newly created gusset feature.

16. Make a linear pattern of the gusset.

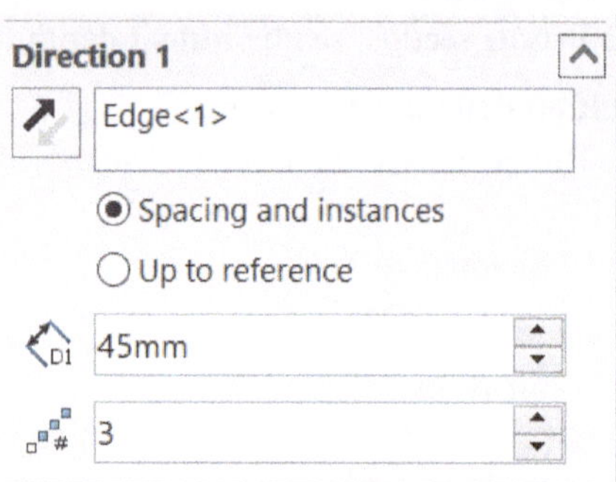

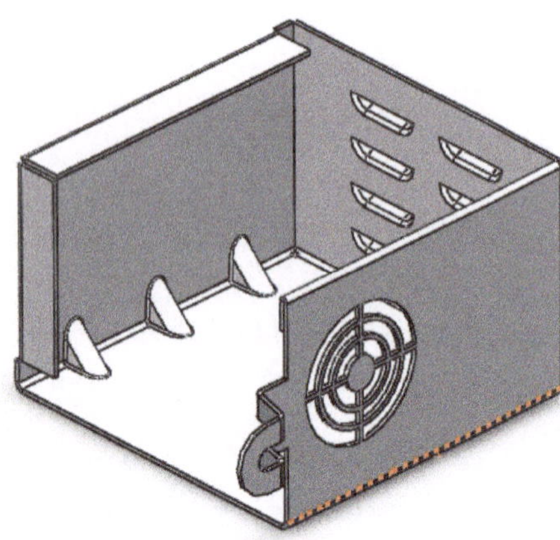

17. Click the **Mirror** tool on the **Features** tab of the CommandManager.
18. Expand the FeatureManager Design Tree in the graphics window and select the Right plane.

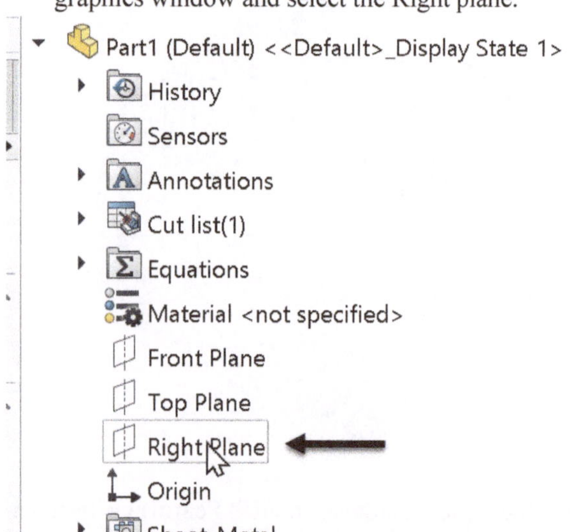

19. Click in the **Features to mirror** selection box and select any of the gussets from the linear pattern; the entire linear pattern is selected.
20. Click **OK** to mirror the linear pattern about the right plane.

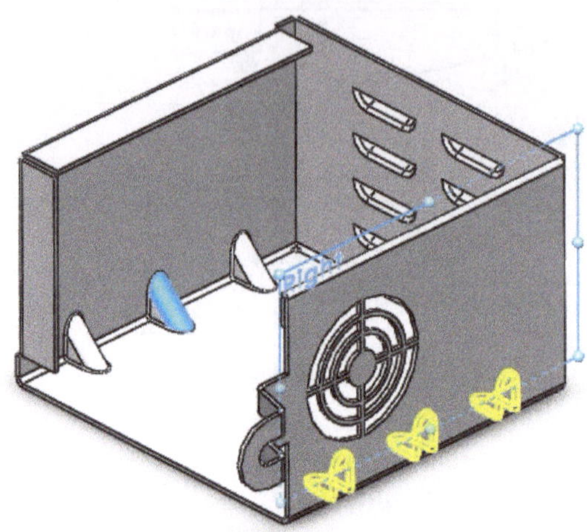

Making a Fill Pattern

1. Draw a sketch on the top face of the base flange.

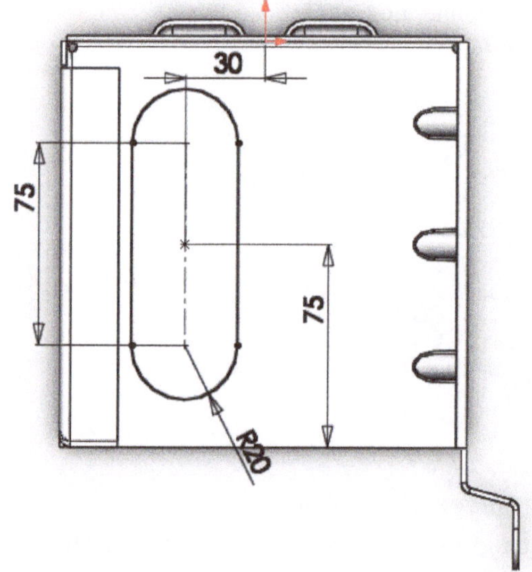

2. Click **Exit Sketch**.
3. To make a fill pattern, click **Features > Linear Pattern > Fill Pattern** on the CommandManager.
4. Select the sketch to define the fill boundary.
5. On the PropertyManager, under the **Features and Faces** section, select **Create seed cut** and select the **Polygon** icon.
6. Set the options in the **Features and Faces** section, as shown.

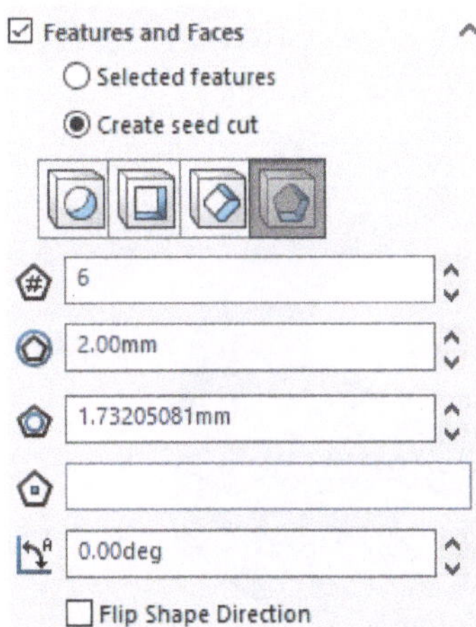

7. Under the **Pattern Layout** section, select the **Perforation** button.
8. Type-in 8 in the **Instance Spacing** box.
9. Set **Stagger Angle** to 46.
10. Set **Margins** to 1.

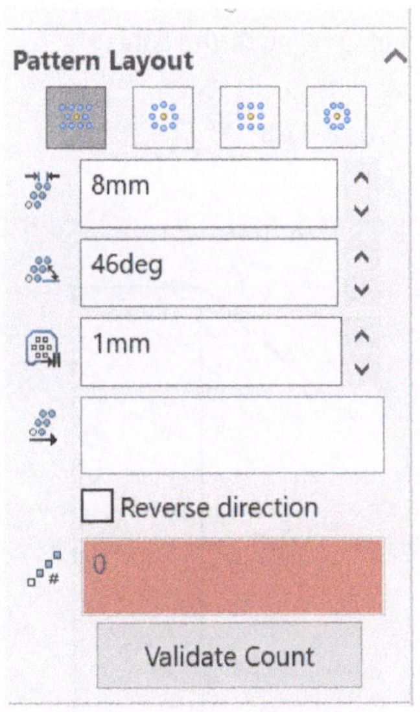

11. Click **OK** to make the fill pattern.

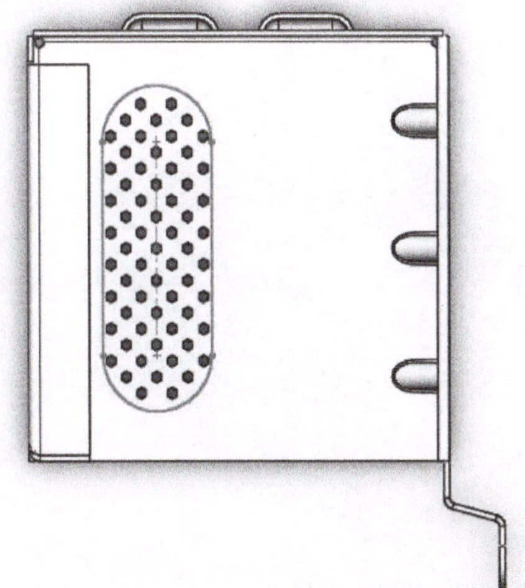

12. Mirror the fill pattern about the right plane.

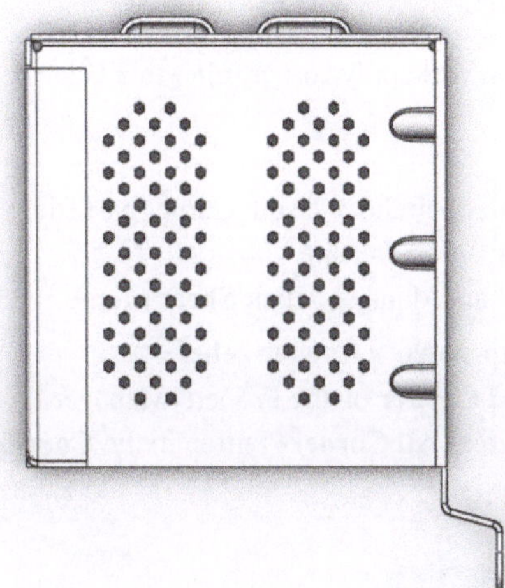

View the Flat Pattern

1. To view the flat pattern, click **Sheet Metal > Flatten** on the CommandManager.

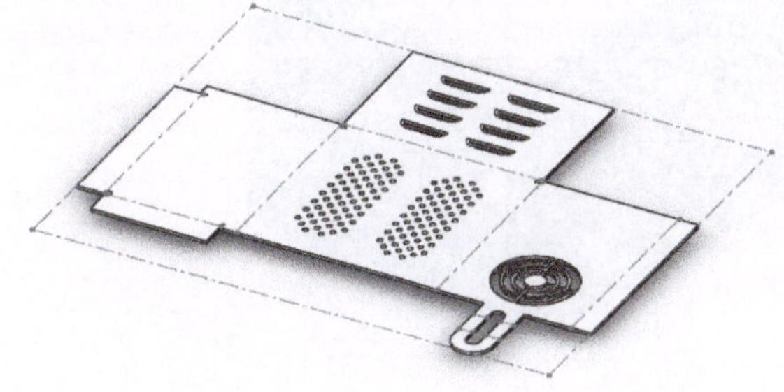

2. Again, click the **Flatten** button to switch back to the model view.

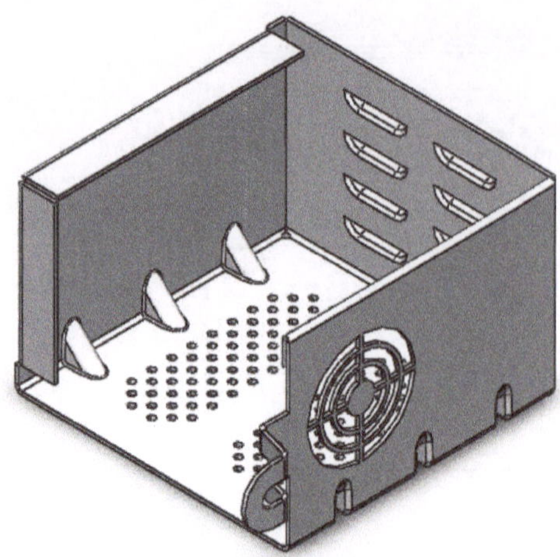

3. Save the sheet metal part.

TUTORIAL 2

In this tutorial, you will apply corner relief to 3 Bend corner.

1. Download and open the 3_Bend_Corner part file from the companion website.
2. On the CommandManager, click **Sheet Metal > Corners drop-down > Corner relief**.
3. Select **3 Bend Corner** on the PropertyManager.
4. Click the **Collect All Corners** button in the **Corners** section.

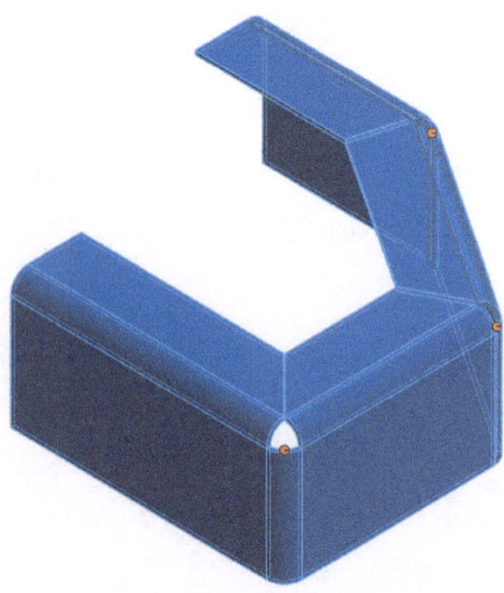

5. On the PropertyManager, under the **Relief Options** section, select **Circular**.
6. Type 4 in the **Slot Width** box available in the **Relief Options** section.
7. Click **OK** on the PropertyManager.

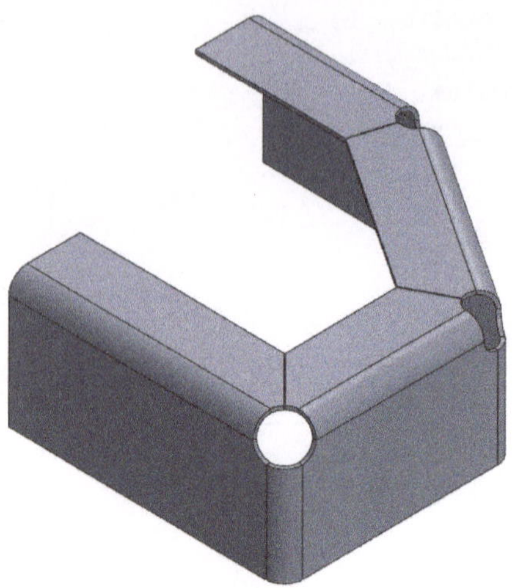

TUTORIAL 3

In this tutorial, you will create a normal cut.

1. Open a new part file.
2. On the CommandManager, click the **Sheet Metal** tab > **Base Flange/Tab** .
3. Click on the Front Plane.
4. Create the sketch, as shown.

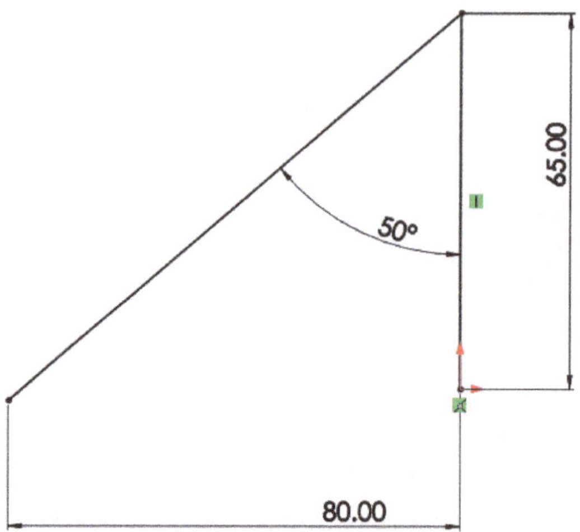

5. Click **Exit Sketch** on the CommandManager.
6. On the PropertyManager, expand the **Direction 1** section.
7. Select **Mid Plane** from the **End Condition** drop-down.
8. Type **80** in the **Depth** box.
9. Click **OK**.

10. On the CommandManager, click the **Sheet metal** tab > **Extruded Cut** .
11. Click on the vertical face of the flange.
12. Create a rectangle and add dimensions to it, as shown.

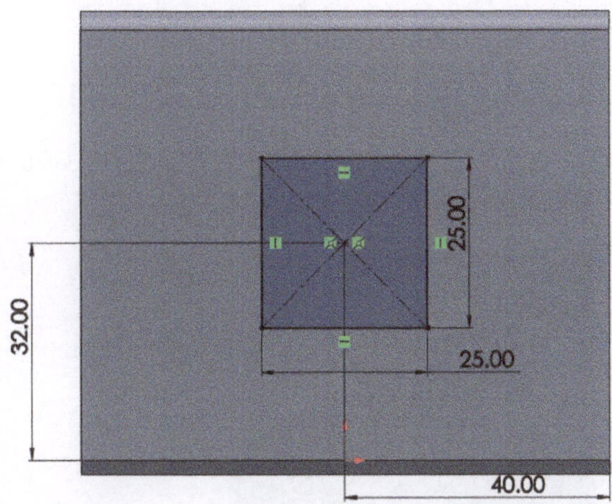

13. Click **Exit Sketch** on the CommandManager.
14. On the **Cut-Extrude** PropertyManager, click **Direction 1 > Through All**.
15. Check the **Normal cut** option.
16. Click **OK**.

17. In the FeatureManager Design Tree, click on the **Cut-Extrude1** feature, and then select **Edit Feature**.
18. On the **Cut-Extrude1** PropertyManager, uncheck the **Normal cut** option.
19. Click **OK**; the side faces of the cut feature are not normal to the sheet metal face.

To make the cut faces normal to the sheet metal face, SOLIDWORKS provides you with the **Normal Cut** tool.

20. On the Menu bar, click **Insert > Sheet Metal > Normal Cut** .
21. Select anyone of the side faces of the cut feature; all the side faces of the cut feature are selected automatically.

22. Click **OK** on the PropertyManager; the faces are made normal to the cut feature.

23. Save and close the file.

TUTORIAL 4

In this tutorial, you will create a tab and slot feature. The **Tab and Slot** tool helps you to create tabs on one body and slots on another. A typical Tab and slot feature are displayed, as shown.

1. Open a new SOLIDWORKS part file.
2. Create a rectangular sketch on the Front plane, as shown.

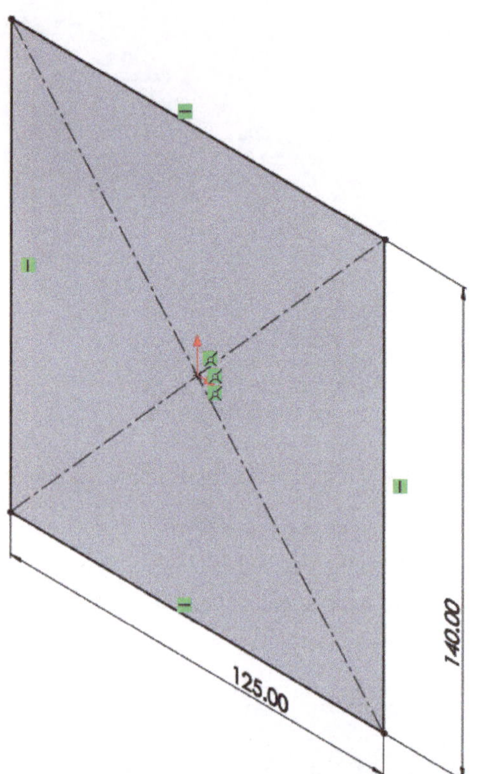

3. Activate the **Base Flange/Tab** tool, and then create a tab, as shown.

4. Create a line on the tab feature, as shown.

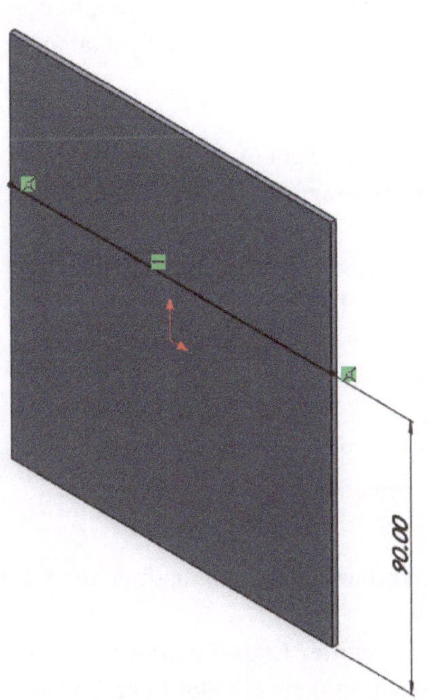

5. Activate the **Base Flange/Tab** tool, and then create a flange of 50 mm distance.

6. On the Menu bar, click **Insert > Sheet Metal > Tab and Slot** .
7. Click on the linear edge, as shown; the tab edge is defined.

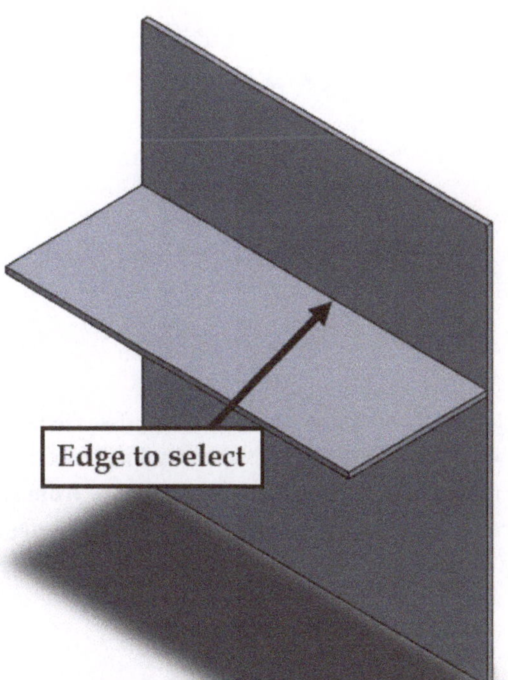

8. Rotate the model, and notice that the slot face is defined.

Notice that the **Start Reference Point** and **End Reference Point** are selected automatically. If you want to change the reference points, click in the corresponding selection boxes on the PropertyManager. Next, select the opposite endpoint of the linear edge.

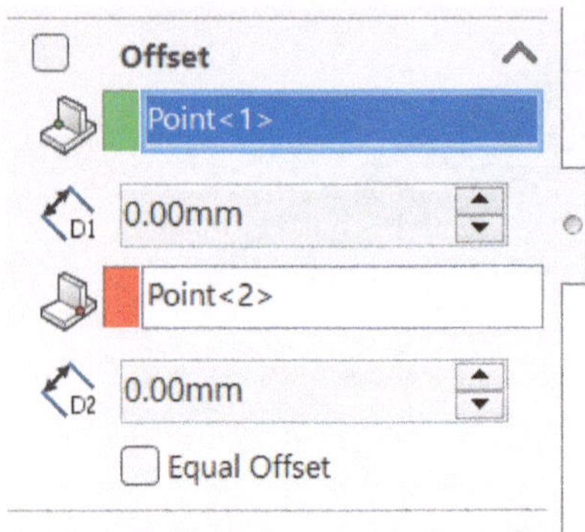

Check the **Offset** option if you want to offset the tabs and slots from the start and end reference points. Next, you need to type in a value in the **Offset distance from start reference point** and **Offset distance from end reference point** boxes.

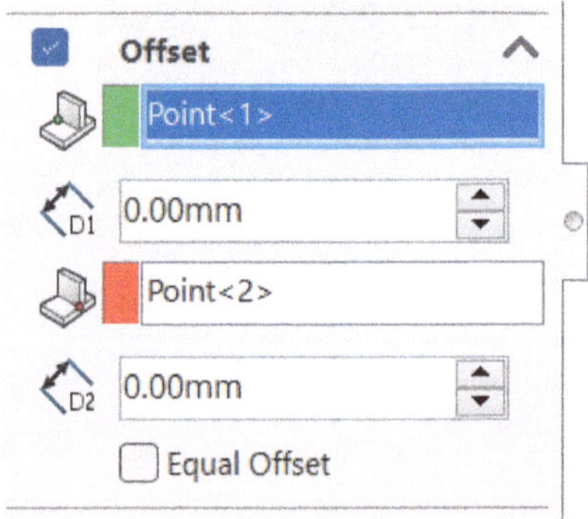

9. In the **Spacing** section, select the **Equal Spacing** option.
10. Type **5** in the **Number of Instances** box.

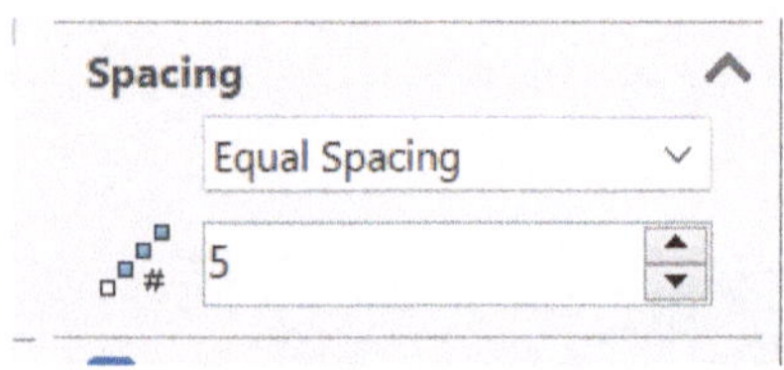

You can also select the **Spacing Length** or the **Center Align** option.

The **Spacing Length** option defines the distance between consecutive tabs or slots along an edge.

The **Center Align** option aligns tabs/slots centrally relative to the selected edge or reference geometry.

11. Type 12 in the **Length** box in the **Tabs** section.

12. Next, select **Up To Surface** from the **Height** drop-down. This option extends the tab height up to the slot surface.

You can also define the height of the tab by using the **Blind** or **Offset From Surface** option.

The **Blind** option is used to specify the tab height by entering a value in the **Tab Height Value** box.

The **Offset From Surface** option offsets the tab from the slot surface by the value you enter in the **Tab Offset Value** box. Check the **Reverse Direction** option to reverse the offset direction.

13. Click the **Chamfer Edge** option from the **Edges Type** section.
14. Type 1 in the **Chamfer Edge Treatment Value** box.
15. Leave the default value in the **Slot Length Offset**, and **Slot Width Offset** boxes under the **Slot** section.

You can use the **Normal Cut** option if tab is at an angle to the slot.

Normal Cut Cleared

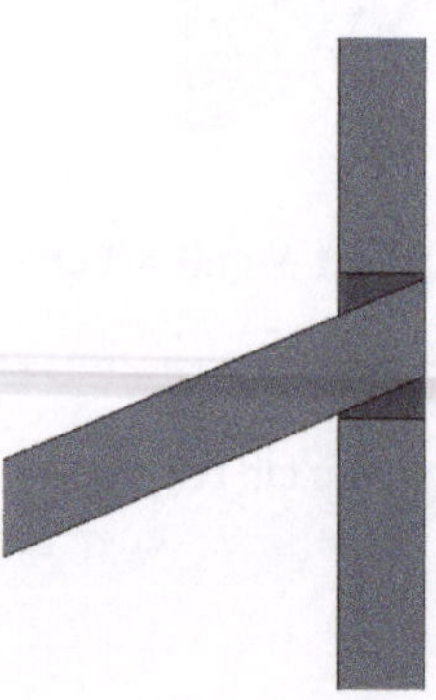

Normal Cut Checked

Next, specify the slot corner type by selecting any one of the buttons available under the **Corner Type** section. There are four corner types:

Slot Sharp Corner: Creates a slot with sharp corners

Slot Fillet Corner: Adds fillets to the corners of the slot. You need to specify the **Slot Corner Fillet** Value.

Slot Chamfer Corner: Adds chamfers to the corners of the slot.

Slot Circular Corner: Adds circular cutouts at the corners of the slot.

16. Click **OK** to create the tab and slot feature.

17. Save and close the part file.

TUTORIAL 5

In this tutorial, you will create a **Swept Flange** feature. The **Swept Flange** tool allows you to create a sheet metal feature by sweeping a profile along the path.

1. Open a new SOLIDWORKS part file.
2. On the CommandManager, click **Sketch** tab > **Sketch**.
3. Click on the top plane.
4. On the CommandManager, click **Sketch** tab > **Arc** drop-down > **Centerpoint Arc**
5. Select the origin point of the sketch.
6. Move the pointer downwards, and then specify the start point of the arc, as shown.

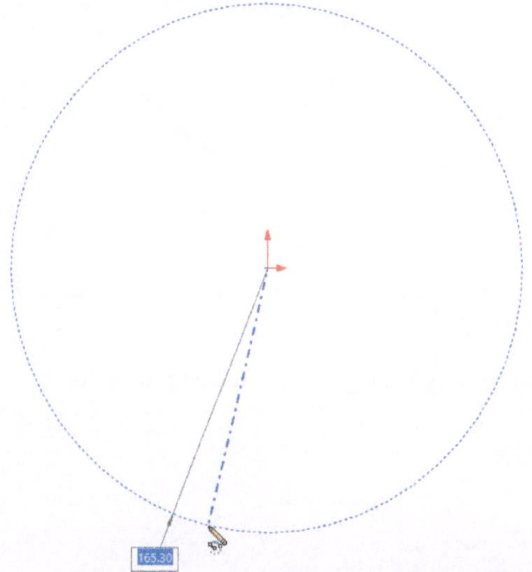

7. Move the pointer in anti-clockwise, and then click to define the arc's end point, as shown.

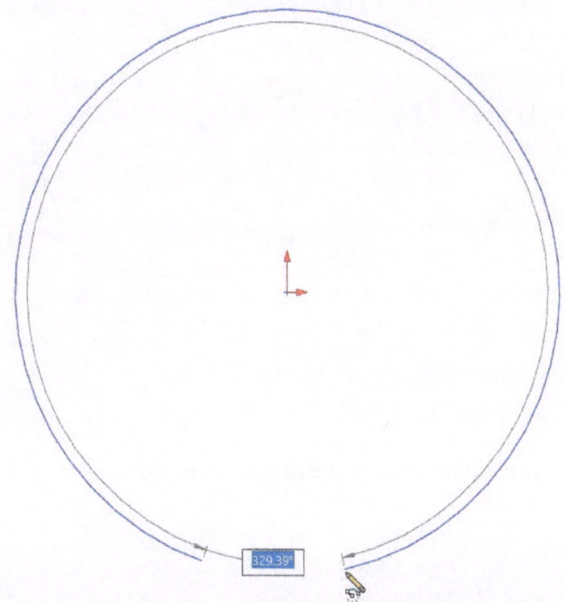

8. Create a vertical centerline, as shown.

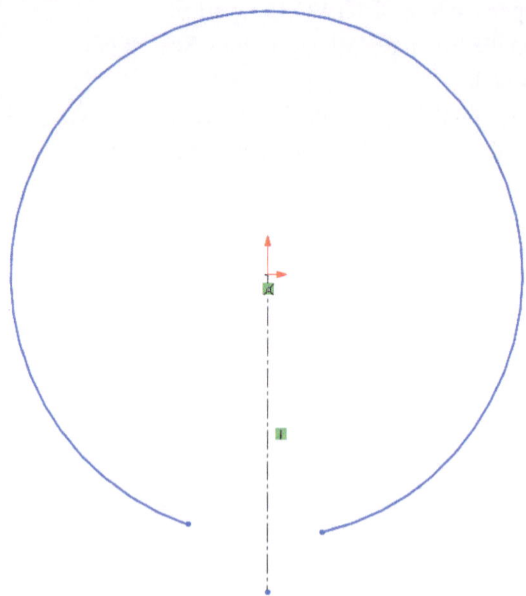

9. Press and hold the Ctrl key, and then click on the two endpoints of the arc and the centerline.
10. On the PropertyManager, click the **Symmetric** icon.
11. Click **OK**.

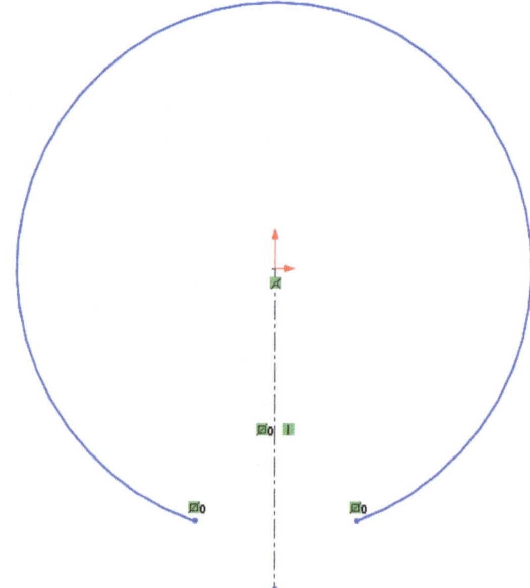

12. Add dimensions to the sketch, as shown.

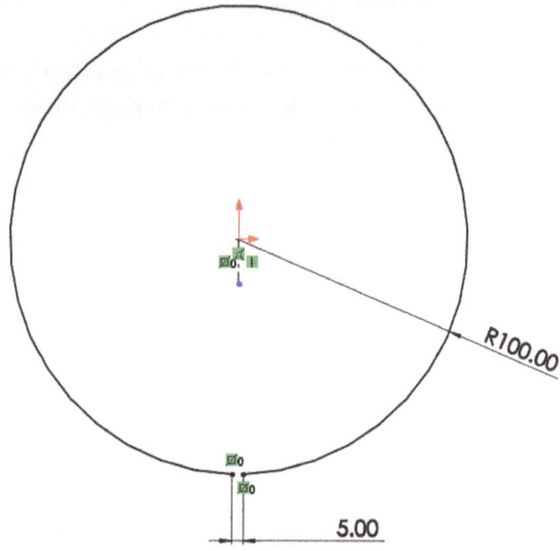

13. Click **Exit Sketch** on the CommandManager.
14. Change the **View Orientation** to **Isometric**.
15. On CommandManager, click the **Features** tab > **Reference Geometry** drop-down > **Plane** .
16. Select the arc and anyone of its endpoints.
17. Click **OK** on the **Plane** PropertyManager.
18. Start a new sketch on the newly created plane.
19. Draw the sketch profile, as shown.

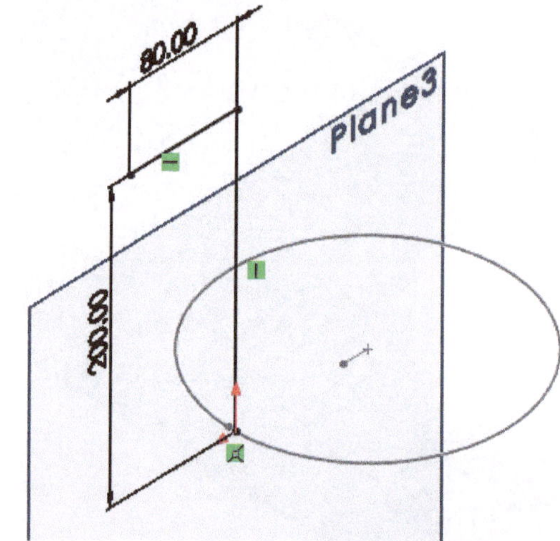

20. Click **Exit Sketch** on the CommandManager.

Next, you need to activate the **Swept Flange** tool and create the swept flange. By default, the **Swept Flange** tool is not displayed on the CommandManager. To add this command to the CommandManager, right click on the CommandManager, and then select **Customize**. On the **Customize** dialog, click the **Commands** tab and select **Sheet Metal** from the **Categories** list. Next, click and drag the **Swept Flange** button from the Buttons area, and then release it on the CommandManager; the **Swept Flange** button is added to the CommandManager.

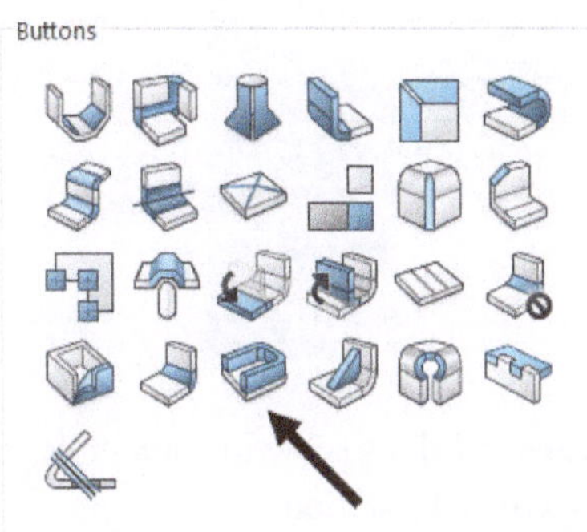

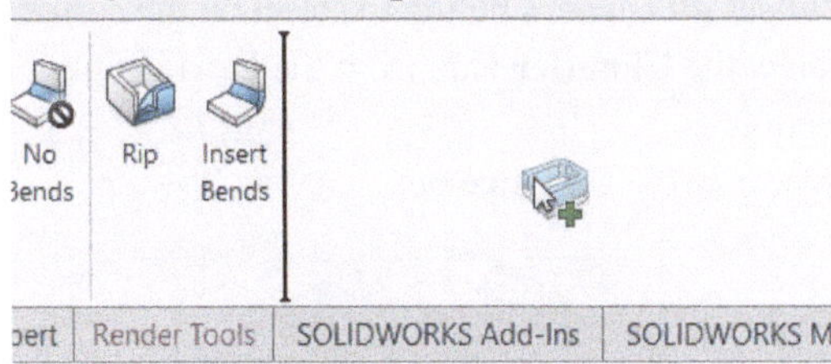

21. On the Menu bar, click **Insert > Sheet Metal > Swept Flange**.
22. Select the profile and path from the graphics window.
23. Click **OK** to create the swept flange.

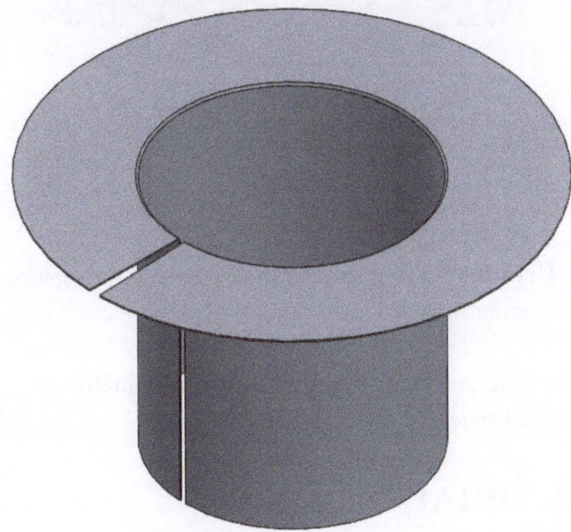

24. Save and close the part file.

TUTORIAL 6

In this tutorial, you will create a **Corner Trim** feature.

1. Download and open the Corner_trim part file from the companion website.

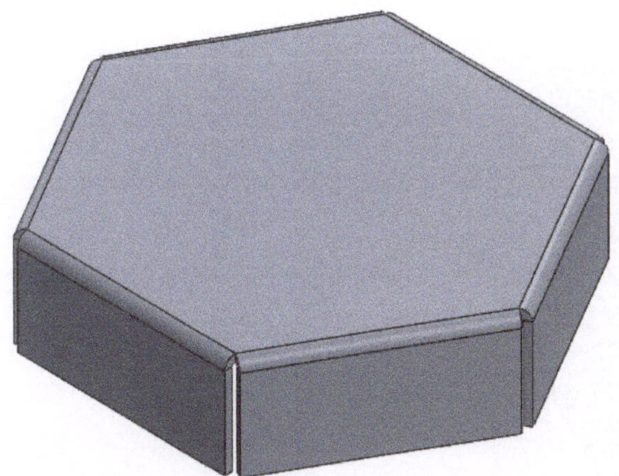

2. On the CommandManager, click **Sheet Metal > Flatten**.

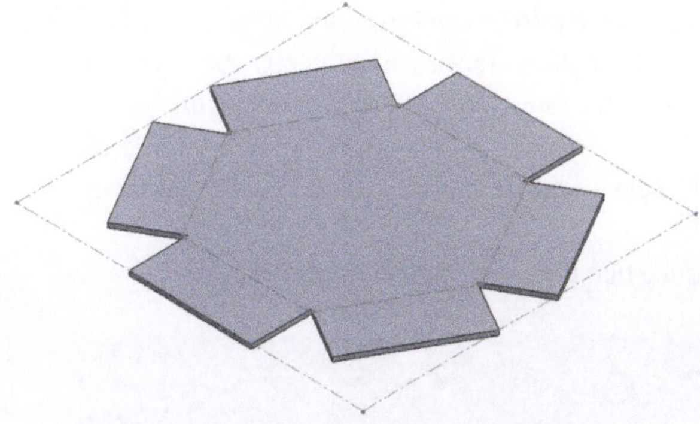

3. On the CommandManager, click **Sheet Metal** tab > **Corner** drop-down > **Corner-Trim**.
4. Select the corner edges one-by-one (or) click the **Collect all corners** button.
5. Select **Circular** from the **Relief type** drop-down.
6. Change the View Orientation to Top.
7. Zoom-in to anyone of the corners and notice preview of the corner trim. By default, the center of the relief is located on corner.

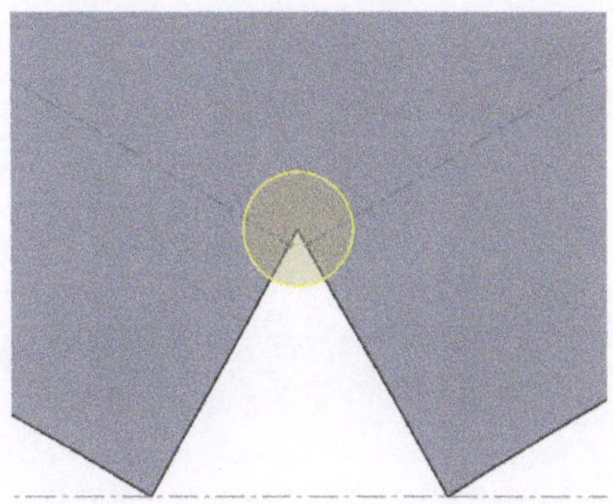

8. Check the **Centered on bend lines** option to move the center to the intersection of the bend lines.

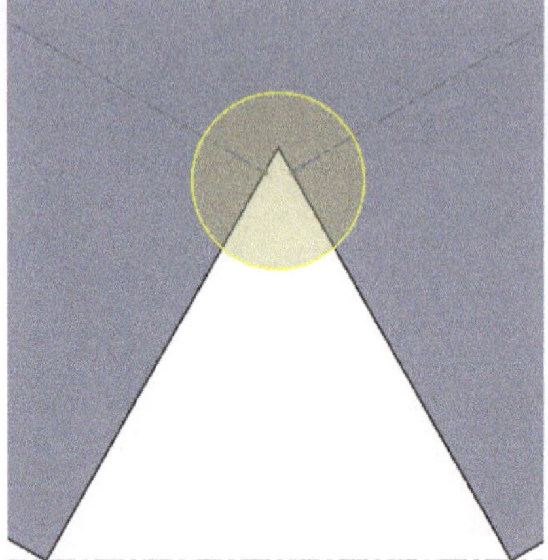

9. Change the **Radius** value to 5.

Notice the **Ratio to thickness** option below the **Radius** box. This option allows you to specify the relief size by entering the ratio value to the sheet metal thickness.

10. Select **Square** from the **Relief type** drop-down.

Notice that the relief is changed to the square.

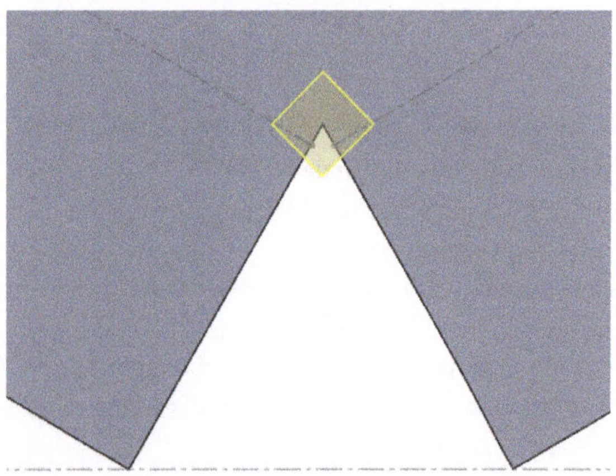

11. Check the **Add filleted corners** option.
12. Type 1 in the **Fillet radius** box.

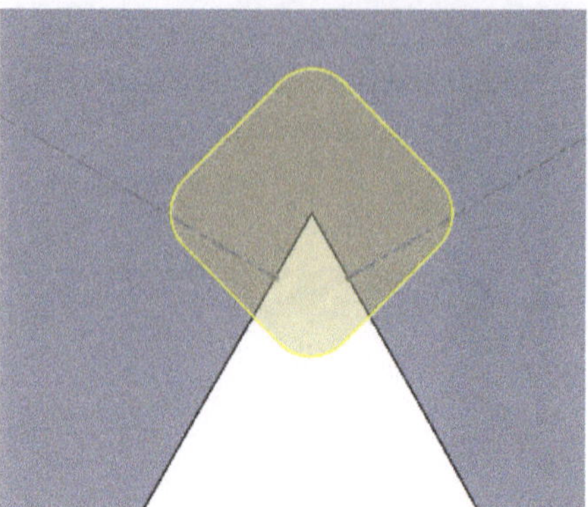

13. Click in the **Corner Edges** selection box under the **Break Corner Options** section.
14. Select the sheet metal corners to break (or) click the **Collect all corners** button to select all the corners.
15. Select the **Chamfer** icon from the **Break type** section.
16. Type 5 in the **Distance** box.

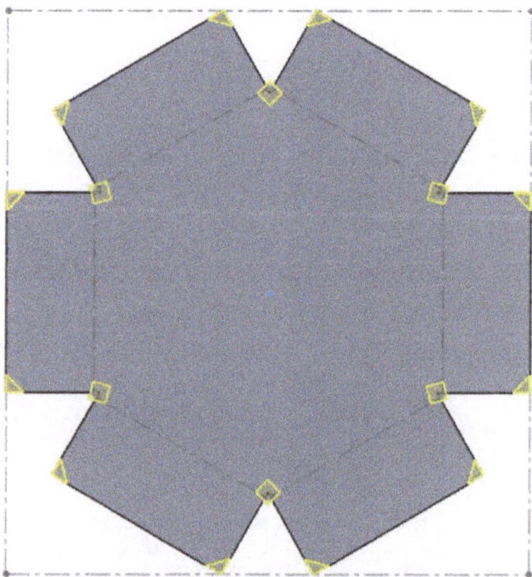

17. Click **OK** on the PropertyManager.
18. Click the **Flatten** icon on the CommandManager to exit the flattened state.

Notice that the corner trims are visible only in the Flattened state.

TUTORIAL 7

In this tutorial, you will convert an imported solid body into a sheet metal part.

1. Download the Tutorial_7. STEP file from the companion website.
2. On the SOLIDWORKS window, click the **Open**

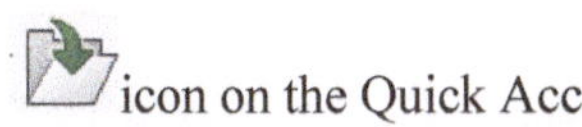 icon on the Quick Access Toolbar.

3. Browse to the location of the downloaded file, and then double-click on it.
4. Click **OK** on the **SOLIDWORKS Design** message box.

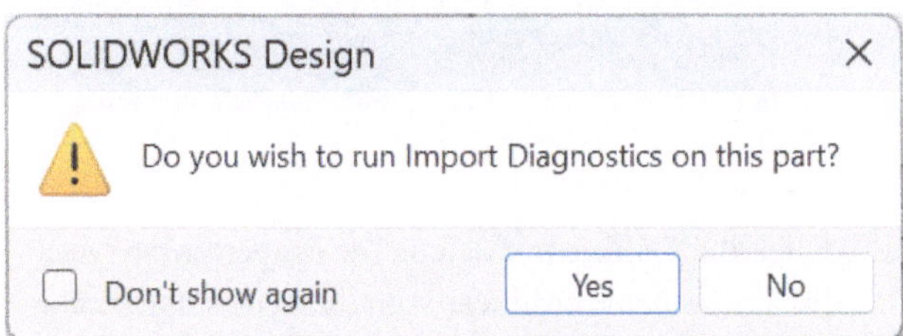

5. Click **OK** on the **Import Diagnostics** PropertyManager.
6. On the CommandManager, click the **Sheet Metal** tab

> **Convert to Sheet Metal** .

7. Click on the horizontal sheet metal face, as shown; the fixed face is defined.

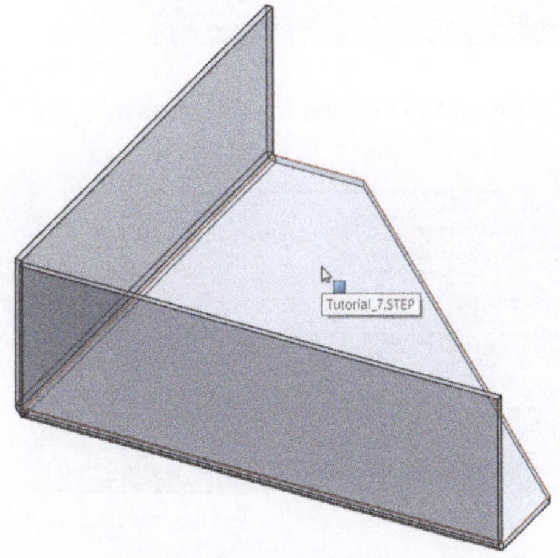

8. Set **Sheet thickness** to 2.
9. Set **Default radius of bends** to 2.
10. Click the **Collect all Bends** button in the **Bend Edges** section.
11. Click **OK**.

Notice that the **Flatten** icon on the CommandManager is now available. You can flatten the sheet metal model and create drawings.

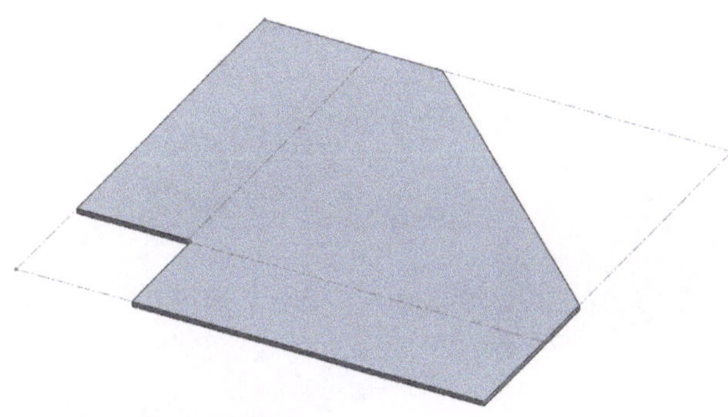

TUTORIAL 8

In this tutorial, you will create a multibody sheet metal part.

1. Start a new SOLIDWORKS part file.
2. Create a new Base tab feature, as shown. The sheet metal thickness is 2 mm.

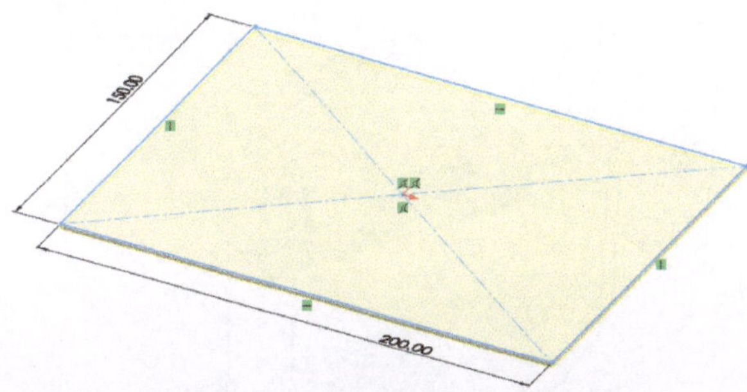

3. Create edge flanges of 40 mm length, as shown.

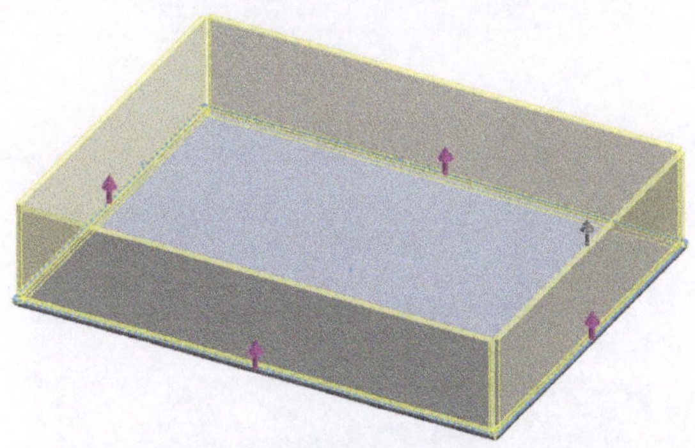

4. Activate the **Base Flange/Tab** tool, and then click on the edge flange's outer face.

5. Change the view orientation to the right plane.

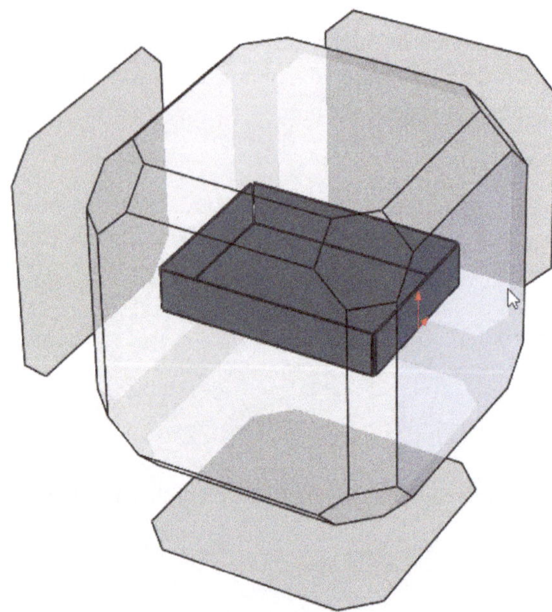

6. Create a rectangle, as shown.

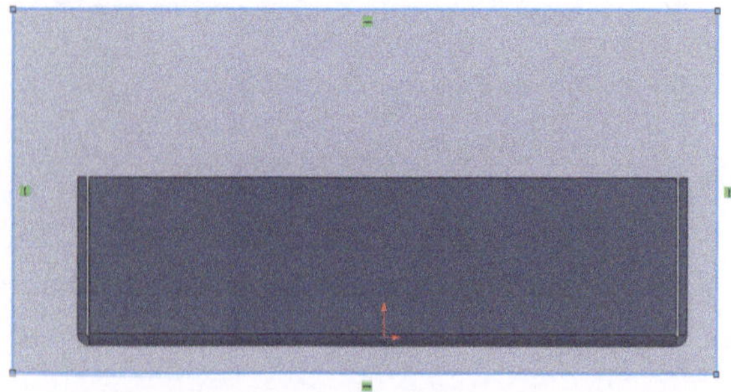

7. Press and hold the Ctrl key and then select the bottom edge and the rectangle's bottom horizontal line.

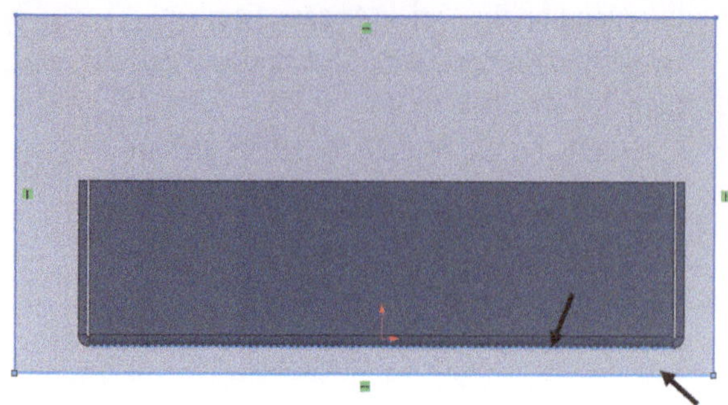

8. Click the **Collinear** icon the PropertyManager; the line is made collinear with the bend's horizontal edge.
9. Likewise, make the vertical line collinear with the side edges, as shown.

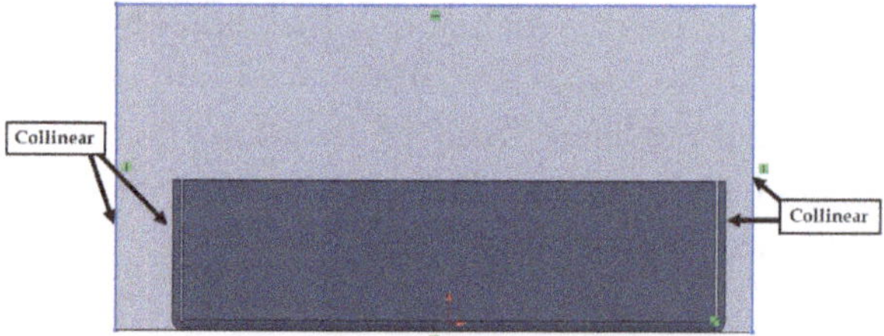

10. Add dimension to the vertical line, as shown.

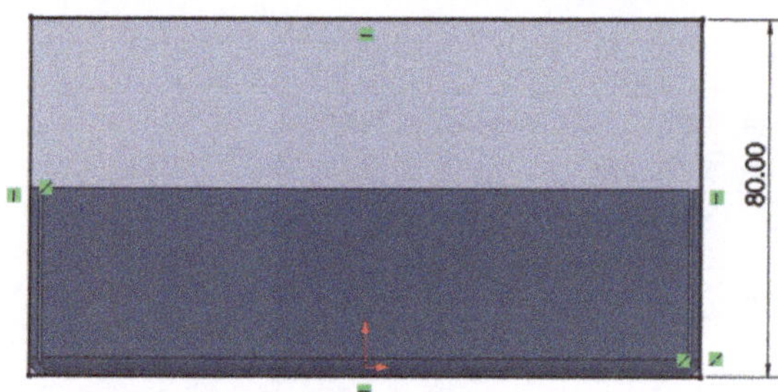

11. Click **Exit Sketch** on the CommandManager.
12. Change the **View Orientation** to **Isometric**.
13. On the PropertyManager, uncheck the **Merge result** option.
14. Check the **Reverse Direction** option.
15. Click **OK**; the tab feature is created as a separate body.

16. Expand the **Cut list** and **Sheet Metal** folders.

Notice two sheet metal bodies inside the **Cut list** and **Sheet Metal** folders.

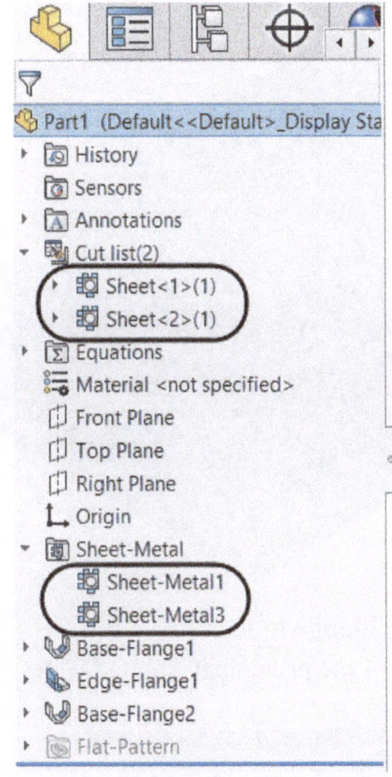

17. Change the View Orientation to Left.

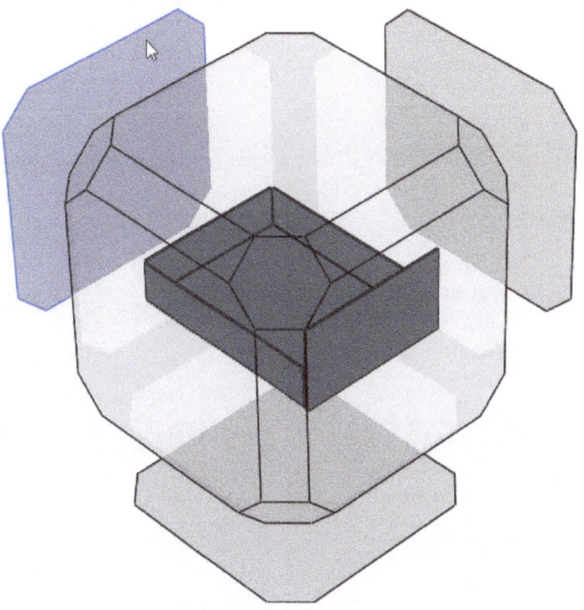

18. Activate the **Base Flange/Tab** tool.
19. Click on the edge flange face.

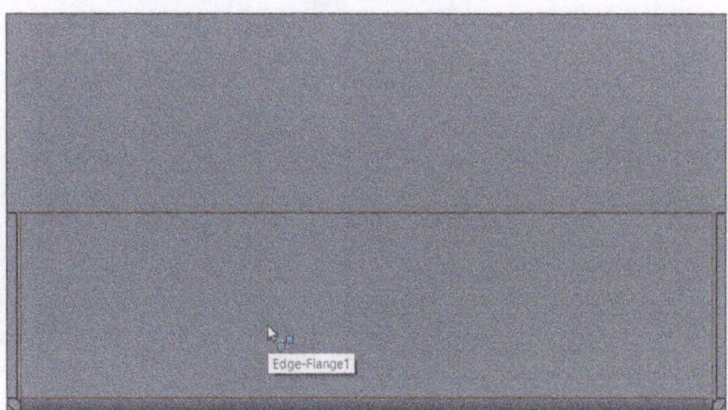

20. Activate the **Corner Rectangle** tool.
21. Click on the first and second corners, as shown.

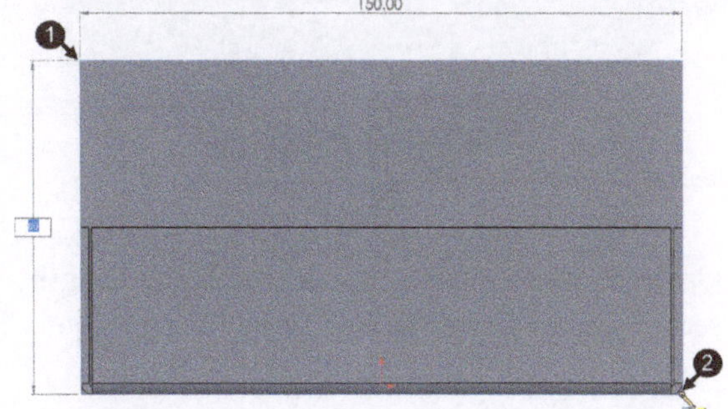

22. Click **Exit Sketch** on the CommandManager.
23. On the PropertyManager, uncheck the **Merge result** option.
24. Check the **Reverse direction** option.
25. Click **OK**.

    Notice three sheet metal bodies inside the Sheet

Metal folder in the FeatureManager Design Tree.

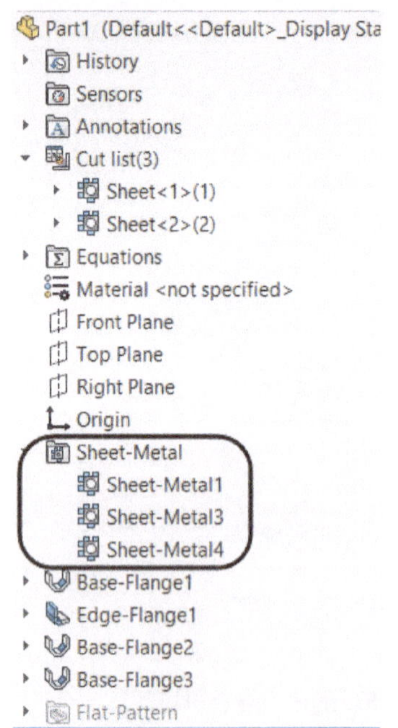

26. Activate the **Edge Flange** tool.
27. Click on the edge of the third sheet metal body, as shown.

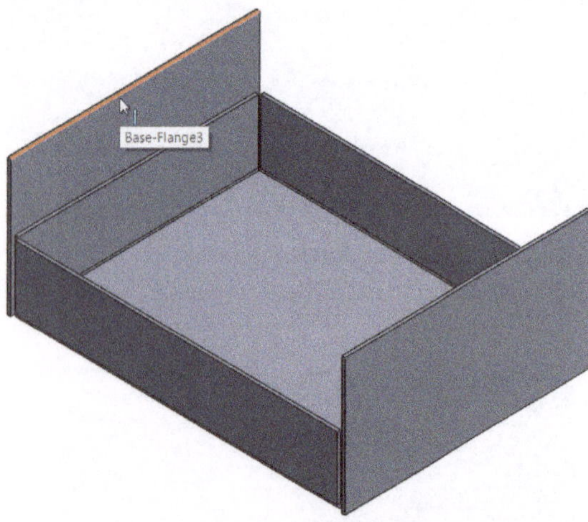

28. On the PropertyManager, under the **Flange Length** section, select the **Up To Edge And Merge** option from the **Length End Condition** drop-down.
29. Select the edge of the second tab feature, as shown.

30. Click the **Material Inside** icon under the **Flange Position** section.
31. Click **OK** on the PropertyManager.

32. Activate the **Edge Flange** tool.
33. Click on the edge of the previously created edge flange, as shown.

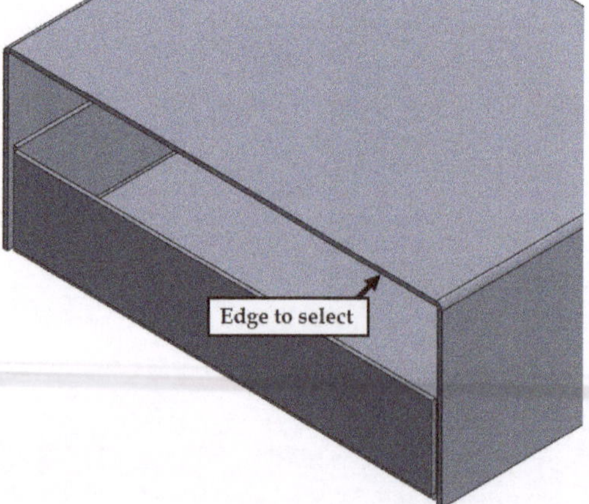

34. On the PropertyManager, select **Flange Length > Up To Vertex**.
35. Zoom to the bottom portion of the sheet metal part, and then select the vertex of the tab, as shown.

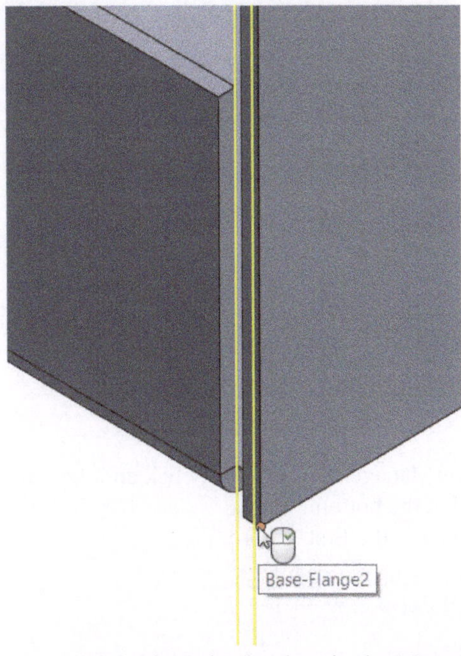

36. Click in the Selection box in the **Flange Parameters** section, and then select the edge on the backside, as shown.

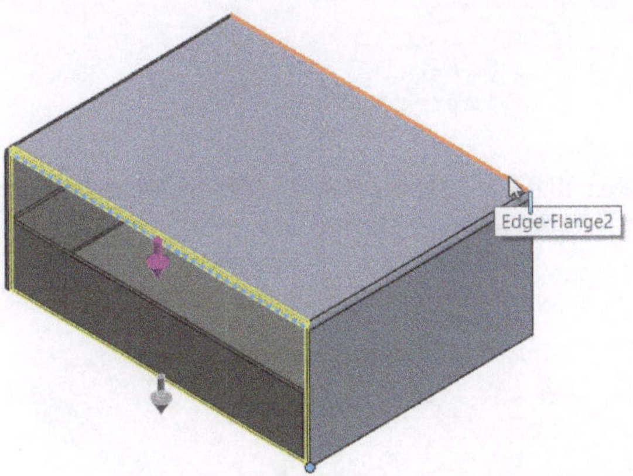

37. Click the **Bend Outside** icon in the **Flange Position** section.
38. Click **OK**.

TUTORIAL 9 (MODIFYING FORMING TOOLS)

In this tutorial, you learn to modify an existing sheet metal forming tool.

1. Start a new sheet metal file and create a base tab feature, as shown.

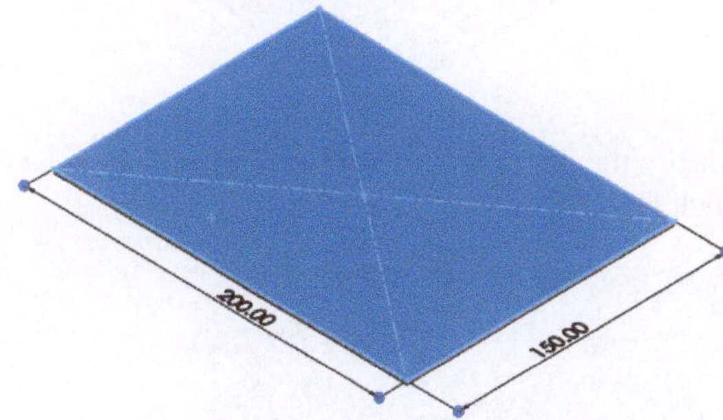

2. Click the **Design Library** tab on the right pane.
3. On the **Design Library** pane, expand the **design library > forming tools > lances** folder.

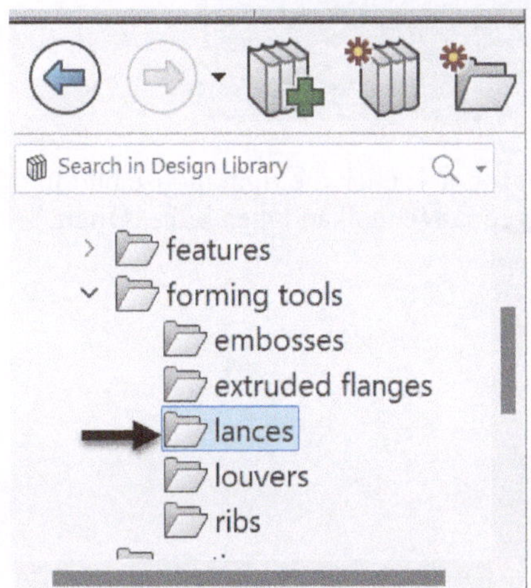

4. Click and drag the **90-degree** lance tool.

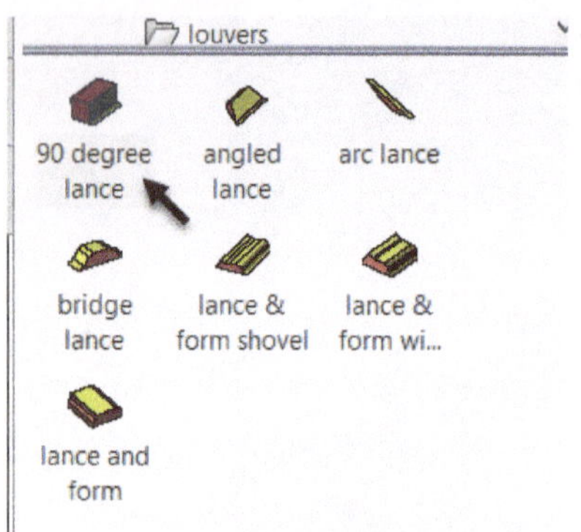

5. Release it on the horizontal face of the sheet metal feature.

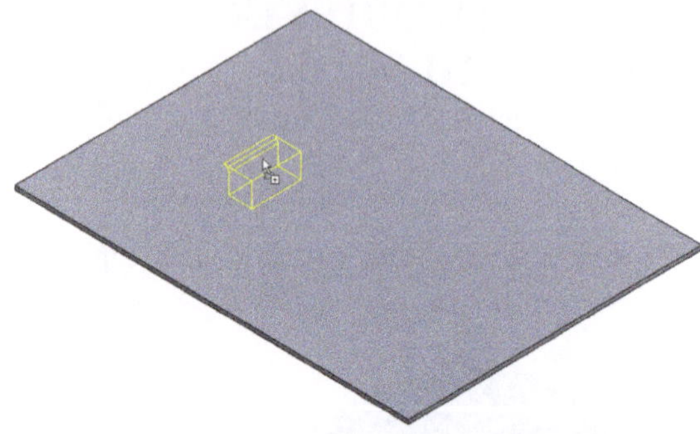

6. Specify the desired value in the **Rotation Angle** box.
7. Click **OK**.

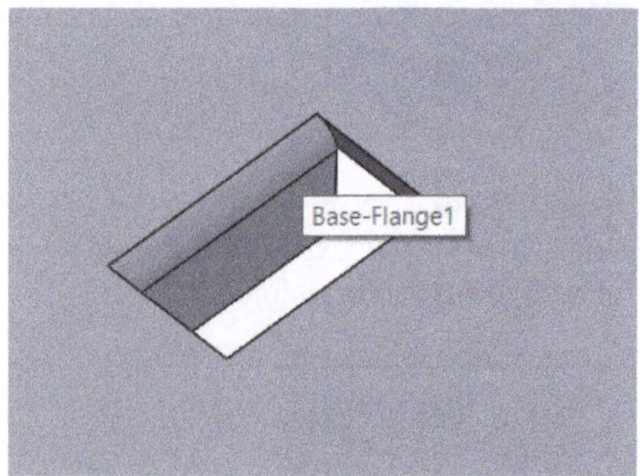

8. On the Design Library, click the right mouse button on the **90-degree lance** tool, and then select **Open**.

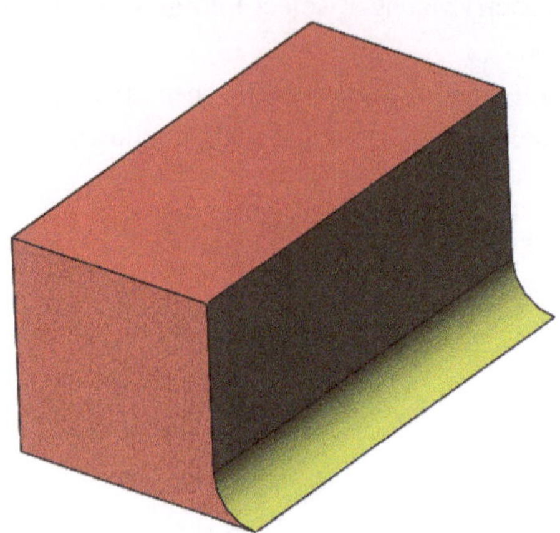

Notice the different colors on the part file. The red color represents the faces to be removed in the sheet metal part. In contrast, the yellow color represents the faces to be kept.

9. In the FeaturManager Design Tree, click and drag the bar located at the bottom.
10. Release it below the first feature.

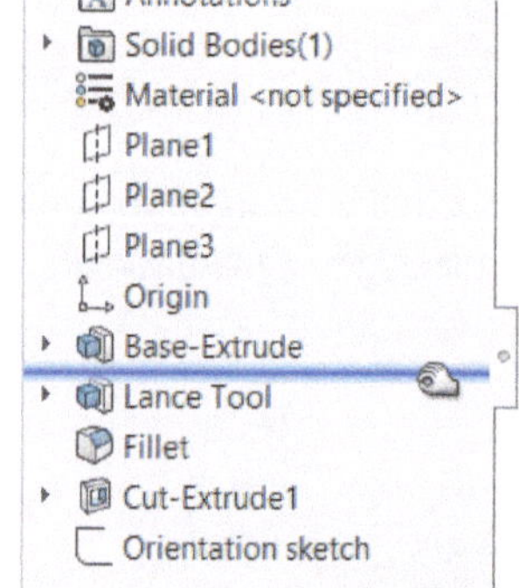

Notice that a base was created as the first feature. Later, the forming tool was created on it.

11. In the FeatureManager Design Tree, click and drag the bar, and then release it below the Lance tool feature.

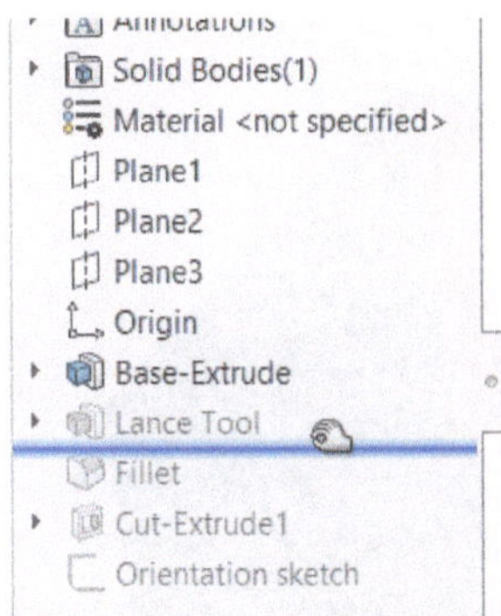

The Extruded Boss was created to define the basic shape of the forming tool.

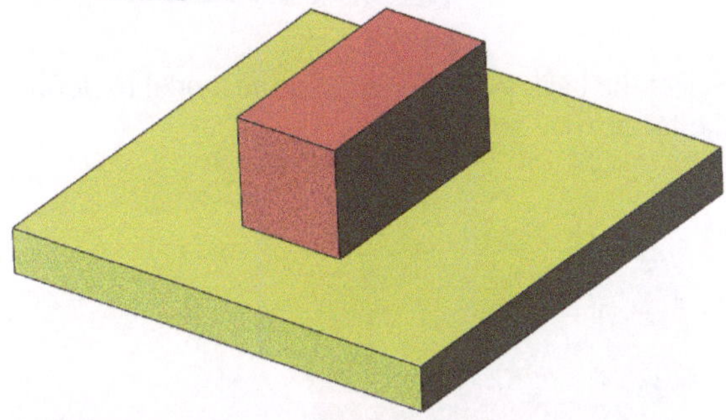

12. Likewise, drag the bar below the Fillet and Cut-Extrude features. The Cut-Extrude feature was created to remove the base feature.

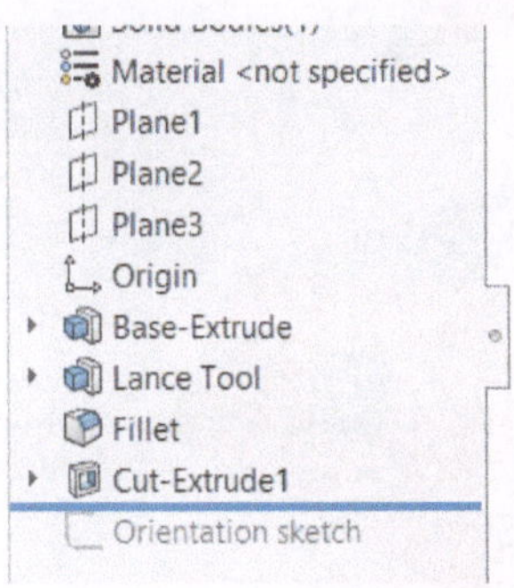

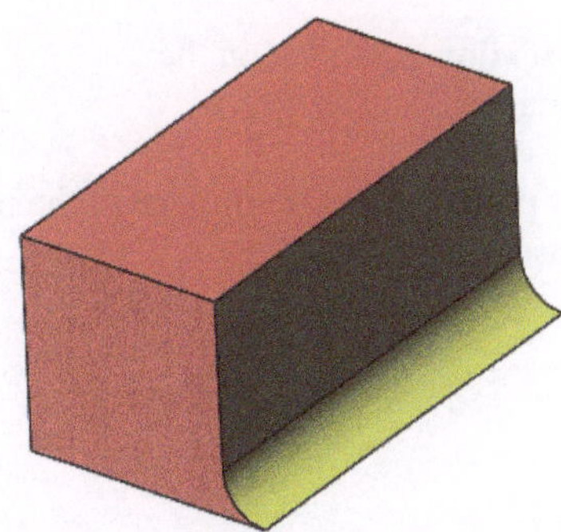

Now, you need to modify the Lance tool feature to change the basic shape of the forming tool.

13. Expand the **Lance Tool** feature.
14. Click on the **Lance Tool Sketch**, and then click **Edit Sketch**.

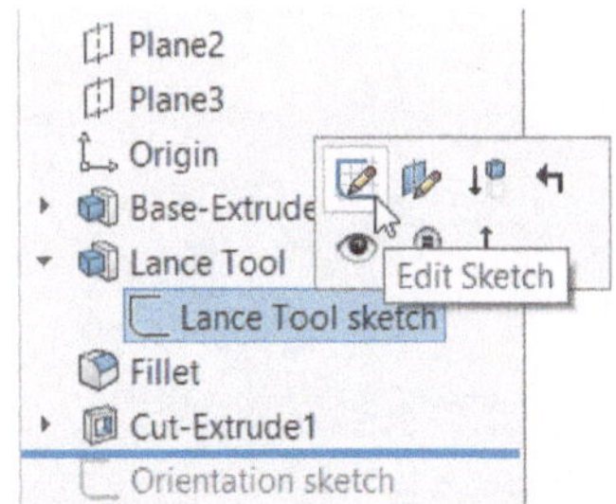

15. Create a line by specifying its start and endpoints, as shown.

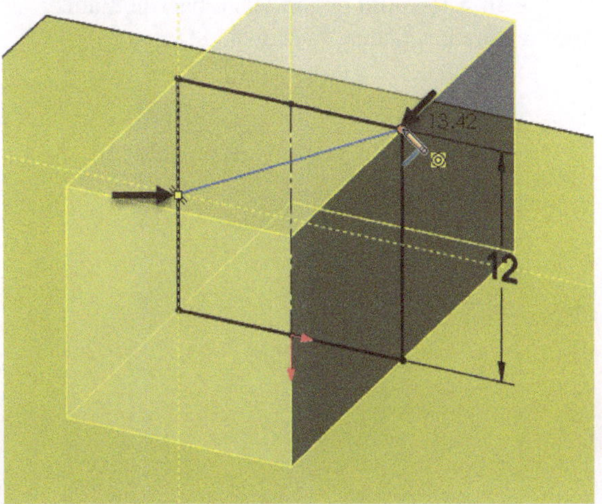

16. Trim the unwanted lines, as shown.

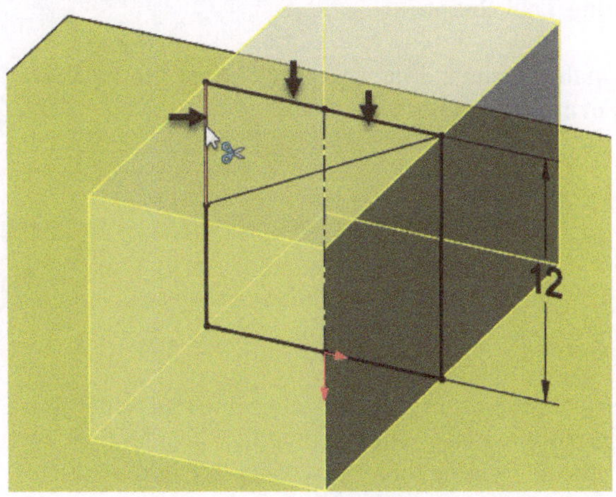

17. Add dimension to constrain the sketch, as shown.

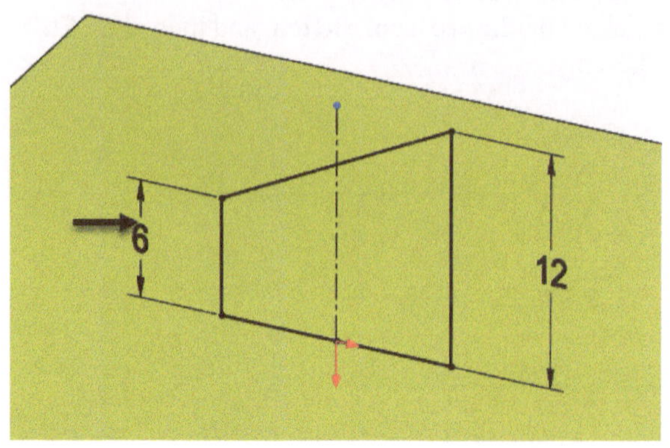

18. Click **Exit Sketch** on the CommandManager.
19. Click **Edit > Rebuild** on the Menu bar; the Lance Tool feature is updated, as shown.

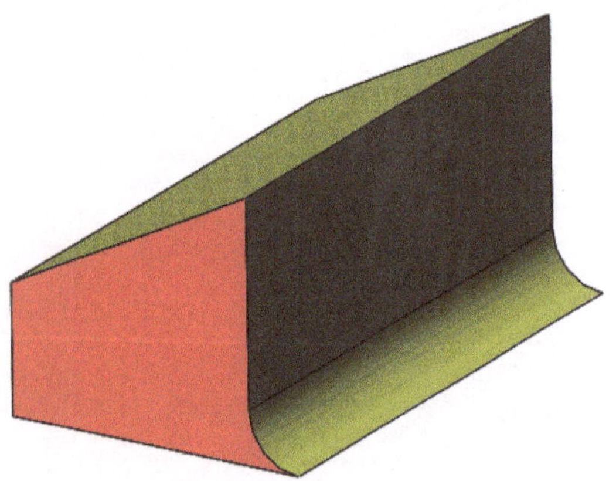

Next, you need to redefine the forming tool using the **Forming Tool** command.

20. On the CommandManager, click **Sheet Metal** tab > **Forming Tool**.

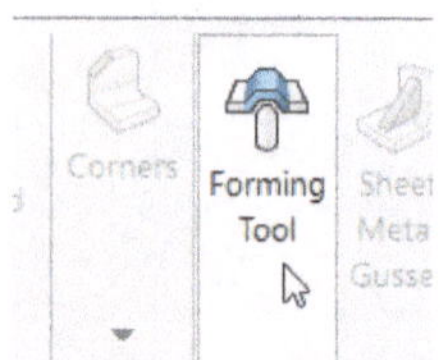

21. Select the bottom face of the forming tool to define the stopping face. The stopping face decides how deep the forming tool will, when placed on a sheet metal part.

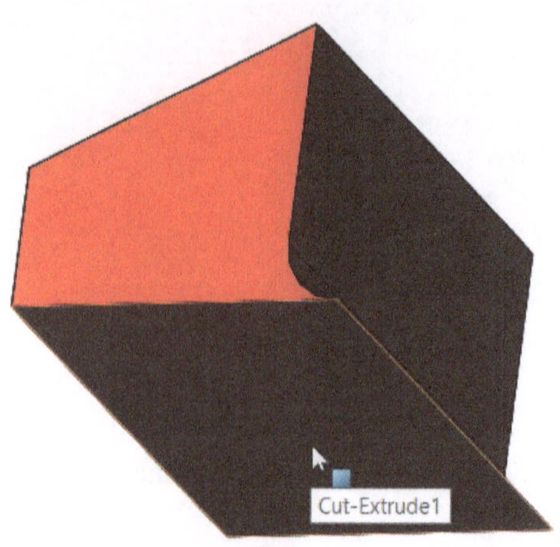

22. Select the back and side faces of the model to define the faces to be removed.

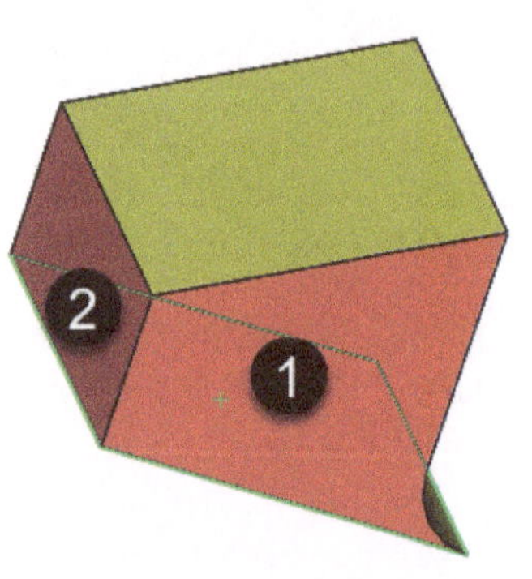

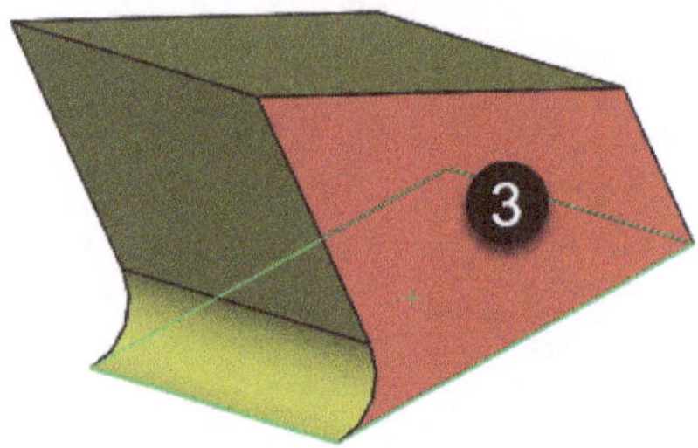

23. Click the **Insertion point** tab on the PropertyManager.

Notice the center point on the bottom face of the model is selected as the insertion point.

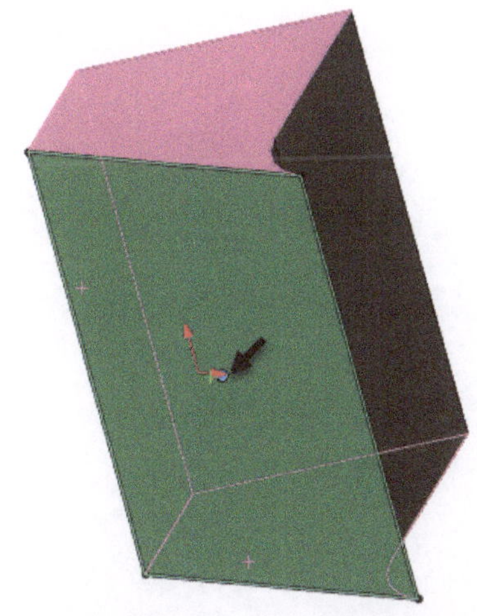

24. Click **OK** on the PropertyManager.
25. On the Quick Access Toolbar, click **Save > Save As**.

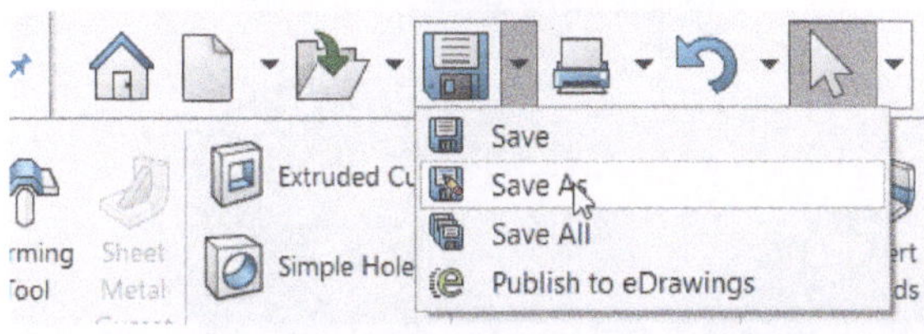

26. Type 90 degree lance-modified in the **File name** box, and then click **Save**.
27. Click **Close** on the top-right corner of the graphics window.
28. In the sheet metal part file, click the **Design Library** tab on the right pane.
29. On the **Design Library** pane, expand the **design library > forming tools > lances** folder.
30. Click and drag the **90 degree lance- modified** tool.

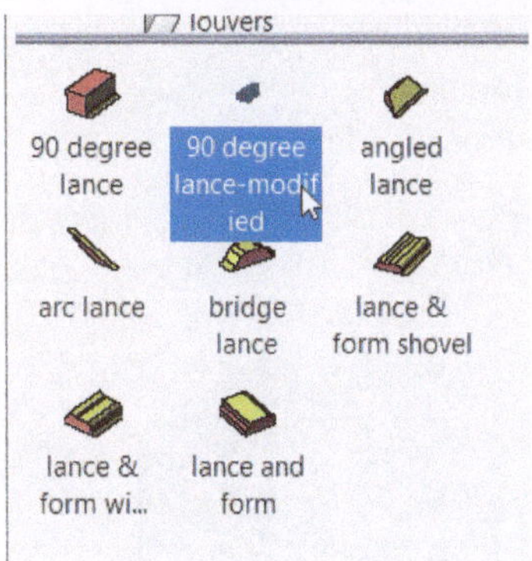

31. Release it on the horizontal face of the sheet metal feature.
32. Click **OK**.
33. Rotate the model and notice the difference between the original and the modified forming tools.

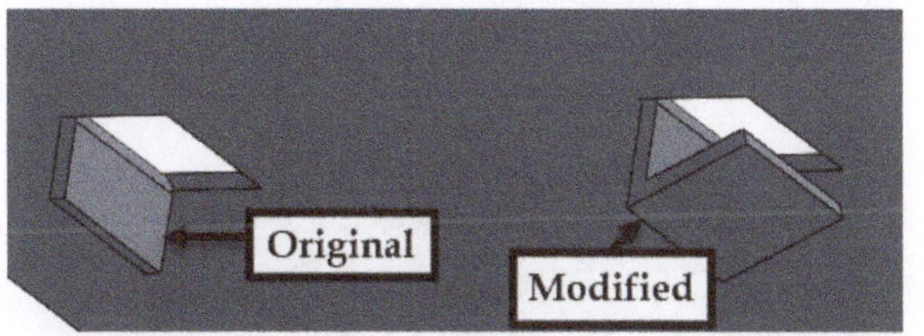

34. Save and close the part file.

TUTORIAL 10 (THE RIP AND INSERT BENDS COMMANDS)

In Tutorial 7, you have learned to convert a solid part into a sheet metal part using the **Convert to Sheet Metal** command. However, you can use the **Rip** and **Insert bends** commands to rip the edges of a part file and convert it into a sheet metal model.

1. Start a new part file.
2. Create a rectangle on the Top plane.

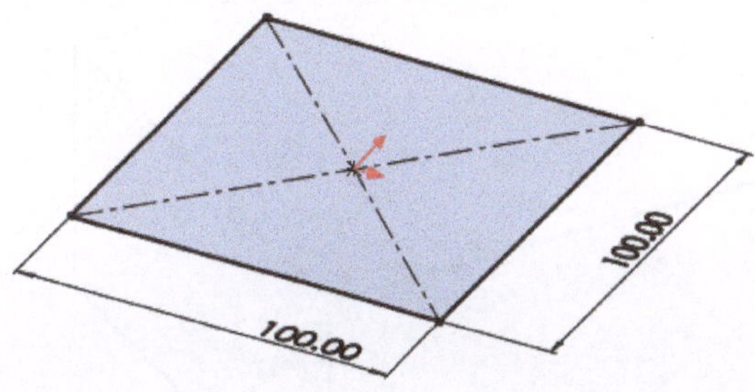

3. On the CommandManager, click **Features** tab > **Extruded Boss/Base**.
4. Select the rectangle.
5. On the **Boss-Extrude** PropertyManager, expand the **Direction 1** section.
6. Type 50 in the **Depth** box.
7. On the **Boss-Extrude** PropertyManager, check the **Thin Feature** option.
8. Type **2** in the **Thickness** box.
9. Check the **Cap ends** box.
10. Type **2** in the **Cap Thickness** box.
11. Click **OK** on the PropertyManager.

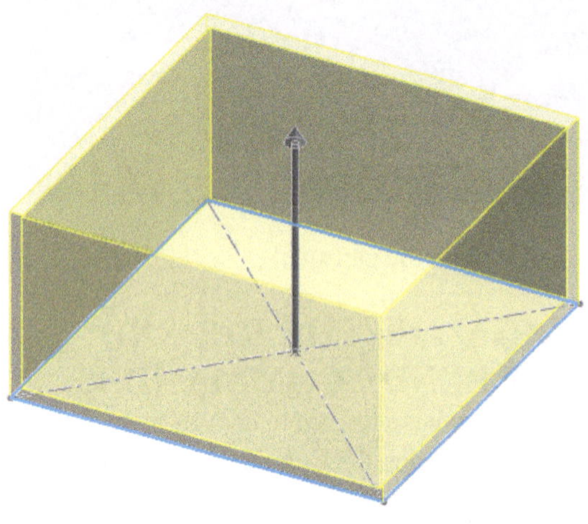

12. On the **View Heads Up** toolbar, select **Display Style > Hidden Lines Visible**.

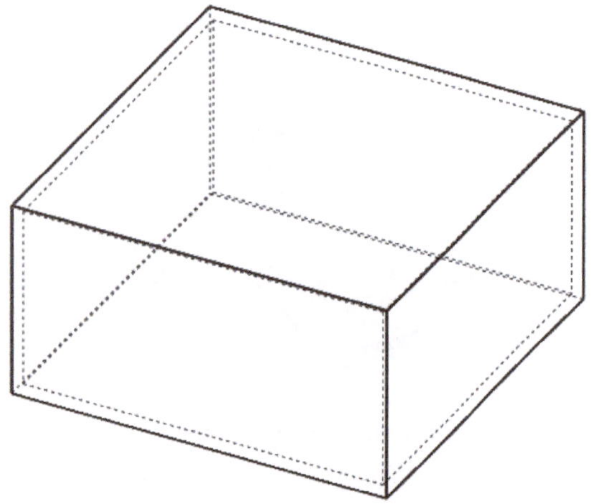

Notice that the model is hollow from the inside.

13. On the **View Heads Up** toolbar, select **Display Style > Shaded with Edges**.
14. On the CommandManager, click **Sheet Metal** tab > **Rip**.

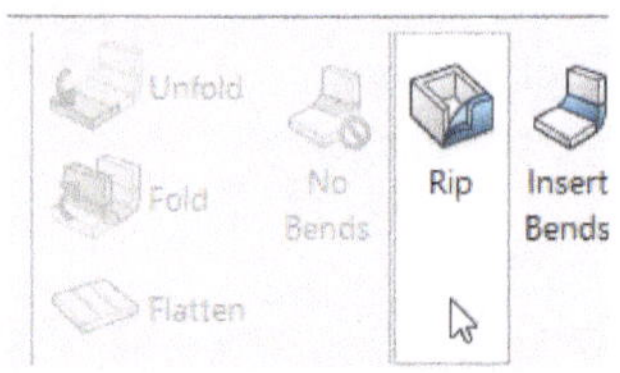

15. Select all the vertical edges of the model.

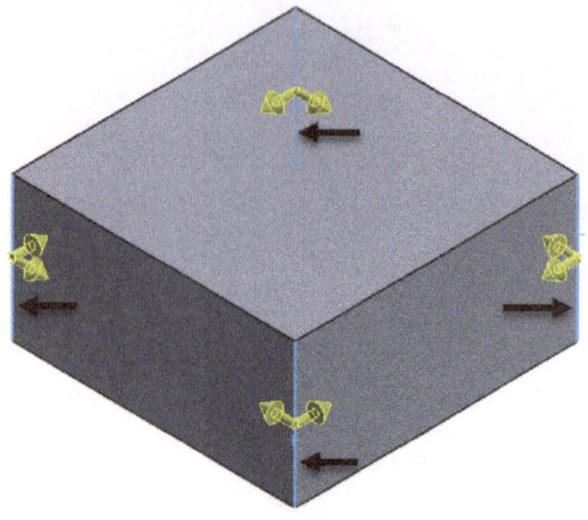

16. Select the top-left and top-right edges.

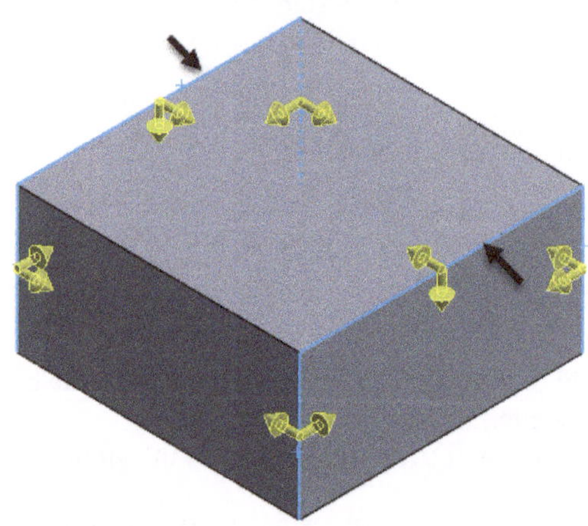

Notice the two arrows on the selected edges. They define the directions in which the edges will be trimmed. If you select only a single arrow, the edge will be trimmed in the selected arrow's direction.

17. Type 0.1 in the **Rip Gap** box.
18. Click **OK** on the **Rip** PropertyManager.

Zoom-in to a ripped edge and notice the edge is trimmed equally on both sides. Also, a small gap is created in between the ripped edge. The gap depends on the value that you specify in the **Rip Gap** box.

Note that you can also rip face using a sketched line.

19. In the FeeatureManager Design Tree, click and drag the bar, and then release it above the **Rip** feature.

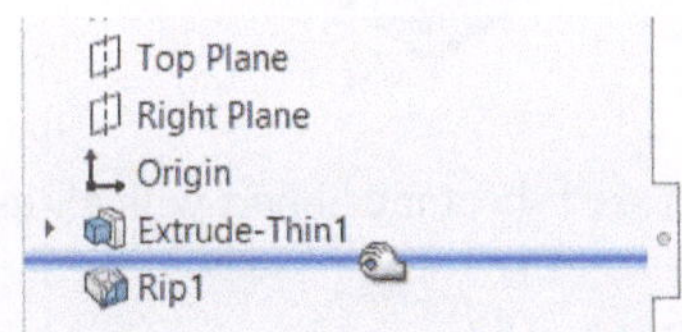

20. On the CommandManager, click **Sketch** tab > **Sketch**.
21. Click on the top face of the model.
22. Create a line by selecting the midpoints of the edges top-left and top-right edges, as shown.

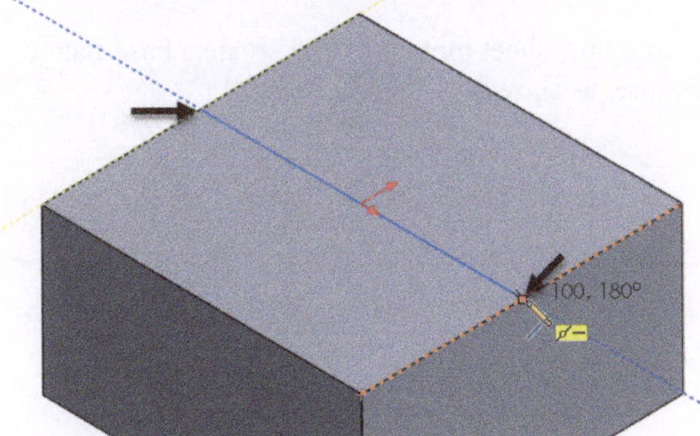

23. Click **Exit Sketch** on the CommandManager.
24. In the FeatureManager Design Tree, click and drag the bar, and then release it below the **Rip** feature.

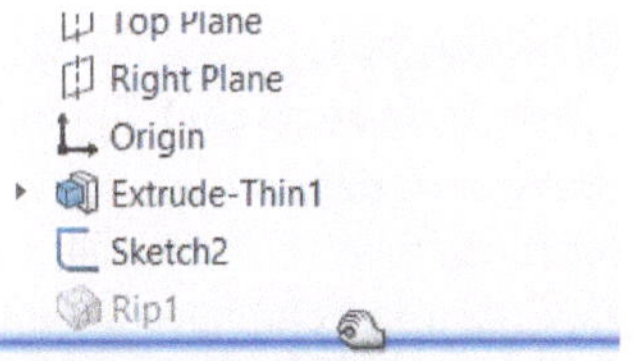

25. Click the right mouse button on the **Rip** feature, and then select **Edit Feature**.
26. Select the sketched line and click **OK**.

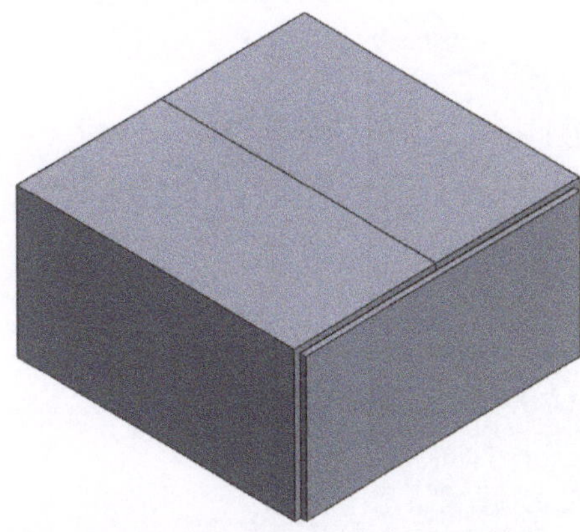

Inserting Bends

After ripping the edges, you need to use the Insert Bends command to insert bends to the model.

1. On the CommandManager, click **Sheet Metal** tab > **Insert Bends**.

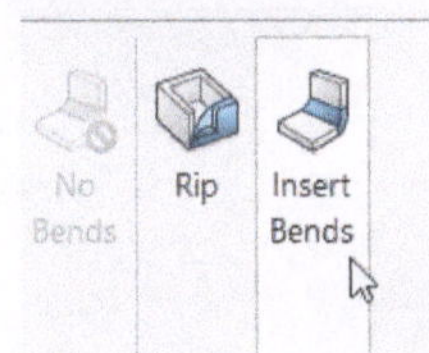

2. Rotate the model and select the bottom face of the model.

3. Type **2.5** in the **Bend Radius** box.
4. Select **Rectangular** from the **Auto Relief Type** drop-down available in the **Auto Relief** section.
5. Type **0.5** in the **Relief Ratio** box.
6. Leave **Rip Parameters** empty as you have already created the rips using the Rip command.
7. Click **OK**; the **SOLIDWORKS Design** message box pops up, showing that the Auto relief cuts were made for one or more bends.
8. Click **OK** to insert the bends.

Notice the four new features added to the FeatureManager Design Tree.

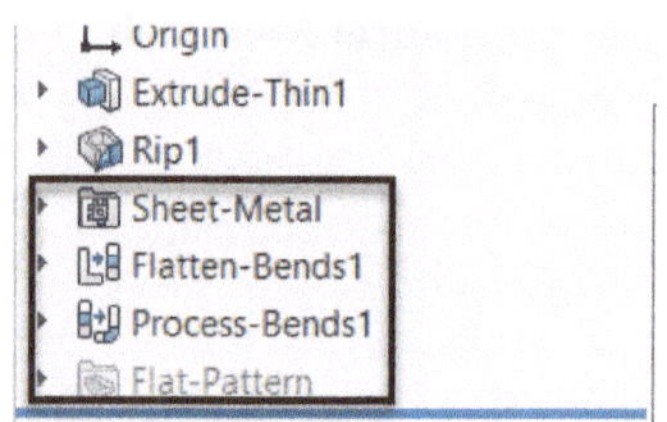

9. Click the right mouse button on the **Sheet Metal** feature, and then select **Edit Feature**; the **Sheet Metal** PropertyManager appears. It displays the settings and parameters that control the sheet metal part.
10. Click **OK** on the **Sheet Metal** PropertyManager.
11. Expand the **Flatten-Bend** feature and notice that all the sharp corners converted into bends using the **Insert Bends** command are listed.

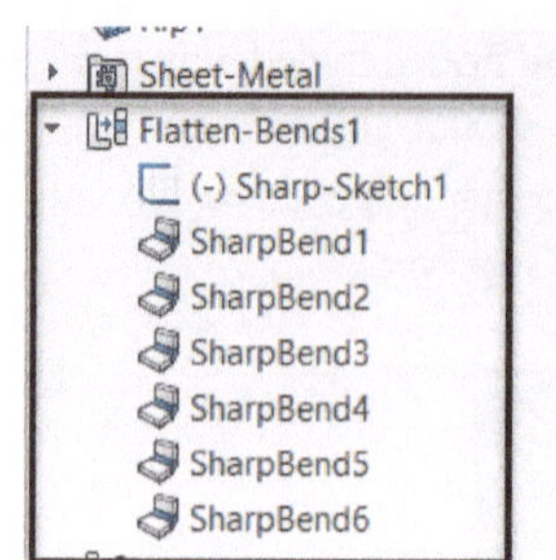

You can edit the bend radius and bend allowance of the sharp bends by right-clicking on the **Flatten-Bend** feature and then selecting **Edit Feature.**

12. Click the right mouse button on the **Process Bends** feature, and then select **Edit Feature**.

You can view the processed sheet metal part with all its bends.

13. Click **OK** on the PropertyManager.
14. Save and close the sheet metal part file.

TUTORIAL 11 (Create Flanges on the Bend Edges)

In this tutorial, you create flanges on the bend edges.

1. Start a new sheet metal file and create a base flange feature, as shown.

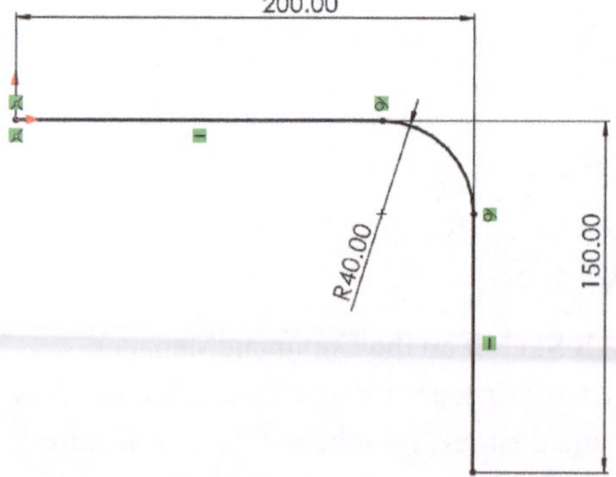

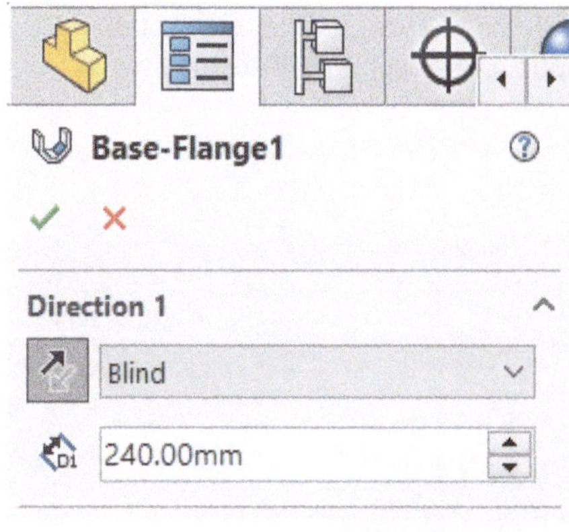

2. Add 50 mm radius fillets to the edges, as shown.

3. On the CommandManager, click **Sheet Metal** tab > **Edge Flange** .

4. Right click on any one of the sheet metal edges, as shown.
5. Select the **Select Tangency** option from the shortcut menu. All the edges tangent to the selected edge are selected.

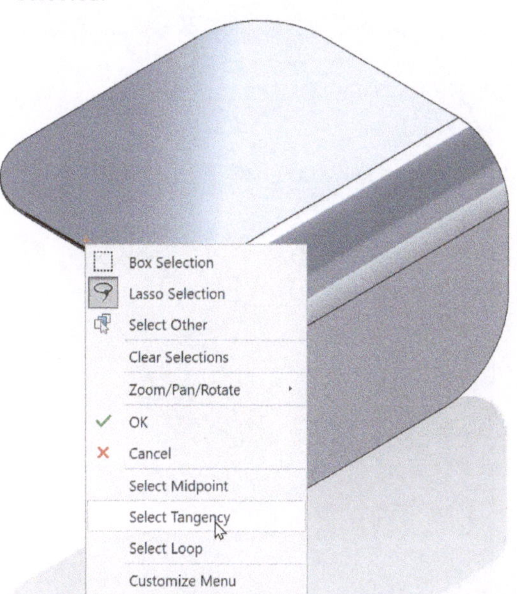

6. On the PropertyManager, type **15** in the **Length** box available in the **Flange Length** section.

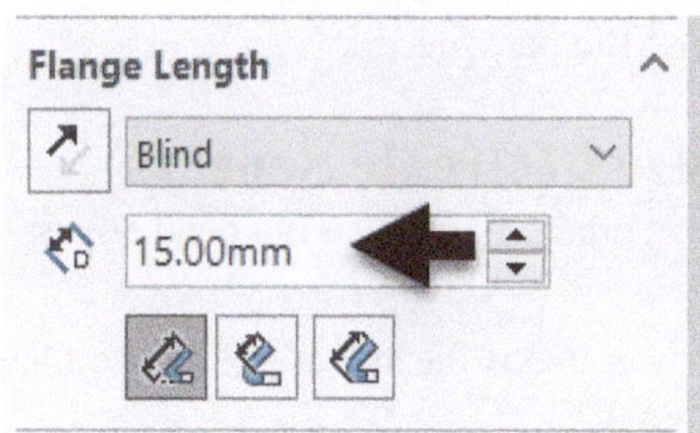

7. Click **OK** on the PropertyManager.

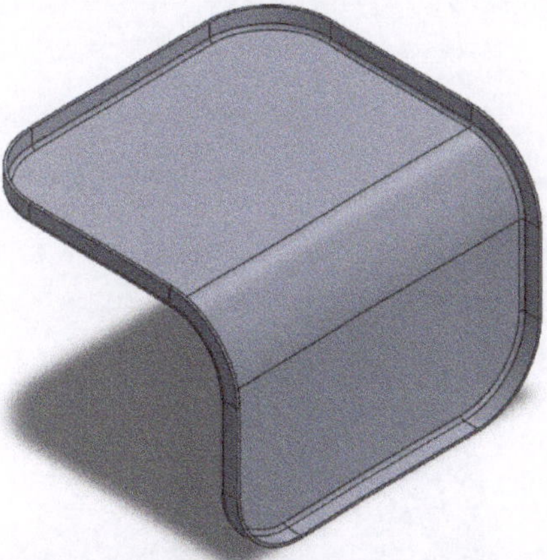

8. On the CommandManager, click **Sheet Metal** tab > **Flatten** . The sheet metal part is flattened.

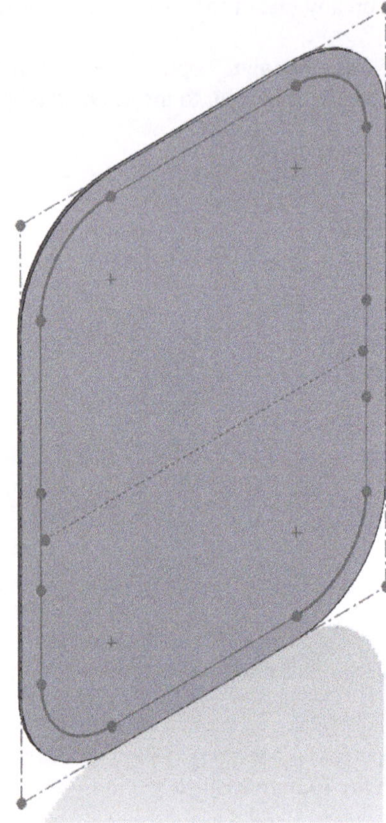

9. Save and close the part file.

TUTORIAL 12 (Create Sensors)

In this tutorial, you create flanges on the bend edges.

1. Start a new sheet metal file and create a base flange feature, as shown.

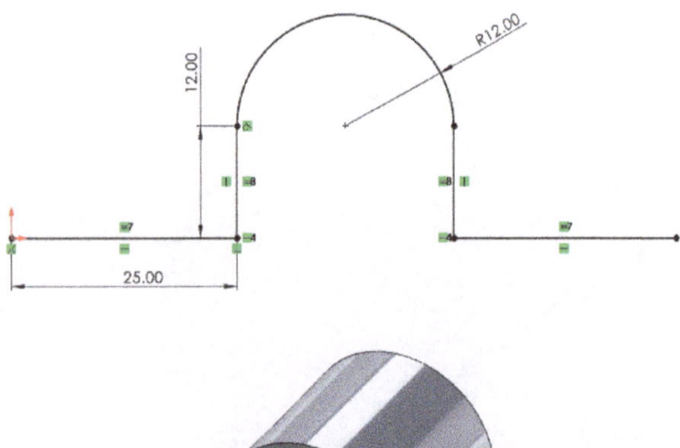

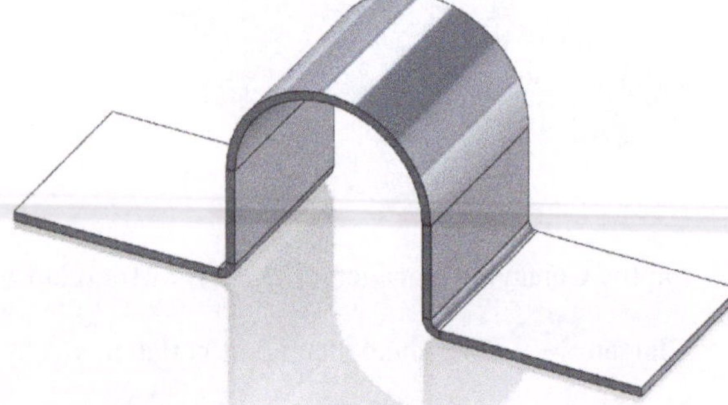

2. In the FeatureManager Design Tree, right-click on the **Sensors** node and select **Add Sensor**.

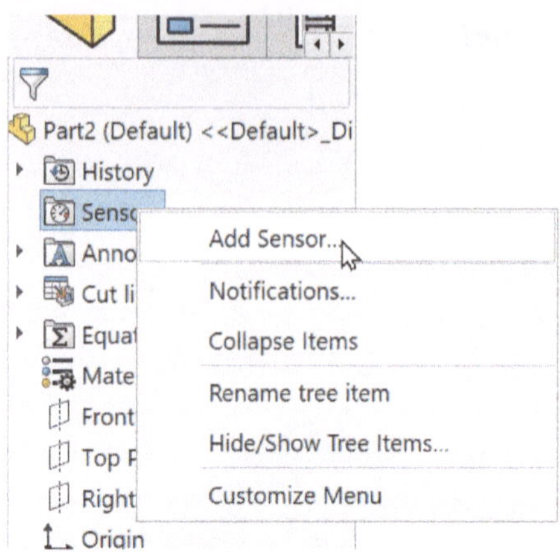

3. On the Sensor PropertyManager, select **Sensor Type > Sheet Metal Bounding Box Properties**.
4. Under the **Properties** section, select the **Sheet Metal Bounding Box Width** option from the drop-down.
5. Select the sheet metal geometry from the graphics window; the width value of the sheet metal bounding box is displayed on the PropertyManager.
6. Check the **Alert** option.
7. Select **Notify me if the value > is not exactly**.
8. Type **22** in the value box displayed below the drop-down.

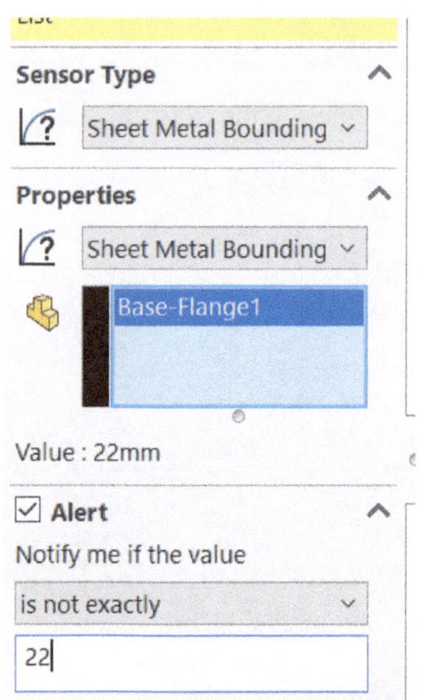

9. Click **OK** on the Sensor PropertyManager.
10. Click on the Baseflange feature in the FeatureManager Design Tree; the dimensions of the flange are displayed in the graphics window.

11. Double-click on the width dimension of the sheet metal part.
12. Type **25** in the value box and click in the graphics window.

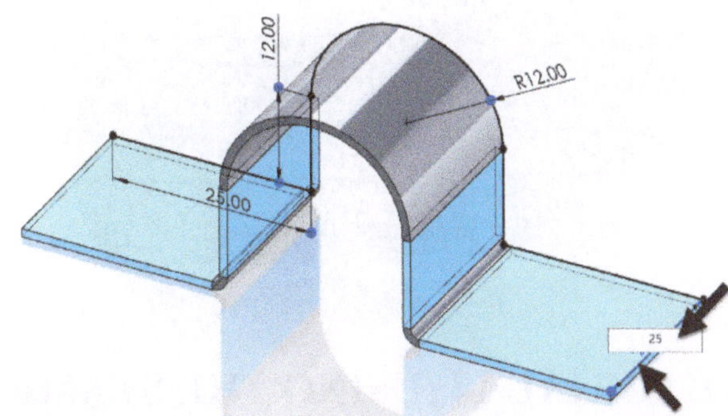

Notice that a warning message is displayed in the **Sensor** node on the FeatureManager Design Tree.

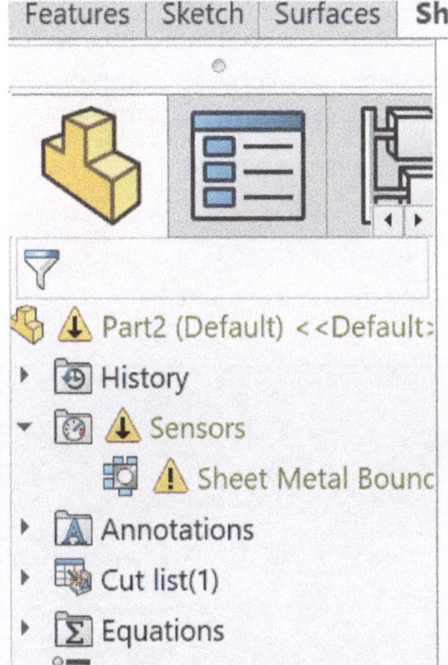

TUTORIAL 13 (USING THE RIP COMMAND FOR THIN CYLINDRICAL OR CONICAL BODIES)

In this tutorial, you will learn how to use the Rip command to convert a thin cylindrical or conical solid body to a sheet metal part.

1. Start a new part file.
2. Create a circle on the right plane.

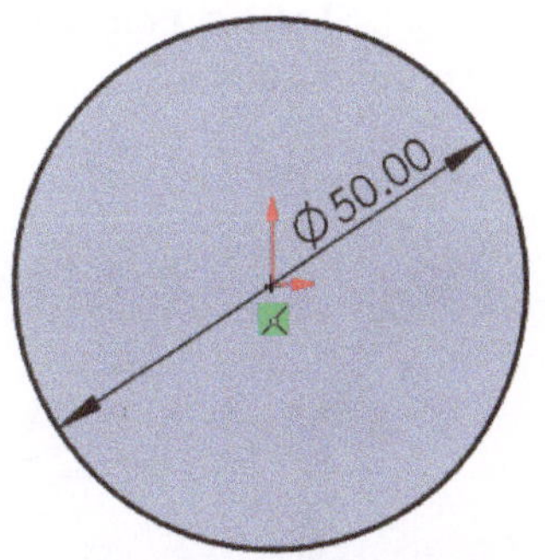

3. On the CommandManager, click **Features** tab > **Extruded Boss/Base**.
4. Select the circle.
5. On the **Boss-Extrude** PropertyManager, expand the **Direction 1** section.
6. Select **End Condition > Mid Plane**.
7. Type **100** in the **Depth** box.
8. On the **Boss-Extrude** PropertyManager, check the **Thin Feature** option.
9. Type **2** in the **Thickness** box.
10. Click **OK** on the PropertyManager.

11. On the CommandManager, click **Sketch > Sketch** and select the end face of the hollow cylinder.

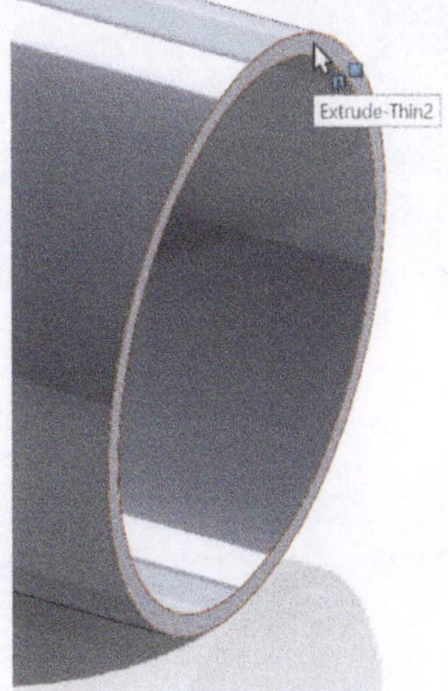

12. On the CommandManager, click **Sketch > Point** and click on the outer circular edge of the hollow cylinder.

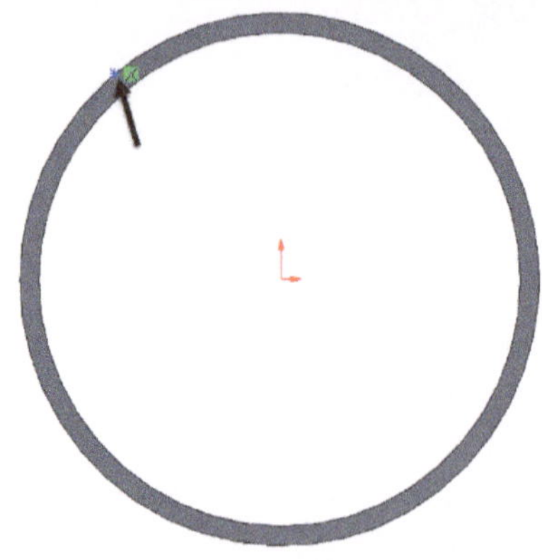

13. Click **Exit Sketch** on the **Sketch** tab of the CommandManager.
14. On the CommandManager, click **Sheet Metal > Rip**.
15. Select the outer edge of the model, as shown.

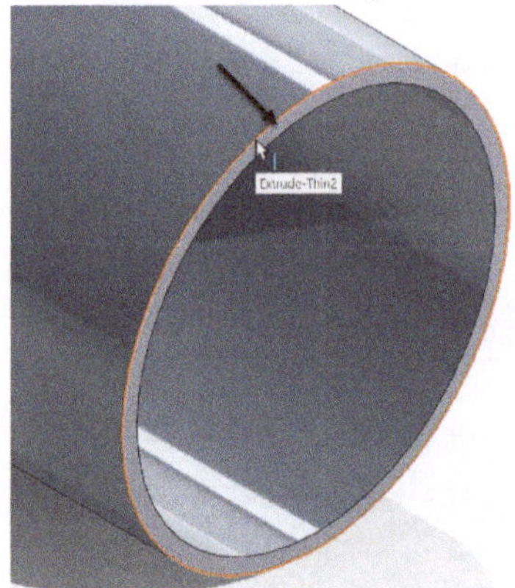

16. Select the sketch point located on the selected edge, as shown.

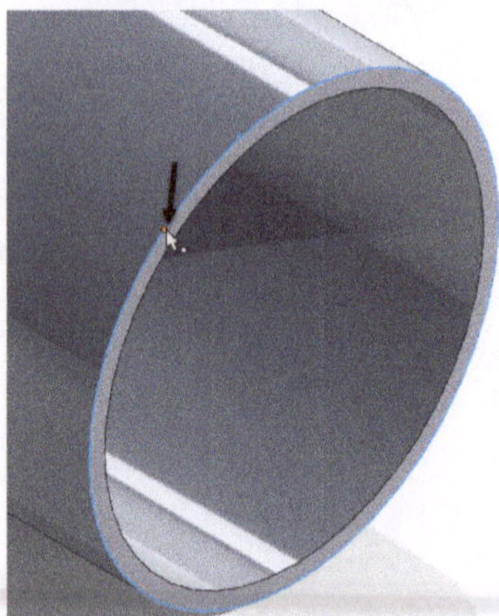

17. Type **2** in the **Rip Gap** box.
18. Click **OK**.

TUTORIAL 14 (USING THE STAMP COMMAND)

In this tutorial, you will learn how to use the Stamp command. The **Stamp** command creates parametric forming tools for sheet metal components using sketches. You can define parameters in a sketch to stamp or form sheet metal without creating a separate part file (.SLDFTP) with predefined sketches and features.

1. Start a new part file.
2. Create are rectangle on the top plane.

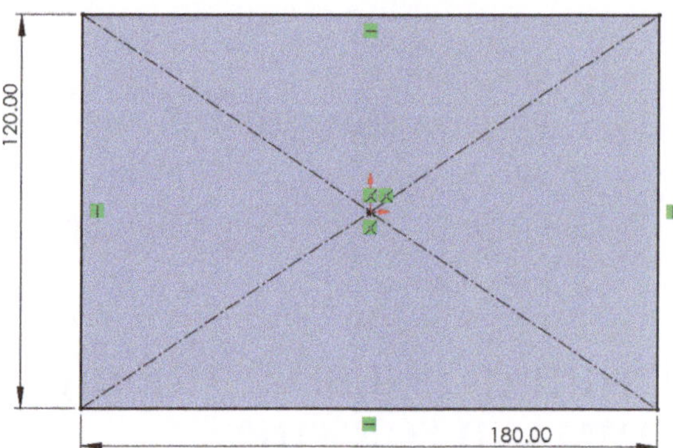

3. Create a new Base tab feature, as shown. The sheet metal thickness is 2 mm.

4. On the CommandManager, click **Sheet Metal > Stamp** and select the top face of the sheet metal part.

5. Create a rectangle and add dimensions to it, as shown.
6. Click **Exit Sketch** on the CommandManager.
7. On the PropertyManager, type 6 in the **Depth** box.
8. Type 1.5 in the **Die Radius** and **Punch Radius** boxes, respectively.

Die Radius:
In stamping, the die radius is the curved edge on the stationary die's surface, shaping sheet metal. Crucial for determining the final shape, it influences bend curvature and smoothness during stamping.

Punch Radius:
Conversely, the punch radius on the movable punch's surface affects the sharpness of bends and overall precision in forming sheet metal to the die's shape. It's a vital factor in determining the final appearance and quality of the stamped part.

9. Check the **Punch Side Corner Radius** option and type **1.5** in the **Radius** box.
10. Click **OK** to create the stamp.

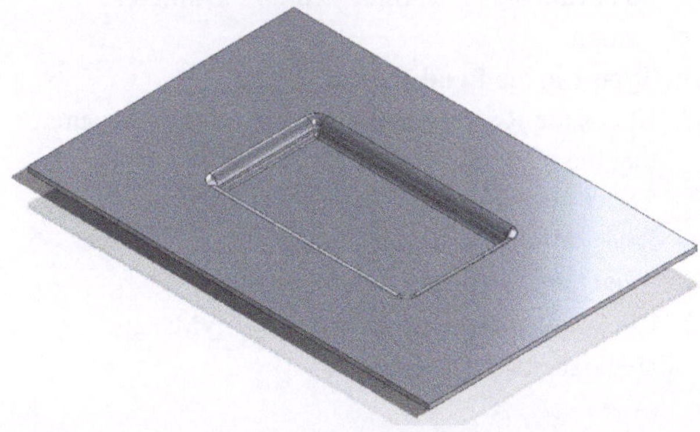

TUTORIAL 15 (CSWPA SAMPLE QUESTION)

In this tutorial, you will create the sheet metal given the CSWPA sample question. You can download the sample question PDF by using the link given below:

https://www.solidworks.com/certifications/cswpa-sheet-metal

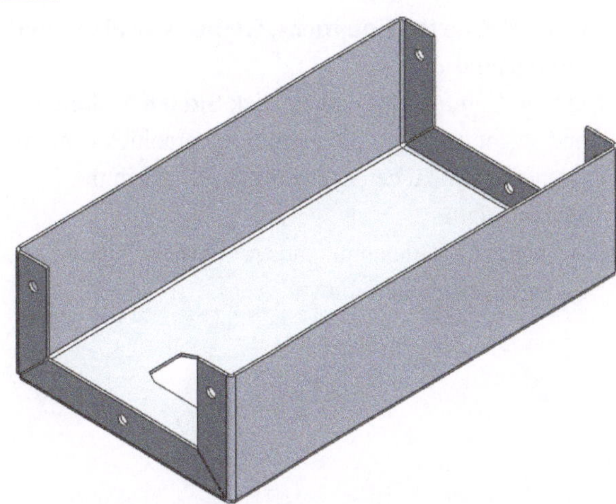

1. Start a new part file.
2. At the bottom of the window, set the **Unit System** to **MMGS**.

3. On the Menu bar, click **Tools > Equation**.

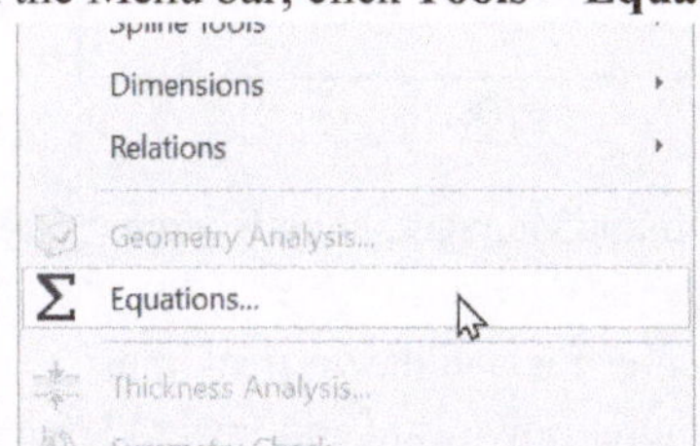

4. On the **Equations, Global Variables, and Dimensions** dialog, click in the field under the **Global Variables** node, and then type **A**.
5. Type **180** in the **Value/Equation** field next to the **A** field.
6. Likewise, create other global variables with the values, as shown.

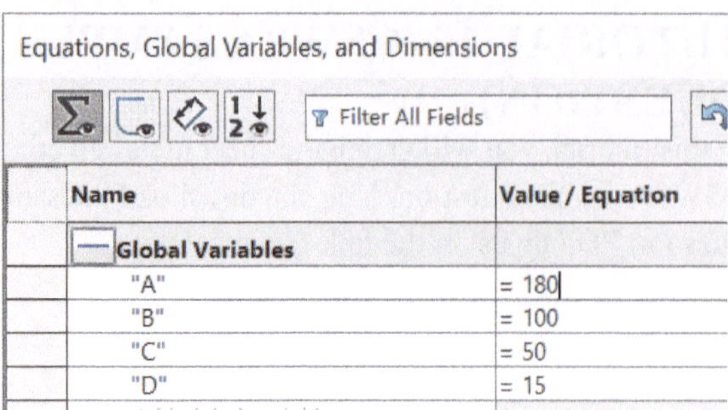

7. Click **OK** on the **Equations, Global Variables, and Dimensions** dialog.
8. On the CommandManager, click **Sketch > Sketch** and select the Front plane from the graphics window
9. Create a vertical centerline passing through the sketch origin.
10. Activate the **Line** command and create a horizontal and vertical line, as shown.

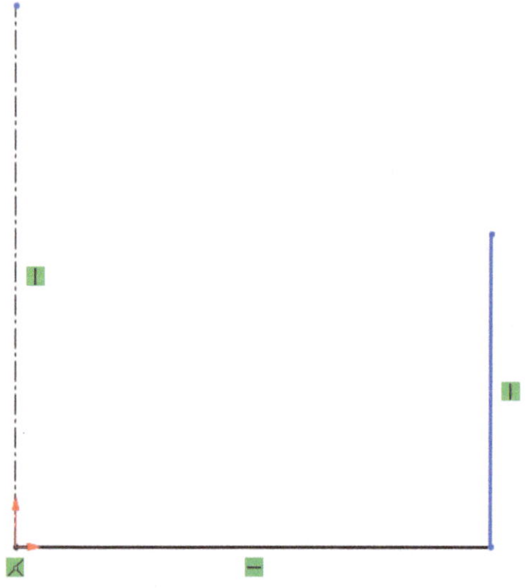

11. On the CommandManager, click **Sketch > Smart Dimension**.
12. Select the centerline and the vertical line.
13. Move the pointer downward and toward left.
14. Click to place the dimension.
15. On the **Modify** box, select the dimension value and type =.
16. Select **Global Variables > B**.

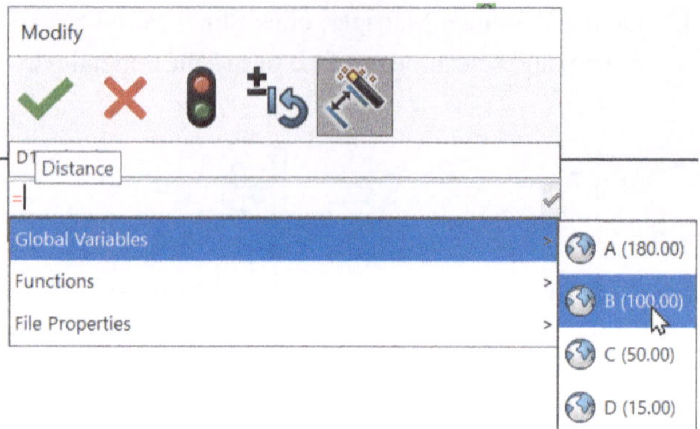

17. Click the green check on the **Modify** box.
18. With the **Smart Dimension** command active, select the vertical line.
19. Move the pointer toward right and click.
20. On the **Modify** box, select the dimension value and type =.
21. Select **Global Variables > C**.

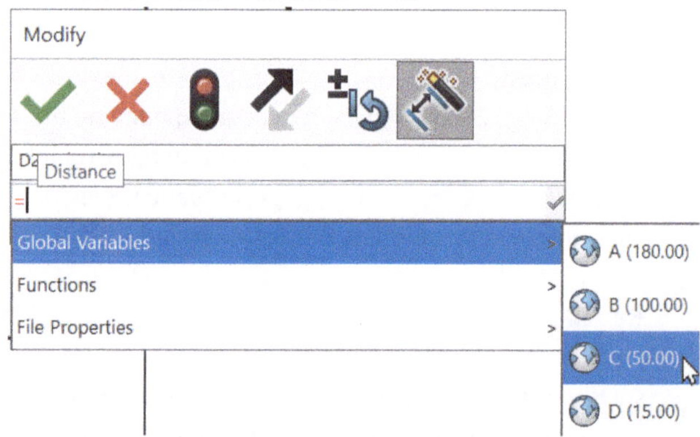

22. Click the green check on the **Modify** box.
23. Click **Exit Sketch** on the CommandManager.
24. On the CommandManager, click **Sheet Metal > Base Flange/Tab**.
25. Select the sketch from the graphics window.
26. On the PropertyManager, type **1.2** in the **Thickness** box available in the **Sheet Metal Parameters** section.
27. Type **1** in the **Bend Radius** box.
28. Check the **Reverse Direction** option to make sure that the material is inside the sketch.
29. Select the value in the **Depth** box and type =.
30. Select **Global Variables > A**.
31. Type /2 to divide the A value by two.
32. Click the green check on the PropertyManager to create the base flange.

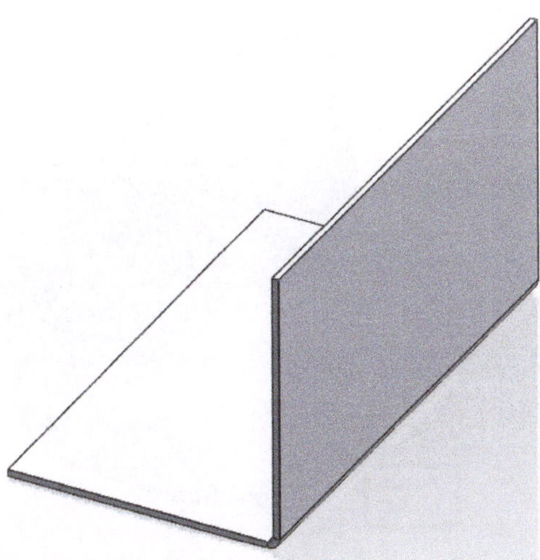

33. On the CommandManager, click **Sheet Metal > Edge Flange**.
34. Select the inside edge of the vertical portion of the sheet metal.
35. Move the pointer inside up to a random distance and click.

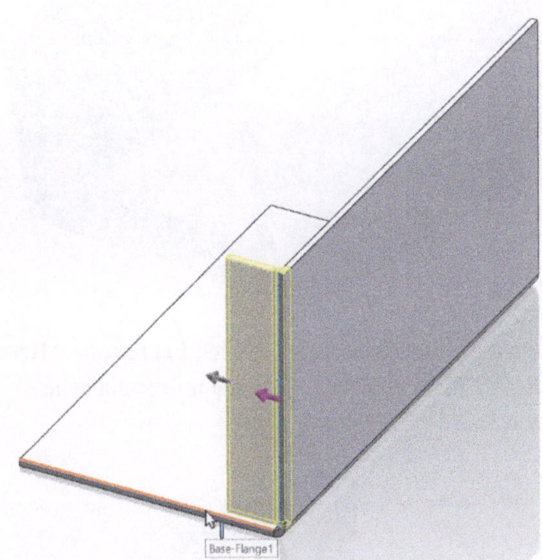

36. Likewise, select thee inside edge of the horizontal portion.

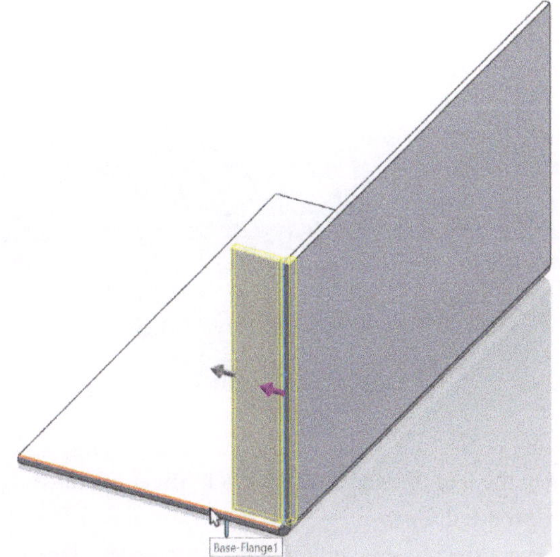

37. Type **0.5** in the **Gap Distance** box under the **Flange Parameters** section.
38. In the **Flange Length** section of the PropertyManager, select the value in the **Length** box and type =.
39. Select **Global Variables > D**.

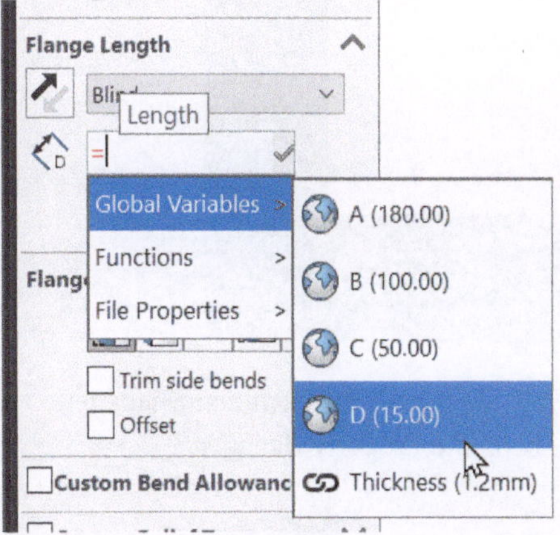

40. Click the green check next to the **Length** box to accept the global variable.
41. Under the **Flange Position** section, check the **Trim side bends** option.
42. Click the green check on the PropertyManager to create the edge flanges.

43. On the CommandManager, click **Sheet Metal > Extruded Cut**.
44. Select the outer face of anyone of the edge flange.
45. Create two circles and add dimensions to it, as shown.

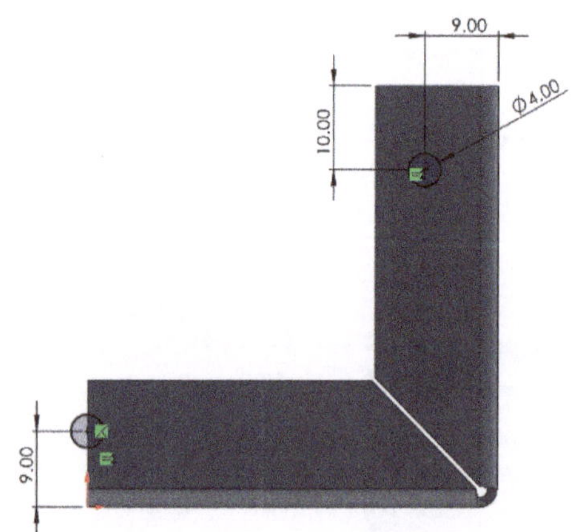

46. Click **Exit Sketch** on the CommandManager.
47. Click **OK** on the PropertyManager.

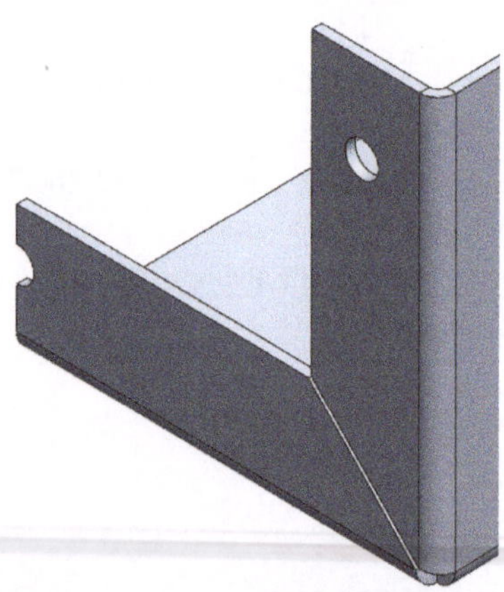

48. On the CommandManager, click **Features > Mirror**.
49. Rotate the model and select the mirror plane, as shown.

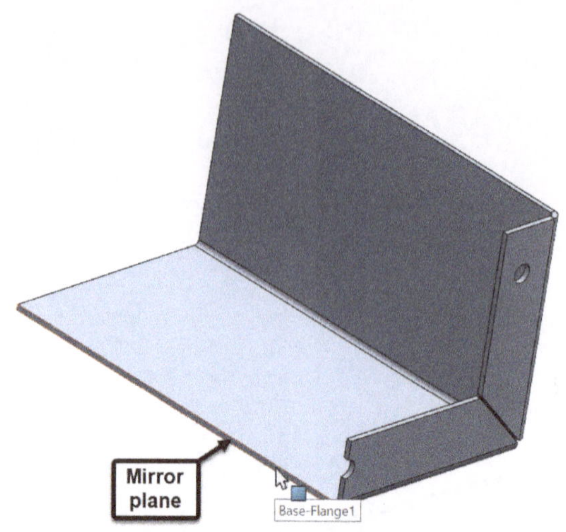

50. On the PropertyManager, click **Bodies to Mirror** and select the entire sheet metal body.
51. Click **OK** to mirror the sheet metal body.

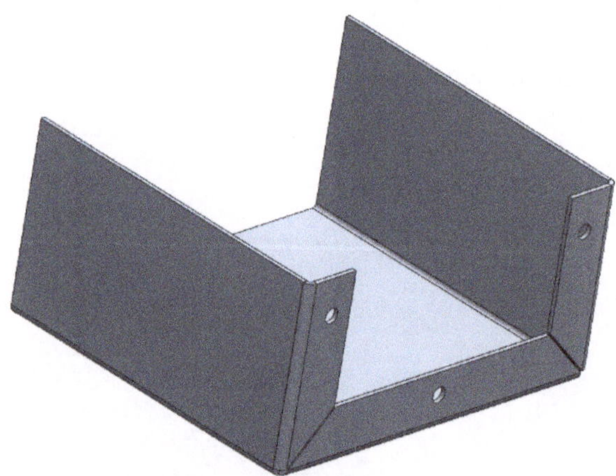

52. On the CommandManager, click **Features > Mirror**.
53. Rotate the model and select the mirror plane, as shown.

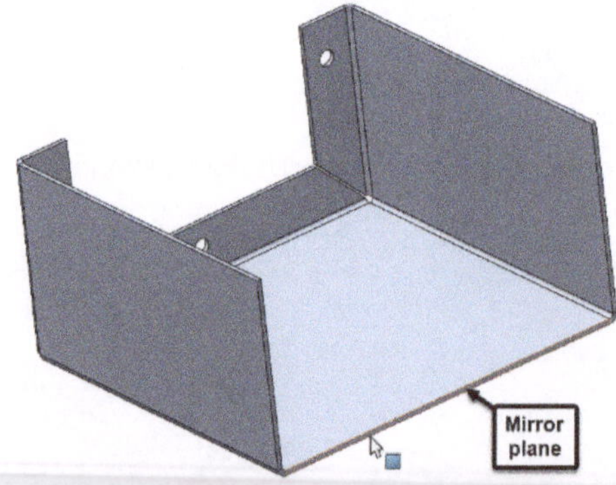

54. On the PropertyManager, click in the **Bodies to Mirror** selection box and select the entire sheet metal body.
55. Click **OK** to mirror the sheet metal body.

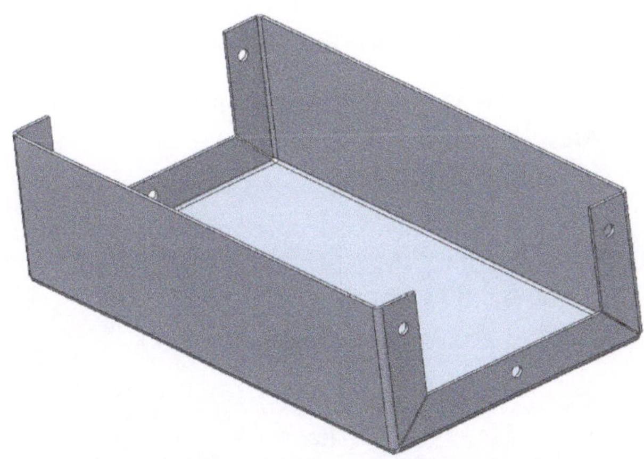

56. On the CommandManager, click **Sheet Metal > Extruded Cut**.
57. Rotate the model and select the bottom face.
58. Create a centered rectangle and add dimensions to it, as shown.

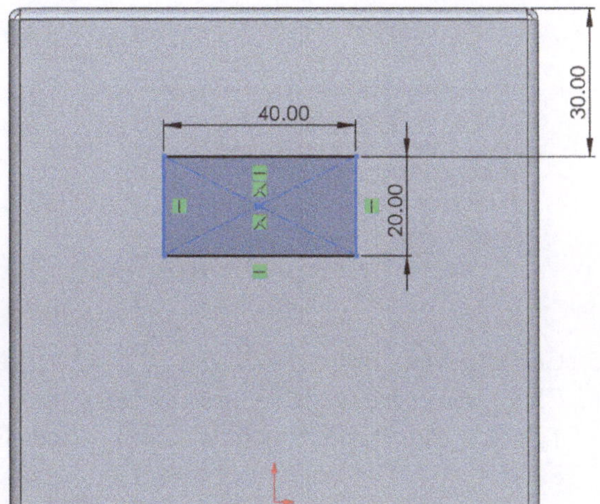

59. Press and hold the CTRL key and select the center point of the rectangle and the sketch origin.
60. Click the **Vertical** icon under the **Add Relation** section of the PropertyManager.
61. On the CommandManager, click **Fillet** drop-down > **Chamfer**.
62. On the PropertyManager, select **Distance-distance** option.
63. Uncheck the **Equal distance** option.
64. Type **5** and **2.5** in the **Distance 1** and **Distance 2** boxes, respectively.

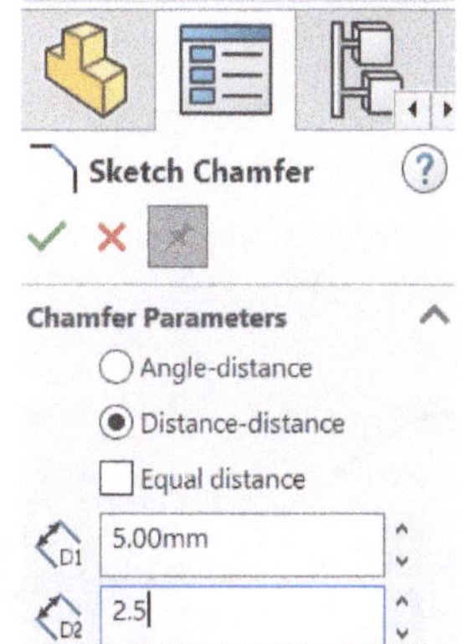

65. Select the lower horizontal line of the rectangle.
66. Select the left vertical line of the rectangle; a chamfer is created at the lower left corner.
67. Likewise, create three more chamfers by selecting the horizontal and vertical lines, as shown.

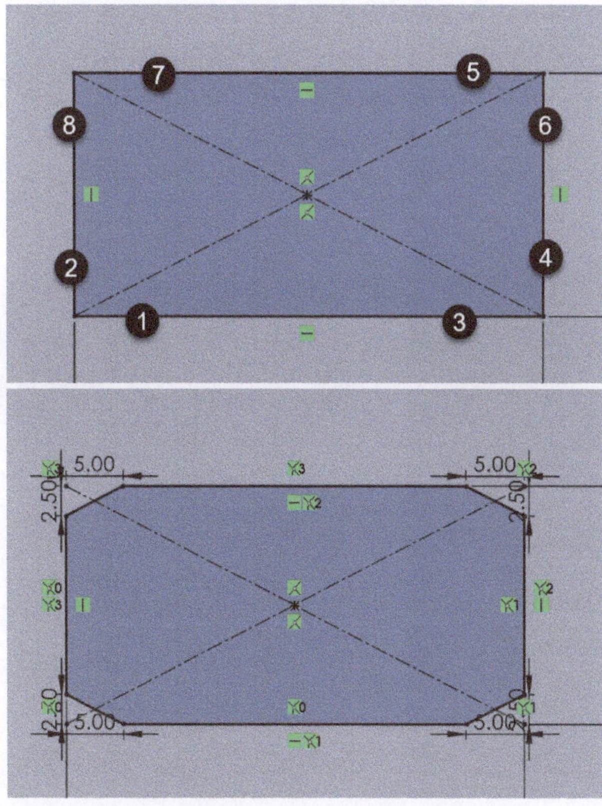

68. Click **OK** on the **Sketch Chamfer** PropertyManager.
69. Click **Exit Sketch** on the CommandManager.
70. Click **OK** on the **Cut-Extrude** PropertyManager.

71. In the FeatureManager Design Tree, right-click on the **Material** node and select **Edit Material**.

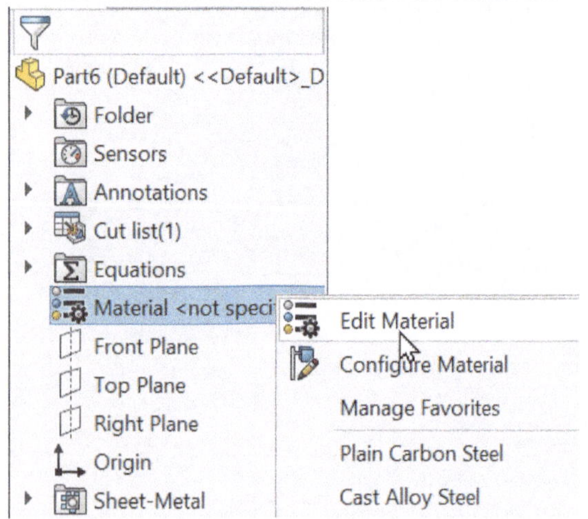

72. On the **Material** dialog, expand the **Aluminium Alloys** folder and select the **1060 Alloy** material.

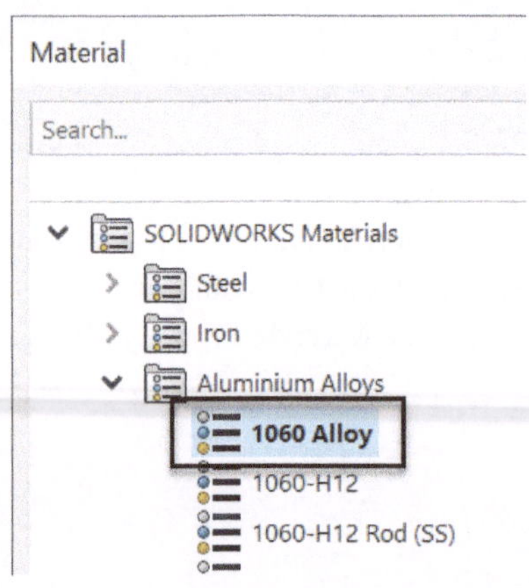

73. Click **Apply** and **Close** on the **Material** dialog.
74. On the CommandManager, click **Evaluate > Mass Properties**; on the **Mass Properties** dialog, the **Mass** is displayed as 125.6.

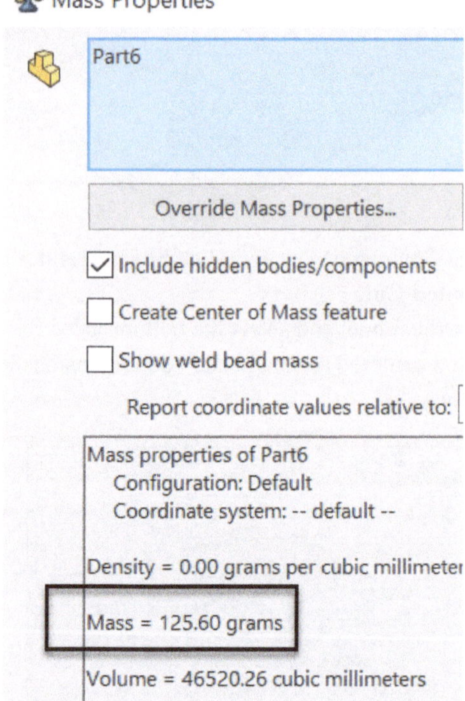

75. Close the **Mass Properties** dialog.
76. Click **Save** on the Quick Access Toolbar.
77. Type **C7_Tutorial15** in the **File name** box and click **Save**.

TUTORIAL 16 (CSWPA SAMPLE QUESTION 2)

In this tutorial, you will update the parameters of the part created in Tutorial 15.

1. Open the file created in Tutorial 15.
2. In the FeatureManager Design Tree, right-click on the **Equations** node and select **Manage Equations**.

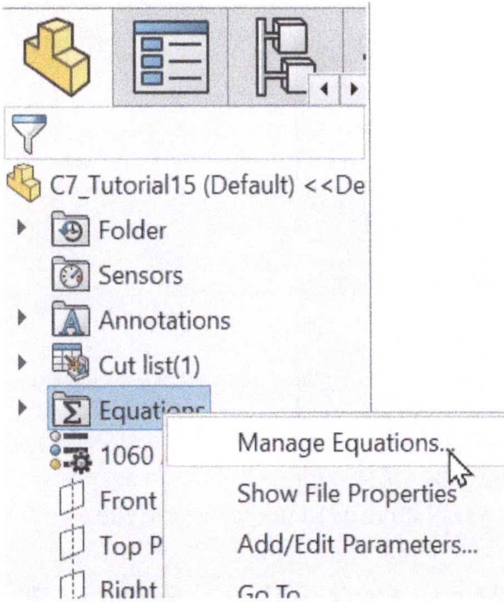

3. On the **Equations, Global Variables, and Dimensions** dialog, select the value in the **Value/ Evaluation** box next to the **A** global variable.
4. Type **200**.
5. Likewise, change the **B**, **C**, and **D** values to **110**, **40**, and **18**, respectively.

Equations, Global Variables, and Dimensions

Filter All Fields

Name	Value / Equation
Global Variables	
"A"	= 200
"B"	= 110
"C"	= 40
"D"	= 18
Thickness	= 1.2

6. Click **OK**; the model is updated.

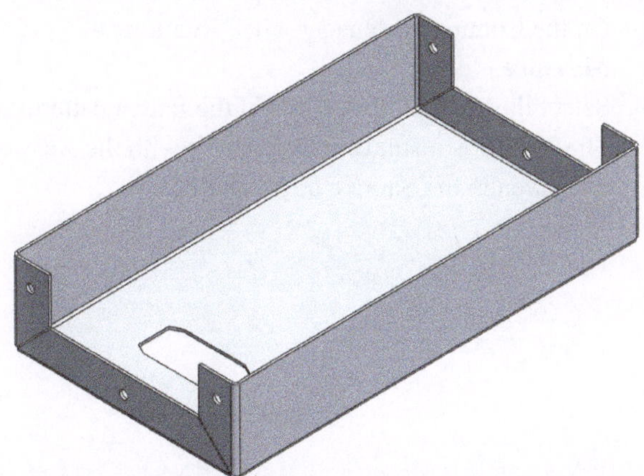

7. Click **Evaluate > Mass Properties** on the CommandManager. The **Mass** value is updated to 133.37 gms.
8. Close the **Mass Properties** dialog.
9. Save the file as C7_tutorial16 and close it.

TUTORIAL 17 (CSWPA SAMPLE QUESTION 3)

In this tutorial, you will create the flat pattern of the part created in Tutorial 15.

1. Open the file created in Tutorial 15.
2. In the FeatureManager Design Tree, right-click on the **Sheet Metal** folder and click **Edit Feature**.

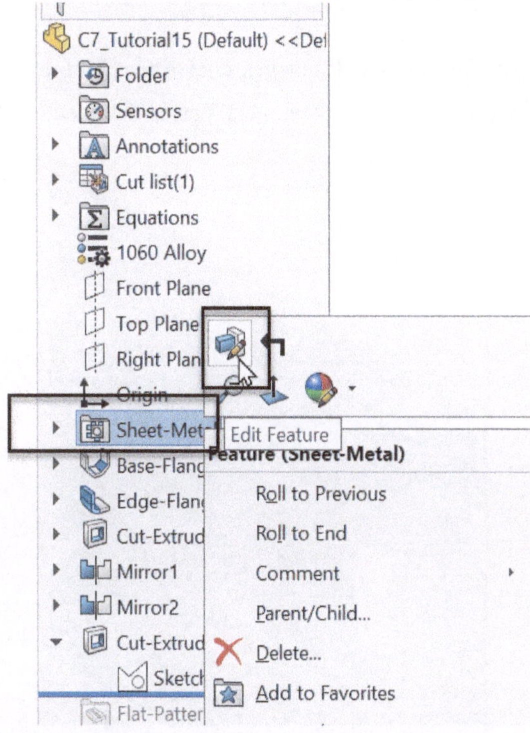

3. On the **Sheet Metal** PropertyManager, check the **Bend Allowance** option.
4. Type 0.4 in the **K** box.

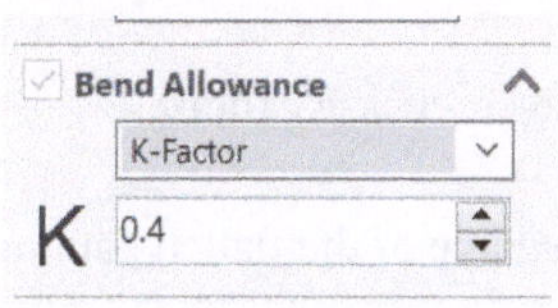

5. Click **OK**.
6. In the FeatureManager Design Tree, click and drag the bar located at the bottom.

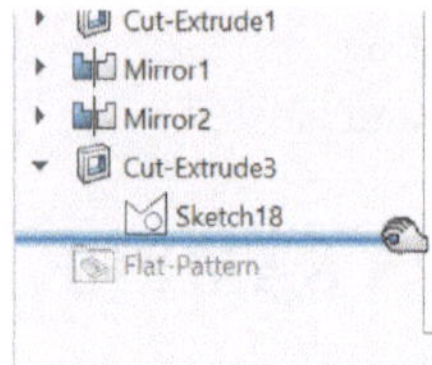

7. Release it below the **Flat Pattern** feature; the flat pattern is activated.

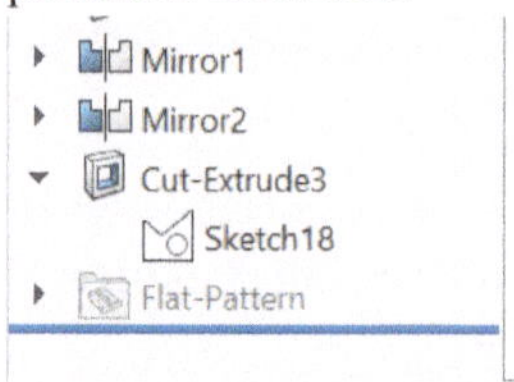

8. On the CommandManager, click **Sheet Metal > Flatten**. The sheet metal part is flattened.

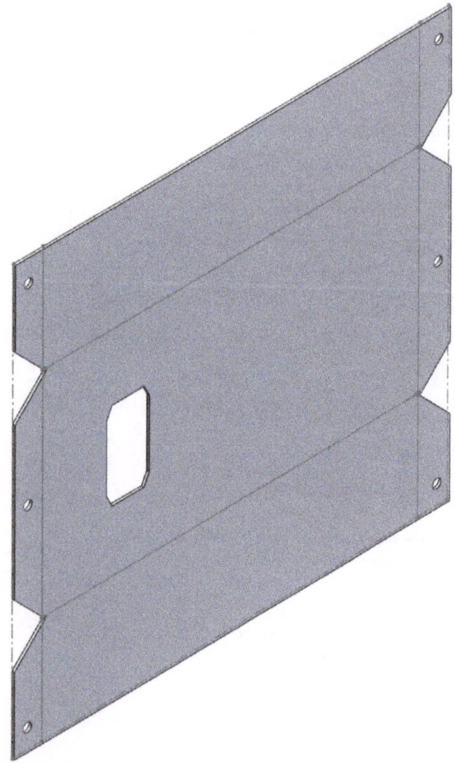

9. On the CommandManager, click **Evaluate > Measure**.
10. Select the vertical dotted line of the flatten pattern. The 195.85 is displayed. Compare it with the Answer key given in the Sample question PDF.

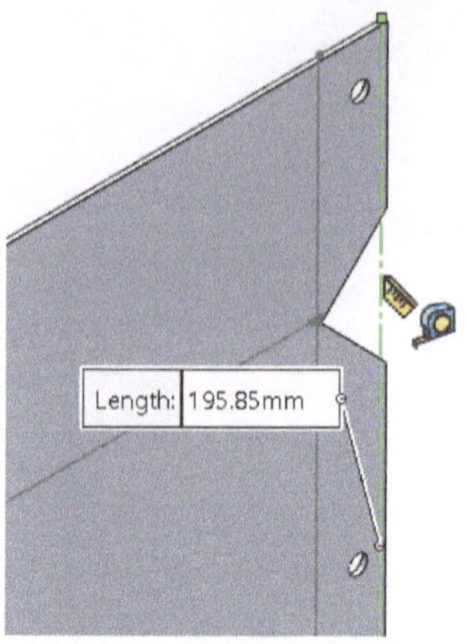

11. Save it as C7_tutorial17 and close the file.

TUTORIAL 18 (CSWPA SAMPLE QUESTION 3)

In this tutorial, you will create the flat pattern of the Tutorial 16 part file.

1. Open the file created in Tutorial 16.
2. In the FeatureManager Design Tree, right-click on the **Sheet Metal** folder and click **Edit Feature**.
3. On the **Sheet Metal** PropertyManager, check the **Bend Allowance** option.
4. Type 0.32 in the **K** box.
5. Click **OK**.
6. In the FeatureManager Design Tree, click and drag the bar located at the bottom.
7. Release it below the **Flat Pattern** feature; the flat pattern is activated.
8. On the CommandManager, click **Sheet Metal > Flatten**. The sheet metal part is flattened.
9. On the CommandManager, click **Evaluate > Measure**.
10. Select the vertical dotted line of the flatten pattern. The 185.55 is displayed. Compare it with the Answer key given in the Sample question PDF.

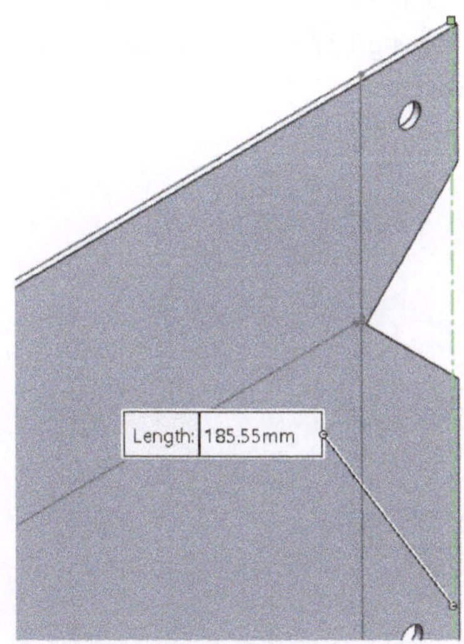

11. On the CommandManager, click **Sheet Metal > Flatten** . The sheet metal part is unflattened.
12. In the FeatureManager Design Tree, expand the Cut List folder and click the right mouse button on Sheet1.
13. Select **Properties** from the shortcut menu; the **Cut-List Properties** dialog appears.
14. On the dialog, view the **Bounding Box Area** value and compare it with the Answer key.

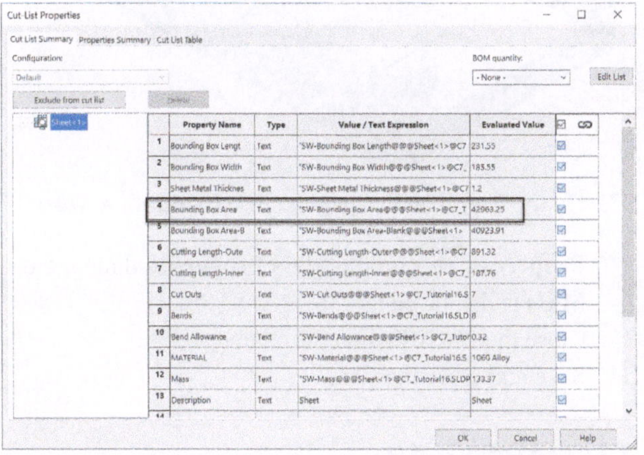

	Property Name	Type	Value / Text Expression	Evaluated Value
1	Bounding Box Lengt	Text	"SW-Bounding Box Length@@@Sheet<1>@C7	231.55
2	Bounding Box Width	Text	"SW-Bounding Box Width@@@Sheet<1>@C7_	185.55
3	Sheet Metal Thicknes	Text	"SW-Sheet Metal Thickness@@@Sheet<1>@C7	1.2
4	Bounding Box Area	Text	"SW-Bounding Box Area@@@Sheet<1>@C7_T	42963.25
5	Bounding Box Area-B	Text	"SW-Bounding Box Area-Blank@@@Sheet<1>	40923.91
6	Cutting Length-Oute	Text	"SW-Cutting Length-Outer@@@Sheet<1>@C7	891.32
7	Cutting Length-Inner	Text	"SW-Cutting Length-Inner@@@Sheet<1>@C7_	187.76
8	Cut Outs	Text	"SW-Cut Outs@@@Sheet<1>@C7_Tutorial16.S	7
9	Bends	Text	"SW-Bends@@@Sheet<1>@C7_Tutorial16.SLD	8
10	Bend Allowance	Text	"SW-Bend Allowance@@@Sheet<1>@C7_Tutor	0.32
11	MATERIAL	Text	"SW-Material@@@Sheet<1>@C7_Tutorial16.S	1060 Alloy
12	Mass	Text	"SW-Mass@@@Sheet<1>@C7_Tutorial16.SLDP	133.37
13	Description	Text	Sheet	Sheet

15. Click **OK**.
16. In the FeatureManager Design Tree, right-click on the **Cut-Extrude** feature and select **Delete**.

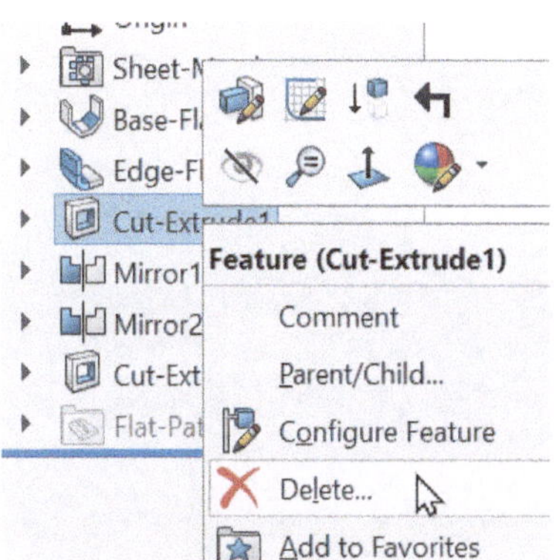

17. Check the **Delete absorbed features** option from the **Confirm Delete** dialog and click **Yes**.
18. Click and drag the bar located at the bottom of the FeatureManager design Tree. Next, release it above the two Mirror features.

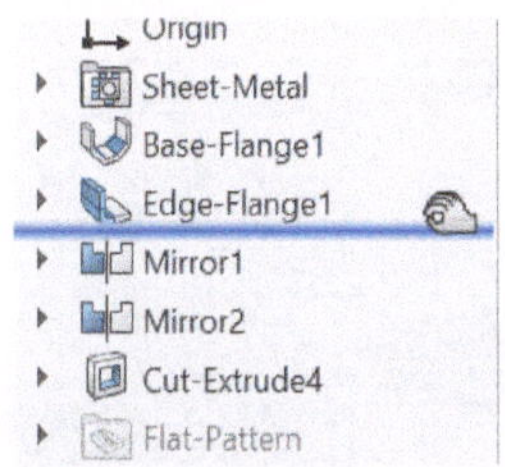

19. On the CommandManager, click **Sheet Metal > Hem**
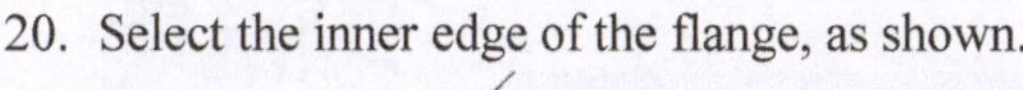.
20. Select the inner edge of the flange, as shown.

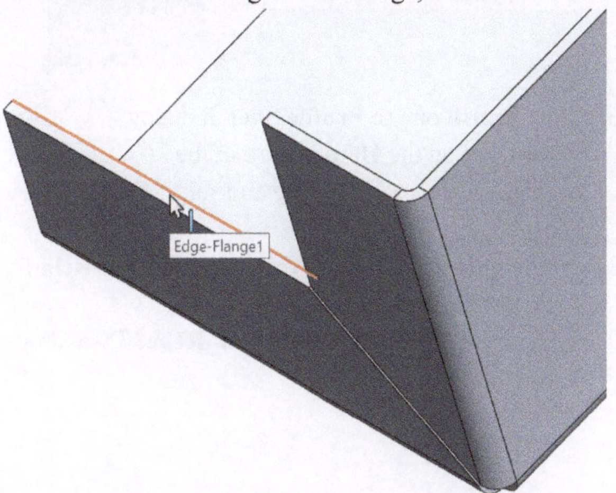

21. Click the **Open** icon under the **Type and Size** section.
22. Type **10** and **1** in the **Length** and **Gap Distance** boxes, respectively.
23. Click the **Edit Hem Width** button to open the sketch of the hem feature.
24. Click and drag the endpoint of the line toward left.

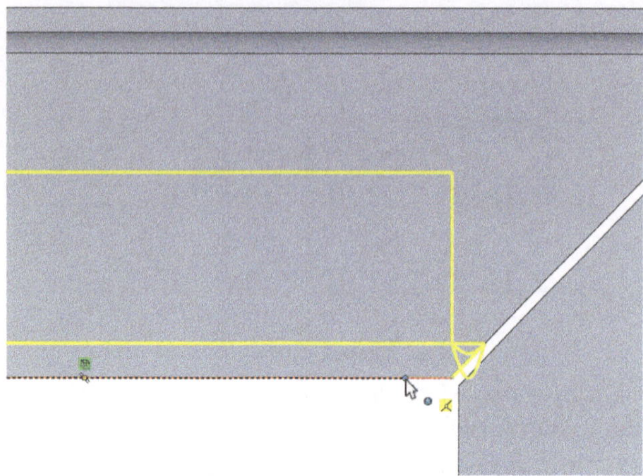

25. Add a dimension between the endpoint of the line and the vertex, as shown.

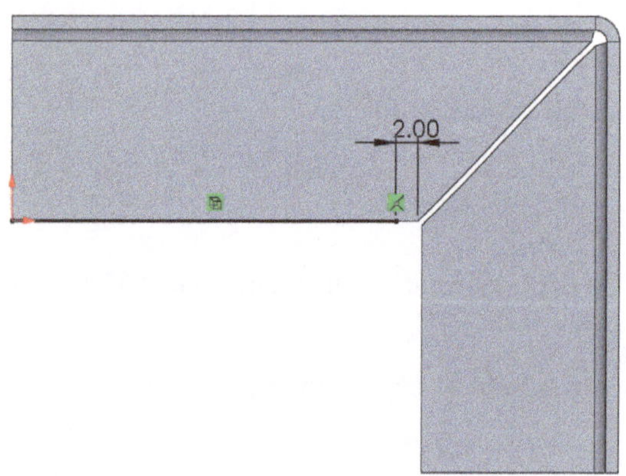

26. Click **Finish** on the **Profile Sketch** dialog.
27. Right-click on the **Hem** feature in the FeatureManager design Tree and select **Edit Feature**.
28. On the PropertyManager, check the **Custom Relief Type** option.
29. Select the **Tear** from the **Custom_Relief Type** drop-down.
30. Click **OK**.

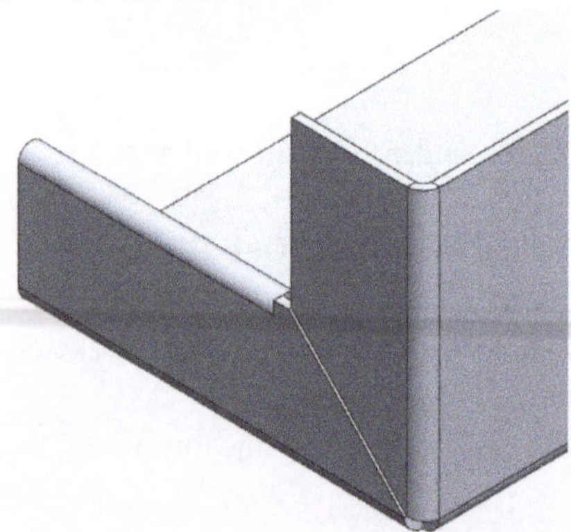

31. Click and drag the bar located at the bottom of the FeatureManager design Tree. Next, release it below the **Cut-Extrude** feature.

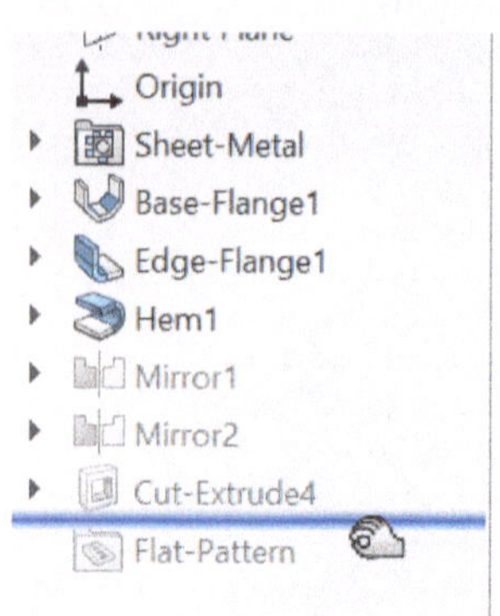

The model is updated, as shown.

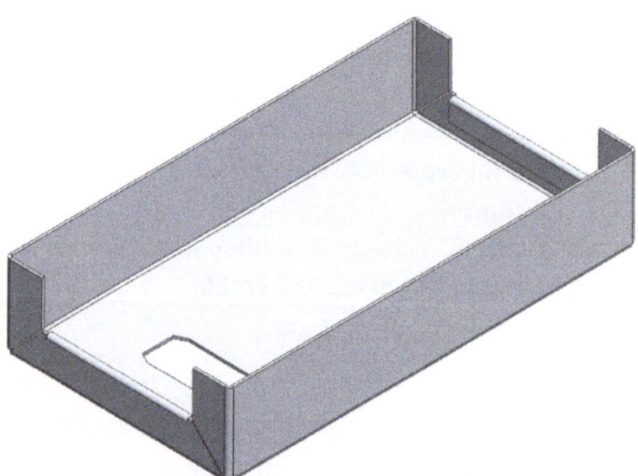

32. On the CommandManager, click **Evaluate > Mass Properties** ; on the **Mass Properties** dialog, the **Mass** is displayed as 138.13.
33. Close the **Mass Properties** dialog.
34. Save and close the file.

TUTORIAL 19

In this tutorial, you will create a **Bend Notch** feature.

1. Download and open the Bend_notch part file from the companion website.
2. On the CommandManager, click **Sheet Metal > Flatten**. The sheet metal part is flattened.
3. On the CommandManager, click **Sheet Metal > Bend Notch** .
4. Select the bend lines from the flattened sheet metal part. You can select the individual bend lines or click

the Collect all bends button to select all the bend lines of the Sheetmetal part.

5. Select the notch type from the Notch type drop-down. There are three options available: **Triangular**, **Circle**, and **Rectangular**.

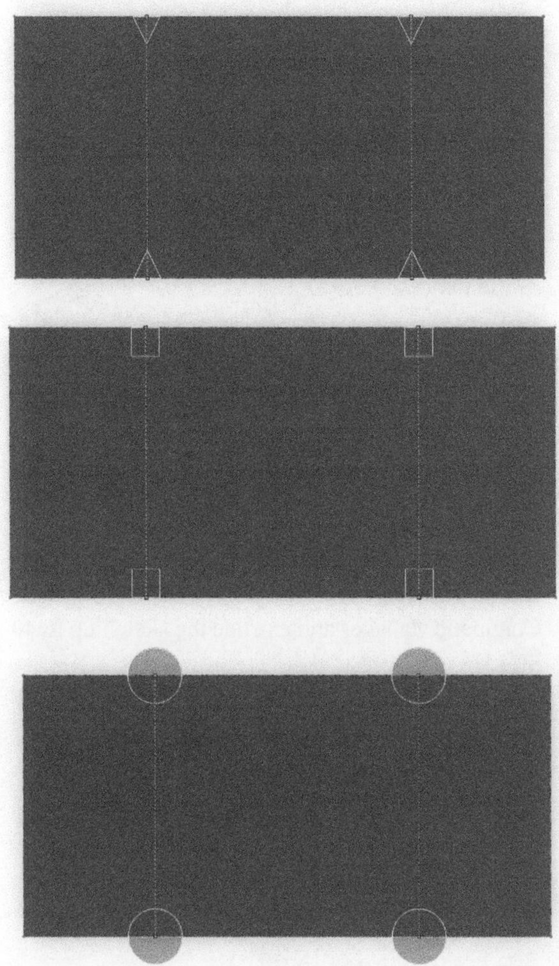

6. Specify the notch dimensions by entering values in the **Width** and **Depth** boxes, respectively.
7. Click **OK** to apply notches.

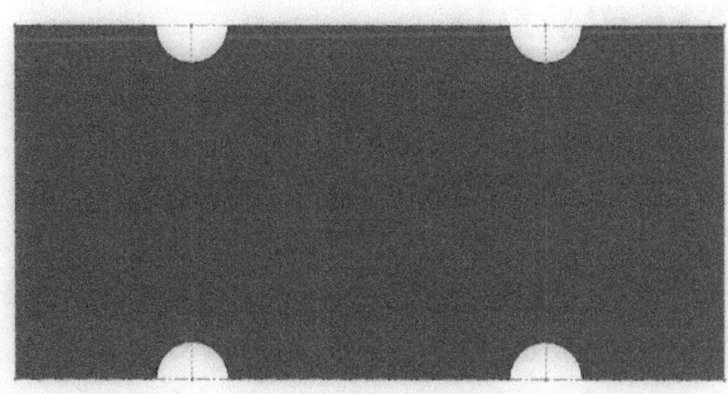

Chapter 8: Top-Down Assembly

In this chapter, you will learn to

- Create a top-down assembly
- Insert fasteners using Toolbox
- Create advanced mates

TUTORIAL 1

In this tutorial, you will create the model shown in the figure. You use a top-down assembly approach to create this model.

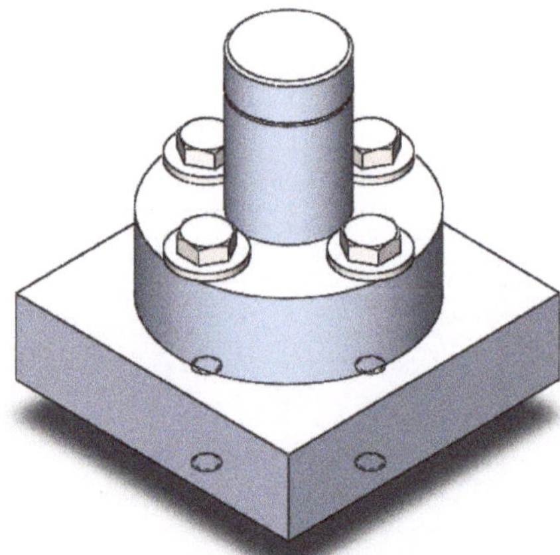

Creating a New Assembly File

1. Click the **New** icon on the Quick Access Toolbar, select the **Assembly** icon, and click **OK**.

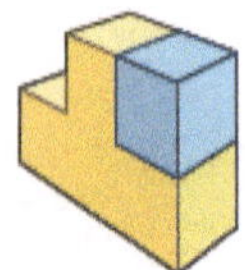

2. Click **Cancel** on the **Begin Assembly** PropertyManager.

Creating a component in the Assembly

In a top-down assembly approach, you create assembly components directly in the assembly by using the **New Part** tool.

1. On the CommandManager, click **Assembly > Insert Components > New Part**.

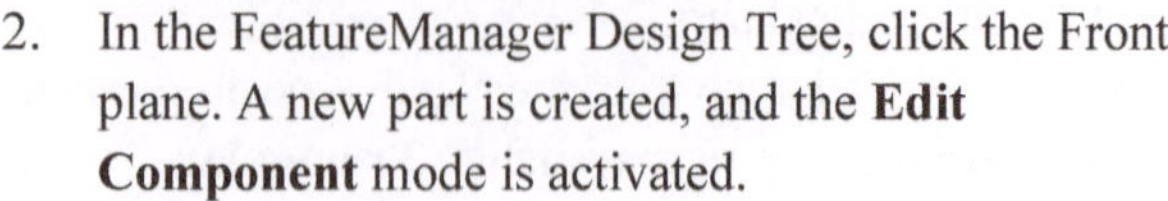

2. In the FeatureManager Design Tree, click the Front plane. A new part is created, and the **Edit Component** mode is activated.
3. Click **Exit Sketch**.
4. Click **Sketch > Sketch** on the CommandManager and select the Top plane from the FeatureManager Design Tree.
5. Create the sketch, as shown below.

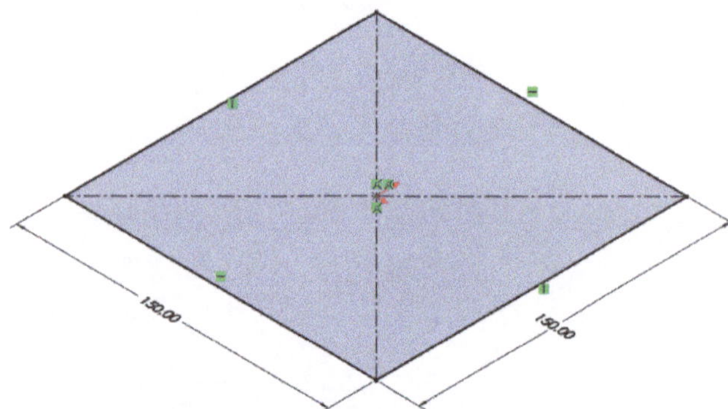

6. Click **Exit Sketch**.
7. Click **Features > Extruded Boss/Base** on the CommandManager and extrude the sketch up to **40 mm**.

8. Start a sketch on the top face and draw a circle of **50 mm** in diameter.

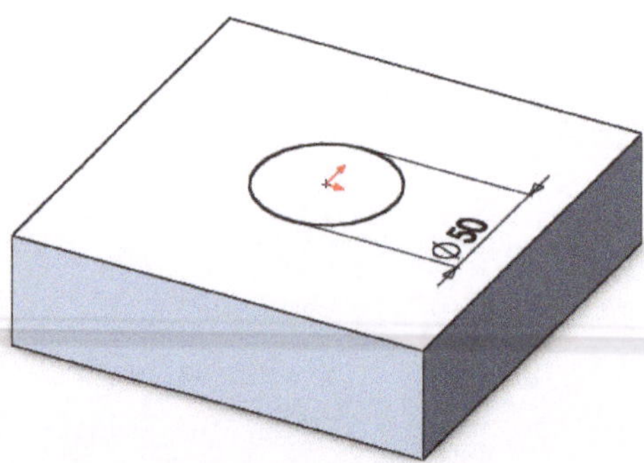

9. Click **Exit Sketch**

10. Extrude the sketch up to 95 mm distance.

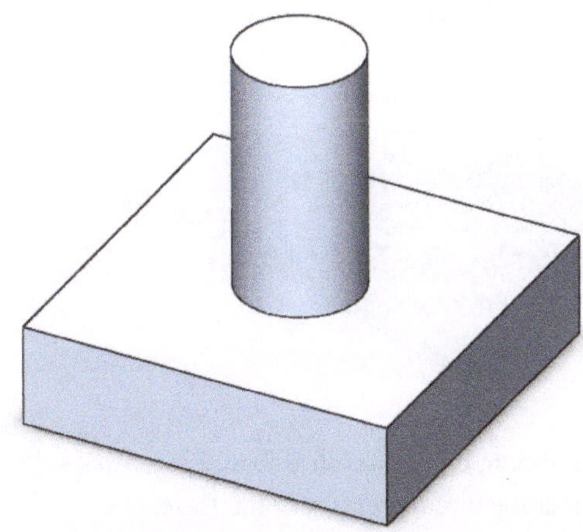

11. On the CommandManager, click **Features > Hole Wizard** .
12. On the PropertyManager, click the **Legacy Hole** icon.
13. On the PropertyManager, select **Type > Counterbored**.
14. In the **Section Dimensions** section, modify the dimensions as shown.

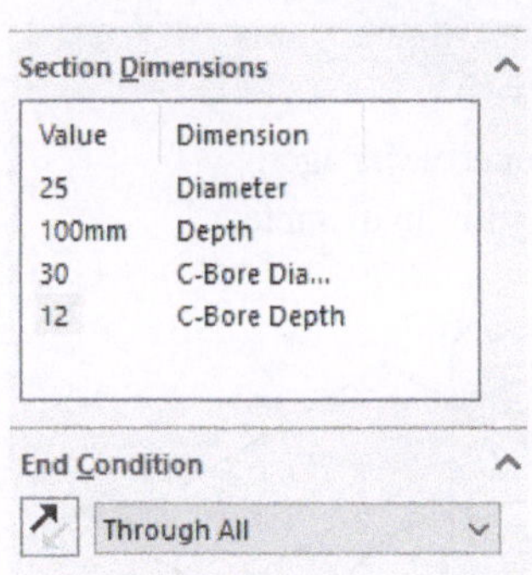

15. Set the **End Condition** to **Through All**.
16. Click the **Positions** tab and click on the top face of the second feature.
17. Select the origin point of the 3D sketch.

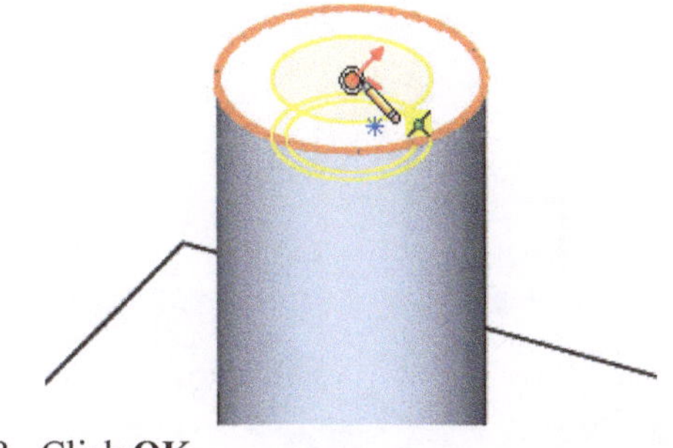

18. Click **OK**.

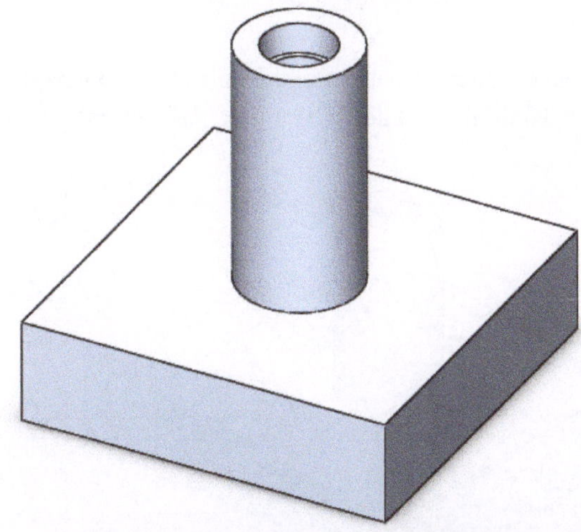

19. Create a through hole of 12 mm diameter on the first feature.

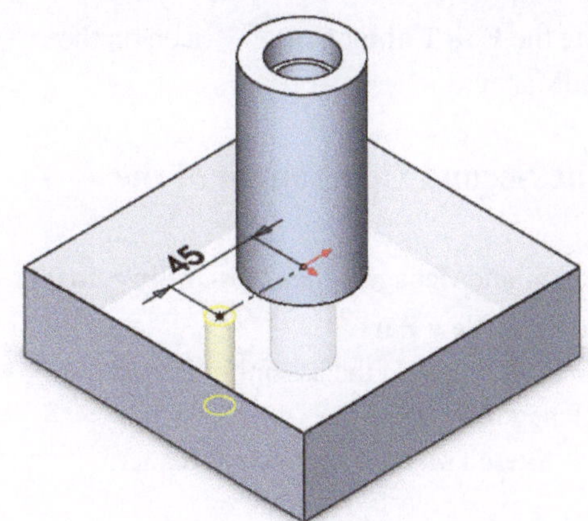

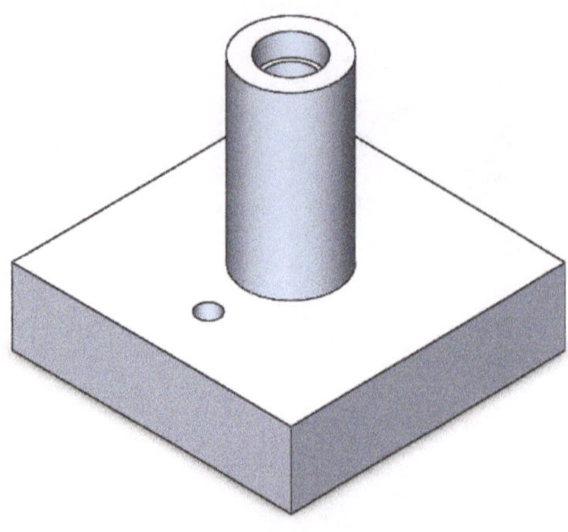

20. Create a circular pattern of the hole (refer to Chapter 6 > Tutorial 4 to know about Circular pattern).

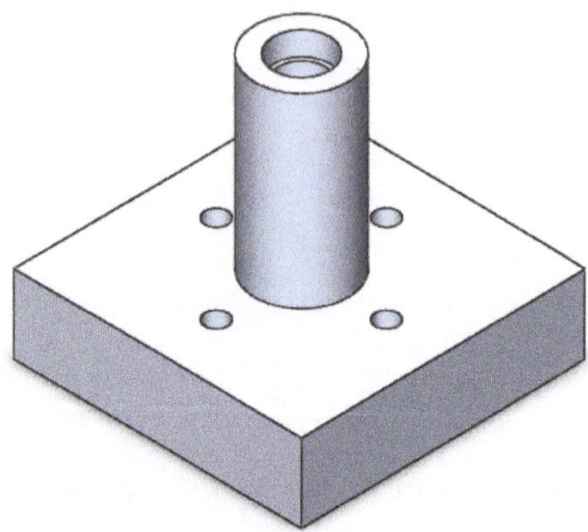

21. Deactivate the **Edit Component** icon on the CommandManager.

Creating the Second Component of the Assembly

1. On the CommandManager, click **Assembly > Insert Components > New Part** .
2. Select the Front plane of the assembly from the FeatureManager Design Tree.
3. Click **Exit Sketch** on the CommandManager.
4. Click **Sketch > Sketch** on the CommandManager.
5. Select the top face of the Base.

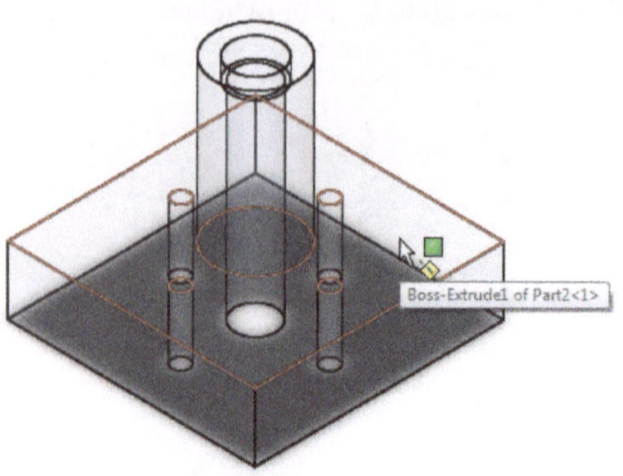

6. On the ribbon, click **Sketch > Convert Entities**  and select the circular edges of the Base.

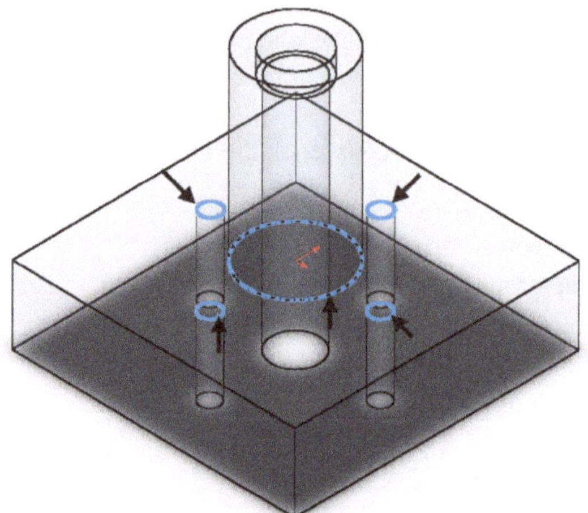

7. Click **OK** on the PropertyManager.
8. Draw a circle of 120 mm in diameter.

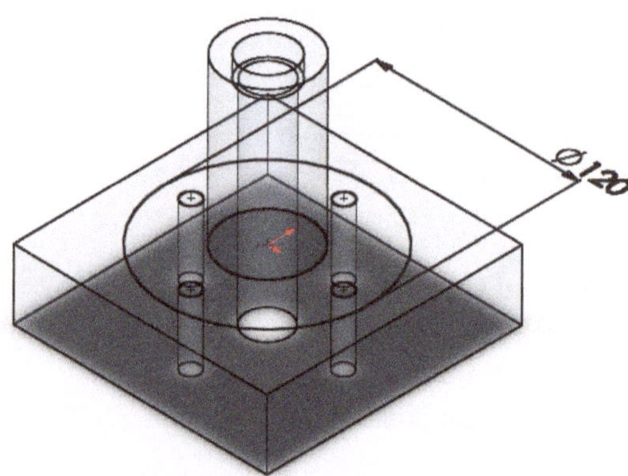

9. Click **Exit Sketch**.
10. Click the outer circle, right-click, click the down-arrows located at the bottom of the shortcut menu, and select **Contour Select Tool**.

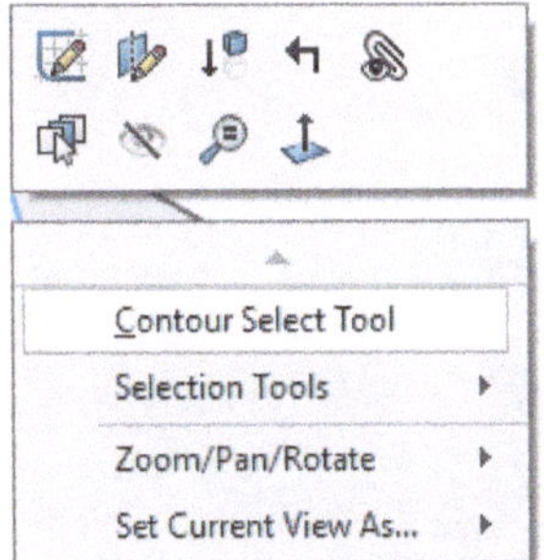

11. Click in the region enclosed by the sketch.

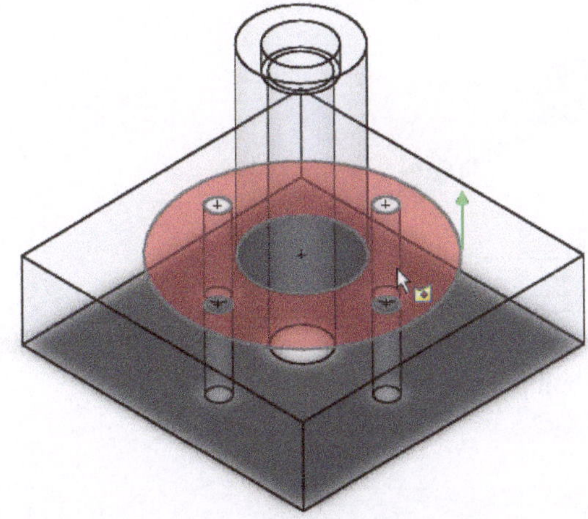

12. Activate the **Extruded Boss/Base** tool and extrude the sketch up to 40.

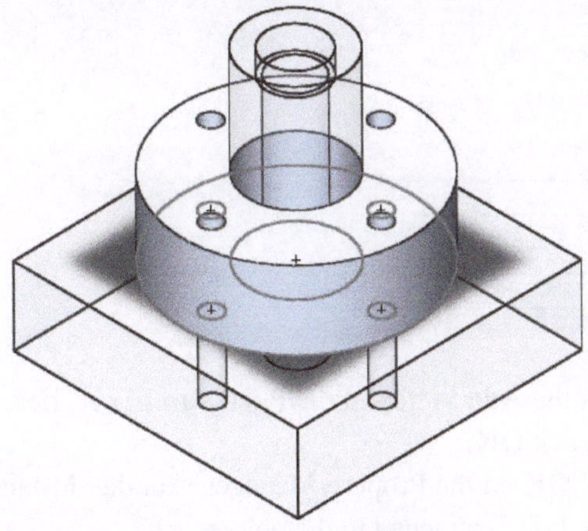

13. Exit the **Edit Component** Mode.

Creating the third Component of the Assembly

1. On the CommandManager, click **Assembly > Insert Components > New Part**.
2. Select the Front plane of the assembly from the FeatureManager Design Tree.
3. Draw a sketch, as shown in the figure.

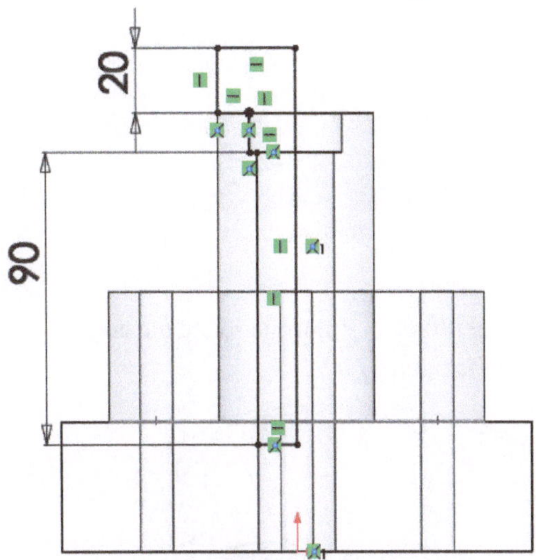

4. Click **Exit Sketch**.
5. Activate the **Revolved Base/Boss** tool and revolve the sketch. (refer to **Chapter 2 > Tutorial 2** to learn about the Revolved Base/Boss tool)

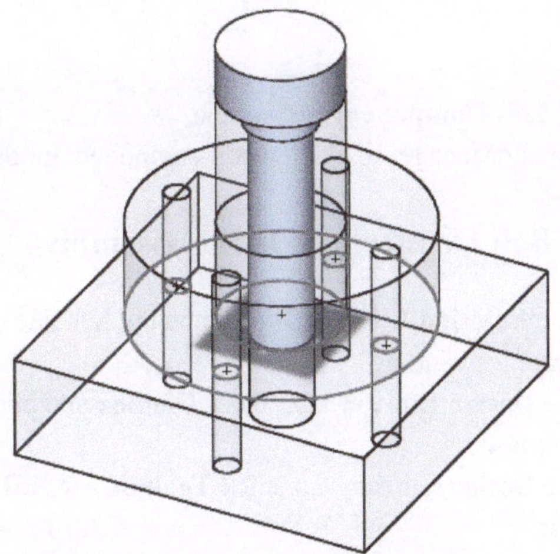

6. Activate the **Chamfer** tool (on the CommandManager, click **Features > Fillet drop-down > Chamfer**) and chamfer the edges, as shown in figure.

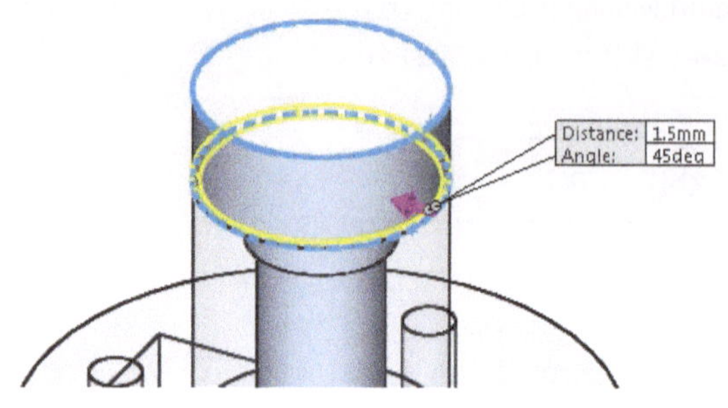

7. Activate the **Fillet** tool and round the edges, as shown in the figure.

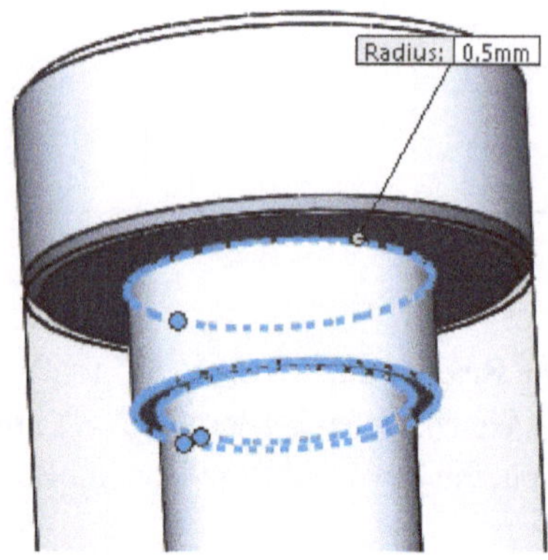

8. Click **Edit Component** on the CommandManager to exit the edit component mode.

Adding Bolt Connections to the assembly

1. Click the **Design Library** tab on the left side of the graphics window.
2. On the **Design Library** tab, select **Toolbox** and click **Add in now**.
3. On the **Design Library** tab, click **Toolbox > ANSI Metric**.
4. Under the **ANSI Metric** folder, click **Bolts and Screws > Hex Head**.
5. Click **Heavy Hex Bolt-ANSI B18.2.3.6M** and drag it into the graphics window.

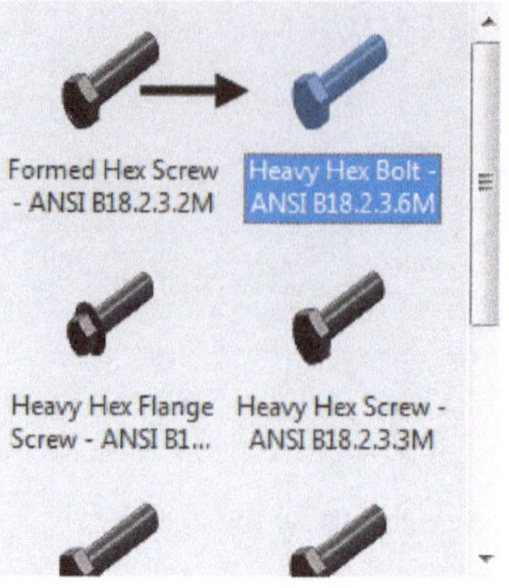

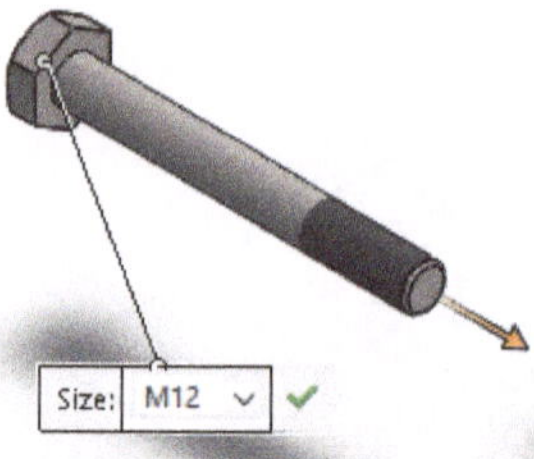

6. On the **Configure Component** PropertyManager, set the bolt properties as shown.

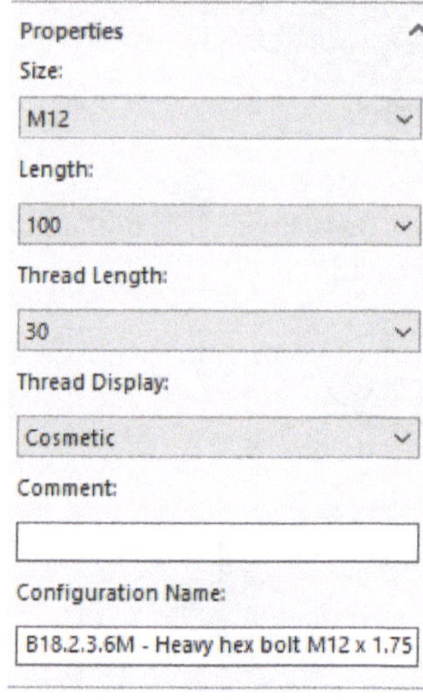

7. Click the **Add** button in the **Part Number** section and click **OK**.
8. Click **OK** on the PropertyManager. Another instance of the bolt is attached to the pointer.

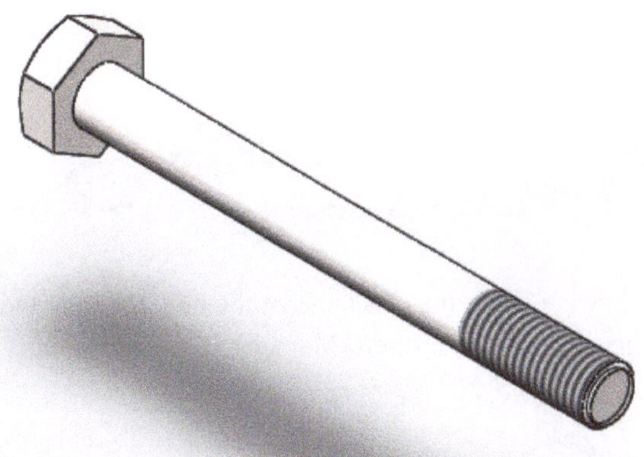

9. Click **Cancel** × to stop inserting more bolts.
10. On the **Design Library** tab, click **Washer > Plain Washers**.
11. Click the **Regular Flat Washer** and drag it into the graphics window.
12. Set the washer size to **M12** and click the **Add** button under the **Part Numbers** section of the PropertyManager.
13. Click **OK** on the **Part Number** dialog.
14. Click **OK** and **Cancel**.

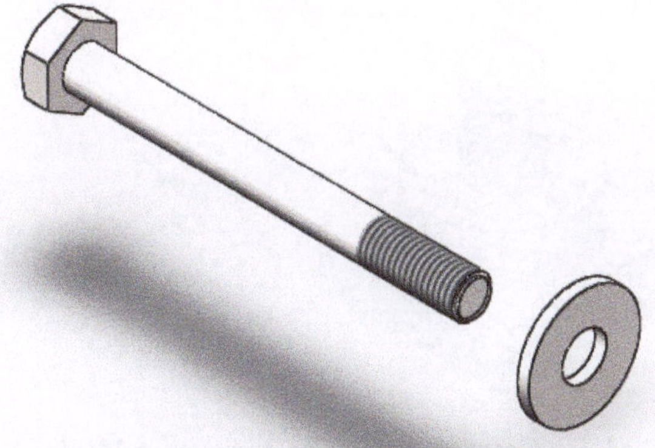

15. On the **Design Library** tab, under **ANSI Metric**, click **Nuts > Hex Nuts**.
16. Click and drag **Hex Heavy Nut** into the graphics window.
17. On the **Configure Component** PropertyManager, set the nut properties as shown.

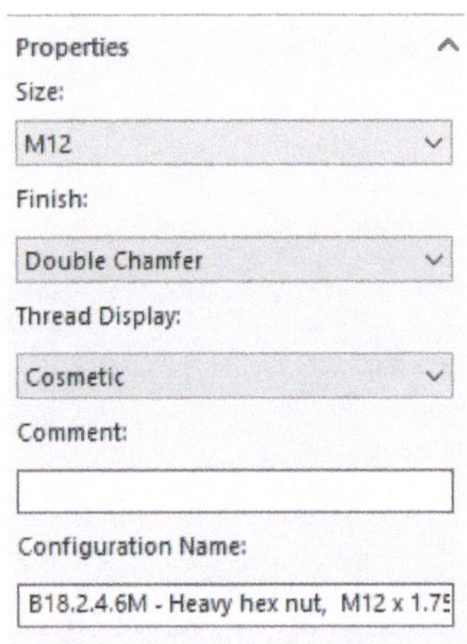

18. Click the **Add** button under the **Part Numbers** section of the PropertyManager.
19. Click **OK** on the **Part Number** dialog.
20. Click **OK** and **Cancel**.

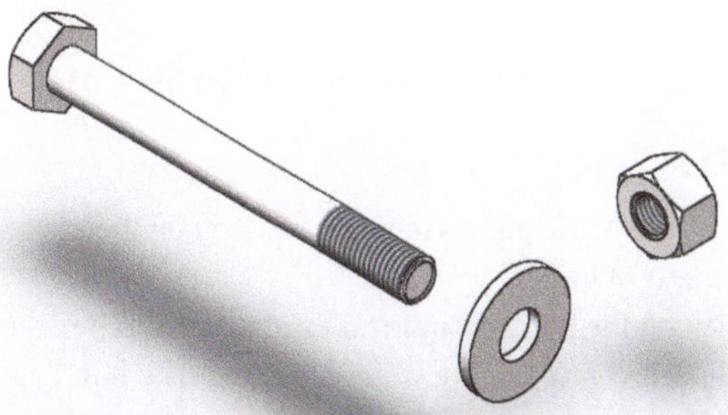

21. On the CommandManager, click **Assembly > Insert Components > New Assembly** . A new sub-assembly is inserted into the assembly.
22. In the FeatureManager Design Tree, click and drag the bolt, nut and washer into the sub-assembly.

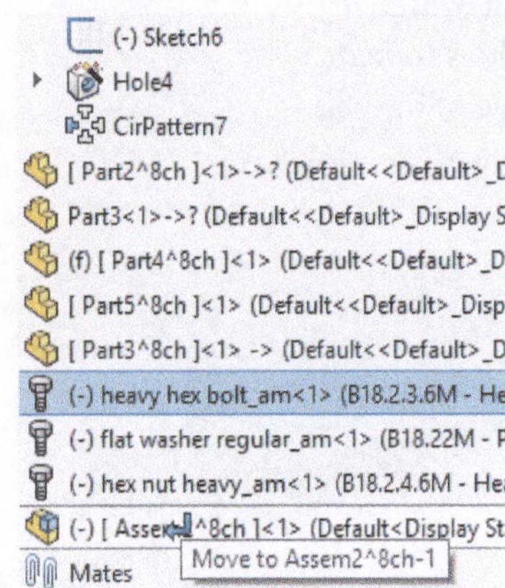

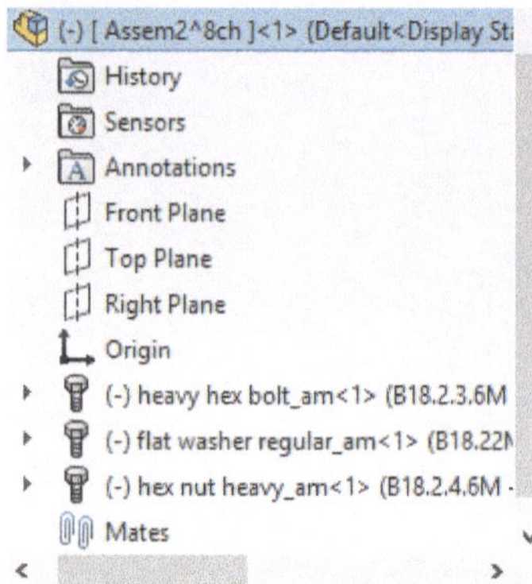

23. Right click on the sub-assembly and select **Open Subassembly**. The Sub-assembly is opened in another window.

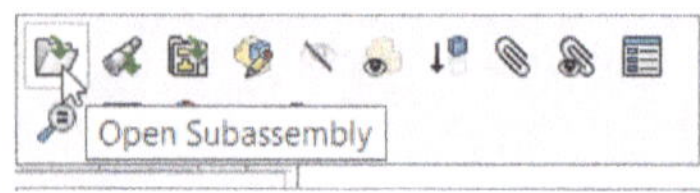

24. On the CommandManager, click **Assembly > Mate** .
25. Click the **Multiple mate mode** icon on the PropertyManager.
26. Click on the bolt's cylindrical face, and then click the cylindrical faces of the washer and nut. The bolt face is selected as a common mate entity.

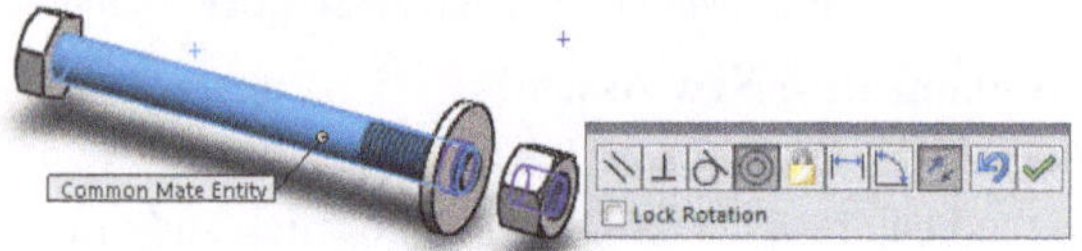

27. Click **Add/Finish Mate**.
28. Click in the **Entities to mate.**
29. Select the flat face of the bolt.
30. Select the flat face of the washer.

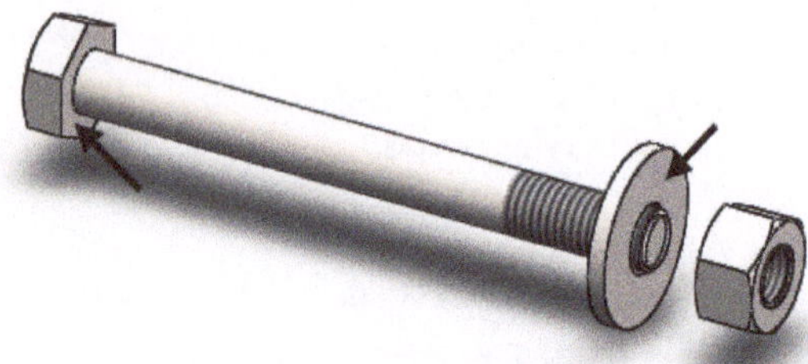

31. Click **Flip Mate Alignment** , and then click **OK** on the **SOLIDWORKS** dialog.
32. Click **Add/Finish Mate** .

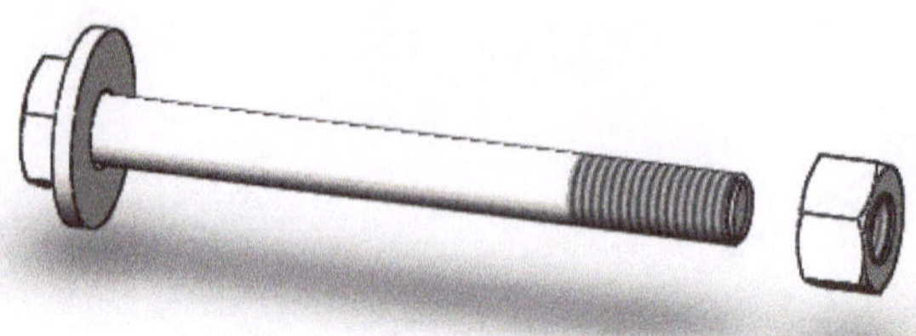

33. Likewise, align the end faces of the bolt and nut, and click **OK** on the PropertyManager.

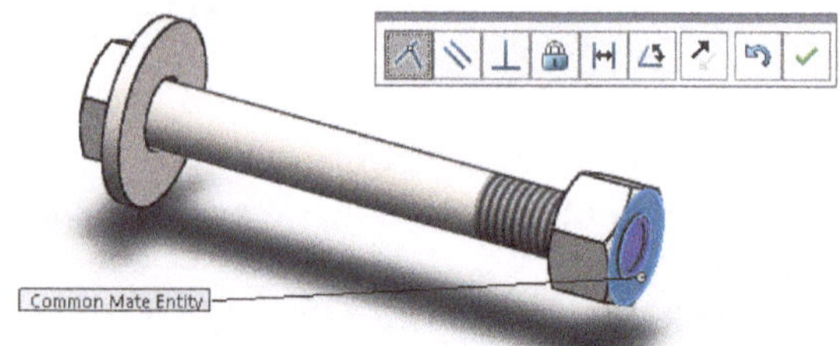

34. Save and close the sub-assembly.
35. On the CommandManager, click **Assembly > Mate** .
36. Click on the flat face for the washer and the part with holes.

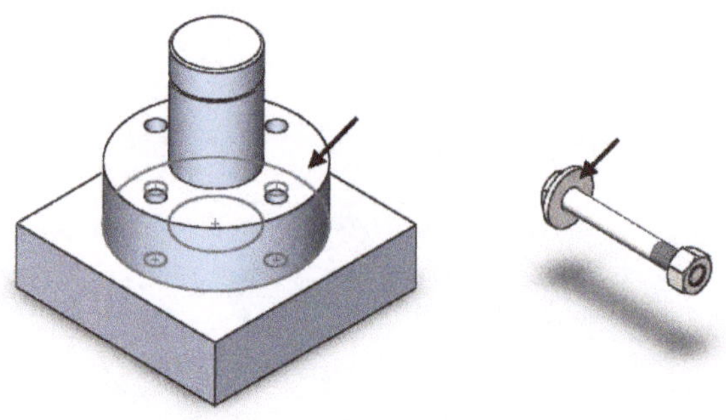

37. Click the **Coincident** icon and click **Add/Finish Mate** .
38. Click the Cylindrical face of the bolt and circular edge of the hole as shown.

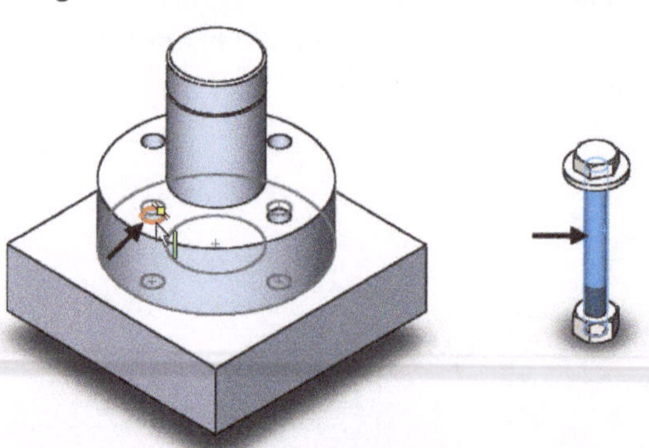

39. Click the **Concentric** icon, check the **Lock**

Rotation option, and click **Add/Finish Mate** .

40. Click **OK** on the PropertyManager.

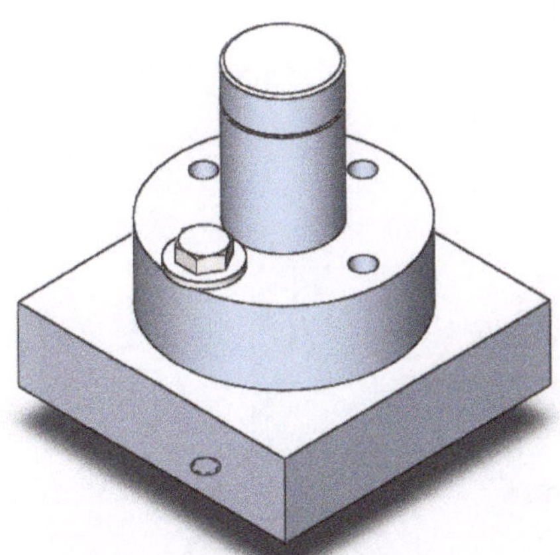

Patterning components in an assembly

1. On the CommandManager, click **Assembly > Linear Component Pattern > Pattern Driven Component Pattern** .
2. Select the sub-assembly from the FeatureManager Design Tree.
3. On the **Pattern Driven** PropertyManager, click in the **Driving Feature or Component** box.
4. Select the CircularPattern of the first component from the FeatureManager Design Tree.

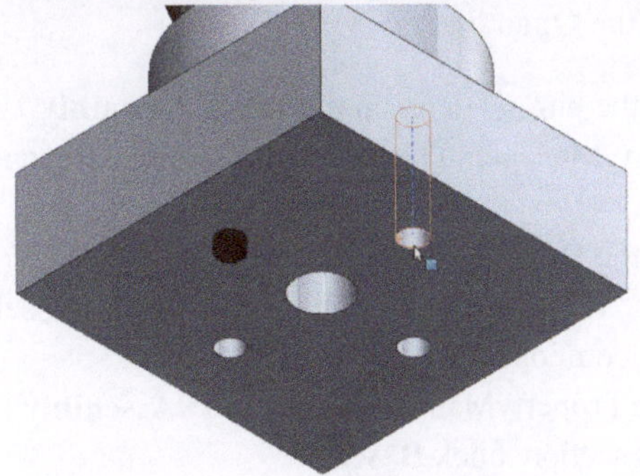

5. Click **OK** on the PropertyManager.

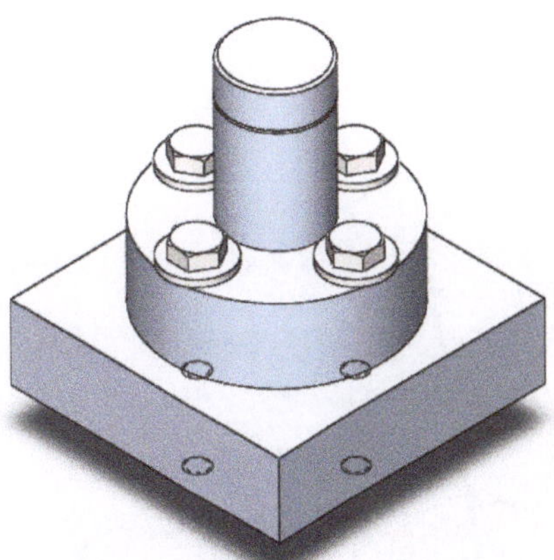

Sectioning an Assembly with Transparency

1. On the View Heads Up Toolbar, click the **Section View** icon.
2. On the PropertyManager, select **Zonal** from the **Section Method** section.
3. On the PropertyManager, select Front Plane from the **Section 1** section.

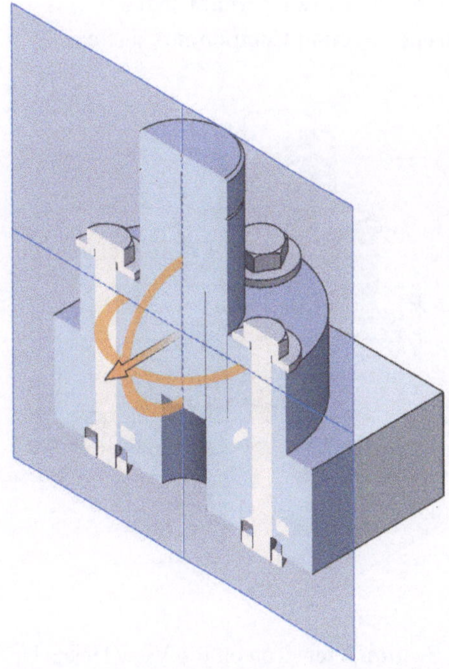

4. On the PropertyManager, check the **Transparency Section Components** section.
5. Select the components to turn transparent, as shown.

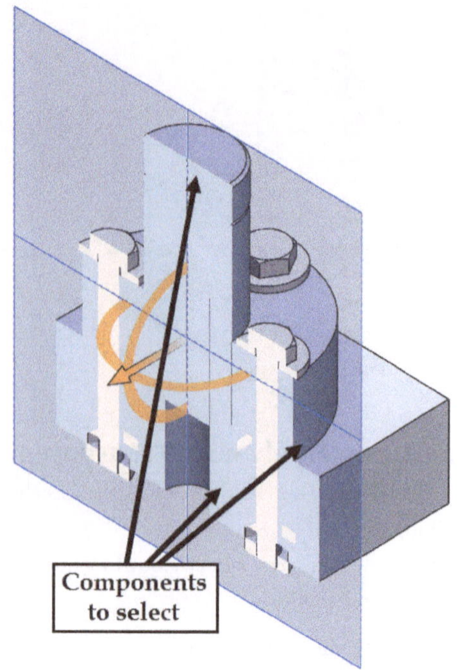

6. Adjust the **Section Transparency** in the **Transparency Section Components** section.
7. Click **OK**.

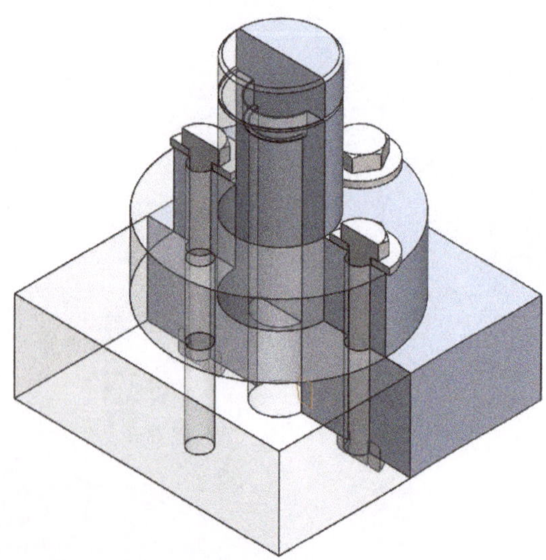

8. Click the **Section View** icon on the View Heads Up Toolbar.
9. Click the **Save** icon on the Quick Access Toolbar.
10. Click **Save All** on the **Save Modified Documents** dialog.
11. Type Ch8_tutorial1 in the **File name** box and click **Save**.
12. Select **Save internally (inside the assembly)**, and then click **OK**.

TUTORIAL 2

In this tutorial, you create a slider-crank mechanism by applying advanced mates.

1. Create **Slider Crank Assembly** folder.
2. Download the part files of the assembly from the companion website. Next, save the files in the **Slider Crank Assembly** folder.
3. Start a new assembly file.
4. Close the **Open** dialog.
5. Click the pin icon on the **Begin Assembly** PropertyManager. This keeps the PropertyManager active.
6. Click the **Browse** button on the PropertyManager.
7. Browse to the **Slider Crank Assembly** folder, select all the components, and click **Open**.
8. On the PropertyManager, in the **Part/Assembly to Insert** section, click **Base**.
9. Click in the assembly window to position the Base component.
10. Likewise, position the other components in the assembly window.
11. Click **OK** on the PropertyManager.

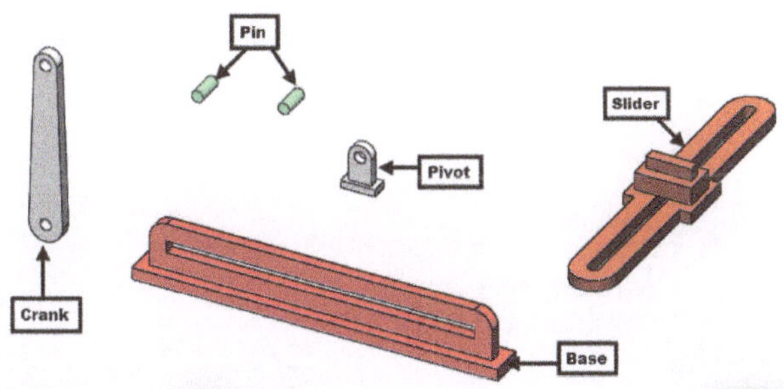

Creating Smart Mates

1. Press the Alt key and click on the face of the slider, as shown.

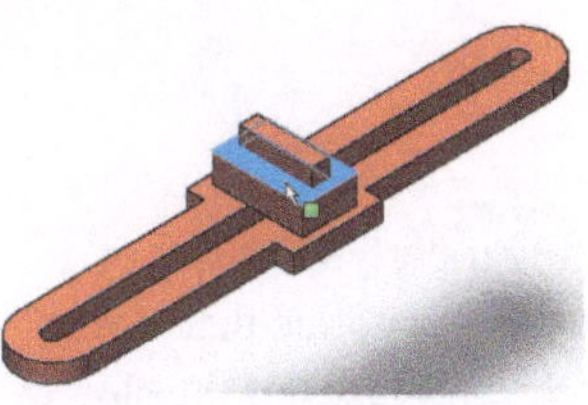

2. Keep the Alt key pressed and drag the component onto the face of the Base as shown.

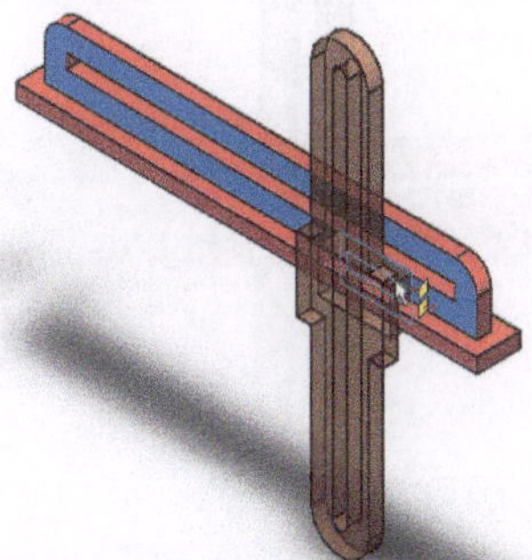

3. Release the left mouse button and notice that the Mates toolbar appears with the **Coincident** icon selected.
4. Click **Add/Finish Mate** to create the **Coincident** mate between the two faces.
5. Drag the slider up and rotate the view as shown.

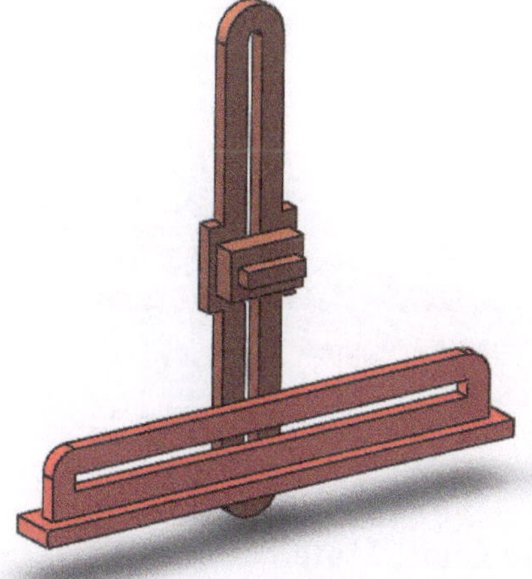

6. Click the face of the slider.

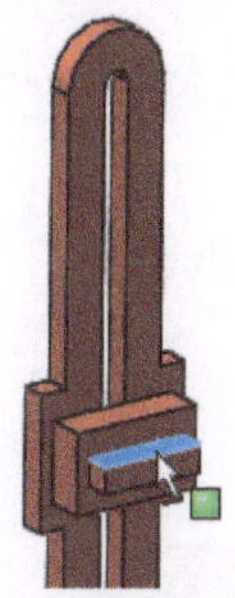

7. Press and hold the Alt key and drag the slider onto the face of the Base as shown.

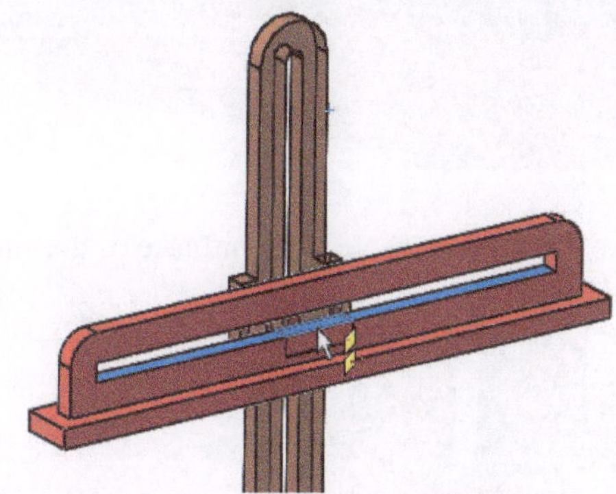

8. Click the **Flip Mate Alignment** icon.
9. Click **Add/Finish Mate.**
10. Click and drag the slider and notice that it can intersect with the base.

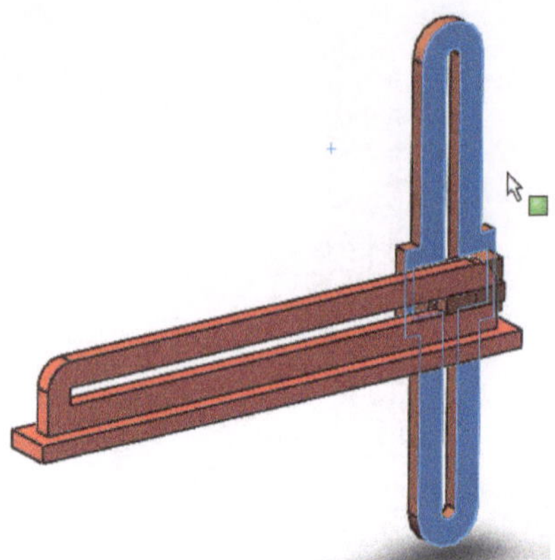

Creating the Limit Mate

1. On the CommandManager, click **Assembly > Mate** .
2. On the PropertyManager, click the **Advanced** tab and click the **Distance** icon.
3. Select the end face of the Base as shown.

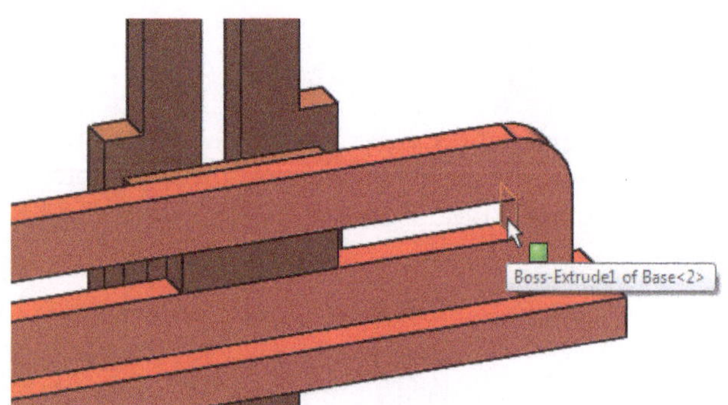

4. Rotate the view and select the end face of the slider as shown.

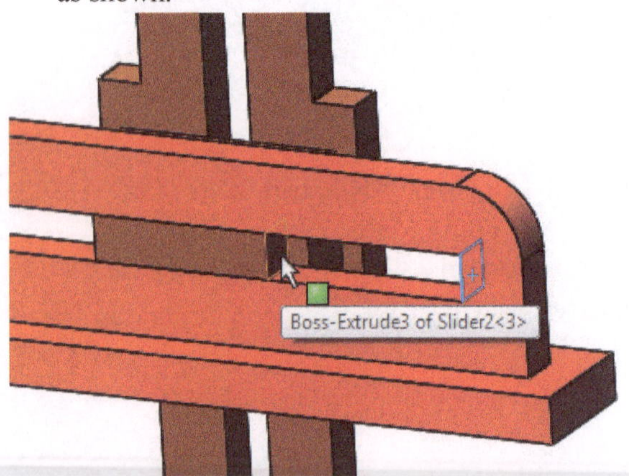

5. Set the **Distance** value to 1 mm.
6. Set the **Maximum Value** and **Minimum Value** to 459 and 1, respectively.

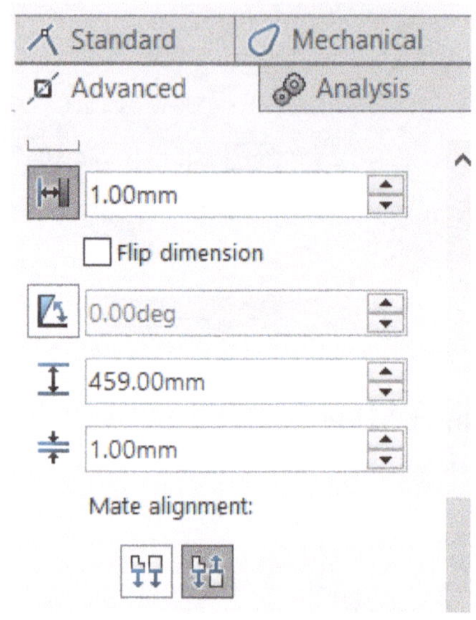

7. Click **OK** twice on the PropertyManager.
8. Click and drag the slider and notice that it is constrained between the end faces of the slot.

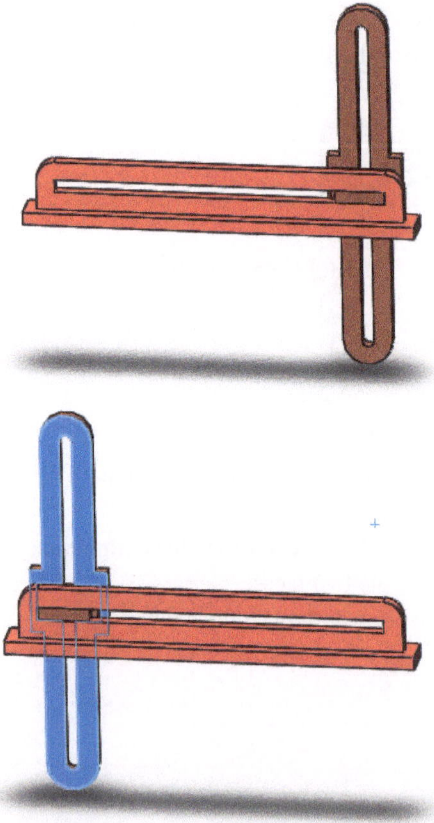

Creating the Slot Mate

1. On the CommandManager, click **Assembly > Mate** .
2. On the PropertyManager, click the **Mechanical** tab

and click the **Slot** icon.

3. Set the **Constraint** to **Free**.
4. Select the cylindrical face of the pin and the flat face of the slider slot as shown.

5. Click **OK** on the PropertyManager.
6. Click the **Standard** tab and click the **Coincident** icon.
7. Select the flat faces of the pin and slider as shown.

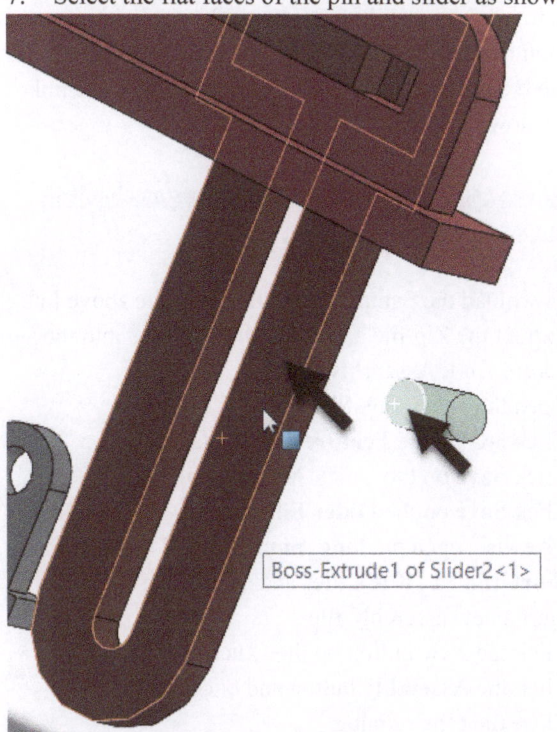

8. Click **Add/Finish Mate**, and then click **OK**.
9. Click and drag the pin and notice that it is constrained along the length of the slot.

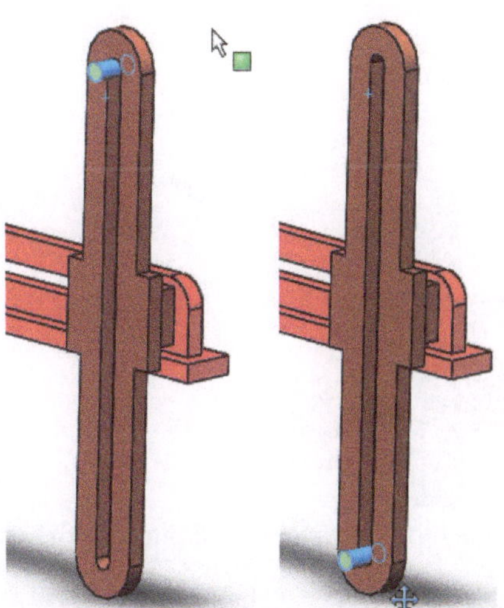

10. Press the Alt key, click and drag the upper hole of the crank.

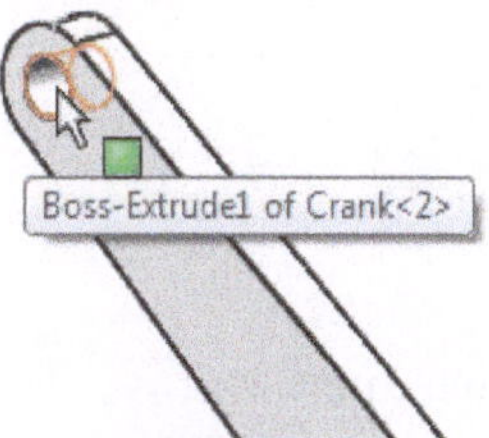

11. Release the pointer onto the cylindrical of the pin.

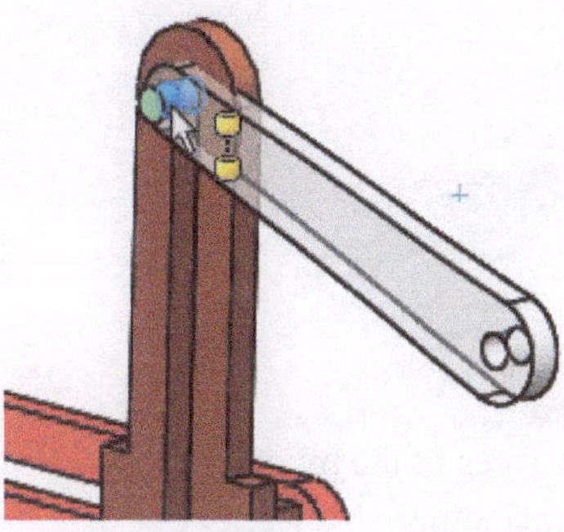

12. Click **Add/Finish Mate** to add the **Concentric** mate between the hole and pin.
13. Use the **Mate** command to add the **Coincident** mate between the end face of the pin and flat face of the crank.

14. Assemble the other instance of the pin with the crank.

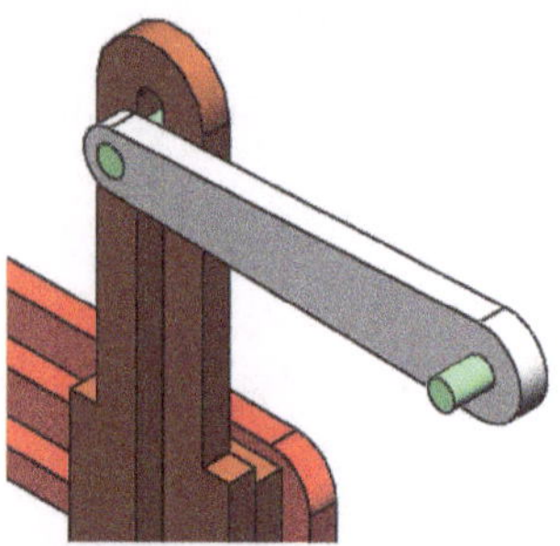

15. Assemble the pivot with the pin.

16. Make the bottom faces of the pivot and base coincident with each other.

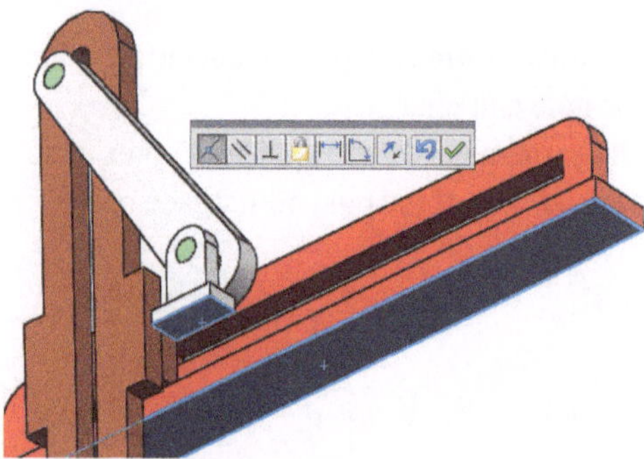

17. Make the Right planes of the pivot and base coincident.

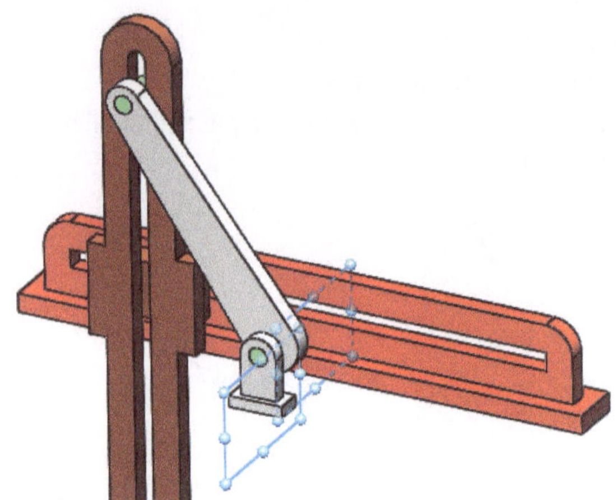

18. Click and drag the crank and notice that the slider moves along the slot.
19. Save and close the assembly and its parts.

TUTORIAL 3 (CSWA Assembly Modeling Sample Question)

In this tutorial, you will create assembly given in Question number 7 and 8 in the CSWA mechanical design Sample Exam. You can download the PDF from the link given below.

https://www.solidworks.com/certifications/mechanical-design-cswa-mechanical-design

1. Download the Sample Exam file from the above link.
2. Extract the Zip file and move the part files into the **Chain Link Assembly** folder.
3. Open the chain_link.SLDPRT
4. Click **NO** on the **FeatureWorks** dialog.
5. Click **Save** on the Quick Access Toolbar.
6. Click **Save** on the **Older File** dialog
7. Likewise, open the **long_pin.SLDPRT** and **short_pin.SLDPRT** files and save them.
8. Start a new assembly file.
9. Click the **New** button on the Quick Access Toolbar.
10. Click the **Assembly** button and click **OK**.
11. Close the **Open** dialog.
12. Click the pin icon on the **Begin Assembly** PropertyManager. This keeps the PropertyManager active.
13. Click the **Browse** button on the PropertyManager.
14. Browse to the **Chain Link Assembly** folder, select **long_pin**, and click **Open**.
15. On the PropertyManager, in the **Part/Assembly to Insert** section, click **long_pin**.

16. Click in the assembly window to position the **long_pin** component.
17. Click the **Browse** button on the PropertyManager.
18. Select the **chain_link** part file and click **Open**.
19. Select the **SOLIDWORKS Colors/Textures Only** option on the **Convert Appearances** dialog and click **OK**.
20. Click in the graphics window four times to place four intances of the chain_link part file.
21. Click **Cancel** on the PropertyManager.

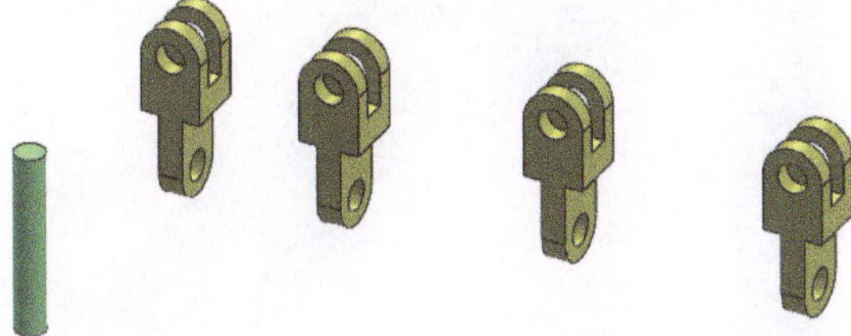

22. At the bottom of the window, set the **Unit System** to **MMGS**.

23. On the CommandManager, click **Assembly > Mate** .
24. Select the circular faces of the **chain_link** and the **long_pin**, as shown.

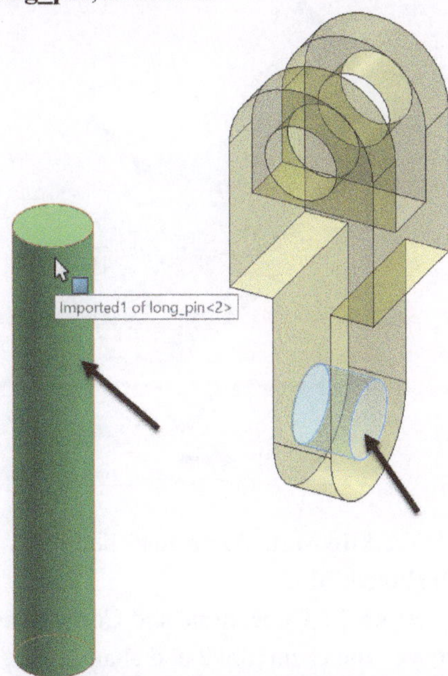

25. Click the **Concentric** icon, and then click **Add/Finish Mate**.
26. Click on the top face of the **chain_link** and the **long_pin**, as shown.

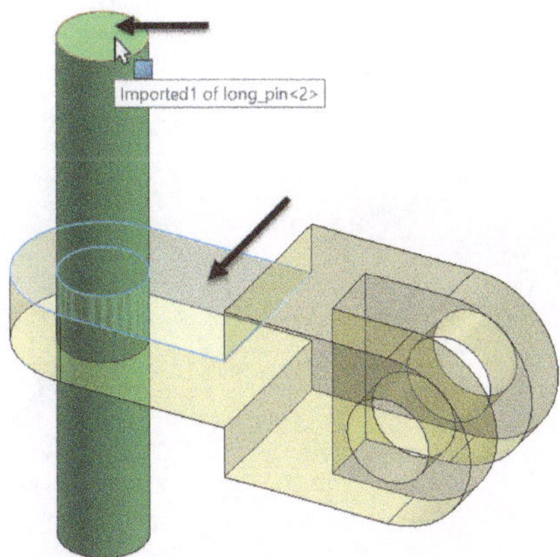

27. Click the **Coincident** icon and then click **Add/Finish Mate**.
28. Select anyone of the Front orienting faces of the **chain_link**.

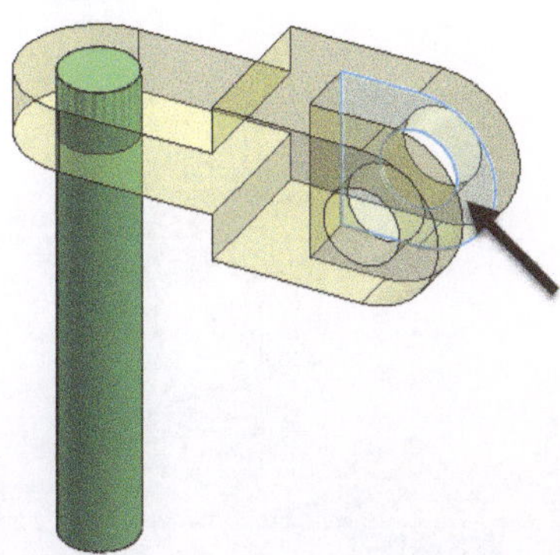

29. Expand the FeatureManager Design Tree and select the Front plane.

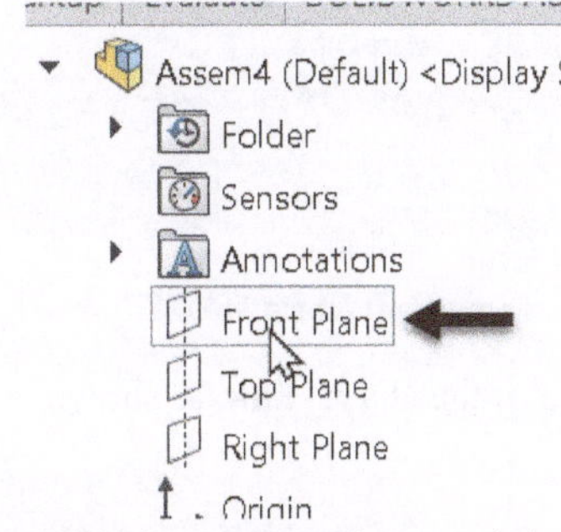

30. Click the **Parallel** icon, and then click **Add/Finish Mate**.
31. Select the circular faces of the two **chain_link**, as shown.

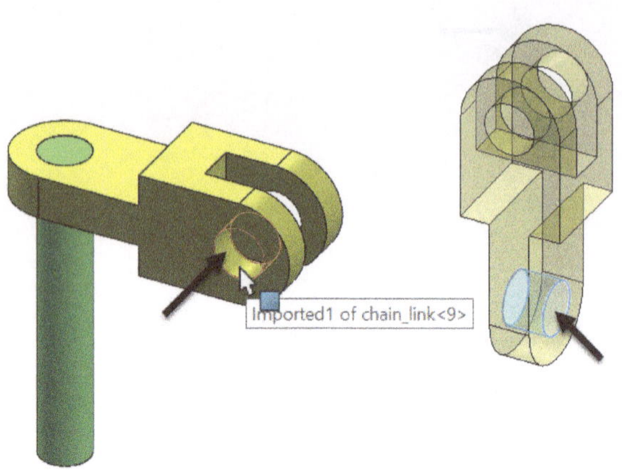

32. Click the **Concentric** icon, and then click **Add/Finish Mate**.
33. Click the right mouse button on the top face of the first **chain_link** part file and select **Select Other**.

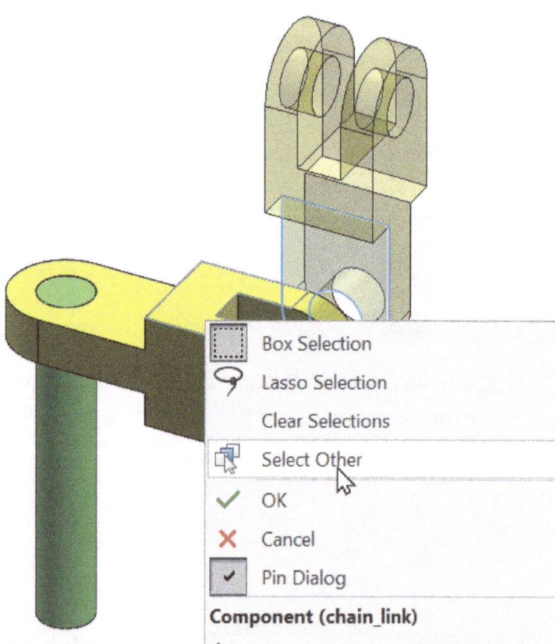

34. Click the inner face of the **chain_link**, as shown.

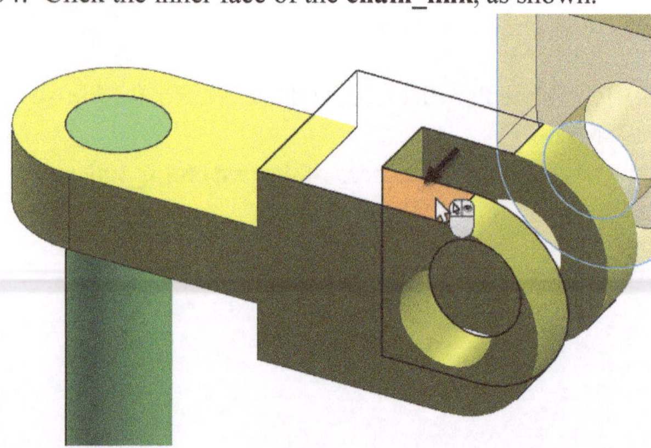

35. Click the **Coincident** icon and click **Add/Finish Mate**.
36. Click on the flat face on the second **chain_link** that is oriented toward right.
37. Press and hold the left mouse button and drag the selected face downward; the **chain_link** is rotated in the downward direction.

38. Select the faces of the chain_links that are oriented to top.
39. Click the **Angle** icon and type **25** in the **Angle** box.
40. On the PropertyManager, uncheck the **Flip dimension** option.

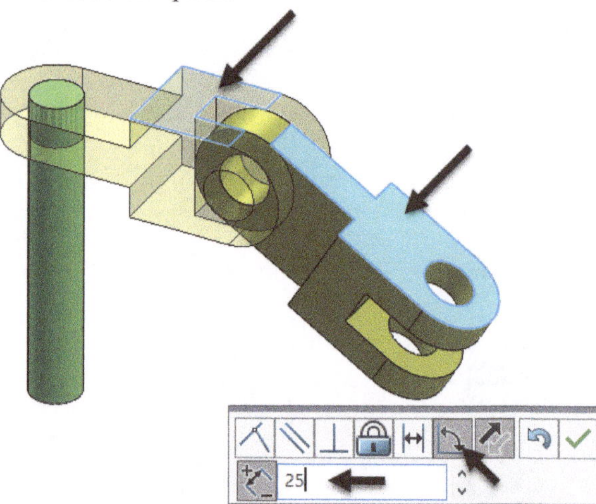

41. Deactivate the **Flip Mate Alignment** button.
42. Click **Add/Finish Mate**.
43. Likewise, create the **Concentric** and **Coincident** mates between the chain_link2 and chain_link3, as shown.

44. Rotate the model and select the faces of the two chain_links, as shown.

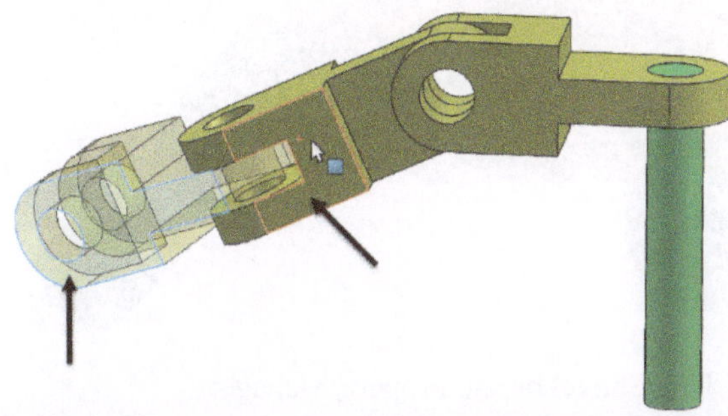

45. Click the **Angle** icon and type **125** in the **Angle** box.
46. Uncheck the **Flip dimension** option.
47. Click **Add/Finish Mate**.

48. Likewise, create the **Concentric** and **Coincident** mates between the chain_link3 and chain_link4, as shown.

49. Select the faces of the two chain_links, as shown.

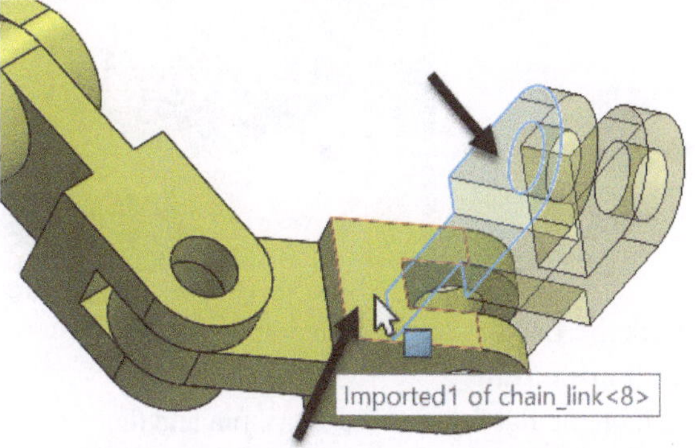

50. Click the **Angle** icon and type **130** in the **Angle** box.
51. Click **Add/Finish Mate**.

52. Click **Close** on the PropertyManager.
53. On the CommandManager, click **Assembly > Insert Components** .
54. Close the **Open** dialog.
55. Click the pin icon on the **Begin Assembly** PropertyManager. This keeps the PropertyManager active.
56. Click the **Browse** button on the PropertyManager.
57. Browse to the **Chain Link Assembly** folder, select **short_pin**, and click **Open**.
58. Select the **SOLIDWORKS Colors/Textures Only** option on the **Convert Appearances** dialog and click **OK**.
59. Click in the graphics window three times to place

three intances of the short_pin part file.

60. Click **Cancel** on the PropertyManager.
61. On the CommandManager, click **Assembly > Mate** .
62. Select the cylindrical face of the short_pin.
63. Select the circular face of the hole of the chain_link, as shown.

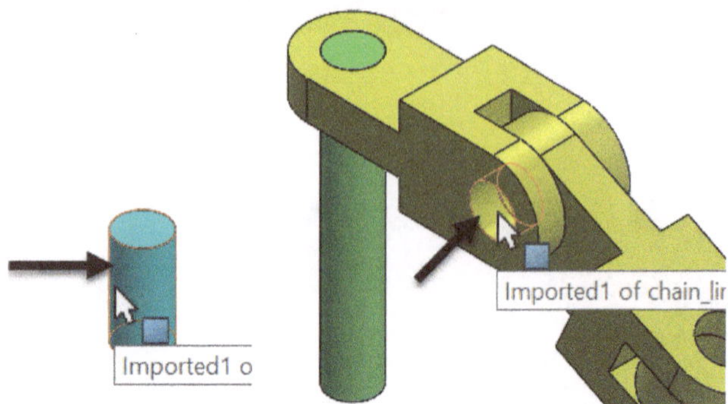

64. Check the **Lock rotation** option and click **Add/Finish Mate**.
65. Click on the flat faces of the short_pin and the chain_link, as shown.

66. Click **Add/Finish Mate**.
67. Likewise, create the **Concentric** and **Coincident** mates between the other chain_links and short_pins, as shown. Make sure that the **Lock rotation** option is check while creating the **Concentric** mate.

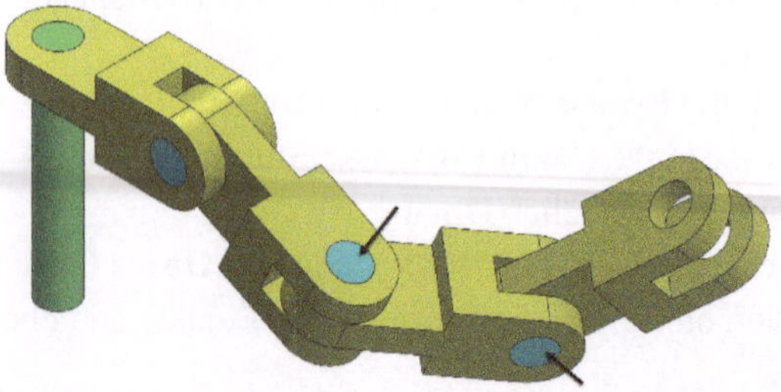

68. On the CommandManager, click **Assembly > Insert Components** .
69. Browse to the **Chain Link Assembly** folder, select **long_pin**, and click **Open**.
70. Click in the graphics window to place the long_pin part file.
71. Create the **Concentric** and **Coincident** mates between the other chain_link and long_pin, as shown. Make sure that the **Lock rotation** option is check while creating the **Concentric** mate.

72. Click **Cancel** on the PropertyManager.
73. On then CommandManager, click **Evaluate** tab > **Mass Properties**.
74. View the **Center of mass** and close the **Mass Properties** dialog.
75. On the Menu bar, click **Tools > Equation**.

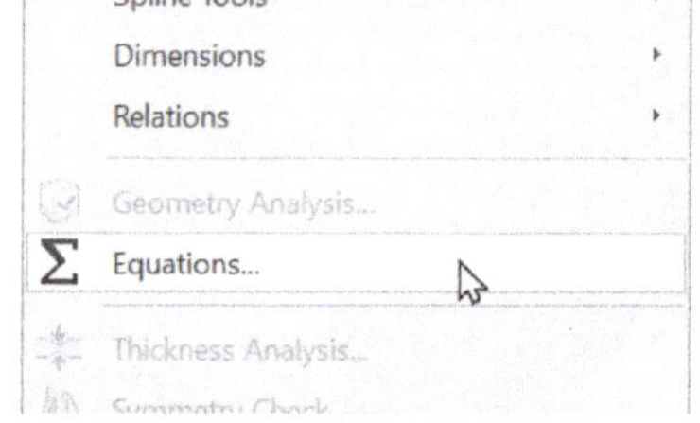

76. On the **Equations, Global Variables, and Dimensions** dialog, click in the field under the **Global Variables** node, and then type **A**.
77. Type **30** in the **Value/Equation** field next to the **A** field.
78. Likewise, create other global variables with the values, as shown.

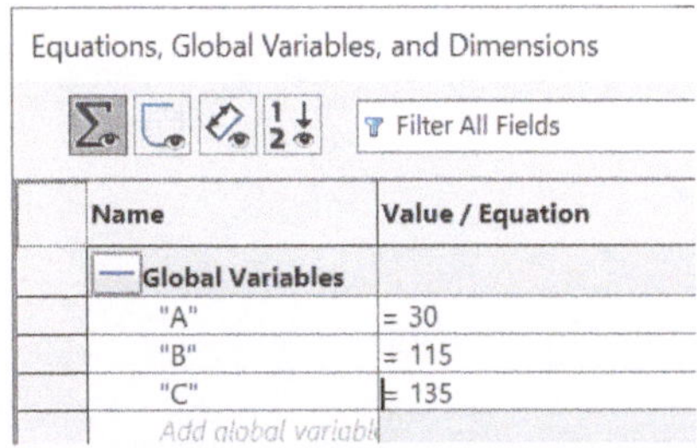

79. Click **OK**.
80. On the CommandManager, make sure that the **Instant3D** button is activated on the **Assembly** tab.
81. In the FeatureManager Design Tree, expand the **Mates** node and select the first **Angle** mate; angle value is displayed on the assembly.

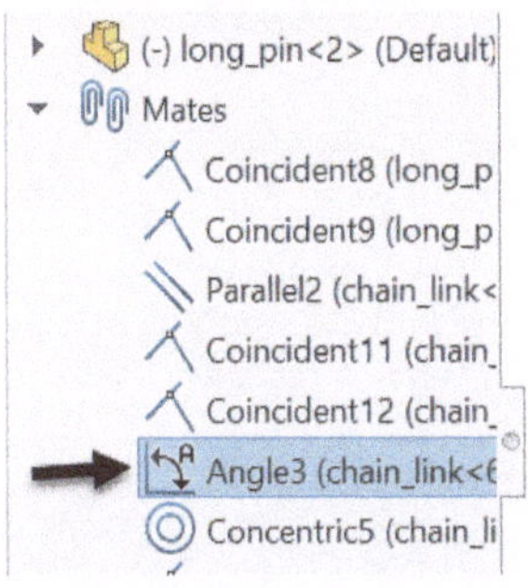

82. Double-click on the angle value to display the **Modify** dialog.

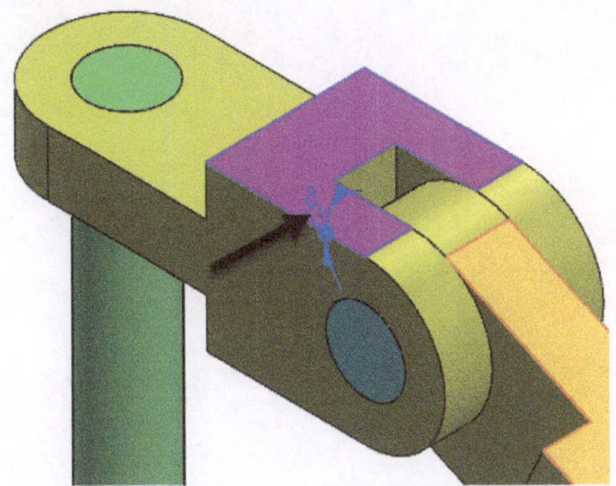

83. On the **Modify** box, select the dimension value and type =.
84. Select **Global Variables > A.**

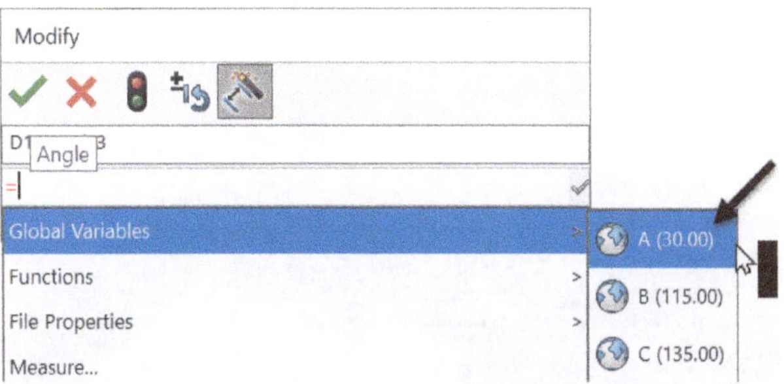

85. Click the green check on the **Modify** box.
86. In the FeatureManager Design Tree, under the **Mates** node and select the second **Angle** mate; angle value is displayed on the assembly.
87. Double-click on the angle value to display the **Modify** dialog.

88. On the **Modify** box, select the dimension value and type =.
89. Select **Global Variables > B.**

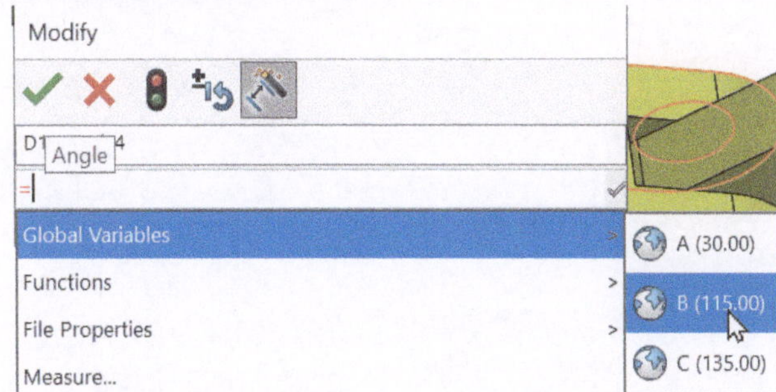

90. Click the green check on the **Modify** box.
91. In the FeatureManager Design Tree, under the **Mates** node and select the third **Angle** mate; angle value is displayed on the assembly.
92. Double-click on the angle value to display the **Modify** dialog.

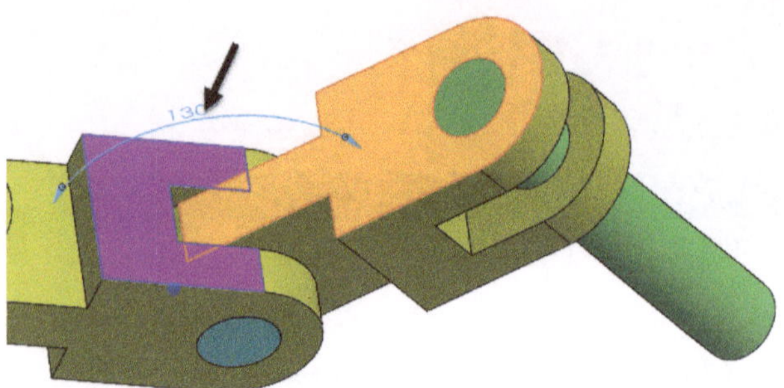

93. On the **Modify** box, select the dimension value and type =.
94. Select **Global Variables > C**.

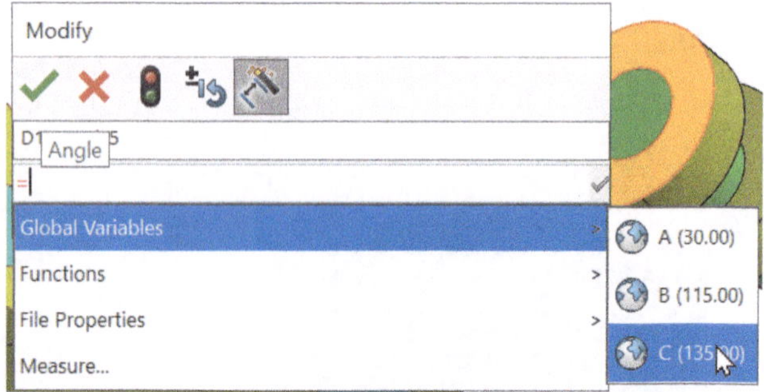

95. Click the green check on the **Modify** box.
96. On the menu bar, click **Edit > Rebuild**.
97. On then CommandManager, click **Evaluate** tab > **Mass Properties**.
98. View the **Center of mass** and close the **Mass Properties** dialog.
99. Save and close the assembly file.

Chapter 9: Dimensions and Annotations

In this chapter, you will learn to

- Create Centerlines and Center Marks
- Edit Hatch Pattern
- Apply Dimensions
- Place Hole callouts
- Place Datum Feature
- Place Feature control frame
- Place Surface symbol

TUTORIAL 1

In this tutorial, you create the drawing shown below.

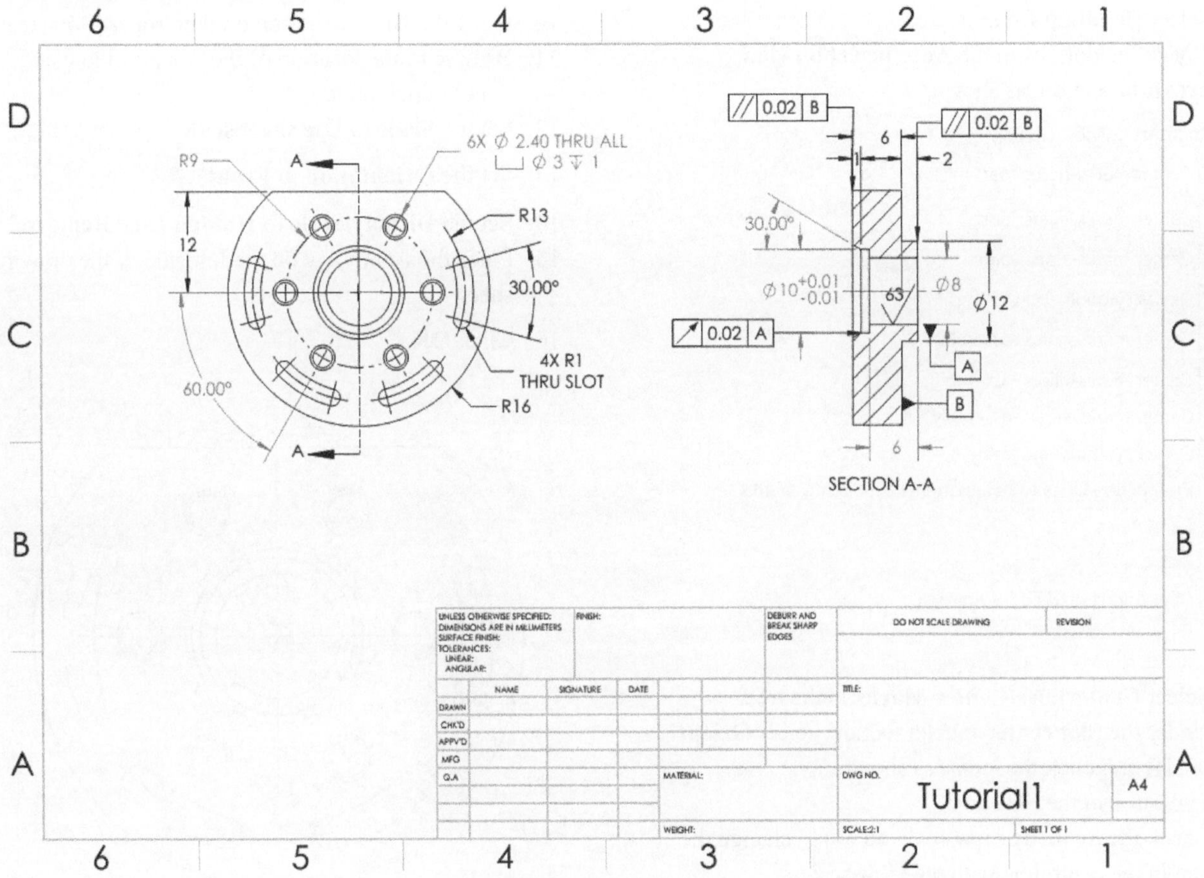

1. Download the Adapter Plate file from the Companion website.
2. Open a new drawing file using the **Sample** template.
3. Click **Cancel** on the **Model View** PropertyManager.
4. In the FeatureManager Design Tree, click the right mouse on Sheet1 and select **Properties**.
5. On the **Sheet Properties** dialog, select **Sheet/Format Size > A4 (ANSI) Landscape**, and then click **Apply Changes**.

Creating a Model View with Center Marks

1. On the **Quick Access Toolbar**, click the **Options** icon.
2. Click the **Document Properties** tab on the dialog and select **Detailing** from the tree.
3. Check the options in the **Auto insert on view creation** section, as shown.

Auto insert on view creation

- [x] Center marks-holes -part
- [ ] Center marks-fillets -part
- [x] Center marks-slots -part
- [x] Dowel symbols -part
- [ ] Center marks-holes -assembly
- [ ] Center marks-fillets -assembly
- [ ] Center marks-slots -assembly
- [ ] Dowel symbols -assembly
- [x] Connection Lines to hole patterns with center marks
- [ ] Centerlines
- [ ] Balloons
- [ ] Dimensions marked for drawing

4. Select **Centerlines/Center Marks** in the tree.
5. Under the **Slot center marks** section, select **Orient to slot** and click the icons, as shown.
6. Type-in 1 in the **Size** box.
7. Check the **Scale by view scale** option to change the gap in the centreline with the view scale.

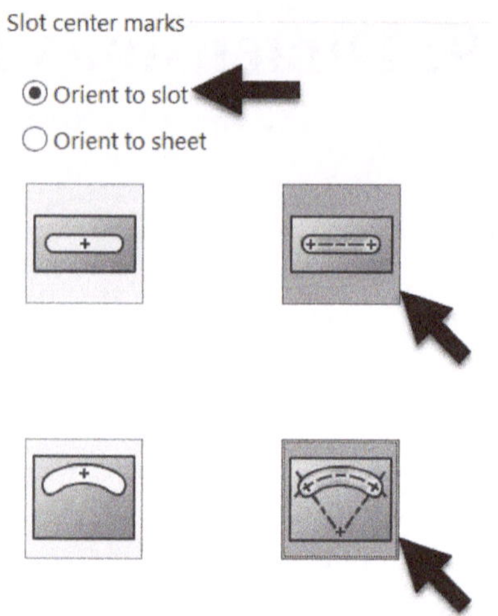

8. Click **OK**.
9. Click **Drawing > Model View** on the CommandManager.
10. Click the **Browse** button on the PropertyManager.
11. Browse to the location of the Adapter Plate and double-click on it.
12. Set the **Scale** to **Use sheet scale**.
13. Set the **Orientation** to **Front**.
14. Set the **Display Style** to **Hidden Line Removed**.
15. Place the front view on the left side of the drawing sheet.
16. Click **OK**.

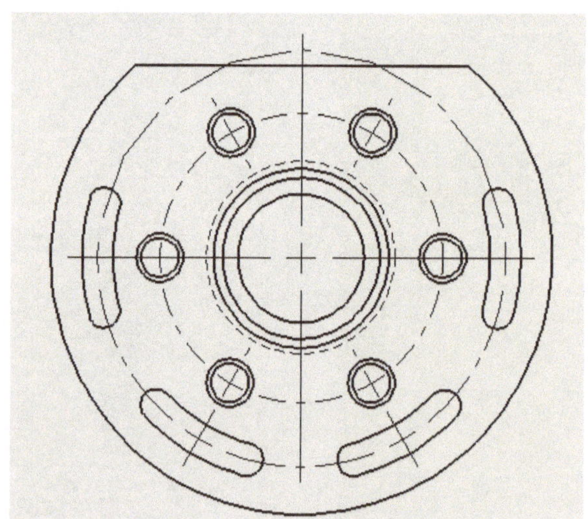

17. Select the view and press **Delete**.
18. Click **Yes** on the **Confirm Delete** dialog.
19. On the **Quick Access Toolbar**, click the **Options**  icon.

20. Click the **Document Properties** tab on the dialog and select **Detailing** from the tree.
21. Uncheck the options in the **Auto insert on view creation** section and click **OK**.
22. Create the front view and notice the difference.

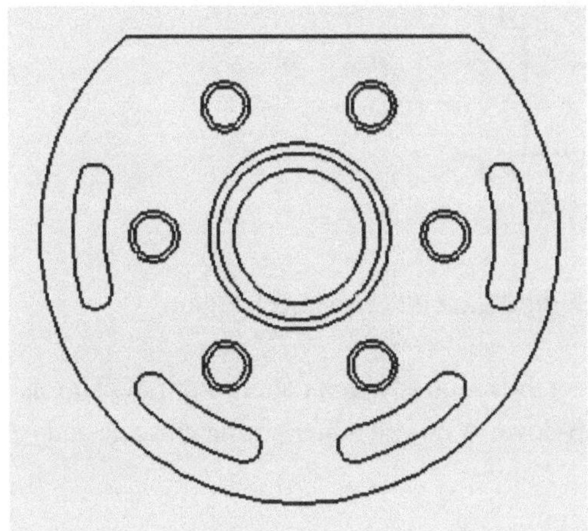

23. Click **Drawing > Section View** on the CommandManager.
24. Select the center point of the front view.
25. Click **OK**.
26. Place the section view on the right side.

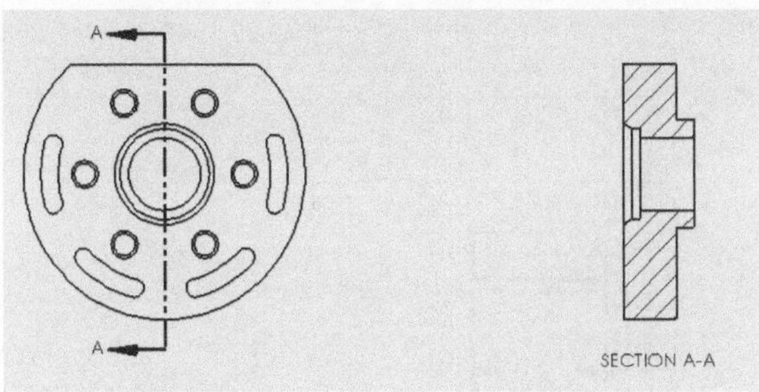

Creating Centerlines and Center Marks

1. Click **Annotation > Centerline** on the CommandManager.
2. Select the parallel lines on the section view, as shown below. The centerline is created.

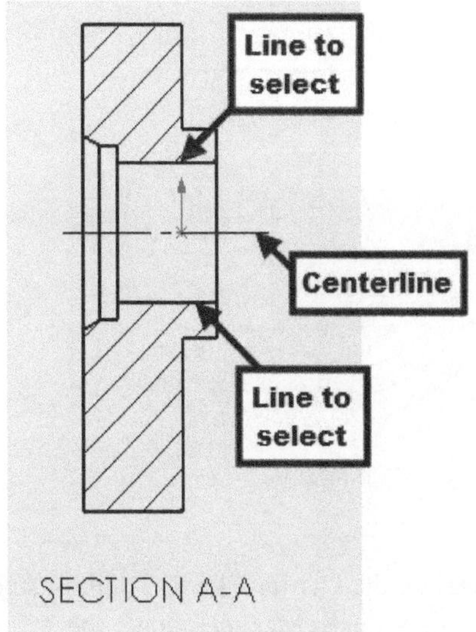

3. Click **OK** on the PropertyManager.
4. Click **Annotation > Center Mark** on the CommandManager.
5. On the PropertyManager, under the **Manual Insert Options** section, click the **Circular Center Mark** icon.
6. Select the outer circles of the counterbore holes

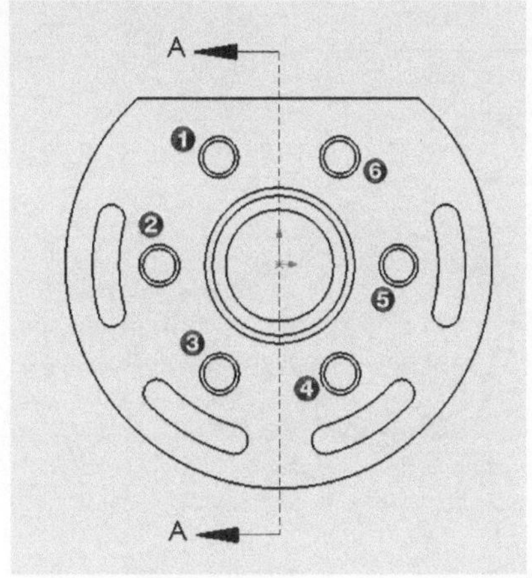

7. Click **OK** on the PropertyManager.

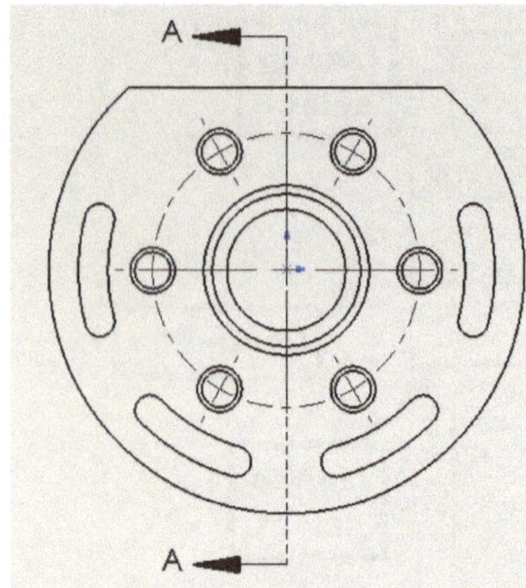

8. Activate the **Center Mark** command.
9. On the PropertyManager, under the **Auto Insert** section, check **For all slots**.
10. Select the front view.
11. Uncheck all the options in the **Options** section.
12. Click the **Arc Slot Ends** icon under the **Slot center marks** section of the PropertyManager.
13. Activate the **Slot Ends** icon.
14. Click **OK**.

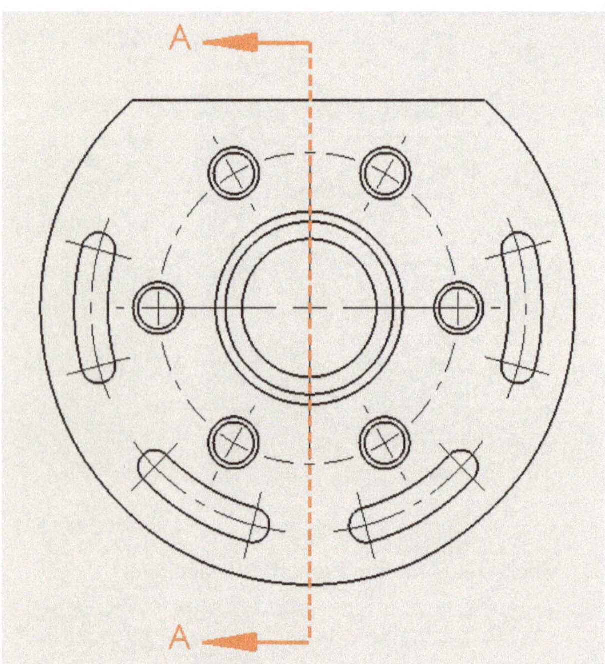

Editing the Hatch Pattern

1. Click on the hatch pattern of the section view. The **Area Hatch/Fill** PropertyManager appears.

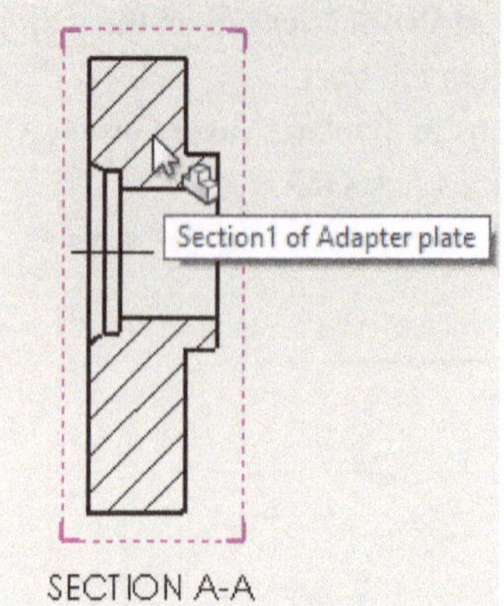

2. Uncheck the **Material crosshatch** option.

You can select the required hatch pattern from the **Hatch Pattern** drop-down. You can adjust the hatch scale and angle.

3. Click **OK** .

Emphasizing the Outline of the Section View

1. Select the section view from the drawing sheet.
2. On the PropertyManager, under the **Section View** section, check the **Emphasize outline** option: the outline of the section is thickened.

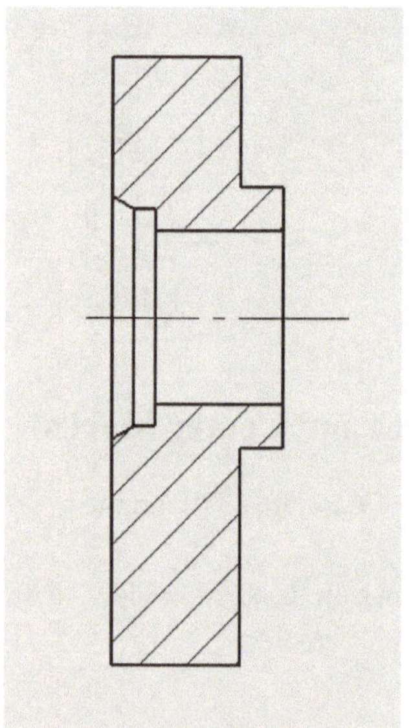

3. Click on the **Options** icon on the Quick Access Toolbar.
4. On the **System Options** dialog, click the **Document Properties** tab.

5. Click **Line Font** in the tree located on the left side.
6. Select **Type of Edge > Emphasized Section Outline**.

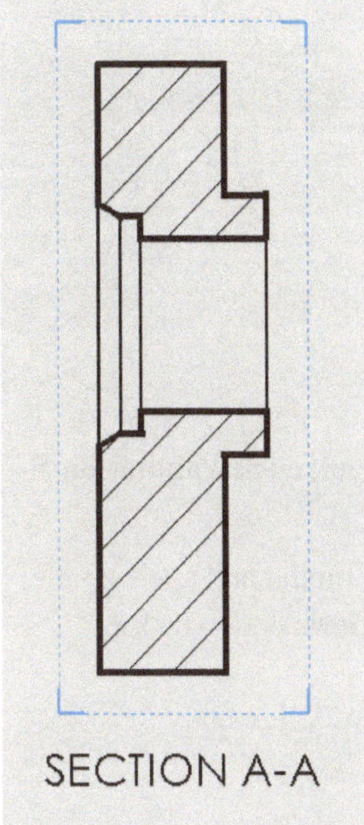

7. Select 0.5 mm from the **Thickness** drop-down.
8. Click **OK**; the thickness of the emphasized outline is changed.
9. Uncheck the **Emphasize outline** option in the **Section View** section.
10. Click **OK** on the PropertyManager.

Applying Dimensions

1. Click **Annotation > Model Items** on the CommandManager.
2. Select **Source > Entire model** and uncheck the **Import items into all views** option on the PropertyManager.
3. Click on the front view.
4. Click **OK**.
5. Drag and arrange the dimensions as shown.

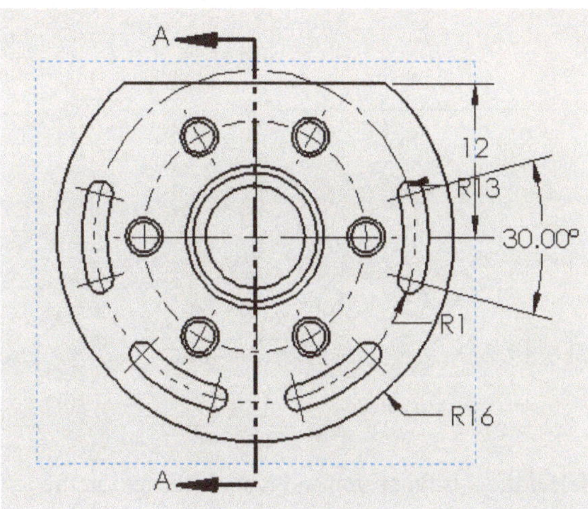

6. On the CommandManager, click **Annotation > Hole Callout** ⌴⌀.
7. Select the counterbore hole and position the hole callout as shown.

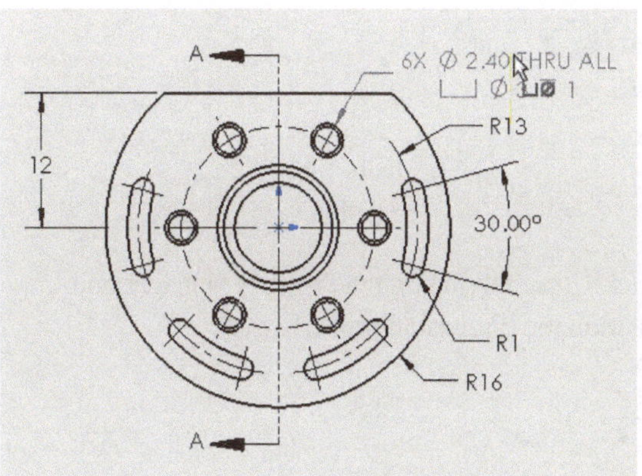

8. On the CommandManager, click **Annotation > Smart Dimension**.
9. Select the center marks of the holes.
10. Move the pointer in the region between the holes and click to position the dimension.

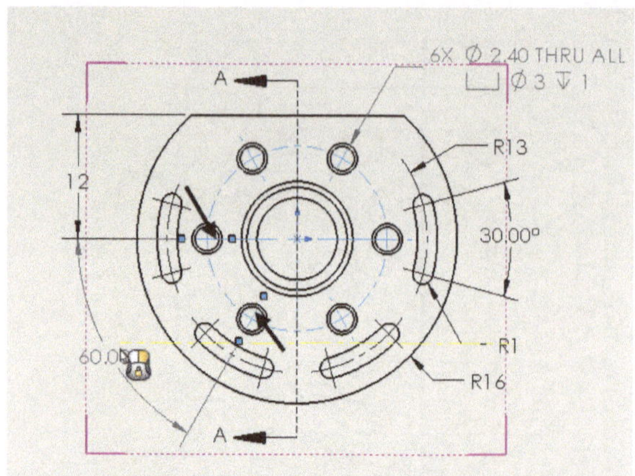

11. Select the R1 dimension and type-in the text in the **Dimension Text** box on the PropertyManager.

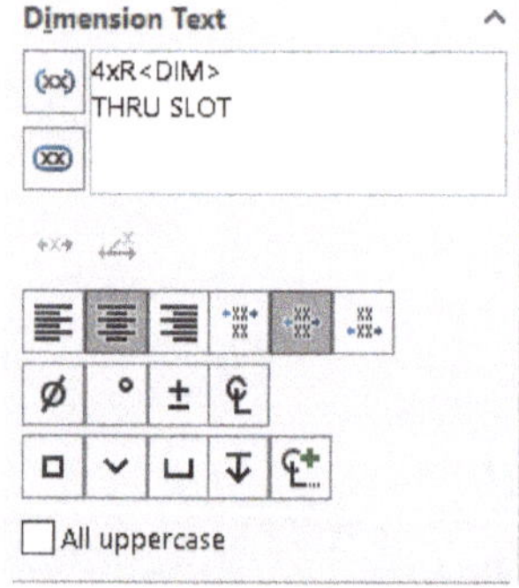

12. Click **Close Dialog** on the PropertyManager and position the dimension properly.

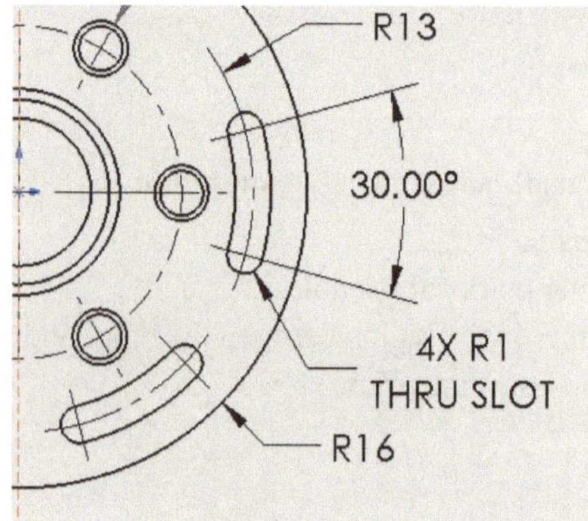

13. Dimension the pitch circle radius of the counterbore holes, as shown.

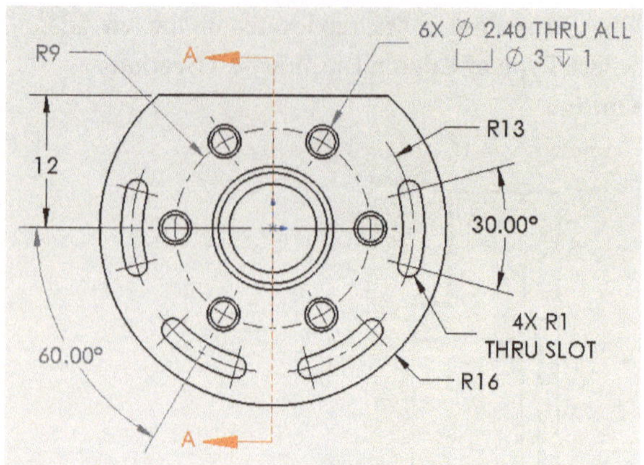

14. On the CommandManager, click **Annotation > Model Items** .
15. Select **Source > Entire model** and uncheck the **Import items into all views** option on the PropertyManager.
16. Click on the section view. Click **OK**.

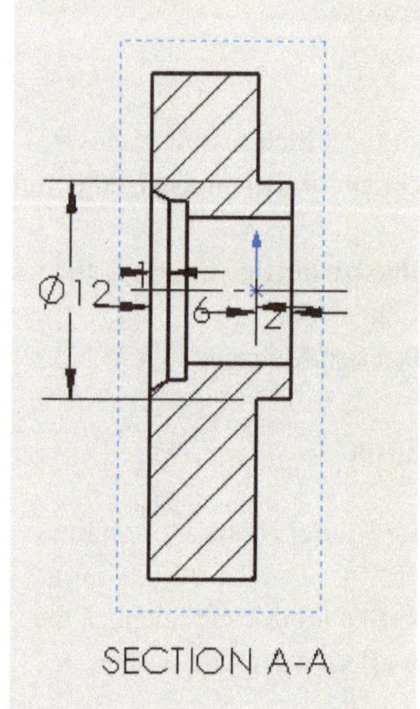

17. Click and drag the dimensions as shown.

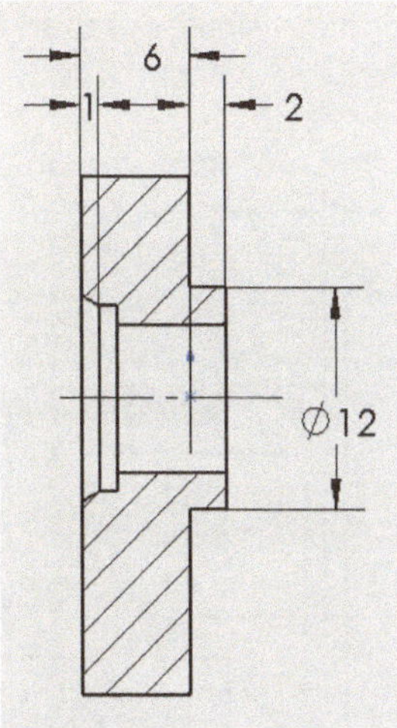

18. Select the 2 mm dimension and notice the highlighted origins.
19. Click and drag the endpoints to the new locations as shown.

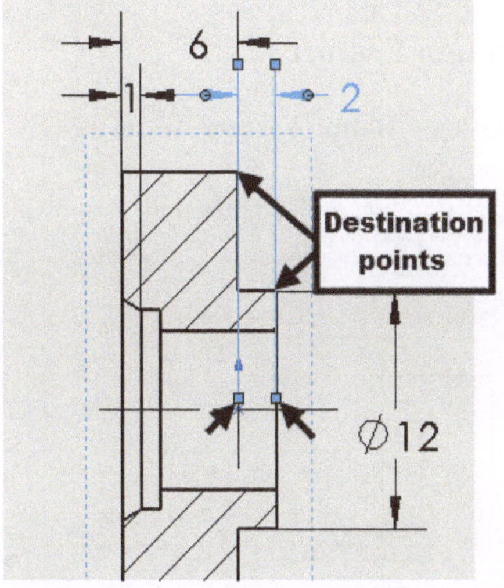

20. Likewise, modify the origins of other dimensions as shown.

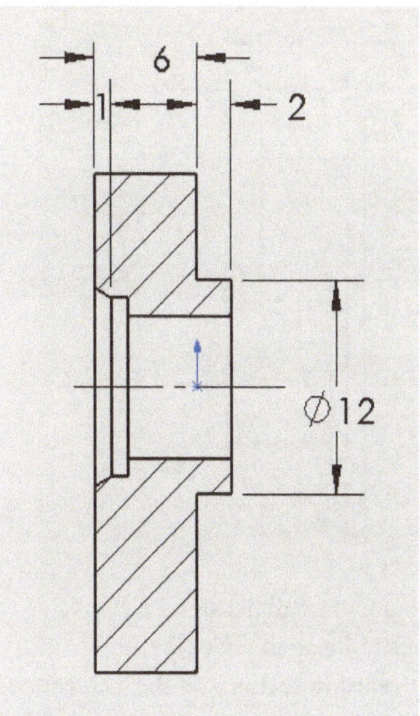

21. Activate the **Smart Dimension** command.
22. Select the lines, as shown.
23. Move the pointer toward the right and click to place the dimension.

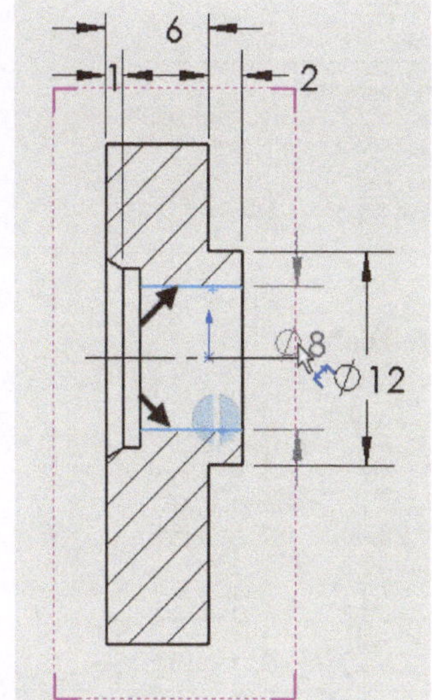

24. Likewise, add the counterbore dimension.

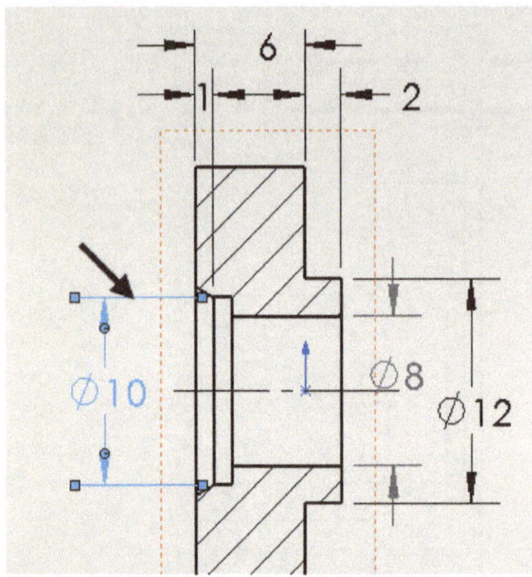

25. Select the counterbore dimension.
26. On the PropertyManager, under the **Tolerance/Precision** section, set the **Tolerance Type** to **Bilateral**.
27. Set the tolerance parameters as shown.

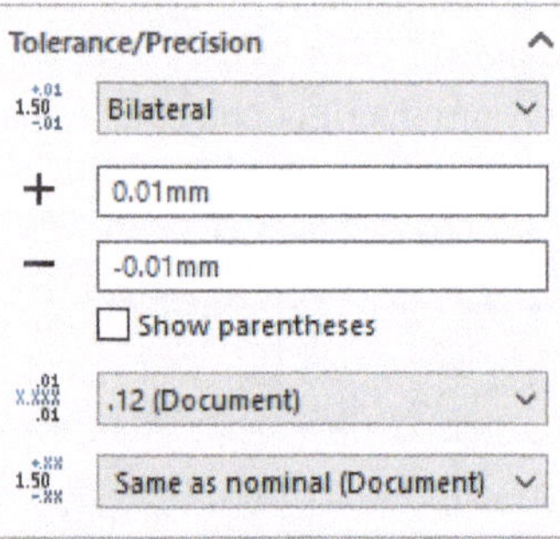

28. Click **Close Dialog**.

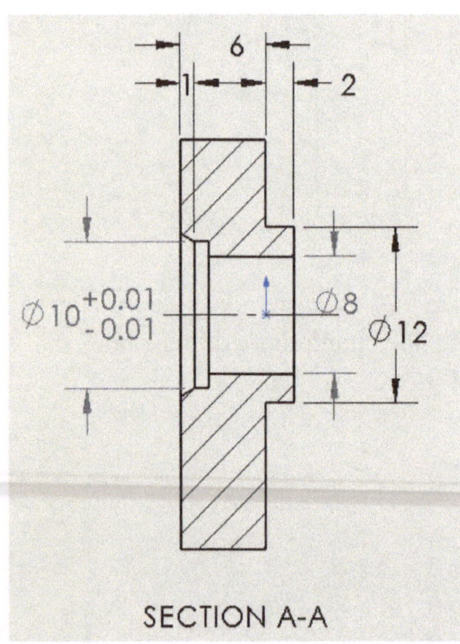

29. Likewise, apply the other dimensions, as shown below.

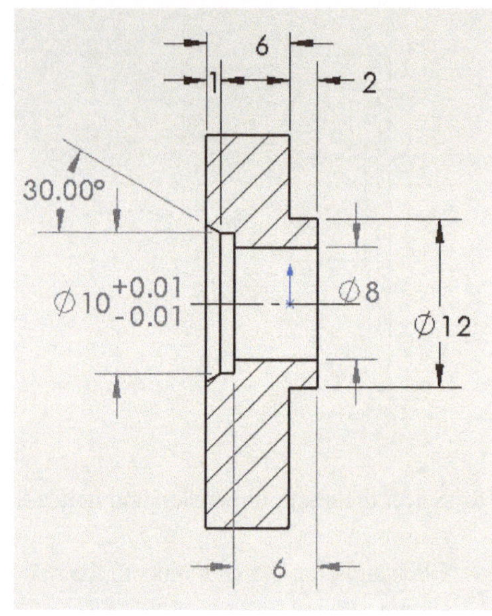

Placing the Datum Feature

1. Click **Annotation > Datum Feature** on the CommandManager.
2. Select the extension line of the dimension, as shown below.

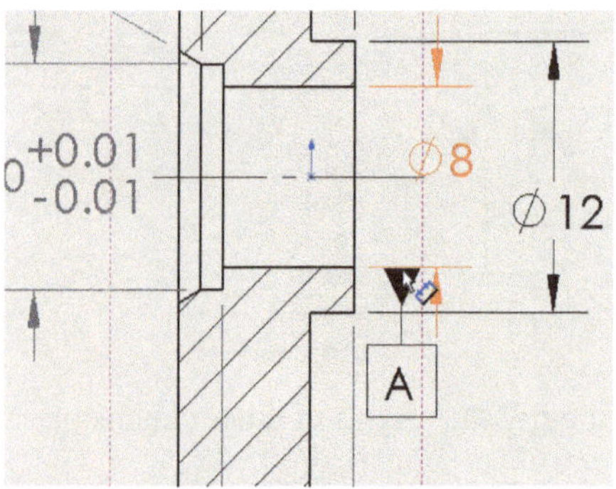

3. On the PropertyManager, click the **Filled Triangle with Shoulder** icon.
4. Move the cursor downward and click.
5. Likewise, place a datum feature B, as shown below. Click **OK**.

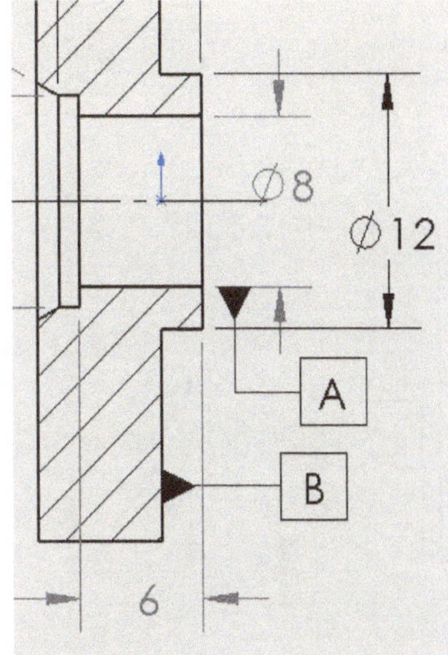

Placing the Feature Control Frame

1. Click **Annotation > Geometric Tolerance** on the CommandManager.
2. Select a point on the line, as shown.
3. Move the cursor horizontally toward the right and click.

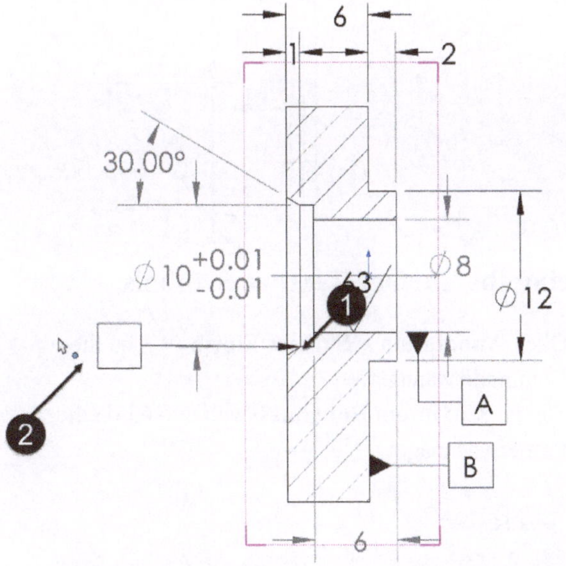

4. On the Tolerance dialog, click the **Circular Runout** button.

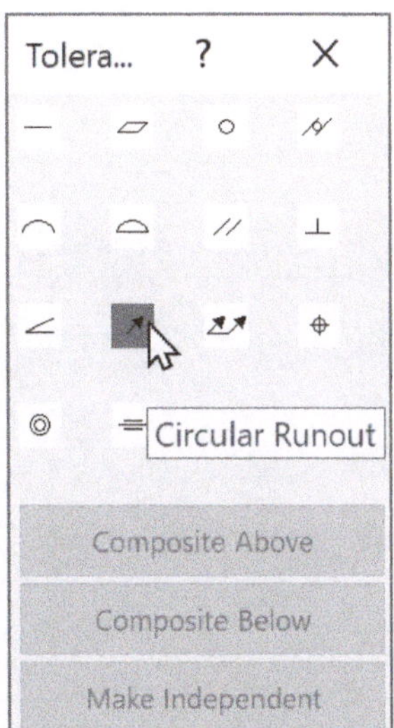

5. Type-in **0.02** and **A** in the **Tolerance** box.

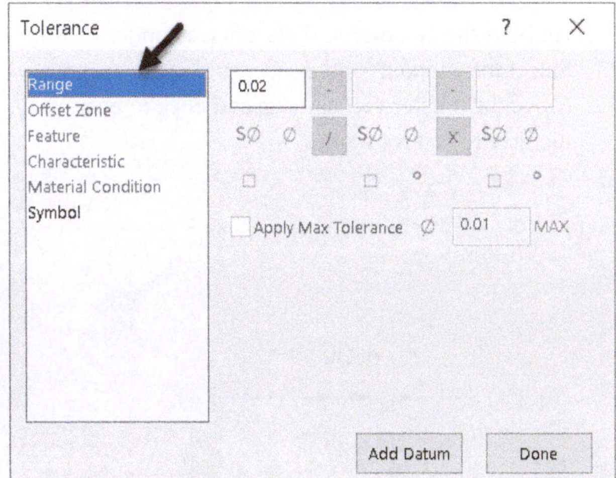

6. Click **Done**.
7. Select the feature control frame and click the plus symbol displayed at the right side.
8. Select the **Datum** option from the menu.
9. Type **A** in the **Datum** dialog and click the **Done** button.

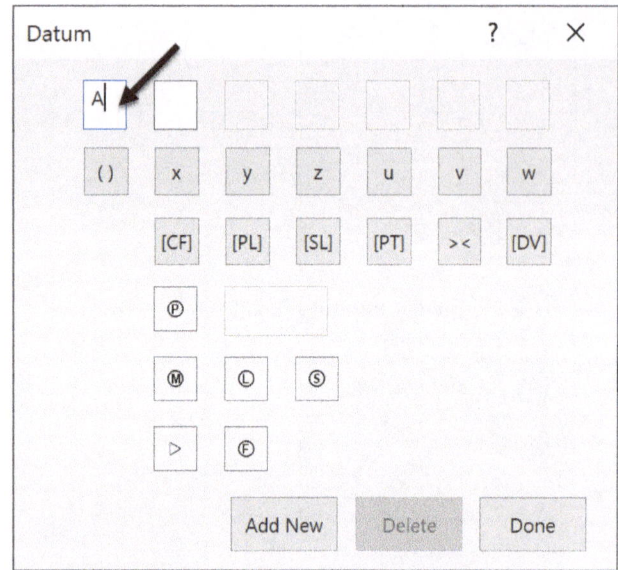

10. Activate the **Geometric Tolerance** command.
11. Select the endpoint of the edge, as shown.
12. Move the pointer vertically up and click to position the feature control frame.

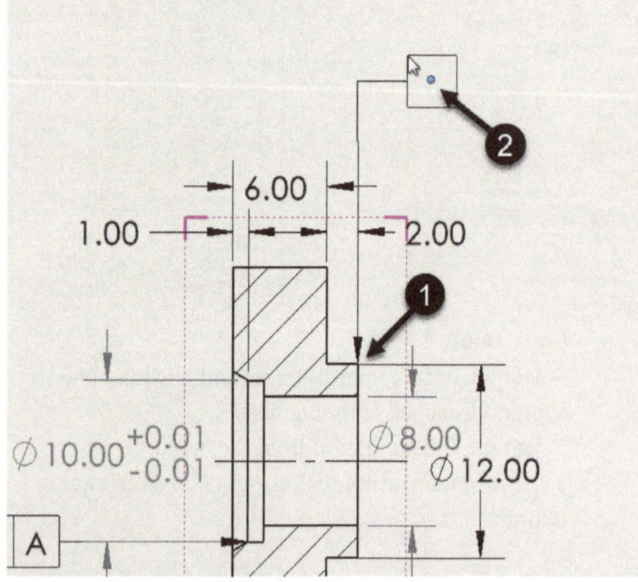

13. On the dialog, click the **Parallel** icon.
14. Type-in **0.02** in the **Tolerance** box.
15. Click the **Add Datum** button.
16. Type **B** in the **Datum** dialog and click **Done**.

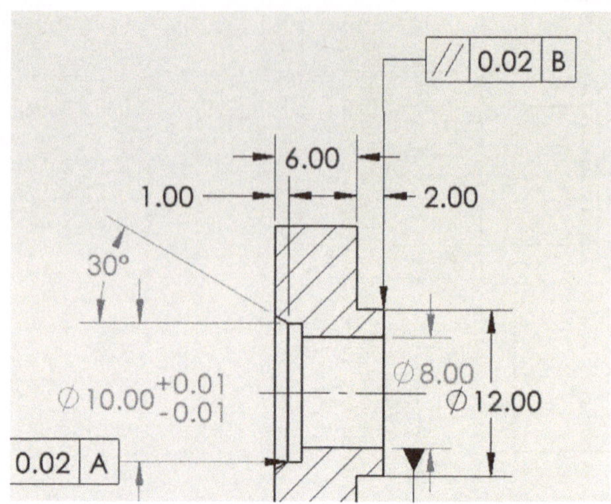

17. Likewise, add another feature control frame and click **OK**.

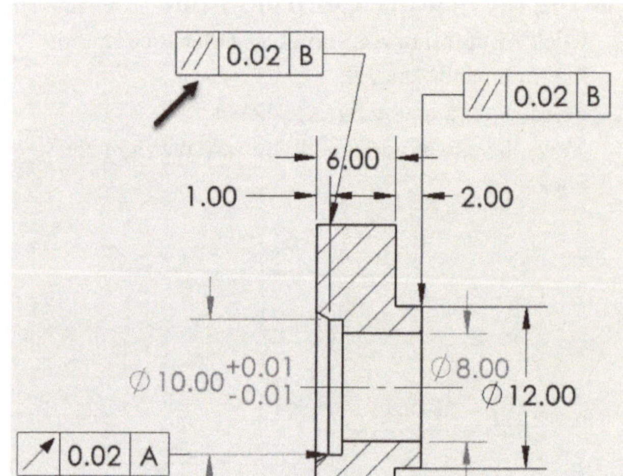

Placing the Surface Texture Symbols

1. Click **Annotation > Surface Finish** on the CommandManager.
2. Set the **Maximum Roughness** value to 63 on the PropertyManager.

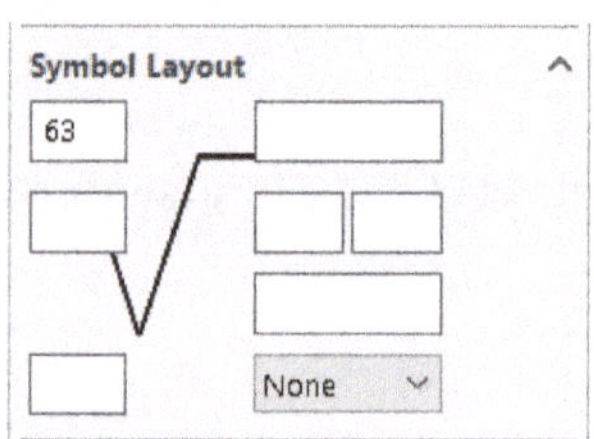

3. Click on the inner cylindrical face of the hole, as shown below.

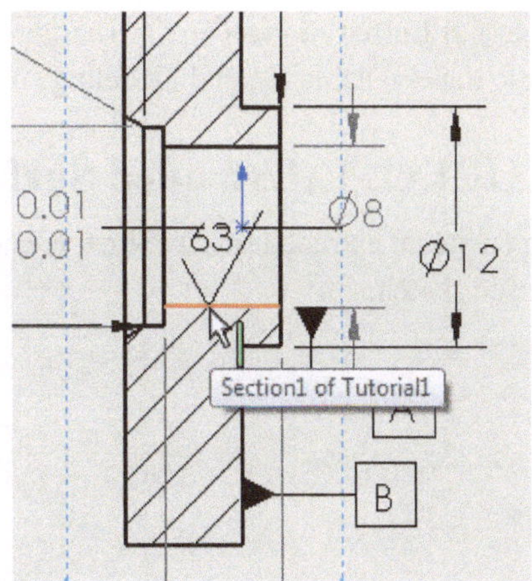

4. Click **OK**.
5. Save and close the file.

Chapter 10: Surface Design

SOLIDWORKS Surface modeling tools can create complex geometries that are very difficult to create using solid modeling tools. Also, you can use these tools to fix broken imported parts. In this chapter, you will learn the basics of surfacing tools that are mostly used. The surfacing tools are available on the **Surfaces** Command Manager. You can also find these tools on the menu bar (click **Insert > Surface** on the Menu bar).

If the **Surfaces** CommandManager is not displayed by default, you can customize it. Right-click on any of the tabs of the CommandManager and select **Surface** from the shortcut menu.

SOLIDWORKS offers a robust set of surface design tools. A surface is an infinitely thin piece of geometry. For example, consider a box shown in Figure. It has six faces. Each of these faces is a surface, an infinitely thin piece of geometry that acts as a boundary in 3D space. Surfaces can be simple or complex shapes.

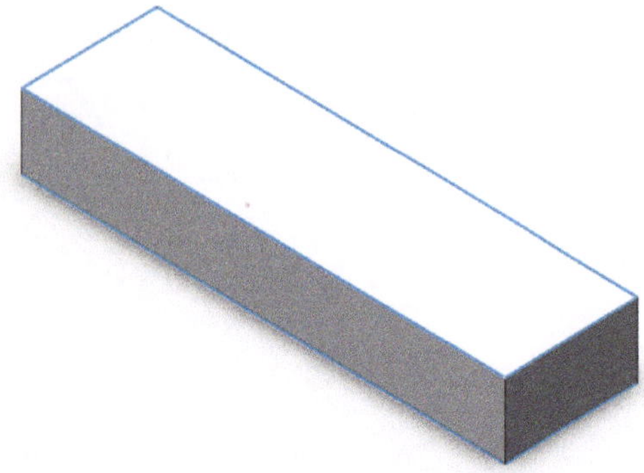

In solid modeling, when you create solid features such as an Extruded Boss or a Revolved Boss, SOLIDWORKS creates a set of surfaces forming a closed volume. This airtight closed volume is considered as a solid body. Although you can design a geometry using solid modeling tools, the surface modeling tools give you more flexibility.

Creating Basic Surfaces

In this section, you will learn to create basic surfaces using the **Extruded Surface**, **Revolved Surface**, **Swept Surface**, and **Lofted Surface** tools. These tools are similar to that available in solid modeling.

TUTORIAL 1 (Extruded Surfaces)

1. To create an extruded surface, first, create an open or closed sketch.

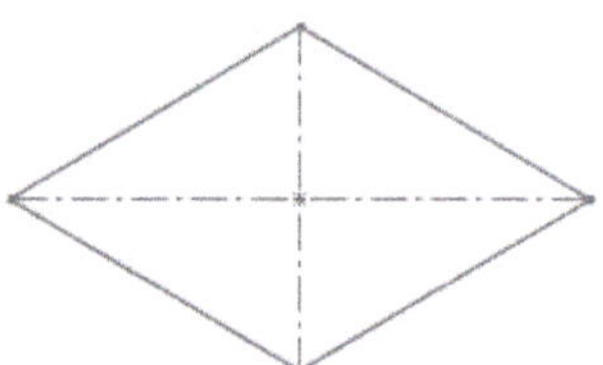

2. Click the **Extruded Surface** button on the **Surfaces** Command Manager.
3. Select the sketch. The **Surface-Extrude** Property Manager appears and is similar to the **Boss-Extruded** Property Manager.
4. Enter a value in the **Depth** box available in the **Direction 1** section.
5. Click **OK** on Property Manager to create the extruded surface. You will notice that the extrusion was not capped at the ends. You can check the **Cap end** option to cap the ends

TUTORIAL 2 (Revolved Surfaces)

1. To create a revolved surface, first, create an open or closed profile and the axis of revolution.

2. Click the **Revolved Surface** button on the **Surfaces** Command Manager.
3. Select the sketch. The preview of the revolved surface appears.
4. Enter the angle of revolution in the **Direction 1 Angle** box and click **OK**.

Even if you create an enclosed surface, SOLIDWORKS will not recognize it as a solid body. You will notice that the **Mass Properties** button is not available in the **Evaluate** Command Manager. It means that there exists no solid body. You will learn to convert a surface body into a solid later in this chapter.

TUTORIAL 3 (Swept Surfaces)

1. To create a swept surface, create a sweep profile and a path.

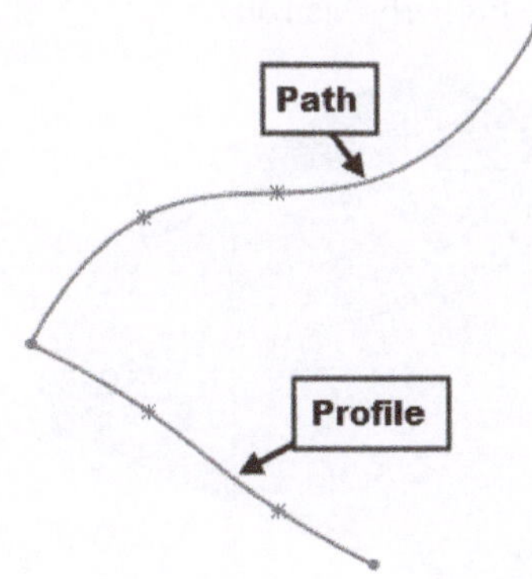

2. Click the **Swept Surface** button on the **Surfaces** Command Manager (or) click **Insert > Surface > Sweep**.
3. Select the sweep profile and then the path from the graphics window.
4. Click **OK** on the Property Manager.

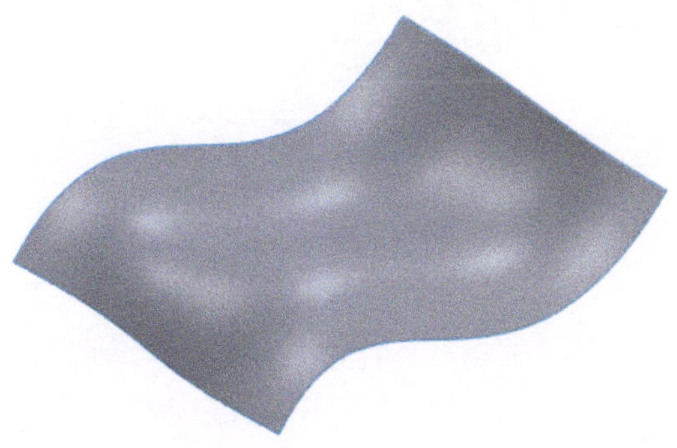

Various ways of creating swept surfaces are given next.

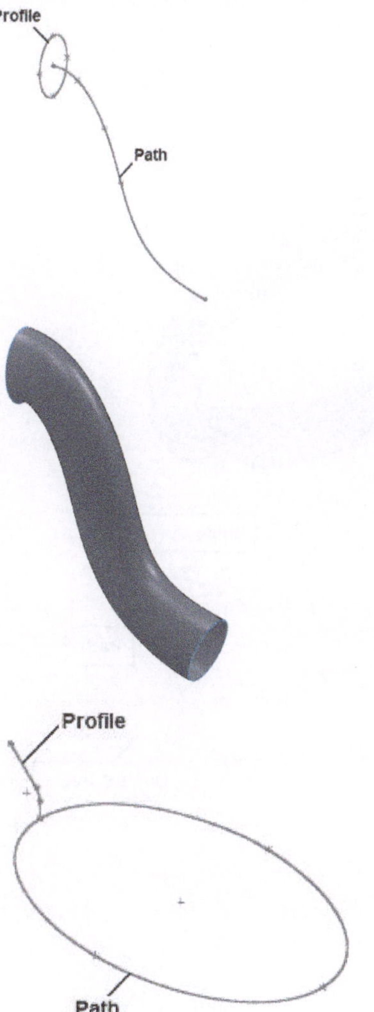

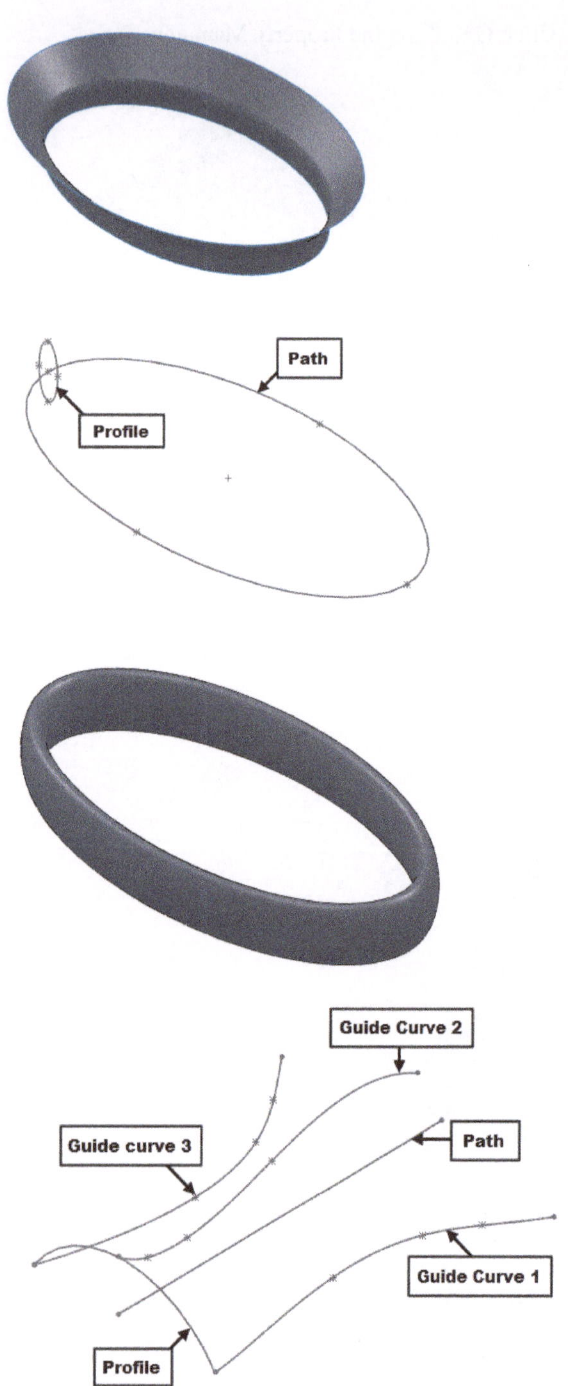

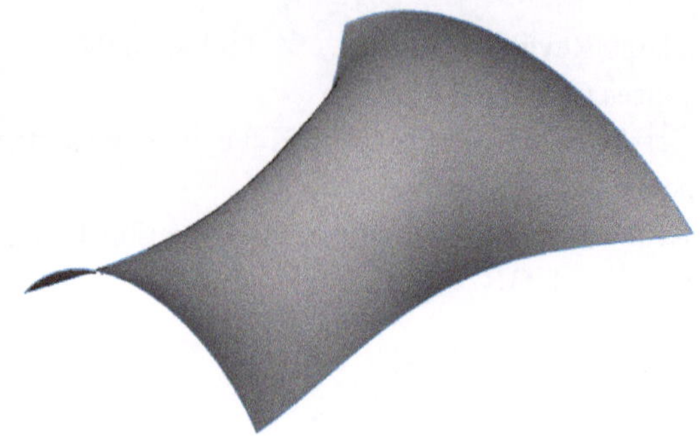

TUTORIAL 4 (Lofted Surfaces)

1. To create a swept surface, create two or more profiles.

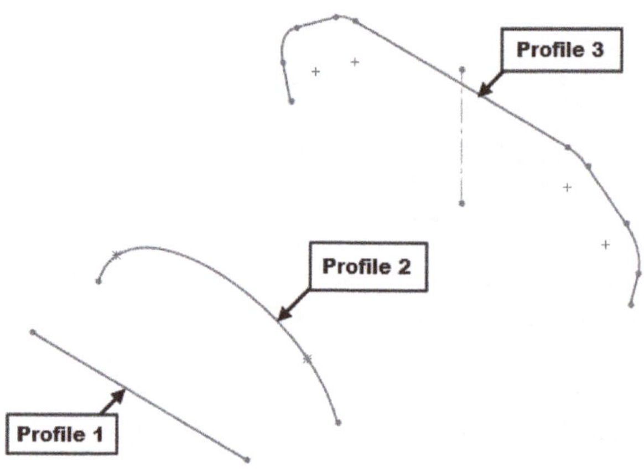

2. Click the **Lofted Surface** button on the **Surfaces** Command Manager (or) click **Insert > Surface > Loft** on the Menu bar.
3. Select the loft profiles from the graphics window.
4. Click **OK** on the Property Manager.

Various ways of creating lofted surfaces are given next.

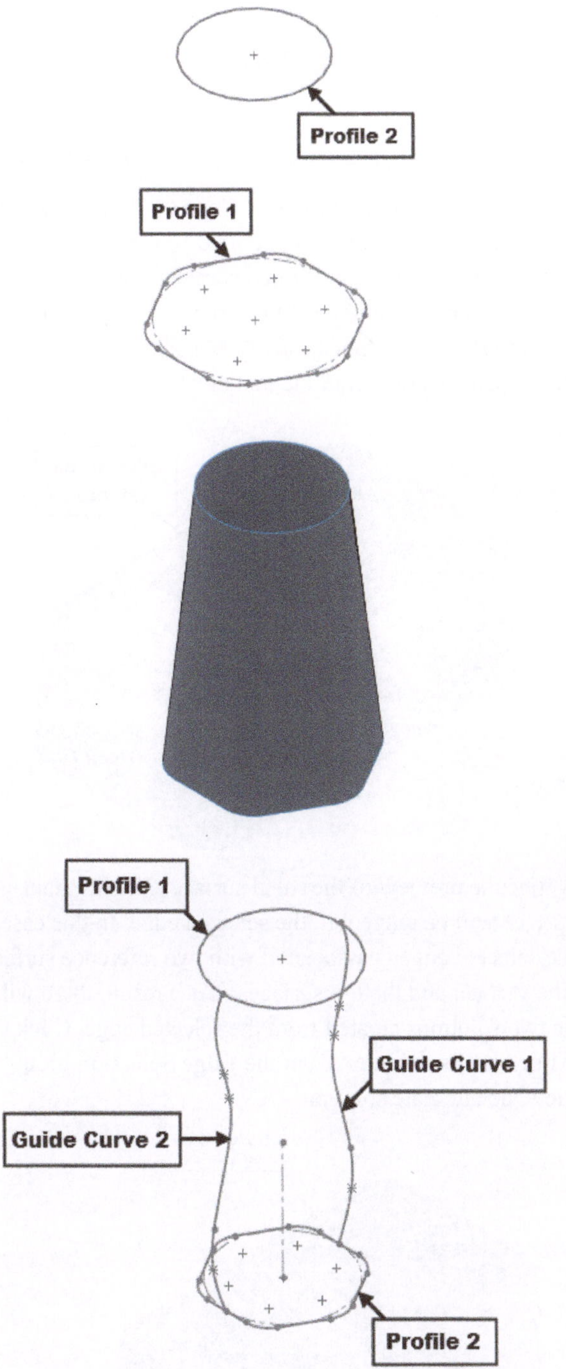

TUTORIAL 5 (Planar Surfaces)

1. To create a planar surface, click the **Planar Surface** button on the **Surfaces** Command Manager (or) click **Insert > Surface > Planar**.

The PropertyManager prompts you to select the bounding entities. You can select a closed sketch or closed loop of edges.

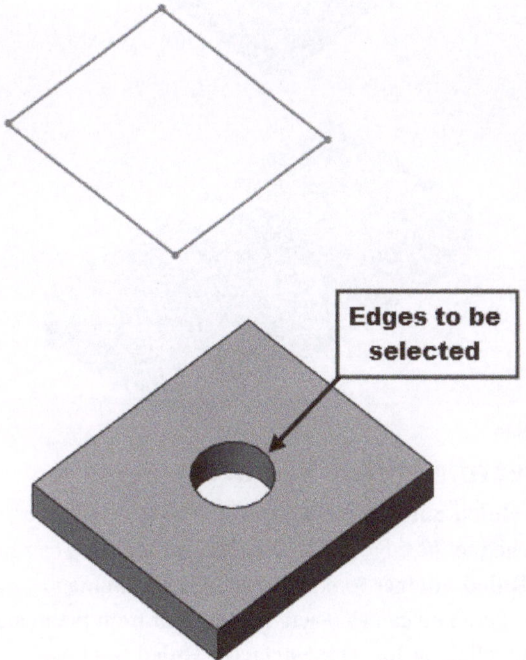

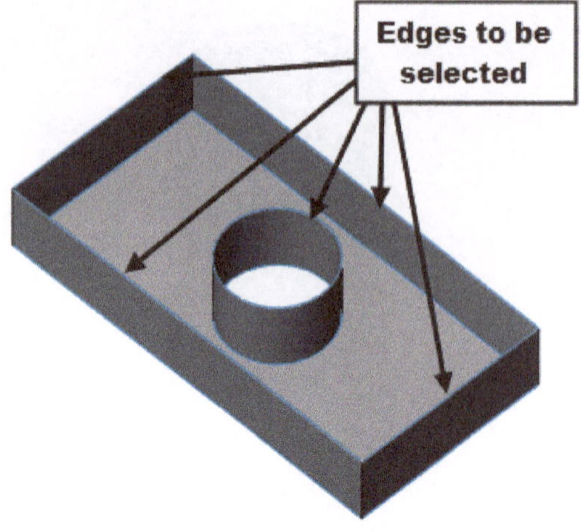

2. Select a closed sketch or a closed loop of edges.
3. Click **OK** on the Property Manager. The planar surface will be created.

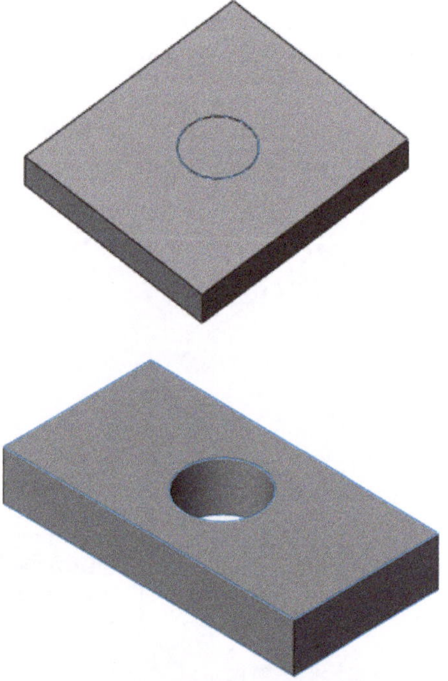

Creating Ruled Surfaces

The **Ruled Surface** tool allows you to create surfaces attached to the edges of an existing surface. You can find the **Ruled Surface** tool on the **Surfaces** Command Manager. You can also activate this tool from the menu bar by clicking **Insert > Surface > Ruled Surface**.

You can create five types of ruled surfaces using the options in the Property Manager. These five types of ruled surfaces are discussed next.

TUTORIAL 6 (Creating a Ruled Surface using the Tangent to Surface option)

1. To create a planar surface, click the **Ruled Surface** button on the **Surfaces** Command Manager (or) click **Insert > Surface > Ruled Surface**.
2. To create this type of ruled surface, select the **Tangent to Surface** option from the **Type** group of the **Ruled Surface** Property Manager.
3. Select an edge from the model.

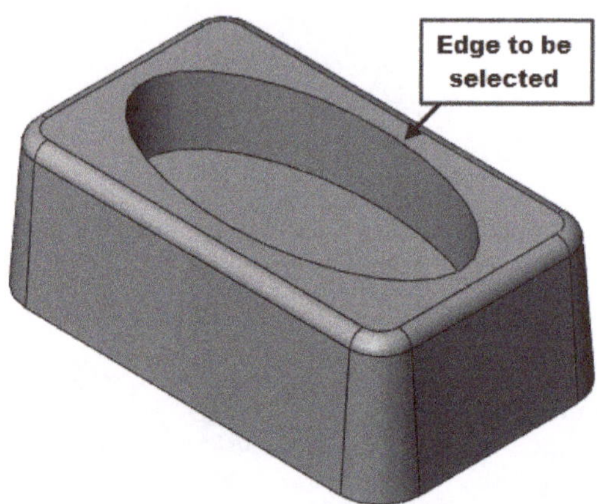

Notice the preview of the ruled surface. The resultant surface will be tangent to the selected edge. In this case, the selected edge is associated with two reference surfaces (the vertical and the top surfaces). As a result, there will be two solutions created from the selected edge. Click the **Alternate Face** button from the **Edge Selection** group to view the alternate solution.

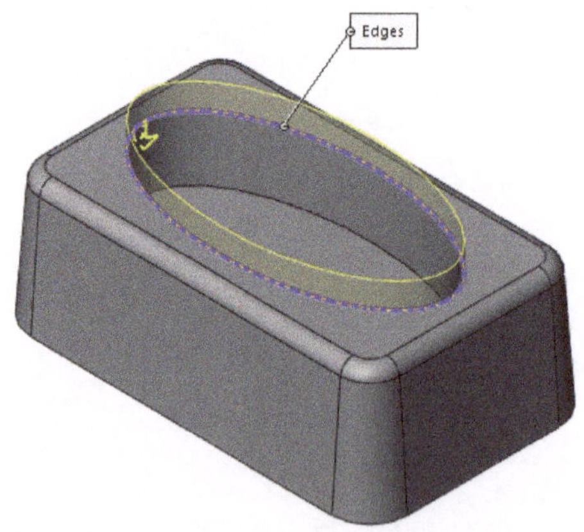

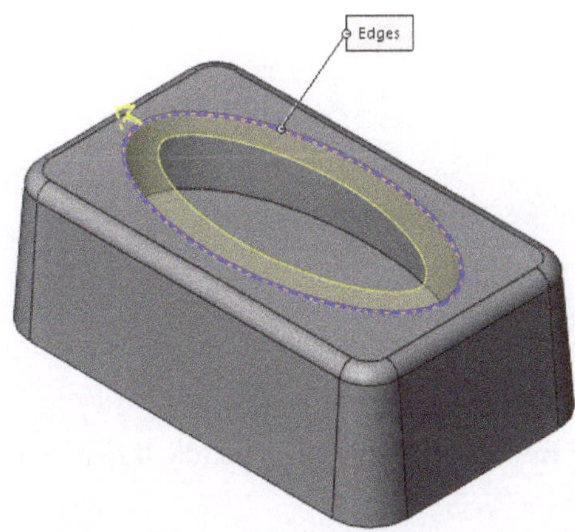

4. Enter a distance value in the **Distance** box of the **Distance/Direction** group.

You will notice two options- **Trim and Knit** and **Connecting surface** options available in the **Options** group. These options are useful while creating multiple ruled surfaces at a time. The **Trim and Knit** option, if enabled, trims and knits the continuous ruled surfaces. The **Connecting surface** option creates a connecting surface at the sharp corners of the ruled surfaces.

5. Click **OK** to create the ruled surface.

TUTORIAL 7 (Creating a Ruled Surface using the Normal to Surface option)

1. To create this type of ruled surface, select the **Normal to Surface** option from the **Type** group of the **Ruled Surface** Property Manager.
2. Select an edge from the model.

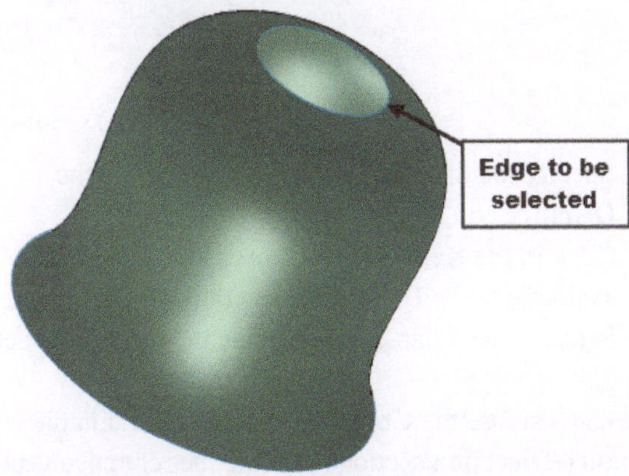

3. Enter a distance value in the **Distance** box of the **Distance/Direction** group.
4. Click the **Reverse Direction** button in the **Distance/Direction** group to reverse the direction, if required.
5. Click **OK** to create the ruled surface normal to the surface on which the selected edge lies.

TUTORIAL 8 (Creating a Ruled Surface using the Tapered to Vector option)

1. To create this type of ruled surface, activate the Ruled Surface command (On the CommandManager, **Surfaces > Ruled surface**) and select the **Tapered to Vector** option from the **Type** group of the **Ruled Surface** Property Manager; some additional options appear in the **Distance/Direction** section.

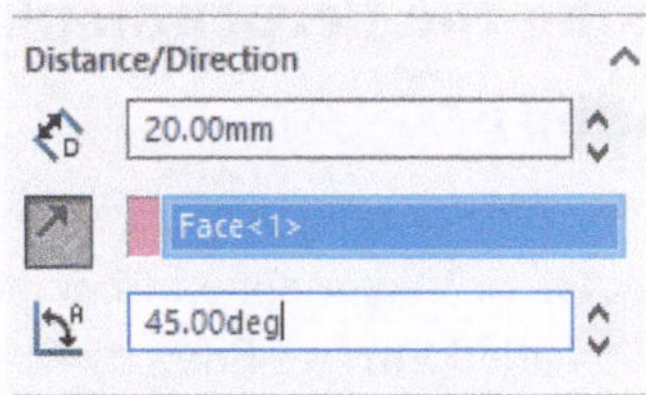

2. Select an edge from the model.
3. Click on the **Reference Vector** box available in the **Distance/Direction** group.
4. Select a face from the model to define the reference vector.

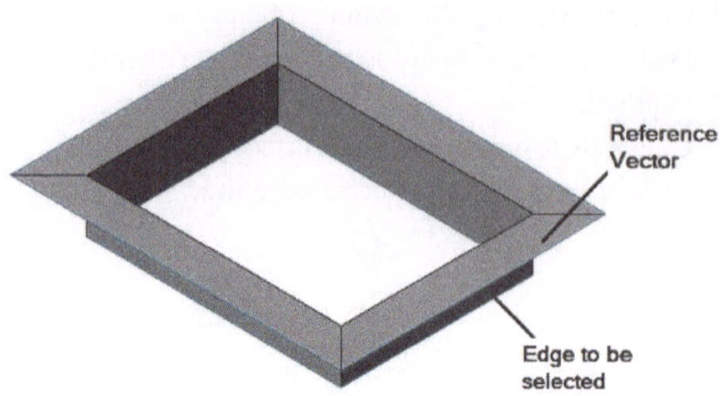

5. Specify the distance of the ruled surface in the **Distance** box.
6. Specify the ruled surface's taper angle in the **Angle** box available in the **Distance/ Direction** group.
7. Click the **Reverse Direction** button, if required.
8. Click **OK**.

The following figure shows the ruled surface created at a taper angle of 60 degrees.

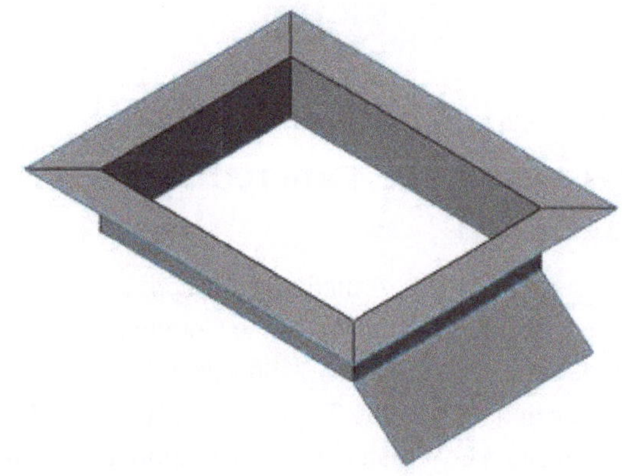

TUTORIAL 9 (Creating a Ruled Surface using the Perpendicular to Vector option)

1. To create this type of ruled surface, select the **Perpendicular to Vector** option from the **Type** group of the **Ruled Surface** Property Manager.
2. Select a face or an edge to define the reference vector.
3. Select an edge from the model.

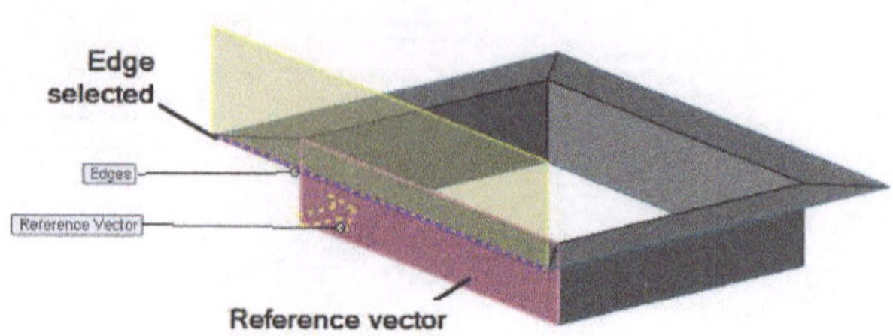

4. Specify the distance of the ruled surface in the **Distance** box.
5. Click the **Reverse Direction** button, if required.
6. Click **OK**.

TUTORIAL 10 (Creating a Ruled Surface using the Sweep option)

This option creates a ruled surface by sweeping the selected edge along a reference vector.

1. To create this type of ruled surface, select the **Sweep** option from the **Type** group of the **Ruled Surface** Property Manager.
2. On the **Ruled Surface** PropertyManager, click in the **Edge Selection** box.
3. Select an edge or loop of edges from the model.

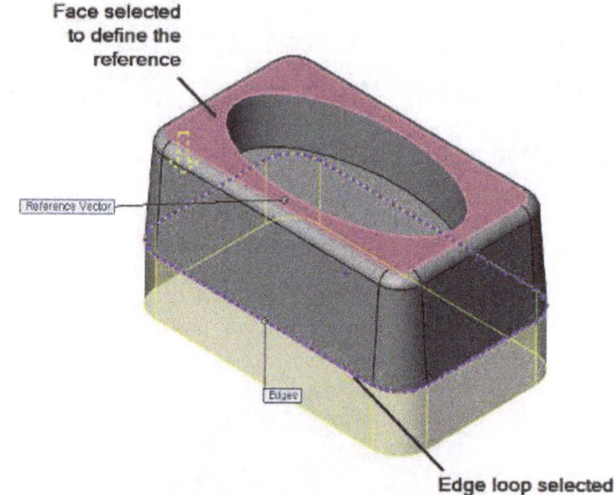

4. Specify the distance of the ruled surface in the **Distance** edit box.
5. Click in the **Reference Vector** selection box available in the **Distance/Direction** section.
6. Select a face or an edge to define the reference vector.

You can also use the **Coordinate input** option in the **Distance/Direction** section to define the reference vector.

Coordinate input

X 1

Y 0

Z 0

7. Click the **Reverse Direction** button, if required.
8. Click **OK**.

TUTORIAL 11 (Offset Surface)

1. To create a planar surface, click the **Offset Surface** button on the **Surfaces** Command Manager (or) click **Insert > Surface > Offset**.
2. Select the faces to offset.

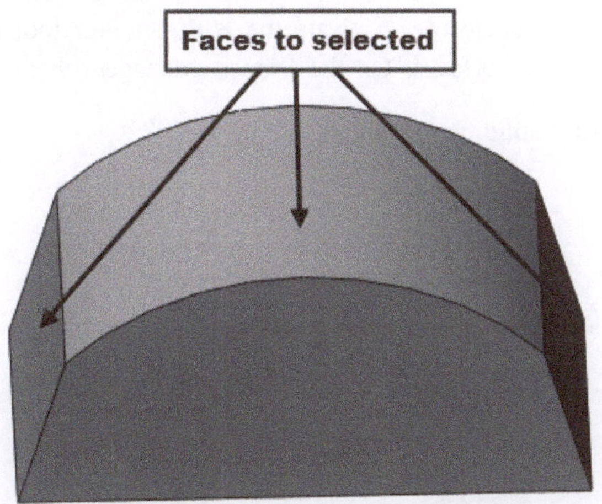

3. Specify the offset distance in the **Offset Distance** edit box.
4. Click **OK** on the Property Manager. The offset surface is created.

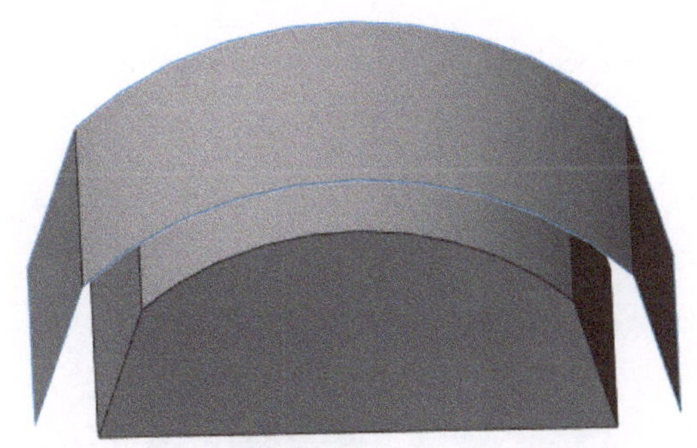

TUTORIAL 12 (Knitting Surfaces)

The surfaces which you create act as individual surfaces unless they are knitted together. The **Knit Surface** tool lets you combine two or more surfaces to form a single surface.

Surface Bodies(2)

Surface-Extrude3

Surface-Extrude4

1. To knit surfaces, click the **Knit Surface** button on the **Surfaces** CommandManager (or) click **Insert > Surface > Knit**.
2. Select the surfaces to knit.

The **Merge entities** option available in the **Selections** section is used to merge the overlapping or redundant surfaces.

The options in the **Gap Control** group are used to knit the surfaces with small gaps. The **Knitting tolerance** box is used to define a tolerance value for the gaps. The gaps within the specified tolerance value will be knitted. You can also specify the gap range by using the sliders in the **Gap Control** group.

3. After specifying the required options, click the **OK** button to knit the surfaces.

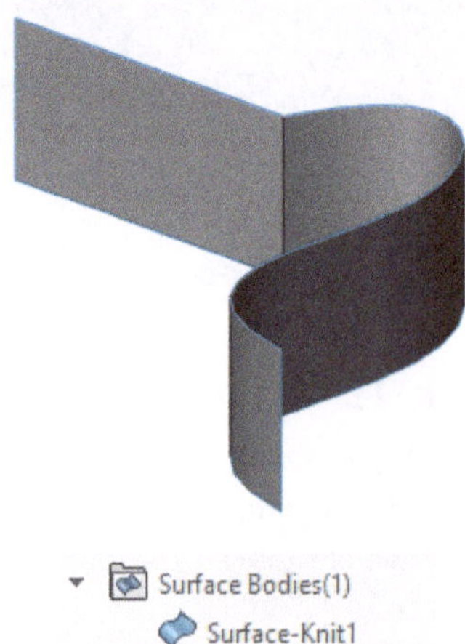

In some cases, you may need to extract the surfaces of the solid body. You can use the **Knit Surface** tool to extract the surfaces of the solid body. Hide the solid body to see the extracted surfaces.

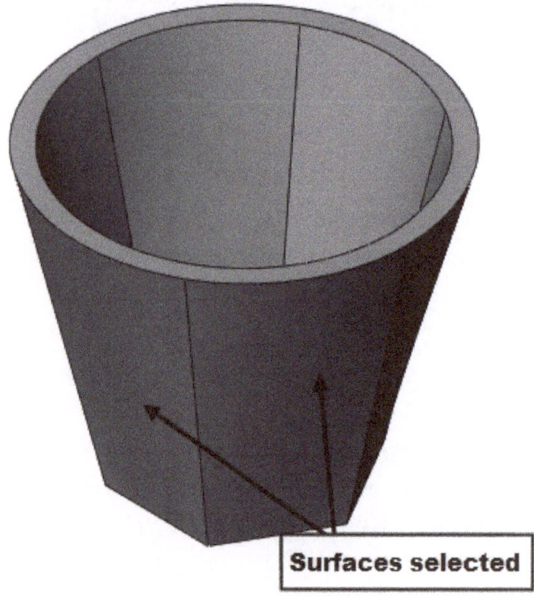

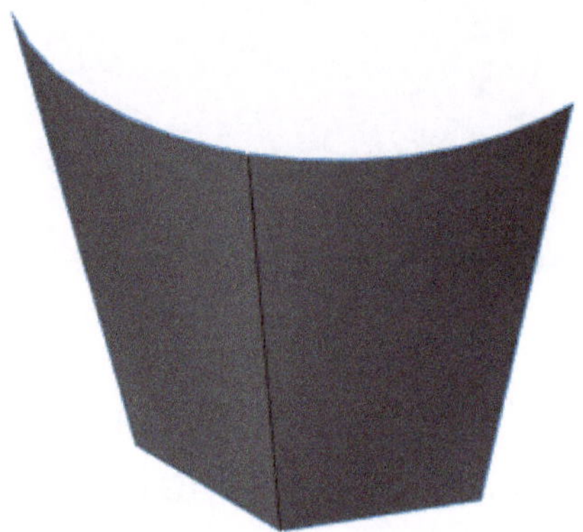

Creating a Solid by Knitting Surfaces

You can convert surfaces forming a closed enclosure into solid using the **Knit Surface** tool. Create surfaces forming a closed enclosure. Activate the **Knit Surface** tool and select the surfaces. On the PropertyManager, check the **Create Solid** option, and then click **OK** ✓ .

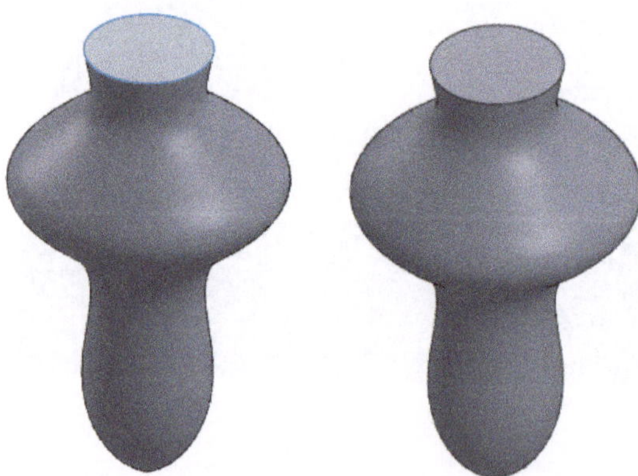

TUTORIAL 13 (Trimming Surfaces)

You can trim surfaces using the **Trim Surface** tool. The surfaces are trimmed using a trimming tool. The trimming tool can be a surface, plane, or a sketched entity.

1. To trim a surface, click the **Trim Surface** button on the **Surfaces** Command Manager (or) click **Insert > Surface > Trim**; the **Trim Surface** Property Manager appears.

You can trim a surface using the **Standard** and **Mutual** options available in the **Trim Type** group. The two trimming methods are discussed next.

Trimming a Surface using the Standard option

2. To trim a surface using this option, click the **Standard** option in the **Trim Types** group.
3. Select **Keep selections** on the PropertyManager.
4. Select the trim tool and surface to keep.

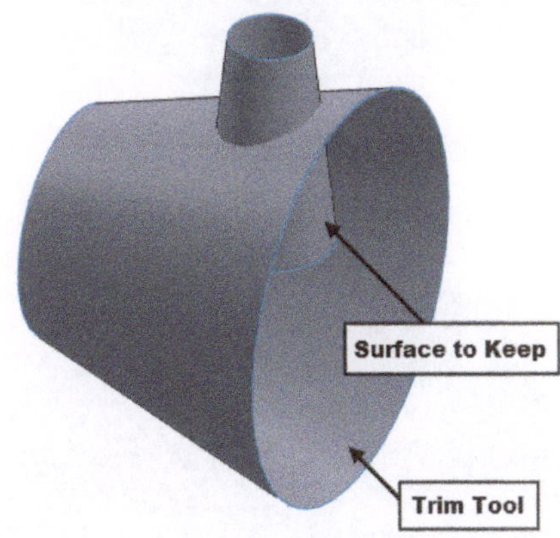

If you select the **Remove selections** option in the **Selections** group, you need to select the surface to remove.

5. Click **OK** to trim the surface.

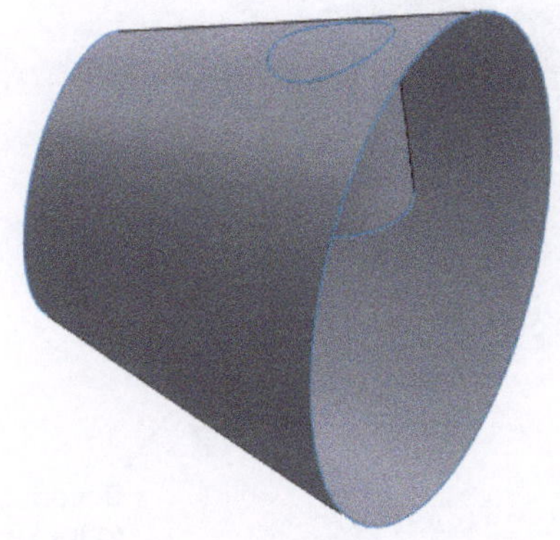

You can also trim a surface using a sketch.

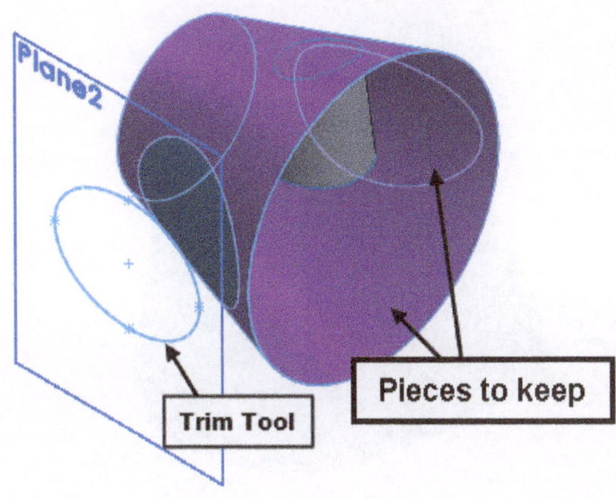

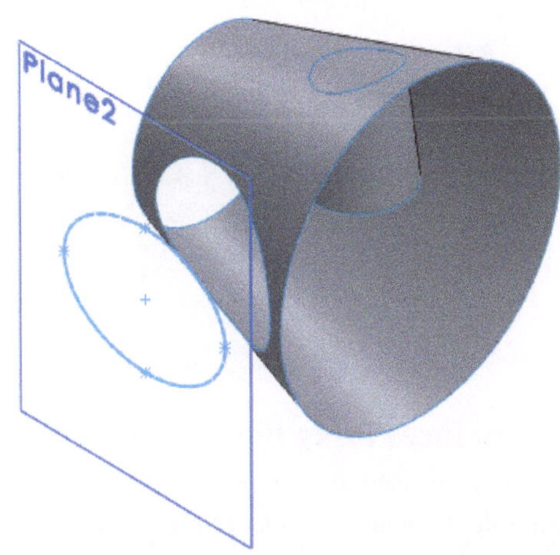

You can also use a surface as a trim tool that does not extend completely along the surface to be trimmed.

In this case, the **Surface Split Options** will be useful. If you use the **Natural** option, the split will occur following the natural extension of the trim tool.

If you select the **Linear** option, the split will be a straight line to the nearest edge.

If you select the **Split All** option, multiple split lines will appear. You can decide which portion of the surface to keep or remove.

Trimming Surfaces using the Mutual option

The **Mutual** option is used to trim multiple surfaces at a time. For example, you can use this option for the following case.

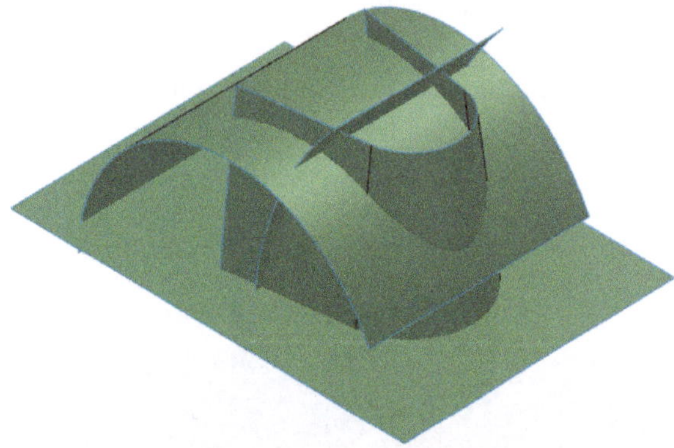

1. To trim surfaces using this option, select the **Mutual** option from the **Trim Type** group.
2. Select the required surfaces from the model (All surfaces in this case).
3. After selecting the required surfaces, select the **Keep selections** or **Remove selections** option.

If you select the **Keep selections** option, you need to select the surfaces to be kept. If you select the **Remove selections** option, you need to select the surfaces to be removed. In this case, you select the **Keep selection** option.

4. Click in the next selection box of the PropertyManager.
5. Select the surfaces to be kept.

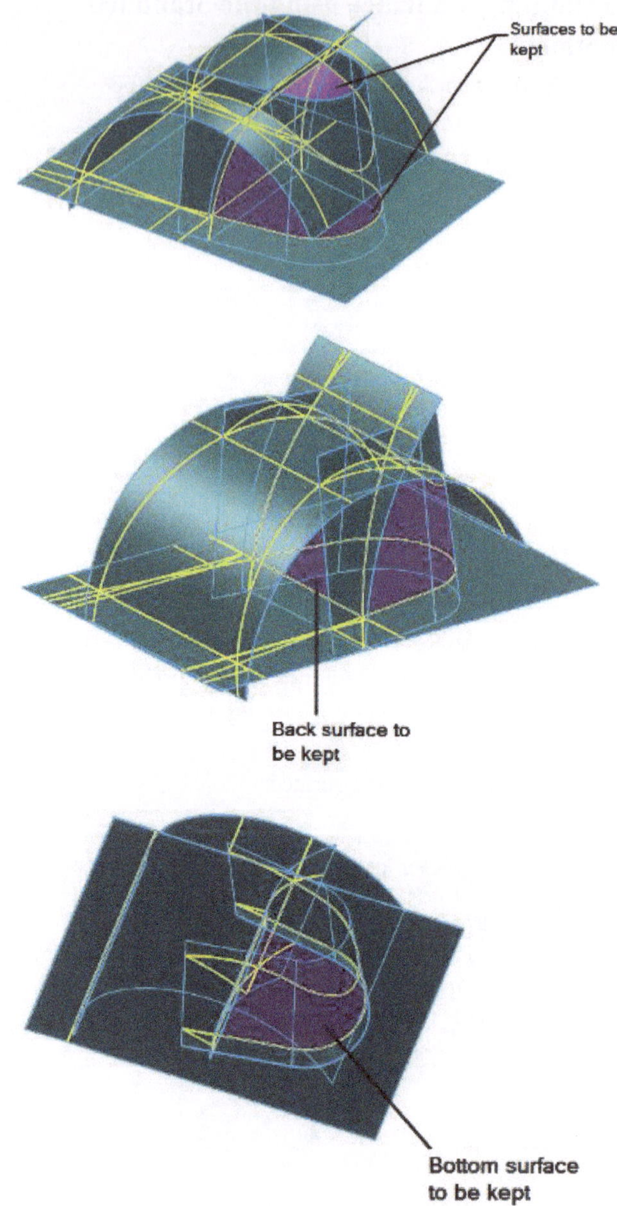

6. Click **OK** ✓ to trim the surfaces.

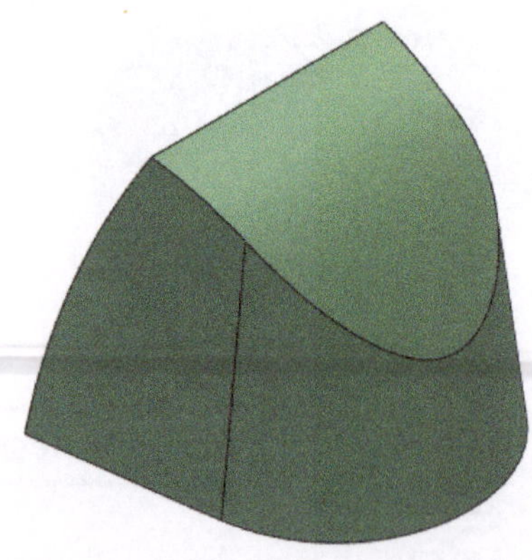

TUTORIAL 14 (Extending Surfaces)

During the design process, you may sometimes need to extend a surface. You can extend a surface using the **Extend Surface** tool.

1. To invoke this tool, click the **Extend Surface** button on the **Surfaces** Command Manager (or) click **Insert > Surface > Extend**.

The parameters used to define an extended surface are available on this PropertyManager. You can select an edge, multiple edges, or an entire surface to extend.

Single Edge

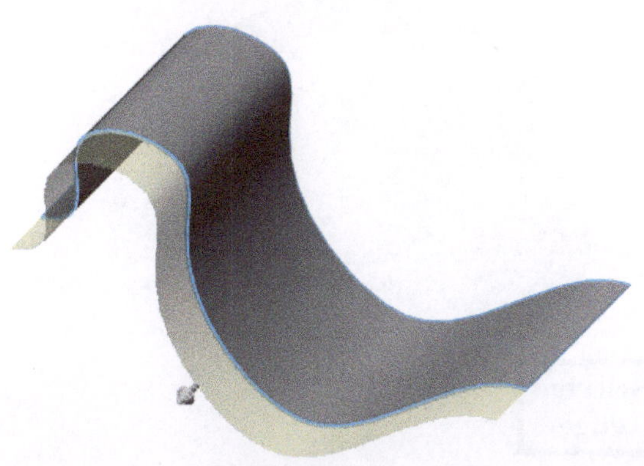

Multiple Edges

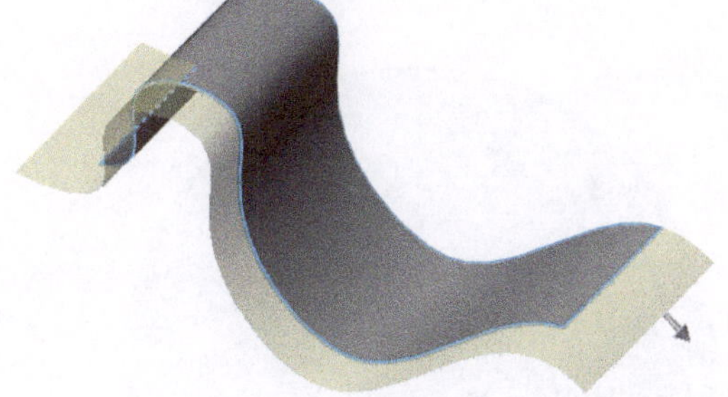

Entire Surface

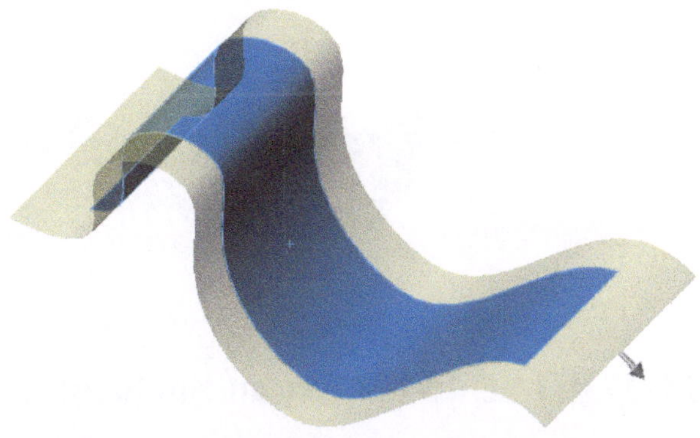

2. Select an edge from the surface body.
3. Select the **Distance** option and type a value in the **Distance** box. If you select the **Up to point** option, you can define the distance by selecting a vertex or point. The **Up to surface** option is used to define the distance by selecting a surface.

When the surface you have selected is not planar, you can decide the type of extension by using the **Extension Type** options. Use the **Same Surface** option to extend the surface by maintaining the curvature of the original surface. If you select the **Linear** option, the extended surface will be created tangent to the original surface.

Same Surface Extension

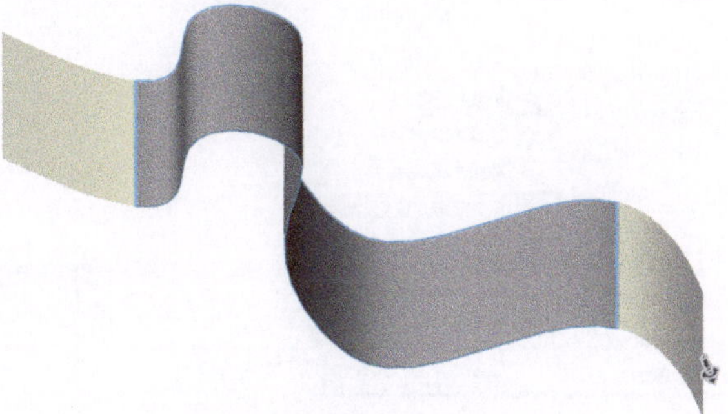

Linear Extension

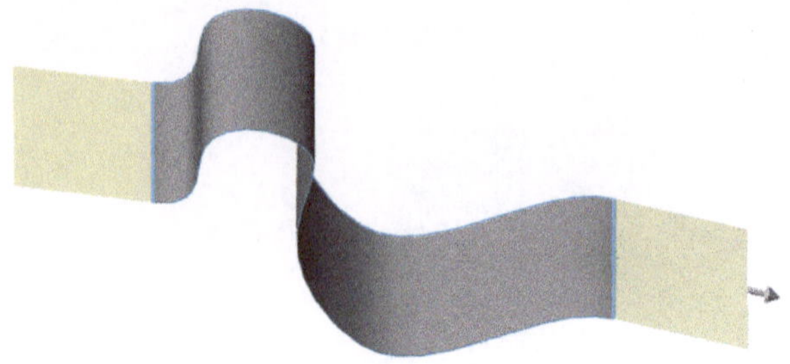

4. Click **OK**.

TUTORIAL 15 (Offset on Surface)

You can offset the edges of a surface using the **Offset on Surface** tool.

1. On the ribbon, click **Sketch > Offset On Surface**.

Tip: *If the* ***Offset On Surface*** *tool is unavailable on the CommandManager, right click on the* ***Sketch*** *tab of the CommandManager, and then select* ***Customize.***

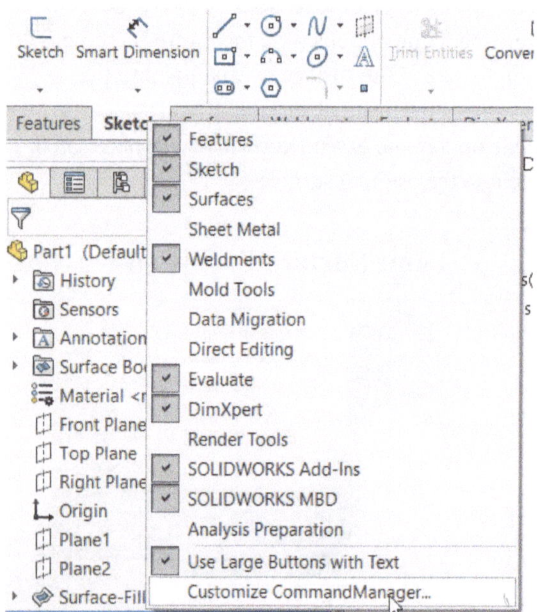

On the ***Customize*** *dialog, click the* ***Commands*** *tab and select* ***Sketch*** *from the* ***Categories*** *list. Next, click and drag the* ***Offset on Surface*** *command. Keep the left mouse button pressed, move the cursor onto the CommandManager, and then release the mouse button; the* ***Offset On Surface*** *command is available on the CommandManager.*

2. Click on the surface.

3. On the PropertyManager, select the **Offset type** (**Geodesic Offset** or **Euclidean Offset**).

The **Geodesic Offset** option creates an offset curve with the shortest distance between the selected edge and the curve. The offset distance is measured along the supporting surface.

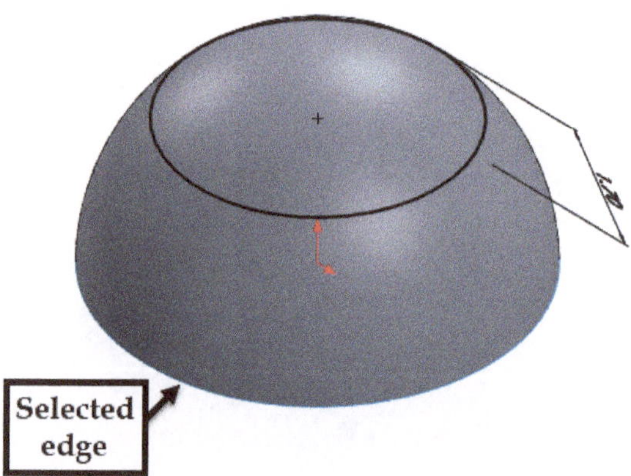

The **Euclidean Offset** option creates an offset curve by measuring the offset distance in the linear direction. It results in a longer offset distance.

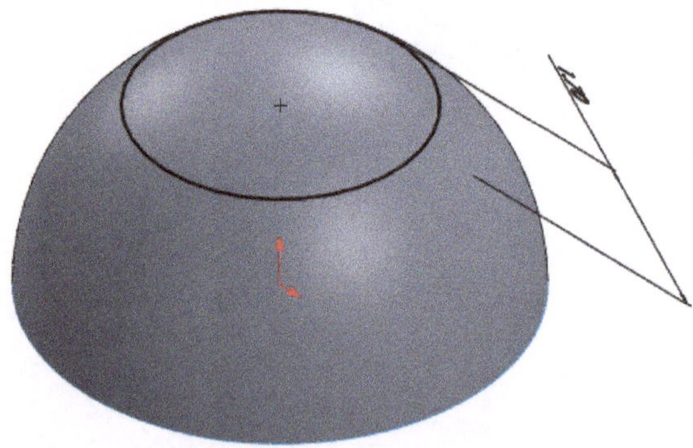

4. On the PropertyManager, type in a value in the **Offset Distance** box.
5. Click **OK**.

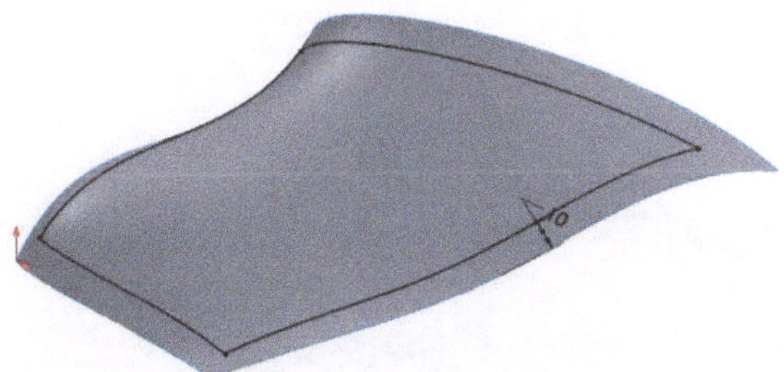

A 3D Sketch is created on the selected surface body.

6. Press Ctrl+Z on your keyboard to undo the **Offset On Surface** operation.
7. On the CommandManager, click **Sketch > Offset On Surface**.
8. Type 5 in the **Offset Distance** box of the PropertyManager.
9. Select the edges of the surface, as shown.

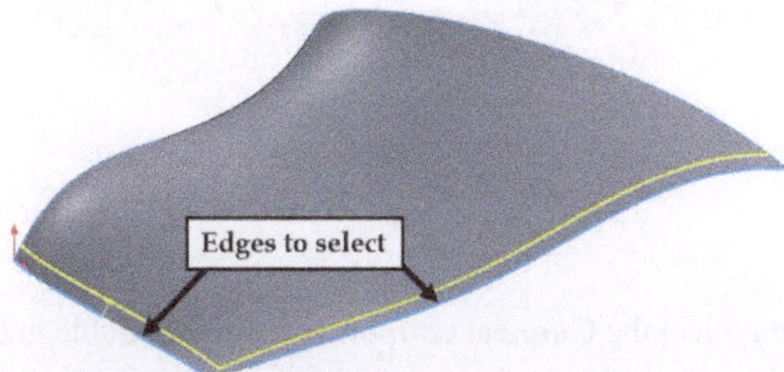

10. Click **OK** on the PropertyManager.
11. Click the **Exit Sketch** icon located at the top right corner of the graphics window.

TUTORIAL 16 (Untrimming a Surface)

You can untrim a trimmed surface using the **Untrim Surface** tool.

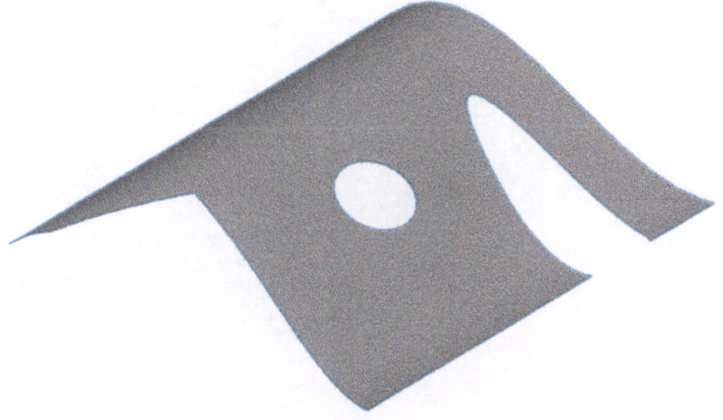

1. Click the **Untrim Surface** button on the **Surfaces** Command Manager (or) click **Insert > Surface > Untrim**.
2. Select the edges to be untrimmed.

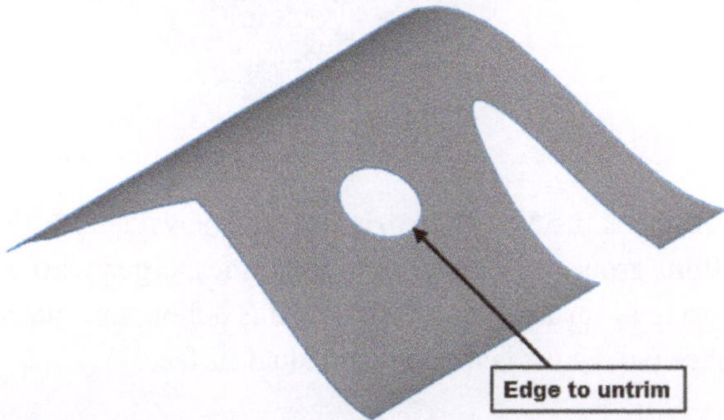

3. Click **OK**.

If you select the edge, which is intersecting the surface's boundary, the untrim surface is created within the boundary. Make sure that the **Edge untrim type** is set to **Extend edges**.

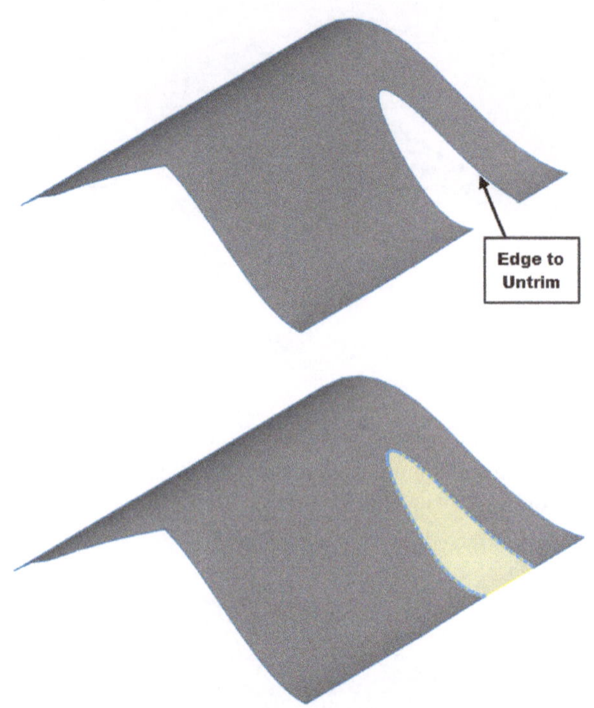

If you check the **Merge to original** option available in the **Options** group, the untrim surface will be merged with the original surface. If you uncheck this option, the untrim surface will be created as an individual surface.

When you untrim the external edges, you have control over the surface created. You can extend the untrim surface beyond the surface's boundary by entering the extension percentage on the PropertyManager.

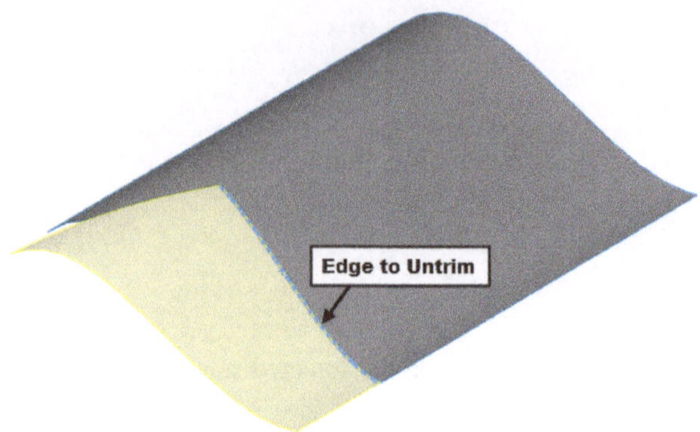

If you select the external edges adjacent to each other, the untrim surface will be bound by the selected edges.

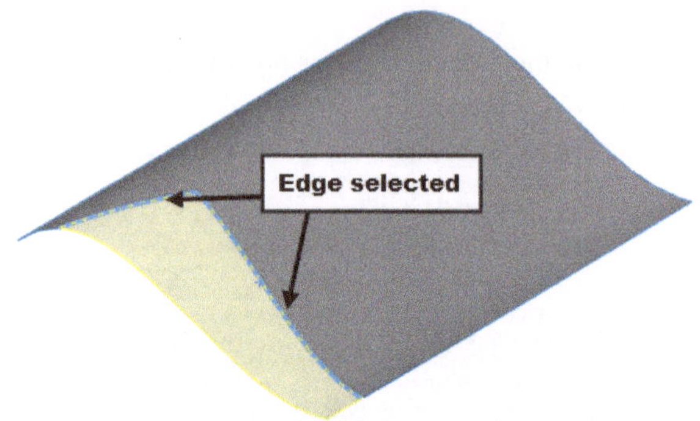

If you select the **Connect endpoints** option available in the **Options** group, only the portion necessary to connect the two endpoints is created.

You can use the **Untrim Surface** tool to untrim an entire surface. Also, the PropertyManager has options to untrim the internal, external, or all the surface edges.

TUTORIAL 17 (Deleting Holes)

1. To delete a hole, select it from the model and press the **Delete** key. The **Choose Option** dialog appears.

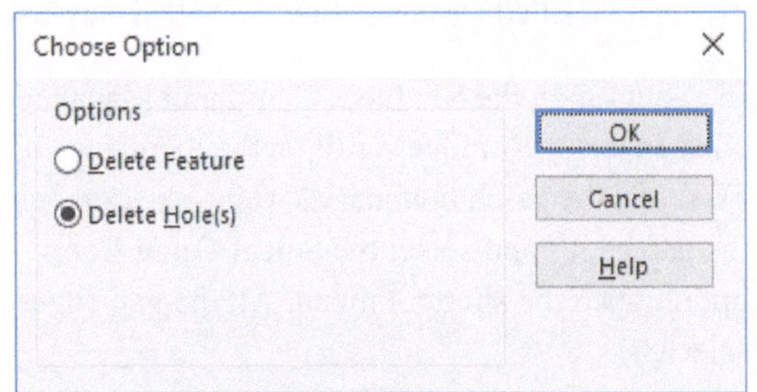

2. Select the **Delete Hole(s)** option and click **OK**.

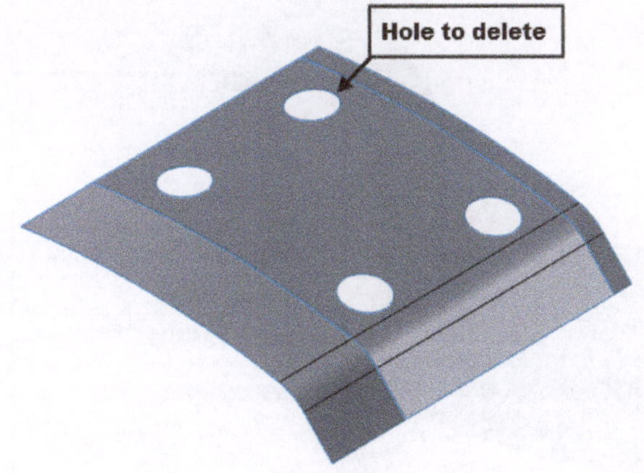

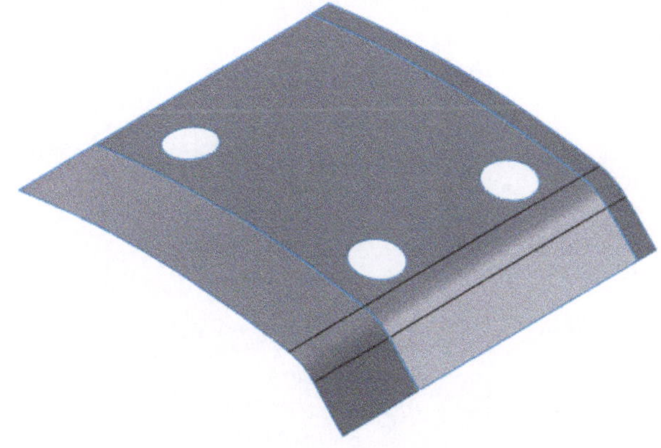

You will notice the **Delete Hole** feature in the FeatureManager Design Tree.

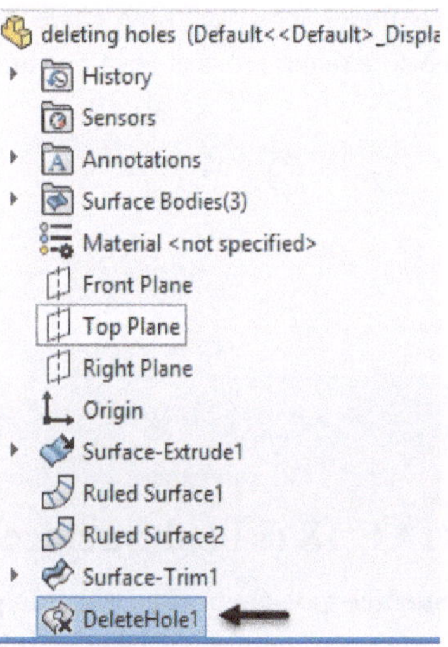

If you want the hole to be back, you can delete the **Delete Hole** feature from the FeatureManager Design Tree. You can also edit the **Delete Hole** feature. Click on the **Delete Hole** feature and click **Edit Feature**.

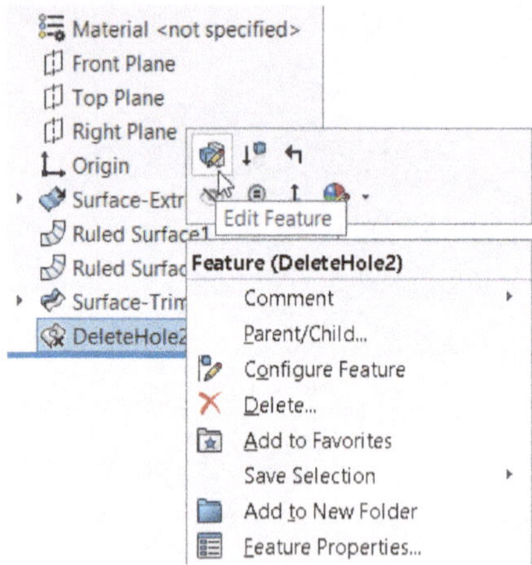

The PropertyManager shows the list of holes that were deleted. You can add more holes to the list by selecting them from the model. You can also remove the hole from the list. Make sure that there is at least one hole in the list.

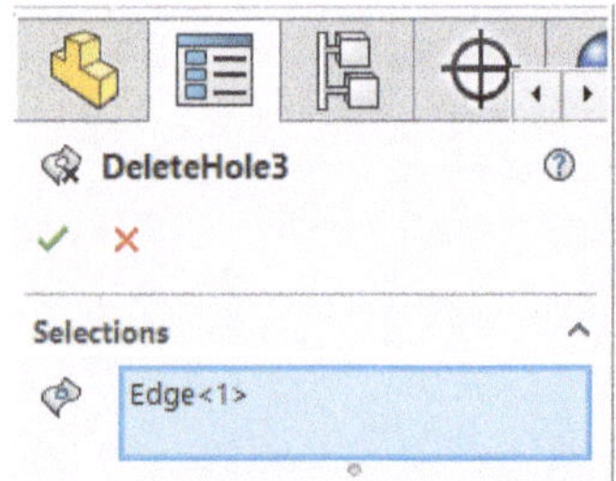

TUTORIAL 18 (Filled Surface)

The **Filled Surface** tool can be used either to patch holes in models or to create complex surfaces. While patching surfaces, the **Filled Surface** tool gives you more options than deleting holes or untrimming. It provides more control over the definition of the resultant patch. For example, consider the model shown in the figure. You can see that a face is missing. In a case like this, both the **Delete Hole** and **Untrim Surface** tools fail to fill this gap. The **Filled Surface** tool will be used in this case.

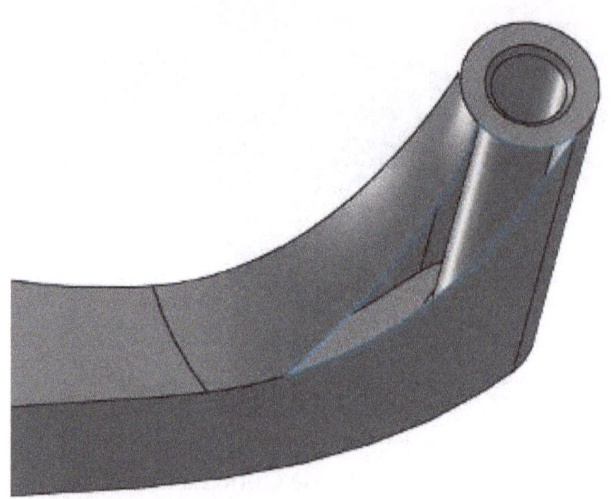

1. To create a filled surface, click the **Filled Surface** button on the **Surfaces** Command Manager (or) click **Insert > Surface > Fill** on the menu bar.
2. To select the patch boundaries, right-click on one of the gap edges and select the **Select Open Loop** option from the shortcut menu. All the gap edges are selected.

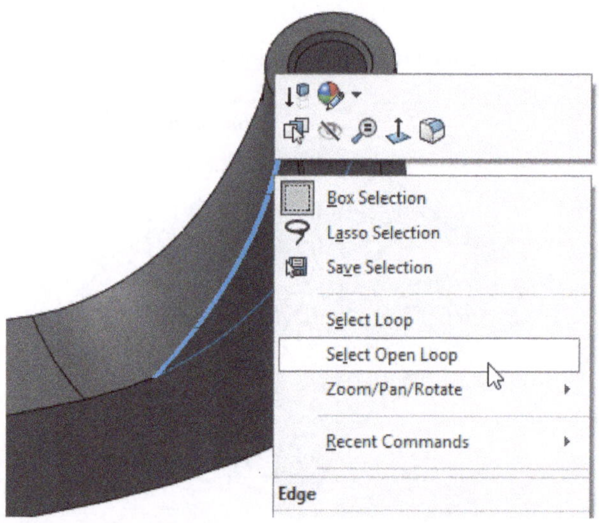

3. Select an option from the **Curvature Control** drop-down. It defines the curvature continuity of the fill surface.

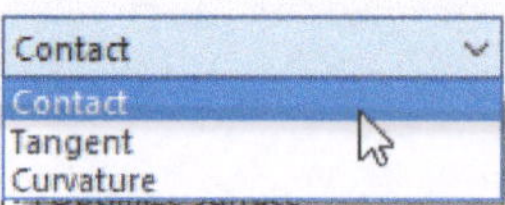

The options in this drop-down are **Contact**, **Tangent**, and **Curvature**. Most of the gap edges should be tangent to the surrounding faces.

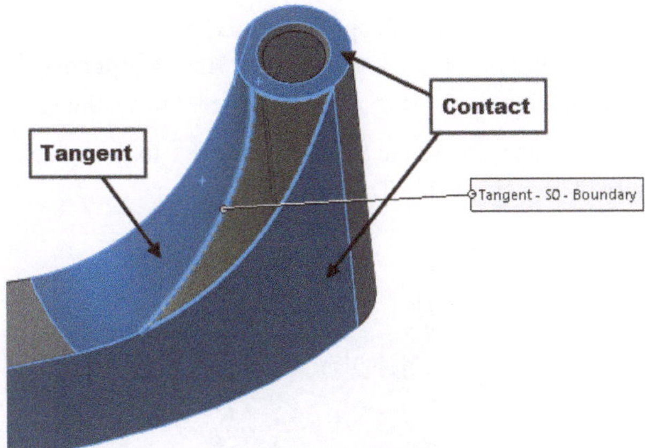

The **Apply to all edges** option is used to apply the curvature setting to all edges.

4. Click **OK** to create the filled surface.

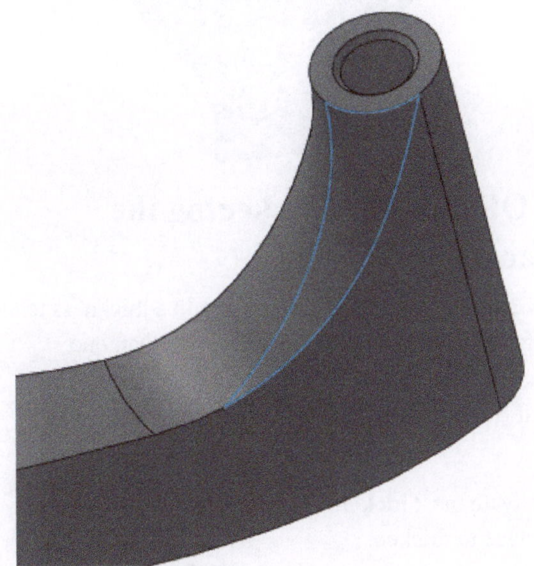

TUTORIAL 19

You can also use the **Filled Surface** tool for creating a new surface.

1. Activate the **Filled Surface** tool and select the patch boundary.
2. Click in the **Constraint Curves** selection box and then select the constraint curves.

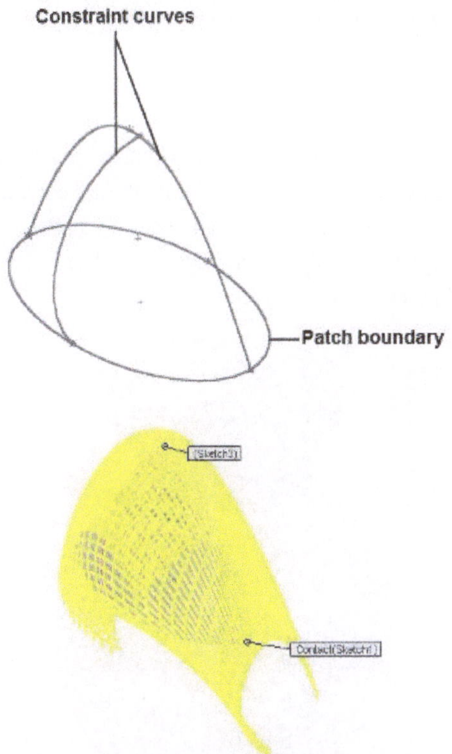

3. Specify the curvature setting (**Contact**, **Tangent**, or **Curvature**).

The **Optimize Surface** option available in the **Patch Boundary** group will create a simple surface very quickly. If you uncheck this option, the **Resolution Control** slider will appear. You can use this slider to define the resulting surface. You can remove wrinkles or other imperfections from the surface. However, the surface will be created very slowly. It is recommended that you use the **Optimize Surface** option for quick results.

4. After specifying the required settings, click **OK** to create the filled surface.

TUTORIAL 20 (Converting a Surface to Solid)

Creating a solid from a surface can be accomplished by simply thickening a surface. You can also create a solid if the surface encloses a volume. For example, consider the surface shown in the figure. It encloses a volume. However, there is only one surface body listed in the FeatureManager Design Tree.

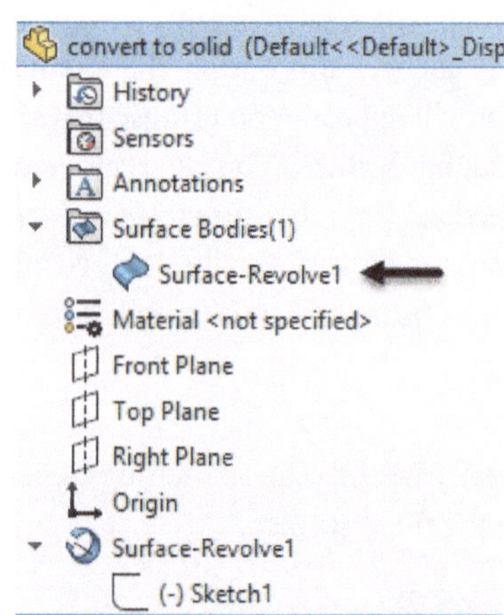

1. To make this surface into a solid, click the **Thicken** button on the **Surfaces** Command Manager.
2. Select the enclosed surface.

You will notice that the **Create solid from enclosed volume** option is enabled. This option is available only when you select an enclosed surface.

3. Check the **Create solid from enclosed volume** option.
4. Click **OK** to create a solid.

You can use the **Mass Properties** tool (On the CommandManager, click **Evaluate > Mass Properties**) to check whether the surface is converted into a solid or not. You can also use the **Section View** tool available on the View Heads-Up Toolbar.

TUTORIAL 21 (Thickening the Surface)

The **Thicken** tool can also be used to add a thickness to the surface. If the geometry contains more than one surface, then make sure that they are knit together using the **Knit Surface** tool.

1. Activate the **Thicken** command and select the surface to thicken.
2. Type-in the thickness value on the PropertyManager.
3. Define the thickness side using the **Thickness** buttons. Select the **Thicken Side1** button to add thickness outside the surface. The **Thicken Side2** button is used to add thickness inside the surface. The **Thicken Both Sides** button is used to add thickness to both sides of the surface.
4. Click **OK**.

Thickness Side1

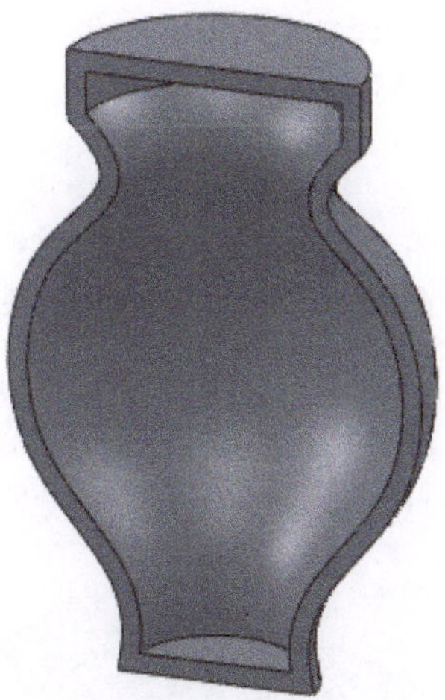

Thickness Both Sides

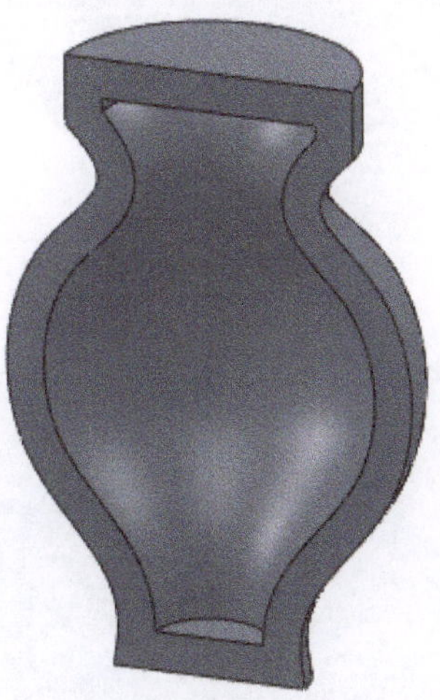

Thickness Sides2

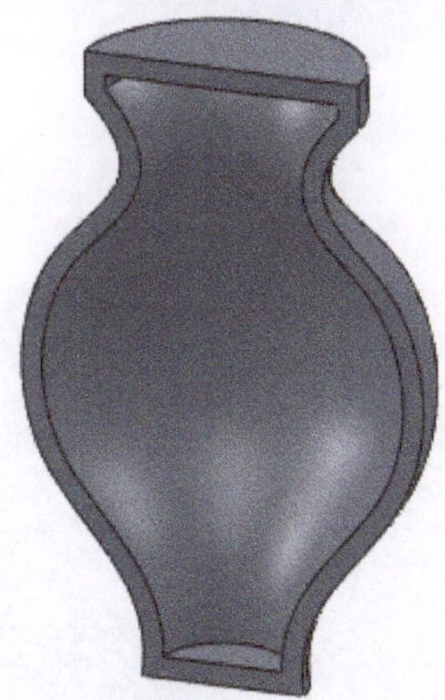

TUTORIAL 22 (Deleting Faces)

You can delete unwanted faces from a model. In the case of a solid, you can delete a face and make it a surface model.

1. To delete a face, click the **Delete Face** button from the **Surfaces** Command Manager.
2. Make sure that the **Delete** option is selected in the **Options** group.
3. Select the face to be deleted.

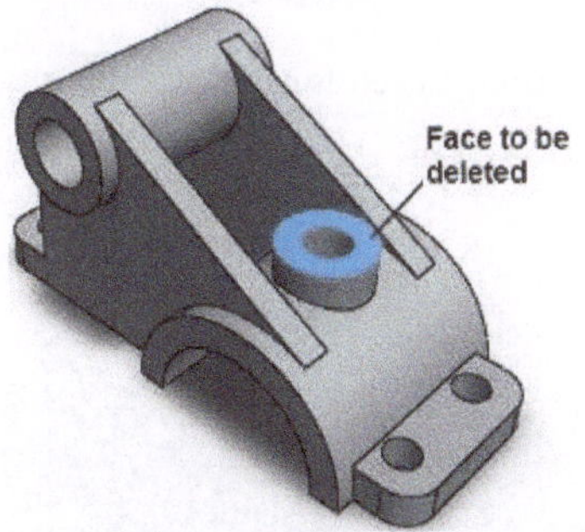

4. Click **OK** to delete the face.

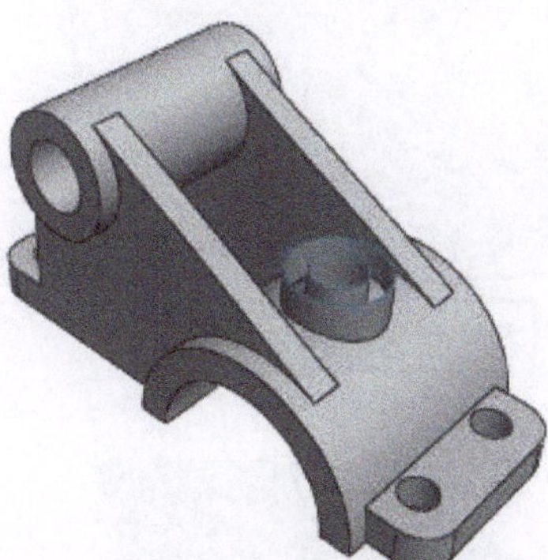

You can also use the **Delete and Patch** option available in the **Options** group. This option will be useful for the following type of cases.

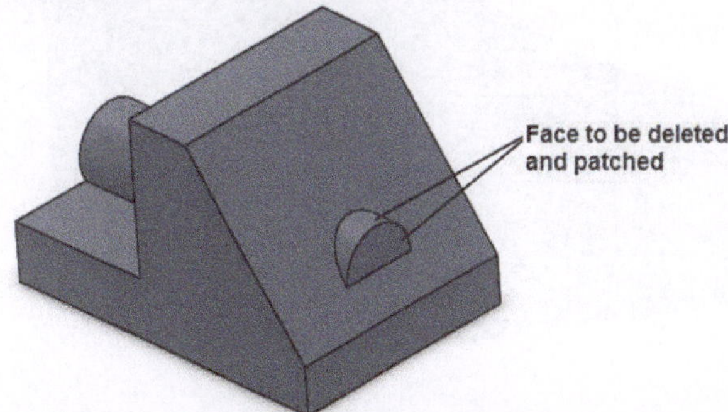

1. Select this option from the **Options** group and then select the faces to be deleted.
2. Click **OK**.

The **Delete and Fill** option is used for the following type of cases.

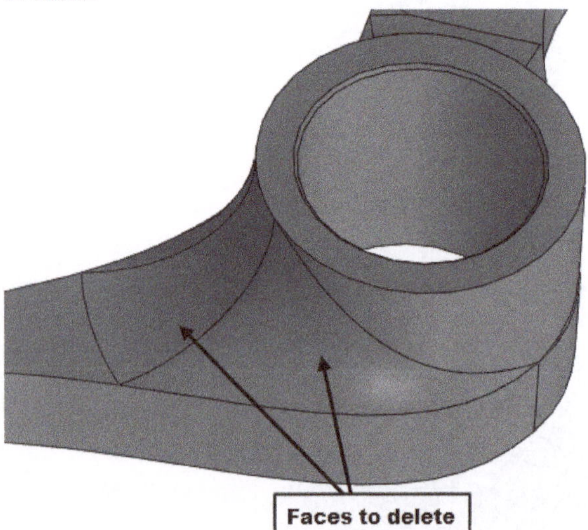

The resulting face is shown next.

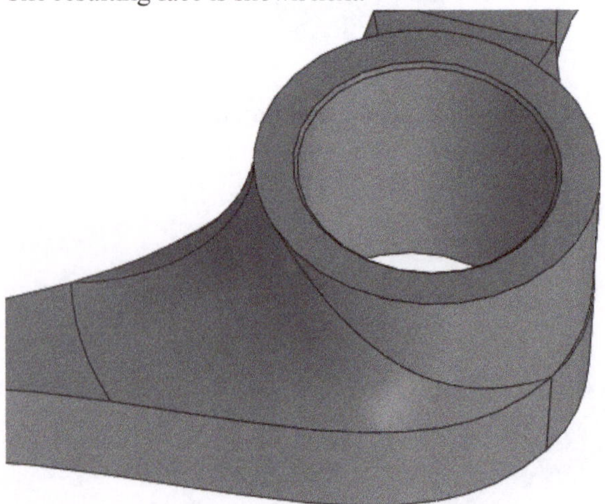

TUTORIAL 23 (Replacing Faces)

The **Replace Face** tool replaces a face or group of faces with another face or group of faces.

1. To replace a face, click the **Replace Face** button on the Command Manager (or) click **Insert > Face > Replace** on the Menu bar.
2. Select the target faces for replacement.
3. Click in the **Replacement Surface** selection box and select the replacement surface.

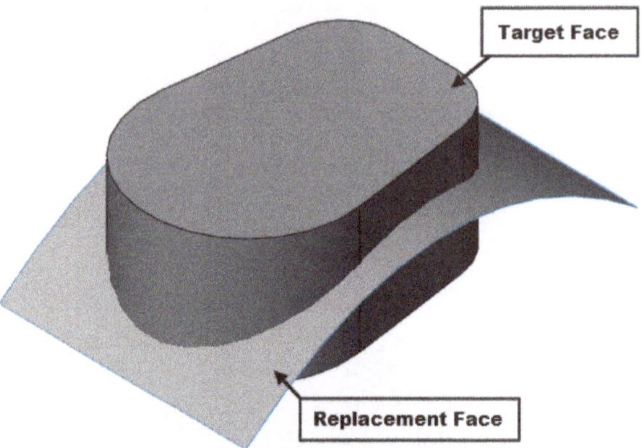

4. Click **OK** to replace the surface.

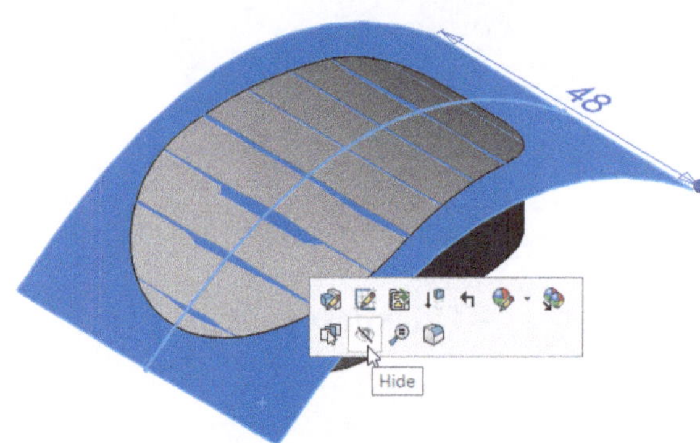

TUTORIAL 24 (Cutting with Surfaces)

You can cut a solid with a surface using the **Cut with Surface** tool. For example, you can cut the solid shown in the figure using a surface and create a complex face on the top.

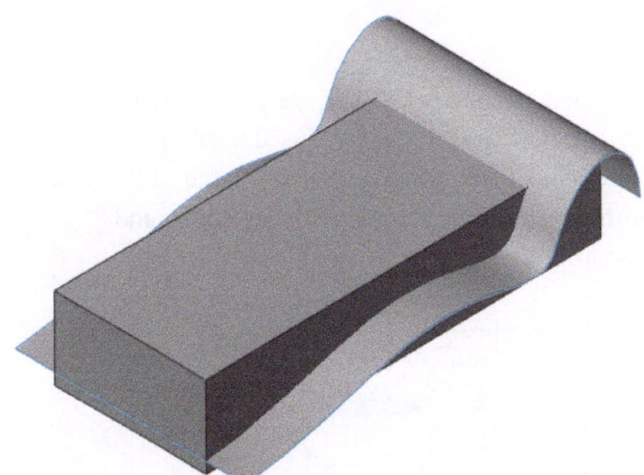

1. To cut a solid using a surface, click the **Cut with Surface** button on the **Surfaces** Command Manager (or) click **Insert > Cut > With Surface** from the Menu bar.
2. Select the cutting surface.

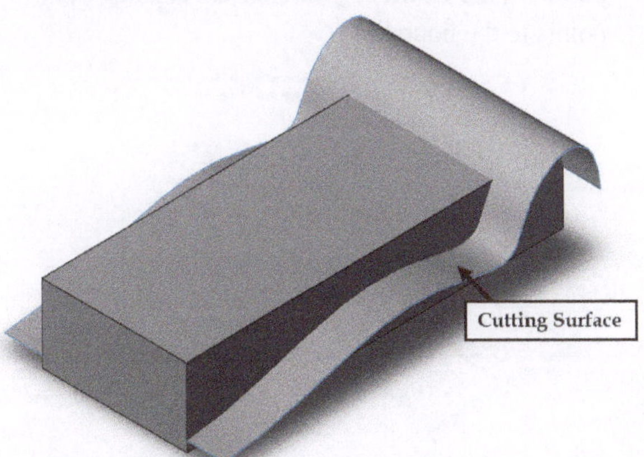

3. Specify the direction of the cut using the arrow that appears on the surface.
4. Click **OK**. Hide the extruded surface to view the result.

The **Bodies to Keep** dialog appears if the cut results in more than one body. Select the **All bodies** option (or) the **Selected Bodies** option and select the bodies to keep from the list. Click **OK** to cut the solid.

TUTORIAL 25 (Thickened Cut)

You can also use the **Thickened Cut** tool to cut a solid with the surface.

1. Click the **Thickened Cut** button on the **Surfaces** CommandManager (or) click **Insert > Cut > Thicken**.
2. Select the cutting surface.

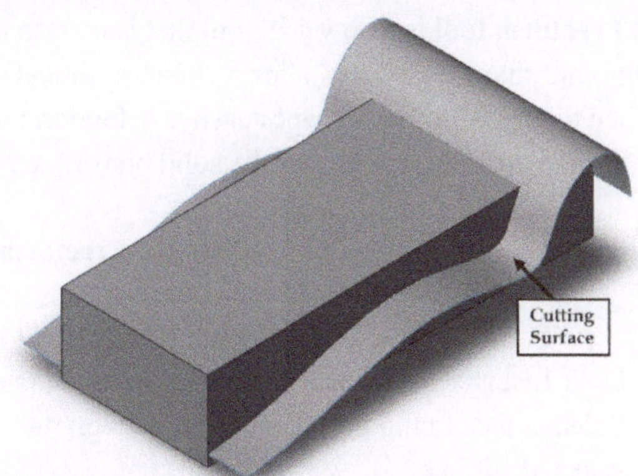

3. Specify the thickness side by clicking anyone of the icons in the **Thickness** section of the PropertyManager.

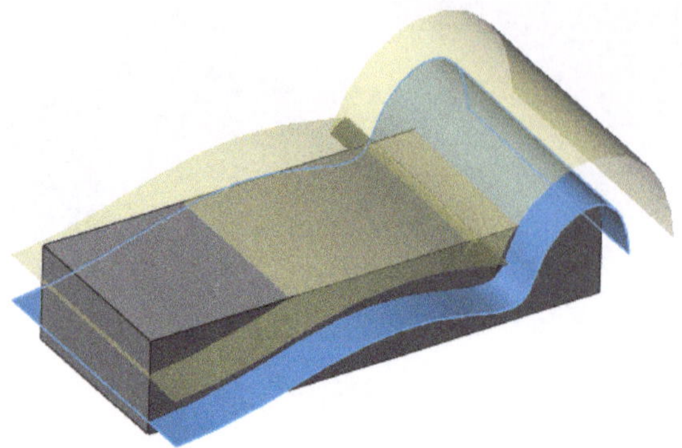

4. Specify the thickness value in the **Thickness** box available on the PropertyManager.
5. Click **OK**.

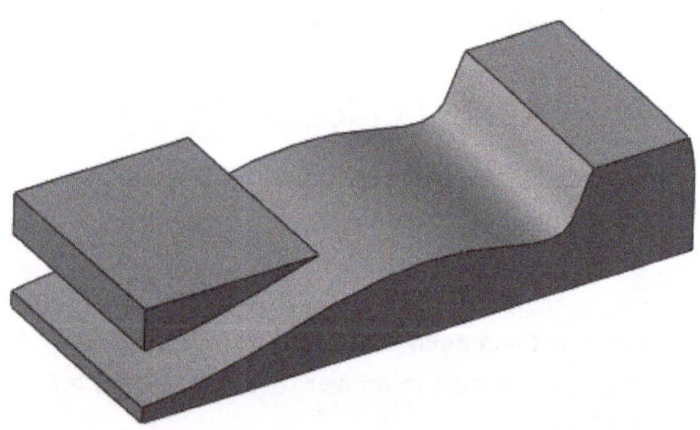

TUTORIAL 26 (Freeform Surfaces)

The **Freeform** tool is a powerful tool that is used to create ergonomic shapes. This tool allows you to push and pull a surface to create complex shapes easily. A freeform shape can be created using the face of the solid body or surface.

1. To create a freeform surface, click the **Freeform** button on the **Surfaces** Command Manager (or) click **Insert > Surface > Freeform** on the Menu bar.
2. Select a face to modify. A mesh appears on the selected surface.

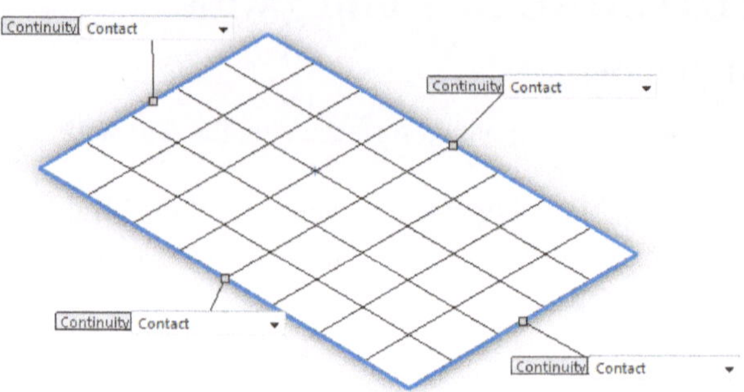

Also, the **Continuity** callouts are attached to the surface boundaries. These callouts are used to control the boundaries of the face. The options in the callouts are **Contact**, **Tangent**, **Curvature**, **Moveable**, and **Moveable/Tangent**.

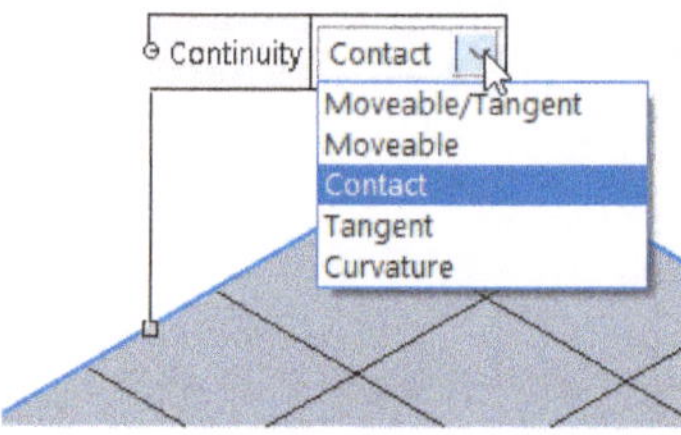

3. Select **Moveable** from the **Continuity** drop-down. The boundary acts as a control curve.
4. On the PropertyManager, click the **Add Points** button in the **Control Points** group and add control points to the boundary.

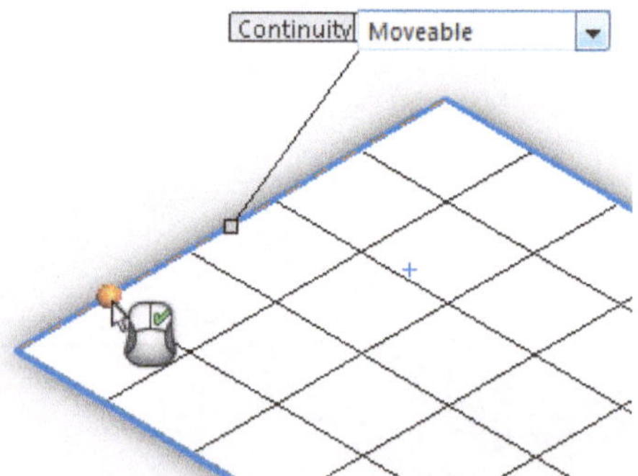

5. Click the **Add Points** button again or press ESC.
6. Select a control point on the boundary. A reference triad appears, as shown.

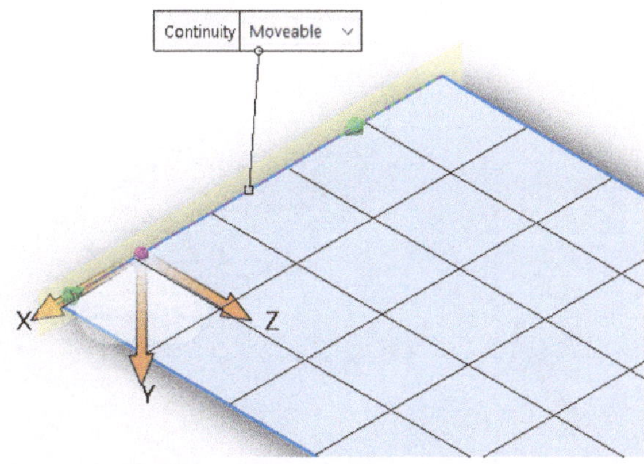

7. Click and drag the Y-axis of the triad and notice the surface. You can use the scale to move the control point precisely.

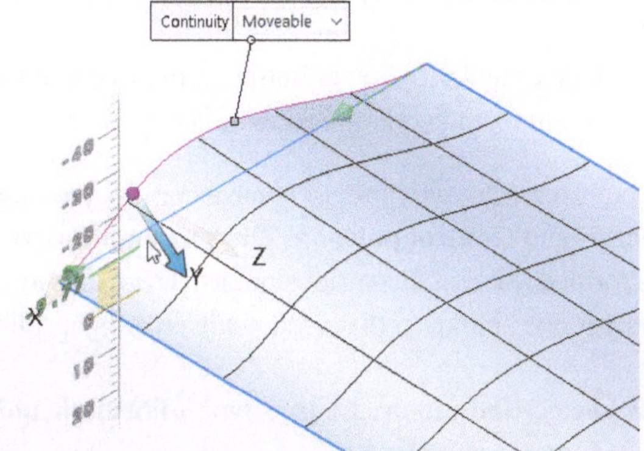

8. Likewise, drag the Z and X axes to modify the surface.

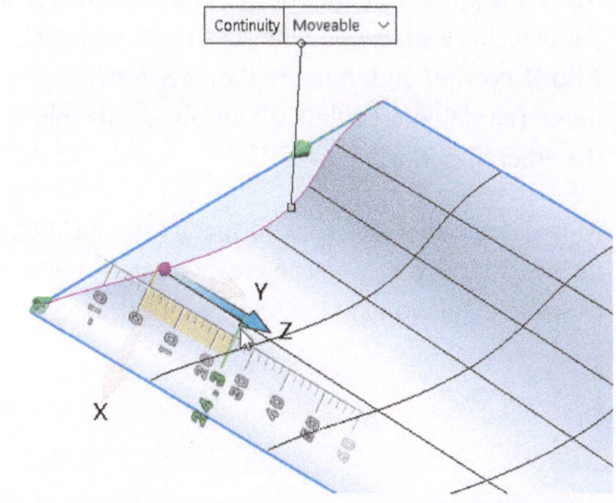

Moving the Control Point in Z-direction

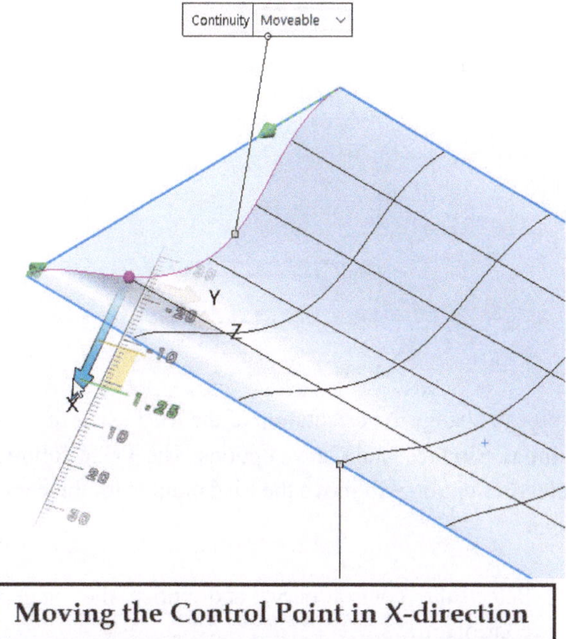

Moving the Control Point in X-direction

9. Click and drag the origin of the triad.

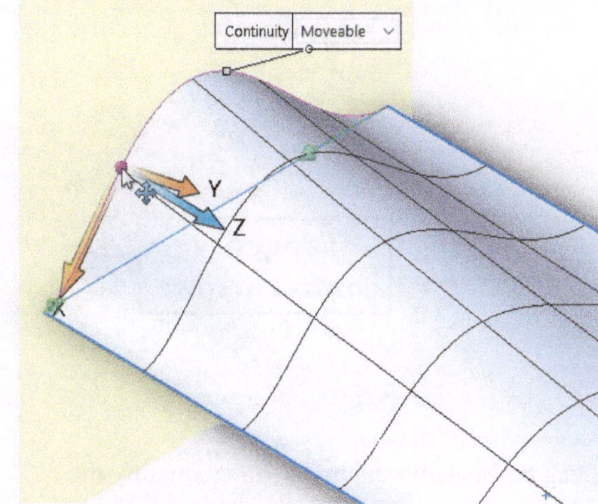

Click **Undo** on the PropertyManager, if you want to return to the previous state of the surface.

The behavior of the triad can also be controlled using the options in the Property Manager.

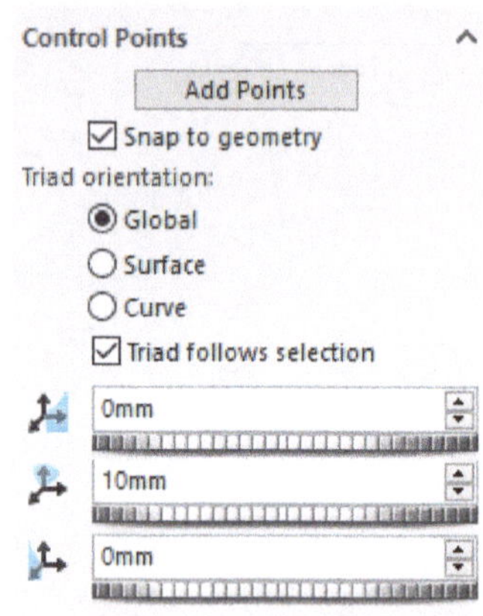

You can change the orientation of the triad using the **Global**, **Surface**, and **Curve** options. The **Triad follows selection** option will move the triad along with the control point.

10. Select the control curve and notice the tangency control arrows.

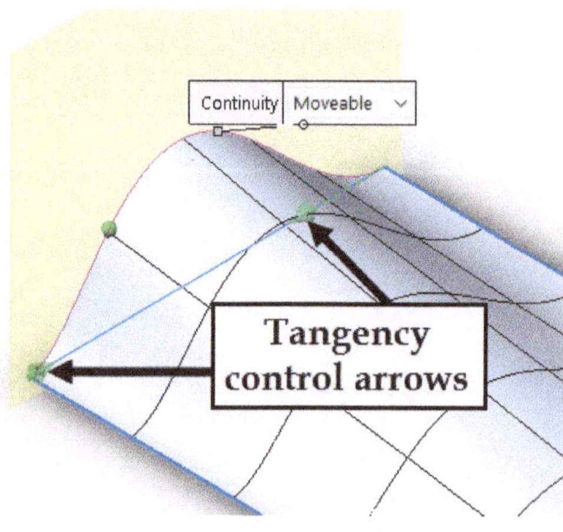

11. Drag the tangency control arrows to modify the curvature.

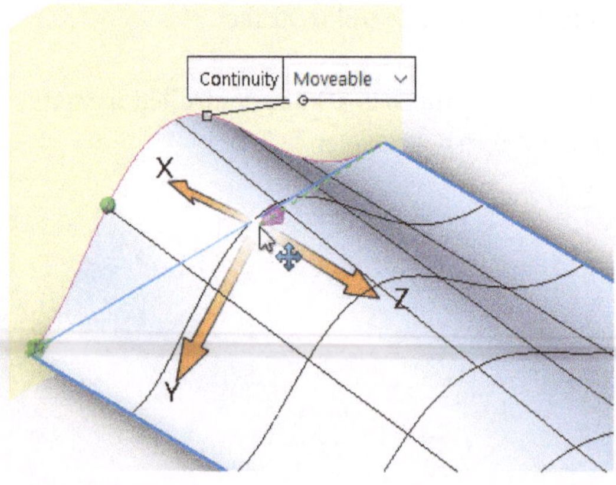

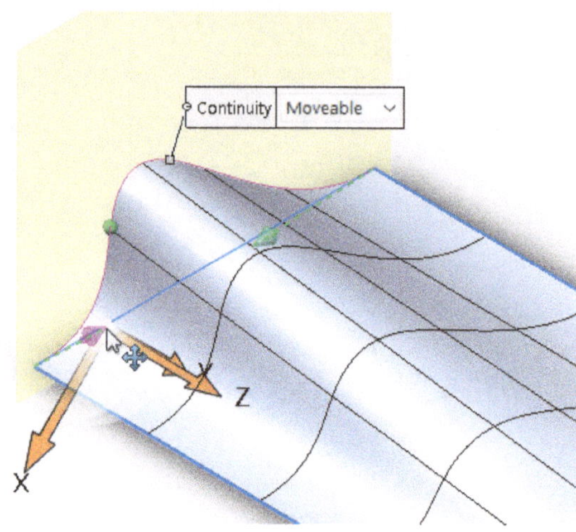

After modifying the surface, if you have changed the option in the Continuity callout by mistake, the modifications will be lost.

12. Click the **Add Curves** button in the **Control Curves** group to add control curves on the surface.

You can create two types of control curves- **Through points** and **Control polygon**. The **Through Points** curve is formed, joining the various points. The **Control polygon** is similar to that used while creating a spline.

13. Select the required curve type (**Through points** or **Control polygon**).

14. Move the pointer on the surface. You will notice that a green curve appears on the surface. If you click the **Flip Direction** button in the Property Manager (or) press Tab on your keyboard, the curve will appear in the other direction.

15. Move the pointer and click to specify the location of the control curves. You can create as many curves as possible by clicking at the required locations.

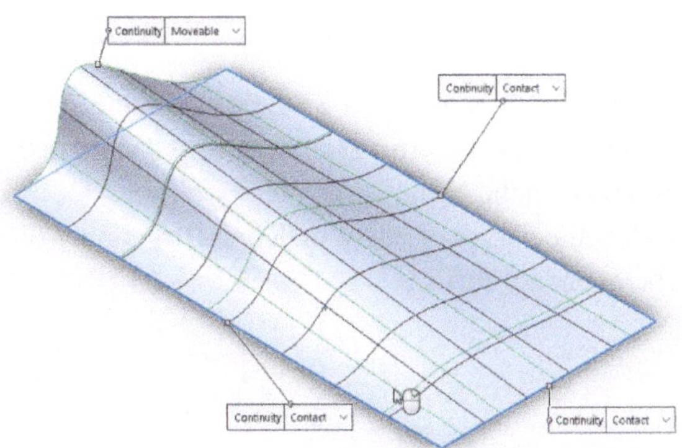

16. Click the **Add Curves** button again or press ESC.
17. Add control points on the control curves by using the **Add Points** button.

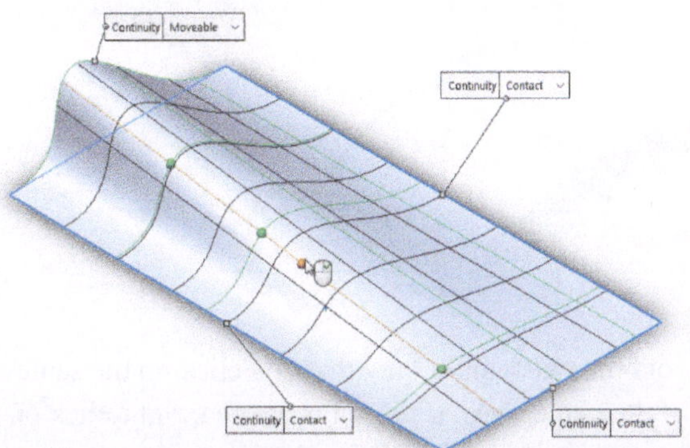

18. Click the **Add Points** button again or press ESC.
19. Select the required control curve; the control points appear on it. Push and pull the control points to modify the surface.

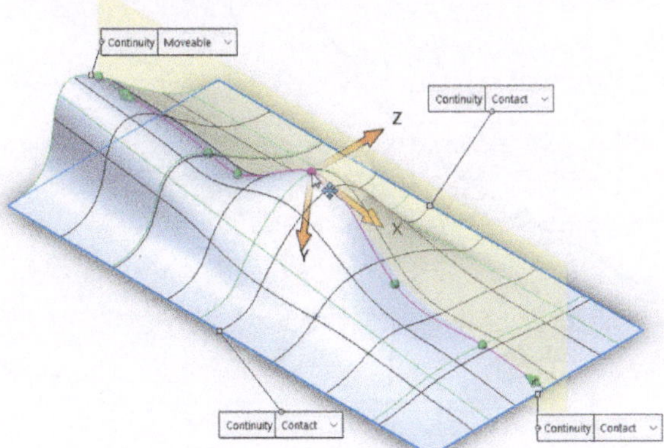

While modifying the surface, if you want to change the control curve type (for this example **Though points**), you can select the required option from the **Control Curves** section. The control curve type will be changed.

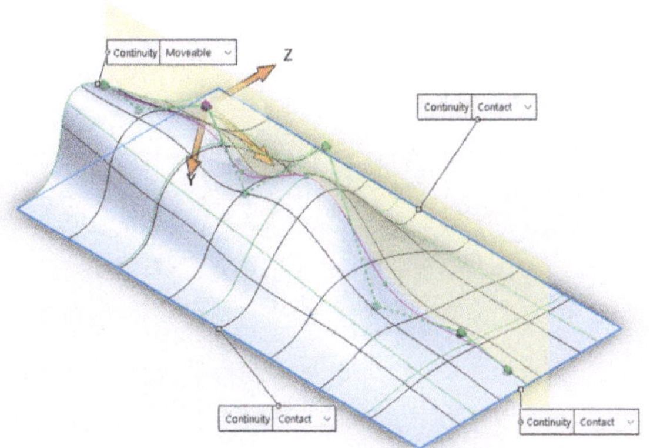

The **Display** section in the Property Manager can be used to modify the display.

20. Drag the **Face transparency** slider to change the transparency of the surface.
21. Drag the **Mesh density** slider to refine the mesh.

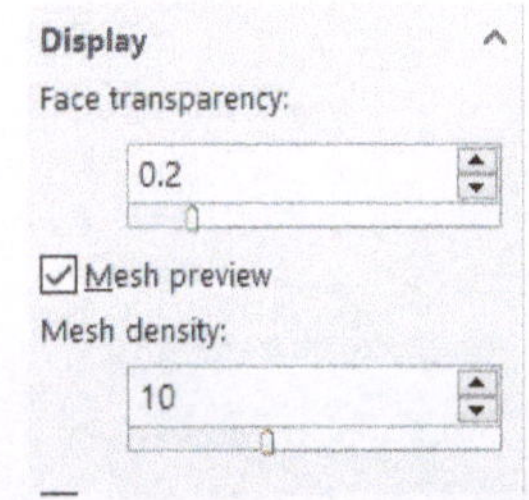

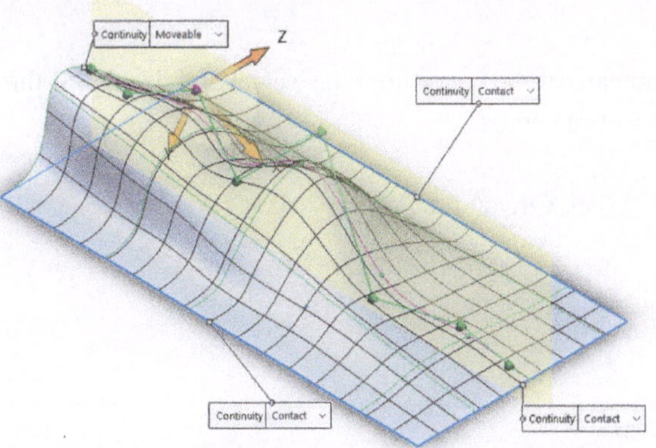

22. Display zebra stripes by checking the **Zebra stripes** option.

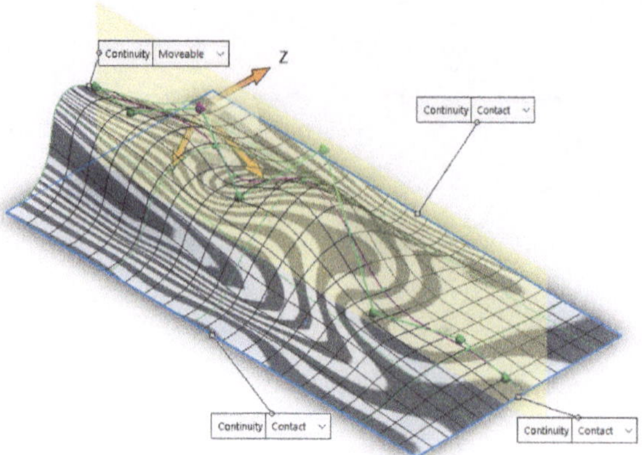

23. Uncheck the **Zebra stripes** option.
24. Check the **Curvature combs** and the **Direction 1** option. The curvature combs appear in the first direction.

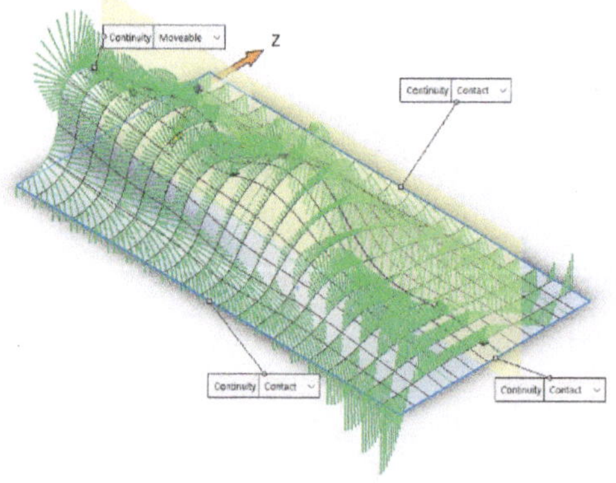

You can set the curvature type, scale, and density of the curvature combs

25. Click **OK** on the Property Manager.

TUTORIAL 27 (Boundary Surfaces)

The **Boundary Surface** tool is very similar to the **Lofted Surface** tool but allows you to create surfaces that can be tangent or curvature, continuous in both directions.

1. To create a boundary surface, click the **Boundary Surface** button on the **Surfaces** Command Manager (or) click **Insert > Surface > Boundary Surface** on the Menu bar.
2. Select the curves or edges to define **Direction 1** of the boundary surface.

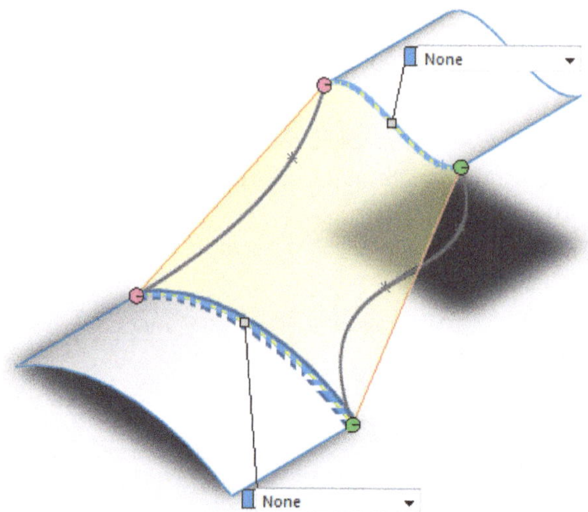

To avoid the twist, make sure that you click on the same side of the two curves. If a twist is created, right-click on any one of the edges in the **Direction 1** selection box and choose the **Flip Connectors** option.

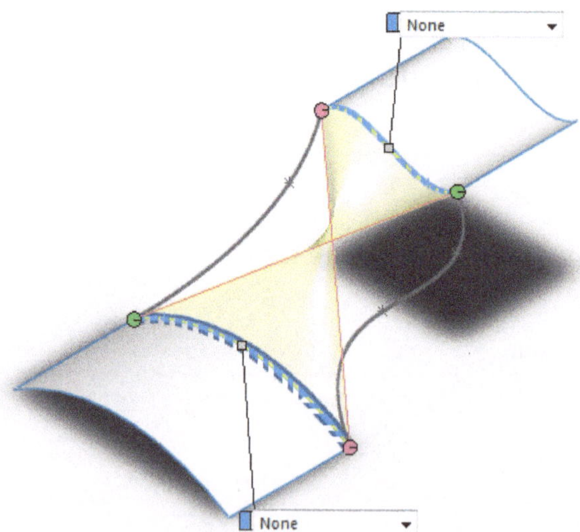

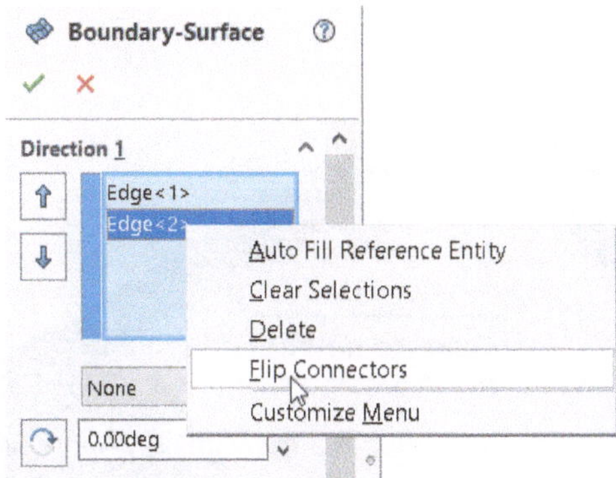

You can specify the way the boundary surface will be connected to the selected edges. To do so, select the required edge from the **Direction 1** selection box. Next, select the **Tangent type** option.

3. Select **Edge 1** from the **Direction 1** selection box.
4. Select the **Tangency To Face** option from the **Tangent type** drop-down (for this example).
5. Specify the tangent length in the **Tangent Length** box or by dragging the arrow displayed on the curve.

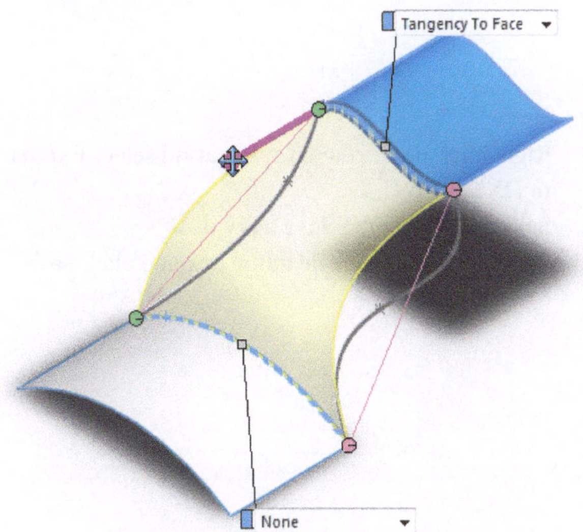

6. Select **Edge 2** from the **Direction 1** selection box.
7. Select the **Curvature To Face** option from the **Tangent type** drop-down (for this example).

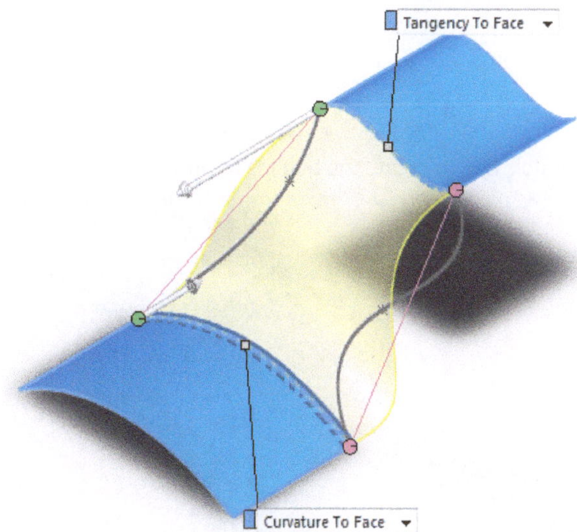

8. Click in the **Direction 2** selection box.
9. Select the guide curves.

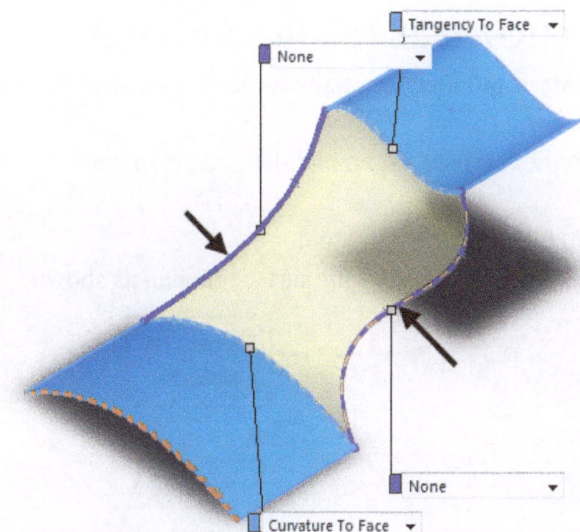

You will notice that the **Tangent type** drop-down is replaced by the **Tangent influence** option in the **Direction 1** group. It is just another way to specify the tangent value.

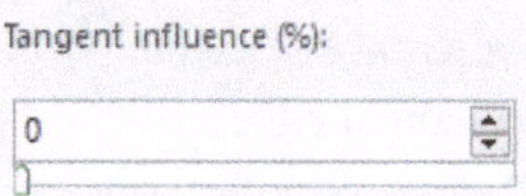

Also, the **Curve Influence Type** drop-down appears under both the **Direction 1** and **Direction 2** groups. Select the required option from this drop-down.

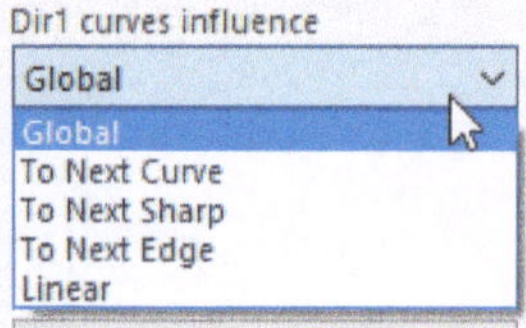

10. Click **OK** to create the boundary surface.

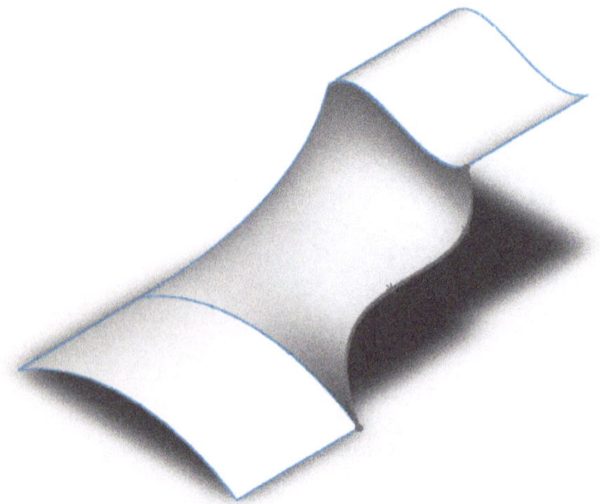

TUTORIAL 28 (Flatten Surface)

The **Flatten Surface** tool flattens the surface model.

1. On the **Surface** CommandManager, click the

Surface Flatten tool.
2. Select the faces from the surface model, as shown.

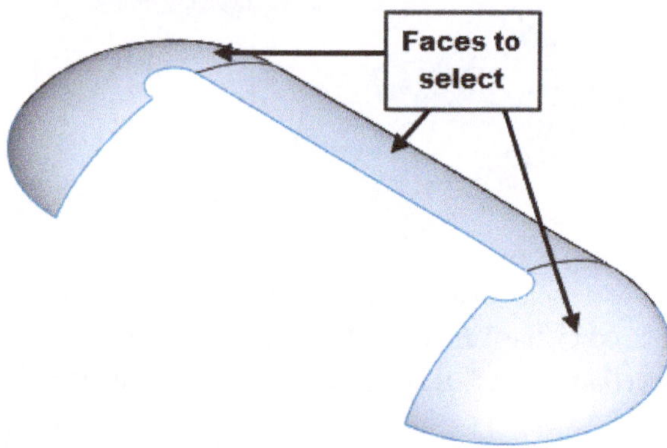

3. Click in the reference selection box.
4. Select the horizontal edge.

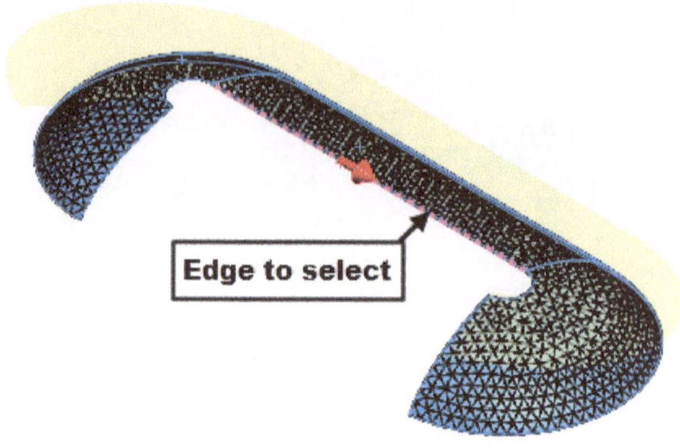

5. Click **OK** .

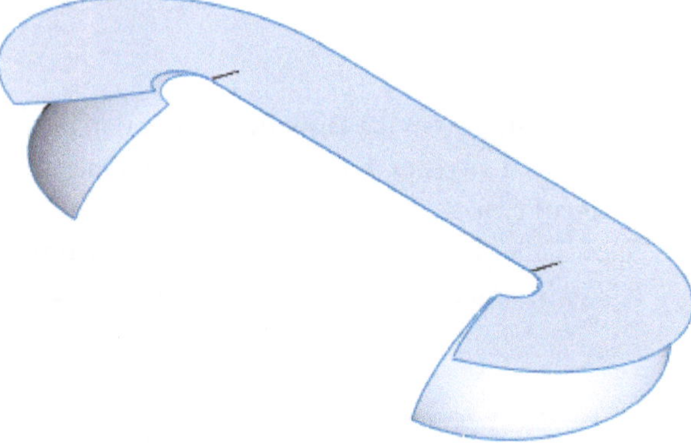

6. Right click on the flatten surface and select **Export to DXF / DWG**.
7. Select **Dxf** from the **Save as type**.
8. Type a name in the **File name** box and click **Save**.

Chapter 11: Mold Tools

In this chapter, you will learn the basics of mold tools in SOLIDWORKS. Creating mold is very complex, but the in-built mold tools in SOLIDWORKS make it easy for you.

In SOLIDWORKS, mold tools are located in the **Mold Tools** CommandManager. You need to customize the Command manager to display this CommandManager. Click the right mouse button on any of the tabs in the CommandManager and select **Mold Tools** to display the mold tools.

TUTORIAL 1

In this tutorial, you will design a mold for the part, as shown.

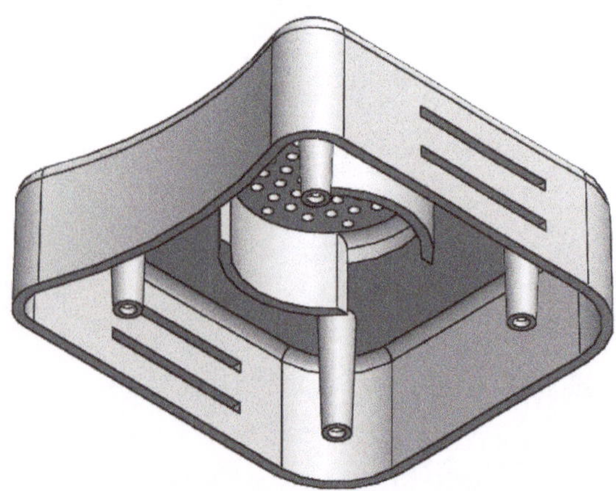

Performing Draft Analysis

1. Download the plastic part from the companion website and open it in SOLIDWORKS.
2. Click the **Draft Analysis** 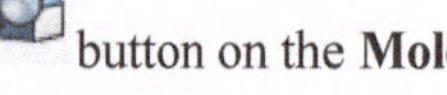 button on the **Mold Tools** CommandManager.
3. Select the Top plane from the FeatureManager Design Tree to specify the Direction of Pull.
4. Set **Draft Angle** to 1 degree.
5. Click **OK**.

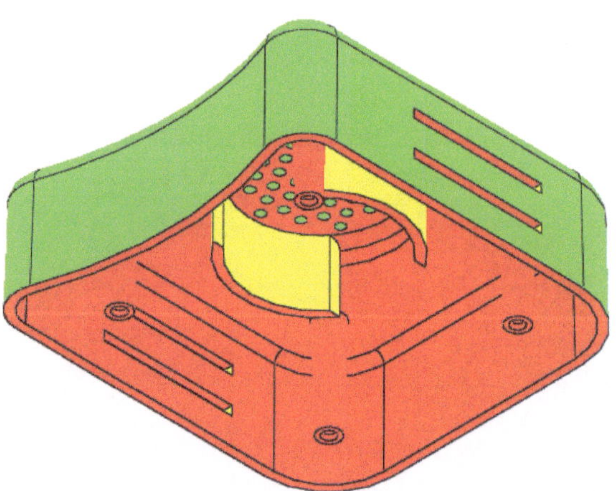

The faces displayed in green color are having a positive draft. Whereas the faces highlighted in red color are having a negative draft.

6. Place the pointer on the outer faces of the part and notice the positive draft angle.

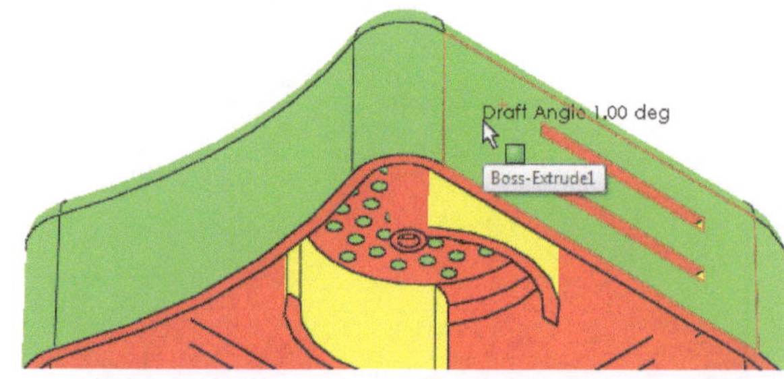

7. Place the pointer on the faces highlighted in yellow color. Notice that the draft angle is zero. You need to apply a draft to these faces.

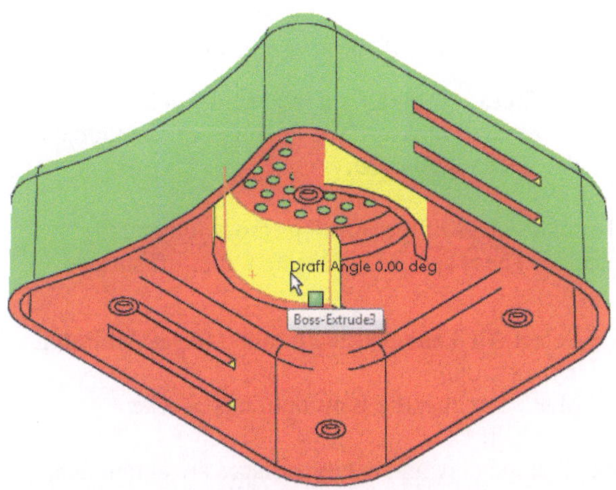

8. On the CommandManager, click **Mold Tools > Draft** .
9. Select the bottom face of the model to define the Direction of Pull.
10. Select the faces highlighted with yellow color.
11. Type 1 in the **Draft Angle** box.
12. Click **OK** on the PropertyManager.

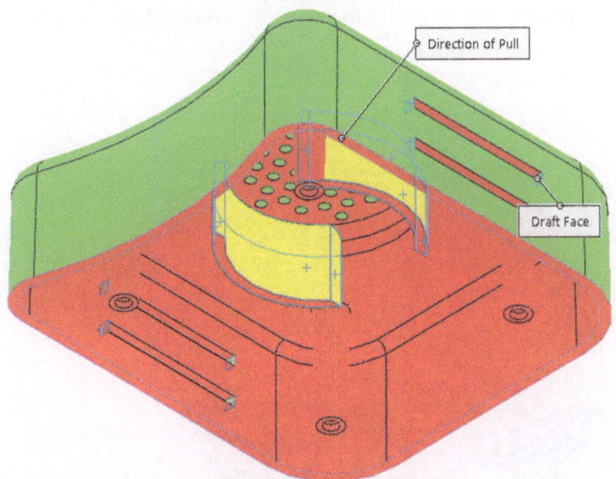

Notice that all the inner faces are red in color, and the outer faces are green.

13. Turn OFF the **Draft Analysis** button on the CommandManager.

Applying the Shrinkage allowance

Molded parts will shrink after they are removed from the mold and allowed to cool. To compensate for the shrinkage, you can scale the model to make it slightly larger.

1. To apply a scale feature, click the **Scale** button on the **Mold Tools** CommandManager.

In the **Scale about** drop-down available on the PropertyManager, you can specify the scale factor about the centroid, origin, or coordinate system of the model.

2. For this tutorial, set **Scale about** to **Centroid**.
3. Check **Uniform scaling**.

Note

You can scale the model uniformly or non-uniformly. To scale the model uniformly, check **Uniform scaling**. To scale non-uniformly, uncheck **Uniform scaling** and enter scale factors in the X, Y, and Z directions. The non-uniform scaling will result in a deformed shape of the model.

4. Enter 1.02 as the **Scale Factor**.
5. Click **OK** to scale the model.

Notice that the scale feature is listed in the FeatureManager Design Tree. The scale feature will not affect the size of previously existing features or sketches.

Inserting Mold Folders

SOLIDWORKS adds mold folders to the FeatureManager Design Tree after creating the mold. However, it is recommended that you add the mold folders before creating the mold.

1. On the CommandManager, click **Mold Tools > Insert Mold Folders** .

Creating a Parting Line

A parting line acts as the boundary between the positively and negatively drafted faces of a part. It divides the model into a core and cavity. Also, the two halves of the mold come into contact at the parting line.

1. To create a parting line, click the **Parting Lines** button on the **Mold Tools** CommandManager.

The parting line uses the draft analysis tool to determine the positively and negatively drafted faces. To create a parting line, you need to specify the direction of pull.

2. Select the Top plane from the FeatureManager Design Tree to define the direction of pull.

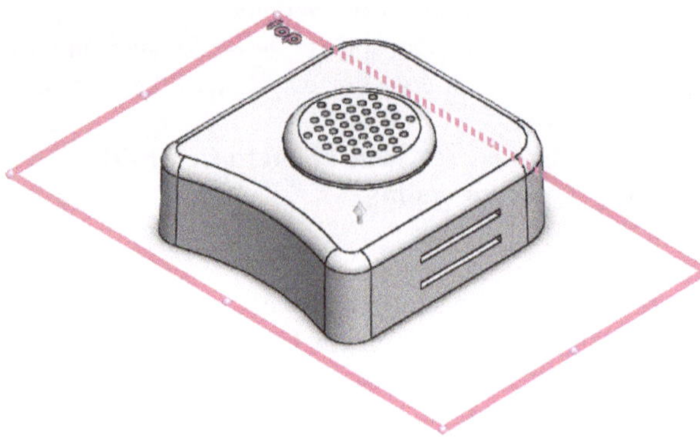

3. Set **Draft Angle** to 1 degree.
4. Make sure that the **Use for Core/Cavity Split** and **Split faces** options are checked.

The **Use for Core/Cavity Split** option is checked to use the parting line to create the core and cavity. Note that if there are multiple parting lines created, the **Use for Core/Cavity Split** option identifies the parting lines for splitting the mold.

5. Click the **Draft Analysis** button on the **Parting Line** PropertyManager. The parting line appears on the model.

The parting line is created at the point where the positively and negatively drafted faces come together.

6. Click **OK** on the PropertyManager. The parting line is created and is displayed in the FeatureManager Design Tree.

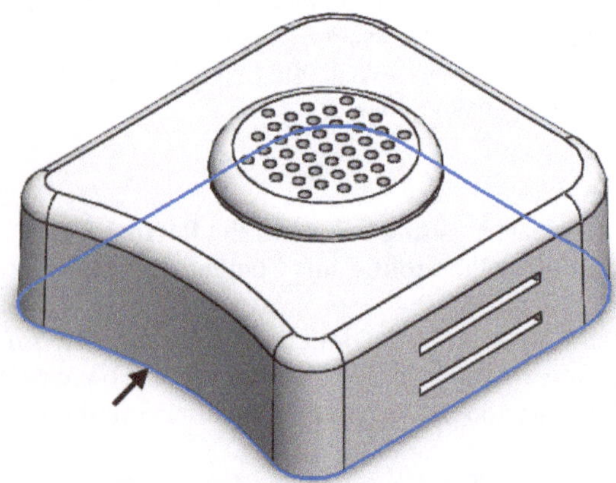

Next, you need to create the shut-off surfaces

Creating Shut-off Surfaces

Shut-off surfaces are necessary when the part being molded has openings on it. To create the model's opening, the two halves of mold called core and cavity will have to touch each other. A shut-off surface is needed to define the face where the core and cavity will touch.

1. To create shut-off surfaces, click the **Shut-off Surfaces** button on the **Mold Tools** CommandManager. The openings on the model are detected automatically.

The inner edges of the openings are automatically selected. These are used to create a shut-off surface.

2. Select **All Tangent** from the **Reset All Patch Types** group.
3. Make sure that the **Knit** option is checked.

Note that the core and cavity surfaces are automatically created along with the shut-off surfaces. The core surface acts as the boundary between the core and the part. The cavity surface acts as the boundary between the cavity and the part.

The **Knit** option combines or knits the shut-off surfaces to the core and cavity surfaces.

4. Rotate the model and notice the redundant loops on the mounting boss holes.

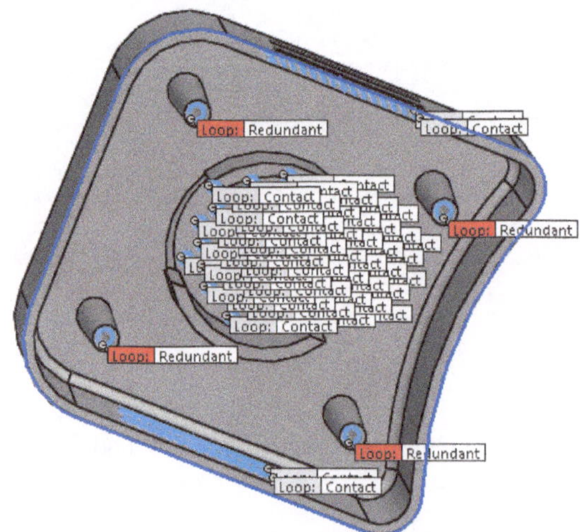

5. Press the Shift key, zoom in, and click on the loops highlighted as redundant. The redundant loops are deselected.
6. Click **OK** to create the shut-off surfaces.
7. To display the results, click the right mouse button on the **Solid Bodies** folder in the FeatureManager Design Tree.

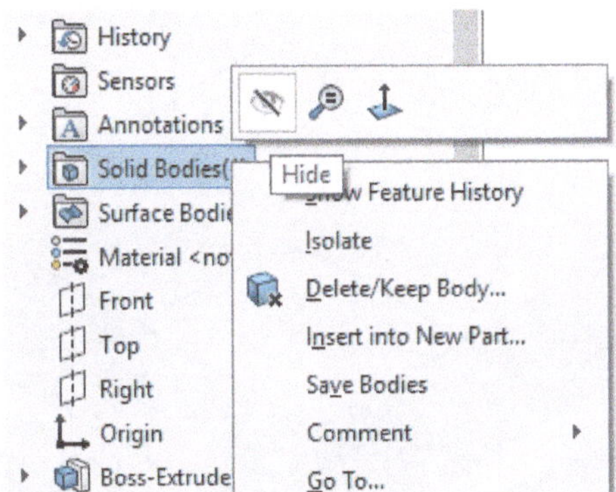

7. Click **Hide** on the Pop-up menu displayed; the core and cavity surfaces are displayed.
8. Expand the **Surface Bodies** folder in the Feature Manager and hide any surfaces to see the other surface.

Core Surface

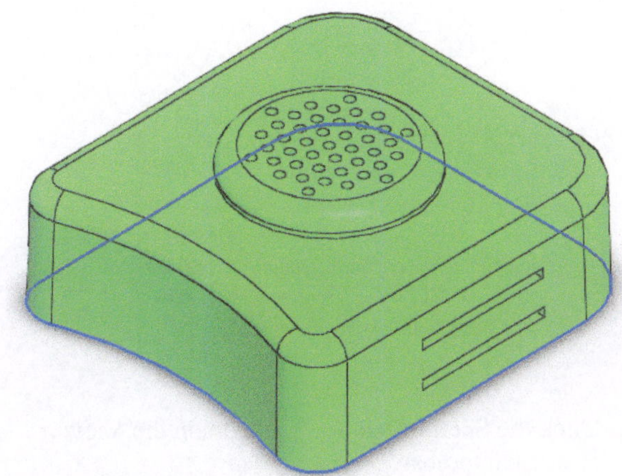

Cavity Surface

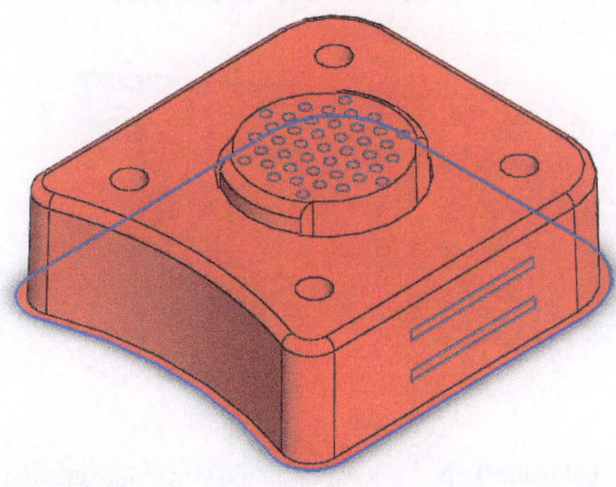

Next, you need to create parting surfaces. To do so, you need to hide the core and cavity surfaces and show a solid body.

Creating Parting Surfaces

The parting surfaces extend away from the part and act as a contact surface between the core and the cavity blocks.

1. Click on the **Solid Bodies** folder and select **Show**.
2. To create parting surfaces, click the **Parting Surfaces** button on the **Mold Tools** CommandManager.

Now, you need to define the method to create the parting surface.

3. Select the **Perpendicular to pull** option. Notice that the parting line is selected automatically.
4. Select the **Smooth** icon from the **Parting Surface** group.
5. Type-in 40 in the **Distance** box located at the top in the **Parting Surface** section.
6. In the **Options** section, check the **Manual mode** option. Notice the dotted handles on the parting surface.

You can drag these handles to adjust the parting surface.

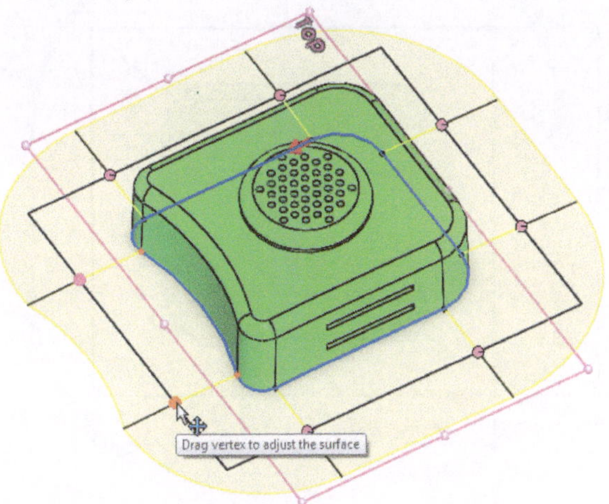

7. Click **OK** to create the parting surface.

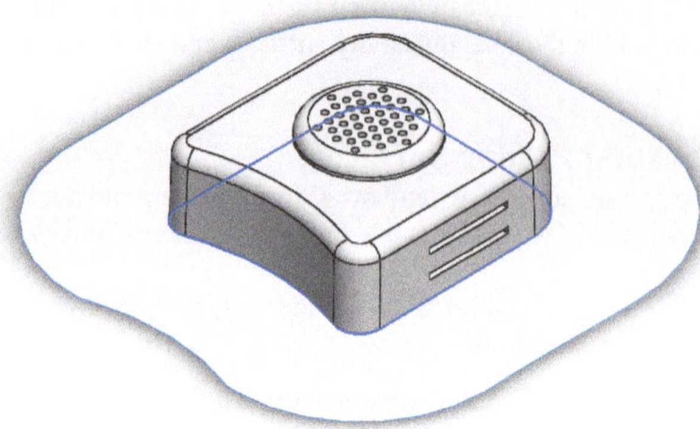

Next, you need to create the mold.

Creating the Tooling Split

First, you need to create a plane that will represent the interface between core and cavity blocks.

1. Click the **Tooling Split** button on the **Mold Tools** CommandManager and select the parting surface.
2. Create the sketch, as shown in the figure. You have to make sure that the sketch covers the part completely.

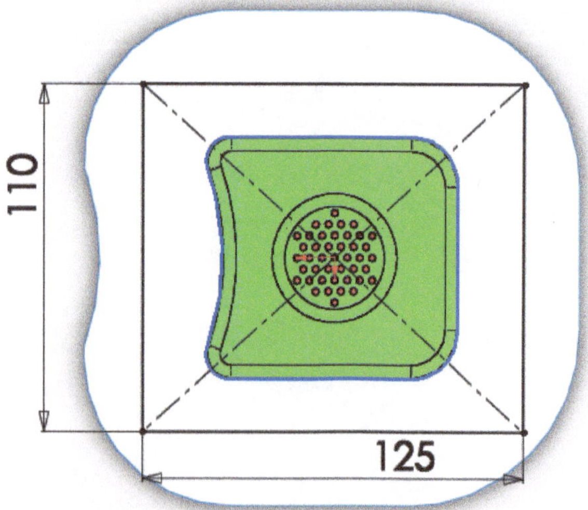

9. Exit the sketch.
10. Specify the **Depth in Direction 1** as 40 in the **Block Size** group.
11. Specify the **Depth in Direction 2** as 10 in the **Block Size** group.
12. Click **OK** to create the mold.

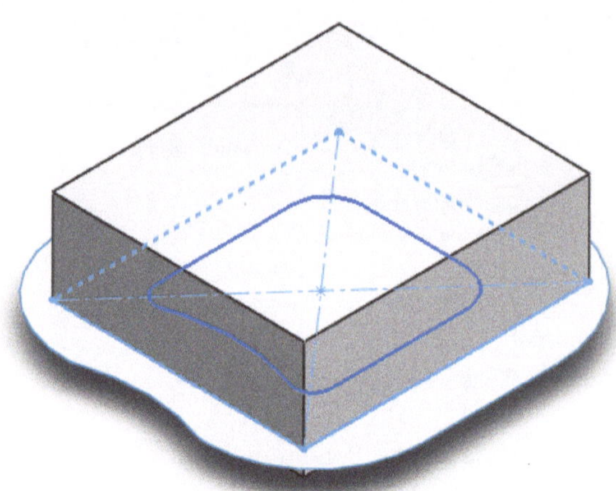

13. Hide the part body, parting surface, core surface, and cavity surface.

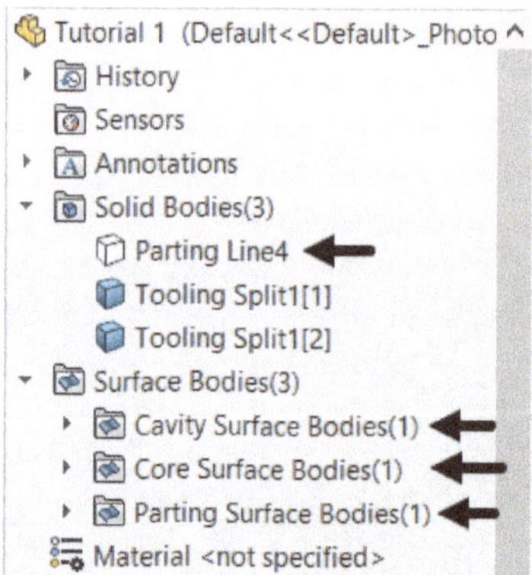

14. Click the **Section View** icon on the View Heads Up toolbar.
15. Click the **Right** icon on the PropertyManager.
16. Drag the arrow and notice the gap in the mold. The gap will be filled with the material to create the geometry.

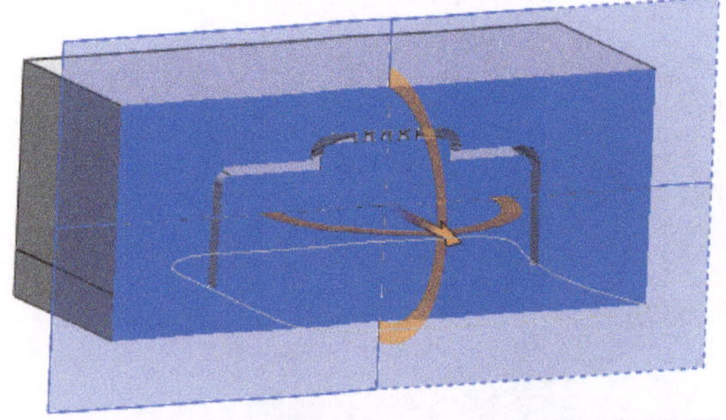

17. Click the **Top** icon on the PropertyManager and drag the arrow. Notice the gap inside the mold.

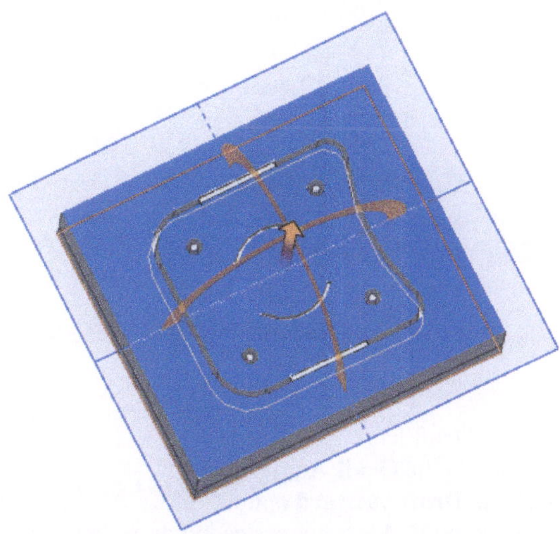

18. Click **Cancel** on the PropertyManager.
19. In the FeatureManager Design Tree, expand the **Solid Bodies** folder, click the right mouse button on the tooling split, and select **Change Transparency**.
20. Likewise, change the transparency of the other tooling split.

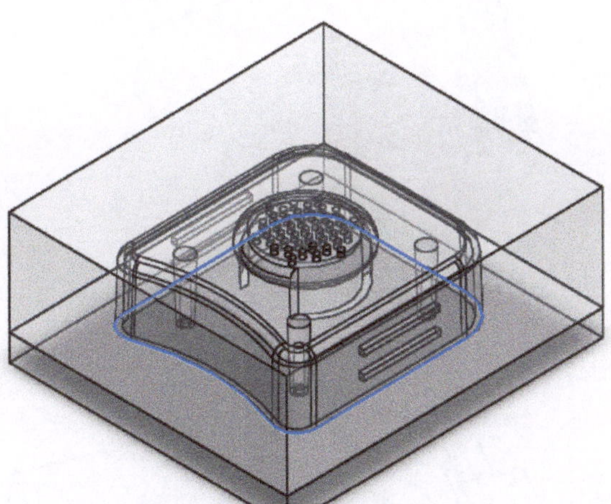

21. Click the right mouse button on any feature of the part body and select **Show**.

Performing the Undercut analysis

The undercut analysis is performed to detect the portions of the part that cannot be molded using the primary direction of pull.

1. Hide the tooling splits.
2. To perform undercut analysis, click the **Undercut Analysis** button on the **Mold Tools** CommandManager.

Note that the direction of pull is already specified, and you do not need to specify it in this case.

Notice the colors displayed on the geometry. Refer to the **Undercut Faces** section on the PropertyManager to get a good understanding of these colors.

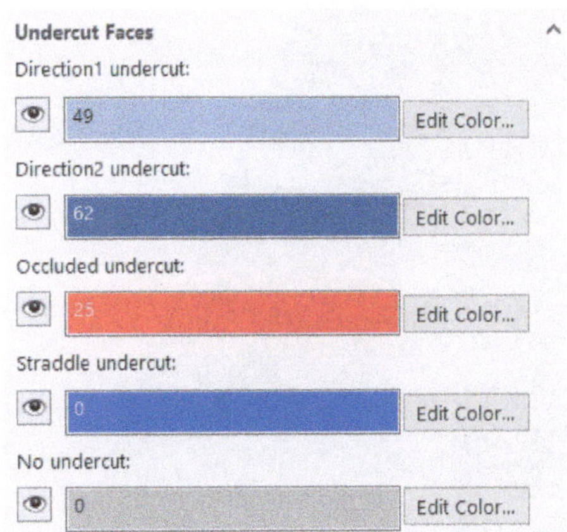

The **Direction1 undercut** faces are one which are not visible from the first pull direction. A single arrow in the graphics window indicates the first pull direction.

The **Direction2 undercut** faces are one, which is not visible from the second pull direction. A double arrow in the graphics window indicates the second pull direction.

Notice the red faces of the model. These are defined as occluded undercuts, which are not visible from either pull direction.

3. Click **OK** on the PropertyManager.

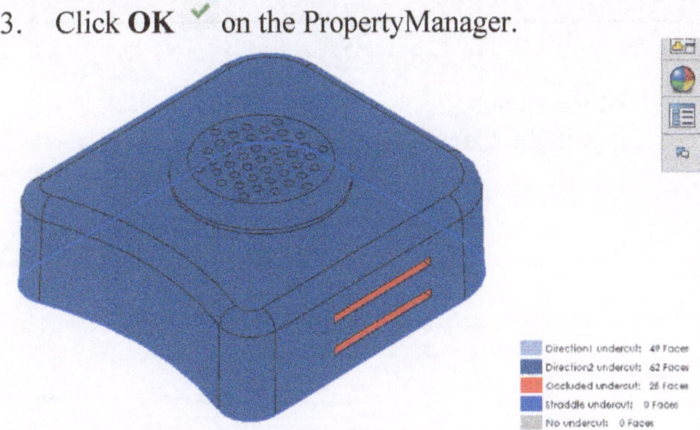

Next, you need to create side cores.

Creating side cores

1. Turn OFF the **Undercut Analysis** button on the CommandManager.
2. To create a side core, click the **Core** button on the **Mold Tools** CommandManager.
3. Select the inner face of the model, which is having openings.

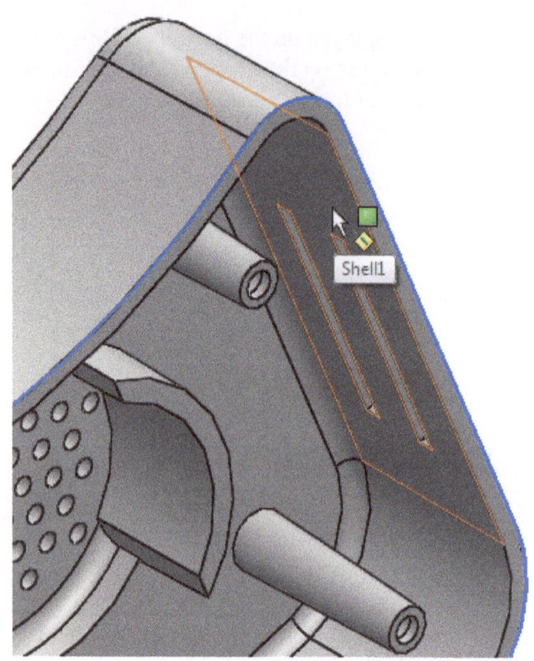

4. Show the lower tooling split.
5. Create the sketch, as shown in the figure.

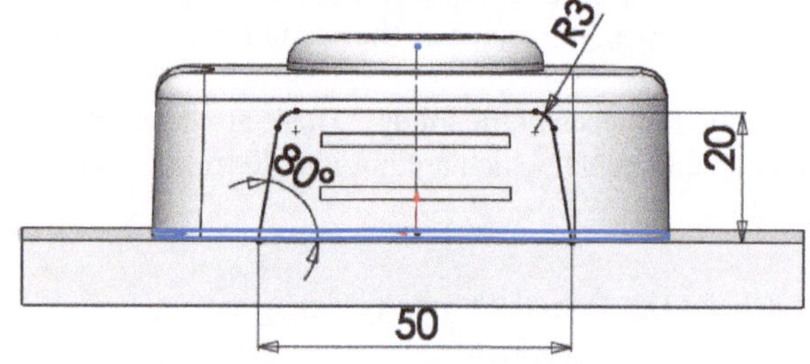

6. Exit the sketch.
7. Click in the **Core/Cavity body** field.

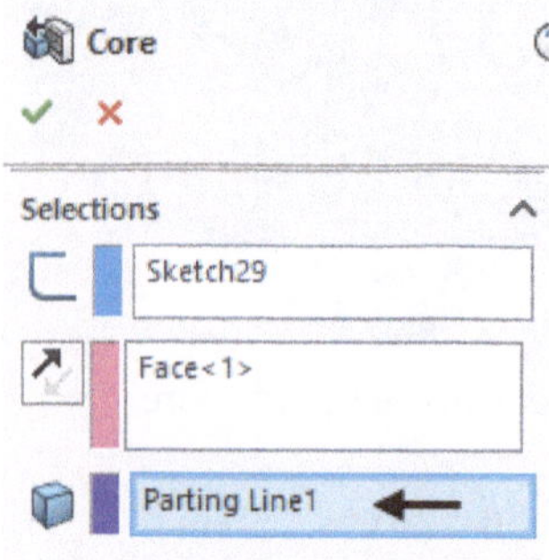

8. Select the upper tooling split from the **Solid Bodies** folder in the **FeatureManager Design** tree.

Tutorial 1 (Default<<...
History
Sensors
Annotations
Solid Bodies(3)
Parting Line1
Tooling Split1...
Tooling Split1...
Surface Bodies(3)
Material <not spe...
Front

9. Click the **Draft** icon.
10. Type-in 4 in the **Draft Angle** box.
11. Check the **Draft outward** option.
12. Select **Through All** from the second drop-down in the **Parameters** group.
13. Uncheck the **Cap ends** option.
14. Click **OK** to create the side core.
15. Hide the other bodies and display the side core body.

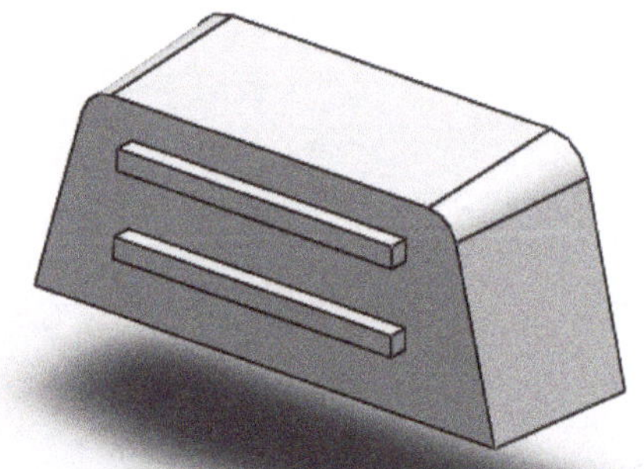

14. Likewise, create another side core for the other openings.

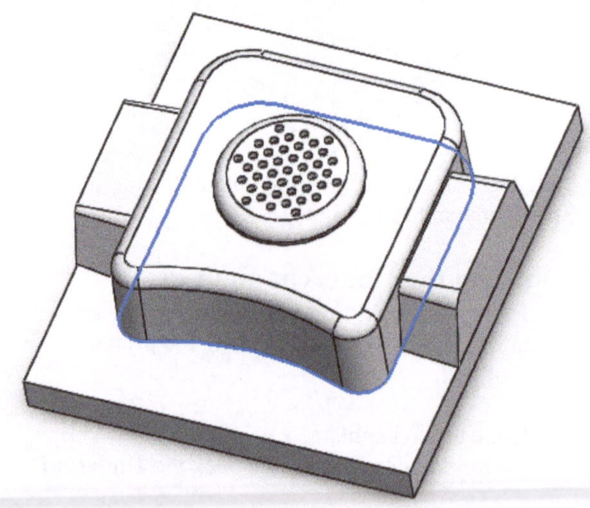

15. Show all the solid bodies.
16. On the CommandManager, click **Direct Editing > Move Copy Bodies** .

17. Select the upper tooling split and click the **Translate/Rotate** button on the PropertyManager.
18. Uncheck the **Copy** option.
19. Click and drag the Y-axis of the manipulator.

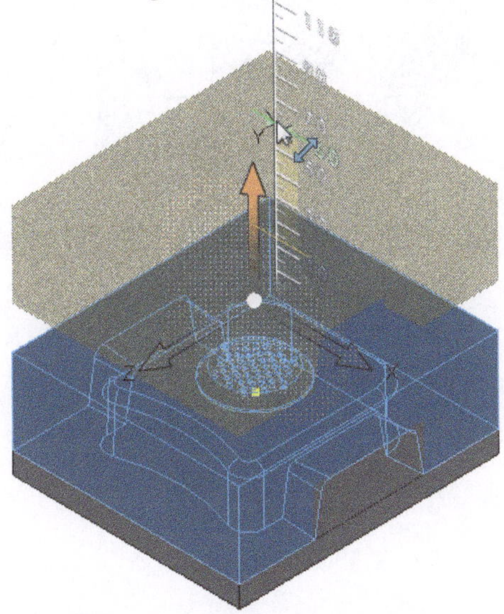

20. Click **OK**.
21. Likewise, move the bodies as shown.

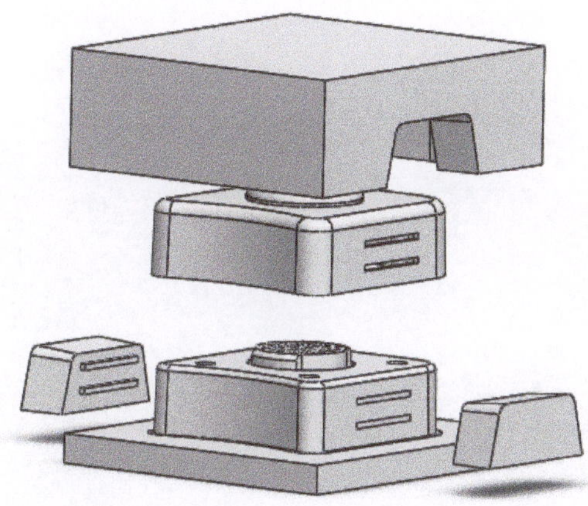

22. Save the part file.

Creating your own surfaces

1. In the **FeatureManager Design Tree**, click and drag the bar located at the bottom.
2. Release it above the tooling split. The tooling split, and cores are suppressed.

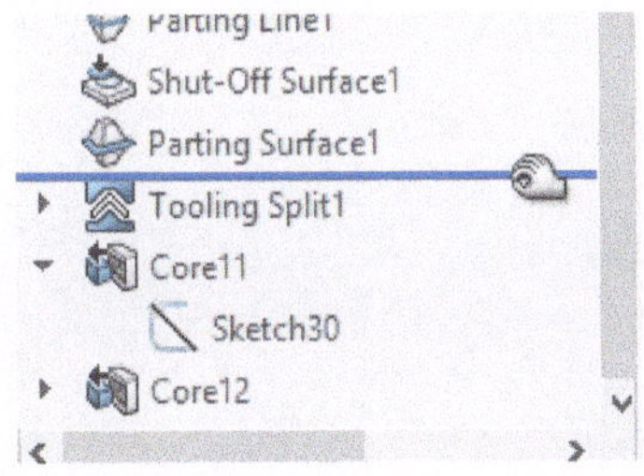

3. Hide the part body and show all the surface bodies.
4. Draw a circle on the top face of the cavity surface, as shown.

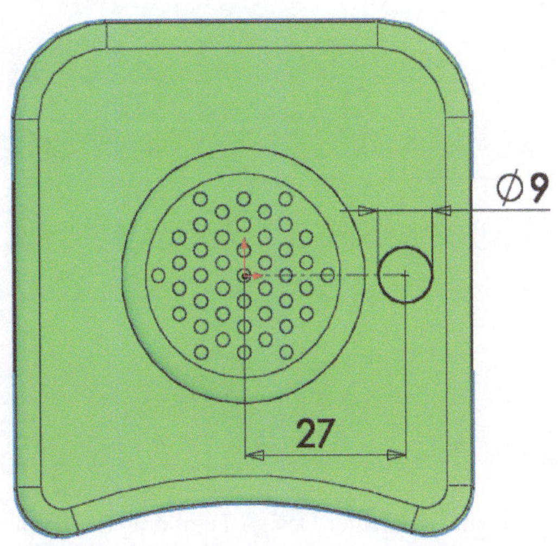

5. Create an extruded surface with the capped end and draft angle.

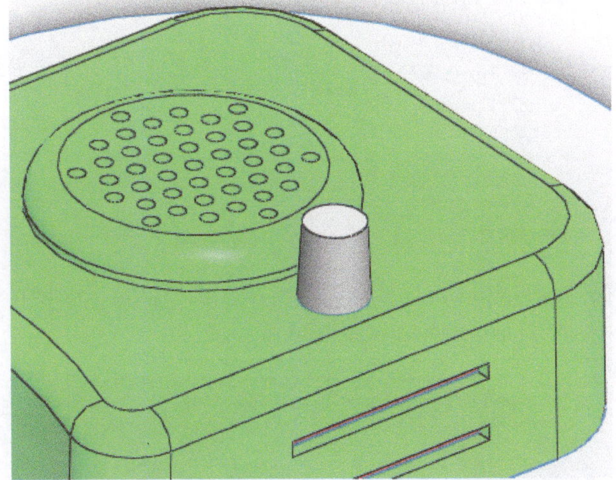

6. Hide the Core surface.
7. Trim the Cavity surface, as shown.

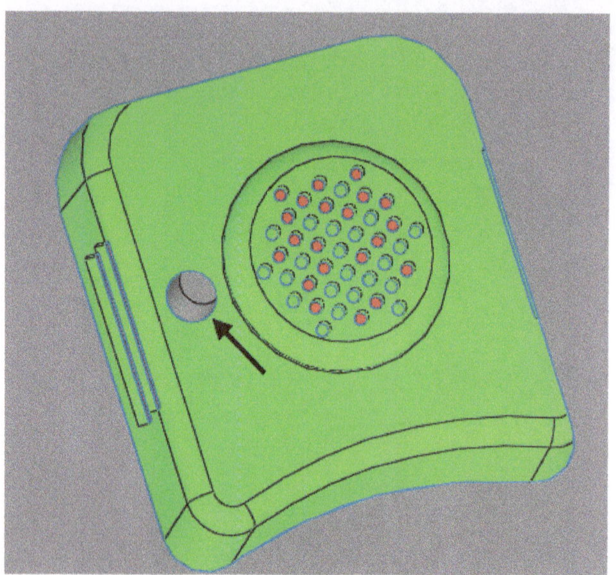

8. In the FeatureManager Design Tree, drag the bar and release it below the cores.
9. In the FeatureManager Design Tree, click on the Tooling Split and select the **Edit Feature**.

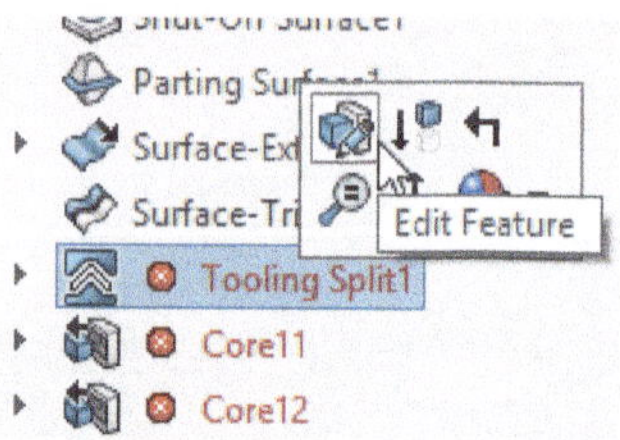

10. On the PropertyManager, click in the Cavity selection box and select the extruded surface.

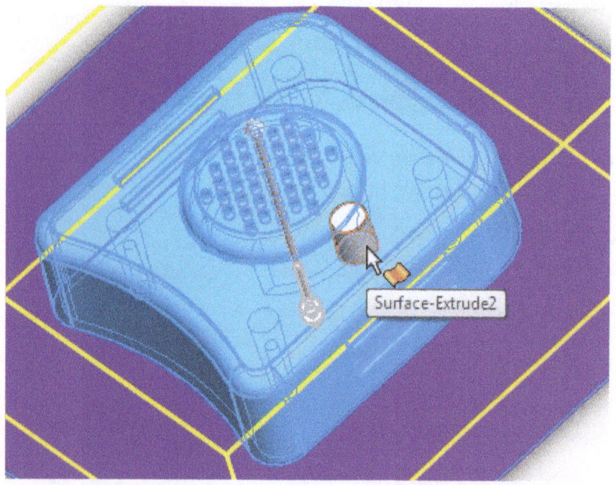

11. Click **OK**.
12. Show the cavity solid body and notice the difference.

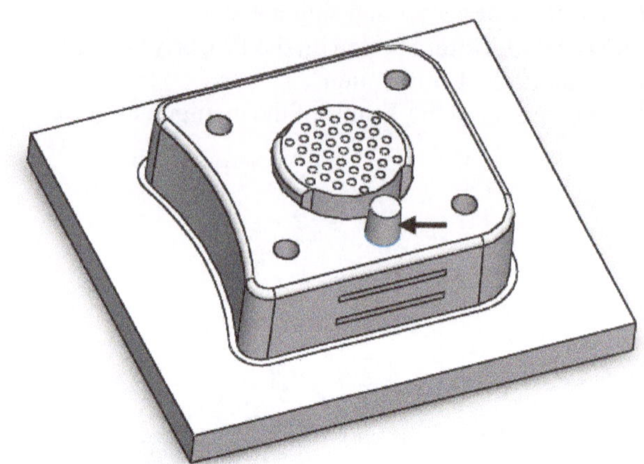

13. Save and close the file.

Chapter 12: Weldments

SOLIDWORKS provides a set of tools for creating welded frames and structures. In addition to creating welded frames and structures, you can use these tools for different applications. In this chapter, you will learn all of the tools used to create weldments. You will also learn to create custom weldment profiles and add them to your Library.

The weldment tools are located in the **Weldments** Command Manager. You need to customize the CommandManager to display this CommandManager. Click the right mouse button on the CommandManager and select **Tabs** > **Weldments** from the shortcut menu.

TUTORIAL 1

In this tutorial, you create a simple weldment, as shown in the figure below.

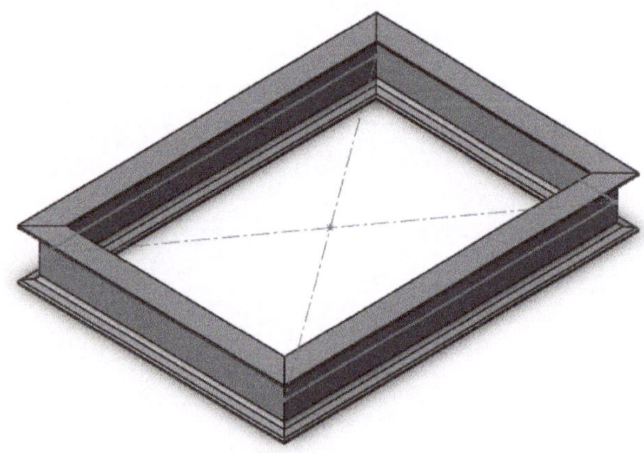

1. Start a new part file.
2. Click the **Options** button on the Quick Access toolbar.
3. Click the **Document Properties** tab on the **Options** dialog.
4. Click the **Units** node.
5. Select the **MMGS (millimeter, gram, second)** option.
6. Click the **OK** button to close the dialog.
7. Create a layout sketch on the top plane, as shown.

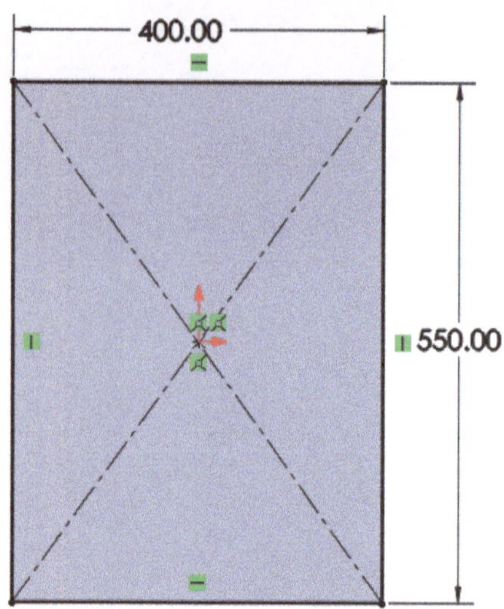

8. Exit the sketch.
9. Click the **Weldments** tab on the Command Manager.
10. Click the **Structural Member** button in the **Weldments** tab.

In this **Structural Member** PropertyManager, you need to define the parameters of the structural member.

11. Select **iso** from the **Standard** drop-down.
12. Select **sb beam** from the **Type** drop-down.
13. Select **80X6** from the **Size** drop-down. Next, you need to define the position of the structural members.
14. Select the left vertical line and bottom horizontal line of the layout sketch. A structural member is created in the selected sketch segment.

You will notice that **Group1** is listed in the **Groups** selection box. Also, the selected segments are listed in the **Path segments** selection box of the **Settings** section.

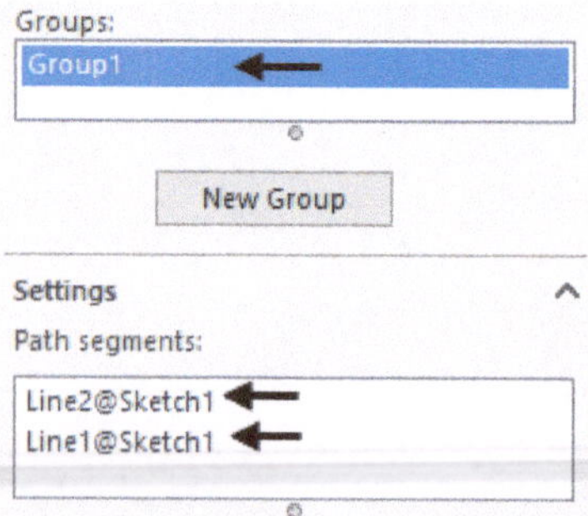

If you click the **New Group** button, a new group will be created. If you select the line segments from the layout sketch, they will be listed under the second group. Note that the size and parameter settings will be applied to all the groups. If you change the structural member's size, it will be applied to members of all the groups.

15. Select the other two segments of the layout sketch.

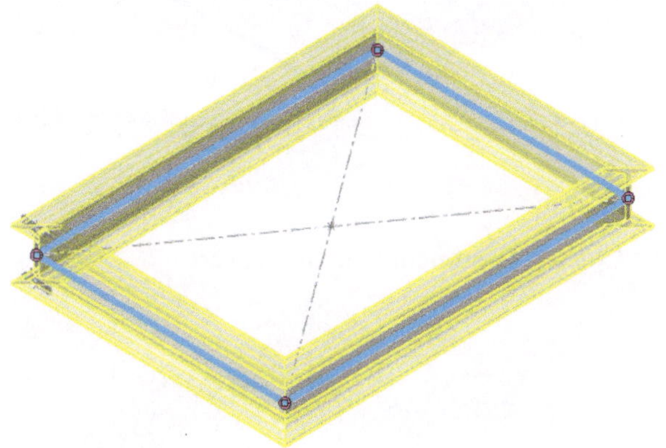

You can control the structural members' end condition by using the **Apply corner treatment** option in the **Settings** section. By default, this option is checked. As a result, the corner treatment is applied between the structural members. If you uncheck this option, the corner treatment will not be applied.

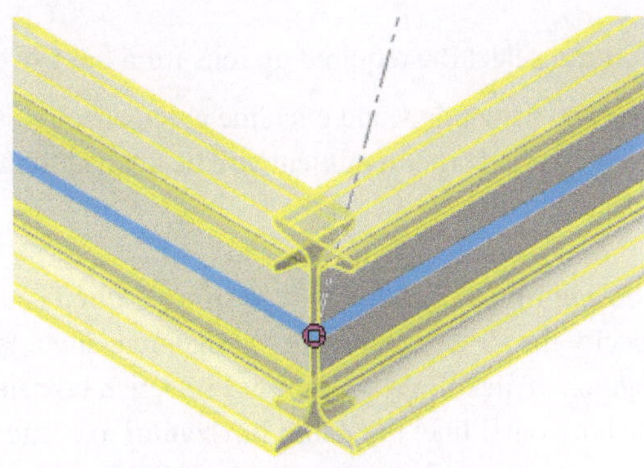

You can change the type of corner treatment using the icons available below the **Apply corner treatment** option.

By using these icons, the corner treatment can be applied to all the structural members. If you select the **End miter** button, the **Merge miter trimmed bodies** option will be available. This option is used to merge the trimmed bodies into a single body.

If you select the **End butt1** or **End butt2** button, the **Simple cut** and **Coped cut** buttons will be available. The **Simple cut** button is used to create a simple cut between the structural members. The **Coped cut** button creates a cut, which takes the shape of the cutting surface.

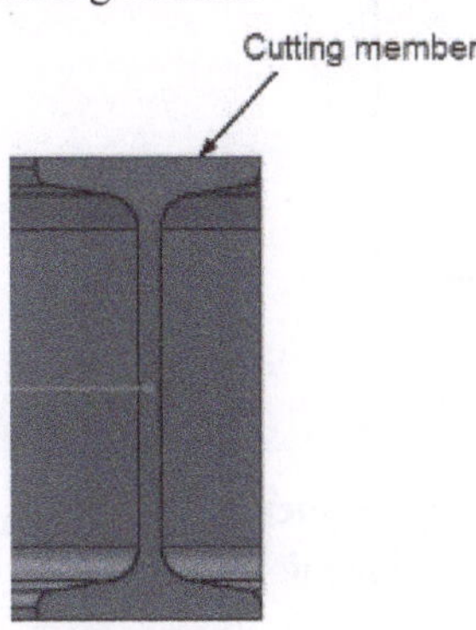

Simple Cut

Coped Cut

The **Gap between connected segments in same group** box is used to specify gaps at the corners of the structural members of same group.

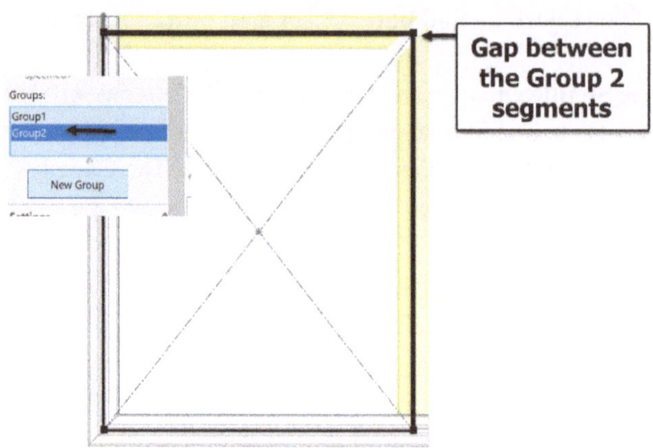

The **Gap between different group segments** box is used to specify gaps between the segments of different groups.

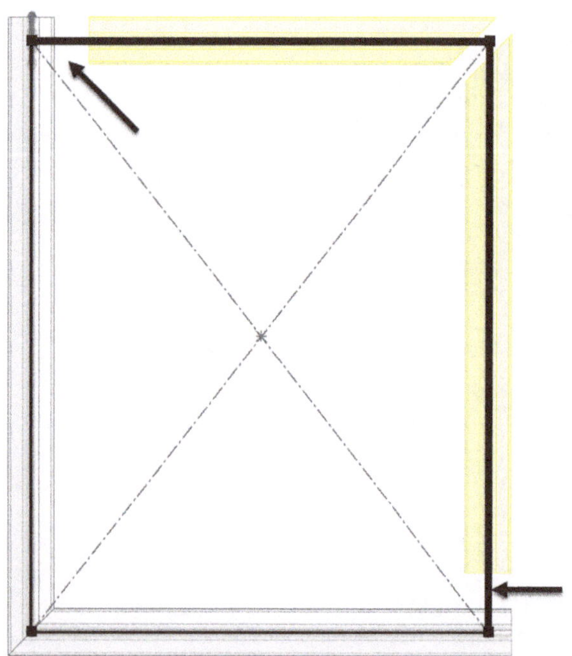

If you want to apply the corner treatment individually, click on the corner point you want to change.

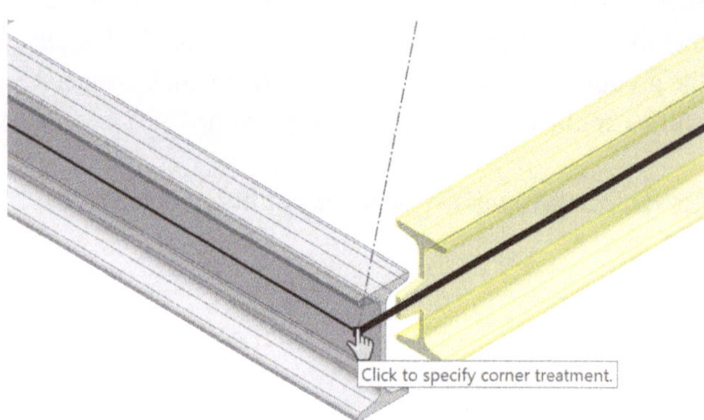

The **Corner Treatment** window appears.

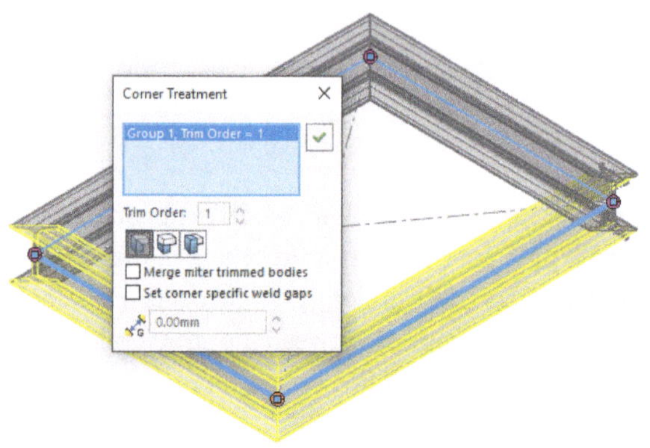

You can select the required options from the **Corner Treatment** window and click the green check on the window; the corner treatment will be applied to the selected corner.

The **Alignment** option in the **Settings** section is used to specify the structural member's alignment about the line segment. Click in the **Alignment** selection box and select the horizontal line; the **Align horizontal axis** and **Align vertical axis** options get active.

The **Align horizontal axis** option aligns the horizontal axis of the beam cross-section with the line segment.

The **Align vertical axis** option aligns the vertical axis of the beam cross-section with the line segment.

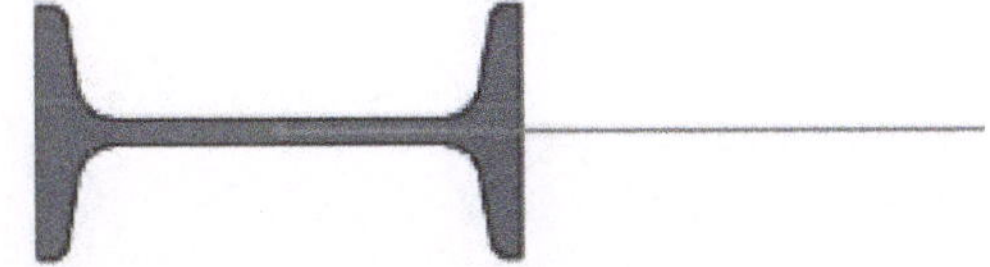

The **Rotation Angle** box allows you to align the structural member at an angle to the line segment.

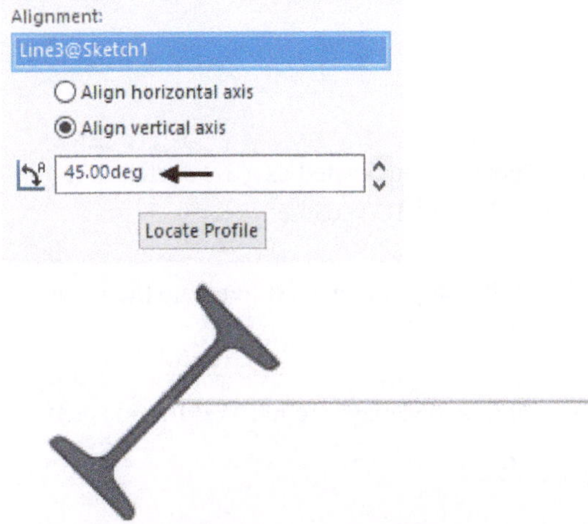

The **Locate Profile** button allows you to locate the profile of the beam cross-section in the graphics window.

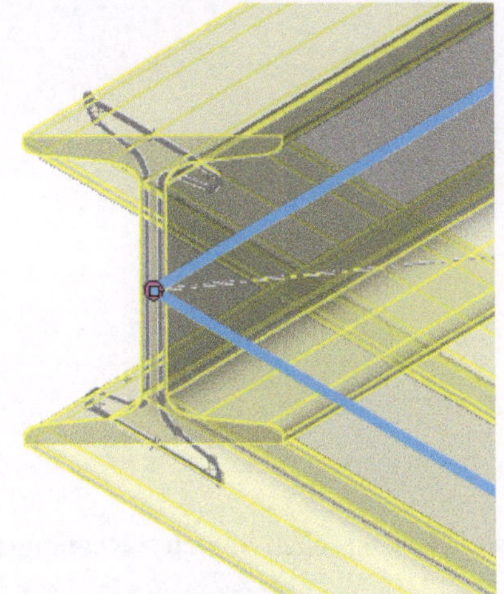

You can change the position of the profile by clicking any other point on the profile.

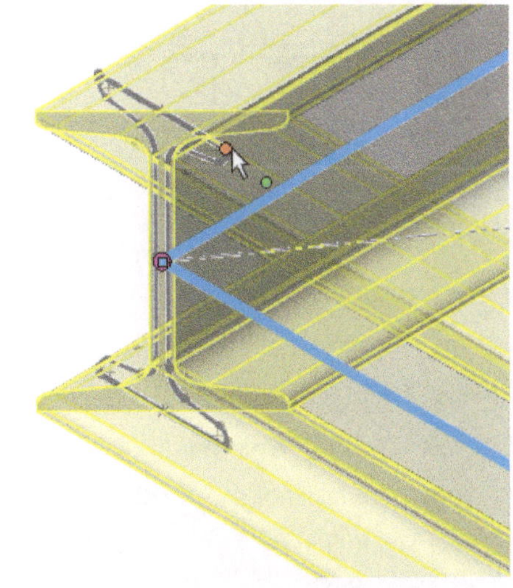

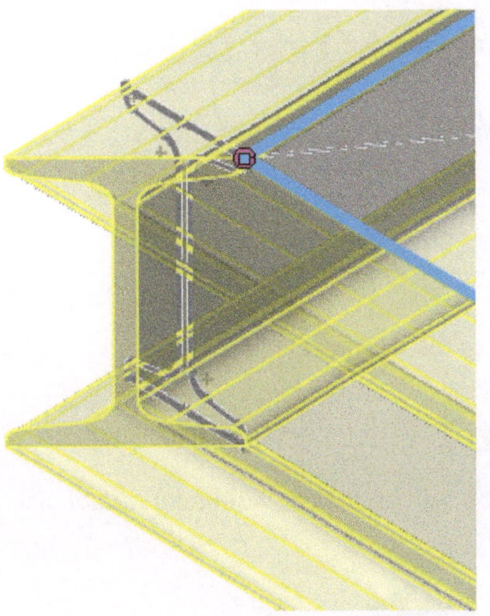

You can also use the **Mirror Profile** option and mirror the profile about the **Horizontal axis** or **Vertical axis.**

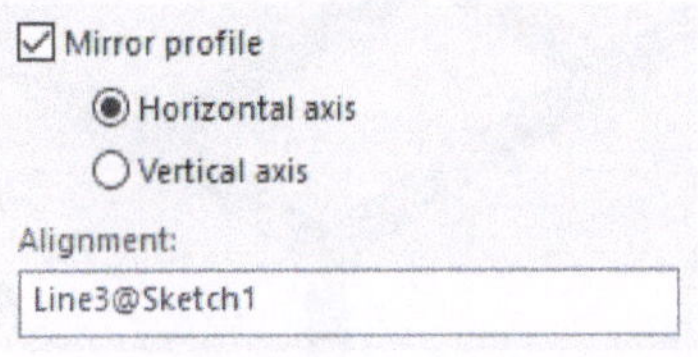

16. After specifying all the settings, click **OK** on the **PropertyManager**.

Notice the two features: **Cut list** and **Weldment** are listed in the **FeatureManager Design Tree**.

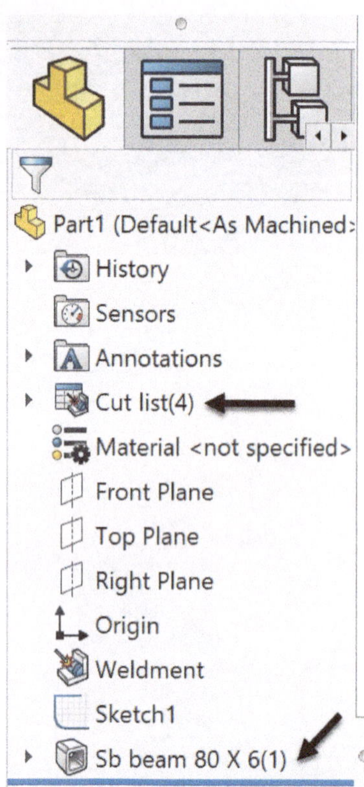

17. Save and close the document.

TUTORIAL 2

In this tutorial, you will create the weldment model, as shown.

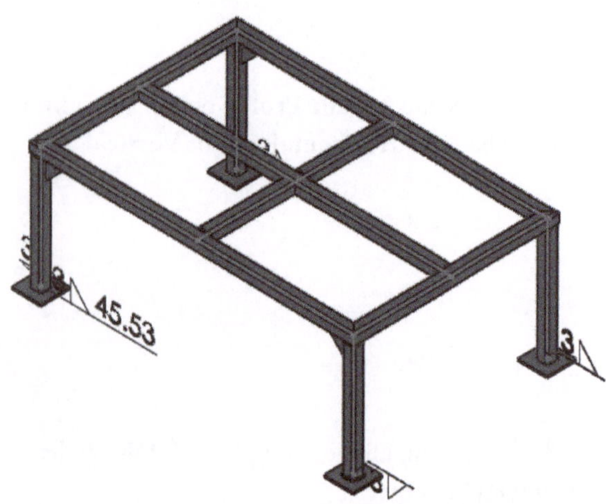

1. On Quick Access Toolbar, click the **New** button.
2. On the **New SOLIDWORKS Document** dialog, click the **Advanced** button.
3. Select the **Part** template and select the **Y-up** option. Next, click **OK**.
4. Create the layout sketch, as shown.

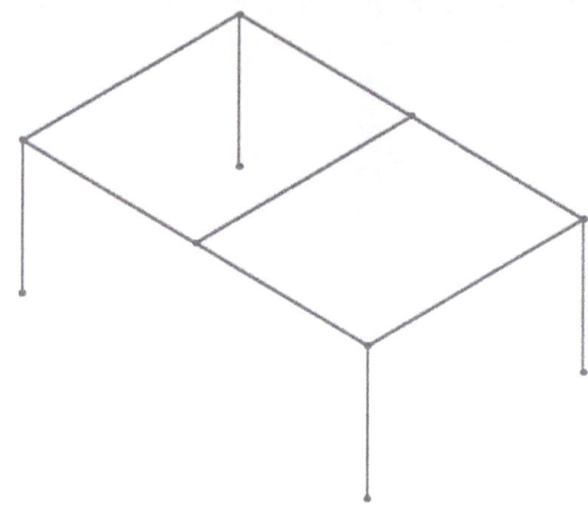

This layout sketch can be created as a 3D sketch or a combination of 2D and 3D sketches.

You can follow the steps given next to create the layout sketch.

5. On the CommandManager, click **Weldments > 3D Sketch** .
6. On the CommandManager, click **Sketch > Line** .
7. Select the origin point, move the pointer up along the dotted lines, and click.

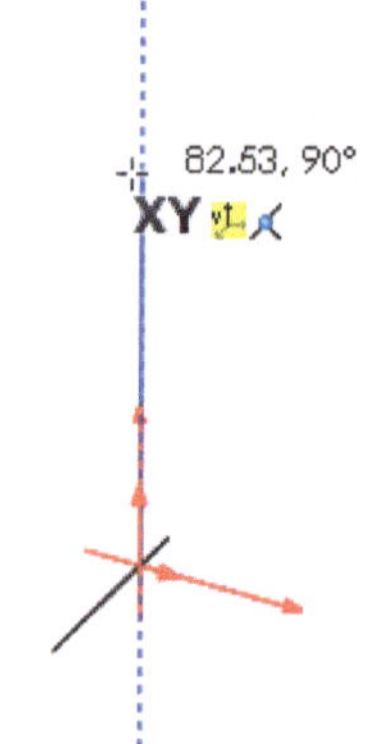

8. On the CommandManager, click **Sketch > Rectangle drop-down > Corner Rectangle** .
9. Select the endpoint of the line to define the first corner of the rectangle.
10. Press the Tab key until the rectangle is oriented, as shown.

11. Move the pointer and click to create the rectangle.
12. On the CommandManager, click **Sketch > Line** .
13. Select the corner point of the rectangle, as shown.
14. Press the Tab key to switch to the XY plane.
15. Move the pointer downward and click.
16. Press Esc to deactivate the tool.

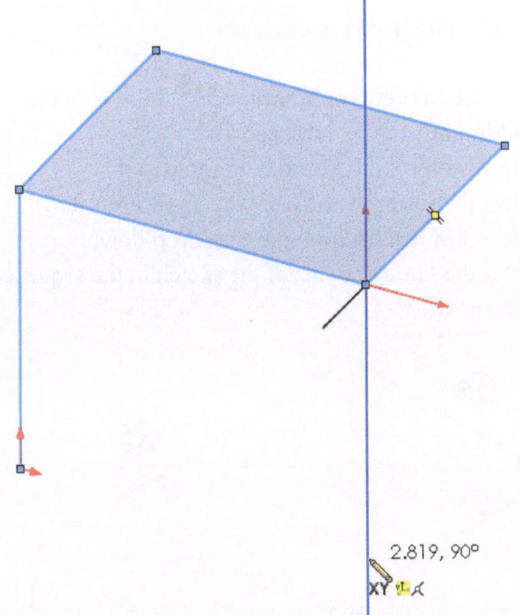

17. Likewise, create other lines, as shown.

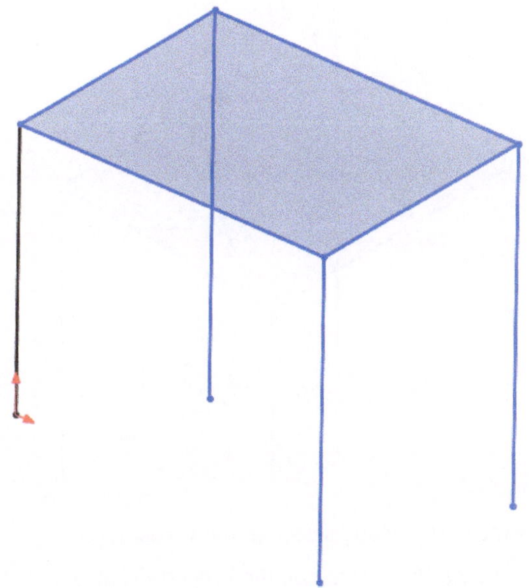

18. Activate the **Line** tool and select the midpoint of the horizontal line, as shown.

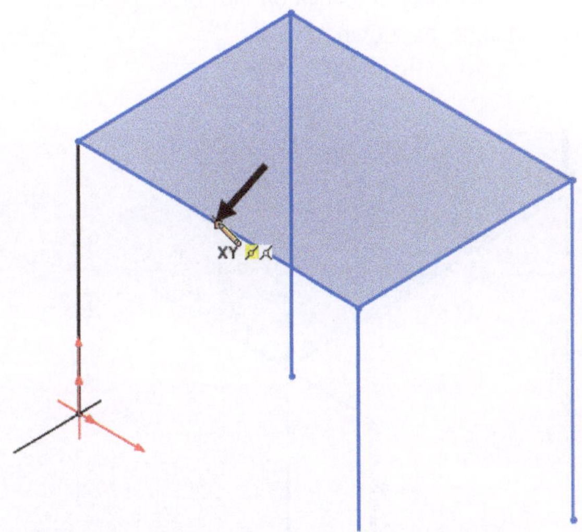

19. Press the Tab key to switch to the YZ plane.
20. Select the midpoint of the other horizontal line and press Esc.

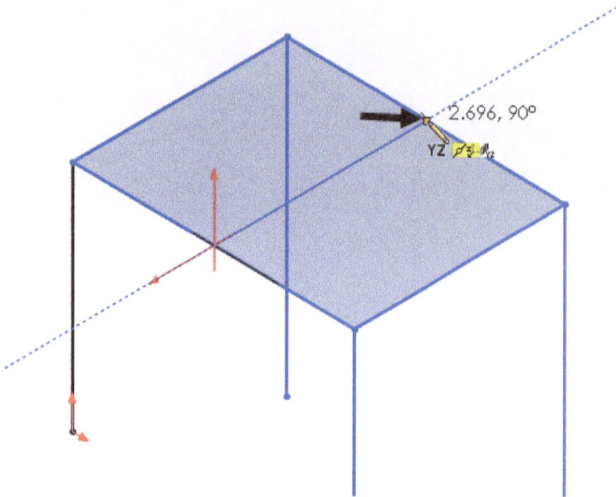

21. Press the Ctrl key and select all the vertical lines.
22. Click the **Equal** = icon on the PropertyManager.
23. Click **OK** on the PropertyManager.
24. Add a 300 mm dimension to any one of the vertical lines.
25. Press the Ctrl key and click on the corner points of the rectangle, as shown.

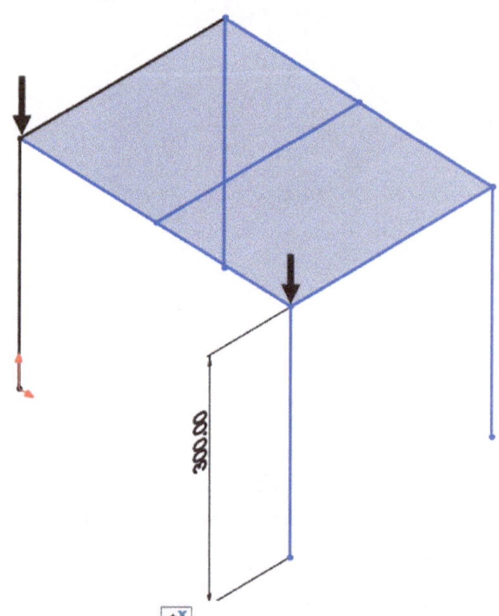

26. Click **Along X** icon on the PropertyManager.
27. Click **OK** on the PropertyManager.
28. Add dimensions to the length and width of the rectangle. The sketch is fully defined and turned into black.
29. Exit the sketch.

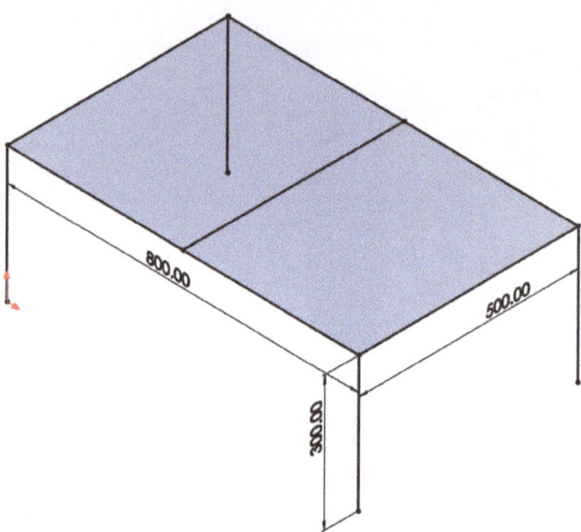

After creating the layout sketch, you need to create the structural members.

Adding Structural members

1. Click the **Structural Member** button on the **Weldment** CommandManager.
2. Select **iso** from the **Standard** drop-down.
3. Select the **square tube** from the **Type** drop-down.
4. Select **30X30X2.6** from the **Size** drop-down.
5. Select the line segments of the sketch in the sequence given next.

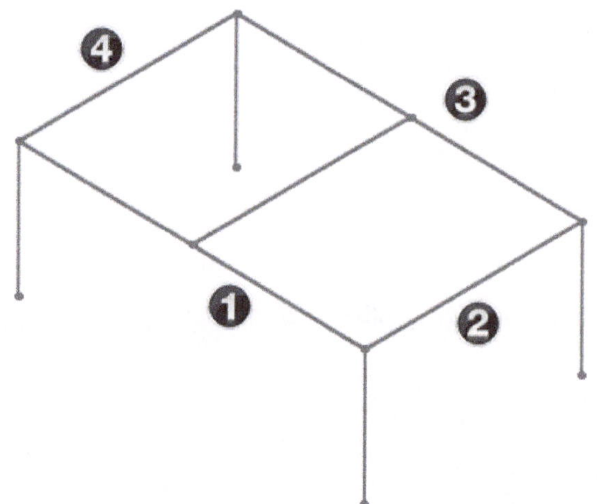

Note that you can select either the continuous or parallel line segments. If you try to select the non-continuous or parallel segment, you will not be allowed to.

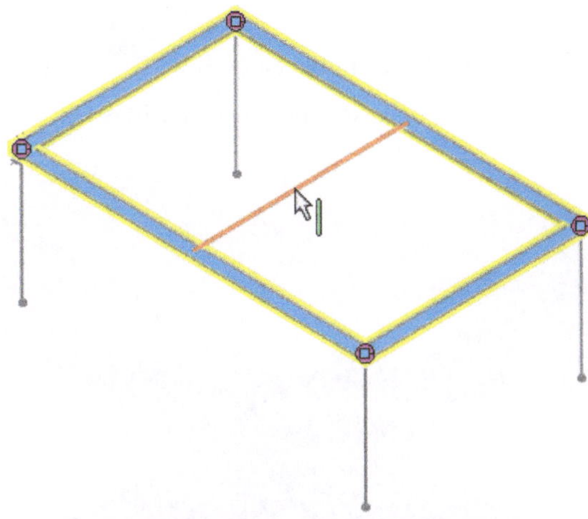

To add structural members to the non-continuous segments, you need to create a new group.

6. Click the **New Group** button below the **Groups** selection box and select the line segments.

Group 2

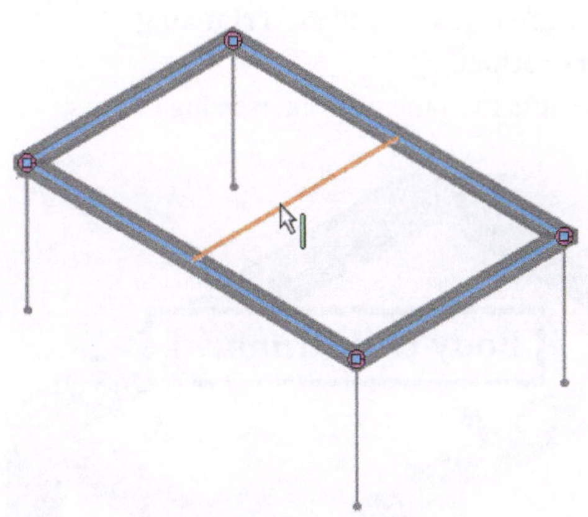

Group 3

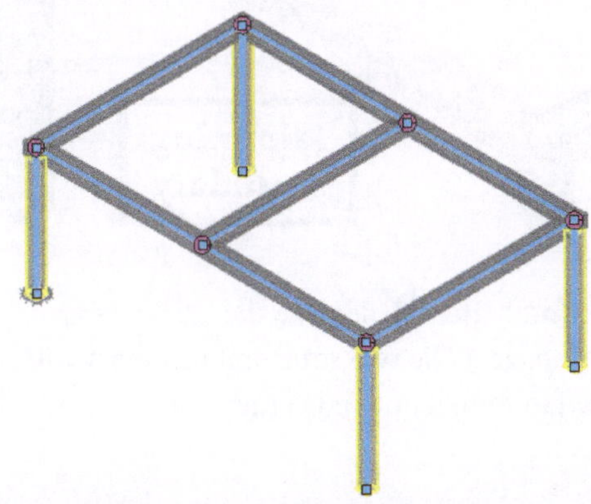

Note that the order in which the structural members are created defines the members that will be trimmed. The structural members that are crossing already created members will be trimmed.

7. Click the **OK** button on the **PropertyManager** to accept the selection.
8. In the FeatureManager Design Tree, click on the **3DSketch** and select **Edit Sketch**.
9. Draw a line connecting the midpoints of the horizontal lines, as shown.

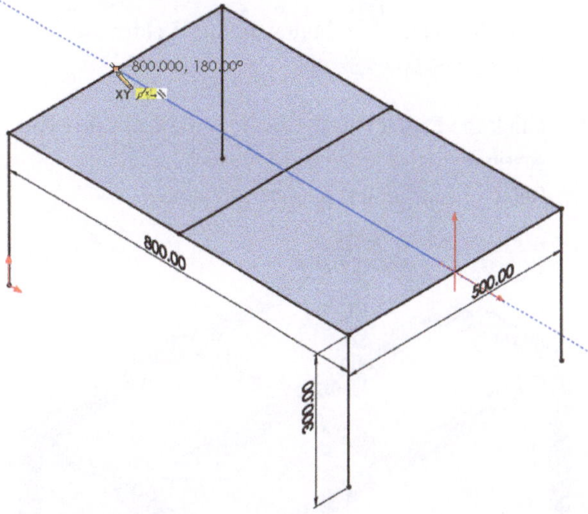

10. Exit the sketch.
11. Activate the **Structural Member** tool.
12. Select **iso** from the **Standard** drop-down.
13. Select the **square tube** from the **Type** drop-down.
14. Select **30X30X2.6** from the **Size** drop-down.
15. Select the line segment and create a structural member, as shown.
16. Click **OK** on the PropertyManager.

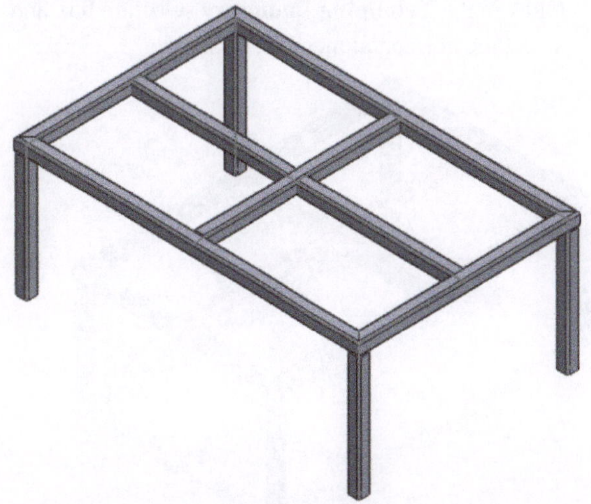

Trimming the Structural Members

The structural members will be trimmed if you have created them as a single instance. However, if you have created the structural members by activating the **Structural Member** tool several times, they will not be trimmed automatically. You need to trim those members by using the **Trim/Extend** tool.

1. To trim the structural members, click the **Trim/Extend** button on the **Weldments** CommandManager.
2. Click the **End Trim** icon in the **Corner Type** section.
3. Select the structural member, as shown.

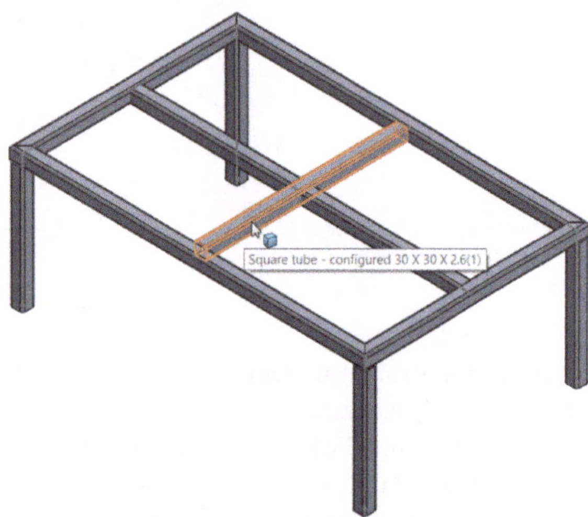

4. Select the **Bodies** option from the **Trimming Boundary** section.
5. Click in the **Trimming Boundary** selection box and select the horizontal member, as shown.

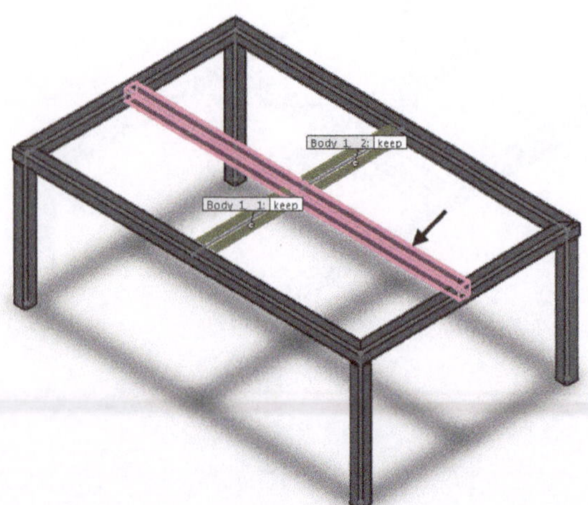

6. Click the **Simple cut between bodies** button.
7. Click **OK**. The structural member will be trimmed.

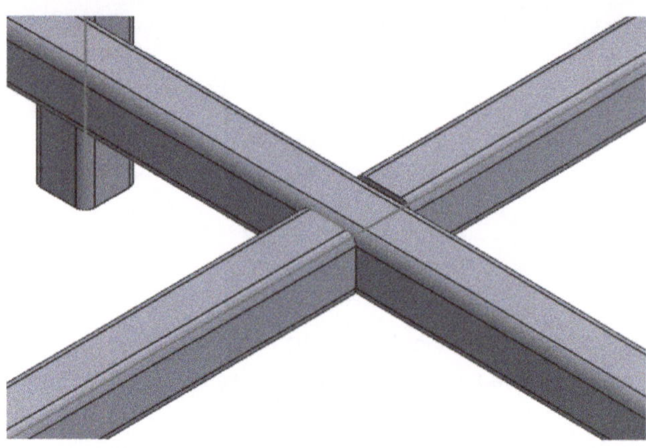

8. Again, activate the **Trim/Extend** tool.
9. Select the body to be trimmed, as shown.
10. Click in the selection box in the **Trimming Boundary** section.
11. Select the structural member intersecting the first body.

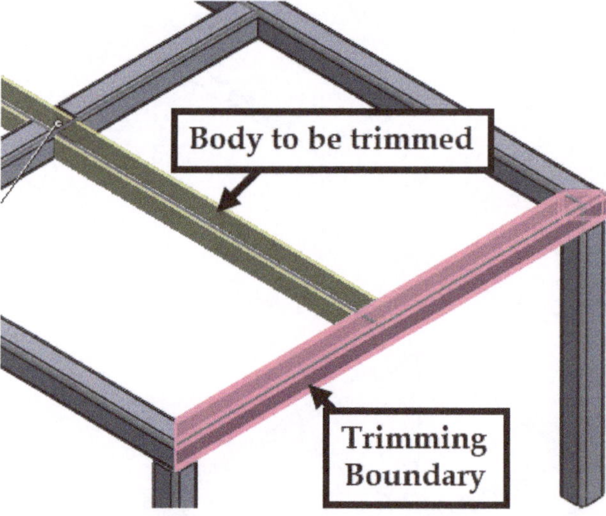

12. Click the **End Miter** icon on the PropertyManager. The two structural members will be trimmed to form a mitered corner.

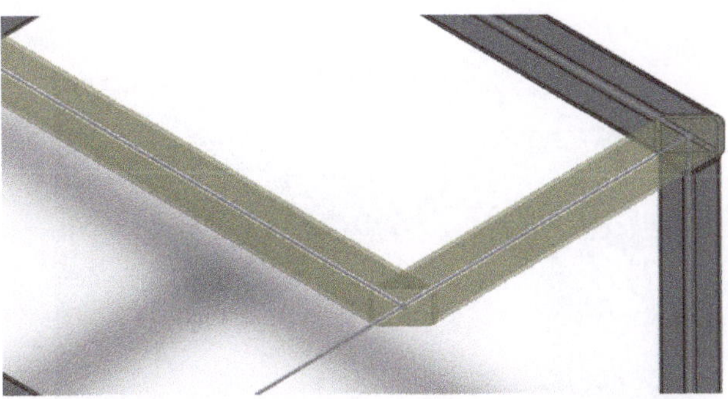

This corner type has two additional options: **Equal angle miter** and **Full flush miter**

The **Equal angle miter** option trims both intersecting members at an equal angle.

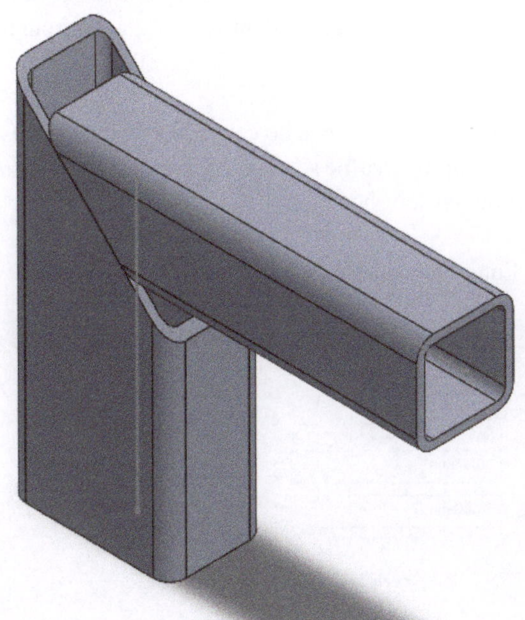

The **Full flush miter** option trims the intersecting members and adjusts the miter angle so that they flush together. This option is useful when the intersecting members are of different sizes and profiles.

13. Click the **End Butt1** icon.

14. Click the **End Butt2** icon.

15. Click the **End Trim** icon on the PropertyManager and select the **Face/plane** option.

16. Select the side faces of the intersecting structural members.

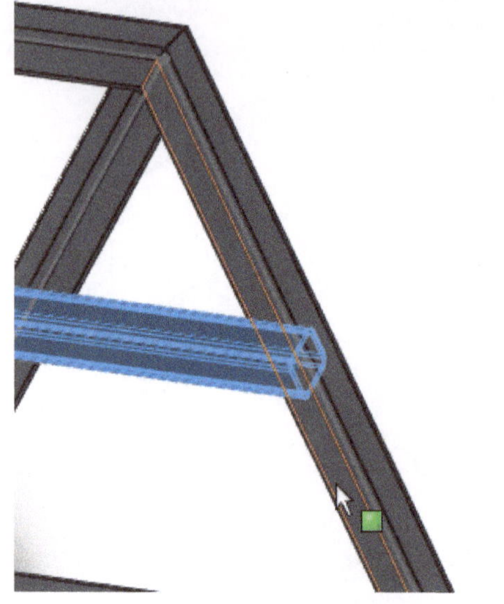

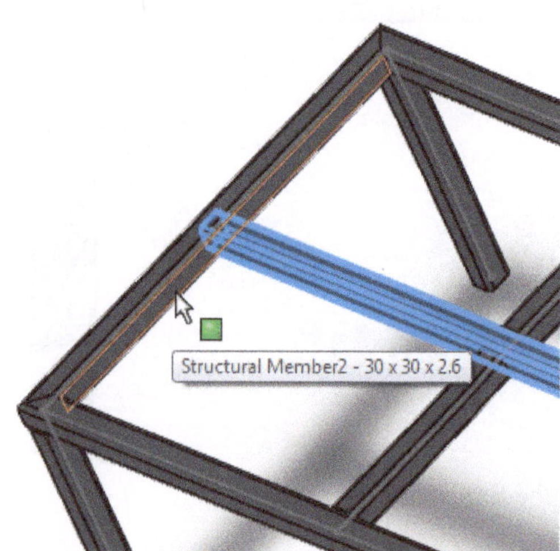

17. Click **OK** to trim the structural member.

Creating Gussets

Gussets are plates used to reinforce corners. Gussets can be created between any two faces that intersect at an angle between 0 and 180 degrees.

1. To create a gusset, click the **Gusset** button on the **Weldments** CommandManager.
2. Select the two faces to join with a gusset, as shown.

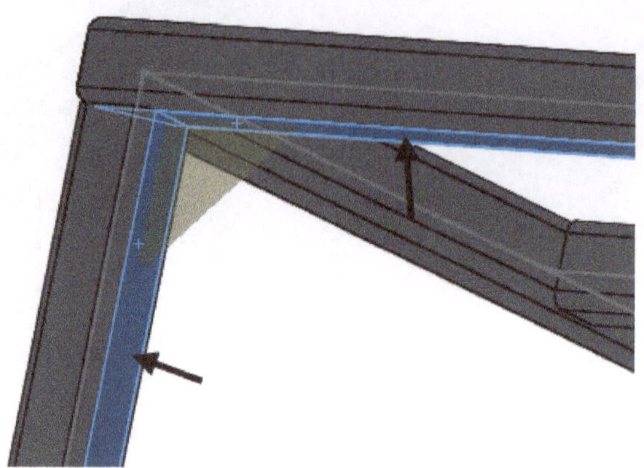

The gusset can be created in a triangular or polygonal shape.

3. Select the **Triangular Profile** icon from the **Profile** section.

The size of the gusset can be controlled by the options available in the **Profile** section. Each option corresponds to the dimension shown on the profile button.

4. Enter the values as shown.

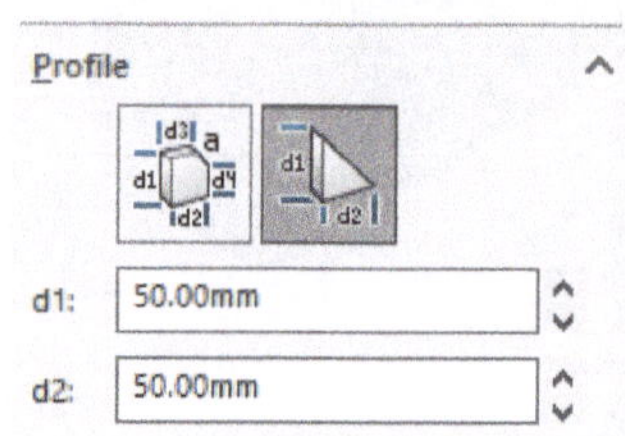

The **Chamfer** button in the **Profile** section allows you to add a chamfer to the inside edge of the gusset.

The thickness of the gusset can be specified using the thickness buttons and the **Gusset Thickness** edit box.

5. Click the **Both Sides** icon and enter **6** in the **Gusset Thickness** box.

The location of the gussets can be defined by using the options in the **Location** section.

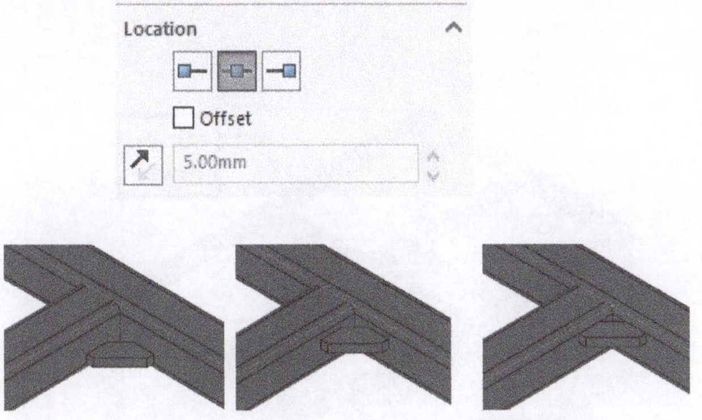

If you want to define the gusset at an offset from the location, check the **Offset** option, and enter the offset value in the **Offset Value** box.

6. Click the **Mid Point** button in the **Location** section.
7. Click **OK** to create the gusset.

You can also use the **Extruded Boss/Base** tool to create gussets with custom shapes and sizes.

Creating Base Plates

1. On the CommandManager, click **Weldments > Extruded Boss/Base**  .
2. Zoom and rotate the model to display the bottom face of the front left column.
3. Select the bottom face of the column.

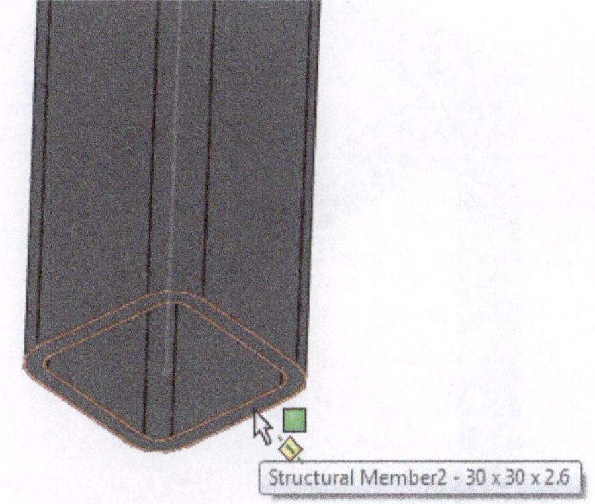

4. On the **Sketch** tab, click **Rectangle drop-down > Center Rectangle** .
5. Select the origin point and create a centered rectangle.

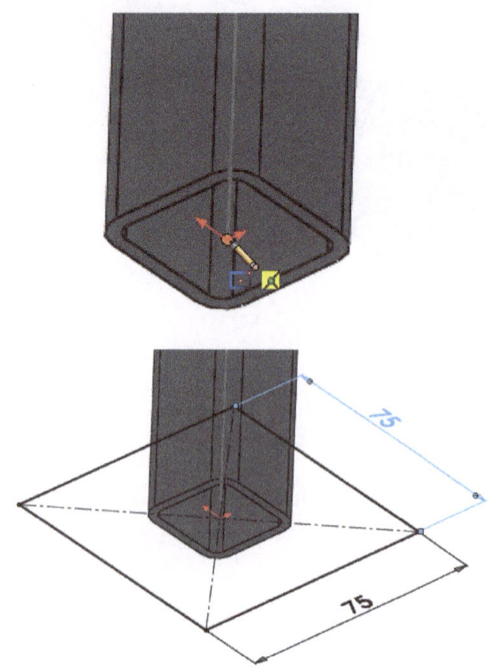

6. Exit the sketch.
7. Leave the **Merge result** option unchecked.
8. Type-in 5 in the **Depth** box and extrude the sketch downwards.

Mirroring Gussets and Baseplates

1. On the CommandManager, click **Weldments > Reference Geometry > Plane** .
2. Select the Top plane from the FeatureManager Design Tree.
3. Select the two points from the layout sketch, as shown.

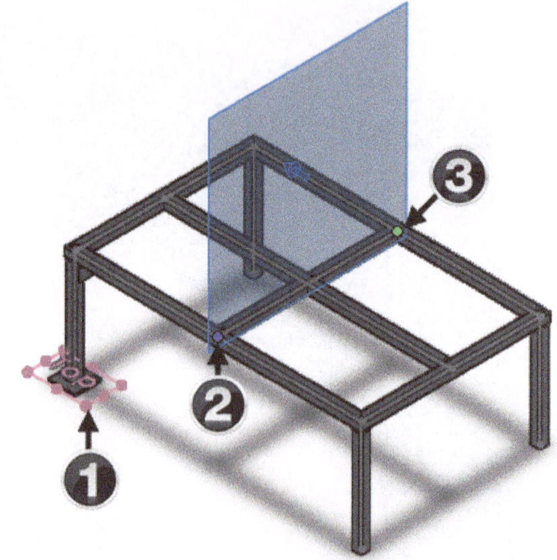

4. Click **OK** on the PropertyManager.
5. On the CommandManager, click **Features > Mirror** .
6. Select the new plane to define the mirror plane.
7. On the PropertyManager, expand the **Bodies to Mirror** section.
8. Select the gusset and base plate, and then click **OK** .

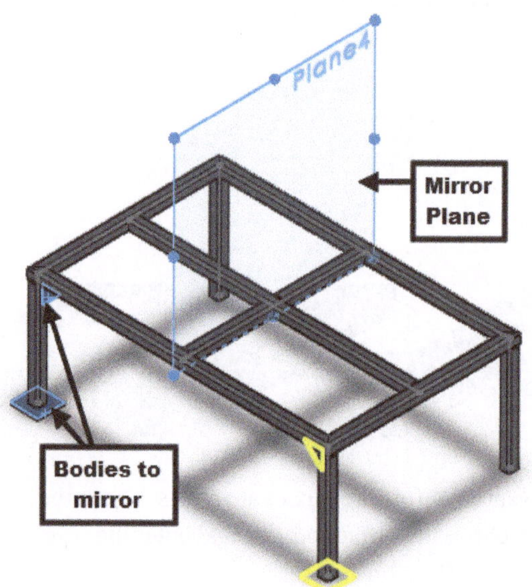

9. Hide the plane.

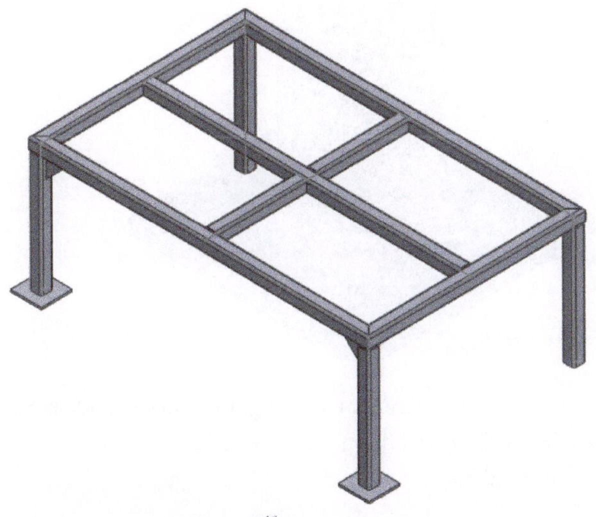

10. Activate the **Plane** tool, and select the Front plane and the point, as shown.

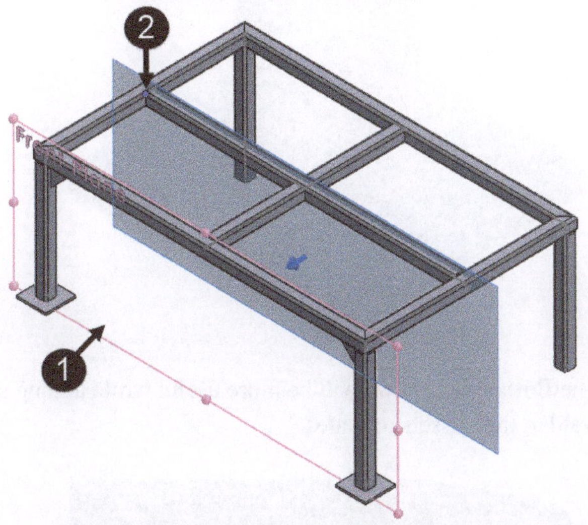

11. Mirror all the base plates and gusset bodies about the new plane.

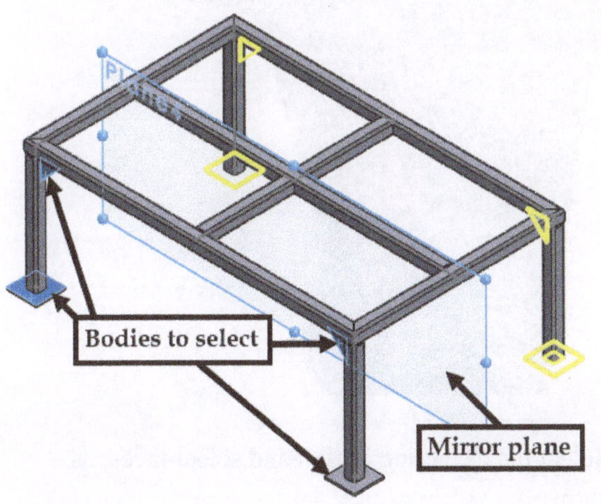

Creating Fillet Beads

You can create fillet beads to add weld information to the model. The **Fillet Bead** is the older SOLIDWORKS tool. The **Weld Bead** tool can be used instead of this tool for performance and new enhancements. However, this tool is explained to know its basic functionality.

1. To create a fillet bead, click **Insert > Weldments > Fillet Bead** from the Menu bar.

You can create three types of fillet beads: **Full Length, Intermittent,** and **Staggered**.

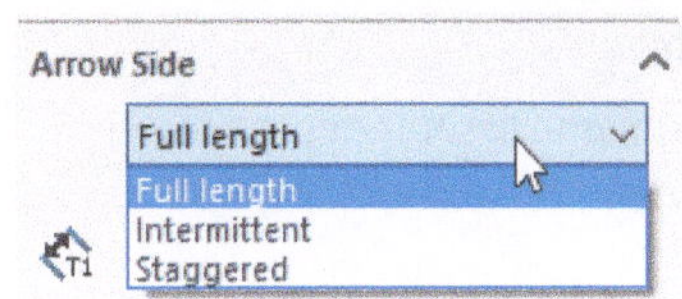

2. Select **Full Length** from the drop-down available in the **Arrow Side** section.
3. Enter **3** in the **Fillet size** box.

Next, you need to select intersecting faces to create a fillet weld between them.

4. Zoom to the base plate of the front right column.
5. Select the top face of the base plate.
6. Click in the **Face set 2** selection box and select a face of the column, as shown.

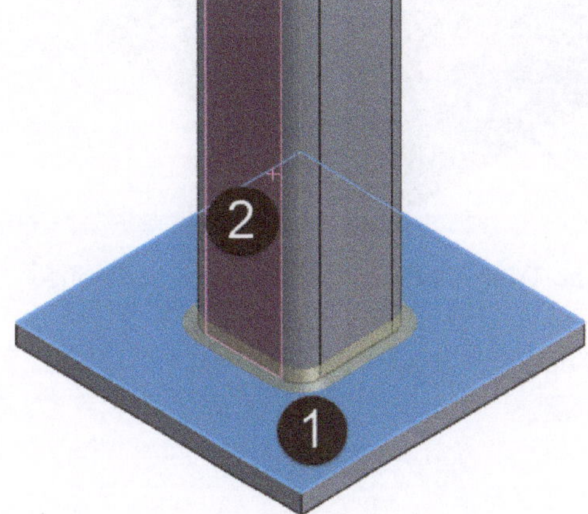

7. Make sure that the **Tangent Propagation** option is checked. You will notice that the bead is created around the structural member.
8. Leave the **Add weld symbol** option checked.
9. Click **OK** to create the fillet bead.

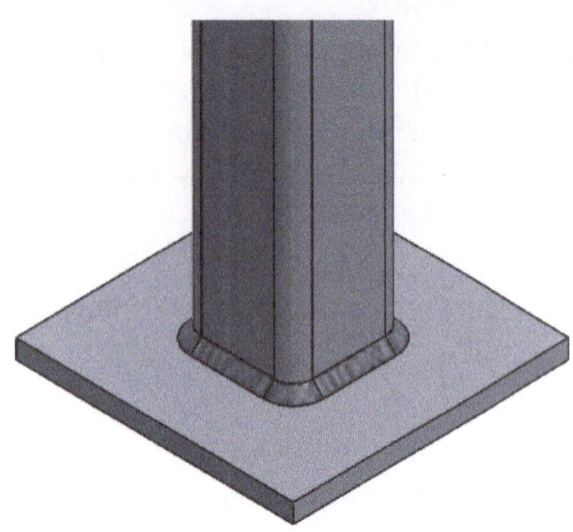

Creating Weld Beads

You can add weld beads to parts, assemblies, or multi-body parts.

1. To add a weld bead, click the **Weld Bead** button on the **Weldments** CommandManager.
2. Zoom to the base plate of the front left column.
3. Select the top face of the base plate.
4. Select the faces of the column, as shown.

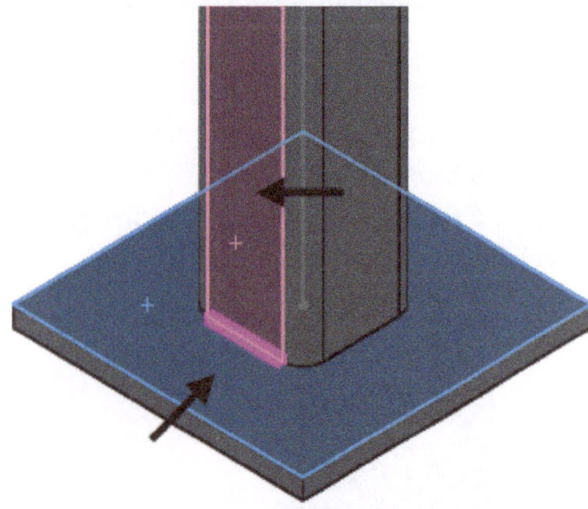

5. Check the **Tangent Propagation** option and notice that all the tangent edges are selected. The **All around** option also gives the same result.

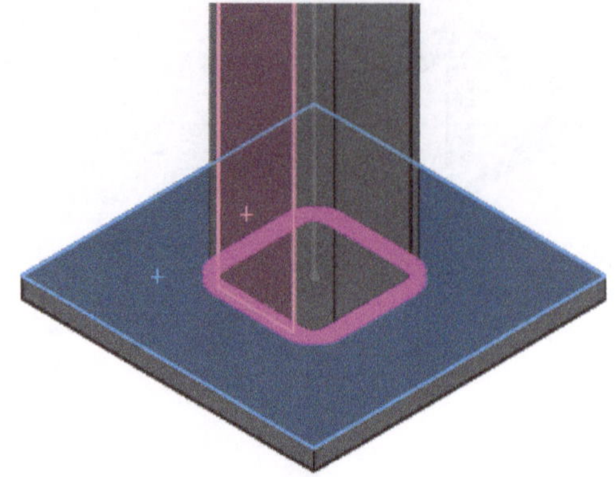

6. Uncheck the **Tangent Propagation** option and select the **Both sides** option. The opposite edge also is selected.

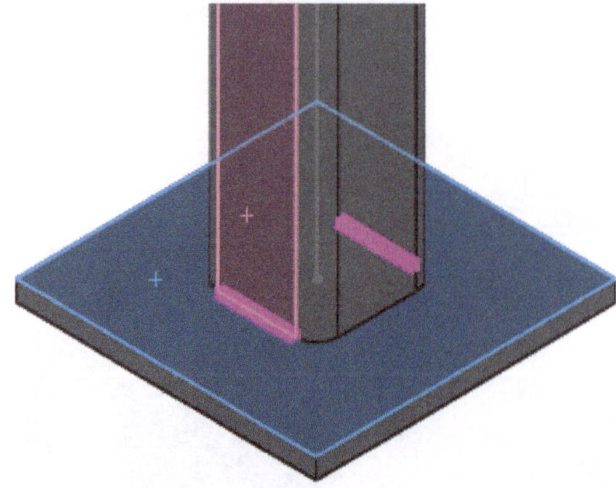

The **Both sides** option will be more useful while adding a weld to the gussets or plates.

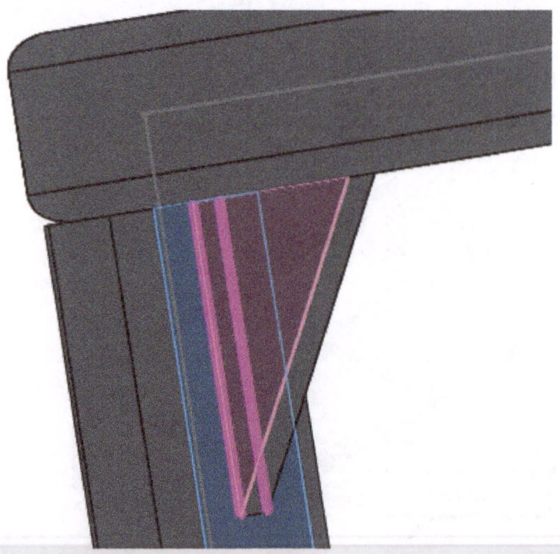

7. Select the **Selection** option and select faces, as shown.

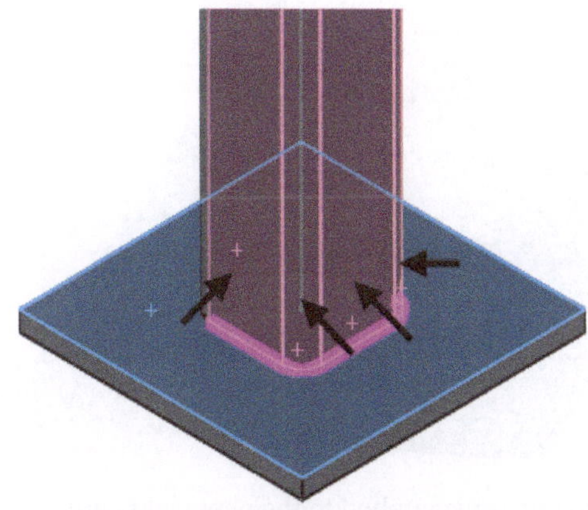

8. Check the **Form/To Length** option on the PropertyManager. Notice two arrows at the start and ends of the weld path.

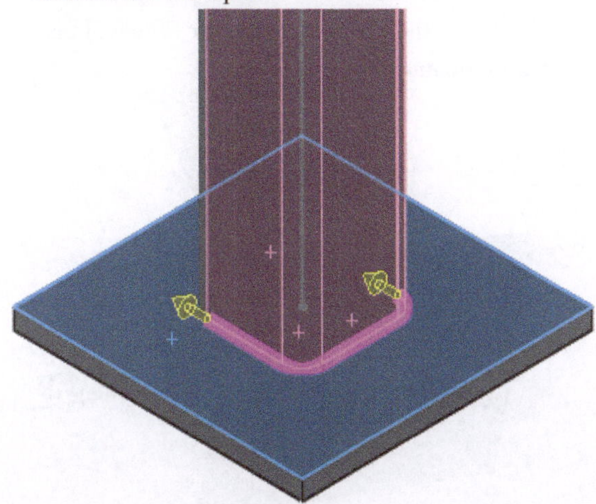

9. Type-in 10 in the **Start point** box and notice that the start point is offset by 10 mm. Also, the weld length is updated automatically.
10. Click the **Reverse Direction** icon next to the **Start point** box. The start and ends of the weld are reversed.

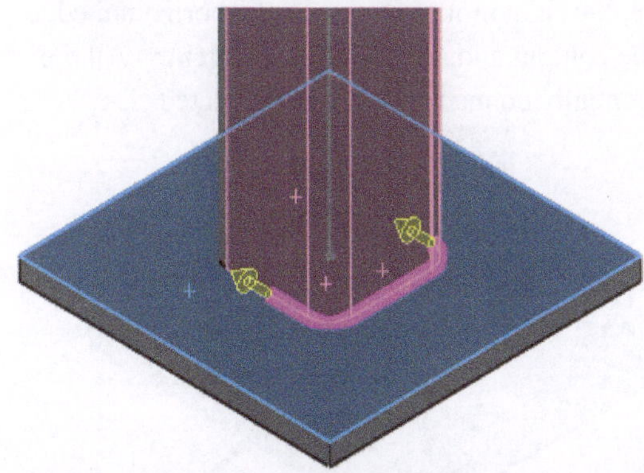

You can also check the **Intermittent Weld** option to create gaps along the weld.

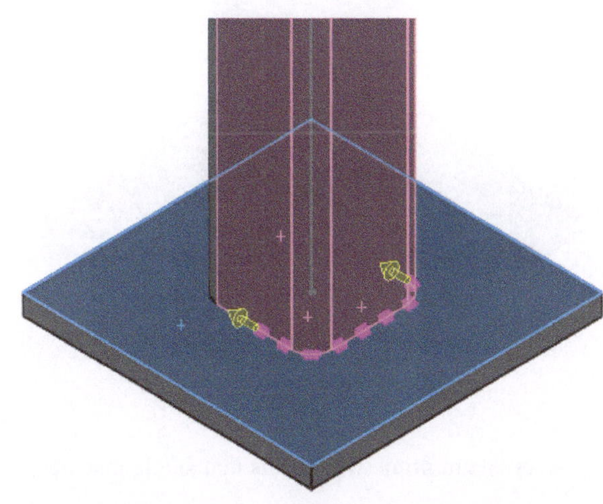

You can create an intermittent weld by specifying the **Gap and weld length** or **Pitch and weld length**.

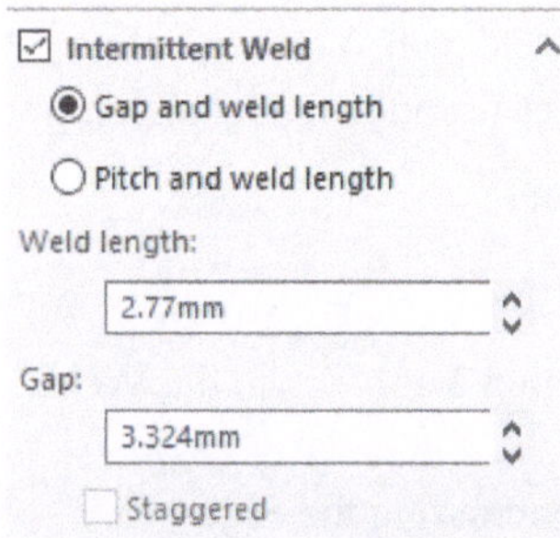

11. Enter 3 in the **Bead Size** box in the **Settings** section.
12. Click the **Define Weld Symbol** button in the **Settings** section.
13. Click the **Weld Symbol** button on the top of the leader.
14. Select the **Fillet** symbol from the flyout.

You can also click **More Symbols** on the flyout to open the **Symbol library** dialog. You can select symbols from a wide range of categories. Click **OK** after selecting the desired symbol.

15. Click **OK** on the dialog. Notice the weld symbol.

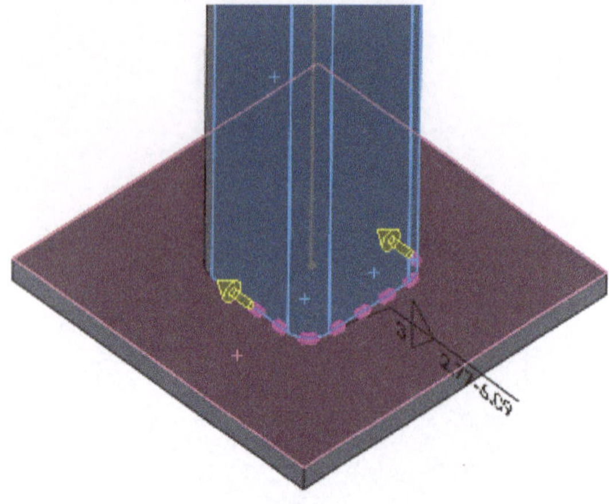

You can create multiple weld paths in a single instance.

16. Click the **New Weld Path** button in the **Weld Path** section.

Now, you need to define the weld path. You can define the weld path by selecting faces from the model or using the **Smart Weld Selection Tool**.

17. Click **Smart Weld Selection Tool** in the **Weld Path** section.
18. Click and drag the pointer crossing the edges, as shown. The edges are selected as soon as you release the pointer.

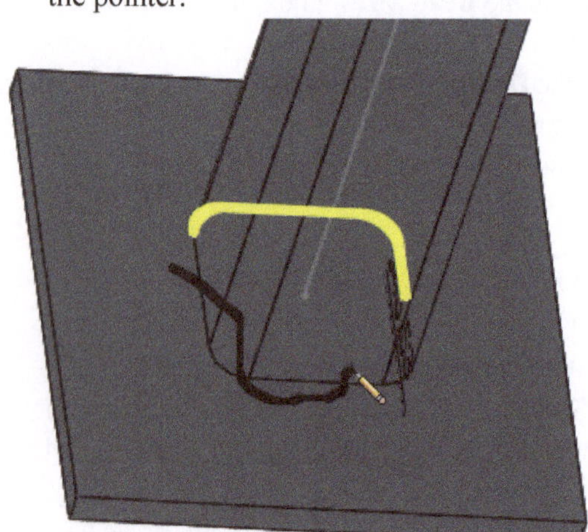

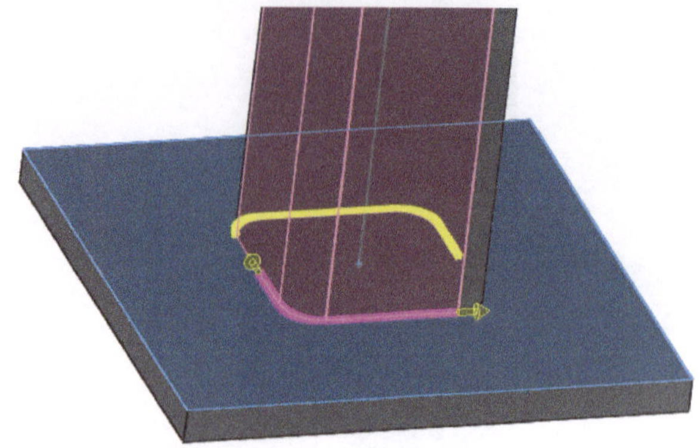

Notice that the offset is applied to the new weld path as well. You can uncheck the **From/To Length** option to remove the offset for the selected weld path.

19. Click **OK** on the Property Manager. The weld is added to the model.

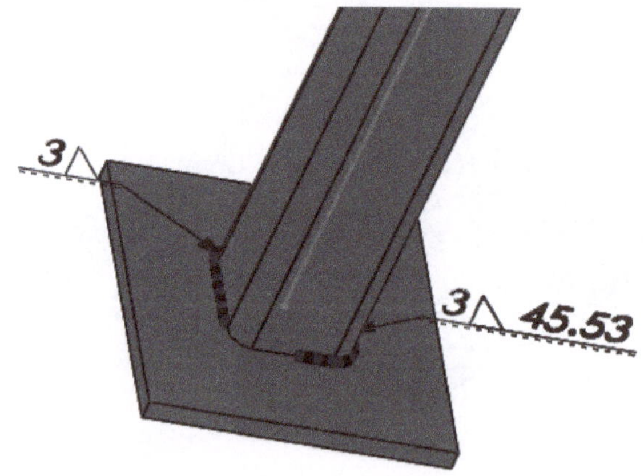

20. Activate the **Weld Bead** tool.
21. Zoom to the base plate of the back-right column.
22. On the PropertyManager, select the **Weld Path** option.
23. Click the right mouse button on the horizontal edge of the column and select **Select Tangency**. All the tangentially connected edges are selected.

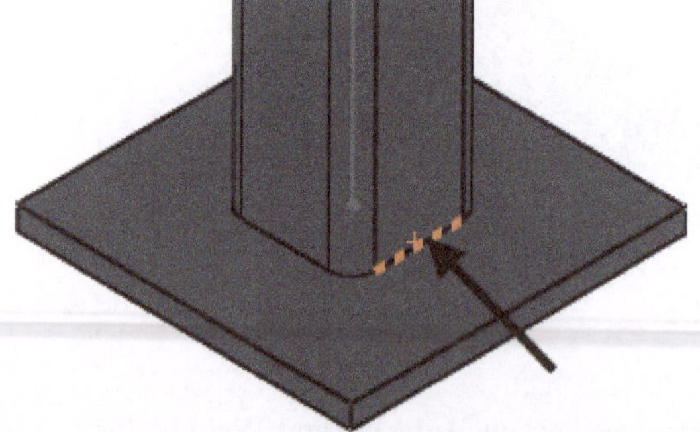

24. Leave the settings on the PropertyManager and click

OK.

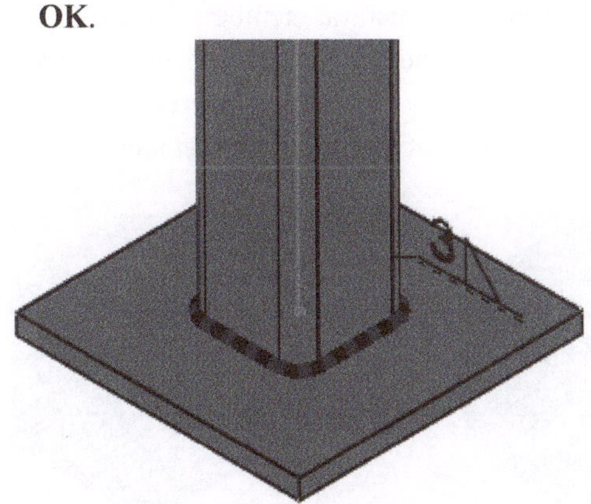

25. Likewise, add the weld bead to the other column.

Notice that there is a **Weld Folder** in the FeatureManager Design Tree. It is added to the FeatureManager Design Tree as you create weld beads.

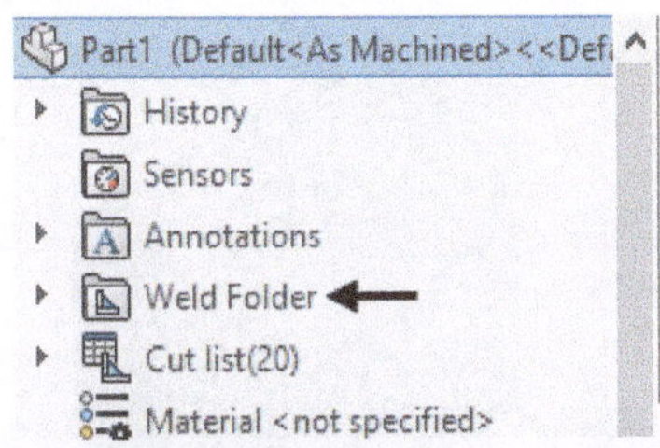

On expanding this folder, you can see the welds that are created.

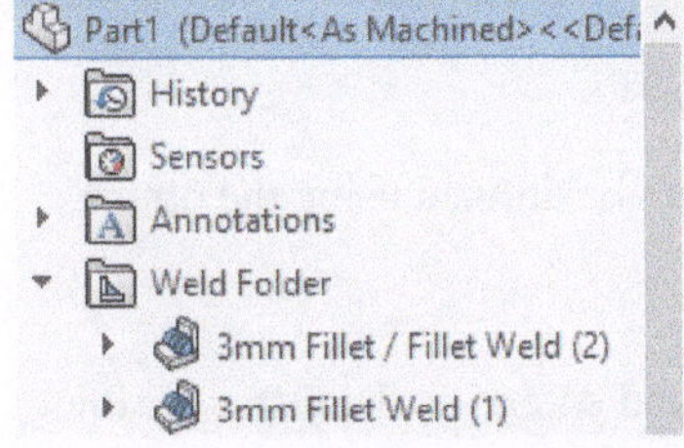

You can edit the properties of the weld by right-clicking on it and selecting **Properties**.

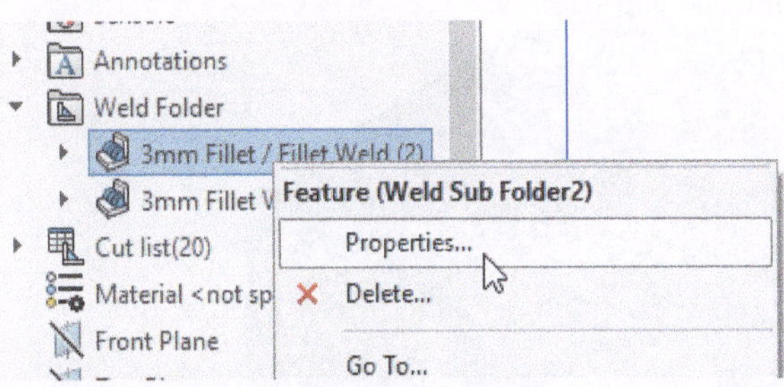

The **Weld Bead Properties** dialog appears.

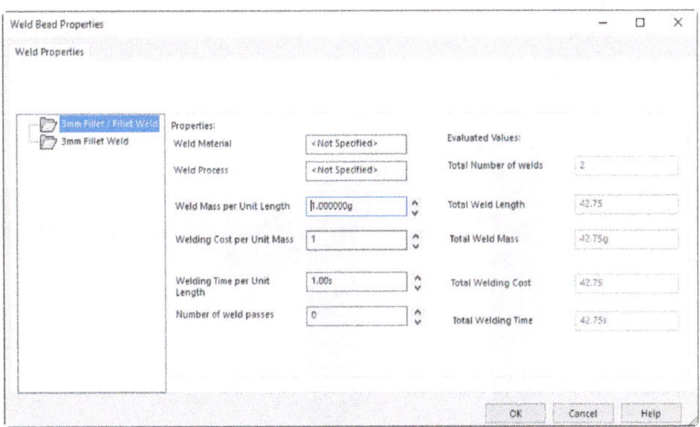

You can change the properties of the weld bead in this dialog. Note that weld beads are for representation same as a cosmetic thread. They do not have any mass properties. When you have calculated the total mass of the model, the mass of the weld bead is excluded from the model. You can add the **Total Weld Mass** value to the total mass of the model.

To edit a weld bead, right click on it and select **Edit Feature**.

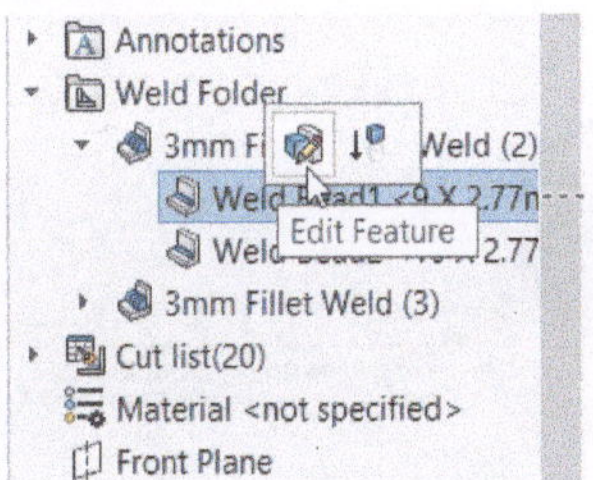

TUTORIAL 3 (Creating End Caps)

End caps are used to close the open ends of the structural members. Note that you can only apply end caps to structural members having linear edges. You cannot apply them to round tubes.

1. Start a new part document and create the model, as shown.

2. To create an end cap, click the **End Cap** button on the **Weldments** Command Manager.
3. Select the end face of the structural member, as shown.

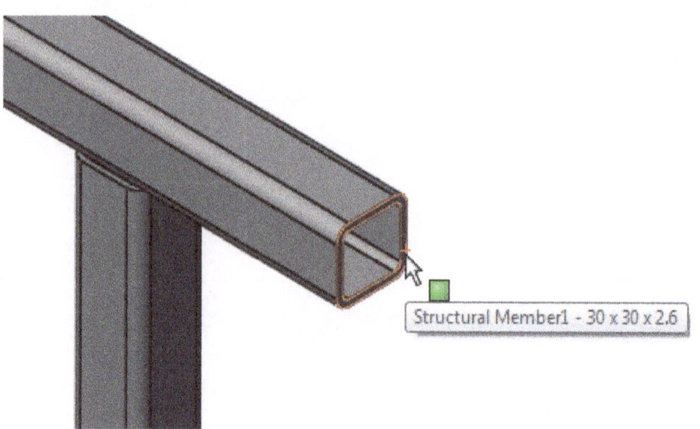

4. Click the **Outward** icon under the **Thickness direction** section. The preview of the end cap appears on the outer face.

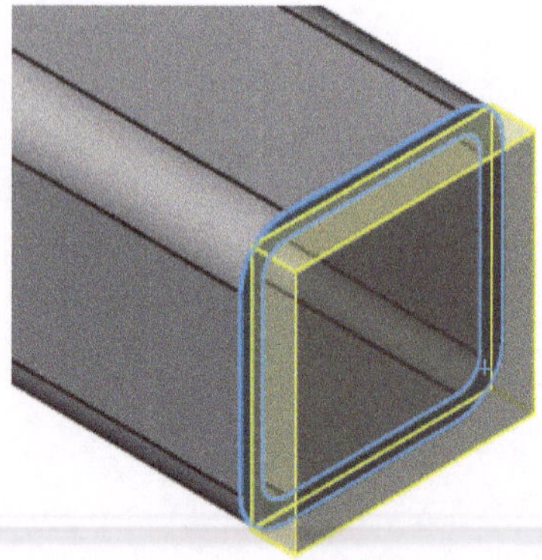

5. Click the **Inward** icon under the **Thickness direction** section. The preview of the end cap appears inside the structural member. However, it will be created on the end face of the member. The inward end cap means that it will be created inside the original length of the structural member.

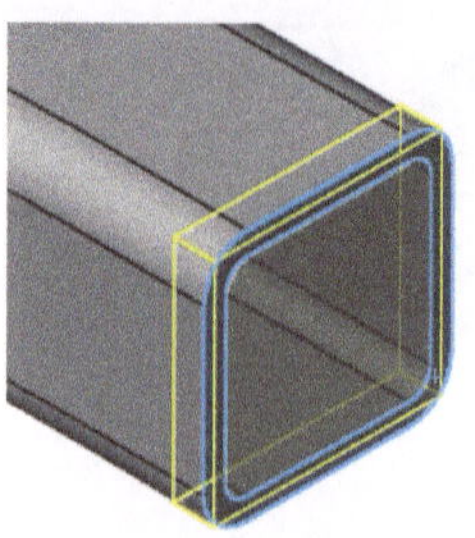

6. Click the **Internal** icon under the **Thickness direction** section. The preview of the end cap appears inside the structural member. You can further inset the end cap by entering a value in the **Inset Distance** box.

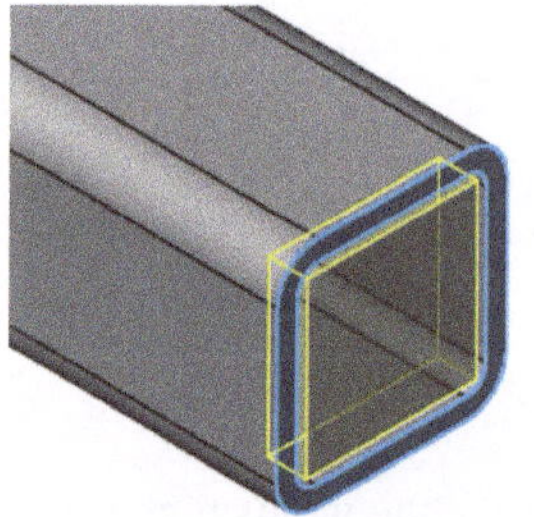

7. Click the **Outward** icon and specify the **Thickness** as **3**.

The size of the end cap can be defined using the options in the **Offset** section.

8. Select **Offset value** and enter 5 in the **Offset value** box. The size of the end cap is reduced by 5 mm. You can click the **Reverse Direction** icon to increase the end cap size.

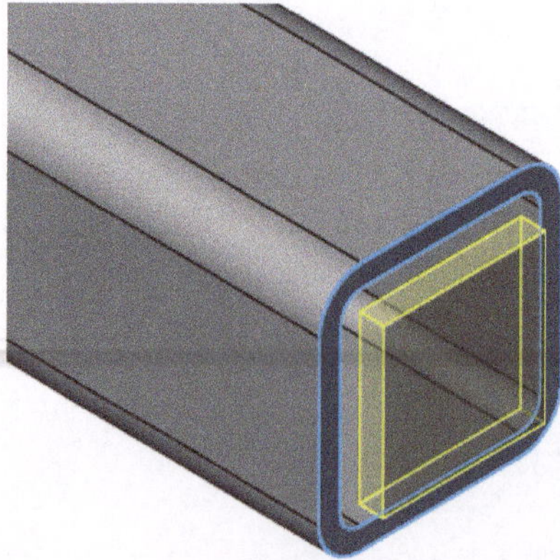

9. Select **Thickness Ratio** and enter 1 in the **Thickness Ratio** box.
10. Deselect the **Reverse Direction** icon. The weldment thickness value reduces the size of the end cap.

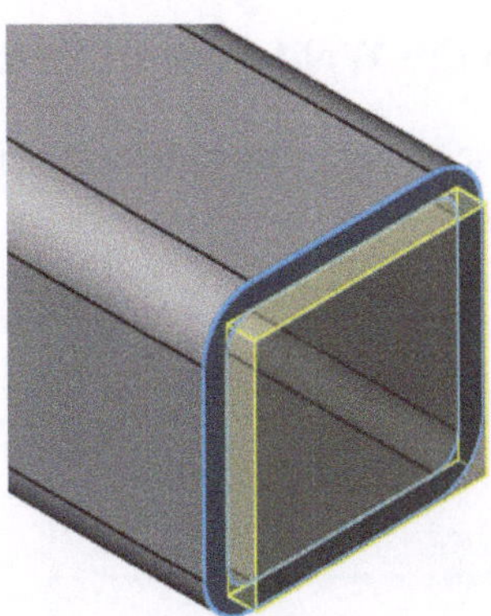

11. Change the **Thickness Ratio** to 0.5. The size of the weldment is reduced by half of the weldment thickness value.

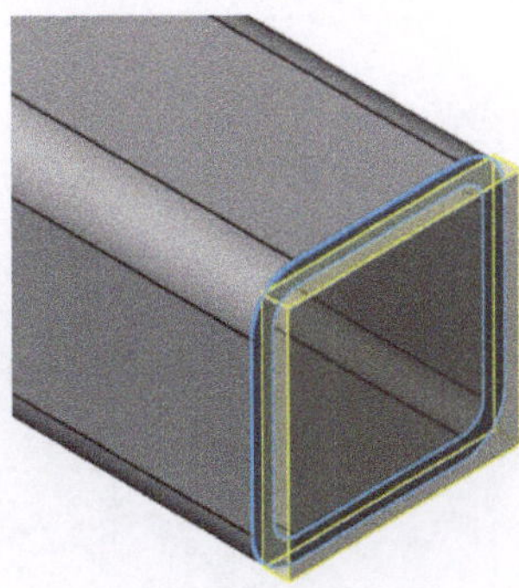

12. Check the **Corner Treatment** option to apply chamfer or fillet the end cap corners.
13. Select **Chamfer** and type-in 3 in the **Chamfer Distance** box.

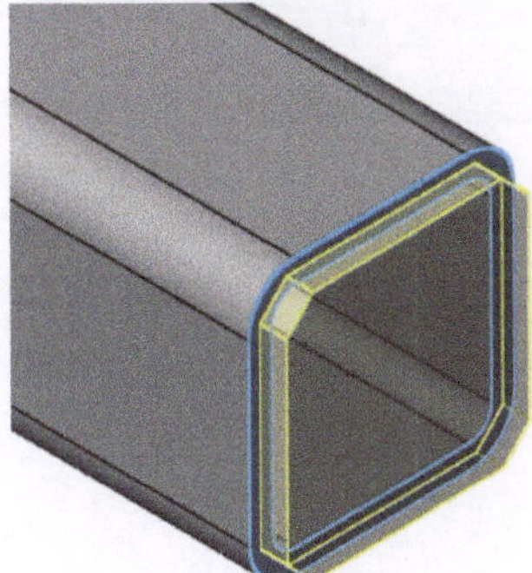

14. Select **Fillet** and type-in 3 in the **Fillet Radius** box.

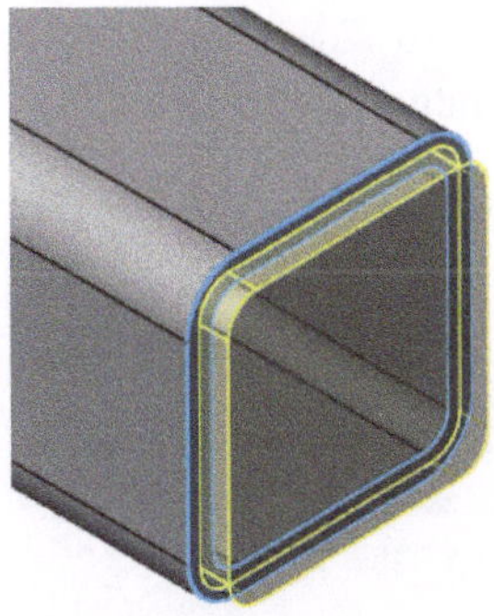

15. Click **OK** to create the end cap.

TUTORIAL 4 (Working with Cut lists)

1. Open the Tutorial 2 file.

Cut lists are used to document weldment designs. They contain information about the type of structural members, the lengths of the individual members, and any other information necessary to manufacture a weldment. SOLIDWORKS automatically creates a cut list as you design a weldment. As soon as a weldment is added, the **Cut list** folder is added to the FeatureManager Design Tree.

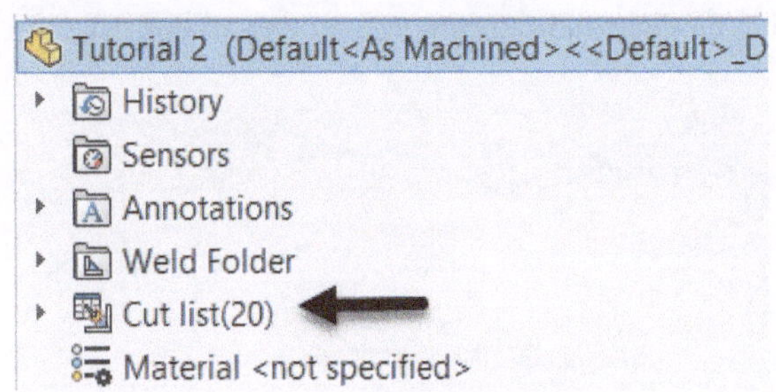

You will notice that the **Solid Bodies** folder is missing. When a structural member is added to the part, it creates a weldment, and the **Solid Bodies** folder is replaced with the **Cut list** folder. As you continue to add weldment features, these features are listed individually within the **Cut list** folder.

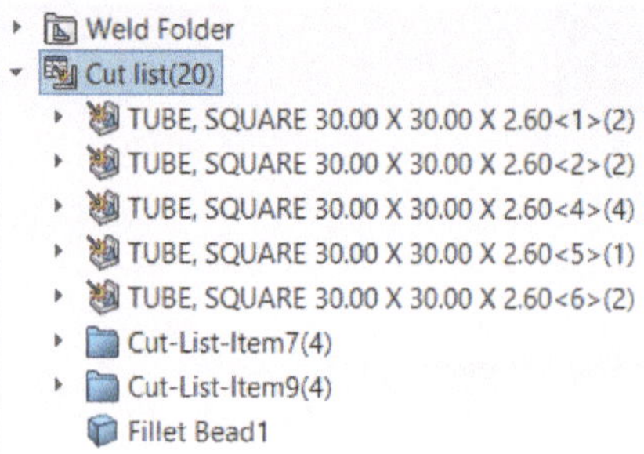

The Cut list is generated and updated automatically as the **Update automatically** option is selected. You can click the right mouse button on the Cut list and deselect this option.

You can see that several subfolders are created within the **Cut list** folder. All the like items, such as plates, end caps, and gussets, are grouped into individual subfolders. Structural Members and weldment components are represented by the weld symbol . Other items are listed in normal folders. You can also reorder these folders by clicking and dragging them.

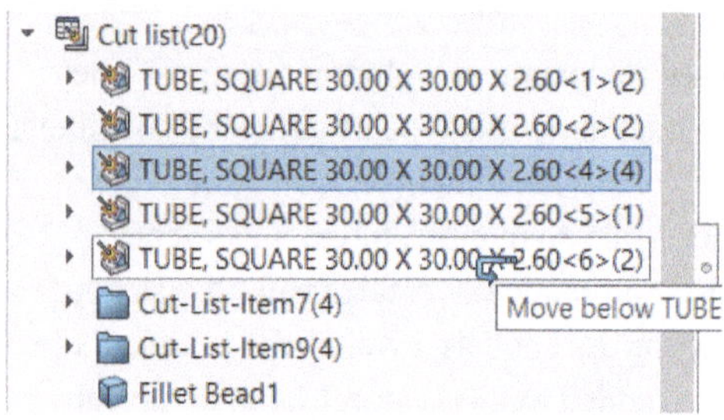

You can also exclude items from the **Cut list** by right-clicking on them and selecting **Exclude from cut list**.

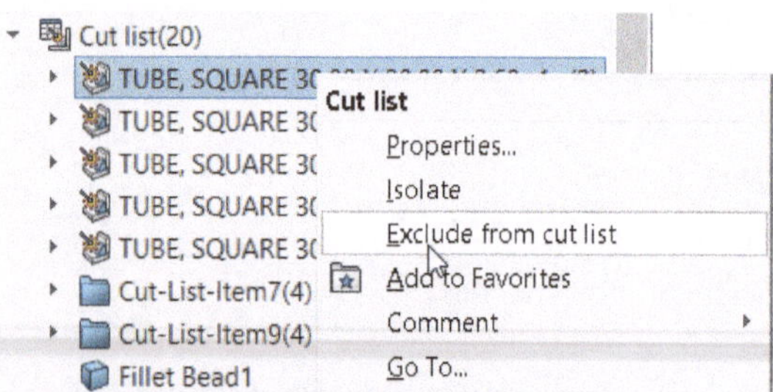

You can also include the excluded items by right-clicking and selecting **Include in cut list**. It is recommended that you make changes to the **Cut list** only after completing the weldment design. If you add any additional members to the model, you will lose all of the changes made to the Cut list order.

Adding a Cut list to the Weldment Drawing

1. Create a drawing by selecting **New > Make Drawing from Part/Assembly**.

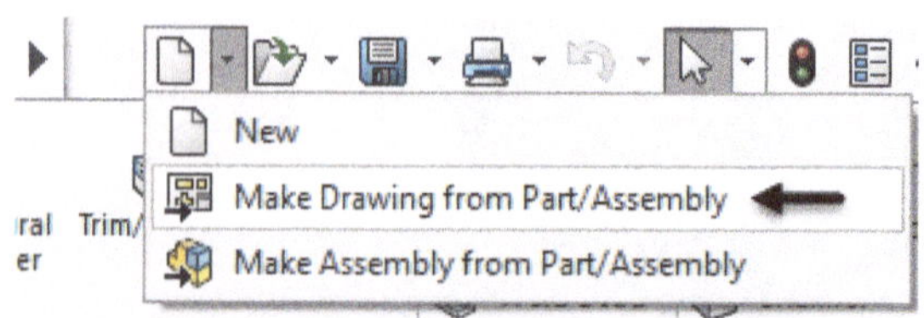

2. Select **A2 (ISO)** from the **Sheet Format/Size** section and click **OK**.
3. On the **Drawing** CommandManager, click the **Model View** tool.
4. Double-click on the Tutorial 2.
5. Place the Isometric view on the drawing sheet.

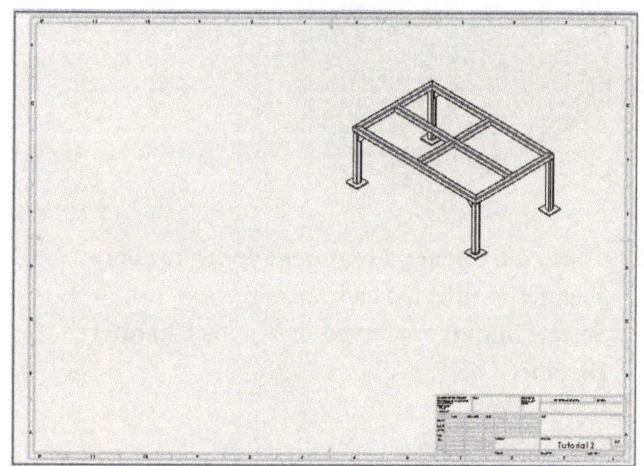

6. Click **Annotation > Tables > Weldment Cut List** on the CommandManager.

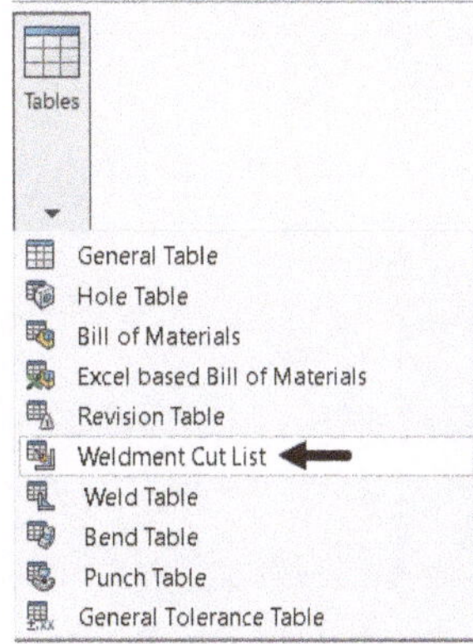

7. Select the view from the drawing sheet. The **Weldment Cut List** PropertyManager appears. The options in this PropertyManager are similar to the **Bill of Materials** one.
8. Click **OK** on the Property Manager and place the cut list table on the drawing sheet.

ITEM NO.	QTY.	DESCRIPTION	LENGTH
1	2	TUBE, SQUARE 30 X 30 X 2.60	830
2	2	TUBE, SQUARE 30 X 30 X 2.60	530
3	4	TUBE, SQUARE 30 X 30 X 2.60	285
4	1	TUBE, SQUARE 30 X 30 X 2.60	770
5	2	TUBE, SQUARE 30 X 30 X 2.60	220
6	4		
7	4		

The **Description** and **Length** may or may not be populated in the cut list. It depends on the type of weldment. The **Description** and **Length** of the structural members are automatically populated. Notice that the **Description** and **Length** of the members such as gussets, base plates, and end caps are not populated automatically. To know about the members that are not populated, you need to add balloons to the model view.

9. On the CommandManager, click **Annotation > Auto Balloon**.
10. Select the view and click **OK**. Notice that the gussets and base plate are annotated with the 6 and 7 number balloons.

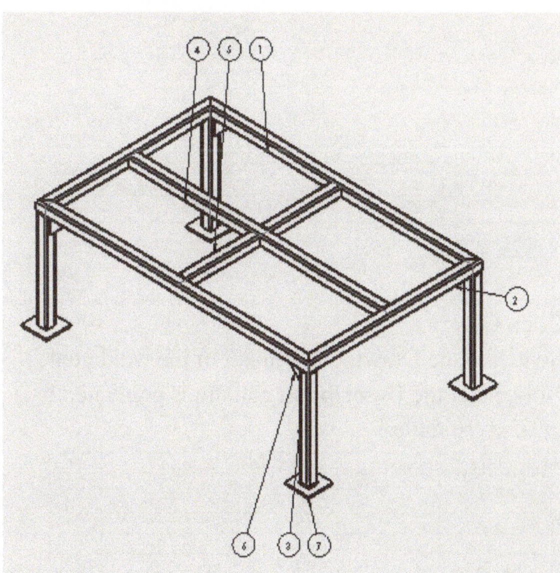

You need to populate these properties manually. To do so, you need to switch to the part document and add properties to these members.

11. Open the part document of the weldment.
12. Expand the **Cut list** folder in the **FeatureManager Design Tree**.
13. Right-click on the **Cut-list-Item7** subfolder under the Cut list folder and select **Properties**; the **Cut List Properties** dialog appears.

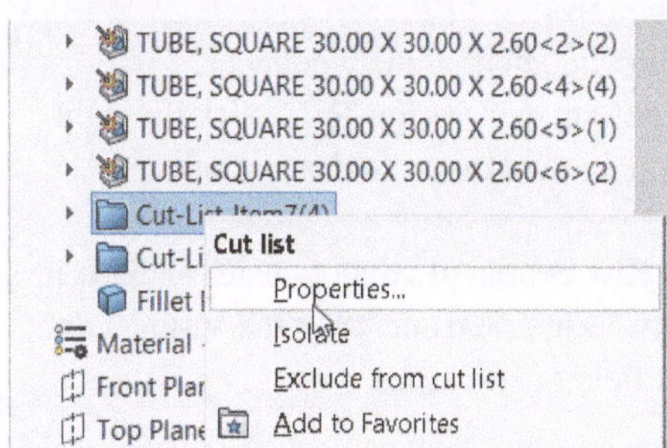

14. In the **Cut List Properties** dialog, enter **DESCRIPTION** in the **Property Value** field and **Gusset** in the **Value/Text Expression** field.

	Property Name	Type	Value / Text Expression
1	MATERIAL	Text	"SW-Material@@@Cut-List-Item7@Tutorial 2.SL
2	QUANTITY	Text	"QUANTITY@@@Cut-List-Item7@Tutorial 2.SLDP
3	Description	Text	Gusset
4	<Type a new proper		

15. Click the **Cut-list-Item8** folder and enter **DESCRIPTION** in the **Property Value** field and **Base Plate** in the **Value/Text Expression** field.

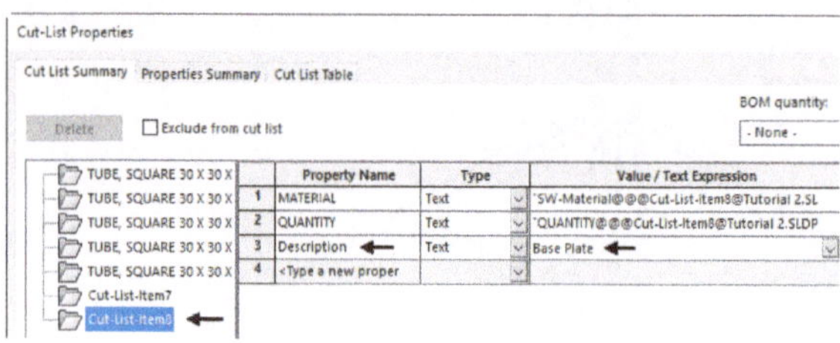

16. Click **OK**.
17. Switch to the Drawing document of the weldment. Notice that the **Description** column is populated in the Cut list table.

ITEM NO.	QTY.	DESCRIPTION	LENGTH
1	2	TUBE, SQUARE 30 X 30 X 2.60	830
2	2	TUBE, SQUARE 30 X 30 X 2.60	530
3	4	TUBE, SQUARE 30 X 30 X 2.60	285
4	1	TUBE, SQUARE 30 X 30 X 2.60	770
5	2	TUBE, SQUARE 30 X 30 X 2.60	220
6	4	Gusset	
7	4	Base Plate	

Adding Columns to the Cut list table

You can add more columns to the cut list table and save it as a template for later use.

1. Place the pointer on the table and notice the row and column headers.
2. Click the right mouse button on the rightmost column and click **Insert > Column Right**.
3. On the PropertyManager, enter **Weight** in the **Title** box and click **OK**.
4. Open the part document of the weldment.
5. In the FeatureManager Design Tree, click the right mouse button on the **Gusset** folder and select **Properties**.
6. On the **Cut List Properties** dialog, enter **Weight** in the **Property Value** field and **48** in the **Value/Text Expression** field.

	Property Name	Type	Value / Text Expression
1	MATERIAL	Text	"SW-Material@@@Gusset<26>@Tutorial 2.SLD
2	QUANTITY	Text	"QUANTITY@@@Gusset<26>@Tutorial 2.SLDPRT
3	Description	Text	Gusset
4	Weight	Number	48
5	<Type a new proper		

7. Click **OK**.
8. Switch to the drawing and notice that the value is not updated in the cut list table.
9. Click in the **Weight** column header.

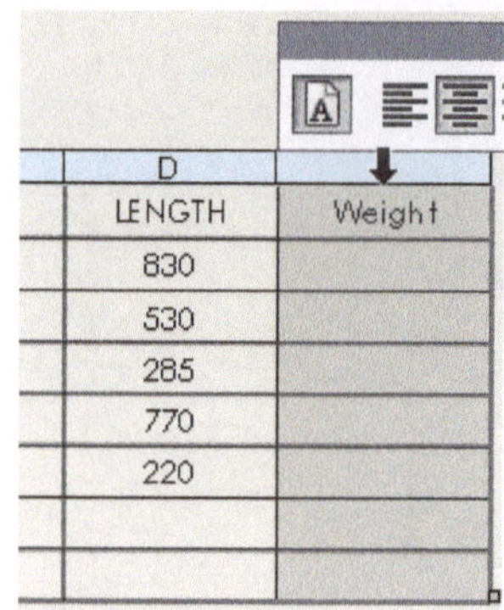

10. On the PropertyManager, select the **Cut list item property**.
11. Select **Weight** from the drop-down menu.

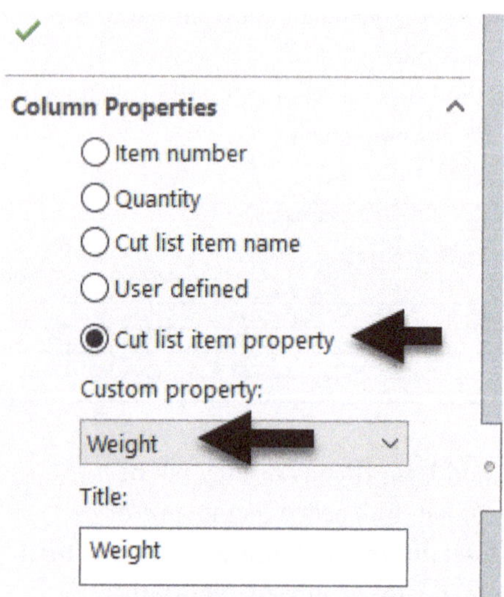

12. Click the green check to update the table.

ITEM NO.	QTY.	DESCRIPTION	LENGTH	Weight
1	2	TUBE, SQUARE 1.18 X 1.18 X 0.10	32.68	
2	2	TUBE, SQUARE 1.18 X 1.18 X 0.10	20.87	
3	4	TUBE, SQUARE 1.18 X 1.18 X 0.10	11.22	
4	1	TUBE, SQUARE 1.18 X 1.18 X 0.10	30.31	
5	2	TUBE, SQUARE 1.18 X 1.18 X 0.10	8.66	
6	4	Gusset		48
7	4	Base Plate		

13. To save the cut list table as a template, right-click on the table and select **Save As**.
14. Type **Custom_cutlist** and click **Save**.

Creating a Bounding box

The bounding box is the smallest box around a weldment. It gives you an idea about the weldment dimensions. You can use the bounding box to add some properties to the Cut list automatically.

1. Open the part document of the weldment model.
2. In the FeatureManager Design Tree, expand the **Cut list** folder.
3. Click the right mouse button on the **Gusset** folder and select **Create Bounding Box**.
4. Expand the **Gusset** folder and notice a 3D sketch inside it.

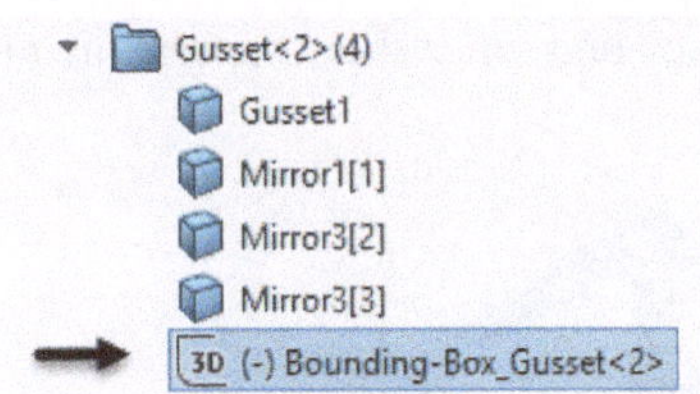

5. Click on the 3D sketch and notice a dotted box around the gusset.

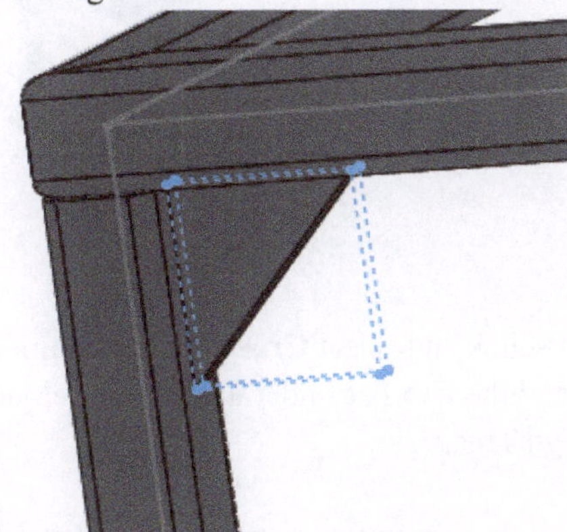

6. Click the right mouse button on the **Gusset** folder and select **Properties**. Notice the thickness, width, length, and volume properties on the **Cut list Properties** dialog.
7. Click **OK** to close the dialog.

You can edit or delete the bounding box by simply clicking the right mouse button on the folder and selecting **Edit Bounding Box** or **Delete Bounding Box**.

Adding a Weld table to the Weldment Drawing

You can show the weld beads or fillet beads of a weldment in a drawing document. You can show them in the form of a Weld table in the drawing.

1. To add a weld table, click **Annotation > Tables > Weld Table** on the CommandManager.

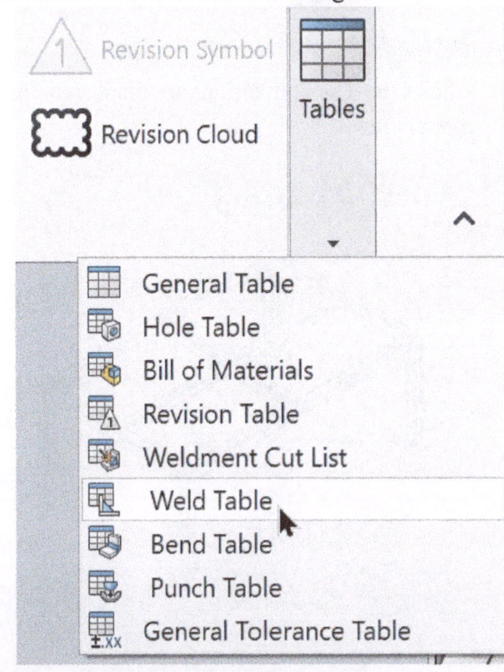

2. Select the Isometric view from the drawing.
3. Click **OK** on the Property Manager.
4. Place the weld table on the drawing sheet.

ITEM NO.	WELD SIZE	SYMBOL	WELD LENGTH	WELD MATERIAL	QTY.
1		◺	23.36		1
2	3	◺	2.77-5.54[23.36]		1
3		◺	19.39		1
4	3	◺	2.77-5.54[19.39]		1
5	3	◺	111.07		2

You can also add weld symbols and other annotations to the model view on the drawing.

Adding Weld Symbols

1. To add weld symbols or other annotations, click **Annotation > Model Items** 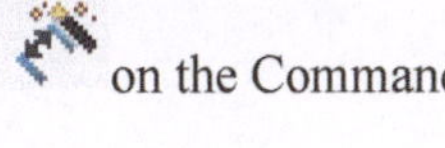 on the Command Manager.

2. On the **Model Items** Property Manager, set the **Source** to **Entire model**.
3. Deselect the **Marked for drawing** icon.
4. Select the icons from the **Annotations** section, as shown.

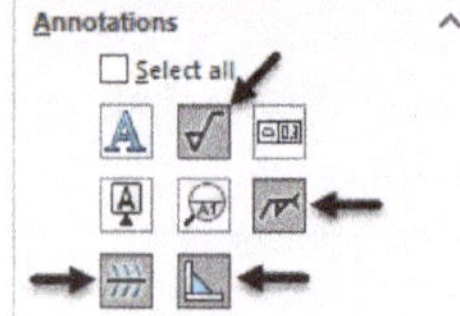

5. Click **OK**. The annotations are displayed on the model view.

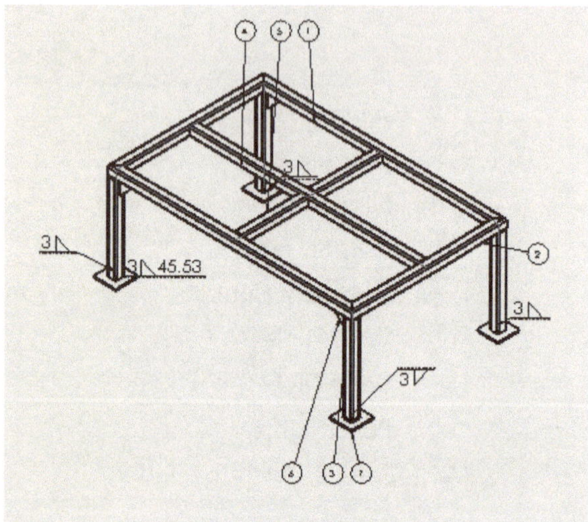

6. Save the Part document and the drawing document.

Creating Sub Weldments

You can break down a weldment into sub weldments to make it easy to manage them.

1. Open a Part document created in Tutorial 2.
2. Right-click on the Command Manager and select **Toolbars > Selection Filter**. The **Selection Filter** toolbar appears at the bottom.

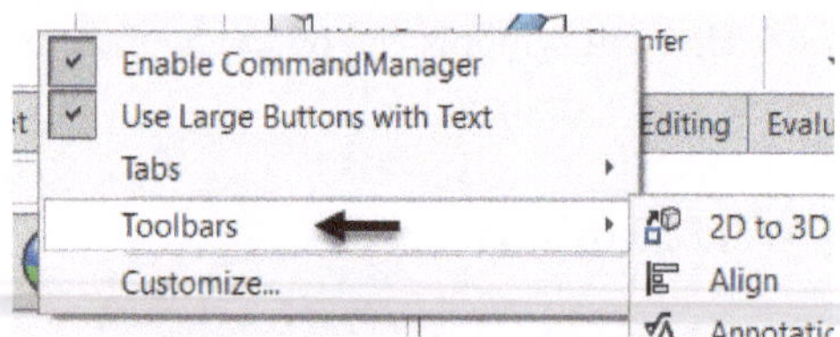

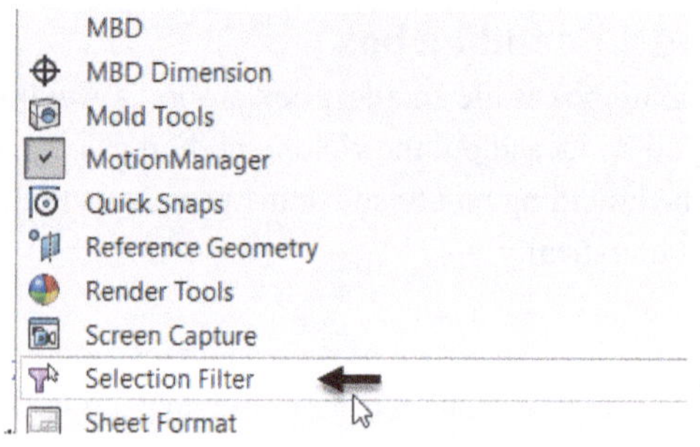

3. Click the **Filter Solid bodies** button on the **Selection Filter** toolbar.

4. Press the Ctrl key and select the structural members, as shown.

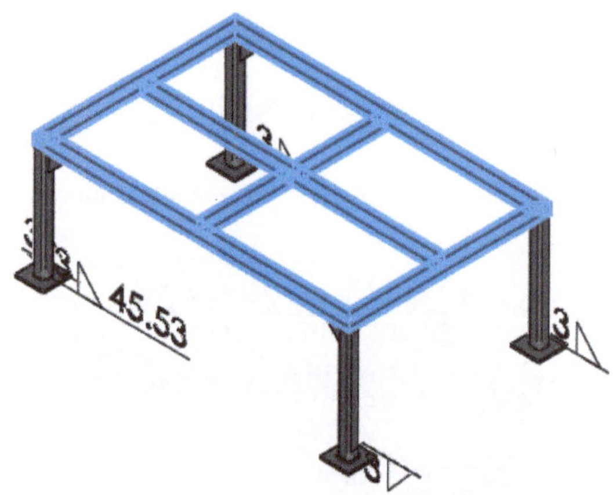

5. Right-click and select **Create Sub-Weldment**.
6. Expand the **Cut list** folder in the FeatureManager Design Tree.

You will notice a new folder under the cut list folder.

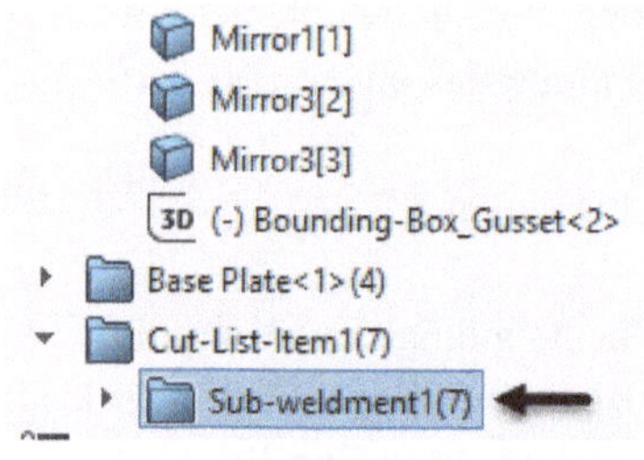

7. Open the drawing document of the weldments model. Place the cut list table on the drawing sheet.

ITEM NO.	QTY.	DESCRIPTION	LENGTH	Weight
1	1			
1	4	TUBE, SQUARE 1.18 X 1.18 X 0.10	11.22	
3	4			48
4	4	Base Plate		

You will notice that the **Description** and **Length** values are empty in the cut list because sub weldments are not recognized as weldment parts. You need to save the sub weldments as a separate weldment part.

8. Switch to the part document.
9. Press the Ctrl key and select the structural members, as shown.

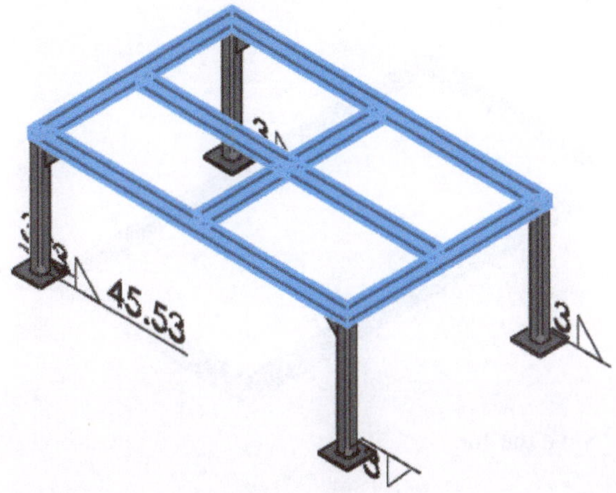

10. In the FeatureManager, click the right mouse button and select **Insert into New Part**.
11. On the PropertyManager, check the **Cut list properties to** option and select **Cut list properties**. This option allows you to insert the cut list table into the drawing.
12. Click **OK** on the PropertyManager.
13. Save the file as Tutorial 2-Sub-weldment1.

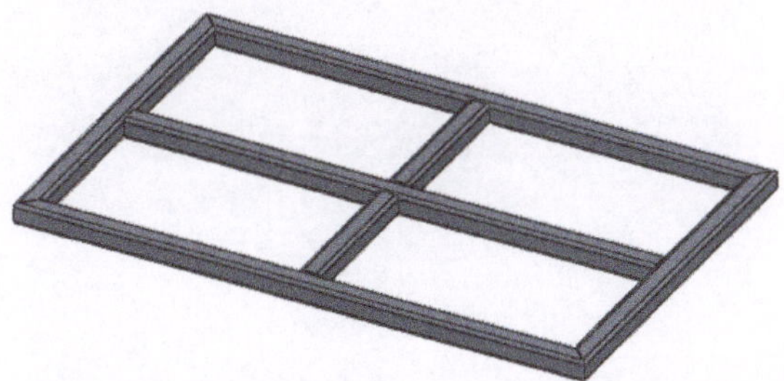

18. Create a drawing by selecting **New > Make Drawing from Part/Assembly**.

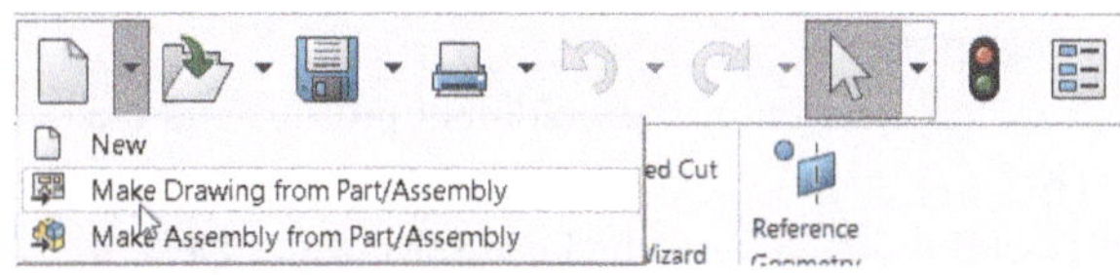

14. Insert the isometric view and cut list table into the drawing.

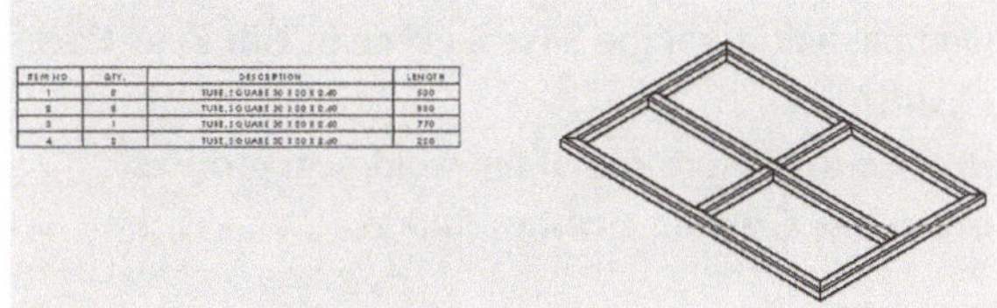

15. Save it as a separate part file.

TUTORIAL 5 (Creating Custom Profiles for structural members)

If you want to create a structural member using a profile not available in SOLIDWORKS, you can create a custom profile.

1. Close the SOLIDWORKS application if opened.
2. Run SOLIDWORKS as administrator.
3. Open a new Part document.
4. Create a sketch on any one of the planes, as shown in the figure.

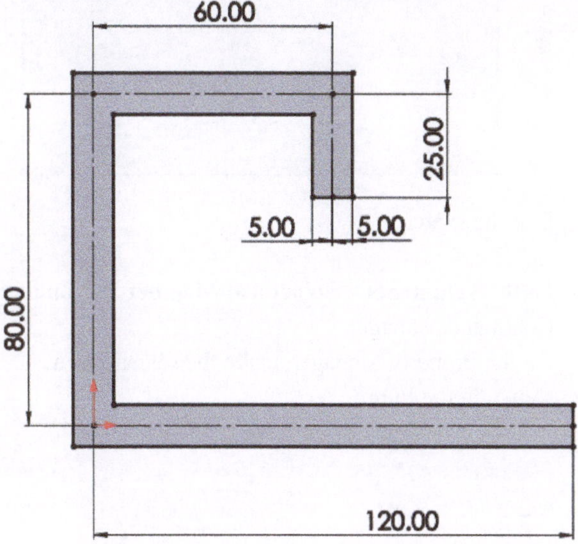

5. Exit the sketch.
6. On the Quick Access Toolbar, click the **Options** icon.
7. On the **System Options** dialog, click **File Locations** in the tree.
8. Select **Weldment Profiles** from the **Show folders**

for drop-down.

9. View the location of the weldment profiles and click **OK**.
10. Select the sketch from the FeatureManager Design Tree.
11. Click **File > Save As** on the Menu bar; the **Save As** dialog appears.
12. On this dialog, set the **Save as type** to **Lib Feat Part (*.sldlfp)**.
13. Browse to the location of the weldment profiles.
14. Create the **Custom Profiles** folder.

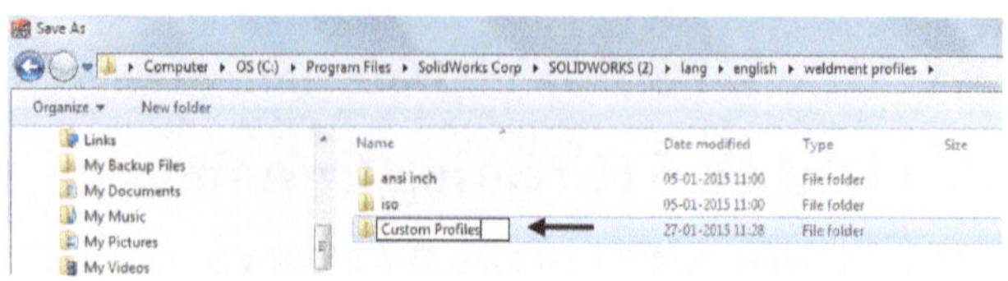

15. Create a subfolder with the name **C-Shape** in the **Custom Profiles** folder.
16. Save the file in the **C-Shape** folder as **C120**.
17. Start a new Part document.
18. Create a sketch on the Top plane, as shown in the figure.

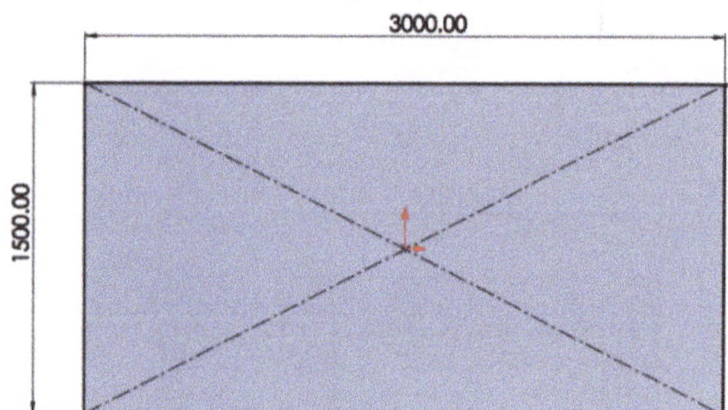

19. Exit the sketch.
20. Click **Weldments > Structural Member** on the Command Manager.
21. On the Property Manager, make the selections, as shown in the figure.

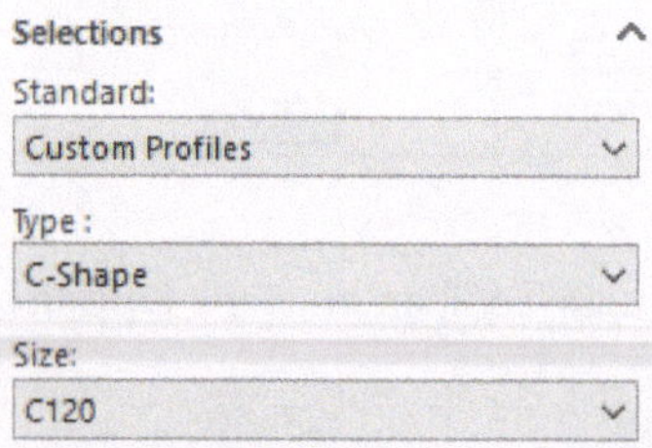

22. Select the line segments from the sketch. The structural members are created.

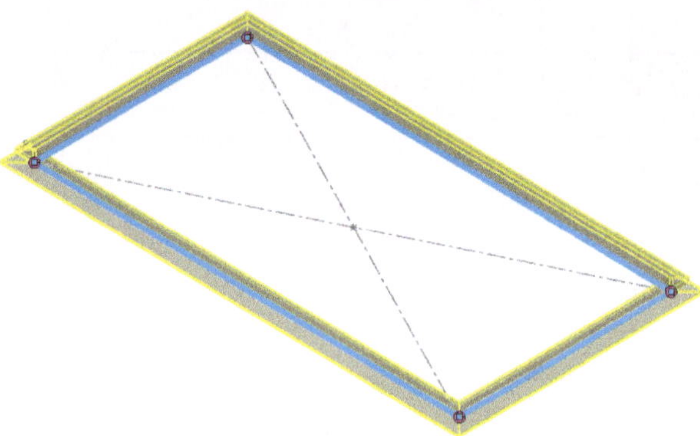

You can also click the **Locate Profile** button and change the position of the profile.

23. Click **OK**.

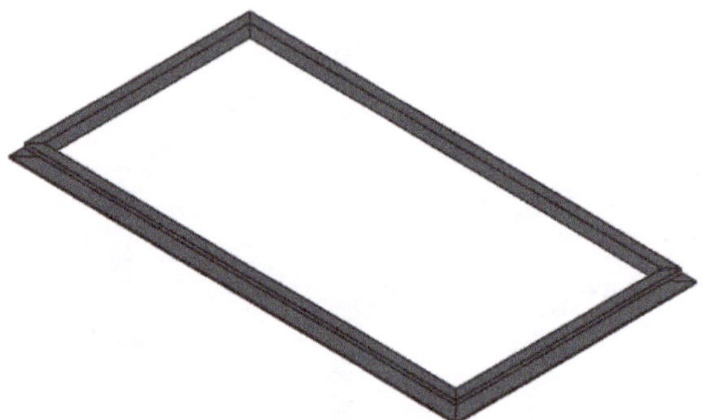

24. Save the file.

Chapter 13: MBD Dimensions

Geometric Dimensioning and Tolerancing

During the manufacturing process, the accuracy of a part is an important factor. However, it is impossible to manufacture a part with the exact dimensions. Therefore, while applying dimensions to a drawing, you need to provide some dimensional tolerances within acceptable limits. The following figure shows an example of dimensional tolerances applied to the drawing.

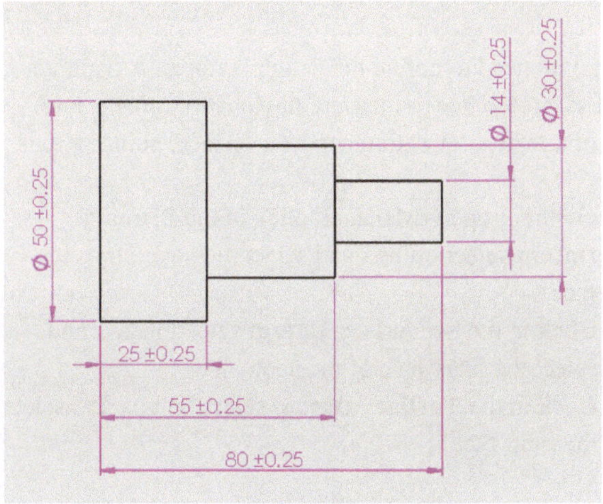

The dimensional tolerances help you to manufacture the component within a specific size range. However, the dimensional tolerances are not sufficient for manufacturing a component. You must give tolerance values to its shape, orientation, and position as well. The following figure shows a note, which is used to explain the tolerance value given to the object's shape.

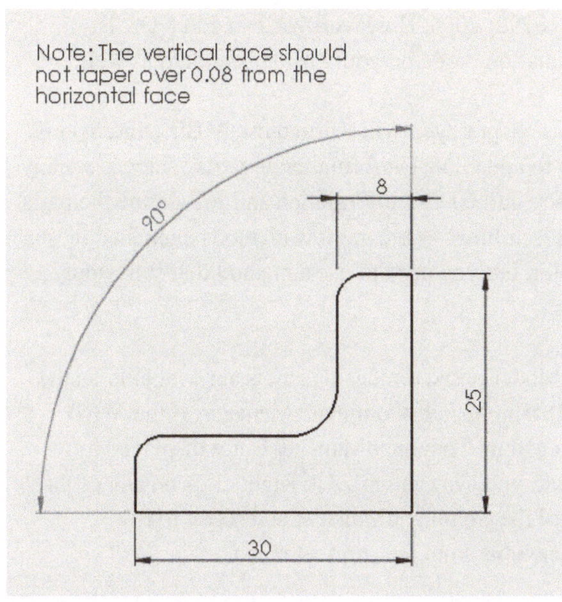

Providing a note in a drawing may be confusing. To avoid this, we use Geometric Dimensioning and Tolerancing (GD&T) symbols to specify the tolerance values to the shape, orientation, and position of a component. The following figure shows the same example represented by using the GD&T symbols. In this figure, the vertical face to which the tolerance frame is connected must be within two parallel planes 0.08 apart and perpendicular to the datum reference (horizontal plane).

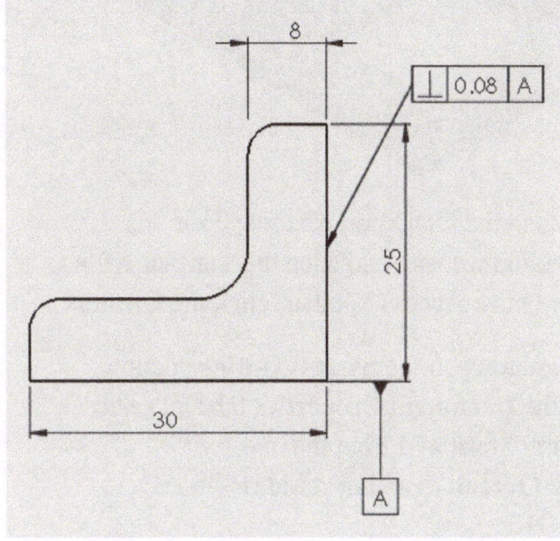

Providing GD&T in 2D drawings is a common and well-known method. However, you can provide GD&T information to 3D models as well. The DimXpert tools help you add GD&T information to the 3D models based on universal standards such as ASME Y14.41 – 2003 and

ISO 16792: 2006. However, you can add GD&T information based on your custom standard as well.

In this chapter, you will learn to use **MBD Dimensions** tools to add GD&T information to parts. There are many ways to add GD&T information and full-define the parts and assemblies. There are few methods explained in this chapter, but you need to use a method that suits your design.

The Model-based dimensions tools are available on the **MBD Dimensions** Command Manager. If the **MBD Dimensions** CommandManager is not displayed by default, you can customize it. Right click on any of the tabs of the CommandManager and select **MBD Dimensions** from the shortcut menu.

TUTORIAL 1 (Auto Dimension Scheme)

This tutorial teaches you to apply tolerances using the **Auto Dimension Scheme** tool. This tool automates the process of adding dimensions and tolerances to the 3D model.

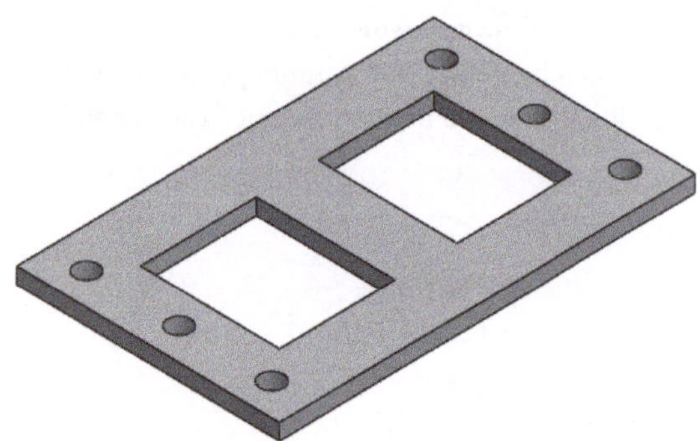

1. Download the DimXpert part files from the Companion website and open the Tutorial 1 file.
2. On the Quick Access Toolbar, click the **Options** icon to open the **System Options** dialog.
3. Click the **Document Properties** tab and select **Drafting Standard** from the tree.
4. Set the **Overall drafting standard** to ISO.
5. Click **OK**.
6. On the CommandManager, click **MBD Dimensions > Auto Dimension Scheme**.

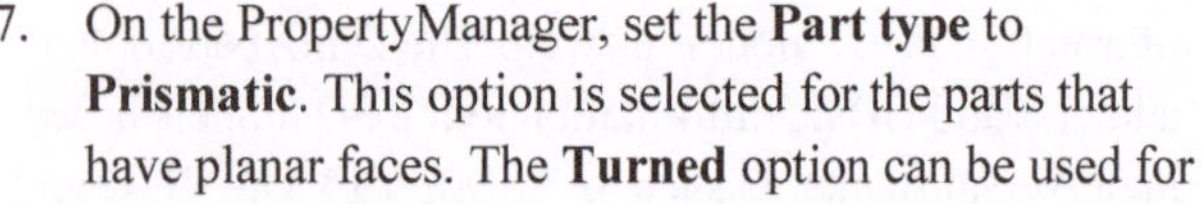

7. On the PropertyManager, set the **Part type** to **Prismatic**. This option is selected for the parts that have planar faces. The **Turned** option can be used for cylindrically shaped parts.
8. Set the **Tolerance type** to **Plus and Minus**.

The **Tolerance type** defines how the features such as holes and cuts are located with reference to the datum feature.

The **Plus and Minus** option adds location dimensions with + and – tolerances.

The **Geometric** option uses Geometric Tolerance symbols to represent the positions of features such as holes and cuts. The type of GD&T symbols used will be based on the **Part type**. For example, if you set the **Part type** to **Prismatic**, the Position symbol will locate a hole. However, if the **Part type** is set to **Turned**, the Circular Runout symbol will position a hole.

Next, you need to define the datum features. A datum is used as a reference to measure the location, shape, and size of a feature. A datum can be a surface, point, or axis.

9. On the PropertyManager, click in the **Primary Datum** selection box and select the geometry's top face.
10. Click in the **Secondary Datum** selection box and select the front face of the geometry.
11. Click in the **Tertiary Datum** selection box and select the right face.

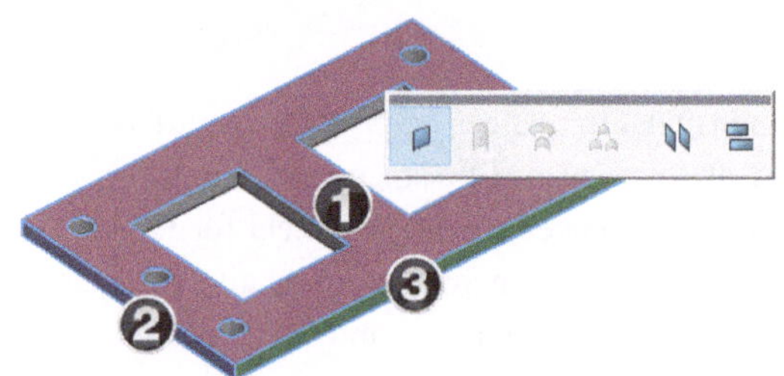

12. Under the **Scope** section, select **All features**.
13. Check all the options in the **Feature Filters** section and click **OK**.

Notice the dimensions added to the 3D geometry. They all have + and – tolerances.

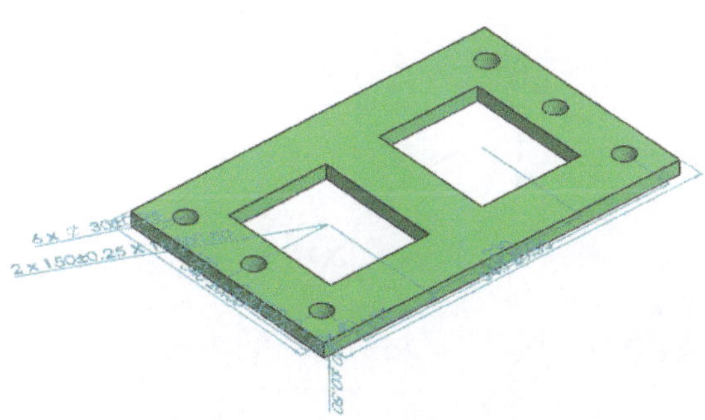

14. Click the **DimXpertManager** tab on the left pane and notice the features listed in it. The **Auto Dimension Scheme** tool recognizes and lists the features to be manufactured automatically.

Notice that the Extruded Cut feature is recognized as a Slot feature. The MBD Dimensions recognizes the features based on the manufacturing language.

15. Right click on the part in the DimXpertManager tree and select **Delete**.

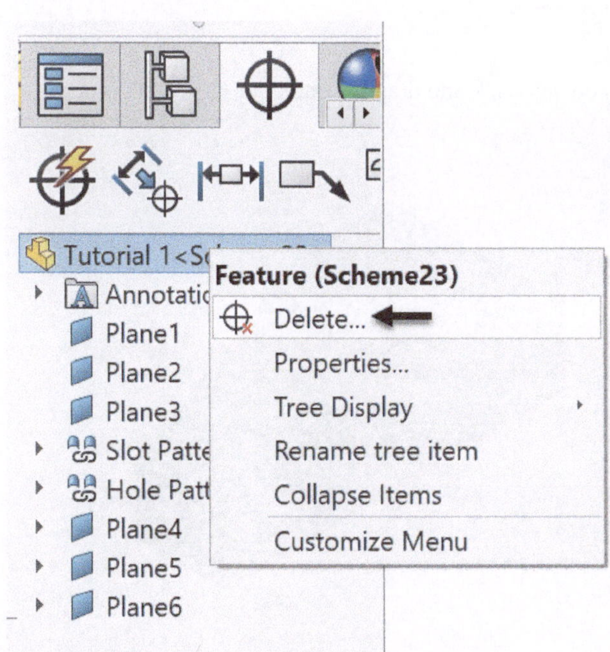

16. Click **Yes** on the **SOLIDWORKS** message to delete all the dimensions and tolerances.
17. On the DimXpertManager tree, click the **Auto Dimension Scheme** icon.
18. Set the **Tolerance type** to **Geometric**.
19. Select the primary, secondary, and tertiary datums. They are the same, as previously selected.
20. Leave the default settings and click **OK**. Notice the dimensions and geometric tolerances added with reference to the datums.

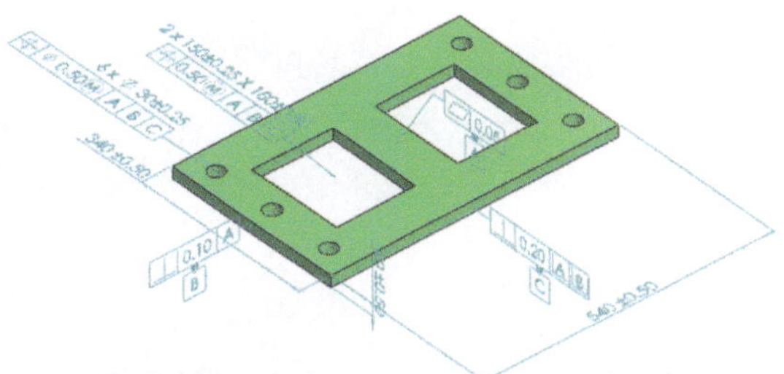

21. Right click on the part in the DimXpertManager tree and select **Delete**.
22. Click **Yes** on the **SOLIDWORKS** message to delete all the dimensions and tolerances.
23. Activate the **Auto Dimension Scheme** tool.
24. Select the primary, secondary, and tertiary datums. They are the same, as previously selected.
25. On the PropertyManager, set the **Scope** to **Selected features**.
26. Click in the selection box in the **Scope** section and select any one of the holes.
27. Select the **Pattern** icon from the Selection toolbar. The entire pattern is selected.
28. Likewise, select any one of the faces of the extruded feature. The extrude features are selected as a pattern.
29. Rotate the model and select the bottom face.

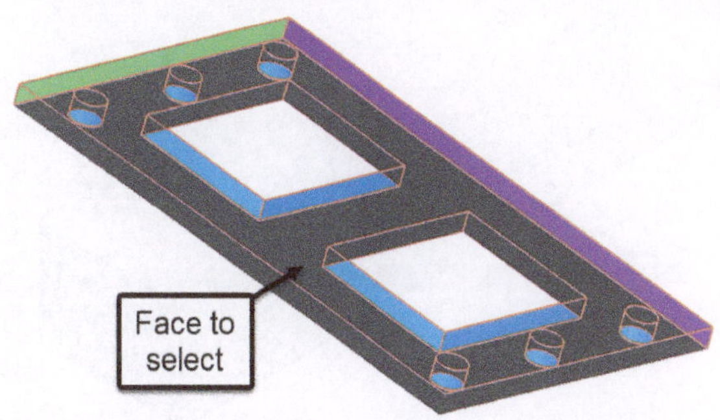

30. Select the **Plane** icon from the Selection toolbar.
31. Click **OK** to add dimensions and tolerance to the selected features only.

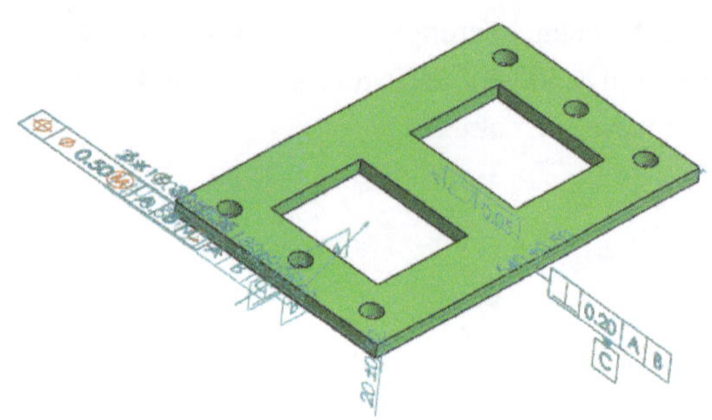

32. Save and close the file.

TUTORIAL 2 (Adding the GD&T Information Manually)

In this tutorial, you will add dimensions and tolerances manually.

1. Open the Tutorial 2 part file.
2. On the CommandManager, click **MBD Dimensions > Datum** .
3. On the PropertyManager, type **A** in the **Label** box under the **Label Settings** section.
4. Select the front face of the geometry.
5. Move the pointer and click to position the datum.

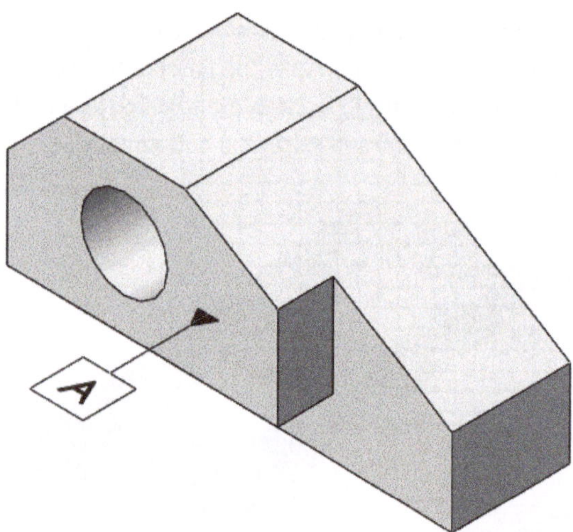

6. Likewise, define the datum B and C, and click **OK**.

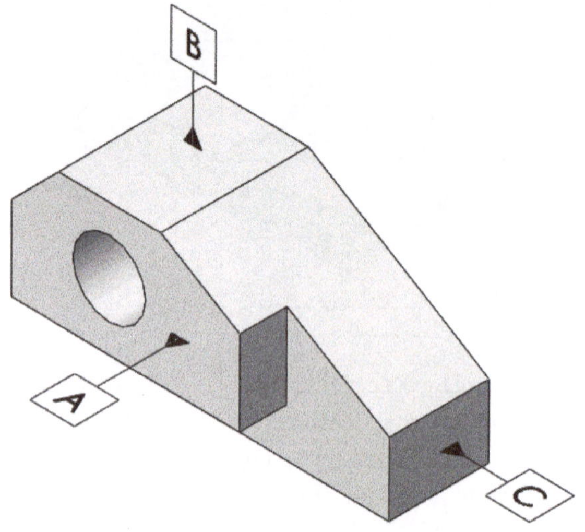

Notice the three plane features in the DimXpertManager tree.

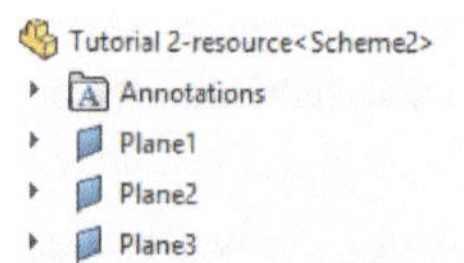

You can click and drag the datum or its origin point.

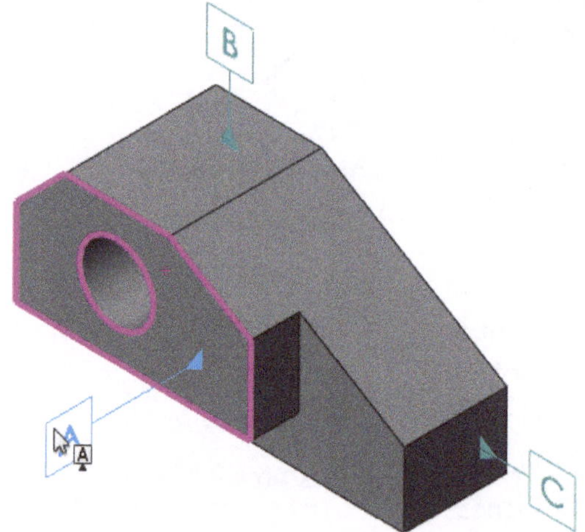

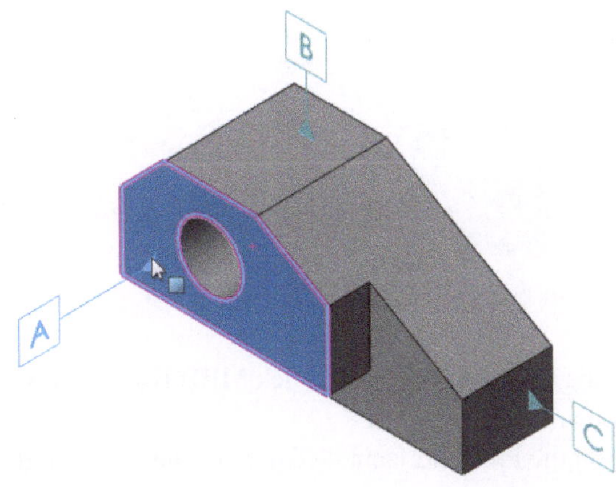

7. On the CommandManager, click the **Show Tolerance Status** icon. Notice that the datum faces are highlighted in green, which means that they are fully defined.

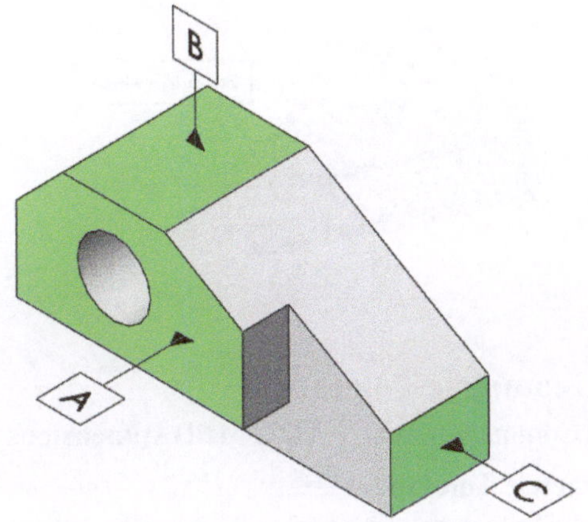

Now, you need to fully-define all other faces by adding dimensions and tolerances.

Adding Size Dimensions

You add size dimensions to the geometry to provide the manufacturing information. These dimensions do not control geometry. Instead, they are controlled by the size of the geometry.

1. On the CommandManager, click **MBD Dimensions > Size Dimension** .
2. Select the hole and place the dimension.

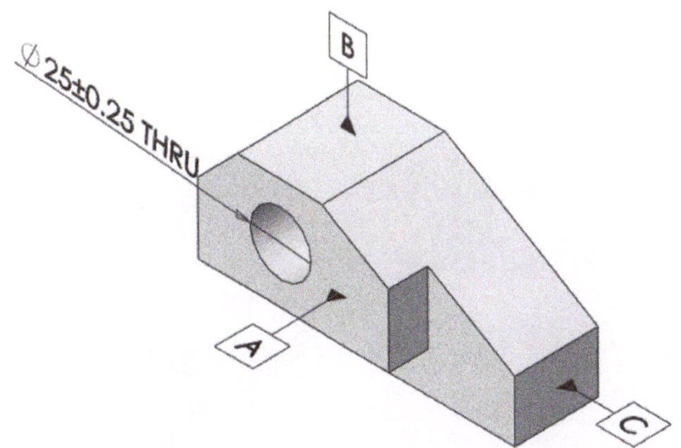

Notice the tolerance values added to the dimension. These are the default tolerance values set on the **System Options** dialog. You can change the tolerance value on the **System Options** dialog. You can also change the tolerance on the **Tolerance/Precision** section of the **DimXpert** PropertyManager.

If you select a single hole from the geometry, all the holes of the same size will be selected, automatically and the hole count will be added to the dimension, as shown.

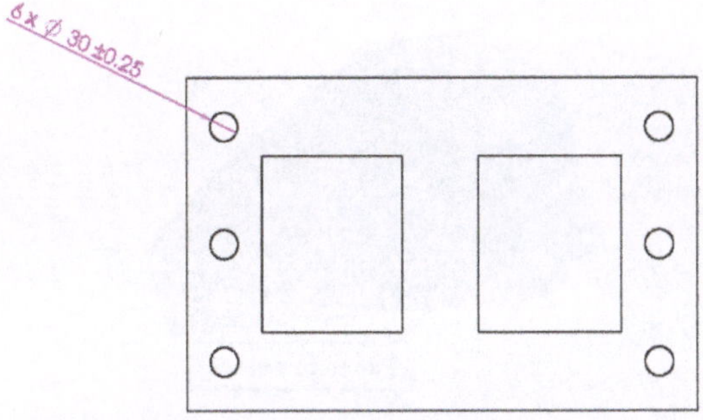

3. Click **OK** on the **DimXpert** PropertyManager.
4. Click the **Show Tolerance Status** icon on the DimXpertManager. Notice that the hole is highlighted in yellow, which means that it is under constrained.

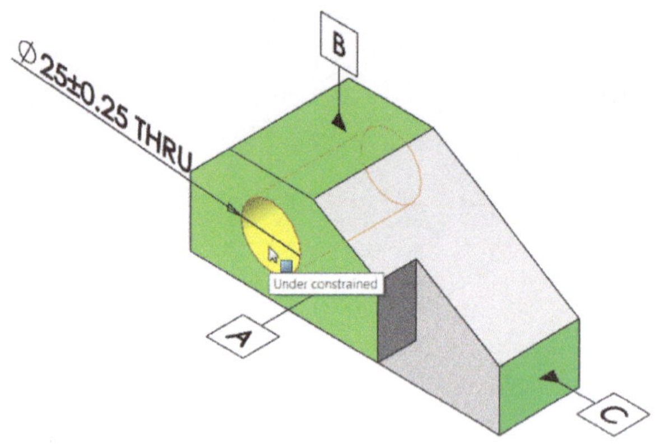

Adding Location Dimensions

You add location dimensions to a feature with reference to a datum.

1. On the CommandManager, click **MBD Dimensions > Location Dimension** .
2. Rotate the model and select its left vertical face.
3. Select the hole and position the dimension, as shown.

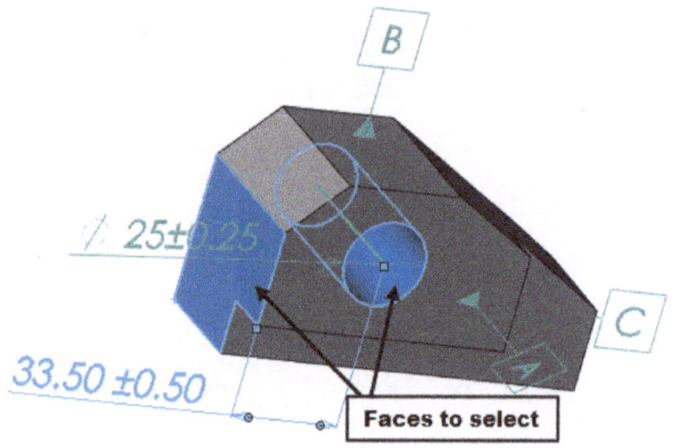

On the **DimXpert** PropertyManager, the **Tolerance Feature** and **Origin Feature** are displayed in the **Reference Features** section. You can swap these features by clicking the **Swap Features** icon.

You can also change the tolerance value in the **Tolerance/Precision** section.

4. Click in the graphics window.
5. Add a dimension between the bottom face and hole. Click **OK** on the PropertyManager.

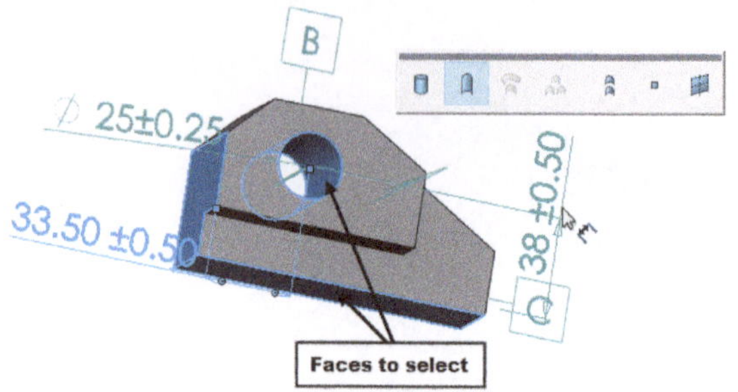

6. On the CommandManager, click **MBD Dimensions > Location Dimension**.
7. Select the lower horizontal edge of the geometry and notice the faces perpendicular to the edge are highlighted.
8. Position the dimension and click **OK** on the PropertyManager.

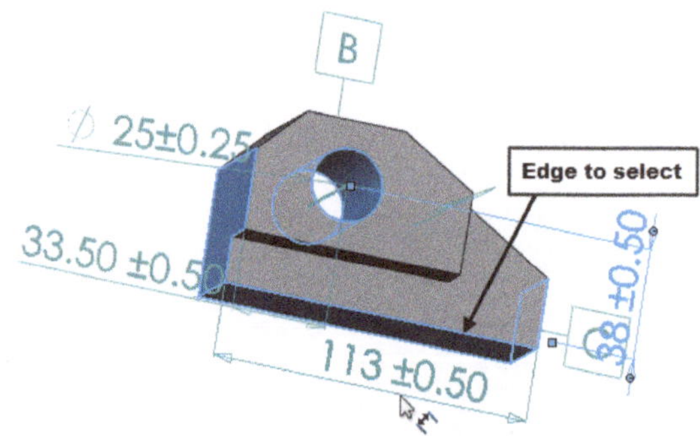

Adding Geometric Tolerances

1. On the CommandManager, click **MBD Dimensions > Geometric Tolerance** .
2. Select the hole and position the tolerance frame.

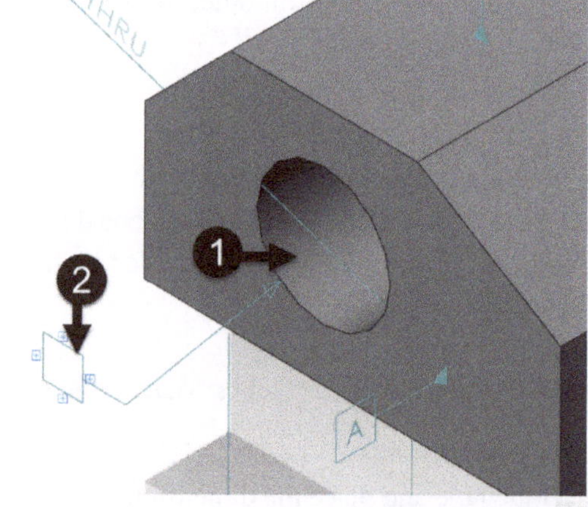

3. On the **Tolerance** dialog, click the **Position** ⌖ icon.

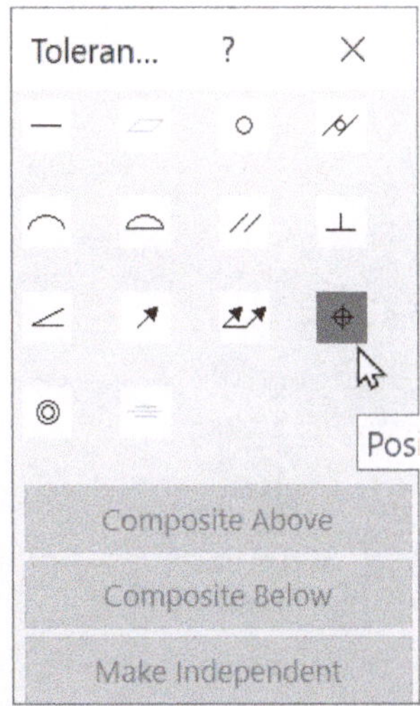

4. Type 0.02 in the **Tolerance** box.

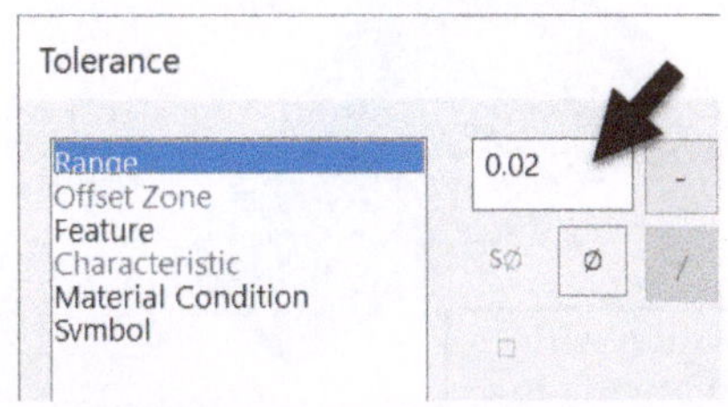

5. Select the **Material Condition** option from the list box and click the **Maximum Material Condition** Ⓜ icon.

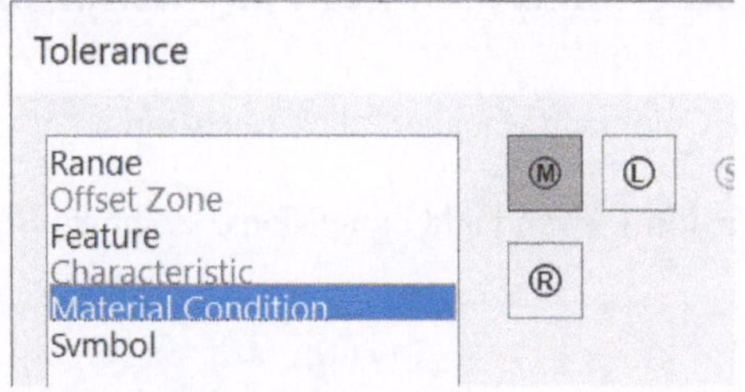

6. Click the **Add Datum** button.
7. Type **A** in the **Primary** box.

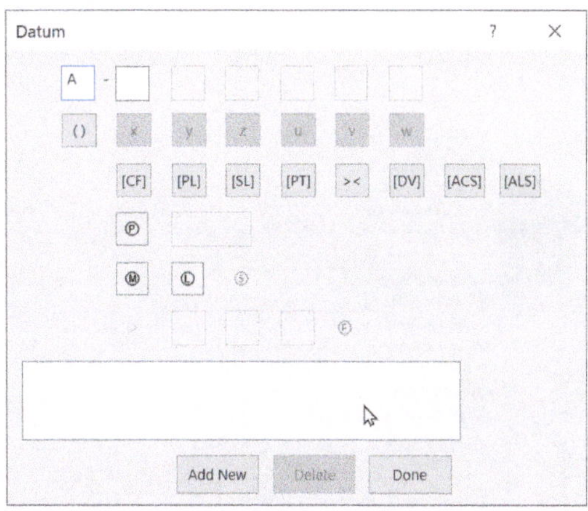

8. Click the **Add New** button and type **B** in the **Secondary** box.
9. Click the **Add New** button and type **C** in the **Tertiary** box.
10. Click **Done** to add the tolerance.
11. Delete the location dimensions, as shown.

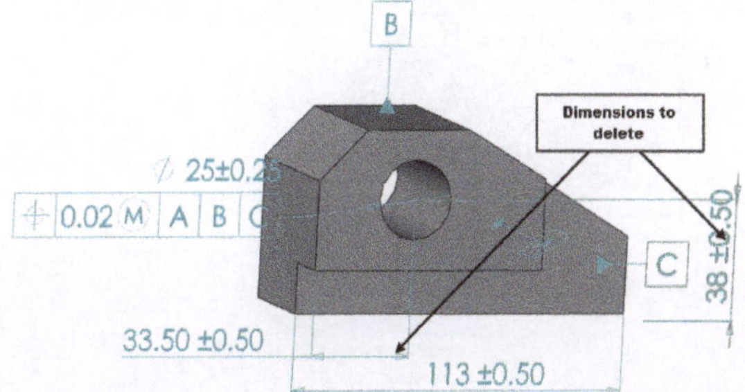

12. Add three tolerance frames to the faces, as shown.

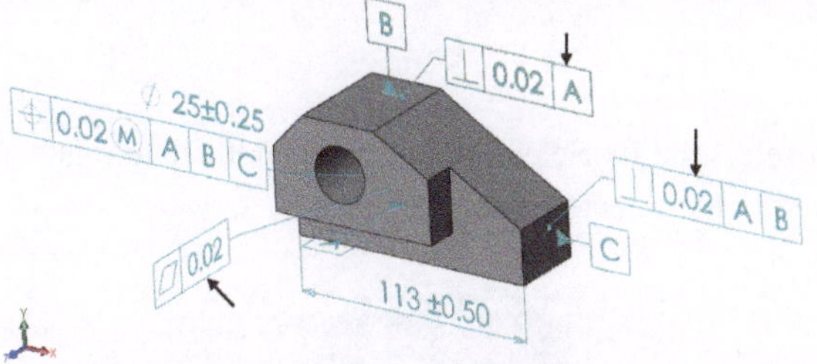

You can change the annotation orientation by clicking the right mouse button on it and selecting **Select Annotation View**. Select a new annotation view from the popup menu. If you select the Front annotation view, the datum's orientation will be changed to the Front plane.

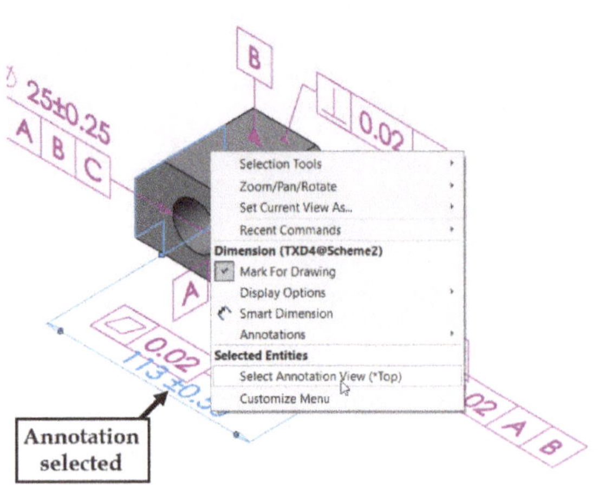

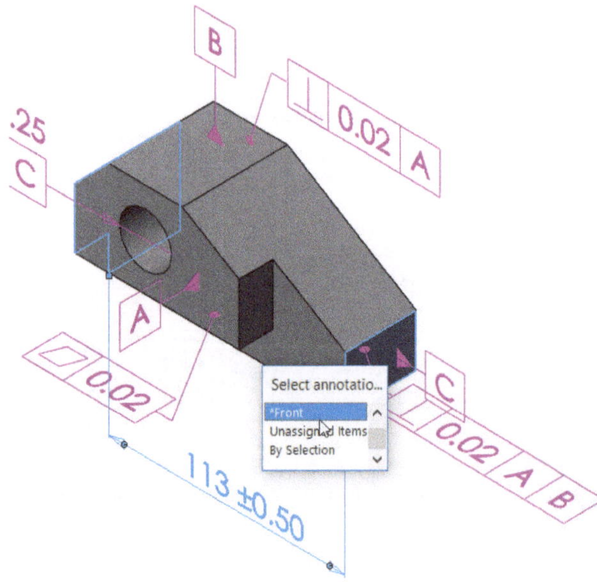

If you select the **By Selection** option, then the datum is oriented to the selected plane.

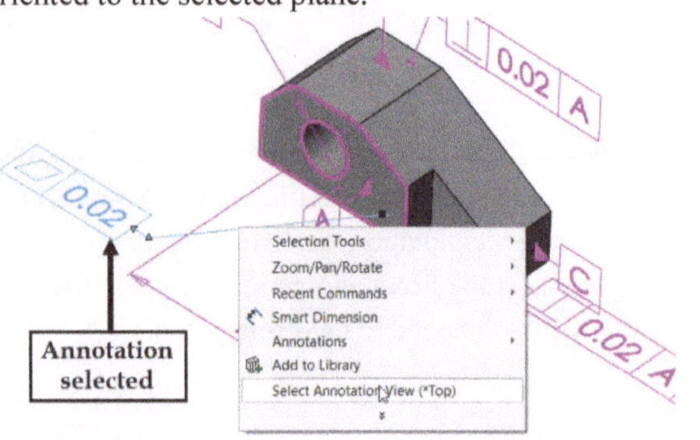

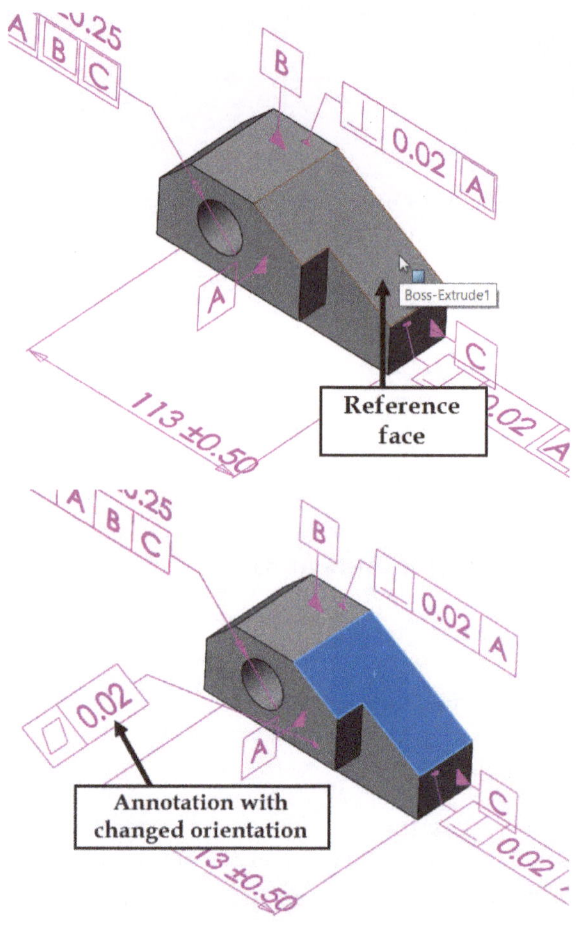

Adding other dimensions to Fully-define the part

1. On the CommandManager, click **Location Dimension** and add dimensions, as shown.

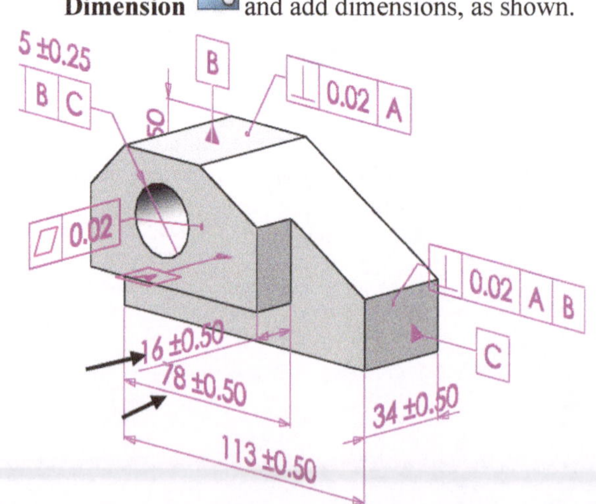

2. Activate the **Location Dimension** tool and click the left vertical face of the geometry.

3. Click the **Create Intersection Line** icon on the Selection toolbar.
4. Select the inclined face and click **OK** on the Selection toolbar.

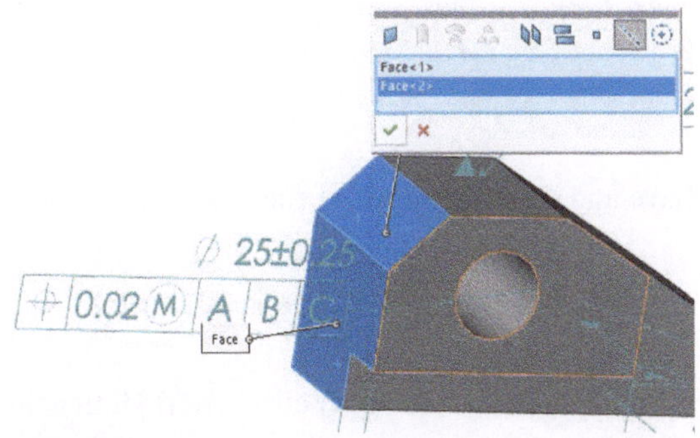

5. Select the top face of the geometry and position of the dimension.
6. On the PropertyManager, click the **Swap Features** icon to change the origin feature.
7. Click **Close Dialog**.
8. Click the **Show Tolerance Status** icon and notice that the inclined face is highlighted in yellow.

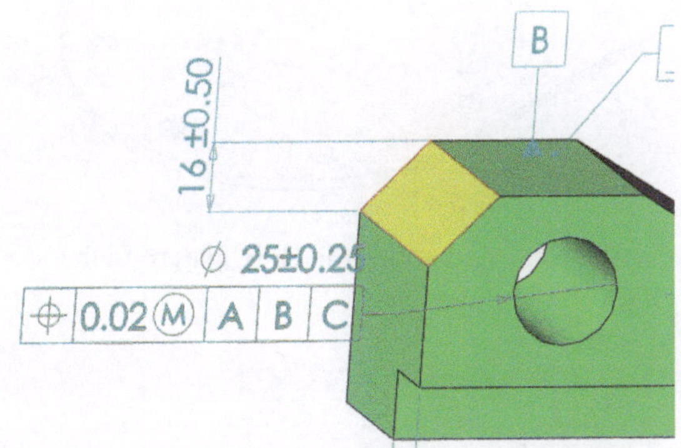

Also, notice that the other inclined face is not fully defined. You need to add dimensions to fully-define these two faces.

9. Activate the **Location Dimension** tool and click the top face of the geometry.
10. Click the **Create Intersection Line** icon on the Selection toolbar.
11. Select the left inclined face and click **OK** on the Selection toolbar.
12. Select the C datum face and position the dimension.
13. On the PropertyManager, click the **Swap Features** icon to change the origin feature.
14. Click **Close Dialog**.

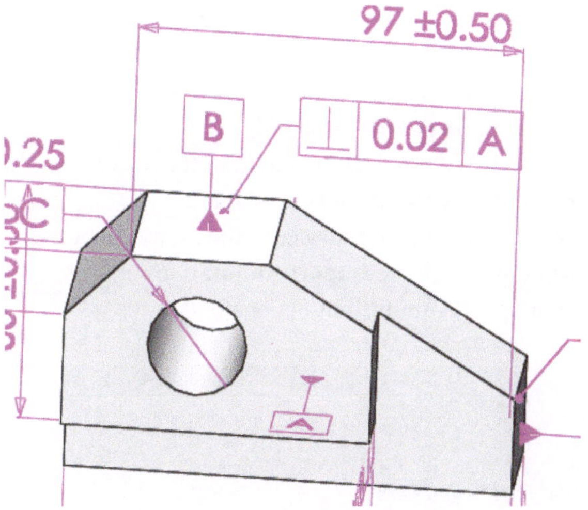

15. Likewise, add the angle and linear dimensions, as shown.

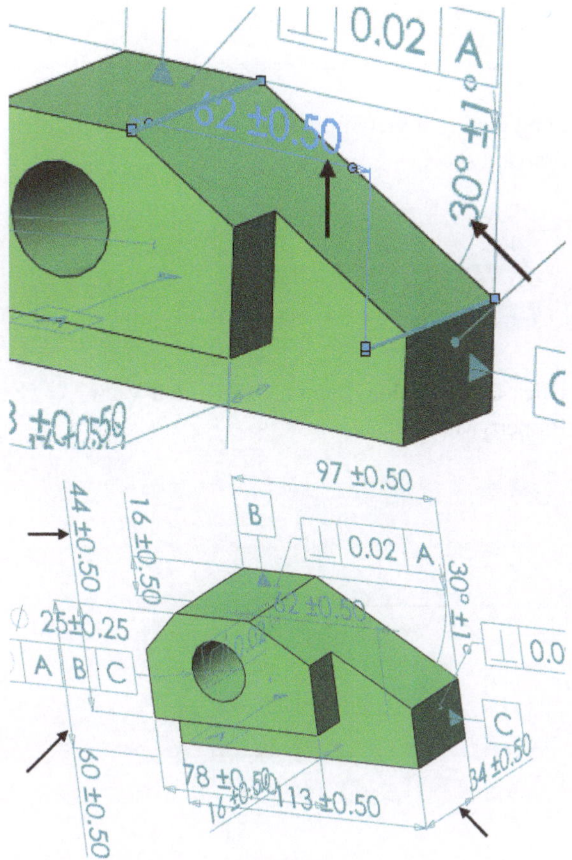

Notice that all the faces of the model turn green after applying dimensions and geometric tolerances.

TUTORIAL 3 (Using the MBD Dimensions Annotations in drawings)

1. Open the Tutorial 2 part file.
2. On the Quick Access Toolbar, click **New > Make Drawing from Part/Assembly**.
3. Select **A3(ANSI) Landscape** from the **Sheet Format/Size** dialog and click **OK**.
4. On the **View Palette** located at the right side of the window, check the **Import Annotations** and **DimXpert Annotations** options.

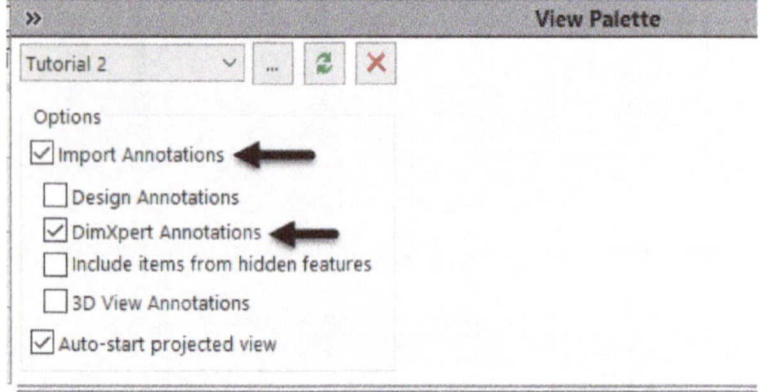

5. Drag the Front view from the **View Palette** onto the drawing sheet.

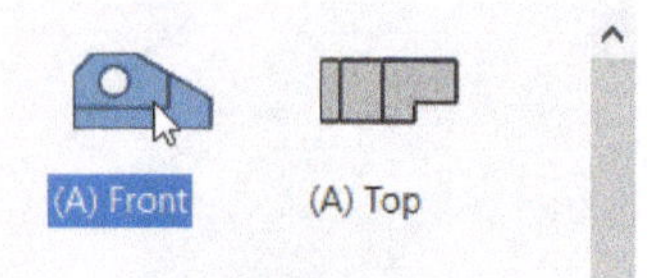

6. Click **Close Dialog** on the **Projected View** PropertyManager.

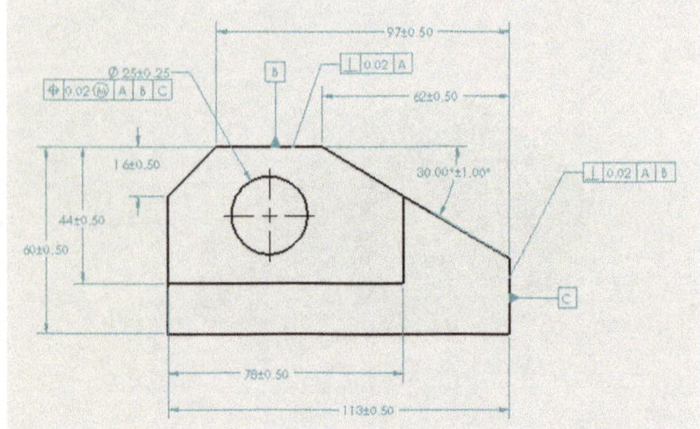

7. Likewise, drag the Right and Isometric views.
8. Adjust the dimensions by dragging them.

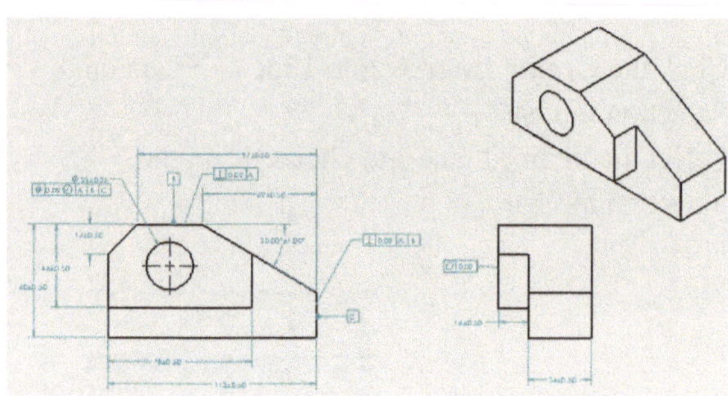

9. Save and close the drawing file.

TUTORIAL 4 (Pattern Feature)

1. Open the Tutorial 4 part file.
2. On the CommandManager, click **MBD Dimensions > Pattern Feature**.
3. On the PropertyManager, select **Linked Patterns**.
4. Select any one of the holes of the curve pattern.

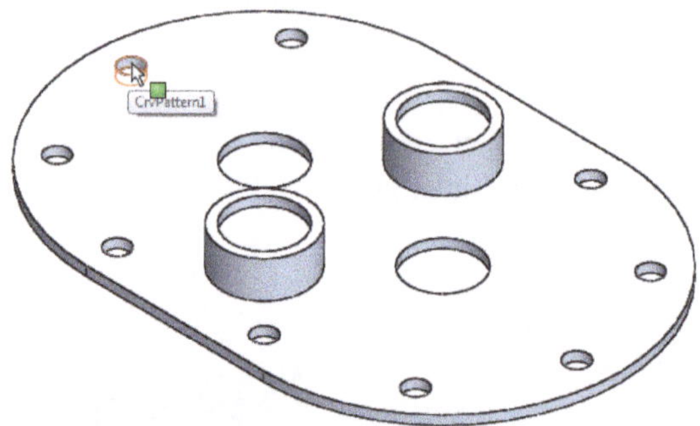

5. Click **OK** and notice the Hole Pattern in the DimXpertManager.

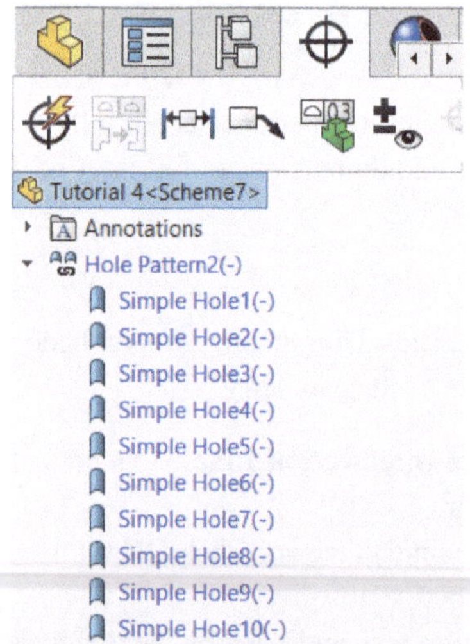

6. Change the instant count of the curve pattern to 10.

Notice that the Hole Pattern in the DimXpertManager is also updated.

7. Activate the **Pattern Feature** command and select any one of the large holes.

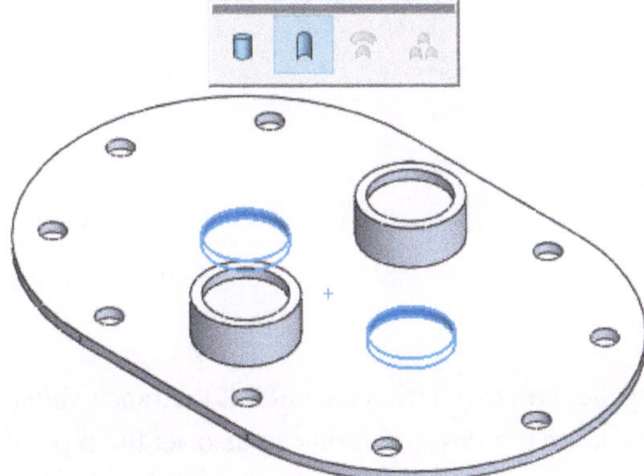

8. The other hole of the same size is selected automatically. Also, the **Manual Patterns** option is active as the holes are created as two separate instances. The **Find all on same face** option selects all the features of the same size.
9. Click **OK**. The Hole Pattern appears in the DimXpertManager Tree.
10. Activate the **Pattern Feature** command and select **Collection**.
11. Select the side faces of the geometry.

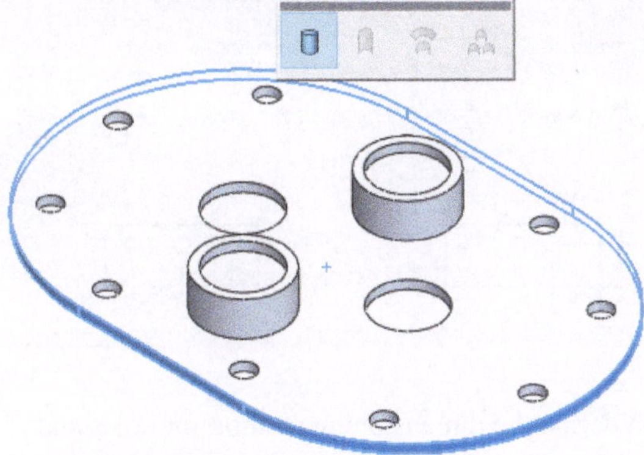

12. Click **OK** on the PropertyManager
13. The **Collection** feature appears in the DimXpertManager Tree. All the faces inside the **Collection** feature appear as a single DimXpert feature. You can add a single annotation to all the faces of the collection feature at a time.

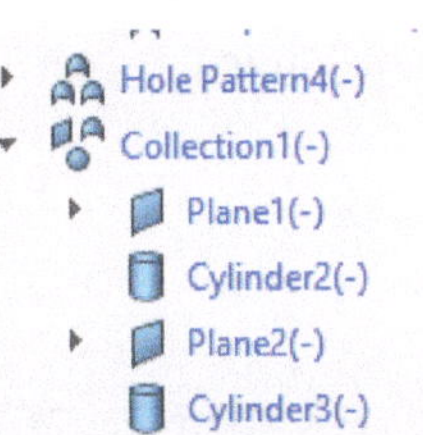

TUTORIAL 5 (DimXpert Options)

1. Start a new Part document.
2. On the Quick Access Toolbar, click **Options** to the **System Options** dialog.
3. Click the **Document Properties** tab and select **Drafting Standard** from the tree.
4. Set the **Overall drafting standard** to **ISO**.
5. Click **DimXpert** in the tree.

The **Methods** is set to **General Tolerance**. This type of tolerance is commonly used with ISO standards. You can define the **Tolerance class** as Fine, Medium, Coarse, or Very Coarse in the **General Tolerance** section at the bottom of the dialog.

The **Block Tolerance** method can be used if you are using the ANSI drafting standard. You can define the decimal values for the length and angle dimensions in the **Block tolerance** section.

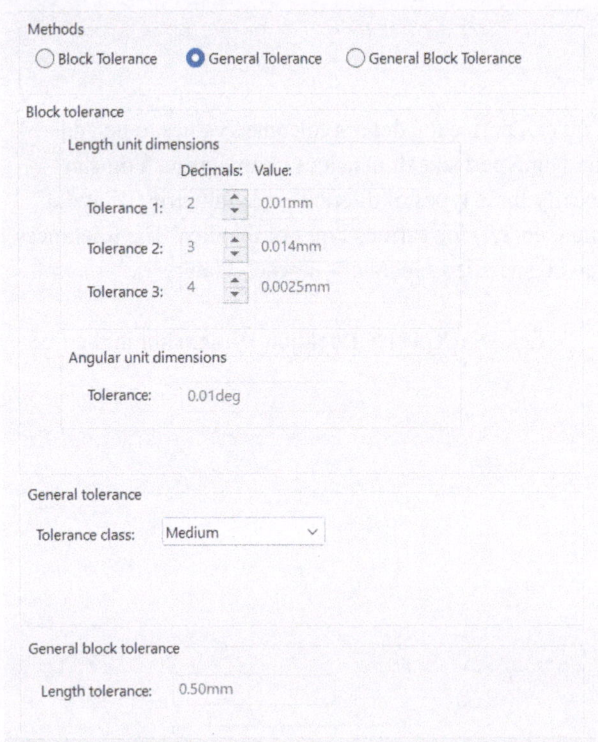

6. Click **DimXpert > Size Dimension** in the tree.

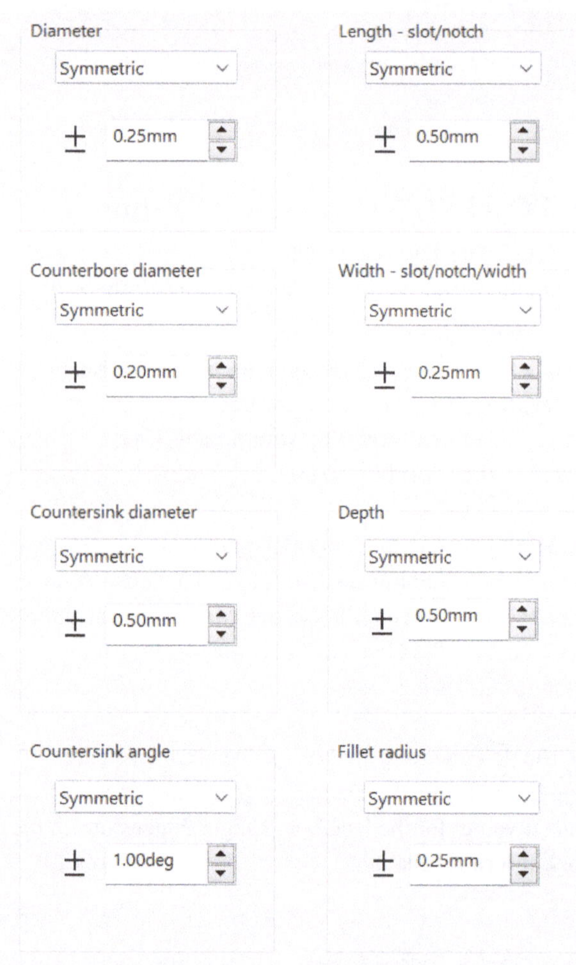

You can define the default tolerance values to be added to the DimXpert size dimensions on this page. You can specify three types of tolerances (Symmetric, Bilateral, and General) for various types of features. The tolerances can be specified separately for each feature.

7. Click **DimXpert > Location Dimension** in the tree.

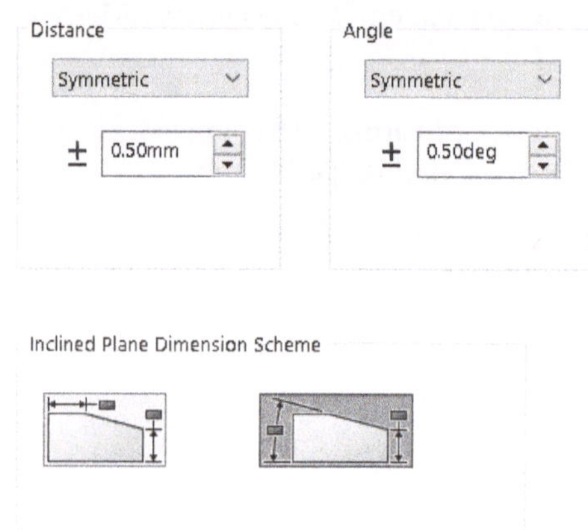

On this page, you can define the default tolerance values for the location dimensions. You can also set the type of dimensions to be added to inclined planes using the **Auto Dimension Scheme**.

8. Click **DimXpert > Chain Dimension** in the tree.

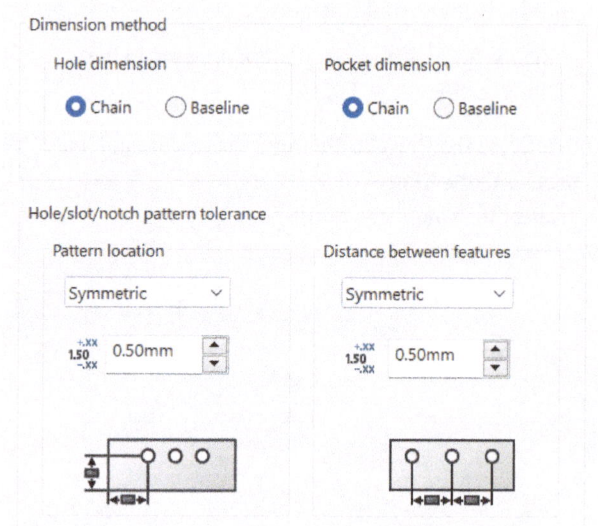

You can define the dimensioning method for holes and pockets using the **Auto Dimension Scheme** on this page. Also, you can define the tolerances for patterns.

9. Click **DimXpert > Geometric Tolerance** in the tree.

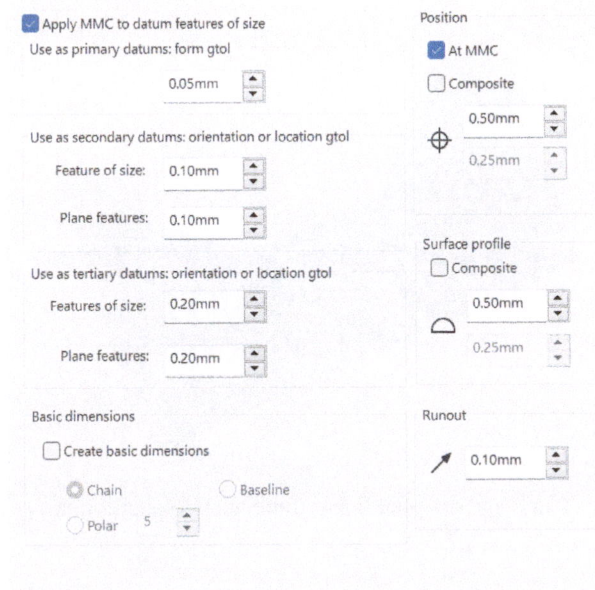

This page allows you to set the default options for geometric tolerances to be added using the **Auto Dimension Scheme**.

Likewise, you can set the default width and tolerance settings on the **Chamfer Control** page.

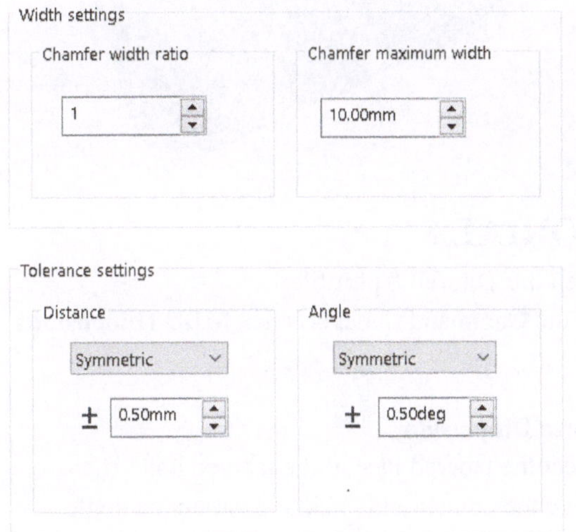

10. Click **Display Options** on the tree.

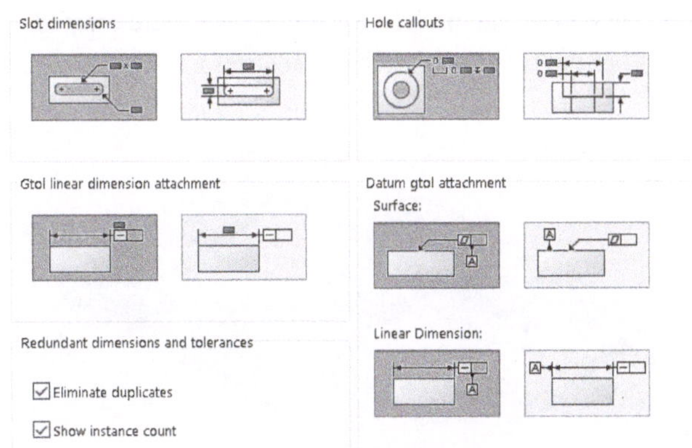

This page allows you to control how the dimensions and tolerances are displayed using the **Auto Dimension Scheme**. Also, you can control the redundant dimensions and tolerances using **Eliminate duplicates** and **Show instance count** options.

11. Click **OK** to close the dialog.

TUTORIAL 6 (Insert Dimensions)

The **Insert Dimensions** tool is used to transform design-oriented sketch dimensions into manufacturable DimXpert dimensions for Model-Based Definition (MBD) workflows.

1. Open the Tutorial 6 part file.
2. On the CommandManager, click **MBD Dimensions > Insert Dimensions** .
3. In the PropertyManager, click in the Features selection box and select the **Boss-Extrude1** feature from the FeatureManager Design Tree or graphics window; the length and width dimensions of the **Boss-Extrude1** feature are displayed.
4. Select the two displayed dimension from the graphics window.

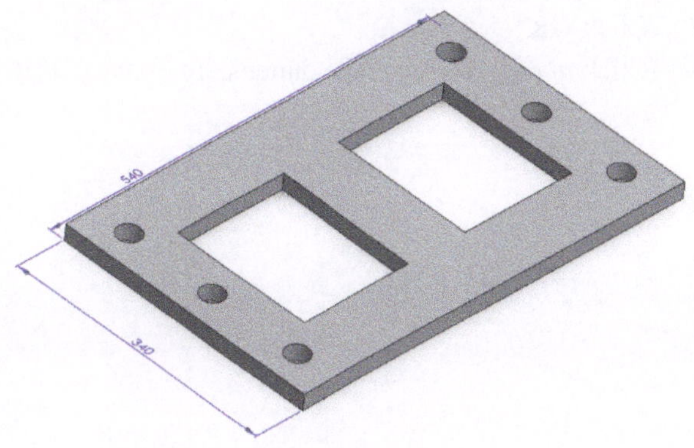

5. Click **OK**; the model-based dimensions are created from the selected sketch dimensions.

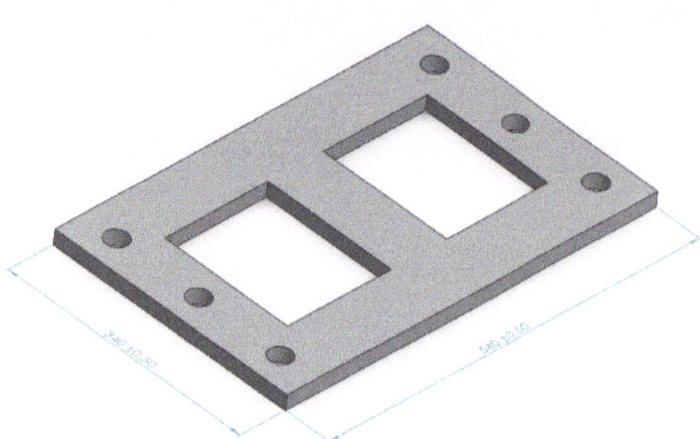

TUTORIAL 7

1. Open the Tutorial 7 part file.
2. On the CommandManager, click **MBD Dimensions** **> Size Dimension**  .
3. Select anyone of the draft faces of the wedge feature.
4. Click the **Create Width/Wedge Feature** icon on the **Selection** toolbar.
5. Select another draft face.
6. Select the end face of the wedge feature.

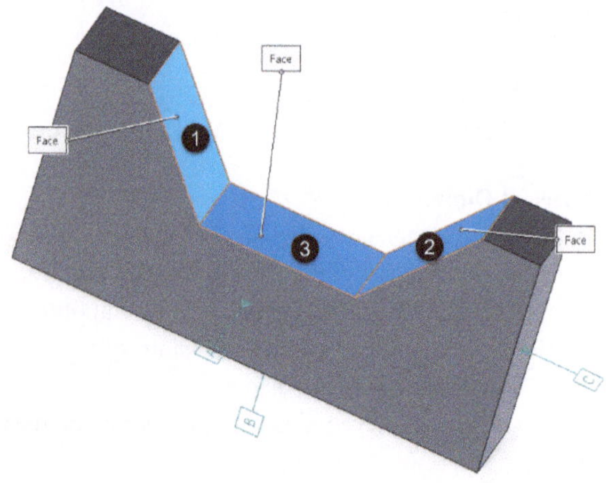

7. Click **OK**.
8. Click to position the angle dimension.

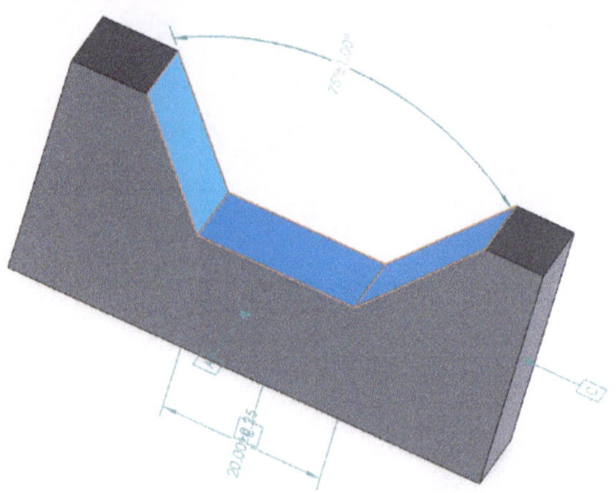

9. Click and drag the linear dimension to position it.

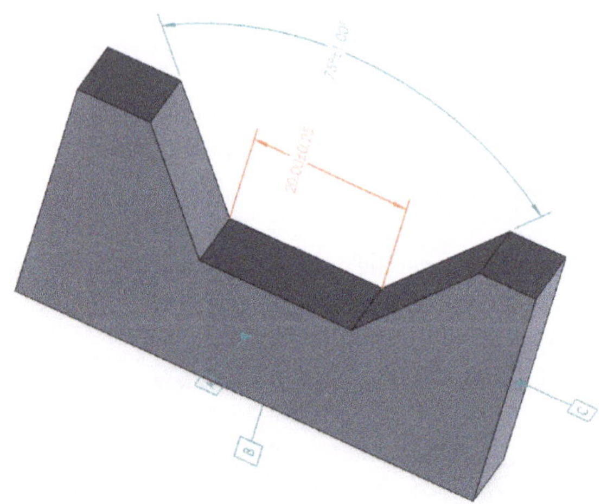

TUTORIAL 8

1. Open the Tutorial 8 part file.
2. On the CommandManager, click **MBD Dimensions** **> Size Dimension** 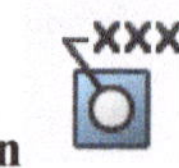 .
3. Select the tapered face of the tapered hole.
4. Move the pointer and click to position the angle dimension.

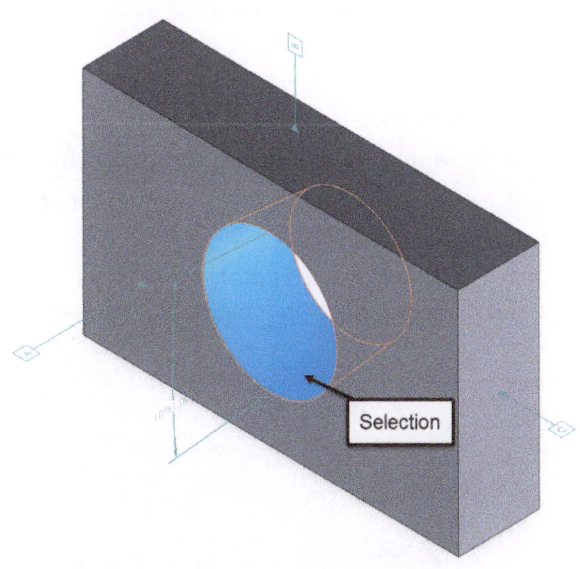

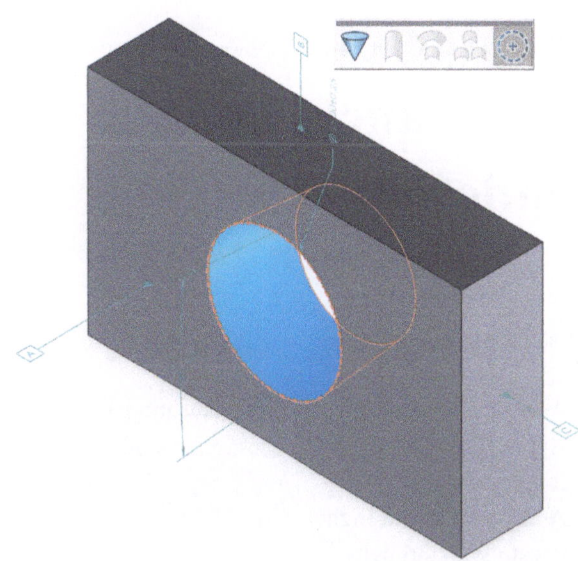

5. Select the top edge of the tapered hole.
6. Click the **Intersect Circle** icon on the Selection toolbar.
7. Select the top face of the tapered hole.

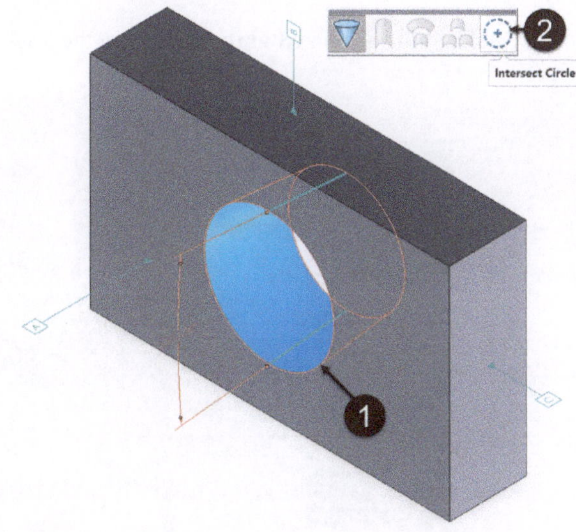

8. Click **OK**.
9. Move the pointer and position the diameter dimension of the hole.

Chapter 14: Appearances and Rendering

In this chapter, you will:

- Add Appearances and Textures to the model
- Apply Backgrounds and Scenes to the model
- Render Images
- Add Cameras and Lights
- Create Walkthroughs
- Add Decals

TUTORIAL 1 (Adding Appearances to the Complete Part)

1. Download the Appearances and Rendering part files from the Companion website and open the Tutorial 1 file.
2. On the View Heads Up Toolbar, click the **Edit Appearance** icon.

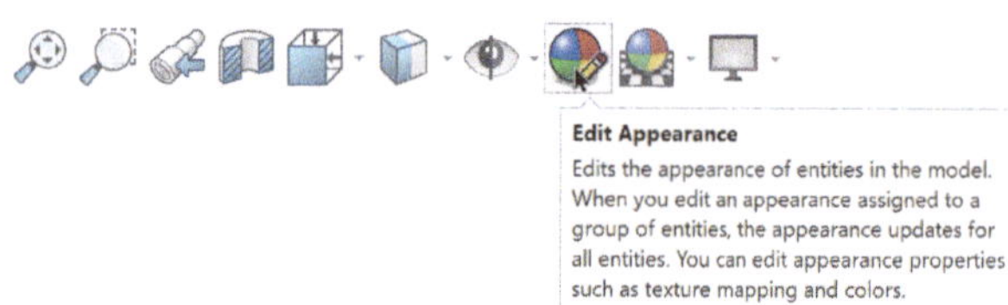

You can also right click on the part in the FeatureManager Design Tree and select **Appearances > Tutorial 1**.

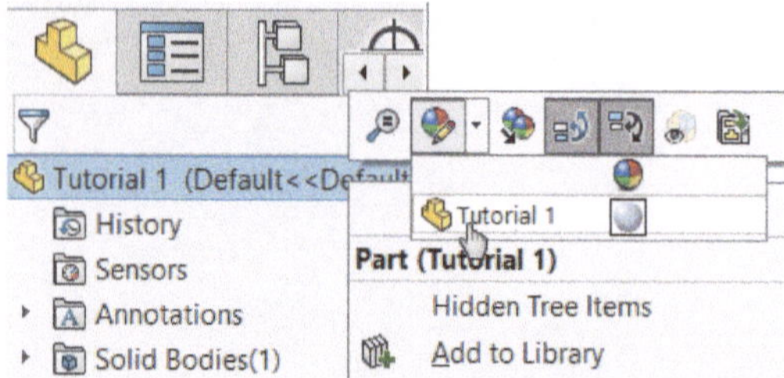

3. Click the **Basic** tab on the PropertyManager. Notice that Tutorial 1.SLDPRT is listed in the **Selected Geometry** section. You can use the **Select Part**, **Select Faces**, **Select Surfaces**, **Select Bodies**, and **Select Features** icons to select different geometry types.
4. Leave the entire part as **Selected Geometry** in the PropertyManager.
5. Click the **Appearances, Scenes, and Decals** tab on the Task pane located on the graphics window's right side.
6. On the Task pane, click **Appearances (color) > Metal > Aluminum**. Notice the various types of Aluminum listed on the lower portion of the Task pane.

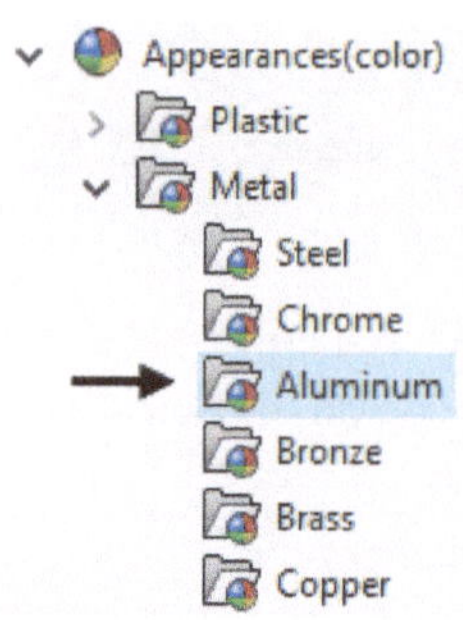

7. Select **blue anodized aluminum** from the Task pane.

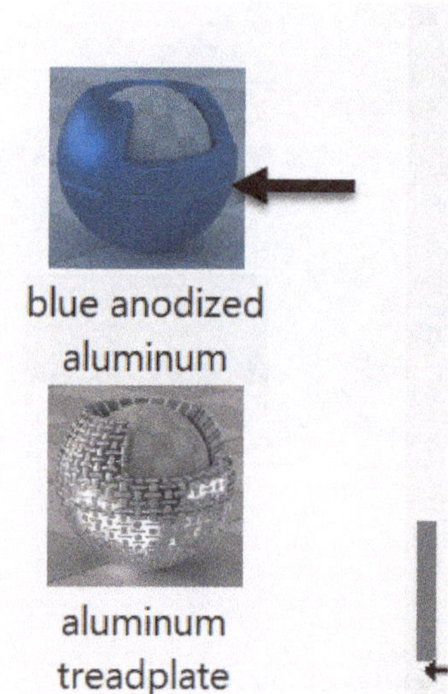

8. Click **OK** on the PropertyManager to apply the selected material to the whole part.

9. Click the **DisplayManager** tab and notice that the material is added to the **Appearances** tree.
10. Expand **blue anodized aluminum** and notice that the material is attached to the entire part geometry.

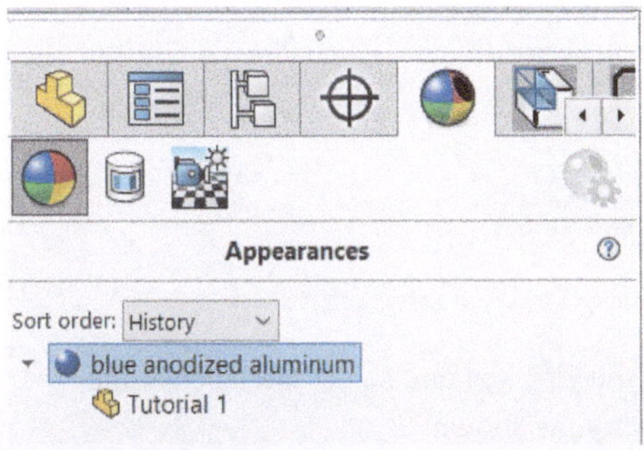

11. Right click on the appearance and select **Edit Appearance**.
12. On the Task pane, click **Appearances (color) > Metal > Copper**. Notice the various types of Copper listed on the lower portion of the Task pane.
13. Select **brushed copper** from the Task pane and click **OK** ✓.

Also, notice the brushed copper on the **DisplayManager**.

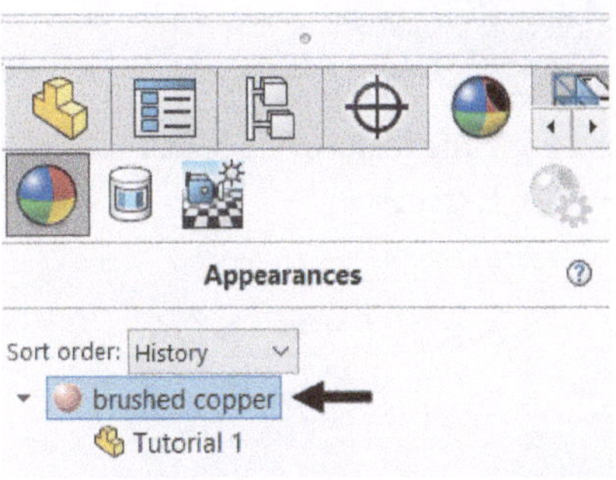

14. Right click on **brushed copper** and select **Remove Appearance** (or) select the appearance and press Delete (or) click on the appearance and select **Edit Appearance**, and then click **Remove Appearance** on the **Selected Geometry** section.
15. Click **OK**.

The appearance is removed from the geometry.

TUTORIAL 2 (Adding Appearances to Faces, Surfaces, and Features)

SOLIDWORKS allows you to apply different appearances to a single part. For example, you can display some faces of the geometry differently from others. To add different appearances to the part geometry, you need to understand the hierarchy in which the appearances are added. For example, if you add an appearance to the entire part and then add a different appearance to a part feature, the feature appearance will be added on top of the part appearance. If you add a new appearance to the feature's face, the face appearance will be added on top of the feature appearance.

1. Open the Tutorial 2 part file.

Now, you need to add appearance to the Boss-Extrude feature, as shown.

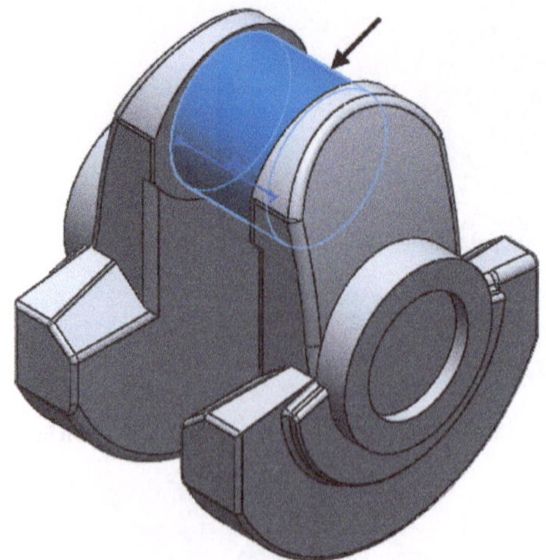

2. Click on the **Boss-Extrude** feature and select **Appearances > Boss-Extrude**.

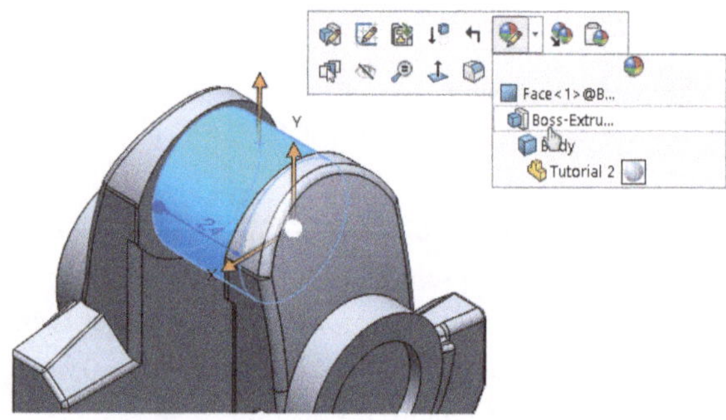

Notice the Boss-Extrude feature in the **Selected Geometry** section.

16. On the Task pane, click **Appearances (color) > Metal > Bronze**. Notice the various types of Bronze listed on the lower portion of the Task pane.
17. Select **cast bronze** from the Task pane and click **OK** ✓.

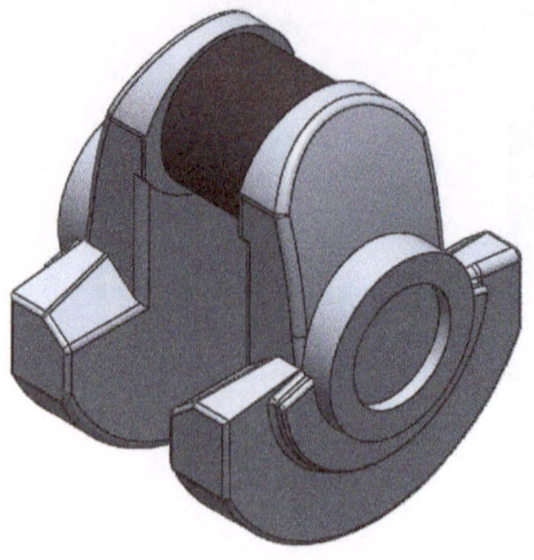

Notice the **cast bronze** on the **DisplayManager**. It is attached to the Boss-Extrude feature

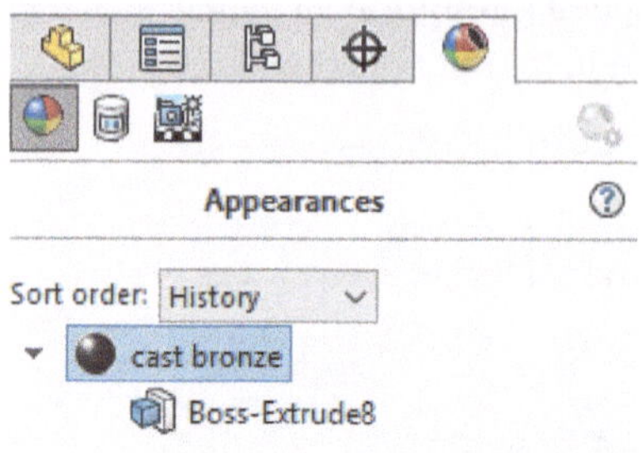

18. Press the Ctrl key and select the faces of the geometry, as shown.

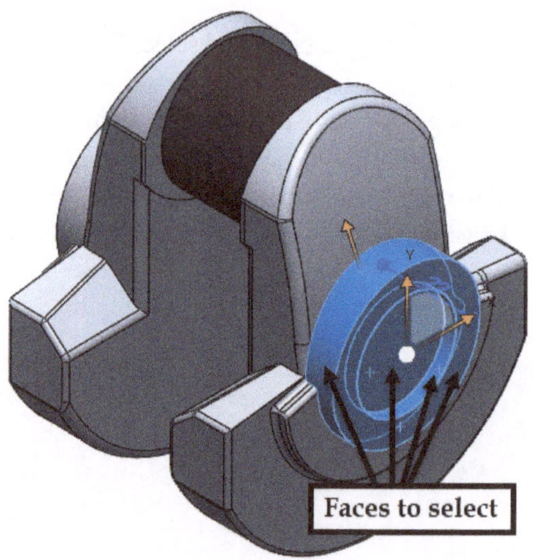

19. On the DisplayManager, right click on the **cast bronze** appearance and select **Attach To Selection**. The appearance is attached to the selected faces.

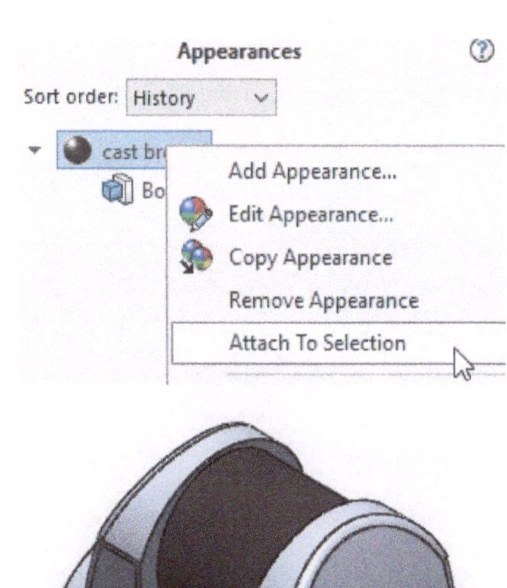

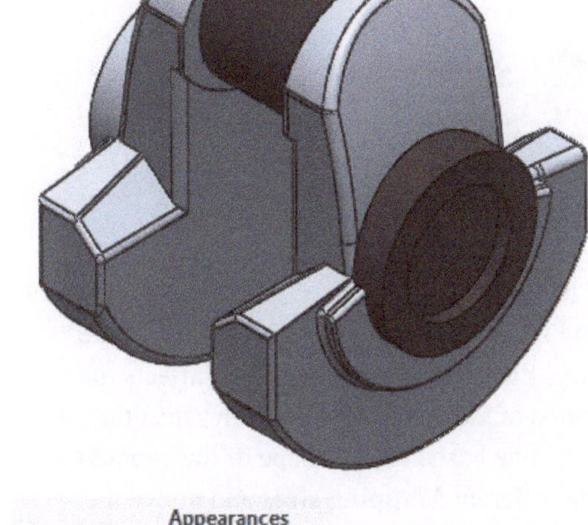

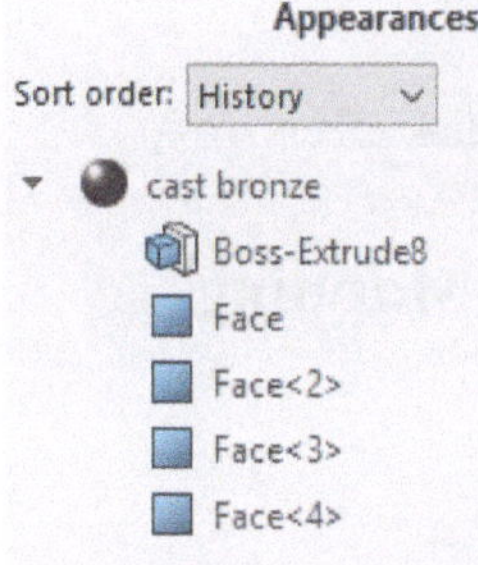

You can also use the Copy and Paste options to apply appearance to the geometry's multiple features/faces.

20. Click on any one of the faces with the **cast bronze** appearance and select **Copy Appearance** (or) right click on the **cast bronze** appearance and select **Copy Appearance**.
21. Select the face as shown and click **Paste Appearance**.

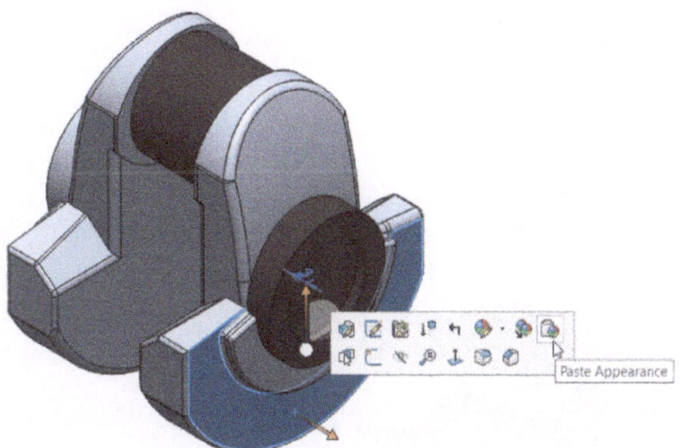

The **Appearance Target Palette** appears on the screen. Place the pointer on the icons of this palette and notice the appearance of the part.

22. Click the Boss-Extrude icon on the **Appearance Target Palette**. The **cast bronze** appearance is pasted on the extruded boss.

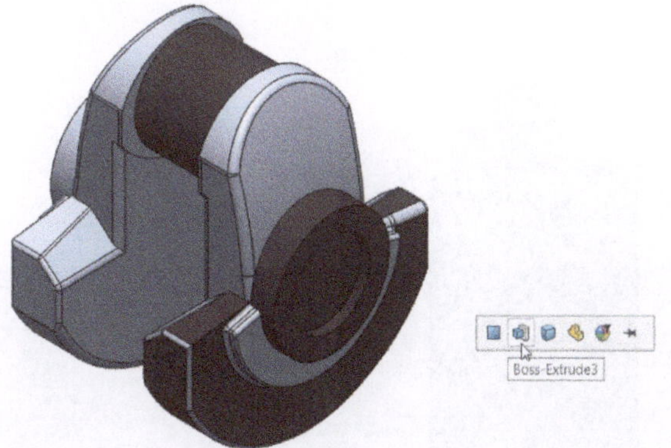

TUTORIAL 3 (Adding Textures)

Textures are two-dimensional images that are wrapped around a 3D model. Adding textures to the 3D model involves selecting an image and mapping it onto the 3D model. As you add a texture, SOLIDWORKS increases or reduces the image size, rotates, and patterns to completely cover the part geometry.

1. Open the Tutorial 1 file.
2. On the View Toolbar, click the **Edit Appearance** icon.

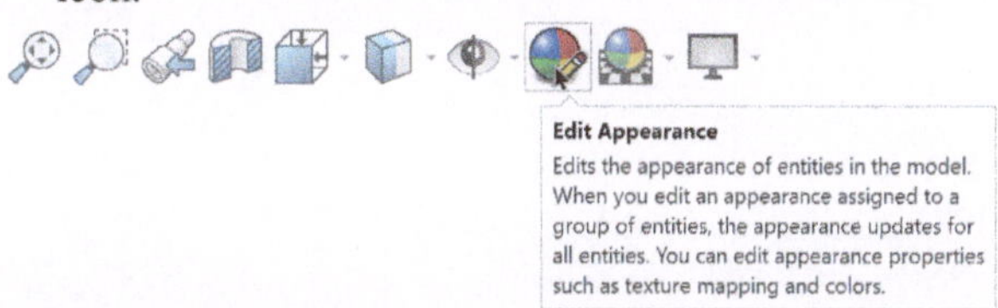

3. Select **texture** from the Task pane.

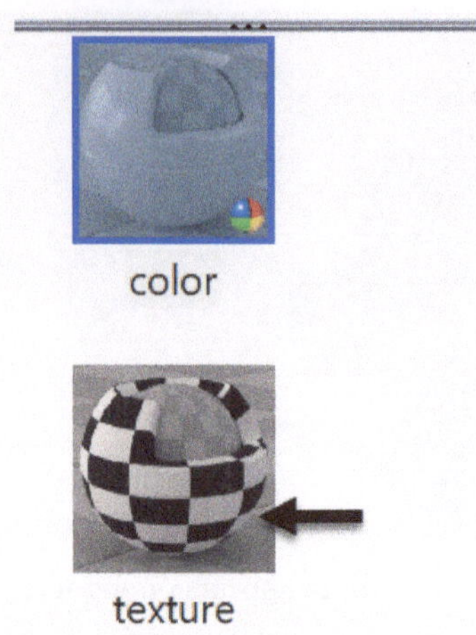

4. On the PropertyManager, under the **Image** section, click the **Browse** button.
5. Go to *C:\Program Files\SOLIDWORKS Corp\SOLIDWORKS\data\Images\textures\metal\rough*.
6. Select **cast** and click **Open**.

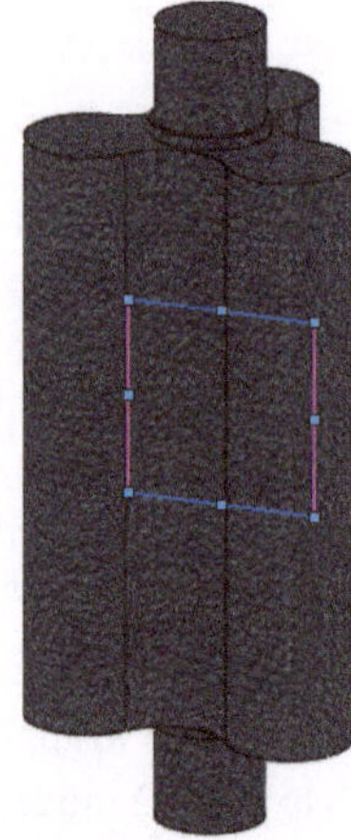

7. On the PropertyManager, click the **Mapping** tab.

The **Mapping** tab has options to select the geometry and set mapping style and size.

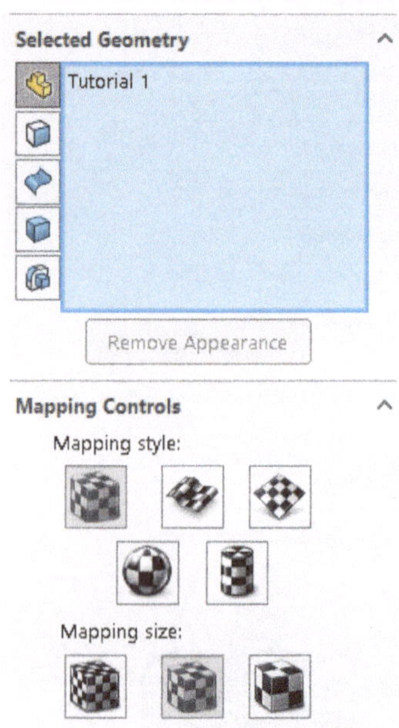

8. On the **Mapping Controls** section, click on different Mapping styles and notice the appearance on the geometry. Each of the mapping styles affects the appearance of the geometry. You can select the Mapping style based on the shape of the geometry.
9. Click on different **Mapping sizes** and notice the difference.
10. Leave the default options and click **OK** ✓.

TUTORIAL 4 (Texture Mapping options)

1. Start a new part file.
2. Create a box, sphere, and cylinder.
3. Select the box from the graphics window.
4. Select **Boss-Extrude-1** from the top left corner.

5. On the **View Heads Up** toolbar, click the **Edit Appearance**.
6. Select **texture** from the Task pane.

7. Click the Browse button on the PropertyManager and go to the location: C:\Program Files\SOLIDWORKS Corp\SOLIDWORKS\data\Images\textures\fabric\loop.jpg
8. Double-click on the loop.jpg file and click **OK** ✓.
9. Likewise, apply the loop texture separately to the other features.

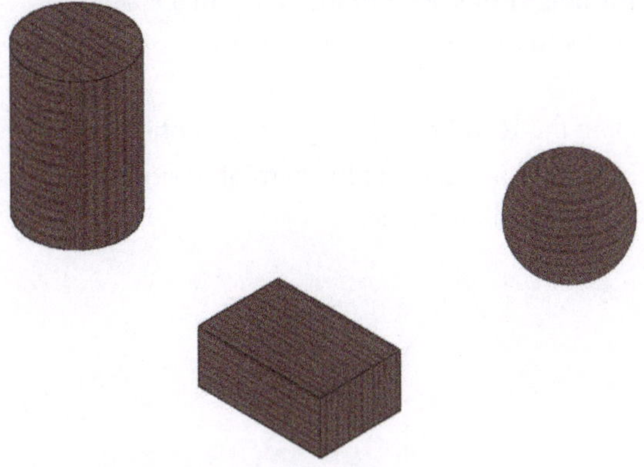

10. Click on the box and select **Edit Appearance > Boss-Extrude**.

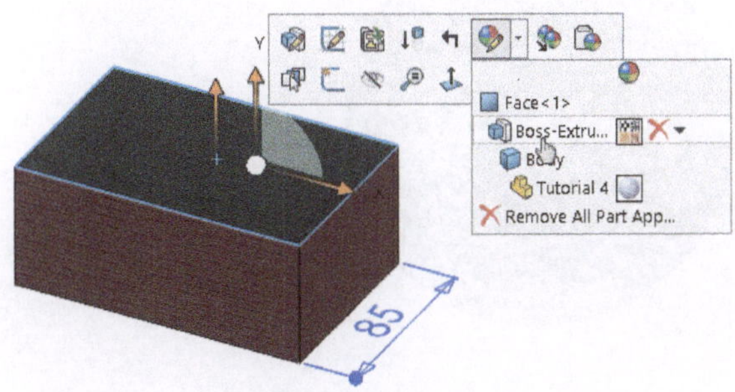

11. On the PropertyManager, click the **Advanced** tab, and then click the **Mapping** tab. Notice that the **Mapping** section's options are the same as the **Mapping style** options in the **Basic** tab.
12. On the **Mapping** tab, select **Mapping > Surface**. This mapping style arranges the image to fit the surfaces of the geometry.
13. On the **Mapping** section, drag the **Horizontal Location** and **Vertical Location** draggers. Notice that the position of the texture image changes horizontally and vertically.

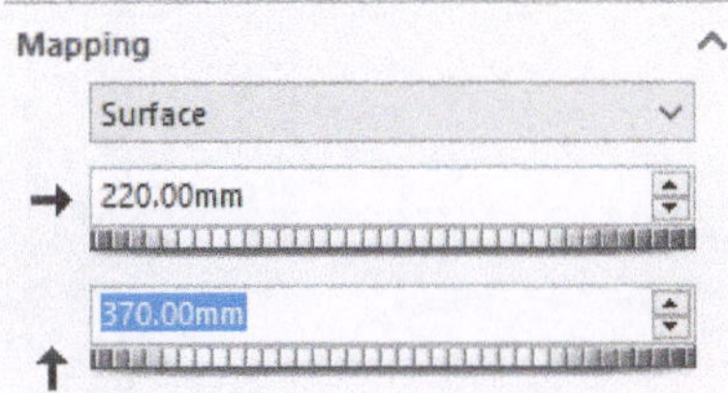

14. Select **Mapping > Projection** and set the **Projection direction** to XY. The texture image is projected onto the feature in the XY direction.

15. Set the **Projection direction** to the **Current View**.
16. Rotate the model and click the **Update to Current** button. The texture is projected based on the current orientation of the model.

17. Set the **Projection direction** to **Selected Reference** and select the vertical edge of the box. The image is projected along the selected edge.

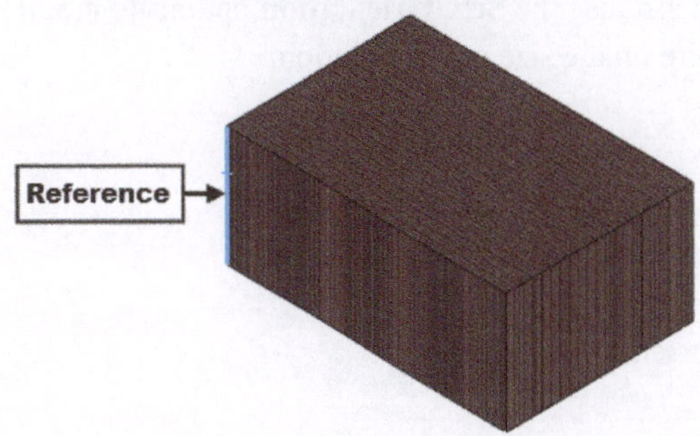

18. Click **OK** ✓ on the PropertyManager.
19. Click on the sphere and select **Edit Appearance > Revolve**.

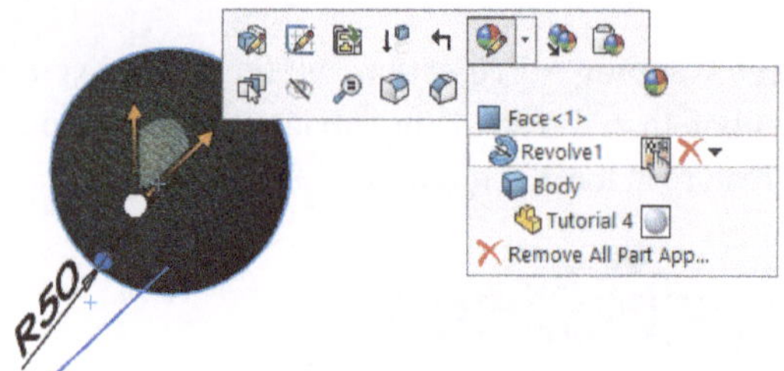

20. On the PropertyManager, click the **Advanced** tab, and then click the **Mapping** tab.
21. On the **Mapping** tab, select **Mapping > Spherical**. This mapping style arranges the image to fit the surface of a sphere.
22. Drag the **Offset Latitude** and **Offset Longitude** draggers on the **Mapping** section. The position of the rectangle changes.
23. Drag the dotted handles of the rectangle to increase/decrease the size of the texture image.

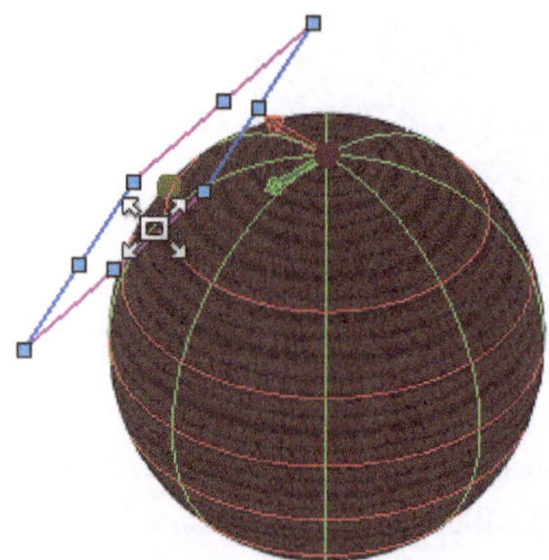

You can also use the **Size/Orientation** options to modify the texture image size and orientation.

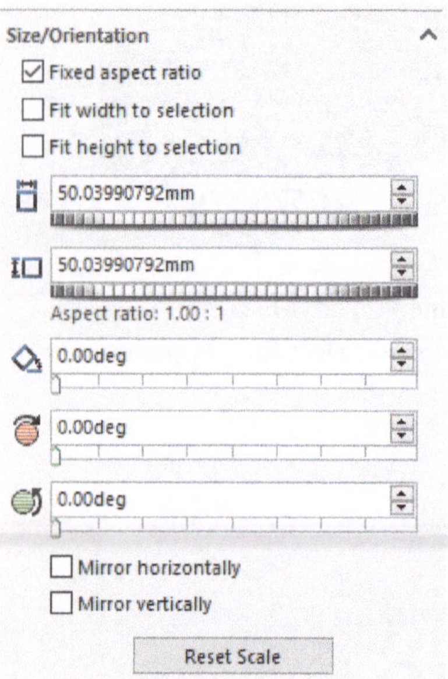

The **Fixed aspect ratio** option locks the aspect ratio of the image.

The **Fit width to selection** locks the image width to its current size. You can change only the height of the image.

The **Fit height to selection** locks the image height allowing you to change only its width.

24. Drag the **Rotation** dragger and notice that the image is rotated about the current position of longitude and latitude.

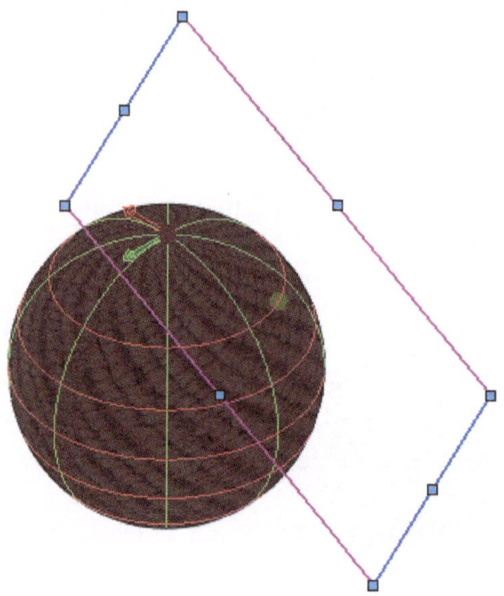

25. Drag the **Axis direction 1** dragger to change its orientation.

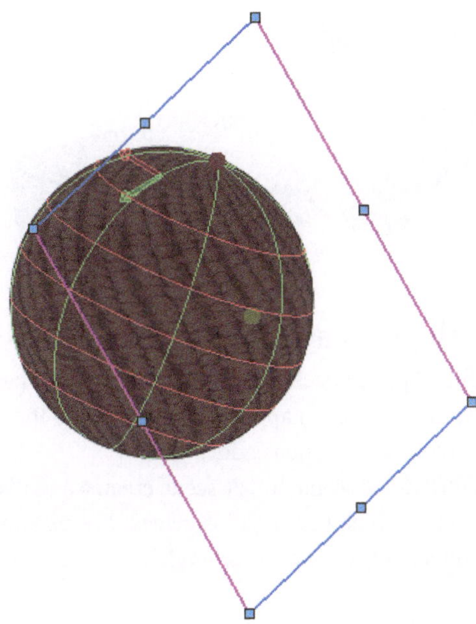

26. Likewise, drag the **Axis direction 2** dragger to change its orientation.

You can use the **Mirror horizontally** or **Mirror vertically** options to mirror the image.

27. Click the **Reset Scale** button to reset the image scale to its default value.
28. Click **OK** on the PropertyManager.
29. Click on the cylinder and select **Edit Appearance > Boss-Extrude2**.

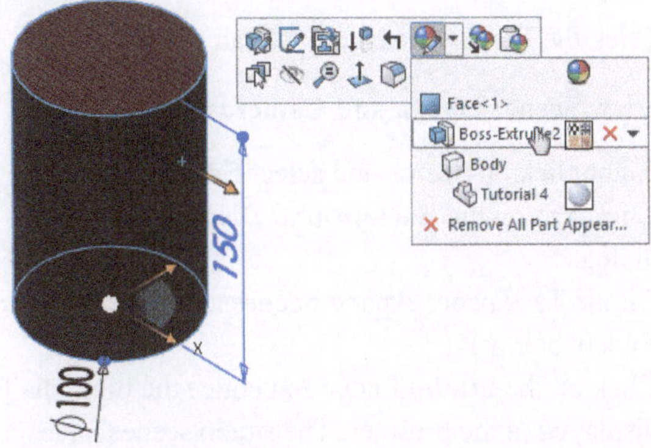

30. Click the **Advanced** tab on the PropertyManager.
31. On the **Mapping** tab, select **Mapping > Cylindrical**. This mapping style arranges the image to fit the surface of a cylinder.
32. Set the **Axis direction** to XY and drag the **About Axis** and **Along Axis** draggers.

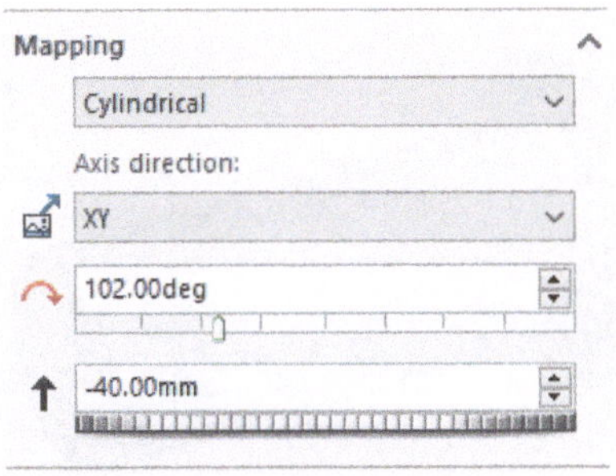

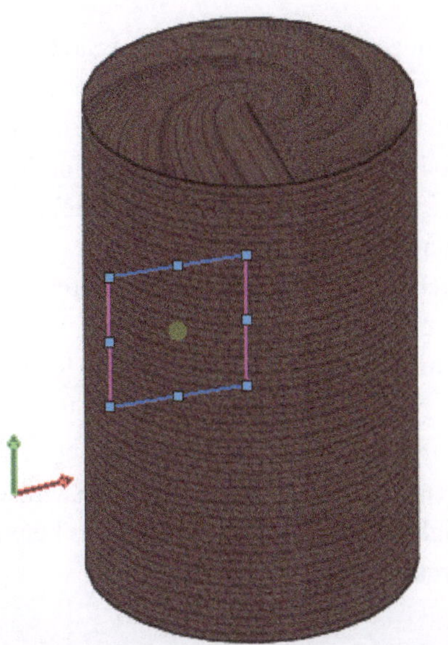

33. Click **OK** on the PropertyManager.

TUTORIAL 5 (Surface Finish)

1. Open the Tutorial 5 file.
2. Apply the **knurl2** texture to the cylindrical face of the geometry. The location of the texture image is C:\Program Files\SOLIDWORKS Corp\SOLIDWORKS\data\Images\textures\metal\machined\knurl2.jpg
3. Click the **Basic** tab on the PropertyManager.
4. On the **Mapping** section, set the **Mapping Style** to **Surface mapping** and **Mapping Size** to **Big mapping size**.

34. Click the **Advanced** tab, and then click the **Surface Finish** tab.
35. Select the **Knurled** option from the **Surface Finish** drop-down. You can also select the **From file** option and specify an image file to define the surface finish.
36. Check the **Dynamic help** option.
37. Place the pointer on the **Knurl angle** and **Knurl height cap** boxes and notice the descriptions.
38. Set the **Knurl angle** and **Knurl height cap** to 90 and 1, respectively.
39. Click **OK** ✔ . The knurled surface finish will be visible in the rendered image. SOLIDWORKS will process the bright areas of the texture image as height and the dark areas as depths.

TUTORIAL 6 (Illumination)

1. Open the Tutorial 5 file.
2. Click on any one of the faces of the geometry and select **Edit Appearance > Revolve**.
3. On the Task Pane, select **Appearance > Metal > Steel.**
4. Select **machined steel** from the lower portion of the Task pane.
5. Click the **Advanced** tab on the PropertyManager.
6. Click the **Illumination** tab and check the **Dynamic help** option. The options on the **Illumination** tab control the illumination of the geometry.
7. Place the pointer on the edit boxes and notice the descriptions.
8. Modify the values on the **Illumination** tab and notice the change in the graphics window.
9. Click **OK.**

Tutorial 7 (Scenes)

After adding Appearances, a Scene is an important part of the rendering process. An appearance is added to the geometry, whereas a scene is added to the SOLIDWORKS environment. A scene creates a realistic environment in which the model is placed. For example, you can add a road scene to a car model.

1. Open the Tutorial 7 file.

2. Click the DisplayManager tab, and then **click View Scene, Lights, and Cameras** .
3. Right click on **Scene**, and select **Edit Scene.**
4. Click **Yes** on the **Background Display Setting** dialog.
5. On the Task pane, expand **Scenes** and notice the folders below it.
6. Click on the **Studio** folder and notice the thumbnails displayed in the browser. The studio scenes have plain or gradient environments and backgrounds.

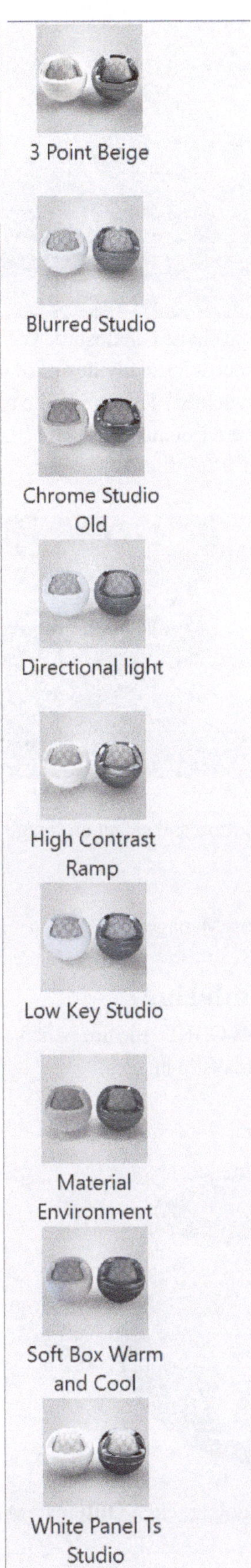

7. Select the **3 Point Beige** scene from the browser.
8. Rotate the model and notice that the background remains static.
9. Click the **Presentation** folder and select the Indoor sub-folder. Next, select **Factory**.

10. Rotate the model and notice that the environment is sphere-shaped and encloses the part completely. You can set the viewpoint at the angle.
11. Click **Cancel** on the **Edit Scene** PropertyManager.
12. Right click on **Scene**, and select **Edit Scene**.
13. On the PropertyManager, select **Background > Color**.
14. Click on the **Dominant color** box available in the **Background** section.

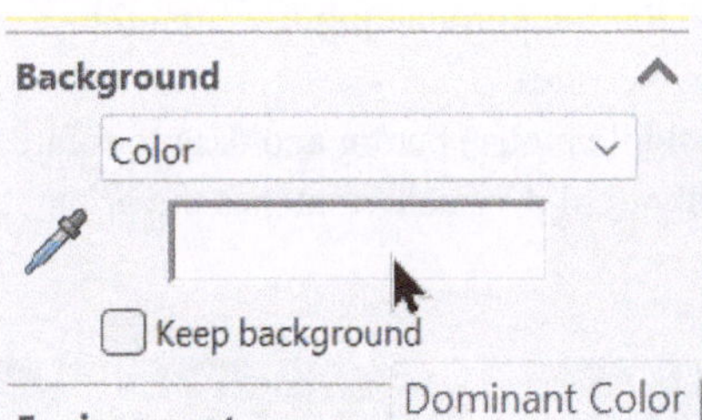

15. On the **Color** dialog, select the Yellow color and click **OK**. The background is changed to yellow.

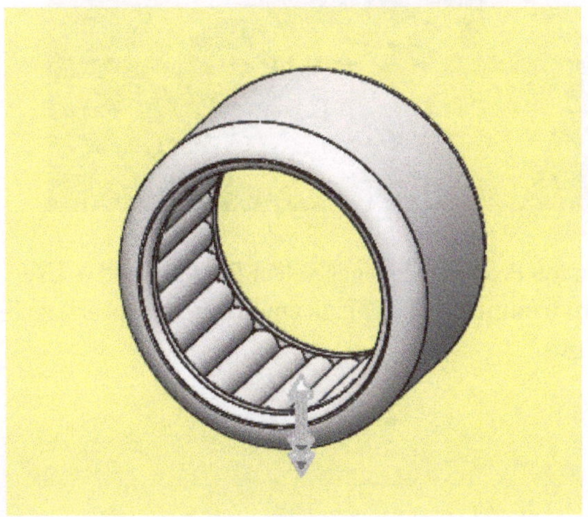

16. On the PropertyManager, select **Background > Gradient**.
17. Click in the **Bottom gradient color** box, select the blue color, and click **OK**. The bottom gradient is changed to blue.

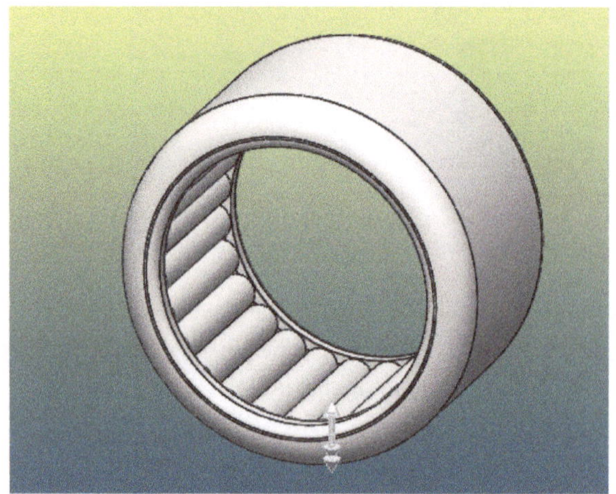

18. On the PropertyManager, select **Background > Image**.
19. Select the Background.jpg and click **Open** (Download the Background.jpg file from the companion website).
20. Hold the middle mouse button and drag to rotate the model freely until it visually matches the orientation, as shown.

21. On the PropertyManager, select **Background > Use Environment**. The default environment appears, as shown.

An environment is a spherical shaped enclosure. The image used in the environment is specially designed and looks similar to the one shown next. The image file types that are commonly used for environments are HDR files and panoramically designed JPEG files.

You can click the **Browse** button and select an image for the environment background.

22. Click **OK** on the PropertyManager.

TUTORIAL 8 (Rendering)

PhotoView 360 is a SOLIDWORKS Add-In, which allows you to create photo-realistic images.

1. Open the Tutorial 8 file.

2. On the Quick Access Toolbar, click **Options > Add-Ins**.

3. On the **Add-Ins** dialog, check the **SOLIDWORKS Visualize** option and click **OK**.
4. On the CommandManager, right-click and select **Tabs > Render Tools**. The **Render Tools** tab is added to the CommandManager.
5. Right-click on the CommandManager, and then select **Customize**; the **Customize** dialog appears.
6. On the **Customize** dialog, click the **Commands** tab and select the **Render Tools** option from the **Toolbars** list.
7. Click and drag the **Render** tool and release it on the **Render Tools** tab of the CommandManager.

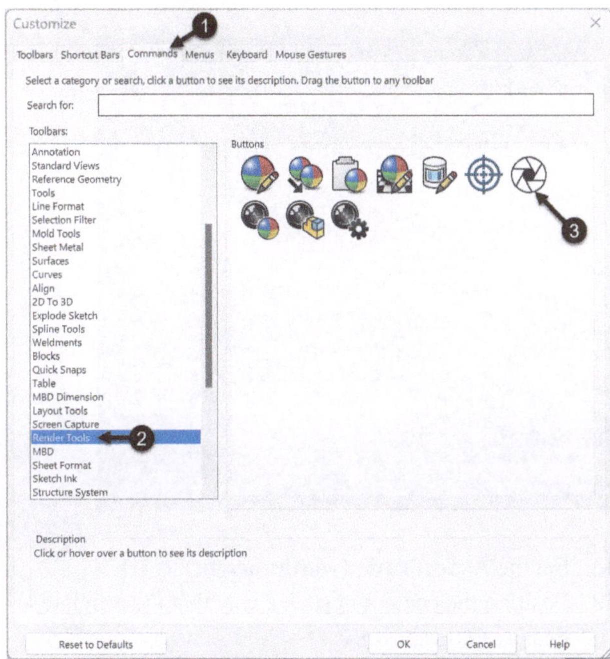

8. Click **OK**.
9. On the CommandManager, click **Render Tools > Edit Appearance**.
10. On the Task pane, select **Appearances > Metal > Aluminum**, and select **polished Aluminum** from the browser.
11. On the PropertyManager, under the **Color** section, click in the **Dominant Color** box and select the light grey color from the **Color** dialog. Click **OK**.
12. Click in the **Secondary Color** box and select white from the **Color** dialog. Click **OK**.

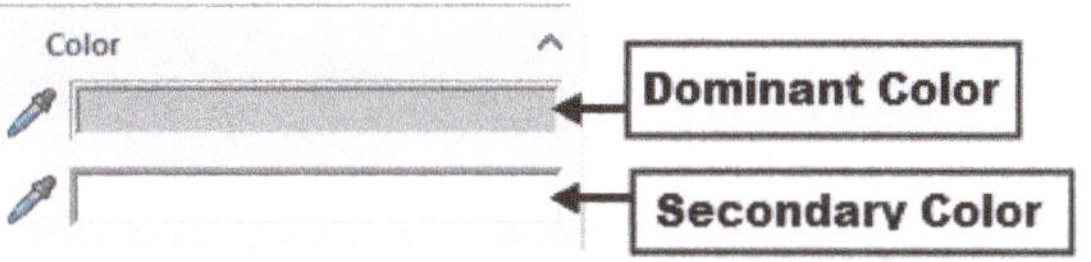

13. Click **OK** on the PropertyManager.
14. On the CommandManager, click **Render Tools > Edit Scene**.
15. On the Task pane, select **Scenes > Presentation > Indoor**, and select **Kitchen** from the browser.

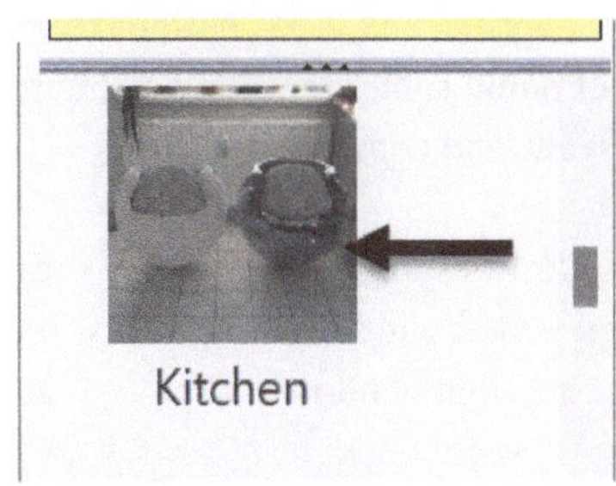

16. Rotate, zoom, and pan the model to position it, as shown.

17. On the **View Heads Up** Toolbar, click the **View Orientation** drop-down and deselect the **View Selector** icon.
18. Click the **New View** icon on the **View Orientation** drop-down.
19. Type **Render1** on the **Named View** dialog and click **OK**.
20. Rotate the model to a different orientation.
21. On the **View Heads Up** Toolbar, click the **View Orientation** drop-down and select **Render1**.

If you are working in the Assembly environment, the **Take snapshot** tool can capture the different view orientations of the model.

22. Click **OK** on the PropertyManager.

Adding Cameras

1. Click the DisplayManager tab on the left pane, and then click **View Scene, Lights, and Cameras**.
2. Right click on the **Camera** folder and select **Add Camera**.

The PropertyManager appears, and it has options to set the camera type, target point, camera position, camera rotation, the field of view, and depth of field.

Also, the graphics window is split in two. You can adjust the camera position in the left window and preview the camera perspective in the right window.

3. On the PropertyManager, set the **Camera Type** to **Aimed at target**. The camera will always show the selected target point regardless of the camera position. The Floating camera type changes the site as you change the camera position and orientation.
4. Zoom out in the left window and notice a camera.

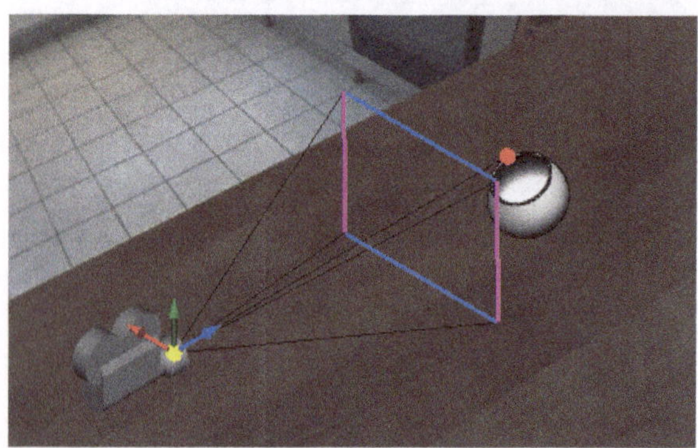

5. Click and drag the red dot attached to the camera. Notice that the target changes as you drag the red dot.
6. Select the outer face of the model to define the target point.
7. Click and drag the yellow dot to change the position of the camera. You can also use the axes of the triad attached to change the camera position.

Notice that the camera focuses on the target point regardless of its position.

8. Expand the **Camera Rotation** section and drag the **Roll(Twist)** dragger to rotate the camera.
9. Set the **Roll(Twist)** angle to 0 degrees.
10. In the **Field of View** section, select different options from the **Standard lens presets** drop-down and notice the area captured by the camera. You can also drag the **View angle**, **Distance to view rectangle**, and **Height of view rectangle** draggers to adjust the field of view.
11. Check the **Drag Aspect Ratio** option and drag the corner of the view box. The aspect ratio of the field changes dynamically.

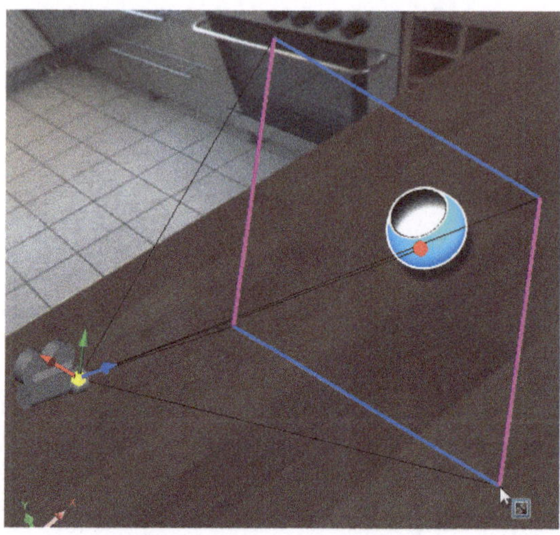

12. Set the **Aspect ratio (width: height)** to **1:1**.
13. Position the camera in such a way that the preview is displayed, as shown.

23. Click **OK** on the PropertyManager.

24. In the DisplayManager tree, expand the **Camera** folder and right click on **Camera1** and select **Camera View**. The view is locked to the camera.

Rendering

1. On the CommandManager, click **Render Tools > Render**. On the PropertyManager, you can modify the width and height of the image.
2. Set the **Format** to **JPEG**.
3. In the **Quality** section, set the **Render quality** to **High**, respectively. Note that the processing time will increase as you increase the image quality.

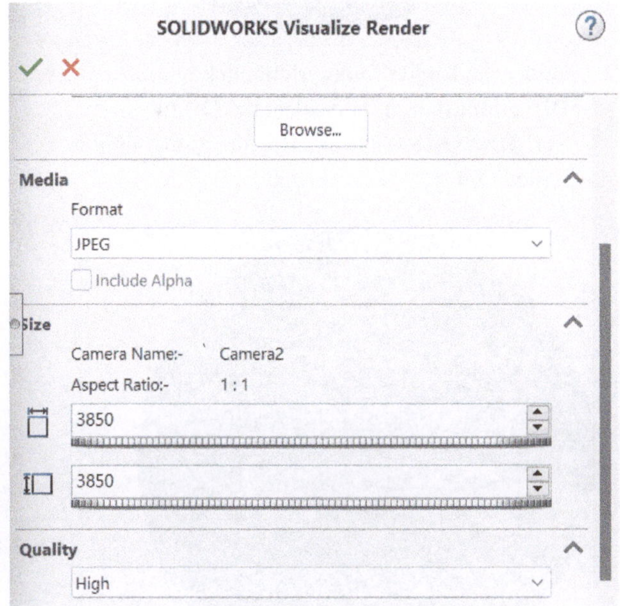

4. Leave the other default options and click **OK** ✓.

The **SOLIDWORKS Visualize Render Progress** dialog appears, and rendering is processed. You can click the **Cancel** button to stop the rendering process.

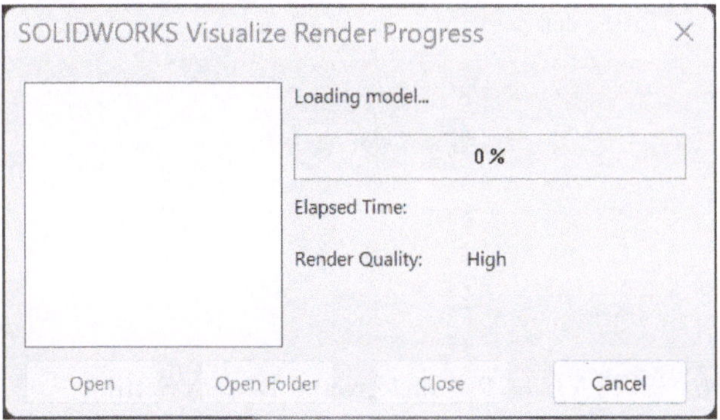

5. Wait until the image is rendered.
6. Click **Open** after the rendering is completed.
7. Save and close the part file.

TUTORIAL 9 (Lights)

Lights are very important in rendering a photorealistic image. They can enhance the image to look more realistic by highlighting some portions and creating shadows. You can access the lights on the DisplayManager tree. Click the **DisplayManager** tab, and then click **View Scene, Lights, and Cameras**. Expand the **Lights** folder and notice the default lights available in the SOLIDWORKS environment.

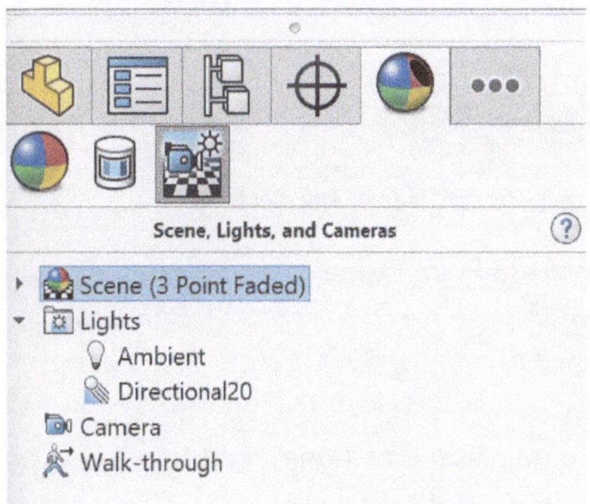

Editing the Ambient Light

By default, the Ambient light is created in the SOLIDWORKS environment automatically. The Ambient light falls on the model from all directions.

1. Open the Tutorial 9 file.

2. Click the **DisplayManager** tab on the left pane.
3. In the **View Scene, Lights, and Cameras** tree, expand the **Lights** folder, and double click on **Ambient**.
4. On the PropertyManager, click the **Edit Color** button, select the red color from the **Color** dialog, and click **OK**. Notice that the red light falls on the model.
5. Drag the **Ambient** dragger to change the light's intensity (or) type-in a value between 0 and 1 in the **Ambient** box.
6. On the PropertyManager, uncheck the **On in SOLIDWORKS** option and notice the difference in the graphics window.
7. Check the **On in SOLIDWORKS** option to turn ON the ambient light.
8. Click **OK** ✔ to apply changes to the model.

TUTORIAL 10 (Working with Directional Lights)

SOLIDWORKS adds a Directional Light to the model automatically. It is used to highlight a portion of the geometry and display shadows. You can add, delete, move, or adjust the Directional Light.

1. In the **View Scene, Lights, and Cameras** tree, right click on the **Lights** folder, and select **Show Lights**. The directional light appears, as shown.

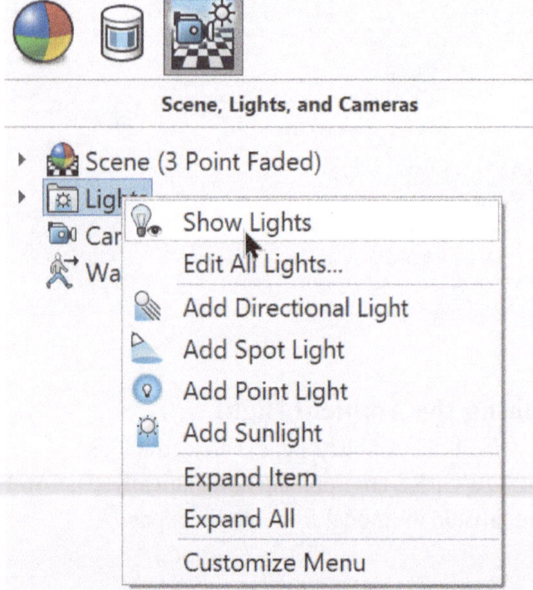

2. Under the **Lights** folder, right click on the **Directional1 light** and select the **Off in SOLIDWORKS** option. The directional light is turned OFF.

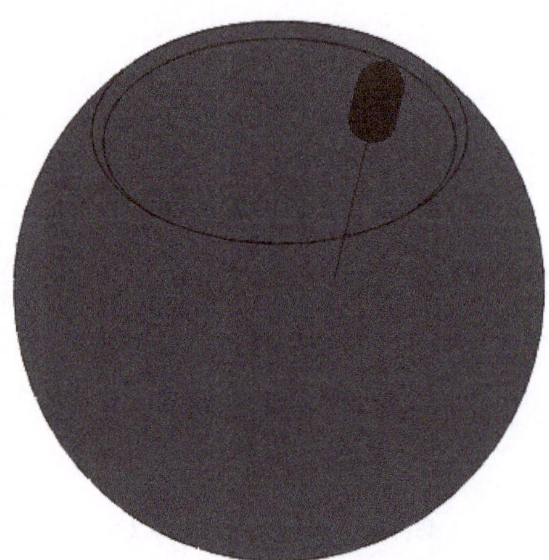

Also, the directional lights change depending on the type of scene.

3. On the CommandManager, click **Render Tools > Edit Scene**.

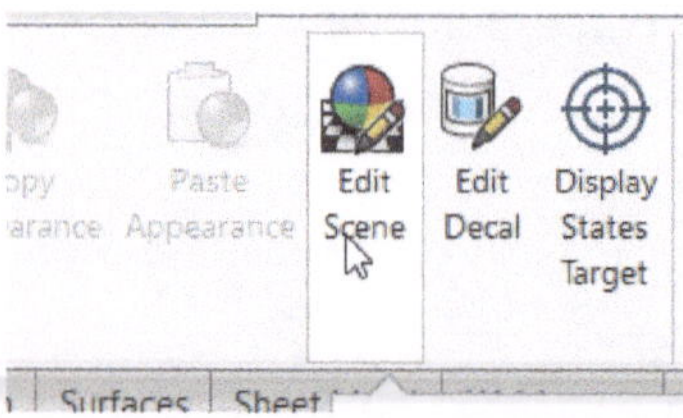

4. Click **Yes** on the **Background Display Setting** message box to automatically update your

background appearance to "**Use Document Scene**." You can also adjust this setting manually at any time by navigating to **Tools > Options > System Options > Colors**.

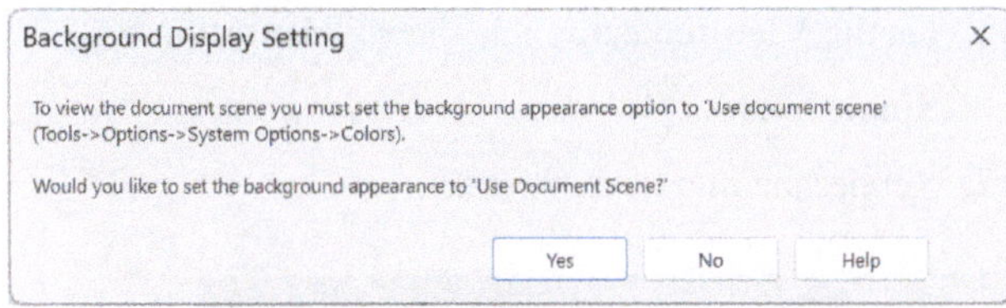

5. On the Task pane, click **Scenes > Studio**, and select the **3 Point Biege** scene from the browser. Notice two directional lights related to the selected scene.

6. Click **OK** on the PropertyManager.
7. On the DisplayManager tree, right click on the **Lights** folder and select **Add Directional Light**. A new directional light appears in the graphics window.

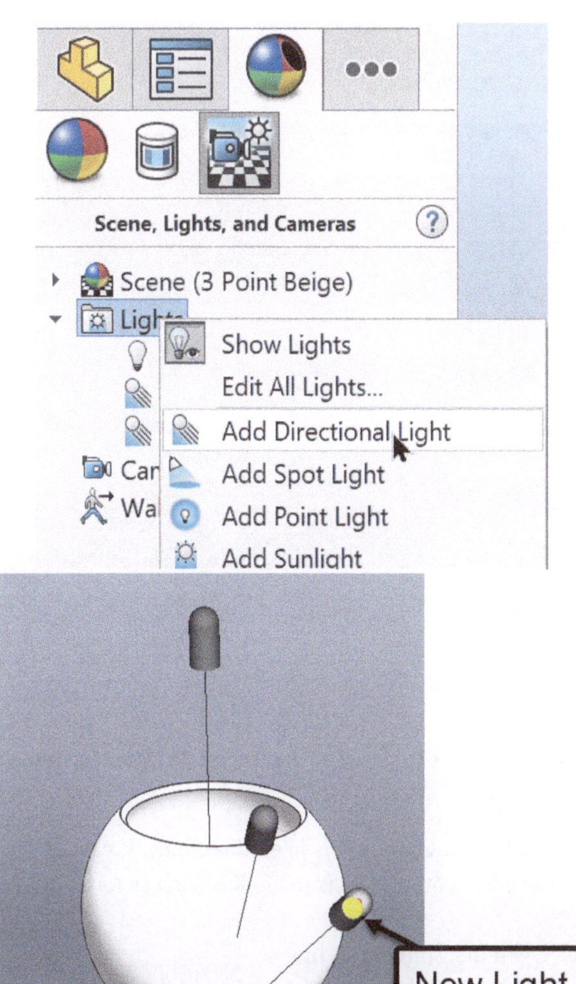

8. On the **Basic** section, check the **Keep light when scene changes** option to retain the light for all the scenes.
9. In the **Light Position** section, drag the **Longitude** and **Latitude** draggers to change the light's position (or) click and drag the light to define its position.
10. Uncheck the **Lock to model** option and rotate the model. Notice that the light is fixed as the model is rotated.
11. Check the **Lock to model** option and rotate the model. Notice that the light rotates along with the model.

You can turn ON/OFF the light by checking/unchecking the **On in SOLIDWORKS** option. You can also change the **Ambient**, **Brightness**, and **Specularity** of the light.

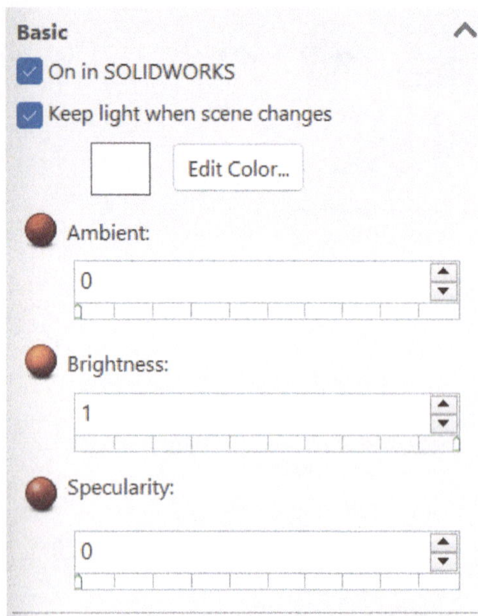

12. Click **OK** on the PropertyManager.

TUTORIAL 11 (Working with Point Lights)

A point light radiates lights in all directions. It can be used to add lighting effects to models such as torch lights.

1. Open the Tutorial 11 file.
2. Click the **DisplayManager** tab, and then click **View Scene, Lights, and Cameras**.
3. Right click on the **Lights** folder and select **Add Point Light**. A red dot appears in the graphics window.
4. On the **View Heads Up** toolbar, click **View Orientation > Four View**.
5. Make sure that the **Link Views** icon is activated on the **View Orientation** drop-down.
6. Click and drag the red dot as shown. You can also use the options in the **Light Position** section.

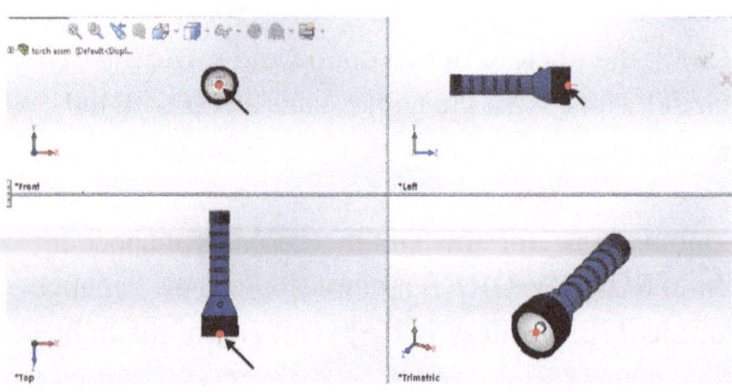

7. On the **Basic** section, check the **Keep light when scene changes** option.
8. Adjust the **Ambient**, **Brightness**, and **Specularity**.
9. Check the **On in SOLIDWORKS** option.
10. Click **OK** on the PropertyManager.
11. On the **View** toolbar, click **View Orientation > Single View**.
12. Render the image, as shown.

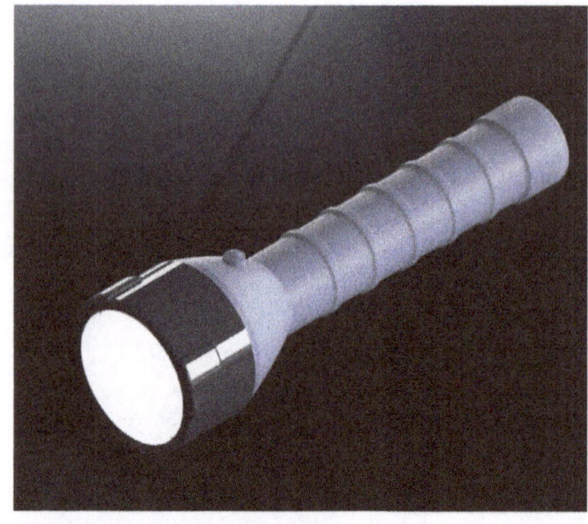

13. Save and close the file.

TUTORIAL 12 (Working with Spot Lights)

Spotlights are similar to directional lights. However, they create brighter and sharp lights targeting a specific area.

1. Open the Tutorial 12 file.
2. Click the **DisplayManager** tab, and then click **View Scene, Lights, and Cameras**.
3. Right click on the **Lights** folder and select **Add Spot Light**. A cone appears in the graphics window.
4. On the **View** toolbar, click **View Orientation > Four View**.
5. Click and drag the red arrow, as shown. You can also use the options in the **Light Position** section.

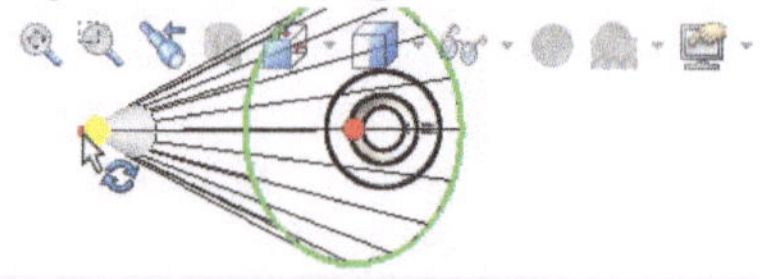

6. Drag the green circle of the cone to reduce its size.

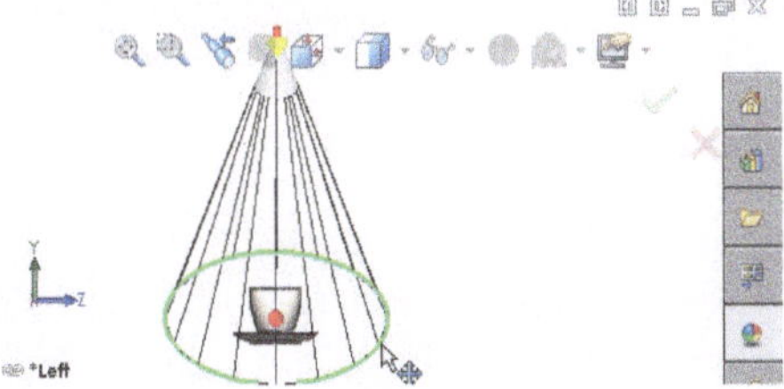

7. Drag the red dot to set the target point of the spot light.

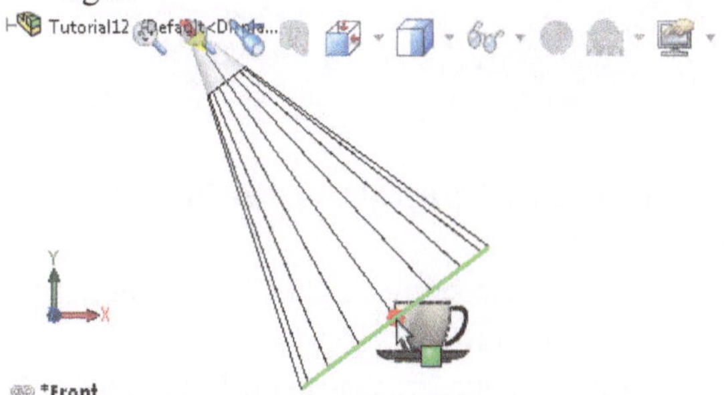

8. Check the **Keep light when scene changes** option.
9. Check the **On in SOLIDWORKS** option.
10. Click **OK** ✓.
11. On the **View** toolbar, click **View Orientation > Single View** .
12. Change the **View Orientation** to **Trimetric**  .
13. Right click on **Scene**, and select **Edit Scene**.
14. On the PropertyManager, select **Background > Color**.
15. Click on the **Dominant color** box available in the **Background** section.

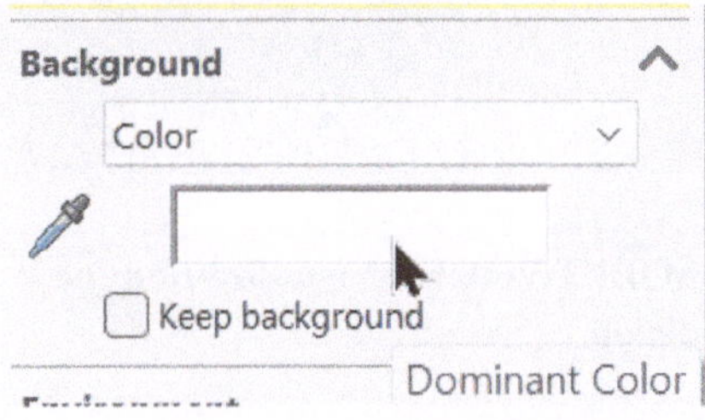

16. On the **Color** dialog, select the Black color and click **OK**. The background is changed to black.
17. Render the image, as shown.

18. Save and close the file.

TUTORIAL 13 (Working with Sun Lights)

Sunlight in SOLIDWORKS represents real-world sunlight and is controlled by the geographic location that you specify.

1. Open the Tutorial 13 file.
2. Click the **DisplayManager** tab, and then click **View Scene, Lights, and Cameras**.
3. Right click on the **Lights** folder and select **Add Sunlight**. The sun appears along with a compass.

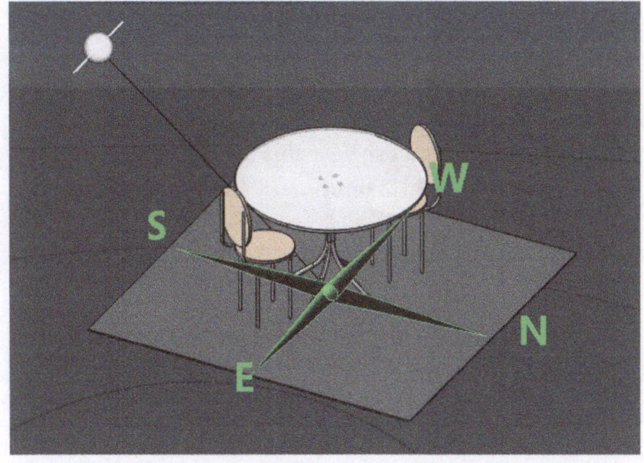

4. Select the right edge of the floor to define the north direction. You can also use a real compass to determine the north direction at your location and then define it in SOLIDWORKS.

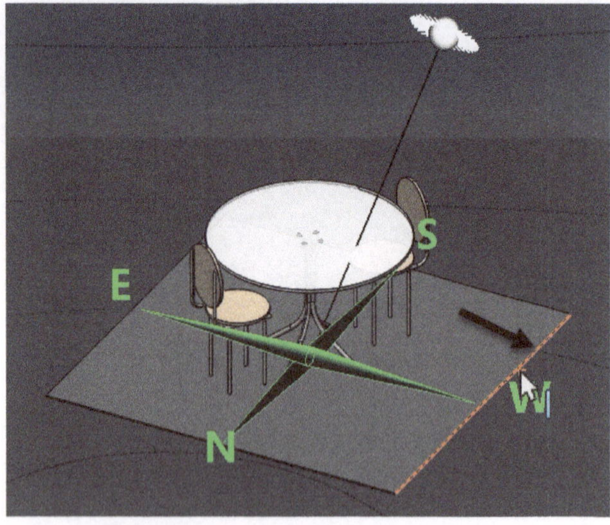

5. Click the **Reverse direction** button next to the **North direction** box. The position of the sun is changed accordingly.
6. Select different locations from the **Location** drop-down and notice the position of the sun. Also, the Time Zone is updated in the **Time zone from GMT** drop-down.
7. Under the **Location, Time, and Date** section, select **Location > Specify Location**.
8. Drag the **North Latitude** and **East Longitude** draggers to define the location. You can use a map as the reference and enter values in the **North Latitude** and **East Longitude** boxes.
9. Select New York from City, NY, from the **Location** drop-down.
10. Set the Date to 07-02-2026.
11. Set **Time of day** to 12:00. Notice that the **Information** section displays all the data related to the location. You can save this information in a file using the **Save Information to file** icon located at the bottom.
12. Click **OK** on the PropertyManager.
13. Click the **Render** icon on the **Render Tools** tab.
14. Click **OK** on the PropertyManager and notice the shadows.

15. Close the **SOLIDWORKS Visualize Render Progress** dialog.
16. In the DisplayManager tree, right click on **Sunlight** and select **Edit Sunlight**.
17. On the PropertyManager, change the **Location** to **Sydney**, and click **OK**.
18. Click the **Render** icon on the **Render Tools** tab.
19. Click **OK** on the PropertyManager and notice the shadows.

20. Close the **SOLIDWORKS Visualize Render Progress** dialog.

TUTORIAL 14 (Walk-through)

SOLIDWORKS Walk-through allows you to visually navigate the design and then create a video for the presentation purpose.

1. Open the Tutorial 14 file.
2. Click the **DisplayManager** tab, and then click **View Scene, Lights, and Cameras**.

3. Right click on the **Walk-through** folder and select **Add Walk-through**. The PropertyManager appears.

Now, select a plane to define the vertical direction.

4. Make sure that the Top plane is selected. The vertical direction is defined as normal to the selected plane/face.
5. Under the **Viewport Settings** section, set the **Viewing height** to 900. The viewing height is offset from the Top plane.
6. Expand the **Motion Constraints** section and select the spline, as shown. The motion path is defined.

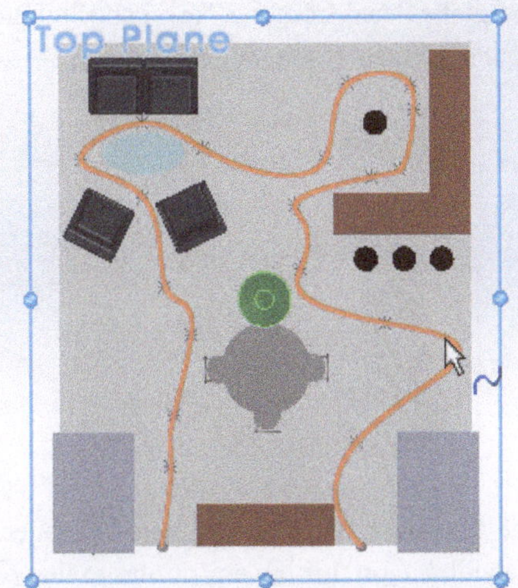

7. Make sure that the **Turn avatar to follow paths** option is checked.
8. Click the **Start Walk-through** button on the PropertyManager.
9. Notice the **Walk-through Quick Start Instructions** and click **OK**.
10. Click the **Show/Hide Map** icon on the Panel. The **Map View** window appears, showing the position of the avatar.
11. Click the **Toggle Constraints** icon on the Panel.
12. Select the spline sketch from the **Lock to Constraint** drop-down on the Panel. The avatar is locked to the path.
13. Click the **Set Home** on the left side of the Panel. The start point of the path is set as home.

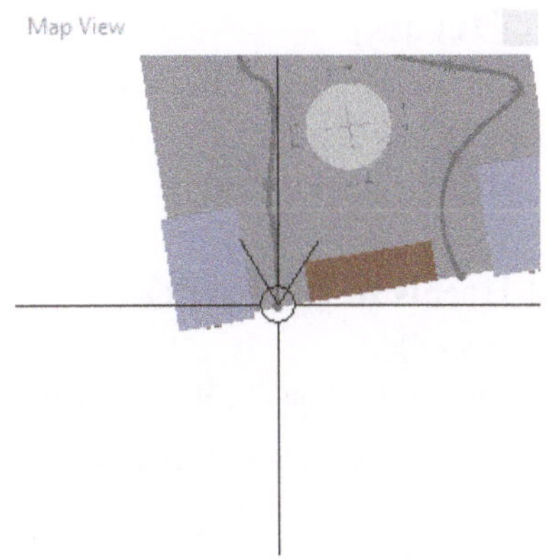

14. Press and hold the **Move Forward** arrow on the Panel. The avatar moves forward along the path. You can increase or decrease the avatar speed using the Rabbit and Turtle icons.

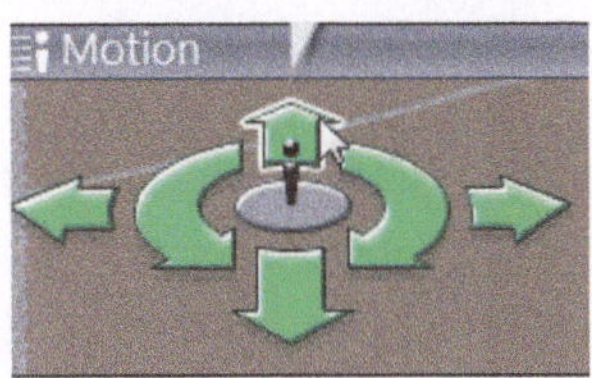

15. Click the **Go Home** icon after reaching the endpoint of the path. The avatar is positioned at the start point.
16. Click the **Toggle Record** icon on the Panel. The **Record** section appears.
17. Click the **Record** icon in the **Record** section and navigate through the model.
18. Click **OK** on the Panel after reaching the end of the path.
19. On the PropertyManager, click the **Play Recording** icon.
20. Close the **Record** panel after the avatar reaches the path end. If the video looks good, then proceed further to generate the video.
21. On the PropertyManager, **Generate Video** icon, type in the name, specify the file type and location.
22. Specify the settings in the **Image Size and Aspect Ratio** and **Frame Information** sections, and then click **Save**.
23. Specify the **Compressor** type on the **Video Compression** dialog, and then click **OK**.
24. Click **OK** on the PropertyManager.

TUTORIAL 15 (Decals)

SOLIDWORKS allows you to add images such as logos to your model by using the Decals option. Adding decals makes the rendered model look more realistic.

Adding the default Decals to the Model

1. Open the Tutorial 15 part file.
2. Click the DisplayManager tab, click the **View Decals** icon, and then click the **Open Decal Library** button. You can also click the **Appearances, Scenes, and Decals** tab on the Task pane and select the **Decals** folder.
3. Click and drag the **Recycling** decal from the Task pane onto the model.

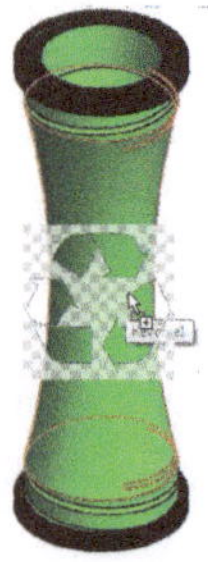

4. Click and drag the corner of the rectangle to change the size of the decal.
5. Click **OK** on the PropertyManager.

6. On the DisplayManager tab, expand the **Decals** tree, right click on **recycle**, and select **Delete**.

Creating your own Decals

1. Download the globe.jpg from the companion website.
2. On the CommandManager, click **Render Tools > Edit Decal**.
3. On the PropertyManager, click the **Browse** button.
4. Go to the location of the globe.jpg file and double-click on it.
5. On the PropertyManager, click the **Save Decal** button.
6. Click **Save,** and SOLIDWORKS creates the *.p2d file.
7. On the SOLIDWORKS Design message, click **Yes** to add the decal file's location to the Task Pane.
8. Click **OK** .
9. On the Task Pane, click the **Appearances, Scenes, and Decals** tab and expand the **Decals** folder. Notice the new folder added to the **Decals** folder.
10. Click on the new folder and notice the Decal in the lower portion of the Task Pane.
11. Select the globe decal from the Task Pane.
12. Drag the globe decal from the Task Pane and place it on the outer surface of the model.

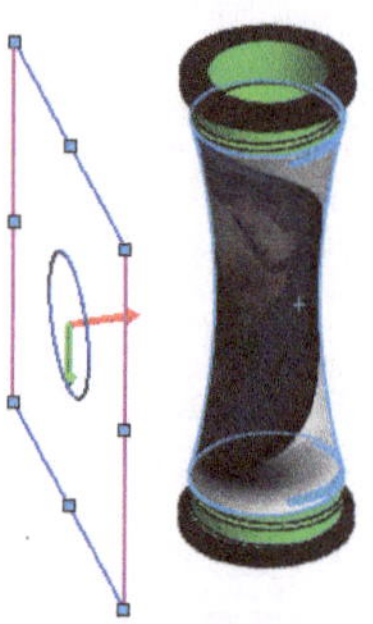

13. Click the **Mapping** tab on the PropertyManager. The options available on this tab are similar to that available on the **Mapping** tab of the texture PropertyManager.
14. Set the **Mapping** type to **Label.**
15. In the **Size/Orientation** section, change the **Rotation** value to **90** degrees.
16. Set the **Width** value to 50.
17. Use the Horizontal Location and Vertical Location draggers to position the decal properly.

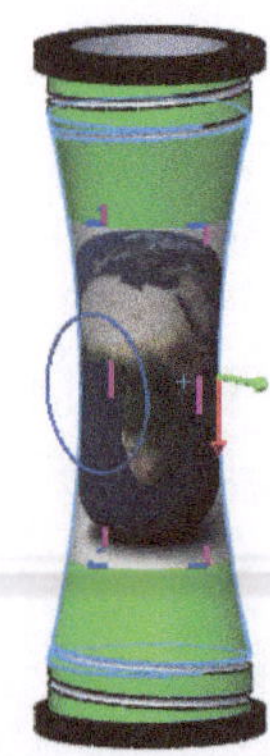

18. Click the **Illumination** tab and check the **Use underlying appearance** option.
19. Click the **Image** tab on the PropertyManager.
20. Under the **Mask Image** section, select the **Selective color mask** option.
21. Click the **Pick color** icon.
22. Go to the **Decal Preview** section and select the white color from the preview image. The color is displayed in the **Selected colors** section and removed from the decal. You can remove it from the **Selected colors** section by selecting and clicking the **Remove color** button.

23. Click **OK** on the PropertyManager.

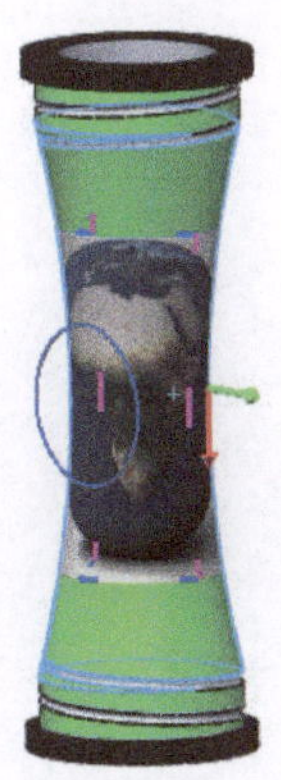

Chapter 15: SimulationXpress

SimulationXpress is a simple to use finite element analysis simulation tool used to analyze stress, deformation, and factor of safety. It is quick and easy to use and effortless to access. It is a small subset of the tools available on the full version of SOLIDWORKS Simulation. However, it has many limitations. One such limitation is that you cannot use it to perform analysis on assemblies. Also, you need to make some assumptions. The assumptions are:

- **Linear material:** A linear material obeys Hooke's Law, i.e., the relationship between the stress and strain is linear.

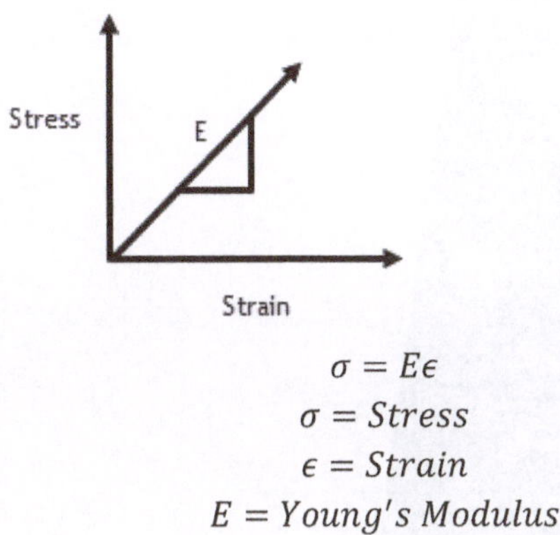

$$\sigma = E\epsilon$$
$$\sigma = Stress$$
$$\epsilon = Strain$$
$$E = Young's\ Modulus$$

To make it simple, the linear materials deform when a load is applied and then return to their initial state upon unloading.

- **Small deformations:** The deformations should be small compared to the size of a part.
- **Static loads:** The examples of static loads are Force, pressure, and gravity applied gradually. They are independent of time.

  Examples of dynamic loads are vibrations, wind loads, moving live loads, and so on.

In this chapter, you will learn the methods and tools to run simple simulations on parts and refine the model to save weight and optimize strength.

The **SimulationXpress Analysis Wizard** tool is available on the **Evaluate** Command Manager. You can also find this tool on the menu bar (click **Tools > Xpress Products > SimulationXpress** on the Menu bar). In addition to that, you need to display the **Analysis Preparation** tab on the Command Manager. To do this, right-click on any of the tabs of the CommandManager and select **Tabs > Analysis Preparation** from the shortcut menu.

TUTORIAL 1

In this tutorial, you perform Finite Element Analysis on a part.

1. Download the Tutorial 1-part file of Chapter 11 and open it.

2. On the CommandManager, click **Evaluate > SimulationXpress.**

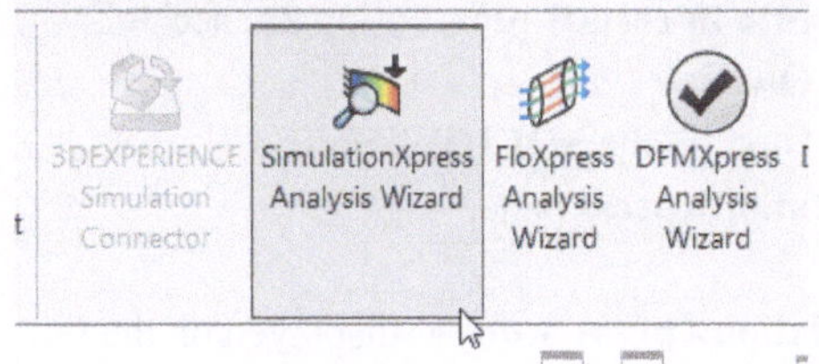

The SOLIDWORKS SimulationXpress pane appears on the right side of the window.

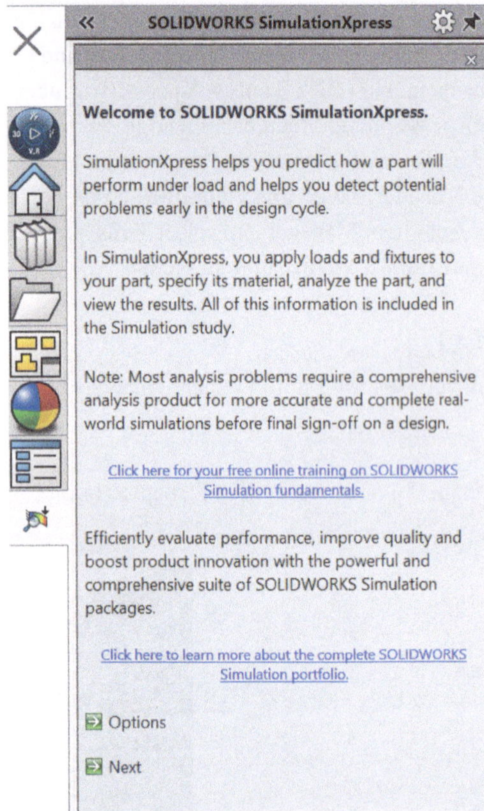

3. Click **Options** located at the bottom.

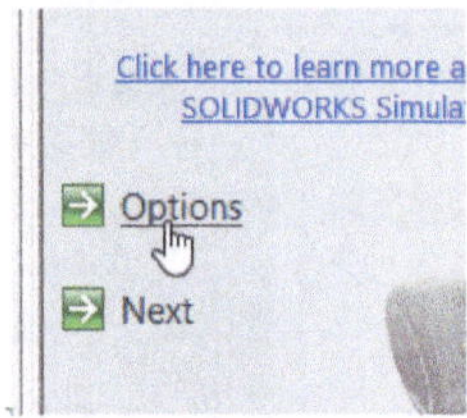

4. On the **SimulationXpress Options** dialog, select **System of units > English (IPS)**.
5. Leave the **Results Location** as default.
6. Leave the **Show annotation for maximum and minimum in results plots** option unchecked.
7. Click **OK**.
8. Click **Next** on the **SOLIDWORKS SimulationXpress** pane.

The **SimulationXpress Study** is displayed on the left side.

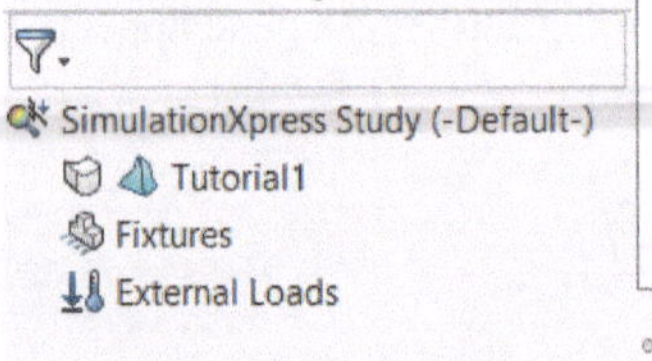

Creating Fixtures

1. Click **Add a fixture** on the **SOLIDWORKS SimulationXpress** pane.

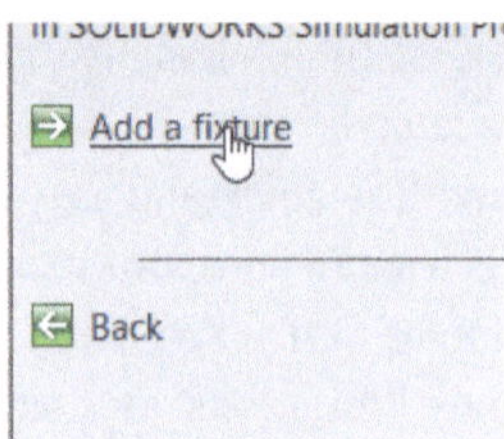

2. Rotate the model and select the holes.

3. Click **OK** on the **Fixture** PropertyManager.
4. Click **Add a fixture** on the **SOLIDWORKS SimulationXpress** pane.
5. Select the back face of the geometry

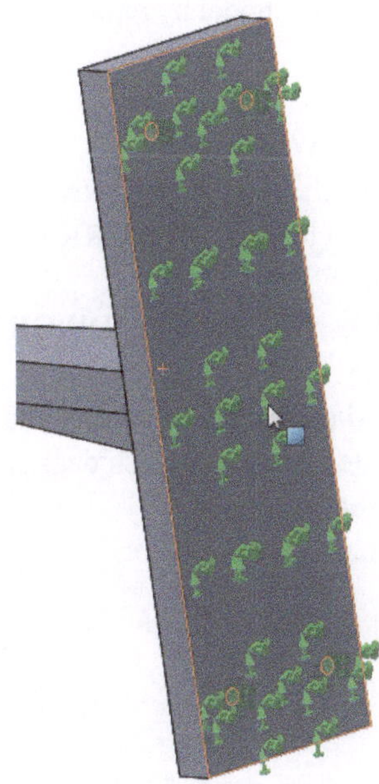

6. Click **OK** on the **Fixture** PropertyManager.

Adding Loads

1. Click **Next** on the **SOLIDWORKS SimulationXpress** pane.

The **Loads** step is activated on the **SOLIDWORKS SimulationXpress** pane.

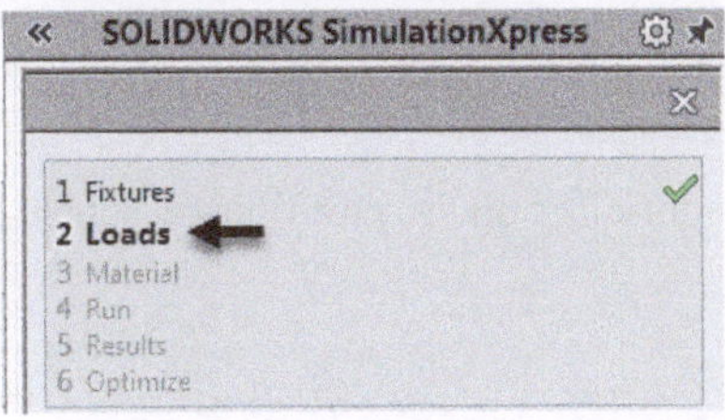

2. Click **Add a force** on the **SOLIDWORKS SimulationXpress** pane.
3. Select the holes, as shown.

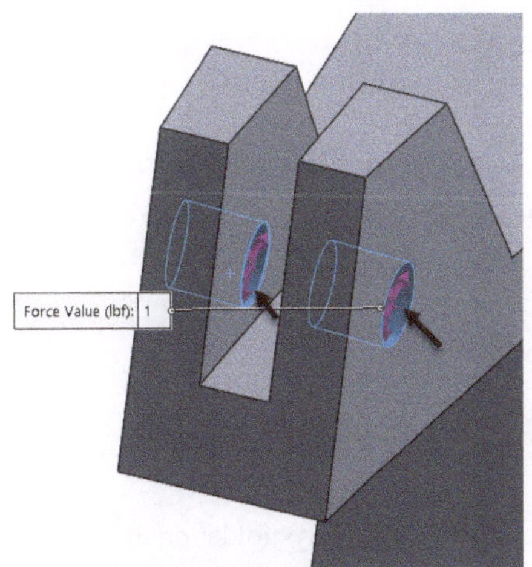

4. Select the **Selected direction** option.
5. Expand the FeatureManager Design Tree and select the Top Plane.

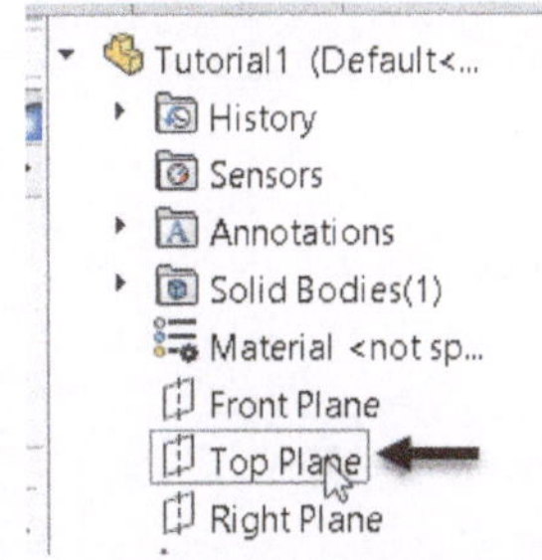

6. On the **Force** PropertyManager, type **450** in the **Force Load** box.
7. Check the **Reverse direction** option.

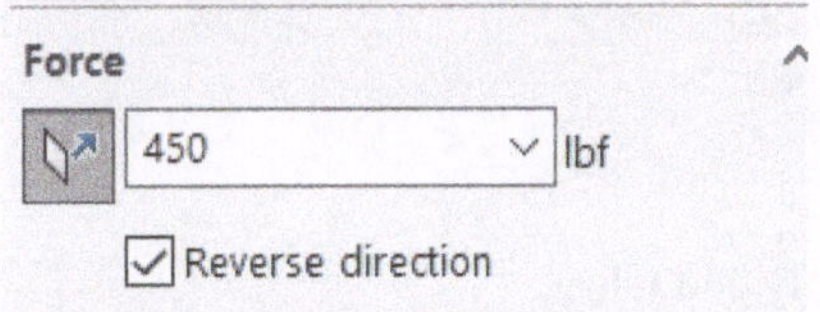

8. Click **OK** on the PropertyManager to apply the Force load.

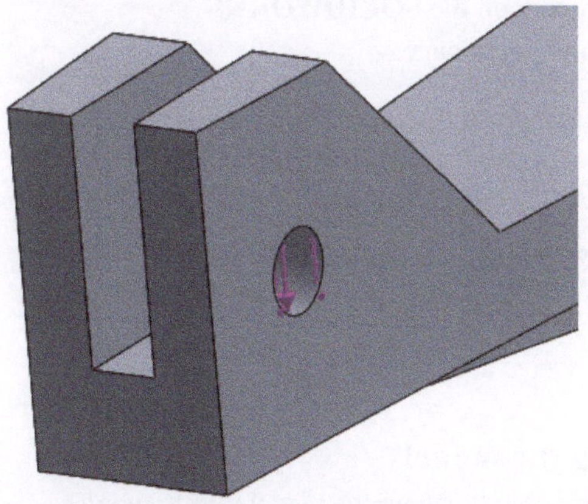

Adding the Material

1. Click **Next** on the **SOLIDWORKS SimulationXpress** pane.
2. Click **Choose Material** on the **SOLIDWORKS SimulationXpress** pane.

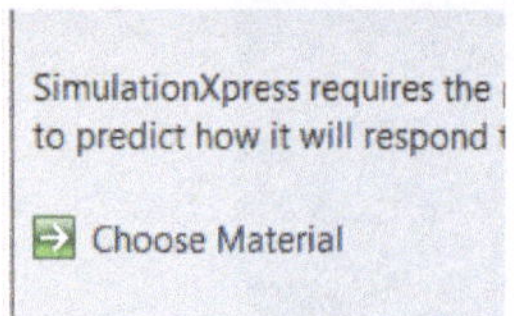

3. Expand the **Aluminum Alloys** folder on the left side of the **Material** dialog.

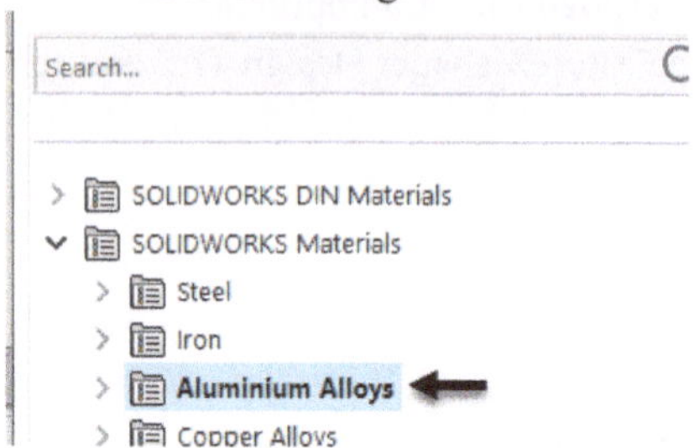

4. Scroll down and select the **6061 Alloy**.

5. Click **Apply** and **Close**.

The **Young's Modulus** and the **Yield Strength** of the selected appear on the **SOLIDWORKS SimulationXpress** pane.

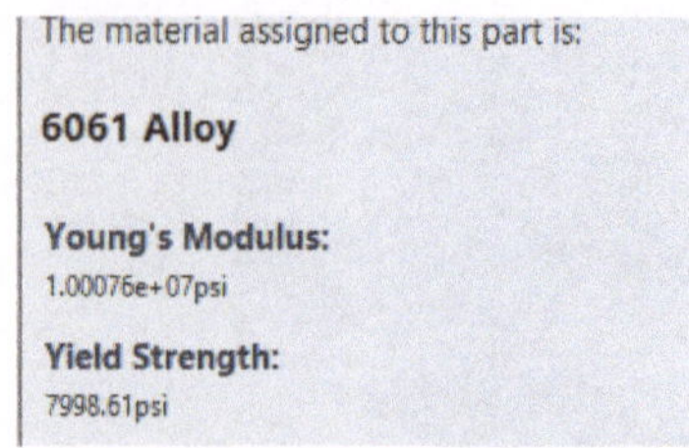

Meshing the model

By meshing, you break up the model into triangular pieces, each piece representing an element. Before meshing, you need to prepare the model by removing small features such as fillets.

1. Click **Next** on the **SOLIDWORKS SimulationXpress** pane; the **Run** step is activated.
2. Click **Change settings** on the **SOLIDWORKS SimulationXpress** pane.
3. Click **Change mesh density** on the **SOLIDWORKS SimulationXpress** pane.
4. On the **Mesh** PropertyManager, click and drag the **Mesh Density** dragger to change the mesh density.
5. Check the **Mesh Parameters** option.
6. Type **0.118** in the **Global Size** box.

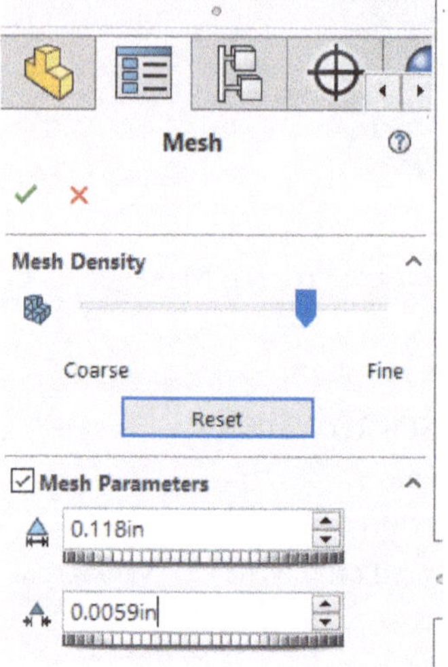

7. Click **OK** on the **Mesh** PropertyManager to generate the mesh.
8. In the left pane, right-click on the part file and select **Show Mesh**.

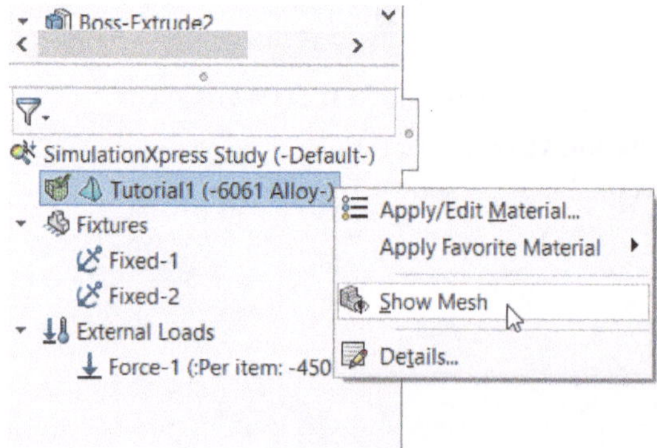

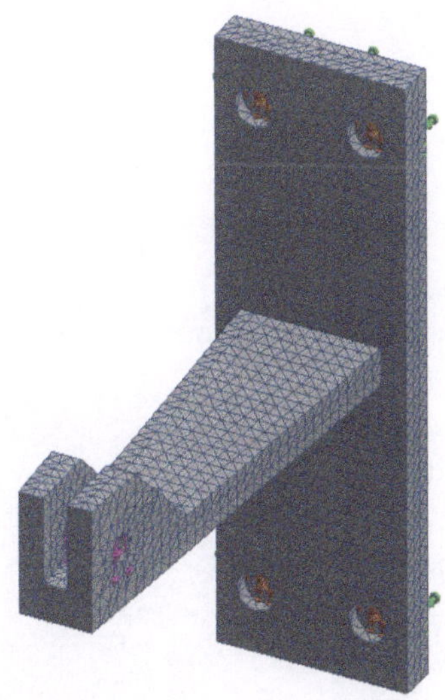

Simulating the Model

Now, you need to check whether the simulation model is setup properly.

1. Click **Next** on the **SOLIDWORKS SimulationXpress** pane.
2. Click **Run Simulation.**

The program runs the simulation and displays the animation of the deformed part.

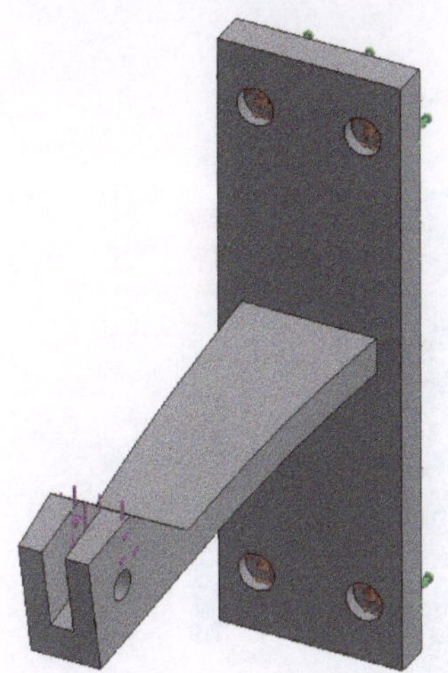

3. Click **Yes, Continue.**

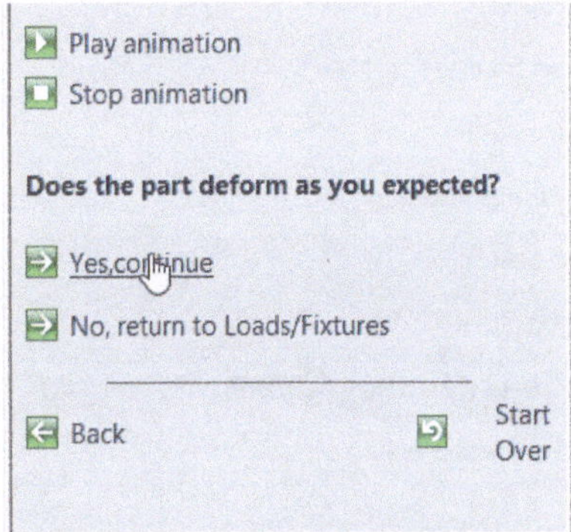

The results of the simulation appear.

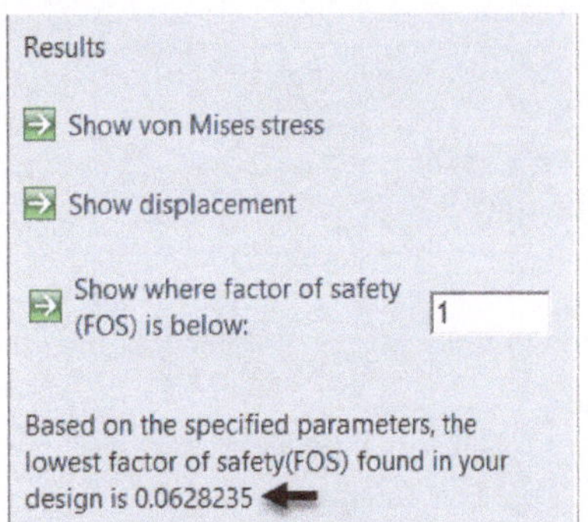

Note that the factor of safety is below 1, which means that the model cannot withstand the applied load. You can solve this by changing the material or load or both. In this case, you change both material and load.

4. Click the **Material** step on the **SOLIDWORKS Simulations** pane.

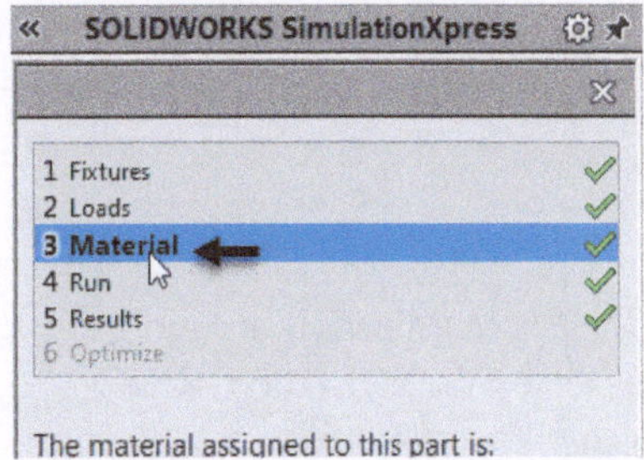

5. Click **Change Material.**
6. On the **Material** dialog, expand the **Steel** folder.
7. Select the **Stainless Steel (ferritic)** material.

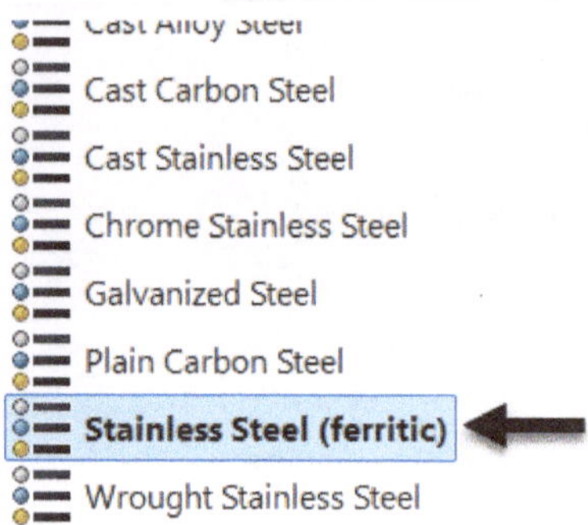

8. Click **Apply** and **Close**.
9. On the left pane, right-click on the **Force** load, and then select **Edit Definition**.

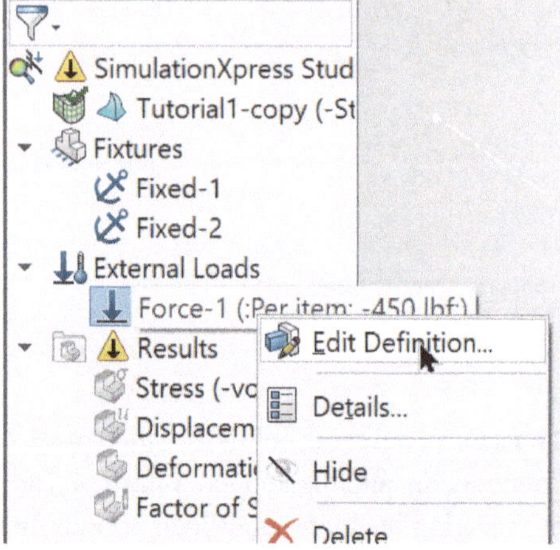

10. Type **50** in the **Force Load** box.

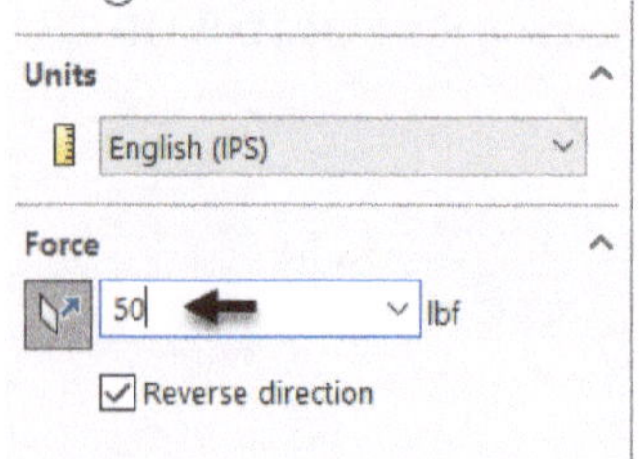

11. Click **OK** on the **Force** PropertyManager.
12. Click the **Run** step on the **SOLIDWORKS Simulations** pane.
13. Click **Run Simulation** on the **SOLIDWORKS Simulations** pane.

Notice that the factor of safety is updated, as shown.

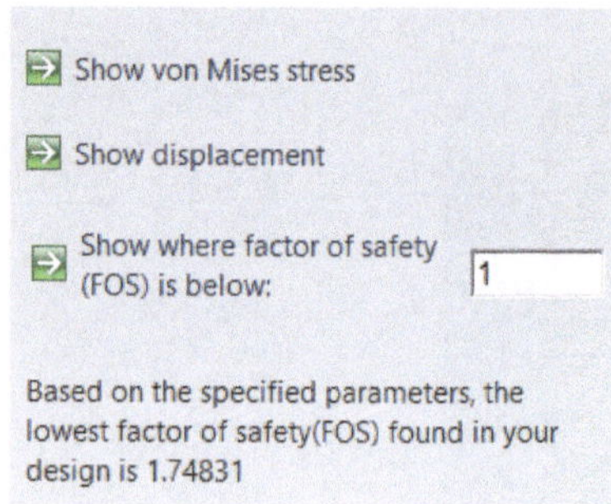

14. Click **Show von Mises stress**.

The result appears, as shown.

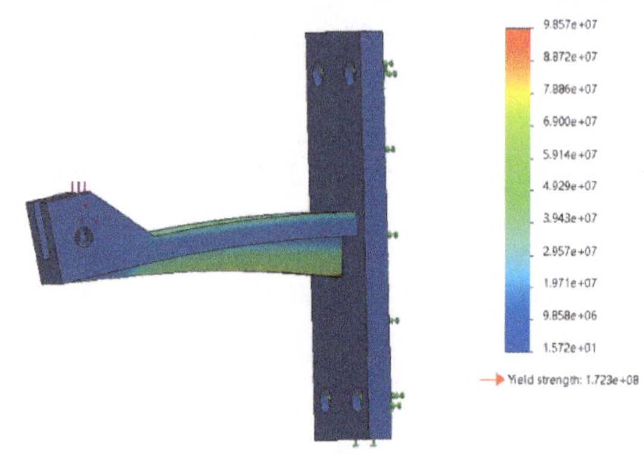

15. Click **Play animation** to animate the von Mises stresses.
16. Click **Stop animation**.
17. Click **Show displacement**.

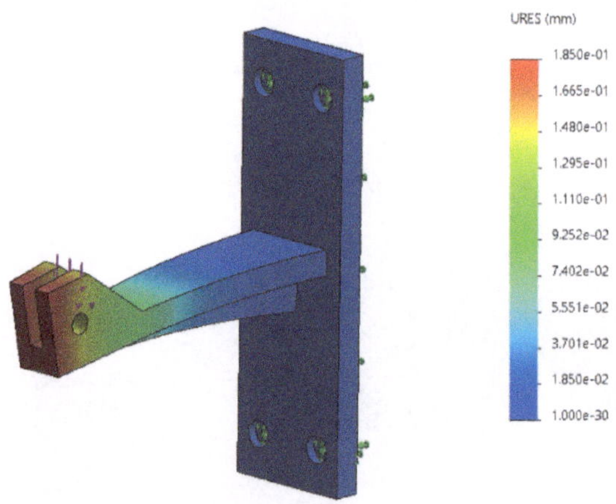

Generating Reports

1. Click **Done viewing results**.
2. Click **Generate report**.
3. On the **Report settings** dialogue, check the **Description** and **Conclusion** options.

You can also check the options available in the **Header Formation** section. After checking the options, you need to enter the information in the boxes displayed next to them.

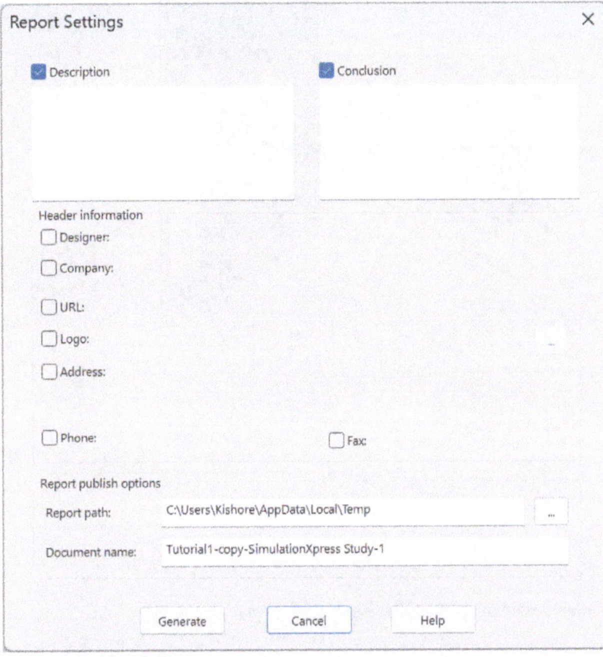

4. Click the **Browse** button next to the **Report Path** box.
5. Browse to the required folder and click the **Select Folder** button.
6. Leave the default value in the **Document Name** box (or) enter the required name.
7. Click the **Generate** button. Solidworks generates a professional report in a word document, and it includes screenshots and simulation data.

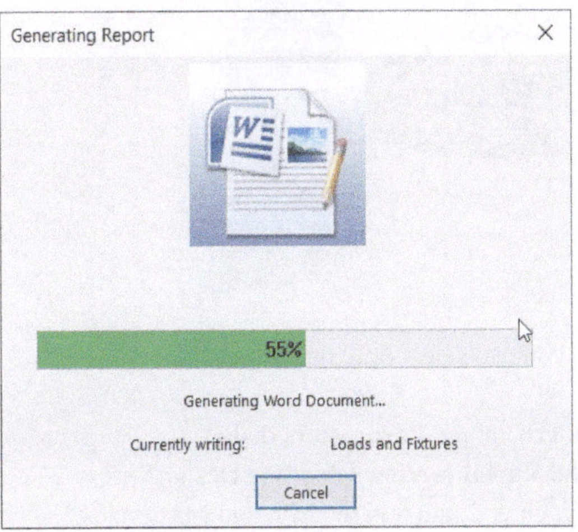

The report includes model information, material properties, loads and fixtures, mesh information, and study results.

8. Click **Generate eDrawings file**.
9. Browse to the required folder and click the **Save** button.

The simulation study is exported to the eDrawings file.

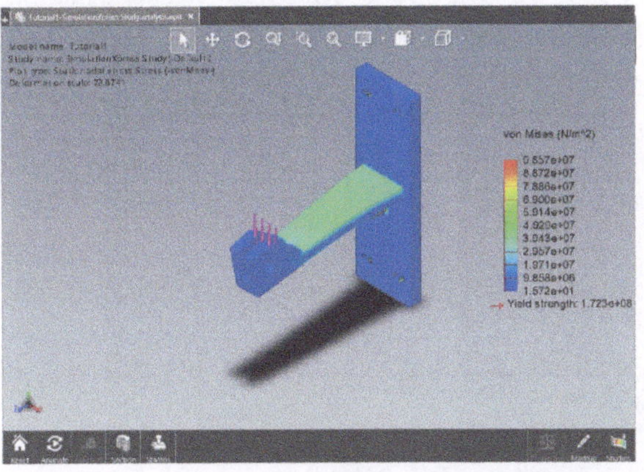

This is a great way to share the file with others using the free eDrawings application. It allows you to zoom or rotate the model and examine the study. You can also click the Studies button located at the bottom right corner to view the simulation analysis tree. You can expand the simulation analysis tree to view the Deformation, Stress, Displacement, and Factor of Safety.

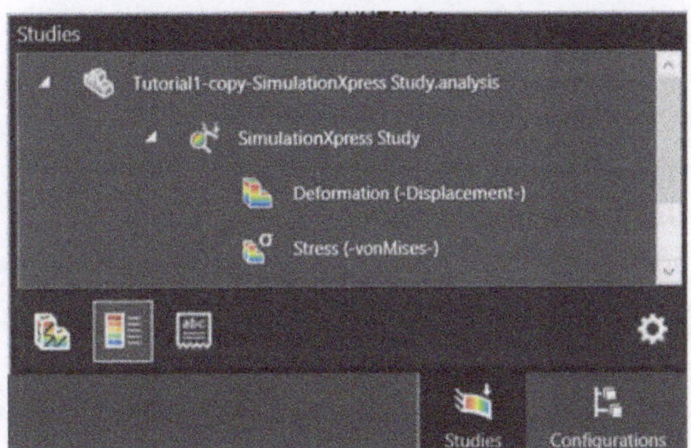

They can also view the mesh by clicking the **Mesh** icon on the **Studies** palette.

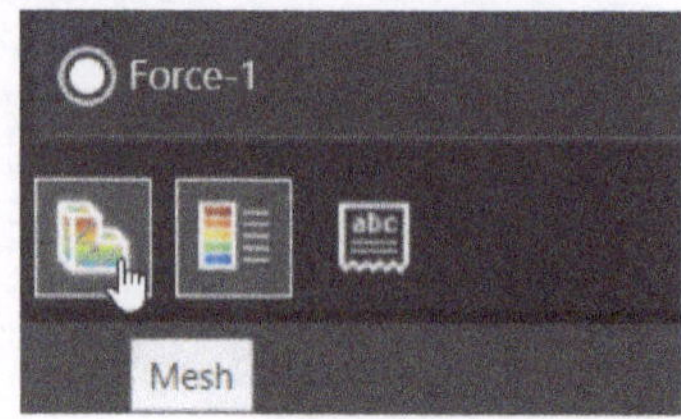

Click **Tools > Markup** on the menu bar. The Markup menu has tools to add comments, dimensions, and labels. These tools will help you to identify any error and mark it up.

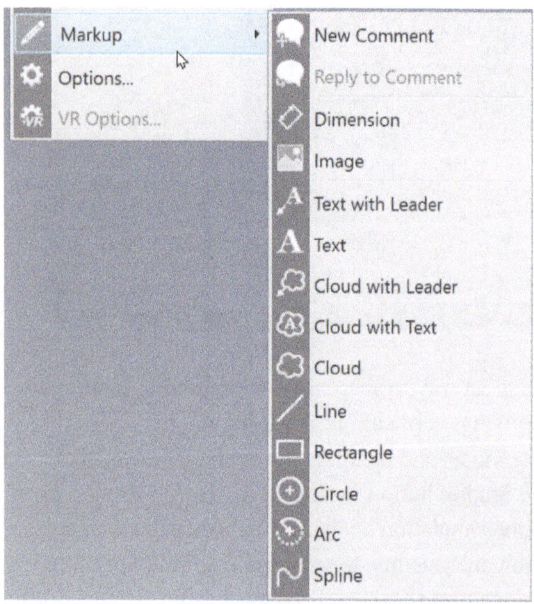

Optimizing the Model

After reviewing the results, you can allow SimulationXpress to optimize the design if the analysis result shows that the model does not meet the required factor of safety. However, if the design exceeds the required factor of safety, you can optimize the design to make it leaner and reduce material cost.

1. Click **Next**.
2. Select **Yes**, and then click **Next**.

All the dimensions of the model appear, and the DesignXpress Study is started.

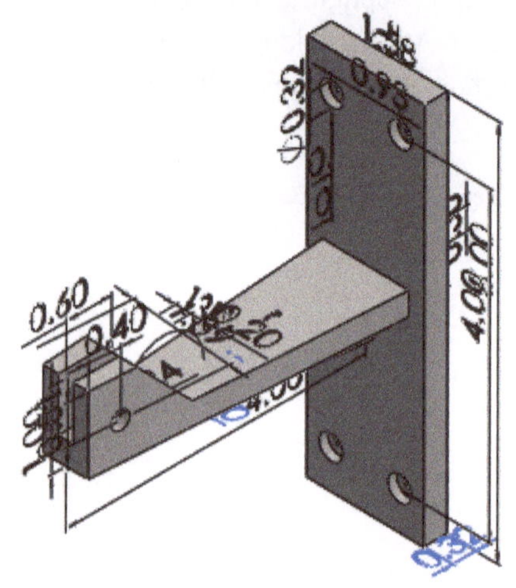

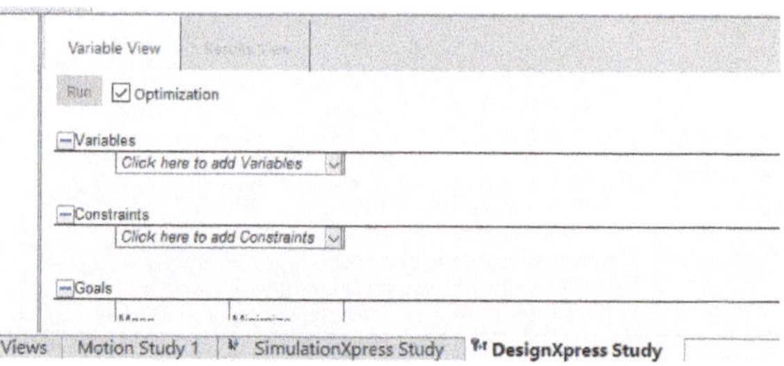

The DesignXpress Study allows you to optimize the design in relation to the factor of safety, maximum stress, or maximum displacement. For example, you can optimize the design to meet the factor of safety of 3.

3. Click **Select a dimension** and select the dimension, as shown.

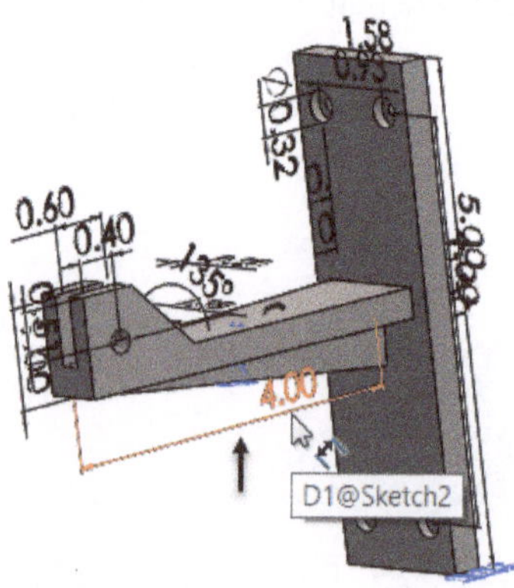

Note that you can select only one dimension.

4. Click **OK** on the **Parameters** dialog.
5. On the **Variable View** tab of the DesignXpress Study, enter 2 and 6 in the Min and Max boxes, respectively.

6. Select **Factor of Safety** from the **Constraints** drop-down.
7. Type **3** in the **Min** box.

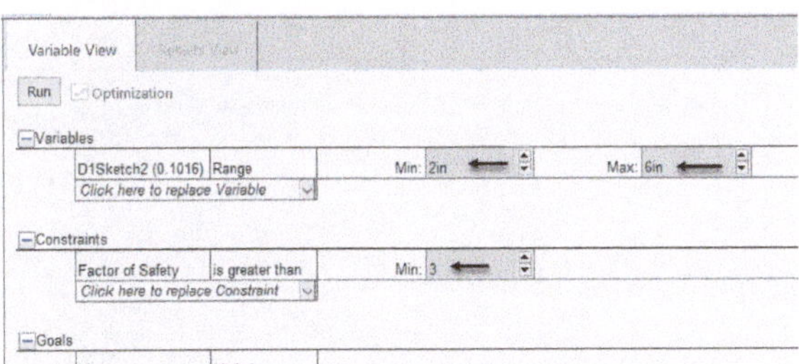

8. Click **Next** until the **Run optimization** option appears.
9. Click **Run optimization**; the DesignXpress Study in Progress dialog appears.

The **Results View** tab displays the results of the design study.

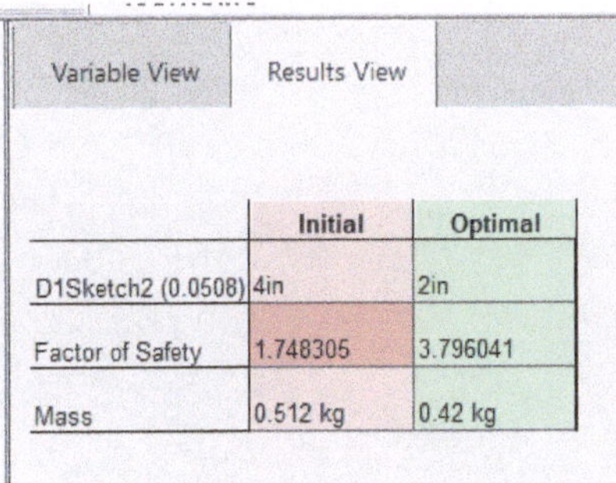

	Initial	Optimal
D1Sketch2 (0.0508)	4in	2in
Factor of Safety	1.748305	3.796041
Mass	0.512 kg	0.42 kg

The resultant design is displayed in the graphics area.

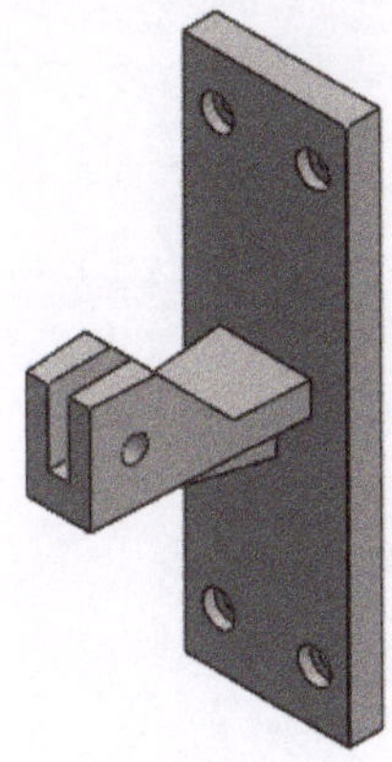

10. Select the **Optimal Value** option from Optimization results.

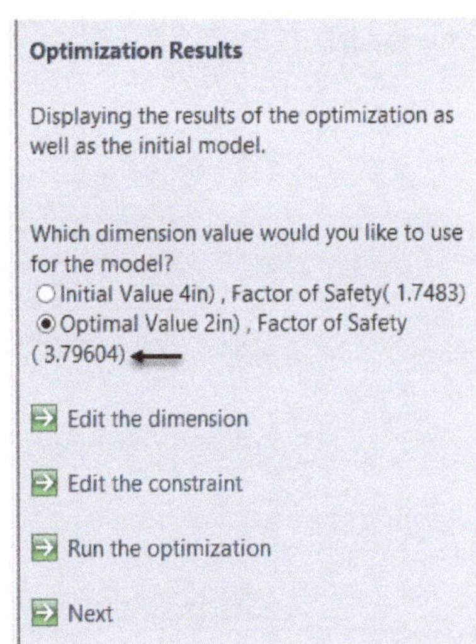

11. Click **Next**; the message appears that the results are out of date.

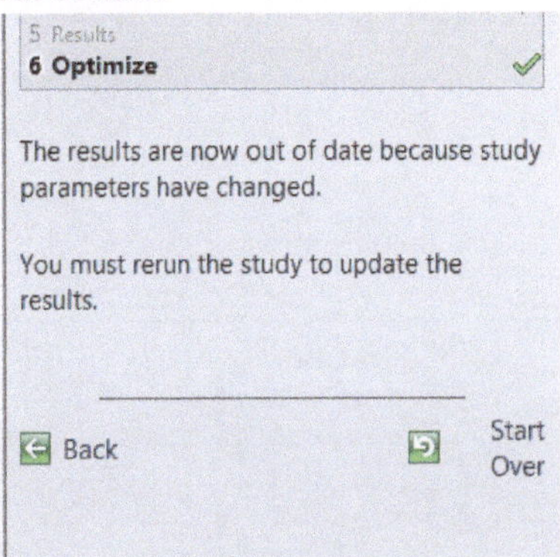

12. Click the **Run** step on the **SOLIDWORKS SimulationXpress Study** pane.
13. Click **Run Simulation**.
14. Click **Next**.
15. Click the **SimulationXpress Study** tab at the bottom of the graphics area.
16. Examine the simulation results from the **Results** section of the SimulationXpress Study.

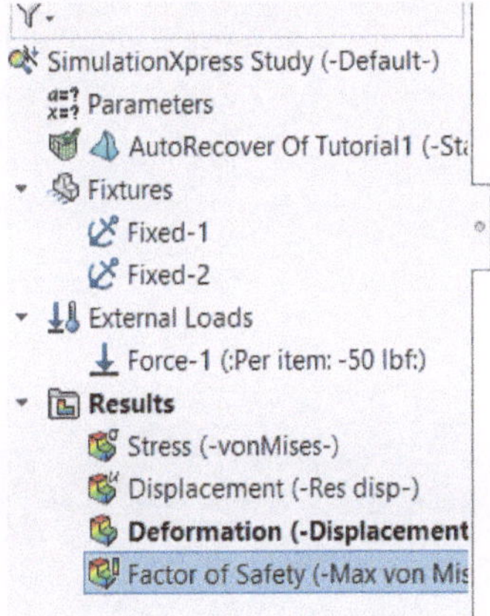

17. Save and close the model.

Index

3D Sketch, 316
Add Relation, 21
Add Sunlight, 371
All Tangent, 304
Auto Balloon, 333
Auto Dimension Scheme, 340
Boundary Surface, 298
Breadcrumbs, 9
Center Rectangle, 29, 323
Centerline, 27, 31, 35
Chain Dimension, 350
Change Transparency, 307
Circle, 18
CommandManager, 6
Convert Entities, 20
Copy Appearance, 357
Core, 307
Corner Rectangle, 31
Corner Treatment, 314
Create Bounding Box, 335
Customize, 11
Cut with Surface, 293
Datum, 342, 351, 352
Delete Face, 291
Deleting Holes, 287
DimXpertManager, 341
Draft, 37
Draft Analysis, 302
Edit Appearance, 365
Edit Background, 14
Edit Decal, 374
Edit Scene, 362
Edit Sunlight, 372
End Cap, 330
End chain, 20
End miter, 313
Exit Sketch, 19
Extend Surface, 283
Extruded Boss/Base, 19, 323
Extruded Cut, 30
Extruded Surface, 272
FeatureManager Design Tree, 7
Filled Surface, 288
Fillet, 32
Fillet Bead, 325
Filter Solid bodies, 336
Flatten Surface, 300
Freeform, 294
Generate Video, 373
Geometric Tolerance, 344
Gusset, 322
Horizontal, 77
Insert Mold Folders, 303
Internal, 330
Inward, 330
Knit Surface, 279
Line, 20, 22
Link Views, 370
Locate Profile, 315
Location Dimension, 344, 346
Lock to Constraint, 373
Lofted Surface, 274
Marked for drawing, 336
Menu, 5
Mid Plane, 37
Midpoint, 78
Mirror, 190, 324
Move Copy Bodies, 308
Move Forward, 373
Normal to Surface, 277
Offset Surface, 279
Options, 312, 367
Outward, 330
Pan, 25
Parallel, 78
Parting Lines, 303
Parting Surface, 305
Pattern, 341
Pattern Feature, 348
Perpendicular, 78
Perpendicular to Vector, 278
Planar Surface, 275
Plane, 324
Play Recording, 373
Power Trim, 23
PropertyManager, 9
Quick Access Toolbar, 5
Replace Face, 292
Resolve Sketch, 76
Revolved Boss/Base, 28
Revolved Surface, 273
Rotate About Scene Floor, 25
Rotation Angle, 315
Ruled Surface, 276
Save, 25
Save Information to file, 372
Scale, 303
Section View, 306
Set Home, 373
Shortcut Menus, 8
Show Tolerance Status, 343
Show/Hide Map, 373
Shut-off Surfaces, 304
Simple cut between bodies, 320
Simulation Advanced, 377
Single View, 371
Size Dimension, 343
Sketch, 17

Smart Dimension, 18, 112, 113
Smart Weld Selection Tool, 328
Specify Location, 372
Status bar, 8
Structural Member, 312, 318, 338
Studio Scenes, 369
Swept Surface, 273
Symmetric, 31, 36
Tangent, 78
Thicken, 290
Thickened Cut, 293
Through All, 32
Tolerance Status, 343
Tooling Split, 306
Trim Entities, 21, 117
Trim Surface, 280
Trim to Closest, 21, 118, 188
Trim/Extend, 320
Undercut Analysis, 307
Untrim Surface, 285
Vertical, 77
View (Heads Up) Toolbar, 8
View Decal, 374
View Orientation, 19, 22, 36
View Scene, Lights, and Cameras, 367
View Selector, 365
Weld Bead, 326, 328
Weld Table, 335
Weldment Cut List, 332
Weldment Profiles, 337
Zoom In/Out, 25
Zoom to Area, 25
Zoom to Fit, 19
Zoom to Selection, 25

Printed at Repro India Ltd.